PSYCHOLOGY TODAY

AN INTRODUCTION

Sixth Edition

CONSULTANTS AND REVIEWERS

Chapter Consultants

Joseph LoPiccolo, State University of New York, Stony Brook
Chapter 13   Human Sexuality

Jay Belsky, Pennsylvania State University
Chapter 14   Early Development

Marvin Daehler, University of Massachusetts
Chapter 15   Cognitive Development

Urie Bronfenbrenner, Cornell University
Chapter 17   Personality and Social Development

Matthew Erdelyi, Brooklyn College
Chapter 18   Psychoanalytic Theories of Personality

Shelley E. Taylor, University of California at Los Angeles
Chapter 21   Health Psychology and Adjustment to Stress

Richard Guzzo, New York University
Chapter 28   Industrial/Organizational Psychology

General Reviewers

Roger Bailey, Southwestern College
John Best, Eastern Illinois University
John Neil Bohannon, Virginia Polytechnic Institute
Susan Donaldson, Indiana State University
Bernard Gorman, Nassau Community College
Robert Johnson, Arkansas State University
Joan Lockard, University of Washington
Thomas Marshall, Fresno City College
John Monahan, Central Michigan University
James Pomerantz, State University of New York, Buffalo
Jeannette Roberts, Miami University
Fred Whitford, Montana State University

Specialist Reviewers

Pietro Badia, Bowling Green State University
Steven Ceci, Cornell University
Susan Fiske, Carnegie Mellon University
Leo Ganz, Stanford University
Leonard Hamilton, Rutgers University
Daniel Leger, University of Nebraska
William Mason, University of California, Davis
Karl Pribram, Stanford University
William H. Saufley, Jr., University of California, Berkeley
Robert Sekuler, Northwestern University
Edward Simmel, Miami University
Barbara Tversky, Stanford University
Brian Wandell, Stanford University
Jeff Wine, Stanford University
Eugene Zechmeister, Loyola University of Chicago

PSYCHOLOGY TODAY

SIXTH EDITION

AN INTRODUCTION

RICHARD R. BOOTZIN
Northwestern University

GORDON H. BOWER
Stanford University

ROBERT B. ZAJONC
University of Michigan

with Part Introductions by
ISAAC ASIMOV

ELIZABETH HALL

RANDOM HOUSE ■ NEW YORK

Sixth Edition
98765432

Copyright © 1975, 1979, 1983, 1986 by
Random House, Inc.

Library of Congress Cataloging in Publication Data

Main entry under title:

Psychology today: an introduction.

   Includes bibliographies and indexes.
   1. Psychology. I. Bootzin, Richard R., 1940-
BF121.P85   1986   150   85-25720
ISBN 0-394-34359-X

Manufactured in the United States of America

Cover design: Jack Ribik

A NOTE FROM THE PUBLISHER

Instructors who teach introductory psychology must choose from a bewildering array of over 100 different texts. Every year, amid tumultuous fanfare and great beating of drums, another dozen or so new candidates come off the press, and each of them promises to be different and better than all the rest. Drowned out by the blare of trumpets is the disquieting news that most of these texts quietly fade away, never to appear in a second or third edition. Only a select few join the ranks of dependable texts, those tried and true best sellers that go through edition after edition.

The books that are chosen by instructors most frequently year after year have two features in common: each has a unique character, and each is flexible enough to change with the times. *Psychology Today* is such a text. It is special and unique, yet it has kept pace with the ever-growing, continually changing field of psychology. Through five editions *Psychology Today* has successfully served the teaching needs of thousands of instructors and the learning needs of more than a million students.

Published in the late 1960s by CRM Books, the first edition of *Psychology Today* took the market by storm, selling more copies in its first year than any other psychology text ever! It was written in a lively, conversational style, designed in an open and inviting magazine format, and sprinkled generously with exciting full-color illustrations. The text was produced in the CRM style by an illustrious crew of thirty-eight academics who provided chapter drafts. These drafts were then rewritten by professional writers to make them more appealing to students.

The fourth edition of *Psychology Today* (published in 1979) was the first edition produced by Random House. It differed from the earlier editions in its improved academic content, which provided solid coverage in all areas of psychology. For the first time, *Psychology Today* appealed as much to faculty as it did to students.

In the fifth edition a team of three distinguished academic advisors worked closely with a professional writer and editor to produce a book that was solid, current, and complete, yet exciting to read and easy to understand.

This sixth edition uses the same approach that was so successful with the fifth edition. We have fine-tuned the book, further strengthening its coverage, and changed the content somewhat to follow current theory and research in the field.

As in the fifth edition, our author team is headed by **Richard R. Bootzin,** professor and chairman of the Department of Psychology at Northwestern University. Dr. Bootzin is a specialist in personality and abnormal psychology and a prominent researcher in the areas of sleep and sleep disorders, principles of behavior change, and mental health evaluation. He is coauthor of *Abnormal Psychology: Current Perspectives,* 4th edition, published in 1984 by Random House.

Gordon H. Bower, professor of psychology at Stanford University, is the second and newest member of our team. A prominent researcher and theorist in the areas of learning, memory, and cognition, his current research interest is the study of emotional influences on cognitive processes. Dr. Bower is coauthor of *Theories of Learning,* 5th edition, with Ernest Hilgard, and editor of the prestigious series, *The Psychology of Learning and Motivation: Advances in Research and Theory,* published annually since 1968. Among his numerous awards and honors are the APA Distinguished Contribution Award and the Albert Ray Lang Professorship Chair at Stanford. In 1984 ten of his former PhD students published a volume entitled, *Tutorials in Learning and Memory: Essays in Honor of Gordon Bower.*

The third distinguished member of our team is again **Robert B. Zajonc,** professor of psychology at the University of Michigan and director of its Research Center for Group Dynamics. Dr. Zajonc, a specialist in social psychology, is known for his research on the effects of mere exposure, social facilitation, family structure and intellectual development, and emotion and cognition. In 1978 he won the APA Distinguished Scientific Contribution Award.

As in the fifth edition, the smooth writing style and even reading level of this book are the work of **Elizabeth Hall.** Ms. Hall is the coauthor of *Child Psychology Today,* 2nd edition, published by Random House in 1986; and of *Adult Development and Aging,* published in 1985. She was Editor-in-Chief of *Human Nature* magazine and managing editor of *Psychology Today* magazine. Her interviews with many eminent psychologists, including Jean Piaget, Jerome Bruner, B.F. Skinner, Erik Erikson, and Bruno Bettelheim, continue to appear in the magazine.

The work of our team is now complete. The sixth edition of *Psychology Today* is one of the most exciting educational tools on the market. We hope that students will continue to enjoy it and to learn from it for many more editions.

Our goals for this sixth edition of *Psychology Today* were the same as those we had for the fifth edition. We wanted to strengthen even further the book's exposition of basic concepts and its expanded coverage of physiology. At the same time we wanted to bring to the book our excitement about the work being done on the frontiers of psychological research today. We also wanted to give students a feel for the way psychology developed by retaining the classical studies that changed the direction of the field. In the pursuit of those goals, we made a number of modifications.

Organization The text still consists of twenty-eight chapters divided into eight parts, but their sequence has been rearranged. Because it is important for students to understand the genetic and evolutionary influences on behavior before they take up the study of behavior itself, we have moved our chapter on Biological Perspectives on Behavior closer to the beginning. The former Part Five, Feeling and Activation, is now Part Four (Chapter 11, Emotions; Chapter 12, Motivation; Chapter 13, Human Sexuality). This change enables students to move without interruption from the study of learning and cognition to the study of emotions and motivation.

Chapter Revisions All chapters have been thoroughly updated and the text carefully examined and rewritten to improve clarity. We have integrated the book—both within each chapter and as a whole—in order to keep relationships within the field of psychology apparent. In a number of cases, our revisions have gone far beyond a simple updating:

- The chapter on the brain has been completely reorganized to help students grasp neuroscience more easily and its coverage strengthened to reflect the newest research and views in the area. (Chapter 3)
- The chapter on biological influences on behavior has been completely redone, and the emphasis has been shifted from animals to human beings. Consistent with revisions in other parts of the book, genetic and evolutionary influences on behavior are extensively covered, and sociobiological theory is carefully explained. (Chapter 4)
- The entire section on learning and cognition has been reorganized to reflect the increased emphasis psychologists place on cognition and information processing. Learning is no longer

presented primarily as a matter of stimulus and response; instead, it is connected with brain function on the one hand and with cognition on the other. The discussion of memory has been heavily revised to present a dynamic picture of memory processes. The coverage of mental concepts has been greatly expanded, as has the material on judgment, problem-solving, and decision making. Exciting new developments in the field of artificial intelligence are integrated into the coverage of cognition. (Part Three: Chapters 8, 9, and 10)

- The chapter on stress has been broadened to cover other aspects of health psychology, one of the newest areas of specialization. Before discussing stress and its effects on health, we examine the attitudes, behavior, and environmental conditions that promote health and aid in the prevention of illness. (Chapter 21)
- The chapter on environmental psychology has been replaced with a totally new chapter, Industrial/Organizational Psychology, in order to cover an area of psychology that is of increasing interest, and one that has direct application to students' lives as they move into the workplace. This chapter, which focuses on the relationship between people and their jobs, covers research and theory on the conditions and effects of employment. (Chapter 28).

Special Features Each of the thirty-one boxed features highlights a topic on the cutting edge of psychology that pertains to the chapter in which it appears, and twenty-two of the boxes are entirely new. The new boxes consider such topics as:

- Alzheimer's Disease (Chapter 3, The Brain and Behavior)
- Expert Humans and Expert Systems (Chapter 10, Cognition)
- Children in the Courtroom: Are They Reliable Witnesses? (Chapter 15, Cognitive Development)
- The Stockholm Syndrome (Chapter 25, Attitudes and Attitude Change)
- Hidden Influence in Daily Life (Chapter 27, Social Influences and Group Processes)

Once again, Isaac Asimov has provided us with a thought-provoking introduction to each of the eight parts of the text.

Pedagogical Aids Each chapter is followed by a summary written in paragraph form. A list of key terms and an annotated list of recommended readings completes each chapter. There is a complete glossary with full definitions in the back of the book, as well as name and subject indexes.

Illustrations New tables and charts have been selected on the basis of their educational value, and the entire illustration program retains the special flair of previous editions. Key physiological drawings in Chapter 3 (The Brain and Behavior) and Chapter 5 (Sensation and the Senses) have been completely redrawn, presenting the brain and nervous system, the eye, and the ear in greater detail and more vivid color.

These improvements and innovations make this text the best edition yet of *Psychology Today.* Students can embark on their introduction to psychology with full confidence that they will find the experience enjoyable and rewarding. It is our hope that instructors will find this new edition a valuable review of past research integrated with the newest research and ideas in the field of psychology.

Acknowledgments We would like to thank the many consultants and reviewers who assisted us in this revision. We are indebted to the consultants who supervised the preparation of both new and revised chapters outside our areas of expertise. Our thanks also go to the specialists who

carefully reviewed and helped fine-tune specific chapters. And, of course, we are deeply appreciative of the time and effort our general reviewers gave to the entire revision. Because their contributions were invaluable to us, we have featured the names of the consultants and reviewers on the title page of this book. Our generous thanks to the graduate and postdoctoral students who labored with us at the research stage of development: John Clapper, Nelson Donegan, Dane Lavin, and Deanna Wilkes-Gibbs at Stanford University; and Pamela Adelmann at the University of Michigan.

Our special thanks go to Mary Falcon, our editor at Random House, who guided the entire project; Susan Tucker, who helped us develop the chapters; Betty Gatewood, Ann Levine, Mary Marshall, and Roberta Meyer, who helped us write some of the chapters; Elaine Rosenberg, who supervised the copyediting and production stages; and Cele Gardner, who was immensely helpful in the art program. The production team at Random House has our gratitude for turning the manuscript into a handsome book: Stacey Alexander, production supervisor; Leon Bolognese, designer; and Kathy Bendo, photo editor.

RRB
GHB
RBZ
EH

CONTENTS

PART ONE

ABOUT PSYCHOLOGY

In 1798, William Wordsworth, writing of a dull and unimaginative clod, said:

*A primrose by a river's brim
A yellow primrose was to him,
And it was nothing more.*

To some people it may seem that this is the picture of a scientist. Science must limit itself, they may think, to the material aspects of that primrose and nothing more. It must avoid poetry, dismiss beauty, and carefully discipline imagination. There can be nothing in the primrose except that which can be weighed, measured, and demonstrated.

And does that not reduce the world to dusty grayness?

Don't you believe it! The methodology of science may be of no use outside a world of numbering and measuring that all can agree on, but even when constrained within those limits, it uncovers wonders and beauty that the undisciplined imagination, unaware of science, could never grasp.

The microscope applied to the primrose petal produces vistas of order and of dainty interrelationships the unaided eye cannot see. Chemistry reveals the molecular structure of pigments that no one could otherwise dream of. Turning to the plant that bears the blossom, there are the complex interrelationships of the components of the photosynthetic mechanism that makes it possible for the plant to turn the energy of sunlight into material structure. The whole is more beautiful than anything Wordsworth ever sensed in a primrose, however impassioned it may have made him feel.

And psychology, too, is a science. It deals with matters that must be numbered and measured, but not in as clear-cut a way. All electrons are absolutely alike. What holds for one, holds for all of them from here to the farthest star. All grains of sand are very much alike. All crystals of salt are very much alike. All tennis balls. In many ways, even all automobiles.

But every human being is different—different in appearance; different in ways of thought; different in perception and reaction.

And yet despite that, you have a headstart in your study of psychology. You may know nothing about electrons, salt, and automobiles, but even if you have never taken a single course in psychology, never read a book about it, you still know a great deal about it. You have spent your whole life with people, learning how to deal with them and react to them, growing interested in and perhaps exasperated by their peculiarities.

When you study psychology you have a chance to organize the knowledge you already have, systematize it, extend it, and understand it more clearly. How interesting that cannot help but be to you.

And not just interesting to you, but tremendously important to the world. If humanity has advanced through its history, it has been through the activity of the human mind, which has brought us material security and every aspect of culture. And if humanity has been placed in danger, it has been through the activity of the human mind, for it is human motivation, carefully thought out and justified by the mind—greed, envy, rage, and lust—that produces the wars, violence, alienation, and cruelties that other motivations—sympathy, love, the desire to give and build and create—fight so endlessly.

And psychology is the organized study of it all. What can possibly be more important to all of us?

Isaac Asimov

UNDERSTANDING PSYCHOLOGY: AN INTRODUCTION

In California a man programs a computer to diagnose illnesses the way a human medical expert does. In Massachusetts a woman interviews executives in large corporations to discover what management techniques put a person in the boardroom. In Colorado a man works with Olympic hopefuls, teaching them to ski down a difficult slope in their imagination. In Alabama a woman teaches a chimpanzee to ask for snacks, games, or company by pressing keys on a computer. In a Florida hospital a man massages the limbs of a baby who was born two months early, talking softly as he rocks the infant and strokes a tiny leg. In New York a woman trains a group of police officers to negotiate with someone who is holding hostages.

What do all these individuals have in common? Surprising as it may seem, they share a very important interest. They are all psychologists. Since its birth about a century ago, psychology has become a wide-ranging discipline that embraces an almost endless array of basic research problems and a broad range of practical matters. Most psychologists would agree that **psychology** is the study of behavior, but the meaning of "behavior" varies among psychologists. To encompass all psychologists, we would have to define **behavior** as including thoughts, feelings, and dreams —anything a person does or experiences.

As this expanded definition indicates, the subject matter of psychology is extraordinarily diverse. Psychologists study behavior in the hope of discovering why we fall in love, how soon a baby can recognize its mother, why some people are creative, why other people become schizophrenic, whether your personality is partially determined before you are born, what happens in hypnosis, how drugs affect human functioning, and whether chimpanzees and dolphins can acquire language. Psychologists investigate everything from how flatworms learn to how a symphony is created, from the seemingly undifferentiated howls of a hungry infant to the complex reactions of an adult to the death of a spouse.

Psychology is not, of course, the only scientific study of human behavior; it overlaps with both the biological and the other behavioral sciences. For example, neurophysiologists and biochemists have made strides toward discovering physiological influences on mental disorders. Anthropologists and sociologists have investigated the customs, manners, morals, and social structures of a wide range of societies, complementing psychology's focus on the individual with a perspective on

groups of people. Some psychologists have begun
to collaborate with researchers in these other
fields, further broadening the scope of the discipline. No corner of our lives escapes the interest of
psychologists, for every aspect of human behavior
—from the moment of conception to the moment
of death—raises issues that are important if we
are finally to understand why human beings do
what they do.

THE GROWTH OF PSYCHOLOGY

It has been more than a hundred years since
psychology broke away from philosophy and physiology to emerge as a separate discipline. In the
past century this young and fertile area of study
has undergone a series of expansions in subject
matter as well as in research methods. During this
period even the basic nature of psychology has
been at issue: Is it the study of conscious experience? The study of unconscious processes? The
study of individual differences, or of observable
behavior? As we will discover when we examine a
few of these basic ideas, these differences of opinion have contributed to the tremendous growth of
psychology (see Figure 1.1).

Psychology as the Study of Conscious Experience

Psychology had its formal beginnings in Leipzig,
Germany, where Wilhelm Wundt founded the first
psychological laboratory in 1879. Wundt is considered the first psychologist, as opposed to the philosophers or physiologists who were also interested in psychology (Boring, 1957). He stringently
limited the subject to the study of conscious experience. Wundt believed that all our conscious experiences are merely intricate combinations of
elemental sensations—that is, intellectual towers
made of sensory building blocks. In much the
same way that a chemist uses certain processes to
discover the basic elements composing all the
complex substances in the world, Wundt attempted to use introspection to find the basic sensations. He trained people carefully in the technique
of introspection, teaching them to observe and
report the "content" or "elements" of awareness in
a particular situation. Wundt also tried to discov-

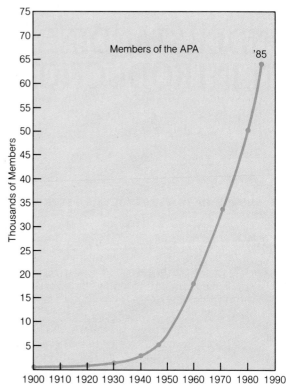

Figure 1.1. The growth of membership in the American Psychological Association over the past eighty-five
years. (Updated from Daniel, 1975.)

er the principles—the "mental chemistry"—by
which those sensations combine to become conscious experience. In essence, Wundt's approach
to establishing a discipline of psychology was confined to analyzing detailed descriptions of how
people perceive things in the world. Psychology
was formally defined as the study of conscious
experience. Would-be psychologists flocked to
Wundt's laboratory from Europe and North America, and the first generation of American psychologists was trained by him (Bringmann, 1979).

Wundt's approach, which fell out of favor in the
early decades of this century, has been coming
back in new form. In recent years our knowledge
about perception, memory, emotion, and cognition (all the processes involved in *knowing*) has
grown immensely, reawakening interest in consciousness and the workings of the mind. In fact,
during the past twenty years psychology has been
in the midst of what might be called a "cognitive

revolution." Today a great deal of psychological theory and research focuses on the workings of the mind. We will discuss the work of these cognitive psychologists in Chapters 8, 9, and 10.

Psychology as the Study of Unconscious Processes

For Sigmund Freud, a physician who practiced in Vienna until 1938, conscious experiences were only the tip of the iceberg. Beneath the surface, he believed, lay primitive biological urges that seek expression but are in conflict with the requirements of society and morality. According to Freud, these unconscious motivations and conflicts are powerful influences on our conscious thoughts and actions; they thus are responsible for much human behavior, including many of the physical symptoms that troubled Freud's patients (R. Watson, 1963).

Since unconscious processes could not be directly studied through introspection, Freud employed an indirect method for their study. In this technique, known as **free association**, a patient said everything that came to mind, making no attempt to produce logical, meaningful statements out of what seemed like absurd or irrelevant thoughts. Freud sat and listened, and then interpreted the associations. Free associations, Freud believed, reveal the operation of unconscious processes. He also believed that dreams express primitive unconscious urges. To learn more about these urges he developed dream analysis, an extension of free association in which the patient free-associated to his or her dreams (Freud, 1949).

While working out his ideas, Freud took meticulous notes on his patients and treatment sessions. He used these records, or case studies, to develop and illustrate a comprehensive theory of personality—that is, of the total, functioning person (Hall and Lindzey, 1978). Freud's theory of personality is discussed in Chapter 18.

In many areas of psychology, Freud's view of unconscious motivation remains a powerful and controversial influence. Modern psychologists may support, alter, or attempt to refute it—but most have a strong opinion about it. (Freud's theories are discussed in Chapters 17, 18, and 23.) The technique of free association is still used by psychoanalysts, and the method of intensive case study is still a tool for investigating behavior.

Psychology as the Study of Individual Differences

A lasting impact on psychology came from a nineteenth-century Englishman's concern with the way in which biology causes one person's abilities, character, and behavior to differ from those of other people. In searching for the determinants of these individual differences, Sir Francis Galton (1869) traced the ancestry of various eminent people. He found that greatness runs in families. (Such a finding was appropriate, for

What makes each person unique? The nineteenth-century English physiologist Francis Galton studied the biological determinants of individual differences and concluded that genius is hereditary. He spent immense time collecting, collating, and analyzing thumbprints in order to identify inherited characteristics.

Galton himself was considered a genius and his family included at least one towering intellectual figure—a cousin named Charles Darwin.) Galton concluded that genius or eminence is a hereditary trait—a premature conclusion. He did not consider the possibility that the tendency of genius to appear in eminent families might well be a result of the exceptional environments and socioeconomic advantages that also tend to run in such families.

The data Galton used were based on his study of biographies. Not content to limit his inquiry to indirect accounts, Galton went on to invent procedures for testing human abilities and characteristics. These tests were the primitive forebears of the modern personality and intelligence tests that most people take at some time in their lives. Galton also devised statistical techniques that are still used today (see Chapter 2).

Although Galton began his work before psychology emerged as an independent discipline, his theories and techniques quickly became central aspects of the new science. His book *Inquiries into Human Faculty and Its Development* (1883) is regarded as having defined the beginnings of individual psychology. Galton's writings raised the issue of whether behavior is determined by heredity or environment—a subject that has remained a focus of heated controversy (see Chapters 4 and 20). Galton's influence can also be seen in the widespread use of psychological tests, in the continuing controversy over their use, and in the statistical methods employed to evaluate their findings (see Chapter 20).

Psychology as the Study of Observable Behavior

A Russian physiologist, Ivan Pavlov, charted a different course for psychological investigation. Pavlov, who received the Nobel Prize in 1904 for his early work on digestive secretions, conducted a series of studies with dogs that were to have a major influence on the development of psychology. In one experiment, Pavlov (1927) set a metronome ticking each time he gave a dog some meat powder. At first the dog salivated the moment it saw the meat powder; after the procedure was repeated several times, the dog would salivate each time it heard the metronome, even if no food appeared.

The concept of the conditioned reflex that grew out of these studies gave psychologists a new tool with which to explore the development of behavior. By applying this concept, in which a response (salivation) is brought about by a stimulus (the metronome) different from the one that first produced it (food), psychologists could begin to account for behavior as the product of prior experience (see Chapter 8). This enabled them to explain certain behavior and certain differences among individuals as the result of learning.

Pavlov was part of a school of Russian neurophysiologists who rejected the introspective approach to psychology in favor of a strictly objective, experimental approach that was to become the hallmark of behaviorism (Kazdin, 1978). Pavlov and his colleagues simply pursued this method of study; it was left for others to turn it into a program for a new psychology.

It is John B. Watson (1878–1958), an American psychologist, who is credited with founding **behaviorism**, the approach to psychology that limits its study to observable responses to specific stimuli—responses that can be measured. He contended that all behavior, even behavior that appeared to be instinctive, is the result of conditioning and that it occurs in response to an appropriate stimulus. Watson (1913) maintained that introspection, the subjective analysis of thoughts and emotions used by Wundt, was as inappropriate in psychology as it was in chemistry. Theology, not psychology, was the proper place for introspection, he argued. The province of psychology was behavior, and its goal was the prediction and control of that behavior.

Watson did not succeed in restricting psychology to the study of observable behavior. In fact, he expanded the field considerably by extending the range of problems and phenomena with which psychologists could deal. In this sense his emphasis on the mechanisms of learning and on the significance of the environment in developing and maintaining behavior were major contributions. By using conditioned reflexes and other techniques for the study of learning processes, Watson also contributed to the development of such areas of psychological investigation as learning (see Chapter 8), memory (see Chapter 9), and problem solving (see Chapter 10).

Although Watson defined and solidified the behaviorist position, and many other learning theorists such as Clark Hull, Edward Tolman, and Edwin Guthrie contributed to it, it was B. F. Skinner, the contemporary American psychologist, who refined and popularized it. Skinner both narrowed the specific predictive claims of behaviorism and broadened its social implications.

Skinner sought to show that the consequences of behavior provide the basic mechanism for predicting and shaping future behavior. He even wrote a utopian novel, *Walden Two* (1948), to indicate how learning principles might be applied to an entire society.

Skinner exerted great influence on both the general public and the science of psychology. His face became familiar to nationwide television audiences, and his book *Beyond Freedom and Dignity* (1971) was a best seller. Walden Two communities have been formed in various parts of the country (Cordes, 1984), and many people toilet train their children, lose weight, quit smoking, and learn new skills using methods inspired by Skinner.

Skinner has been widely criticized, for many are convinced that "manipulative" conditioning could limit personal freedom; however, others have applauded him as a social visionary. The theories and methods developed by Skinner have permeated psychology. Behaviorist-inspired techniques vie with traditional psychotherapy for primacy in the treatment of various psychological disorders. The techniques of reinforcement, or controlling the consequences that follow behavior, have become increasingly popular in education, and Skinner's teaching machine was the forerunner of modern programmed education. Moreover, a vast number of today's psychologists use Skinner's research methods to obtain precise findings in their laboratory experiments (Herrnstein, 1977).

As we have seen, psychology has expanded from an infant discipline characterized by a focus on conscious experience to a vast modern science that embraces the study of all behavior. This brief survey is far from comprehensive, touching as it does on only a few of the most important contributions to the scope, substances, and methods of psychological investigation. A look at the practice of psychology today will give some further idea of the field's expansion.

PSYCHOLOGY TODAY

Psychology's roots can be traced back to ancient Greece and to speculations about the nature of sensation, perception, reason, emotion, dreams, and memory (Klein, 1970). Developments in many countries over many years have contributed to the modern science of psychology, which now flourishes around the world: in Germany, where Wundt established his laboratory; in England, where Galton worked; in Russia, where Pavlov discovered the conditioned reflex; in Japan, where the discipline is still relatively new; and in numerous other countries.

Psychology has gained wide public acceptance in the United States, and this support has encouraged the broad scope of research and study in the field. Of the estimated 260,000 psychologists in the world, about 102,000 live in the United States. And the rapid growth of American psychology has been matched by a similar growth in psychology around the world. While American psychology still dominates the world scene, several other countries have proportionately as many psychologists as the United States, where there are 300 psychologists for each million inhabitants. These countries are all Western industrialized societies; they include Spain, Finland, Israel, the Netherlands, Belgium, and Denmark (Rosenzweig, 1984). One way to grasp the discipline's present diversity is to look at the major fields of specialization in which American psychologists engage.

Fields of Specialization

The national professional organization for psychologists, the American Psychological Association (APA), was founded in 1892 to advance the science of psychology by encouraging research, increasing professional competence, and disseminating psychological knowledge (APA, 1981). In 1985, the APA had more than 64,000 members, most of whom belonged to one or more of forty specialized divisions. Twenty-four of these divisions have more than 1,000 members, and their relative sizes are shown in Figure 1.2. Some members belong to several divisions, but the list gives an idea of the variety of psychologists' interests. The following brief descriptions of problems and research taken from some of the major specialties further indicate the diversity of concerns among psychologists, whose interests run from the firing of a single brain cell to the formulation of public policies.

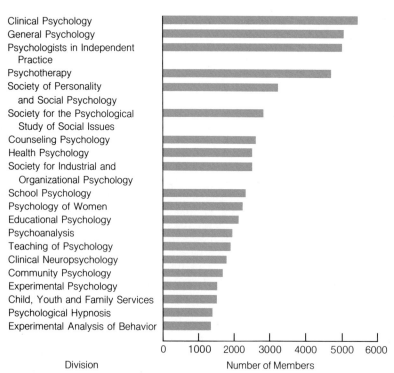

Figure 1.2. Membership in the twenty largest divisions of the American Psychological Association's forty-four divisions in 1985. Note that a psychologist may be a member of more than one division. Members of the psychotherapy division may also be members of the health psychology division and/or the clinical psychology division.

Experimental and Physiological Psychology

Have you ever been trying to read an article assigned by your economics instructor and been distracted when your roommate tuned in a radio talk show? Caught in this common but annoying situation, most of us find it impossible to follow the article we had been reading. We either request that the offending program be turned off, leave the room to read elsewhere, or put aside the assigned article. Nobody, we say, can do two things at the same time. Yet experimental psychologists have trained students to read and understand stories while at the same time they copied dictated sentences, which they also understood—showing that it *is* possible to do two things at once (Hirst, Neisser, and Spelke, 1978). The skill was difficult to master, and the students required a number of training periods before they could follow both trains of thought. And such divided attention has been displayed outside the laboratory: air traffic controllers and simultaneous translators at the United Nations could not handle their jobs unless they had some mastery of divided attention.

Divided attention is only one concern of **experi-** **mental psychology**, which investigates basic behavioral processes that are shared by various species. Although experimental psychologists generally use laboratory experiments to pursue their study, it is not the use of the controlled experiment alone that distinguishes psychologists who pursue this specialty; rather, it is the basic nature of the process studied, which may be sensation, perception, learning, memory, problem solving, communication, emotion, or motivation.

Experimental psychologists have sought answers to such questions as: What is the basis for the love between mother and baby? Can animals reason (see Figure 1.3)? What is the role of the brain in memory? How do visual experiences during infancy affect later vision? Not all experimental psychologists study human beings. Some work with rats; others use mice, kittens, monkeys, or even octopuses to study such questions.

Psychologists study animal behavior for a number of reasons. Some psychologists are simply interested in learning more about the behavior of a particular species; in zoos, for example, a knowledge of animal behavior helps keep animals healthy and aids breeding programs aimed at preserving endangered species. Other psycholo-

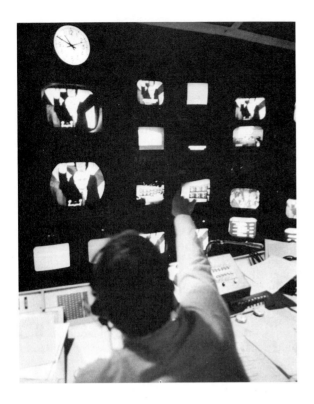

Experimental psychologists have shown that the ability to divide our attention among several different stimuli —as in this television control room—is a skill that can be learned.

gists are interested in how species are interrelated and in the evolutionary significance of certain behavior. As we will see in Chapter 4, any animal's behavior determines whether it will survive in a given environment, and this relationship between an animal's behavior and its environment is important in the species' evolution. Still other psychologists study the behavior of animals to learn more about human behavior. For example, the discussion in Chapter 17 shows how a baby's love for her or his mother has been explored by raising rhesus monkeys in different ways (Harlow and Harlow, 1966). Similarly, research with rats has helped explain the strong connections we make between food and illness. For example, most of us have at some time eaten an unusual food, say lobster thermidor, and then become nauseated. But some people find they can never again eat the dish that they believe made them ill. The sight or even the thought of a lobster shell filled with

Figure 1.3. Do animals think?

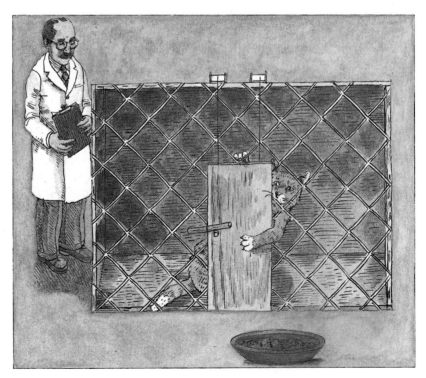

chunks of lobster meat in a rich, sherry-flavored sauce makes their stomachs churn. John Garcia's (Garcia and Koelling, 1966) experiments with rats have shown that these rodents learn similar associations—indeed, that making the connection helps the species to survive—and that learning is a more complicated phenomenon than Pavlov's experiments with dogs had led psychologists to believe.

Recently, a group of experimental psychologists has become increasingly interested in an interrelated set of problems concerning the human mind. These problems, which fall in the domain of "cognitive science," range all the way from the psychology of language (a uniquely human capacity) to questions centering around computers, such as the possibility of artificial intelligence. For example, some experimental psychologists are trying to program robots to identify objects in their environment, in the hope of creating the machine equivalent of vision.

Other experimental psychologists focus on the underlying physical basis of behavior. Researchers in the fields of **physiological psychology** or **neuropsychology** attempt to untangle the connections between the nervous and endocrine systems and behavior. There has been a recent explosion of interest in the way that the brain works. The researchers in this area, which is called **neuroscience**, investigate the workings of sensory systems, the effects of brain damage on behavior, and the effects of various brain chemicals on psychological phenomena such as memory, pain, and motivation.

Most experimental and physiological psychologists work in academic settings, where the freedom of inquiry allows basic research, which aims to advance knowledge, to flourish. However, most experimental psychologists nowadays receive special training in mathematics and computer sciences, and the rapidly growing computer industry has been hiring many holders of advanced degrees in psychology. Psychologists who specialize in **psychopharmacology**, studying the relationship between drugs and behavior, sometimes work in industry as well. Many are employed by pharmaceutical companies to assess the psychological effects of drugs. Other psychopharmacologists explore the connection between psychopharmacology and various mental disorders. Much of this research takes place in basic and medical research laboratories; it is directed at identifying drugs that affect specific receptors in the brain—

receptors that may be involved in such problems as pain, anxiety, depression, memory loss, and schizophrenia.

Developmental Psychology

As children pass from infancy to childhood, their understanding of the world expands enormously. One task a child must master is that of understanding that other people do not see precisely what he or she sees. This growth in the realization that the world is made up of many people, with their own viewpoints, thoughts, and feelings, has been studied extensively by developmental psychologists. One aspect of this development was demonstrated when a developmental psychologist sat at a table with a child and together they looked at white cards. Either the child, the experimenter, or both wore colored glasses; the psychologist's glasses had yellow lenses, the child's had green lenses. About half the three-year-olds always predicted that the experimenter saw the card as they did—green or white—but six-year-olds always predicted exactly how the card would appear to the psychologist (Liben, 1978).

The work of developmental psychology is not confined to the study of children. All aspects of behavioral development over the entire life span are the concern of **developmental psychology**. Every psychological concept—learning, memory, motivation, perception, personality, thinking, and so on—can be examined from the standpoint of its change and development through life. Some developmental psychologists specialize in studying the capabilities of the newborn infant. Others concern themselves with the development of these capabilities in the child, and still others focus on changes through adulthood. There has been increasing interest in the developmental tasks connected with aging, and the past decade has seen the rapid growth of a life-span developmental psychology, which focuses on age-related behavioral change from birth to death (Goulet and Baltes, 1970).

As we shall see in Chapters 14, 15, 16, and 17, the questions posed by developmental psychologists cover a range of topics as broad as psychology itself. How soon can babies perceive depth? Why are the sleep patterns of infants so different from those of adults? How do children develop a concept of self? Is the acquisition of language simply a matter of biological maturation, is it the result of learning, or does it grow out of social interaction?

One bad experience with escargots, and we may never want to eat them again. Experiments with animals have suggested that this aversion to foods that have made us ill has probably had survival value for our species.

And why do all normal children accomplish such a difficult task with seeming ease? How do genes and learning interact in the development of psychological differences between boys and girls? Is the development of conscience dependent upon the way parents discipline a child? How does sexual maturation affect the self-esteem of adolescents? Why do people differ in intelligence quotient (IQ) scores? Is a person's degree of masculinity or femininity stable, or does it change in various phases of life? How does aging affect memory and problem solving? And how do people come to terms with death?

Developmental psychologists work in a wide variety of settings: as consultants to children's television programs; in federal programs such as Head Start; in private practice; in institutions, where they may do psychotherapy with emotional-ly disturbed children; in industry, where they may try to determine how an employee's attitude to work changes with age; and in schools, where they may work with children who have learning problems. Most of them, however, work in university settings conducting research on developmental processes.

Personality Psychology

Some people are highly competitive, hostile when thwarted, and behave as if they were always racing the clock. This pattern of behavior, called Type A, is associated with the development of heart disease, even when such traditional predictors as family history, smoking, high blood pressure, and high cholesterol levels are controlled. Type A people seem to have a strong need to maintain control in stressful situations (Glass, 1977). Although Type A people are often quite productive and frequently outperform Type B people, who tend to be relaxed and who do not feel the continual pressure of time, in some situations the Type A personality pattern can lead to trouble. In one experiment (Brunson and Matthews, 1981) people with Type A and Type B personalities were asked to solve various problems and to think out loud as they worked at the solutions. After the subjects had solved several of the problems, the experimenters gave both groups a series of insolvable problems. By the time the fourth insolvable problem had been presented, the subjects with Type A personalities were frustrated and annoyed, saying that the task was too hard and they lacked the ability to handle it. They seemed to give up, sticking with the same incorrect answer despite the fact they had been told it was wrong. Type B subjects, on the other hand, were unhappy and bored when given the series of insolvable problems, but they continued trying to find a solution and seemed optimistic about their eventual success.

This study of the relation between personality and behavior is an example of research in **personality psychology**, a field in which individual differences in behavior are studied. Such differences reflect the fact that not all people react the same way in the same situation, and personality psychologists attempt to explain why this is so. They also try to discover why people tend to behave in a fairly consistent manner in various situations. It is this combination of differences among individuals and consistency within individuals that creates personality, so that each of us is known for having a specific set of characteristics, our own ways of behaving, of getting along in the world, and of interacting with others.

As Chapter 17 indicates, personality psychologists are interested in how personality develops, whether it changes over time, and if so, how. They want to know whether individual traits and temperament are inherited or the product of the environment. Personality psychologists explore individual differences in aggression, compassion, obedience to authority, sociability, independence, and adherence to ethical codes. From such investigations have come various theories of personality, which are discussed in Chapters 18 and 19, and explanations for different ways of adjusting to life's stresses, which are discussed in Chapter 21.

Most personality psychologists work in academic settings. However, some who specialize in the assessment of personality work in psychiatric hospitals, where they diagnose patients, or in industry, where they assist in personnel selection.

Social Psychology

Human life is primarily social; in fact, the human being has been called the "social animal" (Aronson, 1972). In today's society one effect of living in groups is exposure to mass media—including the ever-present television. Widespread public concern has arisen over the possibility that watching violence on television causes children to become aggressive and violent themselves. Many experiments by psychologists indicate that when children watch aggressive acts on film or television, they may imitate the violence they have seen if an appropriate situation arises in the laboratory shortly afterward. Other studies have found a small but consistent relationship between watching violent television and later aggression in daily life. As yet, however, there is little evidence to show that TV violence *causes* aggressive behavior in children or adolescents (Freedman, 1984). Instead, children who are already aggressive seem to seek out violent television programs. But television can teach new ways of behaving aggressively, as when a film or TV program portraying an unusually violent act is followed by a rash of the same pattern of violent behavior. Attempts to assess the connection between violence in the mass media and aggressive behavior are typical of the sort of research done in the field of **social psychology**, which is concerned with the behavior of

people in groups. Social psychologists are especially interested in the influence of other people on the individual.

Each of us is enmeshed in a network of social relationships with people we encounter at work, at school, in the neighborhood, and within our family. Social psychologists study the ways in which these relationships develop. They want to know who likes whom—and why. They are interested in the attitudes that people have toward social issues and in the way those attitudes are formed and changed by society. They also want to know how those attitudes affect our thought processes. For example, in one study (Judd and Kulik, 1980) college students read statements on women's rights, capital punishment, and majority rule in South Africa and indicated whether they agreed or disagreed with them. The next day the students were asked to write out as many of the statements (such as "The Equal Rights Amendment should be supported by all who believe that discrimination is wrong" and "Majority rule would only complicate the lives of most South Africans") as they could. Students judged statements more rapidly and remembered them better when they either were highly consistent with their own attitudes or clashed violently with them, indicating that our social attitudes affect how rapidly we think and how well we remember certain types of information.

Social psychology has become an extremely wide-ranging field of psychology. Among the topics studied are friendship formation, romantic attraction, perception of other people, social influence, behavior in groups, bargaining, and conflict (see Chapters 25 through 27), with psychologists always searching for the way these aspects of life are affected by the situation—and especially by what others do or say. Social psychologists are particularly interested in the relevance of their research to society; in 1936 they founded the Society for the Psychological Study of Social Issues, which focuses on human problems in the group, the community, the nation, and the world.

Social psychologists generally work in academic settings, but not always in the psychology department. Some social psychologists who are interested in group processes and decision making can be found in schools of business, and others work in industry. The rising interest in applying social psychology to concrete problems has attracted social psychologists into political and legal settings and the health fields.

Educational and School Psychology

Since in many colleges and universities student evaluation of instructors plays a part in determining faculty salaries and promotions, it is important to discover the basis for students' judgments. In one study (Naftulin, Ware, and Donnelly, 1973), adults enrolled in a course were asked to judge the teaching ability of a guest instructor, who was actually an actor. The actor delivered his lecture in a fascinating manner, but its content was garbled, self-contradictory, illogical, and full of non sequiturs and nonsense words. Yet these adult students, who were psychologists, psychiatrists, social workers, and educators, rated the bogus instructor as a highly capable teacher. The teacher's lack of knowledge and absence of scholarly ability had no effect on the ratings, supporting the proposition advanced by other psychologists (Kulik and McKeachie, 1975) that students judge teachers, not on their mastery of the subject, but simply on how well they talk.

Student evaluation of teachers is only one concern of **educational psychology**, which investigates all the psychological aspects of the learning process. At just one professional conference, educational psychologists presented research on creative thinking in fifth graders, gender differences in mathematical ability, television's effect on study habits, anxiety in education, teachers' effects on students' behavior, the identification of gifted children, attention in learning-disabled children, and a host of other topics. Most educational psychologists work in colleges or universities, where they conduct research and train teachers and psychologists. A few work on curriculum development, materials, and procedures for schools, and in government agencies, business, and the military.

Educational psychology differs considerably from **school psychology**. Most school psychologists work in elementary and secondary schools, where they assess children with learning or emotional problems and work out ways for parents and teachers to help them. School psychologists also administer personality, intelligence, and achievement tests in the schools.

Industrial and Organizational Psychology

In most areas of life, physical attractiveness is an asset, but when it comes to getting a job, it can be a hindrance—if you're a woman. When people rated job applications for vacancies in an insurance firm, attractive women who applied for managerial jobs were discriminated against in ratings of their qualifications, decisions to hire them, and starting salaries. In addition, the more attractive the woman, the more stereotypically feminine she seemed to the raters. On applications showing similar backgrounds, qualifications, and interests, unattractive women and attractive men did much better than attractive women, receiving

Industrial psychologists would be interested in knowing the ways in which a country club setting influences workers. Does productivity increase, or are there negative side effects that accompany such a tempting environment?

higher ratings and generally being recommended for the position. When the application was for a clerical job, attractiveness paid off for both men and women, with attractive applicants of either sex consistently rated higher than unattractive applicants (Heilman and Saruwatari, 1979).

The workings of personnel departments and the factors that influence job selection are among the topics considered in **industrial psychology** and **organizational psychology**, in which the relationship between people and their jobs is studied. Work occupies a large part of our waking hours, and psychologists have given increasing attention to the conditions and effects of employment. They investigate employee morale, job-related stress, the qualities that make a good boss, how to enrich jobs, and ways to make working hours more flexible. In **human-factors psychology** the psychologists consider the purpose of a particular machine or environment and the capabilities of the probable user, then devise the most convenient, comfortable, and efficient design that matches the two.

Less than half of all organizational and industrial psychologists are found in colleges or universities; the majority work in business or industry, in government agencies, or as consultants to business or government. Some of these psychologists practice **personnel psychology**; they screen job applicants, evaluate job performance, and recommend employees for promotion. Other industrial and organizational psychologists specialize in **consumer psychology**, studying the preferences, buying habits, and responses to advertising of consumers. Such psychologists might, for example, study ways to persuade people to conserve energy, advise on the design of a new container for salad dressing, or conduct surveys to determine the market for a new product. We discuss many topics in industrial and organizational psychology in Chapter 28.

Clinical Psychology

Depressed people are often pessimistic. They feel lonely, guilty, and bored, and see no hope that their condition will get better. In fact, their friends and relatives sometimes say that if depressed individuals took a more optimistic view of life, they would soon get better. Researchers have found, however, that much of the pessimism of depressed people is realistic (Lewinsohn et al., 1980). In this study a group of depressed individuals and two

groups of "normal" people took part in a series of social interactions. Afterward, the subjects were asked (1) how positively or negatively they had reacted to the others; and (2) how positively or negatively they thought the others had reacted to them. The "normal" individuals tended to believe that they had made more positive impressions on others than they actually had, but the depressed individuals tended to rate the impressions they had made fairly accurately. Their results led the researchers to conclude, "To feel good about ourselves we may have to judge ourselves more kindly than we are judged" (Lewinsohn et al., 1980, p. 212).

The study, diagnosis, and treatment of abnormal behavior is the province of **clinical psychology**. About half of all clinical psychologists work in hospitals or clinics or have private practices. Clinical psychologists have developed diverse ways of treating various disorders. In studying the basis of any disorder, they look for possible biological, biochemical, educational, and environmental causes.

Some clinical psychologists who practice **community psychology** have the primary aim of preventing mental disorders. Their ultimate goal is to change the aspects of the environment that lead to disorder; they can be found in outpatient clinics, advising community workers on how to handle psychological problems, staffing emergency services, and supervising halfway houses and hot lines.

Emerging Specialties

As the field of psychology develops and our knowledge of human behavior broadens, psychology is applied to new areas of human life. Some psychologists have begun to specialize in **health psychology**, or **behavioral medicine**, the branch of psychology that deals with how people stay healthy, why they become ill, and how they react when they are ill. Health psychology's aim is to understand the relationship between the mind and the individual's physical condition. The role of emotional stress in heart disease and ulcers is widely known, but only within the past few years has the effect of psychological factors in other diseases—from colds to cancer—been suspected. Among the issues that concern health psychologists are attitudes toward health, the possibility of community campaigns to change attitudes and behavior, the

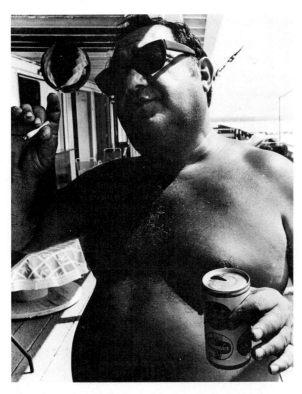

Identifying the psychological factors that may lead some people to overeat or drink too much is one concern of health psychologists.

role of social support in the treatment of illness, and the prevention of health problems via changes in lifestyle such as weight control programs, smoking cessation programs, and increased exercise.

Another new field of specialization is **environmental psychology**, the study of the relationship between people and their physical settings. As human beings live in the world, they modify their environment, but they are also modified by that environment. Environmental psychologists investigate such influence, studying such problems as the effects on city dwellers of crowding, noise, or the perception of danger. Some environmental psychologists explore the effects of building design upon social interaction or the quality of life. In one such study (Holahan, 1982), environmental psychologists investigated the feelings of university students about their living conditions. They found that students who lived in high-rise dormitories were much more dissatisfied with their living quarters than were students who lived in low-rise

dormitories, and that students who lived on the higher floors in the high-rise buildings were the most dissatisfied of all. Apparently, other students found the higher floors of these dormitories relatively inaccessible, so they tended to stay away, making it more difficult for students who lived on these floors to meet people and to make friends.

A third emerging field is that of **forensic psychology**, whose practitioners apply psychological principles to the problems of law enforcement and the courts. Many forensic psychologists are found in psychology or specialized law programs in academic settings, where they research problems concerning eyewitness testimony, jury selection, the process of jury decision, and the testimony of expert witnesses (Loftus, 1979; Pennington and Hastie, 1981). Some forensic psychologists work in community mental health centers, where they consult with the police, the courts, and prison officials. Others work in police departments, where their duties run from screening recruits and training officers in how to handle family quarrels, crowds, suicide threats, and hostage crises to helping officers who have emotional problems and assisting in the investigation of crimes. The assistance of forensic psychologists in criminal investigations may involve using clues to construct personality profiles of probable criminals or hypnotizing defendants, victims, or eyewitnesses to enhance their memory, as discussed in Chapter 7. (Although hypnosis is generally accepted as an investigative technique, the results are not always reliable and most courts refuse to accept information gained in this way as evidence.) Some forensic psychologists work in prisons, where they provide counseling and psychotherapy to inmates.

A fourth field of specialization that has recently developed is **program evaluation** and policy research, in which psychologists evaluate the effectiveness and cost of government programs meant to alleviate social problems. Such evaluation can help to prevent waste and make sure that programs are actually moving a community toward specific goals. Psychologists' training in experimental methods enables them to measure and compare the factors that affect a particular program and the results they lead to. Although economists, political scientists, and sociologists are also involved in the evaluation of programs and policies, many psychologists—including those who practice **quantitative psychology**, which specializes in measurements and statistics—are engaged in evaluating programs for the Congressional Bud-

Extrasensory perception

Have you ever thought about a distant friend and then found a letter from that person waiting in your mailbox? When this happens, many people swear that it is an instance of **extrasensory perception (ESP)**—knowledge about the environment that does not arrive through a known sensory channel. In truth, the connection between your thoughts and the letter is probably accidental; you have undoubtedly thought of your friend on several other occasions without receiving a letter and have forgotten those occasions—while this one stands out in your mind. Some psychologists, however, are convinced that extrasensory abilities exist. Their efforts to study ESP fall in the domain of **parapsychology** ("beyond psychology").

Parapsychologists divide ESP into three forms: telepathy, precognition, and clairvoyance. In telepathy, or mind-reading, thought is transferred from one person to another without being overtly communicated via speaking or writing. Precognition refers to the ability to see the future. And clairvoyance involves the knowledge of events not detectable by normal senses. A clairvoyant person could, for example, sense the suit and number of a playing card sealed in an envelope; a telepathic person could "read" the suit and number by sensing the thoughts in someone's mind. Yet another phenomenon related to ESP is psychokinesis (PK), the ability to move objects without touching them.

The basic question is whether ESP and PK actually exist. Many scientists believe they do not exist, and that any reported incidents can be explained by natural laws, coincidence, or trickery. But some scientists remain undecided. They are willing to concede that ESP and PK *may* exist—they simply point out that no one has yet proved that they do.

EXPLANATIONS OF ESP

Many events that are reported as instances of ESP can be explained without resorting to parapsychology. For example, married couples often swear that on occasion they read each other's thoughts. How is this possible? People who live together for years have a store of common memories. When both people think of the same topic simultaneously, the coincidence is probably due to some barely noticed sight, sound, or smell that triggers the same memory in both minds. Watching a TV drama, they might see a car resembling one owned by friends, so that when the wife says, "We ought to ask Susan and Michael over this weekend," the husband says (with good reason), "I was just thinking about them." When we try to account for apparent instances of ESP and PK, we should search for the simplest possible explanation.

Explanations that contradict the basic principles of science will also be greeted with skepticism by most scientists. For example, the neuropsychologist Donald Hebb (1974) writes that while telepathy is not inconceivable, believers violate basic scientific

get Office and the General Accounting Office of the federal government; others evaluate programs in the field of education. The increasing need to make every dollar count is bringing program evaluations into the fields of health care, employment, transportation, energy conservation, and criminal rehabilitation.

Psychology: Basic and Applied Science

This look at major fields of specialization makes it plain that psychology is both a basic and an applied science. In **basic science**, knowledge is acquired for its own sake to advance our under-standing of the nature of things; the potential usefulness of the knowledge gained is not a consideration. In **applied science**, findings from basic science are used to accomplish practical goals. Most biologists and physicists, for example, practice basic science; most physicians and engineers practice applied science. Psychologists may practice either—or both. Some psychologists who do basic research study a particular topic because they are aware that any knowledge gained will be relevant to practical problems. A developmental psychologist who studies the ability of infants to perceive patterns is doing basic research. His purpose has nothing to do with the design of crib toys, but if his findings are applied by a psycholo-

laws when they say that distance makes no difference in the transmission of thoughts. In the same way, precognition violates what scientists know about time: so far, there is no scientific explanation for how someone could jump ahead to see the future and then jump back to tell about it. Psychokinesis violates what scientists know about space, since there are no known ways that an individual could move an object by sheer force of thought.

Moreover, before we attempt to explain incidents of ESP and PK, we must be able to validate their occurrence. Most apparent events involving ESP or PK have few witnesses, and verification is virtually impossible after the event. Researchers have also had difficulty verifying ESP and PK in the laboratory.

THE PROBLEM OF SCIENTIFIC VALIDATION

Scientific investigations into the existence of ESP and PK have been conducted in the United States since the early 1900s. Joseph B. Rhine, the best-known researcher in the area, tried to use scientific methodology to prove the existence of ESP. For example, Rhine tested people for telepathic abilities by having a "sender" focus on each card in a special deck, one at a time. A "receiver," locked in a distant room, stated which card he thought the sender had turned up and was thinking about. Studies of this sort produced mixed results: some researchers found subjects who could correctly identify more cards than would be expected on the basis of chance, but other researchers could not find any subjects able to do this. Ultimately, Rhine (1974) expressed his own doubts that telepathy could be verified through acceptable scientific procedures, although he never doubted the existence of the phenomenon.

Most scientists do not accept the results of experiments that support ESP or PK, because these findings can rarely be repeated. A basic principle of scientific research is that one scientist should be able to repeat another scientist's experiment and obtain the same results. But experiments in this area have yielded contradictory findings, an indication that the experiments may not have been carefully designed. In some cases the researcher may not have eliminated all the nonpsychic ways that information could be passed to the subject. In other studies the researcher may have failed to consider his or her own influence on the subject.

In still other cases, the problems of design seem to have been related to the apparent fragility of ESP and PK. An individual who seems to show ESP or PK on one day will be unable to demonstrate the ability on the next day. Does this mean the first test results are invalid? Believers in ESP and PK argue that such research cannot be consistently repeated because these abilities demand a friendly atmosphere for their emergence—but that the test results may still be valid. Critics disagree. The instability, they say, may simply show that the earlier study was improperly designed. Or the earlier results may simply have been the result of chance; even the most unlikely event, whether it is throwing "heads" a thousand times in a row or winning a million-dollar lottery, is statistically possible.

gist in her job as a consultant to a toy manufacturer, the science becomes applied. Similarly, a social psychologist who studies the friendships among a group of office workers—who likes whom, how much, and why—is doing basic science. If she discovers that one member of the group has no friends at all and another has so many friends he hardly has time to work, the psychologist might try to understand and explain the situation, but she would not try to alter it. She would leave that to a clinical or industrial psychologist who practices applied psychology.

The use of basic research findings in applied science is relatively common. For instance, psychologists who have studied the learning process in animals have discovered that involuntary responses (such as salivation or eye-blinks) can result from one kind of learning, but that voluntary responses (such as pressing a lever) can result from another kind of learning (see Chapter 8). Recently, other psychologists have extended this basic research and discovered that many involuntary responses (skin temperature, muscle tension) could be brought under voluntary control through the process of biofeedback (see Chapter 7). Useful applications have resulted: for example, individuals with tension headaches have learned to reduce their discomfort by controlling muscle tension, and individuals with spinal-cord injuries have learned to retrain their muscles.

Sometimes the process works in the opposite direction, too. Students interested in applications of psychological knowledge may eventually find themselves developing an interest in psychology as a basic science. For example, a student who has an alcoholic parent may become interested in the process by which any individual becomes addicted to any substance. A student who wants to find more efficient ways of studying may become intrigued by the way memories are organized in the brain. And a student who is struggling with an unwanted ten pounds may decide to investigate the ways cues in the environment affect not only eating behavior but other behavior as well.

PSYCHOLOGY AS A VOCATION

Some students find they have more than a casual interest in psychology and wonder about a possible vocation in the field. As we have seen, psychology is practiced by men and women in a number of professions, and various professions have different educational requirements.

Whether they are engaged in basic research to uncover fundamental laws of behavior, in applied research to solve specific problems, or in providing counseling and therapy to people suffering from psychological problems, the majority of psychologists have earned a PhD in the discipline of psychology. To earn a PhD, a psychologist must complete a four- to six-year graduate program in a department of psychology at a university. Typically, this program includes broad exposure to the theories and findings of psychology, a special focus on a subdiscipline (e.g., developmental or social psychology), and extensive training in research methods. Each PhD candidate must complete an original research project of fairly wide scope, under the direction of experienced researchers on the graduate faculty, and must then submit the findings as a doctoral dissertation.

Students who want to become clinical or counseling psychologists must either meet the requirements for the PhD or enroll in a professional school of psychology (which may or may not be associated with a university), where they must meet the requirements for a PsyD (doctor of psychology), a degree that places more emphasis on

Table 1.1 ■ Full-Time Employment Setting for Selected Subfields at the Doctoral Level: APA Members with Full-Time Positions

Selected Subfields	Employment Setting									
	University		Four-Year College		Medical School		Other Academic		Schools and Other Educational	
	N	(%)	N	(%)	N	(%)	N	(%)	N	(%)
Clinical	910	(9.8)	149	(1.6)	540	(5.8)	66	(0.7)	123	(1.3)
Counseling	658	(27.2)	122	(5.0)	22	(0.9)	66	(2.7)	116	(4.8)
Developmental	515	(57.4)	114	(12.7)	48	(5.3)	22	(2.5)	15	(1.6)
Educational	608	(58.5)	99	(9.5)	26	(2.5)	51	(4.9)	104	(10.0)
Experimental	549	(55.3)	120	(12.1)	19	(1.9)	19	(1.9)	0	(0.0)
Industrial/ Organizational	409	(27.0)	47	(3.1)	0	(0.0)	0	(0.0)	0	(0.0)
Schools	148	(18.9)	16	(2.0)	1	(0.1)	0	(0.0)	497	(63.5)
Social	680	(59.5)	196	(17.2)	40	(3.5)	25	(2.2)	0	(0.0)
Other Subfields Not Listed	1,171	(36.5)	307	(9.6)	237	(7.4)	116	(3.6)	21	(0.7)
All Subfields	5,647	(26.5)	1,171	(5.5)	932	(4.4)	366	(1.7)	876	(4.1)

Note: Row percentages are given. The application of fractional weights and rounding may result in total percentages and *N*s that differ slightly from the sums of subgroup percentages and *N*s. In each case, *N*s have been rounded to the nearest whole respondent.

Source: From Stapp, J., and R. Fulcher. The employment of APA members: 1982. *American Psychologist*, 1983, *38*, 1298–1320. Table 1 appears on page 1309.

application and less on research. Clinical psychologists also complete specialized training in diagnosis and psychotherapy as well as a year of training at an institution that has an internship program. (See Chapter 24 for the relationship between clinical psychology and other mental health professions.)

In recent years, the employment outlook for psychologists with doctoral degrees has been relatively good. According to a survey of psychologists conducted by the American Psychological Association, fewer than 1 percent of psychologists with PhDs were unemployed and seeking employment in 1982 (see Table 1.1). Over one third of all psychologists were employed in higher education; most of the rest worked in business, government, hospitals, or other institutional settings. Since that time, the proportion of psychologists (particularly clinical and counseling psychologists) in independent practice has increased substantially.

Many students are interested in psychology but do not want graduate training. In the last decade or so psychology has become one of the most popular majors in the college curriculum, chosen by thousands of students who have no intention of completing a graduate degree. According to the National Center for Education Statistics, although only 2,780 doctorate degrees in psychology were awarded in 1982, 41,031 bachelor's degrees were awarded. To a considerable extent, psychology has become a general major, like English or history —intriguing, informative, and a useful basis for many careers and interests.

LOOKING AHEAD

Reading this book and taking an introductory psychology course will not make you a psychological researcher or qualify you to conduct psychotherapy. But you will learn a good deal about the ways in which biological, environmental, and psychological factors shape human behavior.

This introduction to the study of behavior will acquaint you in Chapter 2 with the methods psychologists use in research. Part Two explores the role of the brain in behavior and the role of our genetic inheritance; it also delves into sensation,

| Employment Setting | | | | | | | | | | | | | |
| Independent Practice | | Hospital | | Clinic | | Other Human Service | | Business, Government, and Other | | Not Specified | | Total | |
N	(%)	N	(%)	N	(%)	N	(%)	N	(%)	N	(%)	N (100%)	
2,888	(31.1)	1,894	(20.4)	1,319	(14.2)	482	(5.2)	798	(8.6)	115	(1.2)	9,284	
337	(13.9)	226	(9.3)	174	(7.2)	447	(18.5)	217	(9.0)	33	(1.4)	2,418	
26	(2.9)	25	(2.8)	16	(1.7)	41	(4.6)	69	(7.7)	7	(0.8)	897	
5	(0.4)	2	(0.2)	5	(0.4)	46	(4.4)	95	(9.1)	0	(0.0)	1,041	
5	(0.5)	23	(2.3)	0	(0.0)	0	(0.0)	250	(25.2)	7	(0.7)	992	
20	(1.3)	5	(0.3)	5	(0.3)	14	(1.0)	1,013	(66.9)	1	(0.1)	1,514	
23	(2.9)	2	(0.3)	29	(3.7)	14	(1.8)	44	(5.6)	9	(1.2)	784	
10	(0.9)	6	(0.5)	7	(0.6)	13	(1.1)	160	(14.0)	5	(0.4)	1,143	
56	(1.8)	155	(4.8)	209	(6.5)	154	(4.8)	743	(23.2)	35	(1.1)	3,204	
3,369	(15.8)	2,338	(11.0)	1,763	(8.3)	1,213	(5.7)	3,389	(15.9)	212	(1.0)	21,277	

perception, and the varieties of consciousness. Part Three considers the basic aspects of behavior, with special emphasis on learning, memory, and problem solving. Part Four investigates motivation, emotion, and sexuality. Part Five traces human development in all its complexity: physical, cognitive, and language development, and the foundations of personality and social behavior. Part Six describes theories of personality and the assessment of personality and intelligence. Adjustment, behavior disorders, and approaches to treatment are the subjects of Part Seven. Finally, in Part Eight, we look at social behavior, discovering what psychology can tell us about, and do for, society.

This book may sharpen your taste for further exploration in psychology. If you choose to go on in the field, it should provide a solid foundation for future studies. If your interest remains casual, this text should at least enrich and augment your understanding of some of the forces that influence your life.

SUMMARY

1. Although the field of **psychology** has changed and broadened over the past century, it is still best defined as the study of behavior, provided that **behavior** is understood to include thoughts, feelings, and dreams—anything a person does or experiences. Psychologists study every aspect of human behavior from conception to death.

2. Psychology broke away from philosophy and physiology in 1879 when Wundt founded the first psychological laboratory in Leipzig, Germany. Wundt defined psychology as the study of conscious experience. To Freud, unconscious processes were also an important area of study, and he used the **free associations** of his patients to get to underlying unconscious experiences. The study of individual differences was added to psychology by Galton. He invented the forebears of modern personality and intelligence tests and devised statistical techniques that are still used today. With the research of Pavlov, a Russian physiologist, psychology became the study of observable behavior and the role of learning came to dominate the discipline. **Behaviorism**, the study of observable and measurable responses to specific stimuli, was founded by Watson, an American psychologist. Skinner refined and popularized behaviorism, narrowing its predictive claims and broadening its social implications.

3. The major fields of specialization indicate the broad range of psychologists' interests. **Experimental psychologists** investigate basic behavioral processes shared by various species, using controlled experiments to investigate the nature of sensation, perception, learning, memory, problem solving, communication, emotion, or motivation. Experimental psychologists who attempt to untangle the connections between the nervous and endocrine systems and behavior are called **physiological psychologists** or **neuropsychologists**. Experimental psychologists who study the relationship between drugs and behavior are known as **psychopharmacologists**. **Developmental psychologists** study all aspects of behavioral development over the entire life span. **Personality psychologists** study the relation between individual attitudes and behavior. **Social psychologists** study the behavior of people in groups, paying special attention to the influence of other people. **Educational psychologists** investigate all the psychological aspects of the learning process, while **school psychologists** work with children who have learning or emotional problems and administer personality, intelligence, and achievement tests. **Industrial psychologists** and **organizational psychologists** study the relationship between people and their jobs. Some of these psychologists, called **human-factors psychologists**, design machines or environments that match the capabilities of their users; others, called **personnel psychologists**, screen job applicants, evaluate job performance, and recommend employees for promotion. Other industrial and organizational psychologists specialize in **consumer psychology**, studying the preferences, buying habits, and responses to advertising of consumers. **Clinical psychologists** are engaged in the study, diagnosis, and treatment of abnormal behavior. Some clinical psychologists, known as **commu-**

nity psychologists, aim at preventing mental disorders; they are found in the community, at outpatient clinics, emergency services, halfway houses, and hot lines. Other clinical psychologists, known as **health psychologists**, focus on preventing and treating diseases that involve psychological factors. **Environmental psychologists** study the relationship between people and their physical settings. **Forensic psychologists** apply psychological principles to the problems of law enforcement and the courts. **Program evaluators** and **quantitative psychologists** assess the effectiveness and cost of government programs meant to alleviate social problems.

4. In **basic science**, knowledge is acquired for its own sake to advance our understanding of the nature of things; its usefulness is never a consideration. In **applied science**, findings from basic science are used to accomplish practical goals. Psychology is both a basic and an applied science.

5. Most psychologists have a PhD in psychology, which requires completion of a four- to six-year graduate program in psychology at a university, including a dissertation based on an original research project. Clinical or counseling psychologists may complete a PhD or enroll in an internship program.

KEY TERMS

applied science
basic science
behavior
behavioral medicine
behaviorism
clinical psychology
community psychology
consumer psychology
developmental psychology
educational psychology

environmental psychology
experimental psychology
extrasensory perception (ESP)
free association
forensic psychology
health psychology
human-factors psychology
industrial psychology
neuropsychology
neuroscience
organizational psychology

parapsychology
personality psychology
personnel psychology
physiological psychology
program evaluation
psychology
psychopharmacology
quantitative psychology
school psychology
social psychology

RECOMMENDED READINGS

AMERICAN PSYCHOLOGICAL ASSOCIATION. *Careers in psychology*. Washington, D.C.: American Psychological Association, 1985. Prepared by the major national organization of psychologists. This booklet describes the subdisciplines and various career opportunities within psychology.

BORING, E.G. *A history of experimental psychology* (2nd ed.). New York: Appleton-Century-Crofts, 1950. The classic comprehensive presentation of the history of psychology from antiquity to the twentieth century.

HEARST, E. (Ed.). *The first century of experimental psychology*. Hillsdale, N.J.: Lawrence Erl-

baum, 1979. A collection of contributed chapters that traces the history of specific topic areas. Contains photographs of most of the important figures of experimental psychology.

HOTHERSALL, D. *History of psychology*. New York: Random House, 1984. A very readable history of psychology from the ancient Greeks to modern times, with a particular focus on major historical figures.

WATSON, R. I. *The great psychologists* (4th ed.). Philadelphia: Lippincott, 1978. Describes the contributions of great psychologists from the Greek philosophers through modern times.

DOING PSYCHOLOGY: METHODOLOGY

In recent years we have heard much disturbing news about the abuse of children by family members and child-care workers. The public is alarmed, and government officials, educators, and health care workers are growing increasingly concerned. Can anything be done to prevent child abuse? Can we even predict which families are likely to have this problem? Clearly, there is a need for new research into this troubling area of human behavior. Some facts about child abuse are known, but we still do not know the reasons why reports of the problem have been increasingly so dramatically.

Where should the researchers start? As in many similar situations, they face certain fundamental issues.

1. How should we define child abuse? Can we agree on what constitutes an incident of child abuse?
2. Does the behavior seem to occur at random, or can we find some pattern—some kind of uniformity or regularity—in the way it happens? When it occurs at a high rate, can we find other phenomena that also seem to occur in conjunction with it? For example, is child abuse highly associated with other phenomena such as alcoholism in the parents, a high unemployment rate in the community, or premature birth in the children?
3. Can we develop hypotheses about the causes of the behavior and systematically test them?

The researchers' problem is to plan ways to validly address these issues, and formulate their questions in researchable terms. First, they may need to be specific about who is doing the behavior. ("Who are the child abusers?" is a large question that may be hard to answer; "What is the average age of the child-abusing mother?" is a smaller question, possibly answerable and probably of interest.) Second, the researchers must decide exactly how and under what conditions they are going to measure the behavior they are studying. Third, they must arrange the measurements they have obtained according to some plan that will allow them to analyze and summarize these data.

Many times, though not always, the results of psychological research are directly applicable to real-life problems. "Real-life" surveys of child abuse in the community may show high associations with other phenomena such as maternal alcoholism; these studies will help researchers predict which types of families have a high likelihood of developing the problem in the future. Similarly, case studies of families with premature babies may show that these infants require more attention than normal-term infants do, and that the parents—who may already be struggling financially or emotionally—may feel an extra strain. We have no magic "prevention pill" for child abuse, in part because the problem has multiple causes.

Cause-and-effect relationships are best established under controlled laboratory conditions using the rigorous *experimental method* (which is discussed later in this chapter), and child abuse is, of course, not a behavior researchers could ethically study directly in a laboratory. Nevertheless, many hypotheses that advance our understanding of child abuse *can* be studied in the laboratory. These include the effects of frustration on aggression toward other people, the roles of models and reinforcement in many forms of behavior, and the identification of variables that affect the extent to which parents will use punishment on children.

How psychologists tackle research projects is the subject of this chapter. Part of the job involves directly observing behavior and, perhaps, attempting to manipulate that behavior via experiments. The other part involves working with ideas about the behavior. These ideas are related to form theories, and the resulting theories, in turn, shape the ongoing process of direct observation and experimentation.

THEORY AND THE EMPIRICAL APPROACH

What do you do when you are curious about an ordinary everyday phenomenon? You set out, in an informal way, to study the phenomenon by observation. Suppose, for example, you know nothing about watches and are shown one for the first time; you are intrigued by what makes the watch tick, and you want to know why its hands move around the circle. If you open the case, watch the works move, and think a bit, you may guess that the movement of the hands has something to do with the spring, for you can see that the watch movement stops each time the spring is unwound. You also notice the regular oscillation of the balance wheel and its relation to the ratchet, which allows the ratchet wheel to move forward just one catch at a time, instead of continuously. You thus discover why the hands move and what makes the watch tick.

In this little piece of research you have achieved the two goals we talked about above. You have found a uniform, regular pattern: the watch movement stops *each time* the spring is unwound. And you have found a relationship between that association and another association: you have discovered that there is a connection between the spring and the movement of the hands. Your method has consisted of direct observation. Could you have tried a different approach? Yes: in addition, you could have set up an experiment to deliberately manipulate one set of phenomena and determine its effect on another set of phenomena. For example, you could have tried stopping the oscillation of the balance wheel, to see what would happen to the ratchet wheel and the "tick" of the watch. Experimentation and direct observation are two modes that are employed in the **empirical approach** to investigation—the approach that is guided by experience.

How Scientists Use the Empirical Approach

In some ways, the empirical research that scientists conduct is similar to your on-the-spot investigation of the watch. But it is more carefully controlled. Researchers use special methods when they make observations of any sort:

they are *tested* in a context (or surroundings) that closely matches the original context. If subjects are tested in different surroundings, they will recall less of the material.

We can apply this theory to our classroom example and form a **hypothesis** about it. As we have noted, a hypothesis is a prediction about how some specific event will turn out, based on implications we have deduced from the overall theory we are testing. Here is the hypothesis: *If the ture room has provided a context within which students learned their material, then stu who have this context available during the ■ The c will do better than students who do not.*

stat this hypothesis, we can conduct an experi-
repec
group
tions of
their own **al Structure**
research i **ment**
the more c
conclusions, m an **experiment** is a test con-
dividuals are *rison* between two conditions.
same phenome the two conditions would be:

In addition, special precau s are tested in their origi-
researchers use the experi s call this the "Same
experiment, researchers try t .
ulate a single factor that *migh* tested in some other
they are studying. Keeping the "Changed Class-
from all other possible factors is q
will see when we discuss the experi
later in this chapter. performance
Yet even though scientific research ce under
carefully controlled than our everyday ex
tions, the two modes of investigation both n neric
use of a close connection between "thinking" a ld
"doing." When we tinker with our environment in
our everyday lives, we think about what we are
doing as we go along. Scientists do this too; they
call the process working with theory.

How Scientists Use Theory

When you try to find out what makes a watch work, you focus on significant processes—those that have something to do with your observations that the hands move in a certain way and that the watch ticks with regularity and a certain constant frequency. You waste little time considering the nature of the wristband or the shape of the crystal,

out what will happen if we change the classroom. And we could call the "Same Classroom" condition a **control condition**; it will help control the conclusions we reach, by providing a standard with which to compare the results we get under the experimental condition. The two conditions are shown in Figure 2.1.

We can make sure (using methods to be discussed later) that the two conditions are the same in regard to all factors except one: the classroom in which the students are tested. And it is we who will cause that one factor to be different. So, if there is any difference in the subjects' behavior under the experimental condition (the "Changed Classroom" condition), we can be confident that we know *why* that difference in behavior came about: it is the result of the factor that *we* changed. The experimental method, if scrupulously followed, allows us to establish a true *causal relationship* between one set of phenomena and another.

The Independent and Dependent Variables

The feature that distinguishes the different conditions in an experiment is called the **independent variable**. We, the researchers, manipulate this variable ourselves (for example, we decide which room a student will be tested in). Thus, this variable is "independent" of the subjects' behavior: changes in it are not caused by the subjects' behavior, but by us.

The behavior we seek to test in an experiment (for example, the students' test performance) is the **dependent variable**. This behavior will "depend" on the independent variable. In our experiment, we suspect that the students' test perfor-

in al context on students' test performance.
is:

1. A
phen
2. That ar
3. And that
that pheno

Faced with a series of
understand, we may b

	Midterm Test
	Same Classroom
	Unfamiliar Room

mance will depend on the room in which they are tested.

Controlling Experimental Conditions: Handling the Independent Variable

How can we make sure that the changed room will be the only significant factor to distinguish the two treatment conditions? First, we must eliminate any variable that might possibly be *confounded* with, or mixed up with, the variable we are interested in.

For example, suppose we discovered that all the students who took the exam in the original classroom also happened to be upperclassmen, and that those who took it in the new classroom happened to be first-semester freshmen. Under these circumstances, another factor would suggest itself as an explanation for higher test scores —namely, that more experienced students tend to do better on tests (as a group) than freshmen. Thus, any conclusion we reached about the impact of the independent variable (room location) might be erroneous. Room location might influence the dependent variable (the test scores), but so might the students' age and experience.

Consider another example. Suppose the second classroom happened to be rather cold, and suppose that students tested in the different, cold room obtained lower test scores. We would not know whether these lower scores had been caused by the change in the classroom (our intended independent variable) or by the frigid temperature (a possibly confounded variable—or, as we sometimes say, a "confounding" variable).

Our choice of environmental conditions for the "Changed Classroom" condition is also important. If at all possible, we will select a room that is markedly different from the customary classroom —one that is unfamiliar to the students in the class and is perhaps located in a distant corner of the campus. We may even use an unusual seating arrangement, or add "props" of some sort, to further distinguish the "Changed" from the "Same" room. Otherwise, if the "Changed" room closely resembled the "Same" room in all important respects, we would not expect the two rooms to be associated with different test scores.

Counterbalancing

If we want to exercise even more control than is possible in our classroom experiment (which will, of course, take place in a naturalistic setting), we can construct a true laboratory experiment. For instance, we can arrange conditions so that each room becomes the "Changed" room for one-half of the subjects who are assigned to the "Changed Classroom" condition. That is, one-half of the "Changed Classroom" subjects will learn in Room A and be tested in Room B; the other half of the "Changed Classroom" students will learn in Room B and be tested in Room A. For all the "Changed Classroom" students, the effects of the particular rooms will then be distributed evenly. The "Same Classroom" treatment condition can be arranged in a similar fashion.

Such a procedure is called **counterbalancing**. It is one means of making sure that variables that are of little or no theoretical interest to the experimenter are evenly distributed across the variables of interest. For example, while "Change" *versus* "No Change" in room location is of interest to the experimenter, the specific location, color, temperature, etc. of a room might not be; so it is desirable to *counterbalance* the specific room locations, in order to avoid the possibility that a specific room location may be too cold or the lighting too poor. With half of the subjects in the "changed" condition assigned to learn in Room A and be tested in Room B, and the other half assigned to learn in Room B and be tested in Room A, we can rule out all explanations having to do with the specific physical properties of Rooms A and B. Such properties will have been equated across "Change" and "No Change" groups.

Other Laboratory Controls

We may, furthermore, exercise tight control over the material the subjects in our experiment are to learn. Procedures are available for controlling the level of difficulty of paragraphs or word lists, and we can use such procedures when selecting the material for our study. Similarly, we can control our choice of testing method, our response scoring technique, the time duration between learning and test, the level of learning, and so on. Considerable laboratory research of this sort has been done (for example, see Ceci and Bronfenbrenner, 1985) and has indeed shown that recall from memory is sensitive to environmental context.

Handling the Dependent Variable

In this experiment, the dependent variable consists of the scores that the students achieve on the midterm test. We must handle this variable carefully. For example, we must be sure that the midterm is scored objectively. If there are answers that require interpretation, such as short essays, we must grade them without knowledge of the condition from which they came. That is, the grader must be "blind" with regard to the origin of the tests: he or she must not know whether a set of test responses comes from a "Changed Classroom" student or a "Same Classroom" student. Otherwise, the grader's expectations regarding the benefits of "changed" *versus* "same" conditions might result in subtle biases, as will be seen below.

Unfortunately, the experimenter can unwittingly introduce biases, usually called **experimenter effects**, into the study. For example, suppose the experimenter and the instructor in the course are one and the same, so that the experimenter knows the subjects personally. Suppose, furthermore, that this experimenter is faced with making a borderline decision about the test performance of a certain student in the "Same Classroom" group. Without intending to do so, the experimenter might give this student's answer the benefit of the doubt and might move the score a notch higher than if the decision had gone the other way.

Although this type of borderline decision might produce just a small effect in one test, if it were repeated over a number of tests its cumulative effect could be large. Thus, a bias would be present that had been introduced by the experimenter. The independent variable would no longer be the only factor influencing the results of the test.

Often, experimenter effects are introduced when the experimenter has specific expectations about the outcome of the research. In some situations the experimenter may subtly convey these expectations to the subject. For instance, when researchers are testing a pain-reducing substance, the plan usually involves comparing the effects of the pain reducer with those of an inert substance. When the experimenter knows which substance each subject is being given, there may be tiny differences in the way the experimenter behaves—differences in tone of voice, facial expression, or physical gestures.

In order to avoid this form of bias, researchers normally use a **double-blind procedure**. The experimenter does not know which substance is being given (that is, which condition is being applied to each subject), nor does the person receiving the substance. Robert Rosenthal (1966) has assembled a variety of evidence for experimenter effects in human and nonhuman studies and has made recommendations for controlling such effects.

Handling Subjects

The term **subjects** refers to the organisms whose responses are being measured in a study. Subjects can be human beings or other animals. In our imaginary experiment the subjects are the students in the class.

Subjects' Expectations

Just as the expectations of the experimenter can influence the outcome of an experiment, so too can the expectations of the subjects. In our example, our students' test performance might be affected if they knew that an experiment was being conducted—especially if they knew what hypothesis was being tested. Students who were assigned to the "Changed Classroom" treatment might re-

Psychologists must deal with subjects' expectations in an experimental situation.

sign themselves to inferior performance and so score lower. Or they might decide to work harder to overcome the hypothesized negative influence of the changed environmental context. It is even possible that their prior knowledge might lead some to react one way and others another way. The problem is that we would not know how they would react: thus our comparison between the two treatments would be unclear.

Generally, when subjects' responses are strongly determined by characteristics of the research setting unrelated to the variable the researchers are primarily interested in (for example, if your students' test scores are more heavily influenced by prior knowledge about your experiment than they are by the room location), we say that **demand characteristics** are operating: certain characteristics of the research setting seem to "demand" or "suggest" a particular response. Subjects' expectations, as we have seen, can be a significant demand characteristic. One common means of minimizing subjects' expectations is to keep the subjects ignorant of the purpose of the study until it is completed. For example, subjects might be told only after the experiment is completed just what the hypothesis is—or, for that matter, just what the nature of the study is.

Control Conditions and the Placebo Effect

In some experiments, particularly medical research, subjects in the experimental condition are given a drug that the researchers are studying, and subjects in the control condition are given an inert substance. The researchers then see how the subjects' responses to the drug differ from their responses to the inert substance.

In such experiments it is important for the researchers to be alert to an effect that may make it more difficult to interpret the results. The control subjects do not know they are taking an inert substance; they *think* the substance they are taking will have certain specified effects. Sometimes they actually do experience these effects. This result is called a **placebo effect**; it must be carefully "dissected out" of the experimental results if the true effect of the drug under study is to be visible.

Some placebo effects are accompanied by actual biological reactions. In one experiment (Levine et al., 1979) patients suffering from pain were given an inert substance. Although the substance itself had no chemical effect, an interesting test revealed that these patients' bodies might actually be responding to the placebo by releasing endorphins—substances produced by the body to reduce pain—and that those endorphins might have a chemical effect. When some of the patients were given naloxone, a substance that blocks endorphins, the placebo-induced analgesia (relief from pain) disappeared. This result suggests that because subjects expected pain relief from the placebo, they had actually had a physiological response, the release of endorphins. Placebo effects are not necessarily just a nuisance factor that researchers must control for; they can be important and interesting phenomena in their own right.

Establishing Equivalent Groups

The subjects in the two treatment conditions come from the total class membership, and they must be equivalent with regard to all characteristics that could have a bearing on their test performance. To illustrate, let us look at what we do *not* want to happen. We do not want all the "good" students in the class to wind up in one condition, such as the "Same Classroom" condition. We also do not want the students to select the room in which they will take the test, for some may actually excel in a changed context and choose that condition.

Overall, we want to establish two completely equivalent groups of students, with no extra factors operating that might affect their performance. Whenever possible, we will need to use the technique known as randomization to accomplish this aim. When randomization is not possible, we can use another technique known as matching.

Randomization Suppose we elect to randomize. Here's how it's done. We randomly divide the students into two groups, and then **randomly assign** one group to the "Same Classroom" condition and the other group to the "Changed Classroom" condition. If we do this, each student will have an equal chance of being placed in either treatment condition. (Techniques for carrying out random assignment are readily available in statistics texts.) Randomization satisfies the need for equivalent groups, and it also satisfies other requirements of statistical analysis that are beyond the scope of this chapter.

Matching Subjects When we cannot randomize, we may still be able to assign subjects to treatment conditions systematically in such a way as to minimize possibly confounding factors. We might identify a subject characteristic that we think could have an important bearing on our experiment—such as the students' academic aptitudes, or how they had done on an earlier pretest. We would then **match** the subjects on that characteristic, so that students in each treatment condition had the same amount of the characteristic.

Matching can be helpful when subjects have a characteristic that might easily distort the results if it were (by chance) distributed unequally in the treatment conditions. As you might suspect, matching can be effort- and time-consuming when large numbers of subjects are being tested. But it can be a beneficial technique when small numbers of subjects are tested. In such a situation, one or two subjects' characteristics could materially affect the overall measure of a group's performance. Matching would ensure that subjects with the critical characteristic were equally distributed over both groups.

THE CORRELATIONAL METHOD

Whenever they can, researchers try to find true causal relationships between sets of phenomena. (The practical benefits are apparent: if we knew what caused a certain type of mental illness, for example, we could take steps to eliminate that cause.) Researchers have a chance to establish true causality *if* they can set up a true experiment: there they can attempt to control all factors that might affect the behavior they are studying, and they can manipulate one independent variable at will.

But does that mean that nonexperimental research—research that takes place outside the laboratory, and/or that involves possible confounding variables—is of no interest to scientists? Not at all. Often the first step toward finding the cause of a phenomenon (such as, let's say, a specific disease) is simply finding what other phenomena occur *at the same time as* that phenomenon. For example, we might find that many people who eventually developed a disease such as coronary artery disease had a history of eating a lot of food containing butter or other animal fats. Our total knowledge about coronary artery disease would have increased. And another benefit would

also follow. It would be unethical to use our knowledge to set up a true laboratory experiment using our new variable (after all, we would not want to *force* subjects to consume substances that we suspected might injure their health). But we could use our data to predict which people would be more likely than others to develop coronary artery disease in the future, and using this argument we might try to persuade people to cut down their consumption of animal fats.

Investigating sets of phenomena that are associated with each other—that is, that occur at the same time—is the aim of **correlational research**. When two sets of phenomena happen together at a rate that is significantly higher than chance, we say there is a **systematic relationship** between them. Much correlational research deals with historical events: events that have occurred naturally and cannot be manipulated, such as gender, race, or age. We cannot impose an earthquake on a town, nor could we ethically create drug addiction in people. But we can study these phenomena when they occur naturally, and find out what other phenomena occur at the same time.

It is important to stress again that because we have not imposed the conditions as we could have in an experiment, we do not know conclusively why these conditions are present. We cannot validly conclude that there is any causal relationship between the conditions; we cannot say that condition A exists as a direct result of condition B. There is always the possibility that they may exist at the same time "by accident," or for reasons totally unrelated to any factors the researchers can identify. Nevertheless, correlational studies help us make detailed analyses of the variables we are studying, so that we can better understand the relationships among them.

OTHER NONEXPERIMENTAL METHODS

Newcomers to psychology often wonder whether having to pay attention to methodology takes away the excitement of doing research. On the contrary, a good part of the attraction of research lies in that very challenge. It takes a clever researcher to look closely at the research question and figure out exactly what techniques will yield valid answers to it.

If these qualities are needed to design experiments and correlational studies, they are even more essential for methods over whose conditions the researcher has less control. In this section we will discuss three such nonexperimental methods: field experiments, surveys, and case studies. Paradoxically, it is the fluidity of these methods, their relative *lack* of control and *lack* of intervention, that makes them valuable. Avoiding the more controlled and artificial conditions that are found in experiments and in many correlational studies, these methods reveal behavior in a more natural setting.

Field Experiments

Field experiments are studies carried out in the "real world." When, as part of their research design for a field experiment, the researchers have to intervene in the flow of "real-world" events, they try to be sure these interventions are of the sort that could easily pass as normal events. This way, the researchers reduce the chances that the research setting may induce demand characteristics that might cloud the results.

An ingenious field experiment was conducted by two psychologists who wanted to study how people's attitudes function in social situations (Freedman and Fraser, 1966). An attitude is a disposition to think, feel, and behave in a certain way about something—either positively or negatively. The researchers' question was: Would people who had initially complied with a request be more likely to comply with a second request? To find out the answer, they first asked a group of housewives some questions about what products they used around the house (this was the small request, and most of the women who were approached agreed to answer the questions). Several days later, the same researcher called the housewives with a larger request: they asked whether these women would allow some men to come into their houses and classify all their household products.

The results were as follows. The housewives who had already agreed to the small request were more likely to agree to the large request, but the housewives who had *not* been asked the small request (the control group of housewives) were less likely to agree to the large request. So the researchers' initial hypothesis was confirmed. (Note, incidentally, that it cannot be determined whether or not this demonstrates that compliance with a small request increases later compliance with a large request. Possibly, compliance with a request of any size increases subsequent compliance. This was not tested.)

You undoubtedly know that the technique used in this experiment is used intuitively by skilled negotiators and salespeople. If they can get a "foot in the door" by inducing a person to say yes to a small request, compliance with a larger request is likely to follow.

Naturalistic Observation

Naturalistic observations are observations of behavior made in natural settings without *any* intervention by the researcher. When we think about this kind of study, we usually envision a naturalist sitting for many hours in a camouflaged hiding place, patiently watching the behavior of an exotic animal. Similar techniques are actually used to observe human behavior. For example, suppose we were interested in the content of spontaneous language in young children. To investigate this, we could establish a situation in which we could eavesdrop on children while they were playing in the absence of an adult.

A problem with many observational studies is the effect of the observer on the subjects' behavior. If the observer's presence profoundly affects the subjects' actions, the study may not succeed in validly testing the hypothesis. When concealment is impossible, the observer often tries to blend into the background and refrains from recording any behavior until her or his presence is taken for granted.

The Survey

Important information also comes from surveys. A **survey** explores a group of people's characteristics, attitudes, opinions, or other behavior by asking a number of the people in the group the same questions. The popularity of surveys attests to our curiosity about the habits of our fellow humans. Very likely, you or your friends have been subjects of a survey. You might even conduct a simple survey of your own by asking your friends if they have previously been respondents in some form of survey.

Surveys range from the familiar political polls and product information surveys to less obvious forms such as investigations of everyday memory lapses. The National Crime Survey, a classic survey, was begun in 1972 by the Law Enforcement Administration Agency (LEAA) to keep track of crime and its impact on society. Every six months, poll takers visited thousands of homes and interviewed residents about their experience with crime during the preceding six months (*Surveying Crime*, 1976). For example, people who were part of the 1980 sample were asked, "Did anyone beat you up, attack you, or hit you with something, such as a rock or bottle?" and "Did anyone try to rob you by using force or threatening to harm you?" If the answer to such questions was yes, the person then was asked about the circumstances, the effects the crime had on her or him, and whether it was reported to the police.

In many surveys it is impossible to question everyone in the group. Typically, a **population** of interest is identified—say, all female voters over forty years old—and a **sample**, a few members of the defined population, is taken to measure the variable. The researchers then make inferences about the population from the sample. The accuracy of these inferences depends on just how well the sample matches the population in its essential characteristics. Survey researchers use various statistical methods to draw samples so that they do match the population in all the characteristics bearing on the questions of interest.

The Case Study

In contrast to the survey, which is a relatively extensive study of a large group of people, the **case study** is usually an intensive investigation of a single individual or a select group of individuals. In most instances, the researcher has decided to study a given individual because he or she manifests some unique characteristic that can contribute a key insight into an aspect of human nature. Sigmund Freud's intensive case studies of patients who came to him for treatment, for example, provided the basis for his theory of personality development (described in Chapter 18). Jean Piaget's theory of intellectual development (described in Chapter 14) began with astute observations of the behavior of his own three children, whom he studied almost from the moment of their birth.

Case studies are essential when our questions concern variables we would find it repugnant to impose. Brain function, for example, is often studied by examining people who have suffered some form of brain damage. There are instances of children who have been born with conditions characterized by severe seizures and progressive mental deterioration, but who can lead a relatively normal life if the damaged brain hemisphere is removed early. Intensive study of children who have had such surgery has given us valuable information about the capabilities and limitations of a single, isolated hemisphere (Dennis, 1980).

ETHICAL PRINCIPLES IN PSYCHOLOGICAL RESEARCH

Whether a research project uses experimental or nonexperimental methods, ethical issues are a matter of concern. Some studies simply cannot be conducted. For example, shutting infants away from human contact for their first few years to determine whether early experience with language is necessary for its eventual acquisition would clearly be unethical. Such a procedure could cause irreparable harm. Although the great bulk of psychological research involves no risk—either physical or psychological—to participants and poses no ethical questions, some cases are not so clear-cut.

The Ethical Guidelines of the APA

Because psychologists have an ethical obligation to protect the dignity and welfare of the people who participate in research, the American Psychological Association (1981) has drawn up a set of ethical principles to guide the conduct of research that involves human subjects. This code sets up several conditions aimed at protecting human subjects, including *privacy, voluntary participation, informed consent*, and *freedom from harm*. All complaints lodged against psychologists are investigated by the APA's Committee on Scientific and Professional Ethics, and when charges are substantiated, the psychologist is suspended or expelled from the APA (Hare-Mustin and Hall, 1981).

Participants in an experiment have the right to privacy. Their thoughts and feelings may not be revealed without their consent. Thus, to use

THE ETHICS OF EXPERIMENTATION ON ANIMALS

In August 1984 people in sixteen cities across the country took part in protest marches. Some of their signs read STOP THE PAIN and STOP THE KILLING. Who are the victims in need of saving? In the eyes of the marchers, they are the animal subjects in scientific experiments.

For generations, medical researchers have used laboratory animals in their experiments. Many of the life-saving drugs and machines we now take for granted could not have been developed without the sacrifice of mice, rabbits, monkeys, and other animals used in scientific studies. No doubt, the protesters are aware of the human gains that have come from animal sacrifices, but they would prefer that science find a way to help people that does not involve cruelty to animals.

How does this ethical and practical problem affect psychologists? In fact, only about 5 percent of members of the American Psychological Association use animals in their work, but for that 5 percent, animals play a vital role in research on learning and many other aspects of human behavior. Why is this so? The study of evolution tells us that humans developed from mammals through the primates,

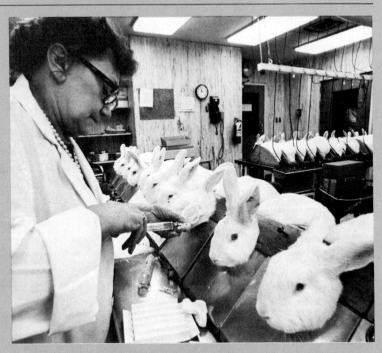

Protests against the painful Draize test, which uses rabbits to determine the safety of cosmetics, are growing.

with the later organisms sharing many physical characteristics with the lower organisms. Psychologists reason that since humans and other mammals share many physical traits, they must also share common principles for learning.

Psychologists reason further that animals are good subjects for studying learning because they cannot talk. Interestingly, language can interfere with our study of simple learning: language exerts so much control over human experience and thought that it may actually modify a person's learning experiences. For example, people can represent an experience in language and then

findings, researchers must keep all personal data private and report their findings in such a way that the identity of participants cannot be determined —whether by ordinary citizens, by the press, by government, or by other scientists.

Participation in an experiment must also be voluntary; a person must be free to decide whether or not to take part. Further, if a subject wants to

drop out of the experiment at any point, she or he must be free to do so.

Before a person can decide whether to participate, she or he must have some sort of information about the experiment. Psychologists are supposed to tell potential subjects what they will have to do during an experiment and whether any harm might possibly come from taking part in the study.

mentally repeat it, or negate it. These acts become part of their learning process. The study of animals shows us how learning can occur without the complications introduced by language, and provides information that can be used to devise hypotheses and models of human learning.

Third, by using animals we can control for genetic influences that can sometimes affect the way organisms respond to various experiences. The genetic inheritance of animals can be controlled by breeding, something that is obviously both impossible and undesirable with human beings. Mice and rat strains used by psychologists have been pure-bred for many generations, minimizing any variation in genetic make-up.

Fourth, by using animals, psychologists can study the learning process in slow motion. People often need only one try to learn the information presented; they provide the researcher with very little opportunity to study a gradual process of change. But animals generally require many trials to learn the same information, thus allowing the researcher to observe and analyze the learning process.

Finally, animals make ideal subjects in research that cannot be performed with humans. For example, a psychologist may study the importance of visual experience by raising one group of rats in complete darkness and another group under normal lighting conditions.

Although researchers may use procedures with animals that would be unethical to use with people, stringent standards govern the treatment of animal subjects. State and federal regulations specify procedures and standards for animal care—housing, feeding, and cleaning. Ethical standards prohibit the researcher from inflicting unnecessary pain. As with human beings, the importance of the research is weighed against the potential harm to the animals involved.

When researchers are suspected of violating these standards, they can be held responsible. In one case, a prominent researcher who had been experimenting on monkeys to find ways of helping stroke victims regain the use of their limbs was charged with cruelty to animals (Holden, 1981). The monkeys had had the nerves in one arm severed, or deafferented, and their good arm had been bound to their bodies to force them to use the deafferented arm. Because monkeys have no feeling in a deafferented limb, it is often injured and the monkeys treat it as a foreign object, perhaps even chewing off their own fingers. An animal-welfare activist who had volunteered to work at the laboratory became concerned at the monkeys' physical condition and at what he regarded as appalling conditions within the laboratory and called authorities. In this case, it was not the research on the animals that was questioned, which has important human applications, but the lack of veterinary care for the monkeys and the living conditions in the laboratory. According to the researcher, he had been on vacation during the period involved, and the workers whose responsibility it was to clean, feed, and care for the animals had not been doing their jobs. When the case came to court, the researcher was exonerated of charges that the laboratory conditions were unacceptable or that he had inflicted unnecessary pain or suffering on the animals. He was, however, found guilty on six counts of cruelty to animals for failure to provide adequate medical care for six of the monkeys, and he was fined $3,015.

Scientific investigation cannot be conducted in an ethical vacuum. Psychological research, which not only affects human beings and animals but depends on them for subjects, must be subject to rigorous ethical constraints.

Thus voluntary participation should be based on informed consent.

Finally, no lasting harm should come from participating in the experiment. Indeed, many psychologists believe that no effects of any kind should linger after the experiment is over and contact between researcher and subject has been terminated.

Ethical Conflicts

In addition to being obliged to protect the people who participate in their research, psychologists are also obligated to try to find the answers to important scientific, psychological questions. At times these obligations conflict. To conduct important studies, psychologists may have to use procedures that involve some risk of physical or psychological harm to some of the participants. For this reason, research involving human subjects is generally reviewed by a panel of other researchers and laypersons who determine whether the subjects will be adequately protected. They also decide whether the experiment will allow subjects to participate voluntarily through informed consent. Such review is required by the U.S. government for all research funded by federal grants, and most universities require such review of all research.

Sometimes a study could not be undertaken if the participants knew its details and purpose. If psychologists want to find out, for example, whether a bystander will report a theft, telling potential subjects about the experiment would destroy its value. Most people would behave the way they think they should behave. In a study (Latané and Elman, 1970) that used deception, researchers staged the blatant theft of a case of beer while the cashier was in the rear of a beverage store. Among people who watched the theft by themselves, 35 percent failed to report it to the cashier. And when two or more people watched the theft, in only 56 percent of the cases did even one of them report it. The discovery of which conditions lead people to report crimes or come to the aid of strangers in distress can have important implications for society.

Using Statistics in Research

When researchers test a hypothesis, whether by experimental or nonexperimental methods, they may end up with masses of observations that mean little in themselves. How do researchers deal with a stack of unanalyzed findings? And how do they figure out whether their experiment has confirmed or refuted their hypothesis? They must tackle the task of reducing their observations to manageable and intelligible form. To do so, they employ analytical procedures drawn from the field of statistics.

One basic statistical procedure involves assembling, classifying, tabulating, and summarizing facts or data, so as to present relevant information about a specific subject in an unambiguous and precise fashion. Using this approach, researchers can reduce large accumulations of data to numbers that are simpler and more informative.

Statistics: The Basics

The first step may be simply to summarize data collected for a sample or a population, to come up with a number known as a descriptive statistic. Your grade point average (GPA) is one example: it is a descriptive statistic that summarizes the results of your past academic efforts. Similarly, the results of the latest Gallup poll summarize public attitudes toward the president's policies. Using these statistics, investigators can say something meaningful about their findings with a few words and figures.

Psychologists often use statistics to describe the behavior of a group in which a single variable is being studied. Suppose you are studying memory, and you want to test the hypothesis that the more time that elapses after a person commits a series of items to memory, the more items that person will forget. Your hypothesis, in other words, is that delay increases forgetting.

Let's say that you design an experiment in which subjects will memorize a list. Your independent variable is the time interval (number of minutes) between the time when your subjects originally learn the list and the time when you ask them to recall it; you suspect that if you change this time interval, your subjects' behavior will change. You recruit 120 students, bring them into the psychology lab, and give them a list of a dozen words to learn. After they have learned the list, you test half of them immediately and the other half one hour later.

Your impression is that the students in your second group, which you have called the Delayed Recall group, have forgotten more words than the first group, which you have called the Immediate Recall group. But your impressions or "hunches" are not enough: saying that one group seems to have done better than another is just a beginning. Without greater precision, you will not be able to compare your results with those of other experimenters on a similar problem, with results from a related study that has been done in the past, or with results you may get in the future.

You want to know whether delay really does increase forgetting or, conversely, whether the lower recall in the delayed condition was simply due to chance, as when you flip a coin five times and happen to obtain all heads. How can you summarize your observations in a way that tells you—and others—the answer to this question at a glance? You may decide to set up a frequency distribution.

Frequency Distribution

To create a frequency distribution for your observations in the memory experiment, your first step is to count the number of subjects in each group whose score is 0—that is, the number of subjects who have forgotten 0 items. You then count the number of subjects whose score is 1 (the number who have forgotten one item), then the number of subjects whose score is 2, and so on.

Next you draw up a table to record the number of subjects in each group who have scored 0, the number who have scored 1, and so on (Figure 2.2). The result is a **frequency distribution**—a representation that shows the relationship between the scores themselves and the *frequency* you have observed (the number or percentage of subjects who make each score).

Tallying a Frequency Distribution

Figure 2.3 shows a number of ways in which your results can be described. Figure 2.3A shows a tally of both groups. The frequency distribution you have made shows that most of the Immediate Recall group made fewer than four errors, whereas most of the Delayed Recall group made more than five errors. Already it is clear that, on the whole, there were fewer errors in the Immediate than in the Delayed group.

Graphing a Frequency Distribution

Frequency distributions can also be plotted graphically. Figure 2.3 shows two ways to graph the frequency distribution table we have just set up. The scores (in this case, the number of words forgotten) are plotted along the horizontal, or *X*, axis (also known as the *abscissa*). The frequency with which each score was made (the number of

Number of Errors	IMMEDIATE RECALL GROUP Frequency	DELAYED RECALL GROUP Frequency
0	2	0
1	7	0
2	15	0
3	27 Mode	1
4	5	3
5	2	2
6	1	6
7	0	11
8	1	23 Mode
9	0	9
10	0	4
11	0	1
12	0	0

Figure 2.2. Memory experiment: frequency distribution table.

students who made each score) is plotted along the vertical, or *Y*, axis (also known as the *ordinate*).

One way to graph the frequency distribution is with a *histogram*, in which a bar graph is used to show the scores (Figure 2.3B). Another method is with a *frequency polygon*, in which the distribution is plotted with points, which are then connected to form a line graph (Figure 2.3C).

The Shape of a Frequency Distribution

The histogram and the frequency polygon both confirm your impression that the Delayed Recall group has forgotten more words than the Immediate Recall group. And these graphs allow you to see the results a bit more clearly than your table did: unlike the table, they show the shape of the distribution.

One characteristic of a distribution is its degree of symmetry. When the results form a *symmetrical distribution*, the polygon or graph does not "lean" or "hang out" to one side or the other. Instead, each side is close to being a mirror image of the other. What causes this symmetry? It may result from the action of some variable—or it may be the result of chance. When, on the other hand, the polygon "hangs out" markedly in one direction

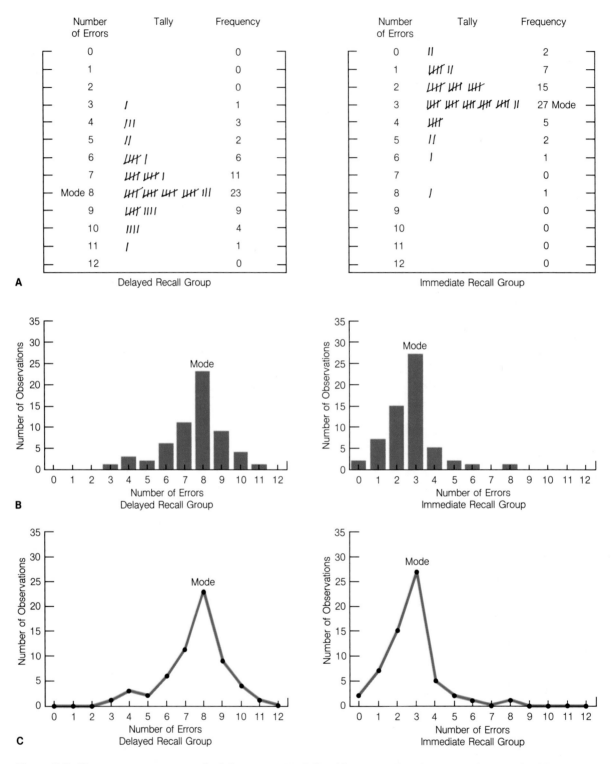

Figure 2.3. Memory experiment: graphed three ways. (A) Tally of frequency distribution, (B) bar graph of frequency distribution, and (C) frequency polygon.

or the other, a statistician would say you had a *skewed distribution*. One "tail" of the distribution is considerably longer than the other: more subjects have obtained scores at the extreme end of one side of the graph than at the extreme end of the other side.

But psychologists are not only interested in the shape of a distribution—the way subjects' scores can be represented graphically. They also want to know about the group's overall performance: the performance, scores, or characteristics of *many* or *most* of the subjects in an investigation. How many words, *on the average*, does a person forget when immediately recalling a list? What is the income of the *typical* college graduate? How many children does the *average* woman plan to have? Here we loosely use the terms "typical" and "average," but we need a way to be more precise about such statements. We need a mathematical way to describe the distribution—a single number that will characterize or sum up the distribution.

Measures of Central Tendency

There are several ways to summarize a frequency distribution. One way is to obtain a **measure of central tendency**—a number that represents the middle of the distribution—and use this measure to characterize the group as a whole. (When we talk about the "middle," we are speaking in terms of averages.)

The psychologist may choose one of three different measures of central tendency—the *mode*, the *mean*, or the *median*—depending partly on how the scores are distributed (Figure 2.4).

The Mode

The **mode** is the highest point of a distribution on a polygon: it is the score that the largest number of subjects have made, or the value that is most frequently obtained. In your Delayed Recall group, the mode, or number of errors most frequently made, was 8; in the Immediate Recall group the mode was 3. Thus, when you use this measure of central tendency to look for "middle" scores in both of your experimental groups, you find some support for your hypothesis: the Delayed Recall group seems to have made more errors.

The mode is useful when we are studying qualitative variables, such as mood state, marital status, psychopathological diagnosis, and so on. The mode of a frequency distribution can also give us a rough idea of whether the shape of the distribution is symmetrical or lopsided. If the mode is very much closer to the extreme of a distribution than to the center, then the distribution is lopsided or skewed.

But the mode is rarely used as a statistical measure. It is only a rough estimate of the distribution's center: it merely tells us which score or category is most frequent—and little else.

The Mean

A more precise measure of central tendency is the **mean**, which is the arithmetic average of the group scores. The mean, in contrast to the mode, can be expressed in fractions or percentages if necessary.

The mean is found by adding all the scores and then dividing the sum by the number of people who took the test (see box). In your study of forgetting, the mean of the Delayed Recall group was 7.6 and the mean of the Immediate Recall group was 2.7; these results again support your hypothesis. Note that the *mean* of the Delayed

Working With Statistics: Calculating The Mean

The mean is equal to the sum of the scores divided by the number of observations.

Conventionally, we abbreviate "sum of the scores" by ΣX, where Σ is the Greek capital letter sigma, meaning "sum," and X is a given score, such as 3 errors, a heart rate of 65 beats per second, or an IQ of 118. The number of observations that are being summed is designated by N. Thus,

$$\text{Mean} = \frac{\Sigma X}{N}$$

MEAN

DELAYED RECALL GROUP

3 + 4 + 4 + 4 + 5 + 5 + 6 + 6

+ 6 + 6 + 6 + 6 + 7 + 7 + 7 + 7 +

7 + 7 + 7 + 7 + 7 + 7 + 7 + 7

+ 8 + 8 + 8 + 8 + 8 + 8 + 8 +

8 + 8 + 8 + 8 + 8 + 8 + 8 + 8

+ 8 + 8 + 8 + 8 + 8 + 8 + 8 +

8 + 9 + 9 + 9 + 9 + 9 + 9 + 9

+ 9 + 9 + 10 + 10 + 10 + 10 +

11 = 454

$$\text{Mean} = \frac{\text{Sum of scores}}{\text{Number of scores}} = \frac{454}{60}$$

Mean = 7.566 = 7.6

IMMEDIATE RECALL GROUP

0 + 0 + 1 + 1 + 1 + 1 + 1 + 1

+ 1 + 2 + 2 + 2 + 2 + 2 + 2 +

2 + 2 + 2 + 2 + 2 + 2 + 2 + 2

+ 2 + 3 + 3 + 3 + 3 + 3 + 3 +

3 + 3 + 3 + 3 + 3 + 3 + 3 + 3

+ 3 + 3 + 3 + 3 + 3 + 3 + 3 +

3 + 3 + 3 + 3 + 3 + 3 + 4 + 4

+ 4 + 4 + 4 + 5 + 5 + 6 + 8 =

162

$$\text{Mean} = \frac{\text{Sum of scores}}{\text{Number of scores}} = \frac{162}{60}$$

Mean = 2.7

MEDIAN AND MODE

DELAYED RECALL GROUP

3, 4, 4, 4, 5, 5, 6, 6, 6, 6,

6, 6, 7, 7, 7, 7, 7, 7, 7, 7,

7, 7, 7, 8, 8, 8, 8, 8, 8, 8,

8, 8, 8, 8, 8, 8, 8, 8, 8, 8,

8, 8, 8, 8, 8, 8, 9, 9, 9, 9,

9, 9, 9, 9, 9, 10, 10, 10, 10,

11

IMMEDIATE RECALL GROUP

0, 0, 1, 1, 1, 1, 1, 1, 1, 2,

2, 2, 2, 2, 2, 2, 2, 2, 2, 2,

2, 2, 2, 2, 3, 3, 3, 3, 3, 3,

3, 3, 3, 3, 3, 3, 3, 3, 3, 3,

3, 3, 3, 3, 3, 3, 3, 3, 3, 3,

3, 4, 4, 4, 4, 4, 5, 5, 6, 8

Median = Exact center score = 8　　　Median = Exact center score = 3

(Because there are an even number of subjects in each group, the median falls halfway between the two circled central scores)

Mode = Most frequent score. In the Delayed Recall group, 23 subjects made 8 errors, and in the Immediate Recall group, 27 subjects made 3 errors.

Mode = 8　　　　　　　　　　　　　　Mode = 3

Figure 2.4. Measures of central tendency.

Recall group happens to be 7.6 errors, quite close to the *mode* of 8 errors. And the same is true of the Immediate Recall group—their *mean* of 2.7 errors also happens to be close to their *mode* of 3 errors. But the mean, as we have noted, is usually a more precise measure than the mode.

The mean is the measure of central tendency most used by psychologists. But it is inappropriate in some instances: it is sensitive to extreme scores, so it can be misleading when the distribution is highly skewed. If one score is extremely high (or extremely low), this unusual score can "pull" the mean away from representing the more truly typical scores.

The Median

One way to eliminate the problem of skewing is to find the median. The **median** divides the entire distribution into halves: when all the scores of a distribution are arranged from highest to lowest, the median falls in the exact center. The median is a useful measure of central tendency in a distribution where a few extreme scores cause the mean to be "pulled away" from the center.

Medians are often used in reporting average incomes: a few large incomes can inflate the estimate for the mean, but they will have no effect on the median. In your study, the median of the Delayed Recall group was 8, while that of the Immediate Recall group was 3.

All three measures of central tendency told you something about the performance of both groups in your experiment—and in an efficient way. Among the subjects in your Delayed Recall group, there was a considerable amount of forgetting (7.6 words, on the average), as compared with the Immediate Recall group (2.7 words, on the average). You can consider these two means as representative of the performance of the two groups.

But how well does the mean of each group represent the performance of the "typical" subject in that group? Are most subjects in each group fairly close to that group's mean, or are many of them relatively far from it? To answer that question, you will have to consider the dispersal, or variability, of scores in each group.

Measures of Variability

Variability refers to the way in which an entire set of scores spreads out from the mean or median. Sometimes scores are clustered closely around the center; if so, the distribution is said to have a *low*

variability. At other times they are widely spread out—in which case the distribution is said to have a *high variability.*

Suppose you give your list of words to a third group of sixty subjects, and in this group the scores turn out to be tightly clustered: twenty-five people have forgotten 7 words and thirty-five have forgotten 8 words. When you add these scores and divide by 60, you will find that this group has a mean that is identical to the mean of your original Delayed Recall group (7.6). But in this third group, the mean predicts the performance of the average subject much better than it does in your Delayed Recall group. The prediction is more accurate because the variability of the new group is much smaller.

The Range

Psychologists use several different measures of variability. The simplest is the **range** of scores, which is calculated by subtracting the lowest score from the highest. In your original study, the Delayed Recall group had a range of 8 points (from 3 to 11). In your new group, in which twenty-five subjects forgot seven words and thirty-five forgot eight words, the range is much narrower—only 1 (from 7 to 8). If you know the mean and the range of scores, you have some idea of how representative the mean is in describing individual scores, and that is what measures of variability provide for the psychologist.

However, the range is not always an accurate measure of variability because it reflects only two scores from the entire group. Suppose two businesses each have ten employees. In the first business, eight employees each make $50,000 annually; the ninth employee makes $20,000 and the tenth makes $80,000. In the second business, the mean salary is the same: one employee makes $20,000, one makes $80,000, two make $30,000, two make $40,000, two make $60,000, and two make $70,000. The range of salaries in both businesses is the same, $60,000. Yet it is clear that there is less variability in the first business, where all but two of the salaries fall close to the mean, so the range does not tell us enough to give us a clear picture of the distribution.

The Standard Deviation

To deal with problems like the one we have just described, psychologists and other scientists often use another measure that takes into account every

WORKING WITH STATISTICS: HOW TO FIND THE STANDARD DEVIATION

Ascertaining the standard deviation is not difficult, although it is tedious to compute without the aid of a calculator. To find the standard deviation:

1. Determine the mean of the scores.
2. From each score, subtract the mean and square the difference. (Scores are squared to eliminate the negative signs that result when dealing with scores that fall below the mean.)
3. Add the squares together.
4. Divide the sum by the number of scores.

5. Take the square root of the value you have obtained. This figure is the standard deviation.

A more succinct way to put it is to translate the formula for finding the standard deviation into words:

$$\text{Standard Deviation} = \sqrt{\frac{\text{Sum of (Score} - \text{Mean})^2}{\text{Number of Scores}}}$$

The standard deviation for the Delayed Recall group, calculated according to the proce-

dure we have described, is 1.57 items forgotten. In the Immediate Recall group it is .96 item. These calculations for the S.D. were done according to the equation for the standard deviation:

$$\text{S.D.} = \sqrt{\Sigma(X - M)^2/N}$$

where (as previously) X is any score, N is the total number of observations, M is the mean, and Σ is the symbol that indicates that we should sum the quantities in the parentheses (that is, we take each score, subtract the mean, square the obtained difference, and add them all up).

---

score in the distribution: the **standard deviation (S.D.)**. To find the standard deviation, we take each score's distance from the mean and square that distance—so that we have a positive number that will not cancel out any of the other scores. After adding the squared differences, we divide that sum by the number of scores, and then take the square root of the answer (see box). We now have a precise mathematical way of describing the degree of "clusteredness" of the scores around the mean. For the Delayed Recall group, the standard deviation calculated in this manner is 1.57 words forgotten, and for the Immediate Recall group, the standard deviation is .96 word forgotten.

Normal Curves

The standard deviation is an important determinant of the shape of the famous "bell-shaped curve"—a distribution you have probably seen in graphs of such data as the heights of American people, their incomes, or their educational levels. The "bell-shaped curve," more scientifically known as the normal curve of distribution, is a curve that

often results when large amounts of data are plotted. For example, imagine that instead of recruiting 120 subjects, you recruited thousands for your experiment in memory. Then imagine that you repeated the experiment on these thousands of subjects hundreds of times, using hundreds of different twelve-word lists. After averaging each subject's performance on all the lists, you would have several thousand scores in your frequency distribution. With so many scores, there would be many more distinctive points to plot on the horizontal axis. For example, you would have some subjects who forgot, on the average, .34 item; others who forgot 11.58 items; and still others who obtained many other scores. You would have a much smoother curve than either of the frequency polygons in Figure 2.3C. Large numbers of observations are more reliable and more systematic than small numbers. For example, 1,000 tosses of a coin are more likely to generate a 50–50 split between heads and tails than 10 tosses.

When all the data from your new experiment are entered on a frequency polygon, the distribution would form a smooth, symmetrical bell-shaped curve, the **curve of normal distribution**

(Figure 2.5). The normal curve is a theoretical curve that represents an infinite number of cases, and it is important because it reliably reflects the distribution of many characteristics of life. If we plotted the IQs, vocabulary, or running speed of the American people, in each case our data would form a normal curve.

Every normal curve reflects certain unvarying relationships among the mean of the distribution, its standard deviation, and the number of observations, cases, or scores in the distribution.

1. The mean, median, and mode are all at the same point on a normal curve, and they all lie at the center of the distribution.
2. Mathematicians have discovered that in any normal distribution, 34.1 percent of the cases fall within one standard deviation of one *or* the other side of the mean. Therefore, 68.2 percent of the cases lie within one standard deviation of *both* sides of the mean, as shown in Figure 2.5.
3. Within *two* standard deviations of both sides of the mean lie 95.4 percent of the cases, and three standard deviations on both sides of the mean encompass nearly all the cases in the frequency distribution —99.73 percent of them.

These properties of the normal curve help us see where each individual's performance lies on the distribution and allows us to make useful comparisons. It happens that scores on IQ tests follow a normal curve, so that knowing someone's IQ score allows you to place him or her within the general population. On IQ tests in the United States, the mean is 100 and the standard deviation is 15. Thus you know that in the general population, 68.2 percent of people have IQ scores between 85 and 115. A person who makes a score of 140 is nearly three standard deviation units above the mean—and is as unusual as a person who makes a score of 60, which is nearly three standard deviation units below the mean. Only one person in a thousand would score higher than 140, and only one in a thousand would score lower than 60.

Variability and the normal curve are also used to help researchers decide whether the outcome of an experiment was due to the independent variable or to chance. For example, in the experiment we have discussed comparing delayed and immediate recall, are the differences we observed due to random variability (chance) or to the real effect of time of recall (the independent variable)? Researchers use the normal curve to calculate the probability of getting an obtained result by chance

Figure 2.5. The curve of normal distribution (normal curve). In a normal distribution of frequencies the mean, the median, and the mode all fall at the middle of the distribution. Don't be deceived into thinking that every standard deviation comprises 34.1 percent of the cases. As we count deviations away from the mean they comprise fewer and fewer cases. The second standard deviation comprises only 13.6 percent of the observations.

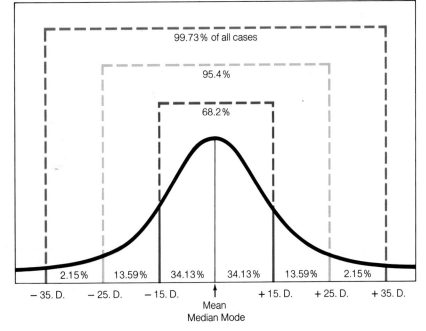

alone, using the assumption that there has been no effect of the independent variable. The assumption that the independent variable has had no effect is called the *null hypothesis*. If the probability is small of getting the observed results by chance alone (less than 5 times out of 100, or .05), the results are said to be "statistically significant." We would then reject the null hypothesis, and conclude instead that the independent variable did have an effect.

Graphing Relationships among Variables

When we spoke earlier about the independent and the dependent variables, we noted that in most investigations, the psychologist is interested in discovering how these two variables are related to each other. The relationship can usually be expressed mathematically.

Graphing a Linear Relationship

Suppose you discover that for every 1 point increase in people's IQ scores, the income they earn is $1,000 higher per year. You could draw this relationship in a graph (see Figure 2.6A). Algebrai-

cally, you could express this relationship as follows.

■ Each person's IQ score can be represented by a distance on the X axis of the graph: the higher a person's IQ is, the farther out to the right on the X axis the point representing that person will lie.

■ Each person's income can be represented by a distance on the Y axis of the graph: the more income a person makes, the higher up on the right on the Y axis will be the point representing that person.

So let us say that Jane Doe has an IQ of 100 and an income of $15,000 a year. We represent Jane Doe with point J on the graph.

Mary Roe, on the other hand, has an IQ of 101 and an income of $16,000 a year. We represent Mary Roe with point M on the graph. If we connect the two points with a line, we see that it is at a 45 degree angle, and its equation will be

$$Y = 100X + 5,000$$

But what if, on the other hand, we find that for every added IQ point, a person's income increases $2,000 a year instead of $1,000? In this case, for every unit increase in Y, we will have 2 increases in X, so the equation will be

$$Y = 200X + 5,000$$

Figure 2.6. Linear relationships.

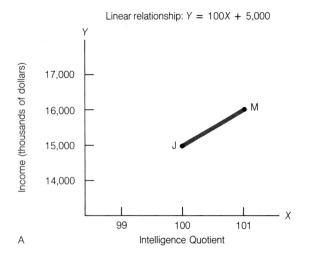

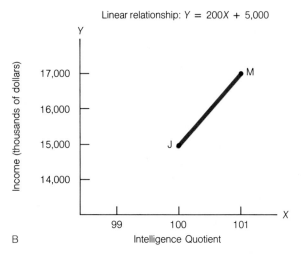

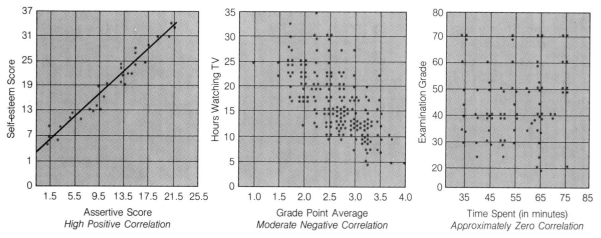

Figure 2.7. Scatter plots showing three types of correlation. (From Spence et al., 1976.)

and the graph will look like Figure 2.6B. This type of relationship is called a **linear relationship** (or **linear function**), because it can be represented graphically as a straight line.

Note, though, that not all relationships are this simple. There are some relationships in which, for every unit increase in one variable (such as IQ scores), there is no constant and predictable increase in the other variable. For example, if we measured a person's problem-solving performance on a test, we would find that as the person became more aroused (as his or her nervous system became more excited), his or her performance would increase—but only up to a point. (We discuss the nervous system in Chapter 3.) When the person's arousal level rose higher than a certain point, his or her performance would decrease. As the person became excessively aroused, in other words, performance would suffer. We are familiar with this effect in cases of panic.

Setting Up a Scatter Plot

When researchers are studying a large number of observations, they sometimes use a scatter plot to organize the data (Figure 2.7). When using a **scatter plot**, the psychologist measures one variable on the horizontal axis and the other variable on the vertical axis; then, using a single point for each observation, he or she plots ratings on the two variables. The resulting figures are called "scatter plots" because they show how the points

scatter over the range of possible relationships (Spence et al., 1976).

Measuring Correlation

The more closely the pattern of dots in a scatter plot approaches a straight line, the more we can detect a correlation, or linear relationship, between the two variables. The most common measure of correlation is the **correlation coefficient**, symbolized by the letter r. The correlation coefficient is a statistic that helps us estimate how well we can predict scores on the dependent variable on the basis of the independent variable—that is, how closely the two are related.

Suppose we want to know whether there is a relationship between intelligence and creativity. Let's say that we have found some highly intelligent people and have taken some measurements of their creativity. If all our highly intelligent people are also highly creative, there is the highest possible correlation, that is, a perfect correlation: r equals 1. If the two characteristics (intelligence and creativity) tend to appear together in most cases but by no means all, the correlation is not perfect, though it is still very high: r may be somewhere around .95. If the association is less close, there is a lower correlation and r will be smaller. If there is no discernible pattern of relationship between the two characteristics, r will equal 0. Some of our highly intelligent people are highly creative, some are somewhat creative, and some are totally uncreative, but there is no way of predicting a person's creativity from his or her intelligence.

Positive and Negative Correlation

When two variables (say, physical punishment by a mother and aggressive behavior by her child) change in the same direction, we say there is a **positive correlation** between them (indicated by a plus sign). The more physical punishment a mother uses, for instance, the more aggressive her child is. It is also possible to have a **negative correlation** between two variables: as one variable increases, the other decreases. Television watching and grade point average are an example: the *more* hours a student spends watching television, the *lower* his or her grade point average is likely to be.

The scatter plots in Figure 2.7 illustrate three classes of correlation.

■ In the first scatter plot the points come close to forming a straight line that relates a person's self-esteem to his or her degree of assertiveness. The scatter plot shows a high positive correlation: we can see that a person's degree of self-esteem is highly correlated with his or her assertiveness—that is, there is a strong relationship between the two variables, so that the higher the self-esteem, the higher the assertiveness.

■ In the second scatter plot, the points show a negative correlation, indicating that students who spend a lot of time watching TV tend to get low grades and those who watch little TV tend to get high grades. But notice that the points are much less perfectly aligned than in the first scatter plot: the correlation is only moderate.

■ The third scatter plot shows the correlation between the length of time required to complete a test in introductory psychology and the student's grade on that test. In this case, the points wander all over the diagram, showing no relationship at all.

The Strength of a Correlation

The correlation coefficient has a possible range that stretches from −1, which indicates a perfect

negative correlation between two variables; through 0, which indicates no correlation; to +1, which indicates a perfect positive correlation. The closer the correlation coefficient is to +1 or to −1, the greater the linear association between the two variables, so the more reliable our predictions will be from one variable to the other.

As we have noted, a perfect correlation (either +1 or −1) indicates that knowing one variable always allows you to predict the other with certainty. For example, if scores on a math test varied directly with IQ, in such a way that a test score of 125 would be gotten by people with an IQ of 125 and a test score of 105 would be gotten by people with an IQ of 105, there would be a perfect positive correlation (a correlation of +1) between test scores and IQ. In real life, of course, people with an IQ of 125 often do poorly. And people with an IQ of 105 often do well; so the correlation—although positive—is not +1. A perfect correlation is not likely to exist between IQ scores and math test scores: you cannot predict with certainty what score a person will get on a math test by knowing his or her IQ.

Correlations come in all sizes, and few ever attain a perfect +1 or −1. For example, the correlation between the height of a parent and the height of the parent's child of the same sex is about +.50, which indicates a moderately strong relationship. The correlation between IQ scores and school grades is about +.45, also moderately strong. The correlation between physical punishment by a mother and physical aggression by her child is about +.20—positive but weak. When a correlation is 0, there is no relationship at all between two variables. For example, the correlation between shoe size and political beliefs is essentially 0.

And now, with our methodological survey complete, we are ready to explore the field of psychology. Although some of the material in this chapter may have seemed esoteric, it lies at the heart of any progress in understanding human behavior. Even a generalist's knowledge of the various methods psychologists use—and of these methods' requirements and shortcomings—will deepen our understanding of the research that is presented in this book and will enable us to analyze it with a more critical eye.

SUMMARY

1. Psychologists are concerned with regularities and uniformities of behavior. They propose **hypotheses**, or propositions to be tested, which may be either derived from **theories** or formulated from observations. Hypotheses may be tested by experimental or nonexperimental methods.

2. An **experiment** compares two conditions that are identical in all respects except for the factors being investigated. The psychologist actively controls the presence, absence, or intensity of the factors, or *variables*, thought to affect the behavior being studied. The variable that is manipulated by the experimenter is the **independent variable**—which is often linked to causes—and the variable that changes when the independent variable changes is the **dependent variable**—which is often linked to effects. In the **experimental condition** the independent variable is manipulated; in the **control condition** it is not. In laboratory experiments the psychologist uses **counterbalancing** to make sure that any variables not of theoretical interest do not affect the outcome of the experiment.

3. The expectations of investigators can influence their findings, introducing **experimenter effects**, or biases, into the study. One way for a researcher to avoid experimenter bias is to use the **double-blind technique**, in which neither the experimenter nor the subjects know which subjects belong to the experimental group and which belong to the control group. Technological innovations can also help prevent bias. Equivalent groups of subjects can be achieved by using randomization or matching techniques to assign subjects to conditions. When the subject's response is determined more by the research setting than by the independent variable, **demand characteristics** are affecting the research results. **Placebo effects** can also affect results.

4. **Correlational research** indicates the degree of relatedness between two variables, after the independent variable has been manipulated by life. **Correlations** are relationships between variables. Although a correlation does not indicate cause and effect, it allows predictions about the likelihood of two things occurring together.

5. In **field experiments**, researchers conduct their research in the "real world." In **naturalistic observation**, behavior is observed and recorded under natural conditions. A **survey** attempts to estimate the opinions, characteristics, or behavior of a **population**, based on the replies of a **sample**, or selected segment, of the population being studied. The accuracy of these estimates depends on how well the sample matches the population in its essential characteristics. Randomized response techniques provide a statistically accurate way to deal with sensitive topics while protecting the privacy of subjects. A **case study** is an intensive investigation of one or a few individuals, usually with reference to a single psychological phenomenon.

6. Certain psychological studies may involve risk of physical or psychological harm to some of the participants. The American Psychological Association (APA) has developed a set of principles to guide the conduct of researchers; this code concerns the subjects' privacy, voluntary participation, informed consent, and freedom from harm. When research cannot ethically be done with human subjects, it can sometimes be performed on animals. State and federal regulations and the APA specify standards for the use of animals in research and procedures for their care.

7. Researchers generally analyze data by means of statistics. Statistics reduce masses of data to simpler and more informative numbers. When studying the behavior of a group on a single variable, a **frequency distribution**, or a representation showing the number of subjects who obtain each given score, is often used. Frequency distributions may take the form of tables, histograms (bar graphs), or frequency polygons (line graphs). A frequency distribution may be *symmetrical* or *skewed*. Another way of summarizing a frequency distribution is with a **measure of central tendency**, which may be

the **mode**, or most frequently obtained score; the **mean**, or arithmetical average; or the **median**, or the score that falls in the exact middle of the distribution. Measures of **variability** indicate how closely clustered the distribution of scores is. The simplest measure of variability is the **range**, which is the difference between the highest and lowest scores. More reliable is the **standard deviation (S.D.)**, a value that indicates the extent to which figures in a given set of data "cluster" around the mean. In a **normal curve of distribution**, the mean, the median, and the mode fall at the same point, and the curve has a smooth bell shape. **Correlation coefficients** show the extent to which a relationship between two variables can be predicted. When two variables change in the same direction, there is a **positive correlation** between them; when one variable increases and the other decreases, there is a **negative correlation**. A correlation coefficient is expressed as a number ranging from −1 (a perfect negative correlation) through 0 (no correlation at all) to +1 (a perfect positive correlation). **Scatter plots** are used to display correlations in graphic form.

KEY TERMS

case study
control condition
correlation coefficient
correlational research
counterbalancing
curve of normal distribution
demand characteristics
dependent variable
double-blind procedure
empirical approach
experiment
experimental condition
experimenter effects

field experiments
frequency distribution
hypothesis
independent variable
linear function
linear relationship
match
mean
measure of central tendency
median
mode
naturalistic observations
negative correlation
normal curve of distribution

placebo effect
population
positive correlation
randomly assign
range
sample
scatter plot
standard deviation (S.D.)
subjects
survey
systematic relationship
theory
variability

RECOMMENDED READINGS

KEITH-SPIEGEL, P. and G. P. KOOCHER. *Ethics in psychology: professional standards and cases.* New York: Random House, 1985. Presents both a preventive and prescriptive approach, giving information and decision-making strategies to help avoid unethical conduct and explaining the monitoring and redress mechanisms available when ethical violations occur.

KENNY, D. A. *Correlation and causality.* New York: Wiley-Interscience, 1979. An important treatise on when and under what circumstances causal statements can be inferred from correlations.

MARKEN, R. *Methods in experimental psychology.* Monterey: Brooks/Cole, 1981. Another fine discussion of methods of conducting and writing up research.

RUNYON, R. P., and A. HABER. *Fundamentals of behaviorial statistics* (5th ed). New York: Random House, 1984. A clear exposition of statistical methods, procedures, and proofs.

SHAUGHNESSY, J. J. and E. B. ZECHMEISTER. *Research methods in psychology.* New York: Random House, 1985. Pointing to the problem-solving nature of research, this book covers a broad range of descriptive, experimental, and applied methods and uses actual studies to illustrate the steps that lead from defining problems to uncovering solutions.

PART TWO

BIOLOGICAL AND PERCEPTUAL PROCESSES

Anything that's too easy isn't very interesting. Children love to play tick-tack-toe, but it is a game that can be quickly and completely analyzed and once that has been done, there is no further point in playing it.

No branch of science is actually *too* easy, but surely psychology, although the most familiar of all sciences, is also the least "easy." It deals, basically, with the human brain, which is built up of 10 billion neurons, and ten times as many subsidiary cells, with each neuron connected to a very large number of others so that the number of neural pathways is too high a number to make easy sense when it is written down.

The three pounds of human brain is much more complex than any three pounds of anything else in the universe that we know of. One brain is much more complicated than one star, which is why we know so much about stars and so little about the brain. What's more, we are trying to comprehend the brain with what? With the brain.

What a challenge!

And it isn't just the brain. It can't be.

Elephants have larger brains than ours, and they are comparatively intelligent animals, but they're not doing well. Of course, we're killing them and destroying their habitat, but they weren't doing well even before that.

Dolphins and whales have larger brains than ours, and they're comparatively intelligent animals, too, but they're limited. They live exactly as they lived millions of years ago.

Chimpanzees, gorillas, and orangutans are very much like us physically and have respectable brains, but none of them are doing well, and they may be heading for extinction even if we leave them entirely alone.

Our brain is remarkable not just for what it is, but for how it has developed. Four million years ago the closest thing to human beings were the Australopithecines, small creatures with brains about the size of modern apes. *But* they stood erect. How that came about, we don't yet know, but they stood and walked exactly as we do and as no ape does.

That freed their arms for other uses. Apes can use their arms as

we do temporarily, but never totally. And never as skillfully, for our ancestors developed large and fully opposable thumbs.

Our ability to manipulate portions of our environment, to make use of tools as extensions of our arms and hands, flooded our brains with perceptions.

Our ancestors, upright on their hindlegs, and with their forelegs reaching, touching, bringing, throwing, twisting, endlessly active, had a premium placed on the increase in size and complexity of brain. There was plenty for a larger brain to do.

In the last million years, then, our brain tripled its size, and probably improved to an even greater extent in complexity and organization. We can speak, we can think in abstractions, we can organize knowledge into science and art into beauty—all because our brain and hand evolved together and in cooperation.

Isaac Asimov

AUDITORY STIMULATION

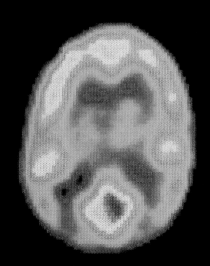

RESTING STATE

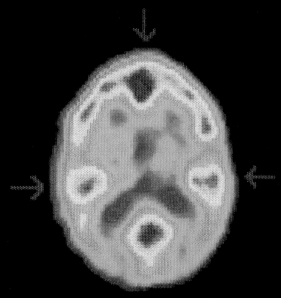

LANGUAGE AND MUSIC

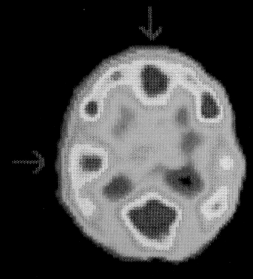

LANGUAGE

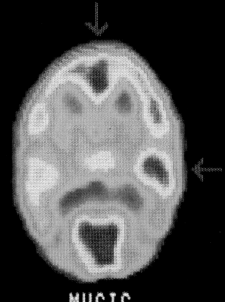

MUSIC

THE BRAIN AND BEHAVIOR

Of all the mysteries of the natural world, one of the most amazing is the brain. The exposed brain —composed of moist, fragile, almost jellylike tissue—resembles a large whitish-gray sponge. To the nonscientific eye, it is quite unimpressive: it is not colorful, and it does not have a graceful shape. Yet this bumpy conglomeration of living cells is an incredibly sophisticated piece of electronic equipment, a machine of great power and precision. Its task is to direct our perceptions, thoughts, imagination, and behavior every minute of our lives.

The brain, like a computer or any other piece of electronic equipment, operates via the switching of electric signals. It also uses chemicals to transmit signals between cells—a feature that makes it different from man-made computers. But while we understand some of these basic brain mechanisms, much else remains unknown. If what's inside our skull is merely an electrochemical machine, how do its switchings and buzzings get translated into our cognitive processes—thinking, planning, learning, remembering—and our emotions? And how are these inner experiences linked to our actions?

At our current level of technical sophistication, brain researchers have few answers to these questions. They know where in the brain some of our emotions and cognitive processes may occur. And they know, in a general sense, how the brain takes in certain types of information from its surroundings, processes this information, and (metaphorically speaking) makes "decisions for action" that are relayed back out to the muscles and limbs of the body as behavioral commands. But it will be some time before we fully grasp exactly how the brain controls our thoughts and actions.

THE EVOLUTION OF A "MACHINE FOR LEARNING"

We do know that the brain is different today from the way it was millions of years earlier in the history of the human species. Like other animals, our species has developed through evolution, a slow process of change in its physical characteristics. Bodily characteristics that have helped individuals survive and reproduce have been handed down through the generations, perhaps even becoming more pronounced over the years. Other less advantageous characteristics have disappeared. The brain, which is part of our physical equipment, has evolved just as the rest of our body has. If a physical change in the brain led to more optimal behavior—such as better hunting, better ways to escape predators, or better ways of attracting a mate—that physical change would survive and be passed along in evolution.

An important feature of human evolution is that our brain has become larger, relative to our body frame, than that of our ancestors. We have retained those portions of the brain that control essential life functions, such as breathing, digesting food, and moving smoothly. But onto these ancient brain areas have been added new areas, specialized for those abilities that have been developed to a unique degree in the human species: thinking, planning, reasoning, remembering, and speaking.

And this brings us to a paradox. If we all have inherited this superbly efficient behavioral control center, specially designed to guide a huge range of behaviors from sleeping to walking, why do we not all behave the same way? The answer is this. For all its complex "hard-wired circuits," the brain is also constructed in such a way that new circuits can be created in a given individual whenever it is advantageous to do so. The creation of these new circuits is probably what we mean by *learning*. Each individual learns slightly different things depending on his or her environment, so each individual behaves slightly differently. (Genetic differences can also cause differences in behavior —a point we will clarify in Chapter 4.) All animals can learn to some degree, but humans are particularly well suited for this task.

In this chapter we will survey the various parts of the brain. We will look at those parts that impose narrow limits on certain behaviors: we all sneeze, for example, in almost the same way, and this pattern of behavior is quite rigidly controlled by the midbrain. We will also look at those parts of the brain that allow each person's behavior to be adaptable, changeable, or "plastic" (as psychologists say): these are the areas that let each person learn unique behavior patterns. To a certain extent, the human brain is "hard-wired," but to a certain extent it is also flexible and "programmable." Throughout this book we will look at the interplay between these two properties of the "brain machine."

THE NERVOUS SYSTEM: MAJOR DIVISIONS

At the basic level, the brain directs our body functions and behavior by sending electrical messages. Some messages go to muscles. They help control our internal systems—the cardiovascular, respiratory, digestive, and reproductive systems —to keep our hearts beating, our lungs breathing, and so on. They also help control our sensory and musculoskeletal systems, directing our eyes to scan the pages of a book, our fingers to fly almost effortlessly over the keyboard of a typewriter, and our legs to propel us through the park on our morning jog. Other messages go to **glands**, organs that secrete chemicals called **hormones** that affect body functions, arouse emotions, and motivate goal-directed behavior.

But regardless of their ultimate destination, all messages from the brain travel by way of the nervous system, an electrochemical conducting network that extends throughout the body. The brain is, in fact, part of the nervous system. Before we explore the brain, therefore, we will consider the structure and general function of the nervous system.

The human nervous system is organized somewhat the way a large army is, when it is engaged in combat with a widely dispersed enemy. In this rough analogy, the brain corresponds to the staff of generals at headquarters, whose job is to think and plan strategic moves. The generals constantly read reports about enemy strength and movements, sent to them from their scouts and front-line soldiers. And they also send out a continuous stream of commands to move troops, supplies, and equipment from place to place. The aim of the army is to cope with a hostile environment and thus survive; the nervous system must cope with the environment in an analogous way.

Like any large organization, the nervous system can be studied at several different levels. We could study an army by studying individual soldiers and what makes them tick; similarly, we will study the nervous system by examining single nerve cells, the basic elements or building blocks of the nervous system. We might also examine the functions of different officers at the general staff headquarters; similarly, we will describe the functions of large segments of the brain.

But before we address these topics, we need to get an overview of the whole army, so that we can see what its major divisions and subdivisions are. An army might be divided into two parts: the general staff and supporting personnel back at headquarters and the line officers and troops out in the field. Similarly, the nervous system can be divided into two parts: the central nervous system (the brain and spinal cord) and the peripheral nervous system (including the somatic and autonomic segments).

The Central Nervous System

Most of the nerve cells, or neurons, in the body are in the **central nervous system (CNS)**, the part of the nervous system that is primarily responsible for the transmission and storage of information. The CNS controls all human behavior, from the blink of an eye to the solution of a complex problem in symbolic logic.

The CNS consists of the brain (the "general staff") and a long cable of communication neurons (the "supporting personnel") known as the **spinal cord**. The spinal cord is covered with a protective membrane and bathed in spinal fluid. Information from the skin and muscles comes into the brain by way of the spinal cord, and motor commands go back out by way of the spinal cord as well. The spinal cord is our primary communications link to the outside world.

Many of the neurons in the CNS are clumped together, forming nuclei, or **centers**, that function as units. Each of these nuclei transmits signals through one or more **pathways**—"cables" made of long parallel axons (structures attached to neurons, analogous to telephone wires). Vastly outnumbering and surrounding the neurons are smaller cells called **glia** ("glue"). Some of the glial cells supply neurons with nutrients from blood vessels. Others wrap around the neurons, insulating them from one another. Think of the glia as insulation that covers telephone wires strung from one army communications center to all its neighbors.

The Peripheral Nervous System

The **peripheral nervous system (PNS)** leads from the central nervous system to all parts of the body. It carries out commands from the central nervous

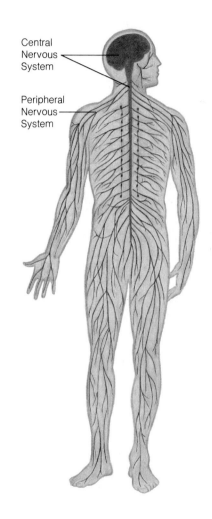

Figure 3.1. The central nervous system (CNS) and the peripheral nervous system (PNS) in the human body. Both of these systems are made up of billions of nerve cells, or neurons, each of which is capable of transmitting a train of chemical-electrical signals in one direction. In the CNS, these neurons form an immensely complex network that organizes, stores, and redirects vast quantities of information. In the PNS, neurons in every pathway carry information either from receptors (such as the sense organs) toward the CNS or away from the CNS to effectors (in the muscles, for example). There is a close match between information going to the CNS and information coming from it. Every muscle, for example, not only receives directions from the CNS to contract or relax but also sends back information about its present state of contraction or relaxation.

system, acting as the major link between the CNS and the rest of the body. The peripheral nervous system consists of **nerves** (pathways containing neural fibers that transmit sensations and motor commands) and **ganglia**, collections of neuron cell bodies found principally along the bony column that encloses the spinal cord. The central and peripheral nervous systems are shown in Figure 3.1.

The peripheral nervous system has two divisions: the somatic and the autonomic.

The Somatic Segment of the PNS

The **somatic nervous system** senses and acts upon the external world. It consists of both sensory and motor neurons. **Sensory neurons** transmit incoming signals to the CNS; these signals originate in receptor cells, located in sense organs such as the eye and the ear. The cell bodies of the sensory neurons make up the ganglia along the outside of the spinal column. Motor neurons, whose cell bodies lie inside the spinal cord, transmit outgoing signals from the spinal cord to neuromuscular cells and glands. The somatic nervous system controls the skeletal muscles, which move the bones and thereby the body.

We usually think of somatic activity as being under voluntary control: pointing a finger or walking, for example, are movements we can control.

The Autonomic Segment of the PNS

The **autonomic nervous system** regulates the internal environment. It, too, contains sensory and motor neurons. The autonomic nervous system controls the visceral muscles (blood vessels, heart, and intestines) and the glands.

We tend to think of autonomic activity as involuntary, for it generally occurs with little awareness or control, as when muscles lining the digestive tract contract or the heart beats. In fact, "autonomic" means "independent," referring to our supposed inability to control these activities. Yet people can learn to modify some of them—heart rate, blood pressure, or skin temperature—when they receive immediate information about the state of such activities at the same time that they are trying to alter them (Stoyva, 1976). This procedure is called "biofeedback," since information

about activity in an organ is "fed back" to the person; in Chapter 7 we will see how the biofeedback procedure works.

The autonomic nervous system is itself divided into the sympathetic and parasympathetic divisions. Both divisions send nerves into almost every gland and visceral muscle in the body.

The Sympathetic Nervous System The **sympathetic nervous system** dominates in emergencies and stressful situations. It responds by increasing blood-sugar level, heart rate, and blood pressure and slowing digestion. Physiological changes such as these promote fast, strong actions, such as fighting or fleeing. You might think of the sympathetic nervous system as being in "sympathy" with our emotions.

The Parasympathetic Nervous System The **parasympathetic nervous system** often has the opposite effect. It dominates in relaxed situations, and its responses tend to conserve energy. For example, after you have eaten a large meal, the parasympathetic nervous system decreases your heart rate and slows the flow of blood to your skeletal muscles, while it enhances your digestion.

This division of labor is not rigid, however. When you are anxious, the sympathetic nervous system responds by increasing your blood pressure and heart rate. But the parasympathetic nervous system also responds; it may cause indigestion, diarrhea, and even urination in extremely stressful situations. The two systems work together in many actions. For example, sexual arousal is the business of the parasympathetic division, but sexual orgasm is a response of the sympathetic division. The relationships among the parts of the nervous system are diagrammed in Figure 3.2.

Neurons

Let us now shift our level of analysis and focus for a while on the individual neuron, the individual "soldier" who functions in many different capacities depending on his location and his role in the army hierarchy. **Neurons** are cells specially adapted to transmit information by means of electrochemical impulses.

Figure 3.2. Diagram of the relationships among the parts of the nervous system.

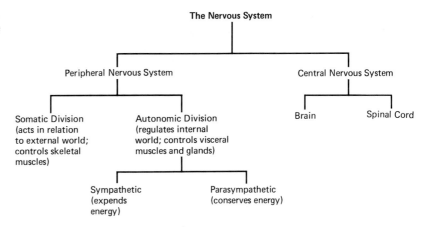

Types of Neurons

Neurons basically perform one of three functions. They may sense information from the environment, as an army scout looks out for enemy troops; they may trigger a response by commanding muscles or glands to move, as an artillery officer fires his cannons; or they may simply pass along or relay to a neighboring neuron information they receive from another neuron, much as a radio operator may transmit an order he receives from general headquarters. These three functions correspond to three categories of neurons: receptor neurons, motor neurons, and interneurons.

■ The job of the **receptor neurons** is to handle stimulation from the environment. These cells, which lie within sense organs, respond to changes in environmental energy. Cells in the back of the eye respond to light, for example; cells in the skin respond to pain or pressure; and cells on the tongue respond to tastes. When receptor cells are stimulated they send signals to the brain. There, the signals may be converted into information about the environment.

■ The job of the **motor neurons** is to carry out the orders of the brain and the spinal cord for muscle contractions; these contractions cause parts of the body to move. As we have noted, some of these movements—chewing, walking, writing, and so on—are under our conscious control. Others, such as breathing, ordinarily take place outside our awareness, though people can sometimes learn to control them consciously.

■ The job of regular **interneurons** is to transmit electrochemical signals from one part of the nervous system to another. Some neurons connect the nervous system with receptor cells, some connect the nervous system with motor neurons, and others simply connect one neuron with another. Many neurons have long fibers, called axons, that are rather like poor, slow telephone wires capable of conveying messages from one point to another in the nervous system.

Parts of the Neuron

Neurons in the central nervous system come in a range of shapes and sizes, but most neurons have features in common. The typical neuron, which looks like the one in Figure 3.3B, has five distinct parts, all enclosed in a thin membrane that resembles the "skin" of a soap bubble. These five parts are the cell body, the dendrites, an axon, a myelin sheath, and the axon terminals.

■ The **cell body** contains the nucleus, which is the cell's energy center. Through chemical reactions, the cell body provides energy for neural action and manufactures the chemicals used to transmit signals.

■ The **dendrites** are many short fibers branching out from the cell body. In most neurons, the dendrites receive signals from other neurons.

■ The **axon** is a long fiber that leads away from

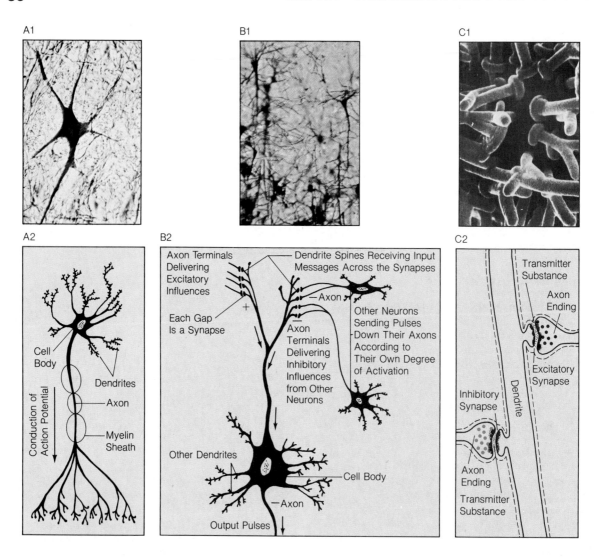

Figure 3.3. The fundamental structures in the nervous system. (Al and A2) A photomicrograph and a diagram of the parts of a single neuron. The dendrites are the receiving end of the neuron; the axon is the sending end. An action potential is transmitted along the axon of a neuron only when its dendrites have been sufficiently excited within a brief span of time. (B1) A photomicrograph of neurons connecting with one another in the cerebral cortex. (B2) A diagram of a typical neuron, representing it as a device that adds up excitatory and inhibitory influences and responds accordingly with a firing rate of so many pulses per second. (C1 and C2) An electron micrograph and a diagram of the structures at the synapse. Note the correspondence between the axon endings and the small protrusions on the dendrites in B2 and C2. When an action potential reaches the end of the axon of a neuron, small amounts of transmitter substances are released from storage areas and cross the synapse to the dendrites of another neuron. The substances from some neurons are excitatory in their effect; the substances from others are inhibitory. If the receiving neuron gets sufficient excitation (and not too much inhibition), it in turn fires.

the cell body, carrying signals to distant regions, where they are transmitted to the dendrites of other neurons or to muscles and glands. It is the axons that form the neural pathways in the CNS.

∎ The **myelin sheath**, which is manufactured for neurons by glial cells, consists of a fatty, whitish substance that surrounds and insulates the axons of many neurons.

∎ **Synapses** are tiny gaps or clefts between neurons, where signals may be transmitted from one neuron to another. The "sending" sides of synapses are axon terminals, specialized structures at the tips of the axon's many branches. The "receiving" sides of synapses are on the tips of the branching dendrites. The two parts of a synapse do not touch; nevertheless, a signal can flow from one neuron to another (see Figure 3.3B).

How Electrical Signals Cross Synapses

Each neuron is, essentially, a tiny battery that has a small background charge (electric potential). To simplify a complex story, neurons communicate with one another by sending electrical charges across the synaptic cleft between them. These charges are sent by way of tiny amounts of chemical substances, called neurotransmitters, which act as messengers. Any substance that is released through the synapses of one neuron and affects another neuron in a specific manner is considered a **neurotransmitter**. (We discuss specific neurotransmitters in detail later in this chapter.)

The neurotransmitters are stored in little sacs within the axon terminals of the sending neuron. When an electrical impulse comes down the axon from the cell body, these substances are squirted out. They flow across the synaptic gap and are taken up through structures analogous to tiny holes in the membrane of the receiving neurons' dendrites. The effect of the neurotransmitter depends on the kind of "holes" that are opened in the membrane: "holes" of different shapes allow different neurotransmitters to flow in. The effect of the neurotransmitter also depends on the kind of connection through which it enters. When the neurotransmitter comes through an **excitatory connection**, the neuron's charge increases. When the neurotransmitter comes through an **inhibitory connection**, the charge is decreased (see Figure 3.3C). In either case, the net result is that the neurotransmitter generates a change in the voltage of the receiving neuron, known as a **slow potential**.

If the voltage, or electric potential, within a neuron grows large enough, it passes a "threshold" and generates a nerve impulse. This impulse is like an electrical pulse that travels down the axon and then splits among the axon's many terminals. Each terminal may then release some neurotransmitter into the synapses it makes with the dendrites of other neurons. Axons are not especially efficient "electrical wires"—they are 10 million times less conductive than copper wire. Yet the nervous system gets the job done with the biological material that has evolved.

The Axon's Rate of Firing

Up to now, for the sake of clarity, we have been looking at the way a single nerve impulse is generated. But this picture is somewhat misleading. Neurons do not sit around completely quiescent, rousing themselves to transmit a single impulse and then lapsing into inactivity again. Instead, they are continually generating electricity and receiving some degree of stimulation from their neighbors. Even during a neuron's "resting phase," it sends small spontaneous impulses down the axon at a steady rate, known as its **resting rate**. If a neuron receives many excitatory signals together, its firing rate tends to increase; if it receives many inhibitory signals together, its firing rate tends to decrease. Most neurons are receiving both kinds of signals most of the time. The signals are combined, and the combination determines the neuron's voltage and its firing rate.

Different firing rates can convey different messages. Many sensory neurons convey information about the intensity of the stimulus affecting the organism; the more intense the stimulus, the faster the neurons fire (Stevens, 1979). Some neurons fire so rapidly that they can transmit about 900 impulses per second. The more rapidly an axon fires, the more packets of neurotransmitters flood into the synaptic gap, and the greater the effect on the receiving neuron. This underlies our ability to detect the intensity of sensory stimuli —to say whether a light is bright or dim, for example, or whether a sound is loud or soft.

Different neural pathways also convey different kinds of information. For example, no matter how a visual nerve is stimulated, whether by light, pressure, or electric shock, the same sensation—a visual sensation— is produced. Similarly, stimulating the nerves of hearing by any method always produces an auditory sensation, and stimulating the nerves of taste by any method always produces taste sensations. The quality of a sensation is determined by the nerve stimulated—not by the method used to stimulate it.

We are interested in neurons because they underlie thought and action. But how might these come about from such simple elements as neurons? We will give two illustrations to indicate the kind of "action-oriented machines" one could build out of chains of simple neurons. First, we'll look at a very simple reflex arc, which will serve to illustrate an elementary action system. Then we will examine how networks of neurons might "compute" the features of a sensory array (e.g., something we see or hear), and how these networks might learn to react adaptively depending on how sensory events stimulate the network.

The Reflex Arc: A Simple Neural Circuit

One function of our nervous system is to provide us with immediate, involuntary reactions or responses to stimuli to prevent our being harmed. These responses are our **reflexes**. We react by reflex withdrawal if something burns or pricks our hand, by reflex closure if we get a cinder in our eye, and so on. It is as though the sensory "scout" were ordering the artillery sergeant to fire off a response

Figure 3.4. (A) A diagram of a two-neuron reflex arc, such as the one present in the knee-jerk response. This is the simplest form of reflex arc. (B) A diagram of a three-neuron reflex arc. The pain reflex, which causes a quick withdrawal from the painful stimulus, is an example of this type of reflex arc. It involves one set each of motor and sensory neurons (as in the two-neuron reflex arc), but in addition, an interneuron is present in the gray matter of the spinal cord. The extra neuron means that the information now crosses two synapses. (Gardner, 1975.)

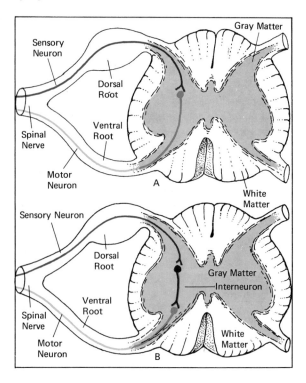

quickly without consulting the "generals" back in the brain, presumably because a fast reaction is needed to prevent more damage.

The signal travels from the sensory receptor to the motor neuron via a circuit of neurons known as a **reflex arc**. A frequently seen example of a reflex arc is the knee-jerk reflex, which occurs when the tendon below the kneecap is tapped. Figure 3.4 shows the simple reflex arc involved in the knee jerk.

However, even this reflex arc is not as simple as you might imagine. It turns out that you can deliberately modify the knee-jerk reflex, by tensing up muscles that oppose the kick. Thus, the brain can send out commands that partly inhibit this reflex.

Other reflexes are more complicated than the knee jerk. In some reflexes, such as removing your hand from a burning surface, many interneurons (neurons that communicate only with other neurons) intervene between the sensory and motor neurons, increasing the number of synapses the signal must cross. The brain can also send inhibitory or excitatory signals to this circuit, to slow or speed up the reaction to the hot surface. For example, people might walk on hot coals or hold their hand over a flame to pass some initiation rite.

The Brain as a Neural Switchboard

Our discussion of reflexes showed that once there are several different inputs to a network of neurons, that network can begin to "calculate" a different response—depending on its exact pattern of stimulation. The brain contains billions of neurons, each of which may have between 1,000 and 10,000 synapses, with which it may receive information from about 1,000 other neurons (Stevens, 1979). Thus, each neuron is part of one or more intricate, interlacing **neural networks**.

Implications of Neural Networks

A constructive way to think about neurons is to visualize each as an element in a computer (Hinton and Anderson, 1981; McCulloch and Pitts, 1943). But the neuron is not like an element in the familiar digital home computer, which manipulates binary signals—signals that have an "on-off," all-or-nothing character. Instead, the neuron is like an element in an analog computer —one that deals with continuously varying quantities, such as voltages or weights.

For simplicity, let us suppose that at any moment, the voltage (and thus the likelihood of firing) at any particular cell in the network is determined by simple arithmetic. A cell's voltage equals the total number of its excitatory receptor sites (excitatory connections) being stimulated by other neurons, *minus* the total of its inhibitory receptor sites (inhibitory connections) being stimulated by other neurons. Because signals are continually arriving, the level of excitation fluctuates. Neural networks are complex switching circuits, continuously computing the level of excitation at all cells.

Take, for example, a single neuron, which we are thinking of as an element in a network. Let's say that this particular neuron receives excitatory impulses through two synapses and inhibitory impulses through a third synapse (see Figure 3.5A). Excitatory impulses add to this neuron's voltage, and inhibitory impulses decrease it. The neuron continually "calculates" its own excitation level, and sends impulses down its axon at a rate proportional to its excitation level.

Now imagine an extremely simple network consisting of five such neural computing elements (Figure 3.5B). Suppose that these elements are faced with two simple stimuli, called A and B. The arrangement of the network permits it to act differently, depending on whether the two stimuli occur together or alone. Neuron 4 receives excitatory impulses from Neurons 1 and 2, and can compute their sum. If Stimuli A and B are sensed so that Neurons 1 and 2 both fire simultaneously, then Neuron 4 will fire and produce a response: it has detected the conjunction of A and B. But note that in this network, Neuron 3 works differently. It will fire at a higher rate *only* if it receives Stimulus A—but *not* Stimulus B at the same instant.

This neural network is able to function logically; it can compute the equivalent of logical conjunction ("A and B"), and it can also compute the equivalent of logical conjunction plus negation ("A but not B"). By connecting many different sensory neurons through a network of interneurons, we could get the network to "compute" and react discriminately to almost any stimulus pattern, expressed as a logical conjunction of "on" and "off" sensory neurons. (We discuss the mechanisms of sensation in Chapter 5.)

In more complex networks (Figure 3.5C), neu-rons that receive sensations might be connected with neurons that eventually evoke actions. For example, the various stimuli (S) might represent specific sights, sounds, or smells, and the response units (R) might correspond to the areas in the brain that can respond by giving the names of these stimuli.

S1, for example, might correspond to a familiar pattern of reflected light; the response unit (or set of units) might identify this pattern as a Dalmatian dog. In such a richly interconnected network one or more circuitous paths can be traced from almost any sensory cell to almost any response cell. The particular response evoked by the stimulation of a sensory cell would then depend on the strength, or efficiency, of the connections between the neurons receiving sensations and those evoking responses.

The Role of Networks in Reflexes and Learning

Human beings are born with many thousands of strong connections built into their nervous systems. These connections, which constitute reflex pathways, provide an infant with adaptive reflexes that are part of the heritage of the species. For example, even a day-old baby will respond to a drop of a sour solution on its tongue by pursing the lips and salivating (Steiner, 1979). By studying such reflexes, researchers can discover how neural networks coordinate sensation and motor responses.

The concept of networks also provides a model that neuroscientists can use when they theorize about the learning process. If the strength and efficiency of the connections within a network can be increased through experience, then we can see how new associations and adaptive behavior could be produced. (In Chapters 8 and 9 we return to the role of networks in learning.) The neural networks in Figure 3.5 are hypothetical, but rudimentary networks have actually been isolated and studied in simple organisms like the sea snail and the crayfish (Hawkins and Kandel, 1984; Wine and Krasne, 1978).

Several current theories of brain function hold that the brain of higher organisms is, in essence, a huge network of computing elements. According to these theories, the elements are connected in much the same way as are those in our hypothetical network, and they can be modified by experi-

A

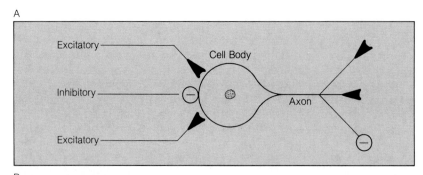

B

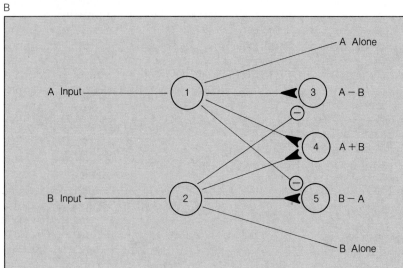

C

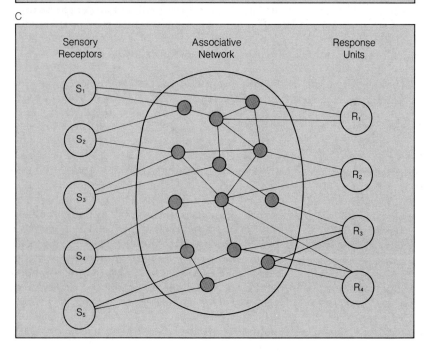

Figure 3.5. The neuron viewed as an element in an analog computer. (A) This neuron receives excitatory impulses through two synapses and inhibitory impulses through one synapse. Excitatory impulses increase the cell's electrical potential, and inhibitory impulses decrease it. At any given moment, impulses are generated along the axon at a rate determined by the sum of the two excitatory inputs minus the inhibitory input. (B) A simple five-neuron network, in which three neurons receive input from two other neurons. Each neuron computes the sum of input it receives. Thus, cell 4 adds its two inputs; cell 3 and cell 5 compute differences in their inputs. (C) A complex neural network, in which neurons that receive sensations (S) are connected with neurons that control responses (R). The pathway between any sensation (sight, sound, smell, taste) and any response goes through an associative network composed of densely interconnected logic elements, in which the sums or differences of excitatory and inhibitory inputs are computed.

ence in adaptive ways. Some of these theories try to show how neural networks could carry out such functions as recognizing familiar scenes and recalling past actions (Hinton and Anderson, 1981; Feldman, 1981).

Neurochemical Transmission

Having now indicated how networks of neurons could compute interesting behavioral functions, let us return to the individual neuron and examine the biochemical nature of its message-sending powers. Recall that neural transmission is basically a chemical process that relies on neurotransmitters. These substances are manufactured in the cell body and then transported to tiny launching sites on the axon terminals.

The efficiency of any synapse in a neural network depends on three factors: (1) how much neurotransmitter is released into the synapse; (2) how much of the transmitter is taken up by receptors in the receiving neurons; and (3) how rapidly the transmitter is cleared away after the impulse crosses the synaptic gap. Neuroscientists have known for a long time that neurotransmitters have a crucial role in passing information along the neural network. But today, neurotransmitters' functions appear to be considerably more complex than once was thought. Eight different biochemicals have been clearly identified as neurotransmitters. And more than twenty-five other substances are known to be active in regulating neural transmission, though they have not been clearly established as transmitters (Schwartz, 1981).

Specific Neurotransmitter Functions

Generally, each neuron uses the same transmitter at all of its synapses. But different transmitters seem to predominate in different parts of the nervous system, and a given transmitter may be involved in different behavioral processes in different parts of the brain. Evidence for such effects has come from studies with drugs. In fact, it has been proposed that virtually every drug that alters mental function does so by interacting with a neurotransmitter system (Snyder, 1984).

Acetylcholine One important transmitter is **acetylcholine (ACH)**, used by the motor neurons of the spinal cord, which carry signals from the spinal cord to muscles and glands. The poison known as *curare*, once used by South American Indians on the tips of their arrows, causes paralysis and death by preventing acetylcholine from acting at the junctions of motor neurons and muscles: victims suffocate when their respiratory muscles stop functioning. Acetylcholine also plays an important role in transmitting signals through the spinal ganglia of the autonomic nervous system. And it is concentrated in the basal ganglia, an area of the brain involved in movement.

Catecholamines The catecholamines consist of **epinephrine** (or adrenalin), **norepinephrine** (or noradrenaline), and **dopamine**. These neurotransmitters play a vital role in arousal of both the sympathetic nervous system and the reticular activating system of the brain. For example, a stressful event causes the outer surface (cortex) of the adrenal gland to release adrenalin, which causes a variety of arousing effects—increased metabolism, increased heart rate, and increased blood pressure. These reactions mobilize the organism to fight or flee in dealing with the stressor. Stressors also cause catecholamines to be released by neurons within the brain's activating system, where they have an alerting, arousing function. The drug amphetamine (whose street name is "speed") enhances the activity of dopamine in brain cells, producing the "speed high" of alertness, restlessness, racing thoughts, and high energy. Prolonged high doses of amphetamine can cause a temporary "amphetamine psychosis" similar to paranoid schizophrenia.

An interesting hypothesis is that schizophrenics have brain cells that are abnormally sensitive to dopamine, so they are always in or near an "amphetamine psychosis." Phenothiazine medications (such as chlorpromazine) that block the action of dopamine often reduce the thought disorders of schizophrenics (Sachar, 1981). Another hypothesis is that psychotic mania and depression are caused by an excess or a deficit, respectively, in the activating neurotransmitters epinephrine and norepinephrine (Sachar, 1981). Antidepressant medications (such as imipramine) which relieve depression appear to act by causing a better supply of epinephrine and norepinephrine in the brain. Other researchers have discovered that gradual destruction of the brain pathways that carry dopamine leads to the development of **Parkinson's disease**, a chronic and often progressive condition that involves involuntary shaking of the limbs and head (Kety, 1979).

ALZHEIMER'S DISEASE

Victims of **Alzheimer's disease** provide a forceful demonstration of the importance of neurotransmitters. This debilitating, progressive brain disease is particularly common among older people, though it can strike younger adults as well. Among people in their sixties, about one in one hundred are believed to have Alzheimer's disease; among those in their eighties, the proportions rises to one in ten (U.S. Congress, 1984). Because at present the disorder is incurable and because the number of older individuals in the population is increasing, Alzheimer's disease is a growing public health problem.

Forgetfulness is usually the first sign of Alzheimer's disease, although not all forgetful people are afflicted. One physician has pointed out that in the sort of forgetfulness that often accompanies natural aging, people forget where they

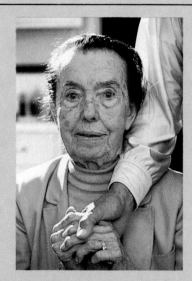

put their glasses; in Alzheimer's disease, people forget that they have ever worn glasses (Schares, 1982). Over a period of several years, forgetfulness in patients with Alzheimer's disease becomes

an increasingly serious memory disorder, accompanied by deteriorating attention, judgment, and personality. The disorder develops slowly: the first symptom noticed by family members may be an inability to write checks or make change. Out walking, the person with Alzheimer's disease may wander away from home and become lost. Eventually, the patient reaches the point where he or she does not recognize family or friends, cannot care for him- or herself, and finally deteriorates physically to the point of death.

Although we don't know the exact cause of Alzheimer's disease, we do know that it is not part of normal aging. In some cases there may be a hereditary element: close relatives of Alzheimer's patients are somewhat more likely to develop the condition than other people (Matsuyama and Jarvik, 1980). It has been suggested

Serotonin Serotonin, a neurotransmitter found in the brain and parasympathetic nervous system, is believed to affect body temperature, sensory perception, and especially the onset of sleep (Iverson, 1979). A large meal makes us drowsy because the absorption of the food temporarily increases the release of serotonin, which inhibits the catecholamine-producing neurons in the reticular activating system.

Endorphins and Pain Relief

Among the twenty-five neuroregulators is a group called **endorphins**, which play a role in the relief of pain. Apparently, the spinal cord and brain release endorphins in response to painful stimulation. The endorphins inhibit the transmission of signals through pain sensory pathways, reducing pain.

The following evidence supports this proposal (Kelly, 1981; Schwartz, 1981; Snyder, 1984):

▪ Endorphins are heavily concentrated in neural centers that are responsible for transmitting pain.
▪ Electrical stimulation of a part of the brain that relieves painful sensations also causes the release of endorphins into pain pathways.
▪ Endorphins appear to mimic the pain-relieving action of morphine, a widely used painkiller. Endorphins and morphine appear to be taken up by the same places in the brain; we might actually say that morphine and other pain-relieving drugs mimic the action of endorphins.
▪ When animals are injected with synthetic endorphins, they seem to feel no pain for a while.

that a slow virus is responsible. But whatever triggers the disease, the behavioral effects appear to be due to a deficiency of the neurotransmitter acetylcholine (ACH). When people die of Alzheimer's disease, their cortex has from 60 to 90 percent less acetylcholine than is found in the brains of people who die from some other cause (Coyle, Price, and DeLong, 1983).

Researchers have found that a structure called the nucleus basalis of Meynert, located beneath a part of the basal ganglia, is heavily implicated in the disease (Coyle, Price, and DeLong, 1983). Nerve fibers from the nucleus basalis project into the cortex and into the hippocampus; the fibers supply both of these areas with an enzyme that synthesizes acetylcholine. In Alzheimer's disease, neurons in the nucleus basalis begin to die, reducing the supply of acetylcholine to the cortex and hippocampus (which, as we shall see, plays an essential role in memory). Neurons in these areas cannot manufacture enough acetylcholine to stimulate their axonal terminals. Starved of this essential transmitter, axons shrink, dendrites atrophy, and the neurons die. In addition, the dying fibers of nucleus basalis neurons appear to provide the basis for placques, flat patches of tissue debris that infest the patient's brain. Other characteristic brain changes include tangles of protein filaments within cell bodies. By the time the patient dies, there is pronounced brain shrinkage.

Recently, researchers have discovered additional brain degeneration and lesions in people who have died of Alzheimer's disease (Hyman et al., 1984). This damage is concentrated in two areas of the hippocampus, which are connected to the nucleus basalis. Cells in these areas are involved in the hippocampal circuit that receives neural signals from the cerebral cortex, elaborates the signals, and returns them to the cortex. This destruction helps explain the memory loss in Alzheimer's: when this part of the hippocampus is damaged or surgically removed, the patient suffers severe memory loss, as we will note in the cases below.

At one time, it was hoped that treatment with acetylcholine would relieve the symptoms of Alzheimer's disease. However, treatment with ACH or the enzymes from which it is synthesized has not been generally successful, perhaps because critical neurons are already dead by the time the disease is diagnosed—usually about five years before the patient dies. During the coming decades, researchers will probably focus on successful early diagnosis of Alzheimer's disease as well as effective treatment. Another possible approach is prevention. Some researchers have turned up slight evidence suggesting that appropriate diet and nutrition—especially dietary supplements of lethicin— may help in reducing the risk of developing Alzheimer's disease (Wurtman, 1982).

Endorphins may help explain findings that at one time baffled physicians. For thousands of years Chinese physicians have relieved pain by inserting needles into designated spots in the skin. This practice, called acupuncture, may stimulate the release of endorphins. If so, acupuncture's success in relieving pain becomes understandable (Carlson, 1981). Similarly, American researchers have been intrigued by the effectiveness of **placebos**—inert "sugar pills" that have no physiological effect on the body—in reducing pain. Perhaps the success of placebos is due to their triggering the release of endorphins through a learning process.

Now that connections between neurotransmitters and mental states have been discovered, some observers hope that we will eventually be able to use synthetic drugs that mimic neurotransmitter actions to relieve pain and cure illness, and to induce peak performance, sharpen memory, and heighten pleasure. But that time seems far in the future. The task of developing such drugs has proved far more difficult than researchers anticipated. For example, the first artificial painkilling substances related to endorphins proved to have the same serious drawback as morphine and heroin: they were addictive. Researchers still hope to discover a synthetic neurotransmitter that is not addictive.

THE BRAIN

The brain is an organ of tremendous complexity. It exerts some sort of control over every aspect of human action—breathing, sleeping, eating, playing tennis, or writing a poem. The brain regulates behavior in three ways. First, it maintains and controls vital internal bodily functions, such as circulation, digestion, and the maintenance of body temperature. Second, it receives sensory information about the external world and may issue motor commands in response to this information. Third, it uses past experience to select or create new ways of responding to the environment.

Studying the Brain

Much of what we know about the anatomy of the brain has been learned by dissecting brains and by examining thin slices of brain tissue under the microscope. Such studies have enabled researchers to establish major anatomic structures, important clumps of neurons, and the connections of major brain pathways. But the next step, relating anatomy to behavior, has been difficult. We have gleaned only limited information by observing the effects of brain injuries caused by accident or disease. Most early observations concerned the effects of damage to the cortex: medical practitioners observed that patients who had suffered strokes or other types of localized brain damage tended to show particular disruptions in behavior. But researchers could verify the relationship between brain damage and behavior only by autopsy after the patient had died, perhaps years later.

Recently, however, technological advances have made it possible to study living brains of both normal and injured individuals. Some techniques even allow us to see inside these individuals' brains and watch them functioning.

Study Techniques: Ablation

Many of the basic relationships noted by early neurologists have been confirmed by modern neurosurgical techniques, typically in experiments conducted with animals with brains similar to ours. The oldest technique is *ablation* or *lesion*, which involves the destruction or removal of precisely localized clumps of neurons or even entire brain structures. Using a book on the anatomy of the animal's brain, the surgeon can remove small, selected structures in the brain either by a scalpel, or by aspiration, or by cauterizing them. Tiny clusters of neurons deep in the brain can be destroyed by placing a thin electrode through a

tiny hole in the skull, moving it to the exact area of interest, and then passing a strong electric current that "burns out" a few millimeters of neural tissue around the tip of the electrode. After the animal recovers from the surgery, it is then given a range of behavioral tests to see what effect that brain lesion has had on the animal's normal behavior.

Later, the animal is sacrificed and its brain examined to verify exactly where the surgical damage has occurred. If a postsurgical deficit is found —for instance, if the animal can no longer distinguish visual forms or shapes—then the scientist infers that the damaged area of the brain was crucially important in helping the normal animal carry out that function.

Stimulation

Another useful technique for studying brain function is to stimulate selected areas of the brain. In one such method, mild electrical stimulation is applied to different areas of the brain: the electricity acts the same way the natural electrochemical impulse does, stimulating neurons to fire. The brain can also be stimulated by chemicals, and scientists have made use of this technique in animals. After implanting a small hypodermic needle in an animal's brain so that the end touches the area under study, a researcher pumps a small amount of chemical through the needle to the area.

EEGs and Event-Related Potentials

In another modern technique, called **electroencephalography (EEG)**, researchers record the brain's electrical activity by placing electrodes on a person's scalp. The typical EEG record shows small, wavelike fluctuations in surface voltage, varying from two to fifty waves per second. The source of these waves is not yet known. They may reflect graded, wavelike changes in specific groups of cells, or they may result from the integrated activity of millions of firing neurons.

EEGs have been used to identify brain disorders, such as tumors or epilepsy, but they can also tell us about the healthy brain. Particular brain waves are correlated with specific psychological states. For example, the EEG varies with a person's state of alertness: an aroused, alert person

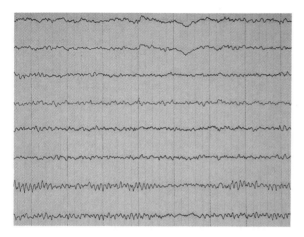

Researchers study records of brain waves by measuring their amplitude (the height of the wave as it appears on the EEG) and their frequency (the number of waves that appear per second). Voltages recorded from the scalp are tiny—just a few thousandths of a volt; they must be amplified to be studied. A normal human EEG pattern is shown here. The top five tracings are a record of Beta waves; the bottom three are Alpha waves.

shows low-intensity, very fast brain waves, but as people relax, their brain waves slow down and become higher in amplitude (see Chapter 7). The correlation between electrical activity and arousal is so strong that the stages of sleep can be identified by EEG recordings, as can episodes of dreaming.

EEGs also reveal how the brain responds to specific events. To detect such reactions, researchers record **event-related potentials (ERPs)** —changes in spontaneous EEG activity in re-

sponse to stimulation, such as a sight or sound. The study of ERPs has supplied useful information about the relationship between the brain and behavior. Some characteristic ERPs have been correlated with such mental phenomena as expectation or surprise. For example, a feature of the ERP known as the **P300 wave** appears to reflect the "double take" of a surprised cortex. The P300, or "surprise," wave arises when a person's expectations are upset (see Figure 3.6). Neuropsychologists are uncertain of the neurological basis for the P300, although it is regarded as a measure of attention and decision making (Parmelee and Sigman, 1983). The records of such specific ERPs give us a small window on the way the brain develops expectancies.

Single-Unit Recording

Not all recordings of brain activity are made with electrodes on the surface of the brain; some involve penetrating the brain itself. Using a technique known as **single-unit recording**, psychologists can place a microelectrode very close to an individual neuron, allowing them to amplify the firing of impulses electronically and record them. Single-unit recording can give a picture of the electrical activity of a single neuron.

Computerized Tomography (CT Scans)

For many years, X-ray pictures of the brain have been used to locate injuries and abnormalities. A single X-ray is difficult to interpret, however, be-

Figure 3.6. Changes in evoked potential following a series of tones. ("beep beep beep"). The influence of expectancy shows up at about 300 milliseconds after the tone. Expected tones ("beeps") yield the top tracing; surprising tones ("boops") inserted into the series of beeps yield the bottom tracing, the P300 wave.

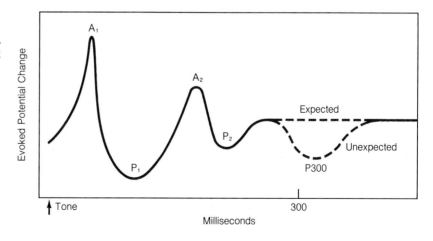

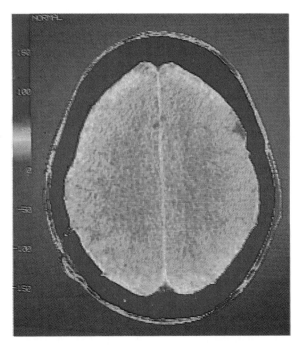

In the CT scan process, a narrow beam of X-rays is passed through the brain from a number of angles. The multiple X-ray pictures that result are fed into a computer that has been programmed with a knowledge of projective geometry. With this knowledge, the computer can reconstruct pictures of single cross sections. When neuroscientists suspect brain damage, they can easily obtain a number of cross sections surrounding the suspected area. Shown here is a CT scan of a normal brain.

cause it squashes together overlapping structures. In the brain, these structures are spread through a three-dimensional sphere, but in a single X-ray, they are pushed into a two-dimensional picture.

To solve this problem, medical engineers have developed a technique called **computerized tomography (CT) scans**, which enables us to reconstruct a single slice, or cross section, of the brain in any depth at any angle. CT scans are fast and noninvasive, and they allow much clearer localization of brain damage or tumors than did earlier X-ray techniques. CT scans also permit neuropsychologists to establish much more accurately the relationship between an injured brain area and a patient's behavioral problems. For example, CT scans can locate the damage caused by a stroke that has been followed by paralysis, language disorders, or loss of memory.

Other Imaging Techniques

The development of CT scans was a giant step toward the goal of relating brain and behavior. Since they were developed, other new techniques have given us a window through which we can observe the living brain's functions. One new technique that provides a picture of brain function, the **position emission tomography (PET) scan**, is based on the biochemistry of the nervous system and involves the use of a radioactive tracer substance. In cases involving suspected degenerative brain disorders, epilepsy, and stroke, diagnosis by PET scans is said to be more efficient than by any other method (Fox, 1984).

In another new technique, known as **nuclear magnetic resonance (NMR)**, the body is enclosed in a magnetic field and radio waves are used to produce images of tissue, biochemical activity, and metabolism. These new techniques promise to enlarge our knowledge of the working brain.

The Brain's Structure—An Overview

The adult human brain, which weighs about three pounds, is composed of numerous substructures with specific interrelated functions. Each layer of

To do a PET scan, researchers inject radioactive glucose into the body and trace the brain's uptake of this substance. More active brain sites take up glucose faster: as the radioactive ions decay, their presence can be translated to create maps of the brain. The scan on the left indicates Alzheimer's disease in a seventy-three-year-old patient; the one on the right shows the normal brain of a person of seventy-two.

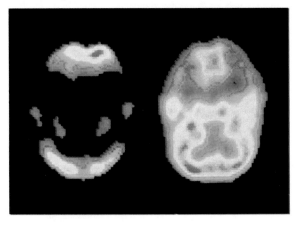

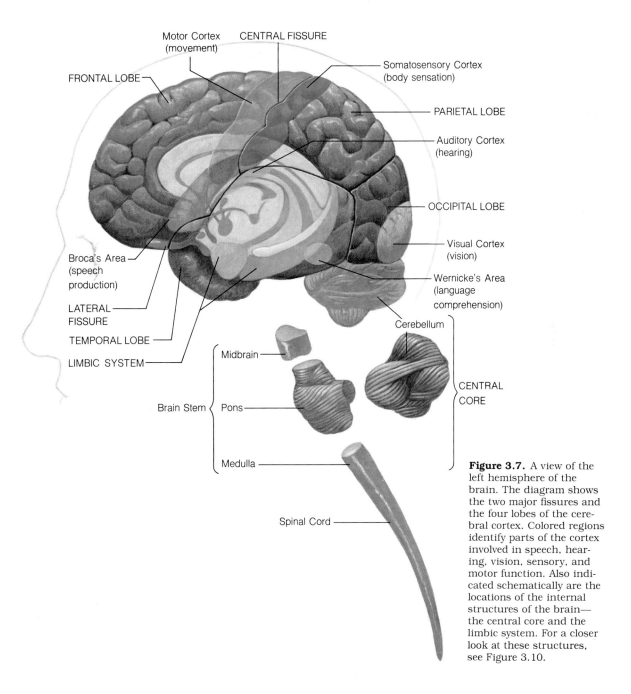

Motor Cortex (movement)

CENTRAL FISSURE

FRONTAL LOBE

Somatosensory Cortex (body sensation)

PARIETAL LOBE

Auditory Cortex (hearing)

OCCIPITAL LOBE

Visual Cortex (vision)

Wernicke's Area (language comprehension)

Broca's Area (speech production)

LATERAL FISSURE

TEMPORAL LOBE

LIMBIC SYSTEM

Midbrain

Brain Stem { Pons

Medulla

Cerebellum

CENTRAL CORE

Spinal Cord

Figure 3.7. A view of the left hemisphere of the brain. The diagram shows the two major fissures and the four lobes of the cerebral cortex. Colored regions identify parts of the cortex involved in speech, hearing, vision, sensory, and motor function. Also indicated schematically are the locations of the internal structures of the brain—the central core and the limbic system. For a closer look at these structures, see Figure 3.10.

this structure represents a consecutive stage in the evolution of the brain. As we will see, different parts of the brain appear to be involved in different types of behavior. This concept is known as **localization of function**.

One way to put the brain's anatomy in perspective is to look at the structure of the entire central nervous system—the brain plus the spinal cord (Figure 3.7). We can visualize the spinal cord as a long tube filled with long nerve fibers. Along this tube, near its top, are, first, the thickening knobs of a structure known as the **brain stem**; then, a ball-shaped structure about the size of a small orange, which is called the **cerebellum.** Perched on the top is a second "orange" that forms the brain's **central core**. Wrapped around this second orange are several layers of "rind": an inner group of structures known as the *limbic system* and an outer area called the *cerebral cortex*. The entire structure makes a sphere about the size of a large cantaloupe. The outer portion of this sphere is divided into two halves, the **cerebral hemispheres**, which constitute what most people think of as the brain. Together the two hemispheres form the **cerebrum**.

The human *cerebrum*, which includes the cerebral cortex and the tissue beneath it, has reached a size that indicates a major evolutionary development. The cerebrum accounts for about 85 percent of the weight of the human brain. We can conceive of the cerebrum as a "thinking cap," which allows us to plan, learn, and reason; its growth reflects the fact that human beings evolved partly by using their wits to outwit stronger predators, to adapt to changing climates, and to solve environmental crises. The growing mass of the evolving cerebral cortex had to be tucked inside a skull that could not expand greatly without making us top-heavy. In the process of evolution, the problem was solved: the cortical tissues were folded up, much as you would crumple a sheet of paper into a ball. If your cerebral cortex were ironed flat, its compression would become apparent, for it would cover the seat of your chair. All those neat, systematic folds allow a giant computer to be packed into a small "melon" you can carry around easily on your shoulders.

The Cerebral Cortex

With the above overview in mind, let us look at the brain's structures in detail. We start with the most recently evolved part of the nervous system: the **cerebral cortex**, composed of gray matter on the outer portion of the cerebral hemispheres. This thin (about one-twelfth of an inch thick), wrinkled covering contains billions of neurons. It is heavily involved in sensation, movement, learning, speech, reasoning, and memory.

Several prominent landmarks on the surface of the cortex are used as guides in locating its regions. Each hemisphere has two deep folds (called fissures) that divide it into four sections known as the **frontal**, **parietal**, **temporal**, and **occipital lobes** (see Figure 3.7). Researchers also use other divisions to refer to different areas or regions of these major lobes.

For convenience we will consider the different cortical areas in terms of their major psychological functions: we may talk about the memory areas, the motor control areas, and so on. The location of specific functions—for example, the conclusion that pattern vision is carried out in the occipital lobe—has generally been established from studies of patients with brain damage. These conclusions actually oversimplify brain function. In most cases, a behavioral ability is supported by a large number of neural structures, so that damage to any of these other areas usually affects that ability. We will, however, try to simplify: we will speak *as if* a given brain locale primarily affected specific types of behavior.

Motor and Somatosensory Areas of the Cortex

Our motor dexterity and many of our touch sensations are handled in neighboring portions of the cortex. This seems like a practical arrangement, since feedback between the two is important for efficient motor functioning.

■ Just behind the deep central fissure, in the parietal lobe, is the **somatosensory cortex**; here the cortex receives and interprets touch and pressure on the skin. It is also the primary area for the sense of bodily position. Damage to this portion of the cortex generally impairs the sense of touch.

■ Across the central fissure, in the frontal lobes, is the **motor cortex**, which regulates our voluntary movements. Damage to this area is followed by weakness or paralysis of specific muscles, depending on the location of the injury.

The amount of cortex devoted to the sensations and motor activities from each particular part of the body has nothing to do with that part's size or muscle mass. Instead, the part's share of the motor and sensory cortex is directly related to the degree of sensitivity or precise motor control exercised by that body part. This relationship shows clearly in Figure 3.8. The body of a little man (often called a "homunculus") has been drawn along the fold; in this drawing, the size of each body part reflects the proportion of the cortex devoted to processing information concerning that part. Notice that the fingers, which can make precise movements, are given a much larger area of the

Figure 3.8. Both A and B represent the right hemisphere of the brain, which controls the voluntary muscles on the left side of the body. (A) A diagram representing the location and amount of cortical space devoted to the motor capacities of various body parts. Areas of the body capable of the most complex and precise movements take up the largest quantities of space in the motor cortex. For example, the eyelid and eyeball (capable of many precise movements) have a larger representation than the face. (B) A diagram representing the location and amount of cortical space devoted to the sensory capacities of various body parts. In the sensory realm, those organs capable of the highest sensitivity have the largest representations in the somatosensory cortex. Relatively direct linkages connect sensory areas to homologous motor areas. (Penfield and Rasmussen, 1950.)

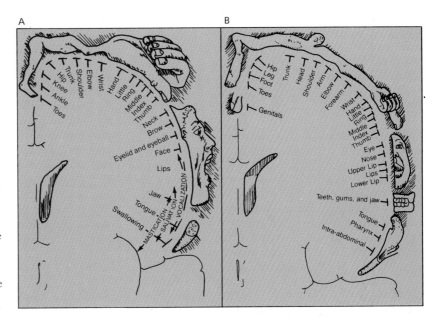

motor cortex than the hip. Similarly, the lips, which make fine movements in speech and are extremely sensitive to touch, have a large area of the somatosensory cortex devoted to them. These large areas correspond to the behavioral capacities that best set human beings apart from other animals—our use of hand tools and our speech.

These relationships have been verified in studies of patients undergoing brain surgery, usually for epilepsy. When weak electrical current is applied to the surface of brain tissue, the neurons beneath the surface fire. Such mild stimulation is painless, and it produces a curious effect. Instead of feeling as if something had touched the brain, the patient feels as if an external stimulus had occurred somewhere on the body. In one classic series of experiments, researchers first stimulated patients in the sensory cortex. The patients claimed they had been touched; the apparent location on their bodies corresponded to a specific location in the cortex. Next, the researchers stimulated spots on the motor cortex; this stimulation caused the patients to move specific skeletal muscles and limbs (Penfield and Rasmussen, 1950).

Simple Visual and Auditory Perception

Our sensory organs differ from each other: an eye bears little resemblance to an ear, and the experience of looking at a painting is nothing like listening to a symphony. Yet although vision and hearing use different sense organs and are processed by different parts of the brain, both senses have the same fundamental task. They must analyze and recognize patterns of stimuli.

Visual Perception The area of the brain most involved in receiving and analyzing visual information is the **visual cortex**, located at the back of the brain in the occipital lobe. Sensory receptors in the eye send information along the optic nerve, through a relay station known as the thalamus (discussed later in this chapter), and on to the occipital lobe.

Research with event-related potentials (ERPs) has helped to establish the importance of the visual cortex in processing sights. When a person sees a flash of light, ERPs appear that indicate neuronal activity in the visual cortex. Damage to this area of the brain confirms such findings: injury to the visual cortex can produce large blind areas in the visual field. People with such injuries may be able to distinguish between light and dark and discriminate movement in this part of the visual field, but they cannot distinguish the shapes of objects.

Researchers have used single-unit recordings, placing a microelectrode in or near a single neuron, to discover how the visual cortex processes information. In one series of studies of cats and monkeys, individual neurons were found to be responsive to highly specific features of visual stimuli. A horizontal line moving across the retina from left to right caused some neurons to fire, but other neurons, in a different area of the visual pathway, fired only in response to a vertical line moving in another direction (Hubel and Wiesel, 1962).

Auditory Perception   The perception of sounds is carried out in the **auditory cortex**, located in the top half of the temporal lobe, which is on the side of the brain below the lateral fissure (above your ear). From each ear auditory signals travel through several relay stations to the temporal cortex. Epileptic activity or electrical stimulation in this area can produce hallucinations of sound, such as buzzes, gunshots, and trickling water (Hecaen and Albert, 1978).

Research with ERPs has also helped to establish the role of the auditory cortex in processing sounds. Sounds evoke marked changes in brain waves recorded at the auditory cortex, indicating a flurry of neuronal activity. Studies have shown a detailed and specific relationship between portions of the auditory cortex and specific sounds. For instance, the musical scale is represented in a more or less orderly fashion along the auditory cortex, with low notes at one end of the auditory cortex, high notes at the other end, and middle notes in between (Woolsey, 1961).

Complex Pattern Recognition   By itself, the neural analysis of shapes and sounds in the visual and auditory cortex produces little meaning. How do we decide that a small, gray furry shape is a cat or that a sequence of four notes is the opening of Beethoven's Fifth Symphony? We must go through a further process, called **pattern recognition**, in which we identify a shape or sound as similar to something we have seen before. Pattern recognition is essential; without it, our perceptual processes would not be very useful.

Some aspects of visual pattern recognition are carried out in the lower part of the temporal lobes. An injury or stroke in this region may create a type of **agnosia**, an inability to recognize some properties or class of objects—colors, letters, or faces. The most dramatic disturbances follow damage in the lower portions of the right temporal lobe and adjacent areas of the occipital lobe. In extreme cases patients may be able to describe a familiar object, say, a hat, when they see it, but cannot name it or describe its function until after they have handled it. More limited damage in the right temporal lobe may leave a person able to recognize familiar faces or pictures, but disrupt the ability to memorize new faces or pictures of objects.

The recognition of auditory patterns also appears to be carried out in the temporal lobe, where the auditory cortex is located. What happens when the top portion of the left temporal lobe is damaged? People can still hear, but they can no longer perceive and understand auditory patterns, whether they are Beethoven's opening notes or the sounds of speech (Kimura, 1973). As we will see, damage in this area affects language ability.

In addition, the parietal lobes, which are above and to the rear of the temporal lobes, are involved in pattern recognition. After damage to the left parietal area, a person may be unable to generate visual images from memory or to answer questions that require the use of such images (such as, what color are the stars on an American flag?) (Farah, 1984). Damage to the right parietal lobe often leaves a person unable to identify patterns by touch. This damage also affects spatial memory and may leave an individual disoriented: for example, a patient may be unable to locate familiar states on an outline map of the United States or may be unable to trace the route home on a street map (Hecaen and Albert, 1978).

The Role of the Temporal Lobes in Memory

Injuries that disturb the capacity for pattern recognition can be seen as disruptions in some aspect of memory: as we have just seen, parietal lobe damage can disrupt visual or spatial memory. However, the temporal lobes are particularly important in memory. Extreme damage to the temporal lobes may be followed by **amnesia**, or memory loss. Patients with amnesia seem unable to retain verbal memories—say, a series of three letters or words—for longer than a few minutes. As long as they repeat the material over and over to themselves, they can remember it. But as soon as their attention is distracted, the words are quickly lost from memory, and the patients have no recollection of ever having heard them (Milner, 1966). In severe cases of amnesia the damage extends beyond the temporal lobe to include the hippocampus, a structure just beneath the cerebral cortex. Later we will explore this sort of memory disorder in greater detail.

Planning and Abstraction

Neuropsychologists have had difficulty locating specific areas responsible for mental processes such as thinking, reasoning, and abstraction. Perhaps the problem lies in the fact that such mental processes as thinking or reasoning are not elementary functions: they require more than the relatively simple, direct neural wiring found in the sensory and motor areas. Complex mental processes probably depend on the coordination of several brain structures.

We do know, however, that a variety of intellectual functions are carried out in the frontal lobes, which are located at the front of each cerebral hemisphere. Because the human frontal lobes occupy a much greater proportion of the brain than those of any other animal, the frontal lobes were once considered the seat of human intelligence. This notion is less popular today, since people with considerable frontal-lobe damage can still perform tasks requiring intelligence. Nonetheless, scientists still believe that the prefrontal area (the portion of the frontal lobes just behind the forehead) is involved in such intellectual tasks as abstraction, planning, concentrating on a single goal, and inhibiting impulsive actions (Hecaen and Albert, 1978).

Animals and people with damage to the prefrontal area are distractible; they react excessively to novel stimulation and are unable to persist in a lengthy plan of action. A person with such damage may, for example, serve dessert before the main course, or may go to the kitchen to refill a basket of rolls and end up doing the dishes, having forgotten the guests seated at the dinner table. These patients often "forget to remember" such information as daily errands, last year's vacation, or lunch dates, but they often remember items or events if they are urged to do so and given plenty of time (Hecaen and Albert, 1978).

The frontal lobes are also involved with mood and emotional reactions, and damage to this area of the brain can lead to behavior that interferes with intelligent action. Some mental patients who have had small amounts of brain tissue destroyed in an attempt to control their violence tend to spend most of their time in apathy and depression, punctuated by brief episodes of euphoria, excitement, and uncontrolled impulses. When excited, such patients may seem out of control and may make inappropriate sexual, vulgar, or caustic remarks (Hecaen and Albert, 1978). Since emotions appear to be generated in the limbic system, psychologists have concluded that the frontal lobes normally monitor and control this more primitive area of the brain. (Later in the chapter, we investigate the role of the limbic system.)

The Two Sides of the Brain

The right and left cerebral hemispheres are roughly mirror images of each other, but they are wired in a paradoxical manner: each hemisphere of the brain receives sensations primarily from, and controls primarily the voluntary muscles of, the *opposite* side of the body. Thus, a stroke that damages functioning in the *right* cerebral hemisphere may cause paralysis on the *left* side of the body. The hemispheres also differ in size: in most people the left cerebral hemisphere is somewhat larger than the right. Even more important for our understanding of the brain, each hemisphere appears to be specialized for particular functions, as shown in Figure 3.9.

Figure 3.9. This drawing, though greatly simplified, suggests the sensory input and the types of information processing handled by the left and right cortical hemispheres of the brain.

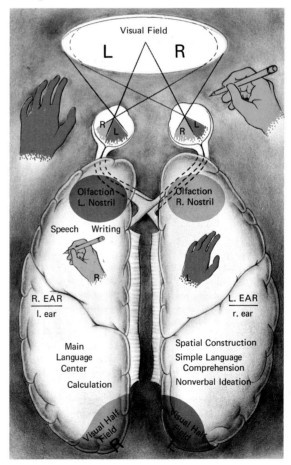

Language and the Left Hemisphere The left hemisphere is usually more adept at processing language, so that damage to this hemisphere often results in severe **aphasia**—disturbance in using, or understanding, spoken or written language. Damage to the left temporal cortex may leave a person with **Wernicke's aphasia**, in which the ability to *comprehend* language is disrupted. The patient may be able to hear and repeat words and sentences, but will be unable to understand their meaning. Or patients may speak fluently but produce meaningless combinations of words—all the while unaware that their speech is garbled (Hecaen and Albert, 1978).

Damage to the rear of the left frontal cortex produces a condition known as **Broca's aphasia**, in which speech *production* is severely disturbed. Although their vocal apparatus is intact, patients with such damage often have difficulty speaking. They seem to have trouble with the structure of language (Gardner, 1978). Their speech is halting; they often omit small grammatical words like "on" and "the," and they may be unable to pronounce a well-known name. The experience of such people resembles the "tip-of-the-tongue" phenomenon, in which you have a person's name right on the tip of your tongue but cannot remember it no matter how hard you try (see Chapter 9). Thus both Broca's aphasia (poor speech) and Wernicke's aphasia (poor comprehension) are caused by damage to areas of the left hemisphere.

The supposition that language is primarily a function of the left hemisphere has been supported by studies of people with normal brains. If sodium amytal, a fast-acting barbiturate, is injected into the artery supplying one of the hemispheres with blood, that hemisphere is temporarily disabled. Using this technique, researchers have found that almost no right-handed person can speak when the left hemisphere is disabled. This finding indicates that among right-handers, speech is located predominantly in the left hemisphere. Among left-handers, 20 to 40 percent have speech located in the right hemisphere, and another group appears to use both hemispheres for speech (Kupfermann, 1981).

Special Abilities of the Right Hemisphere The right hemisphere tends to be specialized for spatial skills, visual imagery, and musical abilities (see Figure 3.9). People with right-hemisphere damage may find it difficult to draw, to find their way from one place to another, or to build a model from a plan (Kimura, 1973). When there is damage specifically to the right temporal lobe, as noted earlier, visual and auditory memory may be disrupted. People with such damage cannot recognize familiar melodies, faces, or pictures, nor can they learn to identify new ones (Kimura, 1973; Milner, 1971).

The right hemisphere also seems to specialize in the control of emotions. When the right hemisphere is damaged, a person may be unable either to produce or to interpret emotional expressions, depending on the area involved (Ross, 1981). If the forward part of the right hemisphere is damaged, the patients are unable to act out the emotions of joy, sadness, or anger, and they may be unable to express these emotions in their voices. In contrast, if the damage is farther to the back of the right hemisphere, patients can generally produce appropriate emotional expression; however, when they look at pictures, they cannot tell whether the people portrayed are expressing joy, sadness, or anger. Nor can they detect such emotions in other people's voices. Not surprisingly, such patients often respond inappropriately in social settings, sometimes confusing harmless jokes with anger (Geschwind, 1979).

Lateralization The establishment of behavioral functions in one hemisphere or the other, known as **lateralization**, exists in all of us. One hemisphere or the other tends to dominate, depending on the type of activity performed. This does not mean that certain abilities are completely localized in either the right or the left hemisphere, but that each hemisphere is more efficient at processing particular kinds of information.

The two halves of the brain seem to store different types of information, but we rarely notice this division in functioning. It escapes our detection because the two hemispheres normally work together as a coordinated unit. The coordination is managed by a large cable of neural fibers called the **corpus callosum**, which carries messages back and forth between the left and right sides of the brain (Sperry, 1964; 1975).

Severing this connection surgically to relieve epileptic seizures seems to produce two separate "minds" in the same body, each seemingly unaware of the other's actions (Gazzaniga, 1977). In the case of most of these patients, only the left hemisphere can speak or write, because it contains the major language-processing area. The right hemisphere cannot speak, though it can communicate somewhat by gesturing with the left hand. (As noted earlier, each hemisphere controls the opposite side of the body.) The right hemisphere does retain some language ability—it understands many words, but it cannot process them as quickly as the left hemisphere can (Zaidel, 1978). Meanwhile, only the right hemisphere (controlling the left hand) can draw objects with their parts correctly oriented and aligned—a skill that requires the perception for spatial relationships.

Because of the way the retinas are connected to the brain, objects in the right visual field are seen only by the left hemisphere, and vice versa. Patients do not notice this splitting of visual awareness in their daily lives, when they can move both eyes over any object in a scene. Researchers discovered it only by using special test conditions that confined visual input to one hemisphere. In such situations, if an object is briefly flashed to the right side of the visual field (so that it reaches only the left half of the brain), the patient can say what he or she has seen. However, if the same object is flashed to the left visual field (going only to the right side of the brain), the person cannot say what has been seen, though he or she can identify by touch alone a similar object from a group of objects hidden from view. In these cases, one-half of the brain does not know what the other half has seen.

The exploration of cerebral hemispheric functioning has been complicated by the existence of left-handed people and two sexes. As we've noted, a large minority of left-handers process language in the right hemisphere or in both sides of the brain. The exact relationship between brain organization and handedness is unclear, but right-handers tend to perform better on language-related tasks, while left-handers tend to be better at the perception of tones and to have superior artistic ability (Herron, 1979).

Gender introduces other difficulties into the study of hemispheric function. Females tend to do better than males in language-based skills, and males tend to do better in tasks of a spatial nature (Springer and Deutsch, 1981). Males are also more proficient at mathematics—but not at arithmetic. Cultural expectations, as well as the different ways in which boys and girls are reared, undoubtedly affect their development of these skills. However, the effects of brain damage in men and women point to a difference in brain organization. When a portion of a man's left temporal lobe is removed, he often develops disturbances in language; removing a portion of his right temporal lobe generally causes disturbances in spatial skills. But this sharp division of function does not appear so clearly among women (Landsdell, 1962). Other researchers have found that language disturbance after damage to the left hemisphere is three times more frequent in men than in women (McGlone, 1978). These findings may indicate that men's brains are more lateralized than the brains of women, and that women may use both hemispheres to some degree in most skills. For practical purposes, the difference between the sexes is not important because the average difference between the groups is small; moreover, some women are better at spatial abilities than most men, while some men are better at language skills than most women (Springer and Deutsch, 1981). For the purpose of understanding the brain, however, such sex-related differences are both puzzling and important.

One attempt to understand the puzzle has been made by Norman Geschwind, who believed that male hormones are at least partly responsible for these differences (Marx, 1982). Geschwind suggested that male hormones slow the growth of the left hemisphere, and that they are responsible for the preponderance of left-handers, reading problems, and superior mathematical ability among males. When researchers pursued his suggestion, they found that among 50,000 seventh graders, those who were extremely gifted at mathematics were twice as likely to be left-handed as the rest of the population and were overwhelmingly male (a ratio of 13 to 1) (Kolata, 1983). Although such correlations support the hypothesis, it remains highly speculative.

The Limbic System

Beneath the cerebral hemispheres and above the central core lies the **limbic system**. Its highly interrelated structures (primarily the **hippocampus**, the **amygdala**, and the **septal area**) ring the top of the brain's central core, connecting with it and with the cerebral cortex (see Figure 3.10).

The limbic system, the second of the three brain layers to develop, evolved about 100 million years ago (Fishbein, 1976). Although the limbic system's original purpose was to analyze odors, it came to have a much wider role. It seems to play a major part in such motivated (goal-directed) behavior as eating, fighting, drinking, self-defense,

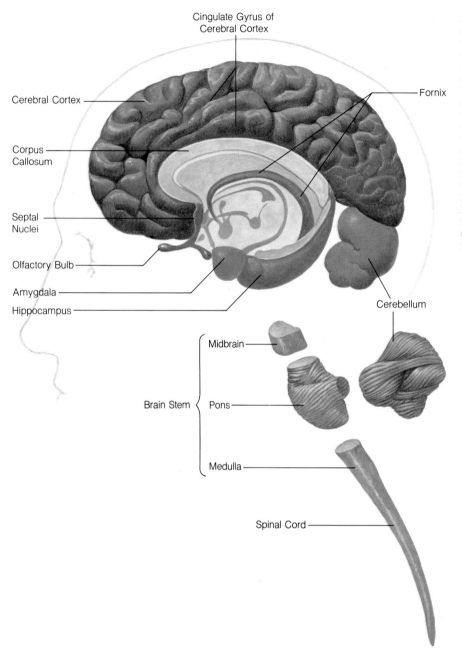

Figure 3.10. The limbic system. Structures within this system play a significant role in a variety of emotional behaviors. Damage to various regions of the limbic system may cause wild animals to become tame, or tame animals to become vicious. Other limbic lesions may radically alter sexual and feeding behavior. The olfactory bulb (responsible for the sense of smell) is closely associated with other limbic structures, suggesting the importance of this sense to several limbic system functions.

and mating (Pribram, 1971). Damage to the limbic system can radically alter such behavior, depending on the area involved. Marked changes in sexual behavior and eating patterns follow limbic system damage, and in some cases the damage makes fierce wild animals docile. As we will see in Chapter 12, these kinds of behavior all have something to do with wants, needs, desires, or emotion. In each case the animal must decide whether to approach or avoid some object (food, water) or some creature (mate, predator).

Pleasure Centers in the Limbic System

The limbic system's role in emotion was highlighted by the discovery of specific areas or pathways that seem intimately connected with reward or "pleasure." The discovery of these "pleasure pathways" came about when James Olds and Peter Milner (1954) found that rats would work to get mild electrical stimulation, delivered through electrodes implanted in certain parts of the limbic system and the brain's central core. The animals would press so as to stimulate their brains several times a second for hours on end. They found this brain stimulation so rewarding that even after starving for twenty-four hours the rats would pass up food in favor of working steadily to receive an electric charge. Such reward centers are distributed along pathways that pass through the limbic system, including the septal area, and also through the hypothalamus, a structure that is part of the brain's central core. But not all stimulation of the limbic area is rewarding. In some parts of the limbic system stimulation is neutral; in other parts of the limbic system and in some parts of the hypothalamus it seems to be painful.

Pleasure centers are not limited to rats; humans who have received similar stimulation in attempts to alleviate serious medical conditions, such as epilepsy, have reported feeling "drunk," "happy," "great," and as if they were building up to a sexual orgasm (Heath, 1963). The most pleasurable sensations are produced by stimulation in the septal area of the limbic system.

The Limbic System's Role in Learning and Memory

Since emotion and interest are controlled by the limbic system, and since emotional interest enhances learning, we can expect that the limbic system will be involved in learning. Once again, the discovery was made in studies of patients with epilepsy (Milner, 1966). In a few patients, parts of the temporal lobes plus parts of the limbic system (the hippocampus and the amygdala) were removed on both sides of the brain in an attempt to control severe seizures. After surgery, these patients seemed unable to lay down new verbal memories. Their intelligence was unaffected; they could remember things that happened before their surgery, and they could converse intelligently about whatever was taking place. But within a few minutes, they had no recollection of matters they had just talked about. The larger the segment of hippocampus and amygdala that was removed, the greater the verbal memory deficit (Hecaen and Albert, 1978). Yet these patients' motor learning

appeared to be intact. Other studies of patients with hippocampal damage have confirmed the importance of the left hippocampus in verbal memory and the right hippocampus in spatial memory and touch (Kolb and Whishaw, 1980). The hippocampus has proved to be so important in memory that such surgery has been discontinued.

The Basal Ganglia

The **basal ganglia** are a group of brain structures that lie beneath the cortex, perched just above the limbic system and the central core. Their principal role seems to be the control of movement, and they act as coordinator between the motor cortex and the thalamus, a structure that is part of the brain's central core. The basal ganglia are deeply involved in the initiation and integration of movement and the maintenance of posture. Using single-unit recording, researchers have found individual cells in the basal ganglia of monkeys where bursts of electrical activity are followed a few milliseconds later by the movement of a specific hand, arm, or leg (Cote, 1981).

Damage to the basal ganglia interferes with muscle tone, posture, and movement. Parkinson's disease, mentioned in the discussion of neurotransmitters, is a degenerative disorder of the basal ganglia. The rhythmical tremors of Parkinson's disease apparently develop when a lack of the transmitter dopamine prevents intact cells from inhibiting neural activity responsible for motor movement. The symptoms of Parkinson's disease can be relieved by the drug L-dopa, which the body converts to dopamine, but L-dopa cannot stop the gradual loss of neurons and the slow deterioration of the patient.

The Brain's Central Core

In both appearance and function, the central core of the human brain resembles the brains of all animals that have backbones. The *central core* was the first layer of the brain to evolve, and it contains structures that carry out functions necessary for survival: sleeping, waking, breathing, and feeding. The structures that make up the central core include the cerebellum, the brain stem, the thalamus, and the hypothalamus (see Figure 3.11).

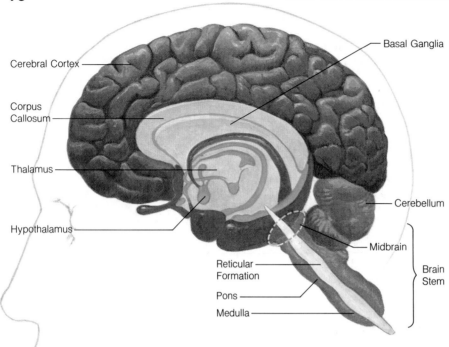

Figure 3.11. The structures composing the central core of the brain. The structures represented in this figure are the first to receive incoming information, and they regulate the most fundamental processes of the body. The reticular formation, which controls the most general responses of the brain to sensory input, is located in the area that connects the brain to the spinal cord and to the rest of the nervous system. The thalamus has a central location in the brain, and the hypothalamus is very close to the pituitary gland, which controls the activity of the other endocrine glands.

The Cerebellum

The *cerebellum* (or "little brain"), which looks like a miniature version of the cerebral hemispheres, is involved in posture and movement. It sits on the back of the brain stem, where it carries out its duties by monitoring information that flows up and down the brain stem. Before transmitting motor commands from the higher brain to the muscles, the cerebellum elaborates this information. It compares these messages with the continuous flow of information that comes in concerning muscle tension and position, reconciles any differences in the messages, and sends them out in a way that ensures smooth and balanced motor response (Eccles, Ito, and Szentagotnaik, 1967).

Damage to the cerebellum may be followed by **ataxia**, a condition in which the patient is afflicted with severe tremors, drunken movements, and a lack of balance. The patient lacks control over simple movements; for example, he or she might accidentally hit a friend in the stomach while reaching out to shake hands.

The Brain Stem

The top of the spinal cord swells to form the *brain stem*, which houses several important structures.

▪ The **medulla** controls salivation, chewing, and facial movements and plays an essential role in such autonomic activities as breathing and circulation.

▪ Above the medulla is the **pons** (or "bridge"), which connects the two halves of the cerebellum. The pons transmits motor information from the higher brain areas and the spinal cord to the cerebellum and integrates movements between the right and left sides of the body.

▪ A small structure called the **midbrain** lies near the top of the brain stem. Through this structure passes all neural information sent between the brain and spinal cord. The midbrain also contains centers for visual and auditory reflexes, including the "startle" reflex to sudden, intense stimuli and "orienting" reflexes that allow us to locate and follow moving objects with our eyes or ears.

The Thalamus

At the top of the brain stem and within the cerebral hemispheres lies the **thalamus**, which consists of a pair of egg-shaped structures. The thalamus links the cerebral hemispheres and sense organs. One of its functions is to act as a relay station, sorting information from the sensory receptors and routing it to appropriate areas of the higher brain. The thalamus also processes information from various parts of the cerebral hemispheres, interrelating it before sending it on to the cerebellum and the medulla. This connective function gives the thalamus a major integrative role in the brain.

The Reticular Formation

The **reticular formation** is a latticework of neural fibers and cell bodies that extends from the spinal cord through the brain stem and into the thalamus. It plays a critically important role in regulating consciousness and attention, arousing the higher brain when information related to survival must be processed. The reticular formation also picks up sensory stimulation that is being passed from the thalamus to the somatosensory cortex and spreads it throughout the cortex. These diffuse messages help alert the cerebral cortex so that its processing of sensory information is more efficient.

Since the reticular formation is linked with consciousness, its activity is reduced during sleep. Anesthetics cause unconsciousness by depressing the activity of the reticular formation, and damage to its cells may be followed by permanent coma (Magoun, 1963). Depressed activity of the reticular formation helps explain why people who are asleep, in a coma, or under anesthesia do not react to sights or sounds. The inactivated reticular formation has ceased to alert the entire cortex of the need to process sensory signals that are flowing into the sensory cortex.

The Hypothalamus

Just below the thalamus lies a small structure, about the size of the tip of your index finger, called the **hypothalamus**. It monitors changes in the body's internal environment and sends out signals that maintain the person's internal state at some balanced optimal level. The hypothalamus influences behavior on which life depends: feeding, drinking, sexual function, emotional and physiological response to stress, and internal temperature regulation. Some of these tasks are carried out through interactions with the endocrine system, the system of glands whose secretions influence a good deal of our behavior.

Many of the functions of the hypothalamus are examples of **homeostasis**, or self-regulation. The body maintains homeostasis as follows: when the body deviates from an optimal physical state, or when substances in the body deviate from a certain norm, the hypothalamus automatically activates processes that restore the body to its original state. A familiar, everyday homeostatic mechanism is the thermostat: deviations in room temperature signal the thermostat to turn the furnace on or off. In a similar fashion, parts of the hypothalamus act as a kind of thermostat to maintain body temperature. When a warm-blooded animal is exposed to cold, signals from the hypothalamus cause blood vessels in the skin to contract, reducing heat loss from body surfaces. Meanwhile, other hypothalamic signals go to the endocrine system, where they instruct a gland called the pituitary to produce a substance that in turn triggers another endocrine gland, the thyroid. Alerted, the thyroid secretes thyroxin, speeding up body metabolism and generating heat to compensate for external cold. High levels of thyroxin induce shivering, which leads to the production of even more heat. Just the opposite process occurs when the animal is exposed to external heat. The hypothalamus mobilizes the body's cooling resources, which dilate body vessels in the skin, secrete sweat, and slow metabolism.

Other hypothalamic areas maintain such homeostatic functions as the regulation of eating and drinking. Destruction of some spots within the hypothalamus are followed by gorging or near-starvation, which produces an obese or an emaciated animal. Destruction of other spots have similar effects on the animal's water intake. (In Chapter 12, we explore the way our bodies regulate these basic needs.) The hypothalamus also plays a role in emotion, such as anger, fear, and sexual arousal; it does so largely through its influence on the autonomic nervous system. (In Chapter 11, we investigate these hypothalamic influences on emotions.)

Besides these influences on motivation and emotional behavior, the hypothalamus also regulates the endocrine system through its effect on the pituitary gland.

THE ENDOCRINE SYSTEM

Although our behavior, emotions, and body functions are controlled by the brain, the brain cannot do the entire job alone. It must also integrate its workings with those of the slower **endocrine system.** The endocrine system communicates by means of hormones, chemical messengers that are produced by the **endocrine glands** and secreted directly into the bloodstream. Some hormones are similar in structure to neurotransmitters, but hormones do not travel across the synaptic gaps between neurons. Instead, they are carried through the bloodstream, which moves relatively slowly. Once a gland has been stimulated, it takes several seconds for the hormone to be produced, released, and transported to its destination.

After hormones are released from an endocrine gland, they influence a wide variety of behavior. But a hormone's action is selective; it is confined to certain target organs that can respond to that chemical. Through their influences on these organs, hormones directly affect physical growth, emotional response, sexual function, the availability of energy, and goal-directed behavior that involves our wants, needs, and desires.

The endocrine system is regulated by the brain, specifically, by the hypothalamus. This regulated interaction is especially apparent in the function of the pituitary gland. The **pituitary gland**, which lies at the base of the brain, has often been called the "master gland" of the endocrine system, because it secretes many hormones that control the output of other endocrine glands. But this master gland is itself controlled by the brain, so the brain is ultimately responsible for the activities of the endocrine system. The brain monitors the amount of hormones in the blood and sends messages to the pituitary via the hypothalamus, ordering it to correct deviations from the proper level. Temperature regulation, which was discussed earlier, is one example of this homeostatic control. Another example is the body's response to stress, which we investigate in Chapter 21.

Our examination of the biological basis of behavior shows the intricate, integrated activity of the brain and rest of the body. As we have seen, the chemical and electrical activity of the brain directs our thoughts, feelings, and behavior. But the world around us also influences the chemical and electrical activity of the brain; we have seen this influence in the neuronal changes produced by sensory stimulation, by learning, by brain injuries, and by changes in temperature. Keeping this continual interaction in mind will help put discussions in later chapters into perspective.

SUMMARY

1. The nervous system integrates information from many sources and translates it into appropriate responses; its work is done by three types of specialized cells, called neurons: **receptor neurons**, which receive sensory information from the environment; **motor neurons**, which control muscle movements; and **interneurons**, which transmit information throughout the body.

2. The *nervous system* acts as a communications network among all body cells. It is divided into the **central nervous system (CNS)**, which consists of the brain and the **spinal cord** and is the major control center for behavior, and the **peripheral nervous system (PNS)**, which relays information from sensory receptors to the central nervous system and sends out messages to muscles or glands. The divisions of the peripheral nervous system are the **somatic nervous system**, which senses and acts on the external world and is generally under voluntary control, and the **autonomic nervous system**, which controls the visceral muscles and glands, and is generally involuntary. The autonomic nervous system is subdivided into the **sympathetic nervous system**, which expends energy in coping with stressful situations, and the **parasympathetic nervous system**, which conserves energy functioning during normal or relaxed situations.

3. Neurons consist of a **cell body**, which contains the cell's metabolic center; **dendrites**,

relatively short fibers that receive information; an **axon**, a long fiber that generally carries impulses (signals) to other neurons; and a **myelin sheath** that surrounds and insulates the axon. Specialized receptor sites on the dendrites, called **synapses**, receive signals from other neurons.

4. Neurons communicate by sending charges across synaptic clefts. An impulse is generated within a cell body and travels down the axon. When the signal reaches the axon terminals before a synapse, **neurotransmitters** (chemicals stored in small sacs at an axon terminal) are released, transmitting a message to adjacent neurons. When the transmitter comes in through an **excitatory connection**, the receiving neuron's charge increases; when the transmitter comes in through an **inhibitory connection**, the charge is decreased. Whether a neuron fires depends on the amount and polarity of impulses it receives.

5. The spinal cord connects the brain and the peripheral nervous system; connected through the spinal cord are **reflex arcs**, the simplest chain of connecting neurons.

6. The neurons in given cortical areas of the brain are connected into intricate neural networks, in which a path can be traced from almost any cell to almost any other cell. A message from one neuron could be sent to, and influence, another neuron, depending on the strength of the connection. Experience can increase the strength of these synaptic pathways or establish new ones, allowing neural networks to learn about the environment and how to deal with it.

7. Most neurons use the same neurotransmitter at all synapses. Different transmitters are predominant in various parts of the nervous system, each affecting different behavioral and psychological processes. Among prominent transmitters are **acetylcholine (ACH)**, **dopamine**, **epinephrine**, **norepinephrine**, and **serotonin**. **Endorphins**, which are similar to transmitters, are similar in structure to opiates and are implicated in relief from pain.

8. The brain consists of three overlapping layers: the central core, the limbic system, and the cerebrum. The **cerebrum**, which consists of the **cerebral cortex** and the tissue beneath it, is involved in higher mental functions: planning, reasoning, and learning.

9. Technological advances are enabling us to learn much about brain activity. **Electroencephalography (EEG)** records the small, wavelike fluctuations in surface voltage. Recording **event-related potentials (ERPs)**, or changes in the brain's electrical activity in response to specific stimulation, has helped to establish brain-behavior connections. In **single-unit recordings** microelectrodes are inserted close to individual neurons to record their firing impulses. **Computerized tomography (CT) scans**, which use multiple X-ray pictures to reconstruct single cross sections of the brain, are a fast, noninvasive way to localize brain damage or tumors. **Position emission tomography (PET) scans** provide colored maps of brain activity through the use of injected radioactive glucose. **Nuclear magnetic resonance (NMR)** produces images of tissue, biochemical activity, and metabolism by using radio waves on a body that has been enclosed in a magnetic field.

10. The **cerebral cortex** is heavily involved in sensation, learning, speech, and memory. In the brain's **parietal lobe** is the **somatosensory cortex**, which is the primary area for the reception and interpretation of touch and positional information. At the back of the **frontal lobe** is the **motor cortex**, which regulates voluntary movements. In the **occipital lobe** is the **visual cortex**, which receives and analyzes visual information; further visual analysis takes place in the parietal lobes. In the **temporal lobe** is the **auditory cortex**, which perceives sound; and these temporal lobes also are involved in memory. Activity in the frontal lobes influences abilities such as abstraction, planning, concentration on a goal, and the inhibition of impulsive actions. The left cerebral hemisphere generally controls the right side of the body, and vice versa. The left hemisphere is involved with language, whereas the right hemisphere is involved in spatial skills, musical ability, and visual imagery. Greater development of functions in one hemisphere or the other is known as **lateralization**. The two hemispheres com-

municate through a thick band of neural fibers called the **corpus callosum**.

11. The **limbic system** is involved in emotional behavior and in goal-directed behavior. It plays a role in feeding, fighting, fleeing, and mating. Pleasure centers have been located in the limbic system, and the **hippocampus** appears to have a role in memory.

12. The **basal ganglia**, a group of brain structures at the end of the brain stem, act as coordinators of movement and posture.

13. The **central core** of the brain carries out the basic functions of survival. The **cerebellum** coordinates voluntary muscle activity and maintains physical balance. The **brain stem** is composed of the **medulla**, which is involved in breathing, circulation, chewing, salivation, and facial movements; the **pons**, which connects the two halves of the cerebellum and is thus involved with the integration of movement; and the **midbrain**, which is a center for visual and auditory reflexes. The **thalamus** sorts information from sensory receptors, routes it to appropriate brain areas, and integrates outgoing information from the cerebral hemispheres. The **reticular formation** has a critical role in regulating consciousness and attention. The **hypothalamus** monitors changes in the internal environment and, through a process of **homeostasis**, maintains equilibrium. It influences feeding, drinking, responses to stress, sexual function, and internal temperature regulation. It also regulates the endocrine system.

14. The **endocrine system** communicates by means of chemical substances called **hormones**. **Endocrine glands** produce these substances, secreting them directly into the bloodstream, which carries them to their target organs. Hormones affect physical growth, emotional response, motivation, energy availability, and sexual function. The **pituitary gland** is considered the master endocrine gland because it secretes many hormones that control the output of other endocrine glands.

KEY TERMS

acetylcholine (ACH)
agnosia
Alzheimer's disease
amnesia
amygdala
aphasia
ataxia
auditory cortex
autonomic nervous system
axon
basal ganglia
brain stem
Broca's aphasia
cell body
centers
central core
central nervous system (CNS)
cerebellum
cerebral cortex
cerebral hemispheres
cerebrum

computerized tomography (CT) scans
corpus callosum
dendrites
dopamine
electroencephalography (EEG)
endocrine glands
endocrine system
endorphins
epinephrine
event-related potential (ERP)
excitatory connection
frontal lobe
ganglia
glands
glia
hippocampus
homeostasis
hormones
hypothalamus
inhibitory connection

interneurons
lateralization
limbic system
localization of function
medulla
midbrain
motor cortex
motor neurons
myelin sheath
nerves
neural networks
neurons
neurotransmitter
norepinephrine
nuclear magnetic resonance(NMR)
occipital lobe
P300 wave
parasympathetic nervous system
parietal lobe
Parkinson's disease

pathway
pattern recognition
peripheral nervous system (PNS)
pituitary gland
placebo
pons
position emission tomography
  (PET) scan
receptor neurons

reflex arc
reflexes
resting rate
reticular formation
sensory neurons
septal area
serotonin
single-unit recording
slow potential

somatic nervous system
somatosensory cortex
spinal cord
sympathetic nervous system
synapse
temporal lobe
thalamus
visual cortex
Wernicke's aphasia

RECOMMENDED READINGS

ASIMOV, I. *The human brain.* New York: The New American Library, 1963. A popular paperback book by the renowned sci-fi writer. With his usual clear, informal style and attention to detail, Asimov describes the nervous system, the endocrine system, the brain, and their behavioral correspondents. Offers some fascinating speculations on the vast potential of the brain.

BLAKEMORE, C. *Mechanics of the mind.* New York: Cambridge University Press, 1977. An introduction to how the mind works and its relationship to the brain. Draws many references to the history of ideas and art.

CARLSON, N. R. *Physiology of behavior* (2nd ed.). Boston: Allyn & Bacon, 1981. A good introductory text on physiological psychology. Explains complex concepts in a clear way.

KOLB, B., and J. Q. WHISHAW. *Fundamentals of human neuropsychology.* San Francisco: W. H. Freeman, 1980. A good description of clinical symptoms and experimental analyses of behavioral deficits caused by damage to different structures of the human brain. It is especially good on clinical neurology.

KANDEL, E. R., and J. H. SCHWARTZ (Eds.). *Principles of neuroscience.* New York: Elsevier/North-Holland Press, 1981. An encyclopedic collection of 52 chapters by experts on most topics in brain science, from the neuron to emotions to cognitions to psychopathology. Difficult, though the most definitive compendium available.

ORNSTEIN, R., and R. F. THOMPSON. *The amazing brain.* Boston: Houghton Mifflin, 1984. Well-written account of the latest developments in brain science, written by two top investigators. Up-to-the-minute coverage of current topics such as physiological bases of memory, language, thinking, and consciousness.

ROSE, S. *The conscious brain.* New York: Knopf, 1975. A British scientist gives a personal account of brain research. Fun to read.

SCHNEIDER, A. M. and B. TARSHIS. *Introduction to physiological psychology* (3rd ed.). New York: Random House, 1985. This text covers the latest developments in the field and provides a highly readable, balanced view of basic research. The experimental orientation challenges the reader to examine conclusions critically, while everyday examples and analogies help make even the most difficult physiological systems easy to comprehend and visualize.

SPRINGER, S. P., and G. DEUTSCH. *Left brain, right brain.* San Francisco: W. H. Freeman, 1981. A discussion of all the recent research on the two hemispheres of the brain, with a well-written discussion of neuroanatomy in the Appendix.

CHAPTER FOUR

BIOLOGICAL PERSPECTIVES ON BEHAVIOR: GENETICS AND EVOLUTION

Jim Springer and Jim Lewis are two men who grew up in different towns but have some interesting similarities. Both grew up in working-class families. Both drive Chevrolets and have vacationed at the same small Florida beach town. Both have worked part time as deputy sheriffs. Both chew their fingernails to the quick, chain-smoke, drink the same brand of beer, dislike baseball, enjoy stock-car racing, and cross their legs in exactly the same way. Both hated spelling but liked math in school; and both like mechanical drawing and carpentry.

That's not surprising, you say? It is true that a lot of these similarities might be due to the two men's social class. But consider this: both married women named Linda, divorced, and then married women named Betty. Both have sons—one named James Allan, the other James Alan. Both owned a dog named Toy. Both live in the only house on their block with a white bench built around a tree in the front yard.

Still not surprised? You think some of these similarities may have been due to generational patterns: during a certain era many people named their sons James or Alan? Or, perhaps, that some of the similarities may be pure coincidence? You

may be right. But before you arrive at a conclusion, here is one last group of similarities between the two men. At the same age each Jim gained ten pounds, for no apparent reason. And ever since the two Jims were eighteen years old, each has had the same pattern of headaches—a combination of tension and migraine that comes on in the late afternoon. They describe the pain in the same way. Their pulse and blood pressure are identical, as are their EEG and sleep patterns. When the two Jims took personality tests, it was as if the same person had taken the test twice (Holden, 1980; Jackson, 1980).

By now, perhaps you are beginning to agree that at least a few of these similarities *may* be due to some factor other than social class, generational trends, or pure chance. What might that factor be? Since the two men grew up in different families and weren't even aware of each other's existence until they were both thirty-nine, we must look for some factor other than family upbringing. The factor we find is the two men's genetic inheritance. The two Jims are **identical twins**: they are the product of a single fertilized egg that divided early in the course of their prenatal development. The two were separated at five weeks, and each was adopted by a different family. Yet both were born with the same set of genetic "instructions," and those instructions seem to have been a powerful factor in shaping the two men's adult behavior patterns.

The object of this chapter is to explore the human genetic inheritance: what it is and how it affects human behavior. As we shall see, the genetic "instructions" we inherit from our parents and our ancestors influence our behavior on two levels. First, those "instructions" lead us to show the common behavior patterns of the human species: walking upright, communicating via language, smiling when we are happy and frowning when we are unhappy, and so on. Second, our genetic "instructions" contribute to the unique behavior pattern of each individual. Have you noticed that you have your grandfather's pattern of sudden, unexplained periods of depression and emotional withdrawal? Or that you laugh very much the same way your mother does? The reasons you do so may, at least in part, be genetic.

It is crucial to note that our genetic programming does not rigidly control our behavior, any more than it does our height or weight. The two Jims are not alike in every detail: they comb their hair differently, like different kinds of music, and have different styles of expressing themselves. Almost all human traits are influenced by environmental factors such as nutrition, our physical surroundings, and the things we learn. In fact, it is precisely because most human behavior is **plastic**—capable of being molded by environmental influences—that we have been able to adjust to new climates, new habitats, and other radical changes in our environment. Such behavioral changes have been crucial to the development of our species. Through learning and cultural transmission, we have changed from the cave dwellers of millions of years ago to the farmers, office workers, astronauts (and so on) of today.

Individuals are unique in part because each one's genetic program is unique in certain ways and in part because of our behavioral plasticity, which leads each one of us to adapt to the environment in different ways. The paradox is that this very plasticity has also been programmed into our behavior patterns by our genetic inheritance! How this all comes about we will see in the sections that follow. But, first, let us look closely at the areas of human behavior where our genetic inheritance is most easily discernible.

INHERITED PATTERNS OF BEHAVIOR

We think of human behavior as heavily influenced by learning, and it is. But learning does not take place in isolation. What we notice and what we learn, what we like and what we dislike, what we find easy and what we find difficult are influenced by our genetic inheritance. That inheritance is passed along from one generation to the next through basic units called genes. Our behavior is the product of an interaction between our environment and those genes.

The importance of genetic factors in our behavior may at first seem a bit hard to accept. We accept the fact that our physical characteristics are inherited: for example, you may have been told that you have your mother's eyes, your grandfather's chin, or your father's height, and you are probably perfectly comfortable with that idea. But we may have more trouble assimilating the notion that we may inherit personality characteristics, such as stubbornness, a sense of humor, or a predisposition to be shy. Suppose you are interested in painting. Did you *inherit* this interest from your parents, or did you just develop it from years of living with people who enjoy art, visit galleries, and surround themselves with reproductions of their favorite works? Clearly, the experiences you have had with art are essential, and without them you would probably never have developed your interest in painting. But researchers have also found an apparent genetic influence on people's capabilities that is over and above any environmental effect (Grotevant, Scarr, and Weinberg, 1977). Psychologists in the field of **behavior genetics** believe that behavior is the result of an interaction between genetic influences and environmental experiences.

Behavior geneticists use a number of methods to discover genetic influences on behavior, including twin studies, adoption studies, and animal breeding experiments. Because genetic effects can be more clearly established with animals, we will look at animal breeding studies first.

Findings with Animals

We cannot select people, ask them to mate, then place their offspring in various environments to see how genetic differences might affect behavior.

But we can do this with animals. In fact, some of the most compelling illustrations of heredity's role in behavior have emerged when researchers have bred animals selectively to accentuate particular behavioral traits.

A number of breeds of dogs show behavioral specialties that have been deliberately fostered through generations of selective breeding. German shepherds have been bred to display ferocious protectiveness; retrievers have been bred to retrieve such objects as game birds and rabbits; beagles have been bred to track animals by their scent. Such selective breeding also seems to affect a dog's personality. When researchers raised litters of beagles, for example, they found that the beagle pups rarely fought with their litter mates and that young or adult beagles seemed relaxed when handled in the laboratory (Fuller, 1983a). Wire-haired terriers, on the other hand, engaged their litter mates in fierce battles and were tense when handled in the laboratory. The beagles were shy in unfamiliar surroundings; the terriers, by contrast, were ready to attack at any threat.

Inherited Learning Abilities

Similar studies have even uncovered genetic influences on insects' ability to learn specific tasks. For example, researchers positioned blowflies so their proboscis was dipped into either water or a salt solution, then gave them a drop of sugar solution (McGuire and Hirsch, 1977). Then after the flies had several opportunities to learn the connection between the sugar solution and the water or salt solution, researchers bred the fastest-learning blowflies together and the slowest-learning blowflies together. They did this for twenty-six generations. When the experiment began, there was only a slight difference between the two groups in their learning speed. But beginning with the fifth generation, the differences widened—until one group of flies was extremely bright and the other extremely dull at making this connection.

Special learning abilities in rats can also be heightened or depressed by selective breeding. After eight generations, a researcher had developed one strain of rats that could learn to find their way through a complicated maze with astounding speed and a second strain that found the task laborious (Tryon, 1940; see Figure 4.1). But the bright rats were superior at only this one task. When they had to escape from water or even when

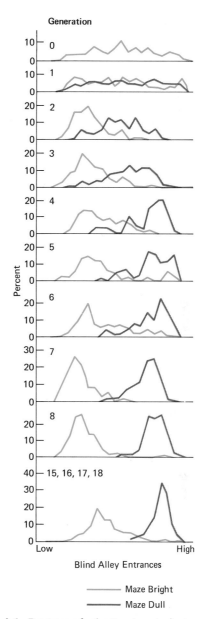

Figure 4.1. Progress of selection in rats for low and high errors in a seventeen-unit maze. By the eighth generation of selection the maze-bright and maze-dull lines were well separated, and further selection resulted in no improvement. (After Tryon, 1940.)

they were placed in a different kind of maze, they learned no faster than the dull rats. Whatever genetic influence had been heightened by selective breeding affected only a small part of the rats' behavior.

Inherited Reactions to Alcohol

Other researchers have selectively bred strains of mice that react differently to alcohol (Horowitz and Dudek, 1983). One strain will drink alcohol at any opportunity; another strain finds alcohol distasteful. A third strain can drink great quantities of alcohol over a lengthy period without becoming addicted, and a fourth strain quickly becomes addicted. A strain has even been bred that becomes highly intoxicated after drinking an amount of alcohol that leaves the behavior of another strain relatively unaffected.

But even among an inbred strain of mice, experience interacts with genetic predispositions. Researchers have developed a strain of mice that will drink alcohol voluntarily when they are young. If they are forced to drink alcohol during this period, they become abstinent when they are nine or ten weeks old. But if they are given a choice of water or alcohol to drink, they will continue to drink alcohol as adults (Kakihana and Butte, 1980).

Findings in Humans

Of course, we cannot breed people to heighten specific traits. But we can study genetic influences on human behavior in several ways. One way is to study twins. We can compare the similarities and differences among sets of identical twins and sets of **fraternal twins** (twins who have developed from two eggs, each fertilized by a different sperm). Fraternal twins are no more alike genetically than any pair of siblings. If identical twins resemble each other with respect to a given trait more than fraternal twins do, then we can assume that some genetic influence is at work. (You may, incidentally, wonder why identical twins have more genetic similarity than ordinary siblings do; after all, ordinary siblings have parents in common. The reasons are discussed later in this chapter.)

Of course, identical twins reared together share a similar environment, and some of the behavior they have in common may have been influenced by that environment; we cannot assume that all their behavioral similarities are due only to genetic influences. For this reason, researchers sometimes study identical twins who were separated shortly after birth, like the two Jims. Twins like the two Jims come from environments that differ in some regards: thus they can tell us even more about genetic influences, be-cause their behavioral similarities must to some extent be molded by their heredity. Very few cases of separated twins exist, however, So these studies are more tantalizing than they are revealing.

Another way we can examine genetic influences is to study adopted children. Adopted children have the same environment as their adoptive parents, but they have inherited nothing from them. These children provide a reverse situation that tells us just as much about genetic influences as do identical twins who have been separated (Scarr and Kidd, 1983).

Finally, we can look at families where certain traits appear more frequently than they do in the general population. We can trace these traits through various degrees of relatedness (parents, children, aunts, uncles, cousins, grandparents) and see whether some genetic influence appears to be operating. From this method we have learned about genetic influences on general aspects of the nervous system and on specific patterns such as drug sensitivity, alcoholism, and depression.

How the Genetic Program Affects the Nervous System

The two Jims had identical pulse and blood pressure patterns and nearly identical EEG and sleep patterns. These functions are all under the control of the central nervous system. What do we know about genetic influences on the way our brain operates? It seems clear that the general pattern of our brain waves is inherited (Claridge and Mangan, 1983). When researchers look at EEGs, which reflect the activity of the brain (see Chapter 3), they find that recordings from identical twins are similar—sometimes even identical—and that they are much more alike than recordings from fraternal twins. This similarity of brain-wave activity occurs when a twin is simply resting and not thinking of any particular subject; it is also found in some components of event-related potentials (see Chapter 3).

Similarly, researchers have found possible genetic influences on individuals' levels of arousal. This is reflected in the level of electrodermal activity—the skin's ability to conduct electrical current, which increases when we are aroused (Claridge and Mangan, 1983). It is also reflected in blood pressure. Compared with fraternal twins, identical twins tend to have similar levels of blood pressure (especially diastolic pressure, the lower of the two blood pressure readings), and their blood pressure seems to react similarly during a stressful psychiatric interview. And data from twin studies are not the only evidence we have for genetic influences on blood pressure. Studies of patients with high blood pressure indicate that a tendency toward high blood pressure runs in some families.

Just how these influences are related to psychological differences among people is uncertain. They may perhaps be related to differences in personality types: as we will see in Chapter 19, psychologists have proposed a biological basis for some characteristics of personality. As yet, however, the exact connections between personality and specific aspects of nervous system functioning remain unclear.

Sensitivity to Alcohol and Other Drugs

A number of studies indicate that genetic factors influence our sensitivity to alcohol. Among identical twins, if one is alcoholic there is a 55 percent chance of the other's being alcoholic also; for fraternal twins, the rate is 28 percent—if the twins are the same sex. In the general population, the risk of sons and brothers of alcoholic men eventually becoming alcoholics is between 25 percent and 50 percent (Schuckit and Rayses, 1979). The researchers who discovered this relationship found that men who have alcoholic siblings or parents metabolize alcohol much more slowly than most people. And in later studies the researchers found that people with alcoholic relatives tend to feel less intoxicated when drinking than other people do (Schuckit, 1980).

Studies of men who were adopted as children have supported the proposal that a susceptibility to alcoholism is inherited. In one study of such men, those whose biological parents were alcoholics had a much higher rate of alcoholism themselves than did other adopted men (Goodwin et al., 1973). The proportion of alcoholism in the adoptive parents was the same for both groups. Apparently, growing up with an alcoholic parent (environment) has less influence on a person's chances of future alcoholism than being born to alcoholic parents (heredity).

Depression

Some studies have shown that our genetic inheritance may influence our susceptibility to depres-

sion. Many researchers believe that depression is a biochemical disorder, so that people inherit genes that contribute to an abnormal biochemistry. As we will see in Chapter 24, many depressed patients respond to one or another antidepressant drug. Because people who respond to one drug often do not respond to the other (and vice versa), some researchers believe that there are two different kinds of genetically influenced depression (Horowitz and Dudek, 1983). In studies of depressed twins, 40 percent of the identical twins but only 11 percent of the fraternal twins also suffer from depression (Allen, 1976). It should be noted, however, that although an individual's basic susceptibility to depression may be inherited, whether or not the disorder will actually develop depends upon the person's life situation.

What Is Transmitted?

What exactly do our parents pass on to us that affects our behavior? As we saw in Chapter 3, our behavior is under the control of the nervous system. The nervous system itself is made up of cells, and each cell is built of chemical substances: proteins and other chemicals, such as sodium, potassium, and calcium. It is the particular forms of protein in our cells that influence the way our body structure and its physiology develop —including the structure and physiology of the nervous system. In one fruit fly strain, for instance, the muscles controlling the wings cannot develop normally—because of the particular kind of protein in each cell. These flies have to hold their wings up instead of at a normal angle; this means that they cannot fly.

What is actually transmitted in genetic inheritance, then, is a pattern of protein formation. After the sperm and the egg meet and the egg is fertilized, the fertilized egg begins to reproduce itself —dividing again and again. Each cell carries the same genetic information, which specifies exactly what forms of protein will be produced within the cell. This information provides a pattern that determines the form of the finished individual —including the characteristics common to all members of that species and the individual's own unique characteristics. Thanks to it, you developed as a human instead of, let's say, a bear: for example, you have five fingers instead of a furry paw, and you stay active all year-round instead of hibernating in the winter. Thanks to it also, you have certain resemblances to other members of your family: in part, due to your genetic inheritance, you may have your mother's upturned nose (let's say) and your father's musical talent.

Genetic Mechanisms

In each cell of a human being's body is a group of tiny threadlike structures known as **chromosomes**. The chromosomes are roughly analogous to tapes containing coded genetic information; they are laid out in "chunks" or "units" of genetic instructions called **genes**. A few human traits are controlled by a single gene. (An example is the disease *phenylketonuria* (PKU), an inability to metabolize phenylalanine, which is a component of some foods.) Most traits, however, are **polygenic**: several genes are required to produce the trait.

A tremendous amount of genetic information was packed into the tiny fertilized egg from which you developed: in that egg's forty-six chromosomes there were approximately 250,000 pairs of beadlike genes. Each cell in your body contains a "copy" of those chromosomes. The copying takes place via a simple, fascinating mechanism. The molecules of **DNA (deoxyribonucleic acid)** from which the chromosomes are constructed are like tiny spiral ladders (see Figures 4.2 and 4.3). When the time comes to make a copy, each tiny ladder simply "unzips" momentarily; a new molecule, like a mirror image, forms opposite each unzipped half of the ladder; and the tiny ladder zips back up.

To a certain extent, we all have similar chromosomes: everyone's genetic information contributes to the development of a human being, including two arms, two legs, a heart on the left side, and all the other fundamental human characteristics. The genetic material for the human species has been handed down through the generations for millions of years. How did this happen? The sex cells that an individual's body produces (a male's sperm, a female's ova) contain chromosomes just as ordinary cells do; and when a sperm from Man A fertilizes an ovum from Woman B, a new individual is created whose "first cell" (the fertilized ovum) contains the same basic genetic instructions that his or her parents had.

But each person's genetic material is also, to an extent, different from everyone else's. There are several reasons why. First, chromosomes can be modified *(mutate)* under certain circumstances, as when the individual is exposed to high doses of radiation. Second, chromosomes can break and be

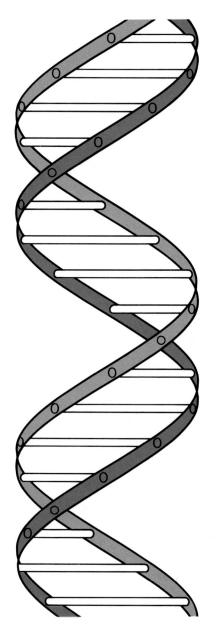

Figure 4.2. The double-stranded helical structure of DNA. The "rungs" of the "ladder" are formed by four different amino acids—adenine, guanine, thymine, and cytosine. The order in which these amino acids appear forms the genetic code.

recombined when the body is copying them to form sex cells. And third, there can be variations in the orderly, almost dancelike process by which the sex cells are formed (see Figure 4.4). During that process the chromosomes line up in neat

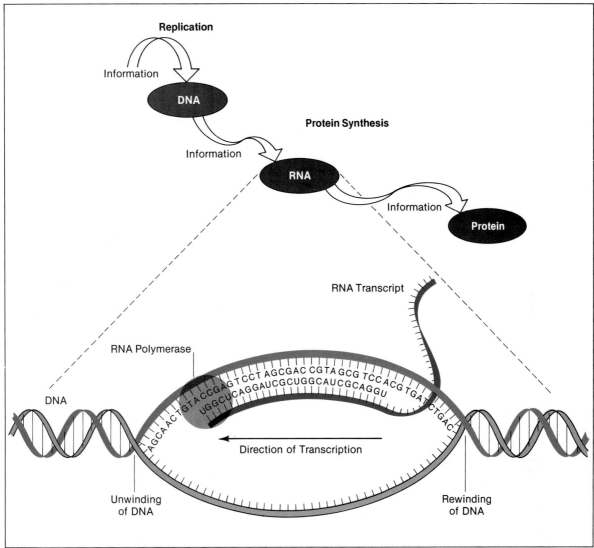

Figure 4.3. The main function of DNA (besides replicating itself) is controlling the synthesis of proteins. Protein synthesis begins with the formation of RNA copied from a sequence of DNA. A double helix of DNA is unwound to give the enzyme called RNA polymerase access to the amino acid sequence, then is rewound when the transcription into RNA is completed. The RNA polymerase, always progressing in only one direction, acts as a catalyst for the formation of a strand of RNA molecules that transcribes an exact sequence of amino acids—always pairing adenine (A) with uracil (U) and guanine (G) with cytosine (C). The newly formed RNA transcript splits off and moves from the cell nucleus into the cytoplasm, where, in a further series of chemical reactions, it transmits the DNA's instructions for the cell to make specific proteins out of the amino acids the cytoplasm contains.

pairs almost the way people line up for a Virginia Reel; but exactly which chromosomes will then go to which "daughter" sex cell varies from one time to the next—so that though all of a particular women's ova are recognizably *her* ova, they are also genetically different from one another.

How Genes Can Affect Behavior

If a genetic change alters the way the nervous system functions, it may ultimately change behavior. There is a gene found in cats, for example, that can cause developmental "errors" in the nerve-

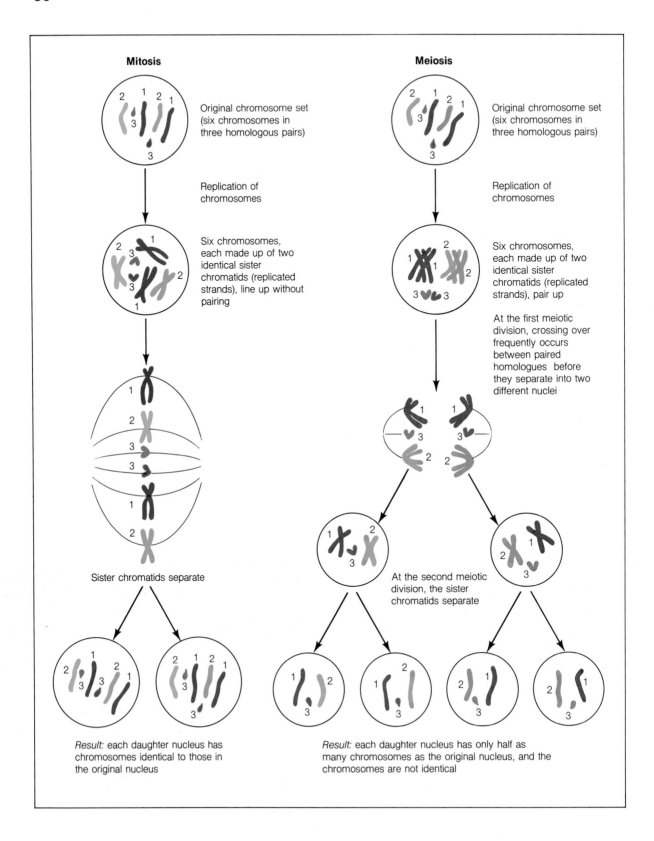

Figure 4.4. Mitosis is the process by which a cell divides to produce two new ordinary cells. Meiosis is the process by which sex cells are formed. Shown here, mitosis versus meiosis in a hypothetical organism that has only six chromosomes. After mitosis, the two daughter cell nuclei have chromosomes identical in number and kind to those in the original nucleus. In meiosis, in contrast, chromosome material may cross from one member of a pair to another, and the result is four daughter nuclei that have only half as many chromosomes, which are not identical to those of the original nucleus. (Adapted from Curtis and Barnes, 1981.)

fiber hookup between the eyes and the brain. A cat with this gene will have crossed eyes and faulty vision.

Genes can also alter the sensitivity of sensory systems. If an animal's sensory threshold is altered by a gene so that it requires more intense stimulation to detect a signal than other members of that species, then the animal's behavior will be affected. Its sight or hearing (depending on which system's threshold is altered) will be poor, and it will react differently in many situations. Genes can also alter the threshold level at which cells can be activated by hormones. If, for genetic reasons, a female dog's cells respond to smaller concentrations of estrogens circulating in her bloodstream than most female dogs require, she will go into "heat" (estrus) sooner, with marked effects on her response to male dogs and perhaps with the birth of more litters of pups over her lifetime.

Single-Gene and Polygenic Transmission of Behavior

When single genes have an effect on behavior, it is because they play a central role in some developmental process that requires dozens of genes—or even thousands—for its expression. We can think of this process as a factory assembly line. Many people on the line help to build a television set. But if any one worker forgets to carry out his or her task, or if that worker damages the set as it goes by, the television set probably will perform erratically, if it works at all (Alcock, 1984).

Sometimes it is difficult to establish whether a genetically influenced behavior is polygenic or a single-gene trait. Reading disorders fall into this class. Children with reading disorders have great difficulty learning to read, even though their intelligence is normal and their environment is sup-

portive. When one identical twin has a reading disorder, the other twin usually—but not always—has the same reading problem. When one fraternal twin has a reading disorder, the chances are less than one in three that the other twin will have the same problem (Scarr and Kidd, 1983). Reading disorders also tend to run in families, with uncles, cousins, siblings, parents, and grandparents often showing the condition. Some researchers have concluded that there are several forms of reading disorders, each with its own genetic influence.

Gene-Environment Interaction in Behavior

It is important to note that genes always affect behavior *indirectly*. Except for a very few traits, such as your blood type, the environment determines just how your genetic inheritance (your *genotype*) is expressed. The way you look and behave (your *phenotype*) is the result of continual interactions between your genotype and the series of environments you encounter over the course of your development.

For example, we can see the effects of gene-environment interaction in handedness. Many

Genes or environment? Henry Fonda's children didn't become actors by chance. Most likely, inherited talent plus the role model provided by their actor-father strongly influenced the career choice of Jane and Peter Fonda.

psychologists once believed that handedness was the result of living in a right-handed culture. But studies of adopted children indicate that genes are also involved in the development of hand preference (Carter-Saltzman, 1980). When parents are left-handed or ambidextrous, the rate of left-handedness or ambidextrousness is much higher in their biological children (72 percent) than in their adopted children (45 percent). Yet the adopted children show a higher rate of left-handedness and ambidextrousness than is found in the general population, indicating that environment is also important.

GENETICALLY PROGRAMMED TRAITS AND ADAPTATION

If you placed a wooden dowel in the hands of a newborn infant and slowly raised it into the air, the baby would probably hold tightly onto the dowel and hang suspended in midair. In fact, some newborn infants can hang by one hand. Human babies are born with this grasping reflex; they tighten their hands around anything placed across the palms or fingers. The reflex becomes stronger during the first few weeks of life, then gradually fades; by the time a baby is three or four months old, it has disappeared. The reflex is a part of our species' genetic inheritance.

What could be the purpose of this temporary reflex? No one is certain, but most scientists believe that the grasping reflex is a remnant of our prehuman past. If our early ancestors carried their offspring on their backs or stomachs, the ability to grasp the mother's fur or skin would keep an infant from a dangerous fall (Prechtl, 1982).

The grasping reflex may no longer be especially useful, but human infants are born with a repertoire of inborn behavior that helps them, even in today's world, to survive during the first few minutes, days, or weeks of life—a period when they have had little opportunity to learn. For example, all newborns have a rooting reflex: if you stroke your finger from the corner of a baby's mouth toward the cheek, the baby's tongue and mouth will follow your finger and the infant may even turn its head in the direction of your motion. This reflex, which disappears within a few months, helps the baby place the nipple in the mouth. A baby will also automatically suck anything placed in his or her mouth.

These reflexes are examples of **adaptive behavior**: they increase the organism's chances of survival. Together, they make it possible for the infant to eat. Any behavior that makes an animal function better in its environment is adaptive. Without adaptive behavior on the part of your prehuman forebears, you would not be sitting here reading this book. In fact, if none of our species' ancestors had behaved adaptively, there would be no human beings today.

Natural Selection

If an organism does not live long enough to reproduce, its genetic information does not get passed along to any offspring. But if the organism can outwit predators, adjust to the climate, survive disease, get food, and survive long enough to have offspring, it will pass along its genetic information —including the genes responsible for whatever behavior made its survival possible. If the organism produces more offspring than the average member of its population and those offspring live to reproduce themselves, we can say that the individual has been naturally selected by the environment. **Natural selection** refers to the individual's reproductive success, which is made possible by its phenotypic advantages over other members of its population. The phenotype, as noted above, is a joint product of the individual's genotype and the environment.

If many individuals in a population carry information for the same successful behavior, the behavior will spread through the population. Eventually, genetic information for that behavior will be present in most members of the population. In our prehuman past, for example, newborn infants who could cling to their mothers' fur were more likely to survive and reproduce. That behavior was apparently so linked to survival that it is now found in almost every human newborn. And this fact points up the opposite side of natural selection: those whose behavior is not adaptive may reproduce at lower than average rates, or may not even live to reproduce. Apparently, newborn prehumans who could not cling to their mothers rarely survived.

The genetic variation in human beings—and in any other population—is vast. Because of this variation, at least some members of a population will have a chance to survive if the environmental conditions change. When conditions do change, it may turn out that behavior that was adaptive in the old environment is fatal in the new. Thus, the frequency of particular alleles in a population group may increase or dwindle rapidly.

For example, an English researcher brought a number of moths into Birmingham, where industrial contaminants have darkened the buildings (Kettlewell, 1955). Some of the moths were white and others were black. The researcher released the moths, and after a period of time caught the survivors. The survival rate among the black moths, who blended with the local background, was twice as high as the survival rate among white moths. When the researcher tried the same experiment in the Dorset countryside, three times as many white moths as black moths survived. This example reflects an interaction between genes and the environment. If a moth does not land on a surface that blends with its color, the moth will not survive. Note, however, that the genetic information that ensures survival in a particular environment is not always so specific; it may be as simple as the propensity to learn a certain thing if the appropriate stimulus comes along.

The Range of Adaptive Behavior

Adaptive behavior in animals has been studied intensively by **ethologists**, scientists who try to explain animal behavior in evolutionary terms. The first ethologists were Europeans trained in zoology; they were inspired by Charles Darwin's assertion that behavioral traits evolve according to the same principles that govern anatomical and physiological evolution. Ethologists observed animals in their natural habitats and analyzed each kind of behavior to determine its adaptive role. Their concerns eventually merged with those of comparative psychologists, who had been comparing the behavior of different species, mostly in laboratory experiments, in the hope of finding similarities that would support general "laws of behavior."

The search for adaptive significance focused on **species-specific behavior**, behavior that is typical of a particular species whose members share a common genetic background and a common environment. This concept integrates the two major influences on behavior, by allowing for both genetic and environmental influences.

Some species-specific behavior is based on an animal's sensory capacities. The bat, for example, locates objects in space by responding to the echoes of high-frequency sounds that it emits while flying. This "sonar sense" explains how bats avoid crashing into obstacles and how they can intercept flying insects in the dark. Honeybees can detect polarized light, which allows them to navigate by the sun, even on cloudy days. Salmons' sense of smell is so keen that they can recognize the odor of the stream of their birth, and so return to the place of their birth to spawn.

Closed Genetic Programs

Some genetic programs for behavior can be changed only slightly by experience. Ernst Mayr (1974) calls such programs **closed genetic programs**; he notes that they are found primarily in animals with short life spans and little or no care of offspring by the parents. These programs may take the form of **fixed-action patterns**, relatively stereotyped and often-repeated patterns of movements. These may range from simple behavior such as pecking to the more complex patterns of courtship. The spider's web, the bird's nest, and the honeybee's hexagonal-celled comb are all produced by fixed-action pattern.

We do not know how such patterns develop because they usually appear in full the first time an animal performs them. Researchers believe that genetically programmed brain mechanisms may be involved; as they note, fixed-action patterns can be evoked by stimulating an animal's brain. For example, when the brain of a laboratory-raised cat is stimulated in a particular area, the animal will kill a rat even if it has never before seen a rat or killed another animal. The cat attacks in a way that is almost identical to the form seen in the wild when experienced cats attack and kill prey (Berntson, Hughes, and Beattie, 1976).

Fixed-action patterns, as well as some more complex behaviors, appear in response to a particular stimulus, known as a **sign stimulus**. Color is the key element in many sign stimuli. Red breast feathers on another bird, for example, are a sign stimulus that encourages attack by a male robin protecting its territory.

Open Genetic Programs

Many behaviors involving signaling among members of the same species are closed programs. But other types of communication within a species are under the control of an **open genetic program**, a program that involves some extensive environ-

Imprinting. A few hours after they were hatched (during a sensitive period), these goslings saw Konrad Lorenz instead of their mother. Thereafter they followed him around as if he were the real mother.

mental influence, such as learning. Mayr (1974) notes that the longer the period of parental care in a species, the greater the opportunity for an open genetic program. Open programs can be advantageous when there is something to be gained by storing more information (via learning) than can be transmitted in the genetic program itself. They can be maladaptive in other circumstances.

Imprinting, the process by which some species of birds and mammals form early social attachments, is an example of an open genetic program. Konrad Lorenz (1965) first found that a newly hatched duckling or gosling will form an attachment, or "imprint," to the first moving object it encounters and will then follow the object. In essence, the baby bird's genetic program dictates that a specific type of learning will take place regarding that first moving object: this object, the program says, is "to be followed" no matter what it is. The baby bird will follow a human being, a box on wheels, or a bird of another species. In the wild the first moving object a duckling sees is usually the mother.

Parents must also be able to identify their own offspring, and many animals do this through other kinds of open imprinting programs. For example, a mother cow licks her calf as soon as it is born. From that time, she can identify her own calf by the smell, and she will reject any other calf.

If for some reason, she is prevented from licking her calf within a short time after it is born, she will reject the calf.

The recognition program of other species does not incorporate learning until some time after the young are born. Swallow parents will accept any chick during the first couple of weeks, but at the end of that time, parents of some species will have gone through a learning process that leads them to accept only their own young.

Animals vary considerably in their learning capacities and in the flexibility they bring to bear on a new situation. Some species learn one behavior pattern readily, yet are extremely inflexible when the situation demands a new pattern. Some show closed programs, which are geared to a stimulus for which there is only one correct response. Researchers believe that in most species there are fixed behavioral responses for predictable aspects of the environment. Some can be seen in humans. For example, you cannot keep your eye from blinking shut in response to a sudden bright light or a puff of air, no matter how hard you try. And if you eat a strange food and afterward become ill, the next time you encounter that food, you will feel slightly nauseated.

But not all the situations animals encounter can be handled with fixed responses. Longer-lived animals may be faced with shifts in available food, shelter, or climate; these shifts require behavioral flexibility, and the animal's responses to the environment are likely to have major evolutionary consequences. Animals deal with unpredictable aspects of their environment by modifying their behavior, a response that requires some plasticity in their nervous system. The more unpredictable the environment in which a species lives, the more easily its nervous system is modified by experience (Fuller, 1983a).

EVOLUTION AND ITS IMPACT ON BEHAVIOR

Years ago, scientists pondered the question of how the earth had come to be populated with so many different kinds of animals. Some biologists were satisfied with the traditional story of divine creation, which says that each **species**, or group of individuals who can mate with each other and produce offspring under natural conditions, was

THE MECHANISM OF EVOLUTION

Much of our knowledge of evolution comes from the study of fossils, which suggest what extinct animals looked like and when they lived. From the study of fossil evidence, scientists have developed several theories of how evolution by means of natural selection took place. These theories are not mutually exclusive; rather, each seems the best explanation of how a particular animal or group of animals developed.

Each theory is built on the assumption that the individual, not the group, is selected by the environment. Evolutionary changes in the group are a by-product of the natural selection of individuals: a species evolves through the reproductive success of individuals whose characteristics are well suited to the species' particular environment. This precise environmental situation, which includes food supply, shelter, climate, and pressure from predators, is known as an **environmental niche**.

In the simplest case, a single evolutionary line can be traced over millions of years—a pattern known as **phyletic evolution**. The evolution of the horse is a good example of this pattern. Today's horses can be traced back more than 60 million years to a small doglike animal known as Eohippus. As the climate and vegetation changed over thousands of years, Eohippus's descendants came to have larger teeth (suitable for eating grass, which was becoming a widely available food) and long legs ending in single-toed feet with hardened hoofs (suitable for run-

ning through grasslands). Despite these bodily changes, Eohippus and its descendants can clearly be seen as lineal ancestors of the horse.

A second evolutionary pattern involves a **branching**, or splitting off, of one evolutionary line from another. This pattern seems to describe the evolution of polar bears, for example, which probably developed as a species after a group of brown bears were separated from the rest of the species during the periods of massive glaciation. Among this group, bears who happened to be born with paler fur were at an adaptive advantage in a snowy environment. Eventually, descendants of the paler bears predominated.

Another pattern of evolution is known as **adaptive radiation**. In this case, a group of organisms with a common an-

The polar bear, evolutionary cousin to the brown bear, represents natural selection at work. In its snowy environment, the polar bear's white fur camouflages it from its prey.

cestor diversify so that they can move into a new environmental niche. For example, once some reptiles happened to develop the ability to produce eggs that did not depend on water for their survival, the reptiles quickly—in evolutionary terms—diversified and moved into a number of new environments on dry land. Although scientists distinguish among these three patterns of evolution, they have common features. Even the comparatively "straight-line" evolution of the horse included some branching, and adaptive radiation can be seen as a combination of the phyletic and branching patterns.

established as a distinct type from its beginning. Other biologists believed that a historical process was involved; this process, by which the various species developed from earlier forms of life, is called **evolution**.

The idea of evolution was not new; it was discussed by Aristotle and other classical writers. But what biologists were searching for was a mechanism that would explain how evolution might have occurred. Then, in the mid-nineteenth century, Charles Darwin produced an explanation: evolution operated through the process of natural selection. (Although Darwin customarily receives sole credit for his contribution, another scientist, Alfred Russel Wallace, simultaneously arrived at the same explanation.) Natural selection, as we have seen, controls which genetic information will be passed along to future generations. As the environment changes, natural selection may favor different traits from those it favored before.

As we all know, Darwin wrote about "the survival of the fittest." But it is important to note that he was not referring to strength, aggressiveness, or uncontrolled competition; he was referring only to reproductive success. A male lion, for example, who spends a good deal of his time fighting may be stronger or tougher than other male lions, but the lion who fights less and copulates more may have better reproductive success, in that his genes will be "selected for," than the highly aggressive lion, whose genes will be "selected against" (Greene, Morgan, and Barash, 1980).

Evolution of the Human Species

More than 13 million years ago, as the forests of East Africa began to disappear, a primate came down from the trees and adapted to life in a new environment—the spreading grasslands. The primates who adapted successfully to life on the ground evolved into our prehuman ancestors.

By about 2 million years ago, these prehuman ancestors of ours were clearly different from other primates. For quite some time they had been able to stand, and by now they were chipping stone into crude tools and eating meat. In fact, *Homo habilis*, as this early ancestor was called, was carrying food and tools to certain places where these prehumans probably butchered their kill. Some scientists believe that these places were "home bases," where family groups slept, shared food, and maintained social ties. But other scien-

tists are uncertain; they believe that the remains of the kills would attract predators, and that *Homo habilis* probably still climbed into a tree at night to sleep.

Whether or not *Homo habilis* established home bases, this ancestor of ours certainly had a larger brain than the primate that climbed down from the East African trees. Without a larger brain, *Homo habilis* would have been unable to hunt effectively in groups and to invent tools. Throughout our prehuman history, large-brained individuals were presumably "selected for"; they were probably better at getting tools, communicating with others, finding food, and avoiding predators (Greene, Morgan, and Barash, 1980).

After a successful existence that may have lasted a million and a half years, *Homo habilis* was supplanted by *Homo erectus*. This ancestor of ours "stood tall"—to his or her full five feet or so—and had a much larger brain. Speech may have first appeared about this time, although we have no way to be certain. *Homo erectus* was definitely not sleeping in the trees; this prehuman built shelters, invented complex tools, and began to wear some kind of clothing. Perhaps most important, *Homo erectus* used fire—an invention that provided the kind of security that allowed home bases and permitted *Homo erectus* to move into colder climates. It widened this species' environmental niche and enabled *Homo erectus* to migrate as far north as Germany.

About 100,000 years ago *Neanderthal* appeared. Neanderthals looked much like present human beings, and they may have invented the first human society. At any rate, their culture had become complex; they made delicate carvings, and they had invented a way to make cloth. They knew something about medicine, and they had developed a religion, complete with cultural rituals. Scientists believe that Neanderthals were not direct ancestors of human beings; in fact, their existence overlapped that of the first human beings by about 20,000 years (Leakey and Lewin, 1977).

The *Cro-Magnons*, who appeared about 35,000 years ago, were the first *Homo sapiens sapiens*, which is our own subspecies. All peoples of the world, no matter what their skin color or physical type, are *Homo sapiens sapiens*. As our ancestors migrated away from the equatorial regions, where dark skin protected against solar radiation, the environment selected for light skin. Away from the equatorial regions light skin was adaptive, because it promoted the production of vitamin D by the comparatively feeble rays of the northern sun. The changed shape of Cro-Magnon's mouth made speech more precise and allowed language to become intricate. All parts of Cro-Magnon's culture became complex, and art was born. Paintings exist today that were painted on the walls of caves by some Cro-Magnon artists.

During this long evolutionary process that selected for upright, large-brained individuals, another process was going on. The pelvis changed to support the additional weight of an upright posture, a change that shrank the pelvic opening. This meant that infants had to be born earlier in their development. What are the implications of being born relatively undeveloped? One consequence is helplessness. Human infants require care for much longer than the young of other primates. But a second consequence of this early birth made us able to exploit our ecological niche more efficiently. The longer period of childhood gave us a protected period in which we could learn the rules of our social group and whatever skills we needed to survive (Leakey and Lewin, 1977). Thus, our long childhood is one of the complicated factors in the evolution of human cultures.

The Sociobiological Perspective

Psychologists are interested in genetics and the evolution of the human species because of their possible influence on human behavior. Much of the evidence we have examined has to do with the influence of genetics on individual behavior, such as intelligence, depression, schizophrenia, read-

ing disabilities, and so on. But psychologists are also interested in **social behavior**, which includes any behavior that involves the interaction of two or more individuals. In social behavior the response of one person depends on the actions of another (Scott, 1983). For the past decade or so a group of scientists known as sociobiologists have been examining the connection between genetics, cultural evolution, and social behavior.

Sociobiology is the study of the genetic basis of social behavior and organizations; sociobiologists attempt to explain the evolution of social behavior in terms of the same genetic mechanisms that govern physical evolution and individual behavior. Sociobiologists apply these principles to such aspects of social behavior as competition, cooperation, altruism, sex roles, the socialization of children, territoriality, and aggression. Because natural selection operates at the individual level, any changes in social behavior are the result of changes in the behavior of individuals; sociobiology suggests mechanisms for this process.

Criticisms of Sociobiology—And the Sociobiologists' Response

When Wilson (1975) first set forth the basic principles of sociobiology, his application of them to human beings set off a storm of criticism. The critics had four major objections to human sociobiology:

■ Human behavior is so plastic, these critics said, that genes could not control social

Why do musk oxen band together in this defensive formation? Sociobiologists suggest that genes for adaptive social behavior are inherited by a species just as genes for physical traits are.

behavior and organizations. There simply is no "human nature." Cultural influences are so rapid and pervasive in humans that genetic evolution is inconsequential by comparison.

■ Human societies are structured to promote the well-being of the society rather than that of individual members.

■ Analogies between human and animal behavior are simplistic. The critics maintained that evolutionary arguments based on animal data cannot be applied to human social behavior.

■ The idea that social behavior and social organizations are adaptive (otherwise they would not have evolved) was seen as wrong. To assume that they are adaptive legitimizes sexism, racism, poverty, war, and all the other social ills of humanity (Fuller, 1983b).

Sociobiologists believe that many of their critics have not understood their position. They point out that all behavior is the result of an interaction between genes and environment. They agree that human beings modify their behavior radically as a result of experience, but assert that the changes are always within certain genetic constraints. And they emphasize that what genes specify is often not a precise effect but a vague propensity toward some response (Greene, Morgan, and Barash, 1980).

How do sociobiologists answer the contention that human societies favor group survival, not individual survival? They do agree that societal forces can affect the individual fitness of members, but they still see groups as furthering individual reproductive success. For example, although primitive warfare eliminates some individuals, it gives the victors access to scarce resources and thus enhances their ability to survive and reproduce in their environment (Fuller, 1983b).

As for the third objection, sociobiologists contend that the behavior of animals often tells us a good deal about the behavior of human beings. They point out that many advances in human physiology and medicine are based on information gleaned from animal studies, and note that all animals with backbones have a similar nervous system (Fuller, 1983b). For example, as we will see in Chapter 17, information from studies of rhesus monkeys was responsible for a major advance in our understanding of babies' socioemotional development.

Sociobiologists further deny that a biological approach to human behavior endorses all social practices that have arisen. Adaptive behavior is not necessarily the "best" adaptation possible; rather, it was merely minimally adaptive at the time it was selected for (Barash, 1980). The present human environment is very different from the environment in which our ancestors evolved; behavior that was adaptive then may well be harmful today. For example, warfare between two tribes armed with spears may have been adaptive, but warfare between two countries armed with atomic weapons is clearly maladaptive. To study aggression and exploitation is not equivalent to condoning these things, any more than studying cancer is an act of support for the disease.

Finally, instead of proposing divisions among human beings, sociobiology downplays ethnic differences and stresses universal aspects of human nature. It has also emphasized cooperative forms of behavior, such as altruism—unselfish concern for the welfare of others.

Explaining Altruistic Behavior

It might seem as if altruism presented an unsurmountable obstacle to sociobiological theory. Altruistic behavior often entails harm to the helper, and since death precludes further reproduction, it is hard to see any genetic advantage in such practices. Yet natural selection, operating on individuals, can explain the evolution of altruism (Greene, Morgan, and Barash, 1980).

Inclusive Fitness How does sacrificing your life to save another increase your own fitness? By indirectly passing along your own genes. "Kin selection"—helping your relatives survive to reproduce—is an important concept in sociobiology. It is related to the concept of **inclusive fitness**—the notion that the reproductive success of an individual is a combination of his or her own personal fitness (passing along genes through offspring) and the fitness of his or her relatives based on their shared genes (Fuller, 1983b). Helping close relatives to reproduce is an indirect way of perpetuating your own genes, since your relatives have a substantial number of genes in common with you. You can regard yourself as a "survival machine," whose job is to promote the survival of your own genes (Alcock, 1984). Or, in Edward Wilson's (1975) words: a chicken is really a gene's way of making more copies of itself.

Sociobiologists say that inclusive fitness explains the suicidal behavior of bees: a honeybee gives up its life to sting an invader, but this act protects the entire bee colony, which is made up of as many as 80,000 sisters, each carrying half of the bee's genes (Wilson, 1978). Inclusive fitness explains why humans make greater sacrifices for their children than for a cousin. The *immediate* cause of their action may be parental love, but "love" is seen as evolution's way of maximizing individual fitness (Barash, 1980). Inclusive fitness can even explain adoption: during most of our evolutionary history, we lived in small groups, in which most of the members were closely related. Adopting an orphaned child helped pass along a portion of the adopter's genes.

Reciprocal Altruism We can also find a solid sociobiological explanation for aiding others in the concept of **reciprocal altruism**, proposed by Robert Trivers (1971). Reciprocal altruism refers to the idea that going to the aid of another person *may* increase the probability that that person will come to your aid in the future—depending, in part, on how risky it is to help you, whether you have already returned a former favor, and how closely your two destinies are intertwined.

In reciprocal altruism, an animal weighs the costs and benefits: if the benefits are likely to be greater than costs, it gives aid. Among the factors that add to the possible benefits of reciprocal altruism are long life span, relative stability of residence, and interdependence in various aspects of life (all increase the chances of encountering the animal in a situation where it can reciprocate). Trivers points to "fish cleaners" as one example of reciprocal altruism. Nearly fifty varieties of small fish enter the mouth and gill chambers of large predatory fish in order to clean out parasites (which the cleaners eat). The large fish rarely eat a cleaner and always signal when they are about to leave the area—even though waiting to give the signal may put them in danger. Their altruism pays off: unless the cleaner fish keep down the parasite population, the large predatory fish will sicken and may die.

According to Trivers, the evolution of reciprocal altruism in human beings is in part responsible for:

- Friendship. Selection favors our liking altruistic people, because altruism increases fitness.
- Moralistic aggression. Injustice and unfairness make us feel indignant, and we often respond to them with aggression out of proportion to the slight. Selection favors our outrage at "cheaters" who do not reciprocate altruism.
- Gratitude and sympathy. Selection favors gratitude, which might be viewed as our emotional evaluation of the cost-benefit ratio of assistance.
- Guilt. Selection favors guilt in order to motivate a cheater to compensate for misdeeds and to behave reciprocally in the future.

In the sociobiological view, human beings are the result of a long process of natural selection. Throughout that lengthy period we have been selected to behave in ways that improve our inclusive fitness (Fuller, 1983b). Sociobiology is more influential than it was ten years ago, but its proposals are rejected by some psychologists. However, the idea that genes and environment interact to produce behavior is generally accepted by most psychologists.

SUMMARY

1. The more unpredictable the environment in which a species lives, the more easily its nervous system is modified by experience. The human nervous system is extremely **plastic**, but human behavior is also influenced by genetic inheritance. Psychologists in the field of **behavior genetics** look for genetic influences on behavior by using twin studies, adoption studies, and animal breeding experiments. Genetic influences have been found on the functioning of the nervous system, on a person's sensitivity to alcohol and other drugs, and on the development of behavioral disorders such as depression and schizophrenia.

2. **DNA (deoxyribonucleic acid)** transmits the ge-

netic code in the form of instructions for the production of protein molecules. Units of information on the DNA string are known as **genes**; genes are located in threadlike structures known as **chromosomes**. Most human traits are **polygenic** and require the occurrence of several genes for their expression. Genes can affect behavior by altering the way the nervous system functions, by altering the sensitivity of the nervous system, or by changing the timing of other developmental events.

3. **Adaptive behavior** is any behavior that increases an individual's chances of survival. **Natural selection** refers to the individual's reproductive success, which is made possible by its genetic differences from other members of its population. Adaptive behavior can spread throughout a population, because individuals carrying the information for that behavior are naturally selected by the environment. Wide genetic variation in a population increases the population's chance of surviving if its environmental conditions change radically. Adaptive behavior in animals has been studied by **ethologists**, who observe animals in their environments, looking for **species-specific behavior**. Species-specific behavior may be governed by a **closed genetic program**, which can be changed only slightly by experience, or by an **open genetic program**, which can be modified by experience. Closed genetic programs are usually found in short-lived animals that receive little or no parental care. Some programs, such as the weaving of a spider's web, take the form of **fixed-action patterns**, which are relatively stereotyped and often-repeated patterns of movements. Whether governed by a closed or an open program, much species-specific behavior appears in response to a **sign stimulus**. **Imprinting**, the process by which some species of birds and mammals form early social attachments, is an open genetic program.

4. According to the theory of **evolution**, each **species**, or group of individuals who can mate and produce offspring under natural conditions, developed from earlier forms of life. Each species has evolved through the reproductive success of individuals whose characteristics are well suited to the species' **environmental niche**. A species may evolve through **phyletic evolution**, **branching**, or **adaptive radiation**. Cultures also evolve through natural selection, with language serving as the genetic code.

5. *Homo sapiens sapiens*, the human species, evolved from a prehuman ancestor known as *Homo habilis*, who could stand erect and make crude tools. *Homo habilis* was supplanted by *Homo erectus*, who built shelters, used fire, and may have been the first of our ancestors to speak. *Cro-Magnon*, the first member of our own subspecies, appeared about 35,000 years ago. During the course of human evolution, large brains were consistently selected for, because their possessors were better at most survival skills than other members of their species. The increasingly upright posture of our ancestors caused the pelvic opening to become so small that infants had to be born earlier in development. Although this change made human infants helpless for a lengthy period, it gave human beings a longer period for learning before they had to survive on their own.

6. **Sociobiology** is the study of the genetic basis of **social behavior** (behavior that involves the interaction of two or more individuals). Sociobiologists believe that social behavior evolved in the same way as our species evolved: through natural selection. One of the basic concepts of sociobiology is **inclusive fitness**—the notion that the fitness of an individual to survive is a combination of his or her own personal fitness and the fitness of his or her relatives based on their shared genes. Because of inclusive fitness, individuals will sacrifice their own lives to ensure the survival of their relatives (who carry a proportion of the altruistic individual's genes). Some altruistic behavior can be explained by **reciprocal altruism**, in which aid given to another individual increases the probability that that individual will come to your aid in the future. Reciprocal altruism is dispensed on the basis of costs and benefits: when benefits outweigh costs, an animal is altruistic even though the individual it assists carries none of its genes. It has been suggested that the evolution of reciprocal altruism is responsible for friendship, moralistic aggression, gratitude and sympathy, and guilt among human beings.

KEY TERMS

adaptive behavior
adaptive radiation
behavior genetics
branching
chromosomes
closed genetic programs
DNA (deoxyribonucleic acid)
environmental niche
ethologists

evolution
fixed-action patterns
fraternal twins
genes
identical twins
imprinting
inclusive fitness
natural selection
open genetic program

phyletic evolution
plastic
polygenic
reciprocal altruism
sign stimulus
social behavior
sociobiology
species
species-specific behavior

RECOMMENDED READINGS

ALCOCK, J. *Animal behavior: An evolutionary approach* (3rd ed.). Sunderland, Mass.: Sinauer, 1984. A broad, biologically oriented discussion of animal behavior processes; thorough and well-written.

DARWIN, C. *The descent of man* (1871). Philadelphia: West, 1902. The evolutionary case for the idea that humans and some other mammals are descended from common ancestors.

DAWKINS, R. *The selfish gene.* New York: Oxford University Press, 1976. This is an engaging and informative review of the new concepts in sociobiology.

DETHIER, V. G. *To know a fly.* San Francisco: Holden Day, 1962. A delightful, readable account of the behavior of flies.

DEWSBURY, D. A. *Comparative animal behavior.* New York: McGraw-Hill, 1978. A comprehensive, up-to-date textbook on animal behavior from the perspective of a comparative psychologist.

LORENZ, K. *King Solomon's ring.* New York: Crowell, 1952. A light, easy-to-read book of essays about Lorenz's many interesting experiences with animals.

TINBERGEN, N. *Animal behavior.* New York: Time-Life Books, 1965. A beautifully illustrated book on animal behavior for the general public, with an excellent running narrative by one of the world's leading ethologists.

SENSATION AND THE SENSES

Imagine a world without sensation. You would exist in a void, where there was neither light nor shadow, and where no sound disturbed the silence. Food would have no flavor, and you would know neither the fragrance of flowers nor the smell of decay. A lover's caress could not excite you, nor could a cooling breeze relieve the summer heat—which you would not feel, no matter how badly sunburned you became. If you picked up a knife, you could not sense it in your hand; if you cut yourself, you would feel no pain. Even walking would be virtually impossible, because you could not tell where your feet were relative to the ground and each other.

Could you live very long without sensation? Your chances would be slim, because without your senses you would have no lifeline to reality. Your senses are specialized neural structures that put you in touch with the external world, enabling you to deal with the challenges of the environment. Whenever there is a large enough change in the environmental energies that impinge on you, your senses capture this change and transform it into information you can use to reach your goals. The change in energy is a **stimulus**; thanks to your senses, you can *respond* to it in some advantageous way.

Each human sense is selective, responding only to a limited range of sensory information. Our sense of vision, for example, responds only to a certain portion of the electromagnetic spectrum —the portion we see as light; we do not sense other portions of the spectrum, such as infrared waves (see Figure 5.1). Yet, as we shall see, our senses are closely adapted to the survival needs of human beings. Other species' senses show the same sort of sensory selectivity. Birds, which hunt for food in daylight, have an acute sense of vision but a poor sense of smell. By contrast, many nocturnal animals, whose waking hours are spent in a darkened world, are color-blind. They have an acute and highly specialized sense of hearing, however: for example, bats avoid obstacles by reacting to echoes of the squeals they emit, and

Sensory stimulation is all around us, but we can usually select the stimuli we wish to respond to. At a street fair, such as this one, we may choose to engage all of our senses at once.

certain moths react to the squeaks of hunting bats that prey on them (while remaining deaf to all other frequencies). Sensory systems are like filters that accentuate or suppress information about the world, depending on the kinds of information the organism needs to survive in its ecological niche.

In this chapter we explore just how our human senses operate. First, we investigate the limits of our senses; we find out how sensation is measured, and how our sensory systems adapt to stimulation. After this discussion of our sensory capabilities, we take up each sense in turn, to see

how it translates stimulation into information the brain can use. In the process, we will see how our senses work as an integrated team.

STIMULI AND SENSATIONS

The external world provides various forms of energy that can impinge on our sensory receptors. Scientists have two ways of measuring this ener-

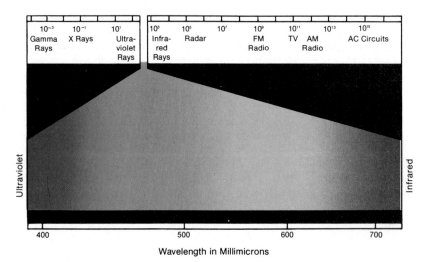

Figure 5.1. The spectrum of electromagnetic energy. The small portion of this spectrum to which the human eye is sensitive is shown expanded at the bottom. The top scale on the large spectrum is a logarithmic scale of wavelength: each step on the scale corresponds to a tenfold increase in the wavelength of the electromagnetic radiation.

gy. They can measure it in physical terms, based on the way the energy influences some mechanical instrument, such as a light meter, a sound-level meter, a thermometer, or a weight scale. Such readings are expressed in units, such as luminance, decibels, degrees Fahrenheit or Celsius, or kilograms. Psychologists are more interested in how people "measure" energy in subjective terms, based on the response it evokes in an organism's sensory system. When they choose this method, they generally describe a stimulus in terms of its subjective attributes, using such words as "brightness," "loudness," "warmth," or "heaviness."

If you ask people to tell you about their psychological reactions to a sensory stimulus, they generally report two things. First, they describe the **quality** of the stimulus, or the kind of sensation it produces: if the stimulus is visual, for instance, they may talk about its color, or if the stimulus is auditory they may talk about its musical pitch. Next they report the **intensity** of the stimulus, or the amount of stimulation it produces in their sense organs: they describe the brightness of a light and the loudness of a sound. These characteristics—color, brightness, pitch, loudness—are psychological aspects of sensations. They are the subjective properties of sensory experience.

Sensory Thresholds and Signal Detection

Detecting a stimulus can be a matter of life and death—for an animal in the wild, say, or a sentry on guard duty. An enemy soldier, creeping stealthily up on a sentry at night, steps on a twig, which snaps. Will the sentry hear the tiny sound—or will it be too faint for his auditory system to pick up? Because the experience of intensity is crucial, psychologists study it in both animals and humans. A researcher who wanted to determine the limits of the human auditory system would try to discover how well it functioned under various environmental conditions. How weak a sound can a person hear? How much must a steady sound be increased for the person to notice the change? How does a person's judgment of a sound relate to the physical stimulus? How do such factors as expectation, motivation, and attention influence these judgments?

Information about human sensory capabilities has been most useful in "human-factors" re-

search, where the aim is to design efficient, "user-friendly" equipment and industrial workspaces. Human-factors psychologists try to design technological equipment so that people can operate it easily without many errors. Most high-technology equipment, such as radar screens or airplane cockpits, requires the human operator to pick up information from displays or monitors, then take some appropriate action. When psychologists design such equipment, they rely on the evidence researchers have collected on sensory capabilities. For example, they take care to design an airplane's altitude meter so that its display can be read accurately by a pilot with average vision: you shouldn't have to have exceptionally sharp eyes to read your altitude off the dial.

The Absolute Threshold

Suppose you had to select a radar operator to monitor radar screens for dim spots of light that represented incoming airplanes. You would want someone who could detect very dim spots of light so that planes would be detected as early as possible. To find such a person you would test each applicant's **absolute threshold**, or the weakest stimulus that produces a detectable sensation. People have different absolute thresholds, and you could measure them by having each applicant watch for a spot of light on a dark TV screen.

First, you would project a very faint light spot on the screen, much fainter than the person can detect. Then you would gradually increase the light's intensity until the person said, "I see it." Or you might start by projecting a clearly visible spot and then gradually decrease its intensity until the person said, "I can't see it any more." To build up confidence in your test results, you would repeat these procedures a number of times with the same person. By convention, the lowest intensity at which a person reports seeing the light *half the time* is considered his or her absolute threshold (see Figure 5.2). The person with the most sensitive eyes (the lowest threshold) would be your choice for the radar monitoring task. Similar considerations would apply if you were choosing a sentry. Putting a deaf person on sentry duty would be disastrous; instead, you would want the person who would hear the rustle of bushes or the snapping of a tiny twig. You would select the person with the lowest auditory threshold for sentry duty.

When conditions are ideal, people's absolute

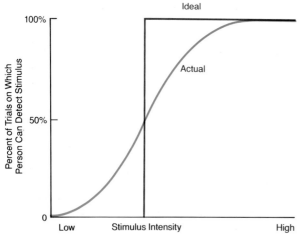

Figure 5.2. Under ideal conditions a specific point would exist at which the intensity of a stimulus was great enough for a person to detect it. Below that point, the person would never detect the stimulus, while above that point he or she would always perceive it. This ideal threshold of sensation is depicted by the red line on the graph. Such ideal conditions never prevail because of intrinsic variability in the stimulus and a person's sensory apparatus. The ability to detect a stimulus is influenced by such factors as fatigue or alertness, motivation, and expectations concerning the signal. As shown by the blue curve on the graph, sometimes low-intensity stimuli are perceived and sometimes not. For comparisons, most psychologists arbitrarily define the absolute threshold as the weakest stimulus that a person can detect 50 percent of the time.

thresholds are quite low, with only minute amounts of stimulation required to produce sensations. For example, the human sense of smell can detect one drop of perfume in a three-room apartment. Your tongue can taste a teaspoon of sugar dissolved in two gallons of water. And on a clear, dark night, the human eye can detect the light of a candle burning thirty miles away (Galanter, 1962).

The Difference Threshold

Suppose a detective investigating a kidnapping has recordings of two telephone conversations about a ransom and wants to know whether both calls were made by the same person. In this case it would be vital that the detective be able to detect slight differences in sounds. This sensitivity is known as the **difference threshold**, or **just no-**

ticeable difference (jnd); the term refers to the smallest change in a stimulus that produces a noticeable change in sensation. The visual difference threshold can be important when an actor is getting ready for a television performance. He or she must apply makeup base and rouge to each cheek so that the shading is subjectively equal and the viewer notices no difference between them. In the laboratory the difference threshold can be measured by a procedure similar to that used with the absolute threshold. You would start with two equal light spots and then gradually increase the difference between them until the person said, "Yes, one spot is brighter than the other." This technique makes it possible to identify the smallest increase in light intensity that a person can detect.

Variations in Performance

Our sensory responses are not consistent. Presented with the same weak stimulus, a person may detect it at one moment but fail to detect it a few minutes or hours or a day later. Why? First, the physical stimulus itself may vary. For example, even if we use the same flash of light on each trial, the number of light particles (quanta) emitted from the bulb and registered by the eye vary from one flash to the next. Second, each person's sensory system varies over time. Random changes in the internal state of the sensory apparatus, and in the person's readiness (e.g., level of attention or fatigue), cause the same physical stimulus to evoke neural responses of different magnitudes at different times. Sensory systems also appear to contain internal "noise"—spontaneous neural activity that goes on independent of external stimulation. Any stimulus, or signal, therefore, is embedded in a background level of "noise," which makes it difficult to distinguish a weak signal amidst this internal noise. Finally, a person's level of motivation may wax and wane, and this can strongly influence judgments of a signal. For example, if you are awakened by a noise in the middle of the night, fears of a burglar will increase your likelihood of hearing any creaking of the house or swaying of nearby trees in the wind.

When people are trying hard to detect weak signals, they occasionally think that they have heard (or seen) a signal when in fact the experimenter has fooled them by giving a "catch trial," in which no signal is presented. These errors are called **false alarms**, a borrowed phrase referring to fire alarms that have been turned in when there's no real fire. Clearly, someone who turns in lots of false alarms on catch trials is not very trustworthy (or "discriminating") in telling us whether or not a signal (or "fire") was actually present. Such a performance lowers our assessment of that person's sensory ability.

Several factors are known to increase a person's tendency to give false alarms. For example, if you strongly expect to hear or see a signal, or if it is profitable to detect all signals and not too costly to turn in false alarms, then when you are unsure about what you have heard, you will probably guess, "Yes, I saw (or heard) a signal." Although such a strategy produces extra false alarms on catch trials, it also increases your likelihood of reporting weak signals. In an attempt to solve the false-alarm problem, researchers developed modern **signal detection theory**, which provides a way to estimate a person's actual sensitivity to signals (Green and Swets, 1966). His or her score is "corrected" by taking into account the tendency to turn in false alarms on catch trials.

Theories of sensory limits and signal detection have important applications in decision making. Much of the machinery of modern society requires people to detect extremely weak stimuli, no matter what external or internal noise may be present. Thus, some work by sensory psychologists is quite useful to society. For example, a radar operator must be able to detect a missile on a radar screen even when the operator is tired or when the blip is faint and difficult to distinguish from blips caused by birds or bad weather. Among radar operators at Strategic Air Command bases, false alarms can have disastrous consequences. Similarly, lawsuits brought by residents against airports must establish just how discriminable and unpleasant the noise levels caused by increased air traffic have become. Understanding influences on sensory judgments and the limits of sensory systems is clearly of major importance.

Sensory Scaling

In order to survive, the sentry we left on guard duty must have sensory systems that can do more than hear a snapping twig against the background of quiet forest noises. He needs to be able to gauge the intensity of sensations as well. Suppose the sentry had to estimate how many enemy tanks were moving toward him, simply by judging the intensity of their collective sound or the intensity of their collective headlights. In this case, the sentry acts as a measuring instrument for the magnitude of sound or light.

Measuring the physical magnitude of a sound or light is a straightforward procedure when we use sound-level meters or light meters. Such meters are calibrated to provide scaled readings of magnitude. But how accurate is the report of a human being? If a person's sensation increased linearly (in direct proportion) with the magnitude of a stimulus (if the sentry experienced two tanks as "twice as loud as" one tank), we could probably trust the person's judgment. However, sensory systems do not work this way. Doubling the sound produced by tanks moving across the terrain does not double a person's sensation of loudness.

Weber's Law

This problem was investigated by Ernst Weber (1795–1878), who proposed a solution in 1834. While studying human sensory processes, Weber found that people notice small changes in a weak stimulus, but that a strong stimulus must undergo a much larger change before they notice it. For instance, if a hiker adds one pound to a backpack weighing 5 pounds, the feeling of heaviness is noticeably increased. But if one pound is added to a seventy-pound backpack, the increase in weight is imperceptible.

For each of the sensory systems there is a specific, unchanging ratio between the intensity of the original stimulus and the amount the stimulus intensity has to be increased in order for the person to experience a just noticeable difference in the sensation; this relationship is known as **Weber's law**. For the human sensory systems that measure weight, for example, the ratio is about one to fifty. If you are carrying a ten-pound backpack and you add one-fifth of a pound of chocolate, you will just be able to notice a difference in weight. But if the backpack already weighs fifty pounds, you will have to add a pound of chocolate before you notice an increase in weight. And if you have a hundred-pound backpack, you won't notice an addition unless it weighs at least two pounds. This one-to-fifty ratio applies only to judgments of weight. Other sensory systems have their own ratios. The human auditory system is less sensitive, with a ratio of one to ten for detecting changes in the intensity of a tone. Most other sensory systems are even less sensitive: the ratio for skin pressure is one to seven; for odor intensity, one to four; and for saltiness of liquid, one to three. The visual system is the most efficient. In most people the ratio for brightness is one to sixty, so even a 102-watt bulb will appear noticeably brighter than a 100-watt bulb. These differences in ratios suggest that some senses have been more important than others in the evolution of our species.

Magnitude Estimates

Weber's law describes the way people detect differences between two or more stimuli. But what about our direct judgment of the intensity of a single stimulus? The psychologist S. S. Stevens (1957) took a simple but direct approach to this issue. He asked his subjects to judge stimuli by assigning numbers that represented their subjective magnitude. For example, if a person thought that a new light seemed twice as bright as a standard light, he or she gave the new light a number twice as large as the standard. Using this direct approach, Stevens found that subjective magnitude increased with the physical intensity of the stimulus, in an equation that involved raising the physical intensity to some power (or exponent). (Recall that in the arithmetic expression 4^3 ($4 \times 4 \times 4$), 3 is called the "power," or the "exponent," of 4.)

The exponent differs for each sensory system. The larger the exponent, the more change a person feels in subjective magnitude as the intensity of the physical stimulus increases a given amount. If the exponent is less than one, then a large range of stimulus intensities is squeezed into a smaller range of subjective magnitudes. Brightness has such an exponent: to double a subjective sensation of brightness, one has to increase the physical intensity of light by a factor of eight. If the exponent is greater than one, then a small stimulus range is expanded into a much greater range of subjective magnitudes. Electric shock is one such stimulus: to double the subjective magnitude of an electric shock, one only has to increase the electric current by about one-sixth its former value. Equipment designers use such results to determine what sort of indicator light or tone will best inform the person operating the equipment about the intensity of air pressure, heat, altitude, or some other physical variable.

Sensory Adaptation

You have probably had the experience of walking from a sunny sidewalk into a dimly lit theater and discovering that you were unable to see which seats were occupied. As your eyes adjusted to the darkness, the temporary blindness passed, and you began to distinguish the seats and the people in them. This process is an example of **adaptation**, an adjustment in sensitivity that gradually occurs after an abrupt change in the level of stimulation. While you were outdoors, your eyes were adapted to sunlight; when you entered the theater, they required time to adapt to the dark.

All sensory systems display adaptation. Some senses, like sight, smell, and touch, adapt quickly, but others, like the sense of pain, adapt very slowly. Adaptation enables our senses to operate efficiently over an enormous range of stimulus intensities. By adapting to the surrounding stimulation, our sensors adjust themselves so they can discriminate small stimulus changes within that range. This adaptation to background stimuli is closely related to Weber's law for noticing differences in stimulus intensity. For example, in darkness (where the intensity of stimulation is low), small variations in light intensity are significant, and so our eyes are extremely sensitive to small changes. But in brilliant sunlight small variations are unimportant and our eyes do not notice them. Another perspective on adaptation is to note that a steady level of stimulation, whether pressure, light, sound, or odor, provides no new information; we adapt by ceasing to notice this constant background of old information. But we still remain alert to changes in stimulation. For instance, a sleeping person adapts to the sound of a playing radio and awakens when the radio volume is abruptly increased.

When part of a sensory system adapts, so that your sensitivity to smell or taste or temperature is partly altered, you may find that sensations are distorted. You can experience this distortion in a simple experiment. Put one of your hands in a pan of icy water and the other in a pan of extremely hot water. Wait a few minutes to give your hands a chance to adapt, then thrust both hands into a pan of tepid water. The initial sensation will be bizarre, because the contradictory messages sent by your two hands will make the water feel hot and cold at the same time.

This experiment demonstrates that the sensations we perceive are determined not solely by the present stimulus but also by immediately preceding stimuli. Baseball hitters rely on this persisting adaptation when they swing a very heavy bat (or several bats) just before going to the plate. Their regulation-weight bat now feels much lighter and they can swing it faster. Similarly, lemonade tastes much sweeter after you rinse your mouth with vinegar but makes your mouth pucker after you eat a sugar cube. The adaptation level to a particular intensity of stimulation seems to aid sensory judgment by providing a frame of reference for evaluating new sensations (Helson, 1964).

THE SENSES

Although most people believe that human beings have five senses, we actually have at least a dozen. We are all familiar with the five senses whose receptors are located in the eyes, ears, nose, tongue, and skin. But few people realize that within the skin are receptors for at least four kinds of sensation (touch, warmth, cold, and pain). This brings our sensory count to eight, but we are not finished. Deep within the ear is an organ that provides our sense of balance, and receptors in the muscles, joints, and tendons tell us about the movement and position of our body. Additional receptors within the brain monitor blood chemistry and temperature.

Each sense organ contains special receptors that are sensitive to particular types of stimuli. No matter what sort of sensation they deal with, however, all sense organs operate according to similar principles. The basic job of all sensory receptors is the same: to convert environmental stimuli into neural impulses, the language of the nervous system. The neural information is then relayed over specialized nerve pathways to specialized sensory areas in the brain. Here it undergoes refined analysis and may ultimately lead to conscious experience and sometimes to actions.

Each sensory nerve seems to provide only its own kind of information to the brain. If you were punched in the eye, the sudden pressure on your eyeball would be experienced as a flash of light. You would "see stars." Why should pressure produce a visual experience? For centuries, scholars debated whether the sort of sensation (heat, light, sound) that was perceived depended on the physi-

cal stimulus or on the sensory nerve that was stimulated. Early in the nineteenth century, Johannes Müller proposed the **doctrine of specific nerve energies**, which states that sensory quality depends on the neural pathways activated by a stimulus, not on the physical properties of the stimulus. Evidence supports Müller's doctrine. No matter how a sensory nerve is stimulated, it signals the same sensory quality (Goldstein, 1984). For example, a weak electrical current applied to the tongue can evoke a sour, sweet, salty, or bitter taste, depending on where the tongue is stimulated. Similarly, electrical stimulation of specific neural pathways or the sensory cortex can evoke hallucinations of sounds or sights.

Sensory pathways and the sensory cortex are highly specialized. We don't "hear lights" or "see sounds" because neural pathways to the visual cortex are connected to receptors in the eye that respond only to light waves, and pathways to the auditory cortex are connected to receptors in the ear that respond only to changes in sound pressure. As we explore each sensory system, this specialization will become clear.

VISION

Vision is one of our richest senses; it provides us with a wealth of information. The eyes receive light reflected from objects in the world, and from this light we perceive shape, color, depth, texture, and movement.

Light, the basic stimulus for vision, is a form of energy that is transmitted in waves. It is a small part of a larger range of such energy, the electromagnetic spectrum. This spectrum also contains radio and infrared waves, ultraviolet light, X-rays, and gamma rays, all of which are outside the range of human visual sensitivity and can be measured only with special instruments. (see Figure 5.1). The electromagnetic spectrum is scaled in units called **wavelengths**, and that portion visible to the human eye ranges from just below 400 nanometers (billionths of a meter, abbreviated nm) to about 780 nm. Even within this range, the human eye is not uniformly sensitive to all wavelengths; it is most sensitive to dim lights from the middle of the visible spectrum.

The Structure of the Eye

The human eye consists of four major parts: the cornea, the iris, the lens, and the retina (see Figure 5.3). Light enters the eye through the **cornea**, the transparent covering in front of the eye. The cornea, which is sharply curved, helps focus the light. Behind the cornea is the **pupil**, the aperture in the center of the eye that appears black. The amount of light that enters the eye through the pupil is regulated by the **iris**, a ring of muscle whose pigmentation gives the eye its color. Reflexive contractions and widening of the iris allow the eye to adapt as the light level changes. When you enter a dark room, the iris opens the pupil so that more light strikes the retina. When you step from a dark theater into the sunlight, you feel a blinding glare caused by too much light striking the retina. In response, the iris constricts the pupil to reduce the entering light.

Light passes through the pupil to a transparent structure called the **lens**. The muscles attached to the lens modify its curvature to focus light rays so that they make a clear image on the **retina**, the surface at the back of the eye. The lens's muscles are generally relaxed during distant vision. For close viewing, they contract reflexively and make the lens thicker, in a process known as **accommodation**: the thickened lens is thus able to focus the image of nearby objects on the retina. If the eyeball becomes abnormally elongated or shortened—say, due to aging—then the image at all distances cannot be focused sharply on the retina even with lens accommodation. In such cases, corrective lenses ("glasses") can be worn. Corrective lenses alter the path of incoming light rays in such a way that the image will be sharply focused on the retina.

From Receptor Cells to the Brain

The retina is an intricate network of receptor cells and neurons, where light energy is converted into neural impulses that can be transmitted to the brain. The major neural structures of the retina and their interconnections take part in a chain of visual processing that begins in the retina, continues in the lateral geniculate nucleus of the thalamus (which, as we learned in Chapter 3, serves as a relay station), and ends in the visual cortex.

The first stage in this chain that leads to vision occurs within the visual receptors. Located near the back of the retina, these specialized cells convert light energy into an electrical potential. The retina actually contains two receptor systems. One system, composed of cells known as **rods**, is responsible for vision in dim light; it signals information about brightness but not color. The other system, composed of cells known as **cones**, operates in increased light and is responsible for detailed vision and for color perception. When light rays strike rods or cones, the rays cause a change in the molecules of a light-sensitive chemical known as a **photopigment**. This change can generate an electrical signal from that cell.

Rods and cones differ in several ways. In terms of sheer numbers, rods far outstrip cones, by 120 million to 6 million. And rods can operate in a dim light that renders cones useless. Moreover, rods have primarily one photopigment, **rhodopsin**, which responds sensitively—but only to the brightness of light regardless of its wavelength. Cones, by contrast, come in three varieties, each type containing a photopigment that captures different wavelengths of light. These three types of cones and their photopigments play a central role in color vision. The rod-cone visual system makes the eye resemble a camera loaded with two different kinds of film: a highly sensitive black-and-white film (in the rods) and a less sensitive, high-resolution color film (in the cones).

Rods and cones are concentrated in different areas of the retina. Cones are highly concentrated around the center of the retina and are the only receptors in the very center of the **fovea**, the retinal area that lies almost directly opposite the pupil. Because cones are so sparse at the sides of the eyes, our vision of objects to either side is color-blind. You can experience this color blindness with a simple experiment. Dump a box of crayons onto the table. While looking ahead of you at the wall, pick up one of the crayons, hold it far enough to one side so that it is invisible, then slowly move your arm from the side to directly in front of you. You will find that you can see the crayon as a dark object in your hand long before you can determine its color (McBain and Johnson, 1962). Because rods are concentrated to the sides of the retina, objects seem clearer in dim light when they are seen from the corner of the eye than when they are seen straight ahead. You can prove this to yourself by going into a dark closet and looking at a very dim object out of the corner of your eye. Now look straight at the object: it may nearly disappear. Also, next time you are looking

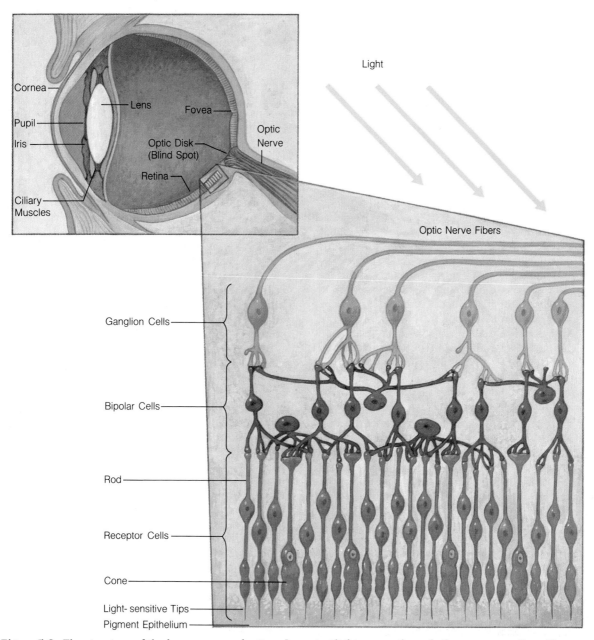

Figure 5.3. The structure of the human eye and retina. Incoming light passes through the cornea, pupil, and lens and hits the retina. As the inset shows, light filters through several layers of retinal cells before hitting the receptor cells (rods and cones), at the back of the eyeball and pointed away from the incoming light. The rods and cones register the presence of light and pass an electrical potential back to the adjacent bipolar cells. The bipolar cells relay the impulses to the ganglion cells, the axons of which form the fibers of the optic nerve, which transmits the impulses to the brain.

at a dim star, note how bright it appears when you look at it out of the corner of your eye.

After the rods and cones have registered the presence of light, they pass their electrical potential through several layers of neurons. These neurons pool and mix the signals from within the retinal area, then send them out through a large bundle of nerve fibers that forms the **optic nerve**. The optic nerve leaves the eye through an area of the retina known as the **optic disk**, as shown in Figure 5.3. Because the optic disk contains no receptor cells, it causes an apparent blind spot in the visual field of each eye. (Using Figure 5.4, you can experience your own blind spot.)

After leaving the two eyeballs, the optic nerves meet at a junction within the brain called the **optic chiasm**, where they are rerouted (see Figure 5.5). Objects in the right visual field are seen only in the left hemisphere, and vice versa. (This anatomical fact was exploited in studies of split-brain patients, discussed in Chapter 3.) After leaving the optic chiasm, the majority of the fibers lead to the **lateral geniculate nucleus (LGN)**, a grouping of cell bodies in the thalamus. (The rest of the fibers are detoured to midbrain structures concerned with the control of eye movements and other visual reflexes.) From the lateral geniculate nucleus, optic fibers travel to the visual cortex, at the back of each cerebral hemisphere, and from there

messages are relayed to still other parts of the brain.

At each of these stages of processing—retinal cells, lateral geniculate nucleus, visual cortex—individual neurons respond only when light falls within a restricted region of the retina. For example, a cell in the lateral geniculate nucleus may respond only if one or more cells in a retinal region about an eighth-inch in diameter is stimulated. This retinal region would be known as the retinal **receptive field** of that LGN cell. Think of an LGN cell and its receptive field as a long cone, with the LGN cell at the apex. Each of the thousands of cells in the lateral geniculate nucleus has such a receptive field, and the fields of adjacent LGN cells overlap considerably. Together, the thousands of overlapping receptive fields form a fine grid that registers light patterns as a mosaic of stimulation encompassing the entire field of vision.

By implanting microelectrodes into individual cells, scientists have been able to trace nerve impulses and discover the kinds of stimuli that trigger responses in neurons within the visual system. Several layers of cells pool signals from the rods and cones, then relay the information to the next layer of neurons, which transmits it along the optic nerve to the lateral geniculate nucleus. Cells have different types of receptive fields. Two common types of receptive fields are the ON-center and OFF-center bull's-eyes shown in Figure 5.6D (see Kuffler, 1953). When stimulated by light falling in the center of its receptive field, an ON-center retinal cell responds with a burst of electrical impulses. But when light falls on the outer rim of the receptive field, the cell either fires more slowly or stops firing altogether. When this light is turned off, the ON-center cell rebounds with a burst of impulses. The receptive field of an OFF-center cell works in the opposite manner. When light falls on the periphery, or surround, the cell sends out a burst of impulses, but when light falls in the center of the bull's-eye, the OFF-center cell's firing is inhibited. If the spot of light is so large that it falls across the entire cell, stimulating both

Figure 5.4. Although you are never normally aware of it, the blind spot is literally blind. To demonstrate this fact to yourself, hold this figure at arm's length, cover your left eye, and focus on the center of the X. Slowly move the figure toward you, staring continuously at the X. At some point, you will no longer be able to see the red spot. This is the point at which the red spot's image has fallen on the blind spot in your right eye. The red spot will reappear if you move the figure even closer. Now cover your right eye and try to use the same procedure to find your left eye's blind spot. What happens? Turn the book upside down and try again. Blind spots are not ordinarily noticed because they are off center, so that one eye fills in much of what the other is missing. In addition, the continual movement of the eyes shifts the area of the blind spot, enabling the brain to fill in the missing information.

Figure 5.5. Pathways for the transmission of visual information from the left and right eyes to the visual cortex. Light from the left visual field—the area on the left side of the fixation point at which you are looking directly—hits the right side of each eye's retina; light from the right visual field strikes the left sides of the retinas. Neural impulses from the right sides of the retinas travel to the left hemisphere of the brain, and vice versa.

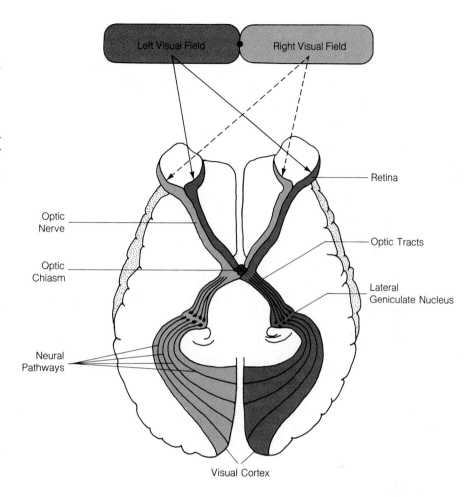

the rim and the center, the two effects tend to cancel each other out (Frisby, 1980).

We do not know why the visual system depends on these bull's-eye-like receptive fields. If we are to perceive the shapes of objects, we must be able to detect the presence of lines, edges, corners, and contours of objects. Yet each retinal receptive field is so tiny that it covers only a portion of the visual field. It seems probable that our vision depends on connecting arrays of these ON-center fields in a network (Lindsay and Norman, 1977). Suppose a single LGN cell collected the impulses from a set of ON-center receptive fields that were arranged, say, in a 45-degree line on the retina. If so, then this LGN cell would respond strongly whenever a 45-degree line fell on that spot on the retina, and the LGN cell would be a "specific line detector." If neural connections further pooled similar 45-degree line detectors from many areas of the reti-

na, the cell would respond whenever a line of that width and orientation appeared in the visual field, no matter where it registered on the retina. It is true that simply detecting such lines is not a great accomplishment for a neural network. But if we can imagine this arrangement, then perhaps it is biologically reasonable to imagine neural networks of ON-center and OFF-center fields that would compute significant features of lines, orientation, edges, corners, and so on. These computations would help the brain begin to identify the shape of the visual pattern it was viewing.

Each successive stage of the visual system—from the retina via relays to the LGN, and then to the visual cortex—probably permits more complex analyses of a visual stimulus. There are many kinds of cells in the visual cortex, each with a particular kind of receptive field. The ON-center and OFF-center fields are only two of the possible

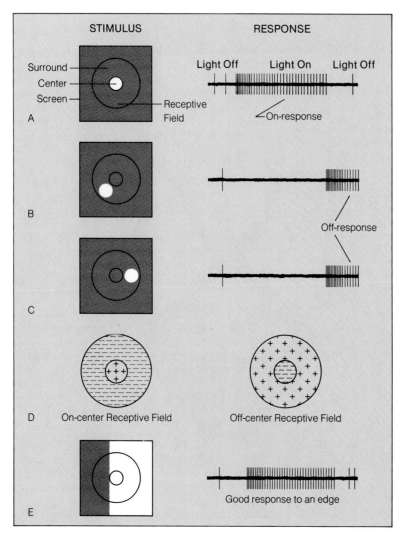

Figure 5.6. Single cell recordings of responses to light stimuli made by a cat's retinal ganglion cell. (A) The basic recording technique involves shining a spot of light (the stimulus) on a screen in a position that corresponds to the center of the cell's receptive field, which in this case causes the cell to emit a vigorous burst of impulses (represented by the cluster of vertical lines under "Light On"). (B and C) Shining the spot of light anywhere on the receptive field's periphery, or surround, inhibits the cell's activity. Only when the light is switched *off* does the cell respond with a burst of impulses. Because of this pattern of firing, this type of cell is described as an ON-center/OFF-surround cell. (D) The center and surround areas of a receptive field are concentric and thus can be plotted by exploring the receptive field with a spot of light. The cell at left has an ON-center receptive field, firing in response to a light shone on its center, as indicated by the plus signs; the cell at right has an OFF-center receptive field. (E) Retinal ganglion cells vary in their responses to edges as well as to light. Here a dark edge is shown falling on the receptive field in such a way that the entire center is receiving a high light intensity while the inhibitory surround is only partly covered. The center responds strongly when it detects the edge because relatively little inhibition is generated from the surround. (Adapted from Frisby, 1980.)

arrangements. In 1981, the neurophysiologists David Hubel and Torsten Wiesel won a Nobel Prize for their pioneering studies of receptive fields in visual areas of the brain. They discovered that many neurons in the visual cortex have receptive fields with elongated ON and OFF regions (Hubel and Wiesel, 1979). Each of these cells responds most strongly to a line at the angle matching the alignment of its ON-center cells (see the examples in Figure 5.7).

Hubel and Wiesel also found cells in the visual cortex that responded only when lines of a particular orientation *moved* in a particular direction. For instance, such a cell might fire rapidly when a vertical line moved to the right across its receptive field and fire only moderately when the same vertical line moved to the left. Finally, some cells in the visual cortex responded in even more specialized patterns. Some cells are sensitive not only to a line's orientation and direction of movement, but also to its width or length. Others respond best to a particular shape, such as a right angle. We might guess that these highly specialized neurons enable us to extract important visual features in our world. In Chapter 6, we will see how they probably contribute to perception.

Color Vision

Our ability to see colors depends on psychological as well as physiological processes. We can experience color only if our retinal cones catch light of a certain wavelength or combination of wavelengths. For example, we usually see light with a wavelength of 470 nm as blue, that of 510 nm as green, and that of 660 nm as red. But this is a simplification, because the experience of a particular color also depends on the intensity of the light, the way it is reflected from a surface, and the color of surrounding objects. The color of any object is not in the object itself, nor is it in the light rays reflected from it. Instead, our color experience results when lights of varying wavelengths stimulate cones with different photoreceptors, beginning a chain of visual processing that eventually excites particular cells in the visual cortex.

How does the visual system translate lights of different wavelengths into the experience of color? People can distinguish about 200 different colors (Coren, Porac, and Ward, 1984). Hypothetically, we could accomplish this sort of discrimination if we had about 200 different kinds of cones scattered about the retina, each cone responsive only to a single color. But such an arrangement would not be very efficient. The density of cones for any specific color would be so low (only 1 in every 200)

that our ability to resolve closely packed color dots would be extremely poor. In actuality, we have very good color acuity, so our color experiences must be created some other way.

During the nineteenth century, two complementary theories, the trichromatic theory and the opponent-process theory, were advanced to explain color vision. Both theories suppose that the human eye has only a few kinds of color cones, and that these cones are like musical instruments that are played on by lights of different wavelengths. Our color experience is determined by the blend or mixture of stimulation of these three basic cone types plus the dark-light information from the rods, much as the ensemble sound of a musical trio depends on the blend of sound from the separate instruments. The two theories differ about which "cone instruments" play in the color ensemble, and how these instruments blend to create our color experience.

Trichromatic Theory and Color Mixtures

The **trichromatic theory** (from the Greek *tri*, meaning "three," and *chroma*, meaning "color")

Figure 5.7. Receptive fields of nerve cells in the visual cortex vary in their responses to stimuli presented at different orientations. As these examples show, some cortical cells respond most vigorously to vertical lines, others to oblique lines, and so on. (Plus signs indicate a receptive-field region that emits an ON response to the specific stimulus; minus signs indicate an OFF response.) (After Hubel and Wiesel, 1962.)

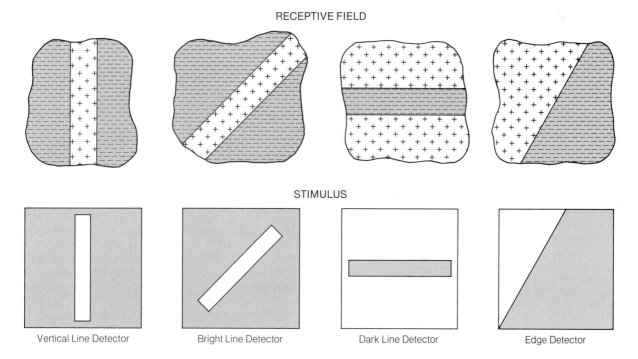

RECEPTIVE FIELD

STIMULUS

Vertical Line Detector   Bright Line Detector   Dark Line Detector   Edge Detector

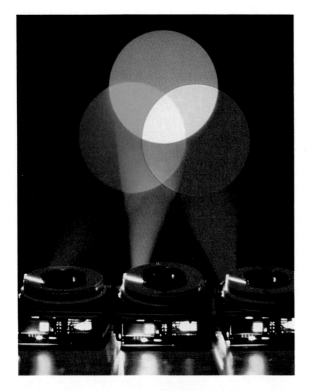

(Top) Additive color mixing by superimposing blue, green, and red lights. Note that when all three are present in equal amounts, white results.
(Bottom) Subtractive color mixing by superimposing blue, yellow, and red filters in a beam of white light. When all three are placed over each other, black results.

was proposed in the early nineteenth century by Thomas Young and later elaborated by Hermann von Helmholtz in 1852. The theory grew out of observations of **additive color mixing**—the mixing of colored lights. Helmholtz found that when he mixed together a blue light and a green light, people did not see tiny spots of blue and of green; instead, they saw a blended color, bluish-green. By combining in varying proportions just three lights —blue, green, and red—Helmholtz discovered he could match virtually any other shade on the spectrum. These three basic colors, blue, green, and red, came to be called **primary colors**.

In the accompanying photographs, you can see some of the results of mixing primary-colored lights. Combining a pure red light with a pure green light produces the color yellow. This reflective color (color deriving from light) is clearly different from what happens when colored paints are mixed. When paints are mixed, we are actually subtracting wavelengths because each pigment absorbs particular wavelengths of the spectrum. The paint color we see is created by the wavelengths that are not absorbed but reflected to strike the retina. But when we mix lights, those wavelengths are reflected. We are *adding* wavelengths, and this additive color mixing has been basic to the trichromatic theory of color vision.

It was a short leap from the results of the experiments with additive color mixing to the **Young-Helmholtz hypothesis** that color vision relies on only three basic kinds of color cones: cones that are sensitive primarily to red, green, and blue. In this view, light of any given wavelength stimulates each of these three types of cones to varying degrees, so that they send out signals of varying amplitudes. And just as the mixing of colored light produces a blended color, the mixture of these signals is integrated by the brain into a unified perception of a single color.

The Young-Helmholtz hypothesis was based on experimental observations and good guesswork. But recent neurophysiological evidence clearly supports the trichromatic theory. The most direct evidence is the discovery of three different types of retinal cones, distinguished according to how strongly they are activated by lights of differing wavelengths (Brown and Wald, 1964; MacNichol, 1964). In Figure 5.8 you can see results from an experiment with the human eye, which demonstrates the way the three kinds of cones absorb light. In this experiment researchers isolated single cones, then measured how much light of spe-

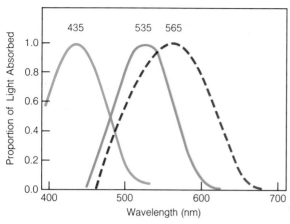

Figure 5.8. Light-absorption curves of the three types of cones. One group of cones is maximally sensitive to short-wavelength (around 435 nanometers), another to medium-wavelength (535 nm), and a third to long-wavelength (565 nm) light. (A nanometer is a billionth of a meter.) The trichromatic theory holds that the perceived color of a light depends on the *relative* intensity of activity caused by that light in the three types of cones.

cific wavelengths each cone took in, or "absorbed" (Bowmaker and Dartnell, 1980). This told the researchers the electrical signal the cone would produce when it absorbed light. After the researchers plotted the relative amount of light of a given wavelength absorbed by the cone, they found that all cones followed one of the three "absorption curves" in Figure 5.8. One group of cones produces the largest response at 423 nm; a second group at 535 nm; and the third group at 565 nm.

Because these three peaks occur at wavelengths that normally appear blue, green, and red, the three types of cones have been called the blue, green, and red cones. But you should note in Figure 5.8 that each kind of cone responds a little to almost any wavelength; it is the *profile* of responses from the three types that provides our color experience. For example, a light of 500 nm evokes a 10 percent response from the blue cones, a 50 percent response from the red cones, and a 75 percent response from the green cones. We would probably see this light as bluish-green. According to the trichromatic theory, activating the three types of cones in different relative proportions is an essential first step in our perception of color. Using our earlier analogy, a color experience would correspond to a certain musical chord played on three musical instruments.

Additional support for the trichromatic theory comes from the fact that people who lack one or more of the cones' three photopigments have predictable types of color blindness. People who lack the pigment that is sensitive to the longest wavelengths cannot perceive the color that those with normal color vision call red. For them, red is indistinguishable from green. The same is true of people who lack the photopigment that responds best to medium wavelengths (those in the green range). Both these groups of people are called **dichromats** (*di* = two, *chroma* = colors), because they seem to have only two properly functioning types of cones. (Tests for dichromatic color blindness are shown in Figure 5.9.) An even rarer and more severe deficiency is complete color blindness. People who are totally color-blind are called **monochromats**. They see the world in shades of gray, as if they were watching a movie in black and white. Presumably, their retinas contain only one kind of cone.

Opponent-Process Theory

The trichromatic theory explains how we see certain mixed colors such as reddish-yellow, bluish-green, and yellowish-green. But it leaves a number of important phenomena unexplained. For example, it does not tell us why we can never see a single spot as a combination of red and green or of blue and yellow. Attempting to solve this puzzle, a nineteenth-century German physiologist, Ewald Hering (1878), suggested that perhaps the brain has a way of "linking together" certain colors, the pairs that are known as **complementary colors**. Complementary colors are those lying opposite each other on the color wheel in Figure 5.10. Green, for example, is the complement of reddish-purple, whereas yellow is the complement of violet-blue.

What happens when a beam of red light is mixed with a beam of green light? An odd thing. Although both our "red" cones and our "green" cones presumably are stimulated, we do not experience reddish-green (as we would experience bluish-green when stimulated by a combination of blue and green lights). Instead, our brains carry out a process known as **color cancellation**: we see a colorless gray or white. Given the "addition" rule of the trichromatic theory and the absorption curves in Figure 5.8, this result is quite unexpected.

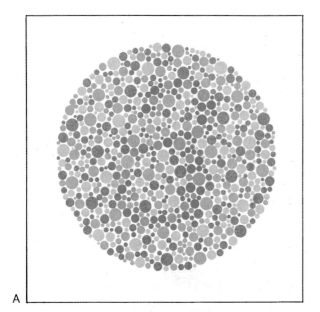 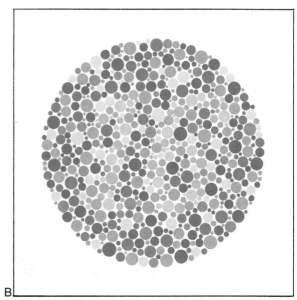

A   B

Figure 5.9. These two figures are used to test for dichromatic (red-green) color blindness. In A, normal subjects will see the number 8 and those with red-green deficiencies the number 3. In B, normal subjects can read the number 16, but most people with red-green deficiencies cannot.

How can we explain the surprising results we get from complementary colors? Experimental evidence has shown that color vision involves much more than the retinal cones. It also involves neurons behind the cones and neurons in the lateral geniculate nucleus. And some of these neurons operate according to a sort of "push-pull" mechanism that differs from the trichromatic mechanism. This "push-pull" mechanism follows an **opponent process**: the neurons are particularly excited by a certain color—but particularly inhibited by the color's complement (DeValois, 1965). (Notice that the trichromatic theory focuses on cones; it says nothing about the possibility of cones cancelling out one another.)

There is now strong evidence that our visual pathways beyond the retina contain such cells: blue-yellow opponent cells and red-green opponent cells (DeValois, 1965). Opponent-process cells have been found throughout the visual pathways, including the lateral geniculate nucleus and the visual cortex (Boynton, 1979; DeMonasterio, 1978; DeValois and DeValois, 1975). An opponent neuron's firing rate depends on the difference between its responses to two types of stimulation. In the case of a red-green opponent cell, the firing rate increases when a red light falls on its receptive field, but decreases when the cell is stimulated by a green light. Other red-green cells have reversed polarity: the cell would increase its firing when stimulated by green, but decrease it when stimulated by red. (The brain can interpret either an increase or a decrease in output from an opponent cell.) The opponent cells are like pan balances for weighing quantities placed on each side of a fulcrum. Such a cell could never "see" red and green at the same time, because if equal red and green signals arrived the scale would balance at the zero point, and the simultaneous stimulation would cancel out. When this happens, no net signal is sent and the person sees "gray." This effect is known as color cancellation.

How could the three types of color cones and the opponent cells be wired together into a system that would create not only color cancellation, but also other aspects of color vision? The psychologists Leo Hurvich and Dorothea Jameson (1957) have worked out a hypothetical wiring diagram that shows how the nervous system might put together these two different mechanisms. Signals sent by the cones are analyzed for color by the opponent-process cells, and the result is passed on to the brain. If the red cones pass many signals to the red-green opponent cell, it will report a "red" sensation; similarly, if it receives many signals from green cones, it will report a "green" sensation. If a light of about 460 nm is sensed, it will stimulate the red side of the red-green opponent cell and the blue side of the yellow-blue opponent cell, with the result that a "purple" colored mixture will be seen. Figure 5.11 describes a number of these interactions between stimulation of the three types of cones and the final color experience.

The opponent-process theory also explains the phenomenon of colored **afterimages**—sensory impressions that persist after the removal of a stimulus. To experience an afterimage, stare intently for forty-five seconds at the lower right-hand star of the flag in Figure 5.12. Now transfer your gaze to a white area, such as a blank sheet of paper. You should see the flag in its correct colors, which are the complements of those shown in the figure. This negative afterimage is apparently caused by temporarily fatiguing the neural responses of your

Figure 5.10. The color wheel. Any two colors that are opposite each other are complementary; that is, combining them (in the proper proportions) produces gray or white. The numbers on the "spokes" of the wheel are wavelengths, expressed in nanometers (billionths of a meter). Spectral colors are shown in their natural order, but not at uniform intervals by wavelength because of space limitations. The nonspectral reds and purples are also shown.

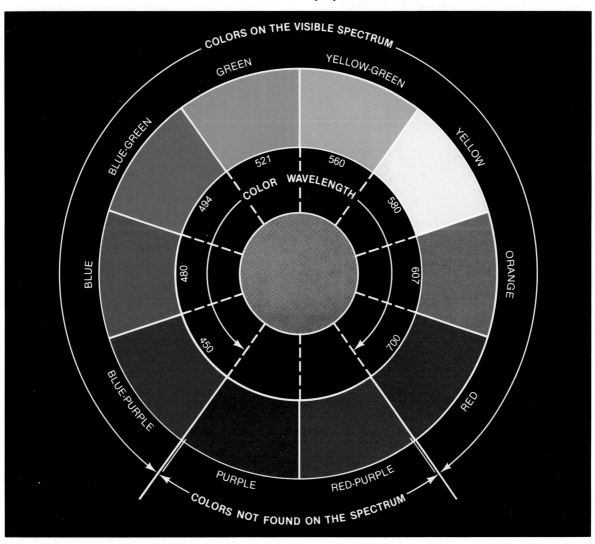

opponent cells to the colors green, yellow, and black. Gazing steadily at the green stripes activated opponent cells in your visual system that are excited by green light waves. After a while these cells adapted to the steady stimulation and began to respond less vigorously. Then you shifted your gaze to the white paper. White light is in fact a mixture of equal parts of all colored wavelengths, including red and green. Ordinarily, the light reflected from this paper would equally stimulate your red and green responses, causing a colorless sensation. But because your green cells were temporarily fatigued, your red cells could respond more vigorously, giving rise to the perception of red stripes.

HEARING

Just as visual receptors in the eyes respond to light, transducing it into neural signals, so auditory receptors in the ears respond to sound waves to produce neural signals. Sound waves are caused by pressure changes in the atmosphere,

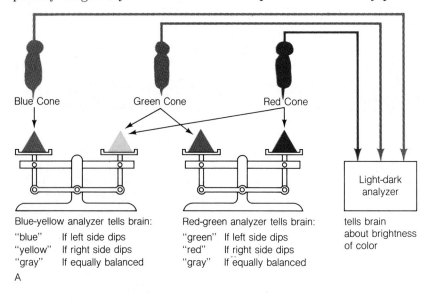

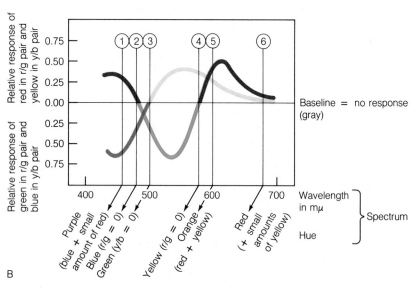

Figure 5.11. The interaction of the trichromatic and opponent-process aspects of color vision. Part A of the figure shows one way in which the three types of cones might give information to color opponent cells. The "blue" cone is actually sensitive to both blue and yellow. The blue-yellow and red-green analyzer cells each produce a moderate output called the "baseline" output when it is not stimulated, or if its two kinds of input are equal. If the blue-yellow analyzer's left side dips—if it produces an output much below baseline (due to a predominance of input from the blue cones)—while the red-green analyzer's right side dips—if it produces an output somewhat above baseline (due to receiving greater input from the red cone than from the green code)—the result will be a mixture of red and blue that the brain will perceive as purple.

This example can be visualized more easily in part B, where it is shown as line 1. This shows the output of the blue-yellow and the red-green color opponent analyzer cells, both of which are taken into account by the brain in perceiving the color of any given patch of light. The other numbered lines show how we see other colors, according to the opponent-process theory of color vision. For example, line 4 shows that when the red-green analyzer is at baseline (which means gray to the brain) and the blue-yellow analyzer responds at above baseline, we see yellow. (After Hochberg, 1978.)

Figure 5.12. The text explains how this drawing can be used to demonstrate the phenomenon of afterimage—a sensory impression that persists after removal of the stimulus that originally caused it. The afterimage will show the flag in its "proper" red, white, and blue colors, thus demonstrating that color opposites are somehow paired in the brain.

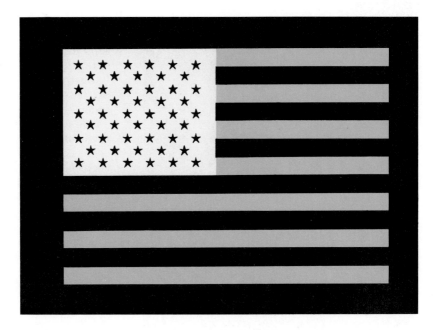

which generate vibrations among the air molecules. The vibrations send waves of compressed and expanded air molecules through the air, striking the eardrum. Then the eardrum is rapidly pushed and pulled by the compressions and expansions so that it vibrates in a pattern that corresponds to the sound.

Sound waves vary in their frequency and amplitude. The **frequency** of a sound refers to the number of waves passing a given point in a given time. It is the number of compression-expansion cycles that occur within one second, expressed in a unit known as a hertz (Hz). The **pitch** of a sound depends on its frequency: the higher the frequency, the higher the pitch. Young adults can hear sounds with frequencies as low as 20 Hz (that is, 20 cycles per second) and as high as 20,000 Hz. As people age, this audible range is reduced, especially at the high-frequency end. Among commonly heard frequencies, the human voice ranges from 120 to about 1,100 Hz, middle C on a piano is 256 Hz, and the highest note on a piano is 4,100 Hz. Most people do not hear the sound of a dog whistle because it produces frequencies greater than 20,000 Hz, but dogs can hear sounds this high.

The other physical attribute of a sound wave is its **amplitude**, or intensity, which can be thought of as the height of the wave, where pressure is greatest. Amplitude, or intensity, is usually expressed in a unit of measurement called the **decibel** (**dB**), which is calculated as a logarithm of the sound pressure level. Perceived loudness nearly doubles whenever the physical intensity of a sound increases by 10 dB (Stevens, 1957). Among common sounds a whisper is generally about 30 dB, normal conversation about 60 dB, and the roar of a subway train 90 dB. Sounds above 120 dB are likely to be painful to the human ear: a sonic boom is 128 dB.

The Structure of the Ear

The ear has three major divisions: (1) the outer ear (the external cuplike portion and the auditory canal); (2) the middle ear (separated from the outer ear by the eardrum and containing three small bones collectively called ossicles); and (3) the inner ear, which includes a spiral-shaped, fluid-filled chamber called the **cochlea** (see Figure 5.13). Three semicircular canals are also located in the inner ear, but they are not part of the auditory system. Rather, they provide cues to body orientation, position, and movement.

When a sound wave enters the ear, it passes down the auditory canal and strikes a membrane known as the **eardrum**, causing it to vibrate just like a drum. On the other side of the eardrum are the **ossicles**, a series of delicate little bones known as the **hammer**, the **anvil**, and the **stirrup** (so named for their shapes). These three bones of the middle ear are linked and suspended in such a way

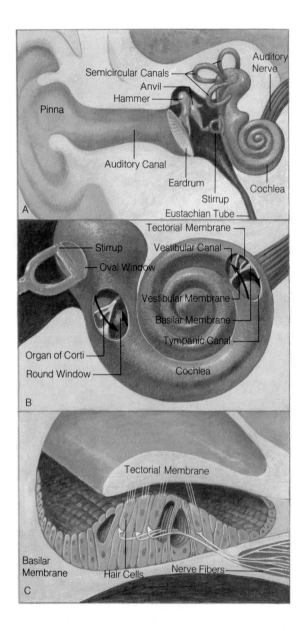

Figure 5.13. Anatomy of the ear. (A) Cross section showing the outer, middle, and inner ear. Sound waves pass through the auditory canal and are transformed into mechanical vibrations by the eardrum. The three small bones amplify this motion and transmit it to the oval window of the cochlea, which is depicted in (B). The motion of the oval window sends pressure waves through the fluid in the cochlea in the directions shown by the arrows. (C) Closeup cross section of the organ of Corti, within the cochlea. Waves in the cochlear fluid cause the basilar membrane to vibrate, which in turn disturbs the hair cells, the receptor cells of hearing.

that when the eardrum moves the hammer, it in turn moves the anvil, which moves the stirrup. This lever action converts changes in sound pressure at the eardrum into mechanical movements. It also amplifies the sound wave as the force exerted at the eardrum is concentrated onto the much smaller area at the tip of the stirrup. This enables the stirrup to apply increased pressure to the **oval window**, a flexible membrane on the side of the cochlea. A second membranous spot on the cochlea, called the **round window**, can be deflected outward (by cochlear fluid) as the oval window is deflected inward. As the oval window vibrates, it pushes cochlear fluid over rows of receptors, called **hair cells**, bending the hairs in a shearing motion. The hair cells are embedded in the **basilar membrane**, a membrane that runs through the cochlea.

Individual neurons are attached to different portions of the basilar membrane, each responding to different sound frequencies. These neurons pass auditory information through a series of relay stations to the auditory cortex, located in the temporal lobe of the brain. Along the auditory pathways are neurons that respond selectively to a particular frequency or pure tone. Within the auditory cortex itself, a significant proportion of the neurons respond neither to frequency nor to intensity, but to such complex sound features as clicks or whistles. Other neurons will not respond to steady tones; instead they fire when frequencies change. Some of these neurons respond only to increased frequencies (a rise in pitch), and others respond only to decreased frequencies (a falling pitch) (Evans, 1974).

Neural Coding by the Ear

We know that a tone's loudness is registered through the total number of nerve fibers that fire as well as through the activation of certain cells by the vigorous shearing of hair cells. Yet we do not fully understand how the brain discriminates pitch. How does it distinguish a high tone from a low one, or tell the difference between F sharp and C? Two distinct mechanisms appear to be involved, one described by the place theory, the other by the frequency theory.

Place Theory

According to the **place theory** of pitch, the particular location (place) on the basilar membrane

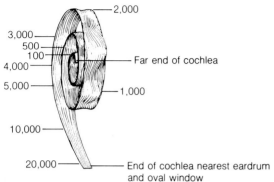

Figure 5.14. The place theory. This diagram shows the basilar membrane as removed from the cochlea. It depicts sound waves traveling down the basilar membrane and indicates the points at which the waves are largest for a number of different frequencies. Because greater displacement produces more stimulation of receptor cells at that site, the brain could use the location of the most rapidly firing receptors as a code for the frequency of the sound.

where a sound wave produces the greatest displacement—hence the most intense stimulation of its cells—signals the frequency of that sound to the brain. A version of this theory was first advanced by von Helmholz and later supported by Georg von Bekesy (1956). Von Bekesy, who in 1961 won a Nobel Prize for his research, discovered that waves of a given frequency do not make the entire basilar membrane vibrate uniformly. Instead, he found, high-frequency waves vibrate the region near the oval window most intensely, and intermediate frequencies cause the greatest vibration farther along the basilar membrane. Low frequencies cause the whole membrane to vibrate at a roughly equal rate. (See Figure 5.14.)

Place theory has been supported by two kinds of data. First, elderly patients who no longer can hear certain high-frequency tones have been found to have damaged groups of receptors along specific portions of the basilar membrane predicted by place theory (Crowe, Guild, and Polvogt, 1934). Second, nerve fibers coming from different regions of the basilar membrane are connected to neural relay stations that are "tuned" to respond most vigorously to pure tones in a narrow band of frequencies (Whitfield, 1968; Liberman, 1982). It is as though signals are sent from a given place on the basilar membrane only when that place is displaced maximally by a sound wave of a special frequency. Third, mild electrical stimulation of small groups of neurons causes a person to experience different pitches, depending on the place along the basilar membrane that is stimulated (Simmons et al., 1965).

Frequency Theory

The second major theory of pitch discrimination, known as **frequency theory**, was advanced by physicist William Rutherford, who saw the auditory system as rather like a telephone. According to frequency theory, the basilar membrane vibrates like a banjo string or like the diaphragm in a telephone, and the auditory nerve functions like a telephone wire relaying these impulses to the cortex. The higher the tone, the faster the membrane vibrates; the more the membrane vibrates, the greater the number of nerve impulses sent up the auditory nerve in a specified time. According to this theory, pitch is determined by the frequency per second of neural impulses sent to the brain.

The real problem with the frequency theory comes from experimental evidence. Recordings from the auditory nerve indicate that neural impulses do proportionally follow sound frequency, but only up to tones of about 4,000 Hz. When stimulated by higher frequencies, the neuron no longer increases its impulse rate as the pitch of the tone becomes higher (Coren, Porac, and Ward, 1984).

Contemporary researchers subscribe to a combination of place theory and frequency theory. High-frequency sounds are best explained by the place theory, especially when we recall that damage to particular portions of the basilar membrane destroys hearing in the high-frequency range. Low-frequency sounds are best explained by the frequency theory, since place theory is unable to explain how we can tell the difference between similar low tones when the entire membrane is vibrating. As for sounds in the middle ranges, perhaps both mechanisms are involved.

Hearing Loss

The capacity to hear any frequency depends on the condition of the receptors (hair cells) in the basilar membrane. If a sound of excessive intensity strikes the ear, the vibrations of the fluids may tear out the hairs, leading to irreversible loss of hearing in that frequency range. Although muscles around the eardrum can dampen, or weaken, the movement of the stirrup in response to high-intensity sound, they cannot prevent damage from continual excessive noise. Consequently, an extensive amount of hearing loss has been caused by modern technology—from factories to jet planes to loud music. In many industries a major dispute between management and labor unions concerns the decibel level that workers can withstand for prolonged periods without suffering permanent hearing loss.

With age many people undergo some degree of hearing loss due to the degeneration of hair cells, the loss of auditory neurons, or stiffening of the moving bones in the inner ear (Corso, 1977). If a person suffers from general hearing loss, a hearing aid that amplifies the sound waves striking the eardrum may be helpful. But there is a problem: most hearing aids amplify all sounds equally, whereas loss occurs most often only in the higher frequencies.

A person with cochlear damage who cannot be helped by hearing aids may be a candidate for a cochlear implant, a new device that transmits electrical impulses directly to nerve fibers, bypassing damaged or destroyed hair cells (Schmeck, 1984). In the most sophisticated implant, a cable containing twenty-two electrodes, each transmitting a different frequency band, is threaded into the cochlea and connected to a small receiver implanted behind the ear. Sounds picked up by the receiver are processed by a pocket-sized computer, which matches the signals to appropriate nerve fibers before relaying them to the implant. Cochlear implants are still considered experimental; although they increase the spectrum of sounds that are heard, they do not as yet restore normal hearing, especially for speech.

THE SKIN SENSES

Our skin is a shield that contains us and protects us from the world. A six-foot man of average weight and body build has about twenty-one square feet of skin surface. This pliable shield keeps out bacteria, holds in body fluids, wards off harmful sun rays, and regulates the temperature of the body core. At various depths within the skin are a number of receptors that connect with neurons to inform the brain about environmental stimulation. These receptors transmit information about four different kinds of skin sensations: touch, warmth, cold, and pain. But not all such receptors are in the skin; touch and pain kinds of receptors are also found in the muscles and the internal organs.

The relationship between the type of receptor and the experience of various sensations is not clearly understood. Although specific nerve endings in the skin appear to transmit only one kind of sensation, microscopic examination has revealed no consistent relationship between the structures of these nerve endings and the type of sensation they transmit. The different skin senses do not appear to have their own specialized receptors. Stimulation of receptors around the roots of hairs appears to be followed by the sensation of touch on the skin, while other receptors seem to respond to pressure within muscles and internal organs. At one time it was believed that only the sensation of pain was transmitted by receptors in free nerve endings in the skin (in contrast to encapsulated nerve endings). But this belief was overturned by studies of the eye. Although almost all the receptors in the cornea are free nerve endings, the cornea is responsive to pressure and temperature as well as pain. Thus the role of nerve endings as sensation receptors is still not clear (Geldard, 1972).

Warmth and Cold

If your skin is touched by a metal rod that is at skin temperature, usually 32 degrees Centigrade, you will not feel any sensation of temperature —either warmth or cold. This temperature, at which there is no sensation, is called **physiological zero**. At temperatures greater than physiological zero, you will feel warmth, and at temperatures lower than that point you will feel cold.

Nor can you feel warmth and cold at every point on your skin. If one square centimeter of skin (an area about the size of your little fingernail) is stimulated with pin points, you will feel a cold sensation at about six spots and a warm sensation at only one or two spots. The separate identity of warm and cold spots is generally accepted: one type of evidence is that stimulating a cold spot with a warm stimulus sometimes yields a cold sensation—a phenomenon known as **paradoxical cold**.

The sensation of hotness appears to be produced by the simultaneous activation of both

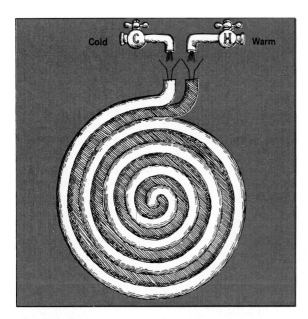

Figure 5.15. With ice water flowing through one of the tubes of this coil, and warm water at about 105° F. flowing through the other tube, the person placing a hand on the coil will feel a burning hot sensation.

warmth and cold receptors in a particular area of the skin, so that information from the two kinds of receptors is mixed. This synthesis of sensation is an example of economical design in the sensory systems. The synthesis can produce "paradoxical hotness," a phenomenon that can be demonstrated using an apparatus like the one depicted in Figure 5.15. Cold water flows through one of the tubes and warm water through the other. If a person touches either of these tubes he or she will perceive the appropriate sensation—either warmth or cold. However, if the person lays an entire hand across the coils so that warm and cold stimulate side-by-side areas of skin, he or she will feel a stinging hot sensation, like that caused by touching a hot oven rack barehanded. This apparatus "fools" the sensory system into sending a message of blistering heat, although the normally appropriate stimulus is absent.

Touch

Pressure-sensitive receptors in the skin are more responsive to changes in pressure than to steady states. Once the skin has been displaced to accommodate a source of pressure, adaptation occurs

and the sensation of pressure usually disappears —rapidly, if the force exerted is small. If this were not true, we would be constantly aware of the gentle pressure of clothes, eyeglasses, rings, and so on.

Sensitivity to touch varies enormously over different portions of the body. Our fingers and lips, for example, are exquisitely sensitive, but portions of the back are relatively insensitive. This variation is reflected in the disproportionately large area of the sensory cortex devoted to the fingers and mouth, as we saw in Chapter 3 (see Figure 3.8).

The sensitivity of the fingers is exploited by blind people who learn to read Braille, a reading code in which each letter of the alphabet corresponds to a specific combination of tiny raised dots (see Figure 5.16). By moving the fingers over the dots, the skilled Braille reader can read at the rate of about fifty words per minute. Relatively few books, magazines, and newspapers are available in Braille, but blind readers may use a machine known as the Optacon, which was invented to allow direct scanning of printed material (Bliss, Katcher, Rogers, and Shepard, 1970). The Optacon converts the visual pattern of the printed letter into a pattern of vibrating points felt through a pad beneath the reader's finger. With this device, a blind reader can reach speeds of twenty to sixty words per minute, depending on practice. Skilled readers apparently attain a high speed by learning to fuse the sequence of vibrating

Figure 5.16. The Braille alphabet. Each combination of dots corresponds to one letter of the alphabet. Based on the Braille cell at the upper left, the first ten letters are formed by distinct arrangements of the top four dots; the next ten letters are made by adding a dot to the lower left; the remaining letters, U to Z, are made by adding a dot to the lower right corner. W is an exception. When printed, the dots are raised slightly above the surface of the page so that blind readers can detect the patterns with their fingertips.

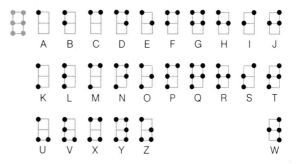

patterns into a unified, distinctive feeling for many common words.

The sense of touch also holds some promise for profoundly deaf people, who may be taught to "hear" through their skin. The psychologists Carl Sherman and Barbara Franklin have been experimenting with a "tickle belt" (Thompson, 1984). They have mounted small rectangular transducers responding to various sound frequencies on a belt that is worn next to the skin. The transducers change sound into brief bursts of electricity, which the wearer senses as vibration. High frequencies are felt at one end of the belt, and low frequencies at the other; a word is felt as a pattern of movement across the belt. Although no more than a few hundred words have been mastered by adults who wear the belt, it is hoped that deaf children, if they wear it from earliest childhood, may be able to develop a larger vocabulary of electric words.

Pain

Pain occurs often on our skin surfaces, but is not limited to the skin. Scientists know little about how pain arises from the interior of the body,

except that such pain seems to be deep, difficult to pinpoint, and often more unpleasant than the bright, localized pain from the skin. Many kinds of stimuli—scratching, a puncture, pressure, heat, cold, twisting—can produce pain. The common property of these stimuli is that they represent a threat—of real or potential injury to body tissue.

Pain sensations reflect subjective judgments. Consequently, they are affected not only by the intensity of the stimulus but also by private factors such as our fears, attention to distracting thoughts, and so on. Partly for this reason, **pain thresholds**, or the stimulation levels at which pain is first perceived, vary considerably from person to person and from time to time. The experience of pain is greatly influenced by our emotional involvement in other activities: in the excitement of combat—whether on the battlefield or the soccer field—perception of pain may temporarily vanish. People who are anxious have lower pain thresholds than those who are not; women tend to have lower pain thresholds than men; and clerical workers tend to have lower thresholds than laborers and miners (Mersky and Spear, 1967). It was once thought that most chronic pain had no organic basis and was probably due to stress or conflict, but this idea has been largely disproven (Liebeskind and Paul, 1977).

Pain can be both physical and emotional. When Mary Decker fell during her race in the 1984 Olympics, the injury she suffered was more than a physical one.

Adaptation to Pain

In the laboratory, people report that skin pain adapts or diminishes with prolonged stimulation as long as the stimulation is not intense. Various studies have shown that people adapt to pain caused by needle punctures, heat, and cold. However, if water is extremely hot (at least 48 degrees Centigrade), there is no adaptation and the pain caused by heat does not diminish (Hardy, Stolwijk, and Hoffman, 1968). Deep pain from nerve irritation (such as a pinched sciatic nerve, which sends pain coursing down the leg from the lower spinal cord) also seems to show little adaptation.

Since pain tells us that something is amiss, it is fortunate that we do not adapt to it immediately. The value of pain as a danger signal is evident when we consider the situation of people who are born without the ability to feel pain. Such people may experience severe burns, broken bones, or even a ruptured appendix without feeling the pain signals that would alert them either to protect themselves against further injury or to seek medical attention.

The Mechanisms of Pain Sensation

For years it was assumed that specialized nerve fibers carried pain signals to specific regions of the brain, as is the case with the other senses. But during the late 1950s studies produced clear evidence that the sensation of pain may occur with or without stimulation of particular specialized nerves. Researchers also found that pain can be greatly relieved by relaxation, deep breathing, or distraction. Furthermore, when people expect that a pill will be a pain reliever, their pain is reduced even though the pill is a **placebo**—an inert substance which has no effect on the body, but which they believe will be effective. This lack of specificity has led researchers to suspect that information about pain is carried by a special *pattern* of neural discharges, and that impulses sent from the cortex can modulate the incoming pain messages from the body.

Psychologists have experimented with a range of methods for relieving pain, using such techniques as hypnosis, mental distraction, relaxation-breathing, and fantasies of pleasant images. A variety of procedures have been somewhat effective in easing both acute and chronic pain. One such technique, developed by the French obstetrician Fernard Lamaze (1972), uses cognitive techniques to reduce pain in childbirth. In the Lamaze method, women learn to carry out three simultaneous activities during birth contractions. Each time a contraction begins, the woman breathes in a particular pattern, chants a nonsense sentence or poem in rhythm with her breathing, and gazes intently at some object. Although the pain of childbirth may not be eliminated, it apparently is substantially reduced for many women.

THE CHEMICAL SENSES: TASTE AND SMELL

The chemical senses of taste and smell are so closely associated that we often confuse their messages. This confusion develops because receptors for these two senses are located close together in the mouth, throat, and nasal cavity, causing smell and taste to interact. Without a sense of smell, the subtleties of food flavor cannot be appreciated. You can discover this for yourself with a simple experiment. Pinch your nostrils shut with one hand and then taste, one at a time, a bite of raw potato, pear, and apple. Can you tell the difference between them? If you first grate these foods to make their texture similar, then blindfold yourself and have a friend give you a taste of each, you may find it impossible to distinguish among them. Since our sense of smell is so important to our sense of taste, it is no wonder that food loses its appeal to people who have bad colds.

Smell

Many people consider **olfaction**, or the sense of smell, to be one of the "lower" senses. This view may stem from the fact that American culture has relatively few commonly used names for smells. Instead, we often give a smell the name of whatever object emits that odor, such as rose, lemon, or orange. But our sense of smell is extremely sensitive, possibly 10,000 times more sensitive than our sense of taste. Some animals have a sense of smell that is at least as sensitive. Police dogs have been used effectively by narcotics agents to sniff packages at post offices and airports in a search for contraband marijuana or hashish. Similarly, bloodhounds track criminals by following an odor trail.

Among human beings, smell serves a vital function: it warns us of possibly dangerous substances, such as gas leaks, smoke, or spoiled food. Odors are also involved with human pleasure. Our use of perfumes, deodorants, and fragrant flowers shows the premium we place on pleasant aromas, and our bulging spice cupboards testify to the importance of odor in our enjoyment of foods. Yet olfaction shows marked sensory adaptation over time. A constant foul odor soon fades from consciousness, as does a pleasant floral perfume dabbed on ourselves or the person next to us.

About 8 percent of the population can detect only a few odors or have entirely lost their sense of smell. Such conditions can be caused by head injuries, influenza, asthma, endocrine disorder, or cancers (Bloom, 1984). For these individuals the pleasures of eating have vanished. All wine tastes like vinegar; ice cream is simply a cold paste; garlic and pepper taste the same. About 25 percent of people who lose their sense of smell also lose interest in sex, apparently because odors formerly played some role in their sexual arousal.

The receptors for olfaction lie in the **olfactory epithelium**, located at the top of the nasal passages and connected to the base of the brain. Millions of hair cells project from the olfactory epithelium, and they are sensitive to molecules of odorous substances that are given off in vapors. The hair cells convert this kind of information into neural impulses. Unlike other sensory receptors, these hair cells are constantly being replaced, and there is a complete turnover of cells approximately every four to five weeks.

Most odors that we smell are organic compounds (compounds that contain carbon), but the exact physical basis of odor sensations remains a mystery. According to the "stereochemical" theory, the quality of an odor is related to the physical size and shape of the molecules that make up the odorous substance. Research by Amoore and Venstrum (1967) has shown that in many cases people do judge as similar odors from substances with similar molecular structures. However, scientists have also found many pairs of substances with similar chemical structures whose odors seem quite different to people. So we still cannot say why people can smell some substances and not others, or why certain groups of odors smell alike; nor can we predict the odor of a new chemical compound from its molecular structure.

Some animals communicate by means of odors. They release **pheromones**, chemicals that trigger some reaction in other animals of that species. Since pheromones travel on air currents, they can communicate over great distances; they move slowly and leave a lingering message because they take a long time to fade away. A major purpose of pheromone production in some species is to attract the opposite sex, and sex-attractant pheromones have been found in many species, including crabs, spiders, moths, fish, amphibians, reptiles, and monkeys (Wilson, 1975). Smell also seems to play an important role in the sexual behavior of monkeys. Vaginal secretions of the female monkey contain volatile fatty acids whose odor stimulates sexual behavior in male monkeys.

The same substances have been found in the vaginal secretions of healthy young women with regular menstrual cycles. Tests have found no effect from these odors on sexual attractiveness or activity in human beings (Morris and Udry, 1978), but their presence may explain the common observation that women who live together tend to synchronize their menstrual cycles.

Taste

As our discussion of smell indicated, when people describe how food "tastes," they include its odor, which circulates from the back of the mouth up to the olfactory receptors. Taste is, however, a more restricted sense than olfaction. An odor can be detected and identified from a distance, but the source of a taste must be in contact with the tongue. Most people can identify and discriminate hundreds of odors, but when odor and other sensory qualities, such as texture, are eliminated, they perceive only four basic taste categories: sweet, sour, salty, and bitter. However, our experience of taste is not as impoverished as that fact might seem to indicate. The gourmet chef and wine-taster will argue that, just as in color vision, a huge range of taste sensations can be composed by mixing and blending these primary tastes in various combinations (Bartoshuk, 1971).

Different areas of the tongue are especially sensitive to each of the four basic taste qualities, as shown in Figure 5.17. These taste qualities seem to be somewhat independent: they can be selectively suppressed and are differently affected by certain drugs. For example, chewing the leaves

Figure 5.17. If you map your own taste buds, you can discover which parts of your tongue are sensitive to different tastes. You will need four glasses, half-filled with water. Into the first, stir a teaspoon of salt; the second, a teaspoon of sugar; the third, two teaspoons of lemon juice or vinegar; the fourth, a half-teaspoon of epsom salts. Label each glass, but hide the labels from yourself and move the glasses around so that you can't tell which glass contains which solution. Using a fresh cotton swab for each glass, dab the solution on various spots around your tongue. You can use a mirror to keep track of your dabbing. Note on the map where you can taste each solution. Between each application of the swab, rinse your mouth out with fresh water. Your taste map should be marked "sour" in the area labeled 1, "bitter" in area 2; "sweet" in area 3; "salty" should be located fairly evenly across the entire surface. (After McBain and Johnson, 1962.)

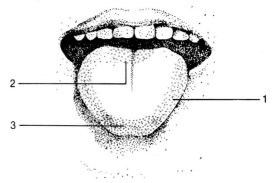

of a certain plant (*Gymnema sylvestre*), briefly makes the tongue insensitive to sweetness, so that granulated sugar feels like sand (Bartoshuk et al., 1969). The drug cocaine temporarily eliminates taste sensations in a certain order: first bitter disappears, then sweet, then salty, and finally sour (Moncrieff, 1966). If you want to experiment with the effects of different substances on taste, try chewing on a piece of an artichoke for about thirty seconds and then take a sip of tap water. You will find that the water tastes sweet. If you sip and swish your tongue in strong coffee for thirty seconds before sipping tap water, the water will also taste sweet, but if you sip very salty water for thirty seconds, the water will taste bitter or sour.

The specific sensation of taste results from stimulation of the **taste buds** in the mouth and tongue. The surface of the human tongue contains about 10,000 taste buds. They contain receptor cells for taste stimuli, and these cells are connected to nerve fibers that carry taste information to the brain. When the dentist injects novocaine into your gums to eliminate pain, the novacaine spills over to deaden the taste nerves from your tongue also, so you become unable to distinguish tastes.

Taste may be a more complicated process than would result if each nerve fiber simply reported on one of the four basic taste stimuli. Researchers have found that in some animals individual nerve fibers respond to more than one kind of taste (Pfaffman, 1955). Perhaps different tastes are produced by particular patterns of neural activity in the thousands of taste nerve fibers connecting tongue and brain (Erickson, 1984).

BALANCE, POSTURE, AND MOVEMENT

In order to move about the world, we must maintain our balance, posture, and orientation in space. Our ability to orient ourselves is produced by the coordination of the vestibular and kinesthetic senses. The information these senses give us lets us know whether we are aligned with the pull of gravity ("right-side up")—even when we are blindfolded. These senses also tell us how far to the side our head and body are tilted.

The Vestibular Sense

The **vestibular sense** contributes to balance. The vestibular sense organ lies in the inner ear, buried in the bone above and to the rear of the cochlea. Its major structures are the three fluid-filled **semicircular canals**, which lie at right angles to one another (look back at Figure 5.13). A movement of the head causes the fluid in the canals to move against and bend the endings of the receptor hair cells, similar to those in the cochlea. The hair cells connect with the vestibular nerve, which runs along beside the auditory nerve on its way to the brain.

Vestibular responses are stimulated by spinning about, walking more rapidly or running, falling, and tilting the body or head. The direction of the head's movement sets up a distinct pattern of hair-cell stimulation in the semicircular canals. The speed of movement is translated into appropriately coded neural messages. Such vestibular stimuli interact with eye-movement systems. For example, spinning rapidly in a circle can cause vestibular nystagmus, an uncontrollable, rapid back-and-forth motion of the eyes. Nystagmus can also develop when a person stops spinning; in this instance it occurs because the fluid in the semicircular canals continues sloshing around for several seconds after the body stops.

Unusual vestibular stimulation can cause motion sickness. The rhythmical bobbing up and down of the body experienced when a boat gets into rough seas or an airplane encounters turbulent air can cause motion sickness. In one study, 53 percent of people who took a simulated ride on seven-foot waves coming at the rate of twenty-two waves per minute became motion sick within twenty minutes (Wendt, 1951). The symptoms of motion sickness may include dizziness, "cold sweat," vertigo, and nausea, often accompanied by vomiting. If you have ever been troubled by motion sickness, you can help prevent it by keeping your head fixed even if your body is moving (which is why experienced mariners advise keeping your eyes fixed on the horizon); it also helps to actively move yourself through the gyrations of your vehicle rather than being moved passively by it (which is why drivers, who can anticipate and move with the car's motion, are less likely than passengers to become sick).

Motion sickness has plagued the space program, with four out of every ten astronauts becoming sick during space-shuttle missions. The motion sickness that follows weightlessness is, however, somewhat different from motion sickness suffered on the surface of the planet. According to the psychologist James Lackner, the vestibular system may be involved in space sickness, but

Motion sickness has been a continual problem for astronauts. The absence of gravity upsets the vestibular system, the kinesthetic system, and the normal activities of the digestive system.

so may the kinesthetic sense (Chaikin, 1984). In space, the brain receives conflicting messages from both these systems. Without the pull of gravity, hair cells in the semicircular canals can no longer tell up from down, and kinesthetic receptors can no longer report body position. However, astronauts who become sick do not report cold sweat or nausea, although they generally vomit. Research in space indicates that the digestive system, which stops its normal peristaltic activity when gravity is removed, may play a larger part in space sickness than either the vestibular or the kinesthetic senses (Chaikin, 1984).

The Kinesthetic Sense

Kinesthesis is the sense that gives us information about our body movement and position. It cooperates with the vestibular and visual senses to maintain balance and equilibrium. The receptor cells for the kinesthetic sense are in nerve endings within and near the muscles, the tendons, and the more than one hundred body joints. Nerve endings in the joints are especially important in sensing bodily movements; which receptors respond depends on the direction and angle of movement. Together, the various kinesthetic receptors give us the feedback we need to regulate our posture and active body movements. Our kinesthetic and vestibular senses help us move about in an efficient and coordinated manner, but we also rely on our eyes to aid our movements. The collaboration of visual, kinesthetic, and vestibular senses indicates once again that the senses generally act as a team.

SUMMARY

1. Our senses are our only source of information about the environment, yet each sensory system responds to only a limited range of **stimuli**, or environmental energy. Stimuli can be measured physically (as with a light meter or thermometer) or psychologically (in terms of subjective sensations). Psychological reports of a stimulus describe its **quality** (or kind of sensation produced) and **intensity** (or the amount of sensation produced).

2. The minimum stimulus required for a person to experience a specific sensation is referred to as the **absolute threshold**. The smallest physical change in stimulus that produces a change in sensation is known as the **difference threshold**, or **just noticeable difference (jnd)**. Human responses to the same sensory stimulus vary for several reasons. The stimulus itself may vary, as may the state of a person's sensory apparatus, variations in neuronal responsiveness, motivational level, and readiness to detect the signal. Expectations about the signal, as well as the consequences of right and wrong guesses, may increase the number of **false alarms**, occasions when there is no signal but the person reports one. **Signal detection theory** provides

a way to correct for false alarms when researchers are estimating a person's sensitivity.

3. The tendency for people to detect small changes in a weak stimulus but only larger changes in a strong stimulus is described by **Weber's law**, which states that the change in stimulus intensity required to produce a jnd is a constant proportion of the intensity of the stimulus. Direct judgments of the magnitude of a stimulus increase as a power function of the physical intensity of a stimulus, with different exponents for the different senses.

4. Following prolonged stimulation, an adjustment in sensory capacity, known as **adaptation**, occurs. Adaptation allows the senses to work discriminatively over a larger range and keeps us alert to changes in the environment.

5. All our sense organs operate on similar principles. In each sense organ are receptors sensitive to specific types of stimuli, and each type of receptor converts environmental stimuli into neural impulses. According to Müller's **doctrine of specific nerve energies**, the subjective quality of sensation depends on the specific nerve being stimulated.

6. The basic stimuli involved in vision are light waves, which are scaled in units called **wavelengths**. The major structures of the eye are the **cornea**, the **pupil**, the **iris**, the **lens**, and the **retina**. Light enters the eye through the pupil and strikes the lens, whose muscles adjust its curvature in order to focus the light and produce a clear image on the retina. In the retina, light is converted into neural impulses by **rods** and **cones**. These impulses travel through several layers of neurons and through the **optic nerve**, which leaves the eye through the **optic disk** on its way to the brain. After meeting at the **optic chiasm**, the optic nerves divide, with most fibers going on to the **lateral geniculate nucleus**, which sends signals to the auditory cortex. At each stage of processing, each neuron responds only to stimuli that fall within its **receptive field** on the retina.

7. Rods provide vision of light and dark, whereas cones (which are concentrated in the **fovea**)

are responsible as well for color vision and detailed vision. Color vision involves two mechanisms. One process, according to **trichromatic theory**, uses three types of cones (most sensitive respectively to the **primary colors** of red, green, and blue wavelengths), with the color percept depending on how many cones of each type are stimulated. According to the **opponent-process theory**, cells at every stage of visual processing beyond the receptors are stimulated by one color and inhibited by its **complementary color**. When receptors are stimulated by both colors simultaneously, through a process of **color cancellation**, we see gray or white. This theory explains the phenomenon of **afterimages**, which are experienced when receptors to particular colors are fatigued.

8. In the auditory system, auditory receptors in the ear convert sound waves into neural signals. Waves of air molecules strike the **eardrum**, causing it to vibrate. The **pitch** of a sound depends upon its **frequency**, or the number of wave cycles that occur within one second, measured in hertz (Hz). The **amplitude** (intensity) of a sound, measured in **decibels (dB)**, corresponds to the point of the wave that produces the most pressure. The eardrum separates the outer ear from the middle ear, which contains the **ossicles**, small bones known as the **hammer**, the **anvil**, and the **stirrup**. The stirrup is attached to the **oval window**, which separates the middle ear from the inner ear. The fluid-filled inner chamber of the ear, called the **cochlea**, contains the **basilar membrane**, in which the sound receptors, or **hair cells**, are embedded. An auditory stimulus causes cochlear fluids to move, bending the hair cells, which produce neural signals that travel to the brain through the auditory nerve. Two complementary theories explain the experience of pitch. **Place theory** states that the site of maximum displacement on the basilar membrane varies with the specific frequency of sounds, indicating pitch to the brain. **Frequency theory** states that tone frequency is converted into the frequencies of neural impulses to the brain, indicating pitch. Most sounds are not pure tones but a mixture of many frequencies: a fundamental frequency and several of its multiples (harmonics).

9. There are four types of skin sensations: pressure, warmth, cold, and pain. Receptors for these sensations, which lie at various depths within the skin, are connected to neurons that relay sensory information to the brain. **Physiological zero** (the temperature of the skin) is the temperature at which a stimulus evokes no sensation of temperature. Separate temperature-sensitive spots on the skin are indicated by **paradoxical cold**, in which the stimulation of a cold receptor with a hot stimulus results in a cold feeling. Receptors of pressure over the body vary in sensitivity. Pain alerts us to real or potential bodily injury, and **pain thresholds** vary among people and over situations.

10. The chemical senses of taste and smell are closely associated. **Olfaction** warns us about potentially toxic substances and provides pleasurable sensations. The hair cells projecting from the **olfactory epithelium** respond to the molecules in odorous vapors by sending neural impulses. Some species communicate by means of **pheromones**, chemicals that trigger some reaction in other animals of that species. There are only four basic categories of taste (sweet, sour, salty, and bitter), which can be detected only through direct tongue contact. The surface of the human tongue has about 10,000 **taste buds**, which contain receptor cells for taste stimuli.

11. The **vestibular sense** contributes to balance, and its major sense organ consists of the **semicircular canals** located above the cochlea. Movement of the fluid in the canal moves the hair cells connected with the vestibular nerve; these hair cells bend and send out signals when the head moves. **Kinesthesis**, the sense of body movement and position, works with the vestibular and visual senses to maintain balance and equilibrium. Receptor cells for this sense are found in nerve endings in and near joints, muscles, and tendons.

KEY TERMS

absolute threshold	false alarms	optic nerve
accommodation	fovea	ossicles
adaptation	frequency	oval window
additive color mixing	frequency theory	pain thresholds
afterimage	hair cells	paradoxical cold
amplitude	hammer	pheromones
anvil	intensity	photopigment
basilar membrane	iris	physiological zero
cochlea	just noticeable difference (jnd)	pitch
color cancellation	kinesthesis	place theory
complementary colors	lateral geniculate nucleus (LGN)	placebo
cones	lens	primary colors
cornea	monochromats	pupil
decibel (dB)	olfaction	quality
dichromats	olfactory epithelium	receptive field
difference threshold	opponent-process theory	retina
doctrine of specific nerve energies	optic chiasm	rhodopsin
eardrum	optic disk	rods

round window	stirrup	wavelength
semicircular canals	taste buds	Weber's law
signal detection theory	trichromatic theory	Young-Helmholtz hypothesis
stimulus	vestibular sense	

RECOMMENDED READINGS

BORING, E. G. *Sensation and perception in the history of experimental psychology.* New York: Appleton-Century-Crofts, 1942. Essential for a historical appreciation of sensation and psychophysics. This classic book is especially noteworthy for its treatment of the attributes of sensation and the historical antecedents of modern color theory.

COREN, S., C. PORAC, and L. M. WARD. *Sensation and perception* (2nd ed.). San Diego: Academic Press, 1984. An up-to-date general text. It adopts the modern information-processing approach to sensory systems and perception.

FRISBY, J. P. *Seeing: Illusion, brain, and mind.* New York: Oxford University Press, 1980. Discusses the psychophysical, physiological, and computer-simulation approaches to the study of vision. The book is richly illustrated with pictures demonstrating various phenomena of vision.

GREGORY, R. L. *Eye and brain: The psychology of seeing* (3rd ed.). New York: World University Library, 1978 (paper). Very readable, fascinating account of the visual system and the way it processes information, arriving at complex perceptions.

GOLDSTEIN, E. B. *Sensation and perception* (2nd ed.). Belmont, Calif.: Wadsworth, 1984. An up-to-date general text on sensation and perception. While emphasizing vision, the book includes coverage of the other senses and contains an interesting chapter on the perception of music.

LEVINE, M. W. and J. M. SHEFNER, *Fundamentals of sensation and perception.* New York: Random House, 1981. Recognizing the great advances made recently in physiological research this text presents a comprehensive treatment of the physiological aspects of the visual and auditory sensory systems.

SCHIFFMAN, H. R. *Sensation and perception* (2nd ed.). New York: Wiley, 1982. A well-written textbook describing each sensory system and its perceptual properties.

PERCEPTION

Suppose you are playing Frisbee with a friend. As she tosses the red Frisbee, how do you pick it out against the background of buildings, grass, and trees? Why does the Frisbee appear as a single object rather than the collection of color points that we might have expected, given what we learned in Chapter 5? How can you tell that the Frisbee is coming at you and not receding? As you look at the edge of the Frisbee skimming horizontally through the air, why do you still see it as round? And when you reach out to catch the Frisbee, how do you know where to put your hand?

Quickly and without conscious effort, you have performed the complex act of *perception*. You have taken sensory data—the image that strikes your retinas—and processed it in your brain to build a meaningful model of the Frisbee: its shape, its distance from you, and its direction of movement. This processing of sensory information from the environment is the work of perceptual systems

that have evolved over millions of years. Our perceptual systems help us adapt to the world; they enable us to extract information from the objects that surround us, imposing order on the complex array of sensations reported by our sense organs.

In order to operate effectively in the world, our perceptual systems must perform a number of tasks. Consider what takes place in our visual system as it perceives a Frisbee. The visual system's first task is to notice that a coherent shape corresponding to some object is in the visual field. Second, the system must identify the features of that object and locate it in space relative to us, and if the object is moving, the system must then judge its movement and velocity. Third, our visual system must be able to maintain a constant perception of the object as it changes in trivial ways—as the lighting on it changes, and as it changes in shading, texture, perspective, and distance from us. And finally, our visual system must be able to

Seeing Without Seeing

On the television screen a group of attractive young people cavort in the California surf, accompanied by the sounds of a singing commercial. Throughout the commercial the words "Drink Ziggy Cola" flash on the screen, but each exposure is so brief that the eye does not detect it. Will sales increase in localities where the flashing command has been superimposed on the commercial, as compared with localities where the commercial has run without the command? If they do, advertisers may decide that they have made effective use of **subliminal perception**. In subliminal perception, sensory information is registered in viewers' visual systems and influences their behavior, but the viewers have no conscious experience of the stimulus. The information can be a sight, a sound, or an odor. It is called "subliminal" to mean below (*sub*) the absolute threshold (*limen*) for conscious awareness.

Psychologists have been trying to establish the validity of subliminal perception, and to determine how it can change our attitudes and behaviors. Dixon (1981) sympathetically reviews a large amount of recent research showing diverse behaviors that can be influenced by subliminal stimuli. Let us look at two recent demonstrations.

One recent experiment (Kunst-Wilson and Zajonc, 1980) looked at preferences established by subliminal stimulation. This experiment relied on an earlier finding by Robert Zajonc that people develop positive attitudes toward familiar things. For example, as a nonsense syllable, a word, a painting, or a piece of music becomes familiar through repeated exposure, people judge it as also becoming increasingly attractive. Kunst-Wilson and Zajonc used this finding in an attempt to establish preferences by subliminal perception. In the first part of their study, these researchers flashed geometrical figures on a screen; gradually, they reduced the length of exposure until it was so brief that the subjects could not say whether a picture or a blank slide had been flashed. In this way, they established an exposure time that was associated with a subliminal perception—the subjects were not aware of seeing the figure.

Then, with a new group of subjects, the researchers flashed a series of irregular black octagons on the screen at this subliminal exposure duration, showing one set of ten octagons to half the observers and a different set to the other half. Afterward, the observers were shown pairs of octagons (one from each set) and asked (1) which of the pair was more liked, pleasing, or attractive, and (2) which octagon they had seen before. The subjects did not remember having seen the octagons; the researchers knew this because the subjects' identification of figures they had seen before was no better than chance (50 percent).

Apparently, the exposure had been too brief to establish

classify the object as similar to earlier objects (Frisbees we have seen in the past), regarding it as a member of a familiar class of objects and recognizing it as a Frisbee. This last process is known as "pattern recognition."

Perception is such an automatic process that beginning students often fail to appreciate what an enormous achievement it is and what complex problems confront the scientist who tries to understand it. For example, students may wonder, "Isn't seeing just a simple matter of the brain's somehow 'picking up' objects from the retinal image, the way we can visually 'pick up' objects recorded in a photograph?" But even that process is complex. If we recall the many steps in the process by which the retina picks up visual stimulation (see Chapter 5), and then ask how the brain might translate that information into objects it can recognize, the difficulties begin to appear.

And the brain does not merely register the array of retinal stimulation in a faithful manner; it also performs an act of construction. It starts with the sensory data and builds on it a meaningful hypothesis about the existence of an object or event. If there are gaps in the the available sensory information, the brain may fill them in as part of the construction process. In fact, many times when we are processing information we fail realize

a conscious memory for the figures. Yet most of the subjects showed some effect of subliminal perception: 60 percent of the time, they preferred as more attractive the octagons they had seen before. Although this is a relatively weak preference (50 percent is chance), it does indicate that some degree of subliminal perception exists, and that it can create a preference for objects that have been made familiar at a level below conscious awareness.

As a second illustration of research on subliminal perception, investigators (Marcel, 1983; Fowler et al., 1981) have found evidence that people can be influenced by flashed words without being aware that they have seen them. The words were flashed so briefly that the subjects were not able to say whether a word had been shown. Yet when the subjects were asked about the meaning of the flashed words, their replies indicated that although they could not say what words they had "seen," they had some awareness of the words' meaning. For example, a person might not be aware that he

or she had seen the word "lady." But when asked to select from the pair "girl/book" the word that was similar in meaning to the flashed word, he or she would choose "girl" —at a level higher than chance.

Psychologists have a running debate about the idea of subliminal perception and about attempts to demonstrate it, such as those above. One problem is that subliminal effects are usually quite small, and they have an exasperating tendency to come and go erratically in different experiments. In addition, the critics of subliminal perception have a more basic disagreement. In line with signal detection theory, they believe there is no such thing as an absolute sensory threshold; it is merely a convenient fiction, defined statistically (see Chapter 5). In particular, critics urge that no special priority should be given to the subjects' reports of awareness, since such reports of weak stimuli have uncertain validity—they are surely somewhat vague, easily biased, and suspect (remember the idea of "false alarms" from Chapter

5). In the view of these critics, if there is no absolute threshold, then it makes no sense to talk about "subliminal perception."

Thus, some researchers simply ignore the question of absolute tresholds. Instead, they look at how different response indicators vary with variations in stimulus intensity (or exposure duration). And they find that different indicators are more or less "sensitive" to stimulus variations in the weak intensity range. In this view, "subliminal perception" is simply a term for any instance in which some behavioral indicator of perception proves more sensitive to changes in stimulus intensity than are typical reports of awareness of the stimulus. And everyone admits there are many examples of this, in which (say) a person's forced guess about the presence of a weak stimulus may be correct more often than chance, even though he or she has no confidence whatsoever in the accuracy of the judgment.

that our perceptual mechanisms can fool us into seeing things that are not there. In fact, if you noticed the missing word in the last sentence or the extra word in the sentence before it, you are very unusual. The context of the entire passage influences the perception of each sentence as a whole; most people read these sentences as if they were unflawed, because the brain constructs a perception of them as they "ought" to be.

But if perception is not simply a reflection of the sensory information picked up by our sensory systems, what is it? Traditionally, **perception** has been defined as an organism's conscious *awareness* and categorization of objects and events in

the environment, brought about by stimulation of the organism's sense organs. But awareness is a subjective term that limits us when we wish to consider perception in animals and young babies, or when we explore topics like subliminal perception, in which a weak stimulus may influence people's behavior without their awareness. For such reasons we need to expand our definition of perception. In our expanded definition, "perception" refers to the entire process by which external stimuli influence whatever thoughts and behaviors of the organism immediately follow those stimuli. Perception may or may not include a person's reports of awareness.

FROM SENSATION TO PERCEPTION

It is impossible to completely separate perception from sensation. Traditionally, sensation refers to the physiological processes by which our nervous system registers stimuli. Perception, by contrast, refers to the processes by which our brains arrive at meaningul interpretations of basic sensations. Research in each field reflects this division. In "sensation" experiments, researchers focus on simple, separate stimuli: for example, they would want to know whether you can distinguish one tone from another. But in "perception" experiments, researchers often focus on the way people interpret more complex patterns of stimuli. They would want to know whether you can recognize a melody that is slowed down or speeded up or shifted to another octave.

What happens in the brain is obviously crucial to our ability to understand what is "out there": the brain organizes and gives meaning to the limited information gathered by our senses. The brain does this by making hypotheses, guessing —on the basis of experience and context—just what that object is that is stimulating our senses. As we saw in the chapter introduction, when sensory information is incomplete, brain processes often create a complete perception by "filling in" missing details. As an illustration, the brain can provide us with **subjective contours**, which are lines or shapes that appear to be part of a figure but actually are not present. When you look at the drawings in Figure 6.1, you will probably perceive the various shapes as having distinct outlines. If you examine the shapes closely, however, you will discover that some of the lines that define them are simply not there. The lines are perceptually present but physically absent. Subjective contours appear naturally when we encounter certain types of stimuli. Our perception of these contours is the result of the brain's automatic attempts to enhance and complete the details of an image (Kanisza, 1976).

Brain processes can do more than provide

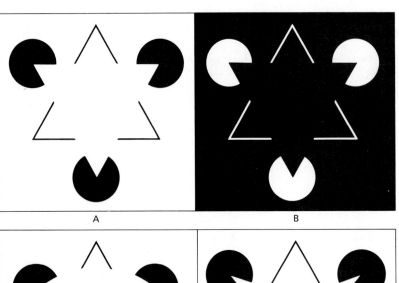

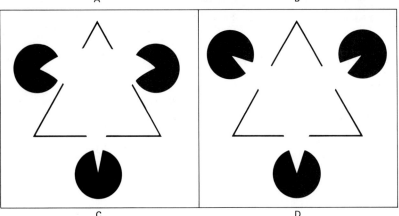

Figure 6.1. Subjective contours. The brain seeks to tie the components of an incomplete picture together by creating the perception of contours that complete the picture. (A) The subjective contours form a white triangle in the middle of this visual image. (B) In this case, the outline of a center triangle is perceived once again, but this time the triangle appears black as the result of the background color. C and D illustrate the fact that subjective contours may be curved as well as straight. (After Kanisza, 1976.)

missing information; they can also compensate for distortions in information *if* the distortion systematically alters the whole visual field in the same way. An experiment performed by G. M. Stratton (1896) offers a striking example of this ability. For a considerable period of time, Stratton wore a pair of spectacles that turned the retinal image upside down. When he first put on the spectacles he had trouble coordinating vision and movement, because he saw everything inverted from top to bottom, with right and left reversed as well. After about a week, however, he adjusted and could walk, read, eat, write, and carry out other activities successfully. Although he adapted so well that he sometimes forgot he was living in an inverted world, Stratton reported the experience as similar to bending over and looking through his legs. When he finally removed the spectacles, the world looked abnormal for several hours, although he did not perceive it as being upside down. In such experiments, adaptation usually does not occur unless the person moves about with the spectacles on and interacts with the distorted environment —a further indication that perception is not a passive but an active process (Rock, 1966).

Brain activity can also create perceptions even in the absence of appropriate sensory stimulation. We sometimes have visual experiences without using our eyes, as in dreams; auditory experiences without using our ears; and so on. In one experiment, subjects wore goggles that eliminated all visual stimulation; they soon began to hallucinate colors, patterns, objects, or scenes (Bexton, Heron, and Scott, 1954).

It seems clear that perception is not simply the detection of stimuli by sensory receptors. Instead, the perceptual process depends on the way the brain organizes those stimuli to create meaning.

Basic Perceptual Organization

The first basic task of any perceptual system is to isolate various objects from their background. This process allows us to perceive the objects in a complex world. We see objects of various sizes, shapes, and colors; we see them as separate units distinguished from other visual units; we see them arranged in space as moving or stationary. We perceive a three-dimensional world, even though the images received by the retina are two-dimensional and upside-down. We perceive a stable environment, although movements of our eyes and body cause constant changes in the stimuli striking the retina. How does the brain accomplish these tasks? We can begin to answer this question by looking at some principles of perceptual organization.

Imagine, first of all, the problems the brain must solve in order to see the simplest visual object—say, a large white spot on a black wall. We can think of the retina as an array of sensitive units that record entering light; the white spot will stimulate a roughly circular set of retinal units. For simplicity, suppose also that the black background does not stimulate cells that surround the circular set.

The puzzle is this: Why doesn't the brain report hundreds of tiny dots of light, each corresponding to a highly stimulated retinal cell? Why does it instead report a unified disk of light? The brain manages this feat by performing a series of calculations. First, cells at the back of the retina fill in the figure by averaging the hundreds of neighboring light points, so that all points within the figure are interpreted as connected. Then neurons behind the retina and in the visual pathways pool together the signals from clumps of retinal cells that (1) lie close to one another and (2) fire at a similar rate. Thus, in perceiving even this simple figure, the brain follows certain "rules" in organizing the sensory information it receives into a meaningful pattern, or **gestalt** (after the German word for *form* or *shape*). As a result, we see a disk of light rather than hundreds of pinpoints. Similarly, we see a natural scene in full color on a television screen, rather than thousands of pinpoints of three-colored dots painted rapidly on the screen.

These organizational processes of the nervous system were a major concern of the Gestalt school of psychology, which developed early in this century. Gestalt psychologists, led by Max Wertheimer, Kurt Koffka, and Wolfgang Kohler, embarked on a series of experiments they hoped would account for perception. Their research led them to believe that the brain's organizational processes were inborn, instead of being learned or modified by experience. This assumption is still controversial. Yet most psychologists accept the Gestalt school's basic premise that the way the brain groups stimuli, such as the points of light in our circle, follows certain rules. We shall summarize these rules in the sections that follow.

Grouping

Grouping is one way of organizing sensory data; we saw this principle in action in our disk example above. What determines whether the brain will group a set of stimuli (as it did with the points of light in the disk), or *not* group that set of stimuli? Several rules relevant to this question are illustrated in Figure 6.2. As you look at the figure, imagine that the dots represent stimulated cones on the retina.

- Part A shows no stable distinguishing organization. If our sensory system registers a set of stimuli like this one, we perceive no organization because dots of equal size are spaced equally across the field.
- Part B demonstrates the rule of **proximity**. Here, some dots have been moved closer together; we perceive a series of four parallel lines.
- Part C demonstrates the rule of **continuity**. Dots that form a single continuous curve are perceived as grouped together. Simply adding a few dots has led us to see two curved lines: the rule of continuity has overruled the influence of proximity. Continuity reflects the tendency of our senses to extrapolate a local trend, extending or projecting it in a smooth or regular direction.
- Part D demonstrates the rule of **similarity**. Because some of the dots are now similar to each other—but different from the rest—we

perceive a cross standing out from the original pattern of dots.

Grouping in Auditory Perception

The rules of grouping apply to all the senses. For instance, both proximity and continuity operate in our perception of a musical composition. We automatically group the notes of a melody according to their proximity in time. Sometimes, however, continuity overrides proximity. If two notes are played close together in time, but are not part of the same continuous melodic line, we do not perceive them as a gestalt.

This effect, based on continuity and similarity, is known as **auditory stream segregation**, and it can easily be demonstrated. You will need a piano or xylophone. Select four descending high notes (call them *ABCD*) and four descending low notes (call them *abcd*). Play them several times in rapid succession, always in the order *AaBbCcDd*. Most people do not hear this pattern as alternating high and low notes, but as two independent streams of notes *ABCD* and *abcd*. The illusion breaks apart if the set of high notes is too close to the set of low notes (so that closeness in time dominates the grouping), or it will fail if the successive notes within each set do not form a simple, continuous stream.

Auditory streaming is common in music; it is used in counterpoint or whenever two melodic

Figure 6.2. A demonstration of some of the gestalt principles of grouping. The pattern of equally spaced identical dots in A is not easily organized. It is seen either as an undifferentiated field or as a set of unstable overlapping patterns. In B a stable perception of parallel lines emerges because of the *proximity* of some dots to others. When some of these lines are made *continuous* with one another in C, dots that are physically quite distant from one another are seen as belonging to a single curved line. In D a very stable organization emerges suddenly because some of the dots have been made *similar* to one another and different from the rest.

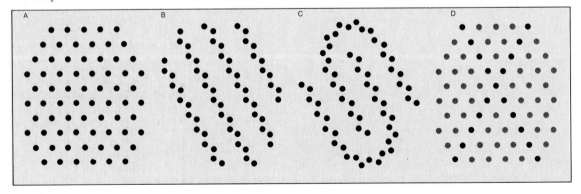

lines are played simultaneously. When we listen to a Bach fugue, we can hear the two simultaneous lines of melody, each with a highly distinctive quality. Different instruments in an orchestra often play different melodic lines, and it is not difficult to pick out and follow any orchestral section—because the brain organizes sound streams by the similarity of the instruments' sounds. At parties where many people talk at the same time, we use auditory streaming in order to follow the voice of one speaker. We can pick out and follow any speaker more easily if his or her voice has distinctive qualities; this fact again illustrates the rule that we group stimuli (this time, spoken words) by their similarity.

Simplicity: The Key to Grouping

All the rules of grouping can be summed up in a single concept: **simplicity** (Hochberg, 1978; Attneave, 1954). We find it much easier to perceive simple patterns than complex ones, no matter which rule of perceptual organization produces the simplicity. For example, Figure 6.3A presents a number of conflicting cues and could be interpreted in several ways. But people invariably report seeing two interlocking circles—which is the simplest way to perceive it. Figure 6.3B is generally seen as a circle covering one large triangle, not as a circle with three triangles or three barbs attached to it. The first explanation is the simpler one.

There is, however, a problem with the simplicity principle. When we look at an ambiguous figure, we cannot always predict which of several alterna-tive interpretations is simplest. Therefore, scientists have sought other principles beside simplicity to predict what will be perceived in some cases. Let us now turn to an illustration of the grouping principle applied to the way we separate a figure from its background or ground.

Figure and Ground

Whatever we look at, whether it is a landscape or a printed page, is seen as divided into dominant objects, or **figure(s)**, and the context in which the objects appear, or **ground**. The figure stands out from the ground like a word on a page: it seems to be more solid and well defined, and it seems to lie in front of the uniform background.

The figure-ground effect can be explained by the principles of grouping. Consider, for example, the way in which you were able to pick out the red Frisbee that was thrown at you in the example at the beginning of this chapter. The red points of the Frisbee were grouped together by the brain (using similarity and proximity), so that the Frisbee was seen as the figure against the ground of the blue sky. Because the red points of the Frisbee are close together and similar in color, they are grouped together to form a figure. The blue points of the sky are grouped together so that the sky is seen as the larger background.

Distinguishing Figure from Ground in Nonvisual Senses

We distinguish the figure from the ground with all our senses. In music, for example, the lead singer

Figure 6.3. Two illustrations of the perceptual tendency toward simplicity. Despite conflicting cues, figure A is seen as two intersecting circles. The circle is among the simplest of perceived forms and provides the simplest means of interpreting this pattern. Figure B is most often seen as a circle covering one large triangle, rather than a circle with three small barbs attached to it. The "one big triangle" interpretation fits and is simpler than the other. Note how the interpretation would change if the barbs were not aligned at the corners of a triangle.

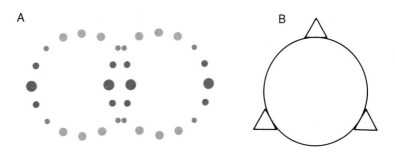

may carry the primary melody ("the figure"), while the background accompaniment is provided by the rest of the musicians (drums, bass, piano, or guitar). A walk through the aisles of a cosmetics department assaults your nose with a jumble of fragrances, but if you catch the odor of your favorite perfume, it suddenly becomes the figure, leaving the other fragrances as ground. By paying special attention to one stimulus out of the many that are available, we can make that stimulus stand out as a figure from its background.

Figure-Ground Segregation Is Innate

The ability to separate objects from background does not seem to depend on the viewer's past experience. About as soon as infants can focus their eyes clearly (from four to seven months), they seem to distinguish figure from ground. During the first few weeks of life, newborns reach out for objects that come close to them, sometimes even grasping them; this reaching reflex then disappears. Not until infants are about five months old will they again reach accurately for objects in their field of vision (T. G. R. Bower, 1976). By this time, infants are beginning to focus their eyes clearly, and their behavior shows clear evidence that they isolate figures against backgrounds (T. G. R. Bower, 1977).

The experience of blind people whose sight has been restored also supports the inborn nature of figure-ground segregation. Almost at once, these individuals are able to distinguish figure from ground, although they are extremely poor at recognizing familiar objects and need prolonged training before they become adept at this skill (von Senden, 1960; Gregory and Wallace, 1963).

Hiding Figures in Ground

Despite our skill at distinguishing figure from ground, we sometimes find it difficult to pick out the figure. For example, an object may not stand out well against the background because its color is similar to that of the background (the rule of grouping by similarity operates here). When a batter steps up to the plate, the white baseball is difficult to see if the center-field bleachers are filled with white-shirted spectators. In fact, this problem was so serious in the past that the major leagues placed large green backgrounds in center-

field stands so that the batters could see the approaching ball.

Camouflage, which works by blurring the distinction between figure and ground, can fool even the experienced eye. Camouflage exploits the principles of grouping by similarity and grouping by continuity. The target figure is either hidden among other figures so that it is difficult to isolate, or else blended into the background so that it is hard to identify. In children's picture puzzles, such as those that ask youngsters to "find the animals hidden in the woods," figures are camouflaged by hiding their contours among other figures. A similar practice of blending the target into the background is used by hunters and the military. Camouflage is also common in nature. Some insects perched on a branch can hardly be distinguished from a twig, and many animals are colored so that they blend into the background scenery, making it hard for predators to see them. One type of lizard, the chameleon, can even change its coloration as it moves from one background to another.

PERCEIVING LOCATION IN SPACE

The principles of grouping and figure-ground segregation describe how we are able to isolate figures or objects from their background—a first task of any perceptual system. But once we have identified a coherent object ("Something's there!"), we are faced with another task: to locate the object in space relative to our body ("Where is it?"). Our bodies have been constructed in a way that enables us to locate objects—that is, judge their position—in three-dimensional space.

Orientation

How do we determine where, in the 360-degree range around us, an object is located? When we are looking straight ahead, we can determine the approximate location of a visual object (relative to our body) by where the object's image falls on the retina. In fact, we turn our head toward an object, and focus our eyes on it, much as we might point to its location relative to our body. This process enables us to place the object in the spatial framework we project before us.

Figure 6.4. Human beings perceive the direction of a sound source by comparing the times at which the sound reaches each of their two ears. You can demonstrate sound localization by blindfolding a seated friend, then tiptoing around the chair, staying about four feet from your friend and snapping your fingers from time to time. Ask your friend to point directly toward the sound source, which you vary by changing your direction occasionally so the sound does not progress in a smooth circle. Your friend is likely to pinpoint the sounds to each side but may confuse sounds directly ahead with those directly behind. This confusion is due to the fact that sounds coming from straight ahead or behind arrive at both ears simultaneously. Now have your friend block one ear by putting cotton smeared with Vaseline in it and repeat the experiment. Your friend is likely to be much less accurate at localizing sounds when only one ear can be relied on. (After Lindsay and Norman, 1972.)

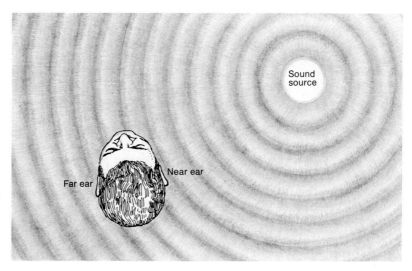

Our sense of touch also participates in locating external objects: we can reach out and touch things and tell where they are relative to our bodies. And in addition, we can use our hearing. We have one ear on each side of our heads; sounds that come from the right side produce sound waves that arrive at the right ear earlier than at the left ear (and vice versa). Consequently, we can locate any sound, determining approximately which direction it comes from. Because the ears are not very far apart, the difference between the sound's arrival time at the two ears is quite small; human beings can detect a difference of about 30 millionths of a second. The farther to one side the sound source is, the greater the time between its arrival at the two ears. The brain uses this difference to calculate the approximate location of the sound source. Sounds coming from straight ahead or behind arrive at the two ears simultaneously, so that their locations are often confused. (For a simple demonstration of sound localization, see Figure 6.4.)

Perceiving Visual Depth

Now that we know the direction in which an object is located, how do we determine the object's depth, or distance from where we are standing? **Visual depth perception**, or the ability to tell how far away an object is, is constructed from several kinds of information.

Binocular Disparity

One source of information for depth perception arises from our anatomy: the eyes, like the ears, are set apart, so that the retinal image received by each eye is slightly different. This difference is known as **binocular disparity**. You can discover how this disparity is involved with depth perception by holding a finger fairly close in front of you, then lining it up with an object that is some distance away. Using one eye at a time, look at both your finger and the distant object. Your finger will seem to jump back and forth against the background, because the difference between the two retinal images is greater for near objects than for distant objects. We use this difference in disparity to judge the distance of an object. As we look at objects with both eyes, their disparity gives a perception of depth, called **stereopsis**.

Monocular Cues

Even if one eye is covered, so that we cannot use binocular disparity, we can still discern depth by relying on **monocular cues** ("mono"—"one," "ocular"—"eye")—information that does not require the cooperation of both eyes. Monocular cues are not as precise as binocular disparity, but they are adequate for depth perception, as you can judge by simply closing one eye and looking around you. The effectiveness of monocular cues is attested to by the success of several airplane pilots and at least one professional baseball player who had only one eye (Regan, Beverley, and Cynader, 1979).

One monocular cue to depth is **motion parallax**, which relies on the relative movements of images on the retina as we move or change position. You can easily demonstrate motion parallax. Look at two objects, one close to you and the other across the room. Eliminate binocular disparity by closing one eye, then move your head back and forth horizontally. The near object will appear to move farther across your visual field than the far object. We use this difference in movement to perceive depth; as we move, things that move less are perceived as farther away from us.

Motion parallax is responsible for a familiar perception that occurs as we drive along an open highway. Trees and telegraph poles beside the road seem to whiz by, but distant mountains appear motionless. As we shall see in Chapter 14, research with infants and young animals indicates that motion parallax enables them to perceive depth shortly after birth, suggesting that the capacity is inborn.

Artists were aware of monocular cues to depth perception long before these cues became the subject of psychological study. Since a painting is static as well as two-dimensional, the impression of depth it conveys must rely on cues that do not

involve motion. Many such cues are illustrated in the Perugino painting reproduced here. One static aid to monocular depth is **interposition**, in which one object partially blocks the view of another object, creating the illusion that the second object is farther away. A second cue to depth is **linear perspective**, which is produced by the apparent convergence of parallel lines toward the horizon. A third depth cue is **relative size**, the relationship between the size of the retinal image produced by

An example of texture gradient as a cue to depth perception.

This Renaissance painting, *Delivery of the Keys* by Il Perugino (1446–1524), uses relatively sophisticated monocular cues to show depth. Linear perspective is illustrated by the lines of the pavement, which converge from front to back. Relative size is illustrated by the difference in size of the background and foreground figures. Interposition is illustrated by the kneeling man's blockage of the woman behind him. Texture gradient is illustrated by the atmospheric haze that makes distant trees and buildings less sharply defined than the figures in the foreground.

an object and the apparent distance of that object from an observer. The larger the retinal image, the closer the object appears to be.

Finally, **texture gradient**, the graduated differences in the appearance of surfaces that occur as distance increases, also provides a cue to depth. In a scene in which texture is obvious, such as the one shown in the accompanying photograph, stones that are near the camera appear larger and coarser, while stones that are in the distance appear smaller and finer. Texture gradient is actually a form of relative size cue. We rely on the same cues to interpret photographs as actual scenes.

Perceptual Constancies

Once we have identified an object and located it in space, our perceptual systems face a third task: how to maintain a stable perception of the object —and, indeed, of the world in general. This task is more complicated than it seems, because each object's exact retinal image constantly varies in size, shape, brightness, orientation, and so on. Yet we achieve a stable percept without difficulty. **Perceptual constancy** refers to this capability, our ability to perceive objects as having certain constant (or stable) properties despite great variation in their appearances.

Perceptual constancy is the perceptual consequence of our confidence in a stable world. It rests on our belief that objects maintain their size, shape, color, and location regardless of how we view them. When our boat approaches the Statue of Liberty, the image cast on the retina by the statue gets larger and the details of the statue become sharper. The retinal shape of the statue changes, and the texture and color of her metallic surface become more distinct. Yet we know that Miss Liberty is no larger than she was when we viewed her from Manhattan, and that she has neither become more detailed nor changed her shape since we climbed on board the boat. Similarly, when we toss a Frisbee back to our friend, we perceive it as maintaining a constant size (not getting smaller); we also continue to perceive it as round, although its retinal image as it glides away may be oval or oblong. Even when there are large moment-to-moment changes in the sensory information we receive from objects in the environment, we tend to ignore them in favor of a world that is constant and predictable.

Size Constancy

One type of perceptual constancy is **size constancy**. The farther away an object is, the smaller the size of the image it projects on the retina; however, we automatically take into account any information we have about the object's distance and translate the projected size into the object's real size.

For a striking demonstration of size constancy, look at the photographs on page 146. In the top photograph, the women are perceived as roughly equal in size, even though the retinal image cast by the woman in the foreground is three times as large as the image cast by the more distant woman. We see them as about the same size because cues in the photograph tell us that the second woman is seated farther from the camera. In the bottom photograph, the woman in the background has been cut out and placed next to the woman in the foreground. Now the disparity is obvious—and startling (Boring, 1964).

Size constancy is such a prevalent part of our world that we usually fail to notice it. When size constancy breaks down, as it does in a well-known phenomenon called the "moon illusion," most people notice and comment on it. As the moon rises on the horizon, it appears enormous, but once it has moved higher into the skies, it appears comparatively small. The terrain extending toward the horizon is responsible for this effect. Putting this terrain between the moon and the viewer signals the moon's great distance; but when the moon is high in the heavens, no such cues to distance are provided. If you look at a rising moon through a tube, thus separating your perception of it from any cues on the horizon, the illusion of great size is destroyed and the moon appears much smaller. Similarly, if you view the moon at its zenith through an artificial horizon drawn on a large transparency, the moon will suddenly seem much larger. Perceived size depends on perceived distance, as it does with the red square in Figure 6.5.

Other Perceptual Constancies

Size constancy is only one important perceptual constancy. Our visual system also maintains constancy with respect to *shape*: the Frisbee skimming horizontally through the air retains its round shape even though its retinal image is oblong. We also maintain *color* constancy: when the sun goes behind a cloud, your frisbee partner's

A

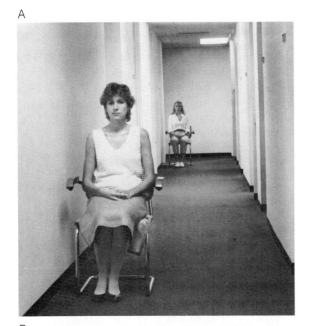

B

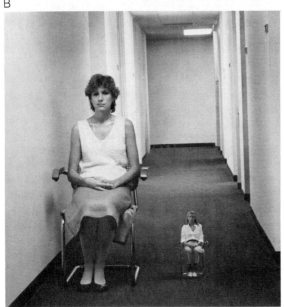

Because we expect two adult women to be roughly equal in size, we attribute the apparent difference between the women in photo A to the distance between them. In photo B, the woman in the background now appears next to the larger woman, and their size difference is obvious.

white shirt still looks white. We maintain *location* constancy: although the trees and houses in your visual field shift as you move your head or run after the Frisbee, the objects do not seem to move.

In each case, the nature of the constancy is similar. We have an unchanging perception based on the relationship between stimuli, despite changes in the sensation provided by the stimuli.

Perceptual Constancies and Geometric Illusions

An **illusion** is a perception that does not correspond to a real object or event; it is produced by physical or psychological distortion. Illusions demonstrate important perceptual processes that go unnoticed under ordinary conditions. By studying illusions in the laboratory, researchers hope to discover more about the way human beings process visual information.

An interesting class of illusions is geometric illusions—line drawings in which the direction, size, or orientation of the parts is perceived incorrectly. Some geometric illusions rely on our natural tendency to view two-dimensional pictures as projections of three-dimensional scenes. Because of size constancy, when we unconsciously scale objects according to their perceived distance, we see an apparent difference in their size.

Geometric Figures

In Figure 6.6, you can inspect illusions of length and depth in their simplest forms. For example, the vertical lines in Figure 6.6A appear to be of different lengths, but if you measure them with a ruler, you can see that they are identical. This figure, called the Müller-Lyer illusion, has features similar to those that indicate distance to the eye. The arrows act like outlines of corners, as illustrated in Figure 6.6B. As a result, the "shorter" line is unconsciously interpreted as being recessed into the page. Because both lines project the same size image onto the retina, the line that is interpreted as being closer is perceived as smaller, in accordance with the principle of size constancy.

Linear perspective cues to depth can create a related effect. In the Ponzo illusion (Figure 6.6C), the converging lines are interpreted as parallel lines that extend away from the observer. Figure 6.6D demonstrates the same illusion using railroad tracks. The horizontal bar that is farther down the track is perceived as larger; once again, size constancy dictates that when two objects project the same size image on the retina, but one

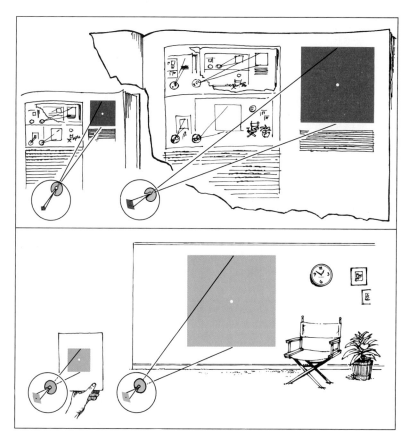

Figure 6.5. The relationship between perceived size and perceived distance can be demonstrated with afterimages—images that persist after the original stimulus is removed. Stare for forty seconds in adequate lighting at the dot in the red square. Then hold a piece of white paper a foot from your eyes and look at the center of it. If you have trouble seeing an afterimage of the square, focus on one spot on the paper. Now move the paper to about two feet in front of your eyes and look at it: the square probably looks twice as large. If you look at a more distant surface, such as a blank white wall, the afterimage will appear to be even larger. The drawings at the left explain why this happens. (top) Normally, the more distant an object is from the eye, the smaller the image projected onto the back of the eye. The brain compensates for this effect by scaling up the apparent size of distant objects. The result is size constancy: objects do not appear to change size just because they move closer or farther. But when the image in the eye is held constant, as it is with an afterimage (bottom), the brain's compensation for changes in distance creates large changes in apparent size.

object is perceived as more distant than the other, the far object is probably larger.

The Ames Room

Striking visual illusions have been created by building models that trick the visual system into misapplying size and shape constancy. The best example is the Ames room, shown in Figure 6.7A. The two women inside the room look dramatically different in size because we perceive the room as rectangular (Ames, 1951), but in fact, as Figure 6.7B shows, perspective and size cues fool the eye. The back wall is farther away on the left side than on the right, which leads us to perceive the women as standing the same distance from us. Once again, size constancy dictates that if two people are the same distance away, but one projects a larger image onto the eye, then that person must be larger.

The Ames room illusion works only if we view the room without adequate perception of depth. As Figure 6.7B shows, the illusion occurs strongly when the observer looks at the room through a peephole; this restriction removes important depth cues such as binocular parallax (the observer can use only one eye at a time) and motion parallax (the observer cannot move around to see the room from different positions). If observers are allowed to explore the surface of the Ames room with a stick inserted through a hole in the wall,

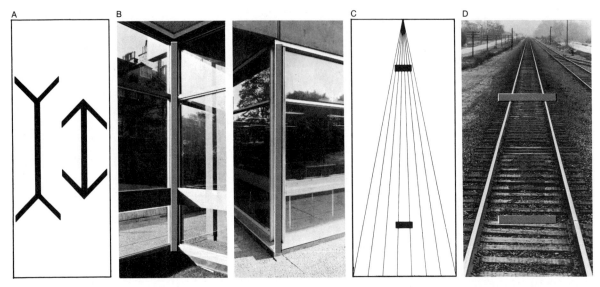

Figure 6.6. Two famous illusions and possible explanations for how they work. The vertical lines of the figures in the Müller-Lyer illusion (A) are identical in length, but they do not appear to be. An explanation for this illusion, suggested in B, is that the arrow markings on the lines in A cause them to be perceived as three-dimensional objects that have corners. The corners seem to induce a size-constancy effect: the vertical line that appears to be distant is perceived as larger. The horizontal lines in the Ponzo illusion (C) are also identical in length. As the photograph in D suggests, this figure, too, could easily be perceived as three-dimensional, and again size constancy would cause the apparently more distant "object" to be scaled up in apparent size relative to the "nearer object." (After Gregory, 1970.)

Figure 6.7. The Ames room. The illusion is produced by trapezoidal windows that run parallel to the sloping floor, making the room look rectangular (A). In B the actual construction of the room is compared with the way the room is perceived. The brain infers that both women standing against the back wall are at the same distance from the eye and interprets the difference between the size of their images as a real difference in size.

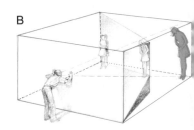

they are less susceptible to the illusion. Gradually, they see the room for what it actually is: a set of trapezoids joined to form acute and obtuse angles —that is, a distorted room. Yet an intellectual knowledge of the room's shape does not prevent the illusion: only active exploration of the room is effective.

In these illusions based on the inappropriate application of size constancy, viewers make incorrect perceptual inferences about distance and size because features of the illusions mimic the patterns of corners, parallel lines, and rectangular rooms that are seen in the world about them. As these illusions show, perception does not simply reflect the world; it also interprets it. The interpretive role of perception is necessary, because sensory input is often sketchy and misleading. By compensating for inadequate sensory information, perception tells us what is out there in the world and where it is in relation to us, helping us to survive in a challenging environment.

PERCEPTION OF MOVEMENT

After we have identified an object at a certain location, our perceptual system must then determine whether the object is moving and, if so, what its speed and direction are. Our perceptual world is characterized by movement—that is, by a continuous, steady change of an object's location over brief time spans.

Actual Movement

Imagine that your eye takes a rapid series of snapshots of a moving object, much as a movie camera takes 16 frames per second. From these frames, how do we decide that an object is moving? First, we have to identify the object as being the same one from one frame to the next; we do this using the principle of object constancy. Next, we judge that the object is moving against a fixed background because in a short time it covers and then uncovers successive parts of the background in one continuous direction. You can tell that your friend is running to the right in pursuit of the frisbee because she successively blocks the background in a line from left to right.

An object's perceived movement is always relative to a background. What happens when the background is homogeneous, as when a spot of light moves across a darkened TV screen? In such a situation we may judge movements from successive changes in the spot's location on the retina or from successive changes in the spot's distance from the edges of the screen.

Any creature soon learns to distinguish between changes in the visual world that are caused by movements in the world and changes that are caused by the creature's own movements. We know when we are in motion, and so we relate the movements of our own bodies to the resulting changes in what we see. When we look from one side of a room to another, what we see changes constantly, but we perceive the changes as resulting from the movement of our eyes and not from movement of the room.

We can also tell that we are moving even though we are not producing the movement ourselves, as when we ride in a car that someone else is driving. As we look out a side window, objects enter our view from the car's front, then leave our view from the car's back end; near objects seem to rush past at a faster pace than far objects. What we see in the world outside the car is motion parallax, a constant flow in what is seen, which produces our perception that we are moving through space (J. Gibson, 1966).

Illusions of Movement

We sometimes perceive motion when no real movement is taking place. In **induced movement**, we judge the motion of an object by changes in its relation to a surrounding frame, which is assumed to remain stationary. It is possible to induce movement in a completely darkened room by surrounding a spot of light with a luminous frame and then moving the frame. If the frame is moved to the right, the spot will appear to move to the left, although it actually remains stationary. Film makers use the technique of induced movement to create the illusion that a driver (and car) are moving along a highway. The car and driver remain fixed in the center of the screen while the background scenery (filmed earlier and projected on a screen behind the actor) swiftly moves past, entering the film frame from one side, flowing across it, and leaving on the opposite side. Induced movement is also responsible for another common illusion. The moon sometimes appears to race through clouds, when in fact the clouds are being blown across the moon's face.

IMPOSSIBLE FIGURES

Our visual system interprets various parts of a scene based on the local cues surrounding each part. This strategy usually succeeds because the brain can mentally patch together its interpretation of parts to form a coherent interpretation of the entire scene. In a real scene these local interpretations put limits on one another's versions, so that we can patch them together into a coherent scene. Computer vision programs often use this principle, For example, a picture of a square box requires certain kinds of corners and surface edges to be linked together in limited ways. The programs thus rely on constraints among smaller parts to produce a larger percept (e.g., Waltz, 1975).

But clever artists can use local cues to make a drawing appear correct when we look at portions of it—but impossible as a whole. Such drawings are called "impossible figures" because the parts do not add up to a consistent whole.

In the trident, or three-pronged figure (see figure A), three prongs can be seen on the left, but only two are suggested by the right side of the drawing. Trace the drawing and see if you can find where the artist has fooled your eye.

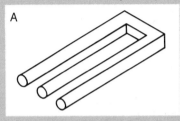

The trident—an "impossible" construction.

In the "impossible triangle" (see figure B), each local part (vertex, or "point" of the triangle) can be interpreted in three dimensions. But as the eye roams from one side and vertex to the next, we interpret the relationships among the triangle's arms differently.

The impossible triangle has been incorporated into M. C.

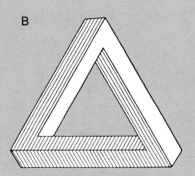

Artist M. C. Escher's "impossible triangle."

Escher's drawing "The Waterfall" (see figure C). The drawing uses two "impossible triangles" linked together, with the waterfall itself forming one side of each triangle. The brick wall surrounding the water canal *appears* to descend; the water appears to flow continuously downward toward the waterfall, and the waterfall appears to plunge into a pool two levels below. But a look at details leads us to perceive the

You can experience another illusory movement by staring at a tiny spot of light in a completely darkened room. After a time, the light appears to move in irregular paths. This phenomenon, called **autokinetic movement**, appears to result from random eye movements and the lack of any external cues for localizing the light. This illustrates the fact that our eyes are often moving, either in large "saccades" or in smaller jumps; furthermore, we are often unaware of these small eye movements. In the autokinetic effect, the extent and direction of the spot's perceived movement can easily be influenced by suggestion and social pressure.

Finally, **apparent movement** can be created by a rapid succession of motionless stimuli that mimics the changes that occur in real movement. One example of apparent movement, the **phi phenomenon**, was described by the Gestalt psychologist Max Wertheimer (1923). Wertheimer pointed out that when lights are switched on in rapid alternation, as in some neon signs, the light appears to move back and forth, although the two lights are actually motionless. The phi phenomenon is the basis for motion pictures. We perceive that people in films are moving, although the stimuli producing the perceived motion are a series of still photographs that flash by at a rate of at least sixteen frames per second. In modern films, frames flash by so quickly that the eye integrates information from the frames to perceive smooth movement. In the early days of film, speeds were far slower and the abrupt transitions between frames was noticeable, giving the impression of rapid, jerky motion.

C

"Impossible" scene drawn by Escher.

pool as being on the same level as the brink of the falls.

In the never-ending staircase (see figure *D*), local cues suggest continuous ascent, but the whole effect is to return us to the same lower point from which we started.

D

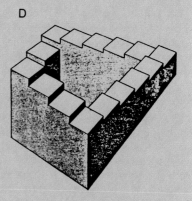

Escher's never-ending staircase.

In neon signs and motion pictures, a rapid succession of visual stimuli reproduces the changes in sensory information that occur in real movement, producing an illusion of movement.

Apparent motion can also produce **illusory aftereffects of motion**. When a train passenger is looking out the window and the train stops, the scenery outside appears to move slowly backward for a time. This aftereffect of motion, called the waterfall illusion, was so named because of the way one of its discoverers (Adams, 1834) came upon it. He found that if he gazed for a long time at a waterfall, then shifted his gaze to the riverbank, he experienced an illusion that the riverbank was drifting gradually upward.

In the waterfall illusion, the apparent movement is always in the opposite direction from the previous real movement. It is probably caused by sensory adaptation, in which the responsiveness of direction-selective cells in the visual cortex is temporarily reduced (Barlow and Hill, 1963). Just as color-opponent cells respond to stimulation by one color and not by another (see Chapter 5), so direction-selective neurons respond to movement in one direction and not in another. If the brain normally detects movement by comparing the outputs from direction-selective neurons, it will become susceptible to the illusion when cells sensitive to motion in one direction adapt and are less responsive to stimulation. Now cells that are sensitive to the opposite motion are stimulated more by a stationary scene, producing the waterfall illusion. The eerie feeling that accompanies this aftereffect probably arises because the visual neurons that detect location have not adapted, so that despite the riverbank's apparent movement, the riverbank keeps its position relative to its surroundings. As a result, the perplexed brain receives contradictory information from two classes of neurons (Blakemore, 1973).

THEORIES OF PATTERN RECOGNITION

Having noticed an object, located it in space, and perhaps determined its movement, our perceptual system is still faced with the task of identifying what kind of thing the object is. We can recognize a pattern either as an instance of some class or category (a bulldog) or as a specific individual (my dog Fido). Similar processes seem to occur in both cases.

One way to understand these processes is to trace the way in which the brain might recognize hand-printed, block capital letters, such as *A, B, P,* and *Z*. There is considerable debate over how it achieves this.

Does the Brain Use Templates?

The simplest way for the brain to recognize capital letters might be to compare them with standard patterns it has stored in memory. Suppose these patterns (called "templates") are similar to a collection of standard printed letters. When a person saw a written letter, he or she would mentally shuffle through this collection of templates, trying out each one to see how well it matched (or "cross-correlated with") the new letter, then placing the new letter in the category whose template it best matched.

In everyday life, just such a process of **template matching** allows bank machines to read checking-account numbers. But this process is successful only when each number conforms exactly to a rigid format for each digit. If the brain had the same requirement, matching would be impossible because people's handwriting is so variable—in size, shape, slant, presence of gaps, extra curlicues, misplaced dots and lines, and so forth.

Psychologists have had difficulty devising templates that would fit all possible ways of hand-printing one letter, yet would not fit other letters —for example, so as to mistake a capital O for a Q.

And that is a relatively simple type of pattern recognition. Think how much more difficulty scientists would have with areas in which pattern recognition is complex.

Feature Analysis

Rejecting global template matching as not very useful, scientists have turned to an approach known as **feature analysis**. The theory behind feature analysis grew out of scientists' intuition that the brain constructs perceptual objects not from complete templates, but from a relatively small collection of features.

Again, suppose the brain is attempting to identify handwritten letters. The key features of these letters would be corners, angles, intersections, curved arcs, lines of various orientation, and the like. These features are much the same regardless of the size and orientation of the letter. They would be connected by a few spatial relationships: angle *X* is *left* of arc *Y*, corner *X* is *above* line *Y*, line *X* is *joined to the left of intersection Y*, and so on. Using these features, it should be possible to create a unique description of each object or pattern to be recognized.

How might the brain analyze the features of a stimulus such as the letter *A*? First, it might construct a description of that stimulus in terms of the stimulus's distinctive features. Then the brain might compare these features to the unique list of features and their relationships that it possessed (in memory) for each letter category. Finally, it would place the stimulus in that category whose feature list provided the best match.

Applying feature analysis to letter recognition in this way, researchers have tried to determine how people visually segment and analyze letters into features and their relationships. A look at the alphabet shows that the letters are made up of distinctive features whose presence or absence characterizes entire sets of letters. For example, *H* and *A* have a horizontal cross-bar, but *C* and *N* do not. By identifying a unique set of distinctive features for each printed letter, researchers can construct a program that would identify any letter and never confuse one with another.

The Pandemonium Model

When the brain has made a description of a stimulus letter's features, its next task is to compare that list of features to those of the various prototypic letters. As it does so, it looks for the best match.

A general model of how the brain reaches this final decision was devised by Oliver Selfridge (1959). According to Selfridge's conceptual framework, known as the **Pandemonium model** of feature analysis, the brain identifies unknown letter stimuli by weighting the various feature matches according to the evidence they provide for each letter, and summing those weighted matches over all features available in the pattern. Using a whimsical metaphor, Selfridge imagined sensory systems as filled with an array of "demons," who function as feature detectors.

The job of each demon (detector) is to check each stimulus letter, to see whether it has that demon's defining feature—for example, to see whether it has a horizontal cross-bar. If that feature is present somewhere in the stimulus, the demon "shouts" (sends a signal) to the next level, which consists of an array of cognitive demons, each responsible for a whole letter (see Figure 6.8). Each cognitive demon accumulates evidence for

the hypothesis that its own letter is the stimulus.

In Figure 6.8 the feature demons are looking at a stimulus letter. (The stimulus happens to be the letter R, but the brain has not yet determined that fact.) The demons have found evidence that this letter has a vertical line, two horizontal lines, an oblique line, three right angles, and one discontinuous curve. As the demons pass along their signals, the cognitive demon for R receives input from five feature demons, the cognitive demon for P gets input from three feature demons, and the cognitive demon for T gets input from only two.

Then, according to Selfridge, each letter demon "shouts" at an intensity that corresponds to the amount of evidence it has received in its favor, setting up a loud noise or din ("pandemonium"). Finally, a decision-making demon selects the loudest shouter (the demon who has the best evidence). Theoretically, the Pandemonium model selects the correct letter the same way your brain consciously identifies marks on paper as the letter R.

How Feature Analysis May Take Place in the Brain

If we apply the Pandemonium model to our own visual processes, we can get some idea of how the brain might use feature analysis. For example, we could consider the feature demons in Selfridge's system as analogous to the receptive fields of cells in the lateral geniculate nucleus and the visual cortex. There would be cells that responded to line segments, to the orientation of line segments, and to intersections (see Chapter 5). Note that all the feature demons work independently and simultaneously (in "parallel"), as do the cognitive demons. This kind of parallel processing is commonly assumed to characterize many sensory systems.

The feature analysis model may explain why we have little difficulty recognizing the face of a politician in a line drawing or a cartoon; such sketches highlight the subject's most prominent features. And Pandemonium models have been useful in developing computer models of pattern recognition (e.g., McClelland and Rumelhart, 1981). They allow psychologists to propose and test a variety of schemes for generating distinctive features and weighing the features' importance. Such schemes are so effective that the U.S. Post Office has experimented with several block-letter reading machines, based on the Pandemonium model, that automatically read addresses.

Figure 6.8. The process by which a feature analysis system recognizes the letter R.

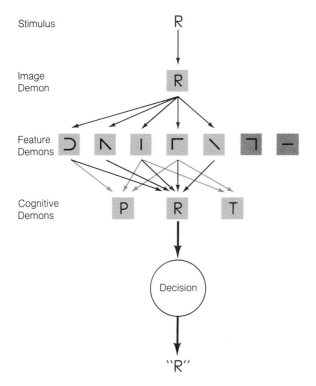

Limits of Feature Analysis

Pandemonium models also have several weaknesses. Suppose, for example, the image demon in Figure 6.8 were given the letter *P*. The cognitive demons for *R* and *P* would then receive the same amount of evidence for their hypothesis; how could the system decide in such cases? One way to get around this problem would be to add the rule that a letter must have *all* its features present, but *only* those features—for example, that an *R* must have a leg and a *P* must not have one. However, this solution immediately raises another question: How is it that we can accurately identify many patterns that have missing parts? Apparently, the final decision the brain makes in such cases uses more sophisticated rules.

Indeed, identifying capital block letters, as our example of the Pandemonium model does, solves only a few of the many problems involved in recognizing visual patterns. In order for a computer to identify handwritten, cursive letters and words, it would probably need a set of graphic features that were different from those for block capitals. But because of the enormous variation in people's handwriting, scientists working on computer models have had difficulty discovering the necessary invariant features and configurations that would make correct, automatic decisions possible.

Yet people manage to decipher the handwriting of most other individuals. How do they do it? Apparently, they go beyond the stimulus itself; they rely on their expectations regarding the content of the written material. In other words, people supplement the sensory information they get through feature analysis with expectations of what the stimulus will be. Some of these expectations derive from the context.

The Importance of Context in Pattern Recognition

Many drivers have had the experience of noting a hitchhiker some distance ahead on the highway, only to discover as they drew nearer that the "hitchhiker" was actually an oddly shaped tree trunk or weathered signpost. Such unsettling experiences confirm the role of expectations in perception and demonstrate that **context**, or the setting in which stimuli appear, helps determine the way we see them.

The power of context led Gestalt psychologists to propose that the brain may identify elementary perceptual stimuli by the role these stimuli play in a global picture, or "gestalt." The gestalt determines the meaning of the parts—an observation that gives rise to the statement, "The whole is more than the sum of its parts." If this is true, feature analysis—in which a perception is built bottom-up, by first identifying elementary parts of a scene—cannot account for all aspects of perception.

Sensory Ambiguity in Visual Stimuli

Sensory data are often ambiguous, allowing the brain to interpret a single set of stimuli in at least two different ways. Usually we resolve the ambiguity by choosing the most likely possibility, using the context as our guide. For example, the two lines at the top of Figure 6.9 are ambiguous stimuli. Placed in the sentence "Fido is drunk," the lines are interpreted as the word "is." However, when they are placed in the number 14,157,393, they become the numbers 1 and 5.

Another type of sensory ambiguity arises with **figure-ground reversal**. Look at Figure 6.10. Do you see a vase? Or a pair of facing profiles? As you stare at it, the two interpretations will probably switch back and forth. In cases like this, when figure and ground are ambiguous, figure and ground alternate so that the perception continues to shift.

Sensory Ambiguity in Auditory Stimuli

Ambiguity can also affect our perception of sounds. The same sound can be perceived as a heartbeat or a bouncing tennis ball; a clattering sound that in one context is interpreted as horses on cobbled streets is interpreted in another context as soldiers clambering up stone steps.

Context is especially important in our perception of speech. When people speak rapidly, it is

Figure 6.9. The stimulus above the handwriting can be interpreted as either 15 or IS, depending on its context.

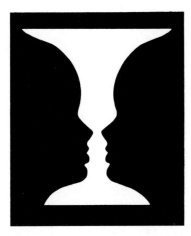

Figure 6.10. This drawing is a classic demonstration of figure-ground ambiguity. What you perceive as figure and as ground depends on a number of factors, including your expectation.

difficult for us to segment a continuous stream of speech into separate words unless we know the topic of conversation. The same sound sequence may be segmented differently, and heard as different messages, depending on the context of the conversation. For instance, part of the sequence, "Have you seen my NU-DIS-PLA?" can be heard as "nudist play" or as "new display," depending on whether you are talking about nudist camps or a computer display terminal.

We use our expectations, as determined by context, to make sense of what we hear in an ambiguous situation or in a noisy environment, such as a loud party. These expectations rely on our past experiences; we learn what kinds of topics or ideas are likely to be expressed in various situations. When we are talking about litter on public beaches, we are unlikely to interpret the segment "How to wreck a nice beach" as "How to recognize speech," but in a discussion of computer speech recognition, the latter interpretation will prevail. In terms of the Pandemonium model, expectations (e.g., expecting the letter to be *R*) increase the bias in favor of certain cognitive demons, so that the decision demon requires less feature evidence to decide in their favor.

Context also helps explain an auditory illusion discovered by Richard Warren (1970). If you play a tape of normal speech but replace a single syllable with a brief cough, buzz, or noise of equal loudness and duration, people will not notice the replacement. Even when they are told to listen for it, they have great difficulty picking it out of the speech stream. Our auditory system apparently becomes so caught up by the utterance that the intruding sound is assimilated into our perception of the word in which it is embedded. The importance of context in this illusion can be demonstrated if you play the tape backwards, destroying its speechlike properties. Now people have no trouble picking out the cough or buzz.

THE INFLUENCE OF EXPERIENCE ON PERCEPTION

A recurrent theme in this chapter has been the role of experience and expectation in perception. Obviously, we derive meaning from the black squiggles printed on this page because of our past learning. Similarly, our expectations influence our perccptions as we read. Your expectations may have blinded you to the misspelled word in the last sentence; earlier, at the chapter's opening, we demonstrated how people may not notice the omission or repetition of a word.

Expectations and previous experience constantly interact to influence our perception of all sensory events, including pain (as we saw in Chapter 5). When we look at an ambiguous figure, we perceive the result of our brain's applying one hypothesis after another to explain the bits and pieces of the sensory array. In applying hypotheses to incomplete figures, we may take some time to interpret the patches of light and dark in the figures.

Before you read on, look at the objects in Figure 6.11. These objects are so difficult to identify that you may sense yourself trying out alternative hypotheses. Now notice what happens to your perception when you receive some hints—"huge animal in a zoo" for Figure 6.11A and "sea cruise" for Figure 6.11B. In such situations, hints help you retrieve hypotheses about these objects from your memory; you can readily adjust and tune these hypotheses so as to fit the ink blobs. A kind of perceptual learning occurs in these cases. People tend to remember automatically the way they eventually succeed in interpreting a given blob; in fact, it becomes difficult for them ever again to see such a picture as the raw, uninterpreted blob it first seemed to them. (In case you're still stumped, part A of Figure 6.11 depicts an elephant; part B is an ocean liner.)

A

B

Figure 6.11. Two ambiguous sensory arrays. To identify the objects depicted here, we are likely to apply and discard various hypotheses as to what they might be. Receiving hints about their identity speeds up this process, as explained in the text. (After Street, 1931.)

Because perception is often a matter of fitting a plausible hypothesis onto an ambiguous sensory array, we can expect that our hypotheses will be influenced by our motivation. Our motives are our wants and interests. They organize our behavior toward a goal, and in fulfilling that function they can influence what stimuli capture our attention. When we have a specific desire, we more easily notice stimuli that we have associated with the satisfaction of that desire in the past. A hungry traveler, for example, notices restaurant signs that he or she would not be aware of just after a meal.

Similarly, even after we notice stimuli, our motives may affect the hypotheses we use to interpret ambiguous stimuli, because such hypotheses are especially available in memory at the moment. Thus, we are more likely to recognize objects related to a given motive—even though the objects are ambiguous or difficult to discern. In one experiment, mothers were tested for word recognition a few hours before their children were to undergo surgery to remove their tonsils (Parkinson and Rachman, 1981). These mothers were understandably anxious about their children's coming surgical ordeal. The researchers tested the mothers' auditory thresholds (see Chapter 5): they had the mothers listen for words spoken softly at the same time that fairly loud music was played. As it turned out, words related to surgery were the easiest for these women to detect: apparently, their worry over the operation made them more likely to try out hypotheses about surgical words. The mothers had no trouble identifying words like "operation," "pain," "bleeding," and "infection," but failed to hear equivalent nonsurgical words, such as "operatic," "pine," "breeding," and "inflection." Thinking about a concept made its verbal label more available.

Our expectations, past experiences, and psy-

chological states combine, "setting" us to perceive the world in certain ways. This readiness to perceive stimuli in a specific way, ignoring some types of stimulation and becoming attuned to others, is called our **perceptual set**. Of course, the perceptual sets of the reader and the hungry traveler are short-lived: they last only until the book is laid aside or a meal is eaten. But some perceptual sets are longer-lasting. Our experiences early in life and those common to our culture lead to enduring ways of perceiving the world.

Early Life Experiences and Perception

We know that certain early experiences can markedly affect our perceptual responsiveness to the world. Some perceptual processes develop only when an individual is raised with exposure to a normal visual environment. Unless human infants have an opportunity to use both eyes in a coordinated fashion during infancy, they never develop normal binocular depth perception. Experience also plays an important role in the depth perception of animals. Kittens raised without light seem unable to perceive depth, and, when tested, will readily venture into situations (such as an apparent "cliff" in the floor) that normally reared kittens avoid for fear of falling (Gibson and Walk, 1956).

At one time psychologists believed that active exploration of the world might be essential for the development of normal depth perception. This suspicion rose from an early finding by Held and Hein (1963), who raised kittens in darkness except for allowing them several minutes per day of visual experience, during which some of the kittens were allowed to move about in the room, whereas others were not allowed to move. When they were tested later, the kittens who had been permitted to move about during the visual experience showed normal depth perception, whereas the kittens deprived of movement during visual experience showed very poor depth perception. But later investigations suggested that depth perception may not be as dependent on active exploration as initially believed. In these later experiments, kittens were kept immobile, but their visual experience consisted solely of watching animated toy cars that resembled mice (an innately potent stimulus for a kitten). The "mouse cars" moved up and down a track in the shape of a figure eight. These kittens developed good depth perception (Walk et al., 1978). Attention to interesting objects that move through different distances may be enough to promote the development of depth perception—or at least to maintain it.

Although babies enter the world with a functioning visual system, early experience plays an important role in the development of visual processing. Abnormal visual experience in the first year can have serious effects on various aspects of human vision (Held, 1979). But with normal visual experience, infants develop depth perception within five months.

Cultural Influences

The normal perceptual experiences of a culture may lead its members to develop perceptual biases. For example, before technology had penetrated into most corners of the globe, people in Malawi could not make sense out of their first sight of black-and-white photographs. Shown a photograph of a dog and told what it was, they were incredulous. Then, when the various features were pointed out ("This is the tail and this is an ear"), they were suddenly able to interpret the shadings before them (Deregowski, 1980). Colored pictures do not present the same problem: people who have never before seen a photograph seem to recognize colored photographs the first time they see them (Hagen and Jones, 1978).

Some psychologists have proposed that cultural factors have great impact on the ways people from different societies view the world. For example, most children in Western societies are exposed to picture books, and these experiences teach them to translate two-dimensional drawings into a three-dimensional world. It may be this special cultural experience that makes us susceptible to the Müller-Lyer illusion, which is based on our tendency to see acute and obtuse angles on a printed page as right angles in the world. People who have not had this special experience, such as members of the Zulu tribe in Africa, are much less susceptible to the illusion (Segall, Campbell, and Herskovits, 1966). Cultural differences in the susceptibility to illusions demonstrate the pervasive influence of experiences on perception.

SUMMARY

1. **Perception** is an organism's awareness of, or response to, objects and events in the environment brought about by stimulation of its sense organs. An adequate perceptual system must be able to isolate objects from their background, locate them in space, judge their movement, maintain a constant perception of the objects, and classify them. Perception is based on an active, constructive inference system that uses certain laws and regularities in the world to interpret stimuli. When sensory information is incomplete, the brain fills in missing details, as when it provides **subjective contours**.

2. The brain's organization of stimulation into perceptual groups follows certain principles. According to Gestalt psychologists, bits of information are organized into meaningful patterns, called gestalts. When presented with an array of stimuli, the brain uses **grouping** to enable us to achieve perceptual **simplicity**. This process allows us to perceive stimuli as coherent objects. The rules of grouping include **proximity**, **continuity**, and **similarity**. Continuity and similarity are at the basis of the effect known as **auditory stream segregation**. Perceptual processes also organize sensations by dividing stimuli into **figure**, regions that represent objects, and **ground**, the context in which figures appear.

3. **Visual depth perception** is the ability to tell

how far away an object is. In **binocular disparity**, the brain uses the slight differences in information received by each eye to infer depth, an ability known as **stereopsis**. We can also detect depth by using **monocular cues** that require information available to only a single eye. Monocular cues include **motion parallax**, differences in the relative movements of retinal images as we change position; **interposition**, in which one object partially blocks our view of another; **linear perspective**, the apparent convergence of parallel lines in the distance; **relative size**, the relationship between the size of the image projected on the retina and the distance of the object from the observer; and **texture gradient**, apparent differences in the density of texture cues of objects as distance increases.

4. Although retinal images of objects change according to the viewer's distance or angle from them, the brain tends to interpret objects as unchanging, according to the principle of **perceptual constancy**. In **size constancy**, the visual system takes into account the fact that the farther away an object is, the smaller the retinal image. Similar compensations are used to achieve constancy in shape, color, and location. **Illusions**, perceptions that do not correspond to real objects or events, are produced by physical or pyschological distortions. Geometric illusions, such as the Müller-Lyer and Ponzo illusions, result from a misapplication of the principles of size or shape constancy.

5. The perception of movement can be caused by our own movements or the movements of objects around us. An object is perceived to move when it changes its location relative to a spatial framework, by covering and then uncovering a line of background stimuli. When we are riding in a car, through motion parallax the constant flow of objects outside the car leads to the perception of movement. When stationary objects appear to move because their relation to a surrounding frame changes, the illusion of movement is known as **induced movement.** **Autokinetic movement** is an illusion of movement caused by unconscious eye movements, which make a stationary spot of light seem to move in the dark. **Apparent movement** can be created by a rapid succession of motionless stimuli. For example, motion pictures use the **phi phenomenon**, in which apparent motion is created by rapidly flashing a series of still pictures of objects changing their locations.

6. In **feature analysis**, perceptual objects are viewed as a structured collection of features, which form the distinctive characteristics that identify the object. However, the brain also uses **context**, or the setting in which stimuli appear, in pattern recognition, especially when the data are ambiguous. Gestalt psychologists stressed the importance of context when they proposed that the identity of basic perceptual stimuli is determined by the role they play in the overall scene.

7. Perception is also affected by our expectations, previous experiences, and motivations, which create **perceptual set**—a readiness to attend to and perceive certain stimuli in a specific way and to ignore other stimuli. Certain perceptual processes, such as size, shape, and depth perception, seem to develop during the organism's early life experience, especially when it includes active exploration of the environment. But active attention to moving visual objects may be enough to promote the development of depth perception. Cultural learning can lead to the development of perceptual biases. For example, the perception of such phenomena as optical illusions and photographs can be influenced by cultural experiences, which tell us how to "read" the three-dimensional reality that is represented by the two-dimensional picture.

KEY TERMS

apparent movement
auditory stream segregation
autokinetic movement
binocular disparity
context
continuity
feature analysis
figure
figure-ground reversal
gestalt
ground
grouping

illusion
illusory aftereffects of motion
induced movement
interposition
linear perspective
monocular cues
motion parallax
Pandemonium model
perception
perceptual constancy
perceptual set
phi phenomenon

proximity
relative size
similarity
simplicity
size constancy
stereopsis
subjective contours
subliminal perception
template matching
texture gradient
visual depth perception

RECOMMENDED READINGS

GREGORY, R. L. *The intelligent eye.* New York: McGraw-Hill, 1970 (paper). Gregory stresses the importance of perceptual inference, arguing that perception is a process of applying simple hypotheses about reality that depend upon sensory experience. The book is particularly strong in the area of visual illusions.

HOCHBERG, J. E. *Perception* (2nd ed.). Englewood Cliffs, N.J.: Prentice-Hall, 1978 (paper). A nicely illustrated update of a popular text. The author discusses research findings within the context of theory and places various problems within a historical framework.

LINDSAY, P., and D. NORMAN. *Human information processing.* New York: Academic Press, 1972. The first half presents a clear, readable account of information-processing analyses of perception. Especially good on how one might build feature detectors out of networks of retinal elements and units in the visual pathways.

ROCK, I. *Introduction to perception.* New York: Macmillan, 1975. This book takes a more cognitive approach to perception. The author adopts a constructivist position wherein perception is treated as a representational process. He argues that it is premature to analyze this process at the neuron level.

ROCK, I. *The logic of perception.* Cambridge, Mass.: MIT Press, 1983. A persuasively written research monograph arguing for the position that perception is a constructive, problem-solving process. Rock has an awesome grasp of the literature on perception; a significant text that is nonetheless accessible to the intelligent general reader.

SEKULAR, R. and R. BLAKE, *Perception.* New York: Random House, 1985. This text uses normal and abnormal experiences of perception as starting points in discussing perception, how it interacts with the senses and how it influences our thoughts and actions. Many simple, equipment-free demonstrations and over 300 photographs and drawings illustrate key concepts.

VARIETIES OF CONSCIOUSNESS

One day in 1962 the Canadian neurologist Wilder Penfield flew to Moscow to examine a new patient, the Nobel-Prize-winning physicist Lev Landau. Landau had been unconscious for six weeks, after an automobile accident left him with severe head injuries. Landau's limbs were paralyzed, his eyes were unfocused, and he seemed unable to see or understand anything. When Penfield recommended a minor diagnostic operation, Landau's estranged wife came to Moscow and visited her husband for the first time since the accident. As she told her unconscious husband about the proposed operation, Landau's eyes focused on her. Suddenly he appeared to see, hear, and understand. Her voice had roused him, and although he still could not speak or move, he had regained consciousness. A hemorrhage in the midbrain was blocking the passage of nerve impulses, but it allowed messages to pass between the brain stem and the uninjured cortex. Consciousness and understanding were present, although motor control and the ability to lay down new memories were lost (Penfield, 1979). As the hemorrhage was gradually absorbed, Landau began to recover, but he never remembered his meeting with Penfield nor anything that happened to him in the months after the accident.

Laudau's story dramatically illustrates a crucial point about consciousness. Consciousness is a separate, discrete function of the brain; it is different from memory, from motor control, and from processes in the lower parts of the brain. Yet, at the same time, consciousness has many aspects. No precise and satisfactory definition of "consciousness" has been produced: if we look at the ways we use the term, we find that it has many meanings (Natsoulas, 1978). It can mean being awake as opposed to being unconscious; or being aware of something in the environment, as when we are conscious of someone's presence; or choosing a course of action in contrast with being driven by unconscious motivation, as when we make a conscious decision. It can mean the flow of sensations, thoughts, images, and emotions —often called the "stream of consciousness"—or it can mean reflecting on that stream of consciousness. It can also refer to different states produced through drugs, meditation, hypnosis, or sleep.

Do all these uses of the word have any element in common? They do: the element of awareness (Natsoulas, 1983). In each of the meanings, we have cited, consciousness is directed toward a different object; but in every case it involves the awareness of some mental process. So the most general, workable definition for **consciousness** is an awareness of the mind's operations.

STUDYING THE NATURE OF CONSCIOUSNESS

Whatever definition we use, consciousness remains subjective—a private world, accessible mainly through introspection. For this reason, many psychologists in past years rejected consciousness as a topic of scientific study. Early behaviorists, whose goal was to establish psychology as an objective, verifiable science, believed that introspection had no place in psychology. They contended that psychology's proper task was to predict and control behavior, not to study inner experience. At that time, the behaviorists' argument was persuasive. Psychologists who were using introspection in their research could not agree on the nature of consciousness, and the behaviorists' proposals offered a new and exciting approach—one that promised to draw a sharp distinction between psychology's roots in philosophy and its aspirations as a natural science. The behavioral perspective soon dominated American psychology. Its ban on the study of mental processes was frequently challenged, but even the challengers agreed that any study of mental operations had to use objective, verifiable methods.

More recently, however, as knowledge about perception, memory, thought, and emotion has accumulated, psychologists have again become interested in consciousness. They are even using methods developed by behaviorists to make new inferences about the workings of the mind. Some researchers have examined the relationship of awareness to brain activity; some have investigated changes in consciousness produced by sleep, hypnosis, drugs, and meditation.

The Unity and Selectivity of Consciousness

Awareness, proposes Anthony Marcel (1983), is only one aspect of consciousness; consciousness also has the qualities of unity and selectivity. Our awareness is not an awareness of the world itself, or of our perceptual expectations and hypotheses (see Chapter 6); instead, we are aware of our perceptions of the world. Thus, when we talk about the "unity of consciousness," we are referring to the integrated nature of experience. For example, we perceive whole words, not just frequencies and intensities of sounds; we derive the meaning of words from the way we synthesize sensory information and perceptual hypotheses.

Likewise, when we talk about the "selectivity of consciousness," we are referring to the fact that our awareness is focused. We can choose our level of awareness; we can deliberately focus on an object's color, shape, identity, or function, or on the fact that we are categorizing objects in a particular way. This selectivity is crucial to our everyday functioning: so many sensations, feelings, thoughts, and memories are accessible at any given moment that attending to all of them would overwhelm us—and perhaps leave us unable to act at all. By screening out much of the information that is available to us, we can pay attention to some things and remain unaware of others. For example, the wide receiver is so intent on the quarterback's signals that he does not hear the screaming spectators in the football stadium.

Consciousness and Brain Activity

For centuries it has been believed that consciousness and brain activity are closely connected. Research supports this notion: stimulating parts of the cerebral cortex can produce conscious, though dreamlike, visual and auditory experiences (Loftus and Loftus, 1980). Yet although the evidence indicates that subjective awareness and brain activity are closely related, the nature of the relationship between mind and body has remained a puzzle. Many neuroscientists (e.g., Rose, 1973) have argued that the distinction between consciousness (or "mind") and the brain is purely semantic. Consciousness, they say, is simply the sum total of brain activity—nothing more.

The psychobiologist Roger Sperry (1977) disagrees with this definition. He proposes an interactional view: mind has a role in directing brain activity, but at the same time, brain activity is necessary for mind to emerge. Despite such insights, however, the connection between consciousness and brain activity remains mysterious.

Indeed, Sperry (1976) feels that it is "one of the most truly mystifying unknowns remaining in the whole of science."

Consciousness Is Limited

A good deal of the brain's activity is beyond our awareness. Although, as we saw in Chapter 3, the brain controls all our body systems, we generally do not notice their workings. For example, we are unaware of digestive activities, changes in blood pressure, or the release of hormones. Other types of brain activity that are initially conscious may eventually become automatic and move out of awareness. When we first learn to drive, we are highly conscious of each task; later, many of the processes involved in driving, such as steering, flipping on a turn signal, or shifting gears, become automatic. This transformation from focused attention to unawareness is typical of most skills we learn by extensive practice, such as typing, playing a piano, or riding a bicycle. The change is so significant that if we *try* to focus our awareness on some aspect of a well-learned skill, we may blunder —type the wrong letter, play a sour note, or fall off our bicycle.

Another example of brain activity that takes place outside our awareness is auditory streaming, which was discussed in Chapter 6. In a crowded restaurant, we have no problem following a friend's words despite the noise of voices, rattling dishes, and background music that surrounds us. We are conscious only of the message we have selected for processing. Nevertheless, the background sounds *are* noticed by the brain. In a simulation of this process, called **dichotic listening,** people wear a set of earphones through which they hear two different but simultaneous messages, one in each ear. When asked to repeat aloud the message received by one ear, most people can do so about as well as they can when there is no competing message being transmitted to the other ear (Cherry, 1953). Afterward, they have no memory of the second message; they cannot even say whether it was meaningful or a stream of nonsense syllables. But at some level of awareness, the second message was heard. People can say whether the "unheard" message was spoken by a man or a woman or both. And if the person's name is inserted into the "unheard" message, he or she is immediately aware of it.

Skill learning and dichotic listening exemplify the selective quality of consciousness. But some aspects of consciousness that remain out of awareness cannot ever reach our attention. For example, we are aware of our vision, hearing, memory, speech, and thinking, but we are not aware of which parts of the brain are involved in these processes (Schwartz, 1978). We are aware of the products of the mind, but not of the mind as a place (Taylor, 1982). This organization may puzzle us, and may lead us to think of the mind as being separate from the body. Nevertheless, it is a useful feature for adapting to the outside world.

Two additional lines of evidence indicate that complex cognitive activity can take place outside of awareness. Both come from patients whose brains are damaged in some way. Since some of these findings may reflect early brain damage from disease, or shifts in function by the brain to compensate for damage (Springer and Deutsch, 1981), we need to be cautious in applying this research to people with intact brains. Nevertheless, the evidence is intriguing, and the observations are consistent with other information concerning awareness.

The first line of evidence relates to the phenomenon which is known as blindsight. People who have suffered damage to the visual cortex, or who have tumors or damage to pathways between the lateral geniculate nucleus and the visual cortex, cannot see, but they can "guess" the direction of light flashes (Poeppel, Held, and Frost, 1973), or point accurately toward objects (Weiskrantz et al., 1974). Although such persons are blind, they still process visual stimuli, but they lack conscious awareness of them. Blindsight indicates that the visual cortex controls our awareness of vision, even though it does not control all functions of vision (Marcel, 1983). Visual stimuli are still processed by the blind, but the person is unaware of them.

A second indication of cognitive activity that is beyond awareness is found among split-brain patients, who have no neural communication between the hemispheres after the corpus callosum is severed. As was described in Chapter 3, when information is flashed to only the left visual field —and thus to the right side of the brain—the patient cannot say what he or she has seen. In Michael Gazzaniga's opinion (1983), our sense of awareness comes from the left hemisphere's attempts to explain the actions of the "multitude of mental systems that dwell within us" (page 536).

Consciousness Has Various Modes

Although not all mental processes are conscious, our conscious life is rich and varied. We can enter many diverse states of consciousness, each with its own distinctive quality of subjective experience (Tart, 1975). Some states occur naturally and are described as existing on a continuum that stretches from normal waking consciousness to dreaming (Martindale, 1981). Between these two poles lie four other states: realistic fantasy, autistic fantasy, reverie, and hypnogogic states.

■ **Realistic fantasy,** which takes a narrative form and is often problem-oriented, is most like normal consciousness; in it we may try out possible social strategies, such as how to go about asking for a raise.

■ **Autistic fantasy** lacks any orientation toward reality; we may imagine a sexual encounter with a rock star or exploits in a fantastic world. Daydreams, with which we're all familiar, may be realistic or autistic fantasy. Whether daydreams are realistic or autistic, individuals differ as to whether they have primarily positive or negative daydreams (Segal, Huba, and Singer, 1980).

■ **Reverie** has neither coherence nor control by the fantasizer, but consists of unrelated images, scenes, or memories.

■ **Hypnogogic states** lie between waking and sleep, and their automatic images may consist of vivid sights or intense sounds.

Dreams are automatic. They are also less coherent than we usually assume: it appears that their structure is often imposed by the waking mind in its attempt to recall them. A large part of this chapter will be devoted to a discussion of sleep, dreams, and the mental processes that are typical of this normally altered state of consciousness.

Some states of consciousness are deliberately induced by hypnosis, drugs, biofeedback, meditation, or sensory deprivation. Each of these states either increases or decreases the level of cortical arousal, which is controlled by the brain's limbic system, a structure linked with emotion and motivation (Martindale, 1981). Although these states differ from one another in many ways, we can use the measure of cortical arousal to place them on a continuum that takes the form of a curve (see Figure 7.1). This method of charting altered states was proposed in a provocative article entitled "A Cartography of Ecstatic and Meditative States" (Fischer, 1971). On this curve, in the direction of decreasing arousal, consciousness shifts from relaxation into tranquillity and then into states associated with meditation. Increases in arousal shift consciousness in the opposite direction,

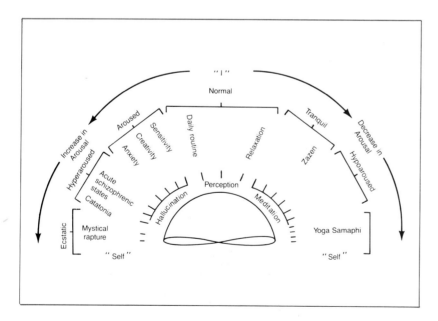

Figure 7.1. Most altered states of consciousness can be classified according to how much they increase or decrease the arousal of the brain's cortex. Thus, altered states can be arranged on a continuum from those associated with very high arousal to those associated with very low. (After Fischer, 1971.)

from the level of daily routine through creativity and into states associated with irrational behavior and ecstasy. These altered states of consciousness will be explored after we examine the state of sleep.

Sleep and Dreams

Few people consider sleep as a stage of consciousness, but despite our feeling that dreamless sleep is a mental vacuum, the mind remains relatively active during sleep. By investigating the nature of mental activity during sleep and dreams, we can get some idea of the sort of complex cognitive activity that can take place outside normal waking consciousness.

The Stages of Sleep

Much of what we know about sleep has come from records of the brain's electrical activity (EEGs), records of eye movements, and records of muscle activity during sleep (Dement, 1979). In a typical sleep experiment, electrodes are attached to a volunteer subject's scalp and face and connected to a device that monitors brain waves, eye move-

ments, and changes in muscle tension while the subject sleeps overnight in the laboratory.

Such studies have revealed the presence of five stages of sleep, through which the sleeper progresses—from wakefulness to deepest sleep and back again to light sleep (see Figure 7.2). This entire cycle occurs about every ninety minutes. The most reliable way to identify sleep is by the character of the EEG: each stage in the process of falling asleep is dominated by certain brain-wave frequencies, measured in cycles per second (Hz), as are sound waves. Beta waves are the fastest; they predominate in the EEG of a person who is fully awake and alert with eyes open. A person who is awake, but relaxed with eyes closed, typically displays a predominance of alpha waves, which are slower. As a person begins to fall asleep (stage 1, Figure 7.3), the pattern of waves changes. Alpha waves drop out and are replaced by slower theta waves. Sleep onset is thought to occur when bursts of high-frequency waves called sleep spindles start to appear (stage 2). As sleep becomes progressively deeper, the extremely slow delta waves become more predominant (stages 3 and 4).

When a person is in deep sleep (stage 4), muscles relax and heart rate and respiration are slow and regular. Because it is difficult to rouse someone from deep sleep, we know little about the nature of consciousness during stage 4. By the time a person is awake, it is difficult to tell whether

Figure 7.2. The kinds of sleep and their durations, as measured from midnight on, during a normal night's sleep of a twenty-five-year-old male. The horizontal axis indicates minutes elapsed. The vertical axis indicates types of sleep. Shaded bars represent periods of rapid eye movement (REM) sleep.

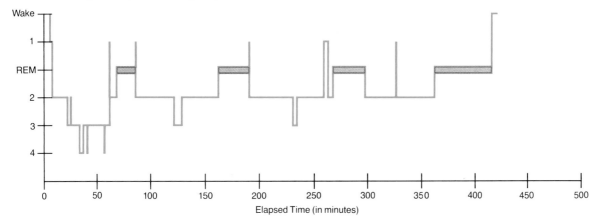

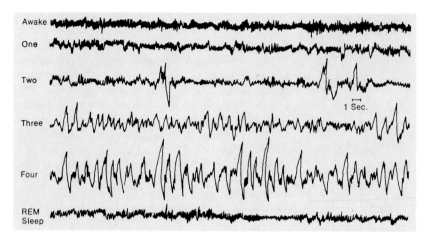

Figure 7.3. Records of the electrical activity of the brain (EEG) in a person in various stages of sleep and in the relaxed waking state known as "alpha." Note that in the deeper stages of sleep the high-frequency, small-amplitude waves give way to lower-frequency, large-amplitude waves. This change is thought to reflect the fact that the neurons in the brain are all firing at about the same level and in about the same pattern. Note also that the EEG pattern in REM sleep is very similar to stage 1.

whatever is recalled from sleep took place during stage 4 or during the wakening period. Yet we know that the brain is active during stage 4, because sleep disorders such as sleepwalking, sleep talking, and night terrors occur during this stage. (For a discussion of night terrors, see the box on page 167.)

Consciousness changes in several ways during sleep. We continue to monitor the outside environment and respond to it, but we are unaware of such watchfulness. Without awakening, we frequently change our sleeping positions. We sleep peacefully through meaningless sounds, but wake quickly to a meaningful sound (such as our name) of the same intensity (Oswald, 1962). This continual monitoring of the environment explains a mother's ability to sleep soundly through a thunderstorm but waken to her baby's faintest cry.

Not all people are able to monitor the environment while seemingly remaining oblivious to it. In some people, this ability is disrupted, and a form of insomnia may develop. Such insomniacs complain that they get little sleep, even though when they are brought into a sleep laboratory their EEGs show normal sleep patterns. If these persons are roused during stage 2 sleep, they are more likely than sound sleepers to say that they were awake when called (Borkovec, Lane, and VanOot, 1981). They give detailed accounts of their thoughts during sleep and can often accurately describe any sounds that occurred while they were sleeping (Engle-Friedman, Baker, and Bootzin, 1985). It appears that these insomniacs monitor the environment as others do, but are unable to shut the stimuli out of their sleeping consciousness.

REM Sleep

As noted earlier, sleepers gradually return from deep sleep to the stage 1 pattern, then begin the descent again to the deeper stages. When they reach stage 1, however, they do not wake up but enter another stage of sleep. At this time, their eyes move rapidly back and forth beneath closed eyelids; thus, the stage is known as **REM (rapid eye movement) sleep.** This stage of sleep, which was first described by Eugene Aserinsky and Nathaniel Kleitman (1953), has proved to be basic to an understanding of sleep and dreams. REM sleep occupies about 22 percent of a person's sleep time, or from one and a half to two hours each night, so that the average person goes through four or five episodes each night. Despite the division of sleep into five stages, the distinction between REM and other stages of sleep (collectively called **non-REM,** or **NREM, sleep**) is the clearest and most important.

REM Sleep and Dreaming

The movement of sleepers' eyes led researchers who were studying sleep to suspect that REM sleep might be related to dreaming. When these researchers woke the sleeping subjects, their suspicions were confirmed: sleepers awakened during REM periods reported dreams with vivid visual imagery at least 80 percent of the time (Webb, 1973). Sleepers wakened during a NREM period rarely reported dreams.

After studies had established the connection

TERROR IN THE NIGHT

A five-year-old child who has been sleeping peacefully suddenly sits up in bed and screams. Her mother rushes in and finds her daughter agitated but still asleep, although her breathing is labored and her pulse is beating wildly. None of the mother's consoling words soothes the terrified child, who seems dazed, talks incoherently, and stares ahead wide-eyed. After a few minutes, the girl's pulse and breathing return to normal and, without ever completely awakening, she returns to sleep. In the morning she has no memory of the attack.

The child's experience is known as a night terror, and it bears little resemblance to the familiar nightmare. Night terrors generally occur within the first two hours of sleep, during stage 4 sleep; nightmares occur much later in the night, during REM sleep. Night terrors are characterized by sudden sharp changes in the autonomic nervous system—increased pulse, respiration, skin resistance, and perspiration; nightmares show only the autonomic changes associated with REM sleep. A person in the grip of a night terror may get up and walk about; a person having a nightmare cannot move because of the muscle paralysis of REM sleep. Finally, night terrors are accompanied by amnesia, but a person can often relate the frightening content of a nightmare at length ("The vampire was chasing me and then I ran down a corridor and opened a door, and it leaped out at me").

Night terrors are most common among children between three and eight years old. This has led sleep researcher Ernest Hartmann (1981) to suggest that they are linked with the development of the nervous system and may indicate a mild neurological disorder due to faulty maturation in the brain stem.

Since these episodes generally disappear by adolescence, other sleep researchers (Mitler et al., 1975) recommend that when night terrors in children have no apparent cause, they should be allowed to run their course. However, parents should make sure that such children sleep in a room where they can come to no harm while sleepwalking.

Stress apparently increases the frequency of night terrors. When the terrors begin after a child's parents are divorced or the child has been in a serious accident, reassurance or psychotherapy may help lessen them (Hartmann, 1981). In severe cases, night terrors can be treated with Valium, which suppresses slow-wave sleep.

between rapid eye movements and dreams, the sleep researcher William Dement (1974) suggested that these movements reflected the movement of the dreamers' eyes while watching a dream unfold. Dement developed this "scanning hypothesis" on the basis of anecdotal reports from subjects in his laboratory. Attempts to verify the scanning hypothesis often involve studies of blind sleepers (Schwartz, Weinstein, and Arkin, 1978). Would blind people "watch" their dreams too? As it turns out, people who are blind from birth go through the same cyclical pattern of sleep stages as do sighted people, and they have periods resembling

REM sleep—but they do not have eye movements. If awakened, they also report dreams, except the dreams are not visual but auditory. However, this may not be the reason for their lack of rapid eye movements: they may have suffered eye damage, altering the electrical activity monitored in the laboratory. It is difficult to test the scanning hypothesis among sighted dreamers because most REM sleep is characterized by a complicated mixture of eye movements, with few clear, testable patterns. REM sleep is clearly more important than the simple scanning hypothesis implies, but its function is not yet clear.

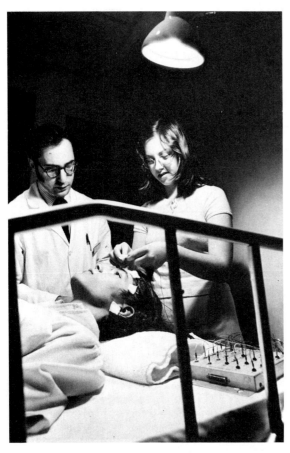

Modern research confirms the long-held belief that altered states of consciousness are related to variation in the activity of the brain. Researchers studying sleep, for instance, routinely monitor a subject's brain waves using electrodes applied to the scalp, as shown here. They have discovered that very distinctive brain-wave patterns are associated with the stages of sleep.

Unexpected Phenomena in REM Sleep

Although the person in REM sleep is obviously not awake, the EEG pattern shows more arousal than would be expected from a sleeper. In addition, there is an irregular and highly varied heartbeat, breathing rate, and increased blood pressure, along with signs of sexual arousal. These physiological signs resemble those of a person who is awake and highly excited. By other measures, however, the person is more deeply asleep than in NREM stages. During REM sleep, people are difficult to awaken and do not respond to touch or sound as quickly as during stages 2 and 3. Despite the aroused physical activity of REM sleep, major body muscles are relaxed—even limp. Because of these contradictory signs, REM sleep is sometimes called "paradoxical sleep": people seem to be awake, yet they are deeply asleep.

In the deepest sleep of stage 4, which is NREM sleep, muscles retain their tone; the body does not move because it has no orders from the brain to do so. During REM sleep, by contrast, there is a loss of muscle tone that temporarily paralyzes the muscles. The body does not move because it cannot (Dement, 1979). The marked drop in muscle tension is a sure sign of REM sleep. It appears that stimulation of a specific part of the brain causes this loss of motor control. When this part of a cat's brain is removed, the animal no longer lies still during episodes of REM sleep. Instead, it gets up, leaps, shows rage or fear, or plays with its paws as if a mouse were between them (Jouvet, 1975). The cat's behavior suggests that the paralysis that accompanies REM sleep keeps us from acting out our dreams.

Is REM Sleep Essential?

On the supposition that REM sleep might play a vital role in human functioning, Dement (1974) deliberately deprived people of the opportunity to dream. For several consecutive nights Dement woke the sleepers each time they entered a REM period. After a few nights it became increasingly difficult to arouse the sleepers as a REM stage began, and the longer they were denied REM sleep, the more often REM sleep appeared. When, on the fifth night, the sleepers were allowed to stay in REM sleep, they experienced a "REM rebound": the sleepers spent twice as much time in REM sleep as they normally would.

Since our bodies automatically compensate for a loss of REM sleep, it apparently fills some psychological or physiological need, but its precise function remains unclear. The restorative function of any sleep stage can be demonstrated only by inference from sleep deprivation studies. Most of these studies have shown personality and behavioral changes, such as aggressiveness, childish behavior, and increased appetite (Webb, 1973). But deprivation of any sleep stage may make a person tired or irritable; we also compensate for lack of stage 4 sleep (Agnew, Webb, and Williams, 1967). It has been suggested that our need for a particular sleep stage depends on the nature of our fatigue—on whether it results from heavy physical activity or from intense intellectual or emotional activity. A study of long-distance runners revealed that stages 3 and 4 sleep increased dramatically for two nights after they had run in a ninety-two-kilometer marathon (Shapiro et al., 1981). Physical tiredness may increase the need for deep sleep, whereas intellectual activity or emotional stress may increase the need for REM sleep—perhaps in part because REM sleep may restore the ability to focus attention (Hartmann, 1979).

There is indirect evidence that REM sleep helps maintain the responsiveness of the brain. Time spent in REM sleep steadily decreases as people age: newborns spend about half their time in REM sleep, infants under two years spend 30 to 40 percent, and adolescents and adults about 20 to 25 percent. As people reach their seventies, there is a further slight decrease in REM sleep (Williams, Karacan, and Hursch, 1974). Some researchers suggest that REM sleep stimulates the brain, enhancing the growth and maintenance of neural tissue (Anders and Roffwarg, 1973). This self-generated neural activity may prepare sensory and motor areas to handle the load of stimulation received from the environment during waking hours. The need for this sort of rehearsal should be greatest in newborns and decrease with age, and this is precisely the REM pattern (Roffwarg, Muzio, and Dement, 1966).

Just the opposite function for REM sleep has been proposed by Francis Crick (who shared the Nobel prize with James Watson for discovering the structure of the DNA molecule) and Graeme Mitchison (Crick and Mitchison, 1983). In this new theory of REM sleep, the brain is seen as requiring an active process of "unlearning" to prevent it from becoming overloaded. As Crick and Mitchison put it, "We dream in order to forget." They agree with other researchers (Hobson and McCarley, 1977) that during sleep the cortex is stimulated by nonspecific signals from the brain stem, and in response, cortical neurons fire, creating dreams. They suggest, however, that in this case the firing modifies neural networks by *weakening* the strength of synapses involved in undesirable activity patterns. In this theory, REM sleep becomes a period of erasure, assuring the brain sufficient neural capacity to meet its waking needs. Whether this theory will replace current views of REM sleep is uncertain, but it is a provocative theory that is sure to receive increasing attention.

Dreams

Just as we all seem to need REM sleep, we all dream—even those of us who claim we never do (Dement, 1979). Most of us judge our dreams by the relatively coherent, interesting, and sexy dreams we remember and tell others about, but dreams collected in sleep laboratories tend to be dull (Webb, 1979). Either we recall dreams selectively, remembering the more exciting ones and forgetting the rest, or else—since the home dreamer remembers only the last dream before awakening—dreams from earlier REM periods are less interesting than the final dream.

What Determines Dreams' Content?

Many of us wonder why we have the particular dreams that invade our sleeping consciousness. Do the environmental events that we monitor during sleep shape the content of our dreams? Studies have found that they do not. Such stimuli as sounds, temperature changes, or touches do not push us into a period of REM sleep nor initiate a dream. But if a sleeper is already in a REM period, stimuli from the environment may be incorporated into the dream's content. When water was sprayed on the faces of some volunteer sleepers, they reported more dreams involving water than did sleepers who were undisturbed (Dement and Wolpert, 1958).

Perhaps our dreams are determined by our problems and conflicts. Sigmund Freud (1900/ 1955) proposed that dreams express the hidden needs and desires of the unconscious mind. He believed that dreams had two levels of content —one obvious and the other hidden. The obvious, or **manifest content,** is a weaving of daily events, sensations during sleep, and memories. However, this manifest content actually disguises the dreamer's unconscious wishes, or the dream's **latent content,** which gives the dream its meaning. These wishes, which often rise from unresolved early emotional conflicts, are regarded by the dreamer as too evil to be expressed openly (Fisher and Greenberg, 1977).

During the past few decades, psychoanalysts have shifted away from Freud's theory of dreams; few still slavishly follow his method of dream interpretation. According to Calvin Hall (1979), dreams are not meant to conceal but to reveal, and their symbolism is not an attempt to veil early

Dreams are mysterious: the dreamer's world is not bound by time or space or by the conventions of waking life.

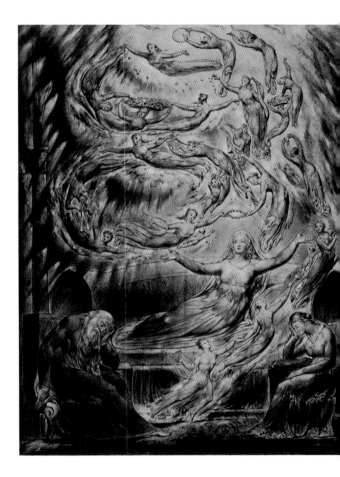

conflicts. However, in their reflection of the unconscious, dreams use visual metaphors. Since people are accustomed to expressing their ideas in words, not images, the visual metaphor seems mysterious.

More directly opposed to Freud's ideas about dreams is the theory that dreams are not mysterious at all but are simply the result of a physiological process (Hobson and McCarley, 1977). In this view, during REM sleep the cortex of the brain is activated by random stimulation. The dream that results is the brain's attempt to "make sense" of many random electrical messages. The fact that we dream four or five times a night on a regular cycle, and that this usually takes place outside our awareness, is consistent with this view.

On the other hand, since dreams often seem to concern themselves with our daily activities and problems, it would seem that random stimulation of the brain is not a complete answer. Studies in sleep laboratories indicate that the four or five dreams that occur during a single night are related and may deal with the same theme or problem (Cartwright, 1977). The night's first dream is the most realistic; the middle dreams are the most distorted and fantastic; the last dream is often focused on solving the problem. Whether the solution carries over into waking life is not known, but perhaps dreams have a problem-solving function.

Attempts have been made to gain awareness and control of dreams. Some people report having dreams in which they become aware that they are dreaming. Such dreams are called **lucid dreams**. One dream researcher who frequently has lucid dreams took part in a study in which dreamers sometimes managed to notify researchers that a lucid dream had begun (La Berge et al., 1981). The prearranged signals included fist clenches and sharp upward eye movements, which were recorded on graphs of eye movements and muscle tension. Some lucid dreamers report that once they become aware they are dreaming, they are able to change the course of the dream.

Is dream control within the grasp of everyone? At one time reports that certain tribal societies actively incorporated their dreams into waking life raised such hopes. It was believed that such groups made a regular practice of cultivating dream consciousness, mastering their dreams, and using them to work out social problems (e.g., Stewart, 1972). However, attempts to scientifically substantiate such practices have as yet failed.

Recalling Dreams

Some people always seem to have a new dream to report; others say that they rarely or never dream. Certain differences have been found between the two groups: those who often recall dreams tend to daydream frequently, to be good at creating visual imagery, and to have better visual memory than do people who rarely recall dreams (Cohen, 1979).

Since nearly all sleepers who are awakened during REM sleep report dreams, researchers have looked for additional explanations. It may be that habitual dream recallers tend to wake up from

REM sleep, whereas those who rarely recall dreams generally waken from NREM sleep (Webb and Kersey, 1967). Mood before sleep has been found to affect dream recall—negative moods increase dream recall (Cohen, 1979), perhaps because the unpleasant mood before sleep leads to poor sleep, which results in the sleeper's awakening from REM instead of NREM sleep.

Another reason for poor recall of dreams may be interference. Dreamers who awaken slowly, or whose attention is distracted as they awaken, are less likely to recall a dream than those who waken abruptly or who are not distracted. In studies, people who were asked to telephone the weather bureau as soon as they woke up and to write down the temperature before they recalled their dreams remembered about half as many dreams as did people who were asked to recall their dreams immediately on wakening (Cohen, 1979). There is some indication that people can increase their recall of dreams. Dream recall may be a skill that develops through an interest in dreams, a custom of paying attention to them, and a habit of telling others about dream experiences (Cohen, 1979).

HYPNOSIS

In the popular conception of hypnosis, the state of a hypnotized person resembles that of a sleepwalker—someone who has lost touch with waking awareness but behaves as if she or he were awake. Yet the sleepwalker and the hypnotized person differ in dramatic ways. On a physiological level, their oxygen consumption and EEG levels differ. During sleep, oxygen consumption gradually decreases, but during hypnosis it remains unchanged (Wallace and Benson, 1972). The sleepwalker, who is in deep sleep, exhibits the slow brain waves of stage 3 or stage 4; but the hypnotized subject's brain waves are those of a waking person. On a behavioral level, actions and memory differ. Sleepwalkers seem unaware that other people are around and will not follow instructions; hypnotized persons are aware of others and will follow most instructions. On waking, sleepwalkers cannot recall any wanderings; on emerging from hypnosis, hypnotic subjects remember the details of the experience unless they have been instructed to forget (Barber, 1975).

Hypnosis is obviously not sleep, but after years

of research psychologists still cannot say exactly what it is. Since hypnosis can be defined only by the behavior of hypnotized people, many psychologists doubt whether it should be considered a separate state of consciousness. And although hypnosis has been successfully applied in medicine and therapy, there is little agreement as to how it works.

Hypnotic Susceptibility

Most people are familiar with the process used to hypnotize a person. The hypnotist induces a trance by slowly persuading the subject to relax, lose interest in external distractions, and focus on the hypnotist's suggestions. Once the subject is relaxed, the hypnotist typically gives a few simple suggestions—such as that the subject's arm will rise. Only after the subject has complied with these easy suggestions will the hypnotist proceed to more difficult ones.

Not everyone can be hypnotized, but some researchers believe that about nine out of ten people can be hypnotized to some degree—if they want to be and if they trust the hypnotist (Williams, 1974). Psychologists measure the trait of hypnotic susceptibility systematically, through tests such as the Stanford Hypnotic Susceptibility Scale. In this test the subject is hypnotized, then the hypnotist offers a series of suggestions, such as "Your left arm will become rigid." Those who are unable to bend their arm more than two inches and who similarly respond to a dozen such suggestions, which include seeing an imaginary fly buzz around the room, are considered highly susceptible to hypnosis.

The Hypnotic State

Since no single objective measure correlates with a hypnotic trance and a hypnotized person shows no specific physiological changes, the status of hypnosis has not been settled. Some researchers, among them Ernest Hilgard (1975), take the position that we simply lack the appropriate measures. It has been only three decades since researchers discovered that rapid eye movements signaled a dreaming state. Until then, although personal experience testified to the uniqueness of dreaming, there was no scientific evidence that classified it as a discrete stage of consciousness. Similarly,

Table 7.1 ▪ Subjective Reports Based on an Inquiry Following Attempted Hypnosis

Inquiry	Affirmative Replies to Inquiry as Related to Hypnotic Susceptibility (Percent)*			
	High (N = 48)	Medium (N = 49)	Low (N = 45)	Slightly Susceptible (N = 17)
Were you able to tell when you were hypnotized?	65	60	47	31
Any similarity to sleep?	80	77	68	50
Disinclination to act:				
to speak?	89	79	68	31
to move?	87	77	64	50
to think?	55	48	32	12
Feeling of compulsion?	48	52	20	6
Changes in size or appearance of parts of your body?	46	40	26	0
Other feelings of changes:				
of floating?	43	42	25	12
of blacking out?	28	19	7	6
of dizziness?	19	31	14	0
of spinning?	7	17	0	6
of one or more of the prior four feelings?	60	60	39	25

*Based on an inquiry following the taking of one of the two forms of the Stanford Profile Scales of Hypnotic Susceptibility, after having scored at least 4 on SHSS-A; the insusceptible are not included.

Source: From Hilgard, E. R. *Divided consciousness: Multiple controls in human thought and action.* New York: Wiley-Interscience, 1977, Table 10, p. 164.

says Hilgard, hypnosis is a state that we can all recognize but cannot yet measure.

In the absence of psychophysiological measures of the hypnotic state, Ernest Hilgard (1977) lists the changes in behavior that hypnotists have long recognized as signs that a subject has been hypnotized. Among them are increased suggestibility; enhanced imagery and imagination, including visual memories from early childhood; compliance with the hypnotist's instructions; avoidance of initiative; and the uncritical acceptance of distortions of reality. Hypnotized persons firmly believe that they are in an altered state, and reports following attempted hypnosis show major differences in the experience of those who are highly susceptible and those who show only a slight susceptibility (see Table 7.1).

However, some researchers contend that these changes do not indicate a special state of consciousness because all of them can be induced outside hypnosis. In support of this view, Theodore Barber (1976; Barber, Spanos, and Chaves, 1974) argues that unhypnotized subjects can do all the feats attributed to hypnotized subjects—if the unhypnotized subjects are given instructions

that motivate them to do the tasks and are assured that they are capable of performing unusual feats. If Barber is correct, the existence of hypnosis as a separate state of consciousness is called into question.

Despite this controversy, what people do and experience under hypnosis demands some kind of explanation. In an attempt to discover whether changes induced by hypnotists are "real," Frank Pattie (1935) hypnotized a highly susceptible woman and told her that she was blind in one eye. The woman agreed that she had lost the sight of one eye, and her behavior indicated that her claim was real. Then Pattie ran a series of tests he had devised, stimulating her eyes in a way that made it impossible for her to tell, without cheating, which eye had been stimulated. If the supposedly blind eye were indeed blind, Pattie would have convincing evidence that hypnosis can actually block the registration of sensory impulses from the eyes. Although the woman insisted that her eye was blind, an extremely subtle test showed that it was not. After placing a red filter over her good eye and a green filter over her "blind" eye, Pattie asked the woman to look at the top line in Figure 7.4. If no

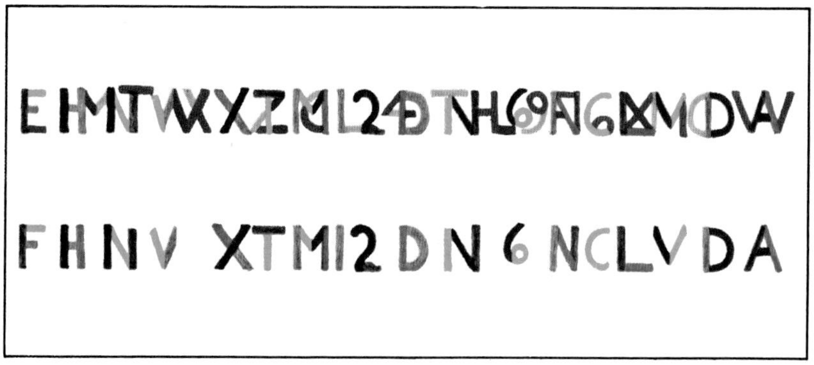

Figure 7.4. The technique used by Pattie to expose a suspected cheater in an experiment on hypnotically induced blindness. The subject was required to look at a line (top) of mixed colored letters and numbers with a red filter over her "good" eye and a green filter over her "bad" eye. The effects of the red filter are shown in the bottom line. If the subject had really been blind, she would have seen only a line of distinct letters and numbers. (After Pattie, 1935.)

sensory impulses from the blind eye were reaching the brain, the woman would have seen only what was visible through the red filter, shown as the bottom line in Figure 7.4. But she saw the entire display. Although she failed this test and was confronted with her failure, she clung to the belief that she was blind in one eye and swore she had not cheated. The sincerity of her claims seemed genuine. Why did she continue to insist that the eye was sightless?

Two explanations have been advanced to account for the woman's belief in her temporary blindness. The first explanation, called the **neodissociation theory** of hypnosis, claims that the woman was in a hypnotic state and, despite the normal physiological response of her blind eye, she was unaware of what that eye was seeing. This theory, proposed by Ernest Hilgard (1973; 1977), is based on the notion that consciousness depends on multiple systems (such as thought and emotion) that are coordinated through hierarchies of control. During hypnosis, those controls shift, and the system that governs behavior during normal consciousness is no longer a part of awareness. Although information continues to be registered and processed, it is no longer represented in consciousness (Hilgard, 1978).

The second explanation, called the **role enactment theory** of hypnosis, contends that the woman had done a skillful job of acting out the role of a hypnotized person as she understood it. This theory holds that hypnosis is not a separate state of consciousness, but is simply an extreme example of role playing. Like actors playing a role, the subjects take the part of a hypnotized person. The experiences they report are those they believe are appropriate for someone under hypnosis (Sarbin and Coe, 1972). Thus, the woman's insistence

that she was blind in one eye was typical of someone acting "as if" she were hypnotized. The question of whether a hypnotized person is in a unique state of consciousness or simply playing a role is also raised by the "regressive" handwriting shown in Figure 7.5.

The two explanations of hypnosis appear to be irreconcilable. However, Ernest Hilgard (1977) suggests that there may be two kinds of "susceptible" people. After comparing their scores on two different hypnotic susceptibility scales, Hilgard suggests that one group of susceptible people is truly hypnotizable and the other group is highly suggestible. Whether neodissociation or role enactment provides a better explanation for hypnosis, the phenomenon is remarkable. It has been used to anesthetize patients during surgery and to treat insomnia, migraine headaches, and psychosomatic allergies. Its value in the treatment of severe pain appears to be unique (Wadden and

Figure 7.5. Signatures obtained from hypnotized subjects with eyes closed under "normal" and "regression" conditions. In the "regression" condition each subject was asked to return to the second grade. Were the subjects temporarily reentering their past, or were they instead acting out an imagined second-grade self? A definitive answer to this question has not yet been found. (Hilgard, 1965.)

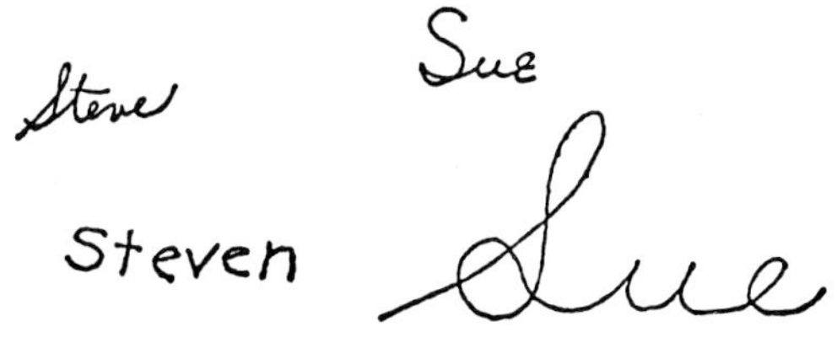

Anderton, 1982). No matter how hypnosis is eventually explained, these effects make it worthy of investigation.

Uses and Abuses of Hypnosis

Hypnosis has been used in therapy, in medicine, and in the courtroom, and as long as its limitations are understood, it can be used profitably in all three places. The use of hypnosis in therapy or medicine primarily affects the person hypnotized, so any misuse has fewer consequences. But when hypnosis is used in a courtroom, it can affect the lives of other people. This makes knowledge of its limitations imperative.

In legal cases, hypnosis is used primarily to enhance memory—the memory of the defendant, whose recall might prove innocence; the memory of the victim, whose recall might identify a culprit; or the memory of the eyewitness, whose recall might establish guilt or innocence. In most cases, courts have refused to admit as evidence information gained by hypnosis, but its use by both defense and prosecution continues to grow.

Yet after reviewing both criminal and civil cases, Martin Orne (1979) has urged caution in the legal use of hypnosis. He points out that people can pretend to be hypnotized and that the pretense is sometimes so skillful that it fools experts. Further, there is no guarantee that information recalled in a hypnotic trance is true. A hypnotized person is uncritical and compliant and, at the hypnotist's suggestion, obligingly fills in requested details. The problem is that many of these details are not recalled but imagined. As we shall see in Chapter 9, due to the nature of human memory, the imaginary details become thoroughly incorporated into the hypnotized person's memory, and she or he becomes convinced that they are real.

Orne sets forth four guidelines that he believes would make the use of hypnosis in legal cases far more reliable than it is today. First, only a specially trained psychologist or psychiatrist, who has received no verbal information about the case, should be used as a hypnotist. Second, the entire encounter between hypnotist and subject should be videotaped so that any suggestions inadvertently implanted by the hypnotist can be detected. Third, no observer should be present during the session, because the reactions of observers to the hypnotized person's statements can shape that person's "recollections." Finally, videotapes of all

interrogations should be available, so that it is possible to check for information that might have been implanted during earlier questioning. Orne believes that if hypnosis is used cautiously and if these instructions are followed, any harm that might come from misinformation will be avoided.

THE SELF-REGULATION OF CONSCIOUSNESS

The clinical applications of hypnosis depend on the suggestions and control of another person: the hypnotist. There are, however, techniques by which we can regulate our own consciousness. These techniques can be used to alleviate many conditions, including pain, psychosomatic disorders, and emotional problems. It is now clear that people can exert more control over their minds and bodies than once was thought possible.

In an early study, investigators monitored the brain waves of a yogi (an expert practitioner of the spiritual school of yoga) as he meditated. Once the EEG tracings started to show a steady flow of alpha waves, the experiment began. A psychologist struck a tuning fork and held it next to the yogi's ear. The stream of alpha waves continued unbroken—indicating that the yogi's brain had not responded to the sound. Nor was there any neural response to the sound of a hand clap, or to the burning sensation of a hot test tube on the yogi's bare skin. His awareness seemed separated from his senses; external stimulation produced no evoked potentials (see Chapter 3; Anand, Chhina, and Singh, 1961).

Since that study was performed, other approaches to the self-regulation of consciousness have been explored in the laboratory; we will consider some of the best-known techniques.

Meditation

The oldest method of self-regulation is **meditation,** a retraining of attention that alters a person's state of consciousness. There are two major paths to the meditative retraining of attention, and each leads to a different state of consciousness. First is the "path of concentration," used in yoga, transcendental meditation, and sufism. In it, the mind focuses on a specific object—whether actual or mental. Second is the "path of mindfulness," in

Figure 7.6. To meditate, it is necessary to empty the mind of distracting thoughts by focusing on a simple pattern or thought that will not lead to distractions. In some forms of meditation the meditator concentrates on a visual pattern such as the mandala shown here, which continually returns the gaze to its center.

which the mind observes itself; this method is used in the meditation techniques of Gurdjieff and Krishnamurti. Buddhism uses both approaches (Goleman, 1977).

In Eastern religions meditation generally becomes part of a comprehensive philosophy of life. Through meditation, the individual progresses systematically through different levels of consciousness, each seen as superior to normal waking consciousness (Paranjpe, 1984). Once the highest state of consciousness is reached, the meditator's life is permanently changed. Normal waking consciousness is transformed: the experiences of self and world are altered, so that personal goals and personal identity lose all importance. To others, the person's behavior and attitudes have become "saintly" (Paranjpe, 1984). Few people attain this state.

Learning to Meditate

People learn to meditate for varied reasons: some seek spiritual growth, others simply seek relaxation or clarity of thinking. In concentrative meditation, the person sits quietly, with eyes closed, focusing attention on one thing. When the person practices transcendental meditation (TM), which the Maharishi Mahesh Yogi developed from classical Indian techniques, the object of attention is a mantra, a sound that the meditator chants over and over. The object of attention can take any

form: short prayers, a picture, a candle flame, a spot in the lower abdomen, a bodily sensation, or a mandala, a design constructed so that the gaze always returns to the center, as seen in Figure 7.6. During this concentrative meditation, when awareness is focused on an unchanging source of stimulation, such as a mantra or a mandala, the effect is to turn off the meditator's awareness of the external world (Ornstein, 1977).

In mindful meditation, attention is on the body, on internal sensations, on mental states, or on the workings of the mind. The normal flow of breathing, the position of the limbs, or a mood can be the focus of attention, but no matter what the choice, its quality or goals are disregarded. During mindful meditation, the object is to open up awareness by realizing the random nature of stimuli that make up reality (Goleman, 1977).

Physiological Changes During Meditation

As a person meditates, his or her body functioning changes to resemble the state of deep relaxation, which is characterized by a slowed metabolism. In one study of people practicing TM, the subjects' oxygen consumption dropped; their breathing and heart rate slowed, their blood pressure fell, and their skin became more resistant to electrical conduction. After comparing these measures with those typical of sleep and hypnosis, the researchers (Wallace and Benson, 1972) concluded that meditation produces a state unlike either sleep or hypnosis.

The physiological changes of meditation resemble those of relaxation, and in many experiments, no differences have been found between the two states (Holmes, 1984). However, brain-wave patterns may distinguish between them. The nature of the change depends in part on the kind of meditation being done. Frequent alpha waves, at eight to twelve cycles per second, are normally found only in relaxed persons *whose eyes are closed*. A meditating person's eyes may be kept open, yet bursts of alpha rhythm appear in EEGs. How is this possible? Studies have shown that when a person's eyes are supplied with uniform visual input (such as that which results when halved ping pong balls are placed over the eyes), the sense of vision vanishes and alpha waves appear. In meditation, the unchanging sensory input from the mantra or mandala may have a similar effect on the brain (Ornstein, 1977). Some studies of meditators practicing TM show increased slow alpha waves (eight to nine cycles per second), along with the occasional appearance of even slower theta waves (Wallace and Benson, 1972). When Zen monks were tested, alpha wave activity appeared within fifty seconds after they began meditating, and as meditation continued, the alpha waves first increased in amplitude, then slowed in frequency; finally, theta waves began to appear (Kasamatsu and Hirai, 1966). Yet their eyes remained open throughout the meditation, and theta waves are not usually found in a person with open eyes. There is, then, suggestive evidence that the state of consciousness attained by highly experienced meditators can affect physiological functioning.

Biofeedback

The apparent control over involuntary bodily processes shown by experienced meditators attracted the interest of scientists. Although studies indicated that meditating yogis did not actually stop their hearts, as had been claimed, the yogis did seem able to slow both their heartbeat and their rate of respiration (Wallace and Benson, 1972). In recent years, with the development of electronic

technology, it has become possible for individuals to learn to control some normally involuntary processes without meditation. The technique is called **biofeedback.** Biofeedback uses electronic devices to monitor some physiological function and provide a continuous flow of information about it. The person being monitored receives the information in the form of lights, clicks, changes in sound volume, or displays on an oscilloscope screen. Given this constant feedback, some persons can, through trial and error, gradually learn to influence the normally involuntary functioning of some bodily system (Yates, 1980).

By helping people to regulate bodily processes, biofeedback has been successful in treating stress-related ailments, as we shall see in Chapter 21. For example, a patient who suffers from headaches caused by muscle tension in the neck and forehead sits in a comfortable chair in a dimly lit room. Electrodes pasted onto the forehead connect the patient to a machine that monitors muscle tension. When muscles in the forehead are relaxed, the patient hears a low tone through earphones. As muscles become tense the tone rises in pitch; the tenser the muscles, the shriller the tone. The patient's job is to keep the pitch of the tone low. By attending to slight body cues connected

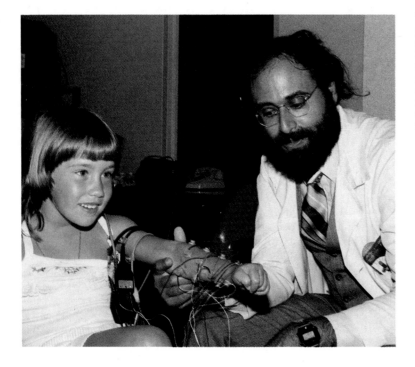

This girl, who suffers from cerebral palsy, has electrodes attached to the muscles of her wrist and hand. She looks at a television monitor, which displays electrical signals that travel from her brain to these muscles. She is learning to control these brain signals through biofeedback and operant conditioning; the aim is to return function to her spastic hand.

with muscle relaxation, he or she slowly learns to maintain a low tone, in the process developing some ability to keep forehead muscles relaxed.

The same general procedure—using biofeedback to learn to control a specific physiological response, then controlling it without biofeedback —has also been successful with migraine headaches, and in retraining muscles following strokes and injuries to the spinal cord (Olton and Noonberg, 1980). Such accomplishments indicate that active learning is going on as people gain control over these involuntary processes; yet learners cannot say *how* they exert control, although some may say that they have put themselves into "another state of mind."

Control through biofeedback is not easy, and some of the first claims about it that gained attention have been questioned. For example, biofeedback has been no more effective than relaxation training for people with high blood pressure, although it is often used as one aspect of treatment. Claims that biofeedback is effective in the self-regulation of alpha-wave production have also been criticized (Miller, 1974). It had been asserted that biofeedback training increased the production of alpha waves and led to a state of calm, blissful euphoria (e.g., Brown, 1974), but later research indicated no reliable connection between alpha-wave activity and such a subjective state (Plotkin and Cohen, 1976). In fact, other studies showed that people generate no more alpha waves through biofeedback than they do by closing their eyes and relaxing (Lynch, Paskewitz, and Orne, 1974).

Although biofeedback has failed to alter consciousness by increasing alpha activity, it appears to have successfully altered consciousness when providing feedback on theta-wave production (Budzynski, 1979). When using biofeedback to reduce the tension of forehead muscles, some people become relaxed enough to produce theta waves and thus to enter the hypnogogic state that lies between reveries and sleep—a state in which EEG tracings bear some resemblance to those of meditating Buddhist monks.

Sensory Deprivation

Meditation and biofeedback involve a kind of attention that shuts out the rest of the world and can alter consciousness. The requirements of some occupations, such as flying intercontinental airplanes or long-distance truck driving, can have a similar effect. For example, many truckers who have driven interstate highways in the western United States have had hallucinations, some of them leading to accidents when the trucker slammed on the brakes to avoid a stalled car that existed only in his mind (Hebb, 1969). Such reports, along with the experiences of shipwrecked sailors and prisoners in solitary confinement, have led researchers to investigate the effects on human consciousness of **sensory deprivation,** in which stimulation (visual, auditory, and tactual) is sharply reduced.

Adverse Effects

The first sensory deprivation experiments indicated that the experience was completely negative (Bexton, Heron, and Scott, 1954). Male college students lay on beds in partly soundproofed cubicles, cut off from the sensory stimulation of daily life. Translucent goggles eliminated the sense of vision, the hum of fans and an air conditioner masked any meaningful sounds, and gloves and cotton cuffs eliminated tactile sensations (see Figure 7.7). After an initial period of boredom, the students became restless, irritable, and unable to concentrate. Many of them hallucinated, some seeing colors or patterns and others seeing objects or scenes (one student reported a procession of squirrels with sacks over their shoulders marching across the snow). Many students found the situation so unpleasant that they refused to continue it, and when they emerged from the cubicles, most showed a temporary disturbance of vision, handwriting, and performance on tests of intellectual functioning.

While these men were in the cubicles, they became susceptible to persuasion. Compared with a control group, sensorily deprived students who heard taped messages advocating a receptive attitude toward extrasensory perception (ESP) were more likely to change their attitudes toward ESP in a favorable direction. Such findings led writers to call the experience "brainwashing." However, subsequent studies indicated that during sensory deprivation people are open to change only on topics that are trivial or on which the person has formed no opinion, and that highly intelligent individuals become hostile to the persuasive message (Suedfeld, 1969).

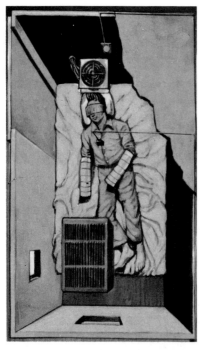

Figure 7.7. In a classic series of experiments on sensory deprivation conducted at McGill University in the 1950s, subjects were isolated in sound-resistant cubicles. Gloves and cotton cuffs prevented input to their hands and fingers; their sense of vision was eliminated; a foam pillow and the continuous hum of the air conditioner and fan made input to the ears low and monotonous. Except for eating and using the bathroom, the subjects did nothing but lie on the bed. Few chose to remain longer than three days.

Beneficial Effects

As further studies on sensory deprivation were conducted, it became clear that the experience was not always negative. Indeed, the stress of sensory-deprivation experiments appears to be in part the result of the subject's expectations. Whether the experiment is carried out under conditions similar to those used in the first experiment or whether the subject is "tanked"—immersed in a tank of highly saline, buoyant water in a dark, sound-proofed room—some people find the experience highly unpleasant, but most find it neutral. Others find it highly pleasant and ask to repeat it (Suedfeld, 1980). In early studies, subjects were led to expect that the situation might be unpleas-

ant or even harmful—they were given medical release forms to sign and "panic" buttons to push if the situation became too stressful. When people go through such threatening preliminaries and are then simply placed in a normally lighted room by themselves for a few hours, they often become disoriented or report unusual experiences —apparently from expectations alone (Orne and Scheibe, 1964).

People who adapt well to sensory deprivation seem to be those who relax and enjoy the sensations instead of becoming anxious. Because sensory deprivation provides a period that is free from distractions and external demands, it has been used in therapy. The isolation gives people a chance to think about their problems and consider possible solutions. Sensory deprivation has been effective in treating obesity and in helping people stop smoking (Suedfeld, 1980). Recently, researchers have begun to report cases in which the procedure has produced long-term reductions in high blood pressure (Fine and Turner, 1982; Kristeller, Schwartz, and Black, 1982; Suedfeld, Roy, and Landon, 1982).

DRUG-ALTERED CONSCIOUSNESS

Changes in consciousness also follow the ingestion of **drugs,** which may be defined as any inorganic substance that can interact with a biological system (Iversen and Iversen, 1975). This definition encompasses such substances as aspirin, antibiotics, and vitamins; thus, the truth is that almost all of us use drugs. In relation to consciousness, however, only **psychoactive drugs,** or drugs that interact with the central nervous system to alter mood, perception, and behavior, are of interest. As we saw in Chapter 3, chemicals have profound effects on behavior, and each drug that changes the chemistry of the brain induces a distinctive state of consciousness (Goleman and Davidson, 1979). Among the psychoactive drugs are such commonplace substances as the caffeine in coffee, tea, and many soft drinks, as well as powerful substances such as marijuana, alcohol, amphetamines, and LSD, which sharply alter consciousness.

Marijuana

Marijuana has a long history of use in Eastern societies and is an accepted psychoactive drug in some cultures that forbid the use of alcohol. Only within the past twenty-five years has it become widely used in the United States. Since the 1960s marijuana has become so common that among Americans older than twelve, one out of every three has tried marijuana and many have become frequent users. The popularity of marijuana has apparently peaked. After climbing dramatically during the 1970s, its use among individuals younger than twenty-five has leveled off (National Institute on Drug Abuse, 1983).

The consciousness-altering agent in marijuana is tetrahydrocannabinol (THC), a complex molecule that occurs naturally in three varieties of wild hemp, or cannabis. The plant can be dried to produce marijuana, or the resin exuded by the flowers of the female plants can be used to make hashish, a gummy powder that is up to ten times as concentrated as marijuana.

The effects of THC vary from person to person, and they appear to be heavily influenced by the setting in which the drug is taken. However, regular users generally agree as to marijuana's effects. The drug appears to heighten most sensory experiences: objects are more distinct, colors take on subtle shading, and drawings or photographs seem three-dimensional; musical notes sound purer and the rhythm stands out; food tastes better and familiar tastes take on new qualities; smells are richer; and sexual pleasure is intensified. A person taking the drug becomes euphoric and may find new meaning in the world or a profundity in mundane events. Time becomes distorted and may even seem to stop. Perhaps as a result, many marijuana users say they become totally absorbed in their drug experience. During these episodes of total involvement, their perceptual, imaginative, and cognitive resources are completely engaged (Fabian and Fishkin, 1981).

Marijuana also has a negative side: it can heighten unpleasant experiences. If a user is already frightened or depressed the drug may intensify the mood, until the user experiences acute anxiety accompanied by paranoid thoughts and may believe that he or she is ill, dying, or going insane. This effect is most likely to appear in an inexperienced user who takes an extremely heavy dose and is unprepared for its effects (Grinspoon, 1977). Cases have been reported in which unsta-

ble people developed psychological disturbances after using marijuana.

Although anecdotal accounts of marijuana's effects are plentiful, no well-controlled research was done on the drug until the late 1960s. One of the early experiments studied college students, some of them experienced users and others who had never used the drug. All the experienced users reported the typical euphoric "high," but none showed impaired intellectual and motor skills. In contrast, only one of the inexperienced subjects got "high," but all of them showed intellectual and cognitive impairment (Weil, Zinberg, and Nelsen, 1968). Other studies have shown that reaction time, attention, time estimation, motor coordination, and driving skills are generally impaired by marijuana but that the experienced user appears to be able to "come down" when necessary to carry out a task (Grinspoon, 1977).

Perhaps the most consistent finding is that marijuana interferes with some aspects of memory. People under the influence of marijuana may be unable to recall some information from memory. Their ability to store information for later recall may also be disrupted, and they often have difficulty remembering information presented only a few seconds earlier. They are more likely to answer requests for such information with material not even presented than are people who are not under the influence of the drug (Miller and Branconnier, 1983). The pattern of memory dysfunction that appears while people are under the influence of marijuana resembles the memory loss seen in patients with Alzheimer's disease (see Chapter 3). This similarity may indicate that marijuana and Alzheimer's disease both affect the same neural pathways (Miller and Branconnier, 1983).

Although some studies claim to find brain damage, fetal malformation, or intellectual impairment from chronic marijuana use, careful examination has found no convincing evidence that habitual use causes such permanent damage (Grinspoon, 1977). The first study (Schaeffer, Andrysiak, and Ungerleider, 1981) of long-term use among Americans found no long-term cognitive effects after more than seven years of extremely heavy use. Intellectual functioning among these ten adults was above average, and was virtually identical with that shown in tests they had taken fifteen to twenty years previously.

A report commissioned by the Institute of Medicine (1982), which reviewed all marijuana research, concluded that marijuana suppressed the production of male hormones and decreased sperm production, but that as soon as men stopped using the drug, the effects were rapidly reversed. However, the report indicated that chronic marijuana use may affect the lungs. Since marijuana smoke contains about 50 percent more carcinogenic hydrocarbon than does tobacco smoke, and since laboratory exposure of human lung cells to marijuana smoke produces changes that are characteristic of early cancer, health authorities are concerned that heavy, prolonged marijuana use could lead to lung cancer. There also appears to be a mild, temporary effect on the body's immune system, so that users might be more susceptible to infection. The amotivational syndrome (apathy, loss of ambition, difficulty in concentrating) does exist among marijuana users, but there is some indication that it may be primarily an accentuation of existing behavior (Maugh, 1982). It appears that the risks associated with short-term marijuana use are slight, but that until more research has been done, we cannot be certain about the long-term effects of regular use.

Stimulants

Drugs that stimulate the central nervous system increase heart rate, blood pressure, and muscle tension. The heart contracts more strongly, blood vessels constrict, the bronchial tubes and the pupils of the eyes dilate, and the adrenal glands go into action (Combs, Hales, and Williams, 1980). The major **stimulants** used to alter consciousness are nicotine, caffeine, cocaine, and amphetamines.

The arousal of the central nervous system by cigarette smoking, the commonest method of nicotine ingestion, is accompanied by a reduction in the amount of alpha-wave production and an increase in the speed of the remaining alpha waves —just the opposite of meditation. EEGs of smokers also show increased high-frequency beta-wave activity. These EEG changes are reversed when users stop smoking, and nicotine withdrawal is often followed by depression, irritation, anxiety, tension, restlessness, drowsiness, and an inability to concentrate. Nicotine-related EEG changes are reflected in behavior: chronic smokers often have trouble sleeping. Studies in the sleep laboratory show that it takes smokers longer than nonsmokers to fall asleep. When smokers abruptly give up

nicotine, they immediately begin to sleep better, despite the discomfort that follows withdrawal of the drug (Soldatos et al., 1980).

Caffeine, another central nervous system stimulant, is found in tea, soft drinks, chocolate, and cocoa, but the commonest source is coffee. Unlike the many drugs associated with recreation, caffeine is associated with work. Since it increases alertness and reaction time, most users feel that it improves their daily performance. But excessive doses of caffeine can lead to restlessness, irritability, and sleep disturbance, and abrupt withdrawal from the drug is often followed by headaches and depression.

Cocaine, a product of the leaves of certain coca plants, is a potent stimulant that is usually taken in the form of a white powder. When it is inhaled, or "snorted," into the nostrils, cocaine is absorbed into the bloodstream through the mucous membranes. It may also be injected intravenously. Although cocaine is both illegal and expensive, in recent years its use has spread. Today more than 25 percent of adults between the ages of 18 and 25 say that they have tried cocaine (National Institute on Drug Abuse, 1983).

Most of the information we have on the effects of cocaine comes from interviews of users (Grinspoon and Bakalar, 1976). One of the few laboratory studies of the drug indicates that a moderate dose produces a euphoria that can last more than half an hour (Resnick, Kestenbaum, and Schwartz, 1977). Users claim that it improves attention, reaction time, and speed in simple mental tasks and that it sharpens memory; they find it helpful for work that requires alertness and a free flow of associations. It also appears to suppress boredom and fatigue. Because of their euphoria, people who have taken cocaine often overestimate both their own capacities and the quality of their work. Because cocaine is a stimulant, it produces a burst of energy, but when the drug wears off, physical exhaustion, anxiety, and depression may follow (Resnick, Kestenbaum, and Schwartz, 1977).

Large doses of cocaine may be followed by hallucinations. For example, users sometimes become convinced that bugs are crawling beneath their skin. This effect is probably caused by a drug-induced hyperactivity of nerves in the skin. Massive injections of cocaine may cause headaches, hyperventilation, nausea, convulsions, coma, or even death. The effects of long-term use can be serious. Perhaps the most widely known effect is irreversible damage to the mucous membranes of the nasal septum, which separates the nostrils. Less well-known is a general poisoning of the system, characterized by mental deterioration, weight loss, agitation, and paranoia.

Amphetamines, generally called "speed," are synthetic drugs. In moderate doses they produce euphoria and energy, increase alertness, and improve reaction time and physical coordination. Anxiety and irritability often accompany the use of amphetamines, but the real danger is amphetamine psychosis, which produces a condition nearly indistinguishable from schizophrenia. For the habitual user to reach a "high," doses of amphetamines must be continually increased, and users may switch from pills to intravenous injections, each containing the amphetamines normally found in about twenty pills. The addict, or "speed freak," injects the drug every three to four hours over a period of nearly a week, then "crashes," and sleeps for several days. Awakening is accompanied by acute hunger and a depression that responds only to more amphetamines. While such massive doses of amphetamines are being taken, amphetamine psychosis may appear. This condition is characterized by paranoia and the compulsive repetition of trivial behavior—for example, one adolescent spent hours counting cornflakes (Snyder, 1979).

Amphetamine psychosis can probably be traced to the drug's chemical structure. Amphetamines resemble certain neurotransmitters; they build up around synapses, leading neurons to fire again and again and exaggerating behavior that is governed by the part of the nervous system where those transmitters function (Snyder, 1979). The resemblance between such amphetamine-based behavior and the behavior of schizophrenics may provide cues that will enable researchers to untangle the genetic, chemical, and environmental causes of schizophrenia, and may perhaps lead to a way of preventing or curing this serious mental disorder.

Depressants

Depressants retard the action of the central nervous system, so that neurons fire more slowly. In small doses they produce intoxication and euphoria, but they also decrease alertness and motor coordination and increase reaction time. Large doses produce slurred speech, unsteadiness, and unconsciousness. The major depressants are alcohol, barbiturates (often known as "reds," "yellow jackets," or "blues"), and tranquilizers, such as Librium or Valium. When taken together, depressants are **synergistic**—that is, the effect of two depressants is greater than the sum of the two drugs' effects. For example, if alcohol is drunk with a barbiturate, the effect is four times (not twice) as great as that of either of the drugs taken alone (Combs, Hales, and Williams, 1980).

Depressants are often taken to relieve insomnia, but because tolerance develops quickly, increasingly larger doses are needed to get the same effect. For this reason, people who require alcohol or barbiturates in order to sleep risk accidental overdose. Depressants also block REM sleep. As a result, when an insomniac tries to sleep without the drug, the REM rebound leads to fitful sleep, filled with restless dreaming and nightmares. The experience is so unpleasant that the individual often returns to the bedtime dose of depressant. Yet continuous use of depressants eventually leads to a pattern of disrupted sleep with frequent wakenings, so that individuals neither sleep well with the depressant nor feel they can sleep without it.

The most common depressant is alcohol. Its initial effects depend on the mood of the drinker and the setting, and may be euphoric or depressing. A couple of drinks often produce a sense of relaxation and well-being, lightheadedness, and a release of inhibitions. It was once thought that people's tendency to say or do things they ordinarily would not do could be traced to the depressive influence of alcohol on the inhibitory centers of the brain. However, laboratory studies indicate that the relationship is not so simple: the drinker's expectations may have a more powerful effect on the release of inhibitions than the amount of alcohol consumed (Briddell et al., 1978; Lang et al., 1975).

Alcohol also affects memory, impairing the ability to process and store new information, although intoxication has a minimal effect on the ability to recall old information (Loftus, 1980). Alcohol's effect on the storage of new information is stronger when a person is becoming intoxicated than when she or he is beginning to recover from the peak period of intoxication.

The long-term effects of alcohol on memory and information processing depend on how much alcohol is generally drunk at a time, not on the total amount consumed over the years. People whose drinking patterns show heavy inebriation on widely separated occasions are more likely to show intellectual impairment than people who spread the same amount of alcohol over longer periods of time. Apparently the brain can handle a drink each day better than it can handle seven drinks on one day followed by six days' abstinence (Parker and Noble, 1977).

Chronic, heavy alcohol use can lead to alcoholism, a major form of mental disorder, which is discussed in Chapter 22. Chronic alcoholics often have memory blackouts: after they have sobered up, they cannot remember what happened the night before. However, social drinkers can also have such blackouts; these are likely to occur when the drinker gulps a lot of alcohol quickly, is extremely tired, or takes another depressant while drinking (Loftus, 1980).

Ironically, withdrawal from chronic, heavy alcohol use can adversely alter the state of unconsciousness. When the level of alcohol in a chronic alcoholic's blood suddenly drops, the alcoholic may enter delirium tremens (DTs). During the three to six days it takes for the DTs to run their course, the individual trembles intensely, sweats heavily, becomes disoriented, and is beset with nightmarish delusions.

Hallucinogens

Hallucinogens—which get their name from their ability to produce hallucinations—have been used to alter consciousness from the beginnings of recorded history (Schultes, 1976). Because some people believe these drugs demonstrate the potential for an expansion of human consciousness, they are also called "psychedelic," or "mind-manifesting." Although hallucinogens are not so widely used as other drugs, one out of every ten Americans older than twelve has taken a hallucinogen at least once (National Institute on Drug Abuse, 1983).

Hallucinogens are found in many common plants, including belladonna, henbane, mandrake, datura (Jimson weed), morning glory, peyote cactus, and some mushrooms. Synthetic hallucinogens include lysergic acid diethylamide (LSD) and phencyclidine (PCP). Although the precise effect of these chemicals on the brain is unknown, some appear to mimic the activity of neurotransmitters and thus they alter the activity of brain cells.

Mescaline, which comes from the peyote cac-

tus, is used by the Native American Church of North America in its religious rituals. The drug produces vivid hallucinations; its effects were carefully described by the British writer Aldous Huxley (1979), who believed that mescaline opened "the doors of perception." Huxley found that his visual perceptions were intensified while he was under the drug's influence—a small bouquet of flowers became a miracle "shining with their own inner light" and full of the significance of all existence.

One of the synthetic hallucinogens, PCP, or "angel dust," may be taken by mouth, smoked along with marijuana, snorted, or injected. In low doses it produces hallucinations, but in large doses it can produce stupor, coma, or death.

The other major hallucinogen, LSD, is one of the most powerful drugs known. Extensive studies have indicated that it is 4,000 times stronger than mescaline. After taking an average dose (100 to 300 micrograms), the user embarks on a "trip" that lasts from six to fourteen hours.

An LSD trip is unpredictable because the situation in which the drug is taken and the user's initial mood, beliefs, and expectations of the drug's effects have a powerful influence on the total experience. Since the drug affects mood, the user may go through a series of intense mood changes. LSD commonly causes a variety of perceptual hallucinations. For most people, the first hallucinations take the shape of simple geometric forms. These abstractions soon change to complex images and then to dreamlike scenes (Siegel, 1977). Perception may be so distorted that familiar objects are unrecognizable. A wall, for example, may seem to pulsate, breathe, or even melt. Sensory impressions become crossed, so that the user may claim to "see" sounds and "hear" sights. The self may seem to split into one being who observes and another who feels. Time may speed up or stretch out interminably.

LSD can have unpleasant side effects; the most common are panic reactions, and they can be terrifying. Panic usually develops among users who try to ignore or shake off the sensations produced by the drug and discover that it is impossible to do so. When the panic is severe, medical attention may be required.

Researchers have found LSD helpful in their study of the brain's biochemical functioning. The chemical structure of the LSD molecule is related to serotonin, a neurotransmitter that may play an important role in the regulation of sleep and emotion. LSD appears to block the effect of serotonin on brain tissue, perhaps by mimicking the neurotransmitter at the neural receptors. This blocking effect may account for some of LSD's effect on behavior, but exactly how the drug works is not known (Iverson, 1979).

SUMMARY

1. **Consciousness** is an awareness of the mind's operations, but consciousness also involves unity and selectivity. An awareness of one's perceptions of the world is an integrated experience that focuses on a particular level of perception, screening out other levels. The precise nature of the connection between consciousness and brain activity has not been established, with some neuroscientists arguing that consciousness is the total of brain activity and others proposing that the mind directs the brain's activity but that brain activity is necessary for the mind to emerge. Much brain activity is beyond awareness, as the lack of awareness that characterizes practiced activities and studies of **dichotic listening** indicate. The natural states of consciousness appear to lie on a continuum that consists of normal waking consciousness, **realistic fantasy, autistic fantasy, reverie, hypnogogic states,** and sleep. Deliberately altered states of consciousness can lead to irrationality and ecstasy when the alteration arouses the nervous system or to tranquillity and meditation when the alteration lowers arousal.

2. Mental activity continues during sleep. During sleep, the outside environment is monitored although the stimuli are shut out of sleeping consciousness. EEGs recorded during sleep indicate five stages of sleep, each dominated by certain brain-wave frequencies. Beta waves are fastest, followed by alpha waves, theta waves, and delta waves. During a night's sleep, a person progresses through the five stages in a regular cyclical pattern that recurs about every ninety minutes. **REM sleep,** characterized by rapid eye movements, occurs when the brain waves return to a state similar to that of a waking person. In **non-REM (NREM)** sleep, the mind's activity consists of drifting, unstructured thoughts and images, but REM sleep is characterized by vivid dreams. The function of REM sleep is unclear. It may allow the brain to adapt to daily experiences, or it may erase neural connections.

3. Some of a dream's content comes from stimuli near the sleeper, but most is supplied by the dreamer's mind. Freud believed that the **manifest content** of a dream derives from daily events, sensations during sleep, and memories, but that the **latent content** consists of disguised unconscious wishes. Most psychoanalysts have either modified or abandoned Freud's theory of dreams. Dreams appear to concentrate on waking problems and may have a problem-solving function. Some people have **lucid dreams,** in which they are aware they are dreaming. People who frequently remember dreams may do so because they wake directly from REM sleep, whereas those who rarely recall them may waken from NREM sleep. Some failure to recall dreams may be due to interference brought on by slow awakening or distracted attention.

4. No specific physiological changes correlate with the hypnotic state. The consequent difficulty of defining hypnosis except by describing the behavior of hypnotized people has caused many psychologists to doubt that hypnosis represents an altered state of consciousness. Two major theories have been advanced to explain hypnosis. **Neodissociation theory** suggests that consciousness depends on multiple systems that are coordinated in hierarchies of control; during hypnosis the controls shift and the system that normally governs behavior is no longer aware of processed stimuli. **Role enactment theory** sees hypnosis as a special case of role playing, in which the subject is guided by the hypnotist and his or her own beliefs concerning the hypnotic experience. Hypnosis is used in medicine, therapy, and the legal system, but its use in court cases requires precautions to avoid the subject's incorporation of fantasy into memory.

5. Consciousness can be self-regulated by meditation or biofeedback. **Meditation** alters consciousness by retraining attention; it produces physiological changes characteristic of deep relaxation as well as distinctive changes in brain waves. **Biofeedback** provides a person with a continual flow of information about some physiological function, which enables the person to learn to alter the monitored function.

6. **Sensory deprivation** alters consciousness by sharply reducing visual, auditory, and tactual stimulation. It apparently leads to a hypnogogic state, which people may find unpleasant, neutral, or highly pleasant.

7. **Psychoactive drugs** interact with the central nervous system to alter a person's mood, perception, and behavior. Marijuana enhances most sensory stimuli and can heighten both pleasant and unpleasant sensations; its effects vary with the person and the setting. **Stimulants,** including nicotine, caffeine, cocaine, and amphetamines, stimulate the central nervous system and speed up other physiological systems. In small doses, most increase alertness and reaction time, but large doses of cocaine can produce hallucinations, coma, or death, whereas large doses of amphetamines can produce amphetamine psychosis. **Depressants,** including alcohol, barbiturates, and tranquilizers, retard the action of the central nervous system, and they are **synergistic.** In small doses they produce euphoria; in large doses they produce unsteadiness and unconsciousness. **Hallucinogens,** such as mescaline, PCP, and LSD, produce hallucinations. Their exact chemical effects on the brain are unknown, but they may mimic the activity of certain neurotransmitters.

KEY TERMS

autistic fantasy	hypnogogic states	realistic fantasy
biofeedback	latent content of dreams	REM (rapid eye movement) sleep
consciousness	lucid dreams	reverie
depressants	manifest content of dreams	role enactment theory
dichotic listening	meditation	sensory deprivation
drugs	neodissociation theory	stimulants
hallucinogens	non-REM, or NREM, sleep	synergistic
	psychoactive drugs	

RECOMMENDED READINGS

DEMENT, W. C. *Some must watch while some must sleep.* San Francisco: W. H. Freeman, 1976. One of the pioneers in modern dream research presents a brief, readable, up-to-date account of what is known about sleep and dreaming. Gives special attention to the relationship between sleep and psychological disorders, including insomnia and mental illness.

HILGARD, E. *Divided consciouness: Multiple controls on human thought and action.* New York: Wiley, 1977. A presentation of neodissociation theory, developed by Hilgard.

KLEIN, D. B. *The concept of consciousness.* Lincoln, Neb.: University of Nebraska Press, 1984. It includes chapters on split-brain research, mystical experiences, and altered states of consciousness.

RAY, O. *Drugs, society, and human behavior.* St. Louis: Mosby, 1983. A lucid, lively, and thorough presentation of drug research and the impact of "recreational" drugs on society. Includes a section on psychotherapeutic drugs.

ORNSTEIN, R. E. The psychology of consciousness (2nd ed.). New York: Harcourt Brace Jovanovich, 1977. Introduces a wide variety of research on human consciousness. It is well written and covers a broad range of topics.

SARBIN, T., and W. COE. *Hypnosis.* New York: Holt, Rinehart and Winston, 1972. An analysis of hypnosis from the standpoint of role theory.

PART THREE

LEARNING AND COGNITION

The physical body (including the brain) is not the only thing that evolves. Ways of thinking evolve, too. The human being differs from other animals in being able to adapt, mentally, to different environments.

Originally, we were hunters and gatherers in the grasslands, but we learned to adapt ourselves to the cold weather of the ice ages, to live in caves, and to use fire. We adapted ourselves to the forethoughful rigors of agriculture and, with extraordinary speed, to the complexities of industrialization.

We can see this in individuals, too. My father spent the first third of his life in a primitive village in western Russia, then came to America and had to learn to make his way in the most complex and advanced city of the world—New York. He managed.

The only mind, of course, that I can examine from the inside is my own. It is hard for me to be objective about myself but, in all honesty, I have always been considered by others to be highly intelligent. (I agree with this assessment, but that is neither here nor there.)

When I entered the first grade, I had already taught myself to read (with some help from older boys) so it wasn't long before I was push-ed along into a more advanced class. Unfortunately, I hadn't taught myself everything, and I suddenly found myself being asked to multiply. I knew that 8 plus 7 was 15 and that 8 minus 7 was 1, but the teacher's insistence that 8 times 7 was 56 had me flabbergasted. I had never heard of multiplication and I could make nothing out of it. I went home humiliated and weeping.

My poor mother was an unschooled immigrant woman and didn't know what I was talking about. My father was at work. My mother, therefore, went next door, got an older girl of about eight, and asked her to explain whatever it was I wanted to know.

The girl dutifully started drilling me in the "1 times," then the "2 times." By the time she began the "3 times," something clicked. I had a little notebook that I used for my school work, and on the back there were conversion tables—so many inches to a foot, so many feet to a yard, so many pints to a quart, and so on. It was all vaguely interesting, but mysterious. There was also a square array of numbers, with columns and rows that were arranged with considerable regularity. I didn't know what it was, but I was already fascinated by numbers so I had studied that array carefully and repeatedly.

Now those numbers came back to me as the girl went through the dull list. I said, "Wait!" I ran for my book, pointed to the collection of numbers on its back and said, "What's that?"

"That's the multiplication table," she said.

"Oh," I said. "Then I know how to multiply," and I sent her home.

In studying the table, I had memorized all the numbers, and now that I looked at it with new eyes, I could see how one could use it to find any multiplication from 1 times 1 to 12 times 12. I didn't even have to simply memorize the products (though I had), for I could see from the organization of the table what multiplication was, and I knew that if I forgot that 8 times 7 was 56 (fat chance!) all I had to do was add seven 8s together, or eight 7s. It would take longer, but I would get the right answer.

And that is the remarkable thing about the human mind. Not that it can force itself to remember dull lists by rote, but that a sudden abstract insight can flash upon it, even at the age of six.

Isaac Asimov

LEARNING

What would life be like if we could not learn? We would not survive for long. Even though our sensory systems could pick up information, we would not be able to retain that information in our brain.

■ If we found a tree full of fruit on Monday, we would have to rediscover it on Tuesday; every time we felt thirsty, we would have to look for a cool stream all over again, no matter how many times we had visited the stream before.
■ There would be no crops to harvest because no one would know that sowing seeds produced grain, that grain ground into flour could be made into bread dough, or that heat could transform the dough into finished loaves.

■ And even if we escaped starvation, we would be easy prey, because we would not know that a pack of hungry wolves might have a taste for human flesh. Nor would we know how to avoid a predator if we did realize we were in danger.
■ If we could not learn, we could not live—and so it is that all animals show learning.

Some organisms, it is true, do not learn very much. Simple organisms live largely by reflexes, meaning that most of their reactions are "hard-wired": when they are confronted with a particular situation, they are genetically prepared to act in a certain way. If conditions change abruptly—for example, if an ice age suddenly causes the climate to become colder—they will be unable to adapt and will die. But as long as their environment remains stable, they thrive—eating, sleeping, mating, and avoiding predators. Within a narrow band of environmental conditions, their "hard-wired" behavior is adaptive.

More complex organisms, by contrast, have a relatively great ability to learn, and there is a relatively small proportion of predetermined, "hard-wired" behavior in their activities. Human beings, in particular, are well equipped for learning new ways to adapt to a changing world because of their large cerebral cortex. When humans are faced with a suddenly cold climate, they can meet the challenge: they can learn to build shelters and fires, or to put on warm clothes. And once a group of humans has discovered such adaptations, these adaptations become part of that group's culture —their ways of living. As useful patterns of behavior, learned adaptations can be transmitted from one generation to the next.

THE NATURE OF LEARNING

Learning is fundamental to all aspects of life. But just what is learning? Behavioristic psychologists view it solely in terms of behavior. For example, suppose a child who is not afraid of dogs is attacked by a vicious dog. And suppose that, later, the child reacts to dogs with fear and agitation. Through learning, the child has developed a disposition to behave fearfully around dogs.

Behaviorists define learning as *a change in an organism's disposition to behave in a certain way as a result of experience.* How can we tell that an organism has learned something? According to behaviorists, the organism reveals that it has learned something by behaving in the indicated way under appropriate test conditions. The child in our example reveals the learned disposition under appropriate test conditions—he shows fear when faced with a dog.

Differing Views of Learning

The behavioral view is helpful when we are studying learning in animals or infants—organisms that cannot use language to describe what they have learned. But some psychologists believe the behavioral view is too limited. These psycholo-

gists, who look at learning from a cognitive perspective, are interested not only in behavior but also in mental processes. They define learning to include *changes in an organism's knowledge about the world that occur as a result of experience.*

Note the word "knowledge" in this definition: from this viewpoint, learning is a cognitive process. If a dog learns to salivate at the sound of a bell, a behaviorist would say that the animal has learned to respond to the bell with a specific behavior—the behavior of salivating. But a cognitive psychologist would say that the dog has acquired some *knowledge* about a lawful regularity: the dog now knows that the bell is usually followed by food (Bower and Hilgard, 1981). In the cognitive view, changes in behavior are just one indicator that learning has established some new internal knowledge structure in the organism's brain.

How Performance Relates to Learning

According to the behavioral *or* cognitive view, we cannot directly observe learning in an organism; we must always infer it from the organism's performance. That performance may involve actions, changes in psychological responses, or verbal descriptions. But the performance itself is not "learning": it only reflects possible learning.

Furthermore, it is important to recognize that not all changes in performance are caused by learning—so changes in performance do not always establish that the organism has learned something. Performance can be temporarily affected by momentary conditions. Most students know this: you yourself may at some time have done poorly on an exam, unable to produce material you felt that you knew. Many factors may have interfered with your performance—fatigue, distractions, emotional upset, competing thoughts, drugs, illness, or lack of motivation.

And performance can be permanently affected by conditions other than learning, such as maturation or advancing old age. Maturation makes young tadpoles start to swim, young frogs start to hop, and human infants start to walk. Such changes in behavioral dispositions do not depend on practice, and they require little experience; in fact, they are thought to be innate. Maturational changes in behavior differ little from one member of a species to another. Learned behavior, by contrast, varies widely among members of a species, according to their individual experiences. For example, chess players and video-game players may each be experts in their own field, but without special training neither is likely to be good at the other's specialty.

Gathering these observations, we can put together a definition of learning that allows for the influence of other factors. **Learning** is *a change in a behavioral disposition that is caused by experience and is not explained on the basis of reflexes, maturation, or temporary states* (Bower and Hilgard, 1981). Learning can take place in three ways.

1. We can learn by direct exposure to the events themselves—by experiencing the events, or acting and seeing the consequences of our actions.
2. We can learn things vicariously, by watching others experience the events.
3. We can learn through language, either by being told directly or by reading.

In this chapter, our focus is on the first two kinds of learning; learning through language will be covered extensively in Chapters 9 (Memory) and 16 (Acquiring and Using Language).

First let us consider how we learn by direct exposure. Just what sorts of things do we—or any other organism—learn?

WHAT DO ORGANISMS LEARN?

Suppose you are dropped down on a distant planet and told to learn everything you can about that world. The sorts of things you will learn correspond roughly to what psychologists see when they study learning in any sort of organism.

Habituation: Becoming Familiar with Specific Stimuli

One of the first things you will do is to learn to recognize particular objects that you encounter on the planet. Eventually, you will learn how these objects can be classified into categories: plants, animals, minerals, and the like. (We will discuss classification and the formation of concepts in Chapter 10.) But to get started, you will have to become familiar with the specific stimuli in your new world.

How will you react to your surroundings before you are familiar with them? Each time you encounter a new or unexpected stimulus you will have a "surprise reaction." Psychologists call this reaction the **orienting reflex**: the stimulus captures your attention and produces a physiological reaction—your heartbeat accelerates, your muscle tension increases slightly, and your skin resistance is lowered. Let's say that the first time you see a small purple plant with long tentacles (common on this planet) you react in this way.

But after you have observed this purple plant for a while, it will lose its novelty and your orienting reaction will weaken. If the stimulus is neither threatening nor especially pleasant, you will get accustomed to it—it will become boring. In technical terms, you have habituated to it. **Habituation** refers to a decrease in the strength of a response after a novel stimulus has been presented for a long time, either in one prolonged stretch or in repeated short bouts. Habituation is the simplest form of learning, and it appears in even the simplest organisms. For example, when a sea snail's gill is touched, the gill withdraws reflexively. But if the touch is repeated, after about the tenth prod the snail habituates and stops withdrawing the gill (Kandel, 1979).

Habituation simply reflects the fact that an organism has become familiar with a particular stimulus. Habituation lasts for a certain length of time: if you attend to other things for a while and then notice the purple plant again, you will react somewhat, but this time you will habituate much more quickly. But habituation does not generalize over different stimuli to any great degree. If some important feature of the object changes—if, let's say, the plant starts waving its tentacles and grabs and eats a large insect—you will once again react with a full orienting reflex. This ability to detect changes in a familiar stimulus implies that your brain does not ignore habituated stimuli; the brain continues to monitor these stimuli, even though they are no longer the focus of attention.

Cognitive Maps

As you learn about the objects on the strange planet, you will also learn where they are located relative to certain landmarks and to one another. You will develop what is called a "cognitive map" of the new environment. Similarly, you have already developed a cognitive map of your own neighborhood: you know where the library is in relation to the pizzeria and where both are located in relation to your home.

Temporal and Causal Sequences

A third type of knowledge you will acquire on your new planet concerns events that follow one another—either because they are in a temporal (time) series, like days of the week or seasons of the year, or because they are in a causal sequence. You will learn that lightning always precedes thunder on this planet, just as it does at home (this is a temporal series). And you will learn that waving a flaming torch causes a ferocious animal to flee (this is a causal sequence).

If you could not learn temporal and causal sequences of events, you would not be able to predict what was going to happen on this planet. You could not explain what had already happened. Nor could you plan and arrange conditions to *make* certain things happen; for example, you could not ward off a ferocious animal. Thus, understanding temporal and causal sequences is crucial to being able to act effectively on your environment.

Perceptual-Motor Skills

Organisms must also learn how to perform activities with skill and precision. For example, if the new planet has less gravity than Earth, you will have to learn the skill of walking gracefully on its surface. This fine-tuning of a perceptual-motor skill involves "knowing how" to do something rather than "knowing that" certain facts are true about the strange planet.

Among the common perceptual-motor skills you may already possess are speaking, golfing, riding a bicycle, or playing a musical instrument. Perceptual-motor skills underlie many human actions. Like habituation, the formation of cognitive maps, and the learning of temporal and causal sequences, they are part of an organism's adaptive repertoire.

Now that we have surveyed the major types of learning, we are ready to investigate them in detail. Except for habituation, the most elementary form of learning that can be imagined is learn-

ing that two events ordinarily follow each other in time. This sort of learning can be illustrated in a procedure called classical conditioning.

CLASSICAL CONDITIONING

A young lawyer who has developed cancer is put on chemotherapy, a treatment whose side effects include nausea. When the lawyer reports to the hospital for her third weekly treatment, she becomes nauseated and begins vomiting as soon as she walks into the hospital. Several days later a similar event occurs. She is shopping in the local supermarket and sees the nurse who has administered the drug to her; a wave of nausea sweeps over her, and she begins to retch.

What has caused the young woman's peculiar reaction? Why should the mere sight of the hospital or the nurse cause her to retch? She has been classically conditioned to *associate* two events —that is, to expect that one will follow the other in time. The first event is that she goes to the hospital and sees people involved with her treatment, such as the nurse. The second event is that she takes a drug that causes nausea. By the process of **association**, the woman has come to connect both the hospital and the nurse (event 1) with her nausea (event 2).

The result is a change in her behavior. At first, she responded only to event 2, the drug—by becoming nauseated. Now, not only the drug, but just the hospital and/or the nurse (event 1) *evokes* or calls forth that same response.

The simple form of associative learning reflected in this woman's experience has been systematically studied by psychologists, because connecting one event with another is related to the way we learn temporal and causal regularities in the world.

The Conditioned Response

Ivan Pavlov (1927), the Russian physiologist who first studied classical conditioning, noticed that the dogs in his laboratory salivated whenever food was placed in front of them. By experimenting (using the apparatus shown in Figure 8.1), Pavlov discovered that if he regularly rang a bell just before he presented food, the dog eventually

Figure 8.1. The apparatus used in early studies of classical conditioning. Saliva dropping from a tube inserted into the dog's cheek strikes a lightly balanced arm, and the resulting motion is transmitted hydraulically to a pen that traces a record on a slowly revolving drum. Pavlov's discovery of conditioned salivation was an accidental by-product of his researches into the activity of the digestive system.

learned to anticipate the food and to salivate each time the bell sounded.

The regular pairing (over time) of the bell and the food led the dog to associate the two stimuli, so that it learned about a temporal series. This learning was demonstrated by a change in the dog's behavior. The salivation that had originally been evoked by the food's presence (event 2) was now evoked merely by the sound of the bell (event 1).

Pavlov believed that the process in the animal's brain that corresponded to the bell became linked to another brain process corresponding to the animal's response to the food, which happened to consist of salivation. Sounding the bell caused excitation to spread to the food response center and caused the dog to salivate (Dickinson, 1980; Rescorla, 1978). Pavlov referred to this process as "conditioning" the salivation response to the bell. Through the conditioning process, an insignificant stimulus (the bell) became highly significant to the hungry dog—just as the sight of the nurse, insignificant in itself, became highly significant to the young woman receiving chemotherapy.

This process is known as **classical conditioning** (sometimes called Pavlovian conditioning). In it, an organism learns to associate two specific kinds of stimuli.

■ The first stimulus (in this example, the bell) starts out as *neutral* with respect to the salivary response. Before the learning experience, it does not evoke any salivation from the dog.

■ The second stimulus (the food, in our example) is one to which the organism has a strong reflex reaction, which exists before the learning experience begins.

Organisms are born with an array of simple reflexes—involuntary responses that are elicited by specific stimuli without any prior learning. When a puff of air is blown into your eye, you automatically react by blinking. Or if you take certain drugs, you will automatically react with nausea and vomiting. Pavlov's experiments focused on the salivary reflex: in a hungry dog (or person), the stimulus of food in the mouth elicits an involuntary response, of salivary secretion from glands in the mouth.

In classical conditioning, a neutral stimulus (the bell in our example) is repeatedly presented as a signal. It is given just *before* the stimulus that normally evokes a reflexive response (in our example, the food). Eventually, the organism learns to *expect* the second stimulus when it perceives the first stimulus. As a result, the first neutral stimulus comes to elicit that same reflexive response even when it is presented by itself, without the second stimulus (see Figure 8.2).

The Basic Terminology of Classical Conditioning

When discussing Pavlov's classical conditioning experiment, psychologists refer to the food in the dog's mouth as an **unconditioned stimulus (UCS)**. The UCS elicits the **unconditioned response**

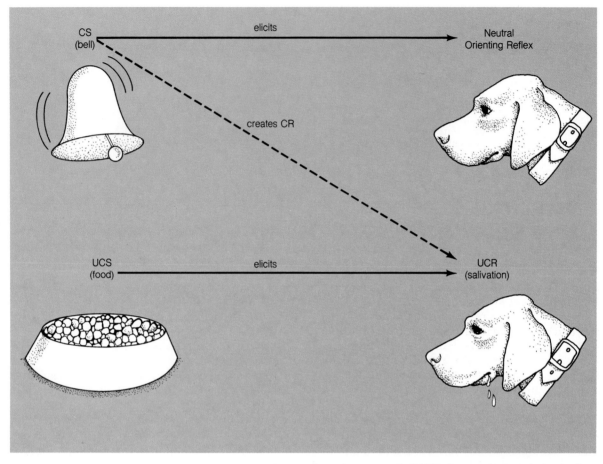

Figure 8.2. The creation of a conditioned response (CR). At first, the ringing bell (CS) elicits only a neutral orienting reflex. Then the bell is paired with food, which elicits an innate, or unconditioned, reflex of salivation (UCR). With repeated pairings, the CS comes to elicit salivation when presented by itself: the subject's expectation of the food, created by the ringing of the bell, causes salivation.

(UCR) of salivation. The term "unconditioned" is used because the dog's response does not depend on any previous experience or "conditioning" with the stimulus—the dog does not have to learn (or "be conditioned") to salivate in response to the food.

The neutral stimulus (the bell) that eventually comes to elicit salivation as a result of repeated association with the food is called the **conditioned stimulus (CS)**. The dog's salivation in response to the conditioned stimulus, in anticipation of the unconditioned stimulus, is called the **conditioned response (CR)**.

Note that salivation is only one of several signs that could be used as a measure of the dog's expectancy of food (its expectancy of the UCS) after it hears the bell (the CS). Another possible sign might be the P300 segment of the brain's event-related potential (ERP), mentioned in Chapter 3. If the expected UCS failed to occur following the CS after the dog had learned to associate the two, the dog would respond with "surprise"—the P300 wave.

Exploring Classical Conditioning

The experiment in which dogs learned to associate food (UCS) with a bell (CS) serves as a prototypical example of classical conditioning. After Pavlov conducted those first experiments, researchers tested all varieties of organisms and tried out a wide variety of stimuli—lights, visual patterns, sounds, whistles, touches, tastes, odors, and internal bodily sensations. They discovered that almost any of these could serve as a conditioned stimulus. And they found that an organism would learn to associate almost any of these stimuli as the signal for any of a wide variety of unconditioned stimuli, such as heat, water, sex, electric shock, puffs of air, or drugs that induced nausea or euphoria.

Learning in Neural Networks

An immediate problem the researchers faced was how to explain what might actually be happening in the organism's nervous system when this learning was taking place. Might the new experience induce actual changes in the nervous system? In Chapter 3 we saw a possible answer to this question. Elementary psychological functions in an organism, such as when the organism responds differently to different patterns of stimulation, might correspond to events caused by alterations within networks of neurons. Experience could increase the strength and efficiency of certain synaptic connections in the network, and through this mechanism the organism could learn new associations and new adaptive behavior. In other words, changes in synaptic transmission along

selected neural pathways could be responsible for classical conditioning.

Imagine a person who picks up a lemon and sucks the juice from it. The lemon juice on that person's tongue is an unconditioned stimulus, which causes the unconditioned response of salivation. Suppose that buried among the millions of neurons in the brain is a set of neurons, like the one in Figure 8.3, that are hooked up so that they connect the taste of a lemon with the sight of one—but the connection is only a weak one. Suppose that in the beginning, the *sight* of the lemon transmits a 1-unit charge to one of the neurons responsible for salivation via this hookup. At this point, the charge is too weak to cause the salivation neurons to fire.

Now suppose that through a learning process, the repeated pairing of the "sight" neuron with the "taste" neuron causes an increase in the efficiency of the synapse between these two neural cells. Suppose that with this modification, the sight of the lemon now transmits a 9-unit charge to the salivation neuron—enough yo fire the salivation reflex. The pairing of sight and taste has now strengthened a pathway that formerly was too weak to be effective; the sight of a lemon can now evoke the salivary reflex. While illustrated with one synapse, the same principles would apply if we were dealing with many synapses connecting large pools of CS and UCS neurons.

Figure 8.3. A neural circuit like the one diagrammed here makes it possible for a relatively weak visual stimulus (here, the sight of a lemon) to become so efficiently transmitted that it elicits the same conditioned response (salivation) as a taste stimulus did originally (lemon juice on the tongue). In associative conditioning, repeated pairings of the taste and sight signals at the interneuron causes the sight synapse to change so that it can transmit a greater potential—a charge of, say, 9 units so that it alone now can elicit the response.

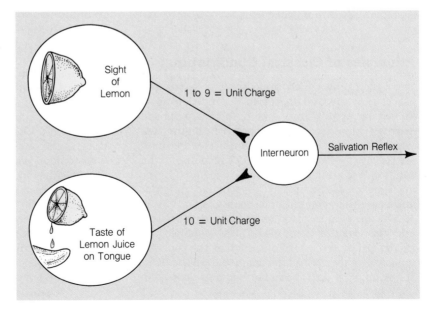

Increasing the efficiency of existing pathways, along the lines of this hypothetical situation, may be the neural basis of most simple associative learning (Hebb, 1949; Hawkins and Kandel, 1984). Learning may also lead to the establishment of entirely new connections, which may be excitatory or inhibitory. Clearly, if experience can alter the efficiency of single synapses or establish new connections, then a complex network of many synapses has many resources with which to learn about its environment and establish effective ways of dealing with it.

Conditioning the Emotions

Classical conditioning seems to underlie many acquired emotional responses of sexual arousal, fear, pride, comfort, nausea, anger, and the like. A response that was once evoked by an unconditioned stimulus is now evoked by some specific conditioned stimulus, which the person has come to associate with the original UCS. For example, babies associate their mothers with food, warmth, comfort, and cuddling, and so feel warm and secure in their mothers' presence. Or babies may associate a physician's office with the pain of hypodermic injections and become fearful the moment they are carried through the door. Motion pictures often exploit conditioned emotional responses in viewers. In horror films, stock stimuli associated with frightening events, such as a dark, windy night, a creaking door, or the howl of a wolf, are used to provoke fear.

Principles of Classical Conditioning

The process by which an organism learns the association involved in classical conditioning is known as **acquisition**, and it follows a typical learning curve like the one shown in Figure 8.4. When the conditioned and unconditioned stimuli are repeatedly paired, the subject's response to the conditioned stimulus generally becomes larger and quicker, as the subject comes more strongly to anticipate the unconditioned stimulus.

The speed of learning reflected in this process and the eventual strength of the response are influenced by several factors, such as the conspicuousness of the CS and the magnitude of the UCR. For example, if the CS is a light, conditioning will be more rapid if a spotlight rather than a 10-watt bulb is used. And if the UCR is nausea, severe nausea and vomiting will lead to faster learning than a mildly upset stomach.

Second-Order Conditioning

Once a conditioned stimulus has been established, that stimulus takes on some of the power of the unconditioned stimulus. If the CS then repeatedly follows a *second* neutral stimulus, the second stimulus becomes associated with the first, and soon begins to elicit the CR by itself. This phenomenon is known as **second-order conditioning**.

For example, suppose that after a dog learns to salivate to the sound of a bell, it is repeatedly exposed to a light followed by the bell. Although the dog gets no meat when it sees the light and hears the bell, the animal will begin responding to the light with salivation, the same response called forth by the unconditioned stimulus. Second-order conditioning is apparently responsible for much of the emotional conditioning involved in attitudes and prejudices.

Extinction

If learning is to be adaptive, the learner must be able to alter his or her expectations when regularities in the world change. Should the unconditioned stimulus no longer follow the conditioned stimulus—as when the dog is no longer fed after the bell rings—the organism eventually stops expecting it. This process is known as **extinction**. As the organism's expectation of the unconditioned stimulus diminishes, the response gradually dwindles, as shown in Figure 8.4, and is finally extinguished.

Extinction helps organisms sort out regularities in the world from the accidental coincidences that plague our lives. Psychologists often tell of a door-to-door salesman who rang a customer's doorbell one day when the kitchen happened to be filled with escaped gas. The spark from the doorbell ignited the gas and blew up the house. Afterward, whenever the salesman pressed a doorbell, he felt a sinking, clammy fear. He persisted, however, and eventually, after he had pressed many doorbells without blowing up houses, his fear disappeared (was extinguished). The process of

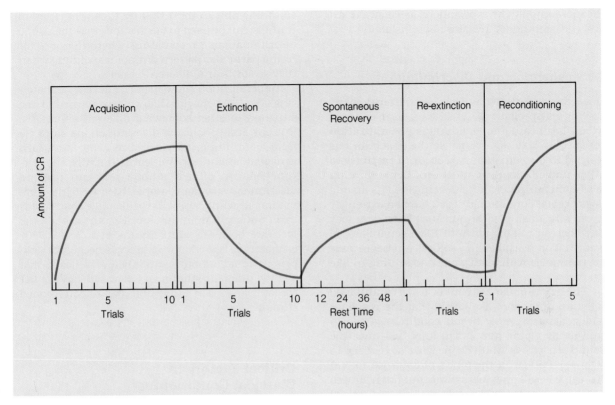

Figure 8.4. The process of classical conditioning, showing the *acquisition* of a conditioned response when the UCS and CS are repeatedly paired; the *extinction* of the conditioned response when the CS is consistently repeated without the UCS; the *spontaneous recovery* of an extinguished conditioned response when the subject is returned to the experimental situation after a rest of several hours; the *reextinction* of the response when the CS is again presented but is not paired with the UCS; and the rapid recovery of the conditioned response, or *reconditioning*, when the CS is again paired with the UCS.

extinction is used by behavior therapists to help clients overcome irrational fears—of snakes, spiders, heights, examinations, the outdoors, and other ordinary objects and situations. In the safety of the therapist's office the client is exposed again and again to the feared object or situation or to a picture or mental image of it. Since no disaster ever occurs in the therapist's office, the fear is gradually extinguished.

Once a conditioned response has been extinguished, it reappears if the organism is removed from the experimental situation for several hours or days and is then reintroduced to it. Suppose we ring the bell again and again without feeding the dog until the animal no longer salivates at the sound. The next day we bring the dog back into the lab and ring the bell again: the dog will

salivate. When the conditioned stimulus (the bell) is presented for the first time upon return to the familiar situation, the conditioned response follows, although not as strongly as it once did. This process, called **spontaneous recovery**, apparently develops because the organism has "forgotten" the recent occasions when the unconditioned stimulus failed to appear on schedule. This time, however, extinction will follow rapidly.

If the unconditioned stimulus is again paired with the conditioned stimulus, the extinguished response will quickly be relearned. The dog will begin salivating after many fewer trials than it originally took to establish the CR. In such **reconditioning**, the new pairings of CS and US appear to "remind" the organism of the expectation it had learned earlier. The stronger the initial learning, the more rapidly the expectations are reawakened and the conditioned response is reinstated.

Generalization and Discrimination

Once the organism has been conditioned to respond in a specific way, as Pavlov's dogs salivated when they heard a tone, **stimulus generalization** may occur. That is, a response the organism has learned in one situation may occur in response to other similar stimuli or situations. Generalization is as common among human beings as it is among dogs or rats. For example, if you have an extremely warm relationship with your Aunt Ellen, you may find that your liking for Aunt Ellen generalizes to women who resemble her, so that you begin your acquaintance with such women expecting to like them.

The more similar a stimulus is to a conditioned stimulus, the more likely it is that the response will generalize to it. If you condition a boy to salivate by giving him lemon juice just after the sound of a tone of 1,000 Hz, he will also respond to a tone of 950 Hz. If the tone's pitch drops to 600 Hz, the boy will probably salivate but not nearly so much, and he may not respond at all to a tone of 250 Hz. This lessened tendency to respond as the resemblance between a new stimulus and a conditioned stimulus becomes fainter is called a **generalization gradient**.

Generalization is important in daily life because it allows us to behave adaptively in various situations. Without generalization, none of us would survive for long, because we would have to learn separately the significance of each minute variation in the world's stimuli. Without generalization, a pedestrian who has learned to get out of the way of cars would be run over by a truck or bus.

Organisms can also be trained to respond differently to similar (though not identical) stimuli, learning to respond to one but not to others. This process, called **discrimination**, results when the unconditioned stimulus regularly follows one stimulus and never follows other, similar stimuli. Suppose that your subject learns to salivate to a 1,000 Hz tone and promptly generalizes his response to tones slightly higher or lower in pitch. If you sound tones at other frequencies without giving him lemon juice but continue to give it when you sound the 1,000 Hz tone, the boy will soon respond discriminatively among the tones,

salivating only to the 1,000 Hz tone. This kind of training can be used to teach subjects to make fine discriminations, responding when they see or hear a particular pattern but not responding when they see or hear a different pattern.

Generalization allows us to be flexible, transferring adaptive behavior that we have learned in one situation to other somewhat different situations. But our ability to learn discriminations stops us from continuing to generalize what we learn across all situations. We learn to notice the relevant features of new stimuli and can respond discriminatively. For example, because of discrimination learning, we will drink milk that smells fresh but avoid milk that smells sour, despite the fact that both are white liquids in a carton. Discrimination is an adaptive process because it enables us to adjust our expectancies. We learn that slightly different stimuli in the world can predict the appearance of quite different unconditioned stimuli.

Critical Factors in Classical Conditioning

Although early researchers concluded that the nervous system was a general-purpose learning machine, their conclusion has not held up. The early assumption that almost any stimulus could be used in classical conditioning crumbled when it became apparent that various factors influence the extent of conditioning—and that, in some situations, conditioning does not occur (Hull, 1943; Mackintosh, 1983).

When does an organism learn? Conditioning is generally rapid, and the conditioned response is strong, when one (or more) of the following conditions is met:

■ The conditioned stimulus is intense or conspicuous, or grabs the organism's attention.
■ The unconditioned stimulus follows soon after the conditioned stimulus, so that the CS acts as an immediate signal.
■ The unconditioned stimulus is of high magnitude (when it consists of large quantities of food, for example, or intense shock).
■ The animal is genetically prepared to connect the particular kind of stimulus (sound, odor, taste) to the innate reaction used as the UCR (see the box on pages 198–199).

When is the organism unlikely to learn? Learning will be poor or will not occur at all if the opposite conditions hold true: if the CS is weak, if the UCS is weak, if there is a wide separation in time between the CS and the UCS, or if the CS is of a sort which the organism is not genetically prepared to connect with the UCS. The association will also be weak if the CS follows the UCS instead of coming before it.

Researchers have been especially interested in discovering the crucial determinants of conditioning. They have discovered that there is more to classical conditioning than a mechanistic "stamping in" of an association between every CS and UCS that occur together. Instead, classical conditioning appears to depend on whether the CS serves as an informative signal that helps the organism predict the appearance of the UCS (Kamin, 1969; Wagner, 1969).

CS–UCS Correlations

In an important experiment, Robert Rescorla (1968) attempted to find out how regularly a CS and a UCS had to be paired if conditioning was to take place. Two groups of dogs were restrained in a box. The two groups received the same number of tones (CS) paired with shocks (UCS), but they differed in how often they received shocks *without* warning (without the signaling tone). Rescorla found that the least highly conditioned animals (the ones that feared the tone the least) were those that had received the largest number of *unsignaled* shocks.

Consider what it means to the animal if it receives a shock in the box *without* hearing the tone as frequently as it receives a shock preceded by the tone. From the animal's viewpoint the tone is not a valid predictor of the shock. Hearing the tone does not reduce the animal's uncertainty, because the animal often receives the shock without hearing the tone. Nor does the sound tell the animal *when* the shock will occur: in Rescorla's experiment, the tone was as likely to occur during or after the shock as before.

In traditional conditioning experiments, do animals do more than simply notice that the CS (tone) often precedes the UCS (shock)? Rescorla believes they do. They also learn that the *absence* of the tone signals the *absence* of the shock; that is, the absence of the tone signals a safe period. Pavlov's dogs were fed when the bell sounded, but they were also *not* fed when the bell did *not* sound. Animals (or people) need both kinds of information if they are to learn the association between the CS and the UCS. Apparently, the brain notes the correlation between the presence versus absence of the two events and, when the events are highly correlated, infers some kind of causal relationship between them. When an animal makes this inference, it expects the UCS after the CS, but does not expect it in the absence of the CS.

The Blocking of Conditioning

Under certain circumstances, the conditioning normally caused by CS–UCS pairings can be blocked entirely. This became apparent in an experiment by Leo Kamin (1969). Kamin conditioned rats to associate a loud noise with a shock: once these rats were conditioned, they showed their fear that a shock was on the way by ceasing to press a lever for food whenever they heard the noise. Then a new CS was added. Each time the noise came on, a light went on over the rats' heads, and both stimuli ended several seconds later with an electric shock.

Would these animals now learn to fear the light? After all, the light also preceded the shock. To find out, Kamin turned on the light by itself, without the accompanying noise. Surprisingly, the rats showed very little fear of the light, and continued to press the lever for food. They had failed to associate the light with the shock. Evidently, prior conditioning to the noise interfered with conditioning to the light—even though, for the rats, the light was as highly correlated with the shock as was the noise.

The experience of Kamin's rats is not isolated. **Blocking** is a reliable phenomenon that occurs in all species and in most conditioning situations. In fact, blocking probably explains Rescorla's earlier finding that conditioning is weak or nonexistent when tones and shocks are poorly correlated. Though the tone was not always present just before the shock, another stimulus was always present: the box in which the dogs were restrained. The shock was more highly correlated with the box than with the tone. Therefore, the dogs may have associated the shock with the box, blocking the formation of any association between the tone and the shock.

What causes blocking? Several interpretations of this phenomenon are being investigated at pres-

TOXIPHOBIA

After Pavlov's ground-breaking experiments, psychologists began trying out similar conditioning experiments with all varieties of animals. They used diverse kinds of stimuli as conditioned stimuli, along with a range of biologically significant stimuli to evoke the unconditioned reflex. A tentative early conclusion was that almost any stimulus to which the organism was sensitive could be conditioned to almost any reaction that was elicited by an unconditioned stimulus. If this were true, researchers argued, then the nervous systems of animals could be regarded as "general-purpose associators," ready to make any possible connection. Such a learning mechanism would be highly sensitive to learning about whatever regularities characterized an animal's world, and, therefore, would be extremely adaptive. Psychologists also believed that for conditioning to occur, the unconditioned stimulus had to follow closely on the heels of the to-be-conditioned stimulus.

The flaws in both beliefs were demonstrated in studies by the psychologist John Garcia and his associates (Garcia and Koelling 1966; Garcia, Ervin, and Koelling, 1966).

They found that some types of neutral stimuli were almost impossible to associate with certain unconditioned responses—yet in other cases, associations could be made easily when as much as twelve hours elapsed between the CS and the unconditioned response. Such results discredit the idea that the brain is a "general-purpose associator" that treats all events the same way in establishing associations among them.

One of the Garcia's experiments showed that the type of UCR that followed the CS determined what sort of learning occurred. Thirsty rats were allowed to drink water from two different spouts. One spout delivered saccharine-sweetened water ("tasty water"). The other spout delivered plain water, but each lick on the spout set off a clicking noise and a flashing light ("noisy-bright water"). The tasty water and the noisy-bright water both served as possible CSs in the experiment that followed.

After both drinking spouts were removed, some of the animals received shocks delivered through the wire floor of the cage; the others were given a dose of X-rays that made them sick to their stomachs. The question was whether the

rats would connect their later distress to the water, and if so, which kind of water (CS) would be associated with which unconditioned response. A few days later the animals were given another chance to drink from the two water spouts. Those who had been shocked avoided the bright-noisy water but eagerly drank the tasty water. Those who had been sick avoided the tasty water but eagerly drank the bright-noisy water. Thus, each group had been classically conditioned, but the CS selected by the animal as a signal depended on whether it had been shocked or made sick to its stomach.

According to Garcia, the evolutionary history of mammals (including rats) has prepared them to connect tastes with stomach sickness and to connect externally caused pain with sights and sounds because such connections have been essential to their survival. In the world in which mammals live, pain is likely to arise from contact with dangerous objects that are seen and heard. But stomach sickness is likely to develop some time after the animal eats poisoned food. If an animal's nervous system is programmed to connect the taste

ent. Some researchers believe that the animals' failure to associate the light with the shock was due to the fact that the animals' attention had been grabbed by the noise, which already predicted the shock. Paying little attention to the light, the animals learned less about it (Trabasso and Bower, 1968).

Other researchers point out that the light gave the animals no new information; it did not in-

crease the predictability of the impending shock above the level that was already given by the noise (Kamin, 1969; Wagner, 1969). With more than one cue signaling a UCS, the animal will rely on the better predictor, and it will block any association between the new CS (light) and the UCS. The original CS had greater validity for the animal. Current research is sorting out the merits of these two hypotheses.

of any food the animal has eaten before a gastric illness with the sensation of feeling sick, the animal is likely to avoid that food on later occasions. And so its chances of survival are increased. Animals are especially prone to associate gastric illness with tastes that are unfamiliar. Apparently, the sick animal scans back in its memory over the things it has recently eaten or drunk and selects the unfamiliar taste as the likely cause —continuing to consider its familiar foods as safe. People who get food poisoning use a similar strategy consciously, to figure out what they have eaten that might have made them sick.

Another surprise in Garcia's experiments was that these novel taste-to-stomach-sickness associations could be established over very long time intervals (12 to 24 hours) between the time the animal had the novel taste (the CS) and the time the animal later became sick (UCR). The occurrence of conditioning over such long CS–UCS intervals completely overthrew researchers' former view that conditioning required that CS and UCS be close in time. (Recall that in nature most causes precede their effects by only a few seconds.) Garcia's findings show, rather, that lengthy CS–UCS intervals can produce conditioning when the animal is biologically prepared to associate unconditioned reactions of a certain type (stomach illness) with earlier stimuli of a specific type (novel tastes).

Taste-aversion conditioning has been used to make coyotes refuse to eat lamb; this approach has been used in western rangelands to cut down predation of grazing flocks. In one experiment the researchers laced chunks of lamb meat with lithium chloride and wrapped them in a sheep hide. After the coyotes ate the meat, they became ill and vomited. Afterward, they not only refused to eat lamb meat but also stopped killing lambs. They would even retch and run away when a lamb came near them. The association was limited to lambs, for the coyotes continued to kill and eat rabbits (Gustavson et al., 1974). The researchers believe that the conditioned coyotes may even convey their taste aversion to their offspring. And the reaction is not limited to coyotes: in another study, wolves who had eaten poisoned lamb meat switched from killing and devouring lambs to cringing their presence (Garcia, Rusiniak, and Brett, 1977).

Human beings seem to be as prepared to connect taste with illness as other mammals are. In a study that paralleled the experiment with Garcia's rats, young cancer patients ate Mapletoff, a distinctively flavored ice cream, just before they received chemotherapy —a treatment that is generally followed by nausea. Several months later three-fourths of the patients rejected the Mapletoff flavor, but among cancer patients in a control group that had not received chemotherapy after eating ice cream, half preferred the Mapletoff to another flavor (Bernstein, 1978). This experiment with cancer patients supports the experience of many people, who find that when they have become ill after eating a distinctive food, the taste or even the thought of the offending food continues to nauseate them, sometimes for years afterward.

Behavior therapists have used a similar form of conditioning to treat alcoholism. The alcoholic patient takes a nausea-inducing drug, with the dose timed so that nausea and vomiting closely follow the drinking of a favorite alcoholic beverage. The patient generally has four to six such sessions; the aim is to condition the patient so that nausea and stomach upset ensue whenever he or she tries to drink alcohol. About half of the patients who go through this program remain abstinent for at least four years, which is an excellent persistence rate for treatments of addictions (Nathan, 1976).

INSTRUMENTAL CONDITIONING

In classical conditioning we learn about the relationship between two events. The events always occur in the same sequence, and they take place no matter what we do. We have no control over them. The dog that salivates at the tone that precedes food has learned that the sound announces the food, but the dog's actions have no effect on the arrival of either stimulus, and it does not consciously order its salivary glands to produce saliva.

In a second form of learning, instrumental conditioning, we learn about another kind of relationship between events. In instrumental conditioning the events still occur in sequence, but this time the relationship we learn, or association we form, is between our own behavior and a particular outcome. In most cases our behavior causes this outcome or consequence. For example, if we are put down on a strange planet, we may learn that when we wave a fiery torch, a threatening predator runs away.

This form of learning is called **operant conditioning**, or **instrumental conditioning**, because the organism's response *operates* on the environment and is *instrumental* in producing whatever rewards or punishments follow it. Most human behavior is learned and performed because of its consequences. To see in the dark, we switch on a light. To get a pencil, we open the desk drawer. To get a snack, we open the refrigerator door. To get a book, we go to the library. To get an A on an exam, we study for the test. We do these things because the consequence is rewarding.

Studying Instrumental Conditioning

Early studies of instrumental conditioning in animals were begun by Edward Thorndike around the turn of the century. In one of his famous experiments Thorndike (1898) would confine a cat inside a wooden box and observe what happened as the cat tried to escape. Each time the cat succeeded in opening the box's escape hatch, the crucial response was strengthened. The cat showed that it had learned the connection between tripping the latch and the hatch's opening (allowing escape) by performing the same response sooner the next time it was put into the box. Thorndike described this process of learning as "trial and error," and concluded that the cat's escape from confinement served as a reward to strengthen or "stamp in" the correct response.

Another major advance in the investigation of instrumental conditioning occurred in the mid-1930s when B. F. Skinner (1938) developed the "operant-conditioning" chamber (see the accompanying photograph). The animal, typically a hungry rat, is placed in such a box. It explores the box until, by chance, it presses or stands on a lever that causes a small pellet of food to drop into a food cup beside the lever. This event causes the animal to begin to associate its lever pressing with the receipt of a food pellet. After a while the rat presses the lever again and gets another pellet, learning a little more about the connection between its action and the arrival of food. In such a situation the animal indicates the strength of its learning by the rate (responses per minute) at

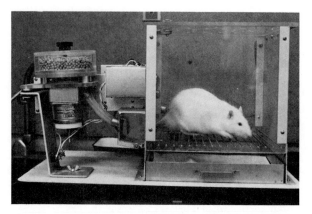

A rat in an operant-conditioning chamber.

which it presses the lever. Soon the animal is pressing and eating steadily until it is full. The lever pressing will now obey the laws of operant conditioning, which we will consider below.

This way of studying instrumental learning is called the "free-operant" method because the animal is in the box continuously and can respond "freely" at any time. The method differs from the "discrete-trial" method, which was used by Thorndike with his cats. In Thorndike's method, the animal is placed in a box or at the starting point of a maze and has one ("discrete") opportunity each time to try to get out or to reach some rewarding goal at the maze's end. By repeatedly placing the animal in the box the researcher can observe the cumulative effect of many trials.

Both the free-operant method and the discrete-trial method are useful ways of studying learning. In either method the subject can make a response that will bring a rewarding consequence, allowing it to learn the connection between its response and the consequence. How quickly or how often the subject performs the response depends on how desirable the consequence seems. As you might expect, behavior that results in pleasant consequences is likely to be repeated, while behavior that results in unpleasant consequences is likely to be suppressed.

The operant conditioning situations described above, such as the "rat in a Skinner box," have become for the learning psychologist what the fruit fly has become for the geneticist: they are extremely simple "preparations" in which large numbers of experiments can be done conveniently, cheaply, and efficiently. The experiments yield regular, lawful results that help us answer many basic questions about learning. Moreover, the results seem to generalize to a large degree across other situations, learned behaviors, and species. Psychologists are not really interested in rats' lever pressing per se, any more than geneticists are interested in how fruit flies naturally multiply. Rather, the experiments are just laboratory tools; the interest and motivation behind their use is almost always to solve certain intellectual puzzles, and to penetrate into certain fundamental mysteries about how all organisms adapt to their world.

Aspects of Instrumental Conditioning

During instrumental conditioning the organism learns an association between its own response and a consequence. How rapidly animals and people learn this association, as well as the strength of their learning, depends on many factors, including the nature of the consequence.

The Role of Consequences in Instrumental Conditioning

The consequences, or payoffs, used in instrumental conditioning are given after the organism's response, and they can be pleasant consequences (benefits) or unpleasant ones (costs).

■ *Pleasant consequences* are usually classified as "positive"; they include rewards, payoffs, and also relief from pain or distress. Such consequences are part of daily life. A typical reward is a money bonus for a job well done; an example of relief from distress is the end of parental nagging after you clean up your bedroom.
■ *Unpleasant consequences* are usually classified as "negative"; they include punishment and also the removal of some pleasant situation. A typical punishment for a child might be a spanking from a parent who thought the youngster had misbehaved; an example of the removal of something pleasant might be a fine for speeding, which removes part of your money.

In animal experiments, researchers generally use biologically significant events, such as food and water, as positive outcomes. These rewards are often called **positive reinforcers**, because they increase ("reinforce") the animal's tendency to repeat a response that leads to them. An animal's desire for these rewards can be varied by changing the quality of the reward and the animal's state of deprivation. Deprivation increases an animal's motivation, or tendency to perform goal-directed behavior, as we will see in Chapter 12; therefore, researchers generally use hungry or thirsty animals in instrumental conditioning experiments. Researchers can also use negative outcomes to study instrumental conditioning: they may use punishments in the shape of mildly painful stimuli, such as foot shock, excessively bright lights, or loud noises. These stimuli are considered **punishments**, because they tend to suppress or decrease the frequency of whatever response has brought them on.

In using rewards and punishments, researchers arrange the conditioning situation so that the animal's instrumental response causes it to encounter a pleasant or an unpleasant event. But they can also arrange just the opposite relationship, so that the animal's instrumental response causes the removal or withdrawal of something —either a pleasant consequence or an unpleasant one. Removing something that is unpleasant provides satisfying relief, so any response that leads to escape from an unpleasant state of affairs will be strengthened. Similarly, removing a pleasant stimulus, as when you take candy away from a baby, causes frustration and dissatisfaction, so the removal acts as punishment.

Operant conditioning procedures have been widely used with human beings to eliminate disruptive behavior and replace it with sociable behavior. For example, a schoolteacher may systematically use praise and attention to reinforce peaceful, socially appropriate classroom behavior in problem children (Kazdin, 1975).

Schedules of Reinforcement

An animal or person does not have to be rewarded each time a response occurs for an operant response to be established or maintained. In a free operant situation the **schedule of reinforcement**, or the basis on which the animal is rewarded, can take any of several forms. Instead of using a **continuous reinforcement schedule**, in which the animal is given a reward each time it presses the lever, researchers may use some form of partial reinforcement, rewarding the animal after only *some* of its responses.

In some **partial reinforcement schedules**, rewards come either after a specific number of responses (a **fixed ratio schedule**) or for the first response after a specified lapse of time since the previous reward (a **fixed interval schedule**). Animals placed on either of these schedules seem to learn the schedule within several hours of exposure to it, and learn to adjust their behavior according to the predictable reinforcement. A hungry animal on a fixed ratio schedule presses a bar at a rapid rate, and for a good reason—the faster it works, the more often it gets fed. Similarly, "piece-rate pay," a fixed ratio schedule, is used with human workers, such as fruit pickers. On the other hand, an animal placed on a fixed interval schedule tends to rest after each reward, waiting until it estimates that the reward is due before responding again.

Not all partial schedules of reinforcement are based on such regular relationships between behavior and reward. Irregular reinforcement can maintain behavior with very few rewards, because the animal can never tell when a reward might be coming. Animals on a **variable ratio schedule** are rewarded after a variable (unpredictable) number of responses. On a variable ratio schedule calling for a reward after an average of ten responses, rewards may come after six, then fourteen, then two, then eighteen responses, and so on, in random, unpredictable order. In a **variable interval schedule**, animals are rewarded for their first responses after a variable period of time has elapsed since the last reward. On such a schedule, there may be two minutes between the first and second reward, then thirty seconds before the next reward, then six minutes, then ten seconds, and so on. On either variable schedule an animal responds more or less steadily, because there is always the chance that the next response will bring a reward.

Behavior that has been maintained on a variable schedule is very difficult to extinguish, because even after all rewards have ceased the animal continues for long periods to expect its unpredictable reward. It is difficult for both people and animals to distinguish between a true extinction situation, in which rewards are never given, and one in which rewards come at highly irregular intervals. The persistent behavior of an animal on a variable ratio schedule is analogous to the actions of a gambler at a slot machine. Because both

Their unpredictability is exactly what makes slot machines so compelling to many people. It is always possible that the next pull of the handle will hit the jackpot.

the amount of reinforcement and its schedule are highly varied, slot machines maintain a compelling attraction for the person pulling the handle. Since the machine pays out unpredictable amounts at unpredictable times, the player continues to hope that the next pull will hit the jackpot. And if a slot machine ceases all payoffs, a long time will pass before the player realizes it.

Learning Superstitious Behavior

Not all learning results from an actual relationship between an act and its consequences. Behavior that just "accidentally" happens to be followed by a reinforcer can also be strengthened. The relationship between the behavior and the reinforcer is coincidental, but the organism quite naturally assumes that its behavior has caused the reinforcement. As a result it responds more often. This kind of learning leads to what is called **superstitious behavior**. Examples of such behavior abound at any baseball game. Batters can be seen tugging at their caps, or tapping the plate or their left foot with the bat three times before they move into the box—rituals they believe will bring them good luck at bat. Most batters hit safely about a quarter of the time; because they are on a variable ratio schedule, each hit they get reinforces their superstitious behavior.

Similar superstitions appeared in pigeons when Skinner (1948a) fed them at very close intervals (about every fifteen seconds) no matter what they were doing. In most cases, the pigeon was likely to be finishing the food and starting to turn away when the next reward was delivered. There was, of course, no connection between the pigeon's behavior and its reinforcement. But when the same behavior was rewarded several times in a row, pigeons developed ritualistic, stereotyped behavior patterns, such as bowing, turning in circles, and hopping from one foot to the other. The birds acted as if they believed that whatever they happened to be doing at the moment the food was delivered was responsible for the appearance of the food.

Generalization and Discrimination in Instrumental Conditioning

Generalization and discrimination occur in instrumental conditioning, just as they do in classical conditioning. A pigeon trained to peck a red plastic disk on the wall ("key") to get food will "generalize" this behavior to pecking an orange key, and its rates of pecking related stimuli form a gradient, just as they do in classical conditioning. It can also be trained to discriminate among keys of different colors, if the trainer rewards responses when the key is one color but does not reward responses when the key is a different color.

Stimulus generalization of operant responses is also common in our daily lives. A young child who has just learned to call the family dog "doggie" may start calling cats and foxes by the same name. Similarly, an adult who customarily drives a sports car with a stick shift will often try to depress the nonexistent clutch pedal when driving a car with an automatic transmission. Generalization sometimes has unfortunate consequences. For example, when a member of a minority group commits a crime, some observers tend to generalize such criminal activities to the rest of the minority group, creating or maintaining prejudice.

Expectancies in Instrumental Conditioning

Not all psychologists have agreed with the view of instrumental learning presented here: that the organism learns an association between its own response and the consequence, *expects* that its response will produce that consequence, and later performs that response if it desires the consequence. (For arguments in favor of this view, see Dickinson, 1980, and Mackintosh, 1983.) Early learning theorists, including Clark Hull (1943) and Edwin Guthrie (1935), did not believe that organisms learned to *expect* anything during instrumental learning. They proposed instead that animals learned direct associations between a stimulus and a response without actually "knowing" or anticipating what consequence the response would produce. If an animal did happen to gain some knowledge of (expectancy about) the consequence, that knowledge would not affect its tendency to make the response.

How can we discover, in an instrumental conditioning situation, whether an animal develops an expectancy for the consequences or acts without knowledge of the consequences? We might begin by conditioning an animal to respond in a manner that brought some positive consequence, such as food. Next, we could change or reverse the value of the consequence so that a formerly pleasant outcome suddenly became unpleasant. If the animal had learned to *expect* that specific outcome but the outcome has in the meantime been devalued, then the animal's tendency to make the instrumental response in the original test situation should be reduced.

When Ruth Colwill and Robert Rescorla (1985) carried out such a study, they found clear evidence that animals indeed seemed to learn reward expectancies during instrumental conditioning. The researchers first placed hungry rats in a small chamber and trained them to make two different instrumental responses: to press a lever and to pull a small chain that hung from the chamber's ceiling. Each response would be made available during different sessions. Both responses were rewarded. Some of the rats got a food pellet when they pressed the lever and a squirt of sugar water when they pulled the chain. For the rest of the rats, the rewards were reversed: they got sweet water when they pressed the lever and a food pellet when they pulled the chain.

After the rats had been conditioned in this way,

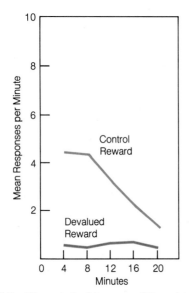

Figure 8.5. After rats had been conditioned to associate sweetened water with nausea, they readily stopped pulling a chain, which formerly had been rewarded by this sweetened water. These results (discussed in more detail in the text) support the view that expectations about the outcome influence an organism's response in instrumental conditioning. (From Colwill and Rescorla, 1985.)

the researchers changed the situation, so that one—but not the other—of the animal's rewards became unpleasant. With the lever and chain removed from the cage, the rats got food and sugar water on alternate days, but on the days when they drank the sweetened water, they were also injected later with a drug that caused nausea. (The animals did not have to work for either "reward.") The effect of this classical conditioning led the rats to avoid the sugar water (just as Garcia's rats did), but since illness had not been associated with the food pellets, they continued to eat them.

After this experience the lever and chain were returned to the cage. Now the animal could make either response, but all rewards were withheld ("extinction") during the crucial testing phase. If, during instrumental conditioning, the rat had learned to *expect* food when it pressed the lever and sweet water when it pulled the chain, then it should avoid the chain because the water had become unpleasant. That is, when the rat considered pulling the chain, it would supposedly think of sugar water, which was now a nauseating substance, so the rat would slack off pulling the chain.

As Figure 8.5 shows, the rats in Colwill and Rescorla's (1985) study behaved in just this way. The animals showed little tendency to make the response that normally brought them an outcome that had become unpleasant. These results support the expectancy view of instrumental conditioning: that is, an organism's anticipation of a rewarding outcome guides and motivates its responses that produce the outcome.

Comparing Instrumental and Classical Conditioning

Instrumental and classical conditioning involve similar phenomena and follow similar laws, so that the five panels of Figure 8.4 illustrate both forms of conditioning. Both instrumentally and classically conditioned responses show acquisition, extinction, spontaneous recovery, reconditioning, generalization, and discrimination. This resemblance is not surprising: after all, in both types of conditioning, the brain is simply learning the correlation between two events in the environment. In classical conditioning, the events are the occurrence of the CS and the UCS; in instrumental conditioning, they are the response and the rewarding consequence.

As these similarities suggest, most factors that influence one kind of conditioning also influence the other. For example, classical conditioning is usually weak or nonexistent unless the interval between the conditioned (bell) and unconditioned (food) stimulus is brief (with the exception of taste aversions). In instrumental conditioning, the longer the delay between response (lever press) and reward (food), the more slowly conditioning progresses. In either case, a long delay makes it difficult for the organism to connect the first event with the second.

But despite great similarities between classical and instrumental conditioning, there are distinct differences in the two procedures.

1. In classical conditioning, the UCS follows the CS whether or not the subject responds to the CS; in instrumental conditioning, the reward occurs only if the subject makes the critical response.
2. In classical conditioning, the subject's response is generally involuntary—it is a reflex elicited by the UCS; in instrumental conditioning, the response is voluntary and not elicited by some UCS (that is, the lever

does not elicit "lever pressing" as if "lever pressing" were a reflex).

3. In classical conditioning, the conditioned response usually resembles the unconditioned response—for example, in Pavlov's experiments, the UCR and the CR were both salivation. But in instrumental conditioning, the conditioned response (pressing a lever) is usually completely different from the customary response to the reward (eating a food pellet). The experimenter can arrange to have almost any operant response bring about almost any reinforcing consequence.

4. In classical conditioning, the response generally involves the autonomic nervous system or other internal organs; in instrumental conditioning, the response generally involves the somatic nervous system. Most classical conditioning experiments train normally involuntary reactions such as changes in salivation or heart rate, while instrumental conditioning experiments generally involve modifying voluntary responses such as pressing or pecking. This distinction is not perfect, however. Some responses—such as an eyeblink—can be either voluntary or involuntary, and they can be conditioned by either procedure. And as seen in Chapter 7, autonomic responses such as heart rate apparently can be modified by biofeedback, a technique that is a form of instrumental conditioning (Shapiro and Surwit, 1976).

Aversive Learning

Instrumental learning is not always a matter of pleasant consequences and rewards. As noted earlier, sometimes the consequence of a response is decidedly unpleasant, or aversive. **Aversive learning** techniques include punishment, escape, and the avoidance of punishment.

Punishment

Punishment involves any unpleasant event (such as shock or denial of privileges) that follows a response and weakens it. If a rat receives an electric shock each time it presses a lever, it will soon stop pressing the lever. There are many kinds of punishment in daily life—spanking children,

jailing or fining lawbreakers, flunking students —and punishment can be a useful means of controlling behavior. Certainly "natural" punishment provided by our natural environment can effectively suppress the repetition of a particular behavior: a child has to touch a hot stove only once. Punishment is effective because the person learns to anticipate the aversive outcome whenever he or she thinks of making a response that has been punished. In order to avoid the punishment, the person inhibits the response (Dinsmoor, 1954; 1955; Mowrer, 1960).

Sometimes punishment takes the form of removing a positive event, as when a small girl who misbehaves is exiled to her room for a half-hour, or when a motorist who is caught speeding is fined. In the first case, companionship is denied the child; in the second, money is removed from the motorist. Elementary school teachers use punishment by denial when they attempt to control disruptive behavior by placing the unruly child in temporary isolation ("time out") (Kazdin, 1975). Similar punishment is used in hockey games, when players who get into fights are removed from play and sent to the penalty box for a specified period of time. In one experiment punishment by denial was used in an attempt to get very young boys to stop sucking their thumbs. Each boy watched a series of animated cartoons and whenever he began to suck his thumb, the film stopped. As you might expect, thumb sucking fell off dramatically (Baer, 1962).

There are disadvantages to the use of punishment. The association between punishment and the behavior can generalize, so that although the undesirable behavior disappears, desirable behavior may disappear as well. A child who is regularly and severely punished for aggression may stop fighting but may also become passive, giving up assertiveness along with aggression. In addition, the punished person tends to dislike and avoid the individual who did the punishing and the situation in which it occurred. For this reason children who are frequently punished by their teachers come to dislike school.

Although punishment clearly tells a person what not to do, it gives no hint as to what the individual should do: it simply suppresses inappropriate behavior, without establishing behavior that is appropriate. For this reason punishment is probably most effective when used in conjunction with positive reinforcement for some alternative behavior, so that as the unwanted behavior is punished, desirable behavior is being reinforced

(Skinner, 1953). For example, a six-year-old autistic girl whose bizarre climbing activities had caused her several serious injuries was given a mild shock on the leg each time she started to climb the furniture. At the same time the experimenter (Risley, 1968) rewarded her with food whenever she sat down quietly or made eye contact with him. In this case the combination of punishment and reward effectively ended the dangerous climbing.

Escape Learning

A second form of aversive learning is **escape learning**, in which the organism learns a specific response that terminates some unpleasant stimulus, so that the organism can escape from an aversive situation. Escape learning is different from learning by punishment: escape learning *strengthens* a response that *removes* an aversive stimulus, whereas punishment *weakens* a response that *produces* an aversive stimulus. Some psychologists refer to the removal of an aversive stimulus (as in escape learning) as **negative reinforcement**, because a response is strengthened (reinforced) by the removal of the unpleasant stimulus. However, this term can be confusing, so we will not use it again in this book.

Escape learning often occurs naturally. When you step out into the bright noonday sun, you immediately reach for your sunglasses, which in the past have removed the unpleasant glare. When you have a headache, you reach for aspirin, which relieves it. Sometimes what is escape learning for one person is positive reinforcement for another. For example, a baby who is generally picked up when he or she cries soon learns that crying is the way to get taken out of the crib. When parents try to break the cycle and extinguish the wails by ignoring them, their infant may cry harder. A particularly prolonged period of crying may so exasperate the parents that they "give in" and pick up the baby. The parents are in an escape learning condition, in which picking up the baby is rewarded with relief from the aversive screams. But the incident simultaneously puts the baby on a variable ratio schedule of positive reinforcement for crying, perhaps training the infant to be a persistent crier.

Avoidance Learning

The third kind of aversive learning, **avoidance learning**, mingles classical conditioning and instrumental conditioning. In avoidance learning a signal announces the impending arrival of some unpleasant stimulus. If the organism makes the correct response, the aversive stimulus does not arrive (it is "avoided"). If the organism fails to respond soon enough, then the unpleasant stimulus comes on and the organism must now respond so as to terminate the unpleasant stimulus.

For example, a buzzer might notify a rat that in five seconds a shock will pulse through the floor of its operant conditioning chamber. If the rat rotates a small wheel on a nearby wall within five seconds, then the shock will not arrive (it will be avoided). If the rat does not respond quickly enough to prevent the shock, then when the shock comes on the animal can terminate the shock and the buzzer by turning the wheel. In this situation the rat's action is presumably motivated by fear that has been classically conditioned to the sound by previous experience with the sound-shock sequence (Mowrer, 1960). Each time the rat turns off the buzzer and prevent a shock, the response is reinforced by the removal of the aversive stimulus. In avoidance training, animals apparently come to expect that their response will lead to safety. Avoidance learning underlies many human activities. For example, we pay our bills on time to avoid late charges, and we take an umbrella to avoid getting wet when it rains.

Learned Rewards and Punishment

Just why an animal—or a person—should be willing to perform a certain behavior in order to get food, water, or sleep is easy to understand. All these things are **primary reinforcers**: that is, they fulfill some basic need of the organism and thus are reinforcing for all members of a species.

According to Clark Hull (1943), any stimulus or event that reduces basic drives or needs (such as thirst or hunger) is an effective reinforcer. This relationship helps a species to survive: it is important for animals driven by a particular need to repeat any behavior that earlier has satisfied that need. But Hull's view of reinforcement as depending on the reduction of drives is too narrow to include the hundreds of emotionally pleasant events that seem to be reinforcing but are unrelated to biological drives. Why, for example, do we seek approval, work for money, and enjoy entertaining activities? Other psychologists have attempted to formulate principles of reinforcement that apply more generally than just to primary reinforcers.

One explanation for the effectiveness of reinforcers that do not satisfy basic drives is that learning, or conditioning, has taken place. When neutral stimuli are consistently paired with naturally positive or negative outcomes, the neutral events (through the process of classical conditioning) take on some of the emotional quality of the natural outcome. Such conditioned stimuli are known as **secondary reinforcers** or **conditioned reinforcers**; an organism finds them as rewarding or punishing as primary reinforcers—at least for a while.

For example, in Pavlov's bell-food experiment the bell would become a conditioned (positive) reinforcer. As another example, the mechanical click as small candies are released into a cup tells a child that a primary reinforcer, food, is on the way. If the child consistently hears the click just before the candies arrive, the sound will become a reward in itself. The child will make some response for a while just to hear the click. Other stimuli can become conditioned punishers if they are paired with an innate punishment. For example, if a parent habitually clears his or her throat in a particular way just before spanking the child, the sound becomes a conditioned punisher, and the child will find the sound almost as unpleasant as the spanking itself.

Experience with such pairings of conditioned and unconditioned stimuli establishes conditioned reinforcers, and experience in situations where the US stops following the CS can extinguish them. Unless the child occasionally gets candies following the click, or a spanking following the throat-clearing, the conditioned reinforcers will lose their power. Of course, partial reinforcement increases the persistence of a secondary reinforcer. If the click is only occasionally paired with the candy, it can maintain its value for a very long time without being backed up by a candy reinforcer (Zimmerman, 1959).

The speed with which a primary reinforcer follows learned behavior in the laboratory is rarely encountered in daily life. In many cases a secondary reinforcer helps bridge the delay between a response and its primary reinforcement. For example, money is a highly effective secondary reinforcer, and people are willing to work for it because they know it can eventually be exchanged for primary reinforcers, such as food or shelter. But money retains this power only as long as it can be exchanged for primary rewards. If it becomes worthless, people will no longer work for it. For example, in Germany during the hyperin-flation of the early 1920s, when a pound of butter cost 1 million Deutschmarks, their money became valueless. People refused it and would work only for the primary reinforcers of goods and services.

Conditioned reinforcers can also be used to establish new behavior, because a conditioned reinforcer can be used in situations that are quite different from the one in which it was established. For example, social reinforcers such as smiles, praise, and approval can effectively change behavior in a wide range of situations—as can social punishers such as frowns.

Although conditioned reinforcers lose their power with animals if they are not periodically paired with the original reinforcers, such extinction does not always occur with people. Certain conditioned reinforcers, such as money, gold, praise, and social power, sometimes seem to become independent of the basic biological rewards for which they stand. When the instrumental "means" become an end in itself, the miser or the power-hungry politician is born. Such people seem to derive their reward from rehearsing in imagination the benefits that supposedly accompany their hoard of wealth, status, or power.

How Skills Are Learned via Instrumental Conditioning

The majority of instrumental conditioning studies seem to involve simple acts. But in daily life most animal or human behavior is complex. Even the simplest response, such as striking a match or pressing a lever, is actually a chain of individual behaviors that are somewhat independent of one another.

To take a simple example, in order for a rat to press a lever, it must approach the lever, rise up on its hind legs, put its front paws on the lever, and push the lever down toward the floor. We may thus analyze the overall "response" into a series of much smaller stimulus-response units that are linked together like beads on a chain. An untrained rat already knows most parts of this sequence (or chain), but the animal rarely executes the entire sequence spontaneously. How does it learn to arrange the parts of the chain? Instead of waiting weeks for the rat to stumble onto the correct chain, the experimenter can use a procedure called **shaping**, an operant conditioning procedure based on reinforcing ever-closer approximations of a desired behavior.

The Shaping of a Skill

The shaping process is effective when the animal is motivated—say, by hunger or thirst—to work for reinforcement. As the process begins, the trainer reinforces the animal's first response in the right direction; next, the trainer gradually requires a closer approximation to the correct response before giving a reward; and finally, the trainer requires a more and more polished execution of the action before giving a reward. At first the rat only has to approach the lever to be fed. Then it must rise off the floor to be fed, and finally it must press the lever in order to be fed. As the rat learns each step in the chain of behavior, the experimenter increases the requirements, refusing to reinforce the rat until it has mastered the next link in the chain. Finally, the animal can carry out an intricate sequence of behavior. Shaping is the name of the general procedure by which complex chains of behavior can be trained.

Through shaping, pigeons have been taught to play Ping-Pong and to tap out simple tunes on a toy piano, dolphins have been taught to "hula" while balancing on their tails, and lions have been taught to ride horseback. In fact, trainers have even taught sea lions to locate and recover antisubmarine rockets, so that recorded information on each rocket's performance can be evaluated by the Navy (Monagan, 1983). Shaping is also an effective way to teach children such skills as printing letters of the alphabet, making their bed, or using the toilet. For example, two psychologists (Azrin and Foxx, 1974) devised a way to toilet-train young children quickly by reinforcing each step in the sequence of walking toward the potty chair, lowering their pants, sitting down, and urinating.

The Importance of Feedback in Skill Learning

Most complex motor skills, such as typing, playing basketball, editing text on a computer, or playing a piano, involve a chain of coordinated perceptual-motor responses. When these skills are being acquired, the most efficient reinforcement consists of immediate **feedback**—information as to whether a response is right or wrong, closer to or farther from the ideal form. For some skills the behavior itself produces direct feedback: the golfer can see whether the putt has gone into the cup, and the tennis player can see whether the serve has landed in the proper court. In other cases the learner may

Practicing in front of a mirror gives a dancer the immediate feedback he needs to correct his movements.

get feedback by watching his or her form in a mirror or by verbal reports from a coach.

Immediate feedback is important because the learner who is trying to improve a motor skill must remember the subtle muscle variant he or she has produced on a given trial and associate it with the quality of the outcome or consequence. The greater the delay between execution of the response and feedback, the poorer the learner's memory of the muscle pattern and of the sequencing of movements that he or she must associate with the outcome. Feedback is also important in learning intellectual skills. For example, learning how to program computers or do proofs in plane geometry is said to progress three or four times as fast with a private tutor as in a conventional classroom because the tutor can provide immediate feedback and correction whenever the learner begins a wrong line of reasoning, thus shortcutting the novice's wasted efforts (Anderson et al., 1984).

By rewarding successive approximations, the tutor can also shape the force or speed with which a skill is carried out. A person can be reinforced for responding gently and slowly, gently and rapidly, intensely but slowly, or any other desired combination. Such selective reinforcement is common when parents show small children how to stroke a kitten gently or brush their teeth with vigor, and it also underlies the acquisition of skills in which timing is crucial—playing a musical instrument, typing, or hitting a baseball.

The Importance of Practice in Skill Learning

Once the rudiments of a complex skill are acquired, performance improves with practice —rapidly at first and then more slowly. As the skill improves, a person must practice for increasingly greater periods to produce a noticeable improvement—whether the learning involves a motor skill such as rolling tobacco leaves into cigars or a cognitive skill such as mental addition. The same relation between practice and performance time has been found in virtually every study of skill acquisition (Anderson, 1980; Newell and Rosenbloom, 1981).

When a person is just beginning to learn a skill, each step in the action absorbs most of his or her attention. After several hours of practice, the learner eliminates errors and strengthens the connections among the parts of the skill. Finally, after long practice, execution becomes smooth and rapid (Anderson, 1980). As we saw in Chapter 7, once this stage is reached, the skill becomes automatic and slips out of awareness; attempts to reinstate parts of it into awareness may even disrupt performance. For example, when a typist or pianist tries to become conscious of just where each finger goes next, he or she slows down and may strike the wrong keys. Many psychologists believe that the speed-up of a skilled motion is accomplished by the learner's condensing a large series of perceptual-motor units into a few "thought-action" sequences (e.g., Anderson, 1982; Newell and Rosenbloom. 1981).

SPATIAL LEARNING

In classical and instrumental conditioning we learn about *sequences* of events, about how one stimulus or response is followed by a particular outcome. But we also acquire another form of knowledge about the world: we learn where in space objects are located, and this is quite independent of the temporal order in which we have experienced those objects. We know where our house is in relation to the rest of the town, where the kitchen is in the house, where the refrigerator is in the kitchen, and so on. This kind of knowledge about the spatial layout of landmarks and objects is acquired by moving around in these spaces and looking, by studying a map, or by having someone tell us where things are. This form of learning is quite distinct from classical and instrumental conditioning procedures.

Some forty years ago, Edward Tolman (1948) explained spatial learning by proposing that organisms learn **cognitive maps**, or internal representations of the way objects and landmarks are arranged in their environment. A map is a collection of associations among sensory objects, describing how they are spatially related to others and to landmarks. At first, Tolman's proposal was unpopular. At the time it was made most psychologists believed that organisms learned only what responses to make to stimuli, and cognitive maps simply cannot be reduced to a small collection of stimulus-response connections. Since then a good deal of evidence has accumulated to support the idea of cognitive maps—and not only in people but also in birds and even the lowly rat.

Chimpanzees have shown an impressive ability at learning cognitive maps. In one experiment, after a group of chimps had familiarized themselves with a new one-acre outdoor enclosure, they took part in an "Easter egg hunt" that tested their ability to remember the location of food hidden within the enclosure (Menzel, 1973). Each chimp was carried around and allowed to watch while pieces of its favorite fruit were concealed in eighteen different locations. When released later, the chimp would run directly to one of the hiding places, eat the fruit, and move on to the next place. The chimps showed that they had some mental representation of the enclosure's layout—they went to the various caches in order of their spatial proximity, not in the order in which they had seen the fruit being hidden (see Figure 8.6). They appeared to use landmarks to remember the hiding places. Their route was planned like that of a traveling sales representative, who organizes the order of customer visits so as to call on all of them while traveling the least possible distance.

When people develop cognitive maps, they apparently form mental images of their surround-

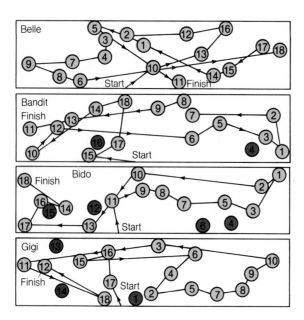

Figure 8.6. These maps show four chimps' performance in finding food that they had seen hidden in a familiar one-acre enclosure. The numbers indicate the sequence in which each chimp saw the food being hidden, while the arrows indicate the sequence in which each chimp found the caches of food. Numbered circles not touched by the start-to-finish line indicate food that was not found. (Menzel, 1973.)

ings, based on various landmarks. When they first enter a new environment, they seem to use landmarks to develop isolated route maps: they chart the path from place to place (two blocks east, turn left at the bakery, then four blocks south, and so on). As yet they have no coherent map of the spatial relationship among the various reference points; they would be unable to take a shortcut or a detour. But as they become familiar with an area, their cognitive maps broaden into survey maps, which cover a wider area and locate various points in relation to one another (Anderson, 1980). However, because people persist in thinking of streets as a grid of horizontal and vertical lines, even when the area includes many curving streets, their subjective maps are generally distorted. Because of this tendency toward simplification, most cognitive maps are filled with errors (Moar, 1983; B. Tversky, 1981).

OBSERVATIONAL LEARNING

Closely related to spatial learning is observational learning, which for humans is one of our most important and prevalent forms of learning. Instead of learning everything through trial and error—by acting and having our successes reinforced and our failures punished—we can profit from vicarious learning, in which we observe what other people do and notice the consequences.

In this way we can acquire knowledge that would otherwise have to come about through direct classical or instrumental conditioning. By observation alone we can learn about the relationship between two stimuli, about the relationship between certain responses and outcomes, or about sequential motor skills, such as how to start a car. Indeed, if we had to learn to drive a car or perform brain surgery by instrumental conditioning, in which punishment for our errors gradually shaped us into drivers or surgeons, the costs to other drivers or to patients would be intolerable.

In observational learning, other people serve as **models**; from them we can learn a complete pattern of behavior in a single observation, instead of laboriously acquiring the pattern bit by bit through trial and error. From watching a model, we can learn a new way of behaving, learn to stop behaving in a certain way, or learn to behave in previously forbidden ways. We may even learn to behave in an old way we had forgotten but recall as we watch the model's performance (Bandura and Walters, 1963). We may store information about a modeled behavior in memory—how to perform a new dance step, how a friend gets dates, how to replace a worn light switch—and use this information to guide our behavior far in the future. Many people imitate parents, teachers, or friends, and some even imitate the behavior of prestigious people they will never meet—movie stars, fictional characters, athletes, or other media personalities. Through observation, people can acquire a full range of attitudes, emotions, and social styles.

Social Learning

We are not born socialized; everything we know about our culture, our traditions, the rules of our social group, and even the behavior that makes each culture distinctive is learned. Much of this knowledge comes from watching others.

Observational learning in a garden: father serves as the model in his daughter's acquisition of a new skill.

Observational learning appears to have powerful effects on the behavior and attitudes of children. In one well-known study youngsters who watched aggressive models showed twice as much physical aggression when they were mildly frustrated as did youngsters who saw no aggressive models before being frustrated (Bandura, Ross, and Ross, 1963). This occurred whether the models were live human beings, or people on film, or cartoon characters. Children who had watched an aggressive live adult model imitated her behavior by pounding an inflated Bobo doll with a mallet, punching it in the nose, kicking it, and tossing it in the air. And children who had watched aggressive adult models on film were more likely to engage in aggressive gun play than any other

group. In another study (Bandura, 1965), children who had watched filmed models go unpunished for aggressive actions later imitated the models, whereas children who had watched filmed aggressive models being punished were unlikely to imitate them. (In Chapter 17 we will explore the long-term effects of televised aggression on children.)

A child's moral standards are probably learned or refined through observation. In one experiment children changed the basis of their own moral judgments after seeing that adults were reinforced for a particular brand of moral judgment (Bandura and McDonald, 1963). For example, children who had formerly judged acts according to the amount of damage they caused switched, as a result of learning, to judging acts on the basis of the culprit's good or bad intentions. In further studies of modeling, children seem to be more influenced by the adult model's actions than by his words. When children watched models who preached high standards but practiced lower ones, the children adopted the model's lower standards for themselves (e.g., Ormiston, 1972). As common wisdom tells us, a parent's actions speak louder than words.

Modeling is sometimes used by therapists to help people learn more adaptive behavior and to give up old behavior that is maladaptive. For example, children have been helped to overcome an intense fear of dogs through modeling (Bandura and Menlov, 1968). These youngsters, who were preschoolers, watched movies of other children playing with dogs and even lying down on the grass and hugging the dogs, with their faces close to the dog's open mouth. The process was most effective when the youngsters watched several models who played with a variety of dogs.

How Observational Learning Works

Observational learning is a central concept of **social learning theory**, an approach to learning that combines traditional learning theory with a concern for human thought processes. According to Albert Bandura (1977), learning is not simply a matter of reacting to stimuli; instead, people apply cognitive processes (thinking processes) to the stimuli they encounter, selecting among these stimuli and organizing and transforming them. In this perspective, stimuli are seen as providing information, and it is people's interpretation of stimuli and not the stimuli themselves that affect behavior. Bandura also emphasizes the cognitive processes by which people regulate their own behavior, by setting goals to motivate and reward themselves.

As an example of Bandura's (1977) approach, he proposes that observational learning consists of four processes: attention, retention, motor reproduction, and motivation. *Attention* paid to the model depends on such factors as the model's attractiveness, engaging personal qualities, prestige, his or her age, race, sex, religious beliefs, and political attitudes, and general similarity to the viewer. Some models are ignored while others are watched closely and imitated. Certain actions, such as distinctive forms of violence and blatantly sexual displays, tend to attract and hold attention. Television and film exploit many of these attention-grabbing factors, which make their models especially effective.

But attention by itself may not be enough. Unless the viewer creates internal images or linguistic descriptions of the model's actions, the behavior will not be *retained* and thus there will be no learning. The easier it is for a viewer to create such mental representations, the better the behavior will be learned and remembered.

Furthermore, unless the learner is able to *reproduce* some approximation of the model's movements, there will be no learning. Observation teaches only the gross movements involved. When a learner is trying to reproduce an action —whether it is shifting gears in a car, handwriting, fly casting, or swinging a golf club—the first attempts will generally lack the fine motor coordination required in the polished action. Because we cannot observe the kinesthetic cues involved in the movement, we must refine such skills by doing them ourselves.

Finally, the *motivation* to imitate any act depends in good part on the consequences that befall the model and how the outcomes he obtains correspond to our needs. We observe, remember, and anticipate the reinforcement or punishment that has followed the model's actions. We are more likely to imitate a model's actions if they are rewarded than if they are punished. Often we learn some modeled behavior but we may not perform it until an appropriate occasion arises. Whether we perform that action at a later time depends on our expectations of the act's consequences in a particular situation. The likelihood of our jumping ahead in a queue or crossing against a red light is affected by whether we see others being punished for such impulsive behavior.

Learning Through Language

Language provides another form of vicarious learning. Most education, including reading this textbook, leads to the creation of symbolic representations that describe or refer to some reality. By reading or hearing about a situation, we can gain a part of the knowledge we would have learned had we experienced the situation directly. Concepts and the relations between them are basic to language, and this aspect of language will be discussed in Chapter 10, Cognition.

We learn the relationships among concepts much as we learn other associations. If someone tells us, "Mary has red hair," we learn to associate the two concepts and expect that when we meet Mary, she will have red hair. We also use language to instruct ourselves and others regarding actions that could lead to some goal, whether the language provides a recipe for soufflé or instructions on filling out a tax form. These aspects of learning will be explored in Chapter 9, Memory, and Chapter 16, Acquiring and Using Language.

SUMMARY

1. **Learning** can be described as a change in a behavioral disposition caused by experience and not explained on the basis of reflexes, maturation, or temporary states. Learning must be inferred from performance because learning cannot be observed directly. Organisms learn about objects and their classifica-tions, about their location in the environment, about temporal and causal sequences, and how to perform various perceptual-motor skills. Such knowledge can be acquired through personal action, observation, or language.

2. Each new stimulus encountered produces an **orienting reflex**, which might be called a surprise reaction. With repeated exposure to the stimulus, **habituation** occurs, so that the strength of the orienting response decreases. Habituation reflects learning to identify a specific stimulus.

3. In **classical conditioning**, when a neutral stimulus (e.g., a tone) is repeatedly presented just before an **unconditioned stimulus** (e.g., food) that normally evokes a reflex, or **unconditioned response** (e.g., salivation), the neutral stimulus comes thereby to elicit that response. Once the previously neutral stimulus elicits an anticipatory, conditioned response, the neutral stimulus is said to have become a **conditioned stimulus** and the response has become a **conditioned response**. Such CS–UCS pairings may lead to learning either by increasing the strength and efficiency of synaptic connections within the nervous system or by establishing new connections. Classical conditioning seems to be responsible for many acquired emotional responses. During the **acquisition** of a conditioned response, the CS causes the subject to expect the unconditioned stimulus to follow. Once a conditioned stimulus is established, it can be used in **second-order conditioning**, in which its pairing with a second neutral stimulus causes the second stimulus to elicit the same response. If the conditioned stimulus is repeatedly presented but no longer followed by the unconditioned stimulus, the conditioned response to that conditioned stimulus will gradually disappear, a process known as **extinction**. An extinguished response will temporarily reappear if, after a rest, the organism is reintroduced to the experimental situation, a process called **spontaneous recovery**. An extinguished response can quickly be relearned if the unconditioned stimulus and the conditioned stimulus are again paired (**reconditioning**).

4. A conditioned response may show **stimulus generalization**, in that the response can be elicited by stimuli similar to the conditioned stimulus. The more similar a test stimulus is to the conditioned stimulus, the more likely it is that the response will generalize to the test, along a curve known as a **generalization gra-dient**. **Discrimination** training refers to a procedure by which organisms learn to distinguish among stimuli: by pairing one CS with a UCS but alternately presenting other stimuli without a UCS, the animal comes to respond readily to the first CS, but not to respond to the other stimuli.

5. Classical conditioning appears to depend on whether the conditioned stimulus enables the organism to predict the occurrence of the unconditioned stimulus better than it could without the aid of the CS. This predictability requires a strong correlation between the CS and the UCS: the presence of the CS must usually predict the presence of the UCS, and the absence of the CS must usually predict the absence of the UCS. If one cue already signals the UCS, organisms rely on this established predictor, a reliance that can block the learning of an association between a second, added CS and the UCS.

6. In **instrumental conditioning**, also called **operant conditioning**, the organism learns to associate its action with the consequences of that action, expects that its action will produce that consequence, and later performs that action when it desires that consequence. Positive outcomes are often called **positive reinforcers**, and they generally strengthen a response. Negative consequences are called **punishments**, and they generally suppress or weaken a response. Escape from unpleasant stimuli produces a positive outcome, and the removal of pleasant conditions produces a negative outcome.

7. In a free operant situation, once the operantly conditioned response is established, the **schedule of reinforcement**, or the basis on which the organism is rewarded, can be changed from a **continuous reinforcement schedule** to a **partial reinforcement schedule**. Rewards may come after a specific number of responses (**fixed ratio schedule**), a specified lapse of time (**fixed interval schedule**), a variable number of responses (**variable ratio schedule**), or a variable lapse of time (**variable interval schedule**). When a coincidental relationship occurs between behavior and reinforcer, **superstitious behavior** may develop. Like classical conditioning, instru-

mental conditioning shows acquisition, extinction, spontaneous recovery, reconditioning, generalization, and discrimination. In instrumental conditioning, the organism learns to expect a given outcome following a given response, and it will alter its performance of that response if the value of the outcome is changed. **Aversive learning** uses unpleasant or aversive stimuli in one of several arrangements. In *punishment,* an aversive event that follows a response weakens that response. In **escape learning**, the organism learns a response that removes it from an unpleasant stimulus. In **avoidance learning**, the organism learns that it can prevent the arrival of an unpleasant stimulus by acting early in response to a warning stimulus.

8. A **secondary**, or **conditioned, reinforcer**, is like a classically conditioned stimulus that signals that a **primary reinforcer** is on the way. With repeated pairings between a neutral reinforcer and the primary reinforcer, the neutral reinforcer takes on some of the same rewarding (or punishing) value as the primary reinforcer, hence it is called a secondary reinforcer. Secondary reinforcers can be used to establish new behavior or to bridge the delay between a response and its primary reinforcer.

9. Skills are often learned through a process of **shaping**, in which ever-closer approximations of a desired behavior are rewarded. As each segment of behavior is learned, it can be chained to earlier segments to form an intricate sequence. When complex motor skills are acquired, **feedback**, which is information about a response and its consequence, provides the most efficient reinforcement. Once the rudiments of a skill are acquired, practice is required to improve performance.

10. Organisms also acquire knowledge of spatial layouts, developing **cognitive maps**, or internal representations of the environment. In observational learning, other people serve as **models**; by watching and imitating them we learn complex patterns of behavior, attitudes, and emotions. Observational learning is a basic part of **social learning theory**, which stresses the role of thinking and symbolic processes in learning about the social world. Observational learning requires attention, retention, motor reproduction, and motivation. Vicarious learning can also take place through language.

KEY TERMS

acquisition
association
aversive learning
avoidance learning
blocking
classical conditioning
cognitive maps
conditioned reinforcer
conditioned response (CR)
conditioned stimulus (CS)
continuous reinforcement
  schedule
discrimination
escape learning
extinction

feedback
fixed interval schedule
fixed ratio schedule
generalization gradient
habituation
instrumental conditioning
learning
models
negative reinforcement
operant conditioning
orienting reflex
partial reinforcement schedule
positive reinforcer
primary reinforcer
punishment

reconditioning
schedule of reinforcement
second-order conditioning
secondary reinforcer
shaping
social learning theory
spontaneous recovery
stimulus generalization
superstitious behavior
unconditioned response (UCR)
unconditioned stimulus (UCS)
variable interval schedule
variable ratio schedule

RECOMMENDED READINGS

HOUSTON, J. P. *Fundamentals of learning and memory* (2nd ed.). New York: Academic Press, 1981. This book emphasizes experimental investigations of learning and memory. It presents the basic data on both animal and human learning, along with the theories that researchers have devised to explain those data.

DICKINSON, A. *Contemporary animal learning theory.* New York: Cambridge University Press, 1980 (paper). Very readable, up-to-date perspective on conditioning and learning. Explains the approach taken in the Learning chapter of this text.

FLAHERTY, C. F., *Animal learning and cognition.* New York: Random House, 1985. Cognitive interpretations of animal behavior, the neural basis of conditioning, and recent work on drugs' effects on conditioning and addiction are discussed in this text. Fascinating material on how the study of animal learning illuminates human behavior issues is integrated throughout. Research on over two dozen animal species is cited.

MACKINTOSH, N. J. *Conditioning and associative learning.* Oxford: Clarendon Press, 1983. The most authoritative recent summary of the theoretical issues in the field. Intellectually challenging.

SKINNER, B. F. *Beyond freedom and dignity.* New York: Knopf, 1971 (paper). This well-written book for the layman illustrates Skinner's views of cultural practices and how behavioral technology might be used to alleviate some of our societal problems. Stimulating, controversial reading.

WATSON, D. L., and R. G. THARP, *Self-directed behavior: Self-modification for personal adjustment* (2nd ed.). Monterey: Brooks/Cole, 1977. This book tells you how to use learning principles to modify your own behavior. It is an interesting how-to-do-it book.

WICKELGREN, W. A. *Learning and memory.* Englewood Cliffs, N.J.: Prentice-Hall, 1977. Good text that describes both animal conditioning and human memory according to an integrated, unified theory. A thoughtful, refreshing perspective on many conventional topics in the field.

MEMORY

Imagine being handed a list of fifty unrelated words, and then after about three minutes' study, recalling them perfectly, forward or backward. A Russian newspaper reporter who was studied extensively by Alexander Luria (1968) found this feat no more difficult than you would find recalling what you had eaten for breakfast this morning. What is more, the Russian, whom Luria called S, could repeat the list without any previous warning after a lapse of fifteen or sixteen years. In such a situation, S would sit with his eyes closed and say:

> Yes, yes . . . This was a series you gave me once when we were in your apartment. . . . You were sitting at the table and I in the rocking chair. . . . You were wearing a gray suit and you looked at me like this. . . . Now, then, I can see you saying . . .

With that, the list would come tumbling out, each word in order and never confused with the words of another list. Foreign languages posed no problem; S once memorized long passages of *The Divine Comedy* in Italian, which he did not speak, and fifteen years later recalled them with ease.

How did S do it? He used mental imagery plus a retrieval plan. Often, when he memorized a list of words, he would imagine that he was walking along a familiar street; for each word, he would mentally place a corresponding image in a distinctive place along the street. To recall the list, all he had to do was repeat the retrieval plan. He would take a mental stroll down the same street and call off each item as he passed it.

Faced with final exams, you might long for a memory like S's. But his incredible memory became a curse as well as a blessing. Over the years, he became unable to forget anything he had learned. He was haunted by the images he had created to help him remember; they intruded into his awareness and made it difficult for him to concentrate on his daily business. He became confused, finding it impossible to follow simple conversations because people's words would trigger a host of associated images that were often irrelevant to the topic. Unable to hold regular employment, he was forced to work at the only job his amazing memory suited him for—that of a performer who displayed his curious ability in one town after another.

S's story tells us something about how memory operates. Even though his odd gift seems unique, the methods he used to remember things were not actually different from those we use every day—they were just much more highly developed. We all have memories that are organized in ways similar to S's. Our memories are intricate networks of associations established through learning, and we access and use these associations in order to bring into consciousness the material we are trying to remember. We will clarify this point as we talk about what memory really is.

WHAT IS MEMORY?

Sometimes, when we think of our memory, we imagine it as a mental "filing cabinet" in which we deposit isolated facts that we want to be sure to retain—such as the dates of the American Revolution, or our mother's birthday, or the errands we must be sure to do on the way home from work. But that is only a partial description of our memory. Our memory encompasses everything we have recently perceived and everything we know or can recollect—about people, places, music, pictures, ways of doing things, languages, emotional feelings, dreams, actions, and skills.

In analyzing memory, William Brewer and J. R. Pani (1983) have suggested that the contents of our memory can be seen as falling into three broad categories.

- *Personal memories* consist of distinct episodes we have witnessed, such as this morning's breakfast. When we remember such episodes, we can "see" the event taking place, and our mental images carry a sense of the past.
- *Generic memories*, by contrast, include memories that are abstract and are not tied to any particular time or place; we do not usually remember where we learned them. They include memories that are primarily semantic, or meaning-related, rather than being scenes. Concepts such as "love" or "constitutional monarchy" are generic memories. So are memories of the meanings and referents of words, such as "icebox" or "Uncle Harry." Generic memories also include perceptual memories of the way things look, sound, and so on—the smell of an apple pie baking, the tune to "The Star-Spangled Banner."
- *Skill memories* consist of cognitive skills, such as our ability to solve quadratic equations; motor skills, such as our knowledge of how to ice-skate or put in a light bulb; and rote verbal sequences we have memorized, such as our own phone number.

Memory is an ambiguous concept. One meaning of the concept refers to a repository of our accumulated knowledge of specific and general things, but another meaning refers to processes —"memorizing" and "remembering." Psychologists analyze the memorizing-remembering cycle into three distinct processes: acquisition, retention, and retrieval. **Acquisition** is the process by which we initially perceive, register, and record information in our memory. If you do not pay attention and register something in the first place, you will never be able to remember it. **Retention** is the process by which we maintain information in storage in our memory; you may register a piece of information such as an address, but it may decay over time, or similar material placed into memory may interfere with its retention. **Retrieval** is the process by which we get information out of storage and bring it back into our awareness. You may register a piece of information and store it, but then find yourself unable to bring it back to mind—until someone gives you a good cue that "jogs your memory."

The Importance of Selective Attention

The gatekeeper to our memory is a process known as **selective attention**. In attending to the world around us, we cannot possibly respond to all the thousands of stimuli that bombard us every second. Instead, we constantly select from the stream of stimuli just a limited number of sights, sounds, and other sensations—and ignore the rest. Only those few stimuli that we select for focused attention will be registered firmly in our memory: the others, registered weakly and unattended to, will quickly fade from our memory.

Consider a common example. You have handled thousands of pennies, but if you are like other people, you have probably registered few of their details in memory. To demonstrate this, put down this book and try to draw from memory the "heads" side of a penny, putting in as many details as possible. (Do it now, then return here.) You may find that you do not draw the penny very well: a coin's size and color are all you need to identify it, so there is no reason to remember other details. Most people, when asked to draw the face of a penny, can locate correctly only about three of its eight or more details.

What guides selective attention? Some factors are universal. For example, the simple properties of the stimulus may make it an attention-getter: anything that is intense, large, loud, or strikingly colorful attracts attention. Also, novelty or deviations from the expected attract attention. A man walking a dog is passed over, but a dog walking a man would get more than a few stares. Other factors in the selection process are very personal. We pay attention to anything that is relevant to our own motives. Stimuli that arouse our *emotions*, whether these signals are violent, sexy, horrifying, or beautiful, attract our attention. Stimuli that affect our *goals* and *self-esteem*, or those of our loved ones, interest us. Events that are relevant to our *interests* also attract our attention. The newspaper story that grabs one person's attention may go unread by someone with different interests.

Memory and Its Time Frames

If a stimulus gets past the "gatekeeper" and you do pay attention to it, your memory processes will begin to operate. The result may be a memory that lasts for just a second or two, a memory that lasts for several minutes, or a memory that lasts for hours, days, or years. What happens when our memory processes operate within these three different time frames?

Sensory Memory

Virtually every moment of your waking life you have memories that are simply the aftereffects of your sensory processes. These fleeting sense impressions, known as **sensory memories**, last for just a tiny interval of time. You can experience a brief sensory impression by taking a small flashlight into a dark closet. Rotate the beam in a one-foot circle in front of you, moving it fast enough so that you "see" a complete circle. The faint, persisting image that allows you to see the circle is called the *visual icon*. It lasts a few tenths of a second after the stimulus disappears. The icon's persistence probably helps us identify visual patterns that are present for only a fraction of a second, such as pictures flashed on a screen. Similarly, our visual world maintains its stability even though we blink frequently as we look about us. This phenomenon is related to our sensory memory.

Similar sensory aftereffects exist for touch and hearing. We rely on auditory aftereffects in conversation: the persisting auditory images enable us to process speech sounds after the speaker has gone ahead with his or her remarks. You may have experienced this aftereffect in a sort of auditory double take that we all perform frequently. If someone asks you a question when you are engrossed in reading, you respond with, "What did you say?" But before the last word is out of your mouth, you rehear the question from your "echo-trace" and go on to answer it.

Short-Term Memory

Many of our sensory memories simply fade almost immediately. But if we pay close attention to a sensory memory, that record enters a more durable phase we call **short-term memory (STM)**. Short-term memory is a temporary form of memory that lasts many seconds; it is also known as active memory or primary memory.

Here is how short-term memory operates. While we are attending to a sensory event (for example, if we hear a friend talking about Ronald Reagan), we may also retrieve associations to that event from more durable parts of our memory (for example, we may retrieve a visual image of Reagan's face). These retrieved associations themselves become active as part of our memory of the event. In essence, we have converted the information from one form to another prior to recording it in memory; this process is called **encoding**. The same thing happens, for instance, if we see the figure 2. We may say the word "two" to ourselves, and record the information as the sound "two."

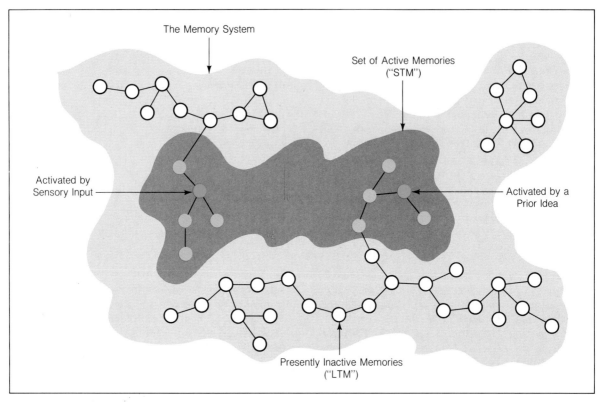

The Memory System

Set of Active Memories
("STM")

Activated by
Sensory Input

Activated by a
Prior Idea

Presently Inactive Memories
("LTM")

Figure 9.1. The diagram provides a schematic way to think about the active and inactive portions of memory and the relationship between them. Memory contains a huge network of ideas or items (represented by the circles) that are linked by associations. At any given moment, a particular idea (dark circles) may be activated or energized, either by a prior mental idea or by a sensory stimulus; these activated items then spread their activation to neighboring ideas to which they are connected. The items and connections inside the inner (shaded) segment are considered to be in active, short-term memory. Inactive, long-term memory is represented by the white circles within the outer segment.

A good way to understand short-term memory is to experience it. Try this: say aloud the letters "*E, K, L, Z,*" and think about them while you are saying them. Doing so sets up **memory traces** (internal records) of the letters, and you will find that you can repeat them from memory. They are available in your awareness and seem to be immediately present—the traces are "active." These spoken letters, which are encoded versions of of the visual letters, are in your short-term memory.

The memories in STM remain active as long as you attend to them, but if you are distracted they will fade within a few seconds. To experience this, try to remember the letters now. Note the difference between the state of the letters as they seem to you now and the impression you had earlier when you were repeating them. Before, they were vivid, and they were available immediately and

without effort. But within a few seconds they faded out of consciousness. Just now, you recalled them slowly and perhaps with some struggle; when you brought them back into consciousness, you may have forgotten some of them or remembered them out of order.

Long-Term Memory

Now try to remember your mother's maiden name. Do you have it as an active trace? Before you remembered it, the name was inactive; it was in what is called **long-term memory (LTM)**, out of your consciousness. Then, when you retrieved it, the name was aroused into your consciousness, into short-term memory. This description is metaphorical. You did not actually move the name from one place (LTM) to another (STM) in your mind, because memory is not a set of places. Instead, a given item can be either active or inactive: it can be in your consciousness, or it can be out of your consciousness for the moment (see Figure 9.1). Psychologists often use the metaphor of memory storehouses as a convenient, shorthand way of expressing the idea that information has been activated into consciousness. But it is important to remember that memory does not really have a spatial or location-oriented quality; it only has varying degrees of activation.

Long-term memory is what most people think of when they talk about memory: the total content of our LTM encompasses that tremendous range of knowledge, ideas, images, skills, and feelings that we have gathered in the course of our experience. All these items of knowledge are inactive for the moment, but they can often be retrieved, given an appropriate request, and "brought into" short-term memory. So short-term and long-term memory have a close, dynamic connection with each other.

How Short-Term Memory Works

You can activate information in your memory (or "bring it into short-term memory") in two ways. You can register stimulus events from the environment, or you can activate information from long-term memory in response to a question or in association to an already active thought (see Figure 9.1). But regardless of how this information becomes active, it may not remain active ("stay in short-term memory") for long. As new items become active, they seem to crowd out earlier items; our consciousness seems able to hold only a few items at one time.

When we wish, we can keep particular information active. If the items have names, we can **rehearse** the names—that is, mentally repeat them to ourselves, as we did earlier with the names of the letters E, K, L, and Z. If the items are sensory images, we can mentally review the images. But if our attention is directed to new material, which then itself becomes active, the intensity, or activity level, of the earlier items begins to decay. Eventually, the earlier items are gone from consciousness; we will be able to retrieve them only if we have retained them in long-term memory.

The brevity of short-term memories is easy to demonstrate. Ask a friend to read aloud an unfamiliar telephone number. To prevent yourself from rehearsing the number, immediately begin to count backward by threes, starting from the number 987 (987, 984, 981 . . .), at the rate of one subtraction per second for about twenty seconds. Now try to recall the phone number: you may find it difficult to do so. (You should repeat the experiment several times, using a different telephone number and a different starting number each time.)

This sort of rapid forgetting has been studied in the laboratory. In one experiment (Peterson and Peterson, 1959), the researchers had individuals read three consonants (such as BXK), then count backwards by threes before trying to recall them. Having a subject do mental arithmetic serves two purposes: it prevents the subject from rehearsing the target items, and it overloads the limited capacity of the subject's short-term memory, so that the subtraction numbers displace the target memories.

As Figure 9.2 indicates, once you begin to attend to other things, items in STM are forgotten with amazing speed. The size of the drop-off grows as you work with more phone numbers; in the consonant experiment, it grew as subjects tried to

Figure 9.2. The results of Peterson and Peterson's experiment to measure the length of time that short-term memory lasts without the aid of rehearsal. Subjects were shown a three-consonant combination (CPQ, for example) that they were to remember; immediately after they saw it, they began to count backward by threes from some number supplied by the experimenter. The longer the experimenter let them count before asking them to recall the letter combination, the less likely the subjects were to recall it correctly.

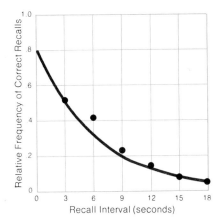

learn and recall more consonant clusters. As additional items are learned, the earlier items interfere with the recall of the most recent items you are trying to remember (Keppel and Underwood, 1962).

Uses of Short-Term Memory

Short-term memory has such a limited capacity, and items in it become deactivated so rapidly, that you might wonder why such a process is part of our memory system at all. Yet short-term (or active) memory has many uses. First, it serves as a sort of temporary scratch pad, allowing us to retain intermediate results while we think and solve problems. When a chess master is planning the next move, for example, he or she develops in STM an imaginary picture of critical parts of the chessboard as they will appear after several future moves and countermoves. Second, short-term memory holds whatever goals or plans we are following at the moment. By keeping our intentions in active memory, we are able to guide our behavior toward those goals.

Third, short-term memory maintains our current picture of the world around us, indicating what objects are out there and where they are located. By constructing and maintaining these world frames, STM keeps our visual perceptions stable. Our process of visual perception actually skitters here and there about a scene, taking about five retinal images, or "snapshots," per second. Yet we do not discard an old image every fifth of a second and construct a new scene of our surroundings. Rather, we integrate information from all the "snapshots" into one sustained image, or model, of the scene around us. As we notice small changes, we update this model, deleting old objects, adding new ones, and changing the relative location of objects. Short-term memory enables us to do this.

Fourth, short-term memory keeps track of the topics and referents that have been recently mentioned in conversation. If I mention my friend John, I can later refer to him as "he" or "my friend" and you will know who I am talking about: the idea of John is still in your active memory, so you can figure out that I mean John and not Scott or David.

Perhaps because short-term memories are so very useful, nearly every computer system for storing information is designed with a kind of short-term memory, located within its central processing unit (CPU). The CPU of a computer system receives data, stores it in memory, retrieves it, performs a variety of calculations, and either stores the result, displays it on a screen, or prints it. These functions are remarkably similar to the functions of our short-term memory. In fact, the parallels are so close that many cognitive psychologists view the computer's CPU as a useful metaphorical model of human short-term memory.

Encoding in Short-Term Memory

When we put information into short-term memory, what format do we use? Each time we attend to information that is already familiar to us, we activate a particular internal representation, or code, for it. This is the encoding process we mentioned earlier.

This internal code may be one that preserves the sensory quality of the information, so that we experience the information as a visual image, an auditory echo, or a memory of a smell, taste, or touch. In most cases, however, we use **verbal encoding**: we may silently name the input, or we may describe it to ourselves. Letters, digits, words, sentences, scenes, and pictures of common objects all have names—and we partially remember them by their names. For example, if we look at a picture of a dog, we can silently encode it by its name "dawhg" (see Figure 9.3).

Even people who lack speech use name encoding. Deaf people who communicate through the hand signs of American Sign Language (ASL) use these signs to represent the names of items in short-term memory. Researchers tested recall from short-term memory among deaf individuals by first visually presenting a series of letters, then asking the subjects to recall them. Some of the subjects were deaf, and others were normal. During recall, the deaf subjects confused items whose signs had similar hand configurations, such as *B* and *Y* or *F* and *L*, while the individuals with normal hearing and speech confused letters according to similarity in sound—*B* and *V*, *F* and *X*, *M* and *N* (Locke and Locke, 1971).

But how is it that we have these internal representations, or codes, at hand and ready for use in establishing short-term memories? Apparently, we refer to a body of knowledge, stored in our long-term memory, that is analogous to a dictionary. This "dictionary" allows us to translate visual

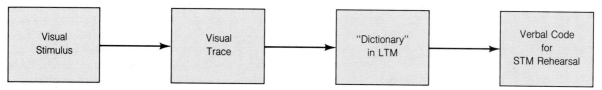

Figure 9.3. Encoding in short-term memory. A visual stimulus is encoded into a visual trace, which is then converted to a verbal code based on the "dictionary" each of us has in long-term memory; the verbal code is then rehearsed in short-term memory.

or auditory input patterns into some other medium or code, such as speech sounds, hand signals, or visual patterns. We use the "dictionary" to encode stimuli before we rehearse and remember them; then, when we prepare to recall them, we use the dictionary backwards, calling up the code and translating it back into the original stimulus form (see Figure 9.3). The content of each person's "dictionary" depends on what he or she has learned in the past.

Advantages and Disadvantages of Verbal Encoding

We can use verbal encoding with almost any sort of material, and it has many advantages. Mentally repeating items' names helps us keep them active in memory. (Perhaps for this reason we tend to have trouble remembering material that is difficult to attach names to, such as a set of abstract paintings.) Verbal encoding may also allow us to reduce material to a few essential, summarizing names or descriptions, so that we can remember it more easily. For example, we can remember a binary series like 1100110011001100 simply as "four alternating pairs of ones and zeros." The briefer the description, the easier it is for us to remember the information. In one study (Glanzer and Clark, 1963), subjects were asked to recite back a random string of eight binary digits. The digit strings that were easiest to remember were those that had shorter verbal descriptions, which subjects apparently had used to encode them.

A disadvantage to verbal coding is that when we recall items, we tend to confuse those with similar-sounding names. Suppose you were given a quick glimpse of the words "sale," "ate," "pane," "eight," "sail," and "pain," and then tried to write out the list in the order in which the words were presented. You would probably interchange some words that had the same sound. When people try to recall names, they sometimes come up with names that have similar sounds, but are wrong. Miss Stubbs becomes Miss Stobbs, and Mr. Sternbach becomes Mr. Sternbeck. Such "sound-alike" confusions are especially frequent when our short-term memory is overloaded: the recalled names are guesses based on a faint trace of what the name "sort of sounded like."

Chunking

During the encoding process, the brain seems to organize incoming information into the largest possible familiar clusters, and then short-term memory deals with each cluster as if it were a unit. These familiar sequences or patterns of elements in short-term memory are known as **chunks**.

Verbal encoding operates according to a chunking process. "Ogd" consists of three chunks (letters), but the word "dog" is just one chunk; "hot dog" is also one chunk, and even "hot-dog bun" is only one chunk. The brain recognizes a chunk of familiar material almost automatically when an appropriately organized pattern is presented. If you hear the sound "dawhg" or see the letters "DOG," for example, you can hardly prevent yourself from perceiving the word "dog."

How Many Chunks Can Be Kept Active?   Exactly how much information we can keep active in short-term memory depends on how the items are arranged. If you test yourself, you will probably find that you can remember seven or eight random digits or letters, *or* six or seven two-letter words or two-syllable words, *or* five to seven familiar three-word combinations, such as "ice-cream cone" or "stars and stripes."

Thirty years ago, George Miller (1956) proposed that short-term memory could maintain no more than about seven chunks without error. Since then, other researchers have found that the capacity of STM depends on characteristics of the information that is being stored in it. The more time it

Figure 9.4A. Study this arrangement of chess pieces for five seconds. Then turn to the empty chess board on page 226 and try to reproduce the arrangement. The amount you are able to recall correctly represents approximately seven of the chunks you have developed for processing information about chess games.

takes to name a series of words, the smaller the number of words that can be maintained in active memory. Apparently, the rehearsal process in STM is not fast enough to prevent lengthy items near the beginning of the list from being forgotten while others at the end of the list are being named during a rehearsal cycle (Baddeley, 1976; Baddeley, Thomson, and Buchanan, 1975).

Nonverbal Chunks These illustrations of chunking have been limited to verbal material, but in daily life we chunk many other kinds of familiar patterns as well. Some of the most useful chunks are visual, as were those of S, the Russian memory expert. Similarly, after a five-second exposure, an excellent chess player can reproduce the entire chessboard shown in Figure 9.4A. Yet the capacity of a chess master's short-term memory is no greater than the average college student's. (You can try to duplicate the chess master's feat using Figure 9.4B.) The masters' superiority lies in their ability to recognize familiar visual configurations, or chunks, on the board. When the pieces are arranged in a random pattern that is unlikely to appear in a game between good players, a chess master is no better at reproducing chessboards than a nonplayer.

Using Chunking to Improve STM In an experiment that explored chunking, an average college student (S. F.) increased his memory span from seven to seventy-nine digits (Ericsson, Chase, and

Faloon, 1980). It took this student 230 hours of practice over a year and a half, but in that period he managed to rival the feats of professional memory experts. How did he do it? As it happened, he was a long-distance runner, and he knew a vast number of facts about racing times. So he simply recoded the numbers he was given into running times for various races: for example, he recoded the number 3,492 as "3 minutes and 49 point 2 seconds, a near world-record mile time." As the study went on, he also added age codes (coding 893 as "89 point 3, very old man") and date codes (coding 1,944 as "near the end of World War II"). In addition to recoding the numbers, he increased his recall by organizing the groups he had constructed from digits into a hierarchy and recalling them in terms of the hierarchy.

Yet this student's phenomenal memory for numbers did not spill over into other aspects of his life. He displayed his record-breaking memory only with numbers and only when he recoded them in a meaningful fashion. His memory for a nonsense series of letters or words remained at about seven units. If he was prevented from recoding the numbers, his STM could handle no more than about seven digits. His training had been limited to number-recoding strategies, and these strategies did not transfer to other kinds of information. Memory is not like a "general-purpose muscle" that, with exercise, becomes stronger at any task.

Forgetting from Short-Term Memory

Items appear to be slowly deactivated from short-term memory through a process of **displacement**, in which new items entering short-term memory seem to crowd out earlier items. A useful way to visualize the way we hold items in active memory is to imagine a circus performer who is trying to spin a group of plates balanced on the end of sticks. The performer sets one plate spinning, then another, then tries to get more and more plates aloft. Each plate is an item in active memory, and its spin represents its level of activation. As new plates are put up, the performer neglects old ones, so that they slow down and become increasingly likely to fall off. Unless the performer periodically refreshes the spin on each plate, it will fall. In increasing the spin of a faltering plate, the performer is doing what we do when we refresh a memory item using our focal attention (see Figure 9.5), for example, by rehearsing the item or reviewing an image.

When the performer does not refresh the spin on one of the plates, its activity slowly decays and it falls off the stick. If this analogy is valid, then we should forget an item if we fail to rehearse it in short-term memory—even if we do not add any new items. Of course, there is virtually no way to test this hypothesis. The kind of situation described—"no rehearsal, no displacement"—is almost impossible to arrange, because people are continually flooding their short-term memories with new information. They look at things, think of associations, plan what they will do next. These perceptions and thoughts create active items that start to fill up short-term memory, displacing the earlier spinning plates. Nevertheless, Judy Reitman (1974) was able to approximate in an experiment the condition of "no rehearsal, no displacement." She concluded that when a person is prevented from rehearsing items in short-term memory, those items do decay somewhat as time passes, even when no new information is presented. However, her research also showed that displacement by similar new material was a far more important cause of forgetting.

Retrieval from Short-Term Memory

If items in short-term memory seem immediately available in our consciousness, then we might assume that when asked about them, we would not have to search for them. This assumption would be wrong. In a series of experiments, Saul Sternberg (1966) showed that we do search for items in STM, and that the more items we have active, the longer it takes to find a specific item. Sternberg's subjects memorized a small set of letters or digits (such as "4, 1, 7") and held them actively in mind while Sternberg presented a se-

ries of test digits. If the test digit was one of the memorized set, the subject pressed a "yes" button; if the digit was not one of the set, the subject pressed a "no" button. This task is easy: the rate of error is less than 5 percent.

Over many trials, using memory sets that varied from one to six items, the pattern of results was consistent. All the subjects answered quickly, in less than two-thirds of a second, even with six items in active memory. But the important finding, the one that tells us most about short-term memory, was that *the time a subject took to decide whether a test digit was one of the memory set increased in direct proportion to the number of items in the set.* Each additional item in the memory set added about 40 milliseconds (one twenty-fifth of a second) to the time a subject needed to make a decision about any number of the set—regardless of whether the answer was yes or no.

Other research indicates that when Sternberg's task is used, the time it takes to search for each item in short-term memory increases with the difficulty of the items. The more difficult the item, the smaller the short-term memory span and the greater the required search time (Cavanagh, 1972). In our spinning-plate analogy, it is as though more complex items correspond to bulkier plates that fall off their sticks more easily.

How LONG-TERM MEMORY WORKS

We have discussed short-term memory as the activated part of our memory system. Let us now look

Figure 9.5. A performer keeping a number of plates spinning on wobbly sticks provides a model of short-term memory. Just as the performer must occasionally spin each plate to keep it from toppling off the stick, so must we rehearse or review a memory item periodically to keep it active in short-term memory.

Figure 9.4B. Turn to Figure 9.4A on page 224, if you have not already looked at it, and study it for five seconds. Then try to reproduce the arrangement shown there on this empty chess board. Your success in doing so will depend heavily on your experience with the game of chess.

at the rest of the memory system, the material that is currently inactive and thus is in long-term memory. Long-term memory (LTM) refers to our relatively permanent knowledge and skills. As we noted at the beginning of the chapter, its range is wide: it includes personal episodic memories, generic knowledge (both semantic and perceptual), and intellectual and motor skills.

Semantic Networks

The semantic portion of our generic knowledge is a particularly fascinating aspect of our memory. Our semantic knowledge is composed of general ideas or concepts such as "dog," "brown," "hair," and "car," along with particular ideas of individuals or places, such as "Fido," "New York City," and "Michael Jackson." These concepts correspond more or less to single words, but the relationship is not exact. Some concepts have many names (synonyms, foreign names, nicknames). Some concepts have no single name: "the person who stole my car" is an example. And some words have a linguistic function but no corresponding concept: for example, what do "of," "an," "to," or "but" refer to?

The concepts in our memory can be of several sorts. They may be simple perceptual qualities ("red," "to the left of"). They can be simple motor functions ("hop," "raise right arm"). Or they can

be defined in terms of their relationships or links to other concepts, much as the meaning of a word in a dictionary is defined in terms of other meanings. One type of link attributes a property to a concept: "Canaries are yellow" attributes the property "yellow" to the concept "canaries." Another type of link relates two or more concepts to each other: when we say "John owns a canary," we are saying that there is an "owning" relationship between John and a canary. These attributes and relationships can be compounded into very complex networks, but they are all, in essence, *associations*. Over time, as we learned about these concepts, we stored them in long-term memory.

We can represent these associations among concepts as labeled links between concept "spots," or nodes, in our memory (see Figure 9.6). Since each concept will have many connections to others, our semantic memory will contain huge networks of these associations. We use these networks to record general or specific facts we learn about the world and also to record specific new episodes.

From this point of view, we can say that when we encounter a new fact or relationship, what we actually do is recognize and activate the corresponding concepts (bring them into short-term memory), and record the relationship between them as a new association (a new linkage). Thus, when we learn new information, we are recording a description of that information by setting up

Figure 9.6. The associative connections in memory between the idea of "canary" and some of its properties. Concepts or ideas are shown within circles and relations are represented by arrows. This diagram is very much simplified; in reality, memory contains many thousands of such concepts and connections in a complex network.

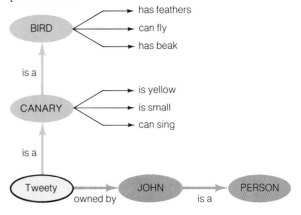

new associations among already-familiar concepts in our LTM networks. If you hear that John owns a canary named Tweety, you take a familiar relationship ("owns") and record in your memory a new association between it and two other familiar concepts ("John" and "Tweety") that you may already have had in memory.

What if you don't know Tweety? In that case, you will have to establish a new concept or entity (named "Tweety") in your memory. In Chapter 10 we'll discuss the ways concepts are acquired, but we can note here that once you have set up the new concept, you will quickly attach all the knowledge you know about it. You know that Tweety is owned by John, and that Tweety is a canary. And by virtue of Tweety's being a canary, you know a large number of things about Tweety, since he or she shares the properties that all canaries have (see Figure 9.6).

Theoretical models of semantic memory made up of such networks fascinate psychologists because the networks have many humanlike powers. For example:

1. To record new information, we simply take familiar chunks (or concepts) and associate them in new configurations—an economical practice for any memory system. All novel information is thus built up from old bits of information arranged in new patterns.
2. We retrieve information according to associations between concepts. The information in any question tells us the points at which we will enter the network of associations. For example, the question "What does John own?" starts our memory search mechanism at the "John" concept in memory, telling us to retrieve the association out of that node identified by the "owns" relationship, and to read off the name of the associated concept at the end of the link (in this case, Tweety).
3. Our conceptual networks give us a basis for thinking, especially for inferring information surrounding new things we learn. From the information that John owns a canary named Tweety, you can infer that Tweety is small, has wings, and can sing, and that John probably keeps Tweety in a birdcage. Why? Because your network told you the properties of birds, and the fact that pet canaries are usually kept in birdcages. You simply derived the information about the

new concept "Tweety" by applying general knowledge that you already possessed about pet birds.

If LTM is like a network of associations, then, let us see how its parts are joined together.

Learning: Strengthening Associations in Long-Term Memory

The incoming information we chunk into familiar patterns in our active memory (STM) eventually becomes less active and is displaced by incoming information that follows it. Yet we remember facts that we picked up minutes, days, or years ago. How did we learn them—that is, tie them into the network in LTM?

Suppose that Jack and Jill are familiar friends of yours, and someone tells you "Jack married Jill." In the process of learning this information, you activate the concepts of "Jack" and "Jill" from LTM, set up a propositional connection between them ("married"), and then strengthen these active connections. As the topic of conversation shifts to other matters, you activate other concepts, so that the earlier concepts ("Jack" and "Jill") and their connection fade from active memory. But this connection will not be totally lost. The longer the new Jack-Jill connection held your attention in the beginning, the stronger the association in your long-term memory will have become. And the more likely it is that you will later be able to retrieve the information if someone gives you a **retrieval cue**—a stimulus that activates some association that is no longer in your consciousness, in this case, "Who did Jack marry?"

We can state this in more general terms: the more a connection is strengthened, the more likely it is to be retrieved in response to an appropriate stimulus (question). Also, the stronger a connection becomes, the more *quickly* it will be retrieved and the more resistant it will be to forgetting.

Strengthening Connections by Rehearsal

Whether an association is strengthened depends in good part on whether we attend to the material to begin with, and how much we rehearse it. Rehearsing material keeps it active in STM; the more time we devote to rehearsal (with the intention of learning the material), the more we strengthen the connections necessary for long-term memory. For example, if we are told that certain information is important or valuable, we generally give it priority in attention and extra rehearsals—and as a result, our memory for it improves.

Information that has strong emotional impact —sudden good fortune, an insult, a crushing failure—is usually kept active in conscious attention for a long period through the influence of our emotional system. As a result, such emotional events tend to establish stronger connections in our memory and tend to be better remembered. Although highly traumatic events are occasionally wiped from memory, such repression is exceedingly rare, despite its prevalence in fiction and films.

Note that not all rehearsal strengthens the memory trace for the material rehearsed. Sometimes we go through a "mindless" kind of rehearsal, called **maintenance rehearsal**, in which we repeat material verbally but fail to strengthen long-term associations (Craik and Lockhart, 1972). In maintenance rehearsal, once an item has been attended to and identified, the brain seems to set the tongue (or its mental equivalent) on automatic pilot, so that the items are repeated without conscious effort or thought. A recent demonstration of mindless rehearsal in college students had them studying digit series and then repeating word pairs one to ten times as a supposed distraction before recalling each digit series (Glenberg and Bradley, 1979). When the subjects were later given a surprise test on the word pairs, they did very poorly, remembering less than 1 percent of the pairs, regardless of how many times they had repeated the word pairs. Apparently, mere vocal repetition without intention to learn causes little long-term memory for those pairs.

The Importance of Elaborative Rehearsal

When we *are* trying to remember material, how does the rehearsal we carry out differ from maintenance rehearsal? One current hypothesis is that we establish long-term memories—that is, we learn—via **elaborative rehearsal**. When people are deliberately trying to learn, they elaborate associatively on the material, finding new connections between the elements, fleshing out the implications of the ideas and their semantic relationships, and embedding the elements into an organizational structure. For example, to remember

that your friend John had bought a canary, you might imagine John feeding his canary, singing along with it, even flying with it. Each connection you imagine brings that connection briefly into STM, setting up more and different associations between the two main concepts (John and canary). The more elaborate the associations, and the more of them a person builds while the material is still active in short-term memory, the better or more persistent will be the long-term memories established by rehearsal.

Many studies have demonstrated that elaborating meaningful connections between elements glues them together in memory. For instance, Gordon Bower (1972; Bower and Winzenz, 1970) had people form mental pictures of meaningful relations that linked pairs of unrelated nouns, such as dog–cigar (imagine a dog smoking a cigar) and chair–canary (imagine a canary sitting in a chair) (see Figure 9.7). Bower then asked them to rate the vividness of their image or the ease with which they set up the relationship, but he said nothing to them about actually learning the word pairs. Later, without warning, he tested the subjects for their memory of the pairs. Most of them showed high levels of recall, remembering about 75 percent of the word pairs. What is more, they outperformed people who had verbally rehearsed the words after being told they would be tested on them. Such studies indicate that just "intending to remember" something is not enough; instead, the extent to which we remember it depends on the amount of relevant elaboration we have carried out.

When we are trying to remember words that

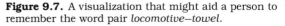

Figure 9.7. A visualization that might aid a person to remember the word pair *locomotive–towel.*

name concrete objects, such as "hammer," "shoe," or "fork," we frequently elaborate the words in terms of the generic image of the object (a typical hammer). In an extensive series of studies, Allen Paivio (1971) found that words or texts that evoke vivid images are easier to learn in almost all situations than are words or texts that refer to abstract concepts, such as "technology," "system," or "familiarity." Paivio proposes that when we learn words for concrete objects, we encode them both visually, in terms of their generic images, and verbally. He believes that we retain the visual memory traces better than we retain verbal memory traces.

Storing Sensory Data

The conceptual networks that we use to record abstract, propositional knowledge in long-term memory are only one way of representing knowledge. As we have just seen, we also store sensory imagery—mental pictures of the appearance of things (Paivio, 1971). Call up a picture of your mother's face or your bedroom in your last home. You will find that these sensory images generated from your memory have a distinctive subjective quality.

We may consider these memory images to have been generated from sensory data structures. We deposited these sensory data structures in our long-term memory as a result of earlier perceptual processing. When we recreate a mental image, we retrieve one of these sensory data structures from our long-term memory and activate it, almost as if we were playing a videotape on our internal television screen.

Sensory images can represent a particular scene (the dog you saw a few minutes ago) or a generic image (a typical collie). All of us have a huge catalog of generic images in long-term memory. We use them for recording specific scenes: as we encounter new examples, we encode them in terms of the generic image with small deviations that reflect the particular example.

People have an exceptionally strong memory for pictures of naturalistic scenes, such as crowds, nature, animals, and cities (see Paivio, 1971). In one study, college students saw 2,560 slides of naturalistic scenes, viewing each for ten seconds. A few days later the students looked at pairs of scenes; each pair consisted of one scene that they had seen earlier and one that was new to them. In 90 percent of the cases, the students accurately picked out the picture they had viewed before (Haber and Standing, 1969). One reason we remember naturalistic scenes so well may be that such scenes have so many distinctive features. We have much more trouble recognizing pictures with few distinguishing features, such as abstract paintings or pictures of cross sections of brain tissue.

Retrieval from Long-Term Memory

Once we have stored away memories, they are of no use to us unless we can retrieve them when we need them. In retrieval, we use a question—some probe or cue—to fetch an appropriate answer from long-term memory. The question triggers the association, bringing the answer into active memory so that we can use it.

Some retrievals, such as reading a word, are effortless and automatic. Other retrievals take longer and often bring memory contents into awareness. Occasionally, the retrieval is such a prolonged internal search that it has many properties of trial and error and problem solving. We will see how researchers study this process.

Direct Measures of Memory

In most laboratory studies of retrieval, memory researchers present the subjects with a small set of self-contained materials to be learned and later administer a variety of memory tests. To illustrate these tests, suppose that you were asked to study twenty pairs of French-English nouns, such as "*pomme* means apple" and "*chapeau* means hat." After you have spent ten seconds studying each of the pairs, your memory can be tested in any of four ways.

■ In **free** (or **unaided**) **recall**, you try to recall the pairs from the list, writing them down in any order you wish. This is the most difficult form of memory retrieval, because the request is so brief—you are simply asked to remember "pairs on the list you just studied." In this case, when you recorded your memories (studied the word pairs), you associated the items to some extent with the context (time and place) in which they were presented, and your memory of that context is your only retrieval cue for the material.

- In **cued recall**, you are given one word of each pair and are asked to retrieve the other word. What does *pomme* mean? What is the French word for "hat"? Cued recall is easier than free recall because the retrieval request is more specific and uses a cue ("*pomme* means?") that closely matches those you actually stored in memory. If the original association is strong enough, you will probably recall the word. You will probably do better recalling from French to English rather than the reverse, because you are more familiar with the English word to be produced, so it is more available.

- In **pair recognition**, you are asked whether *chapeau* means "dog" or whether *pomme* is French for "apple." Like a true-false test, this is easier than cued recall because you do not have to generate the items from memory. All you must do is confirm whether a proposed candidate is in memory.

- In **single-item recognition**, you are asked if you saw the word *chien* in the study list or if "hat" was on the list. This is the easiest task of all. You need not associate the item with its equivalent in another language; all you have to do is check whether the item has an association to the study list and the context of presentation.

Indirect Measures of Memory

When researchers measure the number of items a subject can recall or recognize, they are taking a direct measurement of the subject's memory for that material. They can also measure a subject's memory indirectly, by seeing how rapidly the subject can *relearn* the information he or she may have forgotten. Alternatively, the researchers can *prime* an item: that is, they can prepare the subject by presenting the item some time before the test, and then see how readily the subject perceives that item at the later test.

Relearning Often you can quickly relearn information that you learned once before, even if the original connections have become so weak that you are unable to recall the information, or even recognize it on a test. Even a weak association regains its original strength in memory with just a small amount of relearning or review. Moreover, the more thoroughly you learn something original-

Figure 9.8. A test for priming involves presenting first the most fragmented version of the picture or word (the top version in each series shown here), and then increasingly complete versions until the subject identifies the item. If the subject has been "primed" by being shown the intact item beforehand, he or she is likely to be able to identify the item sooner, in an early fragmented version, during testing. (Warrington and Weiskrantz, 1968.)

ly, the more quickly you will be able to relearn it later. If you study French in school and then fail to use it for a number of years, you will tend to forget it, but if you spend a few weeks in France, you will find that your "forgotten" French returns with just a small amount of study.

Priming In **priming**, either the item itself or an association to the item is presented several seconds or several minutes before your memory is tested, thus priming or preparing you to retrieve the item later. Having seen a picture or word, you will see or read it again more quickly at a later time. For example, the earlier sight of a picture allows you to recognize it later in a degraded picture or in a brief, poorly focused flash that would be insufficient to enable you to identify a totally unfamiliar picture (see Figure 9.8). But because the effect of priming gradually fades, the test must take place before too much time has elapsed.

A person's perception of an item can also be primed by arousing a concept that is associated with it. If you are given a list of letter strings and asked to decide which strings are real words, you will need less time to decide that NURSE is a real word if you have previously thought about DOCTOR (Meyer and Schvaneveldt, 1976). Similarly, after being asked whether *pomme* was on the French-English vocabulary list discussed earlier, you will be much quicker to answer that "apple" was on the same list. These methods work because the activation of one item spreads activation to items that we have related through associations (DOCTOR to NURSE, *pomme* to "apple"), "heating up" the related items in memory so that they are ready for us to perceive them.

Partial Recall

Retrieval attempts may succeed, fail, or partially succeed. An example of partial success that often ends in full recall is the **tip-of-the-tongue phenomenon**. When we have a word or a name on the tip of the tongue, we are certain that we know the word, but we simply cannot pull it out of storage. The condition has been described as "a state of mild torment, something like the brink of a sneeze"; when the word is finally retrieved, there is a feeling of considerable relief (Brown and McNeill, 1966). Experiments with tip-of-the-tongue states have shown that people do have partial information about the target word they cannot recall. This partial information for a word may include its number of syllables and its approximate sound. Such fragmentary information enables us to reject incorrect alternatives to the word (Brown and McNeill, 1966).

Problem Solving in Prolonged Retrievals

The tip-of-the-tongue phenomenon illustrates that memory searches can sometimes be especially long, drawn-out, and frustrating experiences. In prolonged memory retrievals, the process appears to be somewhat like any other search—for a good restaurant, say, or for a library book on a given topic. We may think of the prolonged retrieval as similar to problem solving. The retrieval must always begin from a starting point, which is a partial description of the desired item's characteristics. The description may come from current goals or needs ("I need to find a restaurant") or from a problem that must be solved ("Where did I leave my psychology notes?"). To trigger a success-

ful retrieval, the description we feed into memory should be fairly precise; it should also permit us to check possible answers.

Donald Norman (1982) has suggested that the retrieval process itself can be broken down into four subprocesses. The first is *retrieval specification*: we compose a description of the target memory—for example, "the spot where I left my notes." The second is *matching*: we compare that description against various memories that are in the "library stacks" of our LTM. We then use the third subprocess, *evaluation*, to verify whether a particular memory we have retrieved satisfies the description. The fourth subprocess, *failure diagnosis*, comes into play only if our first attempt at retrieval fails. In failure diagnosis, we figure out a way to alter the description so that a second attempt may succeed.

Such retrieval processes were studied by Michael Williams and James Hollan (1981), who asked a few adults to think aloud as they tried to recall the names of people who had been in their high school graduating class. All of these adults had been out of high school for at least four years. Over a period of four to ten days, they spent about an hour each day searching their memory for classmates' names. At first, they recalled names rapidly; then they began to recall other names more slowly. In addition to the correct names, there were many fabrications—either true names of people who had actually been in other classes, or confused blends of several names.

Once the subjects had progressed beyond the initial rush of highly available names, they used a variety of settings. A subject might try to remember who was on the football team, in the glee club, in the class play; who sat in the next seat in chemistry, who dated whom, and so on. Typically, an image of an acquaintance or some fact about that person would be retrieved before the name. A second strategy was to recall group photographs of the class and try to visualize and identify the people in them. A third strategy was to go down the alphabet, checking whether first names beginning with each letter ("Allen, Alice, Arthur, Betty, Bob, Bill") reminded the subject of some classmate. These strategies generated names of candidates which the subject then tried to verify: Was it Don or Dan or Dick Johnson? Was he in my class or the class ahead of me? Subjects often verified memories by recalling additional evidence about the person, such as activities ("She was on the debating team") or attributes ("He had red hair").

Metamemory

The tip-of-the-tongue phenomenon and the persistent search behind prolonged retrievals illustrate the more general principle that we may "know we know something" without at the moment being able to recall it. These intuitive "feelings of knowing" (or "not knowing") turn out to be reasonably accurate. Studies have shown that people who are unable to recall specific facts ("Who invented the cotton gin?"), but who believe they *would* recognize the correct answer, do in fact generally choose the correct answer on a multiple-choice test (Hart, 1965).

How is it possible for us to know that we know something and yet be unable to recall it? This situation is not as strange as it seems. First, we can make a plausible guess as to whether we have ever been exposed to the information. We know with some certainty that we could not have learned Bruce Springsteen's telephone number or the name of Pope John's mother, but there is other information that we know we are likely to have learned at one time (for example, we may once have heard Muhammed Ali's original name). Second, we may be aware of partial information that is in a tip-of-the-tongue state. Partial information can eliminate alternatives on a multiple-choice test, increasing our chances of selecting the correct answer.

Along with the ability to judge what we know, we also acquire general knowledge about the capabilities of our own memory. We have learned what sorts of things we find easy or hard to remember, and what strategies work for us. We learn how to remind ourselves of things we *want* to remember; and we learn how to test ourselves so we can verify whether or not we actually have committed something to memory. This understanding of the way our own memory system works is known as **metamemory**. It is a knowledge of one's own cognitive processes, and it develops as the child is exposed to many learning and remembering situations. It is part of the changes that occur during cognitive development (see Chapter 15).

FORGETTING FROM LONG-TERM MEMORY

Everyone forgets: the plot of a movie seen six months ago; the menu at dinner last Tuesday night; the date of a friend's birthday; the promise to send an acquaintance a magazine article. What has happened to material that we once knew but now cannot remember? Either the associations we formed for it have become so weak that we cannot recall them, or the associations are there but for some reason we cannot retrieve them.

Retrieval Failures: The Role of Cues

As noted earlier, our memories are based on associations among the relevant ideas. When we lay down memories, we may associate an item of information strongly to one cue but only weakly to another possible cue. This would be like indexing a library book by its topic but not by its author. For example, if you were learning a list of words that included "apple," you might think of it as a *fruit*, associating "apple" and "fruit" strongly. You might also associate "apple" weakly to the general fact of its having appeared on the word list. Later, if the experimenter asks you to recall "words on the list," this request might fail to retrieve "apple" for you, even though a later request to name a fruit mentioned on the list might readily bring "apple" to mind.

A series of experiments by Endel Tulving and his associates (e.g., Tulving and Psotka, 1971) have convincingly shown how powerful the proper retrieval cues can be in reviving memories that are not retrieved by weak cues. How effectively a cue will jog a target memory depends on the way we thought about that target material as we were trying to learn it and also on our surroundings. When we later try to recall the information, we will be most successful if both our surroundings and the way we think about the retrieval cue are the same when we try to retrieve the information as they were when we learned it. The greater the change in the retrieval situation, the poorer our recall of the target memory. This principle is known as **encoding specificity** (Tulving and Thomson, 1973).

For example, when we are at the supermarket, we often find it impossible to recall all the items on our mental grocery list. But when we return to the kitchen at home, we may be reminded of exactly what things we forgot to buy. As we noted in Chapter 8, the likelihood of our giving a learned response is closely tied to the similarity between the test and the learning stimuli; we may have experienced some stimulus generalization, but not enough to allow us to remember our shopping list in the new surroundings. The encoding specificity principle is basically the same idea as stimulus generalization, except that encoding specificity includes the "mental context" available during learning and retention testing.

Effects of the Physical Context

The context cues that guide memory include our physical surroundings, the things we are thinking about, and our internal environment. Studies consistently show, for example, that memory for material learned in the laboratory is about 10 to 15 percent poorer if testing is moved from the laboratory to a distinctly different room. Underwater divers provided a more spectacular demonstration of this effect. Researchers (Godden and Baddeley, 1975) had members of an underwater diving club learn a list of words. Half the members learned the list on dry land; the other half learned the list thirty feet below the surface. When the standard recall test was given, the divers who had learned the list under water recalled more words when they were under water, and those who had learned it ashore recalled more words when they were tested ashore.

Effects of the Verbal Context

Changes in the verbal context of material we have learned can also make retrieval difficult. In one study, subjects saw pairs of words such as "train—BLACK" and "whiskey—WATER," and they were supposed to concentrate their learning on the right-hand words (Tulving and Thomson, 1973). Then the experimenters read a different list of words and had the subjects jot down whatever words they associated with each one (WHITE: horse, hat, black, snow, bandage). Next, the subjects were asked to circle any associates they had written down that had also been on the original list of words. Surprisingly, most subjects failed to recognize many of the associates they had learned earlier! Yet when the subjects were later tested with the original study cues ("train —" and "whiskey —"), they recalled a much higher percentage of the right-hand words from the list.

In this case, the change in the verbal context between the learning situation and the test was so great that the subjects were able to *recall* more words in one context than they could *recognize* in

the other context. Does this outcome conflict with our belief that recognition is easier than recall? Not if we look at the difference between the two situations and apply the principle of encoding specificity. The subjects could successfully recall the right-hand words in a verbal context identical to that in which they had learned the words originally; but they had difficulty recognizing them in a context that was different from the original context. They had probably encoded a word in one way in the learning situation and in a different way in the test situation.

According to one interpretation (Anderson and Bower, 1974), most words have several meanings. In the study context, the subjects may have encoded BLACK according to one set of meanings or associations (e.g., dark steel), but those associations may have been quite different from the ones by which they had encoded "black" (e.g., the race) when later associating to "white" in the word-association exercise. If a subject encodes a test word with one meaning when he or she learns it, but the testing context activates a different meaning, subjects are less likely to recognize the word as one that was presented earlier (Anderson and Bower, 1974).

Effects of the Internal Environment

Changes in a person's internal environment also affect memory. Because of such internal changes, on the "morning after," a person may be unable to recall events that accompanied heavy drinking the night before. These losses of memory may develop in part because a person's internal state—whether sober or drunk, happy or sad—can serve as a retrieval cue (Bower, 1981; Weingartner et al., 1976; Bartlett and Santrock, 1979). In **state-dependent memory**, information that an individual has learned while he or she was in one physiological state is difficult to retrieve when the individual is in a different state. When the original condition is restored, the information can again be retrieved.

Similar effects may appear when the internal state is emotional rather than drug-related. In one study (Bower, 1981), hypnotic suggestions were used to put college students into a happy or sad mood. The students then recalled emotional events of their daily lives, and their recollections were compared with a diary of emotional events they had kept during the previous week. Students who were feeling happy recalled a higher percentage of happy events than sad incidents from their diary, but students who felt sad recalled more sad than happy incidents. Apparently, their current mood more closely matched memory traces that they had laid down when they were in a similar mood; and this matching of moods affected retrieval.

Amnesia

Amnesia is a condition in which a person has a severely impaired ability to remember old material or to learn new material. There are several kinds of amnesia.

The most frequently seen amnesias are those that occur in people who have suffered a concussion or some other head injury that leads to unconsciousness and temporary coma. Some of these people are temporarily unable to recall events just preceding the injury; if so, they are said to be suffering from **retrograde amnesia**, amnesia that is oriented toward the past before the accident ("retro" means "backward" and "grade" means "inclined" or "oriented"). The extent of memory loss in retrograde amnesia varies; a person may forget events that took place minutes, hours, or even days before the concussion.

In most cases of retrograde amnesia, the memories are not lost but are just temporarily inaccessible, so it is a kind of retrieval failure (Russell and Nathan, 1946). It is as though the physiological state of the brain has changed due to the injury, so that the mental context for normal retrieval has changed.

Memories may begin to return within a few minutes or over a period of weeks, depending on the severity of the injury. As memories gradually return, the span of time covered by amnesia lessens. Memories of the distant past are usually the first to reappear (Russell and Nathan, 1946). Sometimes memories of events that occurred seconds before the injury are never recovered, possibly because these memories had not had sufficient time to be fixed into long-term memory before they were disrupted.

Often people awaken from concussion with a headache and complain of feeling disoriented and confused. They can answer simple questions and have a moderately good immediate memory span, but they have great difficulty laying down new memories. This condition is known as **anterograde amnesia**. "Antero" means "forward"; such a

patient is unable to lay down memories from the point of the accident forward in time. Anterograde amnesia seems to indicate problems in encoding information as well as an inability to elaborate new material so that strong traces can be stored in long-term memory. Such amnesics also have some deficits in retrieval from long-term memory (Kinsbourne and Wood, 1975). How long the amnesia lasts depends on the severity of the brain injury. Most patients with head injury have retrograde as well as anterograde amnesia.

Amnesia may also be produced by other types of damage to the brain. For instance, victims of carbon monoxide poisoning usually experience memory loss, with the extent of loss apparently related to the severity of damage to the brain. Patients who undergo electroconvulsive shock therapy (ECT) usually experience memory loss as well. In most cases the anterograde amnesia that follows ECT gradually disappears; the retrograde amnesia usually disappears within seven months (Squire, Slater, and Miller, 1981; Squire and Slater, 1978). When the hippocampal area of the brain is damaged, severe, permanent amnesia follows. We discussed such patients in Chapter 3: if a patient has parts of his hippocampus removed on both sides of the brain, he may as a result suffer severe anterograde amnesia, especially for verbal material.

Amnesia is also seen as a consequence of the brain pathology caused by Alzheimer's disease. As the disease advances, patients become progressively poorer at memory tasks; eventually they become completely disoriented and do not speak at all. Examination of tissue from Alzheimer's patients shows a severe loss of brain cells in and near the hippocampus, with many clumps of uselessly tangled threadlike fibers in these places (Hyman et al., 1984). Damage is concentrated in an area containing a circuit that normally carries neural information from the cerebral cortex to the hippocampus and back again. Cell loss in this area effectively isolates the hippocampus, producing an amnesia much like that of patients with surgical destruction of the area.

The Decay Theory of Forgetting

The oldest theory of forgetting assumes that memory traces erode, or **decay**, with the passage of time. Decay theory presumes that when a new fact is learned or a new experience occurs, a memory

Memories fade with time, but we may remember certain childhood experiences quite clearly even in advanced age.

trace is formed in the brain. As time passes, the strength of the association decays and eventually becomes extremely weak. When this happens, the association will not support attempts at recalling the information. The only way to increase the strength of the association is to make use of, or practice, the information. Decay theory has been used to explain the transience of our fragile sensory and short-term memory stores as well as the gradual loss of our long-term memories.

How useful is decay theory in helping us to understand the loss of long-term memories? The proposal that memories fade with time certainly fits our subjective experiences. Our memory of last week's football game is usually stronger and more detailed than the memory of a game from last season. However, the passage of time is a weak explanation of forgetting. Whether or how soon we forget depends heavily on the characteristics of a particular memory and on the nature of intervening experiences. Research has demonstrated, for instance, that we forget substantially less if we sleep for several hours after we have learned something than if we stay awake (Jenkins and Dallenbach, 1924). A person with Alzheimer's disease who cannot remember what happened yesterday may readily recall certain childhood experiences. And we also tend to remember motor skills over long periods without practice; for example, an

adult who has not been on ice skates for years can generally demonstrate the skill again. These facts are difficult to explain if we assume that decay is inevitable and that it is the main mechanism that produces forgetting.

Interference

A complementary factor promoting forgetting is **interference**; in this case, other material in memory blocks out the sought-for memory. According to the interference principle, we have lost our memory of last year's football game because of interference from all the other events, including football games and similar sports, that have occurred since that time. If we had seen no other games in the past year, the memory might have faded less.

People who learned nonsense syllables just before going to sleep, and so were not subject to interference due to intervening learning, later recalled the syllables better than people who had continued their waking activities. After eight hours the subjects who had remained awake remembered only about 10 percent of the material; those who had slept recalled about 60 percent of it (Jenkins and Dallenbach, 1924).

Research on interference has shown that peo-

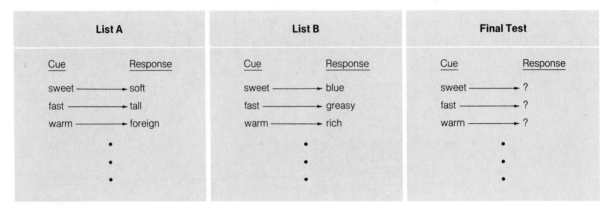

Figure 9.9. Two lists of cue-response pairs of words used to illustrate interference in forgetting. On the final test the subject is asked to recall either the first or the second learned response to each cue.

ple often forget a given association after they have associated the cue term to another, competing item (McGeoch, 1942). In a typical experiment, people memorize a list of paired words, such as List A in Figure 9.9. Then they learn the pairs in List B, which couples the same left-hand cue word with a different right-hand response word. When the subjects are given the cue words in List A to test for recall of the right-hand response words, subjects who have also memorized List B will not remember as many of the response words as do people in a control group who have memorized only List A. When subjects try to retrieve the associated words in the first list, they inadvertently retrieve associated words from the second list, which compete with—and block retrieval of—the words in the first list. Since the interference comes from learning a subsequent list, psychologists call this process **retroactive interference**, indicating that the interference has moved backward (retro-) from List B to List A.

Interference can work in the other direction as well. When people who have learned both lists are tested later for cued recall on List B, they will not remember as many response words from that list as will people who have not memorized List A. When interference moves forward (pro-), it is called **proactive interference**. In other words, proactive interference comes from learning that takes place *before* the target information is learned; retroactive interference takes place during the retention period, *after* the information in question is learned.

It may be that interference does not cause the loss of information so much as it slows down access to the correct associations. In several interference studies with subjects learning paired words, the subjects were not able to *recall* the response words because of interference, but they could *recognize* the cue-response pairs, albeit more slowly (Anderson, 1981; Postman and Stark, 1969). People who were unable to recall many responses to the cues of List A because of retroactive interference were able to recognize most of those cue-response pairs on a multiple-choice test.

The greater the similarity between the two different sets of materials to be memorized, the greater the interference between them during subsequent recall. For example, if you study the biographies of two English poets, similar facts will get confused and interfere with one another (Crouse, 1971). You may have trouble remembering which poet wrote which poems, went to which college, and lived in which town.

Modern researchers (e.g., Anderson, 1983) have concluded that we need both a decay principle and an associative interference principle to account for the full range of facts about forgetting.

Motivated Forgetting

Sometimes our motivation is responsible for our failure to retrieve an item from memory. Conflicting motives can hinder accurate learning and interfere with recall, causing us to distort or forget unpleasant memories.

We may not store information about unpleasant events well because it is discomforting or humiliating to think about or rehearse them. We may decide to put them out of our mind, which itself causes them to accrue less strength in memory. Motivation can also inhibit the retrieval process. We may consciously *suppress* reporting a memory that would cause us to be disapproved or punished (e.g., "Did you steal the cookies?"). Moreover, there is considerable clinical evidence that with repeated denial and suppression, a painful memory can become "repressed" in that we become unable to consciously retrieve it (Erdelyi and Goldberg, 1979). For example, a child may repress his or her memory of traumatic abuses experienced at an earlier age. It is as though the retrieval process is deflected away from approaching those painful memories. At present, the clinical evidence for unconscious repression is far stronger than is the laboratory experimental evidence for it (Erdelyi and Goldberg, 1979).

Motivations also can create distortions, causing us to remember ourselves in a more favorable manner than we deserve, so that our memories become self-serving (Loftus, 1980). We tend to remember ourselves as having done better than we did, as having had greater influence on positive events but being less responsible for bad outcomes, as having made more money, as having had more acceptable opinions, and so on. Our self-serving memories are rarely attempts to deceive others; rather, they are unconscious reconstructions that bolster our self-esteem, so that we can continue to think of ourselves in a positive light (Greenwald, 1981).

Schemas in learning and remembering

Let us return to the issue of how our current knowledge enables us to learn new material. As information enters the memory system, the brain automatically tries to identify familiar patterns or concepts, organizing the information into the chunks we discussed earlier. The organized cluster of general knowledge that we possess about any single topic (object, place, activity, event) is known as a **schema**. With experience, as events are repeated with more or less variation, we can refine and build up a finely articulated hierarchy of schemas about a given topic (Lebowitz, 1983; Schank, 1982; Kolodner, 1983).

For instance, a State Department diplomat might begin storing his experiences under a broad category of diplomatic meetings, subdivided into those meetings with representatives of different countries, such as France, England, and Israel. Meetings with Israeli diplomats might be further classified according to the topics discussed, such as the Camp David Accords with Egypt and negotiations about the withdrawal of troops from Lebanon (Kolodner, 1983). In this way, the diplomat classifies new events by the developing hierarchy, then stores these events in terms of their location in the hierarchy, further described according to their distinctive features.

In this manner, we encode new information in terms of a familiar, generic pattern plus some minor deviations. This method of encoding is economical: it allows us to reuse old knowledge and escape the labor of continually forming novel patterns of associations. Schemas are ordinarily helpful, though, as we will see later, we pay a price for using them—an occasional inaccuracy or distortion in memory.

Schemas and Comprehension

The strong advantage of using prelearned schemas can be demonstrated by having people learn the same material, but arousing an appropriate schema in only some of the subjects. The effects of schemas on comprehension and recall can be powerful, even in the case of simple sentences. Suppose you read the following sentences:

■ The notes were sour because the seams split.
■ The voyage was delayed because the bottle did not break.
■ The haystack saved him because the cloth ripped.

Most people are puzzled by each of these sentences because they cannot retrieve a schema that makes the causal link ("because") understandable. Moreover, most people quickly forget a collection of such cryptic statements. But when an appropriate theme for each sentence is provided, the problems disappear. Add the clues "bagpipe," "ship christening," and "parachutist" before you read the three sentences, and your puzzlement changes to understanding (Bransford and Johnson, 1973).

This exercise demonstrates that in order to comprehend statements or events we witness, we often have to fit a preexisting schema (or collection

IMPROVING MEMORY

Any of us can improve our ability to remember by adopting **mnemonic systems** for assisting memory. Such systems have been known for thousands of years and were practiced by ancient Greek orators. Mnemonic systems organize information so that it can be remembered; they use imagery, association, and meaning to accomplish their purpose, and they make elaborate use of information already stored in memory.

The boost to ordinary memory that mnemonic systems provide will not take the work out of learning: at first, some of these devices may take more time than traditional rote memorization. But people who learn to use these systems gain two advantages. First, they are able to memorize routine material more efficiently, freeing their minds for tasks that involve more thought and creativity. Second, they become better at remembering facts required for tasks involving reasoning and understanding (Higbee, 1977).

MNEMONIC METHODS INVOLVING IMAGERY

Many popular mnemonic systems involve the use of imagery. These methods are based on the principle that it is easier to remember something if the object can be pictured in some way. For example, compare the word combination "gorilla–piccolo" versus "omniscience–euphony." The first pair of words, both concrete nouns, immediately suggests specific images, but the second pair, both abstract nouns, either suggests no images at all or suggests images that have only a remote relationship to the words (Paivio, 1971). Abstract nouns can be remembered through images, but there is always the risk that "choir," chosen as the image for "euphony," will bring "harmony" instead of "euphony" to mind on later recall.

Our memory for pairs of visual images improves further if we weave several images into an interactive scene. As noted earlier, this procedure elaborates meaningful connections between the images. Studies (e.g., Bower, 1972; Bower and Winzenz, 1970; Paivio, 1971) have shown that when a pair of words, such as "pig–ice," must be remembered, people who imagine the words interacting in some way, such as a pig skating on ice will remember the words better than someone who creates unconnected images for both words. The images need not be bizarre to promote memory—ordinary scenes work just as well. But it is helpful to imagine a scene that contains a strong emotional impact (Loftus, 1980).

Why imagery is such a powerful tool of memory is not completely understood. Perhaps visualizing objects acts in memory in much the same way as does elaborating many relations between items to be remembered: each imagined relationship provides one more route or association that helps us retrieve one item when we are cued with the other (Paivio, 1971).

Among the prominent imagery methods are those involving loci and key words.

Methods of Loci One mnemonic system used by the Russian memory expert described at the beginning of this chapter is called the **method of loci**. It involves the use of a series of *loci*, or places, that are firmly implanted in memory—say places along your route home or the rooms of your home. Items to be remembered are placed in imagination along the familiar route.

Another mnemonic system based on a similar principle is the **peg-word system**, which uses ten or more simple words as memory pegs or hooks. Once memorized, these words act as pegs upon which any arbitrary series of items can be hung. For example, each of the ten peg words below stands for one of the numbers from one to ten:

One is a bun.
Two is a shoe.
Three is a tree.
Four is a door.
Five is a hive.
Six is sticks.
Seven is heaven.
Eight is a gate.
Nine is wine.
Ten is a hen.

Each item on a list to be remembered is then visualized as interacting with the corresponding peg word. Suppose the memory task involves a shopping list, consisting of tomato soup, potatoes, spaghetti, and pickles. Imagine tomato soup being poured over a large bun, a potato resting in a shoe, strands of spaghetti hanging over a tree limb, and

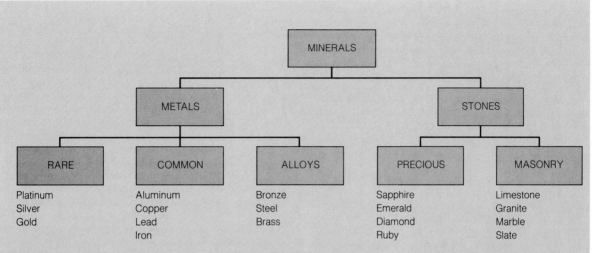

This diagram organizes minerals in a hierarchy, allowing the category labels at each node to serve as retrieval cues. (After Bower et al., 1969.)

pickles sticking like knives into a door. Once you are at the market, it will be fairly easy for you to run through the familiar peg words and recall the images that have been hung on each one (Bower, 1978). This system works effectively because it provides you with a system for storing items and a systematic plan for generating retrieval cues (loci or peg words) at the time of recall.

Key-Word System The **key-word system** has been successfully used to learn foreign vocabulary words. To learn a foreign-to-English association, you find a key English word that is similar in sound to the foreign word, and that can be imagined in association with the translation of the foreign word. For example, if the word you want to learn is *pato* (pronounced "pot-o"), the Spanish word for duck, a good key word is *pot* (sounds like *pato*),

and an effective image is a duck with a *pot* on its head. When you are tested, the word *pato* suggests pot, which cues the duck/pot image, and enables you to recall "duck." To learn the French word for skin, *peau* (pronounced "poe"), imagine Edgar Allan Poe cutting the skin off a chicken. Students who use this keyword method learn almost twice as many words in the same study time as students who use rote memorization. Because some key words are better than others, the system works best if an instruction booklet suggests the key words while students are urged to create their own images (Atkinson, 1975).

ORGANIZING MATERIAL INTO HIERARCHIES
We learn information more easily when we divide it into meaningful groups or categories, then relate these groups or categories to each other. One group may be subordinate to another, or the members may be examples of the other, and so on. Once the material is recorded in memory, the categories themselves serve as retrieval cues for other catego-

ries, making it easier to recall each item.

The power of hierarchical relations to promote memory was convincingly demonstrated when subjects tried to memorize quickly a vast number of words (Bower et al., 1979). The set of 112 words could be divided into four general categories, each composed of about 28 words. For some subjects, the words were arranged in four diagrams, like the one shown here. Other subjects saw four groupings of the same words, but each grouping was a jumbled collection from all four categories. When tested later, the subjects who had briefly studied the organized hierarchies recalled 65 percent of the words, whereas those who had studied the scrambled lists recalled only 19 percent. Hierarchical organization improved retrieval because each higher-level category acted as a retrieval cue for its subordinate classes. If we follow the diagram in memory, we can "unpack" the hierarchy, level by level.

ACTIVE RETRIEVAL
All the techniques we have investigated rely primarily on

Box continued on page 240.

IMPROVING MEMORY

improving the storage of material. But psychologists have also learned that the best way to gain facility at recalling material is to *practice* recalling it, again and again. If you have only a limited time for preparing material you want to recall, set aside a large percentage of your study time for recitation. Try out your memory, see how you perform, and then correct or supplement what you have already learned. In a classic study, Arthur Gates (1917) found that the more time a person devoted to recitation, the more he or she could later recall. Subjects who spent 80 percent of their study time in self-tests of information recalled three times as much material as students who spent all their time at passive study.

THE PQ4R METHOD

The hierarchical method helps organize material so it can be memorized, whereas active recitation fixes it into memory. Such strategies are just one aspect of a broader approach that makes general study time extremely effective, the **PQ4R method** (Thomas and Robinson, 1972). The PQ4R name comes from the steps involved: preview, question, read, reflect, recite, and review.

When you study a textbook chapter, begin with a *preview* of the chapter's topics. Read the summary first. Identify the major sections; then visualize the chapter's organization, making a topical outline, which puts the material in a hierarchical organization. As you read each major section, go through the next four processes.

Based on your preview of the chapter, make up *questions* about the material that is covered. As you *read* each section, try to answer your study questions. This method of actively formulating answers appears to be much more effective than just a careful reading.

Read slowly, *reflecting* on the material as you read it. Try to see how the material relates to information presented earlier in the book and to your other knowledge. When the book lays out general principles or conclusions, try to think of examples that illustrate them. The *question*, *read*, and *reflect* steps of the PQ4R force you to elaborate on the material and relate it to your schemas, which improves memory.

Once you have completed a section, *recite* the answers to the questions you made up for it. Try to recall the major points of each section. The questions should serve as retrieval cues. If you have trouble recalling the information, reread that section.

Finally, carry out a mental *review* of the entire chapter. This step amounts to a repetition of the sectional reviews. Can you recall the major facts in the chapter? Can you answer your questions for each section? These last two steps give you practice in active retrieval.

---

of schemas) onto them. Once we match the statements to elements of a schema, we improve our chances of remembering the information. Similar

effects occur when people are memorizing obscure sketches such as those in Figure 9.10. People remember far more of these obscure "Droodles" if the pictures are interpreted at the time the person studies them (Bower, Karlin, and Dueck, 1975). Without the interpretation, the sketch is just a nonsensical collection of lines; the interpretation calls forth a schema to "fit" onto the sketch, and hence to remember it.

Distortions Caused by Schematic Encoding

Although schemas help us economize on the amount of new material we must learn, we pay for that economy with later distortions in memory. When a particular stimulus is encoded in terms of a schema-plus-correction, we may forget the com-

Figure 9.10. "Droodles." (A) A midget playing a trombone in a telephone booth. (B) An early bird who caught a very strong worm. (After Bower, Karlin, and Dueck, 1975.)

A
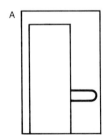

B
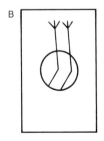

plete correction when we later attempt to recall the information. Consequently, our memory of the particular instance gets distorted in the direction of the general schema (without the correction).

A compelling demonstration of such distortions appeared in a classic experiment by Leonard Carmichael and his associates (1932). People were shown a group of figures accompanied by verbal descriptions, and later asked to reproduce the figures from memory. Their later drawings were greatly distorted, reflecting the labels the researchers had attached to the figures at the original showing. The researchers' labels had triggered schemas by which the subjects had encoded the figures. When a pair of circles connected by a straight line had been called "eyeglasses," the viewers had encoded the figure in terms of an eyeglass schema with slight modifications or corrections. But when the same figure had been called a "dumbbell," the subjects' reproductions of it were distorted in the direction of a typical dumbbell schema, as in Figure 9.11.

Inferences Added in Memory

Memory's primary function is to enable us to learn facts about the world. In constructing a plausible model of the world, we rely on the clues provided by perceptual and linguistic inputs. Because we assume that descriptive language refers to the world, we construct an internal model of the world as a speaker (or writer) describes it (Johnson-Laird, 1983). The effect is similar to a director's mounting a full theatrical stage setting from just the few lines provided by the playwright. We can put on our own "internal play" because the descriptions we hear or read activate our own schemas, which enable us to fill out a described scene. We flesh out the scene by drawing inferences that are only implicit in the description but are part of the information in our schemas.

These inferences are exploited in misleading advertisements, which seem to invite us to make inferences that the advertisers cannot legally assert. Typical ads might tell you: "Gravitrol makes you healthier" (healthier than cyanide?); "Crust fights cavities" (does it win?); "Get through this winter without colds. Take Eradicold pills." Suppose that the FDA has proof that Eradicold pills provide no protection against colds. Can the Eradicold company be prosecuted for false advertising? Technically, it cannot, because the ad does not explicitly assert that the pills prevent colds. But when psychologist Richard Harris (1982) tested people's memories about such ads, 85 percent remembered the inferences the ad makers had hoped to invite—for instance, that Eradicold pills will prevent winter colds. People made such inferences even when they had been warned about the invited inferences in advertising and told how to detect them.

Figure 9.11. Carmichael, Hogan, and Walter designed an experiment to study the influence of schematic encoding on memory. Subjects were shown the line patterns in the middle column of this figure, and these stimuli were described as drawings of various objects. Later, when the subjects were asked to reproduce from memory the patterns they had seen, they made the drawings shown in the right and left columns. You can see how the schemas used to encode the patterns influenced their drawings from memory. (After Carmichael, Hogan, and Walter, 1932.)

Reproduced Figure	Word List	Stimulus Figure	Word List	Reproduced Figure
	Eyeglasses		Dumbbells	
	Bottle		Stirrup	
	Crescent Moon		Letter "C"	
	Beehive		Hat	
	Curtains in a Window		Diamond in a Rectangle	
	Seven		Four	
	Ship's Wheel		Sun	
	Hourglass		Table	

SUMMARY

1. Memory involves acquiring, retaining, and retrieving information. **Acquisition** is the process of perceiving information, **encoding** it (transforming it into the form in which it will be recorded), and registering it in memory. Through **selective attention**, people choose which material will be registered. **Retention** is the process of maintaining information in storage, and **retrieval** is the process by which we get information from storage and use it, perhaps bringing it back into awareness. Memory operates in three different time frames: **sensory memories** are fleeting sense impressions; **short-term memory (STM)** (also known as *active memory*, or *primary memory*) is a temporary form of memory whose contents are available in awareness; and **long-term** or inactive **memory (LTM)** is the repository of permanent knowledge.

2. Short-term memory has many functions: it holds intermediate results while we work on a problem; it holds immediate goals and plans; it maintains our model of the surrounding world; and it keeps track of topics and referents mentioned in conversation. Material in STM is often encoded verbally, although each sensory system has its own form of coding. The limited capacity of short-term memory (about seven items) can be stretched by chunking information into meaningful patterns. The retention span of STM is brief; as new material enters STM, old material is **displaced**. However, old material can be retained through **rehearsal**, or mental repetition.

3. The information structures in long-term memory include personal memories, generic knowledge (semantic and perceptual), and intellectual and motor skills. Semantic knowledge consists of general ideas or concepts as well as particular ideas of individuals or places. The concepts can be simple perceptual qualities, simple motor functions, or concepts defined in terms of their relationships to other concepts, or their associations. Semantic memory contains huge networks of these associations. As these associations are strengthened, the concepts are more likely to be retrieved, are re-

trieved more quickly, and are more resistant to forgetting. Little of the information held in STM through **maintenance rehearsal** is recorded in LTM; long-term memories are established via **elaborative rehearsal**, which forms new associations and embeds material being learned into an organizational structure. Meaningful sensory data are recorded in LTM in terms of generic images with small deviations to reflect particular examples.

4. A question (probe or cue) is used to retrieve material from memory. In test situations, material may be retrieved from LTM by free recall, in which memory is searched with only a weak cue for an entire set of items; cued recall, in which an associated piece of information (a cue) guides the search; or recognition, in which search is minimized because the item itself is the cue for retrieving the context of its earlier presentation. When retrieval is only partially successful, a **tip-of-the-tongue phenomenon** may arise. Prolonged retrievals may consist of retrieval specification, matching, evaluation, and—when retrieval fails—failure diagnosis. **Metamemory**, or our knowledge about our own memory, develops through experience.

5. Information in LTM may be forgotten because of retrieval failure, decay, interference, or motivation. Retrieval failures follow the principle of **encoding specificity**; retrieval will be poor if the physical or verbal context at the time of retrieval differs so greatly from the context at the time of encoding that encoded information is not matched and activated by the **retrieval cues**. In **state-dependent memory**, information that is learned during one internal state (intoxication, sadness) is difficult to retrieve when a person is in a different state (sobriety, happiness); restoring the original state may make the information available. In **retrograde amnesia**, memory is lost for events preceding damage to the brain. In **anterograde amnesia**, following a brain injury or disease, new memories cannot be laid down in long-term memory, perhaps because of encoding problems or an inability to elaborate new material. One account of forgetting asserts that sensory and

short-term memories, as well as some long-term memories, **decay** spontaneously when they are not used, eventually becoming too weak to support recall. A complementary factor in forgetting is **interference**, in which additional material, encountered either before or after the target information was learned, makes that information unavailable. Interference between two sets of material increases with their similarity. Occasionally, memories may be lost through repression, a conscious or unconscious decision to "forget" unpleasant or threatening material.

6. **Schemas**, or the organized cluster of knowledge about any topic, improve comprehension for material that fits the schema, but their use can also lead to distortion in recall. New information is fleshed out and inferences are drawn by relying on information in our schemas.

7. **Mnemonic**, or memory-assisting, **systems** organize information so that it can be remembered. Many mnemonic systems rely on imagery; the reason that visualizing is so effective may be because it causes us to elaborate meaningful connections.

KEY TERMS

acquisition
amnesia
anterograde amnesia
chunks
cued recall
decay
displacement
elaborative rehearsal
encoding
encoding specificity
free (unaided) recall
interference
key-word system

long-term memory (LTM)
maintenance rehearsal
memory trace
metamemory
method of loci
mnemonic systems
pair recognition
peg-word system
PQ4R method
priming
proactive interference
rehearsal
retention

retrieval
retrieval cue
retroactive interference
retrograde amnesia
schema
selective attention
sensory memory
short-term memory (STM)
single-item recognition
state-dependent memory
tip-of-the-tongue phenomenon
verbal encoding

RECOMMENDED READINGS

BADDELEY, A. D. *The psychology of memory*. New York: Basic Books, 1976. An excellent, comprehensive textbook on memory.

KLATZKY, R. *Human memory: Structure and processes* (2nd ed.). San Francisco: W. H. Freeman, 1980. An introduction to memory from a cognitive perspective.

LOFTUS, E. F. *Memory*. Reading, Mass.: Addison-Wesley, 1980. A book written for laypeople that explains how the memory system works and discusses the malleability of memory.

LURIA, A. R. *The mind of a mnemonist*. New York: Basic Books, 1968. A wonderful little book describing a famous Russian memory expert called S, who was studied by Luria for more than thirty years.

NORMAN, D. A. *Learning and memory*. San Francisco: W. H. Freeman, 1982 (paper). A short, exceptionally readable account of memory by a leading cognitive scientist.

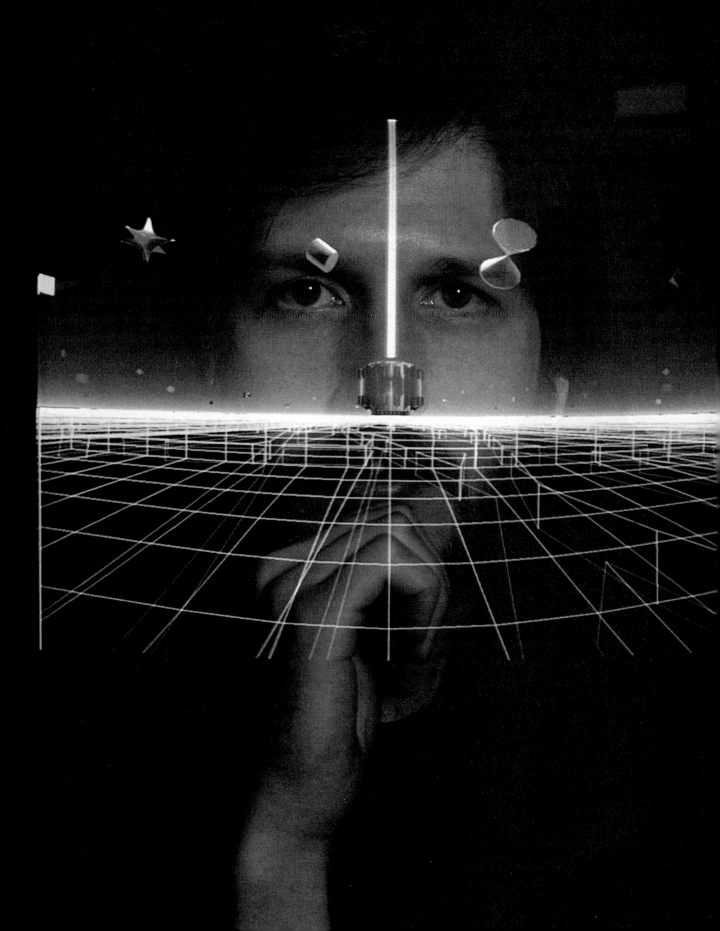

COGNITION

For centuries the disease of scurvy killed more seamen than accidents, warfare, or all other maladies put together. On Vasco da Gama's famous voyage around the Cape of Good Hope in 1497, 100 of his crew of 160 men died of the disease. But two and a half centuries later, James Lind, a physician on the British ship *Salisbury*, found a way to treat the disease (Mosteller, 1981). Lind, who had an infirmary full of scurvy patients, decided to set up an experiment. He combined all the information he had gathered about the disease with other knowledge he possessed, and came up with several hypotheses about possible cures for scurvy. Then he divided his scurvy-ridden patients into six groups and tested his hypotheses by applying a different treatment to each group. The first group got six spoonfuls of vinegar each day; the second got half a pint of sea water; the third got a quart of cider; the fourth, seventy-five drops of vitriol elixer; the fifth, nutmeg; and the sixth, two oranges and a lemon. After a few days, the patients in the first five groups had not improved. But the sailors who had been given a daily ration of citrus fruit were cured—or at least they were

well enough to get out of bed and help nurse the other patients.

How did Lind figure out this solution to his problem? Vitamins were unknown in 1747, so he could not have known that scurvy was the result of a vitamin C deficiency and that citrus fruits were a concentrated source of the vitamin. What made him decide to include oranges and lemons among his miscellany of treatments? He knew that on an earlier English expedition, sailors in one of the ships had received three teaspoons of lemon juice each day and escaped the disease. He took this memory and combined it with another piece of knowledge: lemons and oranges were similar fruits. He then formed a hypothesis—that citrus fruits would cure scurvy—and designed an experiment to test it.

Lind's feat of problem solving is an example of cognition in action—the subject of this chapter. **Cognition** is essentially the process of knowing. It encompasses thinking, decision making, judging, imagining, problem solving, categorizing, and reasoning—all the higher mental processes of human beings. These diverse mental activities may seem to be a jumble of topics without any common elements, but a common ground underlies them all: they all depend on knowledge that derives from learning and memory.

The broad array of processes included in cognition makes it impossible to cover the entire topic in a single chapter. We will, therefore, limit our investigation to four major areas of cognitive functioning: concept formation, decision making, problem solving, and creativity.

CATEGORIES AND CONCEPTS

As we have seen in Chapter 9, much of our knowledge is encoded in our memory in verbal form, so that language is essential to learning, thinking, and remembering. But imagine how impossible language would be if everything had a unique name. If the first slice of bread were called *bofir* and the one behind it *malum,* and so on through the loaf, we would run out of usable phonetic combinations before we got to the end of Wednesday's bread. And think of the number of names we would need to differentiate among the millions of individual hot dogs, pencils, socks, and blades of grass. Fortunately, the mind is lazy. It economizes on the amount of new information that it must notice and store in order to understand events, respond to them, and remember them.

One way the mind reduces its work is by grouping similar objects and events under the heading of a single concept: for example, all instances of a certain type of long-bodied, short-legged, floppy-eared, tail-wagging, tongue-lolling mammal fit under the concept "dachshund." This tendency lets us get by with a single concept and name for the entire lot. Similarly, we do not have to give each individual orange a separate name: all individual oranges fit into the concept "orange." Classifying similar things together by concepts or categories enables us to cope with the task of naming and representing the infinite variety of things in our world.

How do we recognize an object as a member of a category? We check to see whether it shares a number of the typical features, or properties, of that concept. All oranges, for example, share such properties as yellowish-red color, baseball-ish size, spherical shape, nubbly texture, and peelable rind —in addition to their unique, unmistakable smell and taste. When we consider an object that might

be an orange, we check to see whether it has at least a few of these features.

Once we have decided that the object *does* belong in a given class, we can then make inferences about it on the basis of these shared properties. If you are blindfolded and presented with a round, pebbly-surfaced object that smells like an orange, you can predict its other features—color, taste, and so on. Even this simple example shows how categories simplify the world's diversity and reduce the mind's work.

Concept Learning

No one comes into the world with a ready-made stock of concepts; we acquire them slowly, and they reflect our knowledge about the world. Concepts can be learned by direct teaching or by observation. In either process we learn the concept in terms of a collection of features and the relationships among the features.

Teaching a Concept

If you want to teach a child the concept of "orange," you can take the youngster to the local grocery and point out the oranges. Then you can contrast them with apples and pomegranates. Each comparison you make—for example, orange versus pomegranate—points out to the child one or more contrasting features that help to define an orange: for example, the orange's skin is pebbly, and the pomegranate's is smooth. The child will quickly build up an internal representation (or **schema**) of the features that accompany the category "orange."

The child will then be able to generalize the category: that is, he or she will be able to apply the name "orange" to other objects that belong to that class. Also, the child will be able to distinguish an orange from a member of another class, such as an apple or a melon. When these steps have been accomplished, the child will have "abstracted," or drawn out, the relevant features of the concept "orange" from various instances and noninstances of that concept. We say that the child has learned the concept.

Learning Concepts by Observation

Unless we are in the classroom, we learn most of our everyday concepts on our own, by observing instances and noninstances of the concept—not by having other people explicitly define the concept for us. It can be a slow process. A toddler points to a round, yellow fruit and says, "Orange!"; his parent replies, "No, Jimmy, that's a grapefruit." Indirectly, Jimmy is learning to restrict the concept of "orange." He must figure out by himself that the grapefruit's larger size and yellower color make it a noninstance of the category "orange."

Psychologists have conducted many studies of indirect concept learning, in which subjects are asked to infer or figure out a concept but are only told whether particular stimulus patterns (examples) are instances of the concept. In a typical experiment, the subject is shown a bewildering array of stimuli (examples)—perhaps geometric figures that vary in shape, color, and size, or hypothetical people who vary in age, race, marital status, occupation, and educational level. These are stimuli that may or may not be instances of the concept; the subject's task is to figure out what concept or rule will correctly classify the stimuli.

For example, subjects might be told that the FBI has been investigating a series of people, and their job is to figure out what features of a person trigger an FBI investigation. The subjects then read descriptions of a set of people; as they are shown the description of each person, they guess whether it is an instance of the concept (that is, whether this person has been investigated by the FBI). The experimenter then tells the subjects whether the guess is right (see Table 10.1).

From such studies, psychologists have noted several common tendencies (Bower and Trabasso, 1964; Trabasso and Bower, 1968).

1. People have more difficulty learning classification rules if they have to rely on their memory for the way past instances have been categorized. They learn the rules for the category much more quickly if they are allowed to keep a record (Bourne, 1970).

2. People form and test hypotheses about the category (Levine, 1975). They say, "Maybe the FBI is investigating older doctors"; then they test that hypothesis against new instances until it is disconfirmed—at which point they revise their hypothesis.

3. People do not learn much from noninstances of the hypothesis they are testing. A person who is testing an "older doctor" hypothesis gets little new information when he or she is told that a young lawyer has *not* been investigated by the FBI. For the same reason, a child who has seen only examples of nonoranges will be unlikely to learn what an orange is.

4. People have trouble learning concepts or classification rules if these rules are logically complex. The easiest classification rule to learn is one that depends on just a **single feature** or attribute (for example, "doctor"). Next easiest to learn are concepts that depend on two attributes ("old" and "doctor"). In such cases, the easiest classification rule involves the logical pattern known as a **conjunction**; that is, both attributes must be present to satisfy the rule. It is more difficult to learn classification rules that depend on **disjunction**, in which *either or both of two* features determines category membership ("old" or "doctor" or both). And it is most difficult to learn rules that involve exclusive disjunction ("old" *but not* "doctor," or "old" *or* "doctor" *but not both*). Applications of

Table 10.1 ■ Application of Four Classification Rules to Eight Stimulus Descriptions*

Classification Rule	Single Feature	Conjunction	Disjunction	Exclusive Disjunction
Descriptions of "Stimulus" Persons	*"Doctor"*	*"Old Doctor"*	*"Old" or "Doctor" or Both*	*"Old" or "Doctor" but Not Both*
Old male doctor	Yes	Yes	Yes	No
Old male lawyer	No	No	Yes	Yes
Old female doctor	Yes	Yes	Yes	No
Old female lawyer	No	No	Yes	Yes
Young male doctor	Yes	No	Yes	Yes
Young male lawyer	No	No	No	No
Young female doctor	Yes	No	Yes	Yes
Young female lawyer	No	No	No	No

*A "yes" or "no" indicates whether or not that stimulus description would be classified as a positive instance of the rule.

these four rules to our FBI-investigation example are presented in Table 10.1.

Such laboratory studies have told us a lot about the way people form and test out concepts. Underlying these studies are three presuppositions:

1. All instances of a category share certain necessary and sufficient features (for example, all spiders have eight legs).
2. An instance is either clearly a member of a category or clearly *not* a member (for example, pregnant versus nonpregnant female). Logically, this means that all category members fit the category equally well.
3. The boundaries of a category are clear and do not shift.

These assumptions do underlie some **natural categories** (categories made up of some class of objects in the world) such as male versus female human being. The assumptions also underlie most mathematical concepts (such as the concepts "odd number," "square," and "prime number"). However, the same assumptions fail to varying degrees for many other natural categories. And even for logically defined artificial categories like odd numbers, people have a sense that some members of the category are good, or typical, instances (e.g., the numbers 1, 3, and 7), but other members are poor, or atypical, examples (e.g., the numbers 23 and 447) (Armstrong, Gleitman, and Gleitman, 1983). A closer look at how natural categories operate will show why this is so.

Natural Categories: Their Features and Boundaries

Comedian Mort Sahl tells about the robber who stepped up to the bank counter and passed a note to the teller. The note read: "This is a stick-up. Act normal." The nervous teller wailed, "What's normal?"

This joke highlights the vagueness and fuzziness of many natural categories such as "normal," "fashionable dress," or "rock-and-roll." Even such everyday categories as "chair" are vague. What are the necessary and sufficient features of a chair? Legs, a flat surface (the seat), and a backrest? No, because a bean-bag seat is technically a chair, as are a canvas sling, a stool, and an orange crate.

Could we say, then, that the critical feature of a chair is not so much a physical attribute as a *function*: chairs are things that people can sit on? That is not good enough either, because there are doll's chairs, cat's chairs, and marble chairs under marble statues. Perhaps a chair is anything that can support something else. But even that will not do: now our category includes bridge supports, pier supports, poles for birdhouses, and so on. It begins to look as if we cannot identify the necessary and sufficient conditions that qualify objects as chairs.

Most common categories (fruit, houses, students, books, and so on) present similar problems. Natural categories are typically fuzzy; that is, they include some good examples, but these grade into not-so-good examples, so that a given object may be classified in alternative ways (Labov, 1973). Is a tomato a vegetable or a fruit? Is a lichee nut a fruit? Is a bat a kind of bird? Is a whale a fish? Is a virus living? Is a tree stump a chair? Is a well-intentioned little fib a lie? The fuzziness of natural categories tells us something about their structure. Each concept apparently consists of a **prototype**, or central core, which encompasses the very best examples of the concept. The prototype may be thought of as the collection of the most typical features characterizing the category as a whole. Surrounding the prototype are a collection of instances that are more or less typical of the category.

People generally agree on just how typical various instances are. For example, "sofa" and "chair" are good examples of the category "furniture"; "coffee table" and "love seat" are middling examples; "mirror" and "radio" are poor examples. Similarly, "orange" and "apple" are good examples of "fruit," but "kiwi" and "guava" are not typical examples. A category member's degree of typicality influences the way people deal with it. Children tend to learn typical instances faster and earlier than less typical ones. And when adults judge category membership, they are fastest at judging typical instances (Rosch, 1973). Similarly, when adults are asked to name category members, they tend to list the more typical instances first (Battig and Montague, 1969).

Family Resemblances among Category Members

Just what makes an instance more or less typical of a category? Eleanor Rosch and Carolyn Mervis

(1977) investigated this question and found that **family resemblance** was the key: the more closely an instance, let's say "apple," resembled many other category members (other "fruits"), the more typical it was judged to be. To derive a family resemblance score for each instance, Rosch and Mervis asked people to list its attributes: for example, an apple has a skin, is white inside, has seeds, and so on. By averaging the number of the apple's attributes that coincided with attributes of other members of the "fruit" category, Rosch and Mervis came up with a family resemblance score. This family resemblance score correlated almost perfectly with other subjects' ratings of an example's typicality. Instances with low family resemblance scores ("strawberry," "rhubarb") were rated as poor examples of the "fruit" category: people tended to be uncertain about the classification of such poor examples, and, having classified them, they often changed their minds later.

Prototypes of Categories

Psychologists have also investigated the way we learn and use the prototypes that lie at the hearts of our categories. If subjects are shown only instances that vary in minor ways from the central prototype, they quickly come up with a good conception of that central prototype (Anderson, 1980; Bransford and Franks, 1971; Franks and Bransford, 1971). Later, when tested with new instances, these subjects are more certain that an instance is a simple variant of the concept's prototype *if* the instance shares a good number of the prototype's features. The more features a candidate shares with the prototype, the more certain people are that the candidate is a member of the overall category.

The social and personality categories we use every day are called stereotypes. They seem to be constructed like most other natural categories: the category consists of a prototypic instance (a profile of typical features), flanked by members of decreasing similarity. The fuzziness of these categories is reflected in our culture's personality prototypes or stereotypes—the introvert, the extrovert, the hostile child, the lonely person, the bully, and so on: there are extreme and moderate examples of all these types. Similarly fuzzy categories exist for ethnic groups and for psychiatric diagnostic categories, such as mentally retarded and schizophrenic. Indeed, they exist for insanity (or sanity) itself. We discuss social categories in more detail in Chapter 26.

The Importance of Basic-Level Concepts

Most noun concepts fall into a natural hierarchy based on levels of abstraction (see Chapter 9). Thus, a bar stool is an example of a chair, which in turn is an example of furniture—which is an example of a human artifact. A dachshund is an example of a dog, which is an example of a mammal—which is an example of an animal. But when people are referring to ordinary objects in everyday conversation, they tend to use terms that lie somewhere in the middle of the hierarchy—not at the very top or the very bottom.

Eleanor Rosch and her associates (1976) wondered why people choose to label particular items at various levels of the hierarchy. Why do we call this thing a chair rather than a kitchen chair or a piece of furniture? Why do we call that thing a car rather than a sports car or a vehicle? We tend to refer to objects at a particular level called the **basic level**, unless the conversation requires us to say something more specific or more general (see

Table 10.2 ■ Concept Hierarchies

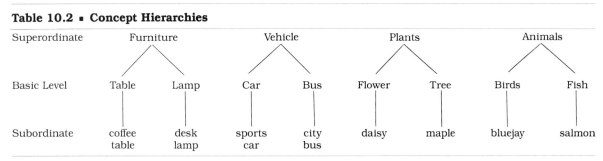

	Furniture		Vehicle		Plants		Animals	
Superordinate	Furniture		Vehicle		Plants		Animals	
Basic Level	Table	Lamp	Car	Bus	Flower	Tree	Birds	Fish
Subordinate	coffee table	desk lamp	sports car	city bus	daisy	maple	bluejay	salmon

Source: Rosch et. al., 1976.

Table 10.2). How do we intuitively select this basic level?

Evidently, we choose the level that conveys the most information. Rosch found that when people were asked to list the distinguishing features of superordinate terms—broad categories at a high level of the hierarchy, such as "furniture"—they listed very few features. But they listed many features for basic-level terms somewhere near the middle of the hierarchy, such as "chair." For subordinate terms—specific items at the lowest rank of the hierarchy, such as "bar stool"—they listed only a few more features beyond those already listed for the basic-level term. The main features that objects shared at the basic level were their *parts*: for example, the main features that tables shared were "legs" and "a flat top" (Tversky and Hemenway, 1984). Basic-level concepts, then, seem to have many features—enough so that they can easily be distinguished from other categories. Yet they are also fairly comprehensive, in that they encompass many cases.

Ad Hoc Categories

Rosch's studies concern common categories, those for which our language has devised a label. But not all the categories we use have labels. People continually make up **ad hoc categories**, spur-of-the-moment categories constructed to handle particular functions, often as part of goal-directed plans. People can readily list "ways to make friends" if they are lonely; "ways to escape being killed by the Mafia" if they are worried about that; "things that can float," and "things that can fall on your head."

Larry Barsalou (1983) found that such ad hoc categories have "good" and "bad" examples, just as common categories do. But ad hoc categories differ from common categories in an important way: typical members may bear little resemblance to other members of the category family. For instance, members of the category "foods to avoid on a diet" (e.g., olives, chocolate cake) would be considered good examples in terms of their calorie count, but not in terms of their sharing features with other diet foods.

A major reason for categorizing people, places, and objects is so that we can make appropriate judgments about them and then decide how to act towards them. On the job we behave differently if we believe we are talking to one of our bosses or

Masculine or feminine? How we categorize people influences our communication with them, so when we meet a person who straddles the boundaries between categories, as Boy George does so well, we may feel uneasy or confused.

one of our subordinates. Obviously, our categories and judgments play a basic role in the decisions we make about how to behave in given situations.

JUDGMENT AND DECISION MAKING

Our life is the history of the thousands of decisions we have made: whether to go to this or that school, take this or that course, go out with this or that person, and so on. Decisions always involve several options or conflicting alternatives—to do one thing or another. If we could know in advance the eventual outcome of each choice, then we'd have no real problem, no miserable indecision, no lack of resolution: we would simply choose that option which led to the preferred outcome. But the world and its future are risky and uncertain, and so we must usually judge how likely it is that different outcomes will occur, before we can even begin to calculate the expected value of the different options among which we must decide.

These preliminary judgments of uncertain events are often more difficult than making a final decision. Thus, modern studies of decision making have looked closely at human judgment and prediction about uncertain events.

The Use of Heuristics in Making Judgments

Uncertainty is part of the human condition. As we have noted, most of our decisions require us to judge the probability of uncertain events. Did this defendant commit the crime? Who will win the election? Will this course be interesting? Will this person make me happy? We have no formal procedure for computing the probability of such uncertain events, and we often lack the complete data that would allow us to make realistic estimates.

Therefore, to assess these likelihoods, people have developed sets of crude assessment strategies known as **heuristics**. Heuristics are essentially "rules of thumb"; they are quick and intuitively sensible ways to judge probabilities, and they frequently give fairly accurate estimates (Tversky and Kahneman, 1983). Among the common heuristics used in judgment are representativeness, availability, and causal scenarios.

The Heuristic of Representativeness

Suppose you read this description of Tom W. and are asked to judge whether he is more likely to be a computer science major or a humanities major:

> Tom W. is of high intelligence, although lacking in true creativity. He has a need for order and clarity, and for neat and tidy systems in which every detail finds its appropriate place. His writing is rather dull and mechanical, occasionally enlivened by somewhat corny puns and by flashes of imagination of the sci-fi type.

> He has a strong drive for competence. He seems to have little feeling and little sympathy for other people, and does not enjoy interacting with others. Self-centered, he nonetheless has a deep moral sense. (Kahneman and Tversky, 1973, p. 138).

First, decide what you think is the probability that Tom W. is a computer science major as opposed to a humanities major. (Do this now before you continue reading.) Next, consider some new information. Suppose you are told that Tom is one of 100 people in a classroom, and 80 of those people are in humanities. Does that change your estimate of the probabilities?

When Daniel Kahneman and Amos Tversky (1973) presented Tom W.'s profile to groups of university students, these students overwhelmingly (95 percent) placed him in computer science at first. And their estimates remained practically unchanged even after they had learned that 80 percent of the class were majoring in the humanities. Why this result, even after the students had gained abstract knowledge about the statistical likelihood of any person's majoring in computer science? That knowledge was apparently overwhelmed by the resemblance of Tom's profile to the popular stereotype (prototype) of the computer science major.

This experiment illustrates the way people use the heuristic of **representativeness**: *people judge the likelihood of an event according to its similarity to the prototype of a given class.* For example, we may predict a person's political beliefs from how similar he or she is to one of three stereotypes: the radical socialist, the middle-of-the-roader, and the archconservative. When people are judging Tom's probable major, they essentially compare him to their stereotypes of computer scientists and humanities majors, then choose the stereotype which he most resembles. In the process, people ignore the overall proportion of the two kinds of majors in the group under consideration.

Misunderstandings Concerning Random Sequences The representativeness heuristic operates when we judge whether a sequence of events is random or systematic. People's stereotype of a random series of, say, births of boys and girls on a given maternity ward, is one which has a large number of alterations and relatively few long runs of a given event. Thus, people will judge BGBGGB as a "more random" and more probable series of births than the sequence BBBGGG or even BBBBBB. But if boys and girls each have a 50 percent chance of appearing, then any sequence of six outcomes is as probable as any other sequence. Therefore, a sequence consisting of all boys is just as likely as a sequence consisting of alternating boys and girls. So strong is people's belief that "randomness equals alteration" that people will judge a short sequence like BBB as far less likely than a longer sequence like GBBBG, which has more alterations (and contains the earlier series). But clearly, any specific sequence of three events is more likely to occur (its probability is $.5^3$) than is any specific sequence of five events (the probability of such a sequence is $.5^5$).

People's failure to appreciate randomness in sequences has helped create the notion of the "hot hand" in basketball players or the "streak hitter" in baseball. If a basketball player shoots three or four baskets in a row, the other players conclude that he is "on" (that something lawful is causing his high hit rate), and try to get the ball to him so that he can shoot more often. The fans agree; in one study of basketball fans, 91 percent believed that a player whose last two or three shots had been successful had a better chance of making the next shot than if the last couple of shots had been missed. But an analysis of hit-and-miss sequences of NBA players closely approximated the sequences we would expect if one shot were completely independent from the next—as, in fact, they are (Tversky, Vallone, and Gilovich, 1984). The common belief in the streak shooter seems to be a superstition that is based on the false impression that any run of hits (or misses) indicates nonrandomness (lawfulness). Since runs often occur in random sequences, there is no way to dislodge this common belief by merely exposing people to additional random sequences.

Similar superstitions appear to underlie the "gambler's fallacy." If you toss a coin, the chances are 50 percent that it will come up heads and 50 percent that it will be tails—*on any one toss*, or each time. If you have tossed a coin ten times and it has landed heads up each time, the gambler will believe that the next toss will turn up tails. The gambler does not realize that each toss is independent; there is no reason to expect that the probability of tails is any higher on the eleventh toss than it was on the first toss. Gamblers fall prey to the same fallacy when they bet on the roulette wheel. They know that the probability of the number 13's coming up on a roulette wheel is 1 in 38. Therefore, many assume that if 13 has not come

up after numerous spins, the "law of averages" makes it likely that 13 will come up soon. In fact, however, one spin of the wheel has no effect on the next spin; the probability of the number 13's coming up on the next spin has nothing to do with the number of preceding consecutive spins that have not stopped on 13. These superstitions reflect our tendency to see a purposeful design or plan behind every series of events, even those generated according to a random process.

Conjunction Fallacies   Another fallacy created by people's use of the representativeness heuristic is the **conjunction fallacy**: a conviction that an example with both a common *and* a distinctive feature is more representative than an example with only the distinctive feature.

Let us say that **C** and **D** denote the common and distinctive features of an example: for instance, let us say that **C** is a visit from our friend Melvin and **D** is a gift of a box of candy from Melvin. Let us also say that the probability of the gift (**D**) is less likely than the probability of the visit (**C**). Notice that for **D**, Melvin just has to get the candy to us somehow —by mail, by hand delivery, or by any other means.

Now, how likely is it that Melvin will arrive in person with a box of candy—that is, what is the probability that **C** *and* **D** will happen at the same time (in conjunction)? Is it more likely than the probability of **D** all by itself—that Melvin will simply get a box of candy to us by *some* means? You may say that the probability of **C** *and* **D** is less than the probability of **D** alone, and if so you are right. You are using a rule of probability that tells us that the probability of the conjunction of both features, Pr (**C** and **D**), must be less than or equal to Pr (**D**), the probability of the least probable feature.

But you would be surprised at how many people make a mistake here. A visit from Melvin (**C**) is highly probable, and it becomes the stereotype by which people judge the likelihood of certain other events. Attracted by this stereotype, people think that the conjunction of **C** and **D** is also highly probable—more probable than **D** alone.

Numerous experiments by Amos Tversky and Daniel Kahneman (1983) have shown surprisingly many circumstances in which people are tripped up by this conjunction fallacy. In one experiment, students read personality sketches of fictitious individuals. One sketch read:

> Linda is 31 years old, single, outspoken, and bright. She majored in philosophy. As a stu-

dent she was deeply concerned with issues of discrimination and social justice, and also participated in anti-nuclear demonstrations. (p. 197)

The students then ranked the likelihood that the person described had later entered one of a series of avocations and occupations. For Linda, the alternatives included:

- Rank the likelihood that Linda is a teacher in elementary school. (Te)
- Rank the likelihood that Linda is active in the feminist movement. (Fm)
- Rank the likelihood that Linda is a bank teller. (Tl)
- Rank the likelihood that Linda is a bank teller *and* is active in the feminist movement. (Fm & Tl)

Most people saw Linda as fitting the stereotype of the active feminist (Fm), but as unlikely to be a bank teller (Tl). Yet 88 percent of them believed that the chances of Linda's being *both* a bank teller and an active feminist were higher than her chances of just being a bank teller. Why? Possibly, when the people saw "feminist" in the bank teller/feminist combination, a significant number of them thought there must be at least some possibility of Linda's fitting into this category. The category resembled the stereotype ("feminist") to some extent, so the people thought it had a relatively high probability.

These estimates violate the most basic rule of probability theory mentioned earlier: the probability of a conjunction of events or features is always less than or equal to the probability of the less frequent event. In other words, Linda cannot become *more* likely to be a bank teller when we *add* the restriction of feminism. Look at the situation in a different context: the chance that a randomly chosen adult is black *and* female clearly must be less than the chance that the person is black (regardless of sex).

The conjunction fallacy is a powerful cognitive illusion; it is based on people's use of a representativeness heuristic that judges the likelihood of an outcome by its resemblance to a likely series or stereotype. Tversky and Kahneman (1983) found that sophisticated experts are about as likely as naive observers to fall into conjunction fallacies. These researchers found such fallacies among physicians judging the likelihood of patients' exhibiting various symptoms, detectives judging the

likelihood that a criminal suspect had committed several related crimes, and political forecasters judging the likelihood of various international events. In fact, the conjunction fallacy shows up everywhere for almost everyone. People seem to believe that likelihoods follow a rule of resemblance to a stereotype rather than the laws of probability. In reality, of course, the laws of probability will win out over resemblances.

Availability

When we use the **availability** heuristic, we estimate the likelihood of any event's occurring on the basis of the availability of supporting evidence in our memory. The more readily we recall such evidence, the more probable an event or proposition seems to us. For example, are there more English words with the letter "k" in the first position ("kangaroo") than words with "k" in the third position ("awkward")? Think about it for a while and make a guess. If you are like most people, you will say that "k" more often appears as the first letter. But in fact the opposite is true (Tversky and Kahneman, 1973). Why do we make this systematic error? Because when we try to retrieve words from memory, words that begin with a "k" (such as "kiss," "king," and so on) come to mind much more readily than words that have "k" in the third position (such as "poke," "sake," and so on). Our mind gets fooled into thinking that the easier it is to generate lots of examples, the more examples there must be.

A similar process is at work when subjects judge that there are more words ending in "-ing" than in "-n-," as well as more words ending in "-ly" than in "-l-." We can retrieve the "-ing" and "-ly" words more easily. So we may persist in this judgment, even though it is clear that every word that ends in "-ing" also ends in "-n-," so that the second set of words contains all the words in the first set, together with all the words that end in "-ne," "-nt," "-ns," and so on. These erroneous judgments show the availability heuristic at work.

Availability can be a useful tool in cases where our past exposure and attention have allowed us to store unbiased information, or when the test question is equally good at retrieving both positive and negative evidence from memory. For example, people can give reasonably accurate judgments of the relative frequency of drugstores versus bowling alleys versus service stations in their city. Similarly, if they pay equal attention, they can accurately judge the proportion of whites, Hispanics, and Asians in their neighborhoods.

But the availability heuristic can also lead us toward biased judgments when the examples we can most easily retrieve are a biased subset of all the examples. A study in which people were given lists of celebrities, then asked whether the list contained more men or women, demonstrates how familiar information can lead to erroneous judgments (Tversky and Kahneman, 1973). When the list included many famous men but less well-known women (John F. Kennedy versus Millicent Fenwick), people judged that the list contained more men's than women's names. But when the women on the list were more famous than the men (Elizabeth Taylor versus Placido Domingo), the judgment was reversed: people said there were more women on the list. Because famous names are more easily recalled (are more available in memory), the relative fame of the people on the list distorted people's recollections. This distortion in memory, in turn, supported a biased judgment of the proportion of men on the list.

Our moods appear to affect the availability of information, influencing our judgments about so-cial events and ourselves. In experiments by William Wright and Gordon Bower (reported in Bower, 1983), both happy and sad subjects were asked to estimate the likelihood that certain events would occur within a few years. Some of the events were personal ("You will be seriously injured in an auto accident") and others were international ("The Arabs and Israelis will stop fighting"). The happy subjects were optimistic, overestimating the likelihood of positive events and underestimating the likelihood of negative ones. The sad subjects showed the reverse bias: their judgments were pessimistic (see Figure 10.1A). When asked to justify their judgments, the happy people retrieved pleasant supporting evidence, tipping the scales in a positive direction; the sad people retrieved evidence that tipped the scales the other way. Similar biases appeared when happy or sad subjects estimated their own abilities, judging whether they would be able to perform a series of challenging tasks that were romantic, assertive, intellectual, or athletic in nature (see Figure 10.1B). Happy people tended to remember their past successes on similar tasks, and sad people tended to remember their failures (Kavanagh and Bower, 1985). The nature of available information apparently influences judgments related to self-confidence and self-esteem.

The availability heuristic also explains the overconfidence we have in **hindsight**. Looking back on events *after* they occur, we fool ourselves into thinking that the outcome was really quite likely, and we can hardly recall how uncertain we

Figure 10.1. (A) The average probability estimates of positive events ("blessings") and of negative events ("disasters") for subjects in a happy, neutral, or sad mood. (Data from Wright and Bower, unpublished.) (B) The average self-efficacy score, or prediction of performance skill across diverse activities, for subjects who were feeling sad, neutral, or happy about themselves. (Data from Kavanagh and Bower, 1985.)

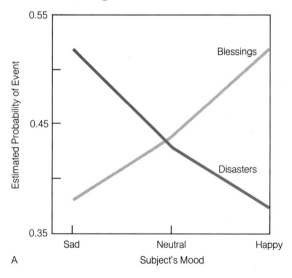

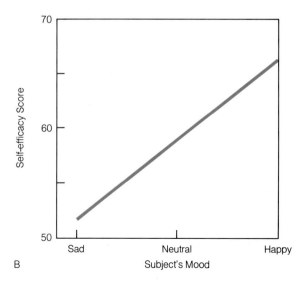

A   B

were about the outcome before the event. Once the event has occurred, it is very available in our mind; hence it later appears in hindsight to have been a very probable outcome. This may explain the confidence of the Monday-morning quarterback who second-guesses the coach's decisions, or the investor who berates his financial advisor for not knowing that the stock market was about to rise or fall.

Causal Scenarios

Another heuristic we use in assessing the future operates when we try to predict a future event with the aid of some credible theory. If we can readily generate a "causal story" that would lead up to the event, then we convince ourselves that the event is likely to occur. In fact, the causal scenario may be a variation of the availability heuristic. Tversky and Kahneman (1983) asked college students to rate the probability that various events would occur within a year. The students believed "an earthquake in California sometime next year, causing a flood in which more than 1,000 people drown" was much more likely than "a massive flood somewhere in North America next year, in which more than 1,000 people drown." The students had, of course, been led into a conjunction fallacy, in which they assumed that a California earthquake *and* a massive flood were more probable than a massive flood by itself. (After all, California is part of North America.) The often-mentioned possibility of earthquake in California came easily to mind, giving the students a scenario in which 1,000 persons could easily drown.

The availability of a causal scenario can even trap experts into conjunction fallacies. For example, during the summer of 1982, when the Solidarity Union was creating political unrest in Poland, a group of professional political forecasters were asked on separate occasions to evaluate the probability of two events:

- A complete suspension of diplomatic relations between the USA and the Soviet Union, some time in 1983.
- A Russian invasion of Poland, and a complete suspension of diplomatic relations between the USA and the Soviet Union, some time in 1983. (Tversky and Kahneman, 1983, p. 307)

The forecasters rated both events as improbable, but judged that a Russian invasion of Poland, followed by the suspension of U.S.–Soviet relations, was more likely than the suspension of U.S.–Soviet relations alone. Because the joint option provided them with a plausible scenario, the forecasters felt it was more likely to happen. This was also an example of the conjunction fallacy.

Causal scenarios can affect our judgment even when we manufacture the scenario. When we are forced to produce an explanation of the way a conjectured event or relation might come about, we often convince ourselves that the event will occur or that the relationship is true. In one study (Bower and Masling, unpublished), subjects were asked to explain a number of far-fetched alleged correlations, such as "The greater the wheat crop in Iowa in the autumn, the greater the weight of the *New York Times* Sunday newspaper that winter," and 'The greater the number of ice cream cones sold during a month in Brooklyn, the greater the number of deaths that month among street vagrants in Calcutta, India." Half the subjects were asked to explain statements in which the correlations were reversed, with "lesser" substituted for "greater." No matter which sort of correlations they judged, these subjects later rated correlations for which they had devised causal scenarios as more likely to be true than did subjects who had never before seen those correlations. Apparently, when the subjects were asked to judge the truth of specific correlations, their earlier explanations were highly available and readily recalled from memory.

We seem to operate by the rule: if we can readily explain something, we should assume that it is true. However, in the process, we ignore the fact that in many areas we can "explain" almost any relationship between almost any two variables. This principle applies not only to subjects who are explaining obscure correlations, but also to scientists who are predicting or explaining events according to their favorite theories.

Anchoring

Our use of heuristics is not the only way in which we can be led to a faulty judgment; we can also be betrayed by our perspective on a situation. In one such effect, called **anchoring**, our judgment is biased by the starting point from which we are making the judgment. Our focus on the starting point (or anchor) leads us to neglect other, relevant information. For example, if a stock-market analyst is asked to predict the Dow-Jones high for the current year after being told last year's *high*, he or she will come up with a higher figure than if told the Dow-Jones *low* for the previous year (Tversky and Kahneman, 1973).

The anchoring effect exerts a powerful influence on many types of judgments, such as reports of grades, health habits, dating patterns, income, and so on. Suppose, for example, that you are asked to estimate the size of a crowd at last night's rock concert. If your questioner says, "How many were there? Was it near 200?" you will give a lower estimate than if the questioner says, "Was it near 50,000?" In response to the first question, you are likely to come up with a number like 2,000, and to the second question, you are likely to come up with a number like 10,000. Your answer will be a mixture of your vague memory for the crowd and the anchor that has been provided by the questioner as an "acceptable answer."

Framing Decisions

The heuristics and biases we have considered are important when we are judging the *likelihood* of events. But curious distortions in judgment may also arise when we consider the *utility* or *value* of a decision's possible outcomes. For example, we tend to evaluate the possible gains or losses an option will bring us relative to our current situation, which we presume to be fixed. We are often unaware that by **framing**, or phrasing, the decision from a different perspective, we can shift our evaluation of the situation. The way a problem is framed can thus affect our decision.

Consider the following problem:

Imagine that the U.S. is preparing for the outbreak of an unusual Asian disease, which is expected to kill 600 people. Two alternative programs to combat the disease have been proposed. Assume that the exact scientific estimate of the consequences of the program are as follows:

■ If Program A is adopted, 200 people will be saved.
■ If Program B is adopted, there is 1/3 probability

that 600 people will be saved, and 2/3 probability that no people will be saved.

Which of the two programs would you favor? (Tversky and Kahneman, 1981).

When the options are phrased this way, in terms of saving lives, most people choose Program A. However, suppose that the same options are framed in a different manner, in terms of losing lives:

■ If Program A is adopted, 400 people will die.
■ If Program B is adopted, there is a 1/3 probability that no one will die, and a 2/3 probability that 600 people will die.

Which of the two programs would you favor? (Tversky and Kahneman, 1981).

Figure 10.2. This schematic diagram illustrates how the subjective value of a decision's outcome varies with the size of potential gains or losses. When the possible outcome of a disease-treatment program is expressed in terms of lives saved, its positive value increases as the number of lives saved increases (upward end of the curve); when the outcome is expressed in terms of increasing numbers of lives lost, the program's negative value increases accordingly (downward end of the curve). So when 600 lives are said to be at risk, subjects are more likely to vote for a treatment program that will save 200 lives than for a program in which 400 lives will be lost, even though the outcome of the two programs is identical—and even if the chosen program places more of the 600 people at risk in saving 200 of them. (After Tversky and Kahneman, 1981.)

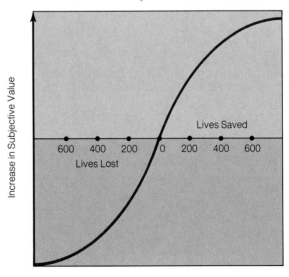

Now the decisions are reversed. Given this frame, people become willing to take the risk they shunned in the first instance, so most choose Program B, even though it risks all 600 lives (see Figure 10.2).

Tversky and Kahneman (1981) sum up the results of research into the framing of decisions by stating that when choices involve possible gains, people tend to avoid risks, but when the choices involve possible losses, they will take risks in order to minimize possible losses. This is the case whether the potential gain or loss involves lives, money, or time; it reflects the fact that most people would rather minimize displeasure (losses) than maximize pleasure (gains). As a result, when programs are framed in terms of certain losses, judgments can suddenly change.

PROBLEM SOLVING

One of the most common uses of thought and reason is in the process of solving problems. Every day we solve hundreds of small problems, and in the process we learn routine actions for handling recurrent problems. Once we have learned these actions, we no longer consider the routines as "solving problems" or requiring "thought"; we begin to "think again" only when an established routine fails. For example, the recurrent problem of doing the laundry is seen as a problem only if all the laundromats are closed by a strike.

It is not always easy to know when a problem has been solved. In the case of **ill-defined problems**, such as writing a good story or designing a beautiful house, there are no agreed-on steps or

---

Table 10.3 ■ Examples of Reasoning Problems Given to Subjects Studied by Psychologists

A. THE HOBBITS AND ORCS PROBLEM
Three hobbits and three orcs stand on one side of a river. On their side of the river is a boat that will hold no more than two creatures. The problem is to transport all six creatures to the other side of the river. However, if orcs ever outnumber hobbits, they will eat the hobbits. How can they all get across the river safely? Remember that someone must row the boat back after each trip across.

B. CREATIVITY
Name as many novel, creative uses as you can for a hammer; for a brick.

C. ANAGRAMS
Rearrange the letters in each set to make an English word:

EFCTA   IAENV   BODUT   LIVAN   IKCTH

D. MATCHING PROBLEM
Sitting at a bar, from left to right, are George, Bill, Tom, and Jack. Use the following information to figure out who owns the Cadillac:

1. George has a blue shirt.
2. The man with a red shirt owns a Volkswagen.
3. Jack owns a Buick.
4. Tom is next to the man with a green shirt.
5. Bill is next to the man who owns a Cadillac.
6. The man with a white shirt is next to the Buick owner.
7. The Ford owner is farthest away from the Buick owner.

E. THE TWO–STRING PROBLEM
Two strings hang from the ceiling in a large, bare room. The strings are too far apart to allow a person to hold one and walk to the other. On the floor are a book of matches, a small screwdriver, and a few cotton balls. How could the strings be tied together?

F. PYRAMID PUZZLE
Place a piece of paper on a table and draw three circles on it, labeling them A, B, and C. On circle A stack four coins—from top to bottom, a dime, a penny, a nickel, and a quarter. Moving only one coin at a time, moving only the top coin in any stack, and moving a coin only from one circle to another, get the coins stacked in exactly the same sequence on circle C. Important restriction: a coin may never be stacked on top of a physically smaller coin; for example, the nickel cannot be placed on top of the dime.

See Table 10.4 for solutions.

Table 10.4 ■ Solutions to Problems in Table 10.3

A. THE HOBBITS AND ORCS PROBLEM
Solving the hobbits and orcs problem involves the twelve steps diagrammed below. The paired boxes represent the two sides of the river, and the numbers indicate how many hobbits (H) and orcs (O) are on each side at each step. The location of the boat is also indicated. Next to each arrow appears the number of occupants of the boat as it crosses the river on a given trip. (From Glass, Holyoak, and Santa, 1979.)

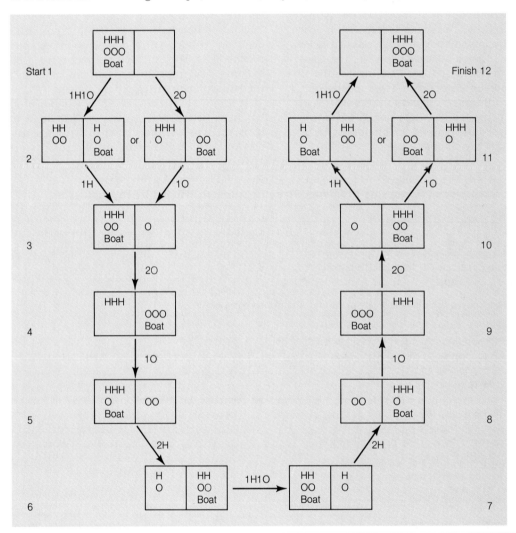

B. CREATIVITY
There is no "correct" solution to this problem. High creativity is shown in the uniqueness of answers and their number.

C. ANAGRAMS
Answers are *facet, naive, doubt, anvil, thick.*

Table 10.4 ■ Solutions to Problems in Table 10.3

D. MATCHING PROBLEM
    Tom owns the Cadillac.

Person	*Shirt Color*	*Car*
George	Blue	Ford
Bill	Red	Volkswagen
Tom	White	Cadillac
Jack	Green	Buick

E. THE TWO–STRING PROBLEM
    Tie the screwdriver to the end of one string and set it swinging. Walk to the other string, grasp it, and wait for the swinging string to come within reach. The two strings may then be tied together. The matches and cotton balls are not needed.

F. PYRAMID PUZZLE
    In the answer, 1 = penny, 5 = nickel, 10 = dime, 25 = quarter; 10–A means move the dime to circle A, and so on: 10–B, 1–C, 10–C, 5–B, 10–A, 1–B, 10–B, 25–C, 10–C, 1–A, 10–A, 5–C, 10–B, 1–C, 10–C. (Adapted from Bourne, Dominowski, and Loftus, 1979.)

rules that will produce a product generally accepted as a solution. By contrast, **well-defined problems**, such as math problems or logic proofs, have a clear structure; there is always a clear standard for deciding whether the problem has been solved.

In the laboratory, psychologists generally study how people solve well-defined problems, because such problems have built-in criteria by which the solutions can be evaluated. Psychologists also concentrate on studying people solving problems that require no special knowledge and can be solved using elementary reasoning strategies. Sample problems of this type are shown in Table 10.3; solutions are given in Table 10.4. For example, in the "hobbits and orcs" problem presented in the table, no special knowledge of boats, hobbits, or orcs is required beyond that given in the problem statement. In this section we concentrate on research investigating how college students solve well-defined, low-knowledge problems.

Stages in Solving a Problem

Psychologists divide the solution of well-defined, low-knowledge problems into four partly overlapping stages: (1) understanding or representing the problem to oneself; (2) planning a sketchy solution to it; (3) carrying out the plan in detail; and (4) evaluating whether the results yield a satisfactory solution (Glass, Holyoak, and Santa, 1979). In discussing these stages, we will combine stages 2 and 3, the planning and carrying out of a solution. But let us first look at stage 1.

Representing the Problem

The way people interpret and represent a problem to themselves may largely determine how easy the problem is to solve. The same problem can often be represented in several different ways, and some representations bring a solution to mind more readily than others. Consider the game of Number Scrabble, which can be described in four short sentences:

1. Each of the digits 1 through 9 is written on a separate card, and the cards are laid out right side up.
2. Two players take turns drawing cards with digits. Each player draws one card per turn and keeps the cards he draws.
3. The first player to draw cards having any three digits whose sum is 15 wins.
4. If all nine digits are drawn without a win, then the game is a draw.

Try playing several games of Number Scrabble with a friend. You will discover that it is extremely difficult to learn a winning strategy, in which you not only draw the correct digits but draw those that keep your opponent from completing the sum of 15 as well.

The problem structure of Number Scrabble is identical with that of Tic-Tac-Toe (or Xs and Os), where you try to connect all elements in a row, column, or diagonal. The numbers in the Tic-Tac-Toe matrix on page 260 show the equivalence:

8	1	6
3	5	7
4	9	2

Furthermore, placing an X (or 0) on a given cell in the table would correspond to the X's (or 0's) player drawing that digit in the card game above.

Note that the sum of the digits in any row, column, or diagonal is 15, the goal in Number Scrabble. Yet most people find Tic-Tac-Toe far easier to play well than Number Scrabble, because they can see their progress (and their opponent's) toward their competitive goals, and they need not keep various sums in their heads. Such are the advantages of a good representation.

Another illustration of the power of a good representation is the "Buddhist Monk" problem.

A monk starts walking along a narrow path up a mountain at sunrise, going at varying speeds and resting now and then. He gets to the top around sunset. After meditating at the Buddhist temple on the summit for several days, he starts out at sunrise and returns down the mountain by the same path, again walking at varying speeds with frequent pauses. Show that there is a spot along the path that the monk will occupy on both trips at precisely the same time of day.

People who try to solve this problem verbally or algebraically find the task extremely complex. But you can devise a simpler proof that such a crossing spot must exist, simply by inventing a second monk who begins to descend the mountain at the same time that the first monk starts ascending. Regardless of the varying speeds of the two monks, it is obvious that the two must meet at some time at some spot along the path.

In such a problem the solution depends on finding a simple representation. Part of what experts learn about a domain of knowledge is how to represent its problems in a fashion that points the way to the easiest solution.

Solution Strategies

To solve a problem, we must often examine a large number of possible options or moves in the search

for a solution. A person's conception of possible moves is known as the **problem space**; problem spaces can be used to characterize people's behavior in solving such problems as proving theorems in logic, making mathematical derivations, and playing games like chess or checkers (Newell and Simon, 1972; Nilsson, 1971). Each time a move is made, the person is seen as moving from one "problem state" to another. For example, suppose you wanted to solve for x in the equation

$$2x + 3 = 13.$$

The problem-solving plan consists of a sequence of arithmetic operations that transform one equation into another:

Starting State	$2x + 3 = 13$
Apply operation	*Subtract 3 from both sides*
New State	$2x + 3 - 3 = 13 - 3$
Apply operation	*Collect constants*
New State	$2x = 10$
Apply operation	*Divide both sides by 2*
Goal State	$x = 5$

In this solution the rules of arithmetic provide you with methods for moving from one state to the succeeding states.

If at each point in the derivation you considered applying all possible legal moves (addition, subtraction, multiplication, division), you would generate a large branching tree, several levels deep, of possible developments to consider in your search. This tree is known as a **search tree**; Figure 10.3 shows a few of the possible branches in this simple algebra problem. In terms of such a search tree, you can reformulate the problem: "Find a sequence of moves in the search tree that will transform the starting state into the goal state."

How might you search through such a tree of possibilities, looking for the sequence of moves that leads to a solution? A minimum strategy is to use simple trial and error (or "generate and test"), considering and checking all possible options that might solve the problem. You might examine all the possibilities at each level in the tree (see Figure 10.3) before proceeding a level deeper; this approach is called "breadth-first search." Or you could first examine all descendants along one branch of the tree ("depth-first search") before backing up to the next higher branch to descend once again (Nilsson, 1971). Using either method,

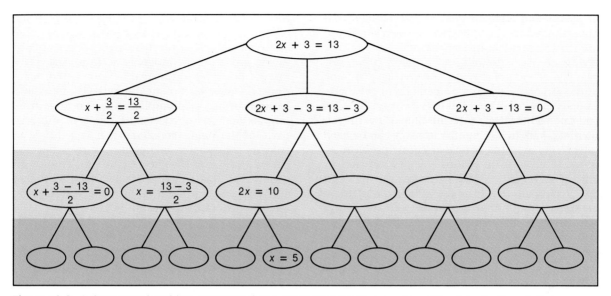

Figure 10.3. A derivational problem represented as a developing search tree of possible states in the solution.

you could blindly exhaust the full range of possibilities in the search tree, looking for a solution.

Depth-first and breadth-first search methods are examples of **algorithms**, mechanical routines that guarantee an eventual solution to a problem if a solution exists. Many efficient algorithms exist in mathematics, such as routines for subtraction, for long division, for solving sets of linear equations, and so on.

The difficulty with the "generate-and-test" algorithm is that for any reasonably interesting problem the number of moves that must be considered is astronomically large. In chess, for example, it is estimated that the problem space of all possible sequences of moves has close to 10^{120} branches; obviously no one could begin to examine more than the barest fraction of such an enormous problem space of possibilities.

If, however, you have some information about the solution path in the search tree, you can use this information to reduce the search space to manageable size. You can use heuristic methods —search methods that rely on plausible guesses about likely solution paths. As we saw in the section on decision making, heuristic methods are rules of thumb, shortcuts, plausible procedures to follow. A good heuristic will probably reduce your search to just those moves that are likely to be successful (Polya, 1957; Wickelgren, 1974). Heuristics do not always work, but when they do, they greatly reduce trial-and-error searching.

Most problems are accompanied by some useful information that can be converted into a heuristic search strategy. The problem-solving context determines which heuristic methods might be most successful.

Search Heuristics: High-Valued Paths Suppose we had some way to assign to each branch of a search tree (see Figure 10.3) a number representing the expected value (gains minus losses) of searching down that path. Then we would merely search down those paths—try out those moves —that carried us along the highest-valued path. This strategy requires a procedure that can first assign values to various search options. For example, in a game like checkers or chess, you can guess the approximate value of a given move on the basis of the game situation that will immediately follow your move. You can estimate the number of pieces you will have in relation to your opponent, the degree to which you will control the board, and so on. After considering and evaluating a number of moves, you can choose the one with the highest value.

The problem with this method is that even though it helps you pick a move, it does not reduce the number of options you have to consider at each step in order to evaluate them. And in many situations it is difficult to evaluate the intermediate states in your search, because you do not know in which direction the goal lies.

Means-End Analysis When using the heuristic

of **means-end analysis**, you choose actions that appear to reduce the difference between where you are (in the problem space) and the goal you are trying to reach (Newell and Simon, 1972). For example, if you are at home and your goal is to be at the airport, you think of methods to get there. Suppose a bus will take you to the airport. How do you catch a bus? Get to the bus stop. How can you do that? Walk to it. A similar strategy can be used to solve for *x* in the simple algebraic problem: to progress toward the goal of having *x* on the left side of the equation and a number on the right side, collect all *x* terms on the left and all numbers on the right. In this procedure you are always reducing the differences between where you are and where you are going, setting up subgoals along the way.

Working Backwards A special form of means-end analysis consists of devising a plan by **working backwards** from the goal state. For example, if my initial goal in logic is to prove statement C, and I know that B implies C, then I realize that if I can prove B, I will be able to prove C. But I notice that A implies B, so I can prove B (and C) either if I can prove A or if A is one of the axioms or "givens" of the problem.

In a practical illustration, suppose your goal is to buy a car. You can do that if you accumulate $7,000. You can accumulate $7,000 if you work summers and weekends during the school year and save your money. You can work during the school year if you get a job. And you can get a job if you apply at the Student Employment Office. So you go there as your first step. Working backwards is a special way of reducing the differences between your current position and the goal, and it is a common reasoning strategy. By reasoning backwards from a distant goal, the problem solver can reach a first step that can be taken now.

Problem Reduction The strategies just mentioned suggest efficient ways of searching a problem tree. They are examples of a more general procedure called **problem reduction**. When we follow a problem-reduction strategy, we break a large problem into a number of smaller problems that are easier or that are within our power to solve. Architects use this strategy in designing a building; a house is a collection of rooms of a coherent style set upon a foundation. By decomposing the overall design problem into a collection of smaller problems (the various rooms, their required sizes and locations), which are refined into

yet smaller decisions, you eventually reach bottom-level decisions as small as where to locate electrical outlets in the bathroom. The standard way to proceed is by progressive deepening, planning at one level (number of rooms) before planning at a lower level of greater detail (number and location of lights). Complications can arise from interactions among decisions made in different parts of the plan: for example, if you decide to enlarge the master bedroom you may have to shrink the size of the guest bathroom. Trading off gains in one place against losses in another is an everyday problem faced by architects, designers, and construction engineers.

Simplification Sometimes a good strategy for attacking a large problem is to begin by solving a similar but smaller problem that is within your powers. Mathematicians frequently use this process, called **simplification**, in order to generalize the solution method to the larger, original problem. A familiar example of problem simplification would be solving the problem of giving a large dinner party for a hundred people by enlarging on the elements in a successful plan for a small dinner party (Anderson, 1980).

Analogy One of the most powerful and frequently encountered problem-solving strategies is one in which the solver draws an analogy between the current problem and another problem from a different but familiar domain that has a similar logical structure (Glass, Holyoak, and Santa, 1979; Sternberg, 1977). In an **analogy**, a parallel is drawn between two systems whose parts are interrelated in a similar way. For example, the flow of electricity through a circuit is somewhat analogous to the flow of water through pipes in a house; the motion of electrons around the nucleus of an atom is somewhat analogous to the motion of planets in our solar system.

Analogies are similar to mental models of the way a physical system works. They require the user to set up a correspondence between the relations and elements in the first system and those in the second, noting, for example, that water in pipes corresponds to electric current in wires; that water pressure corresponds to voltage. If you notice an analogy between the two situations, you may be able to solve problems posed in one domain by considering them in terms of the familiar analogous domain. It is reported that Cyrus McCormick got his idea of the grain reaper by drawing an analogy between stalks of wheat and the hair on a man's head. Noting the function of the barber's hair clipper, McCormick thought of a similar, larger clipper for wheat stalks, and this idea set him on the way toward solving the problem of harvesting wheat mechanically.

Another illustration of analogy in problem solving is the use of worked-out examples. Instructors commonly use this technique when teaching students to solve problems in mathematics, physics, and computer programming. Textbooks often give an incomprehensibly abstract description of a new concept, then follow it with several worked-out problems as examples. When students are asked to use the new concept on a problem, they rarely use the abstract description that appears in the text. Rather, they immediately return to the examples and try to find a correspondence between one of the examples and the problem they are trying to solve (Anderson, Farrell, and Sauers, 1984). Of course, analogies are not available for every problem, and occasionally they may provide misleading suggestions. But in a given domain of knowledge, expert problem solvers have a collection of analogies and know which analogies are useful for various classes of problems (see Gentner and Stevens, 1983).

Evaluating Solutions

Evaluating the quality of a proposed solution is the fourth component of problem solving. When we are solving well-defined problems, we often know immediately whether our answer is correct; for these problems, verifying the solution is a trivial and obvious procedure. Sometimes, however, verification may be difficult—as when a computer programmer must "debug" a program, checking to see whether it is error-free under all conditions.

With ill-defined problems, which have no strict criteria for a good solution, evaluating proposed solutions may be the major task presented by the problem. When students are asked to generate a number of original uses for common objects (a brick, a rubber hose) and to select their most creative suggestions, they rarely select the same ones that an independent panel of experts chooses (Johnson, Parrott, and Stratton, 1968). Novices, it seems, can produce original ideas at all levels of quality but cannot tell the good ideas from the bad ones. Novices often seem to cherish certain ideas —for personal reasons that do not enter into an independent judge's evaluation. People can, how-

ever, learn to judge their creative productions; during their formal education, artists, musicians, and scientists learn to judge the quality of work in their respective professions.

The Influence of Past Experience in Problem Solving

Past experience has a powerful influence on problem solving. If a problem is identical with an earlier problem and the objects used to achieve the goal in the earlier problem are at hand, the past experience is cued from memory and the old solution is simply repeated. This use of old knowledge in new situations amounts to "positive transfer" of learning.

For example, when a lamp stops working, you may find that the same solution you used to solve the problem before—replacing the light bulb—will solve it again. But suppose you replace the bulb and the lamp still does not work. Now the situation presents only a partial match between your experience and the problem. What happens? You attempt to retrieve more information from memory to see if the situation is similar to something that has happened to you in the past. Recalling past lamp failures, you may check the wall plug to see whether the lamp is plugged in, or you may check the circuit box to make sure that the current is on. If neither of these solutions works, it becomes less likely that you will be able to make a match between the problem and past solutions, and if a match cannot be made, no effective action can be taken.

At this point, you may decide that further action is futile and take the lamp to an electrician. But a person with a larger store of electrical knowledge may stop and think about the problem, recalling relevant information about electrical appliances, such as the fact that wires sometimes fray and break and that contact points wear out. Then the person may examine the cord or the socket to see if replacing either the cord or the contact points might solve the problem.

Negative Transfer

The transfer of past relevant experience generally speeds the solution of current problems. But transfer is not always positive. Sometimes our past training leads us to approach new problems in ways that are actually detrimental: for example,

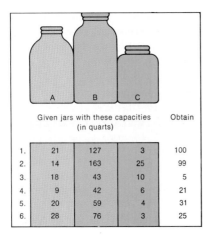

Figure 10.4. Luchins' classic demonstration of fixation in problem solving. In each of the problems in this series you must work out how you could measure out the quantities of liquid indicated on the right by using jars with the capacities shown on the left. Try the series yourself before reading on. After solving the first five problems, nearly two-thirds of Luchins' subjects were unable to solve the sixth. The sixth problem actually requires a simpler strategy than the first five, and it would be easily solved were it not for the fixation established by the first five.

we may have false presuppositions or hidden assumptions about the situation. When we automatically apply an inappropriate strategy to a problem and then cling rigidly to the obviously ineffective approach, we are hampered by **fixation**. Fixation can inhibit or prevent successful solutions.

Fixation due to the transfer of newly acquired habits has been demonstrated many times, for instance, by having people solve a series of "water-jug" problems, as shown in Figure 10.4. If you would like to experience fixation, try working those problems now, before you read on. (Go do it, then return here.) The first five problems in Figure 10.4 can be solved in the same way. Fill the largest jar (jar B), then from it fill the middle-sized jar (jar A) once and the smallest jar (jar C) twice. This method can be stated in a simple formula: B − A − 2C. However, this solution will not work on the sixth problem.

In a series of studies (Luchins, 1946), most people who were *first* given problem 6 solved it readily. However, people who first solved the other five problems and then attempted to solve the sixth problem found it extremely difficult. Two-thirds of these people persisted in using the B − A − 2C formula although it was inappropriate for

the problem. Their fixation was so strong that many gave up, while others staunchly maintained that the formula worked, insisting that 76-28-3-3 = 25.

Fixation can appear in many different forms, such as in faulty presuppositions. Two traditional examples of perceptual fixation are the square composed of nine dots and the six-match problems shown in Figure 10.5. (Try to solve them now, then return here.) The dot-problem task is to connect all the dots by drawing four straight lines without lifting the pencil from the paper. Most people perceive the nine dots as a square and *assume* that the pencil lines must be drawn within the boundaries of the square. Actually, the only way to solve the problem is to draw lines that extend beyond the perceptual boundaries of the square (see Figure 10.7). The six-matches problem

Figure 10.5. Two mind-teasers designed by Martin Scheerer (1963). (A) Nine dots are arranged in a square. The problem is to connect them by drawing four continuous straight lines without lifting pencil from paper. (B) Six matches must be assembled to form four congruent equilateral triangles each side of which is equal to the length of the matches. (If you don't have matches, any six objects equal in length will do.) Check your answers with those given in Figure 10.7.

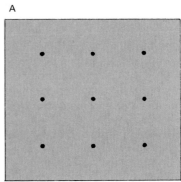

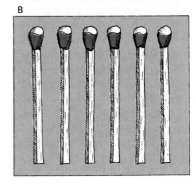

has a similar obstacle: people *assume* that the triangles of the solution must all lie in one plane. However, these problems may be more complex than is supposed; for example, when people are told that the solution requires going outside the square, 80 percent of them still cannot solve it. What is more, after they have been shown the solution, a few still cannot reproduce it. Although these traditional demonstrations may involve perceptual fixation, other factors seem to be heavily involved (Weisberg, 1980).

Another example of fixation, called **functional fixedness**, refers to people's inability to use a familiar object in an unfamiliar way. For example, a person is shown into a room where a candle, tacks, and a box of matches lie on a table (see Figure 10.6). The person's job is to mount the candle on the wall so that it burns properly, using any of the objects on the table. (Try to solve this yourself before looking ahead at the solution.) Tacking a candle directly to the wall will not solve the problem. The matches are in their original box, which emphasizes the box as a container and so encourages the problem solver to fix on this familiar function. As long as the box is seen only as a container, the problem solver will be unable to view it in any other way (Duncker, 1945). But, of

Figure 10.6. A problem used by K. Duncker to demonstrate functional fixedness. He gave subjects the materials shown and asked them to mount a candle on a wall so that it could be used to give light. Try to solve the problem yourself. (The use of the term "functional fixedness" gives you a clue to the solution of the problem that Duncker's subjects did not have.) The solution is given in Figure 10.8.

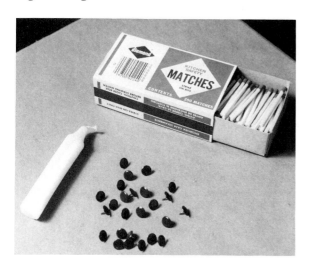

course, if the person can modify the way he or she thinks about the box, a solution appears (see Figure 10.8).

Experiments have also shown that if we use an object repeatedly for some routine function (for example, if we use a hammer for pounding nails), this experience will reduce the chances that we will be able to think of the object as useful for some other needed function (for example, to serve as a weight). Such fixations demonstrate the phenomenon of **mental set**. A mental set is a tendency to repeat a representation of an object and its function that worked in previous situations. When people transfer previously acquired knowledge to new situations where it does not apply, their inappropriate mental sets are responsible for the counterproductive behavior.

Computer Simulation of Problem Solving

Much recent theorizing about problem solving has been cast in the form of programs aimed at making computers solve problems in a humanly intelligent manner. The earliest programs, spearheaded by Allen Newell and Herbert Simon (1972), were written to enable the computer to solve well-defined problems in logic and mathematics, or to play games like chess or checkers. The goal of these **artificial intelligence (AI)** projects is to write a computer program that solves (or fails to solve) problems by following steps similar to those a human being would take. A classic example is Simon and Newell's General Problem Solver (GPS) program, which was based on information collected by having people think aloud as they solved various problems. GPS can solve problems in symbolic logic, trigonometric identities, letter-number code problems, and reasoning problems like the "hobbits and orcs" problem in Table 10.4. For each problem or task, the computer must be provided with information about the objects that will be encountered and the rules that apply to the problem.

GPS uses the problem-space representation discussed earlier; it tries to transform the starting state (e.g., the "givens" in a logic problem) into the goal state (the theorem to be proved) by finding a sequence of legal moves (logic rules). In the search for that sequence, GPS relies on means-end analysis. It begins by comparing the initial state to the main-goal or a subgoal state; if differences are

A 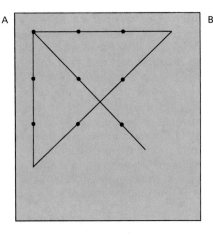 B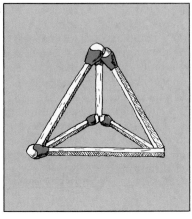

Figure 10.7. Solutions to the mind-teasers in Figure 10.5. The principal impediment in both of these problems is perceptual fixation. (A) The dot problem is solved by extending the lines beyond the dots; most people assume that they must stay within the perceived square structure. (B) The match problem is solved by building a three-dimensional pyramid; most people assume that the matches must lie flat, as they were first perceived.

detected, GPS applies one of the rules in an attempt to reduce the differences. If it cannot apply a desired rule directly, it sets up another subgoal to bring about a state in which the original difference can be reduced. In the process, a search tree of subgoals is generated. Because pursuit of each goal may lead to a proliferation of subgoals, GPS has an executive routine that supervises the developing search tree, evaluates the likelihood of reaching various subgoals, and decides which order to follow in working on them and when to abandon pursuit of a subgoal as fruitless.

GPS has been successful in solving a limited range of problems, and it does so in a way that resembles the solutions of human problem solvers. The program's success has clarified the nature of some human problem-solving techniques (see Newell and Simon, 1972). But GPS also has several flaws. It cannot solve a problem unless the goal is specified as a state in the problem state; this means that GPS cannot solve ill-defined problems, for which clear goal states cannot be specified. Accordingly, other computer systems have recently been designed to tackle some of these difficulties (see the box titled "Expert Systems" on page 269).

Figure 10.8. The solution to the problem depicted in Figure 10.6. Functional fixedness prevents most people from using the matchbox as a candleholder and using the thumbtacks to fasten the box to the wall.

CREATIVITY

Studies of problem solving have avoided ill-defined problems, and cognitive psychologists have generally avoided the scientific study of creativity —simply because objective measurement of results is difficult. Creativity is an amorphous, ill-defined quality. Yet creative ideas are not just plucked out of the air; they depend in good part on the lengthy professional preparation of writers, artists, composers, and scientists. In any field the creative person builds on what has gone before; each new leap begins from the accumulation of old insights. **Creativity** is, in fact, the juxtaposition of ideas in a new and unusual way. But creative ideas must be more than simply unusual; they should also be practical or relevant to a goal.

What Are Creative People Like?

One way to explore creativity is by studying creative people, interviewing and testing them in an attempt to uncover their thought processes. Studies of recognized creative individuals have turned up a number of findings—but few generalizations that are scientifically useful. Creative people daydream more often than uncreative people; they remember their night dreams better, are more susceptible to hypnosis, and are more willing to take risks; they are freer about admitting negative or pathological things about themselves (Martindale, 1981).

The alternative approach to studying creativity is to define creative behavior in a way that enables us to study its appearance in "ordinary people." For example, we can observe average college students as they perform laboratory tasks designed to tap "creative" thoughts. A typical task might be to generate as many original uses as possible for common objects, like a brick or a hammer. Another task might be to produce unusual associations to a word, and yet another might be to think up a good title for a brief essay or story. Using such tasks psychologists have discovered a few things about creativity, and some of their findings are echoed in observations of creative individuals (Barron, 1969). First, verbal tests of creativity correlate highly with tests of verbal intelligence and fluency. Such a finding is to be expected, given the common abilities tapped by both tasks. Second, scores on all verbal tests of creativity are related: people who score high on "novel uses" tests also score high when they are asked to generate lots of unusual or original responses in continuous association to a stimulus word.

The Creative Process

The creative process itself has been divided into four steps: preparation, incubation, illumination, and verification (Wallas, 1962). Not every creative episode involves all four stages, but the majority of them appear to follow this pattern.

■ *Preparation:* The individual formulates the problem, assembling the background material and thinking intensely about it.
■ *Incubation:* Nothing visible occurs. After concentrating intensely on the problem without solving it, the person puts it aside for a while, presumably to let its solution incubate in his or her unconscious mind.
■ *Illumination:* This is the moment of **insight**, when the creative idea is suddenly produced. Creative people are generally at a loss to explain the source of their ideas, but, as we saw in Chapter 7, complex cognitive activity can take place outside our awareness.
■ *Verification:* During this phase, the person checks a solution to make certain that it works. Creative people apparently judge their solutions with more discernment than do the uncreative.

Aspects of the same creative process can be demonstrated even with animals. In one study, chimpanzees showed the need for preparation and the moment of insight (Birch, 1945). When bananas were left far outside the bars of the cage, chimpanzees who had lengthy experience playing with sticks and had previously retrieved objects with one stick, quickly joined two sticks together and raked the food into the cage. Apparently, to gain this insight, a chimpanzee already had to have established a partial match between stored information and the two-stick problem. But after hours of effort, chimpanzees who had no experience with sticks still could not solve the problem.

Increasing Creativity

As long as we regard creative behavior as capricious and spontaneous, it is fruitless to ask whether we can arrange conditions that will enhance it. But if creativity is seen as behavior related to past experiences that appears lawfully in response to the demands of the present situation, we can consider ways to increase it.

A direct approach was taken by Elizabeth Goetz and Donald Baer (1973) with four-year-olds at the University of Kansas preschool center. Working with youngsters who tended to arrange blocks in constricted and unimaginative designs, the researchers began praising the children ("Very good, that's a new and different one") each time the child produced a novel construction. Within a few days the children were producing very elaborate, almost baroque, novel designs with the blocks. When Goetz and Baer stopped reinforcing imaginative constructions and began reinforcing repetitions of the old, constricted designs, the diversity in the

EXPERT HUMANS

Every field, from auto mechanics to music, has its experts, who can quickly solve problems of this field that baffle novices. Just what do the experts know that novices do not? Clearly, the experts have a vast store of knowledge about their field. This knowledge includes many "pattern-means-action" rules, such as the auto mechanic's rule that "pinging in the engine" means "check for loose valve lifters." Bolstering all those pattern-action rules is an elaborate mental model of the car's inner workings (de Kleer and Brown, 1981; Gentner and Stevens, 1983). Such mental models may be partial—a mechanic may have one model for the engine, another model for the car's electrical system. When a problem cannot be solved by a low-level pattern-action rule, the mechanic can run the model, mentally simulating the immediate and remote consequences of particular defects (de Kleer and Brown, 1981; Gentner and Stevens, 1983).

An expert mechanic may also have a particular routine that he or she follows when searching for the cause of a defect. This routine is a kind of search tree, consisting of hypotheses and new tests to be made (e.g., tests of the pressure inside piston cylinders) depending on the outcome of previous tests. This search process is routine but can be adjusted to fit specific situations and hypotheses.

Because experts can recognize huge numbers of meaningful stimulus patterns in

Lining up her next shot, expert golfer Nancy Lopez relies on her thorough knowledge of the sport. The stimulus patterns she sees as she judges her distance from the cup and the condition of the green will help her execute her putt.

their particular domain, they tend to have much better memory than novices for the bits and pieces of information about a specific example (Adelson, 1981; DeGroot, 1965; Egan and Schwartz, 1979). As we saw in Chapter 9, chess experts depend on chunking for their memory of chess positions. The expert can categorize large clusters of information into meaningful chunks, which materially reduces the number of chunks that must be kept active while working on a problem (Chi, Feltovich, and Glaser, 1977). The novice's inability to do this is a major disadvantage: because all problems are unfamiliar, short-term memory is overloaded, important items and subgoals are displaced, and the novice loses track of what he or she is doing. By contrast, the load on the expert's short-term memory is so reduced by automatic chunking that an expert can easily carry on a conversation while going about the problem-solving task almost automatically.

This automatization of the expert's skill is especially apparent under conditions of stress, time pressure, or intense motivation (Baddeley, 1972; Norman, 1982). Stress robs us of mental resources, but automatized habits deteriorate less than actions that require close attention and mental effort. The effects of such stress are familiar to students taking academic exams, and to athletes performing under the stress of competition and public scrutiny. Investigators have pointed out that soldiers in combat regularly demonstrate the negative effects of stress: as many as three-fourths of the soldiers who have handled their weapons effectively in practice may not even fire their weapons during combat (Keegan, 1976). Such deterioration diminishes as people become more expert and are regularly exposed to specific dangers or other stress. Whether they are deep-sea divers or chess masters, they learn to control the anxiety that could otherwise disrupt their performance (Baddeley, 1972).

Expert Systems

When the General Problem Solver (GPS) computer program was designed, researchers believed reasoning was a general skill that relied on just a few powerful methods such as means-end analysis. But today many researchers in the field of artificial intelligence believe that problem solving is seldom a general skill. These scientists contend that experts perform well in their specialty because they have a large fund of knowledge about its specific problems, along with specific techniques to solve them.

Scientists who build artificial "expert programs" give their programs lots of knowledge about a specific domain, such as lung diseases and their symptoms. This knowledge is represented in two ways: as a semantic network of concepts, or schemas (see Chapter 9), and as a set of knowledge rules. Some of these rules are designed to draw inferences. They take the form: "*If* the case in question has certain features, *then* draw particular conclusions." Other rules request tests; they may tell the computer to take a particular action (request a particular test) if a particular pattern of data is observed. When the program diagnoses a medical case, it starts with the reported symptoms, then reasons through a complex chain of "if–then" rules. Finally, the program arrives at several likely diagnoses, ranked in order of their probability, and recommends a medical treatment for each diagnosis.

The Heuristic Programming Project at Stanford University (Buchanan and Feigenbaum, 1978; Clancey, 1983; Feigenbaum, 1977; Shortliffe, 1976) has produced computer programs that simulate experts' judgment in various intelligent tasks. These programs can perform a number of tasks —analyze organic chemical compounds, diagnose lung disorders, and diagnose and prescribe treatment for blood infections and meningitis infections, and so on. This last program, known as MYCIN, contains more than 500 rules, each with a specific "certainty factor" that determines the strength of an association between the patient's symptoms and the indicated disease. The program searches backward or forward through the chain of rules, depending on the information it receives; it often asks for further medical tests to check or refine its hypotheses. Given information about a patient, MYCIN uses the rules to diagnose the disorder and prescribe antibiotics, taking into account the patient's condition, the interaction of prescribed medications with drugs he or she may already be taking, and possible side effects. MYCIN also explains to the physician the reasoning that led to the diagnosis. In tests, MYCIN performs as well as nationally recognized specialists in the field. MYCIN has been used in medical clinics on a limited basis, as has PUFF, a program that diagnoses lung disorders. PUFF's diagnoses agree with those of specialists about 90 percent of the time (Stanford Computer Science Department, 1980).

These computer programs that "think" may give the impression that scientists view thinking as single-minded, dull, mechanical plodding toward an inevitable goal. But what about the frustration we feel when we encounter mental blocks in problem solving? What about our anguish when we waste effort on false starts? What about creativity, inspiration, or insight? In reality, of course, computer programs are filled with false starts and wasted effort, and they fail to solve many problems—but they do not express feelings in response to these snafus. If the computer printed out "I'm frustrated" at each dead-end, or "Drat!" at each momentary failure, we might better appreciate the similarity between artificial intelligence and human head-scratching.

children's designs faded, only to blossom once more when the researchers returned to reinforcing novel arrangements.

Such studies demonstrate the power of social praise in enhancing simple forms of creativity among people of all ages. In response to this type of reinforcement, preschoolers have increased the diversity of their easel paintings (Goetz and Salmonson, 1972); fifth graders have increased their ability to think up novel uses for objects and have boosted their scores on creativity tests (Glover and Gary, 1976); sixth graders have improved the creativity and quality of written stories (Mahoney and Hopkins, 1973); and college students have increased their production of novel associations to stimulus words (Maltzman, 1960). Apparently, social reinforcement conveyed to these students information regarding the teacher's or experimenter's expectations. But the reinforcement of creative responses also seems to have a much broader and more impressive effect: strategies for generating creative answers in one situation generalize to tests in different settings. It is as though practice at thinking up novel uses for a hammer also improves the ability to think of novel associations to other words as well as novel uses of other objects. The ability to search for novel, far-fetched associations probably contributes to creative ideas.

Play is closely related to creativity and the production of imaginative ideas—in adults as well as in children. Exploration and play expose a child to new and varied places, objects, and activities, and the resulting sensory stimulation reinforces exploratory behavior and play (Baldwin and Baldwin, 1981). Throughout life, we explore and play with new ideas; we try out new environments and are reinforced with sensory stimulation. The same sort of natural reinforcement that leads people to watch television, travel, and meet new people can also lead them to invent new products, theories, explanations, and procedures, or to write books, paint pictures, and compose music.

How does exploratory play promote creativity? Our thoughts are often triggered by something in our environment. When we try different ways of arranging the stimuli around us, the new configuration of parts may evoke a novel response from the alert mind. Most technological efforts, for example, would not be possible without the inventor's being surrounded and stimulated by previous inventions. Similarly, writers are stimulated by previously written novels, plays, and poems; composers are stimulated by already existing music; and painters and sculptors are stimulated by existing art. As creative people have often pointed out, they can see further only by "standing on the shoulders of giants" (Merton, 1985).

SUMMARY

1. **Cognition** is the process of knowing, and it encompasses all higher mental processes, many of which are based on learning and memory. The modern study of cognition has drawn from the field of artificial intelligence and views the human being as an active processor of information and manipulator of symbols.

2. Concepts form the basis for our internal representation of the world. Laboratory studies indicate that the easiest concepts to learn depend on a single feature; the next easiest are **conjunctions**, in which two (or more) relevant attributes must both be present; the most difficult to learn are concepts that depend on **disjunctions**, in which either of two features is required, or disjunctions with negation, in which either but not both of two features is required. **Natural categories,** which are classes of things in the world, are typically fuzzy, consisting of a **prototype** (the average, typical example) surrounded by less typical examples. The **typicality** of an example can be predicted by its family resemblance to other instances of the category. Most noun concepts fall into a hierarchy, consisting of the superordinate level (such as "plant"), the basic level ("flower"), and the subordinate level ("daisy"). The **basic level** is the preferred level for thinking because it is both the most discriminating and comprehensive way of categorizing objects. **Ad hoc categories** are used in planning but are not as useful for organizing memory as natural categories, and their members often show no **family resemblance**.

3. In judging events, we generally use **heuristics**, intuitive rules of thumb that often give fairly accurate results. When using the heuristic of **representativeness**, we judge the likelihood of an example by its resemblance to a stereotype or typical ideal example. In some cases reliance on representativeness leads people to ignore other relevant information, such as the overall likelihood of the event or the size of the sample they are considering, and to base estimates of likelihoods on fallacious premises. When using the heuristic of **availability**, we base predic-

tions on a comparison of the current situation with readily recalled situations from the past. When the past information is biased, errors in judgment result. Vividness of past information or our present mood can affect the availability of information. Looking back on events after they have occurred, or **hindsight**, causes a special form of availability; it often leads to biases because of our tendency to believe that events that have occurred were inevitable. When using the heuristic of causal scenarios in judging likelihood, we assume that a readily generated story that could lead up to certain events makes the events likely to occur.

4. The starting point from which a decision is made can also bias judgment, an effect called **anchoring**. Anchoring focuses attention on the starting point, causing us to give it too much weight. Most problems can be posed in more than one way, and a problem's frame, or the way in which it is phrased, can affect the decision. When choices involve possible gains, people tend to avoid risks, but when choices involve possible losses, they become risk takers. By manipulating the **framing** of a decision, we can alter whether it is conceived of in terms of gains or losses, and thus alter the final decision.

5. Studies of problem solving have usually focused on **well-defined problems**, which have a clear structure and accepted solution. They have been studied much more often than **ill-defined problems**, which have no agreed-on rules or solution. The solution of well-defined, low-knowledge problems moves through four overlapping stages: representing the problem to oneself, planning the solution, carrying out the plan, and evaluating the results. The possible moves involved in a solution are known as the **problem space**, and the set of all possible moves at each problem state produces a **search tree**. Sometimes problems can be attacked using an **algorithm**, or mechanical routine that guarantees an eventual solution; when an algorithm is either not available or just too slow, people often rely on some heuristic strategy. **Problem-reduction** strategies include **working backwards** and **means-end analysis**, which involves choosing problem-solving actions that reduce the difference between your position in the problem space and your goal. Another solution strategy is the **analogy**, in which the solver devises a solution based on an analogical correspondence between two systems.

6. Among the impediments to solving problems are **fixation**, the tendency to automatically apply an inappropriate strategy to a problem and then rigidly cling to that approach, and **functional fixedness**, the inability to use a familiar object for an unfamiliar function. Both are examples of **mental set**, or a tendency to repeat a representation of an object and its function that worked in other situations.

7. An example of a computer simulation model of problem solving is the General Problem Solver (GPS), a program that resembles general human reasoning processes and can solve well-defined, low-knowledge problems. GPS uses a problem-space representation of the task and means-end analysis in its solutions, and it has an executive routine that supervises its search.

8. **Creativity** involves the juxtaposition of ideas in new and unusual ways. The creative process generally consists of four steps: *preparation,* in which the problem is formulated, background material is assembled, and intense thinking is carried out; *incubation,* in which the problem is temporarily put aside; *illumination,* the moment of insight when the creative idea occurs; and *verification,* when the solution is evaluated. Reinforcement, in the form of social praise, has effectively increased creative behavior in students of all ages. Exploratory play, which is reinforced by sensory stimulation, also increases creativity.

KEY TERMS

ad hoc categories	analogy	artifical intelligence (AI)	basic level
algorithm	anchoring	availability	cognition

conjunction
conjunction fallacy
creativity
disjunction
family resemblance
fixation
framing
functional fixedness

heuristics
hindsight
ill-defined problem
insight
means-end analysis
mental set
natural category
problem reduction
problem space

prototype
representativeness
schema
search tree
simplification
single feature
well-defined problem
working backwards

RECOMMENDED READINGS

ADAMS, J. L. *Conceptual blockbusting: A guide to better ideas* (2nd ed.). New York: Norton, 1979. Describes strategies of problem solving that teach people how to select the most attractive path from many ideas or concepts. Provides exercises to limber up your mental muscles.

ANDERSON, J. R. *Cognitive psychology and its implications.* San Francisco: W. H. Freeman, 1980. An authoritative textbook written for students with some psychology, presenting a modern view of many topics in memory, concept structure, problem solving, and language. Written by a pioneering researcher in this area.

DODD, D. H., and R. M. WHITE. *Cognition: Mental structures and processes.* Boston: Allyn & Bacon, 1980. A textbook that presents the state of the art of the scientific field of cognition. It is written for someone with a continuing interest and some background in psychology.

GLASS, A. L. and K. J. HOLYOAK, *Cognition* (2nd ed.). New York: Random House, 1985. Using a new model of human information processing as its focus, this is the most comprehensive available overview of the major processes of normal and abnormal cognition. The second edition features new chapters on action, reconstruction of episodes, and incidental learning.

HUNT, M. *The universe within: A new science explores the human mind.* New York: Simon &

Schuster, 1982. A wonderfully readable, lucid, firsthand account of the latest discoveries and theories of cognitive science—the study of how our minds work. The author draws upon two years of interviews with scientists at the cutting edge of this new discipline.

JOHNSON-LAIRD, P. N. *Mental models.* Cambridge, Mass: Harvard University Press, 1983. A research monograph that argues persuasively for the view that people understand situations by constructing mental models of them; reasoning and thinking consists of manipulating the objects in these mental models. Fascinating accounts of many original experiments on comprehension, memory, and reasoning by human subjects.

REED, S. K. *Cognition: Theory and applications.* Monterey: Brooks/Cole, 1982. A textbook on cognition covering a wide range of topics including problem solving and decision making. It places a greater emphasis on the application of cognitive psychology than is typically found in an undergraduate text.

WICKELGREN, W. A. *Cognitive psychology.* Englewood Cliffs, N.J.: Prentice-Hall, 1979. One of the most complete descriptions of the diverse range of topics relevant to modern cognitive psychology, written by a leading theorist. Technical but clear descriptions of phenomena from a unified perspective. Difficult reading but high quality.

PART FOUR

FEELING AND ACTIVATION

A young lady once asked permission to interview me in connection with a book she was writing on "workaholics." A workaholic, I presume, is a person who is addicted to work and who finds it impossible to stay away from it for long. The word is derived through analogy with "alcoholic."

I found the word offensive, however, and refused the interview.

I suppose it is only reasonable to consider me a workaholic, since I do work every day, including Sundays and holidays, and never take a vacation of any kind voluntarily; and I have published 327 books so far, with no signs as yet of slowing up.

Just the same, I don't consider myself addicted, or compulsive, or any of the other words one uses in connection with alcoholics, tobacco fiends, or junkies who find themselves unable to shake the habit. In true addicts, actual physiological and biochemical changes take place when the drug is withdrawn, and there is therefore a *physical* need to continue.

I don't think there are actual physical changes in my body if I goof off for a while. I don't sit at my typewriter or word processor because of any physical hunger; I do so merely because I enjoy it. Dedicated golfers are not called "golfaholics," nor are people who love to fish called "fishaholics," nor are people who delight in stretching out in the sun called "sunaholics."

In fact, if I made no money out of writing, but simply worked away at it as a "hobby" or as an "amateur activity," no one would remark on it, any more than they would if I had a shop in my basement and turned out gimcracks and oddments for my own amusement.

It is the "work" that bothers people, Because most people don't like the work they are forced to do to earn money to live on, and therefore abandon it as soon as they can and for as long as they can, the assumption is that none of us would work longer than we absolutely had to, unless we were physically addicted.

Well, I did not decide to write in order to "make a living" at it. It was my belief, until I approached middle age, that I was going to make a living by being a professor of biochemistry. I wrote only for the pleasure of it. When I began to earn money as a writer, I felt the urge to become a full-time professional writer.

Yet I hesitated at first. Despite the fun and money I got out of writing, I felt shame at abandoning my academic work. It was, after all, so prestigious to be a professor. I couldn't help but feel I had reached a higher social pinnacle as a professor than I possibly could as a writer. But soon I was earning much more money as a writer than I ever did as a professor. Now, at least, I had impressive earnings to justify my writing.

Later, I won awards, and more and more publishers of one kind and another wrote to ask me to do stories, essays, and books. Either because of the sheer quantity of my published output or because it covers an amazing variety of subjects, I had actually become a "personality," so that newspapers referred to me frequently without feeling the necessity of having to identify me. At last I regained the social status I felt I had lost when I left academe. You might conclude that my desire to write has been strongly motivated by a need to achieve money and status. But the truth is, all I ever wanted was to *not* feel guilty at spending all my time enjoying myself.

So call me a "hedonist" if you wish, or "pleasure-mad" or a "playboy." But *don't* call me a "workaholic."

Isaac Asimov

EMOTIONS

Imagine a world in which there was suddenly no emotion—a world in which human beings could feel no love or happiness, no terror or hate. Try to imagine the consequences of such a transformation. People might not be able to stay alive: knowing neither joy nor pleasure, anxiety nor fear, they would be as likely to repeat acts that hurt them as acts that were beneficial. They could not learn: they could not benefit from experience because this emotionless world would lack rewards and punishments. Society would soon disappear: people would be as likely to harm one another as to provide help and support. Human relationships would not exist: in a world without friends or enemies, there could be no marriage, affection among companions, or bonds among members of groups. Our culture's richness would be lost: since people would have no taste for beauty there would be no art, and since people could not be amused or entertained, there would be no music, theater, books, television, or movies. Society's economic underpinnings would be destroyed: since earning $10 million would be no more gratifying than earning $10, there would be no incentive to work. In fact, there would be no incentives of any kind. For as we will see when we discuss motivation (see

Chapter 12), incentives imply a capacity to enjoy them.

In such a world, the chances that the human species would survive are near zero, because emotions are the basic instrument of our survival and adaptation. Emotions structure the world for us in important ways. As individuals, we categorize objects on the basis of our emotions. True, we consider their length, shape, size, or texture, but an object's sensory aspects are less important than what it has done or can do to us—hurt us, surprise us, infuriate us, or make us joyful. We also use emotion-tinged categorizations in our families, communities, and overall society. Out of our emotional experiences with objects and events comes a social consensus that certain things and actions are "good" and others are "bad," and we apply these categories to every aspect of our social life—from what foods we eat and what clothes we wear to how we keep promises and which people our group will accept. In fact, society exploits our emotional reactions and attitudes, such as loyalty, morality, pride, shame, guilt, fear, and greed, in order to maintain itself. It gives high rewards to individuals who perform important tasks such as surgery, makes heroes out of individuals for unusual or dangerous achievements such as flying bombers in a war, and uses the legal and penal system to make people afraid to engage in antisocial acts.

The way emotions shape our personal and social reality is a theme that runs through many chapters of this book. Here we explore the fundamental nature of emotions. We begin by focusing on the ways people manifest their emotional states: their physiological reactions, their behavior, and their subjective experiences.

THE NATURE OF EMOTIONS

If emotions were colors, we would each have a rainbow. We are all familiar with a broad span of feelings, some mild, some intense; they range from the momentary and trivial (embarrassment at being unprepared in class, frustration at an automobile breakdown when we are late for an appointment) to the profound and life-altering (joy when we fall in love, anguish when someone we love dies). Our emotional experiences lend their hues to every moment of our day, and they are so much a part of our life that we can easily empathize with the emotions of others. But as familiar as emotions are, it is not easy to formulate a definition of them—to describe exactly what all these different feelings have in common.

Is it correct to say that all our emotions arise in response to our thoughts at any given moment? No. Although some of our emotions do have cognitive sources (for example, we grieve at the memory of a loved one's death, which is a cognitive source), others have sensory sources (loud sound causes discomfort), and still others have sources that are biological (an injection of heroin causes euphoria). Then can we say that all our emotions are reactions we learn? No. Although learning can teach us some emotions or change them (some people fear all snakes, but others with more knowledge fear only poisonous ones), other emotional reactions seem to be innate. Babies seem to come into the world with a negative emotional reaction to high-intensity stimuli such as loud sounds, bright lights, and pungent odors, and most adults continue to find these stimuli unpleasant. We can become sexually excited without any previous learning or experience, and certain other experiences, such as having a chair knocked out from under us, cause the same emotion in almost everyone.

Emotions, then, are complicated psychological phenomena that we cannot sum up in everyday, commonsense terms. Psychologists have therefore approached them from another angle. They have noted that no matter what the source or the quality of the emotion, all emotions share three basic aspects, or components: **arousal**, **expression**, and **experience**. Psychologists use the term "arousal" to refer to the series of physiological

Shared emotions hold relationships together, and, on a much larger scale, they can help to hold a nation together. On Memorial Day, veterans are honored for the sacrifices they made for the good of their country.

changes—primarily in the autonomic nervous system—that take place when an individual has an emotion. "Expression" refers to behavioral acts that are elicited by the emotion, such as baring the teeth in a moment of rage. "Experience" is the subjective feeling that accompanies the emotion —the individual's perception and realization of the emotional state. As we shall see, these three components are interrelated in complex ways.

Physiological Correlates of Emotion: Arousal

Strong emotions are associated with the activation of the autonomic nervous system. As noted in Chapter 3, the autonomic nervous system usually functions without our awareness or conscious control. Its two divisions, the sympathetic and the parasympathetic, both exert some control over glands and visceral muscles. This dual control generally works in an antagonistic manner: sometimes sympathetic activity dominates parasympathetic activity, and sometimes vice versa. The sympathetic division, which promotes energy expenditure, dominates during situations of emergency or stress; the parasympathetic division, which promotes energy conservation, dominates under conditions of relaxation. Most of the internal changes that accompany such emotions as intense fear or anger are associated with action of the sympathetic division.

When the sympathetic nervous system is activated, certain predictable changes occur. Suppose, for example, you are crossing the street and the sudden loud blast of a car horn startles you. As a result of this emotion-arousing situation, several physiological changes take place:

1. The heart rate increases, sometimes more than doubling.
2. Movement in the gastrointestinal tract nearly stops as blood vessels leading to the stomach and intestine constrict. At the same time, vessels leading to the larger skeletal muscles expand, diverting blood to where it may be needed for fighting or, as in this case, fleeing.
3. The endocrine glands stimulate the liver to release sugar into the bloodstream so that needed energy can be supplied to skeletal muscles.
4. Breathing deepens and becomes rapid. The

In a situation of fear or threat, our sympathetic nervous system is activated; our heart pounds, our stomach constricts, and our breathing becomes rapid. These bodily changes prepare us to cope with danger.

bronchioles (the small branches of the bronchi, the air passages that lead into the lungs) expand, and mucus secretion in the bronchi decreases. These changes increase the supply of oxygen in the bloodstream, which helps to burn the sugar being sent to the skeletal muscles.
5. The pupils of the eyes dilate, and visual sensitivity increases.
6. The salivary glands may stop working, causing dryness of the mouth, while the sweat glands increase their activity, resulting in a decrease in the resistance of the skin to electrical conduction (commonly called the **galvanic skin response,** or **GSR**).
7. The muscles just beneath the surface of the skin contract, causing hairs to stand erect, a condition called "goose bumps" (Lang, Rice, and Sternbach, 1972).

These changes, as we shall see, occur as a result of complex processes, involving neurochemical activity in the brain at the level of neurotransmitters and hormonal pathways (see Chapter 3).

As you leap to safety and the car passes, the opposing effects of the parasympathetic division of the autonomic nervous system reassert themselves. Heartbeat, respiration, glandular secretions, and muscular tension return to normal, and the physiological experience of the emotion subsides.

Measuring Physiological Correlates of Emotion: The Polygraph

With the proper equipment, some physiological changes associated with emotions can be measured. The polygraph, often called a "lie detector," is essentially an "emotion detector": it measures some of the physiological activities related to emotional states. Its use as a lie detector has to do with the fact that people tend to feel guilty or anxious when they are lying. These emotions bring on changes in blood pressure, respiration rate, and the GSR—physiological responses that can be recorded by the polygraph. Typically, the investigator begins with routine questions that establish a baseline response; then the subject's answers to emotionally charged questions are evaluated against this baseline. When the subject's autonomic responses to a particular question show noticeable changes, the interrogator may have reason to suspect that the statement is untrue.

The use of lie detectors is controversial, and for several reasons their findings are generally inadmissible as evidence in most courts. First, there is no distinctive, involuntary physiological response that invariably follows a lie (Lykken, 1981). And conversely, changes in GSR and other responses do not necessarily mean that a person is lying. An innocent suspect's anxiety at being connected with a crime may produce a polygraph tracing that resembles that of a guilty person.

Second, the subject may be able to alter the results of the baseline condition, making subsequent comparisons meaningless. If a suspect makes a strong effort to think about the crime in question when asked for his or her address, for example, the baseline will show responses as strong as those that follow questions concerning the crime. Then, if the subject lies about the crime, the polygraph will reveal no special physiological change.

Because arousal in general and GSR in particular can be affected by many conditions besides lying, caution in their use is well advised. For example, suspects who have forgotten relevant information may become aroused even when they are only being asked about this (possibly quite innocent) memory lapse. Their GSRs will change as if they were guilty.

Emotion and the Brain

Although the physiological changes that accompany emotion are triggered by the autonomic nervous system, that system is ultimately coordinated by the brain.

The Role of the Limbic System   The limbic system, which is among the oldest structures of the brain, is very much involved in emotions. In lower animals it constitutes a very large part of the brain mass. Within the limbic system the hypothalamus is especially involved in emotions. Depending on which area of the hypothalamus is stimulated, the autonomic nervous system will alter heart rate, blood pressure, intestinal contractions, or bladder reactions.

For example, chemical stimulation of the hypothalamus has demonstrated its role in sexual behavior. When estrogen, the female sex hormone, is applied to parts of the hypothalamus, a female rat without ovaries becomes sexually receptive (Davis, McEwen, and Pfaff, 1979). And when testosterone, the male hormone, is implanted in the hypothalamus of a castrated male rat, its sexual behavior is restored (Johnson and Davidson, 1972).

In another example, stimulation of one part of the cat's hypothalamus has been shown to activate the sympathetic nervous system and result in an emotional display that can be interpreted as feline rage. The cat's pupils dilate, the fur along its back and tail stands up, its claws are unsheathed, and it hisses and snarls. If this same area of the hypothalamus is damaged, the cat becomes placid and refuses to fight despite strong provocation. But damage to another area produces a hyperexcitable cat, one that is easily provoked to fight (Kupferman, 1981). Stimulating other parts of the brain leads to behavior associated with other sorts of emotion, such as the "quiet, stalking movements" that are characteristic of cats when they are pursuing their prey (Flynn et al., 1970). All this evidence suggests a connection among brain stimulation, sympathetic nervous system activation, and emotional arousal.

Animals may even be programmed with the potential for displaying emotional behavior that they do not normally exhibit. A cat that has never before shown rage can be induced to do so by stimulation of the lateral hypothalamus. It has been suggested that human beings also possess unused emotional potential; this speculation is supported by cases in which exaggerated emotional behavior has followed damage to certain areas of

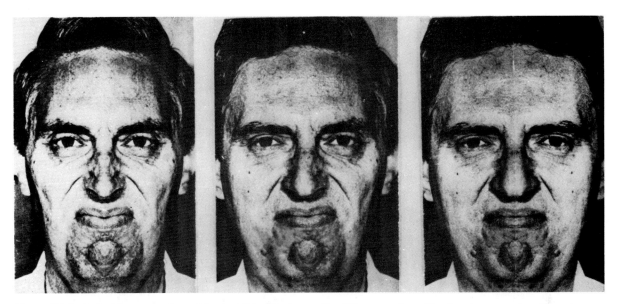

Figure 11.1. Left-side composite, original, right-side composite of the same face. The face is expressing disgust. (Sackheim et al., 1978.)

the limbic system. Children with such brain damage may exhibit impulsive hyperactivity, indiscriminate aggression, and violence. And, as we have seen in Chapter 3, the limbic system is the seat of the "pleasure center," which when stimulated can produce euphoric states.

The Role of the Cortex   The cortex also plays a role in emotion, as noted in Chapter 3; there is now a good deal of evidence that cortical involvement is primarily a function of the right cerebral hemisphere. Patients with lesions in their right cerebral hemisphere, directly opposite the area in the left cerebral hemisphere that controls speech (see Chapter 3), speak intelligibly, but their utterances lack all emotional quality, sounding as if they had been produced by a computer (Ross and Mesulam, 1979). It appears that the modulations in voice that lend an emotional quality to human speech may be controlled by the right cerebral hemisphere, while language content and structure are processed primarily by the left cerebral hemisphere.

This emotional dominance of the right cerebral hemisphere is also evident in the facial expression of emotion. The left side of the face (which is controlled by the right cerebral hemisphere) seems more expressive and communicates emotion better than the right. Researchers photographed faces expressing six primary emotions: happiness, sadness, anger, surprise, fear, and disgust.

After making two negatives of each photograph, they cut them in half and constructed two composite faces for each emotion. The resulting prints looked like intact faces, with two composites for each emotion, one made up of two left sides and the other of two right sides, as in Figure 11.1. Without knowing the nature of the photographs, people judged them for emotional expression and generally said that the left-side composites (controlled by the right side of the brain) expressed the emotion more clearly than did the right-side composites (Sackheim and Gur, 1978). In fact, right-hemisphere damage impairs the display of emotion, for in such patients the facial expression of joy, sorrow, fear, anger, and other emotions is weaker than in patients with left-hemisphere damage or in normal people (Buck and Duffy, 1980).

The Role of Neurotransmitters   Recent evidence suggests that certain neurotransmitters play an important role in emotional reactions (see Chapter 3). For example, it is possible that expressive behavior in emotions may be affected by acetylcholine (ACH), which plays an important role in carrying impulses of the motor neurons of the spinal cord, as they activate muscles of the body. Norepinephrine, on the other hand, has been found to be implicated in moods, and depressive states have been linked to serotonin depletion. Finally, dopamine is now generally recognized as controlling a variety of emotional responses (see Chapter 3), while endorphins are firmly established as effective analgesic agents.

Behavioral Correlates of Emotion: Expression

The physiological processes in emotions give rise to a variety of effects, involving subjective changes and expressive behavior. These effects in turn have subsequent physiological consequences, so that there is a continual interplay among the three emotional correlates.

Behavior that accompanies strong emotion can be observed directly. Moreover, there is general agreement on the meaning of such behavior. Silent movies, for example, depend for their effect on this general agreement. When the villain bares his teeth and clenches his fists, the audience assumes that he is angry; when the heroine furrows her brow and wrings her hands, the audience assumes that she is worried. We learn to recognize such nonverbal behavioral cues very early in life,

and this learning serves as a basis for identifying the states that go with various emotional labels.

A great deal of painstaking research has been done on the nonverbal expression of emotion (e.g., Ekman, 1972; Izard, 1971), and many forms of emotional expression have been identified and classified. The degree of similarity across various cultures is so strong that the role of prominent facial features has been precisely described for at least six emotions, which are expressed by the positions of the muscles in the brow and forehead, eyelids, and lower face (see Table 11.1). The differences in brow and forehead formation for surprise, fear, and anger are illustrated in Figure 11.2. As we shall see, various investigators have speculated that these typical expressions have an evolutionary significance.

If you were to guess which part of the face communicated emotion most accurately, would you choose the eyes or the mouth? In an ingenious experiment conducted nearly sixty years ago, Knight Dunlap (1927) cut apart photographs of faces expressing various emotions, then combined the upper and lower sections of different photos

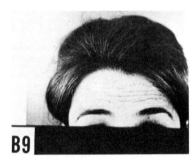

Figure 11.2. Examples of the Facial Affect Scoring Technique (FAST) scoring definitions: the brows-forehead items for surprise (B9), fear (B10), and anger (B12). (Copyright © 1972 by Paul Ekman.)

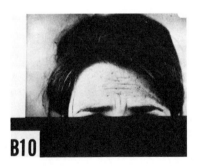

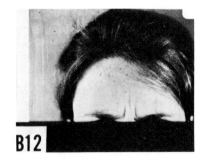

Table 11.1 ▪ Appearance of the Face for Six Emotions

	Brows–Forehead	Eyes–Lids	Lower Face
Surprise	Raised curved eyebrows; long horizontal forehead wrinkles	Wide-open eyes with sclera showing above and often below the iris; signs of skin stretched above the eyelids and to a lesser extent below	Dropped-open mouth; no stretch or tension in the corners of the lips, but lips parted; opening of the mouth may vary
Fear	Raised and drawn-together brows; flattened raised appearance rather than curved; short horizontal and/or short vertical forehead wrinkles	Eyes opened, tension apparent in lower lids, which are raised more than in surprise; sclera may show above but not below iris; hard stare quality	Mouth corners drawn back, but not up or down; lips stretched; mouth may or may not be open
Anger	Brows pulled down and inward, appear to thrust forward; strong vertical, sometimes curved forehead wrinkles centered above the eyes	No sclera shows in eyes; upper lids appear lowered, tense and squared; lower lids also tensed and raised, may produce an arched appearance under eye; lid tightening may be sufficient to appear squinting	Either the lips tightly pressed together or an open, squared mouth with lips raised and/or forward; teeth may or may not show
Disgust	Brows drawn down but not together, short vertical creases may be shown in forehead and nose, horizontal and/or vertical wrinkles on bridge of nose and sides of upper nose	Lower eyelids pushed up and raised, but not tensed	Deep nasolabial fold and raising of cheeks; mouth either open with upper lip raised and lower lip forward and/or out, or closed with upper lip pushed up by raised lower lip; tongue may be visible forward in mouth near the lips, or closed with outer corners pulled slightly down
Sadness	Brows drawn together with inner corners raised and outer corners lowered or level, or brows drawn down in the middle and slightly raised at inner corners; forehead shows small horizontal or lateral curved and short vertical wrinkles in center area, or shows bulge of muscular contraction above center of brow area	Eyes either glazed with drooping upper lids and lax lower lids, or upper lids are tense and pulled up at inner corner, down at outer corner with or without lower lids tensed; eyes may be looking downward or eyes may show tears	Mouth either open with partially stretched, trembling lips, or closed with outer corners pulled slightly down
Happiness	No distinctive brow-forehead appearance	Eyes may be relaxed or neutral in appearance, or lower lids may be pushed up by lower face action, bagging the lower lids and causing eyes to be narrowed; with the latter, crow's feet apparent, reaching from outer corner of eyes toward the hairline	Outer corners of lips raised, usually also drawn back; may or may not have pronounced nasolabial fold; may or may not have opening of lips and appearance of teeth

Source: Ekman, P. Universals and cultural differences in facial expression of emotion. In J. K. Cole (Ed.), *Nebraska Symposium on Motivation* (Lincoln: University of Nebraska Press, 1972). Copyright © 1972 by Paul Ekman.

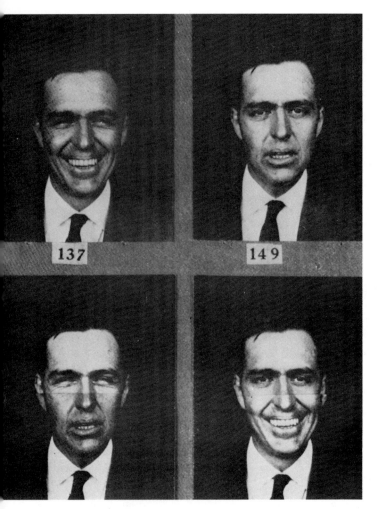

Figure 11.3. Composite photographs of upper and lower areas of faces expressing various emotions (137 shows mirth; 149 expresses pain). (Dunlap, 1927.)

Perceiving and Understanding the Emotions of Others

One does not have to be a talented actor to convey emotion without words. We do it ourselves and respond to it in others, every day, in countless situations. For example, the facial expression of a friend as you describe your problems is likely to betray sympathy, annoyance, impatience, or indifference. The decision to continue or to cut short a tale of personal woe depends in most cases upon the nonverbal reactions of the listener. And faces are not our only clue to other people's emotions. Body language—shrugs, slumps, winces, yawns, laughter, grunts, and more—can successfully convey a broad array of emotions (Duncan, 1969). Think of the figure of Charlie Chaplin as he appeared in silent movies. Chaplin clearly expresses every emotion without words, and he uses his entire body to do so. Happiness? He does a little dance. Despair? His shoulders slump; the corners of his mouth turn down; he grows smaller before our very eyes.

Considering the often subtle differences in the expression of similar emotions, the human capacity for nonverbal communication is impressive. Facial expressions of surprise, for example, can be conveyed with many different overtones. There are various qualities of surprise—questioning, dumbfounded, startled, dazed—as well as various intensities—slight, moderate, or extreme (Ekman and Friesen, 1975). Moreover, facial expressions frequently display blends of such diverse emotions as surprise and joy, anger and fear, amusement and annoyance. If we could not see the faces and gestures of the people around us, we would lose an important vehicle of human communication.

We also gain clues to an individual's emotional state and emotional disposition from his or her voice. It is easy to tell from the tone of voice whether a person is addressing us in anger or with affection; we can readily detect these feelings even if the person is speaking a language that is entirely foreign to us. These emotional qualities of speech are more important than we realize—often even more important than content. "You are a real friend" can take on quite different meanings when it is uttered with feelings of gratitude and when it is uttered with sarcasm.

The importance of these so-called *prosodic* properties of speech became evident inadvertently in the early 1950s when the government was

(see Figure 11.3). When the eyes of a smiling face were combined with a pained mouth, the result was a pained expression—but when the eyes of a pained face were combined with a smiling mouth, the result was a smiling expression. Despite the common belief that we express our emotions through our eyes, it is clear that the lower part of the face—specifically, the muscles around the mouth—dominates our interpretation of another person's facial expressions.

The messages we give to people come not just from our words but from our tone of voice and facial expressions as well. Similarly, a listener conveys a great deal by facial expressions and gestures.

seeking to improve the air-traffic control system. A device was invented whereby more communication between pilots and the control tower could be carried out simultaneously. This invention, needed to accommodate the rapidly growing volume of air traffic, used high- and low-pass filters in the transmission of the radiocommunication between pilots and air-traffic controllers. But instead of accommodating the full range of speech frequencies, the device transmitted only a small middle segment. This limitation made room for more efficient use of the transmission channels, and the voices of the pilot and the controller remained perfectly intelligible. But their voices were bereft of all emotional overtones, like the voices in the Ross and Mesulam study described above, and their speech sounded as if it had been artificially produced. While the invention was technically a success, it was never used in its original form because pilots refused to land to the sound of the computerlike instructions from the control tower. Landing is a traumatic event that involves high risks and high levels of stress. The pilot needs all the confidence he or she can muster at that moment, because all decisions are critical. The pilot wants to know that when the controller says, "You're OK, Jack," things really are all right, and the plane can be brought down safely with full trust in the controller.

Monkeys, apes, and other animals also communicate by means of facial expression and body language. Such communication has been observed in the laboratory as well as in the wild. In one experiment (Miller, Caul, and Mirsky, 1967), rhesus monkeys learned to avoid shock by pressing a bar whenever a panel lit up. Two of the monkeys were then placed in separate rooms, as shown in Figure 11.4. One room contained the shock apparatus and signal light, but no bar that would halt the shock. The other room contained only the bar and a television screen on which the monkey in the first room could be observed. When

Figure 11.4. In Miller, Caul, and Mirsky's experiment, the warning light was followed by shock to monkey A in ten seconds, unless monkey B pressed the OFF switch within the interval. The experimenters reported that monkey B often pressed the switch at the correct time, even though the only communication between the two monkeys was by means of the televised image of the expression on monkey A's face.

the panel in the first room lit up, a look of anguish crossed the face of the monkey hooked up to the shock apparatus; it had no way of preventing the impending pain. The second monkey could not see the warning light, but the first monkey's facial expressions on the television screen apparently told it when the shock was about to be delivered. In most cases, the watching monkey pressed the bar in its own room to keep both monkeys from suffering the shock.

One more point should be made briefly here: the way in which people express their emotions through facial expression, body movement, ges-

Figure 11.5. As this table indicates, there is a great deal of agreement among the members of different cultures about the meaning of facial expressions. This suggests that we are biologically programmed to produce the emotions conveyed by certain facial expressions. (After Ekman, Friesen, and Ellsworth, 1972.)

Photograph Judged						
Judgment	Happiness	Disgust	Surprise	Sadness	Anger	Fear
Culture			Percent Who Agreed with Judgment			
99 Americans	97	92	95	84	67	85
40 Brazilians	95	97	87	59	90	67
119 Chileans	95	92	93	88	94	68
168 Argentinians	98	92	95	78	90	54
29 Japanese	100	90	100	62	90	66

ture, posture, and tone of voice is only one aspect of nonverbal communication. The other aspect, which is required to make communication complete, is the observer's ability to interpret such cues correctly.

Biological Foundations of Emotional Expression

The way human beings express emotion appears to be based partly on innate factors. People from widely diverse cultures show a great deal of similarity in the postures, gestures, and facial expressions they use to convey comparable emotional states, and this fact suggests a common biological foundation. When people in different societies were asked to identify the emotions expressed in a series of photographs of faces (see Figure 11.5), they consistently recognized anger, fear, disgust, surprise, and happiness, regardless of the culture in which they lived (Ekman and Friesen, 1971).

Figure 11.6. Video frames of attempts to pose emotion by subjects from the Fore of New Guinea. (Copyright © 1972 by Paul Ekman.)

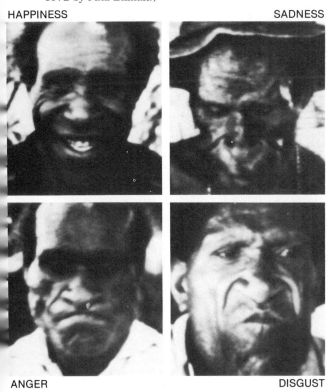

HAPPINESS   SADNESS

ANGER   DISGUST

Even members of New Guinea tribes, who had little previous contact with Westerners and their characteristic patterns of expression, promptly labeled these basic emotions and, as shown in Figure 11.6, had little trouble in displaying them (Ekman, 1980). Apparently there is a universal basis in the human display and interpretation of certain feelings, which suggests a strong biological component.

A further argument for the importance of biological factors in emotional expression is that the capacity for such expression develops early. In one study of infants as young as two months, observed during an inoculation against childhood diseases, the infants showed distinctive facial patterns that could be readily recognized as responses to pain (Izard et al., 1983). In fact, their distress grimace was more pronounced and more distinctive than that of older children. Similarly, although the first social smile appears at about two months, some researchers have found that infants as young as forty-two minutes will imitate emotional expressions quite accurately, sticking out their tongues or opening their mouths in response to an adult's actions (Meltzoff and Moore, 1983), as seen in Figure 11.7. Whether the response is a true imitation or a fixed action pattern like those described in Chapter 4 and part of the species' inheritance (Jacobson, 1979), the response suggests a biological basis for human emotional expression.

Another piece of evidence that is frequently cited in support of the biological underpinnings of emotional expression is the study of a ten-year-old girl who was born deaf and blind (Goodenough, 1932). Obviously the little girl could not have learned emotional expressions by observation, so her behavior was presumed to reflect innate tendencies. When the girl displayed her pleasure upon finding a doll hidden in her clothing, she "threw herself back in her chair. . . . Both the hand containing the doll and the empty hand were raised in an attitude of delight, which was further attested by peals of hearty laughter. . . . Her laughter was clear and musical, in no way distinguishable from that of a normal child." The girl also showed anger in characteristic ways, indicating mild resentment by turning away her head, pouting her lips, or frowning, and expressing more intense resentment by throwing back her head and shaking it from side to side, while exposing her clenched teeth.

The way this child expressed her emotions was remarkably similar to the emotional expression

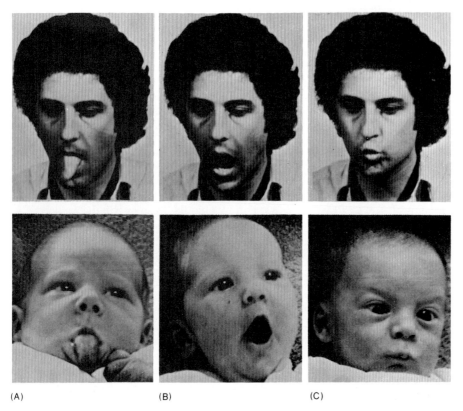

(A)   (B)   (C)

Figure 11.7. Sample photographs from videotape recordings of two- to three-week-old infants imitating (A) tongue protrusion, (B) mouth opening, and (C) lip protrusion demonstrated by an adult experimenter. (From Meltzoff and Moore, 1983.)

Figure 11.8. Innate patterns of emotional expression in dogs. In the top row anger increases from left to right. In the bottom row fear increases from left to right. This illustration is based on sketches by Charles Darwin.

found in most normal ten-year-olds. There were, however, enough differences to lead the researchers to conclude that human emotional expressions are built on innate tendencies that have been altered by a "social veneer." Some later studies of handicapped children have supported this conclusion.

In his classic work *The Expression of the Emotions in Man and Animals* (1872/1967), Charles Darwin asserted that many of our patterns of emotional expression are inherited as part of the distinct behavior pattern of our species because they had survival value. Since there are no fossils of behavior, such conjectures cannot be proved, but the possible evolutionary significance of some expressions is easy to see. For example, when eyebrows are raised in surprise or fear, the individual increases visual acuity; raising the upper lip in rage, thereby baring our teeth, readies us to bite. Other animals also bare their teeth as a threat or when preparing to fight, as shown in Figure 11.8, giving their enemies a warning that may in itself prevent a violent and damaging encounter. According to Darwin, the baring of teeth served a similar function among our ancestors, and this expression that communicates a threat is still characteristic of our species. The current view of evolution suggests that the value of the fear expression is to signal danger to kin or to the entire group of animals surrounding the threatened one.

Moods appear to be as universal as emotions. Moods are different from sudden surges of emotion, because they last longer and their bodily expression is diffuse. For example, depression is accompanied by changes in movement, muscle tone, reaction speed and intensity, and the contraction of particular facial muscles. Darwin believed that the corrugator muscle, which draws down the eyebrow and makes vertical wrinkles in the forehead, was involved in the expression of grief. The universality of the muscle's role in grief was supported by a study with depressed patients, who were first put on an antidepressant drug and two weeks later had changes in the muscle's activity measured. **Electromyographic recordings (EMGs)**, which measure electrical currents caused by slight muscle movements, showed that among patients who had improved while on the drug there was considerably less activity in the muscle, indicating that as depression lifts, the corrugator muscle relaxes (Schwartz et al., 1978).

Learning and the Expression of Emotion

Learning also plays an important role in the expression and interpretation of emotion, especially in establishing the occasions on which certain feelings are seen as appropriate. For example, on hearing a subtle verbal insult, different people may express resentment, fear, disdain, or embarrassment, depending on such matters as their relationship to the speaker (a relative, a teacher, a peer, a stranger); whether they interpret the remark as an insult; and their cultural background. Some cultures encourage the expression of emotions like affection or fear, but others teach their members to suppress such displays. And certain differences in expression and interpretation are also found between cultural groups. For example, in Chinese literature the expression, "He scratched his ears and cheeks," was a signal that a character was happy (Klineberg, 1938). In Western culture this action might be interpreted as indicating that the character was anxious, even distraught. Thus, learning as well as biology plays an important role in both the expression and interpretation of emotion.

But how do people initially learn to express their own emotions and to interpret the emotions of others? Although we noted the early development of emotional expression, we have also seen (in Chapter 8 and Chapter 17) that social isolation in early life can have damaging effects on later social behavior. It has been suggested that this impairment may occur when there is no opportunity for proper social communication to develop (Mason, 1961). Experiments with socially isolated monkeys support this interpretation. In an extension of the research described earlier, in which monkeys communicated fear through their facial expressions (Miller, Caul, and Mirsky, 1967), it was found that monkeys raised in isolation were significantly retarded both in their ability to display facial expressions of fear that other monkeys could interpret and in their ability to respond properly to the facial expressions of normal monkeys threatened by electric shock. The study also indicated that there might be a period in early life that is critical for the proper development of emotional expression. Although the isolated monkeys had been deprived of social contact with other monkeys during the first year of life, they had subsequently spent several years with other monkeys. This social experience evidently came too late to permit the monkeys to learn how to communicate their emotions, despite the fact that they must have feared the shock as much as did the normal monkeys.

Subjective Correlates of Emotions: Feeling

Every emotion is accompanied by an awareness of the feelings associated with it, even though those feelings may be difficult to put into words. When we are happy, for example, we sometimes say that there is a special lift in everything we do, a bouncy feeling. If we are humiliated, we may say that we feel as if we would like to shrink or disappear. Many psychologists who investigate emotions have relied on such subjective reports. Because a specific emotion sometimes does not reveal itself in either facial expressions or overt actions, a subjective report may be the only way to discover if someone is experiencing the emotion at all.

Psychologists have devised special rating scales and measurement techniques to help them record these subjective reports in a systematic way. General agreement among people in rating common experiences (a movie, perhaps) as "hilarious," "disgusting," "sad," or "happy" indicates that our personal emotional reactions to things are shared by many others. Such ratings contribute to an understanding of the degree to which emotional reactions are consistent—or vary—from one individual to the next.

THE RELATIONSHIP AMONG THE CORRELATES OF EMOTION

How do the various correlates of emotion —arousal, behavior, and experience—interact with each other? This question has been a matter of some controversy for nearly a century, and we are just beginning to gain some understanding of the problem's enormous complexity. Do we experience fear because our hearts pound and our hands tremble? Or does our cognitive appraisal of a particular circumstance induce the feeling we call fear, which is then followed by the physiological changes that prepare us for fight or flight? Over the years, psychologists have proposed different answers to these questions, and their experiments have led to a better understanding of the issues involved.

The James-Lange Theory

Our language suggests that the physiological changes accompanying emotions differ in some ways for different emotions. When we are frightened, for example, we say we feel a "knot" in the stomach; when we are nervous, we say we experience "butterflies"; during intense anger, we sometimes refer to a "pounding" in the temples; and when we feel shame, we often describe it as a "blush." This raises the possibility that the emotion experienced at a given moment is simply the result of particular bodily changes.

One of the first psychologists to propose that the ability to identify and label our own emotional states was based on the ability to interpret these bodily changes was William James. His proposal directly contradicted many of the theories of emotion popular in the late nineteenth century. Most other writers argued that events in the environment trigger a psychological state—the emotion —which in turn gives rise to responses by the body. James disagreed:

> My theory, on the contrary, is that *the bodily changes follow directly the perception of the exciting fact, and that our feeling of the same changes as they occur IS the emotion.* Common-sense says, we lose our fortune, are sorry and weep; we meet a bear, are frightened and run; we are insulted by a rival, are angry and strike. The hypothesis here to be defended says that this order of sequence is incorrect . . . and that the more rational statement is that we feel sorry because we cry, angry because we strike, afraid because we tremble. . . . Without the bodily states following on the perception, the latter would be purely cognitive in form, pale, colorless, destitute of emotional warmth. We might then see the bear, and judge it best to run, receive the insult and deem it right to strike, but we should not actually *feel* afraid or angry. (James, 1890)

According to James, then, our perception of a stimulus triggers a pattern of changes in the body. These changes cause sensory messages to be sent to the brain, which produce the experience of emotion. Each emotional state is signaled by a unique pattern. James emphasized visceral reactions (that is, "gut reactions") as central to emotional states. Writing at about the same time, a Dane named Carl Lange proposed a similar theory that specifically emphasized vascular changes (changes in blood pressure). Ever since, the view that emotion is simply the perception of bodily changes has been called the **James-Lange theory of emotion** (Lange and James, 1922).

Cannon's Critique

The James-Lange theory stimulated a great deal of research, much of it designed to disprove that theory's claims. In 1927 Walter B. Cannon presented a powerful critique of the theory based on several arguments. First, he pointed to evidence that physiological changes do not necessarily produce emotions, as the James-Lange theory might predict: when a person exercises vigorously or is injected with adrenaline, she or he experiences the bodily changes typical of strong emotions but does not necessarily *feel* a particular emotion. Physiological change alone, Cannon argued, cannot produce emotion.

Second, the idea that bodily reactions cause us to experience emotion is questionable because emotions are often felt rapidly. We see a bridge collapsing and immediately feel panic; we see an old friend and instantaneously feel joy. How could the viscera, which react sluggishly, be the source of such sudden emotion, as James suggested?

Finally, said Cannon, if the James-Lange theory is correct and our emotions come from interpreting our bodily sensations, it would stand to reason that each emotion would be characterized by a somewhat different set of physiological changes. But, as Cannon's research showed, this does not appear to be the case; many of the same bodily changes occur in conjunction with differing emotional states.

Later investigations tend to confirm Cannon's argument. Although it is possible to make physiological distinctions between certain emotions —anger, for instance, is generally associated with an increase in gastric activity; fear is generally asociated with an inhibition of gastric functions (Wolff and Wolff, 1947)—efforts to find clear-cut physiological differences between some of the more subtle emotions have not been successful. Moreover, even the general patterns of bodily response that have been identified for emotions such as fear and anger vary among individuals and from situation to situation for the same individual (Lang, Rice, and Sternbach, 1972). For most emotions, then, unique physiological changes have been difficult to identify.

Yet Paul Ekman, Robert Levenson, and Wallace Friesen (1983) have been able to distinguish among a number of emotions by using physiological measures. They instructed actors to contract specific facial muscles, one by one, until they had formed the classical emotional expressions. The actors were not told to produce particular emotional expressions, and they were apparently not aware that they were doing so. The purpose of the experiment was to produce precise emotional expressions, not to induce emotional states in the actors. But when the actors' heart rates and finger temperatures were taken, they showed substantial differences that correlated with particular emotions. Their heart rates slowed, for example, when they portrayed disgust, but sped up when they portrayed sadness, fear, or anger. And their skin temperature dropped when they portrayed disgust or fear but climbed when they portrayed anger. Simply assuming the facial expressions of various emotions was accompanied by changes in the autonomic nervous system.

The Facial-Feedback Hypothesis

An approach to emotion that has much in common with the James-Lange theory is the **facial-feedback hypothesis**, which holds that our subjective experience of emotion comes from an awareness of our facial expressions (Izard, 1977). Thus, we feel angry because we scowl, happy because we smile, This approach to emotion has been studied by inducing people to smile or frown or look sad and measuring their physiological arousal and subjective experience.

In one study (Tourangeau and Ellsworth, 1979), researchers told college students that they were interested in measuring physiological responses to subliminal stimuli that had been spliced into a film. The students were attached to a polygraph and told that any movement of their facial muscles during the film would disturb EMG recordings from facial electrodes. Each student was then instructed to extend some muscles and contract others and to hold the muscles in that position during the two-minute film. Although the students were unaware of it, the instructions led them to produce an expression of fear or of sadness. While the students watched either a neutral, a sad, or a frightening film, their heart rate and GSR were recorded, and they reported their subjective responses. This study failed to support the facial-feedback hypothesis. When there was a conflict between the facial expression and the film, the students' subjective reports corresponded with the emotional tone of the film, not with the assumed facial expression. However, the requirement that facial muscles be frozen for as long as two minutes may have affected the students' responses. Perhaps the effort of controlling a particular set of muscles for a long period produces "noisy" feedback that disrupts the emotional responses (see Ekman, Levenson, and Friesen, 1983).

Other studies (Laird, 1974; Laird and Crosby, 1974; McArthur, Solomon, and Jaffe, 1980; Rhodewalt and Comer, 1979) using a similar approach have supported the facial-feedback hypothesis. One researcher (Laird, 1974) reported that a subject who had unwittingly frowned said, "When my jaw was clenched and my brows down, I tried not to be angry but it just fit the position" (p. 480). In addition, when people are asked to deceive an observer by exaggerating or concealing an emotional reaction, their physiological responses (i.e., heart rate, GSR changes) and their subjective experience follow the false patterns they try to communicate to the observers (Kleck et al., 1977; Lanzetta, Cartwight-Smith, and Kleck, 1976; Zuckerman et al., 1981).

The Schachter-Singer Theory

Although physiological arousal may be important in experiencing full-blown emotions, it cannot completely explain their cause. Awareness of an emotion-provoking situation is also an essential component. This was demonstrated in an early study in which 210 people were injected with adrenaline and asked to report the effects (Marañon, 1924). Nearly three-quarters said that they experienced only physical symptoms—a rapidly beating heart, a tightness in the throat—with no emotional overtones whatsoever. The remainder reported emotional responses of some kind, but their descriptions were of what the investigator called "as if" emotions. These people said, "I feel *as if* I were afraid" or "I feel *as if* I were happy." Thus, their feelings resembled emotions but clearly were not what we could consider true emotions. In the few cases in which a genuine emotion followed the injection, the experience seemed to be produced when a person's thoughts combined with the physiological changes. Memories with strong emotional content, such as a father's recollection of a

time when his child was seriously ill, were especially effective. In other words, people did not interpret the physiological state produced by adrenaline as "emotional" unless they imagined an emotion-arousing situation.

Studies like the one just described led Stanley Schachter to propose a **two-factor theory of emotion**. According to this theory, the experience of an emotion is based on a physiological change *plus* a cognitive interpretation of that change. In experiments that explored this point of view (Schachter and Singer, 1962), people received what they thought was a vitamin injection. They believed that they were participating in a study to assess the effects of the "vitamin" on vision. The injection was actually adrenaline, and the real purpose of the study was to see whether people in different situations would assign different labels to the physiological sensations produced by the adrenaline. Those in one group were told that the "vitamin" produced certain side effects, such as heart palpitations and tremors (which are real side effects of adrenaline). People in another group were led to expect side effects not usually associated with adrenaline, such as itching and headache. Those in a third group were told that the injection had no side effects. The situation faced by the first group was similar to that in the earlier study, in which subjects knew that they were receiving adrenaline. Since the other two groups were given no explanation for their physiological arousal, the researchers expected them to attribute their arousal to "emotional" factors.

While waiting for the "vision test," each subject sat in a room with another person, who was a confederate of the experimenters. In some cases, this "stooge" acted in a happy and frivolous manner, throwing paper airplanes, laughing, and playing with a hula hoop. In other cases, the stooge acted annoyed and angry, finally tearing up a questionnaire he was supposed to fill out.

The researchers' suspicions were borne out. People in the two groups that did not expect any physiological arousal, and thus had no way of explaining the sensations they were experiencing, tended to use the emotion shown by the confederate as a label for their own feelings. They expressed euphoria or anger, depending on the emotion displayed by the stooge (see Figure 11.9). In contrast, people who had expected heart palpitations and tremors were less likely to share the confederate's feelings.

Subsequent studies have supported this two-

Figure 11.9. Two of the conditions in Schachter and Singer's experiment on emotion. (A) A subject is misled about the effects he should expect from the adrenaline injection he is receiving. Placed with a companion who joyfully flies paper airplanes around the waiting room, he attributes his state of arousal to a similar mood in himself and joins in. (B) A subject is told exactly what to expect from the injection. Although placed in the same situation as the first subject, he recognizes his physical sensations as the product of the injection and is unmoved by the euphoria of the experimenter's confederate.

factor theory. In one experiment, for example, subjects who had been injected with adrenaline laughed more and harder while watching a slapstick comedy film than did people in a control group who received injections of salt water, a placebo that causes no physiological change. Further, people who were injected with chlorpromazine, a drug that inhibits physiological arousal, laughed less than the control group did (Schachter and Wheeler, 1962). A similar study showed that people behave more aggressively toward a person they dislike (the cognitive factor) if they have been physiologically aroused by exercise (the physiological factor; Zillman, 1971).

Yet the Schachter-Singer theory is not entirely correct, as recent studies have shown (Maslach, 1979; Marshall and Zimbardo, 1979; Reisenzein, 1983). The proposal that physiological change and its cognitive interpretation are both required to produce an emotion is violated by the fact that several depressants produce physiological and behavioral manifestations of depression. These chemical depressants affect all three aspects of emotion: internal physiological response (heart rate, muscle tone, blood pressure decrease); behavior (movements become sluggish, facial muscles droop in a sad expression); and subjective feelings (the individual feels depressed). The action of the depressant on the autonomic nervous system produces the emotion of depression without any "labeling" or other cognitive interpretation on the part of the individual. In fact, many drugs prescribed for patients with hypertension produce depression as a side effect. There is little doubt, however, that when the origin of the emotional arousal is ambiguous, information that is supplied by the environment can have the sort of effects that the Schachter-Singer theory predicts.

The Effects of Cognitive Factors on Arousal and Experience of Emotion

As we have seen, some theorists propose that emotion produces physiological response, some that emotion is the perception of bodily changes, and others that emotion is the interpretation of arousal. Another possibility has also been emphasized. Both the emotional experience and the bodily changes may follow the perception and appraisal of a potentially harmful or beneficial situation (Arnold, 1960). For example, a caged lion causes no emotional reaction among visitors to a zoo, but a lion wandering loose in the park provokes terror. The important difference may be registered during the individual's initial appraisal of the situation.

Other researchers have studied the cognitive processes involved in the initial appraisal of a

The same ostrich that looks tame and even comical wandering around in a zoo becomes a menacing creature when running loose on a city street. This bird escaped from a truck en route to a zoo and scattered passers-by for twenty minutes until it was captured.

situation. For example, in one study people watched emotion-arousing films, such as a graphic portrayal of adolescent circumcision rites of a primitive tribe (Lazarus and Alfert, 1964). While they watched, subjects' heart rates and galvanic skin responses were measured to provide indicators of physiological arousal. Cognition was manipulated by playing special sound tracks designed to encourage various reactions to the film. A "denial" sound track, for example, explained that the participants were actors or that the incidents portrayed were not painful, thus denying the stressful aspects of the movie. Such denial was effective, as Figure 11.10 shows. Galvanic skin response was lower when the denial sound track was played during the film than when the film was shown without a sound track. What is more, the denial sound track lowered GSR even further when it was played before the film was shown. Cognitive appraisal apparently plays a role not only in placing an emotional label on a state of physiological arousal but also in determining the intensity with which the emotion is expressed.

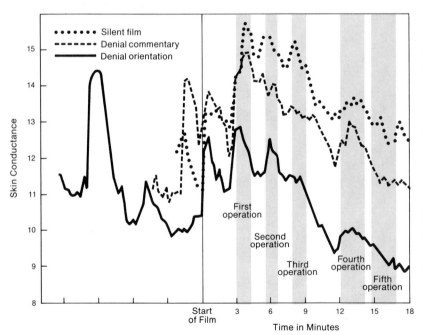

Figure 11.10. The results of an experiment on emotion and cognition by Lazarus and Alfert. They used an anthropological film about puberty rites involving subincision (the cutting open of the urethra along the underside of the penis) as the emotion-provoking stimulus. Changes in galvanic skin response (GSR) were measured as an index of anxiety. All the subjects saw the film. One group (Denial Commentary) heard a sound track with the film saying that the people in the film were actors and the operations were causing no pain. Another group (Denial Orientation) heard the same sound track before they were shown the film. A third group (Silent Film) heard no commentary at all. (After Lazarus and Alfert, 1964.)

The Effects of Expression on Arousal and Experience of Emotion

Most people are accustomed to thinking that whatever behavior accompanies their emotions is a result of their feelings. In other words, they smile because they are happy, clench their fists because they are angry, pace up and down because they are tense. But the relationship between feelings and overt behavior is as tangled as the relationship between physiological response and feelings. Studies have shown that at times emotion-related behavior may be as much a cause as an effect; in certain instances overt behavior may actually help to bring on feelings. If you are tense, then relax your muscles intentionally, you may suddenly discover that you feel less anxious. If you walk with a shuffling, stooped-over posture, you may begin to feel somewhat depressed regardless of your previous mood. Perhaps the behavior gives rise to physiological sensations that we label according to learned categories. That is, we have learned to connect muscle tension with anxiety and the sensation of a stooped shuffle with depression.

Whatever the explanation, the influence of behavior on subjective feelings has been tested in a variety of ways. In a recent study, people listened to a tape played over a set of earphones, with the understanding that the purpose of the experiment was to assess the quality of the earphones under conditions of movement. People in one group were to move their heads up and down and those in another group, from side to side. After listening to the tape, people were asked about the quality of the earphones as well as about their feelings on the issues that were discussed on the tape. People who "nodded" as they listened to the tape more often agreed with the statements they heard than did people who shook their heads (Wells and Petty, 1980). Thus, to some degree, overt behavior can serve as a cause as well as a result of our feelings.

Behavior and Its Emotional Sources

Given the findings discussed in this chapter, how much of our behavior is controlled by emotion and how much by cold rational processes? Clearly, what earlier philosophers called "passions" continue to dominate much of the violent action that occurs today, and a "crime of passion" is still classified as second-degree murder. But the question of how much either emotion or cognition controls behavior is as meaningless as the question of how much behavior is influenced by heredity or environment. Some tasks demand greater cognitive effort, others demand greater emotional capacities. Different people may approach the same situations with varying degrees of emotion, and the same person may approach the same event differently on different occasions.

In many aspects of behavior that we believe are dominated by cognition, emotional factors are often basic and come first. This is especially true of our preferences. We prefer familiar stimuli to novel and strange ones (Zajonc, 1968). In fact, one theory of music appreciation holds that familiarity is the essential factor in determining whether we like or dislike a particular piece of music (Mull, 1957). Western listeners dislike Japanese music when they first hear it, for example. The theory states that we like the familiar music because of our subjective feelings of recognition. We listen to a composition, recognize a particular musical phrase, and correctly anticipate its development. The resulting feeling of familiarity makes the piece attractive. If this is the case—if familiarity is the basis for our liking—then our judgments of familiarity should be more accurate than our judgments of preference. This is not always so. In laboratory studies, people preferred geometric figures they had previously seen in glimpses so brief that they could not discriminate them from similar figures they had never seen (Kunst-Wilson and Zajonc, 1980). Apparently, we like the familiar even when we cannot recognize it as such.

A somewhat similar study showed that the same process that has been observed in the laboratory works in daily life. Smokers of Camels, Chesterfields, and Lucky Strikes smoked cigarettes without being allowed to see what brands they were smoking (Littman and Manning, 1954). A paper label covered the upper half of each cigarette, obscuring its brand name. Half the smokers were asked whether the cigarette was the brand they customarily smoked or another brand. The rest were asked how much they liked the cigarette they were smoking. Smokers were more likely to say they liked their own brand than to identify it accurately. That is, smokers could not tell whether they were smoking their customary cigarette, but their preferences for their own brand clearly indicated that at some level of emotional involvement they could make the distinction.

THE VASCULAR THEORY OF EMOTIONAL EXPRESSION

The problem of emotion is far from solved, and no one has been able to specify the interactions among the physiological, behavioral, and subjective correlates of emotion. Controversy marks the history of research on emotions, and facts that were taken for granted in the past have often been questioned more recently.

Take, for example, the terms "expressing our emotions" and "suppressing our emotions." Both terms imply that an emotion is some sort of internal state that we are impelled either to display or to hide. From this perspective, overt muscular expression becomes the final link in the emotional process—the direct consequence of an internal emotional state. Although Charles Darwin said that no muscular act had ever evolved simply to express an emotion, his theory followed this view. He proposed that our facial expressions of emotion evolved from muscular movements whose function was to facilitate communication among animals. (As we have seen, baring the teeth warns other animals and threatens intruders.) Yet the survival value and direct com-

municative function of given emotional expressions is not always clear. Is it valid to say that teeth-baring serves as a warning, when among human beings and some apes, the baring of teeth also accompanies a grin? And why should an animal display its fear *to* an attacker? Why should surprise be signaled *to* the intruder? Even though these movements may reveal emotion, their adaptive significance is not obvious.

Moreover, can we truly say that facial movements are crucial to human communication? Among all animals, human beings have the richest repertoire of facial gestures, but why should they need it? They also have a much more efficient means of communicating intention and other internal states: language. They can simply *say* what they mean.

Such questions show that the connections between outer expression and inner feelings are vague. Addressing this issue, a little-known French physician, Israel Waynbaum (1907), offered a revolutionary theory of emotional expression—a theory that is in stark

contrast with the views of Darwin and later theorists. Waynbaum's theory was completely ignored and, until recently, was never cited in any of the writings on emotion (Zajonc, 1985). Yet his theory is original and rich in new ideas; it places the study of emotions in a new and useful framework.

Above all, Waynbaum questioned the idea that facial gestures are expressive, and that their primary function is to display an individual's internal state. Instead, Waynbaum looked for other essential functions that facial gestures might serve. His thinking was stimulated by three observations. First, he noted that the entire supply of blood to the brain and face comes from the main carotid artery. Second, he noted that the blood supply to the brain requires the utmost stability; any sudden intense variation sends the organism into shock or coma. Third, he noted that although the face has few moving parts, it has dozens of separate muscles. The logical pattern produced by these facts suggested to Waynbaum that facial gestures might serve a regulatory

SUMMARY

1. Emotions are essential to individual survival, to the maintenance of community, and to the development of civilization. Emotions can arise from biological, sensory, or cognitive sources, and all emotions consist of arousal, expression, and experience. **Arousal** consists of

physiological changes, **expression** consists of behavioral acts, and **experience** consists of the subjective feelings that accompany emotion.

2. Strong emotions are associated with internal changes resulting from activation of the auto-

function: they might control blood flow to the face and therefore to the brain.

Since the brain requires a stable blood flow, and since both brain and face get their blood from the same artery (which separates at the neck into an internal and a facial branch), perhaps the muscles acted as tourniquets on the veins and arteries. The muscles might press against the bony structure of the face, allowing more or less blood to reach the brain. Along with this suggestion, Waynbaum noted that all expressive acts —blushing, weeping, sobbing, laughing—are intimately connected with circulatory processes. Blushing allows blood to rush to the face; tears are supplied by the lachrymal artery, which branches off from the artery that supplies the brain; sobbing activates the diaphragm and modulates oxygen intake; the same is true of laughing heartily. As we have seen, emotional excitement produces circulatory disturbances. Facial gestures might help counteract these disturbances, helping to restore balance to the cerebral blood flow.

When a person smiles, Waynbaum suggested, the major zygomatic muscle (which runs diagonally across the cheek to the corner of the mouth) presses on branches of the facial artery and, together with the slave action of the corrugator muscles (near the eyebrow), momentarily increases blood flow to the brain. This action is beneficial, Waynbaum claimed, and it *causes* a positive subjective feeling. Generally, he argued, a sudden small surge of blood to the brain is positive, and a similar sudden drop in blood flow leads to a depressed feeling. The functions of these relatively small, short-lived changes in cerebral blood flow, said Waynbaum, are mainly restorative. In his view, we do not smile because we feel good; we feel good because we smile. (Note the similarity to the James-Lange theory.)

Waynbaum's idea organizes the disparate facts about emotional expression in a reasonable manner. There are several problems with his theory, because when it was constructed in 1907, scientists knew little about the physiology of the vascular system. But drawing on today's physiological knowledge, we can adjust the theory in a way that agrees with Waynbaum's overall position. Perhaps, for example, changes in our subjective state are not due mainly to the cerebral blood flow itself. Instead, they may be due to sudden changes in the metabolic processes of the brain, or to changes in brain temperature (caused, perhaps, by sudden action of the facial muscles on the returning blood supply).

We might even hypothesize that facial gestures have beneficial effects. Tears contain enkephalins. People with circulatory disturbances often develop depressed moods, and drugs prescribed to reduce cerebral blood flow in people with hypertension often bring on severe depression. Perhaps the metabolic processes or temperature of the brain produce such moods. Either could do so by altering the synthesis and release of neurotransmitters—endorphins, dopamine, serotonin, enkephalins —that are involved in producing emotional states. All biochemical processes depend on temperature, and the synthesis of neurotransmitters probably depends on a very narrow temperature range.

Waynbaum's theory has been ignored for nearly eight decades. But it is clearly testable; in fact, research to test its merits is now under way.

nomic nervous system. The sympathetic division dominates during emotion-arousing situations, and when it is activated, heart rate, respiration, glandular secretion, and muscular tension increase. Some of the physiological activities related to emotional states can be measured by a polygraph. The use of the polygraph as a lie detector is controversial because a subject's physiological responses when lying are not always reliable and because a person can alter the baseline condition, making subsequent comparisons meaningless. The brain coordinates the activation of the autonomic nervous system as it triggers emotional arousal; the limbic system, the hypothalamus, and the right hemisphere of the cortex are involved in the expression of emotion. Certain neurotransmitters also seem to play an important role in emotional reactions.

3. Much of the behavior accompanying strong emotion can be observed directly, and there is general agreement concerning its meaning, with the role of prominent facial features charted for at least six basic emotions. The extent to which people agree in rating a common experience helps establish the degree of consistency in our subjective emotional experiences.

4. Both the expression and interpretation of emotions seem to be based on a combination of inherited and learned factors. A biological basis to emotion is suggested by the fact that diverse cultures show a great deal of similarity in their expression of comparable emotional states, by the early emergence of the capacity for emotional expression in infants, and by the typical emotional displays of a ten-year-old girl who had been born deaf and blind. Some researchers contend that the expression of emotions is built on innate tendencies, which are altered by experience. The role of learning is suggested by the fact that the occasions on which certain feelings are regarded as appropriate vary across cultures and from person to person.

5. A debate continues over the relationship between the bodily changes that characterize emotions and a person's perception of those changes and of the situation that produced them. The **James-Lange theory of emotion** postulates that the perception of bodily changes is emotion. This theory has been challenged because (1) physiological changes do not necessarily produce emotions; (2) the speed with which emotions are felt makes it doubtful that the visceral organs could be their source; and (3) similar bodily changes occur in conjunction with differing emotional states. However, the perception of physiological changes does play a significant role in the experience of emotions. The **facial-feedback hypothesis**, which links the perception of emotion to an awareness of our own facial expressions, has had some experimental support. Cognitive awareness of an emotion-provoking situation is an important component of emotional experience. Schachter's **two-factor theory of emotion** postulates that the labeling of an emotion is based on a physiological change plus a cognitive interpretation of that change. However, the importance of a person's initial appraisal of a situation may precede both the emotional experience and the bodily changes. The behavior associated with emotions is not always a result of the emotions; behavior may sometimes bring on the feelings.

6. It is impossible to say how much either cognition or emotion controls behavior. However, in the matter of our preferences, emotional factors seem to predominate. It has been suggested that we like what we are familiar with, even when we cannot recognize it.

KEY TERMS

arousal	experience	galvanic skin response (GSR)
electromyographic recording (EMG)	expression	James-Lange theory of emotion
	facial-feedback hypothesis	two-factor theory of emotion

RECOMMENDED READINGS

BUCK, R. *Human motivation and emotion*. New York: Wiley, 1976. A broad introduction to the psychological literature on emotion and motivation.

DARWIN, C. *The expression of the emotions in man and animals*. Chicago: University of Chicago Press, 1965. (Originally published, 1872.) This classic work describes emotions and interprets them in terms of evolution and natural selection.

EKMAN, P., and W. V. FRIESEN. *Unmasking the face.* Englewood Cliffs, N.J.: Prentice-Hall, 1975. A thoroughly illustrated treatment of facial expressions that are associated with a wide variety of emotional states.

IZARD, C. E., J. KAGAN, and R. B. ZAJONC (Eds.). *Emotions, cognition, and behavior.* New York: Cambridge University Press, 1984. Recent views on the relationship between emotion and cognition written by the leaders in the field of emotion.

JAMES, W. The emotions. In *The principles of psychology,* (Vol. II). New York: Holt, 1890. A fascinating classic that reviews basic issues and presents and defends what is now called the James-Lange theory of emotions.

SCHACHTER, S. *Emotions, obesity, and crime.* New York: Academic Press, 1971. A compilation of previously published papers related to Schachter's theory of emotion.

SCHERER, K. R., and P. EKMAN. *Approaches to emotion.* Hillsdale, N. J.: Erlbaum, 1984. Biological, psychological, ethological, and sociological views of the emotional processes contributed by experts in these fields who participated in an interdisciplinary workshop.

SELYE, H. *The stress of life.* New York: McGraw-Hill, 1956. Pioneering work on stress, emphasizing the common physiological changes that accompany a wide variety of stresses.

MOTIVATION

Anyone who has ever watched a detective program on television or read a mystery story knows that the way to find out who killed the rich widow is to discover who had the best reason for doing her in. Was it her son, who stood to inherit her $3 million estate? Was it her attorney, who was afraid she had discovered he had been embezzling from her for years? Or was it her stepdaughter, who blamed her for a car accident that had left the young woman crippled? The issue here is the motive—the *reason* the murderer committed the deed. And motives are the concern of this chapter.

Why do people behave the way they do? We can trace the motives behind behavior back to emotions, which we considered in Chapter 11. All our emotional experiences have either a positive quality or a negative quality. We want to reexperience positive emotions and avoid the negative ones. Once we have learned ways to attain positive emotional experiences and to avoid unwanted experiences, we can set goals for our behavior. The widow's son may have committed murder *in order to* achieve the pleasant experience of inheriting millions. The lawyer may have committed murder *in order to* avoid the unpleasant experience of jail or disbarment. In either case, the behavior was oriented toward some goal or desired end state that lay in the future.

Any action that is taken in order to reach a goal is called *motivated behavior*. Motivated behavior occurs in all organisms: a frog sticks out its tongue in order to catch a fly; a student reads a textbook in order to pass a psychology course. How does motivated behavior differ from behavior that is directly connected to an emotion—or, as we said in Chapter 11, is a "correlate" of an emotion? Behavior that is a correlate of an emotion is, essentially, a reaction to an event that is already past: you are embarrassed because you forgot to keep a lunch date; you are angry because someone

299

shoved into a queue in front of you. But motivated behavior is oriented toward what is to come; it is shaped by goals or results that exist in the future.

Clearly, there is a good deal of overlap between motivation and emotion. Emotions may initiate a chain of motivated behavior, as when embarrassment leads you to give a lengthy explanation to account for your forgetting the lunch date; you explain *in order to* gain back your self-esteem. Conversely, motivation can produce emotion. An individual whose path to a goal is blocked feels frustrated, and a child whose half-built sand castle has been destroyed by a careless sunbather may show anger, grief, or rage. But for the sake of clarity, psychologists generally study motivation and emotion as if they were two different and distinct psychological processes. We will handle them that way in this chapter.

MOTIVATIONAL BASES OF BEHAVIOR

How does motivation affect behavior? To begin with, motivation can lead people or animals to initiate some kind of behavior. Because of differing motivation, for instance, one student gets a job as a waiter after school, while another goes out for football; one student who gets a poor grade starts to study harder, while another decides to drop the course. Later, an individual's specific motivation can determine how *persistently* and how *vigorously* he or she carries out the behavior. Motivation can also affect the organization of whole patterns of behavior. For example, the college student whose goal is to own a car might carry out "instrumental" behavior—an act meant to advance progress toward the goal, such as looking for a waiter's job. Later, motivated by the same goal, he or she might carry out "consummatory" behavior —behavior that occurs when the individual attains the goal, such as using the car for shopping or offering rides to friends.

If we put this all together, we can say that motivation affects not only what we do, but how long we do it and how much effort we put into it. Motivation can also shape a series of related actions. We can now define **motive** as *the dynamic property of behavior that causes it to be initiated, gives it organization over time, defines its end states, and influences its vigor and persistence.* We can call the corresponding process **motivation**.

The Meaning of Behavior in the Motivational Context

Suppose our friend Michael has refused to eat dinner, and we are trying to figure out the motivation behind his action. If we know some of Michael's other recent actions, his behavior may start to make sense, and some theme may emerge. We may be able to infer the end state or goal toward which his behavior is oriented, and that end state will reveal to us his motivation.

For example, if we know that he ate a heavy meal only a short time ago, we can infer that his goal is to avoid feeling uncomfortably full. If we know that he customarily fasts one day a week, we can infer that today is his fast day and his goal is to stick with his plan. If we know that he has joined a political hunger strike, we can infer that his goal is to help the group make its point. We are acting on the assumption that Michael's behavior is not random and disconnected. We expect that it is organized by some overall motivation, and we interpret it in this light.

Once we detect the motivational theme that underlies a pattern of behavior, we can interpret a given act as being more likely, more appropriate, or more efficient than any other possible behavior, in terms of the overall pattern. Ruth decides to stay home and study while the rest of us go to the basketball game. How appropriate is Ruth's behavior? We may judge that it is entirely appropriate *if* we also know that Ruth wants to go to law school. Similarly, if we examine what Ruth is studying, noting how its content might help her pass the law-school entrance exam, we can also decide whether her behavior is efficient. Looking at behavior from the perspective of the motivation that guides it gives us criteria against which to evaluate it—ways to see whether it makes sense.

The Interplay of Incentives and Drives

Some motivation is related to biological processes: deficits in blood, sugar, water, oxygen, or salt can lead to behavior changes designed to return the body to a condition of chemical balance. This internally motivated behavior helps the organism to survive. Other motives, such as Ruth's desire to get into law school, have no simple physiological basis. But the entire range of motivational processes, from the simple hunger of the frog to the complex power strivings of Napoleon, do have certain common elements. In all motivated behavior, two factors contribute: external stimuli, which we call "incentives," and internal factors, which we call "drives."

Needs, Drives, and Incentives in Biologically Motivated Behavior

When an organism is deprived of an essential substance such as food or water, we say it is in a state of *need*. This state of deprivation, or need state, eventually triggers the organism's energy, initiating instrumental behavior directed toward obtaining the essential substance. (For example, the hungry lion sets out to hunt for prey.) Once the need has released the organism's energy, it is considered a **drive**. An organism's **primary drives** are produced by emotional and physiological conditions that stimulate the animal to seek fulfillment of basic needs. Eating, drinking, and breathing are examples of behavior based on primary drives, and such behavior regulates basic physiological requirements for a particular organism. As we saw in Chapter 3, this kind of regulation is called homeostasis; it describes the organism's tendency to maintain an optimal level of a physiological requirement by attempting to restore any deviation from the optimal condition (Cannon, 1929). Put simply, when you take off your jacket because you are too hot or put it back on because you are too cold, you are seeking homeostasis.

But that is only half the story. In the most basic biologically motivated behavior—behavior that serves the vital functions of survival and reproduction—organisms also respond to *external motivational stimuli* in the shape of certain cues from the environment, which psychologists call **incentives**. Hungry frogs flick out their tongues at moving black spots, which are external stimuli; during breeding season, gulls sit on eggs in their nest, whether the eggs belong to them or not. Any motive, then, has two components. The first component is the *internal state* that activates and orients the person or animal toward a specific goal such as food or water. The second component is the *external incentive*—which is, in fact, the goal.

The Relation Between Emotions and Incentives

We have established that the incentive is an essential factor in motivated behavior. But what deter-

Driven by hunger, this Ethiopian will walk as far as he must to find food for himself and his children.

mines the incentive value that a particular object will have for a person or animal? That depends on the individual's emotional reactions to that object—and this is true of both biologically motivated and other types of behavior. Positive emotions will elicit approach behavior, and negative emotions will elicit avoidance, withdrawal, escape, or attack. The satisfaction of a need results in a pleasurable emotional reaction; the frustration of a need results in dysphoria (an unpleasant emotional state) and often anger.

Emotions "color" the goal, and so they affect the motivational process that guides the individual's behavior with respect to that goal. When an object is pleasing or when an activity is satisfying, we try to get close to that object or repeat that activity. People who like art will go to museums more often than people who dislike it, and people who like music will go to concerts, buy records, and listen to their favorite radio stations. Alternatively, if a person is afraid of strangers, he or she will avoid public situations; if a person hates the sight of blood, he or she will not contemplate a medical career.

For the most part, the incentives that might organize an ongoing sequence of behavior are not visible. They exist mainly in the individual's mind, as hopes or expectations that outside investigators cannot detect. Yet they are a powerful bridge between a person's emotions and his or her motivational processes. By studying an individual's emotions, we can see how he or she reacts when confronted with various environmental objects or situations, and we can identify his or her incentives. As a result, we can explain behavior that *anticipates* the individual's enjoyment or attainment of those incentives. Again, this is motivational analysis.

MOTIVATION AS A REGULATORY PROCESS

Basic motivational processes are best understood in terms of the functions they serve for the organism. By now it is clear that behavior often has adaptive significance and contributes to the organism's survival. When motivational processes are expressed in behavior such as the flicking of a frog's tongue, they have obvious adaptive significance associated with the regulation of basic physiological needs.

In some basic motivational processes, internal drive states are the most important factor. In others, external incentives have a much more crucial role. The contrast between the way in which the body regulates water balance and the way it regulates weight sheds light on this point.

Thirst and Water Balance

How does an organism know when an adjustment is necessary? And what mechanism is used to make the adjustment? Thirst provides a good example of the way in which these questions can

be answered. An animal's responses to thirst are guided primarily by internal stimuli.

Water is the principal constituent of all living cells and is essential to all physiological processes. Since water continually leaves the body in sweat, urine, and exhaled air, the organism must take in fluids to maintain its water balance. Certain stimuli produce sensations of thirst, telling us to drink, and other stimuli tell us when to stop.

Inducing Thirst

The stimuli that induce drinking come from three different sources. The first is an increased salt concentration in the fluid compartments of the body—inside cells, around cells, and in the blood. Specialized cells in the hypothalamus (see Chapter 3) are sensitive to this change in salt concentration and their activation results in the sensation of thirst, followed by drinking. The location of these cells was discovered by implanting small tubes into various areas of the brains of animals and then stimulating the areas with very small amounts of salt solutions injected through the tubes (Andersson, 1953). Only in certain areas do such injections induce an animal to drink.

Another stimulus for drinking is a decrease in the volume of fluid in the circulatory system (Fitzsimons, 1961). This stimulus involves no change in chemical concentration, but simply a decrease in volume, such as that which results from hemorrhage. Thus, severe bleeding causes intense thirst. The discovery that the brain can recognize a change in blood volume illustrates how physiological mechanisms are involved in drive states (Fitzsimons, 1969). (Recall the vascular theory of emotional expression discussed in Chapter 11.) All blood is filtered through the kidneys. If a kidney senses a reduction in blood volume, it releases a chemical that alters the structure of a substance in the blood. This altered substance then acts directly on the hypothalamus to elicit drinking.

The third major stimulus for drinking is produced by the expenditure of energy or by an increase in body temperature. The mechanism involved is probably identical to that involved when cells in the hypothalamus react to a change in salt concentration. Both energy expenditure and increased body temperature result in sweating, which takes water from the blood as it cools the body. With less water, the concentration of salt in the blood rises, stimulating the "salt-sensing" cells and resulting in the drive to drink.

Satiating Thirst

Long before the body has absorbed water from the stomach and before the blood's salt concentration has returned to normal, thirst disappears and animals stop drinking. Drinking ceases despite a lack of homeostasis because other stimuli report that it is time to stop. One of these stimuli is stomach distention, the feeling of fullness. It has been suggested that cold water satisfies thirst more quickly than warm water because cold water moves out of the stomach much more slowly and thus provides clearer stomach-distention signals to the brain (Deaux, 1973).

Stomach-distention signals are not the only stimuli involved in satiety. If a dog is allowed to drink freely but the water it drinks is prevented from reaching its stomach (diverted through an incision made in its neck for experimental purposes), the dog does not drink indefinitely. It takes in some water, then stops drinking. Soon the dog begins to drink again, but once more it stops. Some "mouth-metering" mechanism appears to gauge the amount of fluid that is ingested and compares it with the amount needed to restore the water balance. If the internal need is not fulfilled, internal stimuli override the mouth messages, and the animal again begins to drink (Bellows, 1939).

But the mouth meter is not essential to maintaining a correct water balance. Animals can learn to press a bar that causes spurts of water to be delivered directly into their stomach and still regulate their water balance although no fluid passes through their mouths (A. Epstein, 1960). Clearly, several physiological mechanisms monitor and control thirst. These mechanisms provide animals with a number of ways to sense the need for water, thus increasing the likelihood that the proper homeostatic condition will be maintained.

Hunger and Weight Regulation

As we have seen, a variety of stimuli, both external and internal, contribute to drive regulation. With drinking, internal stimuli are predominant. With eating, on the other hand, there is a complicated interplay between internal and external stimuli. If you have ever eaten a hot fudge sundae after finishing a large meal, you know that internal hunger signals (such as stomach contractions) had little to do with your actions. The sundae looked and tasted delicious, and these external factors were enough to persuade you to eat it. Exactly how the internal and external factors relate to one another in the control of eating has received a great deal of attention.

Hypothalamic and Other Factors in Normal Weight Regulation

As we saw in Chapter 3, damage to various parts of the hypothalamus has pronounced effects on food consumption. The hypothalamus's role in eating is complex. Some neurons within the hypothalamus fire at the taste and sight of food (Rolls, Burton, and Mora, 1976). Other neurons may monitor the blood's level of sugar, which increases with food intake and decreases with deprivation, as does the level of insulin. The hypothalamus seems to use such information to help regulate food intake and body weight. But internal physiological factors are not the only influence on food consumption. Much of our eating is determined by external factors, including social customs, the look, smell, and taste of food, and the amount of effort required to obtain it.

In view of all these potential influences on eating, it is remarkable that human beings and other animals regulate their weights so precisely. Most people who do not continually monitor their weight manage to keep it within a range of a few pounds, despite great variations in their physical activity and in the caloric value of the foods they eat (Keesey and Powley, 1975). Similarly, laboratory animals with unrestricted access to food regulate their body weights within a narrow range.

Obesity and Weight Regulation

Given that most people seem to regulate their weight effectively, why do some individuals become obese? Obesity is an extremely complex disorder with multiple, interacting causes—both physiological and psychological (Rodin, 1983). Obesity is not simply a matter of overeating; indeed, many obese people eat no more each day than their lean friends (Spitzer and Rodin, 1981). Most obese people seem to have highly efficient metabolic systems that convert calories into energy at a very slow rate; these people require fewer calories to maintain their weight. In addition, as they gain weight and become less active, their metabolism slows even more. (Activity not only uses calories but speeds up metabolism generally, so that when an active person is simply sitting around, he or she uses more calories than does a sedentary person who weighs the same.) When obese individuals diet, their problem may be aggravated, because their bodies respond by slowing the metabolic rate even further so that they need even fewer calories to maintain their weight.

Obese individuals also have higher levels of insulin in their blood than do people of normal weight. Insulin, which is secreted by the endocrine system, enhances the conversion of sugar into fat, making it easier for the body to deposit fat in special cells where fat is stored, known as fat cells. High insulin levels also seem to interact with psychological factors: extra insulin in the blood appears to make people hungrier, make sweet foods taste better, and lead people to eat more (Rodin, 1983).

Unfortunately, obesity seems to be self-perpetuating. For example, as fat cells increase in size, their capacity to store fat increases, and they can become still larger. When the fat cells are so full they can store no more fat, the body may produce more fat cells. But while overeating may add fat cells at any time of life (Faust, Johnson, Stern, and Hirsch, 1978), losing weight does not eliminate fat cells; it only shrinks them. Recent research at Rockefeller University indicates that signals to eat may come from the metabolic state of the fat cells themselves, which may help to explain why it is so difficult for obese people to keep from regaining weight (see Kolata, 1985). These researchers also found that once obese people lose weight, their body chemistry is highly abnormal. Their fat cells are tiny, and if they are to avoid becoming obese again they must limit themselves to 25 percent fewer calories than a person of their height and weight would normally require. Judith Rodin and Janice Marcus (1982) suggest that the increased fat cell size and slow metabolism of obese people are highly adaptive in an environment where food supplies are scarce or food availability fluctuates. But placed in a food-abundant culture, such people—who are primed to overeat —find their fuel-efficient physiology leads to obesity.

Most studies of obesity focus on people who already are obese: as we have seen, once people become obese, their activity decreases, their metabolism slows, and their insulin levels rise. But why do people become obese in the first place? In a study that has followed children from birth to the age of five, William Kessen and Judith Rodin have found that the likelihood of a newborn's becoming an obese preschooler can be predicted by any of three factors: (1) family obesity, (2) an extreme responsiveness to visual stimuli on the first day of birth, and/or (3) an extreme responsiveness to sweet tastes on the first day of birth (Rodin and Hall, 1984). This heightened responsiveness also characterizes many obese adults. They are far more responsive than other people to any food cues (such as the sight or aroma of food), and they are also more responsive to other environmental cues. What is more, when they see or smell food, their insulin levels rise dramatically compared with those of people who are not externally responsive (Rodin, 1983). And as noted above, high insulin levels make people eat more and speed the conversion of food to fat.

But external responsiveness by itself cannot explain obesity, because some externally responsive individuals never become fat, and some obese people are no more responsive to external cues than the average person. Other factors also appear to be important, including insulin, metabolism, learned responses to food cues, social customs, and failure to develop self-control over eating (Rodin and Marcus, 1982). It may be that many externally responsive individuals avoid gaining weight by consciously restraining their eating. One study found that people of normal weight who were chronic dieters tended to be extra-responsive to food and other environmental cues (Klajner et al., 1981), and other researchers have found that people who consciously restrain their eating —whether or not they are overweight—are more likely to keep on overeating once they have broken their restraint and eaten some "forbidden" food (Herman and Mack, 1975).

Motivation and Emotion in Weight Regulation

Why is it that some people respond to external cues and others do not, and why are some external cues more compelling than others? The answer to this question lies in the incentives presented by those external cues and the relationship between incentives and emotions. In order to understand how motivational states arise in connection with a function such as weight regulation, we need to understand what sorts of emotional reactions are produced by the incentives involved.

Let's look at an extremely compelling external cue: a delicious pastry on the table before us. First, the sight of the pastry makes the incentive *salient* (the incentive "leaps out at us"). Next, having the incentive right in front of us makes the prospect of *instrumental* behavior much clearer in our minds. All we have to do, we know, is reach out and take the pastry. And then—most important —the prospect of *consummatory* behavior imposes itself upon us with great force. We cannot help imagining ourselves putting a bit of the pastry in our mouth and tasting it. And as we imagine eating it, we cannot keep from imagining ourselves *enjoying* and *savoring* it.

The enjoyment we are imagining is, of course, an emotional state—one that makes this incentive very tempting. We are likely to respond to the incentive with instrumental behavior, because the attainment of the goal will have emotional consequences—we know and have learned that we will be delighted by eating the delicious pastry. As noted earlier, motives are internal states that organize the organism's energy to drive its behavior toward or away from incentives. These incentives have a positive or negative emotional significance for the organism. How strong the incentives are may depend in part on innate factors; but it may also depend on the particular individual's past experience, which varies from one person to the next.

How much we eat is not just a physiological reaction to hunger. At a banquet such as this, where food is attractive, plentiful, and free, we are likely to eat more than we would at an ordinary meal.

MOTIVES WITHOUT SPECIFIC PRIMARY NEEDS

Activities directed toward satisfying thirst and hunger are obviously related to basic biological needs for water and food. However, people and other animals engage in many activities that seem unrelated to specific biological needs. Some human behavior, such as sky diving and mountain climbing, actually threatens life instead of increasing the probability of survival (see the box on pages 306–307). Such seemingly "unnecessary" behavior, though seldom so hazardous, can be observed throughout the animal kingdom.

For example, one group of researchers (Harlow, Harlow, and Meyer, 1950) found that rhesus monkeys became highly competent in solving various mechanical puzzles (such as undoing a chain, lifting a hook, opening a clasp) that required several steps for solution—despite the fact that they received no reward for their actions. Observing this, the researchers proposed that the monkeys were displaying a "manipulative drive." Other studies led to similar hypotheses about drives, such as a "curiosity drive" (Butler, 1954) and an "exploratory drive" (Montgomery, 1954) for which an activity seems to be its own reward. Human infants and children have a similar propensity to manipulate, explore, and learn about new things in the environment, apparently "just for the fun of it." Whether we look at hamsters running in an activity wheel or people riding bicycles, we find an

WHAT MOTIVATES PEOPLE TO TAKE UNNECESSARY RISKS?

It was nearing noon that Sunday when a stiff, warm breeze suddenly materialized. Brent Hansen, a 29-year-old student . . . had been waiting for it most of the morning. Helmetless, he picked up the control bar of his multicolored hangglider, fastened his harness and ran 100 yards along the top of a 600-foot cliff above "Escape Country" near El Toro, California. But no sooner was he aloft than he got into serious trouble.

Somehow he had become tangled in his harness. "I'm caught, I'm caught," he screamed. But his friends below could only watch as he dove nosefirst into the ground at roughly 40 mph. After three days in the intensive-care unit . . . he recovered, only to hangglide again. (Greenberg, 1977, p. 17)

What makes Brent Hansen and others like him return to a sport that nearly killed him? Whatever it is, it is the same force that sends race-car drivers back to the track and parachutists back to the sky.

When Danger Feels Good
The drawing power of danger has been explained in terms of

opponent-process theory, with a predictable sequence of emotional states appearing in people who court danger. During a parachutist's first jump, the novice is terrified. On landing, terror is replaced by a stunned feeling, which lasts for several minutes, to be followed by normal composure. With experience, the emotions change, but the pattern remains. Although the terror is gone, parachutists may be anxious be-

fore a jump. On landing, they are exhilarated and the emotion may last for hours. Parachutists give this feeling as their reason for jumping (S. Epstein, 1967).

Presumably, other dangerous activities elicit the same pattern of emotional responses: after many experiences, fright is replaced by eagerness, and a relieved daze gives way to jubilation. Just as the dog slowly comes to take pleasure in the cessation of shock, a gradual adaptation to intense emotion enables people to take risks that the uninitiated find overwhelming.

**Risk Takers:
A Personality Profile**
The opponent-process theory explains the changes that make dangerous sports attractive to so many people, but it does not explain why some people are drawn to risks in the first place. When a psychologist looked at the personality profiles of an international group of top athletes, he found that an interest in high-risk sports was accompanied by

apparent drive for activity that is intrinsically rewarding.

In all these drives for activity, internal conditions that help give rise to them are not apparent, as they are in physiological drives (Bolles, 1967), and the activities fulfill no immediate biological needs. Yet these activities undoubtedly have adaptive significance for individual animals, and ultimately for the species, because investigating and manipulating the environment lead to knowledge that can be used in times of stress or danger.

Optimal-Level Theories

It has been suggested that behavior of this sort is based on a built-in tendency to seek a certain optimal level of stimulation and activity. Theories stressing this idea are called **optimal-level theories**. Optimal-level theories are similar to the homeostatic model of physiological drive regulation (Arkes and Garske, 1977). According to these theories, each individual becomes accustomed to a certain level of stimulation and activity, and each desires experiences that are somewhat different

certain personality traits: a strong need for success and recognition; high autonomy and a strong need to dominate; self-assertiveness and forth-rightness; a preference for transitory emotional relationships; a low level of anxiety; a strong sense of reality; and a high degree of emotional control (Ogilvie, 1974). These risk-taking athletes were "stimulus-addictive," for they had developed a need to extend themselves to their physical, emotional, and intellectual limits as a way of escaping from the lack of tension in their daily lives.

A Social-Psychological View: Risk Taking in the Technological Society

Other psychologists maintain that the appeal of risk taking stems from certain conditions within Western society. In a culture that stresses competition and aggression, few jobs provide outlets for these strong drives. Assembly-line workers are drawn to high-risk recreation to distinguish themselves, and as more jobs become routine, members of the middle class are also drawn to high-risk sports

(Klein, cited in Greenberg, 1977).

The Biological Side: High Risks and Brain Chemistry

Finally, an explanation that is more biological than psychological has also been suggested. The results of personality tests administered to more than 10,000 people showed that those who like risky sports also like other intense experiences. Those who seek high sensation are likely to have a number of similar tastes, ranging from sky diving to a variety in sexual partners (Zuckerman, 1978). It may be that physiology helps determine whether a person seeks sensation or security. Researchers have found that people respond differently to various levels of stimulation. For example, the brain reacts to stimulation with bursts of electrical activity called evoked potentials (see Chapter 3). According to Marvin Zuckerman (1978), among some people, the more intense a stimulus, the stronger the evoked potential. Among others, intense stimuli actually diminish the evoked potential. Zuckerman calls the first group "augment-

ers" and the second group "reducers," and found that high-sensation seekers are neither following their peers nor driven by neurotic needs to master anxiety or to reduce sexual tension. Instead, they aim to increase the tension in their lives and need constant variety to reach their optimal level of arousal. Once accustomed to a high level, they may go on to seek even higher degrees of stimulation.

Thus, sensation seeking does not contradict optimal-level theory. It is probable that the difference between augmenters' optimal level and their level of adaptation is not greater than that of others. Augmenters' optimum is simply higher than that of other people. Augmenters continually subject themselves to higher levels of stimulation and excitation than the rest of us. A sky diver is more likely to commute to work on a fast motorcycle than is an accountant. Since augmenters live at a high level of excitation, to achieve an optimal departure from that level, they must attain levels of excitation that would be unpleasant to many people.

from what she or he is used to, but not extremely different. If, for example, people are asked to rate the pleasantness of various temperatures of water after they have adapted to some moderate temperature, they show a preference for temperatures slightly above or below the temperature to which they have adapted, as shown in Figure 12.1 (Haber, 1958). More extreme temperatures, although they do not cause pain or discomfort, are rated as relatively unpleasant. Similar effects have been found in reactions to various tastes. The

experience of ingesting a bitter substance is not always displeasing: small concentrations of bitterness in certain substances are found pleasurable, and so are small concentrations of acidity. It is only as the concentrations become more intense that the experience becomes increasingly unpleasant (see Figure 12.2).

A person's optimal level is apparently based on what that person has become accustomed to. An experienced musician tends to prefer complex sequences of tones over relatively predictable se-

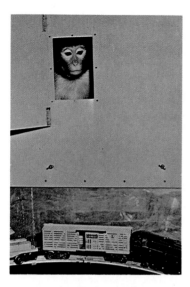

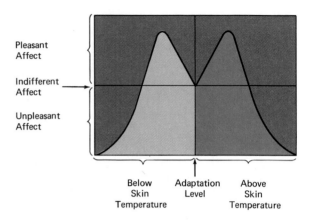

An example of behavior that cannot readily be explained by a drive-reduction model of motivation. A monkey will work hard for the privilege of viewing an electric train, but it would be difficult to say what drive is reduced as a result.

Figure 12.1. The results of an experiment in adaptation. Subjects became adapted to water of the same temperature as their skin and rated the experience as emotionally "indifferent" (represented by the intersection of the vertical and horizontal lines in the center of this diagram). Then they were asked to place their hands in water that was either cooler or warmer than skin temperature and to rate their emotional response to the experience as "pleasant" or "unpleasant." They rated as most pleasant those temperatures that were either slightly warmer or slightly cooler (represented by the two peaks in the diagram) than the temperature to which they had adapted earlier. (After Haber, 1958.)

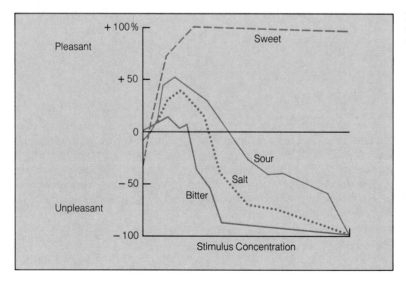

Figure 12.2. Reactions to four tastes at varying substance concentrations. (Adapted from Woodworth, 1938.)

quences, whereas a nonmusician prefers the opposite (Vitz, 1966). Once a person attains a new optimum, she or he adapts to it—and then yet another optimum emerges.

Optimal-level theories are valid only within certain limits, of course. New experiences that are quite different, but positive, are more tolerable than new experiences that are quite different, but negative. A student who expects a D on an exam will be surprised but not unhappy at receiving an A. However, the student who expects an A and receives a D will be miserable. Events that are extremely different from expectations are evaluated less on their magnitude than on their direction (Brickman, 1972).

Opponent-Process Theories

Not all behavior is explained by optimal-level theories. An explanation put forth by Richard Solomon (1980), called opponent-process theory, seems to clarify such phenomena as taste aversion, food cravings, attachment, and addiction. In **opponent-process theory**, there are always two processes involved in acquired motivation—a primary process and a secondary process that opposes the first. The secondary process is a reaction of the central nervous system automatically triggered by the primary process that reduces intense feeling—whether the feeling is pleasant or aversive. For example, when a dog is first exposed to electric shock, it is terrorized: it crouches, whines,

urinates, defecates, and shows signs of behavioral disorganization. When the shock stops, the dog acts confused. If the dog is shocked several times, the pattern of behavior changes. The animal shows less terror, does not urinate or defecate, and often passively accepts the shock. When the shock terminates, the dog seems not confused, but joyful: wagging its tail and jumping are signs of extreme pleasure.

According to the opponent-process theory, the primary emotional reaction begins with the onset of stimulus and ends with its termination —starting and stopping sharply. The secondary opponent process is more sluggish. It starts some time after the stimulus onset and builds slowly, taking time to dissipate. After several experiences, the pattern changes: the primary process (a) remains unaltered but the opponent process (b) is strengthened. Thus, as Figure 12.3 indicates, after a few shocks the dog is not as alarmed as it was at first, because the opponent process (b) has grown until it subtracts from the primary fear reaction. When the stimulus terminates, the pleasure is greater. As the box indicates, the same pattern appears in hanggliding, in which the novice's terror is replaced by the exhilaration of the veteran.

Opponent-process theory can also explain addiction. A novice's reaction to an opiate is a potent "rush," which is succeeded by a less intense but pleasurable state. When the effects of the drug dissipate, the new user may experience a runny nose and eyes, sweaty hands, abdominal pressure,

Figure 12.3. The comparison of the combined effects of the primary process (a) and the secondary process (b). The bottom panel shows the stimulus duration; the middle panel shows the component processes separately; the upper panel shows the difference between the primary (a) and the secondary (b) opponent processes. Note that the change which results from several repetitions of a given experience (good or bad) is entirely due to the changes which occur in the opponent process. The primary process remains unchanged with repeated experiences. (Adapted from Solomon, 1980.)

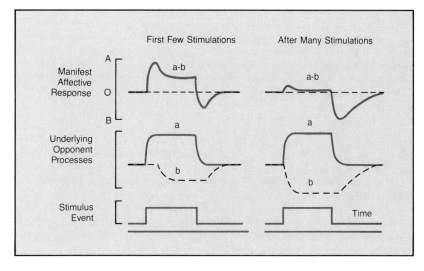

and muscle pains. The discomfort is equivalent to "craving," and it disappears when another dose of the opiate is taken. However, the second dose produces a diminished rush and less euphoria, and the aftereffects are more aversive. Abstinence may eventually result in agony. The rush represents a positive primary process and the aversive state that grows with experience represents a negative opponent process. In an attempt to remove the aversive state, the person again uses the drug, administers higher doses, and becomes increasingly fearful of the time when the effects wear off.

Social Motivation

Beyond the needs that human beings share with other animals for the necessities of life, and beyond the portion of our behavior that is determined by drives to obtain these necessities, unraveling the special nature of human motivation becomes a complex endeavor. One reason for this complexity is the tremendous variation in behavior, goals, and preferences among human beings. For one person, jogging is the road to physical health; for another, it is the way to aching muscles and sore feet. One person's favorite activities are reading books and deciphering ancient manuscripts; another likes nothing better than to play football. Psychologists have sought some way to include such individual differences in accounts of human motivation, and the problem has been approached in several ways. Because these differences derive from the unique social experiences of the individual, and because the incentives are defined by the society, we speak here of *social motivation*.

Achievement Motivation

One method of studying human motivation is based on work done by Henry Murray and his colleagues in the late 1930s. Murray emphasized the role of "psychogenic," or nonphysiological, needs in determining human behavior; he accepted Sigmund Freud's idea that people express their motives more clearly when they are free-associating, saying whatever comes to mind, than when giving direct reports (see Chapter 18). Guided by clinical evidence, Murray and his colleagues devised the Thematic Apperception Test (TAT), in which people write or tell brief stories about pictures that show ambiguous situations (see Chapter 20). The stories are then analyzed for signs of particular motives.

Using the TAT, Murray and his colleagues (1938) identified a list of human motives, among which "achievement," "affiliation," and "dominance" have been most frequently studied. By concentrating on the study of the **achievement motive**, or the capacity to derive satisfaction (that is, have a positive emotional experience) by attaining some standard of excellence, we can see how these motives are measured and analyzed, and how knowledge gained from studying them might have practical benefits.

Measuring Achievement Motivation

To measure the achievement motive, David McClelland, his colleagues, and John Atkinson (McClelland et al., 1953; Atkinson, 1958a) showed people pictures from the TAT. Each person spent about four minutes writing a story that answered the following questions: (1) What is happening? Who are the people? (2) What has led up to the situation—that is, what has happened in the past? (3) What is being thought? What is wanted? By whom? (4) What will happen? What will be done? Typically, each person wrote stories for three or four different pictures to provide a sample of fantasy large enough to score. The scoring system was devised by comparing stories written under achievement-oriented conditions (when each person also took a competitive intelligence test) with stories written under relaxed, noncompetitive conditions.

TAT stories are said to reflect the individual's needs, fears, and wants—feelings that may not be conscious and that normally would not be expressed. To assess individual differences in the achievement motive, people are given the TAT under neutral conditions, and their stories are numerically scored for achievement imagery (Atkinson, 1958b). In stories that score high on achievement, the main character is concerned with standards of excellence and with a high level of performance, with unique accomplishments such as inventions and winning awards, and with the pursuit of a long-term goal or career. High-achievement stories also deal with persistent attempts to accomplish something and with good or bad feelings (pride or shame) aroused by the success or failure of achievement-related activity. In fact, fear of failure is a major negative component of the achievement motive: the greater the fear of failure, the lower the achievement motive. When scoring a story, independent scorers (people who do not know the hypothesis of the experimenter) trained in the use of this method generally reach close agreement.

Comparison of People with High- and Low-Achievement Motivation

Early studies of achievement found that people who showed high-achievement motivation on TAT stories performed better on such tasks as anagram puzzles and addition problems than did people who made low scores. The high scorers also persisted longer at difficult tasks, were more likely than low scorers to recall interrupted tasks (indicating a continuing desire to complete the tasks), and chose "expert" work partners more often than "friendly" ones (because experts were more likely to contribute to success).

In one study that followed from Atkinson's theory (Weiner, 1972), people who scored high in achievement motivation, and who also showed low test anxiety, chose to stand at an intermediate distance from the target in a ring-toss game, thus making the game challenging but not impossible. Subjects with low-achievement motivation and high test anxiety, however, were more likely to stand either very close to the target, where success was assured, or far away from the target, where they seemed to feel that no one could blame them for failing. In daily life, people with high-achievement motivation tend to pursue careers that are difficult enough to be challenging but not so difficult that they will end in failure. People with low-achievement motivation are less realistic. They tend to choose either very easy jobs, where success is certain but the rewards are small, or very difficult jobs, at which they cannot be blamed for failing.

Achievement motivation also affected the way people attempted to explain their successes and failures (Weiner, 1972). People high in achievement motivation usually attributed their performance to internal factors—their successes to high ability and high effort and their failures to lack of effort. People low in achievement motivation were more likely to attribute success to external factors

Performing difficult exercises until they can be done "right" requires more than physical stamina. People high in achievement motivation will persist in spite of discomfort because they believe that greater effort will bring success.

(ease of task and good luck) and failure to an internal factor—the lack of ability. From such results, it is possible to predict how much success a person will anticipate when confronted again with a particular task. For example, a person who attributes her or his success to stable factors (ability and task difficulty) will expect to succeed the next time the task is undertaken. If unstable causes are believed to be responsible, the person is less certain of succeeding at a task again (especially if luck is emphasized).

These differences in the way people view the causes of their successes and failures help to explain behavioral differences that have been found. For example, people who choose achievement-related activities may do so because in the past they have experienced strong positive emotion after success (having attributed it to their own ability and effort). They persist longer in the face of failure than do their counterparts with low motivation, perhaps because highly motivated people think that failure is the result of insufficient effort and that increased effort will lead to success. People low in achievement motivation give up easily because they attribute failure to their own low ability and feel that nothing can be done about it (Brody, 1983).

Achievement Motivation and Economic Progress

McClelland (1961) tried to invoke achievement motivation to explain why societies differ in economic growth. The idea that a community's or a society's economic development may depend on its achievement values is not entirely new. Back in 1904, the German sociologist Max Weber developed such a hypothesis. He suggested that modern capitalism had developed from Protestant values of self-reliance and from the Calvinist belief that if an individual is successful, this constitutes evidence that God has reserved a special treatment for his or her soul—in other words, that the individual is among the "elect."

Whether or not Weber was right, the Protestant ethic is still widespread in modern industrialized countries. In McClelland's investigation of achievement motivation he discovered that the mothers of high achievers had higher expectations for their sons than the mothers of low achievers. They wanted their sons to know their way around the city quite early, to be active and energetic, to try hard for themselves, to make their own friends, and to succeed in competitive tasks.

As additional support for this idea McClelland cited studies that found correlations between achievement strivings that he assumed to exist in a society and economic indicators in that society —for example, the consumption of electric energy in kilowatts per capita. How can a society's achievement strivings be measured? McClelland found an ingenious way. He devised an index of such strivings from an analysis of children's stories: the stories were essentially treated as TAT stories and scored in a similar way. Using this method, McClelland was able to estimate the level of achievement motivation in past societies, going as far back as Greek literature of 900 B.C.

Applications: Managing Achievement Motivation

If the achievement motive is essentially learned, it may be possible to train people to be achievement oriented. Indeed, in one study (McClelland and Winter, 1969), a group of college students were encouraged and instructed to create fantasies of successful achievement, and the training led to greater academic success and higher grades.

In a comprehensive project, David McClelland and David Winter (1969) succeeded in raising achievement-motivation levels among businessmen in a village in India. Their program, called the Kakinada Project, consisted of encouraging the businessmen to create high-achievement fantasies, to make plans that would help them realize the goals of a successful entrepreneur, and to communicate with one another about their goals and their methods of reaching them. McClelland approached the project pragmatically; his aim was to raise the achievement-motivation level among the businessmen rather than to identify the best techniques for doing so. For that reason, he does not know exactly why his program succeeded —whether one technique worked and the others did not or whether all of them helped— but succeed it did. The businessmen became more productive as entrepreneurs, starting several large industries, enlarging their businesses, and hiring more than 5,000 of their neighbors.

Although the scope of the Kakinada Project was small, its success indicates that larger efforts of the same kind could be a major factor in economic development. In a subsequent assessment of this study, McClelland (1978) compared it with a more complicated project that had the immediate purpose of improving the standard of living in another village in India and the long-range goal of teaching the people to help themselves.

The Barpali Village Project, as it was called, was conducted by the American Friends Service Committee. Training and technical aid were provided for digging wells and building latrines, establishing better schools and health facilities, providing information on family planning, improving methods of farming, starting village industries, and teaching the villagers how to repair equipment and to maintain the programs.

Ten years after all American personnel had returned to the United States, the village was revisited and the project evaluated. There was little sign that the Americans had ever visited the village. Most of the wells were unused; the advanced agricultural procedures had been abandoned; the villagers' health was as poor as ever; and the birth-control program was an utter failure (population had, in fact, increased more than in a neighboring village).

In terms of time, money, and enduring effects, McClelland's achievement-training project was far more successful. The Barpali Village Project cost $1 million, lasted ten years, and failed to have any permanent effect on the population. The Kakinada Project, however, cost $25,000, lasted only six months, and resulted in long-term improvement in the villagers' standard of living through self-sustaining programs and expanded employment. While the Barpali Village Project was based on the common-sense idea that people will do things if they are taught how to do them, the Kakinada Project was based on the psychological concept that without motivation, knowledge is unlikely to alter people's behavior.

Sex Differences in Achievement Motivation: The Fear of Success

Studies based on theories of achievement motivation often failed to predict the behavior of women as well as they predicted the behavior of men (Mednick, 1979; Sherif, 1976). Scientists wondered why.

Since girls and women often have higher test-anxiety scores than men do, some psychologists suggested that females were inherently more anxious than males. However, others proposed that socialization was responsible for the difference. As Eleanor Maccoby (1963) pointed out, girls who maintain the qualities of dominance, independence, and striving for success are defying cultural sex-role standards, and if they are successful in their efforts, they are likely to suffer negative consequences. Since women traditionally are not supposed to compete in certain kinds of activity, attempts to succeed in these areas may lead to anxiety.

Studies by Matina Horner (1970; 1972) support this suggestion, for they indicate that sex differences in performance may indeed be the result of culturally imposed sex differences in motivation. Horner proposed that women are motivated to avoid success, and that they fear success because negative consequences often befall women who succeed in traditionally male areas.

Horner devised a way to measure the motive to avoid success, or **fear of success**. Using a version of the TAT that required subjects to complete stories, she found that women showed a significantly higher motive to avoid success than did men.

Horner speculated that the motive to avoid success was aroused when people were anxious about competition and its aggressive overtones. Among women, fear of success seemed related to a belief that success threatened close relationships with men and signified their failure as traditional women. Such women might be expected to marry and have children sooner than women scoring low on the measure, for having a baby can confirm a woman's femininity, remove her from the competitive arena, and reestablish her dependent relationship with her husband. A follow-up study of the same women Horner had assessed found this to be the case (Hoffman, 1977). Indeed, many of these women seemed to have become pregnant when faced with the possibility of success in some area that would put them in competition with their husbands.

Although fear of success provides an intuitively appealing explanation of some sex differences in motivation, the findings do not apply in all situations. Fear of success is not universal among females, and it appears to differ from task to task (Stein and Bailey, 1973). For example, in situations that depend on social skills, women do not fear success as they seem to do when intellectual or athletic skills are critical. Some psychologists (Condry and Dyer, 1976) have suggested that many women write stories saturated with a fear of success because cultural standards lead them to attribute to other women a fear that they do not feel for themselves. However, a different and more objective measure also supports the idea that there are gender differences in the motive to avoid success among undergraduate college students, and that women score higher on the measure (Zuckerman and Wheeler, 1975). It is becoming increasingly clear, however, that many areas that were once men's exclusive domains are attracting women in large numbers. Such a shift is likely to diminish whatever fear of success exists among women.

Other Types of Social Motivation

Although most investigators have focused on the need for achievement, some research has been conducted on other human needs such as the need for affiliation and the need for power. McClelland (1982) reported that individuals who have a strong need for power and who are blocked in their strivings for it develop more physical illness than other people. He contends that a need for power heightens sympathetic nervous system activity, which in turn raises blood pressure. High blood pressure increases the body's output of epinephrine, which eventually reduces the ability of the body's immune system to fight infectious disease.

MOTIVATION AND COGNITION

The environment can provide us with a means of satisfying our goals and needs—or, alternatively, it can generate barriers that frustrate their attainment. Thus, the environment creates conditions that lead to the arousal of powerful motivational states, and our perception and knowledge of these environmental conditions may lead to conflict. A second approach to understanding human motivation is therefore based on the proposition that, just as we seek physiological homeostasis, we also seek equilibrium in cognitive states.

Dealing with Cognitive Imbalance

Our cognitive processes are affected by information, and information inundates us from every possible source—from the environment, from other people, and from our thoughts, dreams, plans, and achievements. Since the information we collect expands at a rapid rate, we must find an efficient way to store it. By storing information in the form of categories, or concepts, and rules (see Chapter 10), we can process it more efficiently. The information that comes our way usually fits some of our categories and some of our rules. If it fits none—that is, if it is inconsistent—we are surprised and disturbed. We are thrown into a state of cognitive imbalance, and we ask ourselves why this item does not fit with anything else we know.

To restore equilibrium we try to resolve inconsistencies in our rules and categories. One way to do this is to find an explanation in the form of a new category or a new rule. For example, if Ann discovers that Jeanne, her best friend, voted for the "wrong" presidential candidate, she will be surprised and feel uncomfortable. Generally, people who like each other like similar things and have similar views (Duck and Craig, 1978)—a rule that we have learned through contact with others. So Ann's state of cognitive discomfort will lead her to seek explanations for Jeanne's vote until she finds some consistency. Under some circumstances Ann may change her own mind about the presidential candidates so as to restore balance. Thus, the state of disequilibrium that is created by the conflict among three cognitions ("I like Jeanne," "I like my presidential candidate," "Jeanne doesn't like my presidential candidate") has motivational consequences. It makes Ann tense, propels her to seek new information about Jeanne and the two candidates, and puts pressure on Ann's political preferences.

Note that, as in the case of other motivational states, the conditions of cognitive imbalance that Ann is experiencing involve (1) an emotional state—in this instance, surprise and discomfort; (2) a drive that gives vigor, direction, and persistence to Ann's ensuing instrumental behavior, aimed at reducing the discomfort; (3) an incentive, which consists of the anticipation of a reduced discomfort; and (4) consummatory behavior that immediately follows the resolution of the imbalance.

These tendencies were incorporated by Fritz Heider (1958) into a theory of cognitive consistency called **cognitive balance theory**. Since the information we receive about people or objects is often inconsistent and contradictory and may lead to opposing inferences, our cognitive processes can easily be thrown out of balance. According to cognitive balance theory the resulting conflict causes us to feel a tension that we seek to resolve. Thus, in this view, pressures from the environment impose on the individual a motivation to regain a consistent view of the world.

Cognitive Dissonance

Heider's theory of cognitive balance attempted primarily to explain changes in a person's attitude toward other specific people and objects. A more general approach to cognitive consistency is that of **cognitive dissonance theory**, which also focuses on people's attempts to avoid cognitive inconsistency, but looks at people's tendency to restore consistency among any of their attitudes, thoughts, beliefs, or perceptions. Leon Festinger (1957), who first proposed the theory, stated that

Figure 12.4. Attitudes are frequently modified in order to resolve contradictions. This motivation for attitude change is called cognitive dissonance. In this figure Mary has expressed two attitudes that are now brought into conflict by Bill's behavior. She cannot "love that man" and "hate those clothes" without experiencing the discomfort of dissonance. A resolution can be accomplished in a number of ways. Mary can start wondering if she really loves Bill after all, or she can broaden her tastes, or she can make such mental rearrangements as, "Good taste isn't really what I'm looking for in a man anyway."

when we hold two contradictory cognitions about our own attitudes, beliefs, or behavior, we are thrown into a state of psychological distress known as *cognitive dissonance*. Because this state is uncomfortable, even painful, we naturally attempt to rid ourselves of it and reestablish internal harmony (see Figure 12.4).

The situations in which dissonance can arise —and the methods used to reduce it—are varied. Suppose, for example, that you need a car to commute to campus. You go to a used-car lot and find two automobiles that you like, a Volkswagen Rabbit and a Datsun. The two cars have about the same number of miles on them and are the same price, the same age, and in equally good condition. You find it difficult to decide between them because both cars seem equally attractive. At last you

settle on the Rabbit. Immediately you are cast into an unpleasant state of dissonance. You liked the Datsun a great deal, but you bought the Rabbit instead and you wonder if you made the right decision. According to cognitive dissonance theory, you would attempt to reduce your distress by adjusting your attitudes toward the two cars. You would try to develop both a more favorable attitude toward the Rabbit, playing up its good qualities and playing down its negative ones, and a less favorable feeling toward the Datsun, focusing on its undesirable features and ignoring its positive ones. Research confirms that this process of rationalization is common. In one early study, people who had just purchased a new car were more inclined to read advertisements for the model they had bought than for those they had considered but rejected, presumably with the goal of reducing the dissonance created by their decision (Ehrlich et al., 1957).

Applications of Cognitive Dissonance Theory

Cognitive dissonance theory has wide applications in the fields of psychotherapy, religion, buying and selling, and politics (Wicklund and Brehm, 1976). For instance, it has been used to explain why people who publicly say or do something contrary to their private beliefs often shift their attitudes to make them conform to their public stance. In fact, the less incentive people have to express the contradictory view, the *more* likely they are to change their original attitudes. Apparently, the lower the incentive, the greater the dissonance created —and therefore the greater the need to restore a state of cognitive consistency.

A classic early experiment (Festinger and Carlsmith, 1959) illustrated this point. People were given the boring task of putting round pegs in round holes and square pegs in square holes for two hours. Then the experimenter asked each person to tell the next person who was to perform the task that the experiment had been fun and exciting. He promised half the subjects one dollar for telling this lie and the other half twenty dollars. After passing on the erroneous information, the original subjects evaluated the degree to which they had enjoyed the experimental task. Those who had been paid one dollar for telling the lie said they enjoyed the task more than did people who had received twenty dollars.

Why did the people who were paid one dollar rate the boring job more favorably than those who were paid twenty dollars? According to dissonance theory, to say something you do not believe ordinarily causes psychological discomfort, but when you have a good reason for lying, you experience little or no dissonance. Therefore, people who received only one dollar and could not justify the lie to themselves "decided" that the task had not been so boring after all, so they had not really lied. People who were paid twenty dollars had a good reason for saying something they did not believe, because in 1959 twenty dollars was a substantial sum. The behavior of the second group created little dissonance and they could readily admit that the task had been dull.

Other Perspectives on Cognitive Dissonance Theory

Dissonance theory assumes that tension must be present when a person experiences cognitive dissonance. But does such tension and discomfort always exist? A good deal of controversy has emerged over this issue, and it appears that whether such discomfort develops depends on the circumstances. Mark Zanna and Joel Cooper (1974) have proposed that tension arises when there is conflict—for example, when we are put in a situation where we must behave in ways that contradict our deep-seated beliefs. If our behavior corresponds to our attitudes, as when we buy a car that we like, no significant conflict exists. But if there is a discrepancy between our attitudes and our behavior, we are indeed aroused by the conflict; we believe our arousal is caused by behaving in a way that goes against our attitudes (perhaps by doing something we are ashamed of). As a result, we change our attitude to reduce the discrepancy and relieve the tension. Such tension is not present when attitudes and behavior match, and therefore no instrumental behavior of consequence is called for.

Cognitive dissonance theory has been challenged on the grounds that in many cases, people can easily accommodate contradictory and conflicting information (Tedeschi, Schlenker, and Bonoma, 1971). But they do not like to *appear* inconsistent. Claiming to like a boring task after receiving a small reward makes a person appear inconsistent—unless that person gives some evidence that she or he does like the task. In such situations, people resort to impression management, in which they manage the impressions others may get of them to appear consistent. Thus, they claim to have enjoyed the task. **Impression management theory** maintains that a person's attitudes remain impervious to the effects of dissonance and that the insufficient reward affects only the *expression* of attitudes to others. (We discuss impression management in more detail in Chapter 26.)

Other motivational consequences of cognitive states were found to be characterized by tension. They were investigated in an experiment that required college students to learn a list of words under painful conditions—they received two shocks on each trial until they learned the entire list (Zimbardo et al., 1969). Although the experiment was ostensibly over once the list had been learned, the students were asked to continue for another session. Half of them were given considerable justification for continuing (the experiment was important to science, to the space program, and so forth). The rest were given poor reasons for participating (nothing might come out of the experiment). When the students who agreed to continue learned the next list, those who had been given little justification learned faster, perceived the shocks as less painful, and showed lower physiological reactions to pain, such as a galvanic skin response (GSR), than students who had been given high justification. The differences in justification manipulated cognitive dissonance among the students in the same way as did paying subjects to lie in the earlier experiment.

In this case, the cognitions in conflict were "I have agreed to suffer considerable pain" and "There will be nothing in it for me, nor will either science or society benefit." Students in the high-justification group felt no such conflict because they believed that there were good reasons for enduring the pain. Apparently, cognitive dissonance can have powerful motivational effects on perception (feeling the shock as less painful), on behavior (learning faster), and on physiological reactions (lower GSRs). According to the researchers, the resolution of dissonance leads people to deny and suppress pain, and this suppression affects behavior and physiology.

Intrinsic and Extrinsic Motivation

The experiment on pain and cognitive dissonance focuses on a distinction between two classes of motivation: intrinsic and extrinsic. Behavior that is undertaken because of some external reward is considered to be **extrinsically motivated**, and behavior that is undertaken because of long-term goals or an individual's established preferences is considered to be **intrinsically motivated** (Deci, 1975). In the pain experiment, students in the low-dissonance group were given external justification for their behavior, thus their motivation was extrinsic. Students in the high-dissonance group had to create their own reasons for enduring pain, thus their motivation was intrinsic.

Behavior that is extrinsically motivated depends upon the external conditions that support it: it persists only as long as external rewards and punishments continue, and it varies with their magnitude. Intrinsic behavior persists despite set-backs and frustrations. Most of our daily behavior is a mixture of both kinds of motivation. Going to college may be mostly a matter of intrinsic motivation, for the goal (a degree) can be reached only after a long period and substantial concentrated effort. But the effort given to daily assignments may be partly motivated by extrinsic factors: praise from the instructor, admiration from peers, and the like.

In some cases, intrinsic motivation may be weakened when extrinsic motivation is also present. This is the case when *overjustification* occurs. The presence of external incentives may lead individuals to revise their conceptions about their real goal, thereby lowering their intrinsic motivation (DeCharms, 1968). For example, someone who looks forward to the crossword puzzle in the daily newspaper may begin working it less often if he or she is paid several times for solving it. In this example, solving the puzzle has moved from intrinsic incentives (pleasure) to extrinsic incentives (money); payment has made work out of play. Note, though, that there is one group of people who react differently to extrinsic reward: people who are high in achievement motivation retain their extrinsic motivation in the presence of extrinsic rewards they cannot control (if, let's say, they get paid sometimes for working the puzzle, but do not get paid other times). Of course, in the case of uncontrollable reward, the individual does not associate the outcome with his or her own effort. Yet people who are low in achievement motivation do not react in this way. Achievement motivation apparently affects our sensitivity to uncontrollable rewards.

Although the assertion that extrinsic motivation can weaken intrinsic motivation has not been fully substantiated (Scott, 1975), the effect of punishment on motivation is becoming clear, with mild admonitions shown to be a more effective means of prohibition than the prospect of severe punishment, apparently because mild punishment leads to the development of intrinsic motivation. The finding has been especially strong in studies of children (Lepper, 1981). In typical experiments, children are told not to play with an attractive toy, and the admonition is either severe (the threat of punishment) or mild (a simple request not to play with the toy). The children are then left alone in the presence of the toy, and in most cases none of them plays with it. When later asked about the toy, children who were threatened with punishment still think it is a nice toy, but those who were merely requested not to play with it now have a low opinion of it. By derogating its value, they find an internal justification for complying with the request, thus resolving any dissonance. What is more, six weeks later these children are more likely to avoid the toy than children who earlier had been threatened with punishment. Children in the latter group had been given a good external justification for not playing with the toy, and it still seemed attractive to them.

A Hierarchical Conception of Human Motives

Our discussion has indicated that in order for theories of motivation to be complete, they must account not only for motives based on physiological needs similar to those of other animals but also for drives that are akin to physiological needs and for motives that cannot be characterized without reference to human cognitive processes. One way to organize these diverse motives conceptually has been suggested by Abraham Maslow (1954), a personality theorist whose work is discussed in Chapter 19.

Maslow believed that human needs, or motives, are organized in a hierarchy. The **basic needs** include fundamental physiological needs (for food, water, and so on) and intermediate psychological needs (for safety, affection, self-esteem, and so on). These needs are also "deficiency needs"—if they are not met, people seek to make them up in some way. Failure to attain a feeling of basic security, social acceptance, or self-esteem can produce pathological discomfort and maladjustment that may be almost as debilitating as physical starvation. The highest motives, called **metaneeds**, have to do with creativity, justice, and what Maslow called "self-actualization" (see Figure 12.5).

According to Maslow, the lower needs take precedence: extreme hunger or thirst is so urgent that severely deficient individuals have no opportunity to worry about social acceptance and psychological security, let alone the creative exercise of their talents. Similarly, people who continually seek social acceptance are not free to create scholarly or artistic works.

Little research has been done to test Maslow's hierarchical concept of motivation. Maslow's theory predicts, for example, that the satisfaction of needs for love and belonging is a necessary precon-

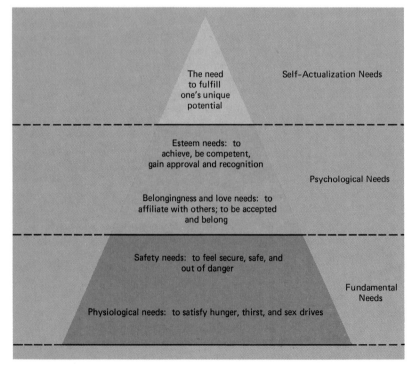

The need to fulfill one's unique potential

Self-Actualization Needs

Esteem needs: to achieve, be competent, gain approval and recognition

Psychological Needs

Belongingness and love needs: to affiliate with others; to be accepted and belong

Safety needs: to feel secure, safe, and out of danger

Fundamental Needs

Physiological needs: to satisfy hunger, thirst, and sex drives

Figure 12.5. This pyramid represents Maslow's hierarchy of needs. According to Maslow, fundamental needs must be satisfied before a person is free to progress to psychological needs, and these in turn must be satisfied before a person can turn to self-actualization needs. Maslow (1970) later added a need for transcendence that is even higher than the need for self-actualization. (After Maslow, 1971.)

dition for altruistic (prosocial) behavior. If this is true, then children who have not yet reached this stage of development, and are mainly concerned with satisfying their safety needs, would not help others as readily as children who are more mature. Using an interview technique, researchers recently found support for this hypothesis among children who suffered a wide range of psychopathology (Haymes, Green, and Quinto, 1984).

Maslow's concept of motivation does draw attention to the complexity of human motivational processes. In addition, it emphasizes aspects of human motivation extending beyond basic survival needs and economic accomplishments. But the need for self-actualization is easily misunderstood; confusion can arise from the belief that each individual has a unique potential that can and should be attained. If people believe that only one occupation, one particular environment, one set of relationships, and one mate will lead to self-actualization, they may become filled with doubt, because no one can ever know whether her or his unique potential has been attained. In reality, there must be thousands of different jobs with which each one of us could learn to be happy, and we could find happiness with any number of different partners. Nor is there any objective way to establish that a person's potential has been actualized.

It is possible that each individual has a unique potential, but it is more probable that the difference between actualizations is small, and that the very best actualization is not far removed from the next best actualization, and so on. People adapt to all kinds of novel situations, but our human tendency to exaggerate the consequences of our decisions—what courses to take, whom to go out with, what car to buy, what job to accept —overlooks our enormous adaptability and our ability to make changes in our environment *after* the decision has been made.

SUMMARY

1. Human behavior is organized and best understood by inferring that it is guided by a purpose and that it leads to an *end state*—a goal or the satisfaction of some need. The property that organizes behavior and defines its end states is called a **motive. Motivation** cannot be observed directly, but must be inferred from behavior.

2. The most basic goal-directed behavior serves the vital functions of survival and reproduction. A motive has two components: an **incentive** (an external motivational stimulus) and a **drive** (an internal motivational factor). Incentives exist mainly as hopes and expectations, but they can be identified by seeing how people react when confronted with rewards and punishments, promises and threats.

3. **Primary drives** are produced by emotional and physiological conditions that stimulate the organism to seek fulfillment of basic needs, there- by restoring homeostasis. In the case of thirst, an organism knows when an adjustment is necessary and which mechanisms make the adjustment. Thirst and drinking are induced by increased salt concentration in body fluids, decreased amount of fluid in the circulatory system, and increased energy expenditure or body temperature. Thirst can be satiated by stomach distention and other physiological mechanisms that maintain the body's water balance. Hunger and weight regulation show the contribution of internal and external stimuli to drive regulation. The hypothalamus helps regulate food intake, but much eating is determined by external factors: social customs; the look, taste, and smell of food; and the effort required to obtain it. Obese individuals often eat in response to external cues; however, a number of other factors (insulin levels, size of fat cells, activity levels, and the interaction of internal and external cues) also contribute to obesity.

4. When a biological need increases, the drive to seek its satisfaction becomes stronger. However, people and other animals engage in many activities that seem to be unrelated to specific primary needs, such as investigating and manipulating the environment. This behavior has adaptive significance, for it leads to knowledge that can be used in times of stress or danger. **Optimal-level theories** propose that such behavior is based on a built-in tendency to maintain a certain level of stimulation, and that people desire experiences that are somewhat but not extremely different from what they are used to. The **opponent-process theory** explains acquired motivations as the result of two opposing processes, with the second (opposing) process being a central nervous system response that reduces intense feeling —whether pleasant or aversive.

5. Social motivation is complex and distinguished by great variation in behavior, goals, and preferences. Social motives can be measured by using the Thematic Apperception Test (TAT); the **achievement motive**, or the capacity to derive satisfaction by attaining some standard of excellence, has been studied extensively in this manner. People who show high-achievement motive generally perform better than low scorers on various tasks and tend to persist longer on difficult tasks. High scorers tend to choose challenging but not impossible careers, while low scorers tend to make unrealistic choices. High scorers attribute success or failure to internal factors, while low scorers tend to attribute success to external factors and failure to lack of ability. People can be trained to be achievement oriented, and a variety of techniques, including the encouragement of high-achievement fantasies, appear to be effective.

6. The level of achievement motivation does not predict female behavior as well as it does male behavior. Women often obtain higher test-anxiety scores than men, and an inherent higher level of anxiety has been suggested as the cause. However, socialization may be responsible for differences in behavior. **Fear of success**, or the motive to avoid success, appears to be more common among women than among men and may be due to culturally imposed sex differences in motivation. Fear of success is not universal among women and does not appear in situations that depend on social skills.

7. Human beings seek cognitive equilibrium in the form of cognitive consistency. According to Heider's **theory of cognitive balance**, we try to resolve any inconsistencies in our concepts by discovering new concepts or by changing our thoughts. According to Festinger's **cognitive dissonance theory**, contradictory thoughts throw us into a distressful state of dissonance, which we may resolve by seeking new information or changing our attitudes. Cognitive dissonance can affect perception, behavior, and physiological reactions.

8. Motivation can be **intrinsic** (undertaken because of long-term goals or preferences) or **extrinsic** (undertaken because of external reward). The introduction of extrinsic motivation may weaken intrinsic motivation, turning play into work. Punishment can affect motivation, with mild punishment being most effective because it leads to the development of intrinsic motivation.

9. Maslow proposed a theory of motivation that accounts for motives based on physiological needs, for drives that are akin to physiological needs, and for motives that cannot be characterized without reference to human cognitive processes. Maslow believed that these various kinds of motives are organized hierarchically and that the lower needs take precedence over the higher needs. **Basic needs** include fundamental physiological needs and intermediate psychological needs (safety and self-esteem, among others). **Metaneeds** are the highest motives, having to do with creativity and self-actualization.

KEY TERMS

achievement motive
basic needs
cognitive balance theory
cognitive dissonance theory
drive
extrinsic motivation

fear of success
impression management theory
incentive
intrinsic motivation
metaneeds
motivation

motive
opponent-process theory
optimal-level theories
primary drive

RECOMMENDED READINGS

ARKES, H. R., and J. P. GARSKE. *Psychological theories of motivation.* Monterey, Calif.: Brooks/Cole, 1977. A broad, basic introductory survey of dominant approaches to motivation in psychology, ranging from instinct through psychoanalysis to attribution theory.

ATKINSON, J. W. (Ed.). *Motives in fantasy, action, and society.* New York: Van Nostrand Reinhold, 1958. An important book that pulls together work done by many investigators on the various methods used to assess and study individual differences in motivational dispositions such as achievement, affiliation, and power. Scoring manuals and self-teaching materials are also included.

ATKINSON, J. W., and N. T. FEATHER. *A theory of achievement motivation.* New York: Wiley, 1966. Focuses on the contemporaneous determinants of achievement-oriented behavior and the marked advances made in psychologists' understanding of that behavior.

DECI, E. L. and R. M. RYAN. The empirical exploration of intrinsic motivational processes. In L. Berkowitz (Ed.), *Advances in experimental social psychology,* (Vol. 13). New York: Academic Press, 1980. A summary of experimental research on the performance effects of intrinsic and extrinsic motivation.

JUNG, J. *Understanding human motivation: A cognitive approach.* New York: Macmillan, 1978. A well-written basic textbook emphasizing individual differences and cognitive factors in human motivation.

McCLELLAND, D. *The achieving society.* New York: Van Nostrand Reinhold, 1961. Addresses the question of the social origins and consequences for society of achievement motivation.

SPENCE, J. T. (Ed.). *Achievement and achievement motives: Psychological and sociological approaches.* San Francisco: W. H. Freeman, 1983. Recent analyses of achievement motivation, with an emphasis on sex differences on the motivational effects in achievement situations.

WEINER, B. *Theories of motivation: From mechanism to cognition.* Chicago: Markham, 1973. A textbook covering, among other topics, drive theory, achievement theory, and—most important—the author's attribution-theory approach to achievement motivation. Presents differences between mechanistic and cognitive theories.

CHAPTER THIRTEEN

HUMAN SEXUALITY

"It's funny because all your life all that stuff is wrong and you're not supposed to let a boy touch you, and then the priest says something and all of a sudden everything is supposed to be all right. But my wedding night was terrible and I cried and cried because I didn't know what I was supposed to do and it did not seem right" (in DeLora and Warren, 1977, p. 197).

Despite the openness about sexuality in this society, the young woman who gave this description of her wedding night to a marriage counselor is not an isolated case. Most of us have learned more about avoiding sex than about enjoying it. We learn the rules our culture has established concerning when and how it is acceptable to express sexual feelings. We even learn what is sexy. In the United States, a small-breasted woman might wish to increase her breast size, but she would never think of stretching her lower lip to appear desirable. Yet among some peoples of South Africa, a pendulous lower lip is an attractive feature (Katchadourian and Lunde, 1975). As a result, although the nature of the physiological response to "effective sexual stimulation" is essentially the same for all human beings, the nature of that stimulation varies greatly from culture to culture. And within a single culture, different learning experiences produce different sexual attitudes.

Because each of us is a sexual being, human sexual behavior fascinates us all. As we explore human sexuality, we shall investigate the factors that influence gender, ways of studying sexual behavior, the nature of the sexual response, some major sexual problems, sex therapy, and the wide variations in sexual behavior. Because many factors that have nothing to do with sexuality influence the nature of our emotionally intense sexual relationships, we shall reserve a discussion of falling in love for Chapter 26.

INFLUENCES ON GENDER

The concept of gender—maleness or femaleness—is composed of many factors, including heredity, anatomy, hormones, and the psychological determination of gender identity. The ability to sort out the respective contributions of these influences on gender is a recent addition to our knowledge of human sexuality.

Genetic and Hormonal Influences

An individual's genetic sex is determined at conception by information carried on one of the twenty-three chromosomes (see Chapter 4) in the father's sperm, which may be either X (female) or Y (male). Since all female germ cells (eggs) contain an X chromosome, an egg that is fertilized by a sperm bearing the X chromosome will be female (genotype XX), but an egg that is fertilized by a sperm bearing the Y chromosome will be male (genotype XY).

In the first six weeks after conception, the sexual development of males and females follows an identical course. Gender first becomes apparent in genetically male embryos (XY), when the gonad begins to develop into testes at about six weeks. In genetically female embryos (XX), ovaries begin to appear some weeks later.

Hormones produced by the tiny gonads determine the way the reproductive organs develop. But the effect of hormones on the fetal brain is equally important. Without male sex hormones (**androgens**), the hypothalamus (see Chapter 3) will develop in a female pattern, set to maintain hormone production in the cyclical pattern that maintains the female reproductive system. When androgens are present, the hypothalamus develops in a male pattern, set to maintain a continual production of hormones.

Yet ovarian hormones are not required for the development of a female. If an embryo receives only a single X chromosome and no Y (a condition known as **Turner's syndrome**), the fetus will develop into an anatomical female, but will have no ovaries and thus will never develop secondary sex characteristics. If an embryo receives a Y but no X chromosome, it will not survive because the X chromosome apparently contains genetic information vital to the development of every fetus. Should the body cells of a genetically male (XY) fetus fail to respond to androgen, the baby will be born genetically male but with the external anatomy of a female (Money, 1963; Money and Ehrhardt, 1972). These children, who have an **androgen insensitivity syndrome**, are reared as girls, and the condition is not generally discovered until late in adolescence when the failure to menstruate leads to a medical examination. From a biological standpoint, the male pattern appears to be an elaboration of the female pattern.

Social Influences: Gender Identity and Gender Roles

With rare exceptions, the child's biological sex, as determined by genes and hormones, is immediately apparent at birth. Up to this point there have been no social influences on sexual development. Following birth, social and cultural forces help to shape a person's gender identity and sexual behavior. They affect how that person relates to other people emotionally and sexually, the things that arouse the individual sexually, and much more.

In Chapter 17 we will see how minor gender differences in behavior are magnified by socialization, and the part played by the environment in the development of gender roles. As a child grows, the child also develops a gender identity, the understanding that he or she is male or female and the inner feelings that accompany the outward behavior of gender role.

Studies of children reared in gender roles that are partially or completely incompatible with their anatomical or genetic sex provide clues as to the influence of upbringing on gender identity. Because upbringing is a powerful force on the development of identity, it has been proposed that when medical reasons make it necessary to change a child's sex, the switch may be done without harm to gender identity up to the age of eighteen months (Money and Ehrhardt, 1972). Yet the major case upon which this theory was built does not appear to be clear-cut. An infant boy's genitals were accidentally mutilated so that he would never be able to function sexually as a normal male. When the child was seventeen months old, surgery was performed to change the child's anatomical sex to female, and the parents reared the child as a girl. At the age of four, the child had adopted a female gender role: "she" played with dolls, was proud of ruffled dresses, and behaved like a "typical" girl. The child seemed to be developing a female gender identity, while her identical twin brother was developing into a "typical" boy. It appeared that upbringing, when combined with a surgical sex change, had overcome the influence of gender and prenatal hormones on gender (Money and Ehrhardt, 1972).

By the age of thirteen, however, the child had developed a masculine gait, was called the "cavewoman" by other children, wanted to become a mechanic, and her fantasies showed some discomfort with her female role. Psychiatrists treating her reported that she was not a happy child and at the age of sixteen, she was having considerable difficulty in adjusting to life as a female (Diamond, 1982).

On the basis of this case, we cannot say that social and cultural influences, powerful as they are, can completely eradicate the combined effect of genes and prenatal hormones. Yet upbringing appears to be extremely powerful. Nine out of ten genetic boys with androgen insensitivity syndrome who were reared as girls developed secure female gender identities (Green, 1981). On the other hand, a recently discovered condition known as Guevodoces syndrome again supports the role of hormones. In this condition, which has been identified in 24 males in the Dominican Republic, an enzyme deficiency prevents genetically normal male babies from showing normal male genitals at birth. As babies and children, these individuals seem to be girls and most are reared accordingly. At puberty, however, their genitals masculinize, and their gender identity seems to make a corresponding switch. How or why this phenomenon takes place is not yet known (Bancroft, 1983).

A great deal of interest has focused on the effect of prenatal hormones in the establishment of gender roles and gender identity. Among girls who were exposed to abnormal levels of prenatal androgens (either because the girls' own adrenal glands overproduced androgens or because their mothers were treated during pregnancy with drugs that raised fetal androgen levels), the exposure appeared to leave lingering traces on gender role but not on gender identity. The girls were born with clear signs of masculinization—for example, a greatly enlarged clitoris that resembled a penis. They received corrective surgery and all were reared as girls. The girls preferred male playmates, dressing in pants to wearing dresses, outdoor games and sports to playing with dolls, and fantasized about future careers instead of about marriage or motherhood. However, the girls' behavior

was within acceptable "tomboy" bounds, most did expect to marry males, and they appeared to have developed female gender identities (Ehrhardt and Meyer-Bahlburg, 1981).

A relatively rare condition called **transsexualism**, in which people develop a gender identity that is inconsistent with their genetic and anatomical sex, provides further evidence of the separation between biological sex and gender identity. Transsexuals feel they are trapped in the body of the wrong sex. Male transsexuals (and most are male) think of themselves as women, want heterosexual relations with men, and sometimes request surgery to "correct" their anatomy. For them, the surgery involves removing the testes and most of the penis and constructing a vagina from the remaining tissue. A series of hormone treatments reduces body hair, and breasts are enlarged by silicone implants. For female transsexuals, surgery involves mastectomy, hysterectomy, and the construction of an artificial penis, accompanied by hormonal treatments. Although male-to-female transsexual surgery produces fairly normal-looking, functional female external genitals and vagina, the corresponding female-to-male operation has as yet been less successful. The "penis" that results from such surgery rarely looks or functions normally.

The advisability of transsexual surgery has recently been called into question, and Johns Hopkins University, which had a major program for transsexuals, has stopped the practice. Some psychiatrists argue that transsexuals are no better adjusted after surgery than transsexuals who do not receive surgery, but others insist that when transsexual candidates for surgery are carefully selected, they adjust well to their new anatomical sex.

Male transsexuals show feminine behavior at an early age—although most feminine boys do not become transsexuals. They like to dress in girls' clothes, play with girls, and avoid rough-and-tumble play and sports in favor of Barbie dolls and similar toys. When female transsexuals were compared with lesbians, researchers found a similar childhood behavior and play patterns, characterized by tomboyism, a preference for male playmates, and a disdain for dolls or motherhood. They were distinguished only by cross-dressing, which appeared after puberty only among the transsexuals. Psychological differences between the two groups were sharp: only lesbians had developed female gender identities and only trans-

Renée Richards, former coach of Martina Navratilova, is a well-known and successful transsexual. However, many transsexuals continue to have adjustment problems after their gender change.

sexuals had a highly negative reaction to breast development and menstruation (Ehrhardt, Grisanti, and McCauley, 1979).

Richard Green (1982a), who has studied transsexuals extensively, indicates that both early socialization and prenatal hormones may well be involved in the development of transsexuality. Despite the influence of early socialization, life with a transssexual parent appears to have little effect in pushing a child toward transsexuality. Studies of children reared by transsexual and homosexual parents show that such children develop gender identities like those of children reared by conventional parents (Green, 1978).

As research of transsexualism shows, social influences on the development of gender are strong, but interact with genes and hormones in a complex and not always predictable way.

HUMAN SEXUALITY: PHYSIOLOGICAL AND EVOLUTIONARY ASPECTS

Between the ages of ten and sixteen, boys and girls undergo the physiological and anatomical changes that make them men and women, capable of conceiving and bearing children. Signs of puberty become visible: they include breast buds and wider hips for girls, a mustache and wider shoulders in boys, pubic and axillary hair and, perhaps, acne in both sexes. Meanwhile, hormones are preparing the body for reproduction. The hypothalamus sends signals to the pituitary gland, which in turn sends signals to glands known as the gonads (the boy's testes, the girl's ovaries) to step up production of sex hormones (primarily androgen in boys, estrogen in girls). In this country most girls begin to menstruate at about age twelve and most boys ejaculate for the first time (often in a "wet dream") at age twelve or thirteen. (The timing of puberty varies considerably from individual to individual: these events may occur as early as age ten or as late as age sixteen.) Most adolescents become fertile a year or two later.

How does the human reproductive system work? A female is born with about 400,000 immature eggs, each enclosed in a tiny sac, or follicle. After puberty, one (or perhaps a few) of these eggs mature about every twenty-eight days. The female reproductive cycle can be divided into three phases (see Figure 13.1). In *Phase I*, the pituitary releases follicle-stimulating hormone (FSH) into the bloodstream. FSH stimulates the growth of a follicle. As this follicle matures, it begins to secrete the hormone estrogen, which causes the lining of the uterus to thicken in preparation for the implantation of a fertilized egg. Then, at mid-cycle, the pituitary releases a sudden burst of luteinizing hormone (LH). LH triggers **ovulation**: the follicle ruptures, releasing a mature egg which drifts out of the ovary to a nearby Fallopian tube and begins its journey down the tube toward the uterus. In

Phase II, the ruptured follicle, which has remained in the ovary, is transformed into a corpus luteum (or "yellow body"). The ovary secretes the hormone progesterone, which will nourish the fertilized egg if the woman becomes pregnant. If the egg is not fertilized, it disintegrates in the uterus, the corpus luteum shrivels, levels of progesterone and estrogen plummet, and the blood-rich lining separates from the wall of the uterus. It leaves the body in the process known as menstruation; this is *Phase III*. The low levels of estrogen in the bloodstream signal the pituitary to produce FSH, and the cycle begins once again. Women remain fertile until menopause, or the cessation of menstruation, which usually occurs sometime around the age of fifty.

In some ways, **spermatogenesis** (the production of sperm) in men is similar to ovulation in women. The male pituitary also releases FSH and LH. (In men, LH is called interstitial cell-stimulating hormone [ICSH], but the two hormones are chemically identical.) FSH and LH (or ICSH), in turn, stimulate the testes to produce sperm, and also to produce the hormone testosterone, which plays a role in sexual arousal. When testosterone levels fall, the pituitary releases FSH

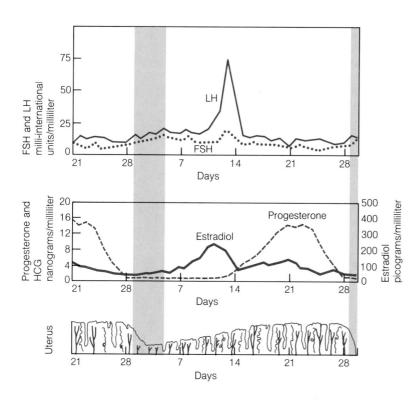

Figure 13.1. (above) Hormone levels during the menstrual cycle. (below) Changes in the uterine lining during a typical cycle. The rise in FSH level early in the cycle causes the ovaries to secrete estrogen. The LH peak brings on ovulation and the development of the corpus luteum. The latter secretes estrogen (estradiol) and progesterone in the second part of the cycle. If conception does not occur, the corpus luteum disintegrates, causing the endometrium to be shed. (Data from Christopher A. Adejuwon of the Population Council.)

and LH, triggering a new round of spermatogenesis. Men produce several billion sperm each year; an average ejaculation contains 300 to 500 million. Sperm take from sixty to seventy days to mature and can be stored in the body for up to six weeks. But the production of sperm is not cyclical, as ovulation is. And men remain fertile throughout their lives, though spermatogenesis may slow in old age.

Human reproductive physiology is similar to that of other mammals. But human sexual behavior is quite different. In most other species, sexual activity is tied to the female's reproductive cycle. The hormones that induce ovulation also cause changes in the female's behavior, called "estrus" (or, colloquially, "heat"). The female rat, for example, goes into estrus about every fifteen days (McClintock and Adler, 1978). If she spots a male of her species, she hops away, twists her head to see if he has noticed, wiggles her ears, and hops again. When the male approaches, she halts, arches her back, and moves her tail to one side, inviting him to mount—which he promptly does. When in estrus, the female rat will mate with any and every available male. When she is not in estrus, however, she will kick and scratch a male that attempts to mount or nuzzle her.

And so it is with most animals. Hormonal cycles determine when and if sexual activity will take place. For the most part, instincts dictate what positions and techniques will be used. There is some relaxation of hormonal control in our primate relatives. On occasion, female apes and monkeys will copulate when they are not fertile, perhaps to appease a dominant male or to maintain a relationship with a male companion. But this is relatively rare.

The human female is sexually unique. In contrast to other females, she can enjoy—or refuse—sex any day of the month, any month of the year. Some women report that at mid-cycle, when they are most likely to be fertile, they are more easily aroused and more likely to initiate sexual intercourse, and they experience orgasm more often. But many say they feel most interested in sex just before or after menstruation, when conception is impossible (McCauley and Ehrhardt, 1976), or that their interest in sex has no relationship to the time of the month. In one study (Hoon, Bruce, and Kinchloe, 1982), researchers asked women to listen to erotic tapes at different points in their menstrual cycle and report how they felt. The researchers established the date of ovulation for each woman and also measured their levels of physiological arousal. They found no mid-cycle peak and, indeed, no pattern. Women who have had their ovaries removed for medical reasons do not experience a drop in sexual interest or satisfaction (Waxenberg, 1969). Nor do women who take estrogen for medical reasons experience an increase in sexual arousal (Sopchak and Sutherland, 1960). There is some evidence that sexual activity can continue without benefit of hormones in men as well. Most men whose testes have been removed (for medical reasons or because they have committed repeated sex crimes) find that their sexual capacity and responsiveness decline. But some remain sexually active years later (Bremer, 1959; Heim, 1981).

This is not to say that hormones have *no* influence on human sexual behavior. A number of studies (summarized in Offir, 1982, pp. 102–106) have shown that high levels of sexual activity are associated with high levels of testosterone, in women as well as men. But this correlation does not prove cause and effect. Increases in testosterone may stimulate sexual activity, or increases in sexual arousal and activity may stimulate the production of testosterone.

What is clear is that for humans, cultural norms, social experiences, and psychological factors are far more important than biology in determining the who, where, when, and why of sex. The relaxation of hormonal controls explains the diversity of sexual practices among different cultures and the variety and subtleties of human lovemaking. Where sex is a strictly procreational activity in other animals, sex can be purely recreational for humans. Where sex is a seasonal event, tied to the female's cycle for most animals, sex can be an everyday event for humans. Compared to other creatures, humans are exceptionally sexually active animals. Thirty or forty years ago, few people knew (or admitted) this.

METHODS OF STUDYING SEXUAL BEHAVIOR

For the first half of this century, most of the data psychologists had about sexual behavior came from the memories and reports of people who had undergone psychotherapy. Today there is a wealth of data on sexual behavior, and it comes from a variety of sources.

Cross-Cultural Studies

The ways in which people learn about, experience, and express adult sexuality also vary widely from individual to individual and from culture to culture. There are cultures that approve homosexual relationships and even encourage them as a sexual outlet before marriage (Davenport, 1965). Other cultures permit masturbation among children, in polygamous marriages, and as an extramarital sexual activity. The average amount of sexual contact engaged in by members of our culture would be considered very low in some societies and very high in others (Ford and Beach, 1951).

Cross-cultural studies have forced a reconsideration of the kind of sexual practices that should be considered "abnormal," "unnatural," or "pathological." The wealth of information that has been gathered makes it harder for us to call many sexual practices that are unusual to us pathological. In general, only two sorts of sexual acts are now considered pathological: those that upset people who feel compelled to practice them (e.g., father-daughter incest) and those that are forced on an unwilling participant (such as rape). Clearly, what is abnormal is relative to the culture in which it is observed, and few practices are considered abnormal in every society.

Nevertheless, cross-cultural studies have also shown that every society imposes some restrictions on sexual behavior. Nowhere in the world are men and women free to do whatever they like, whenever, wherever, and with whomever they please.

Surveys

The first widespread sex surveys were done by Alfred C. Kinsey, a biologist and expert on gall wasps who in 1930 was asked to teach a course on sex education. Unable to find reliable information on sexual behavior, Kinsey decided to collect data himself (Pomeroy, 1966). He and his associates spent the next eighteen years talking to people of different ages, backgrounds, and marital status about their sex lives. The results of interviews with 5,300 American men, *Sexual Behavior in the Human Male* (1948), and with 5,940 women, *Sexual Behavior in the Human Female* (1953), made history—and headlines.

Kinsey's goal was to substitute facts about the sexual behavior of Americans for cultural myths

and to gather data on the population as a whole. His method was to collect sexual histories in detailed, confidential interviews, concentrating on Americans' "sexual outlets" (the number and kinds of sexual experiences they had). Kinsey's most controversial findings concerned premarital and extramarital sex (most men and many women reported such experiences) and homosexual experiences (which he found were far more common than anyone cared to believe).

The Kinsey study relied on volunteers—"self-selected" subjects. It did not include major segments of the population—in particular black, rural, and poorly educated Americans. It did report on what white, well-educated volunteers *said* they did or did not do sexually in America in the 1940s. Until the mid-1960s, Kinsey's were the only comprehensive data on American sexual behavior, and they provided the foundation for most contemporary research on human sexuality.

Observational Studies

Shortly after the Kinsey studies were released, William Masters and Virginia Johnson launched the first observational study of human sexual behavior. Their goal was to concentrate "quite literally upon what men and women do in response to effective sexual stimulation . . . rather than on what people say they do or even think their sexual reactions and experiences might be" (Masters and Johnson, 1966, p. 20). Volunteers were recruited to masturbate and have intercourse in a laboratory where their physiological responses to sexual stimulation could be observed closely. Women, for example, masturbated with an artificial penis equipped with a light and camera. Over twelve years, 694 men and women participated, most of them married couples, allowing the Masters and Johnson team to observe some 10,000 sexual episodes.

The value of these observational studies was limited in that the volunteers, as in the Kinsey survey, may have been atypical. Sexual experiences in a laboratory may be quite different from similar experiences at home in private; and the presence of observers no doubt influenced some aspects of the subjects' behavior. Nevertheless, Masters and Johnson's research has led to a fuller understanding of the human sexual response and of human sexual problems.

Controlled Experimentation

The studies of human sexual behavior we have been describing are essentially descriptive: from them we learn *what* occurs, but not *why*. The influence of various factors on sexual behavior can be examined only through controlled experiments in which specific hypotheses can be tested and discarded.

A study by Julia Heiman (1975) comparing the sexual arousal of men and women in response to pornography illustrates this kind of research. Heiman made direct measurements of physiological signs of arousal in men and women as they listened to tapes of erotic material. The subjects were

Recent research suggests that men and women find explicitly sexual material more arousing than romantic stimuli alone. Women watching a male stripper would be just as likely to get aroused as men watching a female stripper.

divided into four groups: group 1 listened to *erotic* tapes that contained explicitly sexual material; group 2 heard *romantic* tapes that described a tender and affectionate episode in which there was no sexual contact; group 3 listened to an *erotic-romantic* tape that conveyed both explicit sexuality and affection; and group 4 heard a *control* tape in which there was neither sex nor romance.

The physiological measures indicated a clear difference in arousal levels among the four groups. The men and women who heard explicitly sexual material—those in groups 1 and 3—showed high levels of arousal. In contrast, little sexual arousal was recorded among groups 2 and 4.

The results refuted the stereotypical notion that women find romance and affection more arousing than nonemotional sex. Females and males alike showed the same low-level response to the romantic tape as to the control tape. Nor did adding romance to explicit sex (group 3) heighten arousal in women. Thus, by using a controlled experiment, the researcher was able to show that both men and women are aroused by the same kind of erotic material.

As we have seen, there are limitations to every method of studying human sexual behavior. Such studies raise both practical and ethical questions. From a practical standpoint, sexual behavior is so complex that designing an experiment that mirrors sexual response in the world is extremely difficult. From an ethical standpoint, sexual experiments—unless they are part of a therapy program—often evoke intense community reaction and could have unknown effects upon the subjects. For example, showing children pornography in an attempt to assess the effects of childhood experiences on later sexual responses as an adult would clearly be unethical. Because of such problems, few experimental studies have been done on human beings. Experimental studies with animals have provided some information, but such data have limited value because of the difficulty of relating the results to human beings.

THE HUMAN SEXUAL RESPONSE

All healthy men and women are physiologically equipped to respond to sexual stimulation—both physical stimulation (touching and being touched by hands, lips, body, and perhaps objects) and psychological stimulation (provocative sights, sounds, and behavior, and erotic fantasies). Furthermore, as we shall see, men and women experience similar physiological reactions to sexual stimulation.

The Physiology of Arousal and Orgasm

Although no two people react to stimulation in exactly the same way, Masters and Johnson (1966) found that the sexual response in both men and women can be divided into four phases —excitement, plateau, orgasm, and resolution.

During the **excitement phase**, the heart begins to beat faster and the respiration rate increases. Blood flows into the genitals, causing the penis to become erect and the clitoris to swell. Drops of moisture form on the vaginal walls. Women's (and some men's) nipples may become erect, and women may develop a "sex flush" (a reddening, usually beginning on the chest, caused by the dilation of small blood vessels in the skin) over the body.

In the **plateau phase**, the genitals become fully engorged with blood. The clitoris retracts into its hood, though it remains highly sensitive. The entrance to the vagina contracts by as much as 50 percent; the uterus rises slightly, causing the inside of the vagina to balloon. The glans of the penis enlarges and deepens in color. Some fluid (which can contain live sperm) may seep out the opening of the penis as this happens. The testes swell and pull up higher within the scrotum. As excitement reaches a peak, the feeling that orgasm is inevitable sweeps over the individual.

During **orgasm**, muscular contractions force the blood that has been collecting in the genitals back into the bloodstream. The muscles around the vagina push the vaginal walls in and out and the uterus pulsates. The muscles in and around the penis contract rhythmically, causing **ejaculation**—the discharge of fluid, which is called **semen** and contains sperm. For both men and women, the first five or six orgasmic contractions are the strongest and the most pleasurable. In both sexes, the anus also contracts during orgasm, and experiments indicate that by monitoring anal blood flow and anal contractions, researchers will be able to compare the physiological orgasmic responses of men and women (Bohlen, Held, and Sanderson, 1980). Some people also experience intense muscle spasms in their faces

and limbs during orgasm, and some cry out uncontrollably; others show few obvious signs of orgasm.

The body gradually returns to its normal state during the **resolution phase**. Muscle tension dissipates and the genitals return to their usual size and shape.

Masters and Johnson found that the sexual response cycle is physiologically the same for all orgasms, whether produced by intercourse or masturbation. Masturbatory orgasms are often more intense physically, probably because the individual has precise control over the kind and intensity of stimulation. Masturbation may be less emotionally satisfying than intercourse, however (Masters and Johnson, 1966).

The subjective experience of sexual arousal, like the physiology of arousal, appears to be basically the same in men and women. A group of gynecologists, psychologists, and medical students who were asked to read descriptions of orgasm written by twenty-four male and twenty-four female subjects guessed the writer's sex in some cases, but no more often than would be expected by chance (Vance and Wagner, 1976).

Although the pattern of sexual response is the same, there are some physiological differences between the sexes. First, only men ejaculate at orgasm. Second, men experience a **refractory period**—a period of time (ranging from minutes to hours or even days) that must pass after an orgasm before they can become sexually aroused again. In contrast, women may experience **multiple orgasms**, one after another, without going through the resolution phase in between (see Figure 13.2). Although some men have reported multiple orgasms, a close analysis of the reports indicates that their response differs sharply from that of women who have several orgasms within a few minutes (Robbins and Jensen, 1978). In males who report multiple orgasms, the orgasms are spaced over an hour or more, and it appears that these men either have an extremely short refractory period or that they stop an orgasm each time it begins—before semen is ejaculated—allowing the orgasm to proceed to completion only at the final climax.

Stimulation and Arousal

As we have seen, both men and women respond consistently to effective sexual stimulation wheth-

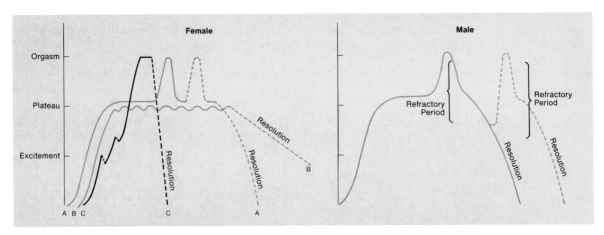

Figure 13.2. Graphs summarizing Masters and Johnson's description of coitus in the human male and female. The four phases are defined in terms of measurable physiological changes. In both sexes excitement leads to a plateau phase that may be maintained for considerable periods without orgasm. The male has only one pattern of response after this: he ejaculates quickly in orgasm, and his arousal decreases rapidly. There is a period after his ejaculation, the refractory period, in which he is incapable of another ejaculation. He may repeat the orgasmic phase several times before returning to an unaroused state. The female may variously have one orgasm or several orgasms in succession (line A), not achieve orgasm at all and return relatively slowly to an unaroused state (line B), or, rarely, have a single prolonged orgasm followed by rapid resolution (line C).

er the source is psychological or physical (Masters and Johnson, 1962). Physiological arousal in response to erotic materials, such as sexually explicit pictures or stories, takes the same form as the arousal that occurs in the initial stages of intercourse (Byrne and Byrne, 1978). But since learning plays a significant role in determining sexual responsiveness, effective sexual stimulation is not the same for everyone.

Touch is the most obvious source of sexual arousal. Certain areas of the body, called **erogenous zones**, are particularly sensitive to touch (the glans of the penis, the clitoris, the mouth, the nipples, the inside of the thighs). Other less obvious areas (the palms, the lower back) also may be highly sensitive. The degree of sensitivity depends on the individual, with one person being almost totally insensitive in an erogenous zone where another is so sensitive that touch is somewhat painful.

Odors exert a powerful influence on mating activity in most animals—even to the extent that placing urine from the receptive female mouse onto the back of a male mouse will incite other male mice to sexually assault the fragrant male (Connor, 1972). Although studies indicate that women are more sensitive than men to odors emitted by the opposite sex, experiments have been unable to establish any clear effects of such

olfactory stimuli among human beings (Rogel, 1978). However, the increasingly popular belief that odors do influence human sexual behavior is reflected in the marketing of odorous substances as aphrodisiacs and in the way perfumes are advertised.

The popularity of erotic films, magazines, and books testifies to the effectiveness of visual stimulation, with both women and men responding to such materials (Heiman, 1975). Fantasies—the pictures in our own minds—may be the most powerful stimulant of all. Males in two studies were able to either decrease (Laws and Rubin, 1969) or increase (Rubin and Henson, 1975) the vigor of their erections through fantasy. In another study, adults who were instructed to imagine sexually exciting situations became more aroused than others who saw explicit slides or read explicit stories (Byrne and Lambreth, 1971). Sexual fantasies frequently accompany intercourse, even among people who are sexually well adjusted and find their partners sexually attractive. For example, 65 percent of suburban housewives reported that they sometimes had erotic fantasies during sexual intercourse with their husbands; 37 percent had fantasies most of the time. Fantasies about imaginary lovers and submission to a dominating male were common. Interviews with these women indicated that their fantasies enhanced their sexual responsiveness (Hariton and Singer, 1974).

Sexual Responsiveness and Aging

Most of us think of sexuality as something that emerges at puberty, reaches full strength in early adulthood, gradually fades with increasing age, and eventually stops. The "sex symbols" of our culture are almost invariably young, attractive men and women, and we often have difficulty imagining that children and older adults are also sexual beings. But surveys and observations have found sexual activity throughout the life span. In the studies of Kinsey and his associates (1948; 1953), men sixty-five and older generally reported having sexual activity about four times a month, typically with their wives. Of the older married men and women in the Kinsey samples, 25 to 30 percent said they supplemented intercourse with another sexual outlet, masturbation. Subsequent studies have found essentially the same thing: most old people who have an available partner maintain relatively vigorous sex lives. Those who are most sexually active tend to be those who also were most sexually active in their youth (Newman and Nichols, 1960).

Some physiological changes do occur with aging; hormone production generally decreases in both sexes and gradual changes in sexual functioning follow. As women and men become older, it takes more intense physical stimulation for a longer period of time to produce adequate vaginal lubrication and penile erection. Elderly men who have sexual intercourse several times a week find that although sex is satisfactory, they do not ejaculate on every occasion. With age less semen is emitted in any single ejaculation, and the intensity of orgasmic contractions decreases. None of these changes diminishes the pleasure of sexual activity; in fact, their effect is to make sexual intercourse last longer than it once did. By showing that there is no physiological reason for stopping sexual activity with advancing age (Masters and Johnson, 1970), modern sex research may have encouraged more people to enjoy sexual activity throughout life.

Sexual Problems and Therapy

There are times when a person cannot be aroused or satisfied sexually. The individual may be tired, preoccupied, drunk, angry at the partner, anxious about "performing" well, or simply uninterested in sex at the time. This happens to everyone on occasion. However, for some individuals it is a recurring experience that can become very upsetting. Any problem that prevents an individual from engaging in sexual relations or from reaching orgasm during sex is known as a **sexual dysfunction**. It is important to recognize that this term applies only to problems in sexual *response*, not to sexual preferences or what are sometimes called, inappropriately in many cases, "deviations" (the choice of unusual sex objects or modes of gratification). For example, a couple who prefers oral-genital sex or mutual masturbation to intercourse is not dysfunctional, so long as both partners are satisfied with their activities.

Sexual Dysfunctions in Men and Women

In everyday conversation the term "impotence" is often used to describe all forms of male sexual dysfunction. Similarly, the term "frigidity" is applied to all manner of female sexual problems, with the implication that the woman is totally unresponsive, cold emotionally as well as sexually. As popularly used, neither term tells us what precisely the problem is. And they incorrectly suggest an invariably permanent rejection of sexuality. One of the goals of sex researchers has been to replace these overgeneralized, pejorative labels with more precise definitions of specific dysfunctions.

Psychologists now reject the term "impotence" and instead use the term **erectile failure** to describe a man's inability to achieve or maintain an erection. Some men have never been able to achieve or maintain an erection (a rare condition known as **primary erectile failure**). Much more common is **secondary erectile failure**, in which men who have experienced no erectile failure with a partner in the past are unable to achieve or maintain an erection in some or all sexual situations. For other men arousal is not the problem. Some acquire an erection easily but ejaculate before they or their partners would like. This is called **premature ejaculation**, and it appears to be the most prevalent complaint among male college students (Werner, 1975). Other men can achieve and maintain an erection but are unable to ejaculate during sex with a partner—a problem called **inhibited ejaculation**. Secondary erectile failure, premature ejaculation, and inhibited ejaculation afflict most males at one time or another. Only when they are extremely persistent and are upsetting to the individual should they be considered dysfunctional.

Some women suffer from **vaginismus**, involuntary muscle spasms that cause the vagina to shut tightly so that penetration by the male partner's penis is extremely painful. In many cases, the vaginal spasms are so severe that sexual intercourse is impossible, and the couple eventually seeks sexual therapy so that their marriage can be consummated. Other women engage in, and often enjoy, sexual intercourse but do not experience orgasms. The term **primary orgasmic dysfunction** refers to the situation of women who have never experienced an orgasm through any means. The expression **secondary** (or **situational**) **orgasmic dysfunction** refers to the situation of women who experience orgasms sometimes, through certain kinds of stimulation (such as masturbation), but not with their primary sexual partner or not during sexual intercourse. Secondary orgasmic dysfunction is a common complaint among female college students (Werner, 1975). As with most of the male problems, difficulties women may have in experiencing orgasm can be viewed as part of normal human variation and are not necessarily considered dysfunctional. Most research (e.g., Kinsey et al., 1953; Hunt, 1974) indicates that about a third of all women do not regularly have orgasms during intercourse. If these women enjoy intercourse, find it pleasurable and arousing, and can reach orgasm through oral or manual manipulation, they are considered sexually normal by most sex therapists (LoPiccolo, 1978).

It is not clear why some people respond freely to sexual stimulation but others do not. Research has revealed that most sexual problems have no physiological basis (Masters and Johnson, 1970). Instead, for some psychological reason, people are unable to abandon themselves to sexual pleasure. Some of these problems may be related to conflicts within the individual experiencing them, while others may be related to conflicts between partners. Therapists often find that many people who seek help for sexual problems were brought up with rigid religious, moral, or social standards concerning sex. Intellectually they may have rejected the belief that sex is wrong, but emotionally or psychologically they have not.

Other psychological sources of sexual problems range from having been the victim of "innocent" ridicule of one's anatomy in childhood to having suffered outright sexual abuse. Fear of failure may also cause sexual dysfunction. An individual may have one disappointing experience, then begin to wonder about his or her sexual adequacy. This anxiety can interfere with free response during the next sexual encounter, and the next, confirming the person's self-doubt. Thus, fear of sexual failure sometimes becomes a self-fulfilling prophecy.

At times, however, physiological factors are responsible for sexual dysfunction. In perhaps 5 to 10 percent of men with erectile failure, hormonal abnormalities may be responsible (Bancroft, 1983). Other conditions, such as severe diabetes, may also be associated with sexual dysfunction in men. Certain prescription medications may also alter the male sexual response. Sometimes it is possible to distinguish between physiologically and psychologically based erectile failure by monitoring bodily activity during sleep. Approximately every ninety minutes during sleep, most healthy males have periods of erection that are associated with REM sleep (see Chapter 7), and these nocturnal erections can be detected by the use of devices that record changes in the diameter of the penis. Men whose erectile failure is due to psychological factors will usually have regular erections during sleep; those whose erectile failure is due to physiological factors will not.

Sex Therapy

In the approach to sex therapy developed by Masters and Johnson (1970), the couple is always treated as a unit by a pair of sex therapists, one male and one female. The focus is on the sexual relationship, on education, on the reduction of sexual anxiety, and on changing sexual behavior. Usually, to lessen the fear of failure, the couple is told not to engage in sexual intercourse for the time being and is assigned "nondemanding" sensual exercises, such as massaging each other. Gradually, more sexual activities are introduced, until at last the couple is permitted to engage in sexual intercourse.

Although many of the techniques developed by Masters and Johnson are still used, both the philosophy and methods of sex therapy have broadened during the past decade. Today sex therapists believe that sex is not always an isolated problem; thus they look at the couple's entire relationship, considering cognitive and emotional factors that affect it and applying techniques from various therapeutic approaches. The couple is helped to resolve conflicts, so that the division of household chores as well as sexual techniques can come within the scope of sex therapy (Heiman, LoPiccolo, and LoPiccolo, 1980).

The conditions of therapy have also changed. There may be only a single therapist, and people may be treated individually or in groups. Educational films and books may be used, and self-help techniques are sometimes prescribed in the treatment of premature ejaculation or orgasmic dysfunctions. Training in directed masturbation is often a part of the treatment for primary orgasmic dysfunction (Heiman, LoPiccolo, and LoPiccolo, 1980).

The fact that the couple is "given permission" to try out new activities by an authority figure (the therapist) may be therapeutic in itself. In most cases, sex therapy is brief (ten to fifteen sessions) but intensive. When the therapy is successful, a couple will find increased pleasure and satisfaction in sexual intercourse. Both partners will also develop a greater acceptance of themselves and of their individual differences.

Sexual behavior

As with other drive-related behavior, such as eating, sexual activities vary with cultural and personal characteristics: just as we develop specific tastes in food, so do we develop specific tastes in sexual partners and in the occasions on which we desire them. Furthermore, what we ourselves do, or refuse to do, often defines for us the bizarre or deviant: although some people consider oral-genital sex natural and pleasurable, others find it disgusting. The line between what one person considers "variations" and another considers "deviations" is a fine and difficult one to draw, and often depends on who is doing the drawing. In sexual preferences and practices, the range of human variability is wide.

Celibacy

Celibacy, or complete abstinence from sexual activity, seems unusual to most people, although some religious orders, such as the Catholic clergy,

have idealized it as a preferred way of life. Until recently, coaches imposed pledges of temporary chastity on athletes in training, in the belief that regular sexual activity saps a person's strength. (There is no evidence for this belief.)

The percentage of people who choose permanent celibacy as a way of life is small. Most people go through periods of temporary chastity—in youth, after the breakup of a marriage or romance, and after the death of a spouse. Since surveys and studies of sexual activity have told us little about sexual inactivity, we know little about how people who have become accustomed to regular sex adjust to life without sex.

Masturbation

Attitudes toward masturbation have changed during the last two decades. Forty or fifty years ago physicians regularly warned youngsters that self-stimulation (or "self-abuse," as masturbation was then called) would cause acne, fever, blindness, even insanity. Today most people know that this is nonsense. According to a survey of more than 2,000 Americans, masturbation is thought to be wrong by only 15 percent of males and 14 percent of females eighteen to twenty-four years old and by 29 percent of males and 36 percent of females over fifty-five (Hunt, 1974). However, most adults are somewhat ashamed and secretive about masturbating. Few admit to their mates or friends that they occasionally stimulate themselves. Apparently the idea lingers that "playing with oneself" is immature behavior, symptomatic of personal inadequacies or of dissatisfaction with one's spouse as a sexual partner.

Yet surveys indicate that masturbation is common. In a survey by Morton Hunt (1974), 65 percent of the men said they had begun masturbating by age thirteen, compared with 45 percent in the sample of Kinsey and his associates (1948). The percentage of women who said that they had masturbated by age thirteen jumped from 15 percent in 1953 (Kinsey et al., 1953) to 40 percent in 1974. Masturbation rates increased most among women, with 82 percent of the women in Hunt's sample reporting that they masturbated regularly. The average rate was about every ten days—twice as often as in Kinsey's report.

Was the Hunt survey truly representative? Though it was sponsored by the Playboy Foundation, it was not a survey of *Playboy* readers. Data were collected from 2,000 subjects by a private research organization. An effort was made to match subjects to the proportions of married and single, black and white, high school and college graduates, urban and rural people in the population at large. Although not a truly random sample, it is more representative than most sex surveys (Offir, 1982, p. 42).

Some theorists believe that early experiences with masturbation help to establish the foundation for adult sexuality. According to this view, self-stimulation is an important part of self-discovery.

Heterosexuality

Probably the most common sexual activity is heterosexuality, a man and a woman stimulating each other sexually. But what couples do together varies from day to day, year to year, and couple to couple. Standard sexual intercourse (penis in vagina) is only one possibility. Many heterosexual couples enjoy petting to orgasm, oral-genital stimulation, anal intercourse, intercourse between the thighs, dressing in fantasy costumes, and other forms of sex play. There is no "normal" position for intercourse itself, which may take place in as many positions as imagination and agility allow.

Premarital Sex

In Kinsey's day, most Americans claimed that they strongly disapproved of premarital sex. Yet 98 percent of men with a grade-school education, 85 percent of male high school graduates, and 68 percent of men with a college education told investigators they had had sexual intercourse before getting married (Kinsey et al., 1948). Nearly half the women in the sample of Kinsey and his associates (1953) had also had premarital sexual experience, and over half of these had had intercourse only with their future husbands.

Since the time of the Kinsey reports, the incidence of premarital sex for men appears to have increased somewhat, particularly among college men. By age seventeen, half the college men in the Hunt sample (1974) were no longer virgins, compared with 23 percent in Kinsey's sample (1948). The biggest change for college men may be in the women they choose as partners. In Kinsey's day, sex partners for most single young men were prostitutes or casual pickups. Today most college men have sex with women they care deeply for and with whom they have a continuing relationship (McCary, 1978).

This behavior may change in the next generation, however. Surveys of adolescents (Hass, 1979; Sorenson, 1973) find that most young men and

In recent years, the incidence of premarital sex has increased. One result of this trend is a rise in the number of teenage pregnancies, leading to conflicting points of view on whether to make birth control information and devices easily available to teens.

women feel that marriage is not a precondition for sex; that couples should find out whether they are sexually compatible *before* they get married; and that sexual intercourse is permissible when a couple have no plans to get married if the two really like each other.

Among women, the incidence of premarital sex has increased dramatically. In the Hunt sample (1974), 81 percent of the women aged eighteen to twenty-four had sexual intercourse before they were married—compared with only 31 percent of the women fifty-five and older. However, the majority of the women in the Hunt survey were no more casual about sex than their mothers had been. Over half had had sex with only one partner. In contrast, the median number of premarital sex partners for men was six.

The double standard persists, with one code of acceptable sexual behavior for men, another for women. In the Hunt sample, 60 percent of the men and 37 percent of the women thought it was all right for men to have sex with someone for whom they felt no strong affection; only 44 percent of the men and 20 percent of the women thought it was all right for women to do so—with men granting women more sexual freedom than women allowed themselves.

Extramarital Sex

About half the husbands and a quarter of the wives in the sample of Kinsey and his associates (1948; 1953) had had sexual intercourse with someone other than their spouse while they were married. To judge from the Hunt survey (1974), the percentage of married men who "play around" has not changed much since the 1940s, but the percentage of married women who do—especially young wives—has. Twenty-four percent of the wives under age twenty-five in the Hunt sample claimed to have had extramarital sexual experiences, compared to 8 percent in the Kinsey sample. But again, women are more conservative. Twice as many husbands as wives have had sex with six or more extramarital partners. According to the Hunt survey, it seems that men are more likely than women to seek extramarital sex without emotional involvement. Women are less likely to separate sexual desire from affection; they tend to embark on affairs only when they are dissatisfied with their marriages.

Although the proportion of people who have extramarital sex is rising, attitudes toward the practice have not changed. More than 80 percent of the couples in the Hunt survey (1974) regarded it as wrong.

Homosexuality

Who is a homosexual? In the United States the tendency has been to label anyone who has had any homosexual experience, however infrequent, as homosexual. However, surveys have shown that sexual experimentation between members of the same sex is relatively common during adolescence (Kinsey et al., 1948). In the view of most psychologists, a **homosexual** is a person whose primary

Homosexuality is a sexual preference for members of one's own gender. No longer classified as a disorder by the American Psychiatric Association, its causes remain unclear despite extensive research.

Table 13.1 ▪ Heterosexual-Homosexual Ratings (Ages 20—35)

Category		In Females (Percent)	In Males (Percent)
0	Entirely heterosexual experience		
	Single	61–72	53–78
	Married	89–90	90–92
	Previously married	75–80	
1–6	At least some homosexual experience	11–20	18–42
2–6	More than incidental homosexual experience	6–14	13–38
3–6	As much homosexual experience as heterosexual experience, or more	4–11	9–32
4–6	Mostly homosexual experience	3–8	7–26
5–6	Almost exclusively homosexual experience	2–6	5–22
6	Exclusively homosexual experience	1–3	3–16

Source: From data in Kinsey et al. *Sexual behavior in the human female.* Philadelphia: W. B. Saunders, 1953, p. 488.

source of sexual gratification is members of the same sex.

This definition was reflected in a seven-point scale created by Kinsey and his associates (1948; 1953) for their surveys. At one extreme (category 0) were people who were exclusively heterosexual; at the other (category 6) were people who were exclusively homosexual. Individuals who were predominantly heterosexual or homosexual but had a passing interest in the other sex were assigned to categories 2 and 4, respectively. Category 3 was for bisexuals, who had about equal interest in members of their own and the opposite sex. In this way, Kinsey set up a continuum of sexual preferences and avoided dividing the world into two opposing camps, one exclusively heterosexual and the other exclusively homosexual. Since the Kinsey scale is based upon counting sexual acts, it may categorize people in a way that does not accord with their self-image. For example, people in category 3 may not feel equally drawn to men and women despite the similarity shown in their behavior.

In gathering statistics on homosexuality, the Kinsey team included reports of both psychological and physical arousal, as well as any erotic contact, whether or not it led to orgasm. The results are shown in Table 13.1. These figures are dated, but they are still the only comprehensive estimates we have of the incidence of homosexual behavior in the general population.

It is likely, however, that the results overrepresent the degree of homosexuality that occurs in the male population. Among the men the researchers interviewed were a large minority with no

higher education, many of whom had prison experience. In addition, they interviewed groups of men from homosexual organizations. A more accurate estimate of the proportion of exclusively homosexual men is between 3 and 4 percent. The estimate of Kinsey and his associates that between 2 and 3 percent of women are exclusively homosexual is probably more accurate, for those interviews contained no biased groups (Gagnon, 1977). Since the Kinsey researchers classified adolescent sexual explorations between people of the same sex as homosexual and since their male sample was biased, their estimates concerning people with varying degrees of homosexual preferences are also too high.

Researchers have found that whether a person is predominantly homosexual or heterosexual has little to do with the body's sexual response (Masters and Johnson, 1979). The same general pattern of arousal, excitement, and release can be identified in male and female homosexuals, in heterosexuals, and in those who respond to both sexes.

Psychologists have advanced two basic hypotheses to explain why some people choose sex partners of the same biological sex; one hypothesis is biochemical and the other stresses social learning. According to the biochemical hypothesis, the level of sex hormones helps to determine sexual preference. Although one team of researchers (Kolodny et al., 1971) found that homosexual males had lower levels of the male hormone testosterone and lower sperm counts than did a comparable group of heterosexuals, other studies have found no difference between such groups, and some studies have found higher testosterone levels among homosexuals (Meyer-Bahlburg, 1977). Studies with women have found normal levels of sex hormones in most female homosexuals, but elevated levels of male hormones in about a third of them (Meyer-Bahlburg, 1979). However, because female hormone levels fluctuate with the menstrual cycle, with the use of oral contraceptives, and with menopause, these findings do not demonstrate a link between male hormones and female homosexuality.

According to the second hypothesis, homosexuality is the product of early learning. One group of researchers (McGuire, Carlise, and Young, 1965) suggested the following developmental sequence:

■ *Step 1*. A "homosexual event" occurs. The individual engages in homosexual play, is approached by an older homosexual, or observes homosexual behavior.
■ *Step 2*. The individual fantasizes about this event while masturbating. Orgasm during masturbation reinforces the homosexual fantasy.
■ *Step 3*. When homosexual fantasies have been reinforced with orgasm, the individual is more likely to engage in overt homosexual behavior should the opportunity arise.

The peer group may play an important role in the development of homosexuality. Homosexuals of both sexes tend to report a preference for the company and the activities of the opposite sex during childhood. The resulting socialization within a peer group of the opposite sex may lead children to adopt the group's sexual orientation (Green, 1980).

Psychoanalytic hypotheses have also been advanced. It has been suggested that many male homosexuals had harsh fathers who did not allow their sons to be close to them. Hence, the sons did not identify with the fathers and did not learn the male role (Saghir and Robins, 1973). Others argue that male homosexuals had aggressive, domineering mothers and passive fathers (Bieber et al., 1962). In this case, too, a son might not form a strong masculine identity.

None of these hypotheses has been adequately documented. There is no more clear agreement on a single explanation of homosexual development than there is on a single theory of overall psychosexual development.

After reviewing a great deal of research on possible psychological and biological causes of homosexuality, Bell, Weinberg, and Hammersmith (1981) concluded that there was as yet insufficient evidence to support any of the many hypotheses that have been advanced. They did note, however, that sexual preference is usually evident by early adolescence; thus, whatever factors are operating seem to exert their influence early. Other recent research (Green, 1982b) has found that boys who display markedly "feminine" behavior from early childhood often grow up to be "effeminate" homosexuals. (This is not to say that all such boys are likely to become homosexuals; of those Green studied, about three-fourths did so. And of course most homosexual men were not noticeably "effeminate" as boys.)

An interactive explanation that combines biochemistry with social learning has been advanced by Green (1980), who suggests that inborn temperamental differences and behavioral predispositions (which may be linked with prenatal hormones) combine with the effects of parents and peer group to produce a child who develops in ways that are typical of the opposite sex. Early in the child's life, the parents make no attempt to discourage behavior that is typical of the opposite sex, the child gravitates to the opposite peer group, and the pattern of homosexual preference develops.

Traditionally, homosexuality has been considered a psychological disorder, but several years ago the American Psychiatric Association rejected the idea that homosexuality is a "disease" or that homosexuals are "sick." However, a number of psychiatrists continue to argue that homosexuality is necessarily a symptom of neurosis, immaturity, personality disorders, or faulty upbringing. The controversy is likely to continue.

The goals for homosexuals in therapy have shifted over the years. In the past therapists assumed that same-sex orientation was the root or symptom of other problems, and they concentrated on transforming homosexuals into heterosexuals despite the general agreement that this sort of conversion was extremely difficult to bring about. Today some therapists let their homosexual clients choose whether they want to change their sexual orientation or to become more comfortable with it. The problem is that, given this choice, many individuals may feel subtly pressured into saying that they want to change. Gerald Davison (1976), for one, argues that a therapist should never try to change a person's sexual orientation. The goal of therapy, he says, should be to enhance interpersonal relationships and perhaps sexual technique, with no reference to sexual preferences.

As for those persons who find their homosexuality a source of distress, therapy to change to a heterosexual response pattern may or may not be successful. Masters and Johnson (1979), who developed a method of sex therapy for homosexuals desiring to change their orientation, reported substantial success in this endeavor. But critics of their research have pointed out that most of those men successfully "converted" by Masters and Johnson's techniques were actually bisexual —either they were already able to function sexually with women some of the time, or they had been able to do so in the past (Coleman, 1982). When the homosexual pattern is exclusive and long-standing, it generally proves difficult to alter by therapy.

Deviant sexual behavior

Some forms of sexual behavior so strongly violate community norms that they are regarded with abhorrence and punished with lengthy prison sentences. In many societies, including the United States, rape and incest fall into the class of deviant sexual behavior, although both have at times been permitted in some cultures. In ancient Egypt, for example, the incestuous marriage of brother and sister was customary, while in wartime the rape of women has historically been considered the right of invading warriors (Brownmiller, 1975). Either rape or incest can result in physical or emotional harm to the victim.

Rape

When sexual intercourse with another person is the result of physical force, threat, or intimidation, it is called **rape**, and most psychologists feel that the primary motive for rape is not sex at all but anger or the assertion of power. In a study of 133 convicted rapists (Groth and Burgess, 1977), just over a third of the attacks were the result of anger; these rapes, which were unpremeditated,

were characterized by violent physical assault, insults, and acts considered degrading by the rapist. The rest of the rapes were an assertion of power; these rapes were planned in advance, fantasized about beforehand, and the rapist stalked the victim, using threats but no more force than was necessary to succeed. According to these investigators, rape—whether motivated by anger or power—can serve many purposes. It compensates for the rapist's feelings of helplessness, reassures the rapist about his sexual adequacy, asserts his identity, defends him against homosexual impulses, bolsters his status among peers, and discharges frustration as well as supplying sexual gratification.

The relative unimportance of sexual gratification in rape is shown by the characteristics of rapists. Most rapists are young, married, or dating women with whom they have sex on a voluntary basis, but either lack or believe they lack the ability to establish a satisfying, loving relationship with a woman (Rada, 1978). In studies (Abel, Blanchard, and Becker, 1978) similar to those used by Heiman (1975) to test male and female arousal to pornography, rapists and a control group of normal men both responded with erections to audio tape descriptions of mutually enjoyable intercourse, but only the rapists responded to descriptions of rape. In addition, a small group of rapists—presumably those who raped as a result of anger—responded sexually to tapes of aggression that had no sexual component. In these studies, normal men's reports of their own sexual arousal corresponded closely to their measured physical responses, but rapists consistently underestimated their own sexual arousal.

Although most rapists are male and most victims are female, such is not always the case. Men who rape other men are generally not homosexuals and are motivated not by sexual gratification but by power, revenge, sadism, status, or affiliation (Groth and Birnbaum, 1978). Their victims generally suffer greater physical injury than do female rape victims, and they are more likely than females to be subjected to gang rapes (Kaufman et al., 1980). Although women have been known to rape men, such cases are extremely rare; most women involved as aggressors in rapes are helping men rape another woman.

Victims of rape at first show acute disorganization, characterized by shock, disbelief, fear, and anxiety. They may lose their appetite, startle at minor noises, develop headaches, insomnia, or

Does Violent Pornography Cause Sex Crimes?

Pornography is intended to create sexual arousal, and nearly 80 percent of Americans have seen some kind of pornography—written material, photographs, or films displaying explicit sexual activity (Abelson et al., 1970). Most adolescents are exposed to such material, generally among groups of peers at school, at home, or in the neighborhood.

Although a number of public commentators have damned pornography as a bad influence on the public, an exhaustive study by a federal commission (Commission on Obscenity and Pornography, 1970) failed to find any ill effects from the availability of explicit films and publications.

But in the past few years, a new case has been made against pornography—this time not against all graphic depictions of sexual activity, but against those that involve violence against women. A number of feminist critics —some of them in an unlikely alliance with such religious groups, as the Moral Majority —have charged that violent pornography makes sex crimes against women more likely. These critics argue that depictions of assault, rape, and murder—the staple of so-called "snuff films"—essentially constitute advertising for violence against women.

Critics cite as evidence for their charges several recent studies that suggest that violent pornography does have a powerful effect on those who are exposed to it. In the most notable of these studies, a group of college men watched

two movies that featured sexual violence against women. Afterward, the men were given an attitude survey. They were found to be more likely to accept violence against women, and to a lesser extent to accept myths about rape, such as "many women have an unconscious wish to be raped" (Malamuth and Check, 1981). It should be noted that the movies seen by the men in this study were mainstream feature films—*Swept Away* and *The Getaway*—not X-rated films. If these comparatively mild depictions of rape and coercion can change men's attitudes, the critics argue, what about the ultra-graphic scenes of torture and mutilation that are part of some X-rated sex films? Are these not likely to have even more potent negative effects?

If violent pornography does have these ill effects, how does it bring them about? Social psychology can provide us with some insights: in joining sex and aggression, these images may act to condition their

viewers to accept the idea that this is a proper pairing (Malamuth and Donnerstein, 1982). Moreover, by presenting women as somehow wanting to be assaulted, the films give out a powerful bit of disinformation. This cognition —"women want it"—is implanted, or reinforced, in the minds of the viewers. And finally, the men on the screen, even if rapists and murderers, act as models for antisocial behavior.

Given these possible negative effects, critics of violent pornography have called for its absolute ban. But this, of course, raises the issue of censorship—a very thorny issue in a society that values freedom of expression. If violent pornography is to be eliminated, who is to define what is "violent"? Since no study has yet demonstrated that exposure to violent pornography actually causes rape, is censorship justified? This issue is likely to be the subject of intense and heated public discussion for some time to come.

fatigue; many have trouble maintaining normal family or occupational life. Some rape victims are plagued by frightening dreams or develop irrational fears (Burgess and Holstrom, 1974). Many are dysfunctional sexually; not surprisingly, after a rape women are often afraid of sex or unable to become sexually excited or experience orgasm. Such sexual dysfunctions may persist for years after the assault (Becker et al., 1982).

Incest

Sexual activity that takes place between closely related persons is called **incest**. Although some authorities apply the term "incest" only to genital intercourse, the term is generally expanded to include oral-genital contact, fondling of the genitals, and coerced masturbation to encompass sexual activity with very young girls (with whom genital intercourse is difficult) and homosexual incest (Meiselman, 1978). In recent years, some light has been shed on this taboo subject; books written by incest survivors and widely reported cases of child sexual abuse have brought out the fact that most children who are sexually molested are abused by their male relatives. Despite increasing recognition of the problem by the public, however, most cases of incest are not reported. Dependent children are rarely in a position to report their adult relatives to the authorities, and even when they do seek help, children who complain of incestuous assaults may not be believed.

Father-daughter incest has been the most intensively studied of all incestuous relationships. It is also one of the most destructive to the child, particularly when it begins when the daughter is very young. Fathers in such cases often have a history of emotional deprivation and psychological inadequacy, and it is not unusual for the incestuous father to molest several of his daughters —often starting with the eldest and proceeding to younger daughters. Not surprisingly, the families in which such relationships develop are often deeply troubled, with much hostility between husband and wife and between parents and children. The mother may condone assaults on her daughters, either actively or passively, and must be seen as partially responsible for the incest by failing to stop it (Mrazek, 1981).

Although early studies of incest associated it with poverty, lack of education, and social isolation, it is now known that incest occurs across the social strata, in all kinds of families—even those that appear normal, happy, and respectable to outside observers. Besides father-daughter incest, brother-sister incest is believed to be fairly common (some authorities assert that it is actually the most common type, but this has never been documented) (Mrazek, 1981). Occurring far more rarely are incestuous relations between mothers and sons, fathers and sons, and more distant relatives, such as grandfathers and granddaughters. Incest between mothers and daughters is exceedingly rare.

Whatever the incestuous relationship, most professionals agree that it is almost always psychologically damaging to the child. Generally, the younger the child and the closer the relationship, the more serious the emotional consequences. The young child, in a helpless and dependent position, is generally unable to say no to an incestuous advance, and he or she is simply not mature enough to cope with the strong conflicting feelings stirred up by sexual relations with a relative —particularly a parent. Therapists often see adult patients who were incest victims in childhood, and these adults often suffer from depression, self-abusive behavior, and sexual dysfunction:

> The late effects of these situations are seen in the tragic feelings of inferiority, non-integrated identity, poor basic trust, repressed anger, . . . and profound difficulties in establishing and maintaining warm, successful adult human relationships. (Steele and Alexander, 1981, p. 233)

Incest, then, often has serious consequences for the child victim—consequences that persist for years.

NEW ATTITUDES AND NEW PROBLEMS

The so-called sexual revolution of the 1960s and 1970s resulted in more openness about sex. Books on sexual techniques became best sellers, mainstream publications allowed more explicit references to sexual matters, and TV and radio talk shows explored sexual themes. Precisely how much people's sexual behavior actually changed during this period is a matter of dispute, however.

But survey evidence, as we saw earlier, suggests that at least some portions of the population are engaging in sexual activity at an earlier age and/or with more sexual partners.

This openness to sexual experience—in particular to experience with multiple partners—may have slacked off somewhat recently, both in the heterosexual and the homosexual populations. With the identification of two serious sexually transmitted diseases, genital herpes and AIDS, some people have chosen a more cautious approach to sexual exploration.

Herpes involves painful blisters on the genitals that develop after sexual activity with an infected person. The condition may recur periodically, and when it is in its active phase, it is contagious. For both sexes, herpes is a painful and unpleasant experience. For women, however, it carries two additional risks: herpes infection is associated with the development of cervical cancer, and it may be passed on to a fetus with very serious consequences (among them birth defects, brain damage, or death).

AIDS is acquired immune deficiency syndrome, a condition resulting from a virus that weakens the victim's immune system. The person then is attacked by opportunistic diseases, such as severe and unusual forms of cancer and pneumonia. In more than 70 percent of the cases, the AIDS victim is dead within two years (Allgeier and Allgeier, 1984). For unknown reasons, most victims of AIDS have been homosexual men. The disease, like herpes, is transmitted sexually, although it apparently can also be spread through exchange of body fluids, such as blood.

These two serious viral diseases—herpes, which is presently incurable, and AIDS, which is so often fatal—have led public health authorities to advise caution in sexual activities. In particular, engaging in sex with casual acquaintances, whose health status is unknown, has been labeled a risky practice. Whether the identification of these two diseases will produce any lasting changes in the sexual behavior of Americans remains to be seen.

SUMMARY

1. Gender is influenced by genetic, hormonal, and social factors. Genetic sex is determined at conception, when an ovum (which always has an X chromosome) is fertilized by a sperm having either an X chromosome (which produces a female) or a Y chromosome (which produces a male). When the testes or ovaries emerge, they produce hormones that complete the process of biological sex differentiation. Social influences on sexual development begin to operate as soon as a baby is born and affect both gender identity and gender role. Social factors seem able to override either genes or hormones, but may not always be able to overcome their combined effect. **Transsexualism**, in which gender identity is inconsistent with anatomical sex, confirms the need to consider gender identity and biological sex separately.

2. At puberty, males and females undergo physiological and anatomical changes that prepare their bodies for reproduction. In mature females, an egg matures during each twenty-eight-day cycle. In Phase I of the cycle, production of estrogen causes the lining of the uterus to thicken in preparation for the implantation of a fertilized egg. At mid-cycle, **ovulation** occurs: a mature egg is released from the ovary. In Phase II levels of the hormone progesterone rise, to nourish the fertilized egg during pregnancy. If the egg is not fertilized, estrogen and progesterone levels drop and Phase III, menstruation, begins: the blood-rich lining separates from the uterus and leaves the body. In males, **spermatogenesis**, the production of sperm, begins with the release of hormones that stimulate the testes to produce sperm and also to produce another hormone, testosterone, which plays a role in sexual arousal. Sperm take from sixty to seventy days to mature, and can be stored in the body for up to six weeks. Men produce several billion sperm a year. In most species of mammals, hormonal cycles determine when and if sexual activity will take place. Human sexual behavior, however, is quite different in that human females are biologically able to engage in sexual activity at any time, regardless of hormonal levels; there is also some evidence that sexual activity can

continue without benefit of hormones in men as well. In humans, cultural norms, social experiences, and psychological factors are far more important than biology in determining sexual activity.

3. The major methods of studying sexual behavior are cross-cultural studies, sexual surveys, observational studies, and controlled experiments. Cross-cultural studies disclose the wide variations in sexual behavior in different cultures and have forced a redefinition of which sexual practices should be considered abnormal. The most important surveys of sexual activity were conducted by Alfred C. Kinsey in the 1940s, and despite some methodological shortcomings, these surveys have provided the foundation for later research on human sexuality. The first observational study of human sexual behavior was conducted by William Masters and Virginia Johnson in the 1960s. Although this study also had shortcomings, it provided some understanding of human sexual response. Controlled experiments can isolate the influences of various factors on sexual behavior, although practical and ethical considerations limit their use with human beings.

4. Men and women respond physiologically to sexual stimulation in parallel ways, and their response can be divided into four basic phases: the **excitement phase,** the **plateau phase, orgasm,** and the **resolution phase.** The subjective experience of orgasm is similar for men and women, but there are some gender differences in orgasm: for instance, men experience a **refractory period** after orgasm, while women may experience **multiple orgasms.** Either psychological or physical stimulation has been shown to arouse both men and women, but effective sexual stimulation varies from person to person. Touch is one form of arousal, and the sensitivity of **erogenous zones** varies with the individual. Visual stimulation is very effective, but the role of odor in human sexual response has not been established. Fantasies may be the most powerful erotic stimulant of all. Despite the physiological changes that accompany aging, enjoyable sexual activity can continue throughout life.

5. Any problem that prevents an individual from engaging in sexual relations or from reaching orgasm is known as a **sexual dysfunction. Erectile failure** refers to a man's inability to

achieve or maintain an erection with a partner. In **primary erectile failure**, a man has never achieved or maintained an erection; in **secondary erectile failure**, a man has reached orgasm in the past but is unable to acquire or maintain an erection at present or in certain situations. **Premature ejaculation** means that a man ejaculates before he or his partner would like. **Inhibited ejaculation** refers to a man's inability to ejaculate during sex with a partner. **Vaginismus** is a condition in which a woman's vagina involuntarily clamps shut so that penetration by her partner's penis is impossible or extremely painful. In **primary orgasmic dysfunction**, a woman has never experienced an orgasm by any means; in **secondary orgasmic dysfunction**, a woman sometimes experiences orgasm but not with her present partner or not during intercourse. Most sexual dysfunction has a psychological basis, but physiological factors—such as hormonal deficits, severe diabetes, and certain prescription medications —can result in erectile failure.

6. People's sexual activities vary with their cultural and personal characteristcs. Although few people choose **celibacy** as a permanent way of life, most people go through periods of temporary chastity. Masturbation is common among both men and women, and relatively few people consider it wrong. Early experiences with masturbation may help to establish the foundation for adult sexuality. Heterosexual interaction, which can take a great number of forms, is probably the most common sexual activity. Although more men than women engage in premarital and extramarital sex, since the 1940s, premarital sex appears to have increased a little among men and a great deal among women. The proportion of women engaging in extramarital sex also is rising, although a majority of people consider such affairs as wrong. A **homosexual** is a person whose primary source of gratification is members of the same sex. Psychologists have advanced a variety of hypotheses—biochemical, learning, and psychoanalytic—to explain homosexual development, but have not reached agreement on any single explanation. As attitudes toward homosexuality have changed, therapy goals for homosexuals have shifted. All therapists once attempted to transform homosexuals into heterosexuals, but many now let

their clients decide whether to change their sexual orientation or to strive for greater acceptance of their homosexuality.

7. **Rape** is sexual intercourse with another person as the result of physical force, threat, or intimidation, and its primary motive is not sexual gratification but anger or the assertion of power. Rape can compensate for a rapist's feelings of helplessness, assert his identity, defend him against homosexual impulses, bolster his status among his peers, or discharge his frustration. Victims of rape may show shock, disbelief, fear, or anxiety; they may have trouble maintaining a normal family or occupational life. Many are dysfunctional sexually, sometimes for years after the assault. **Incest** is sexual activity between two closely related persons. Most cases are not reported because dependent children are seldom in a position to report their adult relatives to authorities and also may not be believed. Incest occurs in all kinds of families and across the social strata; such families are often deeply troubled. Incestuous relationships are almost always psychologically damaging to the child; the younger the child, the more serious the emotional consequences, which often include depression, self-abusive behavior, and sexual dysfunction in adulthood.

8. Survey evidence suggests that at least some portions of the population have been engaging in sexual activity at an earlier age and/or with more sexual partners. However, the identification of two serious sexually transmitted diseases—genital herpes and AIDS (acquired immune deficiency syndrome)—has led some people to take a more cautious approach to sexual exploration.

KEY TERMS

androgen insensitivity syndrome
androgens
celibacy
ejaculation
erectile failure
erogenous zones
excitement phase
homosexual
incest
inhibited ejaculation

multiple orgasms
orgasm
ovulation
plateau phase
premature ejaculation
primary erectile failure
primary orgasmic dysfunction
rape
refractory period
resolution phase

secondary erectile failure
secondary (or situational)
    orgasmic dysfunction
semen
sexual dysfunction
spermatogenesis
transsexualism
Turner's syndrome
vaginismus

RECOMMENDED READINGS

BANCROFT, J. *Human sexuality and its problems.* New York: Churchill-Livingston, 1983. An advanced text which goes into considerable detail on sexual dysfunctions, deviations, gender problems, and so forth.

BREHM, S. S. *Intimate relationships.* New York: Random House, 1985. This research-based text focuses on the process of intimate relationships, beginning with the first attraction and moving through the various issues that may arise, including those in even the most mature relationships.

Clear, up-to-date, and concise discussions of theory and research characterize this text.

FORISHA, B. L. *Sex roles and personal awareness.* Glenview, Ill.: Scott, Foresman, 1978. An up-to-date, lucid presentation of the complex issue of gender role development.

KAPLAN, H. S. *The evaluation of sexual disorders.* New York: Brunner/Mazel, 1982. The most recent work of a well-respected sex therapist, emphasizing diagnosis and new treatment techniques for sexual problems.

KINSEY, A. C., W. B. POMEROY, and C. E. MARTIN. *Sexual behavior in the human male.* Philadelphia: Saunders, 1948.

KINSEY, A. C., W. B. POMEROY, C. E. MARTIN, and P. H. GEBHARDT. *Sexual behavior in the human female.* Philadelphia: Saunders, 1953.The classic "Kinsey studies" of sexual behavior, which provided the first broad survey and comprehensive statistics concerning the sexual behaviors of Americans.

LoPICCOLO, J., and L. LoPICCOLO (Eds.).*Handbook of sex therapy.* New York: Plenum Press, 1978. A comprehensive and mature presentation of the principles and techniques of modern sex therapy.

MASTERS, W. H., and V. E. JOHNSON. *Human sexual response.* Boston: Little, Brown, 1966. Based on observational studies, this was the first thoroughly detailed account of the physiological changes that accompany sexual arousal and orgasm.

ROSEN, R., and E. HALL. *Sexuality.* New York: Random House, 1984. A personalized approach to the study of human sexuality, with an emphasis on common problems.

TALESE, G. *Thy brother's wife.* New York: Dell, 1981 (paper). An account by a well-known novelist and journalist of his investigations into sex in America.

PART FIVE

HUMAN DEVELOPMENT THROUGH THE LIFE SPAN

Whenever something about cloning hits the headlines, there is always a spurt of interest from the public. What if human beings can be cloned? What if a living cell can be scraped off your little toe and its nucleus substituted for the nucleus of an egg cell and the new cell implanted into a woman's womb? In that case, an embryo could develop and a baby be born with exactly your genes. Wouldn't it be you born again? Wouldn't you have a chance of achieving immortality in this way? I suspect that most popular interest in cloning arises out of just this perception of cloning as the pathway to personal immortality.

That is, however, entirely wrong. It is possible for two human beings to have precisely the same set of genes. It happens every eighty births or so when identical twins are born. These twins, however, do not share the same personality; they don't possess a single consciousness. They are two different people. If one twin dies, he or she does not continue living simply because an identical twin survives.

A clone of a human being is not that human being but is rather an identical twin of that human being, and dreams of immortality by such a device are simply fantasy.

In fact, a clone is less than an identical twin in the ordinary sense of the word. To suppose otherwise is to place too much stress on gene content. The gene pattern does indeed fix many things—the color of your eyes, the possession of certain inborn metabolic anomalies, and so on. But not everything is set in concrete at the moment of conception.

The development of an embryo surely depends to some extent on the maternal environment before birth. Expectant mothers can vary in health, in nourishment, in the functioning of the womb and placenta.

Ordinary identical twins do, at least, develop in the same womb under similar circumstances. If a clone were to be formed, a fertilized ovum formed from the nucleus of a grown person would be placed into a womb different from the one in which that grown person developed as an embryo. Even if the person's mother were still available and capable of bearing children, she would nevertheless be some decades older by that time, and conditions would surely be different.

And there is more to development than that. Even if we ignore differences in maternal environment, what about differences after birth—social and psychological differences?

Suppose human cloning had been developed decades ago so that fifty cells of Albert Einstein had been frozen and then, after his death, used to clone fifty Albert Einsteins. Would all of them have turned out to be transcendant scientific geniuses?

Doubtful! Einstein was born into the Germany of Kaiser Wilhelm II, had a rather rough childhood, didn't do well at school in some ways, knocked about in Italy and Switzerland, and so on. The clones would be born in the United States of Dwight Eisenhower, would be lovingly educated and brought up. Can we be sure Einsteins would develop after this great difference of upbringing?

Then, too, whatever the original Einstein did, he did. There was no ground for comparison. Much that the cloned Einsteins might do, however, could prove disappointing, and "unworthy of Einstein." The clones might be unable to bear the strain and prefer to do *anything* rather than science. No, it is not just human genes that count, but the unique set of circumstances surrounding each human being's development.

Isaac Asimov

EARLY DEVELOPMENT

The competent adult who solves problems, makes decisions, works at a job, and develops relationships with other people was once a newborn infant with fleeting memories, whose activities depended primarily upon biological states and inborn dispositions and whose survival depended upon the care of other people. The transition from infancy to adulthood is common to all normal members of the human species. William Shakespeare, Pablo Picasso, Albert Einstein, and your psychology instructor all followed the same general course that characterized your own development: a familiar path that is governed by the combined action of heredity and environment.

This chapter describes what psychologists know about the way heredity and environment work together during the earliest months of life. As we shall see, the process of human development is an orderly sequence of events from childhood to old age, directed by heredity but constantly influenced by the environment. An examination of prenatal development will show the crucial role environmental factors play in a baby's development before it is born. Finally, we shall focus on the human newborn, noting what abilities human beings have at birth, and how quickly they begin to acquire the cognitive and social traits characteristic of their species. Research suggests that the world of the newborn infant is less confusing than we might suspect and that a baby begins acquiring knowledge almost immediately after birth.

THE PROCESS OF DEVELOPMENT

The psychologist who studies the process of human development is faced with two key questions: How do people change—physically, mentally, and socially—as they grow older? And why do these particular patterns of change occur as they do? These two basic questions—the how and the why of human development—are explored by assessing the contributions of heredity and environment and the possibility of sensitive periods in human beings.

349

Developmental Sequences: The Question of How

Anyone who has watched children grow knows that many changes in their behavior are neither accidental nor random. There is an orderly sequence to the development of a young person's behavior in every area of functioning. This development does not cease when an individual reaches adulthood. In all human beings, sequential patterns of development and change continue into old age.

An obvious example of a developmental sequence is that associated with motor development during infancy. By the time babies are about two months old, they can raise the head and chest while lying on the stomach—a feat that enables them to scan a world beyond the crib. Between the fourth and seventh months, hand–eye coordination has improved enough to enable them to reach out and grasp almost any object within range —mother's glasses, father's nose, the mobile dangling overhead. By seven months, they usually can sit up without support, and a few months later they are able to hoist themselves into a standing position while holding on to furniture. At ten months, most babies are accomplished crawlers, capable of wreaking havoc on all low-lying areas of the house. And finally, around the first birthday most infants take their first step—an event that opens a whole new realm of experience. Such orderly sequences appear in the development of cognition, language, and social and emotional development as well, as we shall see in Chapters 15, 16, and 17.

Although all children pass through these sequences of development, each child's timing and style are likely to vary from established timetables. These individual differences arise because any sequence of development consists of averages, or **norms,** established after observing a large number of babies. Such descriptions do not describe the ideal behavior; they simply report the behavior of the mathematically "average" baby. The age at which normal infants master different skills varies widely. Some perfectly normal babies, for example, never crawl, but go directly from sitting and standing to taking their first steps. Walking may begin as early as eight months or as late as twenty. Some babies are talking about everything they see months before other babies have uttered their first word. Yet the concept of developmental sequences remains useful, because it emphasizes the important fact that human development is not random: the progression through the sequences is orderly and predictable.

Determinants of Development: The Question of Why

Although each person goes through similar developmental sequences, individual rates of development differ. What accounts for these similarities and differences among individuals? The answer lies in two interrelated factors: heredity and environment.

Hereditary Factors

As we have noted in Chapter 4, genes affect development throughout life, and every organism has, to some extent, a genetically programmed timetable for its physical maturation. Under normal circumstances, the physical development of an individual's muscles, organs, and nervous system will unfold at a certain pace. Since we are all human, we share similar (though not identical) maturational timetables. At different phases of development, some genes become active and others cease to act. Puberty is a clear example of a genetically timed event, and it appears that genes also affect longevity and the rate at which a person ages (Jarvik, Blum, and Varma, 1972). Heredity, then, has a threefold influence on human development: it influences physical form, behavioral capacities, and the rate of physical maturation.

Does this mean that genes *determine* the rate and pattern of certain developmental sequences? To answer this question, researchers have turned to studies of identical twins. Identical twins are born when a single fertilized egg divides in two, each half having a full complement of the same genetic instructions. (Fraternal twins, in contrast, develop from two separately fertilized eggs and are no more alike than other brothers and sisters.) Because identical twins are genetically identical, researchers have believed that differences between them that emerged during their development could be taken as evidence of the influence of environmental factors. Conversely, if one twin received a certain kind of stimulation from its environment that the other did not, but the twins nevertheless developed at the same rate, then this

Infants around the world develop motor skills at approximately the same age, although the practices of their culture may slightly speed or retard the appearance of a skill. Hopi babies, who spend much of their time bound to cradleboards, walk about a month later than Anglo babies, while African babies walk about a month earlier.

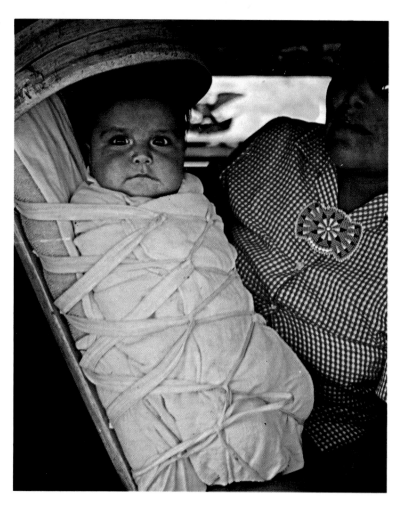

could be taken as evidence of strong genetic influence on the development of a certain behavior sequence.

Research with identical twins has generally supported the supposition that genes affect many aspects of development. For example, case studies of identical twins who were adopted into very different environments found that their rates of maturation, their hobbies, food preferences, choice of friends, and academic achievement were quite similar (Bouchard, 1981). Another way to look for genetic influences on development is to compare similarities and differences in adopted siblings with those of biological siblings. In one such study of adolescents, intelligence test scores of the adopted siblings showed no correlation at all, but test scores of biological siblings showed a correlation of .35, indicating that genes have some

influence on the development of cognitive processes (Scarr and Weinberg, 1978b). Such studies have also found a slight genetic influence on interests and personality differences (Grotevant, Scarr, and Weinberg, 1977; Scarr et al., 1981).

Early studies of twins (e.g., McGraw, 1935; 1939a) indicated that motor development in infancy was heavily influenced by heredity, and studies of children in different cultures tended to confirm this finding. Hopi Indian infants spent their first year bound to cradle boards that severely restricted their movements, yet they walked at about the same age as Anglo infants (Dennis and Dennis, 1940). On the basis of such studies, the assumption was made that environmental differences had little influence on when basic motor skills emerged. Later research was to suggest that the focus on Western cultures had obscured environmental effects on development (Harkness, 1980.)

Environmental Factors

Scientists now know that heredity is never the sole influence on development. Environment is necessarily an important factor in any developmental process, including that of the prenatal period. An organism cannot grow without material from the environment (food) to build its cells and tissues, and the environment continues to influence its development throughout life. In the case of motor skills, development can be accelerated or retarded by the presence or absence of environmental stimulation. Apparently, the ranges of the environmental variations in the earlier studies, mentioned above, had been too limited to reveal this.

We now know that a severe lack of social and intellectual stimulation accompanied by little opportunity for physical activity can retard development. In a foundling home in Lebanon, for example, where children spent most of their first year lying on their backs in bare cribs, virtually ignored by adults, motor skills were so retarded that some infants over a year old could not sit up, let alone walk (Dennis and Sayegh, 1965). However, a simple change of program produced dramatic results among these foundlings. When they were propped into sitting positions and allowed to play for as little as an hour each day with such ordinary objects as fresh flowers, pieces of colored sponge, and colored plastic disks strung on a chain, the babies' rate of motor development accelerated enormously. In fact, foundlings who receive visual and aural enrichment, along with human attention, develop as rapidly—both physically and cognitively—as infants in middle-class homes (Hunt, 1980).

While an impoverished environment retards development, extra experience and stimulation can accelerate motor skills—provided the stimulation is appropriate to the baby's age. For example, in a number of African tribes, infants sit, stand, and walk about a month earlier than American babies. The African babies' precocity does not seem to be the result of genetic differences but of routine child-care practices (Super, 1976). For example, among the Kipsigis of Kenya, babies spend more than 60 percent of their time sitting, often in a care giver's lap; 80 percent of the mothers give their babies deliberate training in motor skills, starting at about five months for

sitting and about seven months for walking. Yet these babies do not crawl early. Among the Teso, however, where babies do crawl early, 93 percent of the mothers train their babies to crawl. Motor precocity is not limited to African groups. Seven-month-old Finnish babies who were given daily training for three weeks learned to creep earlier than babies in a control group (Lagerspetz, Nygard, and Strandvik, 1971).

There are limits to this acceleration of motor development; no matter how much exercise young infants are given, none will walk at six months. In addition, although the age at which babies in these experiments sat, crawled, and walked was significantly earlier than average, the difference is well within the normal range of human differences. In fact, later studies of cradle-boarded Native American babies indicated that they walked about a month later than Anglo babies. Again, this is a significant delay, but within the normal range. The important point is that—within limits— developmental sequences respond to environmental manipulation.

Like the repeated practice of specific skills, generalized stimulation can also lead to accelerated development. This has been demonstrated with premature infants. Nurses and parents tend to regard premature babies as especially fragile and so avoid fondling them as they do normal babies. But physical stimulation may be exactly what these infants need. One researcher (Rice, 1975) encouraged a group of mothers to stroke and gently massage their premature babies for fifteen minutes, then to rock and cuddle them for five minutes, four times a day. At the end of four months, the stimulated babies had shown significant gains in weight, motor reflexes, and mental functioning over a control group of premature babies who did not receive extra handling. In another study (Rose et al., 1980), premature infants who had been massaged, rocked, and talked to while in the hospital nursery showed better recognition memory at the age of six months than premature babies who had not been so stimulated.

These studies suggest that stimulation from the environment not only enhances muscle strength but also facilitates the development of the nervous system. Most infants receive adequate stimulation in their natural surroundings, but infants who grow up under grossly abnormal conditions, such as those in the foundling home in Lebanon, may not get enough stimulation for normal development.

Figure 14.1. Deprivation dwarfism. In one study, the effects of emotional deprivation were observed in a pair of fraternal twins. This drawing, based on photos taken when the children were almost thirteen months old, shows that the female was normal, in weight and stature, but her brother was the size of a seven-month-old. Shortly after the twins were born, the father lost his job and left home. Hurt and angry, the mother displaced her hostility toward the father to the son and soon the boy's growth rate began to decline. It is thought that emotional stress affects the pituitary gland, depressing the secretion of growth hormone and thus stunting growth. When the father eventually returned home and the emotional climate of the household improved, the boy began to grow again. (After Gardner, 1972.)

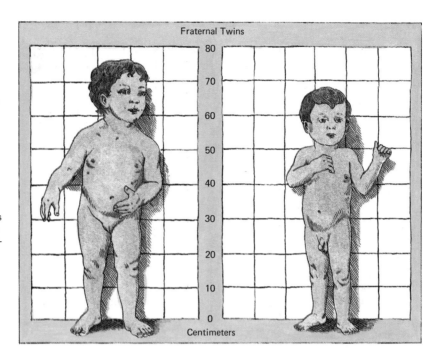

Although severely abnormal environments clearly can have deleterious effects on development (see Figure 14.1), healthy development can proceed in many different environments (Kagan, 1978). Infant intelligence, for example, shows little variation; although some babies reach various developmental levels sooner than others, all normal babies acquire all the cognitive skills of infancy (Scarr-Salapatek, 1976). When infants experience normal freedom of movement and the opportunity to interact with the environment found in most homes, they seem to be only modestly affected by extra enrichment. Thus, there may be an optimal amount of stimulation for optimal development, but it must be appropriate to the baby's age and abilities (White, 1967; 1971). Overwhelming young infants with a profuse display of toys and mobiles and showering them with constant attention does not guarantee the development of precocious children. Instead, an overload of stimulation before the baby is ready for it may be merely irritating or confusing.

Sensitive Periods of Development

The relationship between hereditary and environmental determinants of behavior can be seen in the sensitive periods of development, discussed in Chapter 4. During such periods, an organism is especially susceptible to certain kinds of environmental influences. The same experience before or after this period may have little or no impact. An organism's "readiness" depends on genetically guided maturation; the outcome depends on the environment.

Some psychologists (e.g., Klaus and Kennell, 1967; Hess, 1970) believe that there are sensitive periods in human development. For example, John Bowlby (1958) has suggested that human social and emotional development is marked by sensitive periods. He argues that babies seem to have an innate drive to establish a bond with a parent or caretaker, that love objects selected later in life resemble that person, and that early disruption of the bond can have severe effects on later development. Similarly, the optimal period for language acquisition seems to be between two and thirteen years, and after that time it is extremely difficult to learn a first language.

Many psychologists reject the idea of sensitive periods in human beings. Although most agree that children must reach a level of maturational readiness before they can profit from certain kinds of experiences, they point out that human beings are extremely resilient and can generally overcome

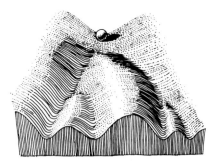

Figure 14.2. Geneticist Conrad Waddington's graphic analogy for the interaction of heredity and environment in development. The landscape represents the possibilities determined by genetic factors, and the path of the rolling ball represents the actual course of development. Such forces on the ball as cross-winds represent environmental factors. The ball can roll down different valleys, depending on the forces that are brought to bear on it, but it cannot easily change from one valley to another once it has started. The analogy is useful in helping us understand how genetic and environmental factors interact to produce different personality traits or different degrees of intellectual ability. (After Waddington, 1957.)

the effects of harmful early experiences. Some children who have suffered years of neglect, shut away in attics, basements, and closets, may recover and become normal adults when they are given adequate environments (Clarke and Clarke, 1979). Negative influences that persist into adulthood most often appear to be the result of continuing bad experiences, not the effect of deprivation during an early sensitive period. The effects of early experience, if the experience is not repeated, usually appear to fade with time. A human child is like a piece of magic plastic with a "memory"; the child can be bent out of shape by severe environmental pressures, but when the pressure is removed, she or he tends to resume a normal shape, functioning without any deep dents (Scarr, 1981a).

The basic point of this section—indeed, of this entire chapter—is that hereditary and environmental influences are two sides of the same coin. Although it is useful to distinguish between them, they can never be entirely separated, as the graphic analogy in Figure 14.2 shows. Despite our inability to separate these determinants, individual differences in development can depend upon genes, upon environment, or upon the combined action of both. Genes can determine the kind of response an individual makes to a particular situation, and the environment can provide or deny

certain types of experiences and can determine the way a genetic influence is expressed. The close collaboration between nature and nurture also applies to developmental disorders that have specific genetic causes. As later sections indicate, the typical course of human development is a combination of heredity and environment.

PRENATAL DEVELOPMENT

Have you ever stopped to think that your own birth was as unlikely as your winning the grand prize in a state lottery? If your parents had had intercourse a day or an hour before or after they did when you were conceived, a genetically similar but quite different individual would be reading this book. If that intercourse had taken place two days earlier or later, the gender of that individual might also be different—or there might have been no pregnancy at all (Hofer, 1981). Of the 350 million sperm released in a single ejaculation, each with a different genetic makeup, only .001 percent will find their way to the Fallopian tube that contains the ovum. And of those sperm, only one will manage to fertilize the ovum. Furthermore, not every fertilized egg produces a new individual. About one out

Although we cannot yet prevent the genetic abnormality that causes Down's syndrome, we can reduce its effects through environmental intervention. Down's syndrome children who receive training in motor skills during infancy perform very well on simple tasks by the time they are three.

of four fertilized eggs fails to implant itself successfully in the uterine wall (Hofer, 1981), and others, once implanted, will be spontaneously aborted, often because of some genetic defect (Babson et al., 1980).

Despite the giant odds against your existence, you were nevertheless conceived. But it required thirty-eight weeks of development to transform that fertilized egg into a newborn baby. You might assume that your development during this fetal period followed a rigid, totally preordained plan, impervious to any environmental influence. In the sections that follow, however, we will see that environmental forces also play a role in development before birth.

Prenatal Growth and Behavior

The development that takes place during the thirty-eight weeks of pregnancy is more rapid than during any postnatal period. The first major developmental sequence unfolds in a largely predictable manner, initiated and guided by genetic factors. Yet even during this early period, environmental factors can make a difference.

Prenatal development is divided into three basic periods: germinal, embryonic, and fetal. During this development, the new organism's structural complexity and behavioral potential steadily increase.

The Germinal Period

Almost immediately after fertilization, the egg begins the process of cell division that eventually produces a human body. At first the multiplying cells are all identical: nerve, muscle, bone, and blood cells cannot be distinguished from one another. But by the end of the first two weeks, the cells have begun to differentiate into three primary layers that will form the various tissues and organs, each layer producing different body systems. Exactly what triggers this process is still a mystery, but scientists believe that the answer may lie in subtle differences in the chemical environments to which different cells are exposed as the cell mass increases in size.

The Embryonic Period

Within three weeks after conception, the organism, called an **embryo,** is about one-fifth of an inch long. Its heart already beats within its worm-like body, although its nervous system has not begun to form (Hofer, 1981). By four weeks it has developed a spinal cord and a two-lobe brain. Many of the major organs have formed, as well as indentations in the head region that will eventually become jaws, eyes, and ears. At about six weeks, the embryo makes its first neuromuscular response, reflexively moving its upper trunk and neck when the mouth area is stroked with a fine hair (Humphrey, 1970). By the end of this period, about the eighth week, the embryo is almost an inch long.

The Fetal Period

For the next thirty weeks, until its birth, the developing organism is known as a **fetus.** In the early fetal period, which lasts until about sixteen weeks, the activity level rises steadily. At nine weeks, the fetus bends its fingers; it also curls or straightens its toes in response to touches on the palm of the hand or the sole of the foot. Gradually, diffuse responses narrow, so that when the mouth is touched only reflexes about the mouth—instead of the entire upper body—appear. Body movements become more graceful, even flowing, and appear less mechanical than at the beginning of the period. Spontaneous movements become frequent and strong, and by the end of this period the mother begins to notice them. As the early fetal period closes the fetus is six or seven inches long; hair may appear on the head and facial features approximate their finished appearance. The major internal organs have attained their typical shape, although they could not keep the fetus alive outside the uterus.

The second fetal period, from seventeen to twenty-four weeks, represents a sharp break with previous development (Hofer, 1981). Fetal activity drops sharply, and when the fetus is stimulated, its response is sluggish. This placid period apparently reflects the maturation of the nervous system, when control of behavior is passing from the spinal cord to the midbrain. When activity resumes, it will be regulated by a different pattern of neural organization. During this time, the brain develops rapidly, and by twenty weeks all 100 billion neurons have developed, although the brain is immature in other respects. At this stage of development, inactivity serves the fetus well, because it is growing so rapidly that its cramped space would not allow the simultaneous movement of all body parts.

From twenty-four to thirty-two weeks, the fetus is again active, but mass action patterns have vanished. Now, a single limb or the trunk moves. Rhythmic activity cycles develop, with peaks and troughs of behavior, so that the fetus appears to sleep and wake. One of these cycles, a ninety-six-minute cycle, appears to be caused by the mother, since it disappears at birth and is approximately the same length as the adult sleep cycle (see Chapter 7). It is a "weak" cycle. The fetus also has a "strong" forty-minute cycle, which lasts until about two years after birth, when it gradually lengthens into the adult ninety-six-minute cycle. Studies of prematurely delivered fetuses have shown that by twenty-four weeks a fetus can cry, open and close its eyes, and look up, down, and sideways (Hooker, 1952). It has developed a grasping reflex, and when a stick is placed in its hand, it is strong enough to support its weight. If born at this time, it has a chance of surviving: 161 days (twenty-three weeks) is regarded as the minimum possible survival age (Kleiman, 1984).

During the remaining time in the uterus, fat forms over the body, smoothing out the wrinkled skin and rounding out contours. The fetus can suck its thumb, cry, yawn, and grunt. Its movements become more coordinated, the transitions from stillness to activity are better defined, and movements are more sustained and vigorous. Although it probably will not be born until thirty-eight weeks, during the last six weeks the fetus seems much like a full-term infant.

Environmental Influences in the Uterus

Although prenatal growth proceeds on a solid genetic foundation, even within the uterus the fetus is not immune from external influences. Perhaps the most important developmental influence is the diet of the mother, from whom the fetus receives its nourishment. Diets deficient in calcium, phosphorus, iodine, and vitamins B, C, and D are associated with high frequencies of malformed fetuses.

Fetal development is also adversely affected by various drugs. A golden rule of obstetric practice is to advise women to take as little medication during pregnancy as possible. The thalidomide tragedies in the early 1960s, when many European women who took the sedative thalidomide during the early weeks of pregnancy produced babies with severely deformed arms and legs, vividly illustrates the consequences of using certain drugs. A parallel instance is the DES tragedies, which are still with us: a high rate of cervical cancer has been found in adolescent daughters whose mothers had taken the drug diethylstilbestrol (DES) early in pregnancy to prevent miscarriage. When daughters in this group who escape cancer later become pregnant themselves, they are twice as likely as unexposed women to have spontaneous abortions (miscarriages), and three times as likely to give birth prematurely (Sandberg et al., 1981). More recently, Benedictin, a drug many women have taken to prevent nausea during pregnancy, has been suspected of causing birth defects —including an increased number of infants with missing limbs, heart defects, and cleft lips (*New York Times,* 1984).

Alcohol also has effects on the fetus, which have been established during the past decade. Alcoholic mothers have three times as many stillbirths as other mothers, and their babies often have **fetal alcohol syndrome,** characterized by mental retardation and retarded growth—both prenatally and after birth (Umbreit and Ostrow, 1980). Some may also have cleft palates, heart murmurs, kidney damage, and eye or skeletal defects (Streissguth et al., 1980). Social drinking also endangers the fetus: its effects, though less striking, are nevertheless apparent. Newborn infants of mothers who averaged five drinks per week during pregnancy seem sluggish and have difficulty adjusting to stimuli (Streissguth, Barr, and Martin, 1983), and as four-year-olds, these children have poor attention and slowed reactions (Streissguth et al., 1984).

Cigarette smoking, too, is known to affect the fetus. Women who smoke during pregnancy tend to miscarry more often than nonsmokers and to produce babies who are, on the average, lighter and smaller than normal (Babson et al., 1980). As four-year-olds, these children have attentional problems (Streissguth et al., 1984), and some studies indicate poorer school performance as seven-year-olds (Landesman-Dwyer and Emanuel, 1979). When mothers both smoke and drink, their newborns perform much worse than other babies on simple operant conditioning tasks (Landesman-Dwyer and Emanuel, 1979).

Caffeine may also be harmful, and in this case, giving up coffee, tea, and cola drinks early in pregnancy does not seem to eliminate the effects. Moderate consumption of caffeine *before* pregnan-

"Give me one good reason to stop smoking."

Your baby.

American Heart Association
WE'RE FIGHTING FOR YOUR LIFE

Pregnancy and smoking is a bad combination. Women who smoke while pregnant run a higher risk of miscarrying or of delivering babies with low birth weight.

cy or before the woman realizes she is pregnant appears to be linked with low birth weight, sluggishness, and irritability in newborns (Jacobson, 1983).

Finally, prenatal exposure to various environmental toxins has become a source of concern. Heavy doses of lead, mercury, or radiation have long been known to damage the fetus, but recent studies have added polychlorinated biphenyls (PCBs), synthetics that are part of many industrial products, to the list. Heavy exposure is known to be followed by premature birth, low birth weight, mild retardation, apathy, and jerky movements. Low levels of exposure have now been associated with poor reflexes, poor neuromuscular function-

ing, and sluggishness in some newborns (Jacobson et al., 1984).

Whether an environmental influence will produce an abnormality in a developing fetus is affected by the dosage, the genetic susceptibility of the fetus, the mother's physical condition, and timing (Tuchman-Duplessis, 1975). Timing is especially important. The first **trimester,** or third, of pregnancy appears to be an especially sensitive period for the development of certain kinds of birth defects because most of the basic organ systems are forming at this time. If organs are already formed —or have not yet developed—a destructive agent may have less serious effects, or none at all. The effect of timing is especially apparent in the case of rubella, or German measles, which can cause blindness, deafness, or mental retardation. Forty-seven percent of the babies born to women who contracted this seemingly minor disease during the first month of pregnancy were seriously affected; 22 percent of the babies born to women who contracted the disease in the second month were seriously affected; and 7 percent of the babies of those who contracted it during the third month were seriously affected (Michaels and Mellin, 1960). Generally, however, the fetus is most vulnerable during the second and third months, because more structures develop during these two months than during any other period of pregnancy.

THE COMPETENCY OF THE NEWBORN

Among the mammals, sensory and motor development varies widely at birth. Some mammals are born with impressive motor coordination and highly acute sensory capabilities. Newborn horses, calves, and guinea pigs are extremely precocious in the sense that they can see, hear, stand, walk, even run within a few hours after birth. Because of this, they are classified as **precocial** species. Others are born almost completely helpless. Kittens, mice, and puppies come into the world blind and physically feeble, totally dependent on their parents for survival. They are classified as **altricial** species.

Like other primates, newborn human babies are both altricial and precocial—a peculiar mix-

THE SPECIAL PROBLEMS OF THE PREMATURE BABY

Premature babies are forced to deal with the world weeks—or even months—before development is complete. Their systems are still immature, they often must be fed intravenously, and they may require the assistance of a respirator to breathe. But their problems are not purely physiological. Their social interactions may also be at risk.

Adults regard premature babies as much less attractive than full-term babies. In comparison with full-term babies, premature babies have smaller eyes and narrower heads, and their noses and mouths are farther apart. When shown drawings of premature and full-term infants' faces, college students described the premature infants as less likable, not as cute, less normal, less likely to be fun, more likely to be irritating, and less likely to make people happy (Reich et al., 1984). If parents respond in the same manner, the important care giver–infant relationship could suffer.

Besides being seen as less attractive, the premature baby also sleeps less and seems less happy than the full-term baby. The premature baby also cries and fusses more, and once the crying begins, the baby is harder to quiet (Friedman, Jacobs, and Werthmann, 1982). As if this stress on the relationship were not enough, the premature baby is also weaker and less alert and has poorer reflexes. Perhaps for all of these reasons, premature infants are more likely to be abused than full-term infants (Friedrich and Boriskin, 1976).

Some of these features undoubtedly affect the way even the most loving parent interacts with his or her child. The slow reactions and diminished alertness may cause parents to believe that their baby is fragile and could be harmed by much activity. At any rate, parents of a premature infant tend to hold their baby less and spend less time with their face close to the infant's face; they also smile, touch, and talk to their baby less than parents of full-term infants (Goldberg, 1978). It has also been found that among premature infants, those who were most alert, responsive, and cuddly at the time they left the hospital were also cuddled more as four-month-olds by their mothers (DiVitto and Goldberg, 1980).

Within a few months, however, most parents step up the stimulation they give their baby. It is as if their baby's sluggish responses make the parents decide that they must work harder and increase their share of social interactions. In one study of three-month-olds, mothers of premature babies were more active with their babies and stimulated them more—though they smiled and laughed less often—than did mothers of full-term babies (Greene, Fox, and Lewis, 1983). Similar differences have been found in mother-infant relationships at four, eight, and twelve months (Crnic et al., 1983).

There are hints, however, that this extra stimulation may be counterproductive. In another study, Tiffany Field (1982) asked mothers not to initiate any activity but merely to imitate the behavior of their four-month-old premature infants. The babies became *more* alert and tended to avert their gaze less often than they had under the mother's usual level of stimulation. Field believes that premature infants may function within a much narrower band of arousal than other infants. When stimulated a little too much, a premature infant's information-processing capacities may become overloaded, so that he or she turns away or fails to respond. But parents of premature babies have to walk a narrow line: if they fail to stimulate their infants enough, they will fail to engage their baby's interest, and development may suffer.

Yet most parents and their premature infants seem to weather the first year successfully. At twelve months, researchers find few differences between pairs of premature and full-term babies and their mothers (Goldberg, 1978). Either the babies have outgrown their earlier behavioral problems, or else the extra effort their parents devoted to stimulating them has paid off in terms of greater social interaction.

ture of incapacity and competence. And among the primates, none of which can creep or walk at birth, human babies are the most helpless and immature. Most human newborns are physically weak and helpless; few can hold up their own heads. Yet when we look at the sensory development of the human infant, we find remarkably mature and well-integrated systems. All the human senses, in fact, are capable of functioning even before birth (Gottlieb, 1976). Thus, human infants may not be able to navigate in their environment at birth, but they can both perceive and be influenced by that environment from the moment they are born.

Reflexes and Motor Skills

Because of their limited motor capacity, most babies appear quite helpless at birth, and for many months they will be completely dependent on their care givers. Yet they quickly master some essential motor skills. For example, within a few days they are eating smoothly, a task that requires the coordination of three separate activities: sucking, swallowing, and breathing. Newborns also come equipped with a set of reflexes that can be elicited by specific stimuli. Some of these reflexes are adaptive and may help babies survive in their new surroundings, as when they close their eyes to a bright light or jerk their limbs away from sources of pain. Others are simply manifestations of neurological pathways in the baby that will later come under voluntary control or will be integrated into more mature patterns of behavior, such as stepping movements of the legs (Minkowski, 1967). Still others may be remnants of traits possessed by prehuman ancestors.

One of the most familiar reflexes is the rooting reflex, a baby's tendency to turn the head in the direction of any object that gently stimulates the cheek or the corner of the mouth. This reflex has obvious adaptive significance for feeding: it helps the baby locate the nipple with her or his mouth.

In the first few weeks of life, babies also have a strong grasping reflex. Sometimes a newborn's grasp is so tight that the infant can hang by one hand. The function of this reflex is not entirely clear, but it may be a remnant of our prehuman past. If our early ancestors carried their offspring on their backs or stomachs, the ability to grasp the mother's fur or skin would keep an infant from a dangerous fall (Prechtl, 1982).

Reaching also appears among newborns. During the first few weeks of life, babies reach out for objects they see, at times successfully grasping them. At about four weeks, this eye–hand coordination is lost, not to reappear for nearly four months (Bower, 1976).

Why do reaching and stepping appear, disappear, then reappear in a different form? Perhaps the initial reflexes are controlled by subcortical brain structures, but when control shifts to the developing cortex, the behavior becomes voluntary and must be learned. The fact that many infant response patterns take this repetitive course of appearance, loss, and reappearance supports this view. However, Thomas Bower (1976) believes that there may be a continuity between these reflexive patterns and later behavior. He points out that when newborns are given practice in either stepping or reaching, the behavior may reappear earlier than expected. Or it may reappear at the expected time but take a more skillful form.

Sensory and Perceptual Abilities

As a species we rely most on our senses of vision and hearing. Smell, taste, and touch—while important—provide a much smaller proportion of human information about the world than they do with other species. One reason we rely so heavily on vision is that we walk upright. Standing, we can see farther in all directions than a species that moves close to the surface of the ground, where smell is a more important source of information.

But this heavy reliance on sights and sounds may develop gradually. A baby's world is relatively confined and, although vision is probably the most important sense for the baby, information from other senses may also play a large role in the baby's world. Much of the infant's information about the world comes through grasping, handling, and mouthing objects. In addition, stimuli we ordinarily pay little attention to, such as slight odors, may give babies a good deal more information than we realize.

Babies come into the world with their senses functioning; they can see, hear, smell, feel, and taste. But the questions that fascinate researchers are: What do babies perceive? How quickly do they come to perceive the world the way adults do? Is a baby's world a chaos of meaningless shapes and noises? Or is it a world of stable objects and distinct sounds?

In recent years a great amount of research has been devoted to finding out just what the newborn infant perceives. These investigations have refuted the notion that a baby's world is essentially disorganized and chaotic, and indicate that infants make great perceptual strides in the first few months. During this brief period, infants become able to handle increasing amounts of perceptual information, to respond more selectively, and to coordinate sensory information with motor ability.

Vision

The visual world of newborn infants is less chaotic than it might be, thanks to the fact that the infant's immature visual system shuts out much of the confusing stimulation. The infant's immature retina, optic nerve, and visual cortex limit visual capability in several ways. First, infants' visual acuity, or clarity of vision, is poor; at twenty feet they see no better than an adult does at six hundred feet (Banks and Salapatek, 1981). Second, their ability to change focus, or to accommodate, is extremely limited, so that most objects appear fuzzy, especially those that are several feet distant or extremely close (Banks and Salapatek, 1983). Finally, their ability to use their eyes together, so that both eyes are looking at the same object, is so poor that newborns are likely to see two of everything. These visual deficiencies rapidly begin to correct themselves. By three months babies can accommodate fairly well (Banks, 1980), by six months they can see as clearly as the average adult, and some time between seven months and a year their visual capacities are fully developed (Cohen, DeLoache, and Strauss, 1979).

Yet despite their visual immaturity, newborns can see a great deal. They can detect contrasts between light and dark (Fantz, 1963) and within a few months will be able to detect subtle changes in brightness. They can perceive movement, and their eyes follow a slowly moving object, although for the first few weeks their tracking movement is jerky. They prefer looking at some things rather than others, and they find patterns more interesting than solid colors (Fantz, 1963). They seem most interested in objects of moderate complexity, but their preferences appear to vary with their state of arousal (Gardner and Turkewitz, 1982).

After studying the vision of newborns, Marshall Haith (1980) summed up their typical behavior in a set of rules: (1) If you are awake and alert and the light is not too bright, open your eyes. (2) If it is dark, search for something to look at. (3) If it is light, search for the edges of some object, using broad sweeping movements. (4) If you find an edge, which distinguishes an object from its background, keep your gaze directed in that area. The fact that infants seem to follow these rules as they look at their world suggests that they come into the world equipped to gather information and that they are motivated to seek actively for it.

Newborns probably see little color in their world because their central retinas are extremely immature and have few color-sensitive cones (Abramov et al., 1982). Most month-old babies are unable to distinguish red and green from yellow (Teller, 1981), but by four months they seem to perceive and categorize colors in the same way that adults do (blue, green, yellow, and red) (Bornstein, 1981).

Because newborns are unable to converge their eyes on an object and have no experience that helps them to interpret monocular cues (see Chapter 6), researchers have wondered just how early infants perceive a three-dimensional world. Binocular vision apparently develops some time between three and six months. Researchers have traced this development by showing to infants paired computer-generated displays of dots—one to each eye (Petrig et al., 1981). The displays are meaningless unless the infants can fuse the two images into a single three-dimensional image. Babies of various ages watched a series of such displays, in which solid forms changed position and appeared to move across the screen. Based on recordings of event-related potentials (ERPs), researchers concluded that by the time babies are about five months old, most have developed three-dimensional vision. Infants apparently begin to rely on monocular cues (such as perspective) as additional guides to depth when they are between five and seven months old (Yonas, Cleaves, and Petterson, 1978).

Apparently, both maturation and experience are necessary for true depth perception. Experience is also necessary before babies can transfer the perception of depth into a warning of danger when placed on precarious heights. The importance of this experience became clear in a series of studies (Gibson and Walk, 1960; Scarr and Salapatek, 1970; Campos et al., 1978) involving the "visual cliff," a platform covered with plexiglass, but patterned and lighted so that it appears to have a "deep" and a "shallow" side (see Figure 14.3). Investigators placed babies on the cliff and

Figure 14.3. The visual cliff apparatus. An infant who can crawl may cross the glass surface over the "shallow" side but is unlikely to venture out over an edge that appears to be a sudden drop or to cross the surface over the "deep" side.

carefully observed their reactions. Young babies seemed to notice the depth, indicating their awareness in the way they explored the plexiglass surface and by a slowing of their heartbeat. Yet they were not afraid, even when placed directly over the deep side. Babies who could crawl seemed frightened: their hearts sped up and they would not cross the deep side of the cliff, even to reach their mothers, who beckoned and held out attractive toys. Human babies apparently develop a fear of heights at about the time they become able to move about. This fear has survival value, for cues of depth can warn them that they are in danger of falling.

Hearing

When newborns enter the world, their ears are often filled with fluid, which may limit hearing. Within a few hours, they react to all major aspects of sound, including pitch, loudness, timbre, and rhythm (Eisenberg, 1970). Most newborns appear able to localize sounds—at least they slowly turn their heads and look in the direction of a sharp noise. This talent soon disappears, only to return in force when babies are about four months old. For example, when researchers shake a bottle filled with popcorn, newborns will slowly turn their heads toward the source of the sound (Field et al., 1980). But the ability slowly declines, and by three months babies make no attempt to look in the direction of the sound. A month later, they are again responding, searching with their eyes for the source of a sound. This pattern may be another example of a change in control from subcortical to cortical brain structures, so that what was once a reflexive movement has become a voluntary coordination of vision and hearing.

Newborns and young infants tend to respond differently to sounds of contrasting frequency or pitch. High-frequency sounds are likely to make a baby cry, and low-frequency sounds generally soothe a fussy baby (Eisenberg, 1970), which is why lullabies are sung to babies around the world. Babies also prefer sounds with the frequency and pitch of the human voice (Webster, Steinhardt, and Senter, 1972).

Newborns not only respond distinctively to speech but also can distinguish between people's voices. In one study, three-day-old babies were given a chance to hear their own mother's voice or the voice of an unfamiliar woman reading a Dr. Seuss story (DeCasper and Fifer, 1980). The device that produced the recorded sound was triggered when the infant sucked on a nipple. The babies' sucking patterns showed that they preferred the sound of speech to silence and that they clearly preferred their mother's voice to that of a stranger.

Taste, Smell, and Touch

Infants' perceptions of taste, smell, and touch have not been studied extensively; because human beings rely on sight and hearing, researchers have devoted their time to these senses. But the research that has been done on taste, smell, and touch indicates that newborns can detect and discriminate basic sensory information through these senses.

Newborns can distinguish among various tastes. We know this because babies less than a day old respond to bitter, sour, or sweet fluids with the expressions we associate with these tastes (Steiner, 1979). A bitter taste makes them stick out their tongues and spit, and many of them try to vomit. A sour taste leads them to purse their lips, wrinkle their noses, and blink their eyes. When they are given a taste of something sweet, newborns smile, suck eagerly, and lick their upper lips. As early as the first day of life, babies have a sweet tooth. Other researchers have found that when newborns are given a sweet liquid, they drink more of it but take longer to do it. Their sucking slows and their heart rate increases, leading researchers to speculate that babies find the taste so delicious that they slow down to enjoy it, and the resulting pleasure excites them, speeding up their hearts (Lipsitt, 1977). Babies' facial expressions in response to various tastes are so consistent that the researcher concluded that their responses are probably reflexive, not learned (Steiner, 1979).

When they are first born, infants' ability to distinguish odors is limited, but within twelve hours they respond to strong aromas. To the odor of rotten eggs or concentrated shrimp, newborns screw up their faces and arch their mouths in an expression of disgust. But to the aroma of butter, bananas, vanilla, chocolate, strawberry, or honey, newborns respond with an eager licking and sucking (Steiner, 1979). By the time they are ten days old, babies' detection of odors has become extremely sensitive. When a pad scented with breast milk was placed on each side of their heads, the babies spent more time turned toward the pad of their own mother. Ten-day-old infants can distinguish the smell of their own mothers from the smell of another woman—and they prefer their mother's odor (Macfarlane, 1977).

Infant Sensory Capacities and Adult Tendencies: An Interlocking System

When we consider the ways in which adults tend to behave with a young infant, it becomes apparent that these tendencies mesh with the newborn's capacities. Newborn visual acuity is best between six and twelve inches, so that a baby

nursing at the mother's breast or being cradled in a care giver's arms is optimally situated for eye-to-eye contact. Newborns prefer sounds in the frequency range of the human voice, and prefer high-pitched voices. In a seemingly automatic adjustment, most adults—even those with no care-giving experience—tend to raise the pitch of their voice when talking to infants, exaggerating their articulation and facial expressions (Stern, 1974).

Infant reflexes also seem designed to fit the tendencies of care givers. Adults perceive crying as inherently arousing and aversive: their hearts beat faster, their blood pressure rises, and their skin conductance increases (Frodi et al., 1978). In order to end the aversive sound, they generally go to the baby's aid. When they do so, they pick up the distressed newborn and raise it to the shoulder. This response not only soothes the baby but places him or her in a state of quiet alertness, when an infant is receptive to stimulation and ready to learn (Korner and Grobstein, 1966; Korner and Thoman, 1972).

The natural fit between the newborn's skills and dispositions and the care giver's inclinations suggests that human evolution has resulted in a system that encourages the survival and development of the infant. The behavioral "tools" for survival seem built into newborn behavior, and the care-giving context promotes the sort of interchange between adult and baby that is necessary if the infant is to flourish.

The Roots of Cognitive and Social Development

The cognitive and social characteristics that define the baby as distinctly human develop from rudimentary capacities for vocalization, movement, and perception. From babbling to language ability, from mysterious smiles to mirth, from an interest in faces to strong social attachments, infants display the progressive development of complex psychological processes. Cognitive and social development will be discussed in detail in subsequent chapters; here, a look at the roots of these most human aspects of development will provide a basis for later discussion.

Looking at Faces

In order to develop vital emotional bonds with care givers, the infant must be able to distinguish them from other people. Although blind babies develop the same sort of bonds as do sighted babies, the ability to perceive faces and to tell one face from another certainly makes the task easier. For that reason psychologists have been interested in the way the infant's perception of faces develops.

When babies about a month old are shown a face, they rarely direct their gaze inside the face (Hebb, 1949); instead they look mostly at the edges of the face and at points of high contrast—like the hairline and chin. By the time they are two months old, they begin to look at features within the face—the nose, the mouth, or an eye (Maurer and Salapatek, 1976). The eyes seem to hold a special attraction for babies of this age—whether the face is moving or still, talking or silent (Haith, Bergman, and Moore, 1977).

At about four months an important transition takes place (Gibson, 1969). Babies start responding to the facial configuration rather than to individual features. They have become aware of the unchanging relations among the elements of a pattern that give it meaning; they are perceiving the whole rather than isolated parts. If they are shown masks of human faces, they look longer at a mask with its features arranged in a normal fashion than a mask on which the nose, eyes, ears, and mouth are arranged bizarrely. Babies clearly prefer normally organized faces to faces with scrambled features (Kagan, 1967; Thomas, 1973).

Now that babies know what a face is supposed to look like, their recognition of faces progresses rapidly. By five months infants can tell one face from another (Cohen, DeLoache, and Straus, 1979); by six months they can tell the difference between male and female faces (Cornell, 1974), and when they are shown a photograph of a face, they can recognize the same face photographed from a different angle (Cohen, 1972; Fagan, 1976). This ability to distinguish different faces rests on a skill adults take for granted: the capacity to abstract those aspects of an individual face that remain unchanged from pose to pose. This is a remarkable ability for a baby who only a few short months ago did not know where the eyes, nose, and mouth belonged.

Once babies are able to distinguish faces, they also begin to distinguish facial expressions. For example, babies can detect the difference between a smiling face and an impassive face. Researchers have been able to establish this infant ability by using holograms, in which images recorded by laser light provide a moving three-dimensional reproduction (Nelson and Horowitz, 1983). These skills are extremely important, because the ability to detect facial expressions is vital to the formation of social relationships.

Imitation

If infants as young as two months old can tell one expression from the other, how soon can they imitate various expressions? Imitation plays an important role in human development. Most psychologists believe that babies begin imitating the facial expressions of others when they are about eight months old; before that time, babies can imitate only actions that they have performed themselves, such as movements of the hands or legs. About eight years ago, however, a great controversy was stirred up by research indicating that two-week-old babies could imitate adults' expressions and movements. Andrew Meltzoff and Keith Moore (1977) reported that babies this young would stick out their tongues, protrude their lips, open their mouths, or open and close their fists in imitation of an adult. Later the same researchers reported that newborns between the ages of forty-two minutes and seventy-two hours showed the same imitative ability (Meltzoff and Moore, 1983).

Meltzoff and Moore (1983) believe that babies have an innate ability to imitate. They argue that when newborns stick out their tongues in response to an adult's protruding tongue, they are somehow mentally representing visual information and sensory information from their mouths, lips, and tongues, matching the two, then imitating the gesture they have seen.

This interpretation of the babies' actions has been challenged by other investigators, who suggest that this early imitation is a response to a sign stimulus, such as those discussed in Chapter 4, and that imitation is an unconditioned, automatic response that babies make to specific stimuli. Baby blackbirds, who automatically thrust up their heads and open their beaks whenever a parent bird lands on the nest, will do the same when any object is thrust toward them (Tinbergen, 1973). In a study by Sandra Jacobson (1979), young babies indeed stuck out their tongues in response to a protruding adult tongue, but they also stuck out their tongues when a small ball or a felt-tip pen was moved toward their mouths, held there momentarily, and then moved away. And babies opened and closed their hands in response to Jacobson's hand movements, but they did the same whenever an orange plastic ring was placed near their hands. Jacobson suggests that sticking out the tongue has an adaptive function related to feeding.

Meltzoff and Moore (1983) have dismissed the idea that these imitative responses are reflexive on the grounds that the babies' actions were not stereotyped; that is, babies showed individual differences in the way that they stuck out their tongues, protruded their lips, and so forth. However, a reflexive response need not be stereotyped; it must only fall within a behavioral range common to the species.

Although some researchers have been unable to replicate the work of Meltzoff and Moore (Koepke et al., 1983; McKenzie and Over, 1983), Field and her colleagues (Field et al., 1982) have found that two-day-old infants can imitate an experimenter's facial expressions. When an investigator modeled a "surprised" face, newborns tended to open their mouths and widen their eyes; when a "happy" face was modeled, newborns tended to widen their lips; and when a "sad" face was modeled, they tended to tighten their mouths, protrude their lips, and furrow their brows. Premature newborns responded with the same sort of imitative expressions (Field et al., 1983). Field and her colleagues agree with Meltzoff and Moore's explanation of the infants' responses, and they point out that such an innate ability is adaptive, in that it is likely to encourage nurturance from care givers.

The baby's smile apparently encourages nurturance because the care giver finds the smile extremely rewarding. But newborns are not yet able to smile in response to their care givers' attentions. Although babies do smile in the first few days after birth, these smiles are not responses to anything that happens in the babies' world; they are responses to what is going on within the babies' physiological systems. For example, babies smile as they are drifting off to sleep after a feeding. Such smiles may have nothing to do with the care givers' ministrations, but the care givers interpret them in this way and so find them rewarding. By six weeks, however, babies *are* smiling in response to a human face, and this smile is believed to strengthen the bond between infant and care giver even further. Such an explanation was suggested long ago by Charles Darwin (1872/1967), who proposed that the smile has survival value for the infant because it evokes a feeling of joy in the care giver. This early smile, which is triggered by the sight of a human face, does not have to be seen as "intentional" on the part of the infant, just as early "imitation" need not have any intent. It would appear that this imitation among newborns is related to such behavior as stepping and reaching—an automatic response that drops out as soon as control passes to the developing cortex.

Self-Awareness

If the baby's first imitations are essentially reflexive, when do babies develop self-awareness—an essential human trait? It has long been suggested that self-awareness emerges only when a person has opportunities to observe others through social interaction (Cooley, 1912; Mead, 1934). According to this assumption, a person reared in isolation would never develop a true sense of self.

If self-awareness depends on social contact, a search for its emergence must begin early, for normal babies interact with others from the moment of birth. This is obvious in hospital nurseries, where when one baby starts to cry, the entire nursery is soon wailing (Sagi and Hoffman, 1976). Babies only a day old not only cry in response to the recorded wails of another newborn but recognize their own recorded cries as well, responding by falling silent and turning their heads to listen (Martin and Clark, 1982). Moreover, the newborns in this study did not cry when they heard the cries of an infant chimpanzee or an eleven-month-old baby. As yet we do not know how newborns can tell when recorded cries are their own and not those of another baby, or why the cries of their peers distress them. Some researchers have suggested that the distress is inborn and is an early precursor of human empathy (Sagi and Hoffman, 1976).

As we saw in the discussion of imitation, intent is not a necessary component of such newborn behavior. Yet there is some kind of rudimentary self-recognition involved when newborns lapse into silence at the sound of their own voices. Research with older babies has shown that a different sort of self-awareness begins to develop during the latter part of the first year and is firmly established in the latter part of the second year. In one study, babies ranging in age from nine months to twenty-four months were exposed to a mirror (Lewis and Brooks-Gunn, 1979). Each in-

This baby's delighted reaction to the reflection is pleasure at seeing another baby; she probably will be two years old before she realizes that the "baby in the mirror" is herself.

fant's mother then surreptitiously placed a spot of red dye on her baby's nose. When returned to the mirror, no baby younger than nine months old showed any awareness that the smudged nose in the mirror was her or his own. But one-fourth of the fifteen- to eighteen-month-olds and three-fourths of the twenty-four-month-olds knew immediately, grabbing for their noses as soon as they looked into the mirror.

The emergence of this sort of self-awareness is influenced by cognitive development, social experience, and linguistic skills. In a similar study of retarded children, most showed no recognition of their mirror images until they were nearly three years old (Mans, Cicchetti, and Sroufe, 1978). When tested in the mirror situation, abused or neglected nineteen-month-olds were significantly less likely to recognize their reflections than were youngsters who had not been mistreated. What is more, neglected or abused infants who did recognize their mirror image tended to be those who had developed a secure, affectionate bond with their care giver despite the abuse (Schneider-Rosen and Cicchetti, 1984). Thus, the quality of interaction between infant and care giver may be important for the development of self-awareness. Finally, when researchers studied autistic children in the mirror situation, they found that, regardless of a child's age, those who had developed linguistic skills were more likely to recognize their images than children who were mute or who did not use speech to communicate (Spiker and Ricks, 1984). These studies support the importance of social interaction in the development of self-awareness.

Although an infant's self-awareness may be rudimentary, psychologists believe that the roots of these important capacities may develop very early in life. Newborn infants notice and react to the world about them, seeking some kinds of stimulation and avoiding others. Their sensory and motor skills serve as the foundation for the development of complex cognitive and social abilities. The studies reviewed here suggest that the foundation of many complex skills may emerge along with sensory and motor coordination. The young infant's abilities to interact with the environment are far greater than was once thought, and babies begin processing information and interacting with others almost as soon as they are born.

SUMMARY

1. Human development consists of the physical, cognitive, and social changes from birth until the end of life. The infant's motor skills, language, cognition, and social behavior emerge in orderly developmental sequences, which can be described in terms of **norms,** averages derived

from observing many individuals. The age at which a particular baby masters any skill may vary widely from the norm. Variations in the rate of development depend on the hereditary and environmental influences that combine to affect all aspects of development.

2. Genetic influences can be established by studying identical twins or adopted children. The environment also affects all aspects of development. Extreme deprivation can retard development, but most homes provide a reasonable level of stimulation so that enrichment is likely to have only small effects. Although the existence of sensitive periods in human development has been proposed, human beings are resilient and negative environmental effects appear to be the result of continuing bad experiences, not simply bad experience during early development.

3. The thirty-eight-week period of prenatal development can be divided into three periods: the *germinal period* (from conception to the fourth week of pregnancy), when cells multiply rapidly and begin to differentiate; the *embryonic period* (from four to eight weeks), when the organism develops a two-lobed brain and responds to stimulation with movements over large body areas; and the *fetal period* (from eight weeks to birth). By twenty weeks, all neurons have formed, and by twenty-four weeks the fetus cries and moves its eyes. Environmental agents can affect the developing fetus, especially during the first **trimester** (or third) of pregnancy, when basic organ systems are developing. Disease, deficient maternal diet, certain drugs, alcohol, cigarette smoking, and environmental pollution can all produce negative effects on the fetus.

4. A newborn infant is both **precocial** (competent) in sensory skills and **altricial** (helpless) in motor skills. Babies are born with reflexes, such as rooting and grasping, that can be elicited by specific stimuli. Some, such as grasping and stepping, show a repetitive pattern: they appear, disappear, and reappear.

Initial reflexes are controlled by subcortical brain structures; when control shifts to the cortex, they disappear and must be relearned. Newborn infants are probably not confused by the environment because of their limited visual abilities, but vision develops rapidly and by six months, babies see about as clearly as adults do. The rules that appear to guide the newborn's visual survey of the world indicate that infants come into the world equipped to gather information and motivated to seek actively for it. By the time babies are four months old, they perceive colors, dividing the spectrum as adults do. The ability to perceive depth develops some time between three and six months. After babies can move around, they use cues of depth to warn them of danger and are frightened by heights. Newborns can locate sounds in space, turning their heads in the direction of a sound; although this ability is soon lost, it reappears at about four months. Newborns respond to tastes and smells with expressions that resemble the responses of adults. Infant sensory capabilities and the way adults tend to behave with young infants suggests that human evolution has produced a system that encourages the survival and development of the infant.

5. At an early age, babies scan the outlines of faces; later they seek eye contact, reinforcing the social bond. At about four months, they begin to respond to the facial configuration, and by six months they can abstract aspects of an individual face that remain unchanged no matter what the viewing angle or facial expression. Newborn babies appear to imitate adults, but the ability may be reflexive and is probably without intent, as the early smile may also be. Some kind of self-recognition is present at birth, for newborns, who cry when they hear the wail of another newborn, fall silent at the recorded sound of their own cries. Self-awareness (as measured by self-recognition in a mirror) appears to depend on cognitive development, social experience, and linguistic skills. It thus seems to be a product of social interaction. Such self-awareness develops slowly during the second year of life.

KEY TERMS

altricial	fetal alcohol syndrome	norms	trimester
embryo	fetus	precocial	

RECOMMENDED READINGS

ABEL E. Fetal alcohol syndrome: Behavioral territology. *Psychological Bulletin*, 1980, *90*, 564–581. A comprehensive analysis of the negative effects of alcohol consumption during pregancy.

CRNIC, K., et al., Social interaction and developmental competence in preterm and full-term infants in the first year of life. *Child Development*, 1983, *54*, 1199–1210. A study of preterm and full-term infants highlighting the different experiences their mothers have interacting with them.

DECASPER, A., and W. FIFER. Of human bonding: Newborns prefer their mothers' voices. *Science*, 1980, *208*, 1174–1176. The fact that from the opening hours of postnatal existence human newborns show a preference for listening to their mother's rather than a stranger's voice raises intriguing possibilities that learning is going on in the womb during pregnancy.

FIELD, T., et al. Discrimination and imitation of facial expressions by neonates. *Science*, 1982, *218*, 179–181. Innovative research methods reveal that babies just a few days old seem to distinguish happy, sad, and angry faces and even imitate these expressions.

LERNER, R., *Concepts and theories in developmental psychology*. New York: Random House, 1986. Using discussions of the controversies surrounding such key issues as nature versus nurture and continuity versus discontinuity to heighten the reader's involvement, this text covers historical and philosophical bases for developmental issues and theories and their relationships to each other. Also includes excellent discussions of research methodology.

PLOMIN, R., J. C. DeFRIES, and G. McCLEARN. *Behavioral genetics: A primer*. San Francisco: W. H. Freeman, 1980. A clearly written, comprehensive review of most of the issues in the inheritance of behavior.

SCARR, S., and R. WEINBERG. IQ test performance of black children adopted by white families. *American Psychologist*, 1976, *31*, 726–739. Provides evidence from a unique study that both genetics and enviroment contribute in important ways to intellectual functioning.

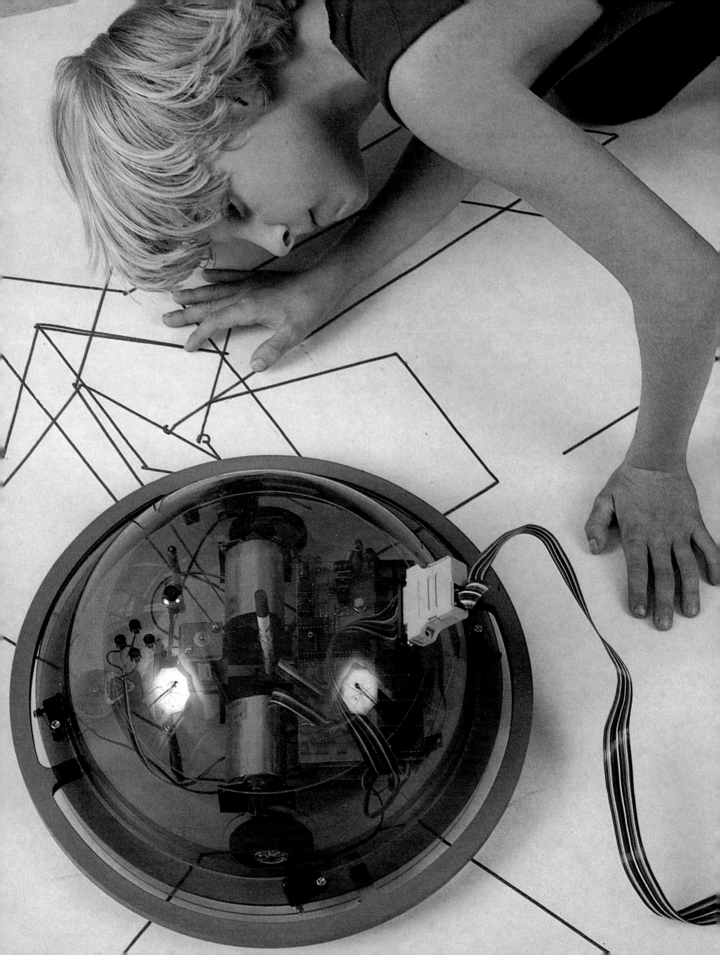

COGNITIVE DEVELOPMENT

Most kindergartners believe that they can make the clouds move by walking and that the sun and moon follow them around. Most preschoolers consider a dog to be an animal but indignantly reject the notion that an insect is also a member of the "animal" class. Is this the way we adults would think? Obviously not: the way young children process information and think about the world is clearly different from the way of a twenty- or thirty-year-old.

But exactly how does children's thinking differ from that of adults? And why? Is the change that occurs as the child grows to adulthood simply a **quantitative change**: Is it merely the result of years of experience, in which the child accumulates memories and experiences so that he or she gradually comes to process new information more swiftly, efficiently, and completely? Or is adult cognition the result of **qualitative changes**: Is it a radical restructuring of the mind, so that the thinking processes of children and adults are different in kind as well as degree? There is no consensus on this issue among psychologists.

Today no one suggests that children are simply miniature adults, as most people believed during the Middle Ages (Aries, 1962). But beyond this fundamental agreement, psychologists take a range of viewpoints.

Some psychologists believe that what seems to be radical change in the child's thought is actually the result of many slow, cumulative changes. According to this view cognitive development is a gradual, continuous process, resembling the growth of a seedling into a flowering plant. Other psychologists believe that children pass through a series of cognitive **stages**: although each stage of development builds on previous ones, the child's thinking patterns at each stage are radically different from thinking patterns at earlier periods. As children mature and gain experience with the world, their mental functions go through a series of reorganizations; after each reorganization, the child passes into a more advanced cognitive stage.

In recent years many psychologists have also tried to discover just what it is that develops in the course of the child's cognitive development. Are the enormous advances that take place in the child's thinking due primarily to rapid expansions in the child's knowledge base—the reservoir from which the child retrieves specific information to apply to tasks or problems? Or do changes take place in the way the child *processes* information? To what extent is the way the child learns and remembers influenced by the development of specific memory strategies? And finally, as children learn about their own mental capacities, does this understanding have an important effect on the way they think? (Siegler, 1983).

We will discuss these issues, as well as the fundamental question of cognitive stages, as we survey cognitive development through infancy, childhood, adolescence, and adulthood. But first, let us turn to one of the giants of psychology, Jean Piaget.

THE PROCESS OF COGNITIVE DEVELOPMENT: PIAGET'S FRAMEWORK

Whatever influences contribute to cognitive development, there is no doubt that the ideas of one individual, the Swiss psychologist Jean Piaget (1896–1980), have served as the catalyst for much of our knowledge about how the child's mind grows. Piaget's careful observations of infants and children have given us a comprehensive account of mental development that has had wide influence on psychologists and educators. For nearly sixty years, Piaget devoted himself to understanding how the child's intelligence becomes increasingly complex, abstract, and subtle, until it is finally transformed into the intelligence of an adult (Piaget, 1952/1966; 1954; 1978; Inhelder and Piaget, 1956). He characterized intelligence as a process by which people actively construct an understanding of reality; he proposed that this understanding—indeed, all knowledge—grows out of interactions between children and objects in the world.

In the course of such interactions, Piaget believed, children encounter discrepancies between what they already understand and what the environment presents to them. As they resolve these discrepancies, their view of objects and events is transformed, and they develop a new, more mature understanding. Piaget saw children as pass-

ing through a series of stages in which they develop new ways of thinking, and he argued that in each of these stages the child's thought is qualitatively different. Vital to this process of intellectual growth are three psychological processes: assimilation, accommodation, and the use of schemes.

Schemes

Babies begin life unable to distinguish between their own bodies and things in the world around them. They have no understanding of the objects (and people) that make up their world, nor do they have any idea of how their own actions affect those objects. But they soon start to acquire this knowledge through a process of exploration and experimentation in which they use recurrent action patterns. These action patterns, which Piaget called **schemes**, include such actions as grasping, sucking, or throwing. They are the infant's form of thought, and they contain organized repeated elements that the infant can generalize to other situations (Gallagher and Reid, 1981).

Infants begin life with a few simple, innate schemes, such as grasping and sucking. It is by using these schemes that infants first come to appreciate much of their world; they understand their environment in terms of things that can be grasped and sucked. A baby girl learns, for instance, that she can grasp a toy duck and lift it in her hand, but that a wall cannot be grasped. Moreover, when the baby girl puts the duck in her mouth and sucks on it, she discovers that its body is soft and pliable—very different from the texture of the crib bar, which she has also tried to suck. From simple actions such as these, infants gradually learn the effects their own movements have on objects, and they also learn some of the properties of those objects.

As children grow older, their schemes for understanding the world become more complicated and less dependent on overt action. The schemes become internalized, so that the child can carry them out mentally. Adding numbers in the head replaces counting on the fingers, and logical reasoning replaces physical experimentation with cause-and-effect relationships. A ten-month-old baby, for example, may explore gravity by dropping peas from her highchair tray and watching intently as each one hits the floor. But an older child, who has come to understand the way gravity

By touching and sucking everything they can reach, babies learn about their world. They also learn that their movements can affect the objects around them.

operates, knows that if any object is released from an elevated position, it will always fall. The scheme that the older child possesses is internalized; that of the infant is not.

Assimilation and Accommodation

According to Piaget, children's thinking is at first isolated into separate schemes. But it becomes increasingly organized, so that related behavior or thought is clustered into systems. The schemes of grasping and looking become coordinated, for example, so that the baby can do both at the same time. As this process continues, the child's thinking steadily becomes more adaptive. The adaptation involves two processes: assimilation and accommodation. Through **assimilation**, the child incorporates new information into old ways of thinking or behaving. Through **accommodation**, the child either modifies old ways of thinking and behaving, or learns new ways that allow him or her to adapt to new objects in the world (Ault, 1983).

We can see how assimilation and accommodation work at a simple level by watching a baby boy—who has been bottle-fed—as he tries to adjust to his first encounter with milk in a cup. The baby is already able to suck competently on a nipple, so at first he tries assimilation, sucking on the cup the way he has always sucked on his bottle. But this strategy does not work, and more milk runs down his chin than enters his mouth. So he modifies, or accommodates, his sucking skills to this new element. Within a few days, he will be using his sucking skills to drain milk from the cup (assimilation), but he will also have modified these skills so that they are more effective for cup drinking (accommodation). His new way of sucking represents a temporary balance between assimilation and accommodation.

Children also use the processes of assimilation and accommodation when they adapt mental schemes to new knowledge. Take, for example, a small girl who knows that a dog is an animal. She will not be able to assimilate insects into her concept of "animal" without some sort of accommodation—in this case, altering the concept of "animal." Perhaps the girl's original concept has required an "animal" to be of a certain size, or to have four feet, or to have a furry coat. But once the girl has broadened the concept, so that it becomes "living things that move," she can assimilate insects into it.

In Piaget's view, cognitive development consists of a continual search for a balance, or equilibrium, between assimilation and accommodation. This process of **equilibration** takes the form of progressive approximations toward an ideal balance that is never reached. Infants start life with relatively simple schemes. As they apply those schemes to the world, they meet new information that cannot be readily assimilated. But through maturation and modification of the schemes as a result of experience, these children become ready to accommodate information they could not have previously handled. When equilibrium is restored through accommodation, the children's thinking advances to a higher level of cognitive organization. As a result, their intelligence grows.

The photos on page 372 show how a child applies a grasping and pulling scheme to a toy, and how she accommodates that scheme by assim-

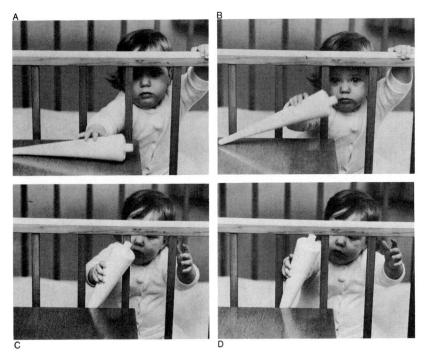

This child possesses a scheme for grasping objects and pulling them to her that does not adequately match the features of the environment that she is now trying to assimilate. Her scheme will not get the toy through the bars of the playpen. An accommodation to her scheme—the addition of turning to grasping and pulling—achieves a state of equilibrium.

ilating features of the environment—the shape of the toy and the space between the bars of the crib. Through this sort of activity, children mature in both their knowledge about the world and their competence in it.

Stages of Intellectual Development

Much of the power of Piaget's view comes from his careful documentation of how children construct their understandings of reality. In his description of intellectual development, Piaget proposed four increasingly complex stages that children always reach in the same order. Whatever labels are attached to them, these periods closely correspond to infancy, the preschool years, later childhood, and adolescence.

■ Through most of the **sensorimotor period**, which encompasses the first two years of life, infants rely on action schemes.
■ After they internalize these schemes, children move into the **preoperational period**, which covers the preschool years. This period is characterized by the development of language and elaborate symbolic play; the children can think, but their thought often

proceeds in a haphazard and seemingly illogical way.
■ The **concrete-operational period** begins to appear about the time children start school. This period is characterized by logical thought—but only in regard to concrete objects.
■ The **formal-operational period** begins around adolescence; this period may continue to develop throughout adulthood, and it represents the culmination of cognitive development. Formal-operational thought is characterized by abstract, hypothetical reasoning, including the ability to assume artificial premises that are known to be false.

The rate at which individual children progress through each of these four stages varies widely, depending on their environment and their genetic makeup. In a suitably rich environment, children gradually acquire the cognitive capabilities that will carry their thinking to a new, more mature stage of intellectual development. Yet the thought processes of the earlier periods are not entirely lost—they are simply reduced in importance. For example, an adult who has mastered formal-operational thinking does not always use it; at times this adult functions at the level of an earlier period. When you ride a bicycle, you use sensori-motor thought; when you become angry at a stalled car that "refuses" to start, you fall back on preoperational thought; and when you double a recipe in order to feed your dinner guests, you use concrete-operational thought.

The remainder of this chapter is devoted to the cognitive changes that occur during these four basic periods and throughout adulthood. The presentation draws heavily on the work of Piaget, but it also includes the research of other psychologists who see development less as a series of stages than as a continuous process.

INFANCY

During the first two years of life, there is an enormous growth in children's cognitive skills, as biological maturation interacts with the children's cumulative experience. As children's minds begin to control their muscles, reflexive actions give way to deliberate movements guided by thought (Kopp, 1982). Memory also develops: the infant who seemed to forget an object as soon as it was removed from sight becomes the toddler who imitates actions seen days, or even weeks, earlier. From a very early age, infants can process complex information, and by the time they are two years old, they have established basic concepts and categories of thought (Harris, 1983). We can trace these achievements by examining three areas of cognitive development during infancy: learning, memory, and the development of the object concept.

The Infant's Capacity for Learning

As noted in Chapter 14, babies are capable of learning from the moment of birth, and perhaps even earlier. Babies less than six months old can learn to suck on a pacifier in order to clear up a television picture (Siqueland and Delucia, 1969). They can also learn to babble in order to get tickled (Rheingold, Gewirtz, and Ross, 1959).

Conditioning and the Newborn

Conditioning techniques are fairly effective with babies—even with newborns. In one operant-conditioning experiment (DeCasper and Carstens, 1981), babies only a few days old learned to turn on a tape recording of a woman singing lullabies and light opera by sucking on a pacifier at a specific pace. Ordinarily, babies suck at nipples in bursts separated by pauses of several seconds, and the researchers based their experiment on this pattern. To hear music the newborns had to learn to wait for a prescribed minimum interval before they began a new burst of sucking. The infants quickly learned to modify their bursts of sucking in order to hear the music. When the connection was removed, so that no matter how the babies adjusted their sucking pattern they could not control the music, they began to grimace, cry, and move about in an apparent display of distress.

It seems that human newborns have the capacity to learn simple connections between their actions and events. But those connections cannot be arbitrary. The most successful conditioning of young infants relies on responses connected with survival, such as head turning and sucking (Sameroff and Cavanaugh, 1979).

Learning for the Fun of It

Once they are more than a month old, babies seem to learn readily. Moreover, solving a problem or discovering the relationship between their own actions and an event in the external world seems to have its own rewards for infants (J. S. Watson, 1972).

The pleasure involved in such an experience seemed obvious in one study of two- to four-month-old infants who were given a chance to control a yellow-and-green mobile. One of these mobiles was suspended above each infant, who lay in a crib with a ribbon attached to one ankle. The other end of the ribbon was attached to the hook from which the mobile was suspended. As the infants moved about, waving their arms and kicking their legs, they learned to connect the motion of one leg with the bobbing of the mobile. As they smiled and gurgled at the moving mobile, their kicks lost any random quality; the infants began to kick the leg attached to the mobile vigorously and precisely—and only that leg. Apparently, they enjoyed controlling the mobile, for they would continue their excited manipulation of the mobile for as long as forty-five minutes (Rovée-Collier, 1984).

Nor is this pleasure in mastery limited to in-

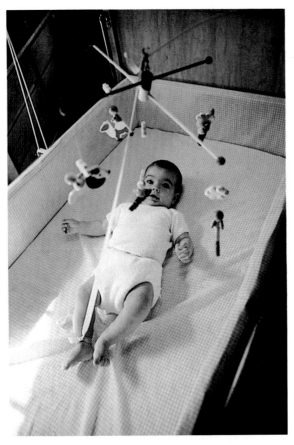

Babies can make their own fun. Several investigators have found that if a mobile is attached to an infant in such a way that the infant's own movements activate the mobile, the infant soon discovers this relationship and coos, smiles, and seems to delight in making the appropriate kick to set the mobile in motion.

fants. In an experiment with fifth and sixth graders (Harter, 1974), the children were asked to solve some word puzzles that varied in difficulty. The youngsters smiled more, and reported far more pleasure, when they solved a difficult puzzle than an easy one. The implication is that human beings of any age—from infancy to old age—derive pleasure from intellectual mastery.

Infant Memory

Unless babies remember what they have seen or heard, they cannot learn. But babies cannot tell researchers whether they remember sounds or objects. For this reason most studies of infant

memory rely on habituation, which we investigated in Chapter 8. Babies are shown a stimulus until they stop looking at it, a sign indicating that they have become bored with the stimulus. The babies are then shown the same stimulus again, along with a new stimulus. If the babies look at the new stimulus in preference to the old one, researchers assume that they are paying attention to the new stimulus because of its novelty. They recognize the old stimulus but not the new one. As babies mature, they habituate more rapidly; two-month-olds remember a stimulus very well if they are allowed to look at it until they lose interest. But when babies are given only brief exposure to a stimulus, and it is removed while they are still looking intently at it, they may not remember it—even if they are six months old (Rose, 1981). Whether the ability to recognize a familiar stimulus improves during the first year of life is uncertain (Rovée-Collier, 1984); however, after babies are a year old, there is little evidence of developmental differences in the ability to retain information once it has been acquired (Werner and Perlmutter, 1979).

Recognition and Recall

From studies using the habituation technique, we can conclude that even a newborn can form a memory of a stimulus, retain that memory for five to ten seconds, and then compare it with a new stimulus. In short, newborns show evidence of the form of retrieval called recognition. Studies have also shown that infants' memory for sounds, three-dimensional objects, patterns, and photographs is quite durable. In one experiment, four- to six-month-old infants were shown a photograph of a human face for several minutes. Two weeks later the babies were brought back into the laboratory and shown the same photograph they had seen before, along with the photograph of a different person. They consistently looked longer at the new photograph than at the old one, demonstrating that they recognized the original photograph (Fagan, 1973).

Babies seem to recognize an object almost automatically. But what about recall? This form of retrieval requires babies to carry out a more active search of their memories, without being cued by whatever they are to remember. Because babies cannot talk, there is little experimental evidence to show the existence of recall among them. However, many such incidents turned up in a study in which researchers asked parents of seven- to eleven-month-old infants to observe their babies carefully and to record instances of recall. Some parents reported that their babies seemed surprised when a household item, such as a bottle of baby lotion, was not in its accustomed place; others said that their babies seearched for people or objects, and many parents said their infants recalled the routine of games (Ashmead and Perlmutter, 1980). In another study (DeLoache, 1980), eighteen-month-old infants who had watched their mothers hide a toy later recalled its hiding place; as soon as the infants were permitted to search for the toy, they found it, although there had been a lengthy delay between the hiding and the search. Just what retrieval cues these youngsters depended on is uncertain, but it appears that younger children need specific, detailed cues in order to remember something, whether it is an object, a location, or an event (Daehler and Greco, 1985). For infants and very young children, the recall situation may have to match the encoding situation so closely that recall becomes difficult to distinguish from recognition. As children pass through toddlerhood, they seem to need fewer and less specific cues, and they can recall information in more varied settings.

Infant Amnesia

Anecdotal evidence suggests that much of what babies see and hear is not permanently retained. Although infancy is a time when an impressive amount of information about the world is learned, few people claim to remember specific events from the first two years of life. Why? Perhaps we cannot remember because we had no language at the time. Permanent memory tends to emerge at about the same time as language ability, and many researchers have suggested that we cannot remember specifics unless we receive verbal labels (see Nelson and Ross, 1980). Or perhaps Freud was right and events from infancy are repressed —in this view, many of our memories cannot be retrieved because of a motivational or emotional block. Still another possibility is that encoding during infancy may be heavily dependent on the context: later situations may rarely be similar enough to provide the cues that would elicit a memory (White and Pillemer, 1979). A fourth interpretation is that the failure to lay down permanent memories is related to the immaturity of neurons in the infant brain (Campbell et al., 1974).

In an experiment supporting this last idea, baby rats eleven to sixteen days old were conditioned to fear a tone by associating the sound with a brief shock (Coulter, Collier, and Campbell, 1976). Six weeks later when they heard the tone again, the rats showed little evidence of fear. Yet rats who had learned to fear the tone when they were seventeen days old were still afraid of it after a lapse of six weeks. This abrupt change in a rat's apparent capacity for long-term memory occurs during a period of rapid brain development, suggesting that infantile amnesia in young rats may be due to the immaturity of brain structures. Like rats, human infants are born with immature neurons and incompletely developed neural circuits. Thus, neural maturation may underlie the emergence of an ability to store information so that it can be retrieved from long-term memory.

Obviously, babies do not forget everything they learn; the problem is to explain why some things are recalled and others forgotten. A series of experiments Carolyn Rovée-Collier (1984) had conducted with human infants suggests that repeated environmental cues may be as important as neural maturation in establishing memories. Three-month-old babies learn to operate a mobile by kicking their feet, in the same arrangement discussed earlier. When fourteen days pass without their having another chance to control the mobile, the babies seem to have forgotten their skill and must learn it all over again. Yet when babies are brought into the laboratory thirteen days after learning to operate the mobile and are allowed to see—but not operate—it, they are as proficient at controlling it on the fourteenth day as they were two weeks earlier.

Strangely enough, it seems to take time for the sight of the mobile to stir infant memory: babies who see the mobile on the thirteenth day cannot operate it an hour later, but by the following day have recalled the skill. In addition, only the sight of the *original* mobile reactivates the memory. Rovée-Collier suggests that when babies seem to forget, it is not because an event has been wiped from memory but because the event has become inaccessible. Given the correct cues, infants would presumably be able to remember it. This effect is not limited to young infants; reencounters with the original stimuli have also improved memory in older infants and children (Cornell, 1984).

Sensorimotor Intelligence and the Object Concept

Most of what babies learn during the first few months consists of simple relationships among objects in the world, and relationships between babies' own behavior and those objects. Such learning, which is the result of the baby's spontaneous activity, is part of what Piaget calls sensorimotor intelligence. Babies learn to act in the world by repeating behavior that gives them pleasure. Throughout the first year these actions become coordinated into larger schemes, which babies begin to use to attain a goal—such as tugging a cloth to reach an attractive toy that is lying on it. It is important to note, however, that infants do not appear to contemplate these actions—they do not seem to think about what they are doing and why they are doing it.

One of the most significant accomplishments of infancy is the development of the **object concept**, which is based on an understanding of **object permanence**, or the awareness that objects continue to exist when out of sight. According to Piaget, very young infants do not seem to understand that their bodies are separate objects in a world of objects. Nor do they appear to realize that objects have a permanent existence apart from the babies' own interactions with them.

The ability to conceive of objects as having an existence of their own emerges gradually during the first two years of life. Until babies are about four months old, they seem to have no object concept at all. They follow a toy with their eyes, and if it is within their reach, they grasp it. But when the object is moved out of sight, the babies act as if it had never been there. They neither search for it nor show any other sign that they are aware of its continued existence.

The first signs of the object concept appear around the fourth month, although some researchers (Bower, 1974) believe it may develop earlier. If an object moves across their visual field, infants between four and eight months turn their head to follow it; they also keep following the object's path after it has vanished from sight. They seem to make a visual search for the missing object. And if only part of a familiar object is visible—if, for example, the handle of a rattle sticks out from beneath a blanket—babies of this age often reach for the toy, suggesting that they realize that the rest of it is attached to the exposed part. At an earlier stage infants would not have

reached for the rattle unless it had been fully visible. Now, however, babies begin to understand that an object may still exist even if it is partially hidden. Their object concept is still rudimentary at this stage. If the object is suddenly covered completely by a piece of paper or a pillow, babies will neither search for the object nor pull it back if they are holding it. When a cloth is dropped over something in their hand, infants seem unaware that the object is within their grasp and often let go of it, withdrawing the empty hand (Gratch, 1972).

From about eight to twelve months, infants will search with their hands for an object that disappears. Suppose a baby girl is shown a desirable toy. While she watches, the toy is put under a pillow. At this stage, she will pull away the pillow and grab the toy. But if she had found the toy under one pillow earlier, she is likely to look for the toy under that pillow, even though it was moved under a second pillow while she watched. This consistent error in searching for an object has been explained in several ways. The baby may associate the toy with the place where it was previously found and thus may fail to remember where the object has just been hidden (Bjork and Cummings, 1984). She may remember, not the place, but the *response* that earlier won the toy, or she may even know where the toy is but be unable to inhibit the earlier learned response that gained her the toy (Bremner and Bryant, 1977).

From about twelve to eighteen months, children can follow all visible movements of an object and find it in the last place it was hidden. When an object is hidden under one pillow and then under a second, a third, or even a fourth pillow, the child can find it. Yet at this age, babies cannot cope with transformations they cannot see. Suppose a small toy is hidden in a matchbox and the box is placed under a pillow. Then the object is surreptitiously slipped from the box and left under the pillow. If the empty box is placed in front of a little girl, she will look inside it for the toy. But she will not search under the pillow, because she cannot consider the possibility that something she did not see might have happened. Not until near the end of the second year do children understand that other people can surreptitiously move an object from place to place (Bertenthal and Fischer, 1983). This development is significant because it indicates that children can now hold the image of an object in short-term memory long enough to search for it, and they realize that other people may be agents who move objects. At this point children can be said to have a fully developed object concept.

EARLY CHILDHOOD

Preschoolers have left the cognitive world of infancy behind them. Their play now demonstrates a capacity for **deferred imitation**, the ability to mimic actions they have observed at an earlier time. They have discovered that symbols can stand for objects and words, and they are rapidly acquiring language. These capacities are signs of new representational skills. Clearly, the intelligence of young children is very different from the action-bound intelligence of infants. But it is also different from the "sensible" thought of later childhood, when children begin to think about concrete objects in logical ways.

At the preschool age, children begin to acquire many cognitive skills that will be important to them in adult life. They learn to count, for example, and to classify objects into general categories. They know that mashed potatoes are "food" and so is hamburger, and that a parakeet is a "bird" and so is a robin. But young children's grasp of these concepts may be deceptive. Their intelligence during this period, in what Piaget calls the preoperational stage, is based on intuition, not logic.

Advances in the Young Child's Thinking

The acquisition of the object concept, which occurs toward the end of the sensorimotor stage, marks the beginning of **representational thought** —the ability to mentally represent objects that are not directly visible. This important cognitive skill is essential to the intelligence of the preschool child, for it breaks the boundaries of immediate perception, allowing the child to imagine things that might happen and to recall things that have already happened.

Now that the child can think in this way, a number of new accomplishments are possible. Language is the most obvious example of this new thought: language can refer to, or represent, objects that are not present. In addition, deferred imitation expands into the rich, symbolic play of

A child's ability to sort rings and boxes according to their size and shape develops between ages two and three. These steps in cognitive development will enable the child to make judgments based on rudimentary logic.

childhood. Children also show insight: when they confront a simple problem, they can think about it for a moment and then solve it.

When they are two or three years old, children can grasp some of the concepts they need to understand the way objects are grouped into classes. Children as young as two can sort a pile of objects (say, dolls and rings) into separate piles. A child this young is likely to put all the dolls in one pile before moving the rings into another: he or she appears to keep only one thing in mind at a time. By the time children are three years old, however, they can keep both classes in mind and can sort the toys by separating first a doll, then a ring, from the pile of objects (Sugarman, 1983). When children can form mental representations of the way objects and classes are interrelated, they may be able to think about the similarity of objects within a class—not simply recognize the class. At that point, they can begin to develop a rudimentary understanding of the logical basis underlying classification.

The glimmerings of a concept of number appear as early as the third year of life. Two-year-olds count, although they may count only as far as two and may invent their own sequence of number words, which they use consistently. As they count objects, they point to them or touch them, and say their number words aloud. Four- and five-year-olds can count a group of objects in many ways; they can start with a different object each time, indicating that they are developing an understanding of the principles that govern counting. They can add and subtract, and they can figure out whether one group of objects contains the same number of items as a second group. If one object is taken from the second group, they will notice it. But young children can do all these things only if the number of objects they must deal with is small, and they must always count them (Gelman and Gallistel, 1978).

Immature Features of the Young Child's Thinking

Through representational thought, preschool children develop an intuitive understanding of many complex tasks, but their intellectual capacities are in many ways still immature. For one thing, their thought is egocentric. This term does not mean that children are selfish, but that they are prisoners of their own viewpoint. Because of their **egocentrism**, preschool children seem to believe that other people see things just as they see them and react in exactly the same way in all situations.

For example, in one study (Piaget and Inhelder, 1956), children were shown a scale model of three mountains in a triangular arrangement (see Figure 15.1). After the children walked around the model and looked at it from all sides, each child sat in a chair facing one of the mountains. Then the child looked at a series of photographs and chose the one that showed what a doll sitting on the opposite side of the model would see. Repeatedly, the child chose the picture showing her or his own view of the landscape. Even when the child was allowed to get up and look at the mountains from the doll's position, the youngster still came back and chose the picture that showed the display from her or his own seat.

Some investigators have pointed out that children's errors when faced with a situation like the mountain landscape may not always be the result of egocentrism. When the experiment is redesigned so that it places less demand on developing cognitive skills, such as language or memory, and more closely parallels incidents in children's dai-

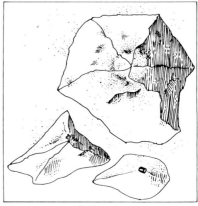

Position A

Figure 15.1. A model used to demonstrate egocentrism. Piaget and Inhelder first had children walk all around the model and look at it from all sides. Then they seated children of various ages at position A and asked them how the scene would appear to observers at other positions. Preoperational children regularly indicated that the scene would appear as it did from position A, no matter where the observer was located. Their thinking did not allow them to mentally reconstruct the scene from a point of view other than their own. (After Piaget and Inhelder, 1956.)

ly lives, their performance improves sharply (Donaldson, 1979; Flavell, Shipstead, and Croft, 1978). When compared with older children, however, the young child's thought is relatively egocentric.

A second immature feature of the young child's thought is known as **complexive thinking** (Vygotsky, 1962), in which the child's thought jumps from one idea to the next instead of unifying a number of ideas around a single theme. This kind of thought is illustrated in the following poem written by Hilary-Anne Farley, age five:

I LOVE ANIMALS AND DOGS

I love animals and dogs and everything
But how can I do it when dogs are dead and a
  hundred?
But here's the reason: If you put a golden egg
  on them

They'll get better. But not if you put a star or
  moon.
But the star-moon goes up
And the star-moon I love. (Lewis, 1966)

Although the thought in this poem frequently
shows connections between adjacent ideas, it has
no overall integration. Evidently, some element in
one idea made Hilary-Anne think of another idea;
some element in the second idea made her think of
a third, and so on. Although every idea is related to
some other, the various ideas are not coordinated
into a meaningful whole. Complexive thinking like
Hilary-Anne's is common in preschoolers, and this
fact helps to explain why a young child might
believe that a tree, which is covered with a substance called "bark," might also be able to "bite"
(Chukovsky, 1968).

Finally, young children's thought is often directed by the distinctive perceptual features of
whatever is before them. Their thinking often
seems excessively guided and directed by external
cues. At times this tendency is helpful, as when a
child attends to the projections and indentations
that determine how blocks fit together. But sometimes perceptual cues can mislead a child; for
instance, when an array of six candies is spread
over a large dish, the child may believe that there
are more candies than when seven candies are
placed side by side. Preschoolers' tendency to rely
on the immediate, highly visible features of objects
and arrays gives rise to a related problem. Often,
these young children focus on the current states of
objects or situations rather than on the transformations these objects or states may have undergone. Faced with a problem whose solution requires the integration of information over time,
preschoolers may have difficulty because their
thought is so dominated by their current perceptions. For example, if a young child watches a
ferocious dog mask placed over the head of a
friendly cat, the child may be frightened until the
mask is removed (DeVries, 1969).

These limitations of young children's thought
form a unified picture. On the one hand, the
children's capacity for representation allows them
to carry on new, complex kinds of mental activity.
On the other hand, because they lack the ability to
organize their thinking into coordinated systems,
young children's thought is egocentric, complexive, and controlled by prominent cues in the environment.

MIDDLE CHILDHOOD

Although some of the thinking of older children is
similar to the intuitive thought of preschoolers,
older children can think in ways that younger
children cannot. About the time they begin school,
children enter what Piaget called the stage of
concrete operations, in which they begin to think
logically about concrete objects and understand
simple transformations of them. In addition, certain developmental differences that appear during
middle childhood, including some that have been
described by Piaget, arise in part from changes in
how children store and organize information in
memory, in part from their growing knowledge
base, and in part from children's increased understanding of the way their own minds work.

A good place to begin our exploration of these
gradual changes is in the child's understanding of
conservation, or the principle that irrelevant
changes in the external appearance of objects have
no effect on certain physical attributes of the
object. Piaget used this phenomenon to illustrate
the development of concrete-operational thought.

The Concept of Conservation

Children's understanding of the conservation of
quantity can be tested in a simple manner. First, a
child is shown two identical containers filled to
the same level with water, as shown in the photographs on page 380. After the child agrees that
there is an equal amount of water in the two squat
containers, the experimenter—calling attention to
his or her actions—pours the liquid from one
container into a tall, narrow container and asks
the child whether the tall and the squat container
now hold the same amount of water. A child who
understands the conservation of quantity will say
that the water in both the tall and the squat
containers remains equal. But a child who lacks
the concept will assert that the tall container has
more water.

A child who has mastered this aspect of conservation is also likely to understand the conservation of number: he or she is certain, for example,
that when two equal rows of marbles are lined up,
spreading out the marbles in one row does not
increase their number, nor does bunching up the
marbles decrease their number. Other similar
concepts that are grasped early in the concrete-

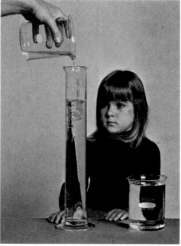

The girl taking part in this demonstration has not yet acquired the ability to understand the concept of conservation of quantity of liquid. She agrees that there is an equal amount of water in the two shorter beakers on the right, but when the water from one of them is poured into the taller beaker on the left, she incorrectly asserts that there is more water in the taller beaker than in the shorter. To develop an understanding of the principle of conservation, the child must be able to coordinate her thoughts about the length and width of the first container, the length and width of the second container, and the change or transformation brought about by pouring the liquid from the shorter beaker into the taller. Preoperational children cannot do this: they consider the state of each container separately, and consequently point to the beaker that "looks like more" as the one that actually "is more."

operational period are the conservation of length and the conservation of mass, illustrated in Figure 15.2. All these transformations involve the conservation of quantity.

It will be several years before the child understands less obvious transformations. One of these is conservation of weight. Another is the conservation of volume: a change in an object's shape does not change the amount of water the object displaces (Piaget and Inhelder, 1941). And although older children understand a growing number of specific concrete operations, they cannot yet understand the similarities among them.

Piaget maintained that an eight-year-old who is

able to grasp conservation is in a qualitatively different stage of cognitive development from a four-year-old who does not understand the concept. As a result of maturation and appropriate

Figure 15.2. Examples of problems for which a child must acquire the concept of conservation. Concrete-operational children interiorize the possibility of making and unmaking the transformations for each task shown here. Thus, they come to see the lengths and quantities as unchanged in each case. Preoperational children, whose thinking is more static, are not able to imagine the transformations required and respond to perceptually striking but irrelevant aspects of the objects in attempting to answer the questions. For example, preoperational children will answer that there are more marbles in the bottom row than in the top one.

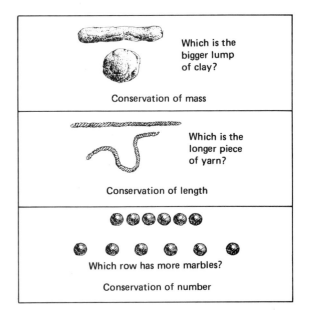

environmental experiences, the older child's thinking has become reorganized and now functions in a logical fashion. The older child's thought is less centered on the immediate perceptual features of a situation, such as the height of liquid in the second container. The child's thought has also become more *reversible:* he or she is able to note that if the water were poured back into its original container, the amount of liquid would still be the same. Or the child may note that the amount is the same because the narrow width of the second, slender container compensates for its height. These responses demonstrate a firm grasp of conservation and, according to Piaget, support his position that the older youngster can mentally reverse a transformation.

Other researchers disagree with Piaget's interpretation of younger children's apparent inability to conserve. These researchers have tried making simple changes in the circumstances of a test: they may, for example, allow the children to pour the water themselves, or they may fail to indicate that the experimenter's actions are important, or they may not ask the children about the quantity of water before its appearance is manipulated. When these simple changes are made, there is an increase in the number of five- and six-year-olds who answer the critical question correctly (Donaldson, 1979; Rose and Blank, 1974). Moreover, it is possible to teach conservation to children who seem to be "nonconservers"—by providing appropriate feedback (Brainerd, 1978), by giving the children training experiences that encourage them to attend to relevant information (Gelman, 1969), or by pairing them with conservers and requiring the pair to arrive at a mutually agreeable solution to conservation problems (Murray, 1972). Taken together, these findings suggest that it is impossible to say with assurance that there are qualitative, stagelike differences in the cognitive skills of preschoolers and schoolchildren (Daehler and Bukatko, 1985).

Supporters of Piaget's theory argue that training studies, and other studies that claim to demonstrate conservation in preschool children, really produce performance that does not depend on the sort of logical thinking with which Piaget was concerned. According to these supporters, qualitative changes in thought are still the best way to explain developmental changes from nonconservation to conservation (Acredolo, 1982). Other observers, however, believe that tests of conservation and other concepts generally involve more

than one cognitive skill. They note that the preschooler's perception, attention, and grasp of language can affect the results—as can a simple desire to give the researcher the answer she or he seems to want; so the change in performance may not be as clear-cut an indication of the reorganization of thought as Piaget believed (Murray, 1972).

Memory Development in Children

Older children also do much better than preschoolers on tasks that involve memory. There are a number of reasons for this improved performance. Older children use memory strategies (techniques for storing and retrieving information) more effectively, they encode stimuli more efficiently, they have an increasingly organized knowledge base into which information can be embedded and with which information can be coordinated, and they have an emerging awareness of how their own memory works and how they can use it to improve their performance on various tasks.

It is helpful to survey the course of this memory development, starting back at the preschool age. In order to remember where an item has been hidden, preschoolers use simple strategies such as looking at objects and touching them (Wellman, Ritter, and Flavell, 1975); when looking for a lost object, they confine their search to locations they have visited after they last used the object (Wellman, Somerville, and Haake, 1979). But by and large, preschoolers fail to display many deliberate strategies that could increase their retrieval of information.

This pattern gradually changes. Rehearsal, the simplest strategy, begins to develop about the time children start school, and by the time children are in the fifth grade, most of them deliberately rehearse material they are trying to memorize. Children are apparently capable of rehearsal before they begin to use it on their own. In one study, researchers watched a group of first graders who were trying to memorize a list of words and noted that some tended to repeat the words softly to themselves, spontaneously rehearsing the items, while others did not. But when the children who had not spontaneously rehearsed a list of items were asked to whisper the names of the items while they waited to be tested, their recall increased and they remembered as many items as the children who had spontaneously rehearsed

CHILDREN IN THE COURTROOM: ARE THEY RELIABLE WITNESSES?

In recent years charges of sex abuse at nursery schools in California and New York have depended on the testimony of child witnesses. But how reliable is their testimony? At one time, psychologists believed that it was virtually worthless. Piaget contended that children found it difficult to distinguish between reality and fantasy, or between dreams and memories; he would have found a child witness unreliable until about the age of eleven or twelve (Piaget, 1929).

Later research, however, indicates that children have no trouble distinguishing between fact and fantasy when describing the actions of other people. In a series of studies, Marcia Johnson and Mary Ann Foley (1984; Foley, Johnson, and Raye, 1983) found that six-year-olds were no more likely to confuse events than adults were. The children knew whether they had made a particular statement or whether another person had said it, and they also knew whether the other person had made a particular statement or had been told to think about saying it. On only one test did the six-year-olds do worse than the adults: the children had trouble distinguishing what they had actually said aloud from what they had only imagined themselves saying.

If children are no more confused about other people's actions than adults, are they as reliable when asked to testify? The answer seems to be, sometimes yes and sometimes no, depending on the circumstances. In one situation, a child may be a more accurate witness than an adult: when testimony depends on noticing some incidental event. If adults are absorbed in following some action or train of thought, incidental stimuli seem not to register. But young children, who do not seem to focus their attention in the same single-minded manner as adults, are likely to see and remember the incidental event. This difference appeared in a study in which Ulric Neisser (1979) was studying selective perception. Neisser asked subjects to watch videotapes of basketball games and to follow the ball closely as it was passed from one player to the next. During the game, a woman carrying an umbrella walked across the court, an incident that was certainly out of place. When the subjects were asked if anything unusual had happened, only 21 percent of the adults recalled seeing the woman with the umbrella. But 75 percent of the six-year-olds remembered seeing her. (Ten-year-olds apparently concentrated as narrowly as did the adults; only 22 percent saw the woman.)

Children are also less likely to make inferences about what they have seen than adults are. Because children have a smaller store of knowledge, they are unlikely to distort information by incorrect expectations or unwarranted inferences (Johnson and Foley, 1984). For example, in one study, adults who looked at a picture of a subway scene usually reported that they had seen a black man holding a razor. Children who recalled seeing the razor always reported—accurately— that it had been held by a white man (Allport and Postman, 1947). In some situations, of course, the child's small store of knowledge will prevent him or her from drawing correct inferences that could be helpful to police.

(Keeney, Cannizzo, and Flavell, 1967). The nature of rehearsal changes with age, and eleven-year-olds go about it in a more organized and efficient way than do eight-year-olds (Ornstein and Naus, 1978).

The more sophisticated form of rehearsal is elaborative rehearsal; when using this strategy, the child links the items with verbal phrases or visual images in order to learn them (see Chapter 9). Children rarely discover elaborative rehearsal on their own; in fact, the practice of creating images that link or integrate items is not consistently found until adolescence. But the ability to use this technique develops much earlier: even four-year-olds can manage to use it when given exact instructions. Until children are about eleven, however, they seem unable to use imagery effectively in a wide variety of situations (Daehler and Bukatko, 1985).

Another common memory strategy of adults is

A child's testimony is also likely to be more sketchy than the testimony of an adult, because children generally remember fewer details. This lack of detail is due in part to the child's smaller knowledge base (the person who knows more about a situation is likely to have a better memory of it) and in part to the child's failure to use various strategies to encode information (Johnson and Foley, 1984).

Witnesses often have to identify suspects. How accurately can children identify a culprit? If we judge by laboratory studies, we would have to say that the younger the child, the poorer the chances of accurate identification (Chance and Goldstein, 1984). Young children are also more likely to make false identifications than adults. But in these studies the subjects looked at photographs and later tried to pick them out of a group; such studies may not tell us much about identification in criminal cases.

When children have to identify a suspect, their performance is likely to vary with the situation. In one study (Marin et al., 1979), subjects had to identify a "culprit" who burst into the room, shouted at the experimenter for fifteen seconds, and then ran out. Five- and six-year-olds were as accurate as college students: both selected the correct culprit 54 percent of the time. In this instance, suggest June Chance and Alvin Goldstein (1984), the children probably saw the situation as more serious than did the college students and therefore paid more attention to the culprit. In all such simulation studies, say the researchers, everyone—child or adult—seems to do an equally poor job of identifying suspects. Chance and Goldstein (1984) point out that children's ability to recognize a face is affected by the same factors that affect an adult's memory; they conclude that no one can say whether these factors have a stronger effect on children than on adults.

Like adults, children find it difficult to identify a person they have seen only briefly, say, when they see a stranger mug someone. However, when the person is familiar to them, as was the case in many of the sexual abuse trials of recent years, the child's identification tends to be highly accurate.

A final problem with child witnesses is one that may cause the most concern. How suggestible is the child witness? Can a clever lawyer use leading questions to get the child to testify incorrectly? Again, the answer seems to be that it depends on the situation. After reviewing the available studies, Elizabeth Loftus and Graham Davies (1984) concluded that when children are testifying about an event they understand and find interesting, they are probably no more vulnerable to suggestion and leading questions than adults. It is important to note that studies have shown that adults are themselves open to suggestion and that leading questions in some cases can change their memory of an event. However, if the child did not understand the event (and so encoded it poorly) or if the child's memory of the event has become relatively less accessible, the child will probably be more suggestible than the adult and more vulnerable to leading questions.

If children are to be used as witnesses, their testimony will probably be most accurate if they are questioned by someone who has no preconceived impression of what actually happened (Dent, 1982). And if children must identify suspects, they will probably be more accurate if the identification is carried out through a one-way window, so that the child does not have to confront the suspect (Dent and Stephenson, 1979).

---

organization, in which material to be learned is grouped, often on the basis of categories. This technique is fairly common among children after they are about ten years old. If items to be learned are presented to preschoolers by category, the children will show improved recall, but they will not organize a scrambled list on their own. Five- and six-year-olds can learn to categorize items efficiently, and when they do so, their recall improves; but when they are given a new list to remember, they fail to use the strategy (Scribner and Cole, 1972). Of course, the better the child's grasp of conceptual categories, the more efficiently he or she will use this strategy.

Much of the improvement that appears in the memory of older children seems due not to an increase in memory capacity but to increased skill in the use of strategies. Indeed, some psychologists (Chi, 1976; Brown, 1975) believe that there is no increase in memory capacity after children are about five. What *does* improve thgoughout childhood, evidently, is the ability to identify incoming information quickly (Dempster, 1981). As children grow older, they probably spend less effort and devote less attention to this phase of encoding; this frees them to become increasingly efficient at storing items. Other improvements stem from older children's increased knowledge and from their growing awareness that memory, including the conscious and practiced use of strategies, is a valuable tool.

The importance of a knowledge base for memory showed clearly in a study by Michelene Chi (1978). Chi discovered that when children know more about a subject than adults do, it is the adults' performance on memory tasks that is inferior. In her study, children who were skilled chess players recalled chess positions much better than adults who were novice chess players. When ten-year-old chess players were asked to reproduce eight middle-game positions that had an average of twenty-two pieces, not only did they recall more chunks of information than did the adults, but they also tended to include more chess pieces in the first chunks they recalled.

Because preschool children seem unaware of the way that memory operates or of its capabilities and limitations, instructing four-year-olds to remember a set of pictures yields no more recall than simply telling them to "look at" the pictures. Eleven-year-olds, by contrast recall many more items when instructed to remember them (Appel et al., 1972). Younger children are simply unaware that such strategies as rehearsal or grouping will help them to remember; even when they are shown how to use a strategy, they drop it as soon as its use is no longer required (Keeney, Cannizzo, and Flavell, 1967). But once a strategy has been taught to older children, they continue to use it. As children come to understand the process of remembering and forgetting, they begin to *plan* to remember, setting a memory goal and using strategies to help them reach it (Flavell, 1977).

Organizing Concepts

Another way to contrast the thinking capacities of older children with those of preschoolers is to compare the way the children organize their concepts about the world. Preschoolers have developed a wide range of concepts, and they can apply symbols, such as "dog," "poodle," or "fox terrier,"

to many related examples of the concept. These concepts are based on the perceptual qualities and functions of objects in the categories; as children gain experience, their concepts increasingly resemble those of adults (Anglin, 1977).

Most of the concepts acquired by very young children are basic-level concepts (see Chapter 10). Throughout the preschool years, knowledge of superordinate- and subordinate-level concepts is gradually acquired (Mervis and Crisafi, 1982). When children enter school, they face the task of organizing these concepts into the hierarchical system that adults use—understanding, for example, that poodles, terriers, and spaniels are all subordinate classes of the basic-level class "dogs," and that dogs, cats, and cows are all subclasses of the superordinate class "animals." This sort of knowledge requires the child to analyze objects on more than one level and to coordinate his or her thinking about objects and how they are related.

When a late preschool child is asked to sort a group of small toys (eight poodles, two terriers, and three cats), he or she can answer a number of questions about the classification. Asked which toys are dogs, the child points to the poodles and the terriers. Asked which are animals, the child points to all three groups. Such a child seems to understand the hierarchy of classes. But another question will reveal that the youngster's understanding is incomplete. Given eight toy poodles and two toy terriers and asked whether there are more dogs or more poodles, the preschool child will say "more poodles." Piaget (1952) explained this response by saying that preoperational children cannot think of both a class and a subclass at the same time; therefore they cannot compare them. But concrete-operational children, said Piaget, have mastered the hierarchy of classes and understand that one class includes another. Despite the distinction drawn by Piaget, many eight- and nine-year-olds fail such tests and, like the preschooler, insist that there are more poodles than dogs (Winer, 1980).

As with conservation, the way the problem is posed affects the number of children who understand it. The key to understanding the relationship between classes and subclasses may go back to Piaget's notion of thinking simultaneously about the class and the subclass. However, other explanations may be equally valid. For example, the question "Are there more dogs or more poodles?" which contrasts a basic-level class with one of its subordinate classes, is unusual. Most comparisons we are asked to make are between classes at the same level of a hierarchy, such as "Are there more poodles or terriers?" When the question is slightly rephrased or when the difference between the basic and subordinate levels is emphasized, children's performance generally shows substantial improvement (Trabasso et al., 1978). Another way of presenting the problem also changes children's performance. When investigators use collective nouns (*forest, band, army*) to describe the general class instead of class nouns (*trees, musicians, soldiers*), the number of children who can answer such questions jumps dramatically (Markman and Seibert, 1976). Ellen Markman (1983) believes that collective nouns emphasize a wholeness among the constituent parts that makes it easier for children to compare classes at various hierarchical levels. As was the case with conservation, the way children process information, particularly how they attend to and encode it, may be at least as important as their logical skill in determining performance on classification tasks.

Limiting ourselves to children's performance in laboratory experiments can lead us to underestimate their ability. Anyone who has watched children for a length of time knows that older children's capacity to coordinate their thoughts into systems extends beyond experimental situations devised by psychologists. Older children have mastered the rules of complicated games, such as Monopoly and baseball. They are less egocentric, in the sense that they are better able to understand that their viewpoints are not the only possible ones. They comprehend the fact that other people's viewpoints may disagree with theirs and are able to coordinate other people's viewpoints with their own. These changes indicate that the thinking of children in the concrete-operational stage has taken on many of the characteristics of adult thought.

Just as advances in memory depend on an increased understanding of the way memory works, so other cognitive advances in childhood depend on **metacognition**, an understanding of the cognitive processes. Indeed, the understanding of memory is an example of metacognition. Because young children lack this understanding of cognition, they neither monitor nor evaluate their own cognitive processes; because of this passive approach to comprehension, they are often unable to realize that they do not understand an instruction, a process, or a game. In one study, when six-year-olds were given deliberately incom-

prehensible instructions concerning the rules of a card game or how to perform a magic trick, they failed to notice when essential information had been omitted—even though they understood that they were helping establish a set of instructions that other children could understand. Eight-year-olds, on the other hand, detected the absence of essential information right away and complained about it (Markman, 1977). The sort of passive information processing that younger children demonstrated in this study helps explain their lack of comprehension in many situations, and the active processing used by older children helps explain their obviously increased understanding of the world.

ADOLESCENCE

As children move into adolescence, a new set of cognitive capabilities, which Piaget called "formal-operational intelligence," starts to emerge. Those who display formal-operational intelligence are able to use scientific reasoning, testing possible explanations in attempts to prove or disprove hypotheses. They can also consider hypotheses that they know to be false, and can reason in abstract terms. As a result, their thinking is far superior to that of the concrete-operational child, and they can solve problems that they could not have handled only a few years before.

However, some people never develop formal thought, and most studies find that only 40 to 60 percent of college students and adults have attained this final level of cognitive development, which Piaget regarded as the highest form of intelligence (Keating, 1980). In some cultures, the ability to reason about hypotheses may not appear at all (Piaget, 1976). Some investigators believe that its development is the direct result of living in a highly technological Western society that stresses formal education (Super, 1980).

Systematic Experimentation

One of the most important new skills of adolescents is the ability to reason scientifically, considering all possible combinations of factors that may have caused an event and, through systematic testing, to eliminate irrelevant ones. A task Piaget

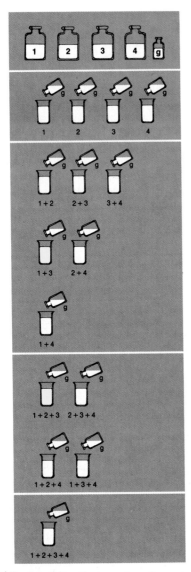

Figure 15.3. A problem that requires the systematic examination of hypotheses for their solution. The chemicals selected by Piaget and Inhelder for this problem have unexpected interactions. It is virtually impossible to determine how the color yellow is produced without trying every possible combination of the liquids, as shown here, and keeping track of the results. Not until children reach the formal-operational period can they conceive of such a procedure. (After Piaget and Inhelder, 1969.)

used to investigate this skill shows the difference between concrete-operational and formal-operational thought. Children are given four beakers of colorless, odorless liquids labeled 1, 2, 3, and 4, as

well as a smaller bottle labeled *g* that also contains a colorless, odorless liquid. Using empty glasses, the children are to find the liquid or combination of liquids that will turn yellow when a few drops from bottle *g* are added (see Figure 15.3). The yellow color is produced when *g* (potassium iodide) is added to a mixture of 1 (diluted sulfuric acid) and 3 (oxygenated water). The liquid in beaker 2 is plain water and has no effect on the reaction; the liquid in 4 (thiosulfate) prevents the yellow from appearing. Since the children are to discover *all* the combinations that produce a yellow liquid, they must try every possible mixture, even if their first or second try results in a glass of yellow fluid.

Faced with this problem, elementary school children often begin in a systematic manner, trying out all the single possibilities. They may test 4 plus *g*, then 2 plus *g*, and 1 plus *g*, then 3 plus *g*. When they fail to produce yellow, they generally say, "I tried them all and none of them works." A few hints from the experimenter may make them realize that they can combine more than one liquid with *g*, but they then drop the systematic approach and begin mixing the liquids haphazardly. But adolescents can systematically consider all possible combinations of the four liquids. Although they may need paper and pencil to keep track of their combinations, they understand how to generate the full set. Since they are capable of conducting systematic experiments, they can also go on to make general statements about their findings and to construct theories.

Hypothetical Ideas and Abstract Thinking

Adolescents also develop the capacity to consider hypothetical situations, reasoning from premises that they know are fanciful. Suppose, for example, that an adolescent and a younger child are asked, "If a man can climb a ladder at two miles per hour, how long will it take him to reach the moon, which is 240,000 miles away?" The younger child is likely to dismiss the question, assume a patronizing look, and declare, "You can't climb to the moon on a ladder." The adolescent, in contrast, can accept the absurd hypothesis and reason out the answer, because the cognitive processes of adolescents are no longer bound by physical reality.

With the ability to think hypothetically comes the ability to understand general principles. Adolescents can, for example, understand the abstract principles of law, whereas a younger child can understand only their concrete applications, as exemplified by the judge, the jail, or the policeman (Adelson, 1975). This new capacity is extremely important: it allows adolescents to study such fields as mathematics, science, economics, and language on an abstract level, and it brings about dramatic changes in their daily concerns. Adolescents may become preoccupied with such notions as ethical ideals, conformity, and phoniness, and they often apply their new abilities to their own thoughts and motives. It is no accident that adolescence is the first phase of life in which individuals begin to think carefully about themselves, their role in life, their plans, and the validity and integrity of their beliefs. Unlike younger children, who deal largely with the present, adolescents are often concerned with the meaning of their past and the direction of their future.

Neither adolescents nor adults apply their new reasoning abilities successfully in all appropriate situations. At times they misunderstand the demands of a particular task; on other occasions they find the problem too difficult. In a study of adolescents, only 2 percent of those who showed formal-operational thought in solving one problem applied formal thought to the entire series of ten tasks, which included such problems as figuring out what factors affect the speed of a pendulum's swing (Martorano, 1977). Other studies have found that even well-educated adults commit all sorts of errors on problems of formal reasoning (Henle, 1962; Wason and Johnson-Laird, 1972). Piaget himself felt that most adults probably use formal thinking only in their own areas of experience and expertise. Astronomers, for example, apply formal hypothesis testing to the calculation of planetary motion, but they may not be able to use it when trying to repair their cars. Thus, specific knowledge and training are as important to cognitive performance as is the general level of intellectual development. Both scientists and auto mechanics may use highly logical, deductive reasoning to solve problems; the major difference between them is the subject matter to which they apply those processes.

ADULTHOOD

There is no fixed line between adolescence and adulthood, no single age at which all people are considered mature. Instead, adolesence fades gradually into adulthood as people begin to take on adult responsibilities, building on the decisions they have made in late adolescence. Adults continue to learn and to understand increasingly complex material, and their cognitive development follows a predictable pattern. Although individuals vary, most people proceed through a similar cycle of intellectual growth and productivity from early to middle to later adulthood.

Cognitive Skills in Early and Middle Adulthood

Since it is impossible to specify the exact age at which a person passes from adolescence to early adulthood and from early adulthood to middle age, we will define early adulthood as the years from twenty to forty, and middle adulthood as the years from forty to sixty. These forty years are a time of peak intellectual accomplishment.

Young adults usually perform better on any learning or memory task than they ever have before, and if success at a task depends on how fast it is completed, they probably do a little better than they ever will again. During early adulthood, people are intellectually flexible. They find it easy to accept new ideas, and they can readily shift their strategies for solving problems. However, age itself is a poor predictor of learning, memory, and thinking ability. These cognitive processes are heavily determined by intelligence, education, and physical health.

Provided individuals remain healthy, their verbal and reasoning skills are likely to improve during middle adulthood. Middle-aged adults continue to learn and to store new information just as they always have. Consequently, they are often more knowledgeable than they were in their younger years. In a study of intellectual performance that followed individuals from birth, average IQ scores were higher in middle age (thirty-six to forty-eight years) than at the age of eighteen (Eichorn, Hunt, and Honzik, 1981), and other studies have found that some aspects of intelligence continue to improve until the age of sixty-five (Horn, 1982). The ability to organize and to process visual information, as in finding a simple figure in a complex one, also improves in middle adulthood. In addition, the ability to think flexibly, shifting the set of one's mind to solve a problem, is likely to be as good as it was in early adulthood. Only when asked to complete a task that involves coordinated hand-eye movements do people tend to perform less well than they used to, because motor skills often decline in middle age (Baltes and Schaie, 1974). In all other ways, however, adults in their middle years are in their intellectual prime.

Cognitive Skills in Later Adulthood

The group of Americans who are more than sixty-five years old has been growing twice as fast as the population as a whole. In 1900, 4 percent of the population was sixty-five or older; today more than 11 percent has reached that age; and by the year 2000, 13 percent will have reached their sixty-fifth birthdays (U.S. Bureau of the Census, 1982). Although many Americans who are past sixty-five are unable to do hard physical labor, they do not necessarily show any significant impairment of intellectual performance. Some physical and cognitive decline generally accompanies the aging process, but healthy older adults make as capable workers as do younger people.

Two problems plague our studies of intellectual performance in later life. First, it is almost impossible to separate the effects of aging from the effects of social change (Neugarten, 1977). That is, the **cohort**, or group of people, born in 1910, for example, has less education than the cohort born in 1960, and the content of their education, because of scientific and social changes, was very different from that received by students half a century later. Second, most studies of older adults may include individuals with mild cases of brain disorders, such as those in the early stages of Alzheimer's disease (see Chapter 3); the scores of these individuals could account for part of whatever cognitive impairment is found and could result in assessments that do not apply to adults who remain healthy. It is estimated that one in every six older adults suffers from some loss of mental ability from these organic diseases, which are often marked by deficiencies in neurotransmitters and by physical changes in the brain (Kolata, 1981). About a third of these people show a severe cognitive loss; the rest show a mild to moderate impairment (Coyle, Price and DeLong, 1983). People with early Alzheimer's disease, for example, do worse than normal elderly at learning word pairs, drawing geometric forms, naming objects and actions, and retrieving information from long-term memory (Rosen and Mohs, 1982).

Keeping such problems in mind, we can explore the changes associated with aging and can consider ways to avert cognitive decline in later years.

Changes Associated with Aging

Of all the changes that accompany aging, perhaps the most characteristic is the tendency to "slow down." This slowness begins with the individual's perceptual processes, for with age, sensory input is reduced. Physical changes in the eye curtail the amount of light that reaches the retina, and hearing loss often develops, particularly for high tones; thus the absolute threshold (see Chapter 5) rises for visual and aural stimuli. In addition, older people with good visual acuity may nevertheless require more contrast than younger adults do to recognize important features of the environment (Kline, Ikeda, and Schieber, 1982). Finally, older adults seem to require more time to process any single perceptual event.

Since the central nervous system processes all information more slowly with age, the older individual reacts more slowly. As the discussion of memory will make clear, older adults seem less able to allocate their available processing resources to specific tasks. Yet this slowing and less effective allocation of resources does not seem to affect all people similarly. For example, some individuals show great slowing in one stage of perceptual processing; others show greater slowing in another stage. This variability may be due in large part to individual differences in disease, nutrition, and life experiences (Walsh, 1982).

Along with slowness, memory impairment is the cognitive change most frequently assumed to accompany aging. In many respects, the memory of an older adult is no worse than that of a younger adult—at least not significantly so. But a number of memory changes do appear with age.

Some of these changes are related to sensory memory. Aging appears to slow down the rate at which the individual assimilates information from sensory memory, so that more information is likely to decay before it can be processed. When younger people are given a brief glimpse of seven unrelated letters, they can usually recall no more than four of them before the letters fade from sensory memory. Older adults consistently do worse than younger adults in this situation, recalling three letters at exposures that allow younger people to recall four, and two letters at exposures that allow younger people to recall three (Fozard, 1980). The same effect is found for sounds. In dichotic listening tasks (see Chapter 6), older people are as accurate as younger adults in remembering information that enters the attended ear, but they recall less than younger people do from the unattended message. Information fed to the unattended ear must be held in sensory memory longer than attended information before it is reported, which means that the message heard by the unattended ear is likely to decay before it can be reported (Parkinson, Lindholm, and Urell, 1980). Studies of visual and auditory memory consistently support the conclusion that older adults process available information more slowly than younger adults do (Kausler, 1982).

When it comes to short-term memory, older people can hold as much information in awareness as younger people do, so that they can remember the name of a person they have just met, or a phone number they have looked up, about as well as they ever did. Moreover, the speed with which information is lost from short-term memory does not change (Kausler, 1982). But when older people are asked to search for information in short-term memory, they are slower than younger adults at finding it. With extended practice, older adults improve as much as younger adults in the speed with which they examine items, but the age gap remains about the same (Madden and Nebes, 1980). Furthermore, when older adults are asked to reorganize information in short-term memory —for example, if they are asked to repeat a list of letters, numbers, or words backward—they tend to perform somewhat more poorly than younger adults (Walsh, 1983). In addition, an older person's short-term memory is likely to be hindered by a task that requires a division of attention.

Outside the laboratory, however, most differences between the short-term memory performance of young and old escape notice. When older adults are carrying out processes that have become automatic, they allocate their attention efficiently; it has been suggested that practiced skills, such as those used by air-traffic controllers, computer technicians, surgeons, and trial lawyers, do not suffer as people age (Hoyer and Plude, 1980).

Does the older adult have problems with long-term memory? We have all heard about the elderly person who recalls events from youth perfectly but is forgetful about things that happened yesterday or last week. But that is a stereotype—and hence misleading. Instead, like adults of any age, older people have the greatest difficulty remembering information from the distant past. Their recall is best for events that happened most recently. The universal nature of this pattern appeared in a study in which researchers questioned adults of different ages for their retention of major news events that had occurred from one month to two years earlier (Warrington and Sanders, 1971). For all age groups, the amount of information recalled declined with the number of months that had elapsed since the event. Memory fades with time, regardless of whether a person is twenty-six or sixty-six.

In another study, adults of all ages were asked questions about movies, sports, and current events. Investigators found that total knowledge increased with age, and that older people were as efficient as young adults at recalling the answers to such questions as "What was the former name of Muhammed Ali?" (Lachman and Lachman, 1980). In fact, older people are faster at retrieving information when they are more familiar with it than younger people are, and just as fast when both groups know the material equally well.

If, however, older adults have not learned the material as well—for example, when they are asked to memorize a list of words in a specified time—they consistently do worse than younger adults. Much of this age difference is probably due to encoding problems: older adults seem to encode selectively, and they often fail to use memory strategies that would have been automatic in earlier times. They can still use these strategies, though, if reminded to do so (Perlmutter, 1983). Some researchers believe that this encoding problem develops because older adults have less attentional energy to spread around—a notion that would explain why practiced activities show no similar decline (Craik and Byrd, 1982).

Information is not simply recalled; it must also be used. Tests of problem solving show that older adults can solve anagrams as well as younger adults; in fact, not age but education and measures of nonverbal intelligence are the best predictors of an adult's problem-solving ability (Giambra and Arenberg, 1980). It is when older adults have to reorganize material that declines appear. Asked simple questions about information they have heard, older people do as well as younger adults. But when they are asked to draw inferences about the material, they do significantly worse, presumably because slowed information processing makes it difficult both to register surface meaning and to reorganize the information so that inferences can be made (Cohen, 1979).

Minimizing Cognitive Decline

Although certain cognitive changes tend to be associated with aging, research shows that none of them is inevitable. A small percentage of elderly people suffer no decline in cognitive functioning, and some elderly people, such as Pablo Casals, Pablo Picasso, Grandma Moses, Bertrand Russell, and Eleanor Roosevelt, have been known for the sharpness of their intellects. Exceptional elderly subjects have also been found in laboratory experiments. Yet other people are failing mentally by sixty. The two indisputable facts about aging are that its effects are widely varied, and that age is a poor way to rate a person's cognitive skills (Fozard, 1980). The best explanation for these large variations is the interaction of biological, environmental, and emotional factors.

One contributing factor is biological. Forty years after finishing school, identical twins are more alike in their cognitive functioning than are unrelated individuals or fraternal twins (Jarvik, 1975). These similarities do not mean that genetic programming inevitably sets a person's timetable for aging. However, identical twins may share a predisposition toward—or resistance to—degenerative diseases that affect cognitive functioning. Whatever the causal link, some of the variation in cognitive decline among the elderly is biologically based.

Equally important are environmental factors —especially the degree to which an older person is physically active and intellectually stimulated (Perlmutter and Hall, 1985). According to some researchers, much of the cognitive decline observed in older people is due to the environmental changes that accompany retirement—changes in the individual's social, economic, and intellectual situation (Labouvie-Vief and Chandler, 1978). If older people continue to use their minds, there is a strong likelihood that their intellectual powers will not be blunted. Expectations and opportunities have as much to do with intellectual performance in old age as they do in any other stage of development.

Finally, a person's emotional state has a profound effect on the aging process. Motivation is known to affect memory, and older people may simply have fewer natural incentives—such as a pending promotion—that would motivate them to remember. In one study of nursing home residents, both men and women showed sharp improvements in their memory when they were given material or social incentives to remember (Langer et al., 1979). And perhaps more important than motivation is the toll that depression, despair, a sense of worthlessness, and a lack of hope can take on physical and mental well-being. The resulting degeneration often results in deepened depression, and a cycle of premature decline sets in. But when people are optimistic, secure, and generally content with their lives, they stand a better than average chance of remaining physically healthy and intellectually adept throughout their later years.

Since biological, environmental, and emotional factors all affect the speed and course of the aging process, some researchers have been attempting to change environmental factors and are looking for ways to avert the cognitive decline that too often accompanies the aging process. Training and simple opportunity for practice have been effective in getting older people to use systematic testing of possible solutions to problems. It appears that when older people are given time to develop their own strategies, they can develop their own cognitive skills and improve their own performance (Giambra and Arenberg, 1980). At the age of seventy-nine, the psychologist B. F. Skinner (1983) discovered that he could diminish, if not eliminate, the memory lapses that had begun to trouble him by rearranging his environment so that it was full of memory cues. When he decides to take an umbrella in the morning, he hangs it on the doorknob as soon as he thinks of it; when he cannot remember a name, he goes through the alphabet, testing each letter; when he gets into a discussion, he keeps his argument on a single track and no longer digresses to make another point; when he is waiting to reply, he either rehearses his point to keep it in short-term memory or jots it down on a pad—in fact, he now carries a notepad and pencil wherever he goes. By relying on files, a tape recorder, a word processor, and plenty of paper and pens, and by making detailed outlines, he has been able to continue his production of professional and popular articles.

SUMMARY

1. Researchers are divided over whether cognitive development is **quantitative**, the result of accumulated knowledge, or **qualitative**, involving a radical restructuring of mind. The foremost exponent of the qualitative view was Jean Piaget, who saw intelligence as a process by which a person actively constructs an understanding of reality. Central to Piaget's theory are the concepts of scheme, assimilation, and accommodation. A **scheme** is an action pattern, which consists of organized repeated elements that are generalized to other situations. As children grow older, their schemes are internalized, and they can carry them out mentally. **Assimilation** is the incorporation of new knowledge into old ways of thinking and behaving. **Accommodation** is the modification of old ways of thinking and behaving that allow the child to adapt to new objects. Piaget saw cognitive development in terms of **equilibration**, or a continual search for a balance between the two processes. In Piaget's theory, intellectual development moves through four increasingly complex **stages**, each involving a qualitative change in thought. The periods roughly correspond to customary periods of development: the **sensorimotor period** (infancy, or the first two years of life); the **preoperational period** (the preschool years); the **concrete-operational period** (childhood); and the **formal-operational period** (adolescence and beyond). The speed with which children move through these periods depends on genetic makeup, maturation, and environment.

2. Babies only a few days old can learn, unlearn, and relearn simple consequences of their actions through conditioning, and the learning is most successful when responses related to survival are used. Babies seem to derive pleasure from solving problems and from discovering their own power over the environment. Studies using habituation have demonstrated recognition in young infants. Although there are no laboratory studies of infant recall, babies show instances of recall in daily life from about the age of seven months. Psychologists have proposed several explanations for our inability to remember events from the first two years of life;

these explanations include the lack of language (representations are not labeled), repression, extreme dependence on context, and the immaturity of neurons. Infants in the sensorimotor period learn through spontaneous activity and apparently do not reflect on what they are doing. During the first two years the **object concept**, or the understanding that objects have an existence of their own, gradually develops. With full development of this concept, babies can represent objects in short-term memory while they search for them, and they realize others may be agents who move objects.

3. A child's intelligence during the preschool years is based on intuition, and during the preoperational period, **representational thought** (which enables children to think about objects that are not physically present) expands rapidly. Preschoolers have developed **deferred imitation**, mimicking in play actions they have observed earlier. During the third year, a concept of number begins to develop, and by the time children are five, they can add, subtract, and figure out whether two groups are equal —but only if the numbers are small and only if they are allowed to count them. The immaturity of preoperational thought shows in **egocentrism** (the belief that others literally see things as they do), **complexive thinking** (jumping from one idea to another without coordinating them), and the control of thought by prominent environmental cues.

4. Older children who have reached the stage of concrete operations can use logical thought about concrete objects. Between the ages of five and seven, children begin to understand the concept of **conservation**, which involves the understanding that simple transformations do not alter an object's quantity and that they may be reversed. During the school years, children show increasing memory skills, which result from their deliberate use of strategies for storing and retrieving information. Another concrete operation that develops during childhood is the organization of concepts into the hierarchical system that adults use. Advances in

cognitive skills depend upon **metacognition**, an understanding of cognitive processes.

5. Formal-operational thought emerges around the beginning of adolescence and involves the ability to think hypothetically and in abstract terms. With formal thought comes the ability to carry out systematic experiments, considering all possible factors and eliminating the irrelevant ones. The capacity to think hypothetically and to understand abstract principles allows adolescents to think about their own thoughts, actions, and motives and to consider the past and the future.

6. Cognitive development during adulthood generally follows a predictable pattern. Early adulthood (from age twenty to forty) and middle adulthood (from age forty to sixty) are a time of peak intellectual achievement, and IQ generally increases into the middle years. Young adults usually perform better than they ever have before on memory and learning tasks and faster than they ever will again. They are also most intellectually flexible. When people remain healthy, their verbal and reasoning skills generally improve during middle adulthood. An adult in the middle years is in his or her intellectual prime; the only decline may be in motor skills.

7. Many people experience little significant impairment of intellectual performance in later adulthood. Because it is difficult to separate the effects of aging from the effects of social change or to be certain that people with mild brain disorders are not included in studies of older adults, studies of cognitive functioning must be interpreted cautiously. The most characteristic change of old age is the tendency to "slow down." Older adults show increased absolute thresholds for visual and aural stimuli and require more time to process a perceptual event. Information is assimilated more slowly from sensory memory so that more information decays before it can be processed. Older people can hold as much information in short-term memory as younger people do, but when they must reorganize the information, they perform less well than younger adults. In addition, short-term memory among the elderly is generally hindered by tasks that require a division of attention, although they allocate attention well to practiced tasks. Long-term memory remains strong for material that has been thoroughly learned, although older adults do worse than younger adults when given a specified amount of time for learning. These age differences may arise because a decline in attentional energy leads older adults to encode selectively, often without using any encoding strategies. When asked to draw inferences, the performance of older adults suffers. When cognitive declines appear, they seem to be the result of biological, environmental, and emotional factors. When older people are reminded to use encoding strategies, their performance on memory tasks improves; training has enabled older people to test possible problem solutions systematically; and providing environmental cues can compensate for mild memory impairment.

KEY TERMS

accommodation	egocentrism	qualitative change
assimilation	equilibration	quantitative change
cohort	formal-operational period	representational thought
complexive thinking	metacognition	schemes
concrete-operational period	object concept	sensorimotor period
conservation	object permanence	stages
deferred imitation	preoperational period	

RECOMMENDED READINGS

ANDERSON, D. R., and R. SMITH. Young children's TV viewing: The problem of cognitive continuity, in F. Morrison, C. Lord, and D. P. Keating (Eds.), *Applied developmental psychology.* Orlando, Fla.: Academic Press, 1984. A review of recent research on preschoolers' attention to and comprehension of television programming. This article focuses on how research on television helps us to understand basic cognitive processes as well as the behavior of children during their television viewing activity.

BRAINERD, C. J., and M. PRESSLEY (Eds.). *Basic processes in memory development.* New York: Springer-Verlag, 1985; and PRESSLEY, M., and C. J. BRAINERD (Eds.). *Cognitive learning and memory in children.* New York: Springer-Verlag, 1985. Two recent books in a series concerned with cognitive development. Chapters focus on memory development from very early childhood through late adulthood and report on the substantial increase in our understanding of children's memory and related cognitive abilities which has occurred in recent years.

DAEHLER, M. W., and D. BUKATKO. *Cognitive development.* New York: Knopf, 1985. This book provides an introduction to the extensive theory and research that currently motivates the study of children and their cognitive development. It includes an overview of major issues and contains numerous references to aid in further in-depth study of the field.

HALL, E., M. PERLMUTTER, and M. LAMB. *Child psychology today.* New York: Random House, 1982. A topically organized introduction to child development. It offers a balanced view of social and cognitive theories as it covers developmental processes from conception through early adolescence.

PIAGET, J. *Biology and knowledge.* Chicago: University of Chicago Press, 1971. Piaget describes the significance of his lifetime work for understanding the human ability to know and the relationship of that ability to human biological heritage.

POON, L. W. (Ed.). *Aging in the 1980's.* Washington, D.C.: American Psychological Association, 1980. A book of contributed chapters on all aspects of aging. Includes chapters not only on cognitive aspects of aging, but also on clinical, neuropsychological, pharmacological, and other issues.

STERNBERG, R. J. (Ed.). *Mechanisms of cognitive development.* New York: W. H. Freeman, 1984. A series of chapters by distinguished researchers concerned with the nature of, and how best to characterize, cognitive development. The book offers several different views concerning the importance of knowledge, psychological processes, and cognitive structures contributing to the phenomenon of cognitive change.

ACQUIRING AND USING LANGUAGE

From its perch on a tree limb, a vervet monkey sees a black silhouette—an eagle—against the sky. Without hesitation, the monkey opens its mouth and gives a sharp bark: "Rraup! Rraup!" Amid a rustling of leaves and a swaying of branches, the other monkeys in the troop drop from the trees and take refuge in the dense underbrush. When the eagle nears the trees, the limbs are quiet and empty. If the monkey who called a warning had seen a leopard, it would have given a different cry, a sort of "chirp"; and if it had seen a snake, it would have uttered a "chutter" (Wilson, 1975). Those signals would have caused the monkeys to climb up a tree, out of danger. These calls allow monkeys to communicate, warning one another of danger and of other important changes in their world. But is the vervet monkey's system of about twenty calls a language? How does the warning call "Rraup!" differ from your physician's warning: "Stop smoking. Now!"

Both the monkey's call system and human language are used to communicate information. But as we shall see in this chapter, the two systems differ in important ways. Human language is an advanced system of social communication that represents the highest achievement of human cognition. In fact, language displays such deep and significant properties of cognition that many researchers believe a better understanding of language could bring us closer to an understanding of the human mind itself (Chomsky, 1975). This connection between language and mind explains why language fascinates psychologists.

Our exploration of language in this chapter is based on the idea that language is a social tool, and that its principal function is to coordinate our actions and exchanges with others in our social group. We first examine the structure of language, investigating how we plan and produce speech, how we understand it, and how we use it to communicate. Then, with an understanding of its structure and uses, we will be prepared to explore the way children learn language and to examine the biological foundations of language. The chapter ends with a consideration of the relationship between language and thought.

LANGUAGE AS A COMMUNICATION SYSTEM

We use human language to communicate information from one person to another ("A truck is approaching") and to influence one another's actions ("Get out of the road!"). Many other species also have simple communication systems: bees dance on the floor of a hive to tell other workers where nectar has been found (Brines and Gould, 1979), seagulls use distinct cries to communicate the location of food or the presence of danger, and howler monkeys, like vervets, have a group of twenty distinct calls—including a signal to other males that a certain territory is occupied (Altmann, 1973). But such animal signaling systems are simple and rigid. An animal's cry is like a knee-jerk reaction to a specific emotional stimulus: the vervet monkey's "Rraup!" is much like the "Ouch!" that escapes our lips when we bang a shin on a sharp corner. By contrast, human language is incredibly flexible and complex.

The Unique Features of Human Language

Human language has several features that distinguish it from animal signaling systems:

- **Discreteness**. Language consists of discrete (separate) units that are strung together into utterances. These separate units are words: for example, the sentence you have just read consists of twelve separate words. Although animal cries are discrete signals, they are not strung together in combination to refer to new things. A seagull cannot give a "fish" cry right after a "clamshell" cry to make a sentence that connects the idea of a fish with the idea of a clamshell.
- **Meaningfulness**. Most of the words in human

languages have meanings, so that they refer to some object, event, or idea. But in contrast to animal communication, where a given sound or signal always has the same meaning, the relationship between the word and the object is arbitrary, depending solely on agreement among a group of people. Seagulls all over the world give the same cry when they see a fish. But the object Americans call a hat is a *chapeau* to the French and a *sombrero* to Spaniards. Children at play can even invent a word and agree that it will have a specific meaning; doing so fits in with their intuitive sense of how human language works.
- **Productivity**. Human language is infinitely productive—that is, we can produce an unlimited number of utterances. Thanks to the system of rules from which our language is constructed, we can combine words in an almost unlimited number of ways to express whatever complex thought we want to communicate. Consider the widely different meanings you can convey using the words "love" and "intelligent." You can say "I love you because you are intelligent," or "I would love you if you were intelligent," or "I don't love you because you think you are so intelligent." How do you get across these three ideas? You follow specific rules that let you combine the words in three different ways to express three different meanings. (We will discuss these rules in more detail later.)
- **Displacement**. In human language the topic of our speech can be displaced—that is, we can speak about something that is not present. We can talk about things that are not immediately in front of us (such as the record player in the next room), things in the past and the future (such as last year's winner of the World Series), and things that are fictitious or hypothetical (such as dragons or a possible manned flight to Venus). Obviously, animals cannot communicate on this level: seagulls cannot converse about hypothetical dangers or fictitious food sources.

These four critical features are found in all human languages. They also appear in written languages, including Braille, and in the silent, gestural language of the deaf. But no animal signaling system possesses them all.

Linguistic Structure

Language is a tool used by human beings—a tool for manipulating the social environment, just as a screwdriver or a saw is a tool for manipulating the physical environment. We can look at any tool from two different points of view: in terms of its structure (its parts and how they are put together), or in terms of its function (how it is used). Here, we will begin with a quick look at language's structure—an area whose study is the province of **linguistics**.

Suppose you are wandering through the jungle and you see a leopard. If you were a vervet monkey, you would tell your companions what you saw by crying "Chutter! Chutter!" But because you are a human being, you do not simply have a reflexive reaction. Instead, you are likely to produce an utterance that will warn your companion about the leopard. How can you convey the thought that a leopard is sneaking up on you? You will come out with a series of utterances, roughly separated into sentences: perhaps "Watch out—a leopard is sneaking up on our left! Don't make any sudden moves!"

Let us look at just one of these sentences, "Watch out—a leopard is sneaking up on our left," and see how you actually go about producing that sentence. We can think of any single utterance as being formed in a number of stages, one stage leading to the next.

1. The first stage is the speaker's intended message or thought: you think about the leopard that is stealthily approaching. Obviously, you cannot communicate this thought to your friend by telepathy; you are going to have to come out with some sort of sentence.
2. The sentence you will eventually come out with is "Watch out—a leopard is sneaking up on our left!" But note that you will not just open your mouth and speak this sentence automatically. Let's analyze the sentence and see what goes into it—what building blocks you must create in order to speak this sentence.
3. The sentence has subdivisions. It has two clauses, "Watch out" and "a leopard is sneaking up on our left." And these clauses are further subdivided into phrases: for example, the second clause contains three phrases, "a leopard," "is sneaking up," and

"on our left." Your brain must somehow translate your thought into these phrases before creating the sentence.
4. Furthermore, each phrase is made up of individual words, and your brain must find these words (for example, "is," "sneaking," and "up") before you can put together the phrases.
5. Each word is itself made up of smaller units of meaning known as **morphemes**. Morphemes include root words as well as common prefixes and suffixes; for example, "unlovely" is composed of the morphemes "un-," "-love-," and "-ly." "Sneaking" is made up of the morphemes "sneak-" and "-ing." Your brain has to choose these morphemes and put them together.
6. Finally, in order to enunciate each morpheme, you must make an overlapping series of basic speech sounds—**phonemes**—such as "sn," "ee," and "ek." Phonemes are the repertoire of speech sounds present in human languages.

If this analysis makes the process of speech seem like a tremendous task, that is because it *is* a tremendous task. Yet we go through all these stages, with ease and tremendous speed, every time we want to put a thought into words.

The sequence of stages is somewhat like the pyramid shown in Figure 16.1. When we generate speech, we progress from the top to the bottom of the pyramid—from the thought all the way down to the phonemes. Conversely, when we listen to someone else speaking, we reverse the process. We hear the sound stream of phonemes, group them as morphemes, then group those morphemes into words, then phrases, then clauses, then sentences—until we finally get what we believe to be the speaker's intended message.

And note one more thing. There are only about forty basic speech sounds (phonemes) in the English language. It is important to recognize how effective, yet economical, our system of communicating by phonemes is. Of course, we need to communicate far more than forty thoughts. Handily, our language system lets us combine and recombine just those forty phonemes to make over 100,000 different units of meaning (words or morpheme strings). Further, it lets us combine and recombine those words to make an infinite number of sentences. All this from just forty basic sounds!

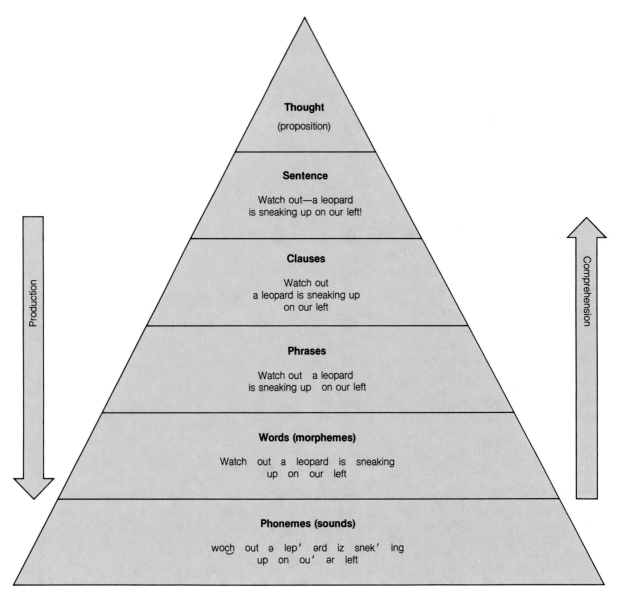

Figure 16.1. An utterance pyramid. Production of an utterance involves moving down the pyramid, from the thought we wish to convey to the phonemes we utter in expressing our meaning. Comprehension of an utterance entails moving up the pyramid, from the phonemes another person utters to the thought he or she is conveying.

Relating Thoughts to Sounds

Our system of language forms a sort of bridge, or chain of relationships, between our thoughts and the sounds we make in order to communicate. We pack our thoughts together and find ways of expressing them in accordance with the **grammar** of our language—the rules that describe the levels of speech in our language and the way those levels are interrelated. We have learned these rules by hearing many grammatical utterances—although we are not aware of having learned the rules and may not even be aware that we know them. First, we follow rules that govern the way we connect our thoughts before we speak them.

Thoughts as Propositions

We usually speak in order to express a thought or convey an intention. But the thought is not the same as the actual sentence we utter. The thought occurs in our consciousness in the form of a **proposition**, consisting of a subject with a predicate. In the proposition "Bill is tired," "Bill" is the subject and "is tired" is the predicate. The subject is the topic we are thinking about, and the predicate is the comment we are making to ourself or to our listener about that topic.

Most of our thoughts are complex. So in order to express these complex relationships in an utterance, we often package several propositions in a single sentence, following the rules of English grammar. For example, after witnessing a street crime, we tell the police officer, "The red-haired man robbed the old woman." This sentence packs together three propositions: the man has red hair; the woman is old; the man robbed the woman. The officer understands our sentence in terms of these three propositions.

The Phrase Level

How did we manage to pack three separate propositions into eight small words? We followed the rules of English **syntax**, which govern the way words and phrases may be combined into sentences in our language. Our sentence consists of a noun phrase ("The red-haired man") followed by a verb phrase, which itself consists of a verb ("robbed") and another noun phrase ("the old woman"). Each phrase in this sentence corresponds fairly closely to one of the sentence's underlying propositions. If a listener can find the phrases, he or she is well on the way to discovering whatever propositions the speaker is trying to convey. The diagram in Figure 16.2 reflects the psychological grouping of a sentence's successive words into phrases.

Again, we follow syntactic rules to combine words into phrases. For example, English (but not some other languages) has a number of rules about word order. A noun phrase may consist of an article ("a," "an," "the") followed by a noun, but the reverse order is unacceptable: we say "the man" but not "man the."

Psychologists are interested in grammatical phrases (which are also called **constituents**), because people treat them as perceptual chunks that have unity and integrity. Speakers tend to utter whole constituents in bursts separated by pauses, and listeners tend to "hear" whole constituents at

Figure 16.2. A phrase-structure tree for a sample sentence. Each node, or fork, of the tree is a "syntactic constituent" that expands into the nodes below it.

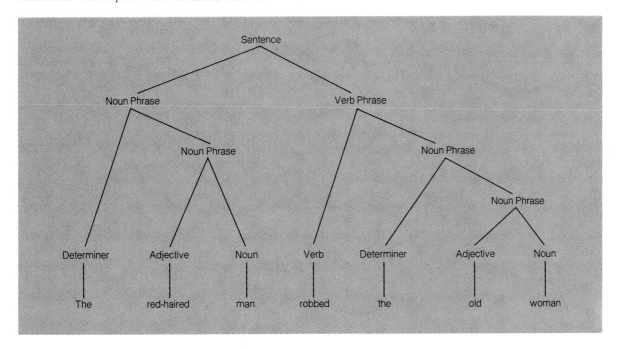

a time. Suppose that as you were listening to the sentence in Figure 16.2, a soft click sounded right after the word "red-haired." Later you would probably believe that the click occurred after the word "man"—at the closest boundary between phrases. And if you studied a number of similar sentences and tried to recall them, you would make the most errors at the boundaries between each phrase and the next. In recalling successive words within a sentence, you would recall words within a phrase rapidly, and then pause to retrieve the next phrase of the sentence (Wilkes and Kennedy, 1969).

People remember the cluster of propositions embedded in a sentence even though they often forget their exact wording. They will remember that the woman was old and the robber was red-haired even if they forget exactly how this was said. The police officer is likely to confuse your original sentence with a paraphrase such as "The man who robbed the old woman was red-haired" —but the officer will not forget your underlying message.

The Word Level

Each phrase in a sentence is made up of words, which in turn are made up of small meaning-units called morphemes. Many words are composed of a single morpheme ("man"). But a complex word like "unreadable" is composed of three morphemes: "un-," meaning "not"; "-read-," meaning "to comprehend written words"; and "-able," meaning "capable of being done." Each language has rules we can use to create and understand new combinations of morphemes. We learn these rules quickly. Very young children often coin new words to fill a temporary gap in their vocabulary, and their coinages follow the rules for composing words from morphemes. For example, a three-year-old boy whose mother was mending his jeans asked, "Is it all needled?" And when watching a man unlock a door, the boy said, "He's keying the door" (E. Clark, 1983). Similarly we have no trouble taking a new noun like "Xerox" and adding the morphemes to make the verb forms "Xeroxing" and "Xeroxed," or the adjective "un-Xeroxable." English has many such morphemes, known as prefixes and suffixes, for inflecting (modifying the form of) words.

Languages also have rules that restrict the ways phonemes, or basic speech sounds, can be put together to make possible words. The word "man," for instance, begins with the consonant sound "m," followed by the vowel sound "a," and then by the consonant sound "n." Phonemes correspond only roughly to the sounds of letters of the alphabet, as you can see by comparing the sound of "a" in "ale," "all," and "Al"; but all English speakers use the phonemes of English automatically even though they have never learned them in school. How do you know that "grok" and "destion" are two words that could possibly be English, but "pbon" and "cgoka" could never exist in English? You have learned the rules governing the way phonemes may be combined in English, although you may be unaware that you know them and could never state them. For example, one of the rules you apply intuitively is that English words may not begin with two "stop consonants" ("t," "b," "p," "d," "k," "g") in a row: "to" and "do" are possible, but not "tdo."

THE COMMUNICATIVE FUNCTION OF LANGUAGE

If we could not get our ideas across to other people and discover what they had in mind themselves, each of us would exist inside a virtually impenetrable shell. Human interaction would be almost impossible, and if people could not interact with one another, societies could not exist, and cultures could not be transmitted from one generation to the next.

Psychologists are interested not only in language's structure, but also in its function, or how it is used—the field of **psycholinguistics**. As a tool for social communication, language coordinates the thoughts and actions of the speaker and the listener. A speaker uses language for a purpose: to arrange a date, perhaps, or to obtain a loan, offer a cup of coffee to a guest, warn an intruder to leave, thank a friend for a gift, or order a child not to touch a fragile vase. The study of the way a speaker uses language to accomplish some goal that depends on a listener's comprehension is known as **pragmatics**.

Designing Our Utterances

Without visible effort we quickly go through the complex process of designing and producing an utterance—from choosing the idea we want to get across to choosing the exact words and expressing them as a series of sounds. Although we are hardly aware of it, we limit our choices of words and expressions to just those that fit our audience, our goals, and the social situation.

The Influence of Context and Goals

An utterance is made in a physical and social context, including the setting (a courtroom, an automobile, the dinner table, a football game), the relationship of the people involved (friends, parent and child, strangers, co-workers), and the content of whatever conversation has preceded the utterance. This physical and social context constrains (limits) what you say and what words you use to say it. And it also limits the number of alternatives your listener must consider in order to figure out what you have said. A general principle guides these choices: "Unless I stipulate otherwise, I can refer only to items that are within our shared knowledge." These items, such as mutual surroundings, beliefs, and recent topics of conversation, make up the **common ground** between the speaker and the listener (Clark, 1984).

Items around us as we talk provide a common ground. To refer to something, I have to construct an expression that will enable you to identify it within our common ground. For example, if there are three men of various ages at a nearby table, I can specify one of them by saying, "the oldest man," but if that same man and two women are at the table, I might pick him out for you by simply saying, "the man." Our choice of words is also constrained by past topics in our conversation. After I refer to John as "the older man," that phrase is locked up for a few minutes; now I cannot use "the older man" to refer to someone else unless I specify that I am changing what the phrase refers to.

The social situation also constrains our speech by dictating a certain style: we whisper in church or during concerts, and the style we use when we are addressing a judge in the courtroom is completely different from the style we use when we are cheering our baseball team. Part of a child's socialization consists of learning what style of speaking is acceptable in various settings.

Finally, we choose our speech to achieve certain goals. We arrange our words so as to have a particular effect on the listener—to persuade, to accuse, to warn, to pledge, to command, to intimidate, to inform, to request, to bet, and so on. An utterance is as much an instrumental act as is opening a door, and for this reason utterances can be viewed as **speech acts** (Searle, 1969). We perform speech acts "properly" only when certain conditions are true. For example, I can properly request information from you only if there is reason to believe that you have the information and I do not, that you are willing to share it with

How we speak depends on where we are and whom we are speaking to. With friends in a restaurant, for example, we may be gregarious and animated.

me, and that you would not do so unless I asked. If any of these conditions are violated, then the request is likely to have overtones of humor or sarcasm.

Not all speech acts are direct; we often use indirect suggestions. To induce a person who has just come in from the cold to shut the door, we may say, "It's cold in here" or "Haven't you forgotten something?" In this context, the listener interprets the utterance as an indirect request—or as the command, "Shut the door." Close friends often use indirection as a private signal. When John says, "I have a headache," for example, Mary knows there probably will be no more romance that evening. And when the hostess says, "I've got to be at work early tomorrow," her dinner guests understand that they have been politely requested to leave. Thus, planning an utterance may be regarded as solving a problem; to solve the problem, the speaker chooses the form that will have the desired effect on a specific listener in a specific context.

Planning Segments of Speech

The speaker does not plan the entire utterance before beginning to produce it; instead it is planned over stretches no longer than a phrase or clause (Dodd and White, 1980). Evidence for such sectional planning has come from studies of errors that people make when they are speaking (e.g., Fromkin, 1973). Slips of the tongue reveal a substitution of sounds among several conflicting words the speaker is considering; they occur because the wrong word has been called from memory. Substitutions almost invariably occur among words that are less than four or five words apart, suggesting that speech is planned in phrases of about six or seven words (Clark and Clark, 1977).

We can see this short-term planning in a slip confined to a single sound, such as "bake my bike" for "take my bike." In this slip (which indicates that a three-word phrase had been planned), the "b" of "bike" has been called up from memory and is available early in the utterance. "Bake my bike" is a slip of the type known as **anticipation**, because the produced sound ("b") was scheduled to appear later in the utterance. Such slips indicate that the process of production itself progresses through the level of phonemes (Fromkin, 1973).

Anticipations are the commonest form of slips. Other slips that involve sounds include **persevera-**

tions, in which a produced sound is erroneously repeated later in the utterance ("pulled a pantrum" for "pulled a tantrum") and **reversals**, in which sounds are exchanged ("food the peech" for "feed the pooch"). Such reversals, called spoonerisms, are named after William Spooner, an English clergyman whose probably deliberate sound reversals customarily produced funny sequences, such as "insanitary specter" for "sanitary inspector," or "I hissed my mystery test" for "I missed my history test."

Understanding Spoken Language

Understanding the utterances of others requires us to extract meaning from a stream of sounds. We must be able to make many kinds of inferences, using our knowledge of the situation, of the world, and of language itself—its regularities of sound, structure, and meaning.

Speakers know what words they are uttering. But consider the problem that listeners face: they have to pick up those words from a relatively complex stream of sound. First they must segment the speech stream into clusters of phonemes, then figure out the words these clusters correspond to, then retrieve the meaning of those words. This is an extremely difficult task. For more than forty years, researchers have been trying to build computer programs that can recognize the words of continuous human speech. But as yet, even the most sophisticated computer programs can recognize only about a thousand words—and then only if the speaker pronounces them carefully, pauses between them, and uses simple sentences (Levinson and Liberman, 1981).

The major problem faced by both brain and computer is that the sound of a word varies with the speaker; it also varies depending on the words that surround it and blend into it. Even when the same person speaks the same sentence on two different occasions, individual words may differ in sound—perhaps because the speaker's emotional state has changed, perhaps because the social situation is more formal (or informal), or perhaps simply because of normal speech variations. For example, from one occasion to the next with the same speaker, the word "cat" may differ more in sound than that same person's pronunciation of the words "cat," "cad," and "cut." Yet human beings handle such variations in the sounds of words with relative ease. How do we accomplish this feat?

Drawing by Stevenson; © 1976 The New Yorker Magazine, Inc.

Phonological (Sound) Clues in Comprehension

It turns out that we are aided by an inborn tendency to hear speech sounds in distinct categories. It is as though the brain has developed some forty phonetic pigeonholes (for sounds like "ba" versus "pa," for example) into which it stuffs the wide variety of speech sounds. A human listener cannot tell the difference between any two sounds that the brain says go into the same pigeonhole, even though one of those sounds may be quite close acoustically to sounds that he or she will perceive as belonging to a different, neighboring pigeonhole (see Figure 16.3). This **categorical perception** helps us deal with the enormous variation in the sound of a given phoneme, because it means that a certain amount of the variation is simply blocked out; we do not notice it.

And there is another reason we can still recognize a word although its sound varies widely: the surrounding context gives us a great deal of help. People appear to process sounds as patterns. We first group them into syllables in sensory memory (see Chapter 9) and then transfer the results into short-term memory. But we do not decipher a word without taking into consideration the words that surround it. In fact, when words taped during a normal conversation are replayed one at a time, they cannot be understood; a listener must hear about five connected words before comprehending the recording (Pollack and Pickett, 1963).

Syntactic Clues in Comprehension

As the speaker is uttering a string of words, the listener is continuously deciding what syntactic role each word plays in the overall sentence —whether it functions as a main noun, as a verb, or in some other role. Listeners use various strategies to make such decisions. For example, the endings of words ("-ing," "-ness," "-ion," "-ity," "-er") often help identify a word's role as a noun, verb, or adjective. If you hear "Boy George is singing the song again, but now his voice is louder," word endings tag "singing" as a verb and "louder" as an adjective. Similarly, when an utterance begins with "is" or "are," the listener can safely predict that a question is coming. Using such strategies to predict the type of words they are about to hear, listeners find it somewhat easier to identify words as they arrive at the ear.

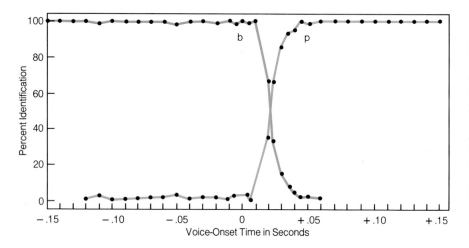

Figure 16.3. This graph shows the results of an experiment that supported the assertion that we make categorical perceptions of similar-sounding phonemes. The phonemes tested here were *b* and *p*. They were found to differ mainly in voice-onset time —that is, the time between the release of the compressed lips and the onset of the sound. Voice-onset time for *b* is 0 second, on average, and for *p* is + .06 second. Yet listeners presented with thirty-two computer-synthesized *b* and *p* sounds that differed only in voice-onset times had no difficulty categorizing the phonemes as either *b* or *p*, even when the difference in voice-onset times in the middle range was only one-hundredth of a second. (Lisker and Abramson, 1970.)

Other syntactic features also aid the listener. For example, if you hear an article (such as "the"), a conjunction (such as "and"), or a preposition (such as "on"), you can assume that a new phrase is on the way (Kimball, 1973). We hold such phrases ("the next morning"; "on our left") in short-term memory until about the point at which another phrase or sentence begins (Clark and Clark, 1977). Then we store the meaning of the phrase in long-term memory and clear our short-term memory, getting ready for the next phrase or sentence. This is why we are likely to forget the exact wording of an utterance and remember only its underlying meanings.

Meaning-Related Clues in Comprehension

Syntactic clues are not always enough to allow us to extract meaning from another person's utterance. Even though we know that "singing" is a verb, or "louder" is an adjective, or "on the left" is a phrase describing location, an utterance may still leave us baffled. And so we also use several broad strategies based on our knowledge of word meanings and plausible relations among things.

▪ We sometimes rely solely on the meaning of the content words in the utterance. For example, if we hear the three words "roses," "sniffed," and "man" in any order, we are likely to assume that the speaker means "The man sniffed the roses," since no other relation makes sense.

▪ We often assume that the first noun-verb-object sequence we identify in the utterance will function as "agent-action-object," as in "The boy hit the ball."

▪ We sometimes identify the main verb and then search through the utterance for words that are required in order for the utterance to make sense. For example, if we hear the verb "put," we know that it requires an actor, an object, and a place where the object is put, as in "The sunbather put lotion on her back."

When words have more than one meaning (river-"bank"; savings "bank"), it appears that we retrieve all the meanings for a fleeting moment. But as the context makes the speaker's meaning clear, the unwanted meanings slip from our short-term memory and are lost. Sometimes the context leads us astray, so that we choose the wrong meaning, and later have to back up and compute a different meaning. If a speaker says, "The punch at the party gave Betty a concussion," the early part of the sentence leads us to focus on "drink" as the meaning of punch; then, when we hear the last words, we have to go back and reprocess the sentence (Dodd and White, 1980). Similarly, listeners have to back up and start again when they hear such sentences as "The old man the boat while the young ride," or "The boat floated past the bridge sank."

The Importance of Knowledge Schemas

We may understand a speaker's every sentence and still be baffled by the entire message. The speaker may assume that it is unnecessary to spell out all references and connections. But if we do not share a common ground with the speaker, or if the speaker's words do not call the appropriate background knowledge to mind, we will find the message incomprehensible.

Imagine listening to the radio broadcast of a cricket match. Without knowledge of the game's terminology and rules, you would be completely baffled by the announcer's description of the game's progress. Our understanding fails unless the speaker's words call to mind an appropriate set of knowledge schemas based on experience. Children who grow up outside the mainstream conventions of American society may be similarly baffled by the scenes and narratives described in typical reading textbooks. Because these children may lack the background knowledge of standard cultural events and situations, their comprehension of materials that rely on this knowledge is often poor, and they tend to do poorly on standard tests of reading achievement (Dillard, 1972; Thorndike, 1973). Let us consider some of the problems involved in understanding the written word.

Understanding Written Language

Special problems arise when we try to comprehend the written word. Instead of decoding a sound stream, the reader has to decode a string of written symbols. But just what do we do when we read? Studies of eye movements suggest that we make a series of eye fixations along each line:

jump, pause (read), jump, pause (read), and so on. We do all our reading with foveal vision (see Chapter 5); reading is restricted to this area because the cones responsible for detailed vision are packed into the fovea. But the fovea is a very small area. You can experience its limitation yourself by fixating on the central X in Figure 16.4 and noticing how many letters or words you can make out clearly on either side of the X (don't move your eyes!). At the usual book-reading distance, people can see about three to five words at each fixation. We also know that the eye can fixate no more than four times per second. Putting these limits together, we might assume a typical reading rate to be between 720 and 1,200 words per minute (Foss and Hakes, 1978).

But as anyone who has tried desperately to read through a stack of assigned books knows, the usual reading rate falls far below this prediction: most adults read from 200 to 400 words per minute. Why do we need so much time? Because reading demands much more than just fixating words. We also have to extract meaning. Once we have learned to read, in fact, letter recognition becomes automatic, and perceptual factors no longer place the limit on our reading speed. Instead, our reading rate is determined by our ability to apply our knowledge of language (semantics —i.e., meaning—and syntax), our general knowledge schemas, our skills at reasoning and problem solving, and our knowledge of typical text structures (Anderson, 1980). Poor readers may not have well-developed knowledge schemas, or they may have trouble calling up knowledge schemas from memory. You can experience such a problem by picking up an advanced textbook in a subject you know nothing about. In such cases, there is no problem with the mechanics of your reading ability; you lack background. This explanation is supported by the finding that people with reading problems continue to have problems when they try to learn material by listening to it (Jackson and McClelland, 1979).

The best predictor of an individual's reading ability in adolescence and adulthood is the

Figure 16.4. Fixate on the X and do not look directly to either side of it. Try to say what words or letters appear on either side. (Foss and Hakes, 1978.)

HOME   PILL   LIST   NECK   (X)   MILK   SHOE   SOCK   BOOK

amount of reading he or she did as a child. Children who were taught to read early by their parents gain an advantage over their classmates that persists for at least six years (Durkin, 1966). Indeed, the amount of reading that takes place in an individual's home and the availability of magazines, newspapers, and books there correlate more highly with reading ability than any other environmental factor (Thorndike, 1973). How much does the pervasiveness of television affect reading ability? No one is certain. Most studies show that the reading of comic books declines when television is introduced—but not the reading of other books. However, two years after television became available in one Canadian town, second- and third-grade children showed a significant decline in reading skills (Murray, 1980).

Dyslexia

When children with normal intelligence and adequate environmental opportunities have extreme difficulty in learning to read, they are said to have **dyslexia**, a term that may cover a variety of reading disorders (Scarr and Kidd, 1983). According to Sylvia Farnham-Diggory (1978), slowness in processing information may be a major factor in dyslexia. For example, dyslexic children seem to identify letters so slowly that before they can recognize one letter, it has been pushed out of sensory memory by the next ones. At the same time these children seem to process sights more rapidly than sounds, so that their attention moves to the next word before they retrieve the implicit pronunciation of the first. Dyslexic children also take longer to name pictures, colors, and numbers than most children, apparently requiring more time to retrieve a label from memory (Spring and Capps, 1974).

Another problem that may contribute to dyslexic children's reading problems is their difficulty in keeping track of the order of words. For example, they do poorly when asked to repeat the order of a few words or digits they have just read. This problem also affects their performance on such nonverbal tasks as repeating the order in which someone has touched a collection of colored blocks (Gibson and Levin, 1975). Because English syntax relies heavily on word order, it is understandable that dyslexic children should have special difficulty in making sense out of English sentences.

The cause of dyslexia is unknown, although some forms of dyslexia apparently have a genetic involvement. For example, one form of dyslexia has been traced to a specific chromosomal site (Smith et al., 1983). In addition, when one identical twin has a reading disability, the other is likely to have it. The correlation is much lower between fraternal twins, whose genetic make-up is no more similar than that of other siblings. However, in many cases only one identical twin is dyslexic, suggesting that the environment must also play some part in the problem (Scarr and Kidd, 1983).

Computer Models of Reading Comprehension

A computer that would help us understand written language would be a boon to problem readers—or to good readers faced with a dense, obscure text. As it turns out, however, only in the past few years have programs that can understand natural language been developed, and these programs have succeeded only within limited areas.

These programs look up the meanings of words in a dictionary and have access to the syntactic rules that specify how words are combined into sentences. One problem is ambiguous meanings, which create far more difficulties for a computer than do complex syntactic structures. For example, in "John threw the ball," "ball" could mean a dance and "threw" could mean that John hosted the event. The computer's dictionary stores multiple meanings of words, but a dictionary cannot specify which meaning to use on any particular occasion. Many sentences have a number of alternative interpretations. One program, for example, came up with four interpretations of "Time flies like an arrow." Can you come up with four interpretations for it?

People deal with a semantically ambiguous sentence like this one by using the surrounding context to decide which interpretation is most likely. But how can we give the computer enough knowledge about appropriate social contexts so that it, too, can resolve such routine ambiguities? This has been a major problem. Understanding language involves applying a vast amount of knowledge about the world. For instance, consider this sequence: "John took the train to Chicago. The conductor punched his ticket while he enjoyed the scenery." If the computer just follows its rules, it will assume that John either stole or carried a train to Chicago. It will also assume that "he" in the second sentence refers to the last male mentioned, thus concluding that the conductor punched his own ticket while he enjoyed the scenery.

Yet you know that "he" refers to John, because you are familiar with the train **script**, or the schema of routine events that occur on trains: conductors punch tickets for passengers. Only if the computer is programmed with the train script will it be able to interpret such sentences. Each aspect of life has its own script—the doctor script, the restaurant script, the lecture script, the telephone script, the circus script, and so on. The problem that faces programmers is the difficulty of making available to the computer the vast number of scripts that people automatically use in language comprehension.

Researchers at the Yale Artificial Intelligence Laboratory have been developing programs that can analyze concepts, enabling the computer to understand various scripts (Schank and Riesbeck, 1981). For example, to interpret the train script, one program would have the computer consult its various definitions for the word "took," and then rely on the semantic features of the nouns in the sentence to determine which definition applies (Birnbaum and Selfridge, 1981). "Train" and "Chicago" in "took the train to Chicago" would tell the computer that the meaning of "took" should be "physically transfer agent by vehicle to location," and that the train script should be used in understanding the passage. By using that script, the computer would be able to figure out that the *passenger's* ticket was punched and that "punch" referred to making a hole in the ticket, not a blow to the head or a sweet drink. But if the first sentence had read "John took an aspirin," the computer would have selected the "ingest substance" interpretation of "took" and would have tried to understand further sentences in terms of an illness script.

Such successes are encouraging. But computers still have a long way to go before they can understand the full complexities of real language —with all of its implicit references to the masses of knowledge we take for granted when we speak.

Rules of Conversation

Our ability to produce and understand sentences is not enough, in itself, to enable us to communicate effectively. Language is a social tool used to exchange information and to coordinate people's activities. To use this tool successfully, we must have a grasp of the conventions that surround the exchanges of language. These exchanges typically occur in conversations.

Our speech is based on the fundamental assumption that speakers and listeners will cooperate in using language. This agreement is unspoken, but it underlies all speech acts. Speaker and listener must first cooperate on the mechanics of speech—talking in a language they both know, following known rules of sentence structure and pronunciation, and speaking loudly enough to be heard. They also cooperate on more subtle but equally important conventions. The listener assumes that the speaker will be informative, truthful, clear, brief, and relevant (Grice, 1975). Even speech between enemies follows all these cooperative rules—except, perhaps, "be truthful."

This **cooperative principle** explains a number of the word choices we make when we refer to objects. If speech is to be clear and informative, speakers will design their utterances so that listeners will be able to figure out what they are referring to. For example, the speaker should not say "It's the white duck," if all the ducks in the pond are white. Instead, a more distinguishing description should be used, perhaps "It's the dirty one on the left."

The Given-New Strategy

One illustration of cooperation in conversations is the use of the **given-new strategy**, which listeners use to figure out the main topic of the speaker's remark (Clark and Haviland, 1977). In most cases, the speaker mentions a concept that already exists in the common ground he or she shares with the listener ("given" information), *before* saying something new about that concept ("new" information). For example, your friend may say, "The guy we met last night is a Phi Beta Kappa." You have no trouble understanding the remark because the speaker has obeyed the convention of placing the known information first, in the "given" position. The "given" information presumably is already in the listener's memory; the speaker is asking the listener to call forth that concept ("the guy we met") and attach the new information to it (being a Phi Beta Kappa).

English has a simple way of tagging a concept as old or new. Without thinking about it, we use the indefinite article "a" to mark a noun as new information and the definite article "the" to mark it as old information (note "the guy" above). Because we are so accustomed to using "a" and "the" in this way, we can be misled when someone presents new information as though it were already common ground. For example, researchers showed people a film of a car accident and afterward asked them questions about it (Loftus, 1979). Some were asked, "Did you see a broken headlight?" Others were asked, "Did you see the broken headlight?" There was no broken headlight in the film, but using the definite article conveyed the idea that the questioner believed there was a broken headlight. A week later, when asked whether there had been a broken headlight in the film, people who been asked about "the" broken headlight were much more likely to recall seeing a broken headlight than were people who heard the question about "a" broken headlight. The earlier small difference in wording had caused people to reconstruct their memories to include the event that had been asked about.

The Conventions of Turn Taking

It is obvious that more than one person cannot speak at once and be understood. To solve the problem of coordinating conversations, we have developed **turn-taking conventions**. When several people are conversing, the speaker may choose who takes the next turn, either by looking directly at someone or by asking the person a question. If the speaker does not select someone, the first person to jump into the conversation has the right to hold the floor (Sacks et al., 1974). Most of us seem to use these signals effectively to keep the conversation flowing; recordings of conversation show that people's utterances overlap only about 3 percent of the time (Sacks et al., 1974).

One way a speaker maintains the floor is to look away from the listener, only occasionally making eye contact. In fact, when speakers are forced to maintain eye contact with listeners, their speech often becomes stumbling, as if processing the facial expressions of others overloaded short-term memory and took up space needed to plan one's speech (Beattie, 1978). Sometimes a speaker wants to hold the floor but needs a few seconds to plan the next remark. In that case, the speaker may say something like, "I have this to say on that topic," or "Let me make this perfectly clear." Others may keep the floor by filling their pauses with something like "ah . . . um . . . you know. . . ."

Speakers who are ready to surrender the floor usually pause, end a sentence with a falling inflection, and often look directly at the listener, as though to say, "I'm finished; now what do you have to say?" Speakers differ in their use of these conventions, but when an individual fails to observe them, he or she may find that it is difficult to

Conversational conventions help both the listener and the speaker, and when they are not observed, both are inconvenienced. British Prime Minister Margaret Thatcher, for example, is often interrupted by a reporter's question before she has finished responding to the last one. Mrs. Thatcher's verbal signals suggest that she has finished speaking when, in fact, she has not.

complete a statement. For example, British Prime Minister Margaret Thatcher sometimes has this problem in press conferences and interviews. She often gives the impression that she has finished speaking, ending a sentence with a falling intonation and looking directly at the listener. This cues the interviewer to ask another question, but the prime minister continues speaking, completing her previous answer. The two utterances overlap, creating the impression that the reporters are being rude, when they may simply be responding to her speech mannerisms. To test this hypothesis, researchers had students view film clips of Mrs. Thatcher's interviews and indicate each time they believed she had finished answering a question. The students reacted the way Mrs. Thatcher's interviewers did; they consistently indicated she had completed a reply just before the interviewer began to ask another question (Beattie et al., 1982).

Other Conversational Conventions

We also coordinate the flow of conversation by performing **adjacency pairs**, in which an utterance by one participant tells the other what sort of response is appropriate. Common adjacency pairs include question/answer, request/promised compliance, summons/answer, offer/acceptance, greeting/greeting, and gratitude/acknowledgment. These pairs form the backbone of many social interactions and help manage turn taking. They also regulate the necessary rituals we use to open and close conversations.

Another set of conventions vital to the maintenance of conversation is the system we use to make repairs when something goes wrong. When a speaker's utterance fails, we may interrupt with, "Pardon, what did you say?" or check out a reference with, "By Hank, you mean Hank Jones, right?" or repair an obvious mistake made by the speaker, "The party is Saturday night, not Friday night." We may make other background responses that help the speaker along without taking away the floor: we may say "um hum" or "I see" or "how interesting," or supply a name or a date the speaker is searching for. We may also use nonverbal cues to indicate our acceptance and attention, perhaps smiling or nodding approval at appropriate places. People differ considerably in the amount of this background feedback they provide a speaker. Individuals who provide an appropriate amount are considered "easy to talk to," perhaps because they give speakers the impression they are talking in an intelligible and comprehensible manner.

LANGUAGE ACQUISITION

If using language now appears a lot more complicated to you than it did before you began this chapter, you are in the right frame of mind to marvel at how children ever manage to learn such a vast, complex system. Their acquisition of language represents a towering intellectual achievement, yet they seem to do it almost effortlessly. In only a few years, children progress from a meaningless babble to a command of their native tongue.

Stages in Language Acquisition

Despite the wide variation in human cultures, children in every society appear to acquire language in the same way (Brown and Fraser, 1963; Bloom, 1970; Brown and Hanlon, 1970; Brown, 1973). One child may begin to use words earlier than another or speak more fluently, but all normal children master the basic features of whatever language they hear spoken.

Prespeech Communication

A baby's first cries are simply signals of distress and not an attempt to communicate. Yet these noises inform parents about the baby's needs and influence their actions. Each infant has about three patterns of crying, distinguished by the pattern of pauses, the duration of the cry, and its tonal characteristics. These basic cries are usually interpreted by parents as signaling hunger, pain, or anger (Wolff, 1969). By the time a baby is seven or eight months old, he or she may have learned to control a parent by crying. In such cases the baby often cries without tears or abruptly begins and ends the crying bouts (McCall, 1979).

Other sounds soon appear, and by six months babies babble, chanting sequences of sounds that resemble syllables. Much early babbling is apparently motor play; deaf babies babble just as hearing babies do. Soon after six months, however, deaf babies stop babbling, probably because they have not been stimulated by hearing human speech. In early babbling, infants make sounds from all languages, and the babbling of Chinese babies, for example, is indistinguishable from the babbling of American babies. Gradually, children develop control over the sounds that they make and begin to imitate the sounds and intonations of others.

Infants also use gestures to communicate. At about ten months, babies begin to seek help from adults. For example, the infant may look at a toy that is out of reach, look at a nearby adult, stretch a hand toward the toy, look again at the adult, and make a fussing sound that increases in volume if the adult does not respond. Now the infant has demonstrated both an intent to communicate and a realization that agreed-upon signals can be used to communicate desires (Bates, 1979). This realization marks the beginning of speech acts.

Babies also express their intentions by the patterns of pitch changes in the sounds they make, and they can signal happiness, commands, requests, or questions (Tonkova-Yampol'skaya, 1973). Toward the end of the first year, their intonation patterns begin to resemble the patterns in the speech they hear around them. Now Chinese babies babble in Chinese cadences, and American babies babble long sequences of sound with the changes in pitch typical of English sentences (Bates, 1976). The baby's mastery of pitch and emphasis systems is an important step in the development of language, because intonation is a grammatical device that changes the meaning of utterances—it can even reverse their meaning, as in the sarcastic "A fine friend you are."

First Words

As babies grow, so does the number of things they begin to notice and want to express. To meet these needs, babies continually refine their communicative system, and this process develops naturally into the one-word stage of language. Parents continually name objects for infants, and by the time their first birthday approaches, many children have produced their first words. Generally, these words are the names of objects; the baby now realizes that objects are worth talking about and that objects have names (Nelson and Nelson, 1978). The baby's first words refer to the immediately tangible and visible; the child's language does not yet exhibit displacement, a feature of adult language discussed earlier. At this stage children understand many more words than they produce.

Limited to one word at a time, infants rely on what they have learned about intonation to communicate their desires. For example, an infant who has learned the word "door" can, by changing the intonation, make a declaration ("That's a door"), ask a question ("Is that a door?"), or state a demand ("Open the door!") (Menyuk and Bernholtz, 1969). Such one-word utterances can be understood only in context. If a toddler stands in front of a closed door and her favorite stuffed animal is on the other side, it is safe to assume that the emphatic "Door!" means "Open the door." If the door were open, the utterance could mean "Close the door." The success of these one-word utterances depends on the ability of listeners to infer the child's intentions from his or her intonations and gestures in the particular context. These clues remain important as the child's command of language grows. Even among adults, tone of voice and body language often provide essential clues to the meaning of spoken language.

Children in this early stage of language acquisition often stretch the meaning of a word, applying it to objects or actions for which they have no words; this process is called **overextension**. Up to a third of a child's early words are extended in this fashion (Nelson et al., 1978), and the overextension is generally based on the appearance of an object. For example, a small girl who has learned the word "bow-wow" may overextend it from dogs to all four-legged animals. When she learns a new word, say "moo" for cows, she no longer has to use the word "bow-wow" for cows. Eventually she will have separate names for all animals (E. Clark, 1983). This also works the other way: as children's ability to perceive distinctions among things in the world increases, the stage is set for them to learn a new label.

Overextension often does not indicate a confusion of meaning, because children who overextend a word in speaking rarely confuse it in comprehension. For example, a child who calls most animals "bow-wow," will always point to the dog and never to the sheep when asked to find the "bow-wow" in a picture of animals (Gruendel, 1977). Children are forced to overextend their limited vocabulary because they do not have all the words they need to talk about all the things in their world.

Although children at this stage have a basic vocabulary, they have not yet acquired language. Language requires that the child be able to combine words according to certain rules (the rules of grammar). Grammar cannot emerge until the child has reached a certain level of neurological maturation. But just as crawling prepares infants to walk, one-word utterances prepare them to speak with increasing grammatical complexity, and thus to communicate about more things in their expanding world.

First Sentences

Between eighteen and thirty months, children begin to put two words together. This new development indicates, among other things, an improvement in short-term memory. They do not pause between the two words, and they speak with a falling intonation that spreads over the entire utterance. Because of the two-word limit during this stage, however, their sentences are stripped to essentials: the little function words—articles, prepositions, and conjunctions—are omitted. Such utterances resemble telegrams, so they are known as **telegraphic speech** (Brown and Bellugi, 1964). For example, if a little boy in the two-word stage wants his mother to read him a book, he can say, "Mommy book," or "Read book," or "Mommy read," but he cannot yet produce the slightly longer version, "Mommy read book." Just as he did during the one-word stage, the boy means more than he can say. He can, however, put together a pair of two-word utterances to express his thoughts, such as "Kitty book. Mommy read" (Scollan, 1979).

Now the rudiments of grammar start to appear in the child's speech. Children do not merely slap together any two words in their utterances; instead they rely on semantics and context to establish permissible word combinations. They develop a number of small patterns (such as actor plus action), but most of those patterns fit comfortably into the basic rules of English word order: "subject-verb-object." Thus, most two-year-olds will say "eat cake" but not "cake eat." Eventually, all the small patterns will be absorbed into the general rules of English word order, but this does not happen until children have moved out of the two-word stage (Maratsos, 1983). Two-year-olds continue to use intonation, which was already present at the one-word stage, and can indicate meaning through vocal emphasis. A two-year-old can say, for example, "*Daddy* coat," emphasizing the first word to indicate possession ("This is Daddy's coat), or "Daddy *coat*," with emphasis on the last word to indicate location ("There is Daddy's coat") or action ("Daddy, put on your coat").

Yet these childish sentences are not simply shorthand versions of sentences heard from adults. Rather, the child appears to construct utterances by following some simple rules. This procedure leads to unique sentences the child would never have heard from an adult. By carefully studying the utterances produced by children of different ages, psycholinguists have been able to piece together changing sets of rules that describe children's utterances at various stages of language development (McNeill, 1970). Even the form of a unique sentence like "All-gone sticky" from a little boy who has just washed his hands can be predicted by knowing what rules he is following.

Two-word utterances can express an immense range of propositions. Although the basic categories of propositions shown in Table 16.1 are based on data from children around the world, the entire list could be compiled from the speech of two-year-olds in any language. Regardless of the culture in which they are reared, two-year-olds express the same range of concepts in their two-word sentences. These concepts provide the basis for all human language; much of the child's later language development is primarily an elaboration and refinement of these basic ideas.

Acquiring Complex Rules

Children learn syntax by building on their knowledge of word meanings. This learning takes place within specific settings in which a parent makes a simple utterance referrring to some aspect of the immediate environment. Imagine a little boy playing in the living room one evening, surrounded by his parents and the familiar sights and sounds of his home. He encodes the scene around him in terms of very simple concepts for objects, actions, and relations among them: "Doggy on chair," "Daddy has hair," "Mommy feeds me," and so on. Now Mommy says, "Your daddy is asleep on the couch." The child hears her utterance and automatically assumes that she is referring to the here-and-now. He sees the situation and tries to match up the words in that string with the kinds of things he perceives around him.

Table 16.1 ■ Categories of Meanings Expressed in the Two-Word Stage

Category of Meaning	Description
Identification	Utterances such as "See doggy" and "That car" are elaborations on pointing, which emerged in the preverbal stage, and naming, which began in the one-word stage.
Location	In addition to pointing, children may use words such as "here" and "there" to signal location—as in "Doggy here" or "Teddy down." To say that something is in, on, or under something else, children juxtapose words, omitting the preposition—as in "Ball [under] chair" or "Lady [at] home."
Recurrence	One of the first things that children do with words is call attention to, and request, repetition—as in "More cookie" or "Tickle again."
Nonexistence	Children who pay attention to the repetition of experiences also notice when an activity ceases or an object disappears. Utterances such as "Ball all gone" and "No more milk" are common at this stage.
Negation	At about age two, children discover that they can use words to contradict adults (pointing to a picture of a cow and saying, "Not horsie") and to reject adults' plans (saying, "No milk" when offered milk to drink).
Possession	In the one-word stage children may point to an object and name the owner; in the two-word stage they can signal possession by juxtaposing words—as in "Baby chair" or "Daddy coat."
Agent, Object, Action	Two-word sentences indicate that children know that agents act on objects. But children at this stage cannot express three-term relationships. Thus, "Daddy throw ball" may be expressed as "Daddy throw" (agent-action), "Throw ball" (action-object), or "Daddy ball" (agent-object). Children may also talk of the recipient of an action by using similar constructions—saying, "Cookie me" or simply "Give me" instead of "Give me a cookie."
Attribution	Children begin to modify nouns by stating their attributes, as in "Red ball" or "Little dog." Some two-word sentences indicate that children know the functions as well as the attributes of some objects—for example, "Go car."
Question	Children can turn types of sentences described here into questions by speaking them with a rising intonation. They may also know question words, such as "where," to combine with others—as in "Where kitty?" or "What that?"

Source: Adapted from Brown, R. *A first language: The early stages.* Cambridge, Mass.: Harvard University Press, 1973.

The process is helped enormously by the special ways that adults speak to small children: they talk slowly, replace difficult sounds with easy ones, substitute nouns for pronouns, and use simple sentences with carefully placed pauses and inflections. Although this special way of speaking has been called **motherese**, it is used fairly consistently by all adults in speaking to very young children (deVilliers and deVilliers, 1978). Generally, the simple sentences of motherese directly reflect the underlying conceptual structures. For example, attributes of objects are expressed as adjectives and placed in the sentence next to the noun they modify ("brown doggy").

We know from studies of adults learning specially made-up ("artificial") languages that they can learn much more quickly if the artificial word strings are grouped into phrases, and if descriptions of one object are grouped together rather than being mixed up with descriptions of another object (Moeser and Bregman, 1973; Morgan and Newport, 1981). Such a language-learning process has been simulated in computer programs. One of these programs enabled the computer to acquire a reasonable grasp of many rules of English word order and inflection following 850 exposures to sample sentences of the language (Anderson, 1983). In a program that simulated the way a child learns language, the same researcher (Anderson, 1983) had the computer learn vocabulary as well as syntax. With 6,000 trials (considerably less than a twenty-four-month-old child's experience), the computer had learned 142 words and could generate utterances like "Daddy eat cookie" and "No more apple juice."

Gaining Mastery of Complex Rules

By the time children enter kindergarten, they apply most grammatical rules correctly. They acquire their largely unconscious knowledge of rules by noticing patterns and regularities in adult speech, then generalizing them. We can think of children as applying perceptual strategies to the language they encounter (Slobin, 1973).

One of these strategies is "Pay attention to the end of words." Children appear to learn suffixes (endings like "-ed," "-ing," "-s") more easily than they learn prefixes (like "un-," "in-," or "pre-"). In one study (Kuczaj, 1979), preschoolers heard a series of sentences in which the same nonsense syllable ("-ip") was always applied either at the beginning or the end of words. For example, some children heard "The boy drove the ip-car" while others heard "The boy drove the car-ip." The situation was set up so that with some children "ip" always meant "big"; with other children it always meant "red." But whether "ip" meant "big" or "red," children who heard the syllable used as a suffix discovered its meaning far more easily than children who heard it used as a prefix. An example of a specific rule that children acquire by paying attention to the end of words is the rule for forming plurals in English: add an "s" or "z" sound to the singular form of the noun ("dog/dogs").

In learning grammar, children must not only grasp the underlying rules for combining words into sentences but must also learn exceptions to the rules. Because many grammatical rules have exceptions, this second task can be difficult. Three- to six-year-olds often commit errors by extending a grammatical rule to cases in which it does not apply (Bellugi, 1970; Slobin, 1973). Such errors show that children have discovered certain language rules and that they are systematically using them, even in cases where the rule does not apply.

Such **overregularization** is similar in name and notion to the overextension of word meanings by the younger child. It is also extremely common when children apply the rule governing past tense in English. Very young children memorize some common but irregular past verb forms, such as "broke" and "went," without realizing that past tense usually follows a simple rule and that these forms are actually exceptions. But later, once they have discovered the rule of "Add '-ed' to the verb when talking about events in the past," they apply this rule everywhere, even to irregular verbs. Suddenly they begin saying such things as "Daddy goed to work" and "It breaked," even though they had used the right words in the past. Children of five or six may apply the rule to the correct irregular past forms and say such things as "wented" or

"ated," but by the time they are seven most no longer overregularize verbs (Kuczaj, 1978). At this point, when they are about to use an -ed form, they may first check whether it is an exception; if not, they follow the general rule for past tense (Anderson, 1983).

Children go through a similar sequence with plural nouns. After they learn to add the "s" or "z" sound to the singular form, such incorrect plurals as "foots," "mans," and "mouses" creep into their conversation. Often these forms are followed by a double plural—"mens" and "mices"—before children return to the original correct form.

Although parents may be startled when their child suddenly seems to slip back and starts to talk less correctly, such behavior actually represents progress in children's analysis of language. The errors show that they are learning rules that reflect the regularities they have noticed in the speech of others.

Explaining Language Acquisition

Obviously, normal children are neurologically equipped to figure out the structure of any human language. As long as they live in a society that uses language to communicate, children seem to learn language readily. But exactly how do they go about this enormous task? Psychologists generally agree on the factors influencing language acquisition, but differ in which factors they emphasize.

According to the biological view proposed by the linguist Noam Chomsky (1972; 1975; 1979), the acquisition of language is primarily a matter of brain maturation and the child's exposure to appropriate speech. Chomsky believes that all languages of the world share a common underlying deep structure that is based on special faculties of the human brain. As we have seen, all languages make some similar distinctions relating to how phonemes are combined into words, words into constituent phrases, and phrases into sentences. When children acquire their native language, Chomsky argues, they are aided by an inborn knowledge of these universal language structures, and this knowledge is different from general cognitive abilities. According to this view, what children have to learn is how the language of their particular culture expresses, or "transforms," this underlying universal structure.

Some behaviorists, especially B. F. Skinner (1957), have sharply disagreed with Chomsky and instead explain language acquisition as simply "verbal behavior"—another example of operant conditioning. They argue that because mothers use words to express affection as they care for their babies, the mothers' speech becomes reinforcing. Eventually, babies are reinforced by their own utterances, which match the sound of their mothers' speech. In addition, parents and other adults reinforce youngsters with attention and approval when they begin to label objects in the world (Bijou and Baer, 1965). When children learn to say things that other people can understand, the child has a way to communicate his or her needs and desires. And so this accomplishment is also reinforcing. Because grammatically correct constructions get desired results, the child tends to repeat them.

Social learning theorists believe that reinforcement is not enough to explain the process; they contend that imitation plays a major role. Parents act as models for their children, and the children imitate both the words and the general rules they hear (Bandura, 1977). Children apparently can imitate general rules; researchers have been able to use modeling to help two-year-olds learn the future tense. When a child asked, "Where it go?" the researcher responded with the future tense, saying, "It will go there" and "We will find it." The new form quickly appeared in the children's speech (Nelson, 1977).

Reinforcement and imitation clearly play a role in language acquisition, but many psychologists believe that some additional principles are still needed to account for the process. For one thing, parents and other adults reinforce children's language in ways that must seem inconsistent to the child. Adults generally reinforce children for the content or truth of their speech, not for correct grammar. For example, when a little girl wanted to indicate that her mother was also female, she said, "He's a girl." Her mother replied, "That's right" (Brown, Cazden, and Bellugi-Klima, 1968). But a child who says "Friday is my birthday" will be corrected if the birthday falls on Saturday. Such anecdotes do not disprove the role of reinforcement in language acquisition; they merely reflect "noise" in the training process. Children are reinforced for so many utterances that occasional incorrect feedback does not impede their growing grasp of language.

Children clearly cannot learn syntax by imitation that consists of the exact copying of a specific response or utterance. The sort of imitation involved in language acquisition consists of learning and applying a rule instead of learning to copy a string of words. The child abstracts a general rule from a set of examples. In some cases, following the rule leads the child to produce nonwords, words the child has never heard before. The child who says, "I seed two mouses" or "I drinked milks" is clearly not imitating an adult's exact words. Instead the child has abstracted rules for past tense and plurals from a variety of examples. Experiments with computer simulations have shown that such a process is plausible (Anderson, 1983).

In recent years several researchers have examined how social interactions of infants support their language development (Bates, 1976; Gleason and Weintraub, 1978). These researchers believe that language use, rather than the grammatical aspects of language, is the key to language development. In their view the social uses of language provide the basis that underlies the development of first words and the semantic functions of telegraphic speech. Young children begin to acquire language by using the context of a situation to figure out a speaker's intentions, eventually learning the rules that govern speech acts. For example, infants may learn something about the nature of human conversation from early exchanges with a parent, in which the parent at first supplies both sides of the conversation. Similarly, in early interactions and games, infants learn to take turns, to make eye contact, and to indicate that they are paying attention. They also learn various scripts that can be transferred to other situations (Bruner, 1983). In these ways, the social interactions of infancy lay the foundation on which language is built.

BIOLOGICAL FOUNDATIONS OF LANGUAGE

Whether researchers stress biology, learning, or social interaction in their explanations of language acquisition, they agree that our ability to use spoken language is closely related to our biological structure. The human vocal organs, breathing apparatus, auditory system, and brain are highly specialized for spoken communication (see Figure 16.5).

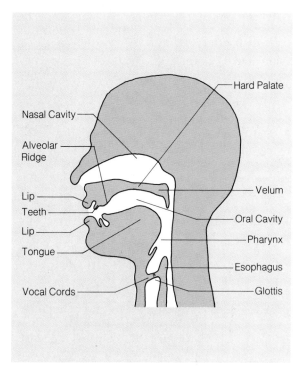

Figure 16.5. Parts of the human vocal apparatus. Air expelled from the lungs vibrate the vocal cords, which can stretch or contract to produce high or low frequencies (pitches). The vibrating cords cause the column of air in the pharynx and oral cavity to vibrate like the air in a pipe organ. By moving the tongue, velum, and lips, we can alter the nature of the sound produced. For example, pressing the tongue against the hard palate so the sound is forced up through the nasal cavity produces the nasal sounds *n*, *m*, and *ng*. (Clark and Clark, 1977.)

Vocal and Auditory Specialization

In human speech the lungs expel air through the throat and mouth; the vocal cords vibrate like violin strings to create sound in the larynx and throat, which act like a pipe organ; the tongue, palate, lips, teeth, and facial muscles work together to pronounce vowels and consonants. Stop a moment, put your hand on your throat, and read this sentence aloud. Feel how these structures move flexibly and how your windpipe resonates.

Just as our vocal apparatus is well adapted for producing widely varied speech sounds, so our hearing is well adapted for perceiving those sounds. As noted in Chapter 14, infants only a few weeks old can detect the difference between "ba"

and "pa" (Eimas and Tartter, 1979). Further, babies only a few days old prefer human voices over other sounds; they will respond more to music that includes singing than to the same music without voices (Butterfield and Siperstein, 1974). It seems that infants are neurologically prepared to process speech sounds, a process that occurs in the brain (see Chapter 3).

Brain Specialization

For most people, language functions appear to be controlled by the left hemisphere of the brain. As we saw in Chapter 3, the brain is lateralized for language, and when the left cerebral hemisphere is injured, an individual's ability to produce and understand language often suffers. Researchers have demonstrated this localization of language function by testing patients undergoing brain surgery. When a patient's left hemisphere is anesthetized, he or she cannot speak or sing the words of a familiar song but has no trouble humming the tune. By contrast, when only the right hemisphere is anesthetized, the patient cannot hum the melody but can recite the words (Gorden and Bogen, 1974).

Signs of lateralization have been detected even in newborn infants; when babies hear passages of speech or consonant-vowel sounds, their brainwave recordings show more activity in the left hemisphere than in the right. And when the babies hear musical chords or bursts of sound, their brain-wave recordings show greater activity in the right hemisphere (Molfese and Molfese, 1979; 1980). Such studies suggest that special left-hemisphere mechanisms for analyzing speech may serve as the foundation for learning language.

Should an infant's left hemisphere be injured, however, the right hemisphere takes over the language function; at this age, the still-developing brain is highly adaptable. Very young children whose left hemispheres have been surgically removed (to prevent debilitating seizures) appear to develop language abilities that come close to normal (Lenneberg, 1967; Smith and Sugar, 1975). In one study (Dennis and Whitaker, 1976), nine- and ten-year-old children whose left hemisphere had been removed before they were five months old had almost normal language. However, they had not yet learned to understand passive sentences (e.g., "I was paid the money by the boy"). This deficit indicates that some aspects of language develop quite slowly if children have only a right hemisphere.

Some theorists have taken the usual right-hemispheric specialization of language as support for the hypothesis that language is a distinct faculty for which specific parts of the human brain have evolved. This specific-faculty view contrasts with the hypothesis that the brain is a general-purpose induction machine that can learn whatever associations, regularities, and skills are important, including the elaborate rule system of language.

The "general-purpose" view of hemispheric lateralization of language would hypothesize that the left hemisphere starts out larger and with denser neuronal connections, because the typical individual is right-handed (due to genetic determination). This larger, denser cortical tissue can then take on the most challenging learning task facing the infant, the acquisition of language. In this view, because the left hemisphere is occupied with language learning, nonlinguistic abilities such as musical, pictorial, or spatial skills are learned and performed predominantly in the right hemisphere. But at the moment, these remain speculations about which psychologists disagree.

Is There a Sensitive Period for Language Learning?

One argument for the claim that language ability is different in kind from our other cognitive abilities is based on the notion that there is a sensitive period during which we must learn our first language—a period that begins at about age two and ends at puberty. According to this hypothesis, after puberty a person would find it difficult, if not impossible, to master a first language. Eric Lenneberg (1967) believed that language function gradually becomes lateralized in the left hemisphere between birth and puberty. He proposed that this gradual lateralization explains the existence of a sensitive period for language. Some evidence supports this position. When brain damage disrupts children's ability to talk, they are more likely than adults to recover completely, presumably because lateralization was not complete at the time of their injury.

Other evidence suggesting a possible sensitive period comes from a few cases of abused children reared without exposure to normal language. The case of Genie, a California girl who grew up in almost total isolation (see Chapter 2), indicates that acquiring a first language in adolescence may indeed present special problems (Fromkin et al., 1974). Genie was nearly fourteen when she was rescued from her miserable situation. She had spent her days strapped to an infant's potty chair, her nights harnessed in a sleeping bag that acted like a straitjacket. She lived in a room by herself, and her only social contact came when her silent, almost blind mother spooned baby food into her mouth. No one spoke to the girl, although her father often growled or barked like a dog at her. She had never fed herself; she could neither talk nor stand.

After being discovered, Genie spent six months in a rehabilitation center before she was placed with a loving foster family. She was given intensive language training, and her progress in language acquisition was studied by psycholinguists (Fromkin et al., 1974). By the time Genie was eighteen, she could understand normal language but could not produce some of its basic structures. Her speech was rule-governed and productive; she used some prepositions, and she spoke of people and objects that were not present. But her language lacked the rich fluency found in the speech of the average schoolchild. Genie's case seems to indicate that although acquiring a first language after the sensitive period is possible, it is extremely difficult. But her special circumstances make it impossible to draw a definite conclusion. Her severe sensory and social deprivation, her malnutrition, and the brutal treatment meted out to her by her parents may have combined to affect her cognitive as well as her linguistic development. Language, as we know, can only build on the foundation of general knowledge.

Another line of evidence relevant to the sensitive-period hypothesis comes from studying people who are learning a second language. If a true sensitive period exists, then a new language should be learned more easily before puberty than afterward, and the person's grasp of the second language should be better. In one review of second-language studies, this prediction was borne out, but the differences between language acquisition before and after puberty were not as dramatic as would be expected if a prepuberty sensitive period existed (Krashen, 1975). In another review of similar but more carefully controlled studies, the researcher found no evidence of a sensitive period

(Ervin-Tripp, 1974). In fact, the older the individual, the faster she or he learned the second language—although younger children were less likely to have an accent in the new language. Finally, among English-speaking families that moved to the Netherlands, adolescents learned Dutch the fastest. Preschoolers were the slowest to learn; they acquired the language much more slowly than their parents (Snow and Hoefnagel-Höhle, 1978). Thus, evidence from second-language acquisition does not support the hypothesis of a sensitive period or the idea that language is a biologically specific capability. The question remains open.

Can Other Animals Learn Language?

Many people have wondered whether human language is a unique development, distinct from the signaling systems used by other animals. Some researchers have tackled this question by asking whether chimpanzees could learn the equivalent of human language if they were exposed to the same sort of rich training environment that children encounter. Because the chimpanzee's intelligence is slightly less powerful than human intelligence, these primates seemed like a good choice for such an experiment.

Chimpanzees lack the vocal apparatus for speech, and so every attempt to teach them spoken language has failed (Hayes and Hayes, 1951; Kellogg and Kellogg, 1933). But chimpanzees can make hand signals. Beatrice and Allen Gardner (1969; 1975) took advantage of chimpanzees' manual dexterity and began teaching American Sign Language (ASL)—a language used by deaf people—to Washoe, a female chimpanzee. Washoe's training began when she was about a year old, and after four years she had learned to use 132 signs in appropriate situations. Some of her mistakes were overextensions, resembling those children commonly make, as when she applied the sign for bruises and scratches to red stains, a tattoo, and her first sight of the human navel. By the time Washoe had learned ten signs, she began to use them in combination, such as "Hurry open," "Please sweet drink," and "Gimme key." However, unlike children, Washoe paid little attention to word order and seemed to lack a grasp of syntax. For example, if she wanted to be tickled, she would sign either "you tickle" or "tickle you" (Klima and Bellugi, 1973).

Other psychologists have used different meth-

Washoe, a chimpanzee, was taught to communicate in sign language. Eventually she was able to learn more than a hundred signs, but she never mastered grammar.

ods of language instruction with chimpanzees. One chimpanzee named Sarah learned to use small plastic symbols of varying colors and shapes to represent words (Premack, 1971*a*; 1971*b*). Sarah learned to ask for things or answer questions by arranging symbols on a special magnetized board. Another chimpanzee named Lana learned to type simple messages on a computer-controlled keyboard (Rumbaugh, 1977). Each time Lana struck one of the fifty keys that represented words, its unique geometric design appeared on a lighted screen in front of her. Unless she adhered to word order, the computer rejected her sentences. Lana learned not only to produce rudimentary sentences but also to "read" what her trainers wrote on the screen and would carry out appropriate actions, such as going to fetch food said to be in another room.

For a while it appeared that chimpanzees were well on their way to language. But then, psychologist Herbert Terrace and his associates (1979) analyzed several hours of videotaped conversations involving their chimpanzee Nim. Terrace concluded that their chimpanzee's progress bore little resemblance to a child's acquisition of language. Nim had learned 125 signs and regularly combined them in utterances—some as many as nineteen signs long. But Nim's longer combinations were a grab bag of every sign that could apply to a situation, and were no more complex (syntactically or semantically) than his shorter combinations. When repeated signs were eliminated, so that "tickle tickle Nim tickle Nim tickle" became two signs long instead of six, the length of Nim's "corrected" utterances averaged only 1.6 signs. Most of Nim's sentences were imitations of his teacher's statements, and the chimpanzee rarely expanded on a teacher's utterance as children generally do. Further, Nim showed no evidence that he understood turn taking in conversations, a basic rule that children master before they begin to talk. When Terrace then examined films of the "talking" primates of other researchers, he found a similar pattern of imitative signing.

Terrace's announcement was followed by other reexaminations of the evidence. An analysis of Lana's typewritten utterances showed that almost everything she produced would fit six stock sentences, into which nouns or verbs could be substituted, depending on the situation (Thompson and Church, 1980). Lana's instructors had already come to similar conclusions. They decided that Lana—and other "talking" chimpanzees—had

gone no farther in acquiring language than the average nine-month-old child (Savage-Rumbaugh, Rumbaugh, and Boysen, 1980).

In these reanalyses, neither Terrace nor Lana's instructors had said that chimpanzees *could* not learn language, only that they *had* not. Thus, they reopened the important issue of whether language acquisition is unique to people. Chimpanzees seemed to use signs primarily to get rewards; their production of correct hand signs when shown an object or its picture did not show that they had grasped the idea that objects have names (the **referential** use of symbols). Instead, like the pigeon pecking keys to get corn, they may have learned only that a certain act (making the sign) in a specific situation produced a particular reward.

Around their first birthday, human children begin pointing to objects or holding them out to an adult while vocalizing. Their goal is to draw the adult's attention to the object. Such gestures precede the child's realization that things have names and that names can be used to communicate about objects without necessarily requesting them. Sue Savage-Rumbaugh and her colleagues (1983), who earlier worked with Lana, have suggested that chimpanzees lack these gestures and without them cannot learn the referential connections on which language is based. With much effort she and her associates have now taught two chimpanzees, Sherman and Austin, the referential behavior that children seem to learn easily and spontaneously. These researchers believe that Sherman and Austin have now acquired an appropriate base for a language system and may be able to learn syntactic combinations of those symbols in the future. If they eventually do succeed, chimpanzees will have acquired many of the critical elements of language.

Language and Thought

Throughout this chapter we have assumed that language builds on a basic conceptual system. The child first learns perceptual concepts and relations, then learns the names for these concepts. But think for a moment about George Orwell's novel *Nineteen Eighty-Four* (1949), in which the government sharply reduces vocabulary in the belief that subversive thought is impossible when there are no words to express it. Was Orwell right?

Do language and conceptualization interact, with each affecting the nature of the other?

How Language Affects Thought

Orwell spelled out some ominous implications of the view that language sets the boundaries of what we are able to think about, even determining whether or *how* we can think about objects and events. More recently, people have attempted to change implicit attitudes toward women by removing sexist language from books and advertising. The trend toward nonsexist language is in part a conscious effort to change our thought by changing our language. Similar motives underlie the removal of pejorative ethnic names from the language.

The idea that language determines thought was expounded eloquently by Benjamin Lee Whorf (1897–1941). When children acquire a language, Whorf believed, they simultaneously acquire a "world view," because what their language allows them to talk about determines the way in which they can perceive the world. According to Whorf (1956), different languages influence thinking in different ways; therefore, people with different languages think about the world differently. For example, English has a single word for snow, but Eskimos—who live in an environment where snow is extremely important—have more than twenty specific words for different types of snow. If language determines our perception, then when Eskimos look out on a fresh snowfall, the way in which they perceive the white substance should differ from the perception of speakers of English.

This view implies that the richness of the Eskimo's vocabulary forces an Eskimo to notice the condition of the snow—whether it is slushy, powdery, or crusty—and that the narrowness of the English snow vocabulary encourages the English speaker to overlook these distinctions. Yet when snow condition is important, as it is for the subgroup of English speakers who ski, a specialized vocabulary develops and many words for snow come into common use (Brown, 1958). The vocabulary of English does not make us blind to such differences. Therefore, the fact that languages differ in their number of distinguishing words does not support the hypothesis that our language determines what we can perceive.

Vocabulary is important, even if not in the way that Whorf proposed. It is impossible to master certain fields without their particular vocabularies (Clark and Clark, 1977). For example, surgeons could not learn the anatomical facts that guide every operation if their teachers had no vocabulary for expressing distinctions among the hundreds of muscles, nerves, and organs of the body. Having new words for novel information also affects the way in which we learn and remember (Dodd and White, 1980). In Chapter 9, we saw that labeling an ambiguous figure as "eyeglasses" caused it to be remembered differently than when it was labeled as "dumbbell" (Carmichael, Hogan, and Walter, 1932). Apparently, words determine how we encode information in memory.

Our memory for the aspects of a particular domain can also be improved by the richness of our vocabulary for that domain. For instance, unless you are a skier, your memory for the exact condition of snow outside the building would probably be worse than an Eskimo's. The importance of highly differentiated labels in memory was shown when Roger Brown and Eric Lenneberg (1954) asked students to name twenty-four color chips that varied slightly in hue (see Figure 16.6).

Figure 16.6. This array of color chips is used in color-naming experiments like that of Brown and Lenneberg (1954). See how closely you and a friend agree on which chips correspond to "pure blue" and "pure red" versus "teal blue" and "brick red." People usually agree more closely on the names of focal colors.

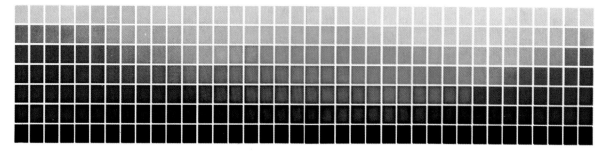

Some colors were highly "codeable" in the sense that students labeled them quickly and tended to agree on the labels. Other color chips were more difficult to code, with students taking more time to produce longer labels and often disagreeing about them ("bluish green" versus "teal blue"). A second group of students took a color-memory test. After viewing four color chips, they later looked at all twenty-four chips and tried to point out the four they had seen. The students remembered highly codeable colors far better than colors that were difficult to code. They seemed to be using easily remembered labels as cues that helped them remember the chips they had seen. In a similar test Zuni Indians, whose language does not have separate words for yellow and orange, made more errors than English speakers in remembering that they had seen yellow and orange chips (Lenneberg and Roberts, 1956).

How Thought Affects Language

Such findings lead us to conclude that language does not seem to determine thought in the far-reaching way that Whorf proposed. The linguistic differences he stressed are not nearly so significant as he believed. In fact, most psychologists now believe that language limits thought only to a small extent, and that some types of thought (e.g., in deaf mutes) may be completely independent of language (Furth, 1966). The pendulum of opinion has even shifted to the opposite belief: that univer-

sal thought processes create universal aspects of language.

The search for linguistic universals that depend on human perceptual and cognitive capacities has focused on color terms, mainly because they are easy to compare across languages. Various cultures use different systems for naming colors, with some cultures distinguishing many hues in their language and others distinguishing only a few (Berlin and Kay, 1969). For example, English uses eleven basic color categories, but speakers of Ibibio in Nigeria have four basic color terms, and speakers of Jale in New Guinea only two. Do people in various cultures carve up the color spectrum in a completely arbitrary way?

Research indicates that they do not. Instead, the structure of the human visual system determines the way we perceive the color spectrum (see Chapter 5). In the case of color, perception and thought impose regularities on human language (Miller, 1978). In a group of twenty languages, the number of color terms differed, but all languages selected their color terms from the list of eleven basic color categories used in English (Berlin and Kay, 1969). What is more, when these color terms occur in different languages, they always occur in the same order (see Figure 16.7). This order is easier to understand if we think about it in terms of the history of languages. The first two terms to enter a language are the equivalents of black and white—the most fundamental perceptual distinction. The next color term to enter a language is red; this is followed by yellow, green, and blue;

Figure 16.7. This diagram illustrates the logical relations among color names in different languages, with the names arranged from left to right in order of use. If a language had only three color terms, they would correspond to English black, white, and focal red; all other colors that English speakers distinguish (toward the right in the figure) would be assigned one of those three labels. If a language had six color terms, these would correspond to the English terms toward the left—black, white, and red, as before, plus yellow, green, and blue—with the other color terms toward the right being assigned one of those six labels. Color terms tend to be introduced into a language in historical sequence from left to right.

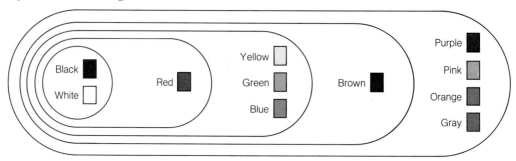

these by brown; and finally by purple, pink, orange, and gray. Thus, a language having only three color terms would have those corresponding to white, black, and red (all other colors that English speakers distinguish would be assigned one of these three labels); a language with six color terms would retain those corresponding to white, black, and red, and would add yellow, green, and blue.

Certain basic colors are more conspicuous than others to all people; these "focal colors" form the basis for the ordering of color terms in Figure 16.7. Even if a language does not name some of the focal colors, its speakers still find those colors distinctive, and they find it easy to pick up names for them from another language. These findings indicate that there are natural, universal color categories: people see colors in the same way (Berlin and Kay, 1969). In a language with only six color terms, purple may fall under the label "blue," but people of that culture still see purple as differing from red in much the same way that we see this difference. Infants apparently perceive differences among focal colors long before they learn the labels their culture has for them (Bornstein, Kessen, and Weiskopf, 1976). Apparently, color categories, like many other linguistic categories, reflect certain basic characteristics of human beings. Although people in different cultures apply different labels to things, language is not just an arbitrary set of conventions. At least some aspects of language are shaped by universal processes of perception and cognition.

SUMMARY

1. All human languages exhibit **meaningfulness**, **discreteness** (distinct units), **productivity** (capacity to combine units into an infinite number of statements), and **displacement** (ability to refer to distant objects and events). Many animal species communicate in some fashion, but no form of animal communication has all these features; human language is unique.

2. The study of language structure is the province of **linguistics**; the study of how people actually use language is the province of **psycholinguistics**. The system of regularities governing language production and comprehension is known as **grammar**—the rules that describe the levels of speech in our language and the way those levels are related. The rules of **syntax** govern the way words and phrases are combined to form sentences. The meaning of most sentences is composed of several **propositions**, which reflect a number of topic-comment assertions. Sentences are expressed in **constituent** phrases, which are in turn expressed by combinations of **morphemes**, which can be divided into the overlapping sounds of **phonemes**.

3. Social communication is the basic function of language, and the study of linguistic function is known as **pragmatics**. Producing an utterance involves a series of cognitive processes, in which a speaker determines the ideas to be communicated, selects the syntactic form and words, holds the words in memory, and finally expresses them in sounds. The context of an utterance places constraints on what is expressed, what words will be used to express it, and the way the words will be combined. The shared knowledge of speaker and listener, or **common ground**, is part of the context. The speaker's goals also influence the planning of a **speech act**, in which choosing the form that will have the desired effect is similar to solving a problem. Slips of the tongue, which reveal that an utterance is planned a phrase at a time, include **anticipations, perseverations**, and **reversals**.

4. Comprehending speech requires the listener to use memory and make inferences based on the knowledge of context and language. Their **categorical perception** of phonemes helps listeners process speech at the level of discrete syllables. Syntactic features and meaning-related clues, based on content words, allow the listener to predict what will come next in the sentence; calling forth an appropriate set

of knowledge schemas is vital for total comprehension.

5. Our reading speed is determined by our general knowledge schemas, our skills at reasoning and problem solving, and our knowledge of syntax and semantics. **Dyslexia** (reading disorder) may be caused by slowness in processing information and/or a difficulty in keeping track of word order. Computers have been programmed to understand a limited amount of natural language, applying syntactic rules to meanings of words looked up in a built-in dictionary. In order to provide for computer programs, **scripts**, or event-schemas, for various domains must be included in the program's knowledge base.

6. An unspoken **cooperative principle** underlies communicative language. Speakers and listeners cooperate in using the **given-new strategy**, by which the listener integrates the new information in an utterance with old information stored in memory. Conversations flow by means of rule-governed patterns, such as **turn taking** and **adjacency pairs**, in which the first speaker's utterance determines the form of the reply.

7. Children acquire language rapidly, mastering their native tongue within two to two and one-half years. The first cries of babies, which are signals of distress, are succeeded within a few months by babbling. As infants grow, they also communicate through gestures and intonations, and at about ten months they appear to realize that agreed-upon signals can be used to accomplish their intentions. During the one-word stage, children often **overextend** the meaning of words to cover objects or actions for which they have no label. As they move into the two-word stage, children rely on **telegraphic speech**, using simple word patterns and intonation to indicate meaning. A child learns syntax by matching the utterances of others to his or her conceptualization of a scene. While acquiring grammatical rules,

children tend to go through a period of **overregularization**, extending a grammatical rule to instances in which it does not apply.

8. Psychologists differ in which factors of language acquisition they emphasize. In the biological view of Noam Chomsky, the acquisition of language is primarily a matter of maturation; special neural structures for acquiring language are built into the human brain. Behaviorists believe that language acquisition is simply verbal behavior—an example of operant conditioning. Social learning theorists believe that reinforcement plays some part, but that rule learning via imitation is the key to language acquisition. Other researchers believe that pragmatics play a key role in language development, with language emerging out of social interaction between infant and care givers.

9. Human beings are equipped to make a great diversity of vocal sounds and to perceive a wide variety of sounds, indicating that language is related to human physiology. Because the left hemisphere dominates for language abilities in most people, it has been suggested that language is a distinct cognitive ability. But many psychologists believe that language is simply one aspect of general human cognitive abilities. Researchers disagree as to whether there is a sensitive period for language development in human beings.

10. Benjamin Whorf proposed that our native language may determine the way in which we think about objects and events and may limit the matters we are able to think about. However, most evidence indicates that while language may influence memory and possibly perception, language does not determine them. Some types of thought appear to be independent of language. Indeed, many theorists believe that universal characteristics of human thought processes may create universal linguistic structures.

KEY TERMS

adjacency pairs	grammar	productivity
anticipation	linguistics	proposition
categorical perception	meaningfulness	psycholinguistics
common ground	morphemes	referential
constituent	motherese	reversals
cooperative principle	overextension	script
discreteness	overregularization	speech act
displacement	perseverations	syntax
dyslexia	phonemes	telegraphic speech
given-new strategy	pragmatics	turn-taking conventions

RECOMMENDED READINGS

AKMAJIAN, A., R. A. DEMERS, and R. M. HARNISH. *Linguistics: An introduction to language and communication* (2nd ed.). Cambridge, Mass.: The MIT Press, 1984. A good introduction to language structure and use from the perspective of linguistics. Covers many "psychological" topics.

CLARK, H. H., and E. V. CLARK. *Psychology and language: An introduction to psycholinguistics.* New York: Harcourt Brace Jovanovich, 1977. Surveys the field of language and psychology. It reads very well and is illustrated nicely. Emphasis is given to the mental processes involved in the comprehension of language.

DAVIS, F. *Eloquent animals: A study in animal communication.* New York: Coward, McCann and Geoghegan, 1978. This book is about communication in animals, including apes, birds, and whales. It is a personal account of animal research provided by someone who visited various research sites.

FARB, P. *Word play.* New York: Bantam Books, 1975 (paper). A delightfully entertaining tour of all the ways we use words to carry out human functions; good discussions of humor, sarcasm, metaphor, and verbal play.

FOSS, D. J., and D. T. HAKES. *Psycholinguistics: An introduction to the psychology of language.*

Englewood Cliffs, N. J.: Prentice-Hall, 1978. This book covers a great deal of research on language and language comprehension.

GARDNER, H. *The shattered mind.* New York: Random House, 1976 (paper). A captivating account of disturbed speech in many clinical cases of patients who have suffered brain injury.

MILLER, G. A. (Ed.). *Communication, language, and meaning.* New York: Basic Books, 1973. Highly readable introductory chapters written by experts on most of the interesting topics surrounding communication and language.

SCHANK, R., with P. CHILDERS. *The cognitive computer: On language, learning, and artificial intelligence.* Reading, Mass.: Addison-Wesley, 1984. A popular book for the layperson, written by a leading theorist in artificial intelligence, describing the problems and achievements of attempts to get computers to learn, understand, and use language the way people do. Contains hopeful speculations about future uses of computers in intellectual activities.

SLOBIN, D. *Psycholinguistics* (2nd ed.). Glenview, Ill.: Scott-Foresman, 1979 (paper). An elementary introduction to the way psychologists study language; despite its age, still one of the most accessible introductions to the field.

PERSONALITY AND SOCIAL DEVELOPMENT

It is commencement day, and 500 new college graduates are launched in life. Although they look similar in their caps and gowns, they are 500 unique persons, each with a distinct history and outlook on life. Some are outgoing, others shy. Some are assertive and ambitious, other easygoing. Some are quick to try anything new, others prefer what is familiar. In any number of ways we can identify differences that distinguish each of these people from the others. These individual differences, as we shall see, are a product of biology, of the family, and of the social world in which each person has grown.

The term that psychology uses to encompass the distinct qualities that make each person unique is **personality**, which we can define as the organization of a person's cognitive, motivational, and social characteristics. The development of a person's personality encompasses all the changes that take place in these characteristics over the course of his or her life, together with the continuities that have existed all along. Our personality influences most aspects of our social, emotional, and cognitive behavior. It affects, for example, our bonds with other people, our conformity to sex roles, our tendency to behave aggressively or cooperatively, and our moral and intellectual development.

Psychologists are extremely interested in personality both as a result and a cause of human development. In one study, for example, researchers followed the lives of a group of college men for fourteen years. By the time a man had reached his early thirties, his achievement, motivation, and feelings of competence seemed to depend on events in his life: the course of his career, his marital satisfaction, and his relationship with his parents (Mortimer, Finch, and Kumka, 1982). But these life events that seemed responsible for the men's feelings of competence in turn depended on

425

how self-confident the men had been as college students. Personality factors had helped these men to actively create certain events—which, in turn, affected the men's personalities.

Personality and the social and emotional development of an individual are intimately intertwined. What is more, psychologists are discovering that personality's influence extends beyond the social sphere: our personality characteristics may influence even our health and longevity. In this chapter we shall look at personality as both effect and cause: how we become what we are, and how what we are determines what we become.

PERSPECTIVES ON PERSONALITY AND SOCIAL DEVELOPMENT

Researchers have come up with several theories that seek to explain personality. Some of the theories, like Freud's, are now many decades old and exert less direct influence on research than they once did. However, as researchers add to and refine what we already know, old theories are sometimes reinterpreted in the light of new evidence. In the past few years studies in this field have explored topics as varied as the effects of premature birth, the role of the father in his children's development, and the impact of a job on the adolescent boy or girl. We will discuss some of these new findings in this chapter.

But before we turn to the newer findings, we will consider the major approaches to personality and social behavior that psychologists have taken. Among them are the biological perspective, Freud's psychosocial theory, the cognitive-developmental perspective, and the behavioral perspective. Although we will describe the various theories separately, researchers and practitioners in this field usually draw on the ideas and findings of several—or all—of these perspectives. This trend toward the integration of theories has been particularly marked in recent years.

The Biological Perspective

A biological basis for personality development has not been as firmly established as has the biological basis for other human capacities. However, some aspects of personality show clear traces of biologi-

cal influence. How do researchers detect the presence of biological influences on personality? A favorite method is the study of twins, in which researchers compare identical twins with fraternal twins. Identical twins have the same genetic background, but fraternal twins are no more alike genetically than any pair of siblings. Therefore, if identical twins are significantly more alike in some aspect of behavior than fraternal twins, researchers assume they have found evidence of biological influence.

Genetic Influences on Temperament, Sociability, and Task-Oriented Behavior

One aspect of personality that is influenced by biology is **temperament**, the individual's pattern of activity, response to stimuli, susceptibility to emotional stimulation, and general mood (Buss, Plomin, and Willerman, 1973). Differences in temperament are apparent among newborn infants, and twin studies have shown biological influences as early as two months—the youngest twins studied (Torgersen and Kringlen, 1978). Heredity seems to have its strongest influence on physiological functions—such as sleep and feeding patterns and the infant's level of excitability. Some babies sleep and eat more readily than others, and some babies respond to a very slight stimulus—a light, a sound, a touch—but others respond only if the stimulus is fairly intense. Some babies are more physically active than others; they are restless and wave their arms and legs about, while other babies seem placid and move more slowly. Some babies fuss and cry a lot; they are irritable and hard to soothe once they begin to fret.

By the time babies are eight or nine months old, genetic influences on sociability appear. Some babies are especially "cuddly" and sociable; others do not like to be held closely. Within another year or so, these differences in sociability are expressed in different ways and in response to different events. Differences in the way babies respond to cuddling become differences in the way toddlers cooperate with other people, how upset they become when left with a stranger, and whether they are likely to strike up a conversation (Goldsmith and Gottesman, 1981).

A final area in which twin studies have found biological influences is called "task-oriented behavior." In babies, this difference shows up primarily in the length of time an infant pays attention to some object. But during the preschool period, biologically influenced differences appear in how long children persist at a task, how hard they will work toward some goal, and even how well they do on tests of intellectual competence (Matheny, 1980).

Similar personality differences appear in laboratory studies, in observations of children at home, and in parents' ratings of their youngsters' personalities. In one study of twins, parents' ratings of one- to five-year-olds indicated that identical twins were much more alike than fraternal twins in attention span, sociability, talkativeness, activity, mood, and their zest for life (Cohen, Dibble, and Graw, 1977). And parents of identical twins who mistakenly thought their children were fraternal twins saw their personalities as being as similar as those of identical twins.

The Emergence of Biologically Based Differences over Time

What are we to make of the fact that biologically based differences among infants seem to increase, rather than decrease, over the preschool years? Shouldn't genetic influences on behavior be apparent at birth? Not necessarily. Like body size, eye color, and sexual maturation, some biologically influenced behavior appears only later in development. Similarly, behavior that is present at birth may not indicate a biological predisposition at all; sometimes the environment begins to act on an infant before birth. As we saw in Chapter 14, when an mother takes drugs, smokes, or drinks, her baby's development is affected. And newborn infants often show the temporary effects of anesthetics or a difficult birth (Carey, 1983).

Finally, as we saw in Chapter 14, human beings never develop in a particular way because of heredity alone; environment—family, peers, a certain social setting—always act on the child's inherited nature. Sometimes an inherited tendency will not even appear unless the child encounters specific conditions, and sometimes a biologically based behavior will disappear unless environmental conditions sustain it (Gottlieb, 1983).

The Interplay of Biological Factors and Environment

We can see how heredity and environment might interact by looking more closely at the effect of a baby's temperament on his or her development.

The baby's temperament has a considerable effect on the way parents and other people treat the baby. And the way parents treat the baby in turn affects the way the baby's personality develops. An alert baby with a long attention span probably gets much more parental contact and stimulation than a baby who pays little attention to the surroundings (Crockenberg and Acredolo, 1983). The extra stimulation is likely to lead the baby to pay even more attention to events in the world and perhaps to learn more about them. A baby who responds to cuddling with smiles and coos probably gets picked up and held more often than a baby who squirms or frets at such treatment.

The demands of a "difficult" baby, one who cries a great deal or who does not eat or sleep well, place the family under stress. Some parents react to a difficult baby by letting the infant "cry it out," so that they are less responsive to the baby's needs. Other parents try to forestall unpleasant episodes, perhaps by making certain that feedings are never delayed or by picking up the baby at the first hint of distress. Which path the parents choose may depend on other aspects of the home situation. In one study, Susan Crockenberg (1981) found that when the mothers of difficult babies had to cope by themselves without any kind of social support, they were not very responsive to their babies. As a result, the emotional bond between infant and mother often suffered. But when mothers of difficult babies had a good deal of support from highly involved fathers, grandparents, or older siblings, they tended to be responsive to their babies. A secure relationship developed between these babies and their mothers. In this case the same difficult temperament led to different outcomes, with different effects on the baby's personality.

Temperament and stress can interact in other ways. Infants who are highly emotional are not especially likely to develop unreasonable fears as two-year-olds—that is, unless they are placed under stress. One kind of stress that many toddlers encounter is the birth of a sibling. In one study, highly emotional youngsters who were confronted with the birth of a sibling developed intense fears and worried frequently—and their reaction persisted for an entire year (Dunn and Kendrick, 1982).

Prematurity is often considered a biological problem, but it, too, has different results, depending on the environment in which the baby grows up (Parke and Tinsley, 1982). In one study of fifty premature babies, those who had received extra

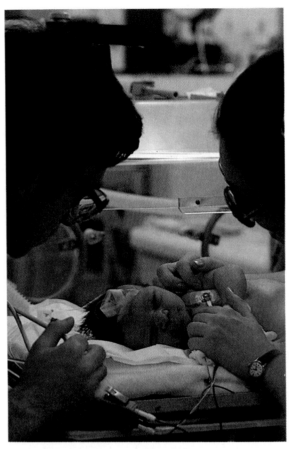

This prematurely born infant is receiving medical care from her doctors and emotional care from her parents. Such stimulation helps to foster healthy development in at-risk babies, especially if parents continue to provide special attention at home.

attention from their parents were found, as two-year-olds, to have developed better than babies who received less attention (Cohen and Beckwith, 1979). The babies who had been looked at, picked up, talked to, and cuddled more often were ahead of the others, both mentally and socially. Other studies have shown that at-risk babies (those who are premature or whose birth was complicated by medical problems) from middle-class families seem to "catch up" developmentally with other children, while those from lower-class families do not (Bronfenbrenner and Crouter, 1983). Since middle-class parents are known to interact more frequently with their infants than lower-class par-

ents do (Tulkin and Kagan, 1972), this finding is not surprising. Differences in caring for premature infants are not confined to social class; in one study, they were also related to ethnicity. Among mothers in the same social class, black and Cuban-American mothers reacted less anxiously to tape-recorded cries of premature infants than did Anglo-American mothers. Anglo mothers found the cries more "distressing, urgent, arousing, and sick-sounding" than the other mothers did (Zeskind, 1983). Presumably, the Anglo mothers would be more likely to pick up and try to comfort the baby, an action that might stimulate the infant's development. It is important to remember that biological development takes place in, and is significantly affected by, a social context.

Freud's Theory of Psychosexual Development

Sigmund Freud's **theory of psychosexual development** has had a dominant influence on research into personality and social development. Although many of Freud's ideas, as originally stated, have not been supported by substantive empirical investigation, his insights have stimulated some of this century's most important investigations into personality and social development.

Freud (1933/1965) maintained that from earliest infancy we are motivated by powerful biological instincts to seek pleasure and that at different ages, different parts of the body, called **erogenous zones**, become the focus of this pleasure. As these instinctive demands clash with the demands others make on us, we gradually learn to control our instincts and develop socially acceptable behavior.

According to Freud, from birth to adolescence children pass through five stages of psychosexual development: the oral stage, the anal stage, the phallic stage, a latency period, and the genital stage. In each stage, the child's interest is focused on the erotic pleasure that is derived from a different part of the body, and the shifts from one erogenous zone to another are directed by biological mechanisms. Freud argued that the adult personality results from the ways in which pleasurable impulses are channeled at each stage of development.

During the **oral stage**, which occupies the first year of life, the baby's mouth is the primary source of sensual pleasure. During the **anal stage**, in the second and third years of life, the child's attention shifts to the anus and the pleasures of holding in and pushing out feces. Almost immediately, however, the child encounters the social demands of toilet training. Freudian theorists regard toilet training as a crucial event, the first attempt to impose social requirements on the child's natural impulses.

The **phallic stage** of psychosexual development covers the years from about three until five or so, when the child's attention is focused on the genitals and the pleasures of fondling them. It is at this stage that the child finds out about genital differences between the sexes. This discovery precipitates the **Oedipal conflict**, which Freud saw as the most important conflict in the child's psychological development. Children perceive themselves as rivals of their same-sex parents for the affection of the parent of the opposite sex. A boy's wish to win his mother for himself puts him in conflict with his father. A girl's desire for her father's love makes her long to shut out her mother. As we shall see, the resolution of the Oedipal conflict has important consequences for the development of sexual identity and morality.

From the phallic stage, children move into the fourth stage, a **latency period**. Until puberty, children's sexual impulses remain in the background, and they busy themselves exploring the world and learning new things. With the hormonal changes of puberty, sexual feelings reemerge and the **genital stage** begins. The focus in this final stage of psychosexual development is on the pleasures of sexual intercourse.

Although Freud's ideas have had a profound effect on psychological thought, they have also been criticized as unscientific. Some psychologists contend that there is no proof that all children go through Freud's stages, for example. But even those who argue with Freud's specific theories agree with his emphasis on the family as a crucial determinant of early personality development. Freud believed that the relationships and processes that take place within the family lie at the core of psychological development. Our personalities, our feelings for others, and our attitudes toward others are formed in our early relationships with parents and siblings. Today, however, psychologists are less certain that what happens in the first few years casts a child's personality into a permanent mold. Radical changes in environment at any age are generally followed by major changes in behavior.

The Cognitive-Developmental Perspective

Like Freudian theory, the cognitive perspective on how personality and social behavior develop is based on the concept of developmental stages. But instead of emphasizing the conflict between demands for gratification and the requirements of society, cognitive theorists emphasize thinking, reasoning, and role taking. Cognitive theorists are especially interested in **social cognition**, the child's understanding of the social world and the process by which the child comes to understand why people (including himself or herself) behave the way they do in social situations. As a child develops, he or she gradually acquires information about the thoughts, viewpoints, intentions, and emotions of others. How the child interprets other people's actions then influences his or her own behavior in social situations (Shantz, 1983).

In the cognitive-developmental view, the child's social behavior reflects his or her understanding of the social world, and that understanding parallels the child's understanding of the physical, or nonsocial, world. This linkage of social behavior and cognitive maturity was heavily influenced by Jean Piaget's approach. The baby's sense of self, for example, is closely connected with development of the object concept, which was discussed in Chapter 15 (Bertenthal and Fischer, 1978). As cognitive skills develop, children are able to construct social schemes (conceptual frameworks) about social situations; these schemes are analogous to schemes about the physical world, and they enable children to know the social world and act within it. The scripts that guide our interpretations of language are one sort of social scheme (see Chapter 16). At first, babies treat people and objects alike, but as infants begin to distinguish themselves from the environment, they construct schemes for social interaction. Each person's unique schemes then contribute to the development of his or her personality.

The cognitive perspective emphasizes the active child—a child who constructs an understanding of the world through his or her actions upon it. As children advance through the stages of cognitive development, they develop increasingly complex schemes for social interaction. During the sensorimotor stage, their social behavior is primitive. It begins with a simple recognition of familiar persons and an early attachment to the mother or other person who cares for the child. To develop a sense of autonomy (independence), the child must develop a sense of the self as a being who is able to act on the environment in a planned and voluntary manner (Lee, 1976). This capacity for planning requires the child to engage in representational thinking and to use symbolic representations of objects and events. For example, a two-year-old may pick up a toy hammer to imitate Mother hanging a picture or Father repairing a chair. Such imitative role playing is essential for social and personality development.

Another cognitive ability seen as important in social and personality development is **role taking**. The infant is egocentric, seeing the world only from her or his own perspective. But the concrete-operational child can take the perspective of another person and can imagine what that person might be feeling. This operational capacity allows the child to develop elaborate social schemes that include the active roles of other people and the reciprocal nature of social interaction.

During adolescence, further connections between cognitive ability and social and personality development appear. As young people move into their teens and become capable of abstract reasoning, they begin to question the beliefs and teachings of their parents and to formulate their own system of values. It is no accident, then, that identity crises occur not during the elementary school years but during adolescence and young adulthood, when we become able to analyze the meaning of our past and the direction of our future.

The Behavioral Perspective

Psychologists have also tried to explain the development of personality and social behavior on the basis of the principles of learning that were presented in Chapter 8. Such behavioral psychologists regard the unique qualities and enduring characteristics of each person as patterns of behavior that have been learned through reinforcement, punishment, or imitation. In this view, development is continuous, not broken into discrete stages. Specific characteristics are acquired in two ways: on the basis of direct experience, in which the person receives reinforcement or punishment connected with particular behavior; or, according to social learning theory, through vicarious experience, in which the person observes and imitates a model's behavior.

An example of behavior acquired through direct experience is the infant's attachment to her or his care giver, which behavioral theorists believe is based on the warmth, comfort, and reduction of hunger that the infant associates with the care

Like grandpa, like grandson: according to social-learning theorists, we learn much of our behavior by imitating that of our parents or other adult models.

giver. This example is an instance of classical conditioning, but behavioral patterns are also acquired through operant conditioning. For example, a preschool boy who is big for his age may learn to achieve his goals by using physical aggression, because threatening or hurting smaller children often allows him to get what he seeks (Patterson, Littman, and Bricker, 1967). Much attention-seeking behavior in children, such as whining, is thought to be acquired in this way —that is, it achieves a desired end and thus is reinforced.

Social learning theorists argue that complex forms of social behavior and the enduring characteristics of personality are probably based on observational learning (Bandura, 1977; Patterson, 1982). Imitating parents and peers allows a child to develop complex patterns of behavior without having to be directly reinforced. For example, children learn male or female roles in part by imitating the parent of the same sex. That is, the child observes the parent and rehearses behavior that will become appropriate as she or he matures. Children also observe the consequences of a model's behavior; when the model is reinforced, children are likely to imitate her or his behavior because they anticipate receiving the same reinforcement themselves (Bandura, 1965).

In contrast to the cognitive perspective, the behavioral perspective emphasizes the impact of the environment on the child. The child acquires behavioral patterns when specific behavior is reinforced—either directly or vicariously. However, some social learning theorists see the child as relatively active in this process (Mischel, 1973; 1979; Bandura, 1977; Patterson, 1982). They believe that reinforcement and punishment serve as information that leads children to develop expectancies about what is likely to happen if a similar situation arises in the future. Children learn to estimate the possible consequences of their action; they also set their own standards of behavior and use these standards to judge (and reward) their own actions. Although these social learning theorists stress the central importance of cognitive activity in personality development, they differ from most cognitive theorists in two ways: (1) they focus on the impact of the environment on the child; and (2) they see behavioral development as continuous rather than as passing through a series of stages.

None of these perspectives by itself provides a satisfactory account of personality and social de-

velopment. Each, however, has led to important advances in our understanding of the processes by which each human being develops into a unique individual. In the following discussions, each of these perspectives—and in some cases all of them —will be used to explain particular aspects of development.

INFANCY

Infancy is usually understood to be the period between a child's birth and the time he or she begins to use language—roughly, the first two years of life (Bower, 1977; Shantz, 1983). During this period important social and personality development centers on the phenomenon of **attachment**, the emotional bond formed between the infant and his or her primary care giver. In later infancy, although interaction between the mother (or other care givers) and the child continues to be important, relationships with peers and others begin to expand the child's social world.

Mother-Infant Interaction

Both Freudian and social learning approaches to attachment explain the emotional bond of infant to care giver as a tie based on nurturance. That is, as the infant learns that the mother is the primary source of food, warmth, and comfort, an attachment to her develops as a positive response to a person who satisfies these needs. Attachment is also viewed as having adaptive significance. According to John Bowlby (1969), attachment helps babies to survive by keeping them near adults who provide them with necessary care and protection.

Although attachment applies to the infant's bond with her or his care giver, the parent also forms an emotional attachment to the infant. It has been proposed that the baby's "cute" appearance, typical of all immature mammals, naturally evokes positive emotional responses from adults (Lorenz, 1943; Alley, 1981).

According to Bowlby (1969), attachment does more than keep a baby alive. It helps infants develop essential social and cognitive skills by providing the emotional security that allows the infant to interact freely with people outside the family (promoting social development) and to explore the world (promoting competence).

The development of attachment appears to go through four phases (Bowlby, 1969; Ainsworth et al., 1978). In the first two or three months, babies respond to anyone and display no special behavior toward their mothers. Then, in the second phase, babies begin to discriminate among people and to respond to their mothers in special ways. At this age, however, babies will not protest if they are left with a sitter. At six or seven months, true attachment develops, and babies actively seek to remain close to their mothers, clinging to them or crawling after them. Now babies show **separation distress**, protesting when they are parted from their mothers and expressing joy at the mother's return. This is about the same time that the object concept begins to develop (see Chapter 15); the baby has become aware that Mother continues to exist when she is out of sight. A month or two after the third stage of attachment develops, babies also show **wariness of strangers**, perhaps responding to strangers with fear or withdrawal, looking away, frowning, or even crying at a stranger's approach. Finally, when children are between two and three years old and their developing cognitive abilities allow them to interpret their mothers' behavior, the attachment relationship becomes more flexible and separation distress vanishes. In this final and lasting stage of attachment, children develop a "partnership" with their mothers.

Psychologists seeking to understand attachment cannot experiment with human babies, separating them from their mothers, for example, to see if they grow up to be maladjusted. Such experiments have, however, been done with monkeys. In the first such experiment, young rhesus monkeys were taken from their mothers and raised with two surrogate "mothers," one made of bare wire mesh and the other covered with soft terrycloth (Harlow and Harlow, 1966; 1969). Although the bare wire "mother" was equipped with a feeding mechanism and dispensed all the monkeys' nourishment, the monkeys became attached to the soft, cuddly, terrycloth "mother," clinging to it, running to it when frightened, and using it as a base from which to explore the world (see Figure 17.1). These studies seem to indicate that comfortable contact is more important than food in establishing attachment—at least among rhesus monkeys.

When the opportunity to form an attachment is completely denied, the effects can be devastating and difficult to cure. Rhesus monkeys raised in total isolation behave in profoundly abnormal ways, clutching themselves and rocking, and later

Figure 17.1 In Harlow's experiments, infant monkeys were presented with a new and frightening object (the mechanical bear) and were given a choice of two surrogate mothers to flee to. Infant monkeys of all ages greatly preferred the terrycloth mother to the wire mother, even though some of the infant monkeys received food only from the wire mother. (After Harlow, 1959.)

becoming apathetic and inactive or else acting in a bizarre manner that resembles schizophrenia. As adults, both their sexual and social behavior are severely disturbed (Harlow, Harlow, and Suomi, 1971).

Rhesus monkeys do recover from most of the effects of isolation if they are placed with younger normal monkeys (Suomi and Harlow, 1972). The younger monkeys gradually draw the isolates into social interaction and play. The nonthreatening behavior of young monkeys helps the isolates make up the developmental deficit caused by their earlier lack of attachment.

Fortunately, few human infants are reared in social isolation, because the effects on the child would be devastating. A secure attachment is important to the development of social competence, and the child who fails to develop such an attachment—for example, one who passes through a series of foster homes—may find it difficult to form deep relationships later in life (Bower, 1977). On the positive side, there are indications that a stable attachment furthers the development of independence and competence in later life (Sroufe, 1977).

Other Social Bonds

Most research on interaction between babies and adults has focused on the bond between infant and mother. But Bowlby (1969) has suggested that babies also become attached to their fathers and other care givers. When researchers finally looked at babies and fathers, they discovered that babies become attached to their fathers at about the same time they develop an attachment to their mothers, and to the same degree (Lamb, 1977; 1978).

Despite the deep attachment between infants and their parents, infants do not have to have a parent in constant attendance to thrive. The *nature* of the interaction between child and parents, not the *amount* of time spent together, appears to be the important factor (Kagan, Kearsley, and Zelazo, 1978; Clarke-Stewart, 1982; Belsky, 1985).

Finally, it should be kept in mind that infants and their families live in a wider social world—a neighborhood, a town or city, and a nation. The importance of social support for mothers has turned up in many studies, where it often seems to make the difference between adequate and inadequate child care. Sometimes this sup-

port comes from the father (Parke and Tinsley, 1982); sometimes it comes from grandparents or other relatives, from friends, or from social agencies. Caring for an infant is a stressful task, so help clearly benefits the mother. What escaped researchers' notice in the past was the fact that whatever helps the mother tends to benefit the baby—and eventually the older child. In another study of teenage mothers, researchers found that when these young mothers lived with their own parents, their children scored higher on intelligence tests and were less likley to engage in antisocial behavior than the children of teenage mothers who lived on their own (Furstenberg, 1976).

CHILDHOOD

Although parents admittedly exert the greatest influence on a child's development, other adults, brothers and sisters, peers, and even television also have an effect. Once the child enters kindergarten and grade school and begins to spend substantial amounts of time away from home, people other than parents become progressively more influential.

As the child grows, the parents' role changes. During the child's infancy, the parent is primarily a nurturing, loving care giver. During childhood, the emphasis changes and parents switch their efforts from physical care to controlling the child's behavior and teaching the child to act in ways that society considers good or acceptable. This process of absorbing society's attitudes, values, and customs is called **socialization**, and it has a profound effect on the child's social and personality development. The goal of socialization is **internalization**—the child's incorporation of society's values to such an extent that violation of these standards produces a sense of guilt. Socialization plays an important part in the development of gender roles and peer relationships, in the control of aggression, and in the fostering of altruistic or other helpful behavior.

Children, Parents, and the Community

Children grow up in families, each unique and each with its own strengths and weaknesses. And families, in turn, live in communities—rich or

THE EFFECTS OF DAY CARE

Nearly a million American children spend a good part of their waking hours in day-care centers (Connell, Layzer, and Goodson, 1979). This time is spent away from parents and under the influence of peers and substitute care givers. Some psychologists—and parents—have worried about the effects of this separation, wondering whether children in day care would be harmed by the experience. Other psychologists have argued that day care helps children develop socially, intellectually, and emotionally (Bruner, 1980).

Is day care harmful or beneficial to a child's development? There is no single answer. After reviewing research on the effects of day care, Jay Belsky (1985) concluded that whether a child is reared in day care or at home is not as important as how the child is cared for. When day care is of high quality, children seem to suffer no ill effects, even if they "leave home" as infants. What constitutes high-quality day care? The most important factors seem to be a well-trained staff with little turnover, and enough care givers so that each child receives individual attention. In low-quality day-care centers, by contrast, employees have little or no training, job turnover is high, and each staff member is responsible for too many children:

researchers have recommended that each adult be responsible for no more than three infants (Kagan, Kearsley, and Zelazo, 1978) or six preschoolers (Clarke-Stewart, 1982).

Some children do seem to benefit from day care (Belsky, 1985). When youngsters from disadvantaged homes are placed in day-care centers that offer a structured program of social and intellectual stimulation, they show greater intellectual gains than similar youngsters who stay at home. Children in day care also seem to get along better with their peers than do children who stay at home; the day-care children are more socially competent, and they cooperate better with unfamiliar children. However, some studies have indicated that children in day care are also more aggressive and impulsive than other children; they are more hostile as kindergartners and less cooperative with adults. This tendency, says Belsky, may be true only in the United States, where such values are prominent in the surrounding culture. In Israel, the USSR, and other societies where competition and individual achievement are less highly valued, day-care children do not seem to be so aggressive, impulsive, and uncooperative.

Another unresolved concern over day care is the worry that

it disrupts the formation of a secure bond between mother and infant. This does seem to happen when infants from high-risk environments are placed in unstable day-care arrangements before they are a year old (Clarke-Stewart and Fein, 1983). But even when care is adequate, this bond may be threatened—at least temporarily. In one study (Thompson, Lamb, and Estes, 1982) a good many middle-class youngsters seemed to develop insecure attachments to their mothers about the time they were put in day care, but in most cases, the bond seemed to be reestablished with time. Other studies (Lamb et al., 1984) have indicated that the bond between parent and infant is related to family circumstances, and any change in the care-giving relationship may be followed by changes in attachment.

As more and more women work at full-time jobs outside the home, the need for day care will increase. The problem is finding *good* day care: care that provides children with the attention, affection, and stimulation they would find at home. Because there are no federal standards for good day care, parents who plan to use day-care centers should observe the center in operation before they enroll their child (Scarr, 1984).

poor, simple or sophisticated, comfortable or chaotic. Both family and community have a decided influence on children's development, as the following examples will show.

Parents of different social classes have different values, different lifestyles, and different resources;

they also bring up their children differently (Kohn, 1979). One major difference has to do with autonomy: middle-class parents place a higher value on self-direction than do working-class parents, who are more concerned that their children conform to expected standards of behavior.

Another class difference in child rearing has to do with discipline: middle-class and working-class parents tend to punish children for different reasons. The working-class mother generally punishes for the *consequences* of her child's misbehavior; for example, she is likely to punish her son for breaking a lamp even if he accidentally stumbled into it. The middle-class mother generally punishes on the basis of *intent*.

Parents' personal lives, as well as their social class, may influence their children's development. When parents experience marital problems and divorce, for example, children's lives are often profoundly affected. And family economic problems can affect a child's development at any age. During the Great Depression of the 1930s, researchers followed the development of children, and discovered that the depression's effects lingered for decades among boys who had been preschoolers when their fathers suffered economic hardships. (Elder, 1979; Elder, Nguyen, and Caspi, 1985).

The world outside the family also affects the developing child. There is, first of all, the sort of school that is available. Does the school give children individual attention and expect them to perform well? Does the school offer ways for parents to become involved in their children's education? Beyond the school lies the larger community, and it, too, may help or hinder children's development. For example, a city that allows large geographical areas to become blighted, "giving up" certain neighborhoods to petty criminals, gangs, or drug dealers, is ensuring that a certain number of its children will grow up in a stressful and dangerous environment (Rutter, 1981).

Acquiring Gender Roles

Sex differences in behavior appear at a very early age, and these differences become magnified during childhood. As children grow, they acquire **gender roles**, adopting attitudes and patterns of behavior that society considers acceptable for their own gender. Some aspects of gender roles are determined by biology (bearing children or impregnating others); other aspects are arbitrary and vary from culture to culture (planting crops and marketing goods). Biology and socialization both play important parts in the development of gender roles, with socialization exaggerating whatever differences exist between the sexes at birth.

The Impact of Biology

Temperamental differences between boys and girls appear to exist at birth, and tend to center on activity, sensitivity to stimuli, and social interaction (McGuinness and Pribram, 1979). For example, when newborn infants were studied in a hospital nursery, boys were awake more than girls and showed more general activity—screwing up their faces, turning their heads, waving their hands, twitching, and jerking (Phillips, King, and Dubois, 1978). The boys had not been circumcised, so their restlessness was not due to physical discomfort. Other studies have shown that three-month-old baby boys fuss considerably more than girls (Moss, 1974); year-old boys tend to play more vigorously than girls (Maccoby and Jacklin, 1974); and year-old boys tend to prefer toys that require gross motor activity.

Such differences in temperament could underlie the consistently observed sex differences in style of play and in aggression. In most studies, preschool boys are more aggressive than preschool girls (Maccoby and Jacklin, 1980), and boys are much more likely to engage in rough-and-tumble play than girls (Blurton-Jones and Konner, 1973). These differences are not large (Hyde, 1984), but they hold true in studies that have been done in various cultures.

Researchers believe that biology affects behavior through the action of male and female hormones on the fetal brain. For example, compared with their sisters, girls who were exposed before birth to male hormones showed much higher levels of rough, outdoor play and a lack of interest in play that involved dolls, babies, and traditional feminine roles (Ehrhardt and Meyer-Bahlburg, 1981). In another study, prenatal exposure to male hormones was linked with increased feelings of aggression in both boys and girls. Boys who were exposed to additional male hormones before birth had significantly higher scores than their brothers on tests designed to measure a person's potential for aggressive behavior, and girls who were similarly exposed had significantly higher scores than their sisters (Reinisch, 1981).

Yet biology does not work alone; instead, a child's predispositions interact with the way parents, siblings, peers, and other adults respond to them and with the physical environment. Thus, initial differences in their levels of activity may cause male and female babies to experience different kinds of care and social interaction.

The Power of Socialization

Despite these possible biological influences, many aspects of gender roles have no relation to biology. If sex differences were primarily genetic in origin, then gender roles would be similar at all times and in all the world's societies. Although masculinity and femininity are always attached to opposite traits and jobs, the attributes of personality and occupations vary from culture to culture (Tavris and Offir, 1977). In the United States, for example, women are considered the emotional and irrational sex, but in Iran women are seen as cold and logical. In the United States, women are supposed to be gossips, but members of one Philippine tribe believe that it is men who cannot keep a secret.

Obviously, socialization is a powerful force in the development of gender roles. It is of primary importance in social learning theory, which sees environmental factors as responsible for the development of **sex-typed behavior**, behavior that is regarded as appropriate for only one sex (Mischel, 1966). The process works through reinforcement, punishment, and observational learning, and the agents of socialization are parents, siblings, peers, teachers, other adults, and the media.

If we can assume that parents treat their own babies as they do unfamiliar babies, then socialization into gender roles begins before the child can walk. In a typical study, parents are put together with a baby they have never seen before. No matter what the baby's age, the parents' behavior changes with the label researchers give to the baby. If they are told the infant is a boy, parents tend to encourage vigorous activity and rarely offer "him" a doll to play with. But if they are told the infant is a girl, they generally present "her" with a doll and rarely encourage vigorous activity (e.g., Smith and Lloyd, 1978).

Similar patterns of behavior seem to prevail when parents are at home with their own children. After reviewing studies of parents and infants, Aletha Huston (1983) concluded that fathers are rougher with their infant sons and play more active, physical games with them. In one study (Fagot, 1978), toddler boys and girls reaped different rewards and punishments for the same behavior. Boys were encouraged when they played with blocks; girls were not. Girls were encouraged when they manipulated objects; boys were not. Girls were encouraged to ask for assistance and to "help"; boys were not. Before their second birthdays, the girls were learning to be dependent and

the boys were learning to be independent. In fact, parents give their sons greater freedom in all areas of life, but watch their daughters closely, apparently in an attempt to protect them. This difference in treatment probably pushes girls toward dependence and conformity (Huston, 1983).

Parents may also act as important socializing agents by providing gender-role models for their children. According to cognitive-developmental theorists, young children begin to classify others by sex on the basis of physical size, hair style, and clothing. Once children develop **gender identity**, an understanding that they are either female or male and will always remain so, they begin to look for models (Kohlberg, 1966). They want to think, talk, and act as others of their gender do, and their parents act as models that help them achieve this goal.

Moreover, most children begin to assume gender roles long before they realize that their sex will never change. According to Sandra Bem (1983), this early adherence to gender roles develops because children construct a knowledge schema for each gender. They then begin to see the world in terms of gender, organizing new information on the basis of their schemas. When they encode information about themselves, they do so in terms of the appropriate **gender schema**. Both Bem and social learning theorists believe that children's gender-role models are not limited to their parents. Children also imitate other children, adults, and television personalities. However, they are especially likely to imitate models who are warm and nurturant, as most parents are (Bandura and Walters, 1963).

Peers not only serve as models; they also push children into their prescribed gender roles. In nursery school, boys who play with dolls or play dress-up are loudly criticized by other boys and girls; girls who play with boys' toys are mostly ignored (Fagot, 1977). When young children are punished by peers for such cross-sex play, they respond by stopping it almost immediately, although when punished for gender-appropriate play, they tend to keep on playing with the toy (Lamb, Easterbrooks, and Holden, 1980). Apparently three- and four-year-olds already know the gender-linked rules for toys and need only be reminded of them.

Teachers also unobtrusively steer children into traditional gender roles. They reinforce independence in boys and dependence in girls. In one study, children were making paper party baskets;

when it came time for the handle to be stapled to the basket, boys were routinely handed the stapler and told how to use it, while girls watched as their teacher took their baskets and stapled on the handles for them (Serbin et al., 1973).

The media—books, magazines, newspapers, movies, and television—also shape gender roles. Movies and television are especially likely to provide a predominance of stereotypical gender models. Such stereotypical models are especially prevalent in children's programming, where women tend to be deferential, passive, and ignored, while men tend to be aggressive, constructive, and helpful. Men's activities bring them tangible rewards, but women who are too active are punished (Sternglanz and Serbin, 1974). As for standard programming, the competent, assertive women who have begun to appear on prime-time television programs are vastly outnumbered by the passive women who appear in reruns. In fact, one researcher found that children who watched lots of television after school and on Saturday mornings were most likely to have stereotypical views of gender roles (Greer, 1980).

Few of us are like the stereotypical creatures in the older television programs, but a good many of us are "masculine" men or "feminine" women—we see ourselves as strong primarily in aspects of personality that are typical of our own gender. In the past decade or so, however, psychologists have begun to study people whose gender roles embrace characteristics of both sexes. These men and women are said to be **androgynous**. They apparently have self-concepts that allow them to match their behavior to the situation; for example, they can be assertive or sensitive to others' needs, depending on which reaction seems appropriate (Bem, 1975). For example, an androgynous person, whether a man or a woman, could fire someone in a way that preserved the person's dignity and feelings.

No one is certain just how androgynous behavior patterns develop, but researchers have tried to find out by asking college students about their childhood (Orlofsky, 1979). Androgynous men's recollections of childhood were similar to the recollections of "masculine" men; both said their fathers had been highly involved in their lives, that they felt relatively close to their mothers, and that neither parent had rejected them. But a difference did appear between androgynous women and "feminine" women. The androgynous women tended to have mothers who modeled achieve-

ment, curiosity, and intellectual values—and encouraged the development of these characteristics in their daughters.

Peer Relationships

In all cultures, children begin to have extensive contact with their peers during the preschool years. Such relationships are important because they are between equals. In relationships with adults, the power runs one way; the child is dependent and the adult has the responsibility of controlling and nurturing the youngster (Hartup, 1983). Through equal interactions with their peers, children learn social skills, developing independence, cooperation, and ways to handle aggression; learn to evaluate themselves in comparison with others, developing a sense of their own identity; and develop a sense of belonging to a group (Rubin, 1980). The importance of peer relationships is shown by the repeated findings that children who are rejected by their peers are more likely than other children to drop out of school, to have later emotional and behavioral problems, and —among middle-class and upper-lower-class boys —to become delinquent (Ullman, 1957; Cowen et al., 1973; Roff, Sells, and Golden, 1972). The role that peers play in socialization can be seen by examining children at play, in individual friendships, and in groups.

Play

Peers and play are closely intertwined. Although play can be solitary, much of it is social and it encompasses a bewildering array of activities. To be considered play, an activity must meet four conditions: (1) it must be pleasurable; (2) it must be an end in itself, not a means to some goal; (3) it must be spontaneous and freely chosen by the player; and (4) it must involve some active engagement on the part of the player (Garvey, 1977).

Play is more than just a pleasant pastime. Its essential role in development has been spelled out by Jerome Bruner (1972). During play, the consequences of a child's actions are minimized, so that learning takes place in less risky circumstances. A four-year-old can practice such adult social roles as pilot, doctor, automobile driver, cook, warrior, parent, or spouse without suffering any of the economic, physical, or emotional consequences

Play is more than fun. In it, a child can practice adult roles in a safe, scaled-down way.

that accompany mistakes made in the actual performance of these roles. In the process, children learn about the conventions of society and about the importance of convention itself—both the conventions of language that allow us to communicate and the procedural conventions that, for example, keep us all driving on the right side of the road. Play also gives children a chance to experiment, trying out combinations of behavior that would never be attempted under the pressures of daily life. Such opportunities allow children to develop a flexible approach to problems and to anticipate new ways of using objects or putting together various subskills to accomplish a goal. Finally, play can serve a very personal function, in which the child works out problems or fulfills wishes through fantasy.

Friendship

Most children have special relationships with one or more of their peers. These friendships change in meaning, depth, and complexity as children grow, and the changes are linked to cognitive development, with friendships becoming increasingly reciprocal.

According to Robert Selman (1980; Selman and Jacquette, 1977), among preschoolers friends are important as playmates and in most cases, children's friends are whomever they happen to be playing with. In the early school years, friendship becomes one-way assistance; a child's friends are valued because they do what the child likes to do. During late childhood comes fair-weather cooperation, in which a child and her or his friend, adapt to each other's needs but loyalty, sensitivity, and intimacy play little part in the relationship. Only in adolescence do intimacy and mutual sharing characterize friendship; friendships change from the cooperation of two individuals to a sense of shared identity (Youniss, 1980).

Groups

Children also socialize one another within the peer group. In any group of children a hierarchy emerges, with some children becoming leaders who dominate the rest. Popularity does not guarantee that a child will be a leader. Studies of nursery-school play groups indicate that children establish dominance through physical attacks, threats, and struggles over objects (Strayer and Strayer, 1976). Aggression may establish a child's dominance, but the most dominant child is rarely the most aggressive child in the group (Strayer, 1977). In these early years the group leader is generally a child who can keep possessions and knows how to use them. Later, the child who can direct play and games becomes the leader. By early adolescence the group is led by the early-maturing child who is good at athletics and has many social skills. Finally, during late adolescence, the group leader is usually an intelligent, popular girl or boy (Hartup, 1983).

Although some psychologists (e.g., Bronfenbrenner, 1970) believe that the segregation of children into age-graded groups (which is encouraged by the structure of the educational system) can erode the power of parental and social value systems, studies indicate that serious conflict between child and adult values is the exception rather than the rule. Research (e.g., Costanza and Shaw, 1966) has indeed shown that a child's susceptibility to peer influence increases with age, but it also shows that the power of the peer group reaches a peak and then gradually declines during adolescence. Nevertheless, there is some evidence that the predominance of peer-group pressure over family ties appears to be a major factor in the entrapment of youngsters in juvenile delinquency and drug abuse (Jessor, 1983a; Pulkkinen, 1982; 1983).

Prosocial Development

Although peer pressure toward antisocial behavior becomes stronger during the school years, children often behave in altruistic ways, sharing their toys or coming to the rescue of another child. Such actions are examples of **prosocial behavior** —action intended to benefit another person, taken without expectation of external reward, and generally involving some cost to the individual (Mussen and Eisenberg-Berg, 1977). When prosocial behavior springs from a combination of emotional distress at another's plight and understanding of her or his needs, it is called **altruism**. As children grow, their concepts of altruism, justice, and morality change, as do the reasons that they give for their moral and ethical acts. These changes are the result of cognitive and social development.

Altruistic Behavior

Preschoolers are reluctant to share their toys or give away candy or money. Spontaneous acts of altruism can be seen in most nursery schools, but between the ages of two and five, there is only a slight increase in prosocial behavior (Hartup, 1983). Researchers have been unable to establish whether spontaneous altruism increases as children grow older (Radke-Yarrow, Zahn-Waxler, and Chapman, 1983).

In some controlled experiments, children seem to become more generous with age. They are more willing to donate pennies, prizes, or candies to "poor children" or to children "who didn't get a chance to play the game." For example, in a longitudinal study, children between the ages of five and ten tended to become more generous with age (Froming, Allen, and Underwood, 1983). However, when children are observed on the playground, where sharing is spontaneous and not promoted by a researcher, children show no indications of becoming more generous as they get older.

Researchers have found out a good deal about the effects of context on altruism. For example, children often behave generously after observing an adult act in an unselfish manner (Radke-Yarrow, Zahn-Waxler, and Chapman, 1983). In addition, reinforcement for altruistic acts is effective. Children who are praised for their generosity often behave more generously, but the form of praise affects children of different ages in different ways. In one study (Grusec and Redler, 1980), eight-year-olds who were praised for themselves ("You are a very nice and helpful person") transferred their generosity to other situations several weeks later, but eight-year-olds who were praised for their acts ("That was a helpful thing to do") did not. However, ten-year-olds were generous in later situations whether they had earlier been praised for their acts or for themselves, perhaps reflecting the older children's greater flexibility in interpreting rules.

Moral Judgment

How do children learn to become altruistic, honest, or helpful? Psychoanalytic theorists believe that moral behavior depends upon the establishment of guilt. When children identify with a parent, they internalize the parent's moral code. Thereafter, each time a child is tempted to violate the parent's standards, the child feels guilty. Social learning theorists believe that moral behavior is a matter of learning, the result of reinforcements, punishments, and delayed imitation.

Such analyses of behavior have little interest for cognitive-developmental theorists, who believe that the study of moral development should focus on changes in the way children think about moral choices and how they justify their decisions. According to Lawrence Kohlberg (1969), who based his theory of moral development on the ideas of

Jean Piaget, children pass through six developmental stages of moral reasoning, with each stage in the sequence growing out of its predecessor. Kohlberg claims that these stages always develop in the same order, that children never skip a stage, and that the stages are universal—they characterize the development of moral reasoning in all societies.

Kohlberg's six stages form three basic levels of moral judgment. In the first, **preconventional level** (stages 1 and 2), the child judges moral issues in terms of pain or pleasure or of the physical power of authority. At the second, **conventional level** (stages 3 and 4), the child—or adult, because most adults reason on the conventional level—decides moral issues in terms of maintaining the social order and meeting the expectations of others. At the highest, **postconventional level** (stages 5 and 6), the person judges moral issues in terms of self-chosen principles and standards based on universal ethical principles and on the ideals of reciprocity and human equality. In Kohlberg's view, a moral decision always involves a conflict in values; hence, what is important is not the decision itself, but the justification given for it. In any moral dilemma, people who are at the same stage of moral development may decide on opposite courses of action.

Criticisms of Kohlberg's Theory: The Question of Sexist Bias   Although Kohlberg's theory is appealing, it has been faulted on several counts. Some critics say there is no clear distinction between stages at any level, nor is there a connection between a person's stage of development and his or her behavior (Kurtines and Greif, 1974). Some critics say that the stages apply only to moral reasoning in constitutional democracies (Harkness, 1980). Another critic, Carol Gilligan (1982), says that the stages have a sexist bias. No girls were included in Kohlberg's original research; he studied only a group of boys between the ages of ten and sixteen. Gilligan believes that women and men learn different priorities. She points out that Kohlberg's ethic of justice, which sees moral problems as rising from competing rights, is very different from women's ethic of care, which sees moral problems as rising from conflicting responsibilities. Because of this difference, says Gilligan, women are automatically rated at lower levels of moral development than men.

In response to these criticisms, Kohlberg and his associates (Colby et al., 1983) have reevaluated the stages in a way the Kohlberg believes will eliminate part of the system's sex-related bias. In this revision of the system, the proportion of people who reach the postconventional stage of reasoning has dropped from 40 percent to 10 percent, and all have completed college. Some psychologists have concluded that the revised system now accurately describes the development of moral judgment among white lower- and middle-class males, but are uncertain whether it can be more widely applied (Fischer, 1983).

Other Sex-Related Issues in Moral Judgments
Despite his insistence on justice as the basis for moral development, Kohlberg has said that people interpret moral rules by taking the role of another (Kohlberg, 1971). In most studies, girls seem to be more empathic than boys, and boys tend to respond to problems with a problem-solving approach instead of with empathy (Hoffman, 1977). However, most laboratory studies show no differences between boys and girls in such altruistic behavior as sharing (Radke-Yarrow, Zahn-Waxler, and Chapman, 1983).

Sex also seems to interact with child-rearing practices to affect the level of moral reasoning among adolescents. In one study, boys and girls tended to respond differently to similar practices by their parents (Leahy, 1981). With boys, authoritarian methods of child rearing led the youngsters to reason at lower levels, while less punitive practices led to postconventional reasoning (as described under Kohlberg's old system). Girls tended to develop postconventional reasoning when parents encouraged them to be independent, but they also reached this level of reasoning even when their fathers exerted a high degree of control and supervision. Both sexes developed postconventional reasoning when the parents were nurturant (accepting, encouraging, and warm).

Children's Ideas of Fairness

No sex differences have been found in children's ideas of equity, or fairness, another aspect of prosocial behavior. The concept of equity is connected to the development of logical reasoning, and children's allocation of rewards for work could be predicted by their scores on tests of mathematical reasoning (Hook, 1978). Preschoolers either operated on self-interest, taking the lion's share no matter how little labor they contributed, or else gave everybody equal shares, no matter how the labor was divided. Between the ages of six and twelve, children gave more rewards to people who worked more and less to people who worked less, but made no attempt to see that rewards were proportional to effort. (A child who did 80 percent of the work might get only 55 percent of the rewards.) Not until children were thirteen did the idea of equity as reward proportional to effort appear.

Cognitive development and moral development are related. In other studies researchers have found a connection between a child's level of cognitive development—judged by the ability to perform Piagetian logical tasks—and her or his level of moral reasoning (Selman, 1976; Kuhn et al., 1977; Harter, 1983); between a child's level of cognitive development and her or his concept of justice (Damon, 1975); and between the ability to understand another's thoughts and feelings and moral reasoning (Moir, 1974). Yet similar conduct can result from great disparities in moral reasoning; precisely how these factors interact in the process of moral development is not clear.

Control of Aggression

Few people expect a three-year-old to be altruistic, but most of us expect youngsters to gain control over their aggressive impulses early. Parents begin imposing restraints on their children's behavior at the first signs of temper tantrums, blows, or the hurling of toys in anger. As they grow, children learn that aggression must be restrained at home and in the classroom, but that it is applauded on the football field. Thus, they must learn where, when, and how to express their aggressiveness.

Children—and adults—show two major forms of aggression: **hostile aggression**, which aims at hurting another person, and **instrumental aggression**, which aims at acquiring or retrieving objects, territory, or privileges (Feshbach, 1964). Because very young children find it difficult to understand that another person might not react to an incident as they do, they rarely believe that other people have negative intentions toward them. Nor do they interpret their own frustration as a threat to their self-esteem. Thus, their aggression is predominantly instrumental. In a study (Hartup, 1974) that followed children for ten weeks, four- to six-year-olds showed more aggression than six- to eight-year-olds, and the differ-

Parents often try to channel children's aggressive impulses into socially acceptable activities—boxing, for example.

ence was primarily due to a decline in instrumental aggression among the older children. As children get older, they also tend to switch from physical to verbal aggression, which is considerably safer.

The Role of Rewards and Punishment

Rewards and punishment affect the amount of aggression children display. Actions that bring a child relief from distress apparently encourage aggression. Much childish aggression comes about because a child's past outbursts of violence have had the desired effect—put a halt to teasing, parental nagging, or the child's being ignored by a parent or teacher (Patterson, 1980; 1982). Aggression can be very rewarding, and the immediate consequences of a child's blows affect whether the child will hit again in the same situation.

In many cases a young child who successfully counterattacks and drives away a bully later becomes an aggressor and attacks a third child

(Patterson, Littman, and Bricker, 1967). Suppose someone takes away a child's toy, knocks down his or her carefully built block castle, or crowds into line in front of the child. Will the youngster respond aggressively? That depends on how she or he has learned to cope with stress and how effective the coping methods have been (Bandura, 1973). One child might seek help, another might try harder, a third might give up, a fourth might hit. Anger or frustration may increase the likelihood of an aggressive response, but neither is necessary.

Cognitive Factors in Aggression

The way children think about a situation also affects the likelihood of their responding aggressively. In any situation, children pick up social cues from the environment and interpret them in the light of remembered information, a series of rules they have developed for such situations, and their own present goals (Dodge, 1981). What makes some children more likely to turn to aggression than other children in the same situation? As part of this process, the child assesses the intent of the other people involved. Aggressive children have come to expect hostility from their peers; the expectation leads them to concentrate on social cues that confirm their expectations. And so, when a child stumbles against them, for example, they interpret the act as hostile, and act accordingly—they push, shove, slug, or insult the offending child. The offender retaliates and an aggressive child's expectations of hostility are confirmed. Next time, the child will be even more likely to ascribe hostile intentions to a peer (Dodge, 1982).

Observational learning also plays an important role in the development of aggression. Children learn aggressive responses from models, and they also learn the probable consequences of these responses. A parent who spanks a child for fighting is modeling aggression and teaching the child that in some circumstances it is appropriate to hit. But parents are not the only model for aggression. Older siblings, peers, other adults, and television and film characters also serve as models.

What Is the Impact of Violence on Television?

Television brings aggressive models into the home, and as soon as infants attend to the glowing tube, they see aggression modeled in cartoons, dramatic shows, sporting events, and the nightly news. By the time they are sixteen years old, American adolescents have seen more than 18,000 murders on television, along with arson, muggings, terrorist activities, and warfare (Smith, 1985). The long-term effects of so much televised violence are uncertain, since children do not imitate every action they observe.

In 1972 the Office of the Surgeon General (1972) commissioned studies of the effects of televised violence, but the research did not establish a definite connection between watching violent programs and aggression in daily life. Ten years later, however, the National Institute of Mental Health (1982) announced that viewing televised violence did cause aggression. Yet after reviewing the research, Jonathan Freedman (1984) concluded that although aggressive children and adolescents were indeed heavy viewers of violent television programs, no one had yet been able to establish the fact that watching violent television programs *made* children or adolescents aggressive.

Other researchers believe that a steady diet of violent television may change a child's standards about violence: the child comes to see violence as more acceptable, more appropriate, and more prevalent in daily life (Parke and Slaby, 1983). This effect is believed most likely to occur when a child sees acts of violence rewarded and justified, portrayed in a realistic manner, and shown as commonplace. For this effect to come about, however, the child's environment must support the interpretation, and the child must lack the experience that would enable him or her to judge standards of televised violence.

Such analyses remind us that neither television nor any other environmental factor works in isolation. In a study that followed American and Finnish children for three years, researchers found that heavy viewing of televised violence was followed by later aggression in daily life—but only in certain situations (Huesmann, Lagerspetz, and Eron, 1984). The most aggressive children identified strongly with aggressive television characters; they believed that the shows they watched were an accurate reflection of life, and they frequently had aggressive fantasies. But certain environmental factors also were closely linked to aggression: these children did poorly in school, were unpopular with their peers, had aggressive mothers, and had parents with little education and low social status. As this study reminds us, behavior results from the interaction of the child's predispositions and experiences; because children have different experiences over the years, no two children will respond to a potentially aggressive situation in precisely the same manner.

ADOLESCENCE

Adolescence is the period between reproductive maturity and the assumption of adult responsibilities. Its beginning is marked by **puberty**, the period of sexual maturation that transforms a child into a physical adult. A major concern during this phase of life is the need to establish an independent identity, and decisions made at this time can have lasting effects on the task. Individual decisions, such as whom to date, whether to have intercourse, take drugs, select a certain major, work part-time, or become politically active, combine to form a more or less consistent core that shapes personality and the course of an individual life (Marcia, 1980). In time, these early decisions influence the major decisions (occupation and marriage, among others) each adolescent eventually faces.

Physical Maturation

Long before the emotional and social conflicts that are associated with adolescence erupt, hormonal changes begin to have their effects on a young person's body. These changes trigger the maturation of the reproductive organs and the development of secondary sex characteristics, such as facial hair in males and breasts in females, a process that generally takes about four years to complete (Peterson and Taylor, 1980). Although the timing of these changes varies considerably with the individual, puberty usually begins between the ages of ten and twelve in girls and twelve and fourteen in boys (Muuss, 1975).

With physical maturation, the urges associated with sexual maturity arise. The first forays into dating are not associated with sexual maturation itself but with peer pressure. Adolescents who fail to date are dropped by their peer group, and studies have found that chronological age (which is related to the peer group) is a better predictor of the onset of dating than is sexual maturation (Dornbusch et al., 1981).

Social Maturation

The sexual maturation heralded by puberty transforms the child physically into an adult. But whether the child is assigned the social status of adulthood after puberty depends on the culture in which she or he lives. In some societies children who have attained reproductive maturity are considered working members of the adult community and may start their own families. For them there is no adolescence, no transitional period between childhood and adulthood (Knepler, 1969; Muuss, 1975). In Western societies, however, children who have passed through puberty are not yet considered adults. Instead, they enter a transitional period that lasts until they are at least seventeen or eighteen years old.

As adolescents come under the influence of their peers, conflicts may develop between the values of their parents and those of their friends. Parents usually have more influence than peers in areas of life related to aspirations, goals, and fundamental moral principles, but peers are more influential in areas related to social norms, such as dress, taste in music, and the use of drugs and alcohol (Hartup, 1983; Jessor, 1983b; Kandel, 1984). For example, an adolescent girl may be strongly influenced by her parents' wish that she go to college, yet pay no attention to her parents' disapproval of smoking marijuana.

But pressure from the peer group to use drugs or alcohol does not invariably draw adolescents into abusing either substance. Adolescent problem drinking, for example, is usually embedded in a problem lifestyle—low academic performance, conflict among family members, and so on. The teenager who drinks heavily rarely does so just because his or her friends drink a lot. In addition, many adolescent problem drinkers stop abusing alcohol once they reach young adulthood—perhaps because they are out of the situation that was associated with drinking (Jessor, 1983a).

Working Teenagers

Although the adolescent has not yet assumed adult responsibilities, many have begun to work at part-time jobs. The proportion of adolescents who are gainfully employed rises from 42 percent among high school sophomores to 63 percent among seniors (National Center for Educational Statistics, 1981). How does the dual responsibility of school and job affect adolescents? In one recent study (Steinberg et al., 1982), researchers found that working more than twenty hours a week seemed to have more costs than benefits for many adolescents. Working made adolescents more personally responsible, but did not increase their social responsibility. Working made girls (but not boys) more autonomous and self-reliant; it raised girls' educational expectations—but lowered the expectations of boys. However, both girls and boys were less involved than other adolescents with family, peers, and school, although their grades did not suffer, and they were more likely to use cigarettes and marijuana. In addition, they became more cynical about the work world and tended to accept unethical business practices. The researchers who conducted this study believe that young adolescents who work more than twenty hours a week may be missing out on important socialization and learning experiences.

Teenage Parents

Work is one adult activity undertaken by many adolescents; another is parenthood. Teenage boys who father babies escape most of the responsibilities of parenthood. But the teenage girl who has a baby usually finds the rest of her life changed —and usually for the worse. This is especially true if she drops out of school, a decision that seems to have a greater effect on her life than whether she marries the father of her child (Zelnick, Kantner, and Ford, 1981).

If a teenage mother quits school, she finds herself unemployed or trapped in a low-paying job. In addition, she is responsible for the care of her infant. After studying adolescent mothers, one researcher concluded that trying to rear the baby by herself is the worst thing a teenage mother can do, and that getting married is only slightly better (Furstenberg, 1976). Adolescent mothers who do best—both psychologically and economically—are the ones who stay home with their parents and return to school. In fact, 65 percent of those who do *not* resume their education are pregnant again within two years (Bolton, 1980).

Most studies have found that adolescent mothers are not very responsive to their babies' needs (Elster, McAnarney, and Lamb, 1983). Their ineffective mothering seems to be a result of their cognitive immaturity, their unrealistic attitudes toward child rearing, the stress that accompanies their unmarried pregnancy, their lack of knowledge about the way children develop, and a lack of social support. The last factor is extremely important, for when an adolescent mother has good

Teenage mothers who choose to keep their babies face many difficulties, especially if they try to raise their babies alone. Those who do best live at home with their parents, while continuing their educations.

social support, many of the other problems can be solved, and the young mother can learn to meet her baby's needs.

Establishing an Identity

Young adolescents are still dependent on their parents for security, guidance, and support. Within a decade, however, most are generally providing for their own needs. Along with the outward signs of independence, such as making their own decisions and becoming financially responsible, most young adults have gained a sense of themselves as separate, autonomous people. The establishment of this separate identity is the major developmental task of adolescence.

As Erik Erikson (1963) has pointed out, the physical, sexual, and social demands on the adolescent may produce internal conflict, an **identity crisis**, that requires the adolescent to develop a new self-concept. To resolve this crisis, adolescents must incorporate their new physical and sexual attributes, developing a sense of continuity between what they were in the past and what they will become. This is what is meant by **identity**: an individual's sense of personal sameness and continuity.

ADULT DEVELOPMENT

Adulthood has sometimes been described as the period of life that begins when we stop growing up and start growing old. It has also been characterized as a period of little change in personality, and many theorists have claimed that among normal adults personality remains quite stable. For example, Freud believed that many of a person's characteristics are established during childhood and that identity is fixed early in adulthood. But society has changed greatly since Freud's day, and for the first time a significant portion of the population is middle-aged or older. In earlier times life expectancy was shorter, and few people survived past the age of forty. Today, there are more than 50 million men and women in the United States—one-fourth of the total population—who are in the midlife period from age forty to sixty. Furthermore, in the year 2010, when members of the post-World War II baby boom join the aging, 16 of every 1,000

Americans will have passed their sixty-fifth birthday. As the population has grown older, developments and changes in personality and behavior during adulthood have received increased attention. As a result, the awareness has grown that adulthood, like childhood and youth, is a period of growth and change.

Work and Personality Development

Taking on a full-time job is itself an important developmental task, and succeeding at work is likely to yield rewards: increased self-esteem and autonomy, for example. Not only the experience of working but also the kind of work a person undertakes influences his or her development. Those whose jobs require thought, judgment, and analysis generally continue to develop intellectually: mental exercise seems to keep the mind in shape, just as physical exercise tones the body.

But the influence of a complex, intellectually demanding job does more than keep a person's wits sharp; it also affects the worker's personality. In one study, workers in the United States and Poland who did complex, self-directed work tended to be open-minded and flexible. In contrast, those who did routine work tended to be intolerant and obedient to authority. A similar effect appeared in a study of working women (Miller, Schooler, Kohn, and Miller, 1979). The kinds of jobs these women had were related to their self-concept, their intellectual functioning, and their attitudes toward others. Best off were the women whose jobs required thought, initiative, and independent judgment. Compared with the other women, these women functioned at a higher intellectual level, had higher self-esteem, and had more open and flexible attitudes toward other people.

At the same time that work influences personality, personality also affects work. In a longitudinal study of California men, those destined to have the most successful careers in middle adulthood could be distinguished from the rest by the time they had reached early adolescence (Clausen, 1981). As adolescents, the future highly successful men tended to be ambitious, productive, dependable, and not self-indulgent.

Other aspects of a person's life also affect his or her success at work. Marriage, a step that most people take in young adulthood, is strongly associated with occupational success in men. Why should marriage give men a career boost? Researchers have speculated that the effect may be due to the strong support married men get from their wives (Mortimer, Lorence, and Kumka, 1982). A wife gives her husband psychological support (she listens sympathetically to his complaints about the boss), social support (she entertains his business associates), and occupational support (she may type his notes or reports, or do his bookkeeping). Do women get a similar career boost from their marriages? Probably not, because few employed women get the same wide-ranging support from their husbands that men get from their wives. However, because relatively few women adhere as yet to the typical male career pattern, no one has studied such effects. The picture may change as more and more women develop career commitments.

Changes in Personal Concerns

People's personal concerns change across the life span; even their gender-related attitudes and behavior alter. In one study (Feldman, Beringen, and Nash, 1981), their stage of family life affected people's feelings of compassion, tenderness, and autonomy. Single men and women were less compassionate, less tender, and more socially inhibit-

ed than were the married. Becoming parents appeared to make people more traditional; women's feelings of tenderness increased, as did men's feelings of leadership and autonomy. But becoming grandparents made grandmothers more autonomous and grandfathers more compassionate and tender.

One of adulthood's developmental milestones is the birth of couple's first child. Psychologists have long known that this event is associated with a drop in marital satisfaction and satisfaction with life in general—especially for women. The dissatisfaction is probably due to the sudden curtailment of economic and personal freedom. In addition, many couples find that spontaneity leaves their marriage.

More recently, psychologists have found that the transition to parenthood is easiest when the marriage relationship is strong and when the father helps care for the child. New studies have found that the adjustment is especially hard on the mother, who often suffers a loss of self-esteem, perhaps because society's standards for the maternal role are high, and the mother has the major responsibility for infant care. Fathers often feel they have lost much of their wives' attention and may have difficulty adjusting to their new role (Alpert and Richardson, 1980), but because socie-

This man need not feel threatened by caring for his baby because society now approves of such behavior for men. In fact, men who share child care tasks with their wives are helping to strengthen their marriages.

ty has few standards for the father's role in infant care, a father's self-esteem is less likely to suffer (Lamb and Easterbrooks, 1981).

People's ways of looking at themselves, of evaluating their own lives, seem to change with age. In one study, Roger Gould (1972) interviewed all the patients in group therapy at a psychiatric outpatient clinic. In a second study he gave questionnaires to 524 white, middle-class men and women who were not psychiatric patients. Among both groups, the same clear differences in the major concerns and key attitudes appeared at various ages. Young adults (age twenty-two to twenty-eight) felt autonomous and focused their energy on attaining the goals they had set. But members of the next age group (twenty-nine to thirty-four) had begun to question their goals, wondering, "What is life all about now that I have done what I am supposed to do?" Those between thirty-five and forty-three continued to question the values they had lived by, but they had also developed a new awareness of the passage of time, asking, "Is it too late for me to change?" With the onset of middle age (forty-three to fifty), adults entered a period of greater stability, of acceptance of the structure of life and of greater satisfaction with their spouses. This last trend continued after age fifty. As people gained awareness of mortality, they came to value personal relationships more highly and to develop a desire to contribute something meaningful to society.

From interviews with more than 2,000 adults, Bernice Neugarten (1976) has also found characteristic psychological changes in adulthood. Among the middle-aged, she found a greater concern with inner life, with introspection, and conscious reappraisal of themselves. They also showed a change in time perspective and looked at life in terms of time left to live instead of the time since birth. This changed perspective led them to an awareness of personal mortality and the recognition of death as inevitable.

Ways of Aging

Making the transition from one phase of adulthood to the next is not always easy. But most people cope with major life transitions—such as the departure of children from the home, retirement from a career, the death of a parent, and the approach of death—without undue stress (Neugar-

ten, 1976). These events become traumatic only when they are not anticipated or when they occur at an unexpected time in the life cycle. Thus, the death of a child is much more stressful than the death of a parent, and divorce when a woman is forty is more difficult to accept than widowhood when she is sixty-five. A study of men who had retired from their life's work (Barfield and Morgan, 1970) found that nearly 70 percent of those who retired as planned were content with their new status, as compared with less than 20 percent of those who retired unexpectedly due to layoffs or poor health.

Older people are often seen by the young in terms of stereotypes that apply only to a minority of the aged—the frail, the sick, the isolated, and the needy. But old people are not a homogeneous group, and their lives differ more than do the lives of the young. People are vigorous for so much longer than they used to be that some seventy-year-olds still consider themselves "middle-aged," and Neugarten (1980) has proposed calling the healthy, active majority of old people the "young-old," reserving the term "old-old" for those who fit that stereotype. Most old people are not lonely; a national survey found a steady decline in loneliness with age, and people who were older than seventy were the least lonely of all (Rubenstein, Shaver, and Peplau, 1979). The elderly were more satisfied with their friendships than the young, had higher self-esteem, and felt more independent than did young adults.

As long as the expected rhythm of the life cycle is not disrupted, most adults cope successfully even with the final stage of life. For example, a study (Lieberman and Coplan, 1970) of elderly people showed that those who were living in familiar and stable surroundings were not afraid of dying, but that those who were about to be admitted to a home for the aged and thus were living in an abnormal, uncertain situation were afraid of death.

Most older adults live in their own households, but those who need extensive care often enter institutions. When older people do enter nursing homes, those who are allowed to retain a measure of independence and choice over their lives seem happier, more alert, and more active than nursing home residents whose needs are automatically taken care of by others (Langer and Rodin, 1976). A sense of autonomy and control seems important even to the end of life.

SUMMARY

1. Various views exist concerning the way that **personality**, or the organization of a person's cognitive, motivational, and social characteristics, develop. According to the biological perspective, some aspects of personality are biologically determined. Differences in **temperament** (individual patterns of activity, susceptibility to stimulation, and general mood) exist from birth, and these biologically determined characteristics interact with experience. According to Freud, human beings are motivated to seek pleasure, and during psychosexual development the focus of this erotic pleasure shifts from one **erogenous zone** of the body to another. Consequently, he called the psychosexual stages the **oral stage**, the **anal stage**, the **phallic stage**, a **latency period**, and the **genital stage**. According to the cognitive-developmental perspective, social behavior depends in part on the child's level of **social cognition**, which refers to a child's understanding of the social world. **Role taking**, or being able to imagine oneself in another's place, plays an important part in social and personality development. According to the behavioral perspective, personality and social behavior follow the principles of learning. "Enduring characteristics" are patterns of behavior that have been learned through reinforcement, punishment, and imitation.

2. During infancy, social and personality development center around **attachment**, the bond between an infant and her or his main care givers. A secure attachment not only helps babies survive but also encourages the development of social and cognitive skills by providing the emotional security that allows the baby to interact freely with others and to explore the world. Once attachment has developed, babies show **separation distress**, protesting at separation from a care giver and showing joy at the care giver's return, followed by **wariness of strangers**. The nature of the interaction between infant and care giver, not the amount of time spent together, is the important aspect of the bond.

3. As children grow, the parents' primary role switches from physical care to **socialization**, in which children absorb society's attitudes, values, and customs. With **internalization**, the child incorporates these standards so that their violation produces a sense of guilt. Family and the wider community also exert a powerful influence on the child's development. Children soon acquire **gender roles**, attitudes and behavior considered gender appropriate in their society. Biology apparently has some effect on gender-related behavior, because temperamental differences between boys and girls exist at birth. These gender-based predispositions interact with the way people respond to children and with the physical environment to produce behavioral differences. Socialization also has a powerful impact on **sex-typed behavior**, behavior that is considered appropriate for only one sex. According to social learning theorists, parents, peers, and other adults use rewards and punishment to steer children toward sex-typed behavior; these people also serve as models of such behavior. Cognitive-developmental theorists believe that identification must follow **gender identity**, the child's understanding that she or he will always be male or female. However, some theorists believe that even before this time, children develop **gender schemas**, organizing new information in terms of these schemas. Instead of being highly sex-typed, some people are **androgynous**; their gender roles embrace characteristics of both sexes.

4. Peer relationships are important because they are between equals. Through interactions with their peers, children learn social skills, learn to evaluate themselves in comparison with others, develop a sense of their own identity, and develop a sense of belonging to a group. Children's play has an essential role in development because it minimizes the consequences of a child's actions and gives children a chance to try out behavior that would never be attempted under the pressure of daily life. Children's friendships change in meaning, depth, and

complexity as children grow. Popularity does not guarantee group leadership, for each group selects its leaders in terms of specific characteristics. A child's susceptibility to peer influence increases with age, peaking in early adolescence and then declining.

5. **Prosocial behavior**, action intended to benefit another person, taken without expectation of external reward, and generally involving some cost, is the result of cognitive and social development. Spontaneous acts of **altruism** appear among children in nursery school, but researchers have been unable to establish whether altruism increases as children grow older. Psychoanalytic theorists believe that prosocial behavior depends upon guilt, which is established when children internalize parental moral codes. Social learning theorists believe that prosocial behavior results from reinforcements, punishment, and delayed imitation. Cognitive-developmental theorists focus not on prosocial behavior but on children's reasoning about moral problems. According to Kohlberg, children pass through three levels of moral development: the **preconventional level**, in which they judge moral issues in terms of pain, pleasure, or the physical power of authority; the **conventional level**, in which they judge moral issues in terms of maintaining the social order and meeting the expectations of others; and the **postconventional level**, in which they judge moral issues in terms of self-chosen principles based on universal ethical principles, on reciprocity, and on human equality. Although cognitive development and moral judgment are related, similar conduct can result from great disparities in moral reasoning, hence the way these factors interact in moral development is not clear.

6. Children must learn how to control their aggressive impulses and where they may be expressed. Aggression among young children is primarily **instrumental aggression**, in which the aim of the child is to retrieve or acquire objects, territory, or privileges. As children get older, they show less aggressive behavior and when it does appear, it is likely to be **hostile aggression**, in which the aim is to hurt another person. Reinforcement, punishment, observational learning, and children's expectations of aggression all affect the amount of aggression children display. Television provides aggressive models, and while aggressive children and adolescents tend to watch a good deal of televised violence, such viewing has not been established as a *cause* of aggression. However, some psychologists believe that televised violence can change a child's standards regarding aggression.

7. Adolescence begins with the onset of **puberty**, the period of sexual maturation. Although some cultures equate adulthood and reproductive maturity, Western societies provide the transitional period of adolescence, which allows young people to try out different roles. The major developmental task of adolescence is the establishment of **identity**: the individual's sense of personal sameness and continuity. According to Erik Erikson, the physical, sexual, and social demands on the adolescent often produce internal conflict, an **identity crisis**, which is resolved by developing an inner sense of continuity.

8. Adulthood is a period of growth and change. Work can affect intellectual development and personality, and personality and life circumstances can affect work. People's personal concerns change across the life span, and gender-related attitudes and behavior appear to be affected by the stages of family life. As people become middle-aged, they develop a concern with introspection, and there is a shift in time perspective that brings an awareness of personal mortality. Most people cope with major life transitions without undue stress; transitions become traumatic only when they are not anticipated or when they occur at an unexpected time of the life cycle. Most old people do not fit the stereotype of the aged, and people are now vigorous until very late in life.

KEY TERMS

altruism
anal stage
androgynous
attachment
conventional level
erogenous zones
gender identity
gender roles
gender schema
genital stage
hostile aggression

identity
identity crisis
instrumental aggression
internalization
latency period
Oedipal conflict
oral stage
personality
phallic stage
preconventional level
postconventional level

prosocial behavior
puberty
role taking
separation distress
sex-typed behavior
social cognition
socialization
temperament
theory of psychosexual
  development
wariness of strangers

RECOMMENDED READINGS

BAUMRIND, D. New directions in socialization research. *American Psychologist*, 1980, *35*, 639–652. A view of child rearing, present and future, from one of America's top researchers on the topic.

BRONFENBRENNER, U., and A. CROUTER. The evolution of environmental models and developmental research. In P. Mussen (Ed.), The handbook of child psychology, Vol. 4. New York: Wiley, 1983. An account of scientific progress in research on human development over the past century and beyond.

CROCKENBERG, S. B. Infant irritability, other responsiveness, and social support influences on the security of infant-mother attachment. *Child Development*, 1981, *52*, 857–865. An example of contemporary research on child rearing: how a mother's social network helps her deal with a difficult infant.

ELDER, G. *Children of the Great Depression*. Chicago : University of Chicago Press, 1974. A study of how growing up in the Great Depression influenced the next generation: a modern classic.

FURSTENBERG, F. *Unplanned parenthood: The social consequences of teenage child-bearing*. New York: Free Press, 1976. The legacy of teenage parenthood in America.

PULKKINEN, L. Self-control and continuity from childhood to late adolescence. In P. Baltes and O. Brim (Eds.), *Life-span development and behavior*, Vol. IV. New York: Academic Press, 1982. An outstanding longitudinal study of the impact of environment on development, including the destructive role of hectic family life.

STEINBERG, L. *Adolescence*. New York: Alfred A. Knopf, 1985. A lively, sometimes humorous, multidisciplinary text that surveys research and theories of individual development and examines the effects of the contexts in which adolescents grow up.

PART SIX

PERSONALITY AND INDIVIDUAL DIFFERENCES

My wife, Janet, has many endearing traits. She is, for instance, a lover of plants and animals. I, myself, don't dislike them, you understand, but if they'll leave me alone, I'll be delighted to leave them alone. (It's an example of our own individual personality differences.)

Just to show you, Janet even loves pigeons, those not very bright birds that seem to be more at home in Manhattan than people are.

Once she noted that a pigeon had discovered our balcony (thirty-three stories above ground level) and she found it impossible not to feed it. Naturally, it came back the next day, and the next, and after a while, it brought its mate. Other pigeons, noting that old Joe was getting fat, followed it and also located our balcony, which came to look like something out of Hitchcock's *The Birds.*

Janet now buys bird seed and various other types of avian comestibles, in huge fifty-pound bags or something and is, I believe, feeding every pigeon in New York (and cleaning the balcony of its accumulation of guano, periodically, with a pick and shovel.)

All these pigeons look alike to me, but Janet can tell them apart at a glance. To her they have distinct colors, peronalities, and patterns of behavior. She talks to them, worries about them in bad weather, and, I think, has grown unaware that they are nonpeople.

Apparently, according to Janet's account, she loved living things from infancy, even though her mother was more like me and wouldn't have animals in the house. As for me, my desire from infancy was to read—even though there were no books in the house. My parents had arrived in the United States as penniless immigrants when I was a three-year-old child. My father found work and there was enough money for food, clothes, and shelter, but that was all. There was no money for books.

I loved to read, having taught myself to do so at the age of five, but my school books were consumed in the first few days of each semester. That left the library, and my father obtained a library card for me when I was six years old. I couldn't get my mother to take me oftener than once a week, and I was only allowed to pick out two books at a time, so that, as a reader, I was continually undernourished.

My father, who had become a candy-store proprietor when I was six, would not allow me to read the magazines on the newsstand because he thought they were unsuitable for a developing mind. It was not till I was nine that I received a special dispensation to read science-fiction magazines, because my father thought (mistakenly) that they were serious essays on scientific subjects—and I was careful not to disillusion him.

Still, there were only three magazines in the field, and they only came out once a month. The undernourishment continued.

Finally, a thought occurred to me. When I read a library book or magazine story that I particularly enjoyed, why not *copy* it, so that I could read and reread it as often as I liked?

I got a notebook and a pencil and began copying. Within the hour I found that it was not a workable idea. At the rate of copying, I couldn't possibly finish a book in the time I could keep it out of the library. Then, too, my hand quickly began to ache. I had to think of something else.

When I was eleven years old, however, I had the idea that changed my life. If there was no time to copy a book, *why not write one of my own?* I could work at it for as long as I wished, since it would not involve a library book that had to be returned or a magazine that had to be put back on the stand.

I began a book about three small-town boys who were going to college. Since I knew nothing about small towns, and certainly nothing about college, my power of invention began to flag, and after eight chapters the project petered out.

However, I had enjoyed writing it, so periodically I would start another book and keep on going until it, too, faded. For six years, I thought of my writing only as providing me with material to read.

Then, at the age of seventeen, a second brilliant notion occurred to me. Why not write a short science-fiction story, one that I could finish, and then submit it for publication? I worked at such a story, on and off, for a year, and submitted it on June 21, 1938. It was rejected, but four months later I managed to sell a story, and after that I never stopped.

Isaac Asimov

PSYCHOANALYTIC THEORIES OF PERSONALITY

Like the man who was surprised to learn that he had been speaking "prose" all his life, you may be unaware that you already know a great deal about the psychology of personality. You know, for example, that if you tell two friends a joke, one is likely to find it hilarious, while the other is likely to miss the point. Ask three people their opinion of the same movie, and their reports are likely to vary, attributing different motivations to the characters, recalling different episodes as important, and stating different themes. Introduced to a young woman, one young man will smile politely and go back to watching the football game; another will shuffle his feet and lower his eyes; and a third will ask for her phone number. Thus, everyday experiences show that each person is unique, with her or his own responses to the world. Moreover, these unique characteristics appear to be stable and enduring.

Such differences among people and the stability of any individual's behavior over long periods are the essence of **personality**. Regardless of their approach, all personality theorists address two key questions: When several people confront the same situation, why do they not all behave the same way? What accounts for the relative consistency of a person's behavior from one situation to the next? These questions inevitably lead to others. Is there something inside that makes people think, feel, and act in distinctive and characteristic ways? Are people driven by biological forces? Do we inherit personality traits from our parents? How do outside forces—our experiences, our relationships, our culture, and the times in which we live—shape us? Are we motivated by unconscious forces, or do we act as we do from conscious choice—or habit? Can we—do we—change over time?

Faced with the extraordinary complexity of human behavior and the wide range of individual differences in personality, theorists have developed radically different explanations in their attempts to answer these questions. The resulting theories, discussed in this chapter and in Chapter 19, are best regarded as complementary—not contradictory—explanations of human diversity. Each theory sheds light on certain aspects of personality and none can satisfactorily account for all aspects. The approaches discussed in this chapter have developed from psychoanalytic theory and research; they emphasize the significance of childhood experience and the power of mental events to determine human behavior.

FREUD'S PSYCHOANALYTIC THEORY

The most influential theorist in the field of personality has been Sigmund Freud (1856–1939). He conceived the first comprehensive theory of personality, and after nearly a century, his theory remains the most detailed and original yet formulated. Critics of Freud—and there have been some vociferous ones—admit that the range of phenomena he identified and explored stands as a challenge and an inspiration to personality theorists. Freud drew on a number of assets to make the rich observations he set down on paper: his remarkable skill as an observer of human behavior; his training in medicine; his background in literature and history, including an extensive knowledge of such materials as jokes and folk tales; and his unusually powerful writing ability. A reader needs no particular training in psychology to be excited, entertained, and educated by some of Freud's major works, such as *The Interpretation of Dreams* (1900/1955), *Introductory Lectures on Psychoanalysis* (1917/1963), and *Civilization and Its Discontents* (1930/1962).

Freud first became interested in personality when he tried to account for certain strange physical problems manifested by some of his patients. Many of them suffered from what seemed to be a neurological defect—for example, paralysis of an arm, loss of sensation in a hand, deterioration of hearing or vision. But Freud, trained as a neurologist, knew that in many cases the defect had no physical origin. When a patient had lost feeling in a hand, for instance, the affected region might be confined to an area that is covered when wearing a glove ("glove anesthesia")—a pattern that does not correspond to any known grouping of nerves.

Freud speculated that such symptoms could be caused by emotional stress. He had been treating these "hysterical" disorders, as they were called, with hypnosis. He soon began a collaboration with Josef Breuer, who had discovered that the symptoms sometimes disappeared if the patient was asked to recall critical events associated with the symptom while hypnotized (Breuer and

Sigmund Freud, the father of pyschoanalysis, startled the Viennese medical community with his theories about the causes of hysteria. His writings on childhood sexuality and personality development remain astute and controversial to this day.

Freud, 1937/1957). One of Breuer's patients was a young woman he called Anna O. While caring for her dying father, she had become exhausted and developed a nervous cough, severe headaches, abnormal vision, and other physical problems. When Breuer visited Anna, she often passed into a trancelike state that she called "clouds." In this state she recounted past experiences, a process she called "chimney sweeping." If she recalled an experience related in some way to one of her symptoms—especially if she seemed to relive the emotions connected with it—the symptoms disappeared, often for good.

After using hypnosis for a time, Freud concluded that it was not an ideal therapeutic procedure. Many patients could not be hypnotized, and although hypnosis offered others relief, their symptoms often recurred. As a result, Freud turned to another technique he called **free association**, in which the patient lay down on a couch and said whatever came to mind. In the course of these apparently aimless statements, themes centering on the patient's important emotional conflicts often emerged. As these conflicts were talked about, the patient began to understand them and to gain mastery over them.

Freud found that although patients with "hysterical" disorders at first could not remember childhood experiences, especially the wishes and fears that seemed to produce their symptoms, hypnosis and later, free association, sometimes brought back the memories. From such evidence, Freud theorized the existence of an aspect of personality, unknown to the mind of the subject, that he called the **unconscious**.

Exploring the Unconscious

The concept of the unconscious is Freud's major contribution to the understanding of human behavior and personality. In his view, the contents of the conscious mind are only a small part of the personality. The mind could be likened to an iceberg: people's conscious thoughts resemble the small tip of an iceberg; beneath the surface—out of the person's awareness—lies the massive unconscious. The unconscious includes instinctual drives and infantile goals, hopes, wishes, and needs that have been repressed, or concealed from conscious awareness, because they cause internal conflict. Freud coined the term **psychoanalysis** to denote a process of "psychological analysis" designed to retrieve elements of a person's unconscious. Freud believed that once repressed memories and feelings were brought into consciousness and carefully examined, the patient would gain insight into his or her behavior patterns—and this insight would put an end to behavior that was disturbed or self-destructive. Psychoanalysis, as developed by Freud, is a constellation of techniques for "making the unconscious conscious." Its goal is not only the recovery of hitherto inaccessible memories but also the uncovering of hitherto inaccessible meanings: a new understanding of one's psychological patterns and structures (conflicts, defense styles, fears, beliefs, interpersonal patterns, and so forth). Uncovering these meanings is what Freud meant by "insight" (Erdelyi, 1985).

Free association turned out to be only one method of reaching the unconscious. The "royal road to the unconscious," as Freud saw it, was provided by the analysis of dreams. A dream, according to Freud, has both a manifest content and a latent content. The **manifest content**, or the events the dreamer relates, is a kind of coded message from the dreamer's unconscious; the **latent content** is the underlying meaning of the dream—which can be decoded by a process of analysis. If properly analyzed and interpreted to the patient, the dream should lead to important discoveries about the patient's psychological difficulties. The following example (summarized from Linder, 1955) illustrates how dream analysis works to uncover conflicts long buried in the unconscious.

Laura, a young single woman, suffered from periods of depression and bulimia—prolonged, uncontrollable eating binges. She had grown up in a troubled family. Her mother, a bitter, quarrelsome woman, was confined to a wheelchair. Her father had deserted the family when Laura was in the sixth grade. In the course of her analysis Laura reported the following dream:

> I was in what appeared to be a ballroom or a dance hall, but I knew it was really a hospital. A man came up to me and told me to undress, take all my clothes off. He was going to give me a gynecological examination. I did as I was told but I was very frightened. While I was undressing, I noticed that he was doing something to a woman at the other end of the room. She was sitting or lying in a funny kind of contraption with all kinds of levers and gears and pulleys attached to it. I knew that I was supposed to be next, that I would have to sit in that thing while he examined me. Suddenly he called my name and I found myself running to him. The chair or table—whatever it was—was now empty, and he told me to get on it. I refused and began to cry. It started to rain—great big drops of rain. He pushed me to the floor and spread my legs for the examination. I turned over on my stomach and began to scream. I woke myself up screaming. (Linder, 1955, p. 93)

The analysis brought out the following: Laura's boyfriend was a medical intern. For some time he had been urging Laura to have sexual intercourse, but she had felt afraid to do so. Laura herself, upon reflection, recognized the woman "in a funny kind of contraption" as her mother. The "examination" that she feared was sexual intercourse. Suddenly she achieved insight into her own fear of sex: she had somehow absorbed the idea, as a child, that sexual activity had been responsible for her mother's handicap. After the analysis of this dream, Laura suddenly began to recall things about her relationship with her mother that she had forgotten. In particular, she began to recall deeply hostile feelings toward her mother. As a young girl she had held her mother responsible for her father's desertion of the family. She recalled that she had played pranks on her mother to "punish" her. On one occasion in particular, her mother had asked her to bring her home some candies from the store. When Laura did so, she refused to give the candies to her mother but instead ate them all herself while her mother pursued her around their apartment in her wheel-chair. This need to gorge herself on what her mother wanted in order to express her hostile feelings toward her was doubtless connected to her continuing problem with eating binges.

This dream analysis is greatly condensed; it barely does justice to the richness of insight that dream analysis may provide. In Freud's own pioneering work *The Interpretation of Dreams* (1900/ 1955), a short, "simple" dream is often followed by pages of analysis. To Freud, even the most cryptic dream could provide multiple clues to what lay hidden in the dreamer's unconscious. Of course, not everyone agrees with Freud on this point; see Chapter 7.

Freud hypothesized that dreams were expressions of unconscious desires and conflicts—not direct expressions, but disguised or censored expressions. He argued that specific mechanisms within the psyche transform the real meaning of the dream, the *latent content*, into the *manifest content*, or the dream we remember upon awakening. One mechanism is *censorship*: in Laura's dream, neither her mother nor her wheelchair is clearly recognizable. There also seems to be a *condensation* of her father (doing something to her mother), her boyfriend the medical intern (who wished to do something to her), and possibly her therapist (a doctor who was probing her in his own, albeit psychological, way). Also present are *symbolization*—the medical exam stood for sexual intercourse—and *plastic-word representation* or *dramatization* (the entire unconscious conflict is made into a vivid story, molded in the concrete language of images, sounds, and body sensation). The peculiar nonsensical or fanciful aspects of many dreams are the result of precisely these

mechanisms, which disguise our inner conflicts (note: "I found myself running *to* him") and make them into apparently harmless stories. Without their disguise, Freud believed, these conflicts would be unacceptably alarming to us.

Unconscious conflicts express themselves not only in dreams; as Freud pointed out, slips of the tongue, accidents, and even jokes may express our most hidden feelings. Thus, the young man away at college who misses his family may type "the weather here has been lonely [lovely]" in a letter home, or he may miss the plane when it is time for him to return to school after the holidays. He may even accidentally break a leg skiing so that he can convalesce at home for several months. These events, like dreams, are disguised expressions of unconscious conflict, in the Freudian view. In his book *Jokes and Their Relation to the Unconscious* (1905/1962), Freud argues that jokes also allow us a means of expressing forbidden feelings. Like dreams, jokes have a manifest content (the joke as related) and a latent content (the underlying meaning the listener "gets" from the joke). When we laugh at a joke, we are often indulging sexual, aggressive, or destructive feelings that consciously we must conceal from others and often from ourselves.

Freud's description of the unconscious and its influence on behavior was one of his greatest contributions to psychology. Although there have been many dissenters from his theories from his day to our own, few would dispute that his thoughts about the human psyche have had a profound influence. In his own time Freud was recognized as a revolutionary thinker, and he attracted many students to Vienna. Soon psychoanalysts were practicing in many countries, including the United States. Until his death in 1939 Freud continued to write voluminously, refining and revising his ideas. In this chapter we must of necessity consider only a few of these ideas, and those only in brief.

Freud's Conceptualization of Personality Structure

Although Freud's view of unconscious conflicts emerged from his work with troubled patients, the idea was based on a coherent theory of personality that he believed explained the behavior of everyone. Freud divided personality into three separate but interacting systems: the id, the ego, and the superego. Each of these systems has its own highly specific role in maintaining normal personality functioning. It may help our understanding of this concept of personality to know that the German word that Freud used for id is *das Es*, which means "it," implying an alien force, something in a person that is not recognized as part of the self. The ego he called *das Ich*, which means "I," the part of the personality recognized and accepted as oneself. "Superego" *(das Über-Ich)* thus means "above the I"; as we shall see, it refers to the moral component that is imposed on the self by society.

Freud sometimes referred to the three systems almost as if they had wills of their own—as if the ego were a rational, self-controlled person at war with an irrational and impulsive person (the id) and a harsh, moralistic person (the superego). This manner of reference, while dramatic and engaging, has received much criticism from psychologists who believe that such descriptions are unscientific. It will avoid confusion if we take the terms in the sense actually intended by Freud —as metaphorical names for the functional (not physical) divisions of the personality. The id, ego, and superego are not persons, places, or physical things; they are the names given to hypothetical mental systems.

The Id

The **id** is that part of the psyche which is primitive and animallike. In Freud's view, it is the only part of the mind that exists at birth. As such, it can be pictured as the "infant" in us that persists throughout life. The id is demanding and hedonistic—it operates according to what Freud termed the pleasure-unpleasure principle: the id wants to obtain pleasure immediately and at all times, and it wants just as definitely to avoid pain. To this aspect of our psyche there are no rules or logic, no doubt, time, or morality. Freud called the id's mode of operation *primary process thinking* —a crude and primitive way of dealing with the world. Dreams, which break rules of space, time, and logic, and which often consist of vivid, bizarre, and irrational images, are good examples of the id at work. They illustrate the imagistic and illogical nature of primary process thinking. Freud also thought that the serious psychological disorders known as *psychoses*, in which an awake person loses touch with reality, represent a return to this primitive, infantile level of functioning.

The Ego

As the infant begins to experience the world, he or she comes to find that it may or may not be a gratifying place. The id's demands, no matter how urgent, are not automatically met. Sometime during the first year of life, the **ego** begins to emerge. This new psychic component has the task of mediating between the id and reality—of finding ways in the real world to satisfy the id's demands. The ego uses memory, reason, and judgment in attempts to satisfy the desires of the id, to anticipate the consequences of a particular means of gratification, and sometimes to delay gratification in order to achieve long-range goals. Because the characteristic task of the ego is coping with reality, Freud termed its principle of operation the *reality principle.*

The ego's functioning contrasts sharply with that of the id. Unlike the id, part of the ego is conscious. It obeys the rules of logic and reason and learns from experience. It can consider matters in abstract terms (in words, for example). This mode of functioning Freud called *secondary process thinking* (Erdelyi, 1985). For an example of ego functioning, consider what happens when a child observes the flame on a stove. When she reaches out to touch the pretty blue flame, she is burned. She therefore learns not to touch the flame (an ego function) even though she still feels the desire to do so (an id impulse).

It should be obvious that the ego's activities are all-important in ensuring our health and safety. Not only does the ego act as a brake on the id's ceaseless demands for gratification; through its attempts to satisfy the id, the ego develops the higher cognitive functions: perception, learning, discrimination, memory, judgment, and planning. Ironically, however, the ego can sometimes do its job too well. By resorting to defense mechanisms, which we shall discuss in more detail below, the ego may distort or avoid reality rather than cope with it.

The Superego

The third psychic component, the **superego**, is that part of the personality which is concerned with meeting the demands of morality and social convention. The superego begins to develop around the age of two or three, the period during which the child is toilet-trained and becomes

FREUD ON THE ID, EGO, AND SUPEREGO

We are warned by a proverb against serving two masters at the same time. The poor ego has things even worse: it serves three severe masters and does what it can to bring their claims and demands into harmony with one another. These claims are always divergent and often seem incompatible. No wonder that the ego so often fails in its task. Its three tyrannical masters are the external world, the superego and id. . . . Owing to its origin from the experiences of the perceptual system, it is earmarked for representing the demands of the external world, but it strives too to be a loyal servant of the id, to remain on good terms with it, to recommend itself to it as an object and to attract its libido to itself. In its attempts to mediate between the id and reality, it is often obliged to cloak the *Ucs.* [unconscious] commands of the id with its own *Pcs.* [preconscious] rationalizations, to conceal the id's conflicts with reality, to profess, with diplomatic disingenuousness, to be taking notice of reality even when the id has remained rigid and unyielding. On the other hand it is observed at every step it takes by the strict superego, which lays down definite standards for its conduct, without taking any account of its difficulties from the direction of the id and the external world, and which, if those standards are not obeyed, punishes it with tense feelings of inferiority and of guilt. Thus the ego, driven by the id, confined by the superego, repulsed by reality, struggles to master its economic task of bringing about harmony among the forces and influences working in and upon it; and we can understand how it is that so often we cannot suppress a cry: "Life is not easy!" If the ego is obliged to admit its weakness, it breaks out in anxiety—realistic anxiety regarding the external world, moral anxiety regarding the superego and neurotic anxiety regarding the strength of the passions in the id.

From Sigmund Freud, *New introductory lectures on psychoanalysis.* J. Strachey (Ed. and Trans.). New York: W. W. Norton. 1965. (Originally published, 1933.)

---

aware that he or she must conform to a number of social rules that govern "good" and "bad" behavior. Its development is more or less complete by the age of six, after the resolution of the Oedipus complex (see below). Thus the superego, like the ego, enables the individual to cope with reality —but a particular kind of *social* reality. (The ego is concerned with the laws of physics and reason: "If I drop a dish, it will fall to the floor and break." The superego is concerned with social rules: "If I drop a dish and it breaks, Mother will be angry and punish me for doing something naughty.") From the promptings of parents and older siblings, the child begins to develop a sense that certain things must not be done because they are wrong. The superego is the repository of all these rules, and it is roughly equivalent to what we call a conscience.

The superego, as Freud conceived it, is partly conscious and partly unconscious. It operates by a combination of primary process and secondary process thinking. Like the ego, the superego can be rational and express itself in words. Yet like the id, the superego can also violate logic and rationality—which should not be surprising, since many moral rules are irrational. The superego can also be as crude and assertive as the id, demanding a certain kind of behavior in spite of reason, convenience, and common sense.

Thus, in Freud's view the psyche contains three distinct structures. The ego must find a way to satisfy the id, which seeks pleasure, without clashing with the superego, which demands socially and morally acceptable behavior. The ego is sometimes seen as the executive agency of the personality, a kind of chairman of the board that must find some way of arranging compromises between the demands of the id and the superego. It is this interplay of pulls and pushes—psychic conflict and its resolution—that Freud referred to as **psychodynamics**.

Psychodynamics

The idea that opposing forces are continually at play in every person is basic to Freud's theory. As we have just seen, the ego has the difficult task of maintaining some kind of equilibrium in this intrapsychic conflict. When things get out of balance—when the demands of physical reality, of morality, or of the passions become too insistent —anxiety results. **Anxiety** is a state of psychic pain that alerts the ego to danger; it is akin to fear. Freud distinguished three types of anxiety, each based on a different source of danger. In **reality anxiety**, which is the closest to what we call "fear," the danger comes from the outside world. A person who sees a shark while swimming in the ocean experiences reality anxiety. In **moral anxiety**, danger comes from the superego, which threatens to overwhelm the person with guilt or shame over some act that has been committed or merely contemplated. In **neurotic anxiety**, the danger comes from the id, when impulses threaten to burst through ego controls and cause the individual to do things that will bring punishment or shame.

The ego attempts to avoid the pain of anxiety in a variety of ways. These may be fairly simple and obvious, such as withdrawing from the anxiety-provoking situation. At the other extreme, when anxiety is overwhelming and inescapable, the entire personality may collapse—as Freud thought happened in the psychoses. But intermediate between these extremes are several strategies by which the ego may defend itself.

Defense Mechanisms

When intrapsychic conflict is acute and anxiety threatens, the ego often resorts to what are called defense mechanisms. **Defense mechanisms** are techniques by which the source of the anxiety is either excluded from consciousness or distorted in such a way as to be less anxiety-producing. Although sometimes we may perceive ourselves making use of defense mechanisms, they operate most powerfully when they are unconscious.

The fundamental defense mechanism, one that keeps threatening thoughts and memories from consciousness and pushes them back into the unconscious, is called **repression**. Repression was one of Freud's earliest discoveries. He observed that without considerable probing, his patients were unable to recall **traumatic**, or psychologically damaging, childhood events. These traumatic memories are concealed from conscious awareness and kept in the unconscious by strong forces. According to Freud, the threats from these unpleasant memories, the expenditures of energy

needed to conceal them, and the anxiety generated in the process are at the basis of neurosis (see Chapter 22). Freud also believed that repression is a part of all other defense mechanisms: the anxiety-producing impulse is first repressed before the other defensive behaviors are engaged in.

One of the most familiar of the defense mechanisms is **rationalization**. In this defense mechanism we give ourselves a plausible explanation for doing (or not doing) something that in fact we are doing for quite different reasons. We may not be conscious of the real reason for our behavior, or the real reason may be unacceptable to us. For example, we may ignore the ragged man on the street who asks us for money by saying to ourselves that he would only spend it on liquor. This allows us to avoid the unpleasant feeling of guilt that we might experience if we thought we had refused to help a deserving person.

Denial is the refusal to recognize a threatening source of anxiety. For example, a boy in high school may plan to become a doctor despite a failing academic record. Even when discouraged by guidance counselors from this career choice, he may go on planning to attend college and medical school, asserting that it will all work out "somehow."

In **regression**, a person returns to an earlier stage of development in response to some perceived threat. In the extreme case an adult may actually return to helpless and dependent infantile behavior. In the more usual sense, however, regression involves distracting ourselves from whatever anxieties we may feel by engaging in comforting childlike behavior—such as eating or drinking too much.

Projection involves turning an inward threat into a threat from the external world; a person who projects unknowingly attributes his or her fears or impulses onto other people. For example, a woman who feels threatened by an impulse to steal items from stores may attribute the same impulse to others and begin to fear that her purse will be stolen and that the clerks will shortchange her.

In **displacement**, a person is unable to express some feelings in the situation that has aroused them and instead vents the feelings on some innocent object. For example, a woman who has been angry at her boss all day may come home and yell at the babysitter or the dog.

Reaction formation, another common defense mechanism, is the replacement of an anxiety-producing impulse or feeling by its opposite; its function is to make a person unaware of the original source of distress. Instead of acknowledging that she dislikes her child, a mother may shower the child with expressions of love. A man who really wants to start fires may become a firefighter and spend his time putting them out. Generally, the stronger the impulse toward socially unacceptable behavior, the stronger the defense against it, so that crusaders who "protest too much" against what they consider reprehensible behavior may be displaying reaction formation.

These common defense mechanisms (and this is not a complete list) may serve a useful purpose at times, relieving minor anxieties and allowing us to meet the demands of everyday life. However, since they all distort reality to some extent, they may impair our ability to cope with things as they are in the world. For example, the would-be doctor may feel relieved to have chosen a career and to have a goal to strive for, but eventually he will have a rude awakening—and perhaps will wish that he had made more realistic plans.

In addition, it should be noted, Freud identified one "positive" defense mechanism—sublimation. **Sublimation** is actually a form of displacement, or the diversion of emotional energy from its original source. But in this case the energy is used in a constructive way. Freud believed that many of the achievements of our culture were fueled by sublimation. For example, in *Civilization and Its Discontents* (1930/1962), Freud suggested that Leonardo da Vinci's urge to paint Madonnas was a sublimated expression of his longing for reunion with his mother, from whom he had been separated at an early age. In fact, Freud thought that civilization itself rested on the sublimation of our sexual and aggressive impulses.

Freud's Psychosexual Stages of Development

Freud was the first psychological theorist to emphasize the developmental aspects of personality and to stress the decisive role of infancy and childhood in establishing the basic character structure of an individual. Indeed, Freud believed that personality is formed by the time a child enters school and that later growth consists of elaborating this basic structure. The discussion in Chapter 17 noted Freud's belief that the child passes through a series of psychosexual stages during the first five years of life, with each stage

originating in the sexual instincts of the personality and organized around one of the erogenous zones of the body. The three early stages, collectively called the **pregenital stage**, are the **oral** (birth to one year), the **anal** (one to two years), and the **phallic** (three to six years) stages. During the phallic stage, according to Freud, the child passes through the Oedipus complex. At this time, the child develops a particularly strong attachment to the parent of the opposite sex, and a corresponding resentment and hatred of the same-sex parent, who appears to the child as a rival for the affections of the desired parent. Freud thought that the young boy, with his intense love for his mother and resentment of his father, would come to fear punishment from his father in the form of castration. The boy would then repress his erotic feelings for his mother and identify with his father, adopting his father's values. A young girl would go through a parallel process. In Freud's theory, it is this identification with the values of the same-sex parent that is responsible for the formation of the superego. After the resolution of the Oedipus complex the child enters a period of **latency** (from about six to eleven years). During this period the child represses his or her sexual feelings—hence, sexuality is latent. At adolescence, hormones encourage sexual interest to reappear, and the young person enters the final stage of psychosexual development, the **genital** stage. Although Freud believed that these stages of personality growth are distinct, he did not assume that children shift abruptly from one stage to another, but rather that the transitions are gradual and the ages approximate.

DEVELOPMENT OF NEO-FREUDIAN THEORIES

As our brief treatment here suggests, Freud's thought was profoundly original. It is hard to overstate the influence his ideas have had, both within psychology and in other disciplines. The importance of childhood to later development, the significance of the unconscious mind, the revelations of dreams—these are but a few of Freud's many contributions. Given his great originality, it is not surprising that Freud attracted a following of powerful and imaginative minds. Some of Freud's students found little to disagree with in their teacher's ideas. Others found themselves

Exploring the Unconscious

A key concept in Freud's theory of personality is the existence of the unconscious as a hidden repository of memories, thoughts, and feelings. In Freud's view, this part of our psyche motivates much of our everyday behavior in ways we are quite unaware of. When Freud's thinking came under the scrutiny of behaviorists and other experimental psychologists, the existence of the unconscious was scornfully disputed. Where or what was this entity, which could not be seen, felt, or measured? Did it perhaps exist only in Freud's mind?

Over the years some intrepid researchers have attempted to determine whether the unconscious does exist. The studies have concerned themselves with memory and with the curious fact that we sometimes can be shown to remember more than we think we do.

One line of research has concentrated on our ability to recover apparently forgotten information from memory. It has been shown, for example, that information that is initially inaccessible to awareness may become accessible over time. In one study, a subject was able to improve his recall of pictorial stimuli over several days by simply trying to do so—by repeatedly thinking over what images he had seen (Erdelyi and Kleinbard, 1978). This very technique—concentration on past experiences in an attempt to retrieve apparently forgotten information—was used by Freud at one one point in his development of psychoanalysis. He found that some patients could recall "forgotten" events from the past simply by focusing their attention on them and trying to remember—or as Freud called it, by doing "the work of recollection."

A second direction research on the unconscious has taken is an attempt to document the dissociation of memory from awareness. What this means is that researchers have found that although we say that we do not remember certain stimuli (as list of words, for example), the stimuli nevertheless seem to have registered in our mind. Experiments show that we remember having seen word *X*, even though we are not aware that we do. In a number of experiments subjects have been shown words flashed so rapidly on a screen as to be essentially invisible (subjects were apparently unaware of them). Yet afterward, when given the first few letters of the word they had "not seen," they would often be able to supply the whole word (Klatzky, 1984). Such examples of subliminal perception—in which we seem to perceive things without being aware that we do—support the idea that we *can* store information mentally without being aware that it is in our mind. This is one essential meaning of "the unconscious." Other research has confirmed this finding. For example, patients suffering from amnesia (caused by advanced alcoholism, electroshock treatments, or brain damage) cannot repeat many words a few minutes after being presented with them. Yet given a cue to help their (apparently nonexistent) memories, they recall about as many words as do control subjects, even though the amnesics are convinced that they are not remembering but merely guessing (Graf, Squire, and Mandler, 1984). They could not recall if they had not, on some level, mentally absorbed and stored the words. If they "remembered" the words without being aware of them, does this not suggest that all human beings potentially may "remember" more than they think they do? And that these deeply shadowed memories may be absorbed in the unconscious?

differing with Freud as they followed their own lines of thought. Some of these introduced modifications in Freud's original theories that are still influential today. We shall discuss five of these neo-Freudian thinkers: Carl Gustav Jung, Alfred Adler, Karen Horney, Erich Fromm, and Erik Erikson.

Jung's Analytic Psychology

Carl Gustav Jung (1875–1961), who in 1913 founded his own school of psychoanalysis (called **analytic psychology**), disagreed with Freud in several major ways. First of all, he had a different view of the unconscious. Jung distinguished between what he termed the **personal unconscious** and the **collective unconscious**.

The personal unconscious essentially corresponds to Freud's notion. Within it, however, Jung did not envision an ego-id-superego structure; instead he pictured the personal unconscious as containing "complexes," which he conceived of as more or less independent clusters of emotionally laden memories and ideas. Jung even thought of these clusters sometimes as separate subpersonalities, which in extreme cases could produce the phenomenon of multiple personality.

The collective unconscious, on the other hand, involves unconscious mental materials that are not of a personal nature but are shared by all of humanity. It is the hereditary aspect of mind. In Jung's view, just as we are born with two ears, one nose, and five fingers on each hand, we are born with certain psychological tendencies—to produce certain myths, dreams, symbols, and so on. The collective unconscious is thus a vast storehouse of psychological propensities inherited from humanity's ancestral past. Jung called the archaic molds responsible for these ideas and images in the collective unconscious **archetypes** and suggested that human beings of all eras and in all parts of the world are molded by them.

The collective unconscious contains more than just frightening images, however; in Jung's view it is also the repository for a kind of mysterious ancestral wisdom and the source of human creativity. Thus for Jung the unconscious had a highly positive aspect; it was not merely the realm of buried, primitive urges, as Freud believed. In fact, Jung thought that one ultimate goal for therapy might be somehow to tap the wisdom of the collective unconscious. This inner exploration, if successful, could bring the patient to a state in which opposing tendencies in the personality (for instance, masculine and feminine, active and passive) are united. In Jung's view this inward quest is dangerous and could lead to madness (psychosis), but it is also the stuff of all great artistic creation. Jung's view, though startling to many Western readers, is a close paraphrase of Hindu-Buddhistic psychology, which holds that the ultimate Guru/God/Buddha is within us. "Be ye lanterns unto yourselves," Buddha said. Thus, many of Jung's ideas have an Eastern or mystical quality, a tendency that set him at odds with Freud.

A second major difference between Jung and Freud is that Freud thought that most significant

Extroversion was, for Jung, a personality type that sought excitement in the outside world.

personality development took place in childhood; Jung did not. Development, to Jung, was a lifelong process, and a person could be expected to grow and change over the years; he was instrumental in bringing to prominence the notion of the midlife crisis. What was to be hoped for, according to Jung, was a process of **individuation**—the development of all the parts of the personality and their integration into a coherent self.

Finally, despite his somewhat mystical approach, Jung contributed several common-sense ideas to psychology. One is that there are two major personality orientations: **introversion**, in which the person directs his interest inward rather than toward the external world and consequently is quiet, reserved, and slow to react to external events, and **extroversion**, in which the person is primarily oriented to the external world and thus is outgoing, sociable, and excitement-seeking. Another of Jung's ideas is that no one kind of psychotherapy works uniformly well with all people or at all times of life—a notion with which most psychologists would agree today. He identified four critical components of therapy, not all of them appropriate at the same time: (1) the confessional (similar to the cathartic technique of Breuer and Freud); (2) insight (such as is gained in psychoanalysis), important because it can lead to self-knowledge; (3) education—it is not enough to have understanding, we also have to learn how to do things once our inhibitions are removed (behavior modification techniques would fit into this category); and (4) transformation—the last great task, to be undertaken after middle age, with the goal of individuation.

Social Personality Theorists

Jung pushed theory in an inward direction, but many of Freud's associates reacted in the opposite way: they rejected what they viewed as Freud's biological viewpoint in favor of a stronger emphasis on sociological or interpersonal factors. Most neo-Freudian thinkers have in one way or another asserted that Freud neglected social and environmental influences on personality development.

Adler's Individual Psychology

Alfred Adler (1870–1937), like Jung, was an intimate associate of Freud. In 1911 he broke away and founded his own school, called **individual psychology**—which, despite its name, emphasized the importance of social factors in personality development.

Adler did not share Freud's belief that human beings are motivated primarily by sexual instincts. Instead, Adler at first claimed that the aggressive drive is responsible for most human behavior. Gradually, however, he came to believe that not the aggressive impulse but the "will to power" motivates human beings. Finally, Adler abandoned the notion of the "will to power" in favor of the idea of "the striving for superiority," making this striving the basis of his theory (Adler, 1930). By "superiority" Adler did not mean social distinction or dominance, but a quest for perfection. His theory has a strongly idealistic quality, for it asserts that "the great upward drive" is the moving force in human life. This conscious striving toward "completion" of the self carries the human

being—indeed, the human species—from one stage of development to the next.

A sense of incompleteness or imperfection in any aspect of life gives rise to feelings of inferiority, according to Adler. These feelings are normal and originate in the childhood realization that adults can do things that children cannot. In their efforts to overcome feelings of inferiority, some individuals succeed in conveying to themselves, and perhaps to others, only the *appearance* of strength and competence. Because they have not improved their actual circumstances, their underlying feelings of inferiority remain. To describe this situation, Adler coined the term **inferiority complex** (Adler, 1931), distinguishing between universal feelings of inferiority and the feelings and actions that characterize a person with an inferiority complex. Adler also placed greater emphasis on conscious motivation than Freud did.

Another of Adler's basic concepts is the idea of **social interest** (1931). He claimed that in addition to seeking individual perfection, each of us is born with a desire to strive for the social good. As we mature, our personal ambition changes to social commitment—provided we have received proper guidance and education along the way. We can compensate for feelings of inferiority and incompleteness by working toward the common good. The ultimate goal of each person thus becomes the perfection of society, and normal people strive to achieve goals that are primarily social in character. The neurotic person, therefore, is one who continues striving toward selfish goals such as self-esteem, power, and self-aggrandizement.

Horney's Theory of Basic Anxiety and Basic Hostility

Karen Horney (1885–1952), a German-born psychoanalyst, sought to modify import aspects of psychoanalytic theory. She accepted such concepts as the importance of early experience, unconscious motivation, and unconscious defenses, but she challenged Freud's biological or instinctive approach to personality development. For Horney (1945), motivation and conflict, even though unconscious, are based on social factors, not on the interplay between biologically based needs and the environment. She attempted to make psychoanalysis a richer and more workable interpretation of human behavior by focusing on the social determinants of conflict and on how neurotic behavior affects social relationships.

While Freud based his theory of human personality on the sexual and aggressive instincts of the id, and Adler on the innate striving for perfection, Horney's theory revolved around what she called "basic anxiety and basic hostility." **Basic anxiety** develops because the child feels isolated and helpless in a potentially hostile world. Young children, discovering that they are weak and small in a land of giants, soon learn that they are utterly dependent on parents for all their needs and safety. Warm, loving, and dependable parents create a sense of security that reassures the child and produces normal development. If the parents severely disturb a child's sense of security—for example, by indifference, erratic behavior, or disparaging attitudes—the child's feeling of helplessness increases, giving rise to basic anxiety. So, unlike Freud and Adler, who based their views of personality development on inborn instincts, Horney constructed a theory based on social and environmental factors.

In Horney's view, basic anxiety is generally accompanied by **basic hostility**, which arises from resentment over parental indifference, inconsistency, and interference. This hostility cannot be expressed directly, because the child needs and fears the parents and must have their love. The resulting repression of this hostility increases feelings of unworthiness and anxiety, and the child is torn between hostility toward the parents and dependence upon them. This conflict between anxiety and hostility leads to the development of three modes of behavior and social interaction: (1) moving toward others, (2) moving against others, and (3) moving away from others.

In the normal personality, Horney believed, these three modes of behavior are integrated and each used in appropriate circumstances. An individual sometimes moves toward other people to gain nurturance and affection; sometimes moves against them to establish dominance and attain goals; and sometimes withdraws to attain integrity and serenity. Neurosis develops when one of these three ways of relating to other people becomes the *only* framework for an individual's social relationship.

For example, someone who only moves toward other people becomes compliant, a kind of doormat, always anxious to please. Such a person seeks security by subjugating himself or herself to gain affection and approval. This self-effacing be-

Karen Horney argued that social factors rather than instinctual drives are the crucial determinants of personality. The young child, weak and dependent, needs to have a steady, loving relationship with his or her parents.

havior buys security by totally repressing basic hostility, thereby leading to psychological martyrdom and intense unhappiness.

The individual who only moves against others attempts to find security through domination, assuming that the establishment of power over others safeguards the self. Resolving the conflict this way vents some basic hostility, but it also suppresses the acknowledgment of basic anxiety.

Horney on Basic Anxiety and Hostility

The typical conflict leading to anxiety in a child is that between dependency on the parents . . . and hostile impulses against the parents. Hostility may be aroused in a child in many ways: by the parents' lack of respect for him; by unreasonable demands and prohibitions; by injustice; by unreliability; by suppression of criticism; by the parents dominating him and ascribing these tendencies to love. . . . If a child, in addition to being dependent on his parents, is grossly or subtly intimidated by them and hence feels that any expression of hostile impulses against them endangers his security, then the existence of such hostile impulses is bound to create anxiety. . . . The resulting picture may look exactly like what Freud describes as the Oedipus complex: passionate clinging to one parent and jealousy toward the other or toward anyone interfering with the claim of exclusive possession. . . . *But the dynamic structure of these attachments is entirely different from what Freud conceives as the Oedipus complex. They are an early manifestation of neurotic conflicts rather than a primarily sexual phenomenon.*

From Karen Horney, *The neurotic personality of our time.* New York: W. W. Norton, 1965. (Originally published, 1937.)

Such a person avoids anything that connotes helplessness or loss of control.

The person who only moves away from others tries to find security by becoming aloof and withdrawn, never allowing close relationships to develop. People who adopt this solution protect themselves from harm, but in the process they give up the possibility of growth and change.

Thus, in each case the neurotic personality is characterized by compulsive rigidity—the repetition of a single mode of behavior no matter what the situation (Horney, 1937). The neurotic behavior described by Horney is often identical to that observed by Freud: rigid, obsessional actions, unconscious hostility toward parents, jealousy of siblings. Horney differed radically from Freud, however, in explaining the motivation for this behavior, seeing it as a product of social relationships rather than as an expression of innate sexual and aggressive instincts. For example, she stripped away the sexual interpretation of the Oedipus complex and replaced it with an explanation based on interpersonal relations. A typical Oedipus situation, in which a child passionately clings to one parent and expresses jealousy or covert aggression against the other parent, becomes, in Horney's view, the result of the interplay between the child's anxiety and hostility (see the accompanying box). To achieve security and to cope with basic anxiety and hostility, a little boy may turn to his mother for comfort, especially if his father arouses the boy's hostility by dominating him or by denying the gratification of his wishes. If the boy finds relief from anxiety, the relationship with his mother is strengthened. Anything that threatens it or competes for the mother's attention (primarily the father) becomes an object of jealousy or covert aggression.

In another area of personality, Horney rejected Freud's analysis of female personality. Freud (1974) believed that women were culturally inferior because they lacked a strong, mature superego. This deficiency, Freud believed, was the result of the little girl's perception of herself as castrated and her consequent "penis envy." Horney retorted that Freud was in a poor position to know what little girls think. According to Horney (1967), it is not little girls who perceive their condition as degraded. Rather, it is little boys—and the men they eventually become—who see females as woefully mutilated and deficient and who have created the self-fulfilling prophecy that has doomed women to inferiority. Any feelings of inferiority in women, believed Horney, arise from their social experiences, which can lead to dependency and a lack of confidence.

Fromm's "Escape from Freedom"

Erich Fromm (1900–1980) based his theory of personality on interpersonal relationships set in a historical context. Taking his fundamental ideas from Karl Marx as well as from Freud, Fromm distinguished between animal nature, consisting of the biochemical mechanisms for physical survival, and human nature, consisting of our ability to reason and to know ourselves. Reason and self-knowledge inevitably set human beings apart from the rest of the animal kingdom and lead to a freedom that permits great creative accomplishment. But fear of isolation and loneliness that accompanies our freedom may lead people to shrink from it.

On the social level, shrinking from freedom leads to mindless conformity and a tendency to submit to dictators and totalitarian governments. On a personal level, it leads to psychotic withdrawal and self-defeating behavior. According to Fromm (1941), we must instead use our freedom, fulfilling our human nature by uniting with others in an egalitarian spirit of love and shared work.

In Fromm's view, the conditions of human existence produce five basic needs: (1) a need for relatedness, which arises from the fact that, in becoming human, we were torn from the animal's primary union with nature; (2) a need for transcendence, or an urge to overcome animal nature and to become creative; (3) a need for rootedness, or for a sense of belonging to the human family; (4) a need for personal identity, or for being distinctive and unique; and (5) a need for a frame of reference, or a stable and consistent world.

Fromm believed that the ways in which these needs express themselves are determined by society, which can change. Personality develops in accordance with whatever opportunities a particular society offers. In a capitalist society, for example, a person may gain a sense of personal identity by becoming rich or may develop a feeling of rootedness by becoming a dependable employee in a large company. For a society to function properly, Fromm points out, it is essential that children's characters be shaped to fit the needs of that society. Thus, in a capitalist system, the desire to save money must be instilled early so that capital will always be available to enable the economy to expand.

However, to the extent that a particular society frustrates the five basic human needs, its citizens will be prone to psychological disturbances. Sick societies produce sick people. Thus, therapy implies not just individual change but social change as well. But change, at both the individual and social levels, is fraught with perils. For example, when the factory system displaced the individual artisan during the Industrial Revolution, the prevailing social character no longer fit the demands of the new society. As a result, although people were free to move in new directions, many felt a sense of alienation and despair.

One of the great dangers inherent in such a situation is that attempts to escape alienation and despair also involve an escape from freedom (Fromm, 1941). Fromm's warning not to let our fear of freedom lead us to abandon the opportunities of freedom is basic to his view of personality. For this reason he is called a humanitarian socialist. Optimistic about the possibility of developing a society that does not inhibit personal freedom,

The young, upwardly mobile professionals who have become known as "Yuppies" are unabashedly interested in making money. As Fromm suggested, they are gaining a feeling of identity by pursuing the material goals of the capitalist society in which they were brought up.

Figure 18.1. Erikson views life as a succession of biological stages, each having its own developmental conflict, whose resolution has lasting effects on personality. Erikson's psychosocial stages represent an extension and expansion of Freud's psychosexual stages, with parallels between the first four stages of each theory. (After Erikson, 1950.)

Stage	1	2	3	4	5	6	7	8
Maturity								Ego Integrity vs. Despair
Adulthood							Generativity vs. Stagnation	
Young Adulthood						Intimacy vs. Isolation		
Puberty and Adolescence					Identity vs. Role Confusion			
Latency				Industry vs. Inferiority				
Locomotor-Genital			Initiative vs. Guilt					
Muscular-Anal		Autonomy vs. Shame, Doubt						
Oral Sensory	Basic Trust vs. Mistrust							

he asserted that taking an active role in determining the future is an essential part of human nature. He thus differed strongly from Freud, who saw human beings primarily as subject to biological laws that determine a destiny they passively accept.

Erikson's Psychosocial View of Personality

Not all psychoanalytic thought is considered neo-Freudian. Some psychoanalytic investigators, who are called **ego psychologists**, consider themselves Freudians who are elaborating his theory. Although they agree with Freud on the existence of the unconscious and the personality structure of id, ego, and superego, they believe that Freud devalued the ego by making the id too important. These ego psychologists take a more optimistic course than Freud did, focusing on the importance of the ego and insisting that it does more than merely try to satisfy the id and superego. Among the ego psychologists, Erik Erikson (b. 1902) has had a powerful influence on theories of personality development.

In line with the emphasis on ego instead of id, Erikson conceives of personality development in **psychosocial** terms. He agrees with Freud that the early years, when a child learns to reconcile biological drives with social demands, establish the individual's basic orientation to the world, but stresses the social rather than the instinctual sexual aspects of development. According to Erikson, a child develops a basic sense of trust during what Freud called the oral period, autonomy during the anal period, and initiative during what Freud called the phallic period. Failure to meet the developmental tasks of these periods leads, respectively, to mistrust, shame and doubt, and guilt. However, Erikson does not adhere to the Freudian belief that personality is unalterably determined in the initial years of life. He sees personality as continuing to develop throughout the life span, placing equal emphasis on the child's efforts to master the skills valued by society, on the adolescent's striving to achieve a sense of identity in that society, on the young adult's quest for intimacy, and on the mature person's desire to guide younger generations and thus contribute to society. Depending on how an individual negotiates these challenges, old age may bring a sense of integrity or despair.

In working out these "eight ages of man" (see Figure 18.1), Erikson expands Freud's concept of identification. He argues that the ego is not content simply to assimilate the values of a parent or other admired person, but strives to form an integrated, autonomous, unique "self," which Erikson calls **ego identity**. He has suggested that establishing an ego identity may be especially difficult in complex societies such as our own, which present the individual with a staggering array of choices in styles of living. In some societies, tradition prescribes the roles the individual

ERIKSON ON GANDHI

. . . I must now confess that a few times in your work (and often in the literature inspired by you) I have come across passages which almost brought *me* to the point where I felt unable to continue writing *this* book because I seemed to sense the presence of a kind of untruth in the very protestation of truth; of something unclean when all the words spelled out an unreal purity; and above all, of displaced violence where nonviolence was the professed issue.

. . . you seem either unaware of—or want to wish or pray away—an ambivalence, a coexistence of love and hate, which must become conscious in those who work for peace.

It is not enough any more —not after the appearance of your Western contemporary Freud—to be a watchful moralist. For we now have detailed insights into our inner ambiguities, ambivalences, and instinctual conflicts; and only an additional leverage of truth based on self-knowledge promises to give us freedom in the full light of conscious day, whereas in the past, moralist terrorism succeeded only in driving our worst proclivities underground, to remain there until riotous conditions of uncertainty or chaos would permit them to emerge redoubled.

You, Mahatmaji, love the story of that boy prince who would not accept the claim of his father, the Demon King, to a power greater than God's, not even after the boy had been exposed to terrible tortures. At the end he was made to embrace a red-hot metal pillar; but out of this suggestive object stepped God, half lion and half man, and tore the king to pieces.

. . . we must admit that you could not possibly have known of the power of that ambivalence which we have now learned to understand in case histories and life histories. . . . it is, therefore, not without compassion that I must point out that your lifelong insistence on the "innocence" (meaning sexlessness) of children is matched only by your inability to recognize the Demon King in yourself.

Source: From Erik H. Erikson, *Gandhi's truth: On the origins of militant nonviolence.* New York: W. W. Norton, 1969.

---

will play as an adult. A young person can count on living much as his father or her mother did, among relatives and neighbors known since childhood. By contrast, the intense struggle waged by adolescents in Western societies to achieve individuality and coherence led Erikson to describe the process as an **identity crisis**.

As this concept suggests, Erikson believes, as Fromm did, that the culture and times into which a person is born have a crucial effect on personality development. Psychosocial conflicts are universal and inevitable. However, at some point a society either eases its members' transition from one stage to another or exploits their fears and doubts. In other words, a society can reinforce growth or discourage it. A person's ego identity, Erikson (1950) argues, is grounded in the identity of the culture.

The effort to create a bridge between the study of individuals and the study of societies led Erikson in unorthodox directions. He worked among America's Sioux Indians to learn how historical circumstances and cultural differences affect child-rearing practices and the development of personality. And he was a pioneer in the field of **psychohistory**, the application of psychoanalytic principles to the study of historical figures. His biography of Martin Luther (Erikson, 1968), for example, focuses on the Protestant reformer's identity crisis. His admiring biography of India's great nonviolent political leader, Mahatma Gandhi, is a psychoanalytic interpretation not only of the man but also of his culture and times. The accompanying quotations from Erikson's book *Gandhi's Truth: On the Origins of Militant Nonviolence* (1969) appear in a section titled "A Personal Word," which Erikson wrote when he discovered that his insight as a psychoanalyst made it impossible to ignore certain flaws in Gandhi's character that might otherwise have been overlooked.

Other Recent Developments in Psychoanalytic Theory

The psychoanalytic tradition continues to stimulate study and controversy within psychology. One subject that has attracted the attention of psychoanalytic circles in recent years has been the origins of personality disorders, ingrained maladaptive patterns of behavior (see Chapter 22). In particular, the syndrome known as narcissistic personality disorder has come in for study. The narcissistic personality, which according to some observers is especially typical of our era, is characterized by a grandiose sense of self-importance, often accompanied by periodic feelings of inferiority. According to one theorist (Kernberg, 1975), this pattern develops as a defense against childhood feelings of rage and inferiority. A contrasting view (Kohut, 1977) sees narcissism as resulting from faulty ego development: the ego has never learned how to temper the demands of the id. These theories have in common with neo-Freudian thinking in general an emphasis on disturbance in relations within the family as a cause of abnormal personality development.

Evaluating Psychoanalytic Theories

Freud's thought has influenced all later attempts to explain personality, but psychoanalytic theories have been controversial since they were first enunciated. The feminist attack on Freud's analysis of female personality represents only one of the areas in which his and other psychoanalytic theories have been criticized.

Criticisms of Psychoanalytic Theory

A basic criticism of psychoanalytic theory has been the difficulty of testing its essential concepts. Some of them are vague and metaphorical and do not lend themselves to an objective formulation. Other concepts are stated as universals, such as Freud's pronouncement that all males must resolve an Oedipus conflict or Adler's dictum that everyone has a drive for superiority. Since the male Oedipal conflict can show itself either by a boy's displaying great love for his mother or by its opposite, when he represses that love and ignores her, the proposition as a whole simply cannot be tested. One portion of the male Oedipal conflict that has been examined—the expectation that the male identifies with his father's masculinity out of fear of him—has failed to pass the test (Fisher and

Greenberg, 1977). Instead, it appears that a positive, nurturant father eases both the boy's identification with his father and the internalization of the father's moral standards.

As a matter of fact, psychoanalytic theories are much better at hindsight than at foresight, and in Chapter 10 we explored the biases of hindsight. A look at the concept of instinct shows how hindsight is employed to explain behavior. We can say, for example, that a person who is continually involved in fights or arguments has a strong aggressive instinct, but only *after* the fact. Before an "instinct" is expressed, it is invisible and hence unpredictable, so that although psychoanalysis can provide logical explanations for the causes of behavior, it seems unable to predict future behavior.

Another criticism of psychoanalytic theories has focused on their heavy dependence on inference and interpretation. In the psychoanalytic view, a person who *never* shows aggression has repressed a basic instinct. Yet an unexpressed instinct cannot be observed; it can only be inferred. In the same way, the meaning of dreams, habits, accidents, or slips of the tongue can only be inferred. Does a woman leave her umbrella or gloves at a friend's house because she unconsciously wants to return there, or has she just been absentminded?

In fact, Freud's description of how personality is formed has not been supported. Studies have not demonstrated, for example, that "oral" or "anal" personalities are formed because of critical events in those stages of development. Nor has any consistent support been found for Freud's proposal that depression in adulthood is a reaction to the loss of a parent or other loved object in childhood (Crook and Eliot, 1980). His description of female personality development has simply not held up. Studies consistently indicate a much smaller difference between male and female personality development and organization than Freud supposed (Fisher and Greenberg, 1977). Freud's notion that women are culturally inferior was based on his supposition that male biology and male psychology constitute the norm for the species and on his observation of the role of women in European society at the turn of the century. Thus, his views of female personality development were bound to the culture of his time.

Psychoanalysis has also been criticized for the small size of the sample on which the theories are based. Most of Freud's published cases were upper-middle-class Viennese women, and on the statements of these adult females with emotional problems, Freud built a universal theory of personality development. Some investigators are uncomfortable with a theory of normal personality development that is based on retrospective childhood accounts of people with emotional problems.

Finally, Freud's metaphorical use of language has led to a reification of his concepts, so that they seem to lead a material existence. Although Freud stressed that he was speaking, not of places or things, but of states of mind, the continued use of metaphor has led to the impression that within each human mind three little creatures—the id, the ego, and the superego—wage a continual battle. Such use of language, though effective in fixing concepts, leads to a gross oversimplification of personality dynamics.

Contributions of Psychoanalytic Theory

Despite these criticisms, Freud has made a lasting contribution to our understanding of human beings. Although he was not a rigorous scientist, Freud was "a patient, meticulous, penetrating observer and a tenacious, disciplined, courageous, original thinker" (Hall and Lindzey, 1978). In fact, psychoanalytic theory has withstood a number of tests. When thousands of studies of psychoanalytic concepts were evaluated, many of Freud's concepts were supported (Fisher and Greenberg, 1977). As Freud proposed, many male homosexuals do seem to have a disturbed relationship with their fathers, who tend to be unfriendly or unapproachable. Children do seem to have an early erotic interest in the parent of the opposite sex; dreams do seem to provide a release for emotional tensions. People who focus on oral activities do tend to be dependent and passive—traits Freud considered "oral" (Masling et al., 1981; Masling,

Johnson, and Saturansky, 1974); those who are preoccupied with anal functions do tend to be parsimonious, compulsive, and orderly—traits Freud considered "anal."

Many basic psychoanalytic concepts, such as anxiety and defense mechanisms, have extended our understanding of human personality. The framework they provide for the explanation of abnormal behavior shows that bizarre and adaptive behavior result from the same developmental processes. As a result, we no longer divide the world into the "sick" and the "healthy," the "sane" and the "insane," but instead see people as falling somewhere on a continuum that shades imperceptibly from adaptive to maladaptive.

Psychoanalytic theory has also expanded our concept of motivation to include impulses, conflicts, or past experiences that have slipped from awareness. Even psychologists who do not accept the concept of an "unconscious" do accept the idea that we have stored much more information about the past than we are aware of. This general acceptance of the notion that much of our thought is unconscious has changed the way we look at art, at literature, and at life itself.

Finally, Freud's methods of psychoanalysis revolutionized the treatment of emotional problems. To Freud we owe the idea that individual psychotherapy (the "talking cure") can, through the relationship of patient and therapist, develop self-knowledge and thus increase the patient's control over her or his actions. Even forms of therapy that reject much or all of Freud's basic theory rely on variations of his technique.

Psychoanalysis has had an enormous influence on the thought of psychologists, psychiatrists, and ordinary citizens. Our tendency to see human behavior as richly determined by our past experiences and as reflecting irrational inner forces is in part the result of Freud's emphasis on both factors.

SUMMARY

1. Personality theorists, no matter what their approach, address two key issues: the consistency of an individual's behavior from one situation to the next and the differences in the behavior of individuals confronted with the same situation.

2. Sigmund Freud's psychoanalytic theory was the first formal theory of **personality**, and it has been the most influential. His concept of the **unconscious** is based on his study of the memories, wishes, and fears that were revealed through **free association**, in which

patients talked about their emotional conflicts; this process of bringing material from the unconscious into the conscious mind he called **psychoanalysis**. Freud found that dreams, jokes, and accidents also reveal unconscious conflicts. Dreams have both a **manifest content** (what the dreamer relates) and a **latent content** (the dream's underlying meaning).

3. According to Freud, the personality includes three separate but interacting systems: the id, the ego, and the superego. The **id** is that part of the mind that exists at birth. It is demanding and hedonistic and operates according to the pleasure principle. The **ego** begins to develop during the first year of life. Its task is to mediate between the id and reality, and it operates according to the reality principle. The **superego**, which begins to develop at the age of two or three, is concerned with meeting the demands of morality and social convention.

4. In the normal personality, the ego is able to satisfy the demands of the id without clashing excessively with the superego. The interplay of these conflicting forces within the mind is known as **psychodynamics**.

5. When psychic conflicts become extreme, the result is **anxiety**, a state of psychic pain that alerts the ego to danger. The ego attempts to avert anxiety in a variety of ways, frequently by the use of **defense mechanisms**. These include **repression**, pushing disturbing thoughts and memories back into the unconscious; **rationalization**, devising acceptable explanations to justify an action; **denial**, refusing to recognize a source of anxiety; **regression**, avoiding anxiety by returning to an earlier stage of development; **projection**, turning an inward threat from anxiety outward; **displacement**, expressing some feeling against an object that has not provoked it; and **reaction formation**, replacing an anxiety-producing feeling by its opposite. Freud also identified one "positive" defense mechanism, **sublimation**, in which emotional energy is diverted from its source and results in a valuable contribution to society.

6. Freud stressed the decisive role of infancy and childhood in determining basic personality structure. He believed that a child passes through a series of psychosexual stages, starting with the **pregenital** stage, which is divided into **oral**, **anal**, and **phallic** stages. After a period of **latency** comes the adolescent eruption of libidinal forces, which stabilize in the **genital** stage.

7. Carl Gustav Jung was one of the first neo-Freudians to break with Freud over theory. Jung believed that there were two kinds of unconscious: a **personal unconscious**, which is similar to Freud's concept, and a **collective unconscious**, consisting of **archetypes**, which are universal themes and images common to all human beings. Jung also believed that development continued beyond childhood.

8. A number of neo-Freudian theorists have modified psychoanalytic theory to acknowledge social as well as biological determinants. Alfred Adler's **individual psychology** emphasized the drive toward perfection as the highest human motivation. He believed that the inability to overcome a childhood sense of incompleteness results in an **inferiority complex**. According to Adler, as people mature they naturally work for **social interest**.

9. Karen Horney's theory of personality is based on the concepts of **basic anxiety**, which arises out of a child's sense of helplessness, and **basic hostility**, which arises from resentment against one's parents, Unexpressed hostility leads to three ways of behaving: moving toward others, moving against others, and moving away from others. In a normal person, these modes are integrated and each used when appropriate.

10. Erich Fromm's theory of personality is based on interpersonal relationships set in a historical context. He believed that there are five basic human needs: for relatedness, for transcendence, for rootedness, for personal identity, and for a frame of reference. Society —which can change—determines the ways in which these needs are expressed. When the social structure gives rise to alienation and despair, attempts to escape them can also lead to an escape from freedom.

11. Erik Erikson, an **ego psychologist**, conceives of personality in **psychosocial** terms and sees personality development as a lifelong process through eight stages. He believes that the ego strives to form an integrated, autonomous, unique "self," or **ego identity**. The struggle of Western adolescents to achieve individuality was described by Erikson as an **identity crisis**. Erikson pioneered in the field of **psychohistory**, trying to bridge the study of individuals and the study of societies.

12. Psychoanalytic theory has been criticized because its essential concepts are difficult to disconfirm, because it is better at explaining behavior than at predicting it, because it relies on inference, because it is based on an inadequate sample, and because its concepts have been reified. Some aspects of psychoanalytic theory have withstood testing, however, and the theory has contributed to our understanding of personality. Concepts such as anxiety and defense mechanisms have shown that bizarre and adaptive behavior result from the same developmental processes. Psychoanalytic theory has expanded our concepts of motivation to include unconscious conflicts. Freud originated the method of individual psychotherapy that revolutionized the treatment of the emotionally disturbed.

KEY TERMS

anal stage
analytic psychology
anxiety
archetypes
basic anxiety
basic hostility
collective unconscious
defense mechanism
denial
displacement
ego
ego identity
ego psychologist
extroversion
free association
genital stage

id
identity crisis
individual psychology
individuation
inferiority complex
introversion
latency
latent content
manifest content
moral anxiety
neurotic anxiety
oral stage
personality
personal unconscious
phallic stage
pregenital stage

projection
psychoanalysis
psychodynamics
psychohistory
psychosocial
rationalization
reaction formation
reality anxiety
regression
repression
social interest
sublimation
superego
traumatic
unconscious

RECOMMENDED READINGS

ERDELYI, M. H. *Psychoanalysis: Freud's cognitive psychology.* New York: W. H. Freeman, 1985. A modern exposition of psychoanalysis that brings it into play with developments in psychology and the neurosciences since Freud.

FISHER, S., and R. P. GREENBERG. *The scientific credibility of Freud's theories and therapy.* New York: Basic Books, 1977. This book provides a detailed review of research on Freudian theory.

FREUD, S. Introductory lectures on psychoanalysis. In J. Strachey (Ed. and Tr.), *The standard edition of the complete psychological works of Sigmund Freud.* Vols. 15 and 16. London: Hogarth Press, 1961 and 1963. (Originally published, 1917.) A readable overview of psychoanalysis by Freud himself.

HALL, C. S., and G. LINDZEY. *Theories of personality* (3rd ed.). New York; Wiley, 1978. This edition of the classic secondary source on theories of personality includes a chapter on contemporary psychoanalytic theory, with an excellent presentation of Erik Erikson's work, and a chapter on Eastern psychology and personality theory.

MADDI, S. R. *Personality theories: A comparative analysis* (3rd ed.). Homewood, Ill.: Dorsey Press, 1976. Classifies personality theorists according to whether their basic assumption relates to *conflict, fulfillment,* or *consistency.* Examines what the theorists have to say about the core and periphery of personality. Presents research on each position and draws conclusions about their strengths and weaknesses.

CHAPTER NINETEEN

HUMANISTIC, BEHAVIORISTIC, AND TRAIT THEORIES OF PERSONALITY

When we began the last chapter, we raised a number of questions about the human personality. First we pointed out something we all intuitively sense: each person appears to have a set of characteristics that seem—at least to some extent—to be relatively stable and enduring and that make his or her personality unique. Take, for example, a man named Roland. Roland is a doorman in an apartment building, and he does his low-prestige job with great dignity. We can predict that when we see him tomorrow morning he will give us a courteous greeting. The question is: What makes Roland the individual he is—why is he polite when another doorman might be surly? Another question is, what makes his behavior consistent over time? In the last chapter we suggested that the behavior patterns of an individual such as Roland might be shaped in part by his environment and in part by certain inner forces. As we described Freud's perspective on those inner forces: he believed they are powerful unconscious drives related to the individual's sexuality.

In this chapter we discuss some other psychologists' answers to these questions. One group, the humanistic psychologists, believe, like Freud, that people's behavior patterns are shaped to a large extent by inner forces—but they believe that those inner forces are positive drives toward love, joy, and creative inner expression rather than dark forbidden impulses the individual would try to repress. An entirely different school, the behavioristic psychologists, have tended to downplay the role of possible inner forces in people's behavior patterns. Some behaviorists have recognized the importance of individuals' unique ways of thinking (cognitive structures). But others have denied the impact of inner forces, or structures, completely, suggesting that only our environment, and what we have learned from it, offer any explanation of the way we behave.

The views of the humanists and the behaviorists are radically opposed, and they have fought a lively battle. The humanists have accused the behaviorists of treating human beings like robots ("Just program them and they will do whatever you want"), and the behaviorists have accused the humanists of vagueness, sentimentality, and cloudy thinking. We will watch this battle and weigh the debate ourselves.

But first we must consider some more basic issues. We said that Roland was a polite, dignified man, and that his behavior patterns could be explained by the interaction of environment and inner forces. (Exactly how we would see this interaction would depend on the theoretical camp we were in.) But do we really have a clear view of

Roland's personality to begin with? Are we sure he will display the same behavior patterns in all situations and at any time—a year from now or ten years from now? Addressing such issues has been the task of still another group of psychologists, known as the trait theorists. The trait theorists believe people do have consistent, enduring personality characteristics. Some other psychologists are not so sure.

TRAIT THEORIES

If you were looking for someone to sell vacuum cleaners for your company, you would probably make your choice on the basis of a hunch you had about the candidates' personality characteristics. You would probably choose an outgoing, sociable person rather than a person who spends more time with books than with people and seldom goes to parties. The characteristics you are looking for—outgoing personality and sociability—are the everyday equivalent of what psychologists call traits. A **trait** is a predisposition to respond in a consistent way in many different situations—in a dentist's office, at a party, or in a classroom. We can only *infer* that this predisposition exists; we cannot dissect it out of a person and look at it. But if we can specify an individual's traits, trait theorists say, we can understand that person and predict his or her behavior in the future.

Trait theories rest on two key assumptions. First, they assume that many traits exist in all people to some degree. Looking, for example, at the trait of dependency, trait theories assume that everyone can be classified as more or less dependent. Second, they assume that we can quantitatively measure the degree to which a trait exists in a person. For example, we could establish a scale on which an extremely dependent person would score 1 while a very independent person would score 10. Viewed from such a perspective, people can be classified on a continuum for any trait. For example, a few people are aggressive in many situations, and others rarely show a trace of aggression; most of us, however, fall somewhere in the middle.

Some psychologists, among them Gordon Allport, regard traits as real entities that exist in the mind. Most other theorists consider traits to be no more than metaphors psychologists can use in describing the uniqueness and consistency of human behavior. When trait theorists search for this underlying consistency, they look for the best way to describe the common features of a person's behavior. A trait theorist would assume that Roland's behavior as a doorman was typical of his behavior in other situations: reviewing all these situations, the trait theorist might try to discover whether Roland was proud, friendly, interested in people, self-confident, or something else. In other words, the theorist would ask, "What is the underlying structure that organizes Roland's behavior?"

Most (though not all) trait theorists believe that a few basic traits are central to individual personality. For example, if a person displayed superficial characteristics such as dependency and a lack of social aggressiveness, these might indicate a more basic trait such as a lack of self-confidence. If a personality is organized primarily around basic traits, then we could say that a person was dependent because she or he lacked self-confidence.

Allport's Classification of Traits

For nearly four decades trait theory was dominated by Gordon W. Alport (1897–1967), a researcher who had a lifelong interest in the uniqueness of each individual. Over the years, Allport (1937; 1961; 1966) developed and refined his theory, but he remained firm in his conclusion that traits accounted for the consistency of human behavior. In his view, the presence of a trait in a person could make a wide range of situations "functionally equivalent" for that person—that is, the person could interpret different situations as calling for a similar or identical response. For example, an aggressive person often would see aggressive behavior as an appropriate response.

The English language provides a vast array of specific descriptions for a countless number of behavioral responses. In 1936 Allport (Allport and Odbert, 1936) searched an unabridged dictionary, noting all the terms that could be used to describe people, and found about 18,000 different words. Even after omitting clearly evaluative terms (like "disgusting") and terms describing transient states (like "abashed"), between 4,000 and 5,000 items remained. Surely, Allport thought, this multitude of descriptions could be reduced to a few essentials.

In his attempt to clarify and simplify these descriptions, Allport described behavior as characterized by three kinds of traits: cardinal, central, and secondary. A **cardinal trait** is a single trait that so pervades a person's disposition that most of his or her acts seem dominated by it. A person whose "ruling passion" was greed or ambition could be characterized by a cardinal trait. Famous historical and mythical figures have given their names to cardinal traits. The term "Machiavellian," after the sixteenth-century Italian political theorist Niccolò Machiavelli, describes a person who persistently manipulates others; the term "narcissistic," after the Greek youth Narcissus, who fell in love with his own reflection, describes a person who is inordinately preoccupied with himself or herself.

Actually, Allport believed that cardinal traits are rare, and that most individuals do not have one predominant trait. Instead, on the basis of their life experiences, people develop a few **central traits**, habitual ways of responding to the world that can be summed up in trait names such as "honest," "sociable," or "affectionate." Less influential are **secondary traits**, characteristic modes of behavior that are less prominent than central traits and are seen in fewer situations. Secondary traits are subject to fluctuation and change; we can see them as generalized tastes and preferences that people display, such as preferences for certain foods or styles of music.

Allport believed that all people could be described in terms of their cardinal, central, and secondary traits. But he also made another key distinction: between traits he considered common traits and traits he considered individual traits. **Common traits** such as aggression, are basic modes of adjustment seen to some degree in all individuals. Because we must all interact in a competitive world, each of us develops our own level of aggression, and each of us can be placed somewhere on a scale of aggressiveness. But since each person is unique, Allport argued, each person also has **individual traits**, which are unique ways of organizing the world that cannot be applied to all people. Allport (1961) later renamed individual traits, calling them **personal dispositions**, since he believed that the uniqueness of individual experience led each person to develop a unique set of dispositions to behave in certain ways. A personal disposition cannot be measured by a standardized test; it can be discerned only by careful study of the individual.

Factor Analysis: Cattell and Eysenck

More recent theorists have concentrated on what Allport called common traits, trying to quantify them in a precise, scientific manner. Their pri-

mary tool in this task has been factor analysis, a statistical method that can be used to identify underlying factors in a number of different situations. (We will discuss factor analysis in detail in Chapter 20.) In applying factor analysis to personality, researchers look for underlying sources of consistency in behavior. Factor analysis is a powerful tool that has the same superiority over simpler statistical techniques that a three-dimensional model of a chemical molecule has over a two-dimensional blackboard diagram.

Raymond B. Cattell has used factor analysis extensively to study personality traits. Cattell identifies a trait as a tendency to react to related situations in a way that remains fairly stable. He distinguishes between two kinds of tendencies: surface traits and source traits. **Surface traits** describe clusters of behavior that tend to go together. An example of a surface trait is altruism, which involves such related behavior as helping a neighbor who has a problem and contributing to an annual blood drive. Other examples of surface traits are integrity, curiosity, realism, and foolishness. **Source traits** are the underlying roots or causes of these behavior clusters, and they are the focus of Cattell's research. Examples of source traits are ego weakness or strength, submissiveness or dominance, and timidity or venturesomeness. Surface traits generally correspond to commonsense descriptions of behavior and can often be measured by simple observation. But since surface traits are the result of interactions among source traits, explanations of behavior are not valid unless they are based on source traits, which are the stable, structural factors that determine personality. Cattell believes that by identifying both kinds of traits and learning to measure them, we will be able to specify the common characteristics that are shared by all people as well as the individual characteristics that distinguish one person from another.

Similar mathematical techniques have led Hans Eysenck to somewhat different conclusions about personality. According to Eysenck (1970), two major dimensions are critical for understanding normal human behavior: extroversion–introversion and neuroticism–stability. An extroverted person is one who is primarily interested in things or people outside his or her self; an introverted person is one whose attention tends to be more predominately fixed on his or her own inner concerns.

Eysenck proposes that these traits have a biological basis. He suggests, for example, that people who are extroverted have a low level of cortical arousal. That is, the extrovert's cerebral cortex is naturally rather quiet, so that she or he seeks stimulating environments, such as loud parties, intense social interactions, and risky situations, to increase arousal. The introvert, however, has a naturally high level of cortical arousal, so she or he seeks situations that minimize stimulation, such as sitting quietly alone. This basic difference has been consistently supported by research. Extroverts fall asleep more quickly than introverts and are less sensitive to pain, suggesting that extroverts operate at a lower level of arousal. As noted in Chapter 12, various studies have found that arousal seems to be related to performance: moderate levels of arousal lead to optimal performance and performance deteriorates when arousal is too low or too high (Yerkes and Dodson, 1908, Broadhurst, 1959; Duffy, 1962). This difference in arousal may explain why extroverts do better on ability tests if they are under time pressure or if they have had caffeine. Just the opposite is true for introverts, who appear to be more highly aroused: they do better with no time pressure and without caffeine (Revelle, Amaral, and Turriff, 1976). However, the time of day when people are tested complicates these results. Extroverts, particularly those who are impulsive, are helped by caffeine in the morning but hindered in the evening. The opposite is true for introverts; they are hindered by caffeine in the morning but helped by it in the evening. Thus, it appears that extroverts and introverts may not differ in general arousal, but in the rhythm of their daily arousal, with introverts being more aroused in the morning and less aroused in the evening as compared to extroverts (Revelle et al., 1980).

Whether or not Eysenck's theory is correct, he has shown that once basic traits have been identified by factor analysis, they can be used in the development of sophisticated theories to account for human behavior.

The Act Frequency Approach: Buss and Craik

In the work of Allport, Cattell, and Eysenck, we saw how psychologists try to discern underlying dispositions in a person by using objective measurements and operational definitions of inferred characteristics. We all tend to judge the personalities of people we know, labeling them with various traits and making such comments as, "He is a jock" or "She is a grind." But of course, we don't use statistical methods. What basis *do* we use for these everyday judgments?

Attempting to understand this process, David Buss and Kenneth Craik (1983) have proposed an **act frequency approach** to personality. Buss and Craik believe we tend to add up all of a person's actions that fit a particular category (say, submissiveness), and then assign a trait to the person on that basis. When we observe a person over a period of time and conclude that he or she is a submissive person (has the trait of submissiveness), we are saying that this person has behaved in a submissive manner more often than most people do. Such a person may sometimes act in a dominant manner—for example, even though this person behaves submissively a dozen times over a two-week period, he or she may also behave dominantly twice—but we still call this person submissive. Note that this approach does assume that the person's behavior is affected by the situation. But it does not specify under what circumstances a person is submissive or dominant.

Buss and Craik emphasize that while the act frequency approach can be used to predict a person's behavior, it makes no attempt to explain how personality differences develop. It says nothing about why one person often behaves in a submissive fashion whereas another often behaves in a dominant fashion.

Evaluation of Trait Theories

Trait theories have been criticized as not very useful in understanding human behavior. Providing a label, say critics, does not provide an explanation. Worse, it may lure us into circular reasoning: if we say that one of the characteristics of friendliness is smiling, we have learned nothing when we are told that John smiles because he is friendly. There is also the danger that once a trait has been labeled, it tends to take on an existence of its own. We think of it as a "thing" instead of simply a shorthand description for a behavioral tendency in a person. Another criticism of trait theory is that it tends to obscure individual differences. And, finally, critics say that there is little evidence that traits persist across situations.

Despite its shortcomings, the trait approach is useful in two ways. First, the names of traits provide a way to describe individual differences in behavior. They allow us to summarize a person's typical behavior and, when there is a reasonable degree of stability, to forecast future behavior in similar situations (Buss and Craik, 1983). Second, traits can be regarded as predispositions to respond *in particular situations* (Revelle, 1983). For example, a person who is high in anxiety may not always be more anxious than other people; but when placed in a situation that gives rise to anxiety, the anxious person may respond more rapidly and more intensely. When psychologists use the concept of traits in this way, they explicitly recognize the interaction of person and situation. This approach to trait theory provides a richer, more complex picture of personality.

A Current Controversy: Personality versus Situational Factors

We know intuitively that there must be some interaction between personality and situation. But exactly what is that interaction? Consider the following situation. Last night you observed Karen at a party. She stood quietly in a corner of the room, seemingly more interested in the books on the wall beside her than in her fellow guests. She spoke in response to direct questions, but her replies were brief, and when the person talking to her wandered away she made no attempt to seek out anyone else. What kind of statement can you make about Karen's personality? That depends on how you explain her behavior. If you think her behavior is due primarily to her underlying disposition, you might say that she is basically shy and insecure. But if you think her behavior is due primarily to the situation in which she finds herself, you might guess that none of Karen's friends is at the party, or that she is tired, or that her past experiences with large parties have led her to expect few fellow guests who share her interest. Among friends or at a smaller party, she might appear sociable and outgoing.

Explanations of Karen's behavior echo the basic questions of personality theory: Why do different individuals behave differently in the same situation? And why does an individual's pattern of behavior remain fairly consistent over the years? Most theories of personality see behavior as resulting from the interaction of person and situation, with some theories emphasizing the situation more than the person and others emphasizing enduring aspects of the person. Trait theorists

have in the past emphasized the influence of disposition.

In 1968, Walter Mischel cast a shadow across the field of personality theory and research. Reviewing one study after another, Mischel showed that correlations between personality-trait measures and behavior rarely exceeded .30.

Mischel thought he had seen enough evidence to conclude that broad personality-trait measures are of little value in predicting behavior outside of test situations. Mischel's argument generated a heated debate.

What is the meaning of the fact that our behavior is generally inconsistent across situations? Does that mean that we are hypocritical or confused? Not at all. It means that we are probably adapting appropriately to the requirements of different situations. The greatest consistency may be shown by people who are immature or who cannot cope with challenging situations. In a two-year study of emotionally disturbed children attending summer camp, children showed the most consistent behavior when they were placed in situations that exceeded their competencies (Mischel, 1984). When under stress, children who had been rated as aggressive consistently became aggressive and children who had been rated as withdrawn consistently withdrew. When situations were less demanding and the children could deal adequately with them, however, there was little cross-situational consistency in their behavior. For example, "aggressive" children showed only a modest consistency in their behavior across less demanding situations, while they still tended to be consistently aggressive when placed under stress. Mischel suggests that lack of consistency probably indicates healthy, competent functioning, in which people are adapting to the demands of the situation.

No matter what theoretical approach to personality researchers hold, their views seem slowly to be converging. We can glimpse the outline of a consensus, in which both consistencies and variations in behavior are recognized: people's behavior patterns are consistent to a certain degree, yet still remain flexible to allow the individual to adapt to a particular situation.

Now let us return to the question of how variability and consistency come about. Is it through learning and responding to the demands of the environment, or is it through inner drives of the individual? The first viewpoint we will consider is that of the behaviorists.

Behavioral Theories of Personality

Since the beginning of this century, American psychology has been concerned with animal and human learning. A number of prominent American psychologists—among them Edward L. Thorndike, John B. Watson, Edward Tolman, Clark Hull, and B. F. Skinner—are known for their research on learning. Naturally, when Freud's ideas became known in American universities, learning theorists took note and some tried to assimilate his work into their own theories of personality development.

Dollard and Miller's Behavior Theory

The most ambitious attempt at assimilation of Freud's ideas was made during the 1940s at Yale University by John Dollard and Neal Miller. Their behavior theory represents an effort to translate the psychodynamic phenomena identified by Freud into the concepts developed by behavioristic learning theorists.

In Dollard and Miller's theory (1950), personality is composed of habits that are made up of learned associations between various stimuli and responses. Neurotic behavior is learned in the same way as any other behavior and is simply an extreme instance of ordinary conflict, in which two motives clash, so that satisfying one motive frustrates the other. Such a situation is called an **approach–avoidance conflict**, and the analysis of it is based on several assumptions (Dollard and Miller, 1950). First, the nearer an organism comes to a goal, the stronger the tendency to approach it. Second, the nearer an organism comes to a feared object or situation, the stronger the tendency to avoid it. Third, as an organism nears an object, the tendency to avoid something that is feared increases more rapidly than does the tendency to approach something that is desired. Fourth, the stronger the drive that is behind an organism's tendency to approach or avoid something, the stronger the tendency will be. The typical approach–avoidance conflict is represented in Figure 19.1, which graphically translates these tendencies into gradients.

Conflict occurs when avoidance and approach tendencies have equal strength. People caught in an approach–avoidance conflict vacillate and can be trapped in a situation that both attracts and

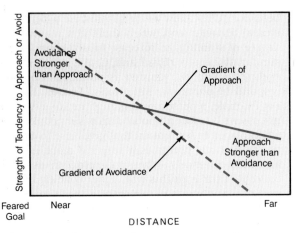

Figure 19.1. Simple graphic representation of an approach–avoidance conflict. The tendency to approach is the stronger of the two tendencies far from the goal, while the tendency to avoid is the stronger of the two near to the goal. Therefore, when far from the goal, the subject should tend to approach part way and then stop; when near to it, he should tend to retreat part way and then stop. In other words, he should tend to remain in the region where the two gradients intersect. (Adapted from Dollard and Miller, 1950.)

repels them. For example, after breaking up, a couple often try to patch up their differences. While they are living apart, the tendency to approach is strong, and they reunite. But living together allows the negative aspects of their relationship to resurface and again they break up, retreating because the tendency to avoid unpleasantness becomes strongest near the goal.

Dollard and Miller's approach was important for two reasons. First, it showed that psychoanalytic observations could be translated into a more testable learning framework. Second, it helped pave the way for behavior therapy—a set of procedures, based on learning principles, for changing neurotic and psychotic behavior. (In Chapter 24 we will consider behavior therapy in detail.)

Skinner's Radical Behaviorism

Although his radical behaviorism is not a theory of personality, through his general influence B. F. Skinner has had a great impact on personality theory. Unlike Dollard and Miller, Skinner rejects such concepts as drive because they cannot be directly observed and must be inferred (Skinner, 1975). Moreover, Skinner sees no need for a general concept of personality structure. He focuses instead on a *functional* analysis of behavior—that is, an analysis of the relationships between environmental events and a particular response. This exclusive focus on the environment is known as radical behaviorism, because it makes no allowance for cognitive or symbolic processes. For example, if a radical behaviorist were asked to analyze the personality of Karen, the girl we saw at the party, he or she would focus on the situation, discussing Karen's various actions purely in terms of past reinforcements she had received in similar situations. In this approach, anyone whose history of reinforcement was identical to Karen's would respond exactly as she did in each situation.

In his analysis of behavior, Skinner (1971) says that internal events, such as thoughts and feelings, can be ignored because they are by-products of external observable events, particularly the consequences that follow a response. Notice that Skinner does not deny the existence of internal events, only their importance in understanding behavior. Consider a man who gets into an argument and punches his opponent in the jaw. Asked why he did it, the man might say he was angry and "felt" like hitting the other person. For Skinner, this feeling is a by-product of previous reinforcement. He would say that it would be more to the point to ask what has happened to the man during previous arguments. If his use of violence has been reinforced (that is, if his opponent backed down, he got his way, or he was admired by others), he becomes increasingly likely to react aggressively in similar situations. To describe him as "aggressive" only sums up his previous history of reinforcement; it says nothing about his "nature." Skinner believes that, because any behavior can be explained by reinforcing events in the past, internal events can be safely ignored.

Arguing that all behavior is controlled by rewards and punishment, Skinner describes, in his novel *Walden Two* (1948), how these principles might be applied to produce a utopian society (see Figure 19.2). He then goes on to analyze contemporary society in *Beyond Freedom and Dignity* (1971), taking the position that individual freedom is an illusion and that the only way to produce a better world is to change the contingencies of reinforcement. Many of today's problems, he suggests, are worsened because society provides rewards for actions that are considered destructive or immoral. For example, corporations make higher profits if they allow their factories to emit pollutants that contribute to the acid rain that is

"After all, it's a simple and sensible program. . . . We set up a system of gradually increasing annoyances and frustrations against a background of complete serenity. An easy environment is made more and more difficult as the children acquire the capacity to adjust."

"But why? . . . What do (the children) get out of it?"

"What do they get out of it! . . . what they get is escape from the petty emotions which eat the heart out of the unprepared. They get the satisfaction of pleasant and profitable social relations. . . . They get new horizons, for they are spared the emotions characteristic of frustration and failure."

Figure 19.2. Can that green-eyed monster of jealousy —as well as other destructive or antisocial emotions —be eliminated, or will such emotions always haunt us? This dialogue from *Walden Two*, Skinner's novel about a utopian society, gives us his answer. Traits and emotions are seen not as inherent biological qualities or essences, but as learned and therefore, *controllable* or *extinguishable* behaviors. Through principles of operant conditioning and reinforcement, Skinner argues, we can engineer a perfect society. Do you agree? (Skinner, 1948.)

destroying eastern lakes and forests than if they install expensive pollution-control devices. Instead of blaming this problem on the personality characteristics of greedy managers, Skinner would suggest that we should change the contingencies reinforcing corporate behavior. If, for example, the tax code made it more profitable to control pollution than to pollute the air, management would quickly clean up the discharge from factories.

Although Skinnerian principles have led to the development of effective ways of changing behavior, most behaviorists do not ignore internal events. As we saw in Chapter 8, social learning theorists acknowledge the importance of cognitive or symbolic activities as determinants of behavior, and cognitive behaviorists, who emphasize the role of cognition as intervening between stimulus and response, take a similar approach (Kendall and Hollon, 1979; 1981).

Society rewards some destructive actions. Shown here, a recent convention of mercenaries, "soldiers of fortune," held in Las Vegas. On the program were speeches, souvenirs, reunions, and an exhibition of the latest killing weapons.

Social Learning Theory

Views of personality based on social learning theory, including those of cognitive behaviorists, differ most sharply from Skinner's radical behaviorism in their belief that the cognitive capabilities of human beings—the ability to reason, remember, and think abstractly—play an important role in determining human action.

Social learning theorists' conceptualization suggests images of human existence that are very different from those of the radical behaviorists. From the radical behaviorists' view, we should look only at two components, environment and behavior, with behavior a relatively passive response to the environment. In the social learning view, by contrast, we should look at the environment, the behavior, *and* the person who is performing the behavior. Each of these three factors influences, and is influenced by, the others (Bandura, 1977; 1978).

According to the social learning theorists, our behavior is indeed partly determined by events in the environment, but it is also determined by cognitive events that are unique for each person. We actively transform the environment. First, we perceive each situation in the light of our own memories, competencies, expectations, self-standards, rules, and values; second, we can alter the situation to suit our desires. For this reason,

social learning theorists and cognitive behaviorists place more emphasis on the interaction between the individual person and the situation than do radical behaviorists.

The Acquisition of Behavior

Social learning theorists maintain that most new behavior is acquired through observational learning, in which we watch the actions of models and vicariously experience their rewards and punishments. As noted in Chapter 8, we can acquire attitudes, emotions, and social styles as well as practical information in this way. For example, suppose that you get a summer job waiting on tables in a restaurant. You carefully watch the most experienced waiter, who is always attentive and friendly with the customers. You mentally rehearse his procedures, from the smile with which he greets each diner to the way in which he presents the check. Then, when you wait on tables yourself, you imitate his attentive, friendly manner.

Social learning theorists do not believe that reinforcement is needed for people to learn by observing models, although reinforcement can make such learning easier. However, once the behavior is learned, reinforcement becomes important if the learner is to repeat the behavior

(Rosenthal and Bandura, 1978). In other words, you may learn the mechanics of taking orders and serving food without receiving any reward yourself, but you are unlikely to retain the experienced waiter's friendly manner or volunteer to handle extra tables unless your imitative behavior is reinforced by a raise, increased tips, or the approval of other waiters. Such reinforcement does not automatically strengthen a given response, as radical behaviorists assume; instead it serves as additional information obtained through direct experience, which gives you incentives to continue patterning your behavior after the experienced waiter.

The Regulation and Maintenance of Behavior

According to social learning theory, once behavior has been acquired it is regulated and maintained by three kinds of control: stimulus control, reinforcement control (both of which are also seen as controls in radical behaviorism), and cognitive control.

Stimulus control means that some particular behavior takes place only when a particular stimulus in the environment evokes it at the appropriate time. In this case, behavior is under the control of the situation, and stimuli in the environment determine whether we are friendly or withdrawn in a specific situation. Stimuli that occur in social situations may be indirect and their message may not always be clear. A person who asks, "How are you?" may only be expressing politeness, not concern, and is not interested in the details of your recent fight with your roommate. The stimuli of facial expressions and gestures often must be interpreted to determine whether certain behavior will be rewarded.

Reinforcement control regulates and maintains behavior by rewarding an individual after she or he has behaved in a particular way. If Jill has frequently been rewarded for aggressiveness, she will tend to react aggressively in most situations in which it is a possible option. Intermittent schedules of reinforcement, in which rewards come only after a varying number of responses, are effective at maintaining behavior long after reinforcement has ceased. That this kind of reinforcement control is effective in maintaining high "addictive" rates of behavior can be confirmed by looking down the rows of slot machines in any

casino, where people stuff coins into slots as fast as they can, many of them playing two or more machines at the same time.

Cognitive control is the process by which our cognitive appraisal and self-reinforcement guide and maintain our behavior. Cognitive appraisal refers to the person's interpretation of a stimulus: according to this view, we respond not to the stimulus itself but to the way we interpret it after we have filtered it through the screen of our memories, beliefs, and expectations. Suppose that while you are giving a talk, you notice several members of the audience get up and walk out. You might view their behavior as evidence of boredom, an interpretation that might make you so anxious that you stumble over the rest of your talk. However, if you interpret the departure as unrelated to yourself, perhaps attributing it to a train schedule or a class meeting, you are likely to be unruffled and continue to make a smooth presentation (Meichenbaum, 1975). Which interpretation you give to the stimulus will be related to your own experiences and beliefs.

Self-reinforcement refers to our tendency to compare our own behavior to an internalized standard and then either approve (reinforce) or criticize (punish) our actions. Self-reinforcement can be external or internal. External self-reinforcement can take the form of rewarding yourself with a new pair of shoes, a movie, or dinner at a good restaurant for any behavior you consider desirable—getting an A on an exam, losing five pounds, cleaning up the attic, or exercising faithfully each day for a week. Internal self-reinforcement is more common; it takes the form of patting yourself on the back for the same sort of activity, or for such accomplishments as playing a piano sonata without striking the wrong keys or completing a marathon run. Such self-reinforcement may account for the sort of modeling that occurs without external reinforcement. Take, for example, the young person who copies Michael Jackson's mannerisms—down to wearing a single white glove. It is possible that for this individual the imagined prospect of being like the admired model will be sufficient reward.

All three types of controls—stimulus, reinforcement, and cognitive—work together. Stimuli that are physically present trigger cognitive representations (images or symbols) of other stimuli, which lead to expectations of reinforcement, which in turn lead to behavior that can lead to direct reward.

Social Learning Theory as a Theory of Personality

How does social learning theory account for the fact that each person reacts to a situation in a unique manner, and the fact that each person's behavior is relatively stable and consistent over time? According to Walter Mischel (1973; 1979), social learning theory can explain both the uniqueness of a person's behavior and its consistency by means of five overlapping and interlocking concepts:

1. *Competencies:* Through learning and experience, each person has acquired a unique set of skills for dealing with various situations.
2. *Encodings:* Each person has a unique way of perceiving and categorizing experience; one person may see a situation as threatening while another sees it as challenging, and each responds accordingly.
3. *Expectancies:* Through learning, each person has acquired different expectations of being rewarded or punished for various kinds of behavior.
4. *Values:* The value a person places on various rewards—such as money, social approval, and good grades—influences the person's behavior.
5. *Plans:* Through learning, each person formulates plans and rules that guide behavior. One person may plan to lose five pounds and then pass up delicious desserts; another may plan to enter politics and then avoid any actions that could later be used against her or him by a political opponent.

These cognitive aspects of personality are seen by Mischel as products of past learning and at the same time as guides for future learning. A continuous interaction takes place between individuals and the situations they confront, an interaction that leads to new learning and to further development of personality.

Social learning theory has developed into a complex system of concepts that attempt to account for the variety and complexity of human behavior. It has a distinct behavioristic flavor, because of its emphasis on observable phenomena and its avoidance of psychoanalytic concepts such as instinct and unconscious motivation. Yet it has moved beyond the radical behaviorist position to emphasize the causal role of characteristically human abilities, such as cognition, the use of symbols, reasoning, and language.

Evaluating Behavioral Theory

The contributions of behavioral theories to the study of personality have been twofold: they have contributed a great deal to the treatment of behavior disorders, and their focus on the objective aspects of personality has changed psychology. The application of behavior therapy to personal problems has resulted in treatments that are faster, cheaper, and often more effective than treatments that have come out of other theoretical approaches to personality. Behavior therapy has been used to end smoking and bed-wetting, to help mentally retarded people become more nearly self-sufficient, to end phobias such as intense fear of snakes, and to draw children out of the isolation of autism (Kazdin and Wilson, 1978). We shall examine such programs in detail in Chapter 24.

The objectivity of behavioral theories of personality stands in sharp contrast to the vague, inferential statements that have come from some other theories of personality. Because behaviorists use clearly defined language and study behavior that can be measured, their claims can be tested and retested. Today almost all research in psychology uses a behavioral methodology, which is based on experimentation, objective measurement, and operational definitions of inferred constructs (Bootzin and Acocella, 1984).

Despite behavioral theories' contributions, they have been criticized. The quarrels of other theorists with behaviorism center on charges that it oversimplifies life, that it is deterministic, and that it can lead to totalitarianism. Because it reduces human action to small, measurable units of behavior and ignores thought and feeling, the behavioristic approach has been criticized as a naïve *oversimplification* of human existence that distorts whatever behavior it measures (London, 1969). The exclusion of thought and feeling by radical behaviorists, it is charged, means that behaviorists refuse to study anything that distinguishes the human species from other animals; hence, their principles are simply not applicable to human beings. By giving a major role to cognitive processes, social learning theory appears to meet these criticisms, but some critics argue that this new behaviorism is still oversimplified. They maintain that a person's personality is determined by more than the easily accessible self-statements upon which social learning theorists have focused.

Behavioristic theories are also criticized because they are *deterministic*, a charge that arises because behaviorists see most human behavior as the product of conditioning. Not free will, they say, but the stimuli that surround us determine what we will do. The position taken by radical behaviorists, in which a person's behavior is primarily a response to stimuli and—in theory—would be completely predictable if only that individual's reinforcement theory were known, is responsible for most such criticism (Overton and Reese, 1973). Social learning theory takes the individual's cognitive processes into account and sees the individual as initiating actions, but it is also deterministic in that it regards our expectations, our perceptions, and even our self-reinforcement as influenced by learning. All scientific study of behavior aims at identifying the causes of that behavior, however; thus, this level of determinism is, in fact, the general scientific position. It is found in most theories of personality with the exception of those proposed by humanistic psychologists, who instead emphasize choice and self-actualization.

Finally, Skinner's idea that all behavior is controlled by environmental rewards—and that we could develop a pleasanter, fairer society simply by designing programs to reinforce socially responsible behavior—is a frightening concept to many people. Skinner's use of the word "control" is generally misinterpreted, however. In *Walden Two*, no one is coerced or forced to behave in any particular way. Instead Skinner uses "control" to mean "predictability" or "lawfulness." For example, a little girl's attempts to ride a bicycle show lawful behavior. She gradually eliminates those responses that lead to falling down and increases the frequency of responses that keep her balanced. She is not coerced into behaving that way, but her behavior is being "controlled" by its consequences. Skinner has acknowledged that the principles of behavior modification could be used by totalitarian governments (Hall, 1972). But he also points out that control works in two directions: individuals may be in part controlled, but they can also exert countercontrol by changing the environment and by using self-reinforcement. In fact, recent behavioral research and theory have taken the position that the individual must be an active participant in any effective attempts to change behavior, and most contemporary applications of behavior therapy are based on self-management and self-regulation.

Each student of psychology will make his or her own evaluation of the criticisms that have been aimed at behavioristic theory. But for a rounded picture of the range of opinion concerning behaviorism, it is important to gain some familiarity with a group of psychologists who have been among behaviorism's sharpest critics. These are the humanistic psychologists, a group who have placed strong emphasis on people's inner drives toward growth, happiness, and creative expression. The humanistic psychologists believe these forces are more crucial in the shaping of people's behavior patterns than are the pressures of their surroundings.

HUMANISTIC THEORIES

Humanistic psychologists emphasize the potential of human beings for growth, creativity, and spontaneity. They stress the uniqueness of the individual and her or his freedom to make choices. The most influential humanistic psychologists have been Abraham Maslow and Carl Rogers.

Maslow's Humanistic Psychology

The guiding spirit behind humanistic psychology has generally been identified as the American psychologist Abraham Maslow (1908–1970). Maslow deliberately set out to create what he called a "third force" in psychology as an alternative to psychoanalysis and behaviorism. He based his theory of personality on the characteristics of healthy, creative people who used all their talents, potential, and capabilities, rather than on studies of disturbed individuals as Freud had done. These healthy people, according to Maslow (1971a; 1971b), strive for and achieve **self-actualization**. They develop their own potential to its fullest, yet instead of competing with others, each strives to be "the best me I can be." Maslow (1966; 1968) believed that most psychologists were pessimistic, dwelling too heavily on the misery, conflict, shame, hostility, and habit that kept people from fulfilling their potential. Instead, Maslow took an optimistic view of human beings, stressing their possibilities and their capabilities for love, joy, and artistic expression. There is an active drive toward health in every person, Maslow believed, an impulse toward the actualization of one's potentialities. But because human instincts are so weak in comparison with those of animals, a person's impulses toward self-actualization can be distorted by society, habit, or faulty education.

Maslow (1955) identified two groups of human needs: basic needs and metaneeds. The basic needs are physiological (food, water, sleep, and so on) and psychological (affection, security, and self-esteem, for example). These basic needs are also called **deficiency needs** because if they are not met, a person, lacking something, will seek to make up for the deficiency. The basic needs are hierarchically organized, meaning that some (such as the need for food) take precedence over others.

The higher needs Maslow called **metaneeds**, or **growth needs**. They include the need for justice, goodness, beauty, order, and unity. In most instances, deficiency needs take priority over growth needs. People who lack food or water cannot attend to justice or beauty. Nor, according to Maslow, can those who lack basic security and self-esteem feel free to consider fairness; to feel deep, reciprocal 'love; to be democratic; or to resist restrictive conformity. Since metaneeds are not hierarchically organized, one metaneed can be pursued instead of another, depending on a person's circumstances. The metaneeds are real, and when they are not met, **metapathologies**, such as alienation, anguish, apathy, and cynicism, can develop.

By studying a group of historical figures whom he considered to be self-actualized—among them Abraham Lincoln, Henry David Thoreau, Ludwig van Beethoven, Thomas Jefferson, William James, Eleanor Roosevelt, and Albert Einstein—Maslow (1954) developed a portrait of the self-actualized person, who shows the personality characteristics listed in Table 19.1. Included in Maslow's studies of self-actualized people were college students and some of his own friends.

Because Maslow (1968) believed that people differed in their capabilities and that some needs were idiosyncratic, his explanation of personality stressed disposition over situation. But he also took into account, in a large sense, the impact of the environment on a person's personality. The values of a culture could have a powerful influence on the development of personality characteristics; so could the degree to which the environment had met the person's needs. Thus, the larger situation would have an impact on the individual's disposition, and in this way, could have a strong though indirect effect on behavior.

Maslow has had a wide influence on American psychology. He has inspired many researchers to pay attention to healthy, productive people and has led many group leaders, clinicians, and psychologists working in organizations to seek ways of promoting the growth and self-actualization of workers, students, and people in therapy.

Table 19.1 ▪ Characteristics of Self-Actualized Persons

They are realistically oriented.	They identify with mankind.
They accept themselves, other people, and the natural world for what they are.	Their intimate relationships with a few specially loved people tend to be profound and deeply emotional rather than superficial.
They have a great deal of spontaneity.	Their values and attitudes are democratic.
They are problem-centered rather than self-centered.	They do not confuse means with ends.
They have an air of detachment and a need for privacy.	Their sense of humor is philosophical rather than hostile.
They are autonomous and independent.	They have a great fund of creativeness.
Their appreciation of people and things is fresh rather than stereotyped.	They resist conformity to the culture.
Most of them have had profound mystical or spiritual experiences although not necessarily religious in character.	They transcend the environment rather than just coping with it.

Source: Maslow A. *Motivation and personality.* New York: Harper & Row, 1954.

The Self Theory of Rogers

Also closely identified with humanistic psychology is the American clinical psychologist Carl Rogers. Like Maslow, Rogers believes that people are governed by an innate impulse toward positive growth. In contrast to Maslow, however, Rogers developed his theory from observations made while practicing psychotherapy, not from studying self-actualized people. Most of Rogers' clients seemed unable to accept their own feelings and experiences. In their youth they had apparently come to believe that unless they acted in distorted or dishonest ways, others would neither like nor love them. So in order to be accepted, they had begun to deny their feelings.

Most children encounter this problem to some extent, says Rogers (1971), because they discover that they are objects of **conditional positive regard**. When they do not conform to family standards or the standards of society, their parents and other powerful people withhold love and praise. A boy who comes to dinner with dirty hands may be told that he is "disgusting" and sent away from the table. If he prefers to stay home and read instead of going over to a friend's house, he may be told that he is a "bookworm" who should get out more. But if he keeps his hands clean and decides to join the local soccer team, he is likely to be rewarded by smiles and compliments. Because conditions are placed on positive regard, a process begins in which the child learns to act and feel in ways that earn approval from others rather than in ways that may be more intrinsically satisfying.

The process continues into adulthood, and to maintain positive regard, adults suppress actions and feelings that are unacceptable to important people in their lives, rather than guiding their behavior by their own spontaneous perceptions and feelings. The result of this process is the establishment of what Rogers calls **conditions of worth**—extraneous standards whose attainment assures positive regard. When an individual is trying to live up to these standards, he or she is likely to misperceive, distort, or deny any experiences that do not meet his or her conditions of worth. If the conditions of worth are rigid, so that the person's behavior is no longer flexible, emotional problems can arise. One young woman whose life followed such a course was persuaded while she was still in high school to give up the idea of a career devoted to helping others. Docility and mildness were part of her conditions of worth;

so, as she always had done, she acceptd her parents' values and rejected her own perceptions and wishes. Within a few years she was engaged to a young man who defined her life for her. But she finally discovered that she was "everything that *he* wanted to be and nothing that *I* was" (Rogers, 1980, p. 209). Realizing that she was ignoring her own perceptions and emotions, she broke the engagement and entered therapy.

The discomfort an individual may undergo when his or her experiences are denied and distorted to this degree highlights the distinction Rogers makes between the organism and the self. He defines the **organism** as the total range of a person's possible experiences; the **self**, by contrast, consists only of the parts of those experiences that the individual recognizes and accepts. Ideally, the organism and the self should be identical, because a person should, in principle, be able to recognize and accept all experience. In practice, however, the organism and the self often oppose each other (see Figure 19.3). For example, the self can deny consciousness to certain sensory and emotional experiences simply by refusing to symbolize or conceptualize them. This idea is similar to the psychoanalytic concept of repression and to its neo-Freudian reformulations. According to Rogers, a person may deny feelings or experiences if they are incompatible with the self-concept. Even an action can be disowned by saying, "I don't know why I did it" or "I must have been carried away."

According to Rogers (1971), psychological adjustment "exists when the concept of the self is such that all sensory and visceral experiences of the organism are, or may be, assimilated on a symbolic level into a consistent relationship with the concept of self." The characteristics of psychologically adjusted, or **fully functioning**, people are openness to experience, absence of defensiveness, accurate awareness, unconditional positive self-regard, and generally harmonious relations with other people.

If the breach between the self and the organism grows too wide, the person may become defensive, tense, conflicted, and unable to relate well to others. Such people are often argumentative and hostile, and they may project their denied feelings onto others. In Chapter 24 we shall see how Rogers' therapeutic methods attempt to heal the split between the self and the organism, so that the person learns to accept all experiences as genuine. Although nearly all people are subjected

Figure 19.3. Carl Rogers believes that the fundamental problem of personality is how to make the self more congruent with the total experience of the organism. It is through the therapeutic relationship, in which the therapist creates an atmosphere of total acceptance, or "unconditional positive regard," that the client may achieve closer—or even complete—congruence. (From Rogers, 1971.)

This, as we see it, is the basic estrangement in man. He has not been true to himself, to his own natural organismic valuing of experience, but for the sake of preserving the positive regard of others has now come to falsify some of the values he experiences and to perceive them only in terms based upon their value to others. Yet this has not been a conscious choice, but a natural—and tragic—development in infancy. The path of development toward psychological maturity, the path of therapy, is the undoing of this estrangement in man's functioning, the dissolving of conditions of worth, the achievement of a self which is congruent with experience, and the restoration of a unified organismic valuing process as the regulator of behavior.

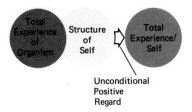

to conditional positive regard, most do not develop so much hostility or defensiveness, or have so much difficulty relating to others, that they require therapy. But what about a person who receives **unconditional positive regard**—someone who reaps approval and acceptance no matter what he or she does? Will such an individual become selfish, cruel, and destructive? After all, it is to prevent such negative behavior that children are punished and police forces are maintained. And what of Freud's assertion that human beings have aggressive or destructive instincts? Rogers maintains that in years of therapeutic experience he has seen little evidence for this pessimistic view. Instead, he has come to believe that the human organism naturally seeks growth, self-actualization, and pleasant, productive relations with others. When not restricted by social forces, a person wants to become what most of us would recognize as healthier and happier.

Evaluation of Humanistic Theories

Humanistic theories of personality have been criticized for being unscientific and subjective. They are considered unscientific because they are based on scientifically unverifiable inferences that are stated in a vague and imprecise manner. For example, how can the various metaneeds be shown to be essential to full human development? And how do we know when a basic need has been gratified? Further, how does one go about testing a person's habit of "transcending the environment," one of the characteristics of self-actualization set forth by Maslow? Or how does one determine the "conditions of worth" that Rogers asserts that each of us develops as a standard of conduct? By recording therapy sessions and analyzing their content, Rogers systematically tested inferences drawn from his theory; for example, he compared self-concept before and after therapy. However, his theory of personality is less open to test. Giving unconditional positive regard to children from birth, for example, might have very different—and less positive—effects than providing unconditional positive regard to people who have become unable to accept many of their feelings and actions.

The second charge against humanistic approaches is that they lack neutrality. For example, Maslow's claim that human nature is "good" has been called an intrusion of subjective values into what should be a neutral science. His study of self-actualized people has been criticized because the sample was chosen on the basis of Maslow's own subjective criteria. How can self-actualized people be identified without knowing the characteristics of such people? But if we already know their characteristics, why list them as if they were the results of an empirical study? Finally, self-actualized people are supposed to be fully developed in all areas of personality, yet some of the people Maslow considered self-actualized are reported to have had severe problems.

Despite such criticism, the work of Maslow and Rogers has had a significant impact on research, therapy, and counseling. For example, it has led many psychologists to concentrate on their patients' or clients' personal growth and to adopt Rogers' concept of unconditional positive regard, letting clients know that they are still accepted even if they behave in self-destructive ways. Along with the concentration on personal growth has come an interest in exploring the limits of human potential through altered states of consciousness (Fadiman, 1980; Tart, 1975). As we saw in Chapter 7, a Western interest in meditation, yoga, hypnosis, and hallucinogenic drugs has increased in recent years, heightened by the impact of humanistic approaches to personality.

In fact, the group therapy movement, which has grown rapidly in the past twenty-five years, can trace its strength and impetus to humanistic psychology. Group therapy is generally character-

ized by a focus on growth and on personal interaction freed from conventional restraints. The humanistic approach has also been responsible for the establishment of personal growth centers throughout the United States; perhaps the most famous of these is the Esalen Institute in California, where Maslow worked until his death in 1970. Carl Rogers has for a number of years been a fellow at the Center for the Study of the Person in La Jolla, California, which is also widely known for its humanistic emphasis.

SUMMARY

1. Most nonpsychoanalytic theories of personality can be classified as either behavioristic approaches, humanistic approaches, or trait theories. These approaches deemphasize unconscious forces as determinants of personality and emphasize observable behavior, learning, and cognitive processes.

2. *Trait theories* of personality are primarily descriptive, emphasizing the extent to which an individual possesses various **traits** (or predispositions to respond in a consistent way in many situations). Gordon Allport believed that traits can render different situations "functionally equivalent." He classified three kinds of traits: **cardinal traits** (a single trait that so pervades a person's disposition that most of his or her acts are dominated by it); **central traits** (habitual ways of responding to the world); and **secondary traits** (tastes and preferences). Any of these traits may be either **common traits**, which are seen to some degree in all individuals, or **individual traits** (also called **personal dispositions**), which make each individual's behavior unique. Some trait theorists have used factor analysis to develop measures of personality's fundamental dimensions. Raymond Cattell obtained a number of **surface traits**, which he further analyzed to yield **source traits**, the underlying dimensions of personality. Hans Eysenck concluded that there are two major trait dimensions underlying personality: introversion–extroversion and neuroticism–stability. Eysenck related personality differences to biological factors.

3. David Buss and Kenneth Craik have proposed the **act frequency approach** to personality, in which traits are seen as summarizing a person's way of responding. Buss and Craik believe that our views of another's personality are based on that person's responses in prototypical situations. Trait theories have been criticized because they are merely descriptive, providing no way of explaining behavior, because theoretical trait constructs tend to be seen as existing on their own, because traits tend to obscure individual differences, and because cross-situational behavior is not consistent. Yet traits allow prediction of behavior in similar situations, have led to the development of sophisticated analytical techniques, and have generated research documenting the stability of personality.

4. The controversy over whether a person's disposition or the situation is more influential in determining behavior has begun to move toward a consensus. Theorists agree that behavior is the result of the interaction between person and situation. Many people behave consistently in similar situations, and although traits seem to lead to a predisposition to respond in certain ways in certain situations, researchers cannot predict behavior in one situation from behavior in another. Our judgment of others appears to be based on the consistency of their response in prototypical situations as well as on our first impressions of them. People appear to behave more consistently in

stressful situations where the demands of the situation exceed their competency.

5. *Behavioral theories* emphasize the situation more heavily than do other theories, viewing personality as a set of learned responses. Dollard and Miller's behavior theory seeks to translate psychoanalytic phenomena into behavioristic terms. In this theory, neurotic conflicts are learned; they are characterized as extreme **approach–avoidance conflicts**, in which two motives clash so that satisfying one frustrates the other. B. F. Skinner's radical behaviorism analyzes behavior in terms of the external conditions that control it, paying no attention to internal events such as thoughts and feelings. Social learning theorists believe that most new behavior is acquired through observational learning, but emphasize human cognitive capabilities. Once acquired, behavior is regulated and maintained by **stimulus control** (a particular behavior takes place only when a stimulus evokes it at an appropriate time); **reinforcement control** (previously rewarded behavior is maintained by intermittent reinforcement); and **cognitive control** (the ability to guide and maintain behavior by providing cognitive appraisal and self-reinforcement). According to Walter Mischel, social learning theory accounts for both the uniqueness and the consistency of human personality. Behavioral approaches to personality have been criticized on the grounds that they oversimplify life, that they are deterministic, and that they can lead to totalitarianism. The contributions of behavioral approaches have been their methods of treating behavioral disorders (behavior modification) and their focus on the objective aspects of personality.

6. *Humanistic theories* emphasize human constructive and creative potential and stress personal growth. Abraham Maslow based his theory on people who had achieved **self-actualization**, those who find fulfillment in doing their best. He believed that there is an active impulse toward the actualization of one's potentialities and identified two groups of human needs: basic, or **deficiency needs** (physiological and psychological needs), and **metaneeds**, or growth needs (which include justice, goodness, beauty, order, and unity). Unfulfilled growth needs can lead to **metapathologies**, such as alienation. Carl Rogers believed that **conditional positive regard** in childhood leads to the denial and distortion of feelings so that we develop **conditions of worth** under which we know we will receive positive regard. Rogers' self theory suggests that people have an innate impulse toward becoming **fully functioning**, or psychologically adjusted. Rogers distinguished between the **organism**, or the total range of possible experiences, and the **self**, or the recognized and accepted parts of experience.

Humanistic theories of personality have been criticized for being unscientific and subjective. The contributions of humanistic approaches include the emphasis psychologists now place on their clients' personal growth, the recent interest in exploring altered states of consciousness, and the strength of the group therapy movement.

Key Terms

act frequency approach	conditions of worth	organism	stimulus control
approach–avoidance conflict	deficiency needs	personal disposition	surface traits
cardinal trait	fully functioning	reinforcement control	trait
central traits	growth needs	secondary traits	unconditional positive regard
cognitive control	individual traits	self	
common traits	metaneeds	self-actualization	
conditional positive regard	metapathologies	source trait	

RECOMMENDED READINGS

HALL, C. S., and G. LINDZEY. *Theories of personality* (3rd ed.). New York: Wiley, 1978. This is the classic text describing different theories of personality.

MADDI, S. R. *Personality theories: A comparative analysis* (3rd ed.). Homewood, Ill.: Dorsey Press, 1976. This textbook classifies personality theorists according to whether their basic assumption relates to *conflict, fulfillment,* or *consistency.* Examines what the theorists have to say about the core and periphery of personality. Also presents research on each position and draws conclusions about its strengths and weaknesses.

MISCHEL, W. *Introduction to personality* (3rd ed.). New York: Holt, Rinehart and Winston, 1981. This recent textbook by a well-known social-learning theorist divides theories into five categories: type and trait, psychoanalytic, psychodynamic behaviorist, social learning, and phenomenological. The book covers theory, assessment techniques, and personality development and change (including therapy). Because of the author's orientation, behavior theories and behavior modification techniques receive more emphasis than usual, and a great deal of attention is paid to empirical evidence, especially from laboratory experiments.

SMITH, B. D., and H. J. VETTER. *Theoretical approaches to personality.* Englewood Cliffs, N.J.: Prentice-Hall, 1982. This book emphasizes individual theorists and presents each person's theory in detail.

PSYCHOLOGICAL ASSESSMENT

Is there any point in taking a special course to try to raise one's scores on the College Entrance Examination Board's Scholastic Aptitude Test (SAT)? Coaching high school students for the SAT has become a multimillion-dollar industry. More than 150 independent firms provide coaching for a fee, and at least 50,000 students take advantage of their services each year. Many high schools also offer some sort of course aimed at improving students' performance on this vital test (Kulik, Bangert-Drowns, and Kulik, 1984). Is all this money and effort well spent, or are students wasting their money, and high schools squandering valuable instructional time, on worthless courses?

The claims of some firms would make it appear that coaching causes SAT scores to skyrocket, but studies indicate that the effects of coaching are modest. For years researchers have been studying the effect of brief coaching and more extensive courses on SAT scores, and an analysis of these studies shows that the average gain is only .15 of a standard deviation (Kulik, Bangert-Drowns, and Kulik, 1984). That gain translates into no more

than a 15-point increase in scores on the SAT, whose scale of scores ranges from 200 to 800 points; at 15 points, the boost is so slight as to have little effect on admissions decisions. Other researchers (Messick and Jungeblut, 1981) have found that the return from time invested in coaching classes diminishes rapidly. Students who have from eight to twelve hours of coaching generally find that their scores increase about 10 points; score increases of more than 20 to 30 points seem to require as much time and effort as full-time schooling.

If the payoff is so small, why do students keep demanding the courses? Primarily because they believe that test results may profoundly affect their lives. SAT scores are not the only factor involved in college admission. And students often overrate the importance of SAT scores: in one survey of nearly 1,500 colleges and universities, more than half said that test scores were not a very important factor in their admission decisions (Hargadon, 1981). But SAT scores may figure importantly in the decision. It is no wonder that students, especially those striving to get into a select college, feel anything they can do that might increase their scores is worthwhile.

Tests play an important role in many aspects of our society. Most of us take our first tests when we begin school and continue taking tests throughout life. We are given competency tests for high school graduation; then we are tested for admission to college, then for admission to graduate school. Nonscholastic tests also have weighty consequences. Most occupational futures are controlled by testing, whether the test is for professional licensing, a civil service job, placement in the armed forces, or employment by a corporation. Tests are also used in the assessment of psychopathology. Even dating services may use some sort of personality test to match their customers. In this chapter we explore a variety of tests: intelligence tests that can discover children with previously unrevealed gifts or needs; aptitude tests, such as the SAT, which can identify students who are academically gifted; and personality tests that can reveal specific psychological problems requiring treatment. In closing, we consider the ethics of testing.

Requirements of a Test

A **psychological test** is an objective and standardized measure of a sample of behavior (Anastasi, 1982), which provides a systematic basis for making inferences about people (London and Bray, 1980). Unless a test is reliable and valid, it cannot measure behavior accurately, and unless it has been standardized, there is no way to determine the meaning of an individual's score. Therefore, reliability and validity are important criteria for judging a test's value, and standardization is essential in judging its utility.

Reliability

A test is **reliable** if it measures something consistently. We trust a yardstick; it can be expected to produce the same measurements whether it is used today or next week, and whether it is used by a carpenter or a plumber. Like a yardstick, a psychological assessment technique is reliable only if it yields the same results with repeated

measurements. When a test is reliable, a group of people can take the test on two separate occasions and their scores will fall in approximately the same order each time.

Different sorts of tests require different measures of reliability. In psychological assessment, three types of reliability are used: **internal consistency reliability**, the extent to which different parts of the test produce the same results; **test-retest reliability**, the extent to which repeated administration of the test to the same group of people produces the same results; and **interjudge reliability**, the extent to which scoring or interpretation by different judges will produce the same results.

A test's internal consistency is important if the test uses many items to measure a certain characteristic. For example, if a test constructed to measure anxiety consists of sixty items, its internal consistency can be assessed by randomly dividing the test in half and comparing people's scores on one half of the test with their scores on the other half. If the test is internally consistent, people's scores on the two sections will be highly correlated. The test must be divided at random, because such factors as boredom, fatigue, or practice can progressively affect the way a person answers the items, so that comparing scores on the first thirty items with scores on the second thirty will not assess the test's reliability.

Test-retest reliability is the extent to which repeated administrations of a test to the same group of people produce the same result. It is especially applicable if the test measures a relatively stable characteristic, such as intelligence or ability. When test-retest reliability is high, a test will yield similar scores when taken on two different occasions, indicating that the test is not particularly susceptible to such temporary influences as stress, illness, or distraction at the time of testing. For example, students who score high on the mathematical portion of the SAT (SAT-M) in February should also score high on the test in November, since mathematical aptitude can be expected to remain constant. Note, however, that not all measures are expected to have high test-retest reliability. For example, a test that measures an unstable attribute, such as attitude or mood, would not be likely to produce similar results each time it is taken. And note that similar scores on the same test are not always an indication of test-retest reliability. Suppose a woman takes an intelligence test on Friday and on the following

Monday takes the same test again. With such a short interval between the tests, her similar scores may be the result of her recalling on Monday a good many answers from the first test's administration.

When a test requires the scorer to interpret a person's answers, interjudge reliability is extremely important. In tests involving psychiatric diagnoses, the grading of essay examinations, or ratings of observed behavior, unless two people can judge a test and arrive at similar scores, an individual subject's score would fluctuate wildly, depending upon who scored the answers. Therefore, before subjectively scored tests can be considered reliable, there must be evidence that any appropriately trained person can administer, score, and interpret them with similar results.

Validity

A test is **valid** when it measures what it purports to measure, and the way its validity is established depends upon the purpose of the test. **Content validity** refers to whether the test actually covers a representative sample of the measured attribute. Unless tests given in school situations, such as a final exam or the Advanced Test portion of the Graduate Record Examination (GRE), have content validity, they are not accurate yardsticks of a student's knowledge of the field. For example, if a

GRE in literature contained only items about French or Spanish poetry, it would lack content validity.

Content validity is sometimes confused with **face validity**, which refers to whether the test *appears* valid to the people taking it. For example, a law school admission test would lack face validity if questions testing knowledge of algebra were included. When tests lack face validity (although they may be valid by other standards), people who are expected to take them may become hostile and refuse to cooperate.

If the purpose of the test is to predict future performance, content validity is not enough. Suppose a city asks applicants for the job of firefighter to take a civil-service examination and fills vacancies on the basis of test results. A test for prospective firefighters must have **predictive validity**; that is, scores on the test must have a relationship to future performance on the job. If people who make low scores on the test do as well at preventing and fighting fires as those who make high scores, the test lacks predictive validity: it is not a good yardstick for personnel selection.

Predictive validity is often difficult to establish, because it may require years to determine, but once a test has been shown to have predictive validity, it becomes extremely valuable. However, test givers must have a clear picture of exactly what the test is predicting. During World War II, it was noted that verbal and reading comprehension

A test has predictive validity if its scores are related to future performance on the job. A test for prospective firefighters, for example, should include the kind of physical feats that firefighters sometimes have to perform.

tests were the best predictors of grades in gunner's mate schools. Yet reading skills and the skills involved in maintaining guns aboard a warship seemed to have little to do with each other. It soon became clear that the predictive validity was based on the teaching and testing method used in those schools, which in turn was based on verbal comprehension. This meant that training success was not necessarily related to success as a gunner's mate. When the Navy switched to actual performance tests, the predictive validity of verbal tests declined sharply, and mechanical aptitude tests became the best predictor of success at gunner's mate schools (Fredericksen, 1984).

A test is also considered to be a valid predictor if it has **concurrent validity**—that is, if scores on the test correlate highly with other existing measures or standards. Concurrent validity is especially useful when a simple test, such as a quickly answered paper-and-pencil test of depression, can be shown to correlate highly with a time-consuming test, such as an extensive interview by trained clinicians.

Finally, **construct validity** refers to whether the test actually measures the theoretical construct it claims to measure (Anastasi, 1982). A construct is a complex image or idea formed from a number of simpler images or ideas. Psychological constructs include intelligence, anxiety, shyness, leadership, mechanical ability, mathematical ability, fatigue, and anger; each of these constructs has a theory that helps us understand what it is. Each theoretical construct has many aspects, so a test with construct validity must be a valid measure of several related criteria. For example, scores on a test of shyness should show a correlation to the number of parties a person attends, to talkativeness in groups, and to ratings of shyness obtained from parents and friends. But shyness scores should not be related to measures of certain other constructs, such as intelligence. Construct validity tests the theory underlying the construct. This makes construct validity the unifying concept of validity: it integrates external standards and internal test content into a framework for testing hypotheses about important relationships (Messick, 1980).

Valid tests, as we have seen, measure what they purport to measure; thus they measure something more than random variability. For this reason, valid tests must show some reliability. Note that although valid tests are always reliable, reliable tests are not always valid. For example, astrological horoscopes are highly reliable; they will always produce the same prediction for the same person. But horoscopes are not valid, because they neither describe personality nor predict future events accurately. Similarly, measuring head size as an indicator of intelligence is highly reliable. Using the same tape measure in the same way will always produce the same head measurement. But head size is not a valid indicator of intelligence because there is no relationship between head size and academic success or scores on intelligence tests. Head size, however, is both a reliable and a valid indicator of hat size.

Standardization

An individual test score tells us very little unless we also know what kind of scores other people have attained. If a person has correctly answered fifty-three of the eighty-eight questions on a test, it is impossible to say whether the subject has done well or poorly unless we know that most people can answer only forty-four questions correctly. Thus, before a test is put into general use, testers develop normative distributions, or **norms**, which show the frequency with which particular scores on the test are made. Norms are established by giving the test to a large and well-defined group of people, called a **standardization group**. The arithmetical average of the standardization group becomes a reference point, and norms indicate how far above or below this average any given score is.

The most common methods of translating "raw" scores (that is, the scores individuals actually make) into scores that are relative to the scores of others are the percentile system and the standard score system.

The **percentile system** divides a group of scores into one hundred equal parts. Since each percentile then contains 1/100 of the scores, a percentile number shows the proportion of the standardization group that is above and below a person's score. For example, a score at the eightieth percentile would be higher than the scores of 79 percent of the rest of the people who took the test and lower than the scores of 19 percent.

The **standard score system** is more complex. Standard scores represent points on a bell-shaped curve that reflects the normal pattern of distribution of scores on almost any test. (The concept of normal distribution was discussed in Chapter 2.) As Figure 20.1 shows, in a normal distribution the

Figure 20.1. The theoretical normal curve (A) and a practical application of it (B). The curves show the proportions of a group or population that fall at various points on a scale. The theoretical curve is useful because it has precise mathematical characteristics from which such relative measures as standard and percentile scores can be calculated. A standard score describes the position of an individual's score in terms of the variance of the group's scores. A percentile score describes the position of an individual's score in terms of the percentage of scores in the group that his or her score exceeds. A single standard score unit corresponds to about 16.4 IQ points on the 1937 Stanford-Binet Test. Knowing this correspondence and knowing the average IQ (approximately 100), one can convert any IQ into a standard score or a percentile score by reading the theoretical curve. (Bottom graph after Terman and Merrill, 1973.)

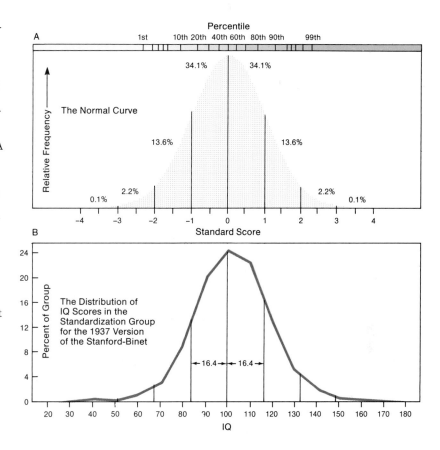

majority of people obtain scores within a narrow range lying somewhere in the middle of the distribution of all test scores. The farther a score is from the middle, or average, the fewer the people who obtain it.

On most intelligence tests (discussed in the following section), raw scores of people within the same age group are converted to standard scores with a mean of 100 and a standard deviation (see Chapter 2) of 15. As a result, about 68 percent of the population achieves scores between 85 and 115; more than 95 percent achieves scores between 70 and 130; and more than 99.7 percent achieves scores between 55 and 145.

If a test is to provide accurate information about the relative standing of a score, the standardization group must represent the population that takes the test. Different standardization groups are needed for different purposes. Thus, the standardization group used when we want to compare an eleventh-grade student's achievement test score with the scores of eleventh graders who plan to attend college is a different standardization group from that used when we want to compare the student's scores with those of all eleventh graders taking the test in the country. Under some circumstances, it is useful to develop separate norms for different groups. For example, a physical fitness test generally has separate norms for males and females, and most intelligence tests have separate norms for various age groups. But in both cases the normative group must represent the population with which the individual is to be compared.

THE MEASUREMENT OF INTELLIGENCE, APTITUDE, AND ACHIEVEMENT

Until this century, mental ability was assessed by simple tests of sensory discrimination and reaction time, which could be measured with precision. Such tests were used because it was considered impossible to measure complex intellectual functions objectively. Then in the first decade of the twentieth century, Alfred Binet (1857–1911) developed the first valid intelligence test. Binet believed that by finding tasks on which performance improved with age, psychologists could directly—and objectively—measure complex intellectual functions. He reasoned that if older children did better on these tasks than younger children, then children who performed better than others of their own age must be mentally older —and more intelligent—than their age mates.

In 1904 Binet began to develop a test that could identify mentally retarded children in the Paris schools so that these children could be taught separately. In collaboration with Theodore Simon, a psychiatrist, Binet devised thirty simple tests that rated children's ability to do such tasks as understand commands, recognize familiar objects, and grasp the meaning of the words. These tests were arranged in order of difficulty and incorporated into a scale. Although Binet's original test was designed for children between the ages of three and eleven, it was extended to adults in 1911 and to infants as young as three months in 1912 (Anastasi, 1982).

By 1908 Binet's tests were being used to predict school performance among normal children (Binet and Simon, 1916). On the basis of their scores, children were assigned a mental age, which corresponded with the average age of children who obtained that score on the intelligence test. Binet originally defined as retarded those children whose normal mental age was two years or more below their chronological age. One problem with this definition was that children aged fourteen who were two years behind their age group were considered to be as retarded as children of six who were also two years behind their age group. To solve the problem, the German psychologist William Stern (1914) came up with a way of assessing children's degree of retardation or acceleration in relation to their peers. He proposed that examiners use a simple index that expressed the ratio of mental age to chronological age, a ratio that became known as the **intelligence quotient (IQ)**. It is computed by dividing mental age by chronological age and multiplying the result by 100 (to get rid of the decimals).

In modern intelligence tests a person's IQ no longer represents the ratio of mental age to chronological age. Instead, it is a standard score with a mean of 100 and a standard deviation of 15 in relation to the person's own age group. Although the scores are still called IQ scores, they are more accurately called "deviation IQs" because they show how far a person's score deviates from the mean of his or her own age group.

Tests take various forms. Some intelligence tests are designed to be administered to individuals, some to groups; other tests measure aptitude or achievement rather than intelligence. The purpose for which the test is given generally determines the kind of test that is used.

Individual Intelligence Tests

Clinicians and school personnel generally prefer to use individual intelligence tests, in which one examiner administers the measure to one subject. In addition to providing standardized information about intelligence, individual tests also furnish a rich sample of the person's behavior. Such behavioral information is often useful in understanding the basis of a child's difficulty or in deciding among alternative programs. Among the individual intelligence tests in wide use today are a version of Binet's test and the intelligence scales developed by David Wechsler.

The Stanford-Binet Test

Binet's test of intelligence has been adapted by psychologists in many countries and revised many times. The American version, called the **Stanford-Binet Test**, was developed at Stanford University by Lewis Terman (1916; Terman and Merrill, 1973); it was the first to incorporate the concept of IQ. The current version, which is used throughout the United States, is made up of various subtests, grouped by age. Some of these subtests probe verbal ability and others assess performance ability. The performance subtests include such tasks as block design, picture arrangement, picture completion, and object assembly. To provide an adequate assessment of ability, the test must be administered by a highly trained examiner who carries out the standardized instructions in a precise manner. It is important for the examiner to make sure the subject feels comfortable and is motivated to do his or her best.

The examiner begins by establishing a proper starting level for the test, usually by asking a few questions from the vocabulary subtest. The aim is to find the child's basal mental age, which is the age for which he or she can answer all test items. If the child being tested seems to be reasonably intelligent, the examiner will probably start with questions that can be answered by a slightly younger child, so that a ten-year-old will first get questions from the nine-year-old level. If the ten-year-old misses some of the items for a nine-year-old, the examiner will drop back to items from the eight-year-old level. Once the basal age is established, the test moves on to the next year, and the session lasts until the child encounters a level at which he or she can answer none of the items.

The WAIS and the WISC

During the 1930s David Wechsler became dissatisfied with the Stanford-Binet Test because it was a poor measure for testing adults, and because it was primarily a test of verbal ability. To overcome these problems he developed a test to be used with adults that measured both performance and verbal ability. This test eventually became the **Wechsler Adult Intelligence Scale (WAIS)**, and after its revision in 1981 it became known as the WAIS-R. Wechsler also developed the **Wechsler Intelligence Scale for Children (WISC)**, which he revised in 1974 as the WISC-R. In the 1960s he developed the **Wechsler Preschool and Primary Scale of Intelligence (WPPSI)**, to be used with children from four to six and a half years old. Its form is similar to the WISC, although some easier items have been added to it.

The WAIS-R, the WISC-R, and the WPPSI are among the most frequently used individual intelligence tests. In all of these tests, items of the same kind are grouped together into a subtest arrangement, such as block design. The subtest scores are in turn combined into separate IQ scores for verbal and performance abilities (Wechsler, 1955; 1958). This method of scoring helps the examiner make a qualitative sketch of how an individual reacts to different kinds of items. Most important, it encourages the treatment of intelligence as a number of related abilities rather than simply as a single generalized ability.

Group Intelligence Tests

Although individual intelligence tests are preferred over group tests, they require skilled examiners and are impractical to administer to large numbers of people. When the Army decided to classify a million and a half recruits during World War I, the first group intelligence tests, the Army Alpha and Army Beta tests, were developed. Revisions of these tests, which are strictly paper-and-pencil measures, are in use today. Because group tests require no manipulation of objects or interaction with another person, the examiner does not have to be highly trained.

Group tests customarily use multiple-choice items, which can be scored by a computer. Their nature makes the scoring entirely objective, whereas the interaction with the examiner that is a feature of individual tests introduces a certain degree of subjectivity. In addition, the mass administration of tests to hundreds of thousands of people enables test developers to standardize the tests on much larger normative groups (Anastasi, 1982).

Because group tests are both convenient and inexpensive, their use has spread throughout schools, businesses, employment offices, and any other situation in which mass testing is useful. Group testing has become routine, with individual tests reserved for cases in which intensive study of an individual is required. Most children are repeatedly given group achievement and aptitude tests at school.

Achievement and Aptitude Tests

Achievement tests were originally constructed to assess the extent of an individual's knowledge about subjects taught in school; **aptitude tests** were designed to find out about an individual's talent or capacity for particular lines of work. Indeed, the intelligence test is one variety of aptitude test. As time passed, however, the distinction between achievement and aptitude tests blurred. What psychologists first thought were tests of aptitude—defined as innate ability or talent—turned out partly to measure different kinds of experience, so that they had to be regarded in some sense as achievement tests as well. Conversely, because achievement tests often turned out to be good predictors of many kinds of occupational abilities, they were also in some sense aptitude tests. Thus, the distinction has come to rest more on the purpose for which a test is given than on its content. When a test is used to evaluate what a person knows, it is an achievement test; when the same test is used to predict how successful the person will be in a particular endeavor, it is an aptitude test.

FAMILY SIZE, INTELLIGENCE, AND SAT SCORES

In 1964 the SAT scores of American high school students began to fall. Each year they dipped lower, until by 1980 the average combined score had fallen 90 points; it had plunged from 980 to 890 (424 on the SAT-V and 466 on the SAT-M). Educators, psychologists, politicians, and journalists tried their hand at explaining the drop in scores. They blamed television, drugs, a waning interest in language skills, a craving for freedom of expression, the quality of teaching, a lack of school discipline, the parents' failure to motivate their children, or an increase in the proportion of students from disadvantaged minority groups.

At the University of Michigan, psychologist Robert Zajonc (1976) proposed a simpler explanation: he suggested that the drop in SAT scores was due in part to changes in the home intellectual environment, and that these changes could be traced to larger families. SAT scores began to fall when the first members of the baby-boom generation took the test, and these were high school seniors who had grown up in larger families. Some research has supported this proposal. When Richard Franke

and Hunter Breland analyzed the association between SAT scores and family size since 1965, they found that birth order and the average number of siblings accounted for 87 percent of the drop in SAT scores during that period (see Zuckerman, 1985).

Why should living in a large family be bad for your SAT score? When children's principal companions are other intellectually immature children, says Zajonc (in press), they are exposed to a diminished vocabulary and to relatively low levels of intellectual interaction, and they observe mostly immature ways of meeting environmental demands. To back up his theory, Zajonc (1976) showed that in large samples taken from the United States and the Netherlands, intellectual performance declined with birth order. The more older brothers and sisters a child had, the lower the youngster's IQ score. In some countries, however, later children did not show this decline. In these countries children within a family tended to be widely spaced; in France, for example, siblings are generally separated by five years. This spacing raises the home intellectual environment and can

cancel the negative effects of being a later-born child. In addition, when a child has opportunities to play "teacher" to a considerably younger sibling, the child teacher's intellectual growth is stimulated (Zajonc, Markus, and Markus, 1979).

Zajonc (1976) was so confident of his theory that he made a prediction: in 1980, as the last of the "baby boom" seniors graduated, SAT scores would stop declining and begin to rise. And that is exactly what has happened. Since 1980 scores have been creeping up a point or two each year, and by 1984 the combined average SAT score had climbed 7 points: the combined average is now 897 (426 on the SAT-V and 471 on the SAT-M).

Recently, Zajonc (in press) made another prediction: SAT scores would continue to rise until about the year 2000, when high school seniors (who are today's four-year-olds) will have a combined average score of between 1020 and 1030. Then, however, SAT scores will begin to drop again. The reason? Since 1981 the birth rate has been rising.

The Scholastic Aptitude Test

Almost every student who reads this book has probably taken the College Entrance Examination Board's **Scholastic Aptitude Test (SAT)**. The test is a direct descendant of the Army Alpha Test and was first administered in 1926. Designed to measure "aptitude for college studies" rather than school achievement or general intelligence, the test has been continually and meticulously revised

and updated. It yields two scores, SAT-V for verbal aptitude and SAT-M for mathematical aptitude. The reliability of both scores is very high: .89 for SAT-V and .88 for SAT-M (Wallace, 1972)—quite close to a perfect correlation, which, as we saw in Chapter 2, would be 1.00. The validity for predicting college grades is .39 for SAT-V and .33 for SAT-M. High school records, which show a validity of .55, are more valid than the two SAT scores as a predictor of college grades. But when all three measures are combined into one index, the correlation with college grades is .62 (DuBois, 1972). These validities are high enough to make the SAT useful in predicting college performance but low enough to make it clear that other factors, such as motivation, are also important determinants of academic success.

Until recently, students who took the SAT received their scores but no information as to the correctness of specific answers. Since 1980, however, students in New York State have been able to get copies of the tests, their marked answer sheets, and the correct answers. Almost immediately, it became clear that a valid, reliable test can contain some wrong answers. As a result, in 1981 the practice was voluntarily extended to the entire country.

New Directions in the Measurement of Intelligence

Dissatisfaction with current IQ tests has led cognitive psychologists to look at intelligence and testing in a different way. They believe that it may be possible to come up with a more meaningful measure of mental ability by incorporating some measure of how people process information into the testing.

Some cognitive psychologists have focused on the cognitive functions of perception, learning, and memory. These psychologists have compared the speed and accuracy with which these individuals carry out these cognitive processes with their performance on standard IQ tests. They believe that a person's performance on an IQ test may be affected by the speed with which he or she retrieves information from long-term memory, or by the speed with which he or she manipulates material in short-term memory. The efficiency with which a person shifts the burden of information processing from one component of the system to another may also affect his or her performance (Hunt, 1976).

Other psychologists have looked directly at reasoning and problem solving, analyzing the way people solve typical analogy items from IQ tests, such as: "*Composer* is to *symphony* as *author* is to:
    statue   work   novel   writing   music."
Robert Sternberg (1981) believes that the process an individual uses to solve such problems can be broken down into components (the steps one goes through in solving the problem) and metacomponents (the mental processes by which one decides *how* to solve the problem and then monitors the solution). Sternberg has attempted to discover which components are critical in an individual's performance on IQ tests. When people's performance on individual test items is analyzed in this way, a good deal of the individual difference in their performance can be explained. For example, people who do well on analogy problems such as the one above tend to focus on the first step, or component, in problem solving, which is encoding. These people start by forming an elaborate representation of the words involved. People who do poorly on such problems, by contrast, tend to spend relatively more time on a later step in the problem-solving process. They focus on making comparisons among whatever representations of the problem they establish (Sternberg, 1981; 1982).

If test makers are to apply this insight productively to IQ tests, they will have to consider enlarging the scope of the tests. Instead of simply requiring correct answers, the tests would have to be designed to assess the various components of problem solving: information processing, mental representation, and specific problem-solving strategies. Moreover, the tests would have to be administered in a computerized setting, so that each person's test performance could be broken down to reveal specific aspects of the way that the individual processes information. Once a problem area was identified, the challenge would be to determine whether the individual actually lacked the particular component or simply executed it inefficiently.

Of course, such a procedure would require lengthy sessions and would be more elaborate and expensive than typical group IQ tests. Thus, Sternberg sees information-processing testing as a complement to, not a substitute for, traditional tests. He recommends reserving it for individuals whose scores on traditional tests indicate the need for a more thorough analysis. As Sternberg's analysis demonstrates, the cognitive approach may help psychologists identify specific weaknesses in the individuals they test. With such information in hand, the psychologists may then be able to offer these individuals training aimed at strengthening those aspects of information processing.

Since Sternberg first applied information-processing theories to the analysis of intelligence, he has developed his ideas into a broad theory of intelligence (1984). His new analysis of intelligence goes beyond the information-processing components of problem solving and takes into account the way in which individuals cope with the demands of their environment.

Another psychologist who is dissatisfied with current methods of measuring intelligence has also developed a theory of intelligence. Howard Gardner (1984) has proposed a **theory of multiple intelligences**. His theory gives equal weight to seven different kinds of intelligence: linguistic, logical-mathematical, spatial, musical, bodily-kinesthetic (skill in using the body), intrapersonal (knowledge of the self), and interpersonal (knowledge of others). Gardner points out that our IQ tests measure only those abilities that are valued in a Western technological culture, and that other cultures have valued different abilities. Five hundred years ago, when few people could read, linguistic skills might not have been given such prominence in the assessment of intelligence. And in Micronesia, the highly rated ability to navigate over hundreds of miles of open sea without chart or compass requires spatial and bodily intelligence as well as an impressive linguistic memory, a kind of intelligence virtually ignored in standard intelligence testing. Even his theory, says Gardner, does not include all aspects of intelligence: he has not incorporated such broad cognitive capacities as common sense, originality, wisdom, and the ability to perceive analogies.

Although Gardner has not yet developed tests to measure all seven of his intelligences, he would like to see such tests developed. If this were done, an individual's various strengths and weaknesses could be assessed early in childhood. Educators could encourage individuals with great strengths to develop their talents and could devise special aids or enrichment programs of some type to help counterbalance other individuals' weaknesses.

Variations in Intelligence

Although nearly 70 percent of the population makes scores on intelligence tests that fall within a narrow range of 30 IQ points (85 to 115), a few people show extreme variations in intelligence, being either mentally retarded or gifted. At present we know more about the causes of mental retardation than about the causes of giftedness, but many aspects of extremely low or high intelligence continue to be baffling.

Approximately 5.6 to 6.7 million people in the United States are mentally retarded. Such a large pool of retarded individuals presents a serious social problem: mental retardation involves a person's adaptive behavior as well as her or his intellectual functioning. These twin aspects of retardation are the basis of the accepted definition of **mental retardation**, drawn up by the American Association on Mental Deficiency (1977):

> Mental retardation refers to significantly subaverage general intellectual functioning existing concurrently with deficits in adaptive behavior, and manifested during the developmental period. (p.11)

Despite the fact that all people whose functioning fits this definition are considered mentally retarded, mentally retarded people vary greatly in the degree of their limitations. Some are able to live productive lives with a minimum of assistance; others may be unable to speak or to take care of themselves. Because of this wide variation, mental retardation is generally divided into four levels—mild, moderate, severe, and profound—with each level determined by estimates of adaptive behavior and scores on standard intelligence tests. Each level of retardation blends into the next, so that there are no clear boundaries between the categories.

More than 90 percent of the retarded are considered to have **mild retardation**. Their IQs, based on Stanford-Binet scores, are from 52 to 67. Although they develop much more slowly than normal children, they are fairly independent by adolescence and most of them can hold undemanding jobs, marry, and have children. People with **moderate retardation** have IQs between 36 and 51 and although they can take care of themselves, they must live in sheltered workshops. They rarely marry or becomes parents. People with **severe retardation** have IQs between 20 and 35, can learn to care for some of their physical needs, and can be trained to perform simple work in sheltered workshops or to do household tasks. They require considerable supervision. People with **profound retardation** have IQs below 20. Although many remain in institutions, they can sometimes carry out a few tasks under close supervision. Some cannot speak, although they may understand simple communication.

The causes of mental retardation are as varied as the differences in the ability of the retarded to function effectively. Among the causes of mental retardation are abnormal chromosomes, inherited metabolic disturbances, infections contracted during the fetal period, toxins, brain damage, severely disadvantaged home environments, and severely deprived institutional environments.

IQ Scores: Nature or Nurture?

Many people have tried to use intelligence tests to obtain answers to the age-old question about whether there are innate intellectual differences among groups, but the quest has not led to reliable conclusions. People whose childhood environment has been quite different from that of the majority of American and European children tend to have lower scores on tests developed in the United States and Europe. This difference, even when statistically significant, is not evidence that various groups differ in innate potential, because a person's score reflects not only her or his genetic potential for intellectual development (nature) but also what she or he has learned from experience (nurture).

Cultural Bias in Testing

If a test is developed for people with a specific cultural background, it cannot legitimately be used for people with a markedly different background. Vocabulary items, which provide the best single estimate of IQ scores, are an obvious example. Youngsters who have always heard an item of furniture referred to as a "couch" will be bewildered when asked about a "sofa," and adults who have never heard the words "symphony" or "precursor" will perform poorly on the verbal portions of an IQ test. Those who have grown up in a community where the primary language is not English will face an even greater handicap.

From time to time, attempts have been made to develop a **culture-fair test**—a test whose items or methods of administration do not depend on familiarity with middle-class experience. These tests generally consist of nonverbal items such as geometric figures, mazes, and block designs. A person may be asked to reason about the relation between geometric figures, to copy designs, or to draw a human figure. However, culture is so interwoven into every aspect of life that devising a test that taps only noncultural aspects is extremely difficult. Most of these tests turn out to depend more

on cultural background than the designers anticipated, and when they are given to children, scores typically increase with the children's socioeconomic level (Anastasi, 1982).

Although it is very difficult to eliminate cultural bias from intelligence tests, it is easy to incorporate it in them. The Counterbalance Intelligence Test, deliberately devised by Adrian Dove, a black, to be culturally biased against whites, demonstrates through exaggeration the effect a person's background can have on intelligence test scores (see Figure 20.2). Obviously, any test that rests heavily on vocabulary terms like those shown in the figure is culturally biased. It would not be fair to judge the intelligence of white middle-class youngsters by their ability to define expressions they have never heard. Yet the makers of IQ tests often include words that are undoubtedly more familiar to white middle-class children than to their minority-group peers.

The issue of cultural bias in IQ tests has been reviewed by George Albee (1978), who pointed out that the tests are generally used to predict academic performance—performance in schools largely run by and for the white middle class, schools that embrace and promote the dominant values of our society. In fact, Terman, who brought Binet's test to the United States and adapted it to American use, limited his selection of items to material from the prevailing school curriculum (Garcia, 1972). Of course, the original purpose of these tests was to predict school performance, and that is exactly what they do best. IQ tests are the best single predictor of school success for children of all socioeconomic levels (McCall, Appelbaum, and Hogarty, 1973).

However, the scoring of IQ tests also seems biased in favor of white middle-class standards of behavior. For example, to the question, "What would you do if another child grabbed your hat and ran with it?" most white middle-class children answer that they would report the problem to an adult. Many black inner-city youngsters, however, answer that they would chase the offender and fight to get the hat back. The first response would be scored as "correct," the second as "incorrect," although neither solution is right for all children under all conditions (Albee, 1978). In addition, the standardization groups for IQ tests are generally composed of white urban children from English-speaking families.

The most obvious victims of cultural bias in IQ tests are the poor and the nonwhite, particularly

---

**The Dove Counterbalance
Intelligence Test**
by Adrian Dove

If they throw the dice and "7" is showing on the top, what is facing down?
(a) "Seven"   (b) "Snake eyes"
(c) "Boxcars"   (d) "Little Joes"
(e) "Eleven".

Jazz pianist Ahmad Jamal took an Arabic name after becoming really famous. Previously he had some fame with what he called his "slave name." What was his previous name?
(a) Willie Lee Jackson
(b) LeRoi Jones
(c) Wilbur McDougal
(d) Fritz Jones   (e) Andy Johnson

In "C. C. Rider," what does "C. C." stand for?
(a) Civil Service
(b) Church Council
(c) County Circuit, preacher of an old-time rambler
(d) Country Club
(e) "Cheating Charley" (the "Boxcar Gunsel")

Cheap "chitlings" (not the kind you purchase at the frozen-food counter) will taste rubbery unless they are cooked long enough. How soon can you quit cooking them to eat and enjoy them?
(a) 15 minutes   (b) 2 hours
(c) 24 hours
(d) 1 week (on a low flame)
(e) 1 hour

If a judge finds you guilty of "holding weed" (in California), what's the most he can give you?
(a) Indeterminate (life)   (b) A nickel
(c) A dime   (d) A year in county
(e) $100.00.

A "Handkerchief Head" is
(a) A cool cat   (b) A porter
(c) An "Uncle Tom"   (d) A hoddi
(e) A "preacher"

Figure 20.2. An extreme example of how an intelligence test may depend on knowledge specific to one culture. A population of urban blacks would score high on this test, and a population of suburban whites would score low. Even when a test's items do not show this kind of obvious culture loading, a test may have validity problems. For example, many subcultures within Western society place great emphasis on competence in test taking. In a subculture where such emphasis is lacking, the validity of almost any test is likely to suffer. (Copyright 1968 by Newsweek, Inc. All rights reserved. Reprinted by permission.)

blacks and Hispanics. However, about a half century ago newly arrived immigrant groups from southern and eastern Europe faced the same cultural bias and made low average IQ scores. In fact, one tester reported that 83 percent of Jews, 80 percent of Hungarians, 79 percent of Italians, and 87 percent of Russians were "feeble-minded" (Kamin, 1976). Today, after roughly fifty years of upward mobility, Americans from these groups attain scores that equal or surpass the national average. In fact, as the United States has become more ethnically diverse, the average IQ level of white Americans appears to have increased by almost one standard deviation (see Chapter 2). With each revision of the IQ tests, the norms have been set at a higher standard in order to keep the mean IQ at 100. After analyzing the available data on all Stanford-Binet and Wechsler tests from 1932 to 1978, James Flynn (1984) concluded that the average IQ increased 13.8 points during that period. Although researchers are uncertain as to the cause of the rise, an increase in test-taking sophistication and the spread of shared knowledge by the mass media may be involved. Groups that have not risen economically, however, have not shown the enormous improvement in average IQ scores that appeared among immigrants from southern and eastern Europe (Sowell, 1977).

Differences among the *average* IQ scores of different races and nationalities do exist. Because heredity and environment are so closely intertwined, it is impossible to conceive of these differences as resulting primarily from either differences in heredity or differences in upbringing and environment. Still, the relationship between the factors continues to fascinate social scientists.

Racial Differences in IQ: The Debate

In 1969 Arthur Jensen, an educational psychologist, asserted that genetic factors might prove to be "strongly implicated" in the fact that the IQ scores of black people are, on the average, 11 to 15 points lower than the scores of white people. Jensen's thesis that differences in IQ are highly heritable, and that therefore racial differences in IQ are due largely to differences in the gene distributions of the populations studied, caused an uproar that has not yet died down.

To understand the arguments for and against Jensen's view, it is necessary to understand two concepts: reaction range and heritability. **Reaction range** refers to the unique range of possible responses that each individual can make to the environment, given his or her genetic makeup. Take the case of height: good nutrition will make each of us taller than poor nutrition will, but under both conditions genetic makeup will dictate that some of us will be taller than others. A person's genes do not specify that he or she will grow to a particular height; rather, they establish a potential range of growth. The actual height a person achieves is determined not only by genes but also by nutrition and other environmental factors—it is a result of both heredity and environment.

The intellectual skills we develop, as measured by IQ tests, also have a reaction range. No matter how stimulating their environments, few people become Albert Einsteins or Leonardo da Vincis. Each person who is not subjected to severe deprivation (which can make anyone mentally retarded) has a range of perhaps 20 to 25 points in which her or his IQ score can vary, depending on the person's environment (Scarr-Salapatek, 1971).

The second concept, **heritability**, refers to the extent to which the observed variation of a trait (such as IQ) can be attributed to genetic differences among *a specific group of individuals in a specific environment*. Take, for instance, the heritability of intelligence. Because many blacks live in an environment that is characterized by poor nutrition, poor medical care, and other factors that constrict the development of intelligence, the influence of these factors decreases genetic influences on intelligence among them. Many whites, on the other hand, live in favorable environments that allow genetic influences on intelligence to have a stronger impact, and allow its development nearer the upper end of the reaction range. Heritability is an estimate that depends on both a specific population and a specific environment. The environment is highly implicated in heritability, and the heritability of a trait changes as the group's environment changes (Scarr and Kidd, 1983). This means that heritability estimates for one group cannot be applied to another. Heritability may be different among blacks and whites, and among middle- and lower-class groups.

It seems clear that there is high heritability for intelligence *within* populations. This conclusion is based on many studies in many different countries. When all the studies done up to 1981 were summarized and correlations obtained between people of different degrees of relatedness, the overwhelming conclusion was that the results reflected a genetic component (Bouchard and McGue, 1981).

When Jensen made his original assertion re-

garding heritability, his work was based on data from a series of studies by the English psychologist Sir Cyril Burt (1966; 1972). Burt compared the IQs of identical and fraternal twins and showed, for example, that when identical twins —who have the same genetic makeup—were separated early in life and brought up in different environments, their IQs as adults were similar. These findings appeared to show that environment played only a minor role in the development of IQ differences. Jensen's side of the controversy, presented first in his 1969 article and later expanded in two books (1973; 1980), can be phrased as follows: if individual differences in intelligence *within* the black and the white populations taken separately have a high heritability, it is possible that the average differences *between* these racial groups likewise reflect genetic differences.

In making his argument, Jensen ruled out a number of environmental factors that have been proposed to explain black-white IQ differences. He made four major points:

1. Even when socioeconomic class of the two races is equated, blacks score well below whites on the average.
2. Environmental deprivation affects Native Americans (Indians) more than blacks, yet Native Americans score higher on IQ tests than blacks on the average.
3. The absence of the father in many lower-class black homes has not been found to account for the lower intelligence level.
4. Characteristics of the test and testing situation, such as cultural bias and the race of the examiner, do not appear to account for the differences in the IQ scores of black children. The same difference occurs on nonverbal tests and on tests administered by black examiners.

Jensen's argument began to founder when his basic data were called into question by Leon Kamin (1974; 1976), who found that no matter how many sets of twins Burt presented, the correlations between IQ and relatedness for each set were the same to three decimal places—a coincidence that seemed virtually impossible. Burt's data have been rejected by most psychologists, and his research has come to be seen as careless (Jensen, 1978), as an example of experimenter bias, or as fraudulent (Hearnshaw, 1979).

But even without Burt's data, the conclusion

that there is high heritability *within* populations (at least white populations) remained strong. Meanwhile, those opposed to Jensen's position have provided a rebuttal based on other grounds:

1. High heritability *within* populations tells us nothing about the cause of differences between populations. A crop grown in rich soil, loaded with nutrients, will produce a heavier yield than the same crop grown in deficient soil. And all crops, no matter what their genetic differences, grow better in good soil. Differences *between* populations could be due primarily to the environment, even though differences *within* populations are due primarily to heredity.

2. Blacks and whites differ in numerous ways besides genetic makeup, such as their living conditions and the degree to which they experience discrimination. Blacks and whites supposedly in the same socioeconomic class actually differ considerably in income, education, and quality of housing.

3. Jensen's assertion that black-white IQ differences are not explained by the environmental factors that he dismisses does not rule out an explanation due to other, as yet unspecified environmental factors. For example, young children commonly eat the lead paint chips that peel from the walls of many slum dwellings; the lead in the paint can cause brain damage, which results in sharp decreases in intelligence. Moreover, pregnant women sometimes develop a craving for paint chips, and research has shown that lead can be transmitted from a pregnant woman to her unborn child (Barltrop, 1969; Scanlon and Chisolm, 1972). Partly because of this transmission and because lead poisoning is common among urban blacks, its effects may be erroneously seen as genetic (Needleman, 1973; 1974). In addition, blacks are more likely than whites to be members of large families, and family size can have a subtle effect on intelligence. Robert Zajonc (1976; Zajonc, Markus, and Markus, 1979) has found that IQ scores are generally lower for children from large families than for children from small families, and lower for later-borns than for first-borns. This birth-order effect is particularly noticeable among children who are close in age to their siblings. Zajonc proposes that

with the arrival of each additional child, the intellectual environment of the family is diluted. The box on page 500 suggests that family size also affects SAT scores.

4. IQ tests are affected by such nonintellectual influences as motivation, anxiety, and test-taking skills. These nonintellectual influences lessen the value of the IQ score as a reliable measure of the differences in intelligence among racial groups.

5. Jensen's critics say that he seems to imply that heredity "fixes" IQ scores within limits, and that he does not take reaction range into account. Data from adoption studies (Skodak and Skeels, 1949; Schiff et al., 1978) suggest that when children are adopted into a higher social class than the one into which they were born, they can develop significantly higher IQs than would be expected if they had been reared by their natural parents. The broad reaction range of IQ and the fact that it can be dramatically affected by changes in the environment was confirmed by Sandra Scarr and Richard Weinberg (1976). These researchers studied black children who had been adopted by white, middle-class couples of above-average intelligence. The average IQ score of these adopted children was 106, well above the average for the entire population and about 15 points above the average IQ of black children reared in their own homes in the part of the country in which the study was conducted.

6. After reviewing all the research, Scarr wrote that she could "see no evidence for the hypothesis that the average difference in intellectual performance between U.S. whites and blacks results primarily from genetic racial differences" (1981, p. 528). After an earlier review, J. C. Loehlin, Gardner Lindzey, and J. N. Spuhler (1975) concluded that on tests of intellectual ability, differences in the scores of members of different American racial and ethnic groups reflect in part the inadequacies and biases in the tests, in part environmental differences and in part genetic differences. The three factors interact, and "differences among individuals within racial-ethnic and socioeconomic groups greatly exceed in magnitude the average differences between such groups" (p. 239). Thus, conclusions about

hereditary racial differences are difficult to evaluate and of little value in making predictions about a person's behavior. Since there is far more intellectual variability *within* populations than *between* them, people should be treated as individuals instead of as stereotypical members of a group.

THE MEASUREMENT OF PERSONALITY

Intelligence tests may help us assess abilities, but a yardstick that measures only cognitive functioning deals with only part of the person. Therefore, we also need personality tests, which explore emotions, motives, interests, attitudes, and values. Such tests are widely used in counseling, clinical practice, and screening for employment. Among the methods used to assess personality are observation, self-report inventories, projective tests, and physiological measures.

Self-Report Inventories

One of the quickest and least expensive methods of measuring personality is the self-report inventory, which shares the assumption and method of intelligence tests. First, personality inventories assume that people possess varying amounts of the trait being measured. Second, because no single item is applicable to everyone, many items are used to obtain a reliable assessment.

A type of personality inventory is constructed by **factor analysis**. This statistical method analyzes responses to a host of possible scale items, and reduces them to highly correlated items that reflect a few underlying factors. For example, Julian Rotter (1966) used factor analysis to develop a scale that measures an individual's **locus of control**, or whether people believe that what happens to them is primarily determined by external or internal factors. People with an *internal locus of control* believe that their own behavior primarily determines their fate, whereas people with an *external locus of control* believe that what they do makes little difference—and that their fate is determined by luck, fate, or powerful people.

Another type of personality test is constructed and developed using the empirical method. In such a test, items are first selected without regard to their possible relationship to a certain trait, such as depression. These items are then administered to an experimental group of people who are known to be high in the trait or traits the test developers want to measure (e.g., high in depression), as well as to another group of people in which the traits are known to be low or absent. Those items that successfully differentiate between the two groups—items that receive one particular answer from most of the subjects high in the trait and a different answer from most of the subjects low in the trait—are retained; the others are discarded.

A third type of personality test is the **rational**, or **deductive**, **scale**. To develop such a scale, the test maker first defines the various constructs that he or she wishes to measure, then writes items that appear to fit the definitions. Naturally, when this method of construction is used, the test reflects the framework of a particular theory of personality. Using such an approach, a scale to diagnose depression has been developed within the cognitive behavioral framework (Beck, 1978).

The Minnesota Multiphasic Personality Inventory

The most widely used personality inventory, the **Minnesota Multiphasic Personality Inventory (MMPI)**, was originally used to aid in the diagnosis or evaluation of mental illness. The MMPI was developed empirically, using groups of psychiatric patients and groups of normal people. Items that distinguished between the two groups were then combined into separate scales (see Figure 20.3).

The authors of the test (Hathaway and McKinley, 1940) began with a set of 550 true-false statements. Many of these items dealt directly with psychiatric symptoms, including delusions, hallucinations, obsessive and compulsive states, and sadistic and masochistic tendencies. But the other items ranged widely over areas such as physical health, general habits, family and marital status, occupational and educational problems, and attitudes toward religion, sex, politics, and social problems.

By following the development of the depression scale, we can see exactly how MMPI scales were constructed. The original set of 550 items was

133 I have never indulged in unusual sex practices.

151 Someone has been trying to poison me.

182 I am afraid of losing my mind.

234 I get mad easily and then I get over it soon.

244 My way of doing things is apt to be misunderstood by others.

288 I am troubled by attacks of nausea and vomiting.

A

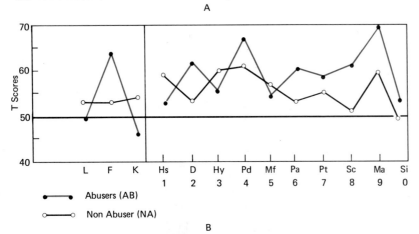

B

Figure 20.3. (A) Sample MMPI items. (B) MMPI profiles for abusive and nonabusive fathers. Note that the two groups obtained different profiles: fathers who abused their children scored much higher than nonabusive fathers on the Depression (D), Psychopathic Deviate (Pd), and Mania (Ma) scales. While it appears that the MMPI can differentiate between abusive and nonabusive parents, further study would be necessary before a more conclusive profile of an abusive parent could be drawn. This research does offer some tentative hypotheses about important personality differences between abusers and nonabusers. (Adapted from Paulson, Afifi, Thomason, and Chaleff, 1974.)

administered to a group of patients with depressive disorders and to a group of normal people. Their answers diverged sharply on about fifty-three items. These fifty-three items, together with a few others that distinguish severely depressed people from those with other psychiatric diagnoses, make up the MMPI-D (for depression) scale. This scale is a highly sensitive indicator not only of psychotic depression but also of less severe forms of depression, of varying mood states, and even of reactions to various methods of psychological treatments. In a similar way, eight additional clinical scales were developed for the original MMPI, as well as a scale rating masculinity and femininity.

The MMPI is an excellent tool for identifying and diagnosing the psychological disorders for which it was constructed (Butcher and Owens, 1978), but it is not useful for measuring normal personality or for screening job applicants. Furthermore, interpretation of the MMPI requires a skilled clinician. Because the MMPI can be easily scored by computer, there has been a tendency for people who are not highly trained to interpret the scores. But such interpretations are not valid, and psychologists have become concerned about this issue. In a recent court case a computer-generated psychological report that was administered and interpreted by a nonpsychologist was accepted in place of a face-to-face psychological evaluation (*U.S.* v. *Bilson*, 1984). Yet a computer profile is not a psychological assessment, just as a report of laboratory tests is not a complete medical examination (Turkington, 1984). To avoid such situations, psychological associations are drawing up guidelines on computer testing.

Projective Tests

Unlike self-report inventories, **projective tests** have not been rigidly standardized. They can be scored objectively, but the overall assessment depends on clinical interpretation. In these tests personality characteristics are revealed by the way subjects respond to and interpret ambiguous material. There are no right and wrong answers. Because there is no established meaning to the test materials, it is hoped that whatever meaning people put into their responses will reveal something about their personalities. Some of the ambiguous test materials are highly abstract images, such as inkblots; others are more concrete images, such as pictures of actual social situations.

The Rorschach Inkblot Test

The projective test best known to the general public is the **Rorschach Inkblot Test**, which invariably turns up whenever psychiatry is dramatized in a movie, book, or play. The Rorschach Test was developed in 1921 by the Swiss psychiatrist Hermann Rorschach (1942). The person taking the test looks at a series of ten symmetrical inkblots that increase in color and complexity, then reports what he or she sees, using free association. Then the examiner asks certain general questions in an attempt to discover what quality or pattern in the inkblots prompted the person's responses (S. Beck, 1961; Exner, 1974). A sample inkblot like those used in the Rorschach Inkblot Test, and a sample response, are presented in the accompanying box.

The Thematic Apperception Test

Another widely used projective test is the **Thematic Apperception Test (TAT)**, which also requires the person to describe what is shown on cards. In the TAT, instead of responding to inkblots, the person responds to a series of ambiguous scenes that involve one, two, or three people. As many as thirty black-and-white scenes may be shown, with specific cards determined by the person's sex and age. Each card is the stimulus for a story: the person is asked to describe the situation, tell what led up to it, tell what each character thinks and feels, and provide an ending.

"IT LOOKS LIKE A MONSTER WITH BIG FEET"

Rorschach inkblots are used in a projective test of personality. In interpreting a person's response to the ten inkblots in the series, examiners pay at least as much attention to the style of the responses as to their content. For example, a person's tendency to see white or shaded areas as meaningful, or to see the blot as a whole rather than as a collection of parts, is deemed significant in scoring and interpretation.

When presented with the inkblot shown here, a young female outpatient free-associated that "it sort of looks like a monster with big feet. A cute little thing. Really a dashing little monster. Such a friendly little guy." Further probing by the examiner showed that the woman was responding to the blot as a whole instead of to only a portion of it, and was concerned primarily with its shape or form, which, while humanlike, was not distinctly human. Interpreting the meaning of Rorschach responses is a complicated task. Despite the fact that formal attempts to establish its reliability and validity have failed, the test remains widely used.

Source: R. I. Lanyon, and L. D. Goodstein. *Personality assessment.* © 1971, p. 50. Reprinted by permission of John Wiley and Sons, Inc., New York.

The stories are usually analyzed on an individual basis; that is, one person's stories are not compared with another's. Harry Murray, who developed the test in 1935, recommended interpreting the TAT stories in terms of his own theory of personality (Murray et al., 1938), but a variety of other systems, including some based on psychoanalytic theory, are also used.

Clinical psychologists agree only moderately well about interpretations of the TAT and predictions based on it. In fact, agreement on TAT interpretations among professionals often does not exceed that among psychology students who have not been trained in TAT interpretation. But all the methods of interpreting the TAT depend on certain assumptions regarding the sort of fantasy that is tapped by the test. Common assumptions are that the subject will identify with the hero or heroine of the story, that the stories will reveal the subject's motives, and that unusual responses are more likely than typical ones to reveal important aspects of personality.

Physiological Measures

Because emotion and physiological functioning are so closely related, physiological measures are sometimes used to establish individual differences in personality. Rising blood pressure is connected with levels of hostility; anger is accompanied by rapid heart rate, increased skin conductance, and high blood pressure; anxiety, by a rapid heart rate, rapid breathing, perspiration, and muscle tension. As we saw in Chapter 11, the polygraph is useful in detecting physiological states connected with emotion. By monitoring changes in blood pressure, EEG, GSR, and EMG (electromyograph, which records changes in the electrical activity of muscles), examiners can establish individual differences in arousal. For example, when studying the way people cope with stress, examiners often measure autonomic levels of arousal in addition to obtaining self-report inventories (e.g., Coyne and Lazarus, 1980).

THE ETHICS OF TESTING

We have seen that tests can be effective tools when properly used. But it is important to remember that they are powerful. In fact, they may change the course of people's lives. A high score on a mathematics examination may result in an accelerated program in math for one student, but a low score on the same exam may mean the denial of admission to college for another.

Like other tools, tests are not always used properly, and their results are not always accurate. Several ethical issues have been raised concerning their use.

One issue has to do with the appropriate interpretation of test results. Many people draw sweeping conclusions from personality and intelligence test scores, forgetting that the tests often measure much less than we think they do and that their results are always a matter of probability. At best, tests provide a good estimate of what they are designed to measure. For these reasons, it is important that a given test be valid for the specific purpose for which it is being used.

A second ethical issue concerns the proper use of test information. Even if test results are valid, the question of how widely the scores should be available is unanswered. Employers, college admission boards, parents of schoolchildren, and the subjects themselves have either demanded, been given, or been denied test results in various situations.

These issues have attracted widespread attention in connection with the placement of children in special education classes, personnel decisions, and truth-in-test legislations.

IQ Tests and Special Education

Children who are labeled mentally retarded on the basis of intelligence tests are often placed in special classes for the "educable mentally retarded." The proportions of blacks and Hispanics in such classes are far higher than their respective percentages of the population; the proportion of white middle-class students in special classes is far lower. A few years ago, for example, there were four times as many blacks and three times as many Hispanics, proportionately, as there were white English-speaking children in California's special education classes (Albee, 1978).

For the most part, it is schools who label children as retarded, and they do it primarily on the basis of IQ scores. Judging subjects on their adaptive behavior (their ability to function in society) as well as on their IQs, Jane Mercer (1972) concluded that a vast number of "retarded" adults should not have been so labeled.

IQ tests and the institutions that administer them are increasingly being challenged in the courts. In one case, a young man sued the New York City Board of Education, claiming that the board had been negligent in denying him an adequate education. At the age of four he had scored one point below normal on an IQ test and had then been put into a special class for the mentally retarded. He was not tested again until he was eighteen, and at that point his score was within the normal range. The jury awarded him the sum of $750,000 (Fiske, 1977).

In a pair of cases, black children in special classes for the educable mentally retarded brought class-action suits that have had opposite implications for the future use of intelligence testing. In the first case, *Larry P. v. Wilson Riles* (1979), the court found IQ tests to be racially and culturally biased and banned the use of intelligence tests for placing children in classes for the educable mentally retarded. In addition to finding the tests biased against blacks, the judge stated that because the tests were standardized on white, middle-class groups, they had not been shown to be valid for blacks. Validation for blacks had been "assumed, not established." In the second case, *PASE v. Hannon* (1980), the court found that the tests were *not* culturally biased and said that they could be used to help place children in special education classes. The judge examined the tests and proclaimed "all but a few of the items on their face appear racially neutral." This judge refused to rule on the issue of validity, saying that the question was not involved in the case. Both cases have been appealed, and although the *Larry P.* case has been upheld by the appeals court (Cordes, 1984), the question probably will not be settled until the issue has worked its way to the Supreme Court.

Psychologists themselves cannot agree on the issues involved in these cases. In each instance psychologists have testified for both sides, and the American Psychological Association, because its membership is so divided, refused to enter either case (Armstrong, 1980). Both judges have been criticized by psychologists. The judge in the first case was reproached for defining an unbiased test as one that yields "the same pattern of scores when administered to different groups of people," because tests are fair when they predict with equal *accuracy* for all groups—not when they provide equal *results* (Bersoff, 1979). The judge in the second case came under fire for declaring a test valid on the basis of his subjective opinion of the

questions, since validity cannot be established so casually (Armstrong, 1980).

For the present the effect of the appeals court decision in *Larry P.* v. *Wilson Riles* will probably be a less frequent use of IQ tests for classification (Cordes, 1984). Although new tests are being developed that attempt to identify academic deficits for instructional purposes, these tests are not yet available. An across-the-board prohibition of intelligence tests would eliminate psychologists' and educators' only valid diagnostic tool.

Truth-in-Testing Laws

It has customarily been difficult for individuals to find out exactly how they scored on intelligence, achievement, aptitude, or personality tests. A guide to test use, *Standards for Educational and Psychological Tests* (APA, 1974), advises that test scores be reported only to people who are qualified to interpret them, a standard that rules out most of the people who take the tests. However, the *Standards* also states that when test results are used in making career decisions affecting people's future, those people have the right to know their scores. This position is similar to the one behind legislation regulating credit bureaus, which gives individuals the right to see information in their credit files. But under this arrangement, only test scores—not copies of the tests themselves or the answers—are available.

New York State's truth-in-testing law (discussed earlier) goes much further, however, stipulating that people who take college admission exams like the SAT may later get copies of the test and its answers. Some psychologists are uneasy about truth-in-testing laws, because they worry that widespread publication of tests could decrease their validity. Indeed, on the assumption that revealed tests may become less valid, Educational Testing Service has increased the number of SAT forms it constructs each year.

There is another aspect of test confidentiality that truth-in-testing laws fail to consider. One reason for test confidentiality has been the protection of the person who takes the test. Keeping test scores confidential was meant to protect people from ridicule and harassment and to prevent the misuse of test results. One problem is the dissemination of test scores outside a company personnel staff, so that information gathered for one purpose is used for another, as when hiring tests are used in considering promotions, changes in work assignment, or selection for training programs. Unless an employee has been informed of the way test results may be used in the future, such multiple usage presents an ethical problem. One way to prevent misuse of information is to destroy old scores as they become obsolete, so that outdated information cannot be used when considering an employee's promotion or termination. However, decisions to clear files are often difficult to make. First, some ratings still have predictive validity as long as sixteen years after they are collected; and second, material that has been used to make personnel decisions in the past may be needed in the future should the company ever become involved in a lawsuit concerning the employee (London and Bray, 1980).

Psychologists are aware that personality and intelligence tests can be used with desirable or undesirable results. In the case of intelligence tests, the undesirable results include the excusing of bad education for minority groups and the labeling of children who lack exposure to the dominant culture as "retarded." Intelligence tests have also had desirable results: they have kept other children *out* of classes for the retarded; they have indicated whether a child's problem was intellectual or behavioral; they have selected gifted children for educational opportunites; and they have given children from disadvantaged families a way out of poverty (Hyman, 1979). And they have done this in a manner that keeps the attitudes of teachers from affecting the decisions. Similarly, tests used to screen employees allow people to be hired or promoted on their own merits and help eliminate disqualification because of employer biases. By providing realistic information about capabilities and dispositions, tests can help people make appropriate social and occupational choices.

But as the debate over ethical issues indicates, knowledge about people entails power over their lives, and tests can be used as potent weapons as well as helpful instruments. If tests are to be used for the benefit of the individual and society, the ethical issues raised by their use will require careful, continuing attention.

SUMMARY

1. A **psychological test** is an objective and standardized measure of a sample of behavior, which provides a systematic basis for making inferences about people. When used properly, psychological tests are efficient tools for selecting students who are academically gifted, for identifying specific problems that require treatment in the mentally disturbed, and for discovering children with previously unrevealed gifts or needs. If a test is to be useful, it must be reliable, valid, and standardized.

2. A test is **reliable** if it yields the same results with repeated measurement. Psychological tests used to measure a certain characteristic or a possibly unstable attitude or mood should have **internal consistency reliability**: different parts of the test must produce the same result. Tests that measure a stable characteristic, such as intelligence, must have **test-retest reliability**, so that repeated administrations of the same test to the same group of people produce the same results. Tests that require the scorer to interpret a person's answers should have **interjudge reliability**, so that scoring by different judges produces the same results.

3. A test is **valid** if it measures what it purports to measure. A test with **content validity** covers a representative sample of the measured attribute. A test with **predictive validity** produces scores that show a relationship to future performance. A test with **concurrent validity** produces scores that correlate highly with other existing measures or standards. A test with **construct validity** actually measures the hypothetical construct, such as dominance, it claims to measure. Valid tests are reliable, but reliable tests are not always valid.

4. Unless a test has been standardized, so people's scores can be compared with those of others, it is of little use. To standardize tests, **norms**, or normative distributions, are established by giving the test to a **standardization**

group of people. Raw scores are converted into standardized scores either by the **percentile system**, which shows the proportion of the standardization group that is above and below a person's score, or by the **standard score system**, which locates a score on a bell-shaped curve that reflects the normal pattern of score distribution. Unless the standardization group represents the population taking the test, standardized scores will not be accurate.

5. Intelligence tests are the most frequently administered tests measuring mental characteristics. On the basis of their test scores, children are given a mental age, which is converted into an **intelligence quotient (IQ)**, which represents the ratio of mental age to chronological age. Individual intelligence tests are administered by one examiner to one subject at a time. The **Stanford-Binet Test**, an individual test based on Binet's original test, contains both verbal and performance subtests that are grouped by age level. The **Wechsler Adult Intelligence Scale (WAIS)** and the **Wechsler Intelligence Scale for Children (WISC)**, also individual tests, treat intelligence as a number of abilities rather than as one overriding ability. Group intelligence tests, which are paper-and-pencil measures, are convenient to administer, but clinicians prefer individual tests because they provide a sample of behavior in addition to standardized information about intelligence. Achievement tests and aptitude tests are distinguished from one another primarily by their purpose. An **achievement test** evaluates what a person knows; an **aptitude test** predicts how successful a person will be in a certain situation. The **Scholastic Aptitude Test (SAT)** is a reliable, valid test that measures a student's likelihood of succeeding in college by assessing verbal and mathematical aptitude. Dissatisfaction with IQ tests has led cognitive psychologists to look for new ways of evaluating IQ. Some of these psychologists are trying to assess differences in the way people process information, and others are trying to assess various types of **multiple intelligence**.

6. **Mental retardation** refers to deficiencies in a person's adaptive behavior as well as to deficiencies in intellectual functioning. Most mentally retarded people have **mild retarda-**

tion, in which IQ is between 52 and 67; they are able to hold undemanding jobs, marry, and have children. **Moderate retardation** indicates an IQ between 36 and 51; **severe retardation** indicates an IQ between 20 and 35; and **profound retardation** indicates an IQ below 20. The causes of mental retardation include abnormal chromosomes, inherited metabolic disturbances, congenital infections, toxins, brain damage, cultural-familial deprivation, and institutional deprivation.

7. IQ scores reflect not only a person's genetic potential (nature) but also what the person has learned from experience (nurture). Because cultural background is so pervasive, **culture-fair tests** have proved extremely difficult to design. IQ tests predict school performance according to white, middle-class standards so that they appear to be biased against the poor and nonwhite. Although differences do exist between the average IQ scores of different races and nationalities, differences may be due primarily to environmental causes. **Heritability** depends as much on environment as on genes, and the environment determines in what part of the **reaction range** genetic influences will be expressed.

8. Self-report inventories assume that subjects have varying amounts of the trait being measured, and many items are used to measure each trait. Some personality inventories are constructed by **factor analysis**, a statistical method that reduces responses to highly correlated items that reflect a few underlying factors; such tests are useful for research on the structure of personality. Empirically constructed personality inventories, such as the **Minnesota Multiphasic Personality Inventory (MMPI)**, are most valuable for diagnostic purposes.

9. **Projective tests** attempt to measure personality through the responses of people to ambiguous material. In the **Rorschach Inkblot Test**, a person uses free association to report what she or he sees in a series of inkblots. In the **Thematic Apperception Test**, a person tells a story about each of a number of ambiguous pictures. Because emotion and physiological functioning are so closely related, physiological measures, such as changes in blood

pressure, EEG, GRS, and EMG, are sometimes used to establish individual differences in personality.

10. A number of ethical questions have arisen in regard to psychological testing, including the proper interpretation of test results and the proper use of test information. The labeling of children as mentally retarded can have a powerful influence on the course of their lives, and a number of legal suits have been brought in an attempt to stop the practice. Truth-intesting laws have been enacted that force institutions to give people who take college admission tests copies of the test, the answers, and their own marked answer sheets. The opposite problem of privacy exists in business, where test information can be used in many ways, and where psychologists attempt to keep test results confidential in order to protect employees.

KEY TERMS

achievement tests
aptitude tests
concurrent validity
construct validity
content validity
culture-fair test
deductive scale
face validity
factor analysis
heritability
intelligence quotient (IQ)
interjudge reliability
internal consistency reliability
locus of control
mental retardation

Minnesota Multiphasic
  Personality Inventory (MMPI)
mild retardation
moderate retardation
norms
percentile system
predictive validity
profound retardation
projective tests
psychological test
rational scale
reaction range
reliable
Rorschach Inkblot Test
Scholastic Aptitude Test (SAT)

severe retardation
standard score system
standardization group
Stanford-Binet Test
test-retest reliability
Thematic Apperception Test
  (TAT)
theory of multiple intelligences
valid
Wechsler Adult Intelligence Scale
  (WAIS)
Wechsler Intelligence Scale for
  Children (WISC)
Wechsler Preschool and Primary
  Scale of Intelligence (WPPSI)

RECOMMENDED READINGS

AMERICAN PSYCHOLOGICAL ASSOCIATION. *Standards for education and psychological tests.* Washington, D.C.: American Psychological Association, 1974. The latest revision of the Association's guidelines for test construction and use.

ANASTASI, A. *Psychological testing* (4th ed.). New York: Macmillan, 1982. This is an outstanding text which covers reliability and validity and surveys tests of intellectual development and personality.

LOEHLIN, J. C., G. LINDZEY, and J.N. SPUHLER. *Race differences in intelligence.* San Francisco: W. H. Freeman, 1975. A careful, balanced examination of the research evidence relevant to the issue of genetic and environmental determinants of IQ differences between racial groups.

WECHSLER, D. *The measurement and appraisal of adult intelligence* (4th ed.). Baltimore: Williams & Wilkins, 1958. A classic discussion of intelligence and intelligence testing.

PART SEVEN

HEALTH PSYCHOLOGY, BEHAVIOR DISORDERS, AND THERAPY

I am a materialist, so I have never been able to argue myself into supposing that there is anything in the brain but atoms and organization. The atoms are organized into molecules, the molecules into cellular organelles, the organelles into neurons, the neurons into synaptic pathways, and so on.

Since I believe this, I can't help but believe further that all mental and behavioral disorders arise fundamentally out of some abnormality of atomic organization at some level, since there is nothing else. I suppose it's logical for me then to assume that any mental or behavioral disorder could be corrected by some form of medication.

As we learn more and more about the biochemical and biophysical makeup of the brain, we can more accurately determine just what chemicals might affect certain receptors in the brain, stimulating them or depressing them according to need.

Certainly, there is precedent. It was only a century ago that we learned that small quantities of vitamins suffice to prevent, or cure, serious diseases. Even more recently, we learned that grave conditions resulted from hormonal imbalances. Still more recently, we have learned that many inborn metabolic errors are the result of gene abnormalities and deficiencies and might be permanently curable if we learn how to manipulate and modify genes.

Medical science is gradually developing a repertoire of chemicals that have effects on mental conditions. The use of tranquilizers in the 1950s, for instance, introduced a near-revolution in psychotherapy.

Can we look forward to a day when we not only find such chemicals in nature but learn to design them to suit our needs; when a psychiatrist will talk to a patient as a matter of diagnosis rather than cure? Once psychiatrists can make experienced estimates as to what is wrong in molecular terms, they can prescribe the necessary curative (or at least ameliorative) medicine.

I, for instance, take Synthroid to substitute for the hormone that my thyroid cannot be relied on to make since half of it was removed in 1972. I also take Inderal to keep my heartbeat regular since a mild heart attack in 1977. Why should I not also take something to keep my acute lifelong acrophobia under control so that I can go out on the balcony of my own apartment, which happens to be on the thirty-third floor?

A consummation devoutly to be wished? I wonder.

Suppose we all took various mild medications periodically to deal with whatever peculiarities waste our time and make us uncomfortable. Then we would all be normal.

But who defines normality? Isn't a little bit of abnormality very useful if it goes along with unusual abilities, unusual ways of looking at the world, unusual artistic or organizational talent, or whatever?

And if it seems that society will be better off without the wild creatures who break into violent and criminal behavior, would the safe way out be to fill our water supplies with appropriate chemicals designed to make us all submissive, meek, and obedient?

Might not the cure be worse than the disease? Might it not be better to endure the occasional dangerous mind, in order to have a full supply of unusual creative ones?

Maybe I'd better keep my acrophobia.

Isaac Asimov

HEALTH PSYCHOLOGY AND ADJUSTMENT TO STRESS

The !Kung of southern Africa believe that accidents, illness, and death are caused by spirits and ghosts. The spirits shoot their victim with invisible arrows, which must be removed if the person is to recover. Healers are individuals who have a special power (called *n/um*) that enables them to enter a trance state, leave their bodies, and fight the spirits for the sick person's soul. In the curing ceremony the family and friends of the victim gather around a fire and the healer dances to the women's songs, often for hours. When the healer's *n/um* heats to a boiling point, he breaks out in a heavy sweat. Trembling, he lays his hands on the sick person and draws the "badness" into himself. Then, with a soul-wrenching cry, he hurls the sickness out of his body into the air.

!Kung healers say that while they are in the trance state, they see the god, spirit, departed relative or friend, or living enemy who caused the illness sitting outside the circle of fire. These visions reflect a belief that *psychological factors* play a role in disease (although the !Kung do not use this term). In one case, reported to the anthropologist Marjorie Shostak (1981), a woman became ill with malaria shortly after her father died. The healer's soul journeyed to the world of the dead and found the father cradling his daughter's spirit in his arms. The father said that he could not bear to be without his daughter. The healer argued that she had a right, indeed an obligation, to live: "Your daughter has so much work to do in life—having children, providing for family and relatives, helping with grandchildren" (p. 293). After a long argument, the father reluctantly agreed to free his daughter. Her spirit returned to her body, and she recovered.

For most of human history, body and soul have been viewed as one. The evidence from archeology and anthropology suggests that, like the !Kung, ancient peoples attributed illness and injury to evil spirits (Rosen, 1972). Treatment consisted of exorcising the invading spirit and reclaiming the victim's soul. As far as we know, the Greeks were the first to depart from this view. Hippocrates (c. 460–377 B.C.), the father of modern medicine, studied the workings of the human body with the scientific detachment of a naturalist studying butterflies or birds. Diseases are the result of imbalances in body fluids, he argued, not of spiritual problems. Mind and body are separate (this view is known as mind–body dualism).

Hippocrates' teachings were abandoned in the Middle Ages. The medieval church taught that sickness and injury were God's punishment for sin. Treatment was focused on saving the victim's soul, often by torturing the body. But mind–body dualism was revived in the Renaissance. New techniques for studying the body (especially autopsies), the invention of the microscope, and the discovery of the cell provided strong support for a strictly physiological theory of disease. In part to associate itself with stunning advances in laboratory science, in part to dissociate itself from the superstitions of the past, the new profession of medicine declared itself the guardian of the body. The mind and spirit (psychological factors) were left to philosophers and theologians. Mind–body dualism dominated the practice of medicine in Western societies for almost 300 years. The idea that a case of malaria might be related to the death of a loved one would have been dismissed as ignorant. Malaria is caused by a parasite that is injected into the human bloodstream by mosquitoes and destroys red blood corpuscles.

In the last decade, however, attitudes towards illness and health have begun to change. The medical profession now recognizes that although psychological factors may not be the direct cause of malaria or other diseases, they may make a person more vulnerable to illness and can play an important role in recovery. Stripped of its mystical overtones, the traditional view that body and spirit are one now has scientific backing. The connections between physical and emotional well-being are the central concern of one of the fastest growing fields in psychology today, health psychology.

THE FIELD OF HEALTH PSYCHOLOGY

Health psychology is the branch of psychology that deals with how people stay healthy, why they become ill, and how they react when they become ill.

Health psychology is based on the view that the mind and body play equal roles in health and illness. This approach differs from the conventional medical model in a number of ways. First, the medical model assumes that biological processes are separate from psychological and social processes, and that the causes and cures of disease are strictly biological. The physician's job is to treat the body, not the mind or the family or the workplace. Second, the medical model focuses on lower-level processes (such as biochemical imbalances) and seeks single-factor explanations of disease (such as the search for a virus that causes cancer). It assumes that all diseases will ultimately be reduced to a single biological cause and a single medical cure. Third, the medical model emphasizes illness. Health is taken for granted, and illness is viewed as a deviation from the norm. The aim of research and practice is to cure diseases once they occur, not to prevent ill health.

Health psychology, by contrast, is based on a biopsychosocial model. It assumes, first, that psychological, social, and biological processes are all important influences on health and illness. How a person thinks and feels, and the settings in which he or she lives and works, have medical consequences. A disease cannot be understood apart from the person and the social context in which it developed. Second, health psychology focuses on the interaction of higher-level processes (cultural values and practices, social institutions and relationships, personal beliefs and habits) with lower-level processes (body chemistry). It assumes that health and illness have multiple causes and multiple effects. Third, this model views health as something to be achieved and maintained, not as the normal "steady state" of the organism. Research and practice focus on promoting health and preventing disease and injury, as well as on curing or controlling problems that have already developed.

The growth of health psychology in recent years reflects changes in patterns of illness and health. At the turn of the century, the leading causes of illness and death in the United States were acute infectious diseases, such as tuberculosis, influenza, polio, and even measles. These diseases are no longer major threats. Inoculations, antibiotics, and improved public sanitation and nutrition have reduced the incidence and severity of many infectious diseases. It is true that sexually transmitted infectious diseases (STDs) have become more widespread since the early 1960s. But other than the STDs, the main causes of illness and death in the United States today are chronic illnesses, especially heart disease, cancer, and diabetes.

There is evidence that many of these chronic illnesses result in part from lifestyle factors, including smoking, overweight, alcohol, and possibly stress. Genetic vulnerability and environmental pollution may also be involved, but to a large extent, modern diseases are associated with problems of behavior. In some cases they can be prevented if people adopt proper health habits early in their lives. And even if an individual does contact one of these chronic diseases, in some cases it can be controlled and the patient can lead a relatively normal life for many years, if he or she adopts appropriate health behaviors. This means that treatment of chronic diseases is not a one-shot, win-or-lose effort, as with infectious diseases. Moreover, it suggests that the patient cannot rely on the physician for a cure but must be an active participant in regaining and maintaining his or her own health. Living with chronic illness has raised a whole new set of psychological issues that few families or physicians faced in the past.

Given the changing profile of health and illness, the growth of health psychology seems all but inevitable. Health psychologists are interested in the attitudes, behavior, and environmental conditions that promote health and aid in the "primary prevention" of illness. They study the effects of stress on the body, and attempt to determine what individuals can do to reduce or avoid stress. They investigate the ways in which people deal with pain and discomfort, and with chronic or terminal illnesses. They also are concerned about the health care system and health policies. In this chapter we will concentrate on the first two goals of health psychology, primary prevention and understanding stress.

PRIMARY PREVENTION

Primary prevention is concerned with maintaining health—by encouraging people to develop a healthy lifestyle and take proper precautions to avoid health risks, and by identifying and counseling those whose health is at risk. But because it is difficult to devise procedures to identify individu-

als at risk, most efforts are aimed at discovering why people develop unhealthy habits and how they can be helped to change them. Primary prevention is difficult for many reasons: health habits develop in childhood and adolescence, typically a time of life when health concerns are low. Many adults are overly optimistic about their health and hence see no need to change behaviors that are hazardous to their continued well-being. And most physicians are not trained to examine or prescribe health behavior until disease is present. Health psychologists face these and many other challenges as they examine the psychological, social, and behavioral factors that affect health.

The major causes of death in the U.S. today are at least in part preventable. About 125,000 deaths from cancer and 170,000 deaths from cardiovascular disease each year could be avoided if individuals stopped smoking (American Cancer Society, 1982; *Oncology Times*, 1984). A mere 10 percent weight loss could lead to a 20 percent decrease in coronary artery disease among middle-aged men (Ashley and Kannel, 1974). Nearly 50 percent of highway fatalities (about 25,000 deaths each year) are the result of drinking and driving. The Center for Disease Control (1980) estimates that about half of all premature deaths (deaths well before age sixty-five) could be prevented if people took steps to maintain their health, such as sleeping seven or eight hours each night, eating balanced meals, and getting regular exercise, and if they avoided health risks: they should not smoke, they should drink alcohol only in moderation, they should have regular examinations (especially Pap tests and breast self-examination for women), they should be sure to buckle seat belts, and they should never drink and drive.

Healthy and Unhealthy Habits: What Are the Causes?

Most Americans know what is good for them, yet our society remains a study in health contrasts. We spend millions on health foods and exercise equipment, yet we spend millions more on cigarettes and alcohol. The number of adults who exercise regularly has increased by nearly 50 percent in the last few years (American Running and Fitness Association, 1981). Yet one in three adult women and one in four adult men are overweight or obese (Stunkard, 1975); about one in ten is an alcoholic or problem drinker (Vischi et al., 1980);

This woman may have started smoking to appear sophisticated, but soon she began to need cigarettes whenever she was under stress. What began as a choice developed into a habit and became an unhealthy addiction.

and 55 million Americans continue to smoke, despite repeated warnings by the U.S. Surgeon General (American Cancer Society, 1982). For every individual who is health-conscious, there is another who is health-careless.

Why do people behave as they do with regard to their health? Healthy behavior is usually a matter of habit (Hunt et al., 1979). Children who are fed three balanced meals a day and are discouraged from eating too many sweets and snacks generally grow up into adults with good nutritional habits; eating moderate amounts of the right foods has become as automatic as brushing their teeth. Children who learn to enjoy playing ball, hiking, swimming, and other sports generally grow up to be physically active adults. They continue to exercise as long as the environment provides opportunities to do so. The best predictors of regular exercise for adults, for example, are a history of athletic participation and access to exercise facilities (Dishman, 1982). Once established, health habits resist change.

Unfortunately, unhealthy behavior can also become a habit. Consider smoking, for example. A young girl accepts a cigarette from her date, thinking it will make her seem older and sophisticated. He approves, and she continues smoking, until gradually she begins to feel uncomfortable without a cigarette in any social situation. In college she finds that smoking "helps" her through long nights studying for exams. Her behavior has been reinforced, socially and physiologically. She quits after a bout with bronchitis, but starts again three months later when she changes jobs. At age thirty she has forgotten the name of her high school date, but she is still smoking. Her behavior is automatic; she lights up without thinking about what she is doing. She may have vague plans to stop one day, but the immediate discomfort she feels when she does not smoke outweighs the threat of developing lung cancer or emphysema in the future. An unhealthy habit has become established. Unfortunately, unhealthy habits are usually pleasurable, often automatic, and sometimes addictive.

Social Factors

Whether an individual develops healthy or unhealthy habits depends in part on social factors. Socioeconomic status determines whether an individual has a personal physician or goes to a public clinic. High-income people who have a family doctor are more likely to take preventive health measures (children receive immunizations, women have regular Pap smears), to see their doctor if they suspect a health problem, and to follow the doctor's orders. Low-income people tend to seek health care only in emergencies.

Sociocultural values also influence health behaviors. Before World War I, for example, it was considered improper for a woman to smoke, and few women lit up in public or private. One side effect of changing norms is that the percentage of females who smoke has increased in recent years (whereas the percentage of male smokers has decreased). The American Cancer Society (1982) projects that in the next decade, lung cancer will overtake breast cancer as the major cause of cancer deaths among women.

Finally, socialization is the source of many unhealthy as well as healthy habits. The effects of parental models can last a lifetime. Young people are far more likely to overeat, drink heavily, and/or smoke if their parents do so (Stunkard, 1979; Moos, Cronkite, and Finney, 1982; Leventhal and Cleary, 1980). Some individuals may be born with a genetic predisposition to alcoholism (Mayer, 1983) or obesity (Kannel and Gordon, 1979); these health problems do run in families. But it is difficult to untangle the effects of heredity from environmental influences. Is a child overweight because his body stores fat more readily than that of a normal-weight child, or because his parents spend most of their time around the kitchen table (modeling) and give him candy when he does as he is told (conditioning)?

Emotional Factors

Attempts to identify personality factors that predispose individuals to unhealthy habits have generally failed (Rodin, 1981). Emotions, on the other hand, do influence health practices. Some individuals react to stress by overeating. If they lose a job or quarrel with a best friend, they go on a binge. Other people react to stress by exercising, working off their anger or frustration—a much healthier response. Some people turn to alcohol after a divorce. They have not spent an evening alone or gone on a blind date in years; a few drinks help them relax. Others go on a diet and lose the extra ten or fifteen pounds they did not worry about when they were married. Some people vow to quit smoking on their fortieth birthday—and succeed. Others decide it is too late to do anything about their health. (They are wrong.)

Cognitive Factors

The role cognitive factors play in establishing and maintaining healthy or unhealthy habits is sometimes overlooked. But researchers in this area have focused on the **health belief model,** which sees attitudes, values, and knowledge as paramount (Hochbaum, 1958; Rosenstock, 1974). According to this model, good health practices depend, first, on whether people actually believe that they are vulnerable to illness and injury; many people do not believe they will ever get sick or be hurt, and so they do not bother to improve their health habits. Young people, especially, often develop a personal fable of immortality. They see heart attacks, diabetes, and cancer as diseases of old age; at sixteen, old age can seem as remote as ancient Greece. Similarly, adults who have never had a serious illness may believe that they have an exceptionally strong constitution or that doctors can fix anything today. But when people do become aware of their vulnerability, this new knowl-

edge can be the first step towards establishing good health habits or breaking bad ones. For example, women are more likely to follow their physician's advice to stop smoking when they are pregnant than at any other time in their lives (Barec, MacArthur, and Sherwood, 1976).

According to the health belief model, good health practices also depend on whether people believe that changing their behavior will reduce the threat to their health. A man whose father has diabetes may be very concerned about developing this disease himself but may not believe that losing weight will improve his chances. (It will.) A woman may worry a good deal about breast cancer but not realize that most tumors are discovered through self-examination.

How Can Health Habits Be Changed?

A primary goal of health psychology is to devise ways to help people break habits that are harmful to their health. Psychologists in this area use a range of intervention strategies, which draw on the principles of learning we discussed in Chapter 8. Some of these strategies are devised to change attitudes, some to change behavior, and some to change cognitions.

Mass Appeals

In recent years we have witnessed many attempts to use the mass media to inform the public of health risks. One example is the annual "smoke out," sponsored by the American Cancer Society, which combines fear appeals with information on how to stop. Media campaigns can change the climate of opinion. Twenty-five years ago many people did not know or believe that smoking was a serious health risk. Today most smokers say that they want to quit. However, there is little evidence that mass appeals cause masses of people to change their behavior (see Meyer et al., 1980).

Therapeutic Approaches

Behavioral therapists believe that unhealthy behaviors are conditioned responses that people often perform reflexively, without thinking. Behavioral therapists may use the technique of *shaping:* the therapist helps the patient develop a

These messages are part of mass-media campaigns aimed at changing people's behavior, but they may be more effective in altering opinions than behavior.

schedule of rewards for successive approximations to the goal of, say, not smoking. Another technique, *modeling,* relies on vicarious shaping and reinforcement. (For more on behavioral therapy, see Chapter 24.)

Cognitive therapies are designed to correct irrational thinking and false beliefs, and to promote self-control—in part by helping a person to become his or her own therapist. The first step is *self-monitoring.* An overweight person might record her food intake, noting what circumstances triggered an urge to eat and how she felt at the time. In this way she brings her automatic behavior into consciousness, becoming aware of her own particular pattern. She may find that she overeats to relieve anxiety, to counteract boredom, or to be sociable. The second step is to design a *contingency contract.* The client and therapist devise a system of specific rewards for achieving goals (attending a play or buying a new dress for losing five pounds) and punishments for failures (no TV or phone calls to friends if the client indulges in chocolate cake).

Most therapists who adopt this approach also employ *cognitive restructuring.* Internal monologues (what people say to themselves) often interfere with the desire to change: a smoker may find himself thinking, "I've tried to quit before and always failed." The therapist teaches the client more adaptive self-talk: "Getting through that meeting without a cigarette was an accomplishment!"

Evaluating the Various Approaches

How successful are these different techniques? In general, behavioral therapies are more effective than mass appeals, and cognitive approaches are more effective than traditional behavioral techniques. But high initial success rates are usually followed by high rates of return to the problem behavior, whether smoking, problem drinking, or overeating (Leventhal and Cleary, 1980; Kaplan, 1984). From 15 to 60 percent of the people who participate in health behavior modification programs relapse. Participating in a program—any program— motivates people to change, but initiating change seems to be easier than maintaining change. For this reason, many health psychologists have turned their attention to preventing youngsters from developing health-destructive habits in the first place. In doing so, they often rely on a combination of social, emotional, and cognitive appeals, in a multimodal approach.

Smoking Prevention: A Multimodal Approach

At least 15 percent of U.S. adolescents describe themselves as "smokers." Many if not most young people experiment with cigarettes. What causes some to acquire this extremely risky habit? Any number of studies show that teenagers are most likely to become smokers if they have a positive image of the smoker, if their peers pressure them to smoke, and if their parents and others whom they admire smoke. Teenagers often see the smoker as sophisticated and rebellious, as willing to take risks and defy authority figures. Smoking conveys this image; not smoking may invite accusations of being a "chicken" or a "sissy." Observing older adolescents and adults (especially parents) who enjoy smoking yet show no apparent ill effects eases youngsters' fears about the dangers of smoking.

Evans and his colleagues (1978) designed a multimodal program for the Houston School District to deal with these underlying motivations. Antismoking materials used in this program are designed to appeal specifically to adolescents. All teenagers know that smoking is risky, but few are concerned about health problems that might arise twenty or forty years in the future. Therefore, Evans concentrates on the current disadvantages of smoking (financial costs, bad breath, and the like). Films that explain the techniques advertisers use to sell cigarettes create a negative image of the smoker as someone who is easily duped. These are backed up by posters that appeal to the adolescent's need for independence: "You can decide for yourself."

Evans also uses older, high-status, nonsmoking peer leaders to model techniques for resisting social pressure. The goal is "behavioral inoculation," a social version of immunization. If individuals are exposed to a weak version of a germ, they develop antibodies to fight a stronger dose. By analogy, if individuals are exposed to weak versions of social pressure to smoke, they develop counterarguments that protect them when they are exposed to intense social pressure. Some of the peer models who appear in films participate in group discussions and practice sessions after the film is shown.

Programs like this have been somewhat successful in preventing teenagers from smoking, or at least delaying the onset of smoking (Leventhal and Cleary, 1980). In this case, some success —convincing 1,000 or even 500 teenagers not to smoke—saves lives.

Social Engineering

The most controversial approach to modifying behavior involves social engineering, or taking action on a societal level to enforce healthy behavior. Lowering the speed limit to fifty-five miles per hour, raising the legal age for drinking from eighteen to twenty-one, and banning smoking in public facilities are familiar examples. Social engineering can work. The decline of infectious diseases in the United States is in large part the result of government purification of public water supplies; it is doubtful that a campaign to convince people to boil their own water would have been as successful (Robertson, 1975). Similarly, when speed limits were lowered in the late 1970s to conserve energy, the number of deaths and injuries on the highways dropped significantly (Fielding, 1978). But social engineering can also backfire. During Prohibition, breaking the law became a national sport. Social engineering collides with individual freedom, something we value highly. Making cigarettes illegal would reduce deaths from lung cancer and heart disease, but many nonsmokers as well as smokers would consider this an assault on personal freedom.

Dissatisfied with the number of people who are helped by individual and group therapies, and mindful of the limits to social engineering, many health psychologists are looking to the schools, the workplace, and the community as natural opportunities to promote healthy habits. Programs may combine restructuring of the environment (creating nonsmoking areas in the workplace, for example, or providing low-calorie and low-cholesterol choices in school or workplace cafeterias; concrete incentives (time off for exercise, reduced health insurance premiums for nonsmokers); social pressure and social support (weight-reduction support groups among employees or lunch-hour aerobics classes) with specific therapies—a multimodal approach to primary prevention.

In this section we looked at some persistent but preventable health risks. In the next section we analyze stress—a health risk that no one can entirely avoid.

STRESS AND HEALTH

The symptoms of stress are all too familiar. Perhaps you have an interview for a job you have always wanted. You arrive five minutes early and take a seat in the reception area. You want to appear confident and self-assured, but your heart is racing, your mouth feels dry, and your hands shake as you reach for a magazine. Perhaps you are a student who is working twenty hours a week, carrying a full course load, and playing the lead in next month's drama club production. As the stress builds, you find that little problems begin to irritate you. Some days you forget to eat; some nights you are so tired you cannot sleep. Or perhaps your father calls to say that your mother is going into the hospital for some tests—but nothing to worry about, he assures you. You try to study, but find yourself reading the same page over and over. Your thoughts keep returning to the fight you had with your mother on Thanksgiving, and you forget the date you made to go to the movies tonight.

Stress is a pattern of disruptive physiological and psychological reactions to events that threaten a person's ability to cope. The symptoms of stress include physiological arousal (increases in pulse rate, blood pressure, and respiration); higher levels of certain hormones; cognitive disorganization (inability to concentrate, obsessive thoughts); and emotional upset (fear, anxiety, excitement, anger, embarrassment, depression). A certain amount of stress is an inevitable part of life. As one physiologist put it, "Complete freedom from stress is death" (Selye, 1974). But acute stress can interfere with emotional, cognitive, and physiological functioning. And chronic stress has been linked to degeneration of overall health, diseases of the upper respiratory tract (colds and flus), allergies, high blood pressure, and a greater risk of sudden cardiac death and heart disease (Jemmott and Locke, 1984).

There are three basic approaches to the study of stress. One is to identify events in the environment that cause physiological and psychological disruption. The second is to analyze the psychological and cognitive factors that shape an individual's response to potentially stressful events. The third is to examine the physiological consequences of stress.

Environmental Stresses and the *Social Readjustment Rating Scale*

At some times in our lives, most of us must cope with extremely upsetting events, such as death, losing a job, or divorce. All of us must deal with the annoyances and problems of daily life; we face traffic jams, noisy—or nosy—neighbors, "cash flow" problems, computer malfunctions, romantic breakups, too much work, too little sleep. Are some events inherently stressful? Is it possible to measure the impact of environmental events on our psychological and physical well-being?

Some years ago, Thomas Holmes and Richard Rahe (1967) asked medical patients to list stressful events they had experienced in the months before they became ill. They were surprised to discover that patients mentioned positive events such as Christmas or getting married and minor problems such as getting a traffic ticket as well as such clearly distressing events as the death of a spouse. Holmes and Rahe concluded that *change* is a major factor in stress. Even welcome events, such as an outstanding personal achievement, force people to make readjustments in their lives. And this causes physiological and psychological wear and tear.

Holmes and Rahe went on to devise the *Social Readjustment Rating Scale* which is shown in Table 21.1. They argued that 150 "life change units" (LCUs) in a single year greatly increased the odds that a person would become ill, and that 300 LCUs made an individual extremely vulnerable. Current research challenges the view that change, per se, causes stress (Glass, 1977.) Nevertheless, Holmes and Rahe devised the first objective measure of stress and directed the attention of researchers to events that do seem to correlate with ill health.

Separation and Loss

Holmes and Rahe found that the three most stressful events for most people are the death of a spouse (100 LCUs), divorce (73 LCUs), and separation (65 LCUs). Other research supports this finding. Premature death rates are consistently higher among people who are widowed, divorced, or single than among people who are married. This connection appears among males and females and among whites and nonwhites, and it is true for almost every cause of death, including heart attack, can-

Table 21.1 ■ Social Readjustment Rating Scale
The amount of life stress a person has experienced in a given period of time, say one year, is measured by the total number of life change units (LCUs). These units result from the addition of the values (shown in the right column) associated with events that the person has experienced during the target time period.

Rank		Mean Value
1	Death of spouse	100
2	Divorce	73
3	Marital separation	65
4	Jail term	63
5	Death of close family member	63
6	Personal injury or illness	53
7	Marriage	50
8	Fired at work	47
9	Marital reconciliation	45
10	Retirement	45
11	Change in health of family member	44
12	Pregnancy	40
13	Sex difficulties	39
14	Gain of new family member	39
15	Business readjustment	39
16	Change in financial state	38
17	Death of close friend	37
18	Change to different line of work	36
19	Change in number of arguments with spouse	35
20	Mortgage over $10,000	31
21	Foreclosure of mortgage or loan	30
22	Change in responsibilities at work	29
23	Son or daughter leaving home	29
24	Trouble with in-laws	29
25	Outstanding personal achievement	28
26	Spouse begin or stop work	26
27	Begin or end school	26
28	Change in living conditions	25
29	Revision of personal habits	24
30	Trouble with boss	23
31	Change in work hours or conditions	20
32	Change in residence	20
33	Change in schools	20
34	Change in recreation	19
35	Change in church activities	19
36	Change in social activities	18
37	Mortgage or loan less than $10,000	17
38	Change in sleeping habits	16
39	Change in number of family get-togethers	15
40	Change in eating habits	15
41	Vacation	13
42	Christmas	12
43	Minor violations of the law	11

Source: Holmes, T. H., and R. H. Rahe. The Social Readjustment Rating Scale. *Journal of Psychosomatic Research,* 1967, *11*, 213–218.

cer, strokes, cirrhosis, hypertension, pneumonia, suicide, and even automobile accidents (Lynch, 1977). In one study, the mortality rate for 4,500 British widowers was 40 percent higher during the first six months of widowhood than the rate for other men the same age (Parkes, Benjamin, and Fitzgerald, 1969). Many children who develop cancer have recently lost someone to whom they were close (Jacobs and Charles, 1980).

Can people actually "die of grief"? Media reports of *sudden death syndrome* suggest that they can.

▪ A sixty-nine-year-old man, returning from a visit to the grave of his wife, who had been buried the day before, bumped lightly into the rear of the car in front of him. While waiting for the police he got out of the car, walked around, got back into the car, and slumped over the steering wheel, dead. (Engel, 1971, p. 774)

▪ Thirty-nine-year-old twins, whom their family described as inseparable, died within a week of each other. The cause of death was unknown.

▪ The twenty-seven-year-old army captain who commanded the ceremonial troops at President Kennedy's funeral died ten days later of "cardiac irregularity and acute congestion." (Taylor, 1986)

Note, however, that sudden death syndrome seems to result from the combination of a severe shock and a preexisting physiological weakness, such as undetected heart disease or infection (Cottington et al., 1980). The overwhelming majority of people survive the death of a loved one, although they may be psychologically and physiologically vulnerable for a time thereafter.

Why are family and friends important to our health? They provide us with tangible support, such as meals when we are sick or when a family is grieving; with information, including practical advice on how to cope with a problem and feedback on our ideas; and with emotional support—the knowledge that we are loved and cared for when our self-esteem is threatened (Schaefer, Coyne, and Lazarus, 1981). Social support seems to mute the effects of stressful events, reducing the likelihood of illness and speeding recovery when we do become ill (Berkman and Syme, 1979).

Occupational Stress

Five of the items on the *Social Readjustment Rating Scale* deal with work. A large literature (summarized in Taylor, 1986) supports the view that stress in the workplace is associated with higher rates of illness and injury. The leading causes of occupational stress are work overload—longer hours, higher standards, and more tasks than people feel they can handle; pressure (demands to achieve); responsibility for others; role ambiguity, or lack of a clear idea of what their job is or how it will be evaluated; and role conflict, brought on when different people make incompatible demands on them; lack of opportunities for developing social relationships; career problems, such as feeling that they are being promoted too fast or too slowly; and lack of control over their work.

People who work in high-stress occupations may pay a high price. Air traffic controllers, who spend their days juggling the flights of giant airliners and whose minor mistakes can mean mass death, are four times as likely as commercial airline pilots to suffer from hypertension and are more than twice as likely to develop diabetes or peptic ulcers (Cobb, 1976). Occupational stress does not necessarily lead to illness, however. Workers may "cope" with stress in the workplace by showing up late, producing less than is expected, sabotaging management efforts to increase productivity, or quitting and looking for a less stressful job.

Traumatic Events

Traumatic events—earthquakes, floods, airplane crashes, fires, rape, assaults and war—result in distinctive patterns of stress. For days, weeks, even years after such an event, victims may relive it in painful memories and nightmares; suffer from extreme fatigue, hypersensitivity to noise, loss of appetite, and diminished sexual desire; and feel "emotionally anesthetized"—unable to respond to affection or to take interest in daily life (Brody, 1982).

Natural or manmade disasters are most likely to cause severe stress when a high percentage of the community is affected and many lives are lost (Glesser, Green, and Einget, 1981). Survivors often feel numb and unable to act. A man who lived through a flood in the West Virginia mining town of Buffalo Creek, which left 125 dead and thousands homeless, describes his immediate reaction: "I just didn't—I really didn't feel anything. Things just wasn't connected. Like I couldn't remember my own telephone number. . . . I couldn't remember where I lived. . . . I was just standing there and it seemed like I really didn't have anything on my mind at the time. Just everything disappeared" (Erikson, 1976, p. 162). Survivors may feel guilty, as if their taking a place on the survivor list had caused others to die. In July 1981, for example, two "skywalks" in the Hyatt Regency Hotel in Kansas City collapsed, killing 113 and injuring 200. In the weeks and

Traumatic events, like this bombing in Lebanon, leave survivors with predictable patterns of stress. They may be "emotionally anesthetized" for a long time afterward.

months after the disaster, people who had been injured actually had fewer emotional problems than did those who were not physically hurt: it was as if the injured people had already "paid their debt" (Brody, 1982).

"Hassles" and "Uplifts"

In recent years a number of researchers have begun to investigate the possibility that mildly stressful events—such familiar and frequent experiences as getting caught in traffic jams, waiting in lines, performing household chores, or losing things—take a toll on health. Daily hassles may have a cumulative effect, or they may make a person more vulnerable when a major life event strikes. Richard Lazarus and his colleagues (Lazarus, 1980) devised a "hassles scale," similar to the *Social Readjustment Rating Scale,* but composed of apparently trivial events. Their preliminary research suggests that everyday hassles are a better predictor of declines in physical health, and of depression and anxiety, than are major life events (Delongis et al., 1982). Lazarus and colleagues are now working on an "uplift measure," to determine if such everyday pleasures as listening to music, playing with one's child, and having a pleasant

dinner with friends act as a buffer against stress (Lazarus, Kanner, and Folkman, 1980).

Stress and Psychological Functioning

One person thrives on deadlines; another is immobilized by them. One person is thrilled by an invitation to speak at a political rally; another is terrified; and still another is bored. One woman views the discovery of a breast tumor as a death sentence and loses interest in daily events; another views this threat to her health as a challenge and finds that daily events take on new meaning. Given individual variations in responses to potentially stressful events, a number of psychologists have come to view the psychological and cognitive elements of stress as paramount.

Psychological Appraisal of Potential Stressors

Richard Lazarus (Lazarus, 1968; Lazarus and Folkman, in press) is a leading spokesman for the view that stress depends not on the event itself, but on how a person appraises the event and his or her ability to cope with the situation. This psychological view of stress contends that when we are faced with new or changing circumstances, we first determine what these events mean. Lazarus calls this process **primary appraisal.** Primary appraisal depends on the person's motives and goals. A student who receives a C on a chemistry exam, for example, may see this event as beneficial ("I never thought I'd pass"), neutral ("I'm only taking chemistry because it's required"), or negative ("I need a B or better to get into medical school"). Negative events are then analyzed for the degree of danger they represent. The student may conclude that he or she has been harmed irrevocably ("Now I'm automatically excluded from the premed program"), threatened ("My chances of getting the B that I need to get into medical school are slim"), or challenged ("I'll just have to work twice as hard and try for an A on the final").

The next step is **secondary appraisal**— assessing whether we have the ability and resources to cope with the situation. A student who is struggling with four difficult courses and a part-time job is more likely to feel stressed than one who has more time to study and a roommate who offers to help. Thus, how much stress individuals experience depends on the balance between their primary and secondary appraisals. If the degree of perceived harm or threat is high and their self-appraisal is low, they will feel considerable stress. But if the threat or harm seems small, and/or the person's coping ability is high, stress will be slight.

The psychological approach has enabled researchers to identify not only the kinds of events that are most likely to create immediate stress but also those that are likely to lead to negative appraisals and additional stress in the future.

Predictability and Control

Whether we experience stress depends in part on whether we believe that events are predictable and that we have some control over what happens to us. During World War II, for example, Londoners, who were bombed with considerable regularity, showed few signs of anxiety. But residents of the surrounding villages, where bombing was infrequent but unpredictable, showed high levels of anxiety and apprehension (Vernon, 1941). Predictable events are less stressful because we can prepare for them. If we know when an aversive event will occur, we also know when it will *not* occur and

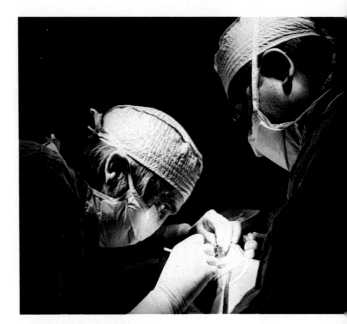

Surgeons may suffer somewhat less anxiety and stress than might be thought. Their high level of training and skill provides the control they need when performing an operation.

thus when it is safe to resume normal activities. When aversive events are unpredictable, anticipatory stress remains constantly high.

The effects of unpredictability have been demonstrated in the laboratory both with animals (Badia, Harsh, and Abbott, 1979; Weiss, 1977) and with human subjects. In one experiment (Glass and Singer, 1972), researchers asked female college students to perform simple verbal and mathematical tasks. While they were doing the tasks, one group of women was subjected to random bursts of loud, aversive noise (at 110 decibels, the level of a motorcycle engine); another group was exposed to the same bursts of noise, but at regular, predictable intervals. A control group was allowed to work in peace and quiet. Then the noise was turned off, and the women were asked to perform more complex tasks, which included seven pages of difficult proofreading and two insolvable puzzles. The women in the group that had been exposed to loud, unpredictable noise earlier in the experiment gave up sooner and made many more mistakes than did the women in the other two groups. The energy they had spent overcoming the distraction and irritation of loud, random noise was energy they could not apply toward the new task.

A feeling of being in control may be even more important than being able to predict events (Thompson, 1981). In another experiment (Glass, Reim, and Singer, 1971), researchers gave pairs of male college students a series of simple tasks to do and exposed them to random bursts of the same 110-decibel noise used in the study just described. One group of students was told that they could stop the noise by signaling their partner but that the researchers preferred that they not do so. The other students were given no means of control. The students in the first group did not take advantage of the signal to stop the noise, yet when they were given a subsequent task they performed much better—and showed significantly less tension—than the students who felt they had had no control over the noise (see Figure 21.1).

In general, it seems that the inability to control or avoid danger can be more stressful than danger itself. During World War II, fighter pilots had the highest casualty rates among flight crews, yet they reported less fear than either bomber pilots or their gun crews, who stood a much better chance

of surviving (Rachman, 1978). Why? Fighter pilots had more flexibility and therefore more control than bomber pilots, who were required to fly in formation. Members of the gun crews, who were comparatively safe but had no control over their planes, were the most fearful of all. As this example suggests, it is the degree of *perceived* control that the person has—not the actual degree of control—that determines anxiety.

Learned Helplessness

The belief that we are unable to do anything to relieve certain types of stress is rooted in folk wisdom, and most of us have repeated such familiar sayings as "You can't fight city hall" or "Better the devil you know than the devil you don't." In addition, our own experiences lead us to express similar sentiments, such as "I can't learn to dance—I have two left feet" or "I'll never get more than a C in this course no matter what I do." Since feelings of helplessness impaired performance in the noise experiment and led to anxiety among flight crews, there is the possibility that feeling helpless in one situation might teach us to be helpless in other kinds of situations.

Experiments with dogs indicate that this may indeed be the case. In an already classic experiment (Overmier and Seligman, 1967), each dog was placed in a sling, where it received a series of shocks. Nothing a dog did had any effect on the shocks, and the animal could not escape. Later each dog was placed in a shuttlebox, consisting of two compartments separated by a low barrier that the dog could easily jump. A series of electrical shocks was then delivered to the dog's feet through a grid on the floor of the box. Instead of leaping into the safe compartment, the dog simply sat and endured the shock. Some dogs never learned to escape, even after they were lifted from one compartment to the other to show them the way. A control group of dogs, which had not been subjected to inescapable shock, learned to escape after the first or second shock. Martin Seligman and his associates propose that the dogs were victims of **learned helplessness,** and that a similar mechanism underlies human depression, a disorder we shall consider in Chapter 22. However, the concept of learned helplessness also provides a way to understand the effects of uncontrollable environmental stress.

Research has demonstrated that learned help-

Figure 21.1. Coping with a stressful environment. In two experiments David Glass and colleagues have shown that exposure to uncontrollable and unpredictable noise had a much greater effect on performance of a subsequent task in a quiet environment than did exposure to controllable and unpredictable noise. More effort is required to adapt to the unpredictable and uncontrollable noise, which leaves the person less able to deal effectively with future tasks.

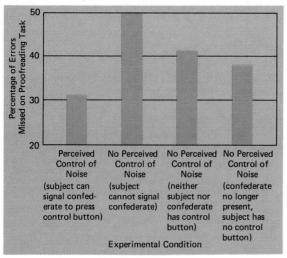

lessness can be an important factor in the failure to adjust to stressful events. In one study (Hiroto and Seligman, 1975), groups of college students were subjected to an inescapable loud tone. On subsequent tasks, when the students could escape from the unpleasant, distracting noise, they made fewer attempts to get away from it and performed the new task poorly compared with students who had earlier experienced a tone from which they could escape. Inescapable noise was not the only means of inducing such helplessness. Students who faced a series of unpredictable failures at a problem-solving task also learned to be helpless. Furthermore, helplessness learned in one situation carried over to the other, so that students who could not escape a tone were also helpless in the problem-solving task.

Although the concept of learned helplessness seems to apply to many situations, it is incomplete. As Seligman and his colleagues (Abramson, Seligman, and Teasdale, 1978) point out, the concept does not explain why some people become helpless when confronted with an aversive event and others who face the identical event do not. Nor does it account for the fact that people generally feel sad or guilty after enduring aversive events that cannot be avoided.

To fill these gaps in the theory, Seligman and his associates have revised their explanation of learned helplessness. According to the new formulation, learned helplessness is not simply the result of a person's belief that she or he lacks control over a situation but depends upon the person's explanations for this lack of control. People are likely to become helpless only when they see their lack of control as due to causes that are (1) permanent rather than temporary; (2) internal (located within themselves) rather than external (located within the environment); and (3) applicable to many areas of their life rather than limited to a single area of functioning.

Stress and Physiological Functioning

Studies of environmental stresses and psychological responses provide us with many examples of the effects of stress on health. But how, exactly, does stress affect the body? How are psychological experiences translated into physiological symptoms?

Selye's General Adaptation Syndrome

Hans Selye (1956; 1976) was a pioneer in the study of stress and physiological functioning. As a medical student Selye learned that each disease has its own particular causes and its own peculiar symptoms (the medical model described at the beginning of this chapter). In practice, however, he noted that patients suffering from a wide variety of diseases often exhibited similar symptoms, including loss of appetite, apathy, and weakness. He suspected that these symptoms were a generalized response to a stressful attack on the body. Years later he tested this hypothesis in the laboratory by exposing mice to extreme cold, prolonged hunger, fatigue, and a variety of toxic substances. He found that all of these stressors produced the same physiological response: enlarged adrenal glands, shrunken thymus and lymph nodes, and stomach ulcers.

Selye went on to propose a "general adaptation syndrome" that applies to humans as well as to laboratory animals. This syndrome can be broken down into three stages: alarm, resistance, and exhaustion. In the alarm stage, an initial shock causes the autonomic nervous system to send adrenal hormones through the body, preparing the glands and organs for action. In the resistance stage, local defenses take over. If the stressor is a virus, antibodies rush to the scene. If the stressor is a psychological threat, the sympathetic nervous system prepares for "fight or flight." The body has mobilized. In most cases the stressor is defeated, and the body returns to normal. If the stress continues, however, the resistance effort exhausts the body's resources, and the organism succumbs to exhaustion. Exhaustion causes physiological damage and sometimes death. If a man falls into icy water, for example, he goes numb (the alarm stage). Then his autonomic nervous system takes over, enabling him to adapt to the cold (the resistance phase). If he stays in the icy water very long, however, he becomes exhausted and may not recover, even if he is rescued.

Selye's research was a milestone, for he went beyond speculations to identify physiological processes that might link stress to illness. But critics (e.g., J. Mason, 1974) believe that he underestimated the role psychological factors play in stress and illness. Moreover, they say that Selye's concept of "exhaustion" is too broad. New research suggests that specific stressors, personality traits, and/or socioeconomic conditions are implicated in specific physiological disorders. Here we will examine in detail three of the leading causes of chronic and terminal illness, filling in the picture Selye sketched.

Stress and Hypertension

An estimated 30 million Americans suffer from hypertension, or high blood pressure. Elevated blood pressure is a common response to stress (Shapiro and Goldstein, 1982). In hypertensive individuals, this response is chronic and dangerous (Galton, 1973).

In the United States hypertension is most common among black males. Research by Harburg and his colleagues (Harburg et al., 1973; Gentry et al., 1982) shows that this one fact conceals multiple causes. Harburg's team studied a large population of males in Detroit. They found that hypertension was more common among white and black men who lived in high-stress areas, characterized by poverty, crime, crowding, and high divorce rates, than among men in low-stress areas. It was more common among blacks than whites in these areas, implicating both their minority status and genetic makeup, and was also more common among blacks who exhibited "suppressed rage," or a tendency to direct anger inward, on psychological measures.

How is "rage" translated into a physiological disability? Because of genetic or other factors, hypertensive individuals may be particularly sensitive to stress (Harrell, 1980). Their blood pressure rises rapidly in response to minor stress, or even the anticipation of stress, and it takes longer to return to normal levels in them than it does in most people.

Stress and Coronary Heart Disease

Coronary heart disease (CHD) is the leading cause of death and chronic illness in the United States today. CHD occurs when the blood vessels that supply the heart are narrowed or closed, blocking the supply of oxygen and nutrients to the heart. CHD has been linked to hypertension, diabetes, smoking, obesity, high levels of cholesterol, and low levels of physical activity (American Heart Association, 1984). Taken together, however,

these risk factors account for less than half of known cases of CHD.

Some years ago, two physicians, M. Friedman and R. H. Rosenman (1974), identified a behavioral and emotional pattern they believed greatly increased the risk of CHD. Friedman and Rosenman labeled those who exhibited this pattern as **Type A personalities;** such individuals are impatient, highly competitive, and hostile when thwarted. Their fast-paced lives are characterized by a continual struggle to achieve more in less time, regardless of the social and psychological consequences for themselves and others, and by the nagging feeling that they could achieve still more. Type As tend to blame themselves for failures that are beyond their control (Brunson and Matthews, 1981). Type B individuals, in contrast, are patient, relaxed, and better able "to roll with the punches."

A longitudinal study of more than 2,000 male executives (Rosenman et al., 1975) found that Type As were twice as likely as Type Bs to develop CHD, and five times more likely to have a second heart attack—even after family history, smoking, hypertension, and high cholesterol levels were controlled for. The link between CHD and Type A behavior is one of the best-documented in the literature on stress and illness.

How does Type A behavior lead to coronary heart disease? There is some evidence that Type As are hyperresponsive (Glass, 1977). When exposed to stress, their bodies respond with exceptionally high levels of sympathetic nervous activity, which causes wear and tear on the heart. Paradoxically, there is also some evidence that Type As are *hypo*reactive, or underreactive, and do not feel the symptoms of fatigue or stress that warn other people to slow down (Carver, DeGregorio, and Gillis, 1981). Both may be correct. Current research is directed at identifying connections between specific elements of Type A behavior and different forms of CHD (Matthews, 1982; Carver and Humphries, 1982).

Are There Links Between Stress and Cancer?

The term "cancer" refers to more than a hundred different diseases, all of which are characterized by a malfunction in the mechanisms that control cell reproduction. The slow, regular duplication of cells that normally goes on is replaced by a rapid production of abnormal cells that invade the body. Some cancers develop rapidly; others develop slowly over a period of ten or twenty years; the course of still others is irregular and unpredictable.

Certain cancers run in families and ethnic groups, a fact that suggests that cancer is, in part, genetic. But members of a family or ethnic group share a lifestyle as well as genes, and one may compound the other. Breast cancer is common among North American women and rare among Asian women. But the longer Japanese-American women live in the United States and the more Americanized they become, the more likely they are to develop breast cancer (Wynder et al., 1963). Cancer has also been linked to stressful life events, especially the loss or disruption of social supports (Sklar and Anisman, 1981). Married people are somewhat less likely to develop cancer than are single people.

A number of psychologists are investigating the possibility that cancer is linked to personality traits. Some researchers (Bahnson, 1981; Dattore, Scontz, and Coyne, 1980) suspect that people who learn to cope with stress through denial and repression (two defense mechanisms discussed further in Chapter 18) are more vulnerable to cancer than those who deal with stress more directly. Others have suggested that personality factors may influence the sequence of events once cancer has appeared (see Levy, 1983). According to this view, combative individuals who are angry about developing cancer and hostile toward physicians and nurses live longer than those who are passive and accepting. Depression may increase vulnerability to cancer by reducing immunocompetence, or the body's ability to protect itself from invaders (Jemmott and Locke, 1984).

We must emphasize that this research is still in the exploratory phase. To date, there is no firm evidence linking cancer to personality traits. Suppose researchers did find that cancer victims tend to be passive. How would we know which came first? Denial may be a *response* to cancer, not a precipitating factor. It is important to avoid "blaming the victim" for a disease over which he or she has no control.

Coping with stress

Coping is the process of managing external and internal pressures that might otherwise lead to

stress. Successful coping depends on a combination of problem-solving ability and emotional self-regulation (Cohen and Lazarus, 1979). A person is coping well if he or she is able to change environmental conditions that are harmful or threatening (problem solving); to adjust to painful but unavoidable realities; and to regain emotional equilibrium after an upset, maintaining a positive self-image and continuing satisfying relationships with others (emotional self-regulation).

Hardiness

S. C. Kobasa (1979) studied successful and unsuccessful coping in a group of business executives. Using a checklist similar to the *Social Readjustment Rating Scale*, she singled out executives who had encountered a large number of potentially stressful events in the preceding three years. Then she determined which of the highly stressed executives had experienced health problems during that period and which had not. When the two groups were compared, distinct differences in personality and behavioral style emerged. Highly stressed but healthy executives had a strong sense of commitment and became deeply involved with people and activities. They felt in control of their lives, taking credit for their successes and blame for their failures. They welcomed challenge and tended to see new activities and changes in routine as opportunities for growth.

Kobasa concluded that the combination of commitment, control, and challenge makes a person "hardy." Hardy individuals seem able to transform potentially stressful situations into less stressful experiences. They tend to appraise both new situations and their own ability to cope in positive terms. As a result, they take direct action, learn more about people and events than they would if they avoided the situation or denied the problem, and are therefore better prepared to deal with new situations in the future. Although Kobasa's study has been criticized on methodological grounds (Ganellen and Blaney, 1984), it does provide a positive counterpoint to portraits of unhealthy coping styles—such as Type A behavior.

Controlling Arousal

What can be done to help individuals who are not hardy by nature to cope with stressful events so as

Tension and anxiety are reduced by exercises that relax the muscles.

to reduce both externally and internally imposed wear and tear? The growing literature on stress and physiological functioning has inspired a number of therapies designed to reduce physiological arousal. The most common approach is relaxation training.

In **progressive relaxation,** which was developed by Edmund Jacobson (1938; 1964), the individual tenses and then releases different muscle groups in sequence. During this process the individual learns to relax deeply the muscles of the body. For example, the first step might be to bend the left hand as far back as possible and to notice the pattern of strain in the back of the hand and up the arm. After maintaining that position for about ten seconds, the person is told to let the hand relax completely (a procedure Jacobson called "going negative") and to notice the difference in sensation at the points where the strain had been felt. The object of this training program is to teach the individual how each muscle group

feels when relaxed and to provide practice in achieving further relaxation. Once a person can discriminate patterns of muscle tension from those of relaxation, she or he no longer is required to tense the muscles before relaxing them. Instead the muscles are relaxed from whatever level of tension they have reached.

An abbreviated form of progressive relaxation is an important part of a procedure used in behavior therapy, called systematic desensitization, which will be described in Chapter 24. By itself, progressive relaxation is an effective treatment for a variety of stress-related disorders. For example, studies have found that progressive relaxation effectively reduces general tension and anxiety (Borkovec, Grayson, and Cooper, 1978); relieves insomnia (Borkovec et al., 1979); and reduces high blood pressure (Jacob, Kraemer, and Agras, 1977).

A second relaxation procedure, called **autogenic training,** which depends upon self-suggestion and imagery, was developed by Johannes Schultz and Wolfgang Luthe (1969). They devised this technique after observing that during hypnosis people seemed to be able to induce physiological changes in themselves. A suggestion to a hypnotized person that an arm is getting heavy often elicits changes in the arm's muscle potential, indicating that the arm is becoming very relaxed. Schultz and Luthe speculated that a person did not need hypnosis to elicit physiological changes, but could achieve the same effects with language. To accomplish this, the individual repeats suggestions, such as "My arm is heavy. I am at peace. My arm is heavy." Each attempt to relax lasts from thirty to sixty seconds. After an individual has learned to make the whole body "heavy," she or he follows similar procedures to induce warmth, control heart rate, respiration, and abdominal warmth, and cool the forehead. Both progressive relaxation and autogenic training were found to be effective treatments for insomniacs (Nicassio and Bootzin, 1974).

A third technique for reducing physiological arousal is **biofeedback.** As described in Chapter 7, biofeedback is a form of operant conditioning designed to make people aware of an unconscious physiological response so that they can learn to control it. The patient is hooked to a machine that translates some bodily activity into light or sound patterns that the person can identify. For example, heart rate might be converted into a tone that becomes louder when the person's heart rate rises and softer when his or her rate decreases. Then, through a process of trial and error, the patient attempts to control this response. One patient may find that slow, regular, deep breathing lowers his heart rate; another, that deliberately trying to relax her muscles produces the desired change. The constant feedback enables many people to become quite skilled at controlling what used to be an automatic, unconscious response.

A number of researchers have reported that biofeedback is successful in reducing the incidence and severity of tension headaches and migraines, lowering blood pressure, and treating Reynaud's disease (in which a reduced flow of blood to the extremities produces cold, pain, and in extreme cases gangrene) (Sterman, 1978; Yates, 1980; B. Brown, 1980). But reviews of a large number of experiments suggest that biofeedback is no more effective—and much more expensive—than simple relaxation techniques. Indeed, some critics believe that changes in arousal attributed to biofeedback are the result of other factors, such as relaxation, an enhanced sense of control, suggestion, or perhaps a placebo effect (Turk et al., 1979).

Stress Management

Stress management programs are workshops designed to alter cognitive and behavioral responses to stress (Meichenbaum and Jaremko, 1983). This approach is based on the view that stress is not a simple matter of stimulus and response; it also is affected by a person's appraisals of the situation and of his or her ability to cope.

Stress management programs typically begin with education. Participants are taught about the role of cognitive appraisal in creating and maintaining stress, and they are given techniques for identifying the sources of stress in their lives and their own patterns of coping. In the second phase of the program, participants are introduced to an array of new techniques for coping with stress. Most programs employ the cognitive-behavioral strategies we mentioned earlier in our discussion of changing health habits, such as positive self-talk and contingency contracting. Most also include relaxation techniques, and many offer training in specific skills as well. Individuals who often feel that they are being "pushed around" by others will be given assertiveness training; people who often feel overwhelmed by demands on their time will be given help in time management. Partici-

pants are encouraged to "inoculate" themselves against stress by planning ahead and developing several strategies for dealing with situations they find particularly difficult (Meichenbaum and Turk, 1982). In the third phase, participants practice new coping skills in real-life situations, then report their experiences to the trainer and the group for feedback and suggestions.

This multimodal approach has been used successfully to treat headaches and high blood pressure, to train Type A individuals to use Type B coping skills, and to reduce such health risks as problem drinking and obesity, which often turn out to be responses to stress.

Environmental Intervention

Some environments, such as hospitals and nursing homes for the elderly, are inherently stressful. In requiring inhabitants to follow preestablished

Living at home permits this elderly woman to control her activities and to maintain a sense of freedom. People in nursing homes often lose this freedom and begin to feel helpless.

Vietnam Veterans: A Special Case?

Manmade disasters—especially war—may provoke more severe stress reactions than natural disasters do (Glesser, Green, and Einget, 1981). Combat veterans often suffer from "shell shock" and "combat fatigue." A soldier may break down after an engagement in which he has had a close brush with death and in which a number of his buddies were killed. But the breakdown usually follows months of fear, deprivation, extreme cold or heat, lack of sleep, and narrow escapes. Often soldiers do not feel the effects of war until they have returned to civilian life.

Studies of Vietnam veterans show an exceptionally high rate of post-traumatic stress disorder. According to Dr. Arthur S. Blank, Jr., director of the Vietnam Veteran Counseling Centers, between 350,000 and 400,000 of the 3.7 million Americans who served in Vietnam are still suffering from mild to severe forms of the disorder (in Lyons, 1984). Symptoms include nightmares, vivid flashbacks to scenes of horror, chronic startle reactions, and a tendency toward violent aggression. In some men these symptoms did not appear until months after they had returned to civilian life; many are still suffering the aftereffects of the war.

Why is post-traumatic stress more common among veterans of the war in Vietnam than among veterans of World Wars I and II? J. I. Walker and J. O. Cavenar (1982) suggest four

reasons: (1) Most soldiers were shipped to Vietnam alone, rather than in groups, and once there, they were transferred frequently. They were unable to develop the group ties and social supports that serve as a buffer against stress. (2) Public opposition to the war and the lack of an all-out campaign to win the war created an atmosphere of purposelessness. Soldiers who fought in World Wars I and II knew that they were "fighting the good fight"; the public was behind them. Vietnam soldiers did not have this unanimous support. They did not return to cheering crowds and victory parades, as veterans of the two world wars had, for the simple reason that there was no victory. (3) High rates of drug use in Vietnam tended to hide psychological problems from military psychiatrists. Soldiers "treated themselves" with drugs; they did not receive the counseling they might have received otherwise. (4) Many soldiers were shipped home suddenly, with little or no time to ease the transition from combat to civilian life. In many cases neither they nor their families and friends wanted to discuss the war. Society expected them to pick up their lives as if nothing had happened.

In addition, the soldiers who went to Vietnam tended to be younger than the men who fought in other wars. The average age of soldiers in World War II was 26 years; the average age of soldiers who fought

in Vietnam, 19.2 years (Lyons, 1984). They went to war during the stage of life when most young people are putting together an identity and working out commitments to occupations and intimate relationships. They spent this period of their life on the battlefield. For many, the result was identity diffusion. On their return, many felt "I'm changed," "I don't fit in," "I'm twenty and I came back fifty." Unresolved identity issues are resurfacing as these men approach midlife.

For many years after the United States withdrew, the special problems of Vietnam veterans went unrecognized. Vietnam veterans, it was thought, were no different from other members of the so-called "hippie" generation who were turned on to drugs and turned off to traditional occupations. The American Psychiatric Association did not recognize post-traumatic stress disorder as a distinct syndrome until 1980. The climate of opinion has changed, however. The Veterans Administration and the public at large are more sympathetic to their problems. In the words of Robert O. Muller, president of Vietnam Veterans of America, "Vietnam veterans are less likely to be seen as crazy, out-of-control time bombs, and this enhances the probability that veterans will seek treatment, and benefit from it" (in Lyons, 1984).

routines, nursing homes inevitably deprive the elderly of personal freedom. Research shows that the loss of control can lead to feelings of helplessness and hopelessness, aggravating the stresses of aging and illness. Restructuring the environment can restore control, improve coping, and perhaps improve health.

E.J. Langer and J. Rodin (1976) worked with ninety-one residents in a nursing home for the aged, whose ages ranged from sixty-five to ninety. After dividing these people into two groups, the investigators encouraged people in the first group to take responsibility for their belongings and to make decisions about how they spent their time. Those in the second group were encouraged to leave decisions and responsibility to the staff. People in the first group, for example, were allowed to choose a plant and care for it themselves, and to decide which night they would like to see a movie. Those in the other group were given plants that the staff chose and cared for, and were assigned a movie night.

Three weeks later, according to ratings by the residents themselves and observations by the staff, 93 percent of the group that had been encouraged to take more control of their environment showed overall improvement; they were more active and felt happier. Only 21 percent of the group that had been encouraged to rely on the staff were judged to have improved.

Eighteen months after they had rearranged conditions in the nursing home, the researchers returned and assessed the health and well-being of the people in both groups (Rodin and Langer, 1977). The old people who had been encouraged to take responsibility were still more vigorous and active than those who had been encouraged to leave decisions to the staff. Furthermore, there had been a lower death rate in the first group: 15 percent, in contrast to 30 percent for the other group.

These findings are of great potential importance in shaping our policies and practices not only in homes for the elderly, but also in the workplace and in schools. It may be that preserving a feeling of control and responsibility will add years of happy, more vigorous activity to our lives.

SUMMARY

1. **Health psychology** is the branch of psychology that focuses on why people maintain or neglect their health, how and why they become ill, and how they react when they become ill. In contrast to the traditional medical model, health psychology assumes that psychological, social, and biological processes all play important roles in health and illness; that most illnesses have multiple causes and effects; and that health is something to be achieved, not something to be taken for granted.

2. The growth of health psychology reflects the changing patterns of health and illness in our society. Chronic illnesses that result in part from lifestyle are more common today than acute, infectious diseases. To some extent these chronic disorders are preventable, or at least controllable.

3. The aim of **primary prevention** is to discover why people develop unhealthy habits (such as smoking, overeating, or problem drinking), and how these can be changed. Social factors (socioeconomic status, cultural norms, and socialization), emotional factors (styles of coping with disappointment, for example), and cognitive factors (including attitudes, values, and knowledge of health risks) all play a role in establishing and maintaining good or bad health habits. The **health belief model** holds that people's habits depend, first, on whether they believe they are vulnerable, and second, on whether they believe that changing their behavior will reduce risks to their health.

4. A number of techniques for eliminating unhealthy behavior patterns have been tested. Mass appeals may change the climate of opinion. Behavioral therapies may establish new responses to stress (through shaping, modeling, and the like). Cognitive therapies emphasize self-monitoring, contingency contracts, and cognitive restructuring to enable the client to act as his or her own therapist. Social engineering may enforce change but infringe on individual rights.

5. **Stress** is a pattern of disruptive physiological and psychological responses to events that interfere with a person's ability to function. A certain amount of stress is an inevitable part of living, but some situations take a higher toll than others. Separation and loss, occupational problems, traumatic events, and an accumulation of "hassles" are major environmental sources of stress. But stress also depends on psychological factors; on whether people believe that they can predict and control events in their environment. Those who believe they cannot control events develop **learned helplessness.**

6. Selye, a pioneer in the study of stress and physiological functioning, held that the body responds to stress in three stages: alarm, resistance, and finally exhaustion if the stress continues. According to Selye, the alarm stage mobilizes the body to cope with danger, but prolonged mobilization can lead to exhaustion and even death. Current research focuses on the relationship between stress and specific diseases, including hypertension, coronary heart disease, and—perhaps—cancer. There is considerable evidence that persons with **Type A personalities**—people who are highly competitive, hostile when thwarted, and always seem to be working against time—are far more likely to develop heart disease than the relaxed, unpressured Type Bs.

7. **Coping** is the process of managing external and internal pressures that at first seem intolerable. According to Kobasa, "hardiness" to the effects of stress results from commitment, control, and flexibility. Hardy individuals enjoy a challenge. Psychologists have devised a number of techniques for assisting people who are not hardy by nature to control their reactions to stress. Three techniques for reducing physiological arousal are **progressive relaxation** (through deep breathing and muscle relaxation), **autogenic training** (based on self-suggestion), and **biofeedback.** Stress management workshops combine these techniques with training in coping skills. Psychologists have also discovered relatively simple ways of restructuring stressful environments (such as nursing homes and hospitals) to give inhabitants more control over events, thus enhancing their ability to cope.

KEY TERMS

autogenic training	health belief model	primary appraisal	secondary appraisal
biofeedback	health psychology	primary prevention	stress
coping	learned helplessness	progressive relaxation	Type A personality

RECOMMENDED READINGS

CALHOUN, J. F., and J. R. ACOCELLA. *Psychology of adjustment and human relationships* (2nd ed.). New York: Random House, 1983. This is a textbook, but it is also a very practical guide to problem solving. The authors present psychological principles relevant to the process of adjustment, and they provide clear illustrations of how the principles may be applied.

KUTASH, I. L., and L. B. SCHLESINGER (Eds.). *Handbook on stress and anxiety.* San Francisco: Jossey-Bass, 1980. An excellent collection of chapters by leading theorists and researchers dealing with a variety of topics on stress and anxiety.

SELYE, H. *Stress without distress.* Philadelphia: Lippincott, 1974. A very readable overview of the field of stress by one of the major figures in the field.

TAYLOR, S. E. *Health psychology.* New York: Knopf, 1985. A comprehensive survey of health psychology. Examines the role that psychological and social factors play in illness and health.

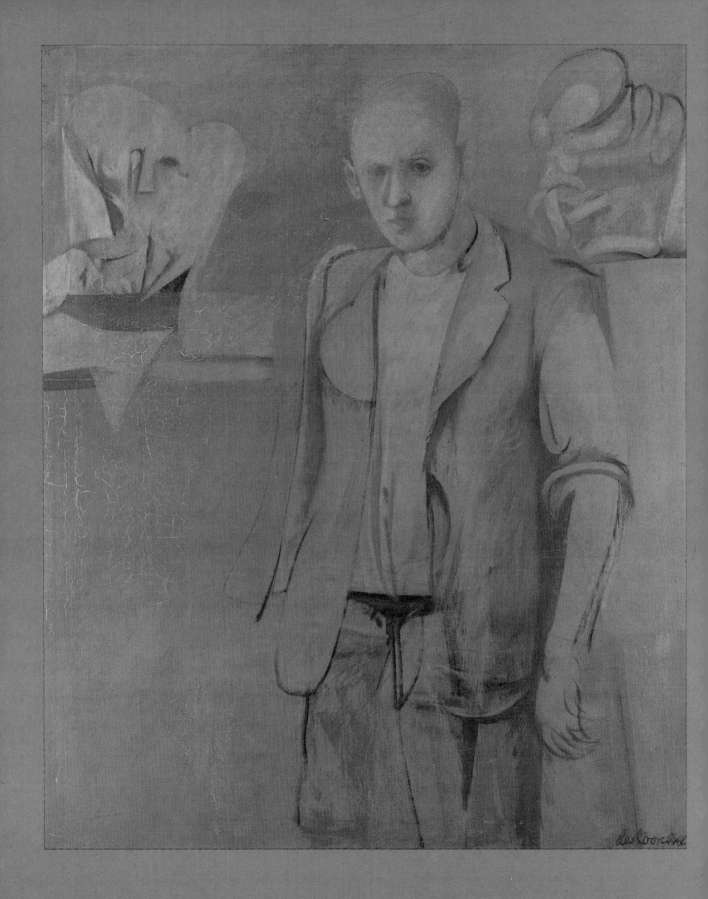

PSYCHOLOGICAL DISORDERS

A scantily clad woman staggers toward you. She is soaked with perspiration, her lips are flecked with foam, her face is contorted, and she can barely speak. If you met this woman in an art gallery, you might think her mad. But if you were standing at the finish line of the Boston marathon, you would probably applaud her courage and endurance. A man invites his friends and neighbors to a party, where he gives them all of his possessions, thus making himself a pauper. Most of us would consider him demented, yet when this same behavior takes place at a ceremony called the potlatch, it elicits respect and admiration among the members of Native American tribes in the Pacific Northwest. Behavior that appears abnormal in one context can seem perfectly ordinary in another situation. Given such widely different interpretations of the same actions, can we say with any confidence when behavior is abnormal?

DEFINITIONS OF ABNORMALITY

In medicine "abnormality" generally refers to a lack of integrity in any organ's structure or function. A broken bone, an excess of certain sugars in the blood, an ulcer on the wall of the stomach—all are abnormal. For physicians, the line between normality and abnormality is relatively easy to draw. For psychologists and psychiatrists, however, the criteria that divide normal behavior from abnormal behavior are not so easily specified. As we shall see, there are several ways of defining psychological abnormality, and some of these definitions may change from one society to another and from time to time in the same society.

Norm Violation

Each society has a set of **norms**—rules that prescribe "right" and "wrong" behavior—by which its members live. These norms cover every aspect of life, from whom one may marry and when to what food may be eaten and where. In American society, scantily clad, sweat-soaked women who attend art galleries and men who give away all their possessions have violated cultural norms.

Since norms are absorbed in childhood during the process of socialization, people take them for granted. Although nearly every one of their actions is governed by some norm, people notice a norm only when it is broken—and if the violation is bizarre, they label the violator as abnormal. Thus, the man without a jacket who enters an expensive restaurant will be lent one by the management, the barefooted person who enters will be turned away, but the person who comes in naked will be arrested and will probably receive a psychiatric examination.

Norms change over the years, sometimes gradually and almost imperceptibly, but at other times the change is accompanied by friction. For example, one aim of the Gay Liberation Movement is to convince society to change its norms so that homosexuality is regarded as normal behavior. Despite loud resistance from certain sections of society, these attempts have had some success and reflect the fact that American definitions of normality have broadened over the past few decades —especially in regard to sexual conduct. As a result, the range of behavior that is considered abnormal has shrunk somewhat.

Since norms can change drastically, they may seem an inappropriate basis for the definition of normality. Yet they remain the dominant standard because they have been so deeply absorbed that they seem natural, right, and proper, and violations automatically seem abnormal. Norms may even be grounded in the evolutionary history of the species. Since a social group cannot exist without some kind of norms, their development may have some survival value. A danger in using only norms to define abnormality is that they may enforce conformity as "good" and mark the nonconformist as automatically "bad."

Statistical Abnormality

A related, but somewhat different, way of defining abnormality is to call it any substantial deviation from a statistically calculated average. People whose behavior conforms with that of the majority are considered normal; those whose behavior differs greatly are abnormal. This statistical definition automatically encompasses norm violators, because the majority of people follow cultural norms.

The greatest attraction of the statistical definition of abnormality is its simplicity, and it continues to be used in some areas of psychological functioning. For example, the diagnosis of mental retardation is in large part statistical: people whose scores on intelligence tests fall below the range established as average are considered retarded.

Although a statistical definition of abnormality does make such diagnoses simple, this view of psychological functioning also presents problems. Using statistics to define the bounds of normality leaves us without any way to distinguish between the desirable differences of genius and creativity and the undesirable difference of psychological disorder. Indeed, "average" human behavior may not be the sort that society would like to encourage. If we were to apply a statistical yardstick, people without symptoms of psychological disturbance would be considered abnormal.

Personal Discomfort

A less restrictive approach to the definition of abnormality than either norm violation or statistical rarity is that of personal discomfort, in which people judge their own normality and only those who are distressed by their own thoughts or behavior are considered abnormal. This approach is now being used by many psychologists and psychiatrists in regard to homosexuality, and the diagnosis of psychological disorder is reserved for homosexuals who are seriously unhappy with their sexual preference (American Psychiatric Association, 1980).

This approach allows genius to flourish, encourages harmless eccentricities, and gives no problem in the case of homosexuals. However, like other definitions of abnormality, the criterion of personal discomfort is open to criticism. Identical behavior patterns can make one person miserable and bother another only a little—or not at all, so that limiting the definition to personal discomfort leaves us no yardstick for evaluating that behavior. In addition, when behavior harms other people or disrupts society, personal contentment is not a sufficient measure of normality. For example, some rapists and murderers may be perfectly content with their way of life, and a man's delusion that he has an enormous fortune might make him happy but is likely to disrupt the lives of the people with whom he transacts business.

Maladaptive Behavior

An approach to abnormality that overlaps both norm violation and personal discomfort is maladaptive behavior. If a person's behavior results in repeatedly getting fired at work, alienating family and friends, or simply not being able to get out of bed in the morning, most people would agree that he or she shows some psychological disturbance. In many cases the accompanying personal distress

Unable to cope with the demands of a job and the tasks of life, severely disturbed people may live in the streets, as this "bag lady" does.

will lead the person to seek professional help. This is not always the case, however; sometimes people who are behaving very maladaptively may not recognize the problem. When people cannot hold a coherent conversation or handle the simple tasks of living, the diagnosis of abnormality can be made by nearly anyone. Although this approach may work fairly well with people who are completely out of touch with reality, many people who might be considered disordered by themselves or others may still be functioning fairly well in social and occupational settings. The advantage of maladaptive behavior as a standard is that it focuses on a person's behavior in relation to others. The major disadvantage is that in certain cases "adaptive" behavior may be morally objectionable, as when German soldiers and civil servants readily adapted to the demands of the Nazi regime.

Deviation from an Ideal

A fifth way of defining abnormality is to set up a description of the ideal well-adjusted personality —such as that proposed by Carl Rogers (see Chapter 19)—and to regard as abnormal people who deviate from that ideal in any serious way. This sort of definition leaves most of us in the abnormal category, for few people ever achieve this ideal adjustment, no matter how hard they try.

Deviation from the ideal is also an imperfect guideline in our search for a definition of abnormality. This approach leads people who seem to be functioning adequately and who show no serious symptoms of disorder to regard themselves as disturbed and in need of therapy. For example, a woman with many friends and a bright career may seek psychotherapy because she lacks an intense, intimate relationship or because she feels that she is not self-actualized—both standards of adjustment in various theories. Such pursuit of ideal adjustment can make people feel seriously inadequate when they are only imperfect human beings. In addition, since the definition of the ideal personality is as culture-bound and relative as social norms, it is just as weak a foundation as norms for the diagnosis of abnormality.

Thus, although we have five ways of defining abnormal behavior, no one of them encompasses all behavior that might be termed abnormal. In practice, the judgment of abnormality, whether by diagnosticians or by family and friends, is usually based on a combination of standards. Although we can reach high levels of agreement about clearly abnormal behavior, strong disagreements still exist.

CLASSIFICATION OF ABNORMAL BEHAVIOR

Attempts to understand abnormal behavior have led to its classification into various categories. The generally accepted classification is that provided by the American Psychiatric Association: the third (1980) revision of the *Diagnostic and Statistical Manual of Mental Disorders,* commonly called *DSM-III,* which consists of highly detailed descriptions of virtually all known forms of psychological disturbances. The *DSM-III* is meant to assist psychiatrists, psychologists, counselors, and psychiatric social workers in diagnosing patients' disorders so that they can be effectively treated. The *DSM-III* is tied to the **medical model** of abnormal behavior, which views psychological problems in the same way as it views physical problems—as diseases with specific symptoms, causes, predictable courses, and treatments. However, *DSM-III* does not assume that these disorders have a biological cause. Instead, it merely describes mental disorders as fully as possible, without speculating about causes. As we shall see, there is widespread disagreement over the idea of assessing and categorizing abnormal behavior, and the use of the medical model is especially controversial.

Advantages of Classification

By enabling us to communicate about mental disorders, the classification of abnormal behavior has major advantages in both treatment and the advancement of knowledge. To treat a disorder, we have to be able to talk about it, hence the importance of *DSM-III*'s provision of a special language for behavioral disorders. This classification system sorts abnormal behavior into various categories, describing each in detail and giving it a label, such as "schizophrenia" or "bipolar disorder" or "phobia." After comparing a patient's behavior with the various descriptions, a psychologist or psychiatrist names the patient's problem by attaching the label that most closely describes it. If we can describe an individual's problem accurately, we are more likely to be able to predict the future course of her or his behavior and to decide on the appropriate treatment.

In addition, a classification system makes advancements of knowledge about various disorders possible. Without it research would be well-nigh impossible, since researchers would have no way of sorting out the vast array of disordered behavior. By having an agreed-upon label for each distinguishable disorder, researchers and clinicians can exchange information about research findings and clinical experience. An accurate system of diagnosis greatly increases the chances of identifying the causes of various disorders and designing appropriate treatments for them.

Criticisms of Psychiatric Diagnosis

Some theorists feel that the use of terminology based on the medical model is a serious error, because it labels people as "sick," removes them from normal life for treatment in a "hospital," and often maintains or even creates bizarre behavior. Call people "sick" and treat them accordingly, say some social scientists, and they will act out the role that is expected of them. In the view of some critics, abnormal behavior is not an illness but a "problem in living" (Szasz, 1961).

A second criticism of the practice of classifying abnormal behavior is that our labels give the illusion of explanation. To say that a man is highly suspicious because he is paranoid leads us to believe that we understand the cause of his actions. In reality, all the label does is to describe a pattern of behavior—a collection of symptoms whose cause is unknown.

A third criticism of such labels is that they stigmatize people. The label itself can intensify a person's problems by disrupting personal relationships, leading to the termination of employment or making it impossible to get a job, and depriving the person of civil rights. As noted in the criticism of the medical model, the patient may also accept the label and adopt the role of mental patient. In addition, the label creates expectations on the part of mental health professionals.

The issue of labeling came to a head when D. L. Rosenhan published a paper titled "On Being Sane in Insane Places" (1973), reporting the results of a provocative experiment. Eight sane people (three psychologists, a psychiatrist, a pediatrician, a graduate student, a painter, and a housewife) arranged to have themselves admitted to mental hospitals. In order to do so, each person reported a single symptom of mental disorder: in their admissions interviews, the people said they heard voices saying things like "empty," "hollow," or "thud." Otherwise, they gave accurate case histories. Once admitted, the pseudo-patients never again referred to the phantom voices.

Rosenhan reports that although other patients recognized that these people were imposters, the hospital staff did not. Physicians and nurses treated them as nonpersons. (When one patient asked about ground privileges, the doctor replied, "Good morning, Dave. How are you?" and moved on without giving or waiting for an answer.) Normal behavior was viewed as symptomatic. (All of the pseudo-patients took notes, and one nurse, observing her patient, entered in the records: "Patient engages in writing behavior.") The pseudo-patients were released after an average stay of nineteen days with the diagnosis of "schizophrenia in remission." Rosenhan argues that once a person is diagnosed as mentally ill, his or her behavior is forever reinterpreted in light of the diagnosis—by mental health professionals, family and friends, and the patients themselves. But Robert L. Spitzer (1976) argues that erring on the side of caution is good medical practice. How would the public react if a patient were refused admission to a hospital because a physician believed he was faking symptoms of a heart attack or a bleeding ulcer? Unless a person is taking drugs, hallucinations are a symptom of serious mental disorder, a symptom that may disappear and then reoccur. Spitzer believes the hospital staffs acted responsibly by observing Rosenhan's pseudo-patients for a few weeks. The short hospital stays of the pseudo-patients show that the staff responded rapidly to the "patients' " failure to produce further symptoms. So there are two sides to the labeling question.

Finally, diagnosis based on the medical model has been criticized because of its unreliability. When examined by two different professionals, a patient may receive two different diagnoses, being called schizophrenic by one and depressive by the other. With the publication of *DSM-III*, this criticism is no longer as valid as it once was. *DSM-III* has provided a highly specific set of criteria for each disorder—something that was missing from earlier editions of the manual—with the result that its reliability has improved substantially (Spitzer, Forman, and Nee, 1979; Webb et al., 1981).

Despite the difficulty of defining abnormality and the problems involved in psychiatric diagno-

sis, some sort of classification system is necessary, and the *DSM-III* is the most practical system yet devised. In fact, our classification system is not so far off the mark as some critics indicate, for some of the same patterns of psychopathology occur around the world, in both highly industrialized and extremely isolated cultures (J. Murphy, 1976; Draguns, 1980).

This chapter follows the classification system used in *DSM-III*. One notable consequence of doing so is that the term "neurosis" has been discarded as a diagnostic label. In the view of psychoanalytic theorists, **neurosis** is any condition in which a person develops some maladaptive behavior as a protection against unconscious anxiety. **Psychosis** is reserved for conditions in which the person's perceptions of reality are highly distorted. As a result, psychoanalysts grouped all disorders they saw as characterized by anxiety—whether the anxiety was apparent or not—into the single category of neurotic disorders. However, the diagnostic manual is intended for use by mental health professionals of all theoretical persuasions, so the use of a term that has come to imply a psychoanalytic interpretation is not appropriate. Moreover, a number of criticisms have been leveled at the assertion that anxiety is the chief characteristic by which neurotic disorders might be classified together: (1) anxiety has actually been observed in only a few of the so-called neuroses; (2) anxiety is difficult to measure accurately and thus is an unreliable standard for diagnosis; and (3) anxiety is a universal emotion, experienced to some degree not only by neurotics but also by normal people, psychotics, depressives, and sexual deviants (Nathan et al., 1969). In this chapter, following the format of *DSM-III*, we will discuss anxiety disorders, somatoform disorders, and dissociative disorders as independent categories.

ANXIETY DISORDERS

Anxiety is a feeling of dread, apprehension, or fear. It is accompanied by physiological arousal, manifested as increased heart rate, perspiration, muscle tension, and rapid breathing. Anxiety also affects cognition, throwing the individual into a state of confusion and making it difficult for him or her to think clearly or to solve problems.

As we noted above, virtually everyone experiences anxiety at one time or another. Without mild anxiety, bills would not get paid on time, term papers would not get written, drivers would not slow down on foggy mornings, and people would not get medical checkups. In addition, most people have difficulty in coping with some area of their lives. One person may worry about getting cancer at the first symptoms of a sore throat; another may be afraid to make decisions; a third may become tongue-tied in social situations; a fourth may have difficulty spending money. For most of us, such anxieties do not severely limit activities or interfere with daily life. If we wish, we can adjust our routines to avoid situations that we find difficult. We can turn down a high-pressure job that would make us anxious or take the bus if flying makes us nervous. While these evasions entail some inconvenience, life is still livable.

For some people, however, one situation—or many—becomes a major source of anxiety, taking up more and more time and attention. Anxiety becomes so severe or so persistent that it interferes with everyday functioning—family life, social activities, and work or school. This condition is classified as an **anxiety disorder**.

Generalized Anxiety Disorder and Panic Disorder

Generalized anxiety disorder is characterized by diffuse and generalized anxiety that cannot be managed by avoiding specific situations. The whole personality may be engulfed by anxiety, and the person is nervous, irritable, and on edge. Although the person with a generalized anxiety disorder may have a great many fears and worries, she or he cannot identify their source—a condition that Freud called **free-floating anxiety**.

People who have this problem often show motor tension: they may be jumpy, complain of aching muscles, tire easily, and find it impossible to relax. Their autonomic nervous system is overactive, and they often complain of cold, clammy hands, a racing heart, dizziness, stomach pains, and frequent urination. Such people also expect the worst to happen. They may fear that they will faint or lose control of themselves or worry that members of their family will develop some disease or be hit by a car. Because they are so apprehensive about the future, they become extremely attentive. This eternal vigilance may make them irritable or impatient, and they may find it difficult to concentrate or to fall asleep. In the morning they feel tired rather than relaxed.

From time to time people suffering from generalized anxiety may have **panic attacks**, brief periods during which tension and anxiety become completely disabling. Usually these attacks last from fifteen minutes to an hour. Individuals may report a shivering sensation. The heart begins to pound loudly, perspiration flows, and breathing becomes difficult. A feeling of inescapable disaster overcomes them. They try to escape, but no place offers safety. When the attack subsides, they feel

People with a generalized anxiety disorder may feel threatened by environmental stimuli that would not bother other people. Being surrounded by mirrors, for example, may prove so disorienting that a panic attack results.

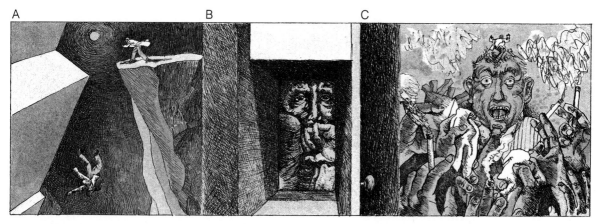

Figure 22.1. An artist's representation of three phobias: (A) fear of heights, called acrophobia; (B) fear of enclosed spaces, called claustrophobia; and (C) fear of dirt, called mysophobia. (After Vassos, 1931.)

drained. When no specific stimulus precedes the panic attack, it is called a **panic disorder**. Sometimes, however, panic attacks come in response to a specific stimulus, in which case they are classified as phobias.

Phobic Disorder

When anxiety is irrationally centered on some specific object or situation, it is called a **phobia**. The focus of anxiety may be a stimulus that is slightly dangerous, such as snakes, dogs, elevators, or high places, or it may be some situation that carries no danger at all, such as a fear of being alone or of being in public places where escape might be difficult (see Figure 22.1). This fear, called agoraphobia, is the most common phobia among people seeking treatment and can utterly disrupt an individual's life. A person who suffers from agoraphobia is likely to have a panic attack in any public place, so that she or he may become a virtual prisoner, afraid to leave the safety of home.

Phobias sometimes develop after an initial association of fear with some stimulus. For example, one woman developed an automobile phobia after being a passenger in a car that was struck broadside by a truck that ran a red light (Wolpe, 1973). After spending a week in the hospital with knee and neck injuries, the woman felt frightened while being driven home. Within a few weeks, she became extremely anxious in a car whenever another vehicle approached from either side, and her panic became severe when the car she was in made a left turn in front of approaching traffic. She was also

anxious when walking across streets, even when the traffic light was in her favor and the nearest car was a block away.

Phobias have two somewhat distinct effects. First, there is the anxiety associated with the phobia and the consequent avoidance of situations in which the feared object will be present. Second, there are the complications in a person's daily life, which must be rearranged to accommodate the phobia—a maneuver that requires time and trouble. If the person feels guilty or ashamed of the phobia, as some do, there is the additional effort of hiding the phobia from others, so that the anxiety connected with the feared object is compounded by the fear of being found out.

Obsessive-Compulsive Disorder

An **obsession** is an involuntary, irrational thought that occurs repeatedly. An obsession may be mild, as in those instances when we cannot stop wondering whether we remembered to turn off a faucet or lock a door before leaving home. In some cases, however, an obsession becomes so persistent that it markedly interferes with daily life. Severe obsessions often have a violent or sexual quality to them, such as the desire to burn down the house or rape a neighbor, which makes the person feel guilty and horrified as much by the content of the thought as by its persistence.

A **compulsion** is an action that a person uncontrollably performs again and again, although she or he has no conscious desire to do so. The act is often senseless, such as looking under the bed several times before going to sleep or locking and unlocking the door several times before going out. There are two general categories of compulsions: checking rituals, such as looking under the bed; and contamination compulsions, such as hand washing (Rachman and Hodgson, 1980). A person may show little anxiety when carrying out a compulsion. However, if she or he is prevented from carrying out the compulsive ritual, the person becomes extremely anxious.

Such ritual behavior is often both obsessive and compulsive. Constant hand washing, for example, may be caused by an obsessive preoccupation with germs. Although we all can remember times when a song lyric ran persistently through our minds, no matter what we did to get rid of it, or when we checked several times to make sure that the alarm clock was set, these minor obsessions and compulsions pass. A pathological obsession or compulsion continues—day after day, year after year.

Somatoform disorders

Somatoform disorders are characterized by the persistence of somatic, or physical, symptoms that do not have a physiological cause. Somatoform disorders are quite different from psychosomatic ailments like those discussed in Chapter 21, in which psychological factors, such as stress, cause or complicate actual physiological disease. Thus, a person in a stressful situation who develops ulcers does not suffer from a somatoform disorder. Two typical somatoform disorders are hypochondriasis and conversion disorders.

Hypochondriasis

Hypochondriasis is the preoccupation with bodily symptoms as possible signs of serious illness. Although the hypochondriac is perfectly healthy, she or he lives with the conviction that cancer, heart disease, diabetes, or some other particular disorder is about to develop. Hypochondriacs do not imagine their symptoms, but each vagrant twinge or cramp, each headache, each skipped heartbeat, is taken as a sign that major disease has struck. The hypochondriac is likely to read everything in the popular press concerning

health, to adopt strenuous health routines, or to consume vast quantities of vitamins and other medicines. Since physicians generally give them a clean bill of health, hypochondriacs change doctors frequently, looking for one who will confirm their own dire diagnoses.

Conversion Disorders

In **conversion disorders,** which were mentioned in Chapter 18, a person develops some physical dysfunction—such as paralysis, blindness, deafness, or loss of sensation in some part of the body—that has no organic basis and apparently expresses some psychological conflict. Although no medical evidence supports these afflictions, they are not under a person's voluntary control. For example, a hand might become completely numb, as in "glove anesthesia," but sensation might be clearly felt in an area directly above the wrist (see Figure 22.2). If the numbness were actually a result of neurological dysfunction, the line between sensitivity and numbness would not be so clear-cut. Such symptoms often appear or disappear suddenly. Many "miraculous cures" in which patients who have been paralyzed suddenly leave their wheelchairs and walk, or people who have been blind suddenly are able to see again,

Figure 22.2 A patient who complained to a doctor that his right hand had become numb might be diagnosed either as suffering from damage to the nervous system or as a neurotic suffering from hysteria, depending on the exact pattern of his numbness. The skin areas served by different nerves in the arm are shown in A. The "glove anesthesia" shown in B could not result from damage to these nerves.

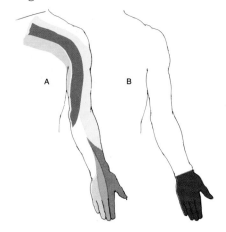

come about because the original dysfunction was the result of a conversion disorder.

There is, however, a major diagnostic problem in distinguishing between some conversion disorders and the early stages of actual neurological disease. In fact, many people who are diagnosed as having a conversion disorder are later found to have developed neurological disorders. For example, a group of 122 patients were followed, half of them diagnosed as having conversion disorders and the other half as having anxiety or depression disorders. At the subsequent examination, more than 60 percent of the patients diagnosed as having conversion disorders had developed signs of organic brain disorders, as compared with only 5 percent of the patients with anxiety or depression (Whitlock, 1967). In another study, a ten-year follow-up of forty people who were diagnosed as having conversion disorders found that 25 percent were misdiagnosed. Again, in most cases the problem was organic brain disorder (Watson and Buranen, 1979). One reason for these misdiagnoses is that neurological disorders are difficult to detect and diagnose in their early stages. While some patients are misdiagnosed as having a conversion disorder, the reverse diagnostic problem is also likely: that is, many patients who are diagnosed as having physical disorders may actually have conversion disorders. Conversion patients believe they have medical, not psychological, problems, and therefore are likely to go to physicians for help. Furthermore, many physicians may associate conversion disorders with dramatic symptoms such as glove anesthesia or blindness, permitting less dramatic cases such as numbness or blurred vision to be diagnosed as physical disorders (Jones, 1980).

DISSOCIATIVE DISORDERS

As the name implies, **dissociative disorders** designate the dissociation, or splitting off, of certain kinds of behavior that are normally integrated. Among the dissociative disorders are amnesia, fugue, and multiple personality.

Amnesia is the partial or total loss of memory concerning past experiences, such as an automobile accident or a battle. Psychogenic amnesia can be differentiated from organic amnesia in several ways. It appears suddenly, often following severe stress, and disappears just as suddenly. It is selective in nature. And the forgotten material can often be recovered under hypnosis.

The dissociative disorder called **fugue** ("flight") is related to amnesia. Individuals in a fugue state flee from the home as well as the self. They may be absent for days or months or years and may take up a totally new life, later remembering nothing of what happened while they were in the fugue state.

A rare and extreme form of dissociation is **multiple personality,** a division into two or more complete behavior organizations, each as clearly defined and distinct from the others as the two personalities of the main character in Robert Louis Stevenson's story *The Strange Case of Dr. Jekyll and Mr. Hyde.* Two actual cases of multiple personality, *The Three Faces of Eve* and *Sybil,* have been widely publicized in films and books, but the disorder is so rare that fewer than 100 cases have been reported (Rycroft, 1978). There has, however, been a dramatic increase in the number of cases reported in the past ten years. Cases of multiple personality often seem to involve personalities that take extreme forms: one personality may be conformist and "nice," while the other is rebellious and "naughty." Severe child abuse seems to be a common feature in the backgrounds of individuals with multiple personality. Most report severe physical abuse and sexual molestation during childhood (Greaves, 1980), as in the following case:

> Sue Ellen Wade was admitted to the county psychiatric hospital for the first time when she was 37 years old. She complained of depression over her inability to control "impulses to self-destruct" that were forced upon her by someone she referred to as "Ellen." Over the previous six months Ellen had tried to kill her on more than one occasion, once making her swallow a large quantity of tranquilizers, and another time making her fall down the stairs of her house. Ms. Wade complained that she had been struggling for many years against Ellen, whom she described as "another self." Ellen periodically "took over" the patient's "real self" and made her do "horrible things." Ms. Wade said that Ellen had been going out with other men, spending afternoons away from the home in motel rooms, and flaunting her promiscuity in front of her husband. Ms. Wade said that her real self, Sue, was a very diligent and conscientious mother, homemaker, and part-time

secretary. . . . In later psychotherapy sessions, Ms. Wade [described] two years at an orphanage where she complained of severe mistreatment at the hands of the staff. She claimed she was beaten, had her head held under water in the bath, was forced to sit on her knees with her arms held in the air for hours at a time, and was frequently locked in a dark closet. . . . During this time, Ms. Wade developed an imaginary "friend" whom she called "Ellen." . . . Ellen was able to resist in ways that [Sue] was not. Ellen frequently yelled at and hit back at her tormentors when they tried to touch her. From this point on, Ellen was an alternative personality. (Spitzer et al., 1983, pp. 37–39)

Since multiple personality is sometimes called "split personality," it is often erroneously confused with schizophrenia, because the word "schizophrenia" comes from Greek words for "to split" and "mind." Schizophrenia, as we shall see, refers to a separation of ideas, emotions, and perceptions within a single person—*not* to the development of separate personalities.

MAJOR AFFECTIVE DISORDERS

The defining feature of the **affective disorders** is a disturbance in mood. Everyone is subject to mood changes, and emotional response, or **affect**, is usually influenced by the events of everyday life. Fluctuations in mood are a matter of concern only when they are so exaggerated as to interrupt normal functioning and to cause severe and prolonged distress.

Major Depression

All of us have had periods of sadness or disappointment, and perhaps have suffered from feelings of guilt, loss of appetite, and lack of sexual interest. Usually such feelings are experienced in response to a negative situation in our lives: the loss of a job, an argument with a friend, a poor mark on an exam. Sometimes the upset comes for no apparent reason; it seems as if we just "got up on the wrong side of the bed." These symptoms of normal depression do not differ in kind from abnormal, or major depression, but they do differ drastically in degree.

Major depression consists of one or more major depressive episodes with no intervening episodes in which people feel extremely elated or unnaturally euphoric. The course of a major depressive episode often follows a fairly smooth curve with a gradual onset, taking weeks or months to appear, lasting for several months, then ending as it began, slowly and gradually.

A person in a major depressive episode shows, radical changes in mood, motivation, thinking, and physical and motor functioning. During such an episode a person's behavior shows the following characteristics: *depressed mood,* which may be described as utter despair, loneliness, or simply boredom; *feelings of worthlessness and guilt,* in which the individual sees her- or himself as lacking intelligence, physical attractiveness, health, or social skills—whatever attributes the person values, most; *reduced motivation,* in which interest and pleasure vanish from formerly valued activities; *disturbances of appetite, sleep, and sex drive,* in which a person either cannot eat or sleep or else eats and sleeps to excess, and almost invariably loses interest in sex; *psychomotor retardation or agitation,* in which people commonly seem overcome by fatigue and move slowly and deliberately or else become agitated, wring the hands, pace, fidget, or moan incessantly; *reduced energy,* so that the person feels exhausted all the time; *difficulties in thinking,* in which cognitive processes slow and there is difficulty in thinking, concentrating, and remembering; and *recurrent thoughts of death or suicide,* which sometimes do culminate in suicide.

Some of these characteristics of major depression are illustrated in the following patient's description:

I began not to be able to manage as far as doing the kinds of things that I really had always been able to do easily, such as cook, wash, take care of the children, play games, that kind of thing. One of the most . . . I think one of the most frightening aspects at the beginning was that time went so slowly. It would seem sometimes that at least an hour had gone by and I would look at my watch and it would only have been three minutes. And I began not to be able to concentrate. Another thing that was very frightening to me was that I couldn't read any more. And if awakened early . . . earlier than I needed to, I sometimes would lie in bed two hours trying to make myself get up because I just couldn't put my feet on the floor. Then

Major depression leaves a person feeling unable to do tasks as simple as washing dishes or clearing a table.

when I did, I just felt that I couldn't get dressed. And then, whatever the next step was, I felt I couldn't do that. (Educational Broadcasting Corporation, 1975)

Such severe depression is a major problem in the United States, with about 3 percent of men and from 4 to 9 percent of women diagnosed as having major depression. The percentage of Americans who will have at least one major depressive episode sometime during their lives is 8 to 12 percent for men and 20 to 26 percent for women (Boyd and Weissman, 1981). Depression is also the most frequent problem seen in outpatient psychiatric clinics, where it accounts for one-third of all patients (Woodruff et al., 1975).

Bipolar Disorder

Although patients with bipolar disorder have depressive episodes, they also have manic episodes, periods of intense, unrealistic elation. **Bipolar disorder** is characterized by the episodic nature of these extreme moods. The first sign of bipolar disorder is almost always a manic episode of intense euphoria, excitement, and activity; this is followed by a depressive episode. A person in a manic episode shows an *elevated mood*, com-

posed of euphoria mixed with irritability; *hyperactivity* in physical, social, occupational, and often sexual functioning; *sleeplessness* without any decrease in energy; *talkativeness,* with loud, rapid, and continual speech; *flight of ideas and distractibility,* with racing thoughts that abruptly switch from one topic to another; *inflated self-esteem,* in which people see themselves as extremely attractive, important, and powerful; *reckless behavior,* including shopping sprees, reckless driving, careless business investments, and sexual adventures; and *irritability,* which in some cases overcomes the euphoria.

The addition of manic episodes is not the only characteristic that differentiates bipolar disorder from major depression. The two syndromes differ in many respects (Depue and Monroe, 1978; Hirschfeld and Cross, 1982). Bipolar disorder is much less common than major depression, affecting an estimated .4 to 1.2 percent of the adult population (American Psychiatric Association, 1980). Bipolar disorder usually appears before the age of thirty; major depression can occur at any time of life. The two disorders also show different demographic profiles. Unlike major depression, bipolar disorder occurs with equal frequency in the two sexes, and while major depression is more prevalent among the lower classes, bipolar disorder is more prevalent among the upper classes. People who are married or have intimate relationships are less prone to major depression, but have no advantage with respect to bipolar disorder. Another difference is that people with major depression tend to have histories of low self-esteem, dependency, and obsessional thinking, whereas the personalities of people with bipolar disorder are typically more normal. The course of the two disorders is somewhat different; in bipolar disorder, episodes are generally briefer and more frequent than in major depression. Finally, bipolar disorder is more likely to run in families than is major depression, which suggests that genetic factors may be more important in bipolar disorder than in major depression. These differences have led researchers to conclude that these two disorders, similar as they may at times appear, spring from different causes (Nurnberger and Gershon, 1982).

SCHIZOPHRENIA

Schizophrenia is a group of disorders characterized by thought disturbance that may be accompanied by delusions, hallucinations, attention deficits, and bizarre motor activity. It is a **psychotic disorder**, one that is characterized by a generalized failure of functioning in all areas of a person's life. Schizophrenia was originally called *dementia praecox*, or "premature mental deterioration," by Emil Kraepelin (1902), who devised the first comprehensive classification system for mental disorder. Kraepelin believed that such behavior was due to a disease of mental deterioration that began in adolescence. Ten years later, however, the Swiss psychiatrist Eugen Bleuler pointed out that many patients displaying these symptoms do not continue to deteriorate and that the illness itself often starts after adolescence has passed. Bleuler believed that Kraepelin's term only made diagnosis confusing, so he substituted the term "schizophrenia" to indicate a "psychic split," or the dissociation of various psychic functions within a single personality. Emotions may be split from perception and be inappropriate to the situation; words may be split from their usual meanings; motor activity may be dissociated from reason. In Bleuler's words, "The personality loses its unity" (1911/1950, p. 9). However, schizophrenia should not be confused with multiple personality, which is a dissociative disorder. Although depression is the most prevalent mental disorder, schizophrenia is the most common cause of hospitalization for mental illness in the United States.

Symptoms of Schizophrenia

Although thought disorders are often the predominant symptom, the schizophrenic person generally displays a variety of other abnormalities, including disorders of perception, emotion, and motor behavior. All schizophrenics display some of these symptoms some of the time, but no schizophrenic displays all the symptoms all the time.

Disorders of Thought

In most schizophrenics, there is a split among various ideas or between ideas and emotions. Normal people mentally link concepts and symbols and establish logical connections with a main idea that they wish to express. They might think, for example, that they are hungry and would like to eat a steak. The concept of hunger is joined to the concept of steak, and a relationship is set up

between the two: namely, steak satisfies hunger. The incoherence or dissociation in the thought processes of the schizophrenic, however, interupts such relationships. Concepts, ideas, and symbols are sometimes thrown together merely because they rhyme. Such a series of rhyming or similar-sounding words is called a **clang association**. The following transcript of a conversation between a doctor and a schizophrenic patient, who produced rhymes in about half his daily speech, illustrates clang associations.

DOCTOR: How are things going today, Ernest?
PATIENT: Okay for a flump.
DR.: What is a flump?
PT.: A flump is a gump.
DR.: That doesn't make any sense.
PT.: Well, when you go to the next planet from the planet beyond the planet that landed on the danded and planded on the slanded.
DR.: Wait a minute. I didn't follow any of that.
PT.: Well, when we was first bit on the slip on the rit and the man on the ran or the pan on the ban and the sand on the man and the pan on the ban on the can on the man on the fan on the pan.
  [All spoken very rhythmically, beginning slowly and building up to such a rapid pace that the words could no longer be understood.]

In addition to showing interruptions in the logical connections of words, schizophrenic thought sometimes is characterized by a tendency to dwell on the primary association to a given stimulus (called **perseveration**). More often, there is a loosening of associations, so that each sentence is generated from some mental stimulus in the preceding sentence, thus wandering further and further from the central idea (called **overinclusion**). This tendency to slip from one track of thought to another can lead to syntactically correct communication that conveys almost no information, as in the following letter, written by one of Eugen Bleuler's patients:

Dear Mother,
I am writing on paper. The pen which I am using is from a factory called "Perry & Co." This factory is in England. I assume this. Behind the name of Perry Co. the city of London is inscribed; but not the city. The city of London is in England. I know this from my school days.

Then, I always like geography. My last teacher in that subject was Professor August A. He was a man with black eyes. I also like black eyes. There are also blue and gray eyes and other sorts, too. I have heard it said that snakes have green eyes. All people have eyes. There are some, too, who are blind. These blind people are led about by a boy. It must be very terrible not to be able to see. There are people who can't see and, in addition can't hear. I know some who hear too much. One can hear too much. (E. Bleuler, 1911, p. 17)

The dissociation of concepts also produces delusions, one of the most common thought disorders among schizophrenics. **Delusions** are irrational beliefs that are maintained despite overwhelming evidence that they have no basis in reality. They take several forms. Some are delusions of grandeur, in which an individual believes that she or he is some famous person like Napoleon or Jesus Christ. Some are delusions of persecution, in which the individual believes that others, often extraterrestrial beings or secret agents, are plotting against her or him. Some are delusions of sin and guilt, in which the person believes that she or he has committed some terrible deed or brought evil into the world. There also may be delusions of control, in which the person feels under the power of other people or mysterious forces. Very characteristic of schizophrenia are delusions that one's thoughts are being controlled or tampered with. There are three types of such delusions:

1. *Thought broadcasting*, the belief that one's thoughts are being broadcast to the outside world so that everyone can hear them.
2. *Thought insertion*, the belief that other people are inserting thoughts, especially obscene thoughts, into one's head.
3. *Thought withdrawal*, the belief that other people are removing thoughts from one's head.

As the above suggests, the delusions of schizophrenia are often extremely bizarre. The schizophrenic may experience a number of fantastic delusions simultaneously, as revealed in this young woman's speech:

Mick Jagger wants to marry me, I don't have to covet Geraldo Rivera. Mick Jagger is Saint Nicholas and the Maharishi is Santa Claus. . . . Teddy Kennedy cured me of my ugliness. I'm pregnant with the Son of God. I'm going to marry David Berkowitz and get it over with. Creedmoor [a mental hospital] is the headquarters of the American Nazi Party. They're eating the patients here. Archie Bunker wants me to play his niece on his TV show. . . . I'm Joan of Arc. I'm Florence Nightingale. . . . Divorce isn't a piece of paper, it's a feeling. Forget about zip codes. I need shock treatments. The body is run by electricity. My wiring is all faulty. A fly is a teenage wasp. . . . Israel is the promised land, but New Jersey is heaven (Sheehan, 1982).

Disorders of Perception

A distinguishing characteristic of schizophrenia is a distorted view of reality. Although this distortion is in part the result of disturbed thought processes, it is directly related to the fact that schizophrenics seem to perceive the external world in an altered manner. They consistently report **hallucinations**, or distortions of sensory perception—most commonly, auditory, somatic, and tactile hallucinations. Auditory hallucinations may take the form of insulting comments on the schizophrenic's behavior; tactile hallucinations may be felt as tingling or burning sensations; and somatic hallucinations may be reported as the sensation of snakes crawling under the abdomen (American Psychiatric Association, 1980). Visual, gustatory, and olfactory hallucinations are less common; in fact, visual hallucinations may be a symptom of drug poisoning (as in alcoholism), and olfactory hallucinations are often experienced by epileptics.

The hallucinations of schizophrenia differ from the imagery of normal people in two ways: they are spontaneous and apparently uncontrollable, and the schizophrenic perceives them as real. The pattern of tactile hallucinations experienced by one woman during a schizophrenic episode is shown in Figure 22.3. This woman felt that patches of her flesh were being stretched, sometimes as far as twelve inches from her head, and at other times contracting into her head. The sensations varied in intensity and occasionally caused acute pain. She was so frightened by these strange sensations that her personality, thought, and actions were affected in a devastating manner (Pfeifer, 1970).

In dreams, we often experience physical states that are impossible to achieve while awake. Severely disturbed people may experience delusions or hallucinations which they believe are real.

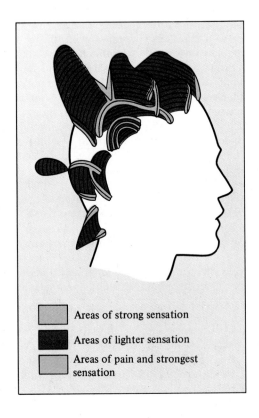

Areas of strong sensation

Areas of lighter sensation

Areas of pain and strongest sensation

Besides having hallucinations, schizophrenics experience other perceptual abnormalities. Laboratory tests show that schizophrenics have difficulty estimating size (Strauss, Foureman, and Parwatikar, 1974), time, and the positioning of their own hands and feet. According to one current theory (Maher, 1977; Maher and Maher, 1979), perceptual abnormalities are the fundamental problem in schizophrenia. In this view, schizophrenia involves a loss of the normal ability to attend selectively to stimuli in the environment. Flooded with information from all the senses, the person's mental organization short-circuits. Descriptions from schizophrenic patients themselves seem to support this notion:

> Things are coming in too fast. I lose my grip of it and get lost. I am attending to everything at once and as a result I do not really attend to anything.

Figure 22.3. A schizophrenic woman's drawing of her own tactile hallucinations, showing the areas of sensation and their associated strengths. (After Pfeifer, 1970.)

My thoughts get all jumbled up. I start thinking or talking about something but I never get there. Instead I wander off in the wrong direction and get caught up with all sorts of different things that may be connected with the things I want to say but in a way I can't explain. People listening to me get more lost than I do. (McGhie and Chapman, 1961, pp. 104, 108)

Disorders of Affect

Like other aspects of functioning, the emotional responses of schizophrenics are disturbed. Schizophrenics frequently show inappropriate emotional responses, or none at all. A schizophrenic might become angry when done a favor, weep when told a joke, or show no evidence of emotional response at all. In the last case, the schizophrenic's face remains immobile and the voice becomes a monotone. Again, the external situation or stimulus fails to trigger an appropriate response.

Disorders of Motor Behavior

The schizophrenic may behave in bizarre ways, or, more often, may perform repetitive and inappropriate acts. One patient might spend hours rubbing his forehead; another spend hours slapping her leg; still another might sit all day on a couch tracing the pattern of the fabric. In some cases,

there is no physical activity at all; the patient is said to be in a catatonic stupor, remaining in one position for hours at a time, responding to neither persons nor things.

Disorders of Identity

In schizophrenia, the sense of individuality is often so disturbed that individuals seem uncertain as to who they are, and they become preoccupied with the question of their identity.

Disorders of Volition

Schizophrenics nearly always display a lack of interest in self-directed activity and are unable to initiate or to complete a project. When volition disappears, a schizophrenic's resulting inability to make decisions or choices may lead to almost complete inactivity.

Disorders of Relationship to the World

Schizophrenics often withdraw from involvement in the world's activity, becoming preoccupied with their own thoughts (see Figure 22.4). Interaction with other people is almost totally absent, and schizophrenics may act as if other people did not exist. To the observer, schizophrenics may seem to be living in their own world.

Figure 22.4. These paintings were done by a male schizophrenic with paranoid tendencies. Both illustrations are characterized by the consistent symbolism of watchful eyes, grasping hands, and the self as subject matter. In the first painting, which reflects a subdued emotional state, there is a strong emphasis on the eyes, with a figure watching over the shoulder. The torso of the central figure is surrounded by hands, and the figure in the background is reaching out. The second painting, elaborate in composition and vivid in color, reflects a more active emotional state. Again there is an emphasis on the eyes and on the hands, represented by tentacles and claws.

The Course of Schizophrenia

Schizophrenia does not manifest itself in the same way in all people, and no one patient shows all the disorders described in the preceding section. The disorder has been divided into five major subtypes, which are described in Table 22.1. However, schizophrenia generally follows a regular course that moves through three distinct phases: prodromal, active, and residual.

The Prodromal Phase

Before schizophrenia becomes active, the person may go through a phase of deterioration called the **prodromal phase**, in which she or he becomes increasingly withdrawn, eccentric in behavior, and unable to carry out daily functions. Emotions slowly become inappropriate or nearly absent, and those close to the person notice a distinct change in personality. The prodromal phase may be brief, or it may last for years, in which case the deterioration in behavior is so gradual that the person may be entering the active phase before the family notices the severity of the disorder. Just such a slow deterioration was attributed to John W. Hinckley, Jr., the man who wounded President Ronald Reagan in an assassination attempt. Testifying in Hinckley's defense, one psychiatrist said that Hinckley had gradually withdrawn during his adolescent years and was schizophrenic.

The Active Phase

During the **active phase**, the person shows some of the psychotic symptoms discussed in the preceding section. Delusions, hallucinations, disorganized speech, catatonic stupor, or any of the other symptoms mentioned may appear. The active phase often begins when a person in the prodromal phase encounters a particularly stressful situation (American Psychiatric Association, 1980).

The Residual Phase

After a period in the active phase, most schizophrenics enter the **residual phase**, in which behavior is much as it was during the prodromal phase. The person may continue to show diminished emotions and be unable to hold a job, but behavior is far less bizarre. Should any delusions or hallucinations persist, they are weakened and have less power to disturb the individual. Some schizophrenics pass through the residual phase and go on to complete recovery, but many lapse back into the active phase. A longitudinal study that followed more than a thousand schizophrenics indicated that 25 percent became able to function normally; 10 percent remained permanently in the psychotic, or active, phase; and between 50 and 65 percent alternated between the residual and active phases (M. Bleuler, 1978).

Table 22.1 ■ Five Types of Schizophrenia

Disorganized (hebephrenic) schizophrenia	Individuals live in private worlds dominated by hallucination, delusions, and fantasy. Behavior is almost completely unpredictable, and speech may be unintelligible. Most severe disintegration of personality.
Catatonic schizophrenia	Individuals show either excessive, sometimes violent, motor activity or a mute, unmoving, stuporous state. Some catatonic schizophrenics alternate between these two extremes, but often one or the other behavior pattern predominates.
Paranoid schizophrenia	Individuals have delusions of persecution, grandeur, or both. Paranoid schizophrenics trust no one and are constantly watchful, convinced that others are plotting against them. May seek to retaliate against supposed tormentors.
Undifferentiated schizophrenia	Individuals are schizophrenic but do not meet the above criteria, or else they show symptoms of several subtypes.
Residual schizophrenia	Individuals are not in an active phase of schizophrenia, but show residual symptoms.

INFANTILE AUTISM

Autism means, literally, "self-ism." Autistic children live in a world of their own, from which other people are excluded. The first sign of infantile autism is a lack of social responsiveness in babyhood. Autistic infants do not like to be cuddled, as other babies do. When picked up they become stiff and rigid (or in some cases, go limp). They seldom cry—or laugh. Parents sometimes describe them as "good babies" because they do not demand attention.

. . . Peter didn't look at us, or smile, and wouldn't play the games that seemed as much a part of babyhood as diapers. While he didn't cry, he rarely laughed, and when he did, it was at things that didn't seem funny to us. He didn't cuddle, but sat upright in my lap, even when I rocked him. But children differ and we were content to let him be himself. (Eberhardy, 1967)

As they grow older, this aloneness becomes more pronounced. Such children recoil from physical contact and avoid eye contact.

Only rarely could I catch [Peter's] eye, and then I saw his focus change from me to the reflection in my glasses. It was like trying to pick up mercury with chopsticks. (Eberhardy, 1967)

If autistic children do form attachments, it is usually to inanimate objects.

Many autistic children are mute; they never speak. Those who do learn to speak often develop *echolalia*—they echo words, phrases, and snatches of songs they may have heard on TV, with no apparent desire to communicate. A few do make some attempt to communicate but betray their isolation by referring to themselves as "you," "he," or by their proper name. Often these speech deficits are the result of mental retardation. Autistic children who show signs of intellectual development and attempt some speech have a much better prognosis than those who do not (Rutter and Lockyer, 1967).

Around age two and a half, many normal children suddenly exhibit a concern with regularity and sameness. They want their toys to be in the same place, their meals to be served on the same plate, and so on. With autistic children this becomes an obsession. They insist on eating their breakfast in a rigid order: egg first, vitamin second, toast third. They become extremely agitated if a toy is not placed in the *exact* position on the shelf it occupied before. If anything in their environment is disturbed in any way, they throw tantrums.

Autistic children engage in repetitive, ritualistic motor patterns—such as rocking, hopping, hand flapping, or spinning—for hours on end. When involved in these private games, they seem oblivious not only to the outside world but also to their own physical state. They refuse to eat, even when they have gone twenty-four hours without food (Lovaas et al., 1979). Self-mutilation is common.

Finally, the autistic child's lack of interest in people is often matched with a fascination with objects. One father describes his son:

His little hands hold the plate delicately, his eyes surveying its smooth perimeter, and his mouth curls in delight. He is setting the stage. This is the beginning of his entry into the solitude that has become his world. Slowly, with a masterful hand, he places the edge of the plate on the floor, sets his body in a comfortable and balanced position, and snaps his wrist. The plate spins with dazzling perfection. It revolves on itself as if set in motion by some exacting machine . . . as indeed it was. . . . For a moment, his body betrays a just-perceptible motion similar to the plate's. His eyes sparkle. He swoons into the playland that is himself. . . . (Kaufman, 1975, p. 43)

On occasion this fascination with objects can be a bridge to adjustment. Peter, whose mother we quoted above, became a skilled piano tuner in adolescence and shows signs of being able to develop into a happy, self-supporting—if socially isolated—adult (Eberhardy, 1967). Peter is the exception, however. Only about 5 percent of individuals who were autistic infants develop the skills to become self-sufficient adults (DeMyer et al., 1981).

Recently, some researchers have suggested new ways to identify patients with a good chance of recovery (Andreasen and Olsen, 1982; Strauss, Carpenter, and Bartko, 1974). Generally, patients with predominantly positive symptoms (those involving the presence of something—delusions, hallucinations) are more likely to improve than are those with predominantly negative symptoms (those involving the absence of something—lack of affect, speech, emotional response). Patients with the latter pattern of symptoms are likely to have experienced a long, slow slide into schizophrenia over several years, and they often develop the disorder in its more severe form. Other recent research (Lewine, 1981) has found that men are more likely to develop this pattern than are women; not only are they more likely to be more seriously affected, but they usually develop the disorder earlier—before the age of twenty-five. This distinction between positive and negative symptoms has led some researchers to speculate that there may be two kinds of schizophrenia, one of which may be more closely linked with inherited brain dysfunction. (We shall consider this question in more detail in Chapter 23.)

SOCIAL DISORDERS

The disturbances described thus far include some of the major mental disorders. Although it is impossible to encompass all disorders in a single chapter, several additional classes of disturbance are important enough to warrant a brief description. Because they often create social complications and involve longstanding habits of thought and behavior, personality disorders, sexual deviance, and disorders of substance use might be considered together as social disorders.

Personality Disorders

When personality traits become so inflexible and maladaptive that they impair a person's functioning, they are known as **personality disorders**. The individual with a personality disorder often does not recognize that it exists or that her or his behavior is at all deviant or disturbed. This inability to recognize the disorder comes about because the problem behavior is part of the person's personality, so deeply ingrained as to be second nature and accepted as familiar character traits. Often adopted at an early age to cope with specific stress in the environment, the pattern of deviant behavior is difficult to change. Frequently these people have little motivation to change their behavior, since their actions generally cause more discomfort to others than to themselves. Although *DSM-III* outlines eleven different types of personality disorders, we shall consider only one—the antisocial personality. There are two reasons for focusing on antisocial personality disorder: it has been the most intensively researched, and it is the personality disorder on which there is the greatest diagnostic agreement.

The **antisocial personality**, or **sociopath**, is one who is indifferent to the rights of others. Such people appear to be blind to moral considerations, to have no conscience, and to be untouched by a whole range of emotions shared by the "normal" population. Yet the intellectual faculties of sociopaths are intact, and their abilities to reason and to perform tasks are unimpaired. Sociopaths show antisocial behavior by early adolescence, and this antisocial quality pervades most behavior. To be diagnosed as a sociopath, a person must display at least four of the following nine qualities: aggressiveness, impulsiveness, recklessness, deceptiveness, involvement in criminal activities, inability to hold down a job, inability to maintain a lasting sexual attachment, failure to act as a responsible parent, and failure to honor financial obligations (American Psychiatric Association, 1980).

In attempting to develop a reliable diagnosis, *DSM-III* confines itself to verifiable behaviors. But many experienced researchers have emphasized more subjective characteristics (e.g., Cleckley, 1976). They have observed that the most striking characteristic of this disorder is the absence of emotion in social relationships. The sociopath is simply indifferent to other people and preys upon them with no more feeling than if he or she were picking an apple from a tree. Thus, the sociopath shows no guilt over the most callous murder and no sadness at the death of a parent or friend. The remarks of one such person, Dan F., show this absence of normal emotions (McNeil, 1967). Thinking over the death of his best friend from leukemia, Dan decided that he felt nothing about the loss of his friend, that he wouldn't miss his mother or father if they died, and that he "wasn't too nuts" about his brothers and sisters either. Despite such a lack of emotion, the sociopaths' impulses are at times positive: they may buy presents for a friend or give money to charity; but the motivation for these acts has as little feeling behind it as their casual shoplifting or embezzling. Although usually intelligent, cunning, and clever, sociopaths seem to have little insight into the disorder and are slow to learn from experience. No matter how often they face prison terms, social sanctions, expulsions from school, and loss of jobs, sociopaths tend to repeat the very behavior patterns that have brought punishment down upon them.

Sexual Deviance

Definitions of sexually deviant behavior have changed over the past few years. *DSM-II*, the previous edition of *DSM-III*, was published in 1968, and it defined as sexually deviant any "individuals whose sexual interests are directed primarily toward objects other than people of the opposite sex, toward sexual acts not usually associated with coitus [sexual intercourse], or toward coitus performed under bizarre circumstances" (American Psychiatric Association, 1968, p. 44). Just twelve years later, the only kinds of sexual behavior classified as disorders in *DSM-III* are "those deviations from standard sexual behavior that involve gross impairments in the capacity for affectionate sexual activity between adult human partners" (American Psychiatric Association, 1980).

The change shows a recognition by the American Psychiatric Association that social attitudes vary, and so do sexual practices. Nevertheless, there is still some sexual behavior that psychologists and psychiatrists consider "abnormal" in our society and in others. The most common are:

The message on this man's bag is an incisive statement about the nature of sexual masochism.

- **Fetishism**: sexual gratification that is dependent on an inanimate object or some part of the body other than the genitals.
- **Transvestism**: sexual gratification obtained through dressing in clothing of the opposite sex.
- **Transsexualism**: gender identification with the opposite sex.
- **Exhibitionism**: sexual gratification obtained through exhibiting the genitals to an involuntary observer.
- **Voyeurism**: sexual gratification obtained through secret observations of another person's sexual activities or genitals.

- **Pedophilia**: sexual gratification obtained through sexual contacts with children.
- **Incest**: sexual relations among members of the immediate family.
- **Rape**: sexual relations achieved by threatening or using force on another person.
- **Sadism**: sexual gratification obtained through inflicting pain on another person.
- **Masochism**: sexual gratification obtained through having pain inflicted on oneself.

Mild forms of such "abnormal" behavior can appear among sexually "normal" individuals without being diagnosed as deviant. For example, many people become sexually aroused by the sight of lacy underwear or by swimming in the nude, and both the woman who is aroused by displaying her breasts in a low-cut dress and the man who is aroused by the display are behaving in a normal fashion. Such behavior is considered a serious disorder only when it is a person's sole or primary means of achieving sexual gratification.

Substance Abuse

As long as a person's use of a drug, whether tobacco, alcohol, marijuana, cocaine, or any other consciousness-altering substance, remains within reasonable bounds—when the drug is used and not abused—the practice does not fall under the category of psychological disorders. But when a person comes to depend upon one of these substances, so that her or his life is primarily devoted to getting and using the drug, the condition fits all the definitions of abnormality discussed in this chapter. Although there are as many varieties of substance abuse as there are drugs, we shall focus on only one—alcohol abuse.

Alcoholism is the most serious drug problem in the United States, and alcoholism is a major subcategory of mental disorder. Current estimates are that there are between 7.5 and 10 million alcholics in the United States (U.S. Department of Health and Human Services, 1981).

Alcohol abuse carries a high social and personal cost. The social damage of alcohol abuse takes many forms: family disruption; decreased job productivity due to inefficiency, accidents, absence, and low morale; death, injury, and property damage from alcohol-related automobile accidents; and increased medical care for alcoholics. The American Hospital Association estimates that approximately half of all occupied beds in United States' hospitals are filled by people with ailments linked to the consumption of alcohol (United States Department of Health and Human Services, 1981). In the economic area, alcoholism has great costs to the American economy. The personal costs of alcoholism are severe psychological and physiological deterioration.

As we saw in Chapter 7, alcohol is a depressant, suppressing inhibitions and allowing people to do or say things they ordinarily would not. Some people feel good when they drink, others become depressed, and others lose all anxiety or guilt over their past, present, or future behavior. In large quantities, alcohol causes disorders of sensation and perception, can lead to dangerous, self-destructive behavior, and is capable of producing coma and death.

The feeling of well-being achieved in "social drinking" can be a first step toward alcohol abuse and a psychological dependence on the drug.

Alcoholics build up a tolerance for alcohol; to experience the original feeling of well-being, or freedom from anxiety, they must increase their intake of alcohol. Often drinkers develop such a psychological dependence on alcohol that they feel normal only when they have been drinking and experience severe, painful symptoms if they stop. The slide into alcoholism generally follows the same sequence of behavior. A study of 2,000 alcoholic men showed that the sequence begins with periodic excessive drinking, then progresses through blackouts, sneaking drinks, losing control over the amount of alcohol drunk, remorse over drinking and rationalization of excess alcohol consumption, enforcing a change in drinking patterns in an attempt to solve the problem, morning drinking, alcoholic binges lasting for several days, and the onset of alcohol-related physical ailments, the centering of life around alcohol, and the admission of defeat (Jellinek, 1946).

Because of the toxic effects of alcohol on the body and the malnutrition that so often accompanies chronic alcoholism, alcoholics are likely to develop diseases affecting the liver, brain, and nervous system. Prolonged alcoholism leads to degenerative brain disease. A chronic alcoholic whose blood alcohol level drops suddenly may experience delirium tremens, better known as DTs. This reaction is actually a withdrawal symptom. Patients with DTs tremble, perspire heavily, become disoriented, and suffer nightmarish hallucinations. These last from three to six days, after which the person may vow never to take another drink—a vow that in many cases is broken soon after discharge from the hospital or treatment center.

ORGANIC DISORDERS

Various explanations have been offered for the development of psychological disorders, and Chapter 23 will present them in some detail. From Kraepelin on, many theorists have believed that mental disorders such as schizophrenia or depression are due to organic dysfunction of the brain. Much evidence supports this idea. But many social scientists feel that such mental disorders are due to psychological factors, emotional disturbances, and environmental stress. About certain disorders, however, there is little argument; they are directly traceable to the destruction of brain tissue or to biochemical imbalance in the brain. These disorders are known as **organic brain syndromes** and are classified as a separate category in *DSM-III*. Included in the list are: presenile and senile dementia; alcoholic psychoses such as delirium tremens; intracranial infections such as encephalitis and tertiary syphilis; other cerebral conditions such as epilepsy, cerebral arteriosclerosis, and brain trauma; endocrine disorders; metabolic and nutritional disorders; systemic infections; and drug or poison intoxication.

Because physical and mental health are so closely related, it is often difficult to determine whether a particular behavioral disturbance is due to organic dysfunction or to emotional factors. Most organic brain disorders are accompanied by five major symptoms: impairment of orientation (awareness of who and where one is); impairment of memory; impairment of other intellectual functions, such as comprehension, calculation, knowledge, and learning; impairment of judgment; inappropriate affect. However, most of these symptoms are also present in schizophrenic patients, in patients with conversion disorder, and even in depressed patients. Thus an accurate diagnosis of organic brain syndrome is not easy.

EPIDEMIOLOGY OF MENTAL DISORDER

Epidemiology is the study of the range of occurence, distribution, and control of illness in a population. The incidence of mental disorders is particularly difficult to measure because many people with psychological problems do not seek treatment. The National Institute of Mental Health (NIMH) recently reported on a survey of 20,000 Americans in five communities across the nation (*New York Times*, 1984; *Newsweek*, 1984). In an interview that lasted up to two hours, each subject was asked 200 questions about specific symptoms. On the basis of this survey, NIMH estimates that 13.1 million Americans suffer from anxiety disorders (including phobias, obsessive-compulsive behavior, and panic attacks); about 10 million abuse alcohol or other drugs; another 9.4 million suffer from affective disorders (chronic depression or manic depression); about 1.5 million are schizophrenic; and 1.4 million would be diagnosed as antisocial personalities. Altogether, about 20 percent of Americans are currently suffering from psychiatric disorders, but only one in five has sought help for his or her condition.

Demographic Variability

Not all segments of the population show the same incidence of mental disorders. Such factors as age, sex, marital status, and social class appear to affect a person's chances of developing some psychological disturbance.

Age

Psychological disorders seem to be concentrated in young adulthood. The incidence of emotional problems drops by 50 percent after age forty-five; in fact, the lowest rates of mental disorder are found among Americans over age sixty-five.

Sex

The rates of mental disorder are about the same for men and women, but the sexes are prone to different disorders. Men are much more likely to suffer from alcohol and drug abuse and from antisocial personality disorders. Women are much more likely to suffer from depression or anxiety disorders. Women are also twice as likely to seek professional help.

Marital Status

Marital status appears to have an effect upon the likelihood of psychological disturbance. People who are married are less likely than others to have psychological disorders, but people whose marriages break up are the most likely to have disorders. The highest rate of mental disorder is reported among separated and divorced persons; the next highest among single persons; the next highest among widows and widowers; and the lowest among married men and women. Yet marriage itself may not be the important factor. It may be that disturbed people are more likely than others to stay single or to fail at marriage.

Social Class

Social class is a broad category that encompasses such variables as ethnic group, occupation, marital status, and religion. Most studies have found a clear relationship between social class and reported mental disorder. In nineteen of twenty-four studies, the lower the social class, the higher the incidence of serious mental disorder (Kolb, Bernard, and Dohrenwend, 1969). Two major explanations have been advanced to account for this difference: first, life in lower social classes is more stressful than life in the middle and upper classes and thus produces more mental illness; and second, as people develop serious mental disorders they tend to withdraw from others and their ability to function in society deteriorates. As this happens to people in the middle and upper classes, they drift downward into lower social classes. Both stress and the downward drift are probably involved in this relationship between social class and psychological disorders.

Cross-Cultural Variability

Earlier we noted the role of social norms in defining abnormal behavior. A comparison of the symptoms of mental disorder in various cultures is of great interest to psychologists because it can help them to differentiate between changing environmental factors and unchanging basic elements of mental disorder. Other cultures also report disorders similar to schizophrenia, bipolar disorder, and anxiety disorders. In fact, some form of most disorders appears in most cultures, but the symptoms appear to vary across cultures. For example, although in many cultures schizophrenia is characterized by social and emotional withdrawal, auditory hallucinations, general delusions, and inability to react, the style of the symptoms varies from one culture to another (H. Murphy et al., 1961). Among schizophrenic Christians and Moslems, religious delusions and delusions of destructiveness are common, but Asians are most likely to develop delusions that involve jealousy.

It is clear that cultures may supply the material for delusions, but the extent to which differences in symptoms directly reflect differences in culture is difficult to measure. It is probably safe to conclude that no disorder is completely immune to cultural influence, and that no serious disorder is entirely a creation of cultural and social forces. It also appears that psychoses are less influenced by culture than are other disorders, and that symptoms involving thought, perception, and emotion show less variation across cultures than do symptoms involving a person's role and social behavior (Draguns, 1980). Yet the complexity of human behavior continues to confound and confuse even those who study it most closely.

SUMMARY

1. Several definitions of abnormality are used within the field of psychology: **norm** violation; substantial deviation from a statistically calculated average; personal discomfort arising from thoughts or behavior; maladaptive behavior; and deviation from the ideal, well-adjusted personality. None of these definitions encompasses all abnormalities.

2. The generally accepted classification of abnormal behavior is that provided by the American Psychiatric Association in its *Diagnostic and Statistical Manual of Mental Disorders (DSM-III)*. DSM-III is tied to the **medical model**, which views psychological problems as diseases with specific symptoms, causes, predictable courses, and treatments, but *DSM-III* does not assume that these disorders have a biological cause. By enabling us to communicate about mental disorders, such classification has major advantages in both treatment and the advancement of knowledge. The disadvantages are the medical model's labeling of people as "sick," the illusion that naming a disorder explains it, the stigmatizing of people by attaching labels to their behavior, and the unreliability of diagnoses. However, *DSM-III* provides the most practical classification system yet devised.

3. **Anxiety** is a feeling of dread, apprehension, or fear, and when severe and persistent anxiety interferes with daily functioning, the condition is classified as an **anxiety disorder**. **Generalized anxiety disorder** is characterized by generalized anxiety that cannot be managed through avoidance and by **free-floating anxiety** —an inability to specify the source of the fear. **Panic attacks** are brief periods during which tension and anxiety become completely disabling. When no specific stimulus precedes the attack, it is called a **panic disorder**. Anxiety that is irrationally focused on a particular object or situation is called a **phobia**. An **obses-**

sion is a recurring irrational thought; a **compulsion** is the repeated performance of a particular irrational act. Much ritual behavior is both obsessive and compulsive. **Somatoform disorders** are characterized by physical symptoms that have no physical cause. **Hypochondriasis** is the preoccupation with bodily symptoms as possible signs of serious illness. In **conversion disorders**, a person develops a physical dysfunction that has no organic basis. In **dissociative disorders**, the dysfunction is psychological and certain normally integrated behavior is split. The major dissociative disorders are **amnesia**, **fugue**, and **multiple personality**.

4. **Affective disorders** are characterized by disturbances of mood. **Major depression** consists of one or more major depressive episodes with no intervening episodes of euphoria. In a major depressive episode, a person shows radical changes in mood, motivation, thinking, and physical and motor functioning. **Bipolar disorder** is characterized by extreme moods, beginning with a manic episode of euphoria, excitement, and activity, followed by a depressive episode.

5. **Schizophrenia** is characterized by disordered thought accompanied by other abnormalities such as disordered perception, emotion, and motor behavior. Most schizophrenics show a lack of association among various ideas or between ideas and emotion. Very characteristic of schizophrenia are **delusions**, irrational beliefs held in the face of overwhelming disproof, and **hallucinations**, spontaneous sensory perceptions that are unrelated to external stimuli. Schizophrenics also display disorders of **affect**, or emotional response, of motor behavior, of identity and volition, and of their relationship to the world. The course of schizophrenia often begins with a **prodromal phase** of gradual de-

terioration, followed by an **active phase**, in which psychotic symptoms dominate, then a **residual phase**, in which behavior resembles that of the prodromal phase.

6. **Personality disorders** involve inflexible and maladaptive personality traits that impair functioning. The deviant behavior is completely integrated into the individual's life and she or he may be unaware of any disturbance. The **antisocial personality**, or **sociopath**, violates the rights of others without feeling any guilt, lacks all conscience or emotion in relationships, and seems unable to learn from experience. Although definitions of sexual deviance vary with time and place, certain sexual behavior is considered abnormal, including **fetishism, transvestism, transsexualism, exhibitionism, voyeurism, pedophilia, incest, rape, sadism**, and **masochism**. Among disorders of substance abuse, alcoholism is a major subcat-egory of mental disorder and is the country's most serious drug problem.

7. Certain psychological disorders, the **organic brain syndromes,** can be traced to the destruction of brain tissue or to biochemical imbalance in the brain.

8. **Epidemiology** is the study of the range of occurrence, distribution, and control of illness in a population. Establishing the epidemiology of mental disorder is difficult because far fewer people are admittted to treatment than suffer mental disorder. The incidence of mental disorder varies with such factors as age, sex, marital status, and social class. Comparison of mental disorders across cultures helps to distinguish between changing environmental factors and unchanging basic elements of psychological disturbances.

KEY TERMS

active phase
affect
affective disorder
amnesia
antisocial personality
anxiety
anxiety disorder
bipolar disorder
clang association
compulsion
conversion disorder
delusions
dissociative disorder
epidemiology
exhibitionism
fetishism
free-floating anxiety

fugue
generalized anxiety disorder
hallucinations
hypochondriasis
incest
major depression
masochism
medical model
multiple personality
neurosis
norms
obsession
organic brain syndromes
overinclusion
panic attacks
panic disorder
pedophilia

perseveration
personality disorder
phobia
prodromal phase
psychosis
psychotic disorder
rape
residual phase
sadism
schizophrenia
sociopath
somatoform disorder
transsexualism
transvestism
voyeurism

RECOMMENDED READINGS

AMERICAN PSYCHIATRIC ASSOCIATION. *Diagnostic and statistical manual of mental disorders* (3rd ed.) (DSM III). Washington, D.C.: American Psychiatric Association, 1980. The generally accepted classification system which contains detailed descriptions and criteria for psychological disturbance.

BOOTZIN, R.R., and J.R. ACOCELLA. *Abnormal psychology: Current perspectives* (4th ed.). New York: Random House, 1984. A comprehensive textbook that describes the major categories of psychological disorder and presents a variety of theoretical perspectives.

LANDIS, C. *Varieties of psychopathological experience.* F. A. Mettler (Ed.). New York: Holt, Rinehart and Winston, 1964. A collection of autobiographical reports that provide a glimpse into the experience of disorder. A valuable complement to theoretical discussions.

SAHAKIAN, W. S. (Ed.). *Psychopathology today* (3rd ed.). Itasca, Ill.: Peacock Publishers, 1985. An extensive collection of readings by the major theorists and researchers in the field.

ZILBOORG, G., and G. W. HENRY. *A history of medical psychology.* New York: Norton, 1941. A fascinating discussion of the history of madness; a classic in the field.

THEORIES OF ABNORMALITY

A thirty-two-year-old man complained that his thoughts were being repeated in public and that he was being "tortured by rays." He claimed that people who lived on the other floors of his apartment building transmitted abusive messages to him through the central heating system. At times he would stare into the mirror, grimacing at his reflection. On occasion he broke a silence or interrupted a conversation by speaking or singing words that bore no relation to the situation, such as "Emperor Napoleon." He often laughed boisterously and for no apparent reason. He complained about odd sensations in his hair and scalp, saying that they felt "as if they were congealed." Finally, he began to pound on the walls in the middle of the night, waking his family and people in the neighboring apartments (Bleuler, 1978).

Such irrational behavior, delusional thinking, disordered perceptions, and inappropriate emotional responses are signs of serious psychological abnormality. The person who undergoes such experiences is likely to be confused, frightened, and frustrated. Friends and relatives of such a person often feel distressed about their inability to help. What has happened to the person to produce such strange behavior?

Most kinds of abnormal behavior, of course, are far less dramatic than the schizophrenic symptoms we have just described. Many disorders, such as depression or phobias, are enough like "normal" behavior to seem less mysterious and alien to us. But however abnormality manifests itself, its causes have been a matter of interest for thousands of years. Scientists and other observers have developed several theories about the causes of abnormal behavior. As we shall see, each theoretical perspective stresses a different aspect of abnormality, with some centering on the ways the environment can encourage and maintain deviant behavior and others focusing on possible physiological bases of disorders. To understand current theories of disorder, it is helpful to consider the way people in past centuries have viewed abnormality.

S OME THEORIES FROM THE PAST

All through history, deviant behavior—behavior that is strikingly different from that of most people

—has been explained and defined according to the philosophical and religious outlook of a particular society. Most societies attribute psychological disturbance to gods, demons, disease, or emotional stress.

Demonology

Archeological evidence suggests that in prehistoric times people sought explanations for natural events in supernatural forces. Unusual behavior was probably considered the work of spirits or demons. Skulls recovered from certain Stone Age sites show that holes were sometimes chipped in the foreheads of some unfortunate individuals, presumably to allow the evil spirits to escape. This crude attempt at treatment, called trephining, probably resulted in the victim's death most of the time—although some skulls show evidence of healing, indicating that the person survived.

Similar ideas of demonic possession endured for many centuries among the ancient Chinese, Egyptians, Hebrews, and Greeks. In some instances, possession was considered a desirable state; in Greece, for example, the priestess at Delphi was revered, and the cryptic prophecies she delivered were thought to come from a god who was inhabiting her body.

The development of naturalistic explanations for abnormal behavior is commonly associated with the Greeks. Particularly influential were the writings ascribed to the physician Hippocrates (c. 460–360 B.C.). Hippocrates considered all illness, including what we call mental illness, to be due to natural causes. Among his contributions are the first detailed descriptions in Western scientific literature of disorders such as epilepsy, phobia, and postpartum psychosis. Given the state of medical knowledge in his day, some of his theories now seem extremely primitive to us. For example, he believed that the body was composed of four liquids, or "humours"—blood, phlegm, yellow bile, and black bile—each with special characteristics. Hippocrates proposed that too much or too little of any humour could lead to changes in personality and disturbances in behavior. For instance, melancholy (depression) was thought to be caused by an excess of black bile. Despite such crude theorizing, Hippocrates' contribution was substantial. His notion that abnormal behavior had causes within the body was farsighted, as we will see

when we consider the recent discoveries in neuroscience.

In the Middle Ages supernatural explanations for mental disturbance were again put forward —not surprisingly, given the power of religious teachings at that time. While some disturbed persons were treated with prayer and exorcism, however, others were considered simply as ill and were treated accordingly. Commonsense explanations for mental illness—a fever, a blow to the head, the death of a husband or wife—often sufficed. Disturbed persons were sometimes cared for in hospitals or almshouses, or sometimes simply kept at home with their families. A guardian was sometimes appointed for those with no relatives (Neugebauer, 1978).

The notion that deviant behavior was somehow connected with the supernatural had a very long life. During times of social stress and political upheaval, this idea sometimes served as a justification for persecuting certain people for being under the influence of evil spirits. The most notorious examples of this persecution were the witch hunts that took place in Europe between the middle of the fifteenth and the end of the seventeenth centuries. In fact, most people who were harassed, tortured, or killed as witches were not mentally ill. They were often poor, old, socially marginal women and others who were considered misfits in their communities (Spanos, 1978). More than 100,000 people, about 85 percent of them women, were killed in Western Europe's witchhunting era. And America was not immune. In 1692, nineteen people were executed in Salem, Massachusetts, after they had supposedly bewitched residents of the town and caused them to have fits.

Biogenic Theory and the Medical Model

A few lonely voices were raised in protest against witch hunts. One was that of Johann Weyer (1515–1588), a German physician who stated that abnormal behavior is an illness and should be treated by a physician rather than a priest. Another was St. Vincent de Paul (1576–1660), a French priest who placed himself in great danger by declaring openly that those persecuted were simply ill and that it was the duty of Christians to help rather than to persecute them. Thus, it was in the seventeenth century, in the midst of the witch hunts, that illness began to be reemphasized as an explanation for deviant behavior. Not until the eighteenth century, however, during the period known as the Enlightenment, did the persecution of "witches" finally die out. Deviant behavior was once again widely viewed as a result of natural forces.

The view of mental disorder as having a physical, or organic, cause is known as **biogenic theory**. Although an organic explanation had been put forward by various physicians since Hippocrates, the biogenic theory was not firmly established among psychiatrists until the German physician Emil Kraepelin (1856–1926) brought out his *Textbook of Psychiatry* (1923) in 1883. In that book Kraepelin argued cogently for the central role of brain pathology in mental disturbances. He applied the medical model to mental disturbances, adopting the same scientific standards of observation and classification used in studying physical diseases. As noted in Chapter 22, he furnished psychiatry with its first comprehensive classification system, based on distinctions among different types of mental disorders and their clusters of symptoms. Kraepelin's classification system provided the basis for the American Psychiatric Association's first *Diagnostic and Statistical Manual of Mental Disorders* (*DSM-I*, 1952), and the current edition, *DSM-III* (1980), is a descendant of Kraepelin's system (Blashfield, 1984).

By the turn of the century, neurological research was progressing rapidly, and one mysterious mental disorder after another yielded to biogenic explanations. Senile psychoses, toxic psychoses, cerebral arteriosclerosis, and some forms of mental retardation were shown to be caused by brain pathology. Most stunning of all, general paresis, a puzzling disorder marked by the gradual breakdown of physical and mental functioning, was shown to be advanced syphilis.

The successes of the biogenic approach led researchers to treat all abnormal behavior as if it had an organic cause. The influence of the medical model's early success can be seen in the terms we apply to psychological disorders and those who have them: "patient," "symptom," "syndrome," "pathology," "therapy," "cure," and "mental illness" (Price, 1978).

In the past few decades, many psychiatrists have criticized the pervasive influence of the medical model, and perhaps the most eloquent and relentless of the critics has been the American psychiatrist Thomas Szasz. In *The Myth of Mental Illness* (1961), Szasz asserts that most of the disorders that are called mental illnesses are not organic illnesses at all; instead, they are "problems in living" that manifest themselves in behavior that deviates from arbitrary social norms. Szasz argues that by labeling abnormal behavior as "illness," we not only describe the problem inaccurately but deprive individuals of responsibility for their own behavior as well. Although Szasz's arguments have had some influence, the biogenic approach to understanding and treating abnormal behavior continues to thrive. For example, recent research has implicated neurotransmitters in abnormal behavior; these advances will be described in the section on the neuroscience perspective.

Psychogenic Theory

As biogenic theory was making great strides, **psychogenic theory**, which holds that mental disturbances result primarily from emotional stress, was also rapidly gaining ground. It began with the colorful figure of Franz Anton Mesmer (1733–1815), an Austrian physician who thought that the heavens influenced people's mental states. Mesmer held that the movements of the planets control the distribution of a universal magnetic fluid, and that the shifting of this fluid is responsible for the health or sickness of mind and body. In accordance with his principle of "animal magnetism," Mesmer believed that by touching various parts of a person's body with colored rods and a special wand, he could adjust the distribution of magnetic body liquids. His treatment seems to have brought about improvement in many cases, a recovery due to the power of suggestion in curing mental disorders. The discovery of this power was Mesmer's major contribution to psychotherapy. In treating his patients, he used "mesmerism," an artificially induced, sleeplike state in which the subject is highly susceptible to suggestion.

Mesmerism eventually developed into the technique of hypnosis (see Chapter 7), which was adopted and used systematically by two French physicians, Ambroise-Auguste Liébault (1823–1904) and Hippolyte Bernheim (1837–1919), who in turn influenced the famous Parisian neurologist Jean-Martin Charcot (1825–1893). Charcot found hypnosis to be a highly successful treatment for hysteria, the original term for conversion disorders, in which physical symptoms have no corresponding organic causes. It was Charcot's example that influenced Josef Breuer and Sigmund Freud to use hypnosis in treating psychological disorders.

The steps by which Freud progressed from the use of hypnosis to the techniques of psychoanalysis, free association, and dream analysis have been described in Chapter 18. Although Freud's psychoanalytic theory is a general theory of personality, it is also a detailed theory of abnormal behavior (as we shall see in the next section). Other dominant views of abnormal behavior that are based on psychogenic theory include behavioral, humanistic-existential, family, and sociocultural perspectives. As we shall see, psychogenic views have broadened to include the role played by society in the development of disorders. Biogenic views of mental disorders remain strong, focusing on genetic and biochemical factors. Psychogenic and biogenic approaches are presented separately here, but an understanding of mental disorder clearly requires attention to both psychological and organic factors.

THE PSYCHOANALYTIC PERSPECTIVE

Psychoanalytic theory holds that mental disorders arise when the balance among id, ego, and superego has been disturbed by a failure to resolve conflicts and the person encounters additional stress or conflict. As we saw in the detailed discussion of Freud's theory of personality (see Chapter 18), conflicts among the id, the ego, and the superego may produce anxiety. Freud identified three kinds of anxiety. The first is **reality anxiety**, the result of an external danger: a man points a gun at you and says, "Your money or your life!" and you become frightened. The second is **moral anxiety**, caused by the superego's demands for moral behavior and self-punishment for moral transgression: you copy someone else's answers on a test and feel guilty. The third is **neurotic anxiety**, produced when impulses generated by the id threaten to overwhelm the ego and interfere with its functioning: in a noisy quarrel with your roommate you feel a sudden sense of panic arising from aggressive impulses that threaten to break loose and cause you to strike out uncontrollably. To deal with neurotic anxiety, the weak ego begins to use defense mechanisms in an increasingly rigid manner.

The particular defense mechanism that is employed determines the form of abnormal behavior a person displays. The panic attacks that characterize anxiety disorders (see Chapter 22) are seen as the result of desperate attempts by the ego to control the impulses of the id, using repression of those impulses as the major defense. The ego succeeds in pushing down (repressing) the impulse, and, although the anxiety is directly experienced, the true nature of the conflict remains hidden in the recesses of the unconscious.

The defenses employed in other disorders are considerably more complex, and the level of anxiety that is experienced is somewhat less severe. **Obsessive-compulsive disorders** that are characterized by rituals of orderliness or cleanliness, such as continual hand washing, are seen as the product of reaction formation, another defense mechanism. The ego responds to unacceptable impulses to soil oneself, to be dirty and destructive, by outwardly abhorring dirtiness and practicing fastidious cleanliness. Conversion disorders are also seen as a defense against unacceptable impulses. For example, glove anesthesia, discussed in Chapter 18, can be interpreted as a defense against an aggressive impulse to strike someone or a sexual impulse to masturbate.

Freud gave the name "neuroses" to the disorders that he thought involved anxiety. According to his thinking, neurotic behavior is either the expression of anxiety or a defense against it. Since *DSM-III* is primarily descriptive and avoids speculation about the causes of disorders, it does not use the term "neurosis," which is closely identified with psychoanalytic theory.

According to psychoanalytic theory psychotic disorders are caused by severely deficient ego functioning. Psychoses occur when the ego is unable to use defense mechanisms as a shield against unacceptable impulses: the person loses contact with reality and regresses to an early phase of the oral psychosexual stage. The psychotic person suffers from deficient ego functioning in perception, verbalization, and problem solving. In the psychoanalytic framework, a psychosis is not just a severe form of neurosis, but a disorder of a different kind. Neurosis is associated with the overuse of defense mechanisms; in psychosis the ego is so weakened or deficient that it has no effective defenses against the id's impulses. A normal or adequately functioning person, in contrast, has an ego that effectively mediates the conflicting demands of id and superego without resorting excessively to defense mechanisms.

Psychoanalytic theory developed out of the clinical experience of Freud and his students, and it has led to many insightful observations. For example, the psychoanalytic view of depression, first put forth by Freud's student Karl Abraham (1911/1948; 1916/1948), is that depression arises when a person loses a love object toward whom she or he had both positive and negative feelings. The loss can be a real or a perceived loss or rejection. In the face of desertion by the love object, a person's negative feelings turn to intense anger. At the same time, the positive feelings give rise to guilt based on the feeling that the person failed to behave properly toward the lost love object. The rage and reproach remain unconscious and are turned inward, becoming depression. Athough theorists from other perspectives might disagree as to whether anger turned inward causes depression, the early psychoanalytic observation that depression includes elements of anger is now widely accepted.

In Chapter 18 we saw how other psychoanalytic theorists have expanded Freud's theory to emphasize social factors and the role of the ego. Psychoanalytic theory is not static but continues to grow and change in response to the contributions of many psychoanalytic theorists.

THE BEHAVIORAL PERSPECTIVE

Although behavioral theories of personality, which are described in Chapter 19, also see a psychogenic basis to emotional disorders, adherents of the behavioral perspective reject most Freudian concepts.They believe that the learning principles of modeling, classical conditioning, and operant conditioning can explain the development of abnormal behavior. These theorists assume that abnormal behavior is learned in the same way as other behavior. The person with a psychological disorder differs from others because she or he either has learned inappropriate behavior or has never learned the adaptive behavior that most people acquire.

Maladaptive behavior is sometimes the result of modeling, and many people learn to be fearful and anxious in particular situations by observing the anxiety of others (Rosenthal and Bandura, 1978). For example, a boy may develop a fear of dogs because he observes his mother's fearful reactions to the animal and is rewarded with her comfort when he acts in the same way. In addition, some people learn fears through classical conditioning, developing anxiety and phobias following traumatic events, natural disasters, or accidents. For example, all but one of the thirty-five survivors of a gasoline tanker explosion on the Delaware River reported severe symptoms of nervousness, depression, and phobic reactions when at sea as long as four years after the accident (Leopold and Dillon, 1963).

Direct reinforcement can teach behavior that allows people to avoid something unpleasant. For example, a girl who hates going to school may learn either to develop a stomachache every morning or to behave so disruptively in class that she is repeatedly suspended. Both types of behavior are reinforced because both allow her to miss school.

The lack of reinforcement (extinction of adaptive or appropriate behaviors) may also contribute to the development of maladaptive behavior. For example, many behaviorists (e.g., Ferster, 1973; Lewinsohn, Youngren, and Grosscup, 1979) regard depression as a result of a reduction in reinforcement, which may be the result of changes in a person's environment. The amount of positive reinforcement any person receives depends on three broad factors: (1) the number and range of stimuli that the person finds reinforcing; (2) the availability of such reinforcers in the environment; and (3) the person's skill in obtaining reinforcement (Lewinsohn, 1974). If a person retires or loses a spouse through divorce or death, one or more of these factors may be suddenly and dramatically affected, leaving the person inactive, withdrawn, and distressed. To treat depression the therapist adds possible sources of reinforcement to the depressed person's environment and helps the person acquire skills that will increase the chances of obtaining it (Lewinsohn, Sullivan, and Grosscup, 1980).

In recent years, behaviorally oriented theorists have been paying more attention to the role of cognitive events in the development and treatment of abnormal behavior. The cognitive approach emphasizes that the way we interpret events may be almost as important as the events themselves. Thus a poor grade on an essay might produce self-blame and a feeling of failure in one person, the determination to try harder in another, and the conviction that the instructor misgraded the essay in a third. The interpretation placed on the event influences how the person feels about it and how she or he behaves in the future. In this view, depression is a behavioral response that develops when a person consistently interprets events as hopeless through the exaggeration of disappointments, the overgeneralization of criticisms, and the recall of only their unpleasant aspects (Beck et al., 1979).

In the behavioral perspective the development and course of a disorder are considered the result of the interaction between a person's behavior and his or her environment. The impact of environmental stress depends on the person's competencies and deficits. For example, a person who is at risk for schizophrenia has a reduced capacity for acting effectively in a number of important areas. But in an environment of very low stress, such a person may either never develop pronounced schizophrenic symptoms or exhibit them only occasionally. By the same token, a "normal" person, given sufficient environmental stress, may temporarily show the mental disorganization that we think of as typical of schizophrenia. Even bizarre behavior, therefore, such as the behavior characteristic of schizophrenia, is not discontinuous with the complexity of behavior we all experience. The aim of the behavioral approach is to increase the person's abilities and enhance his or her functioning—not to provide a cure for a specifically diagnosed disorder (Liberman, 1982).

Sometimes the environment contributes to feelings of stress and depression.

THE HUMANISTIC-EXISTENTIAL PERSPECTIVE

Another psychogenic approach to psychological disorder is that of the **humanistic-existential perspective**, which includes both humanistic and existential theorists. Humanistic personality theories, such as those of Abraham Maslow and Carl Rogers (see Chapter 19), emphasize the potential of human beings for growth and self-actualization. Although humanistic and existential theorists differ somewhat in their view of disorders, they share a number of basic assumptions: (1) both insist on a **phenomenological approach**—an approach that stresses the individual's own perception of events as opposed to a therapist's interpretation of hidden causes; (2) both stress the uniqueness of each individual; (3) both place great emphasis on human potential; and (4) both stress the individual freedom to make choices, a freedom that makes each person responsible for her or his own behavior.

Humanistic theorists believe that maladjustment develops when a hostile and rejecting family and society thwart the individual's natural drive for self-actualization, thus leading to a negative self-concept. Existential theorists emphasize the establishment of personal values and **authenticity** —living by those values—over self-actualization. For example, Viktor Frankl (1962), an existential psychiatrist, considers the need to find meaning in life the primary human motive. When people are unable to find meaning, they experience **existential frustration**, a major source of abnormal behavior. While acknowledging the biological and psychological components of behavioral disorders, Frankl distinguishes between two major categories of psychological disturbance: anxiety neurosis and obsessional neurosis. He interprets anxiety neurosis as stemming from the neurotic person's guilt over not having pursued any values. In contrast, obsessional neurosis is caused by the inability of a person with values to endure the discrepancy between the real and the ideal. As we shall see in Chapter 24, the role of the existential therapist is to help patients live life as it is (the real) and to help them discover values inherent in life (Frankl, 1975).

A more radical view of abnormal behavior, particularly schizophrenia, is presented by another existential psychiatrist, R. D. Laing (1967). According to Laing, modern society and the modern nuclear family are psychologically destructive environments. By surrounding us with "double messages" and by demanding that we stifle our feelings and pursue meaningless goals, both family and society consistently discourage authentic behavior in favor of inane conventional behavior. Although all of us are subjected to this destructive environment, the demands of the schizophrenic's family are even worse. Within the family schizophrenics develop their particular ways of experiencing, understanding, and behaving in the world. These ways may seem incomprehensible to outsiders, but within the family they are appropriate and can be seen as adaptive in that context. Because members of a schizophrenic's family are not honest with one another, their interaction forces each of them to deny parts of their experiences and to invalidate important feelings (Laing and Esterson, 1971).

Laing came to believe that emotional disturbance is inherent in contemporary Western society and that schizophrenics are victims not only of their families but also of society itself. In fact, he believes that the abnormal behavior of psychotics reflects their attempts to reconcile the self that existed before socialization (the "true" self) with the self created by cultural demands and social sanctions. In this view, schizophrenia is not insanity but "hypersanity," a voyage from our own mad reality into another reality in the existential search for an authentic identity.

It should be noted that the view that schizophrenia is "hypersanity" is emphatically rejected by adherents of most other perspectives. In fact, even Laing has conceded that schizophrenia may be due in part to biochemical disturbances (Sedgwick, 1982). Despite the controversy regarding some of the positions of the humanistic-existential perspective, theorists from this perspective have made an important contribution to our understanding of abnormality by stressing the validity of each person's experience.

THE FAMILY PERSPECTIVE

Adherents of the psychogenic perspectives discussed—psychoanalytic, behavioral, and humanistic-existential—are convinced that a person's family has an important role in the development of abnormal behavior. From the psychoanalytic perspective, early childhood events are particularly critical in the psychosexual development of the child and in laying the foundation of the person's personality. From the behavioral perspective, family members are the major models for behavior and important sources of reinforcement. As a result of family interactions, maladaptive behavior can be learned in the same way as adaptive behavior. From the humanistic-existential perspective, the family is the primary vehicle for transmitting society's values, and within the family the individual learns to conform by suppressing individuality, self-actualization, and authenticity. Although all three perspectives affirm the importance of the family, their primary emphasis is on the psychological processes of the individual. Other psychogenic perspectives, in contrast, focus more directly on the processes of family interaction as the primary determinant of abnormal behavior.

One group of investigators, headed by Theodore Lidz (Lidz et al., 1957; Lidz, 1973), explored the role of family interaction in the development of schizophrenia. After studying schizophrenics and their families for several years, these researchers suggest that two basic family patterns can produce schizophrenics: marital schism and marital skew.

In the **marital schism** pattern, the parents of the schizophrenic were bitterly divided, and the marital relationship aggravated the personality difficulties of each parent. The parents were continually on the verge of separation, and communication between them was reduced to coercion and defiance—both open and carefully masked to avoid a fight. The parents carried their hostility toward each other into their children's lives, with each partner habitually telling the children about the faults and worthlessness of her or his spouse.

In the **marital skew** pattern, the family was calmer but one parent totally dominated the other. The marriage consisted of one extremely dependent or masochistic partner and one strong partner who acted as a parental figure to the weak partner but who generally appeared to be the disturbed member of the pair. the dependent parent accepted or even supported any weakness or psychopathology displayed by the dominant parent. As a result, although the family atmosphere was abnormal, the other spouse's acceptance of the abnormality probably made the environment seem normal to the children (Lidz et al., 1957).

Lidz and his associates concluded that the child faced with the conflict and confusion found in either of these family situations would develop ways of coping that led to problems later in life.

Another theorist, Frieda Fromm-Reichmann, placed most of the blame on the mother instead of on the marital relationship. She believed that the influence of the mother is so crucial in the development of schizophrenia that in 1948 she coined the term "schizophrenogenic mother" to describe a cold, domineering mother who simultaneously rejects and overprotects her child (Fromm-Reichmann, 1974). Such a mother, in conjunction with a passive father who exerts little influence in the family, seems to Fromm-Reichmann to be capable of inducing schizophrenia in her offspring.

A third group of investigators, headed by Gregory Bateson and Don Jackson, examined the family environments of schizophrenics and decided that faulty communication lay at the root of schizophrenia. According to their **double-bind hypothesis**, parents in these families habitually send conflicting messages to their children so that no matter what a child does, the action is wrong (Bateson et al., 1956). An obvious double bind is reflected in the familiar joke in which a mother gives her child two shirts for his birthday and he immediately puts on one of them. His mother looks at him and says, "What's the matter? Didn't you like the other one?"

In the family of the schizophrenic, the double bind works in the following manner. Suppose a mother has great difficulty accepting her child's affection for her, but at the same time finds it hard to deal with any anxiety or hostility she feels toward her child. As a result she *talks* in a loving manner, perhaps telling the child to give her a kiss, but then stiffens her body when the child approaches. The child, perceiving the discrepancy between the mother's speech and her actions, receives contradictory messages. If such occasions are common, the child may never learn to distinguish among the meanings expressed in normal language and behavior. She or he develops the bizarre language and social ineptness characteristic of schizophrenics.

Although examples of double binds are typically vivid, there has been little empirical evidence that they actually are involved in causing schizophrenia. It has been particularly difficult to get investigators to agree about which communications qualify as double binds (Ringuette and Kennedy, 1966). Research that has received stronger empirical support has focused on a broader range of communications and communications among the entire family. Considerable research indicates that families of schizophrenics typically have deviant communication patterns, which have been described as blurred, muddled, vague, confused, fragmented, or incomplete (Hassan, 1974; Lewis et al., 1981; Wynne et al., 1975). In one study (Doane et al., 1981), deviant communication by the parents predicted whether their adolescent children would be diagnosed as schizophrenic five years later. Despite these findings, we cannot say with certainty that schizophrenia results when a "normal" child grows up surrounded by abnormal communication, for some studies have found that anyone who attempts to communicate with schizophrenics ends up sounding confused (Liem, 1974). In other words, it may be the presence of a disturbed child that produces abnormal communication from other family members.

THE SOCIOCULTURAL PERSPECTIVE

Instead of confining the social causes of abnormal behavior to family interaction, the sociocultural perspective, a final psychogenic view, places the primary blame on the entire society. The sociocultural perspective embraces two interrelated views, social stress and social labeling. In the social stress view, abnormal behavior can be caused by the stresses of living in modern society. As noted in Chapter 22, psychological disturbance is linked with social class, so that the lower the socioeconomic class, the higher the prevalence of mental disorder. From the sociocultural perspective, this relationship is caused by such stresses as poverty, discrimination, and the lack of valued roles for people in certain segments of our society, such as the elderly. The effects of economic recessions support this hypothesis. In recent recessions, admissions to mental hospitals, suicides, and deaths from stress-related ailments such as heart disease and cirrhosis of the liver rose significantly as unemployment rose (Pines, 1982).

In the social labeling view, which follows naturally from the social stress view, the link between social class and disorder arises because people from the lower socioeconomic classes are more likely than members of higher socioeconomic classes to be labeled as mentally disordered.

It has been proposed that the "mentally ill" are simply people who have had the label attached to

Social deviance can be mistaken for mental illness. Is the sign-carrier emotionally ill? A mental health professional would have to evaluate his overall ability to function before a proper diagnosis could be made.

them because of behavior that violates social norms (Scheff, 1975). Although much deviant behavior is ignored by society, if such behavior comes to the attention of the mental health establishment, the person may be labeled as disordered. Attaching the label to a person places her or him in the social role of the mentally ill person, and it is probable that she or he will accept it. So labeled, the person is discriminated against for attempting to behave in a normal fashion, perhaps being fired, refused employment, or shunned by others. But the same person is rewarded with attention, sympathy, and removal of all responsibility if she or he will only accept the role.

The label of mentally ill is more likely to be attached to people in lower socioeconomic classes

for several reasons that were discovered in a series of studies (Hollingshead and Redlich, 1958; Myers and Bean, 1968). First, the label automatically accompanies admission to mental hospitals, and disturbed people without money for private care frequently find themselves in state mental hospitals. The middle-class person with the same degree of disturbance is likely to be seeing a private psychiatrist regularly and so escape the label. Second, lower-class people tend to display deep unhappiness by becoming aggressive or rebelling against social norms. Although such behavior is regarded as a "normal" sign of frustration in the lower class, it appears aberrant to mental health professionals, since in their own middle class the appropriate response to such unhappiness is withdrawal and self-deprecation. Therefore, the person from a lower socioeconomic class who goes to a mental health clinic has a good chance of being labeled as psychotic and being hospitalized, whereas the middle-class person is likely to be considered neurotic, a status that is not regarded as "sick." In addition, the psychotic is given small chance for improvement and usually meets those expectations, whereas the neurotic, who is supposed to improve with regular therapy and resume daily responsibilities, is likely to do just that. Thus, socioeconomic class may affect not only a person's diagnosis but the chances of eventual improvement as well.

There are alternative explanations to labeling theory for the social class differences in diagnosis and admissions; we mentioned two in Chapter 22. First, life is likely to be more stressful in the lower social classes than in the middle and upper classes. And second, as people develop serious mental disorders, their work performance is impaired, and they drift downward into lower social classes. A third hypothesis is that the classes have different attitudes toward psychological disturbance. Lower-class persons are more resistant than middle- or upper-class people to the idea that they are psychologically disturbed; therefore, they are more likely to reach a diagnostician only when their symptoms become severe enough to be described as psychotic (Gove, 1982).

Furthermore, the theory that psychological abnormality is a cultural artifact, maintained through labeling, is being called into question. This theory was developed in the 1950s, when hospital stays tended to be long—fostering both the stigma and the social role attached to "mental patient" status. Today, with mental hospital stays

Admission to a psychiatric hospital automatically labels one as "mentally ill." A middle-class person with the same symptoms as a lower-class person may avoid both the hospital and the label.

far briefer, there is less evidence of persisting stigma (Gove, 1982). Although the conditions for labeling have been reduced, the prevalence of mental disorder has remained the same. Since these reforms were motivated in part by an effort to prevent labeling, labeling theory has, ironically, suffered from its own acceptance.

THE NEUROSCIENCE PERSPECTIVE

Ever since Hippocrates suggested that abnormal behavior is a result of too much phlegm or bile circulating through the body, scientists have attempted to find biogenic explanations for psychological disorder. Like psychogenic theories, biogenic theories are varied and stress different aspects of organic functioning. Genes, biochemis-

try, and neurological impairment have all been the focus of biogenic explanations. In many cases, organic causation is clear and undeniable, as when impairment results from brain injury, infection, or tumor. The effects of alcoholism and untreated syphilis, for example, have been mentioned earlier. For a number of other disorders, primarily anxiety disorders, most research has focused on psychogenic explanations. In the case of psychoses, a good deal of research has been directed at establishing some organic basis. Schizophrenia, the most prevalent psychosis, has been the subject of genetic, brain structure, and biochemical research.

Genetic Theories of Disorder

A direct connection between genes and behavior is difficult to document, as noted in Chapter 4, and only a few disorders have been traced directly to specific genetic defects. Chromosomal abnormality has been established as the cause of Down's syndrome and Turner's syndrome, both of which result in mental retardation. But establishing a link between defective gene combinations and a complex disorder like schizophrenia is an extremely difficult task. The main obstacle is the virtual impossibility of eliminating environmental factors—the influence of family and society. In schizophrenia, as in most other situations, there is no simple way to separate genes from environment.

Nevertheless, fragmentary evidence that schizophrenia may be hereditary has come from studies that explore the incidence of schizophrenia in families. It has been discovered, for instance, that the brother or sister of a schizophrenic, with whom she or he shares many genes, is more likely to be schizophrenic than is, say, the schizophrenic's first cousin (Slater, 1968). Studies of identical and fraternal twins also seem to affirm the role of heredity in schizophrenia. In about 40 to 50 percent of the cases, when one identical twin had schizophrenia, the other twin also had it; the frequency among fraternal twins was much lower but still significant—10 to 15 percent, as shown in Figure 23.1 (Gottesman, 1978).

The problem with studies of twins is that most pairs are reared under the same conditions, making it difficult to rule out environmental factors. To overcome the environmental obstacle, researchers have studied children adopted in infancy. Using adoption and hospitalization records in Denmark,

one group of investigators identified a group of 5,500 adopted children and nearly all of their biological parents (Rosenthal et al., 1968). All of the parents who had ever been diagnosed as schizophrenic or suffering from an affective psychosis were traced. The seventy-six children of these parents were matched against a group of adoptees whose parents had no such psychiatric history. The investigators found that 21.9 percent of the seventy-six children showed schizophrenic characteristics, while only 6.3 percent of the control group children showed such characteristics. Three of the seventy-six children already had full-blown schizophrenia; none of the control children did (Haier, Rosenthal, and Wender, 1978). In another study based on the same records, the investigators traced the family histories of thirty-three adopted children who later developed schizophrenia. They found a much higher percentage of schizophrenia among these children's biological relatives than among their adoptive relatives (Kety et al., 1975).

Other studies have looked at children born to mothers hospitalized with schizophrenia who gave their infants up for adoption. In one study that compared fifty-eight adopted children of schizophrenic mothers with a control group of adopted children, more than 15 percent of the children born to schizophrenic mothers, but none of the children in the control group, developed schizophrenia (Heston, 1966).

Although these adoption studies support the view that heredity plays a role in schizophrenia, they do not rule out environmental influences.

Figure 23.1. The concordance rates that accompany various degrees of relationship to a schizophrenic person. A concordance rate of 100 percent would mean that if one member of the related pair is schizophrenic, the other person will be too. Note that if a fraternal twin is schizophrenic, the concordance rate is about the same as that for any other sibling, but that the concordance rate for an identical twin is far higher. (After Gottesman, 1978.)

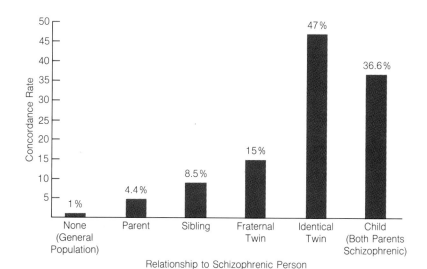

First, adoption is not random. Adoption agencies attempt to match children and adoptive parents on such factors as social class and intelligence. Second, these schizophrenics may have inherited a vulnerability to schizophrenia, but unless certain environmental factors are present, the disorder will not develop. Thus, most researchers believe that, whatever combination of genes is involved, genes alone will not produce the disorder. If schizophrenia were simply a matter of heredity, the concordance rate among identical twins would be 100 percent, not 40 to 50 percent. According to the most widely held view, which is known as the **diathesis-stress model**, genes establish a diathesis, or predisposition, to schizophrenia, but the disorder will not develop unless the predisposition is combined with certain stressful environmental factors. The question is how to identify the children who are most vulnerable to environmental stress and the environmental stresses that are most likely to activate their vulnerability.

High-Risk Studies

Most studies of schizophrenics are retrospective —that is, the study is conducted after a child or adult has become schizophrenic. And this presents some problems. Recollections of the person's childhood behavior and environment by parents, grandparents, or mental health professionals may be colored by their present knowledge of the person's condition. And even if people's recollections about the patient are accurate, it may still be difficult to distinguish cause and effect. Suppose investigators find distorted patterns of communication in the families of schizophrenics. How do they know whether the family has caused the child to become schizophrenic, or whether the child's disturbed behavior has caused problems within the family? Moreover, if the person is institutionalized or is being given drug therapy, some elements of his or her behavior may be the result of the treatment, not the disorder.

Prospective studies are designed to eliminate these problems. The researchers follow a group of children from birth, keeping track of their physiological, psychological, and social histories. If some of the children develop schizophrenia, the researchers then look for connections among genetic factors, environmental conditions, and the development of schizophrenia, comparing these children to matched children who did not develop the disorder.

In the early 1960's Sarnoff Mednick (1970) and Fini Schulsinger launched such a study among Danish children. Since few people in the total population become schizophrenic, the place to look for future cases is among the children of schizophrenics. About 15 percent of these children eventually develop the disorder, compared with less than 1 percent of the general population. Mednick and Schulsinger found 200 normally functioning children of schizophrenic mothers and matched them with a control group of children whose mothers were not schizophrenic.

Their ongoing study has several notable points. First, none of the children had ever been institutionalized nor had they ever experienced any of the other environmental aspects of schizophrenic treatment (such as drug therapy) when the study began. Second, bias could be eliminated from the testing and diagnosis because no one knew which children would become schizophrenic. Third, no one's colored recollections were part of the record; all information was current. Fourth, in addition to the formal control group, the investigators had built in a second control group consisting of high-risk children who did not develop schizophrenia (Mednick, 1971).

By 1971, twenty-seven of the two hundred high-risk children had been diagnosed as emotionally disturbed. When these children were compared with children in the control group and with high-risk children who were not deviant, investigators found five critical differences:

1. The mothers of deviant children were hospitalized earlier in their children's lives and were more severely schizophrenic than the mothers of children who were not deviant.
2. The deviant children were aggressive and disruptive in school.
3. On a word-association test, the deviant children quickly drifted from the stimulus word, so that, given the word "table," a deviant child might reply, "chair, top, leg, girl, pretty, shy."
4. The deviant children showed quite different galvanic skin responses (GSRs; a measure of reactivity); when these children heard a series of irritating noises, for example, their GSRs did not eventually habituate as did the responses of other children.
5. Complications during the mother's preg-

nancy or the child's birth had occurred among 70 percent of the deviant children, but among only 15 percent of the healthy high-risk group and 33 percent of the control group (Mednick, 1971).

Between 1972 and 1974, all the children in the study went through an intensive diagnostic assessment. Among the high-risk group, seventeen were diagnosed as schizophrenic, but only one low-risk child was diagnosed as schizophrenic. However, one difference that had earlier distinguished deviant children in the high-risk group had disappeared. Those in the high-risk group who were diagnosed as schizophrenic did not show more drift on the word-association task than did those who did not become schizophrenic (Griffith et al., 1980).

This project has inspired many other similar projects, and there is now intense activity in high-risk longitudinal research. Later reports from this and other projects have found additional differences. Children at high risk for schizophrenia:

1. commit more criminal offenses (Kirkegaard-Sorenson and Mednick, 1975);
2. show more adjustment problems (Hanson et al., 1976);
3. have difficulty focusing their attention (Asarnow et al., 1977);
4. show maturational lags in the processing of visual stimuli (Herman et al., 1977);
5. have different EEG patterns (Ital, 1977).

Other recent findings have shown further differences among children who later develop schizophrenia. Mothers of these children are more likely to have had childbirth-precipitated psychosis and are more likely to have had unstable relationships with men than are other mothers (Talovic et al., 1980). Also, teachers described boys who would later become schizophrenic as behaving inappropriately in school and being disciplinary problems. Teachers described girls who would later become schizophrenic as apathetic, withdrawn, and isolated (John, Mednick, and Schulsinger, 1982).

It will be another ten years before all of the data from their projects are collected and analyzed. Once the findings are complete, we may have a better idea of which children are at high risk for schizophrenia and what environmental factors and events are most likely to trigger a schizophrenic reaction.

Brain Structure Theories of Disorder

The development of the diagnostic technique known as the CAT scan (computer-assisted tomography) has made it possible for researchers to obtain sophisticated X-ray images of the brains of schizophrenic subjects. Studies using the CAT scan have discovered that schizophrenia is often associated with abnormalities in brain structure. These take the form of enlargement of the brain ventricles, those areas that contain cerebrospinal fluid (Golden et al., 1980). This pattern of brain abnormality, however, is not found in all schizophrenic patients; it is found most often in those who have developed the disorder slowly over a period of years and who have more negative than positive symptoms (Andreasen et al., 1982). (Negative symptoms of schizophrenia, as we saw in Chapter 22, involve the *absence* of some normal behavior, for example, social withdrawal or lack of appropriate affect. Positive symptoms involve the *presence* of an abnormal behavior, such as hallucinations.) The finding of measurable brain abnormalities in one group of schizophrenics and not in another suggests that there may be two different kinds of schizophrenia, one more "biological" than the other. Further research is needed to substantiate this notion, however.

Biochemical Theories of Disorder

If genes are involved in the transmission of some psychological disorders, the problem is to establish how they operate to produce abnormal behavior in some environments. Converging evidence indicates that an important influence may be the body's chemistry. As we saw in Chapter 4, genes are the transmitters of all hereditary information. A single defective gene can disrupt the program for a sequence of necessary biochemical transformations; such a disruption can result in physical or mental disorder. For example, a single defective gene, by upsetting the body's metabolism of phenylalanine, produces phenylketonuria (PKU), with its severe mental retardation.

The hypothesis that mental disorder is caused by some biochemical abnormality can be explored by searching for some biochemical difference between people with a particular disorder and a control group of nondisturbed people. Although this procedure seems straightforward, it is often difficult to carry out. Complications can arise in finding an appropriate control group. The perfect control group would have to live in an environment identical to that of the people who suffer from the disorder, so that the only difference between the subjects and the control group would be the disorder.

However, the biochemistry of human beings is extremely complex, and our understanding of it is far from complete. The medical and life histories, and even the diets, of psychiatric patients are markedly different from those of the members of control groups. Most hospitalized schizophrenics, for example, eat an institutional diet, smoke heavily, get little exercise, and have long histories of drug therapy. Any of these factors can alter a person's biochemistry. Moreover, the extreme emotional and physical stresses associated with having a mental disorder can also cause changes in biochemical functioning (Kety, 1969). When researchers find that the body chemistry of disturbed persons differs from that of nondisturbed people, they must then find ways of determining whether these differences are related to the causes of the disorder or to its effects.

Some progress has been made in distinguishing causes from effects, especially in the biochemistry of schizophrenic disorders. The most promising biochemical approach involves neurotransmitters and is called the **dopamine hypothesis**. According to this view, schizophrenia is associated with excessive activity in those parts of the brain that use dopamine to transmit neural impulses. The major impetus for this hypothesis comes from research on "antipsychotic" drugs (the phenothiazines and butyrophenones), which effectively reduce the primary symptoms of schizophrenia, including thought disorder, blunted emotional responses, withdrawal, and autistic behavior. The drugs work by blocking the absorption of dopamine by the dopamine receptors in the neurons, thereby reducing neural activity in those areas of the brain that use dopamine to transmit neural impulses (Creese, Burt, and Snyder, 1975; Snyder, 1981).

This evidence has been supported by research into the effects of amphetamine and methylphenidate, two stimulants that are known to increase dopamine activity in the brain. As we saw in the discussion of amphetamine psychosis in Chapter 7, these substances can produce temporary psychotic states remarkably similar to schizophrenia (Snyder, 1972; 1976). Furthermore, when either drug is given to schizophrenic patients, their symptoms become even more pronounced (Van Kammen, 1977). A final link has been provided by post mortems. One group of researchers (Mackay et al., 1982) has found increased brain dopamine and an increased number of dopamine receptors in the brains of schizophrenic patients examined postmortem. Many of these patients had been taking antipsychotic drugs, however, which might have produced the results.

The focus on dopamine has revealed a possible link between schizophrenia and Parkinson's disease, an organic brain disorder that produces uncontrollable body tremors. As noted in Chapter 3, Parkinson's disease is caused in part by a gradual destruction of the pathways that normally carry dopamine, and the drug L-dopa, which increases dopamine activity, effectively reduces tremors in patients with the disease. However, L-dopa can also produce symptoms like those of schizophrenia, and antipsychotic drugs often produce a Parkinson's-like movement disorder as a side effect (Paul, 1977).

Although many lines of evidence converge to support the dopamine hypothesis, there is also evidence against it. For example, not all schizophrenics respond to drugs that block the absorption of dopamine; from 50 to 75 percent of patients who receive the drugs during an acute episode show improvement, but the rest do not respond (Gelder and Kolakowska, 1979). In addition, schizophrenics who do respond to these drugs improve gradually, over a period of about six weeks. Yet it takes only a few hours for the drugs to block dopamine receptors in the brain. If schizophrenia were merely the result of activity in these neural tracts, it should improve dramatically within a few hours (Davis, 1978). Dopamine's involvement in the development of schizophrenia is not simple, and we are far from establishing a clearcut cause-and-effect relationship.

A similar approach to the causes of depression has resulted in the **catecholamine hypothesis**. Again, neurotransmitters are involved, and this time the focus is on norepinephrine. (Norepinephrine is one of the catecholamines.) According to this hypothesis, depression results from low levels of norepinephrine in the brain, while high levels of norepinephrine can produce mania. As with the dopamine hypothesis, the supporting evidence is indirect and based primarily on drug effects. Drugs that increase norepinephrine levels relieve depression or produce mania, whereas drugs that reduce norepinephrine levels produce depression or alleviate mania (Schildkraut, 1965; 1972). More recently, it has been suggested that norepinephrine levels by themselves may not produce depression. Instead, an interaction between norepinephrine and excess hormones produced by the thyroid gland may be responsible for depression and mania (Whybrow and Prange, 1981).

Although evidence relating schizophrenia and depression to neurotransmitters continues to grow, psychogenic factors cannot be dismissed. As noted earlier, the social and psychological bases of schizophrenia and depression—as well as other mental disorders—must be taken into account in any complete explanation of the disorder.

One noteworthy attempt at synthesizing psychogenic and biogenic explanations has been the proposal that many factors increase the likelihood of a person's developing schizophrenia, including genes, social class, and family communication patterns (Zubin and Spring, 1977). In this view, a person's vulnerability to schizophrenia depends on the cumulative total of such factors. In addition, the degree of vulnerability might be reduced by improving a person's competence and ability to cope with stressful events.

Such a synthesis reminds us that physical and mental functioning cannot realistically be separated, as we saw in the discussion of stress (see Chapter 21). Since mind is a function of the nervous system, psychogenic and biogenic theories of abnormal behavior are complementary rather than mutually exclusive. Although some biological theorists claim that all mental disorders are organically based, and some behaviorists argue that all abnormal behavior is the consequence of learning, it is extremely unlikely that any one perspective or any one theory will ever be able to account for all abnormal behavior.

SUMMARY

1. Societies have always explained and defined deviant behavior according to their own particular philosophical and religious outlooks. Typical explanations for psychological disturbances have been gods, demons, disease, and emotional stress. Theorists today tend to draw on both biogenic and psychogenic explanations. **Biogenic theory**, which views mental disorder as having a physiological cause, was established among psychiatrists in the late nineteenth century by Kraepelin. The biogenic approach led to the rise of the medical model, which has received a good deal of criticism. **Psychogenic theory**, which holds that mental disturbances result from emotional stress, began with Mesmer, whose major contribution to psychotherapy was the discovery of the power of suggestion in curing mental disorders.

2. Psychoanalytic theory holds that mental disorders arise when id, ego, and superego are out of balance because of unresolved conflicts, and the person encounters additional stress. Conflicts among the id, ego, and superego can lead to **reality anxiety**, when an external danger triggers fear; to **moral anxiety**, when the superego demands moral behavior and self-punishment for transgressions; or to **neurotic anxiety**, when impulses generated by the id threaten to overwhelm the ego. To relieve neurotic anxiety, the ego may use defense mechanisms in an increasingly rigid manner; the defense mechanism chosen determines the form of abnormal behavior that appears. "Neuroses" are associated with the overuse of defense mechanisms to control the id; psychoses occur when the ego is so weak that it has no defenses against the id.

3. Behavioral theorists believe that abnormal behavior is learned in the same way as is all other behavior and that there is a continuity between normal and abnormal behavior. The person with a psychological disorder has either learned inappropriate behavior or failed to learn adaptive behavior. Maladaptive behavior can result from modeling, from direct reinforcement, or from a combination of reinforcement and extinction. Behaviorally oriented theorists who take a cognitive approach believe that the way people interpret events determines their feelings and behavior. Since the development and course of a disorder are considered the

result of interaction between a person's behavior and his or her environment, the aim of the behavioral approach is to increase the person's abilities and enhance his or her functioning.

4. The **humanistic-existential perspective**, which includes both humanistic and existential theorists, makes four basic assumptions: (1) a **phenomenological approach**—which stresses the individual's perception of the world—is necessary; (2) each individual is unique; (3) human potential must be emphasized; (4) the individual is free to make choices and is responsible for her or his own behavior. Humanistic theorists believe that maladjustment is the result of a thwarted drive for self-actualization. Frankl, an existential theorist, divides psychological disorders into anxiety neuroses, the result of guilt over not having pursued personal values, and obsessional neuroses, the result of a person's inability to endure the discrepancy between the real and the ideal. Laing, another existential theorist, believes that disorders are caused by modern society and the modern nuclear family; he believes most people are mad and the schizophrenic is "hypersane" and searching for an authentic identity. Adherents of most other perspectives emphatically reject the "hypersanity" view.

5. The family perspective goes beyond the psychological processes of the individual to focus on the family's role in the development of abnormal behavior. According to Lidz, families of schizophrenics show one of two family patterns: the **marital schism** pattern, in which the parents are bitterly divided; and the **marital skew** pattern, in which a strong but disturbed parent totally dominates a dependent or masochistic parent who supports the dominant parent's actions. Other theorists believe that faulty family communication is at the root of schizophrenia. According to the **double-bind hypothesis**, parents in these families habitually send conflicting messages to their children so that a child never learns to distinguish among the meanings expressed in normal language and behavior.

6. The sociocultural perspective, which places the primary blame for disorders on society, stresses two interrelated views: social stress, in which the stresses of modern society cause abnormal behavior; and social labeling, in which having a "mentally ill" label attached to a person leads to his or her adopting a "sick" role. In both views, compared to people in the middle class, people in lower socioeconomic classes are more likely to show mental disorder because they face more stress, are more likely to be labeled as disordered, and are more likely to resist the idea of being disturbed and therefore avoid early treatment.

7. In the neuroscience perspective, mental disorders have biogenic causes: genes, biochemistry, or neurological impairment. Genetic studies of schizophrenia, in which the disorder is traced in families and which uses studies of twins and of children adopted in infancy, indicate that heredity plays some role in schizophrenia. According to the **diathesis-stress model**, genes establish a predisposition to schizophrenia and environmental stress allows it to develop. CAT scan studies have discovered that schizophrenia is often associated with abnormalities in brain structure. Biochemical studies indicate that neurotransmitters are involved in schizophrenia and in depression. According to the **dopamine hypothesis**, schizophrenia is associated with excessive activity in those parts of the brain that use dopamine to transmit neural impulses. According to the **catecholamine hypothesis**, depression is associated with low levels of norepinephrine in the brain.

8. Physical and mental functioning cannot be separated, and psychogenic and biogenic theories of abnormal behavior are complementary rather than mutually exclusive. Neither perspective, by itself, is likely to account for all psychological disturbances.

KEY TERMS

authenticity
biogenic theory
catecholamine hypothesis
diathesis-stress model
dopamine hypothesis
double-bind hypothesis

existential frustration
humanistic-existential
   perspective
marital schism
marital skew
moral anxiety

neurotic anxiety
obsessive-compulsive disorders
phenomenological approach
psychogenic theory
reality anxiety

RECOMMENDED READINGS

BOOTZIN, R. R., and J. R. ACOCELLA, *Abnormal psychology: Current perspectives* (4th ed.). New York: Random House, 1984. A comprehensive textbook that describes the major categories of psychological disorders and presents the major theoretical perspectives.

MASER, J. D., and M. E. P. SELIGMAN. *Psychopathology: Experimental models.* San Francisco: W. H. Freeman, 1977. A collection of papers in which each author explores the fundamental nature of a different disorder through experimental research.

SNYDER, S. H. *Madness and the brain.* New York: McGraw-Hill, 1974. A highly readable account of the biological bases of mental disorder by one of the leading researchers in the field.

WYNNE, L. C., R. L. CROMWELL, and S. MATHYSSE (Eds.) *The nature of schizophrenia: New approaches to Research and Treatment.* New York: Wiley, 1978. A collection of papers on the latest findings and theories regarding schizophrenia.

APPROACHES TO TREATMENT

A young man, a year out of college and at work at his first job, begins to feel out of sorts and sluggish. He has trouble sleeping and loses his appetite. His increasing fatigue causes his work performance to suffer, and he is reprimanded by his boss. He finds himself drinking more and more heavily in the evenings to relieve the stress of the workday. Finally, he feels unable to get out of bed one morning to go to work. He begins to realize that he has a problem: he is seriously depressed and he is drinking too much.

Once he recognizes that he needs help with his problem, our hypothetical young man is faced with an important choice: to whom does he turn to get the help he needs? To a therapist? If so, to what kind of therapist? Should he choose one whose therapeutic method includes only talk, one who prescribes drugs, or one who gives specific recommendations about changing problem behavior? Perhaps the young man will decide to zero in on the drinking problem and sign up for a meeting of Alcoholics Anonymous. If he is like many of us, he will decide that his problem is not so serious —he will seek the support of friends, family members—or maybe even the bartender at his neighborhood bar.

Psychotherapy comes in many forms, from formal sessions between therapist and client to assistance from a lay volunteer at the end of a crisis hot line. And psychotherapy is not the only form of treatment for emotional problems; other approaches include organic methods, such as drugs and psychosurgery. All these modes of treatment will be considered in this chapter.

THE NATURE OF PSYCHOTHERAPY

Psychotherapy may be defined as a systematic series of interactions between a therapist trained to aid in solving psychological problems and a person who is troubled or is troubling others. In contrast to the advice of family and friends, psychotherapy is a relatively formal arrangement in which the therapist is a paid professional. Psychotherapists may have had any of several kinds of professional training. A **psychiatrist** is a physician (MD) who specializes in the diagnosis and treatment of mental illness. He or she has usually completed a three-year residency in psychiatry. A **clinical psychologist** has earned a doctorate (PhD or PsyD) in clinical psychology and has completed a one-year clinical internship. A **psychoanalyst** is usually a psychiatrist (although she or he can be a psychologist or a lay person) who has had special training in the technique of psychoanalysis and who has been psychoanalyzed as part of the training. A **psychiatric social worker** has earned a master's degree in social work and has specialized in psychiatric social work. A **psychiatric nurse** is a registered nurse who has specialized in psychiatric nursing.

Psychotherapists may use any of a wide variety of therapeutic approaches, depending upon their training, their view of the therapist's role, and their own style. The goal of some psychotherapies is the patient's understanding of her or his motives for behaving in a particular way; the goal of other psychotherapies is to change the patient's behavior directly, paying little or no attention to motives. There are more than 100 different varieties of psychotherapy, each with its own specific program. Some therapists adhere closely to one theoretical perspective. But most therapists, even those who consider themselves as strongly influenced by one body of theory, characterize themselves as "eclectic" practitioners: they make use of the valuable insights of each perspective (Garfield, 1980; 1982).

Whatever the theory behind any particular kind of therapy, there seem to be certain commonalities involved. For example, the therapist offers support along with a willingness to listen to the client's problems and take them seriously. This support and interest from the therapist are so important that clients often report some relief of distress from an initial interview (Howard, 1984).

Another important ingredient in most psychotherapy is hope: the client often comes into therapy feeling demoralized, and the therapist can often combat the person's feelings of hopelessness (Frank, 1961; 1983; Bootzin, 1985). It should be remembered, then, that even though we shall be considering the differences between therapies here, all therapies share much in common.

PSYCHODYNAMIC THERAPIES

The psychodynamic therapies, particularly psychoanalysis, are closely identified with Sigmund Freud. Psychoanalysis is at once a general theory of personality, a theory of psychopathology, and a form of psychotherapy. All therapies that focus on a dynamic interplay of conscious and unconscious elements are derived from psychoanalysis. For a variety of reasons, including economic ones, few practitioners today use standard Freudian psychoanalysis (Korchin, 1976). Although it can be effective, it is a long and expensive process.

Freudian Psychoanalysis

Freud's clinical experience led him to conclude that the source of neurosis was the anxiety experienced when unacceptable unconscious impulses threatened to break through the constraints established by the ego. To fend off these impulses, the patient would resort to defense mechanisms, the most important of which was repression—the "forgetting" of thoughts and impulses that the conscious mind considered shameful or forbidden. Although such impulses could be avoided for a while, they remained alive in the unconscious, provoking anxiety and draining strength from the ego, which expended energy in keeping them submerged. According to Freud, the proper treatment for these anxiety-based disorders was to allow the unacceptable unconscious thoughts to emerge fully into the consciousness, where they could be confronted and "worked through," thus eliminating anxiety and liberating psychic energy for more worthwhile endeavors.

The aim of psychoanalysis is to uncover these long-buried impulses, putting the patient in touch with her or his unconscious, where past traumas and childhood conflicts still live. Various techniques are used to unlock the doors of memory. The client lies on a couch, a relaxing position that helps to loosen the restraints on the unconscious. Once relaxed, she or he free-associates, putting into words whatever thoughts come to mind in whatever order, without imposing self-censorship or logical structure and without interruption from the therapist, whose remarks are kept at a minimum and who sits out of the patient's view.

The therapist and the patient look for clues to the present anxiety in dreams, in which the usual restraints on the unconscious are loosened. But because the unconscious is censored even in sleep, forbidden material appears only in symbolic form. Thus every dream has its manifest content, its plot or story line, and its latent content, the symbolic meaning of the dream, which exposes unconscious conflicts (see Chapter 18). For example, a client who has just had a baby might dream that she had given birth to two boys and that one had died (manifest content). The latent content of the dream, however, may indicate the new moth-

er's ambivalent feelings toward her son, whom she both wants and does not want.

The conscious recognition of forbidden thoughts is not pleasant. Often at this stage in the therapy, clients begin to show signs of **resistance**, or attempts to block treatment. They may pick an argument with the therapist, make jokes, even miss appointments rather than squarely face the unpleasant material. The therapist's ability to recognize and interpret resistance is crucial to treatment, for it enables the client to learn to confront and analyze painful conflicts that would otherwise be avoided.

As the psychoanalysis progresses, the client may respond to the analyst with strong feelings —sometimes love and at other times hostility. Freud interpreted this phenomenon as **transference**, a transfer to him of his clients' childhood feelings toward important people in their lives, particularly their parents. It has become a basic assumption of traditional psychoanalysis that therapy will not be effective unless each client goes

During psychoanalysis, patients must resolve childhood conflicts that originated in their relationship with their parents.

through this stage, called **transference neurosis**, in which the client reenacts with the analyst childhood conflicts with the parents. In the process, the client can bring out repressed emotions, unsatisfied needs, and misconceptions, and can begin to deal with them realistically.

The client attends one-hour psychoanalytic sessions three, four, or five times a week, for several years. In successful psychoanalysis the client eventually breaks through resistance, confronts unconscious conflicts, and resolves the transference neurosis, thereby eliminating anxiety and self-defeating responses to it.

Other Psychodynamic Therapies

Freud's ideas were challenged almost as soon as he got them onto paper. His students Carl Jung and Alfred Adler developed their own theories, as we saw in Chapter 18. Later psychoanalysts also made important revisions in both theory and therapy. One group, of whom the most prominent is Erik Erikson, formed a loosely knit band called ego psychologists. Although they accept a major portion of Freudian theory, ego psychologists reject Freud's assertion that the ego is primarily engaged in finding acceptable ways to satisfy the id's demands. To them, the ego has important functions of its own, such as memory, judgment, perception, and planning. Thus, instead of concentrating on conflicts produced by uncontrollable impulses of the id, ego psychologists, in therapy, tend to focus on ego mechanisms and on how the person learns to cope with stress. Working primarily within the theoretical tradition founded by Freud, ego psychologists use free association, dream interpretation, and the analysis of resistance and transference to lead the client to insight. This adherence to Freudian tradition is not found among neo-Freudians, a group of psychodynamic theorists including Erich Fromm, Karen Horney, and Harry Stack Sullivan, who emphasize social influences and interpersonal relationships.

The many variations on psychoanalysis have been called psychodynamic therapy. Although the therapists who practice such psychotherapy believe that training in psychoanalytic theory and techniques enhances their effectiveness, only a small percentage of them rigorously follow Freud's techniques. Many retain the general psychoanalytic framework, uncovering unconscious motivation, breaking down defenses, and dealing with resistance, but they practice a greatly modified form of psychoanalysis. The couch is generally not used; instead, clients sit up and face their therapists, and the therapists take a more active role, offering interpretation and advice. Most modern psychotherapists tend to emphasize situations in the present, especially personal relationships, rather than events from the distant past. Therapy is briefer and less intensive, and its aim is usually confined to helping the client with a particular problem or problems. Little research has been done on the effectiveness of traditional psychoanalysis (Luborsky and Spence, 1978), but evaluations of modified forms of psychoanalysis will be discussed later in the chapter.

BEHAVIOR THERAPIES

In behavior therapy, the therapist applies learning and other experimentally derived psychological principles to problem behavior (Bootzin, 1975). Basic to the approach of behavior therapy is the belief that the same principles govern all behavior, normal or deviant. Behavior therapists regard psychological problems as learned responses and view problem behavior not as a symptom of unconscious conflicts that must be uncovered but as the primary and legitimate target of therapy.

Behavior therapists also believe that the environment plays a crucial role in determining behavior and that problem behavior is specific to particular types of situations. Consequently, behavioral assessment requires accurate descriptions of observed behavior and the environmental events that accompany it.

Behavior therapists differ from other therapists such as psychoanalysts in the way they deal with the person's inner life. Psychoanalysts tend to regard a person's statements about thoughts and feelings as clues to deep-seated conflicts; but to behavior therapists, emotions and cognitions are simply hidden responses, subject to the same laws of learning as observable responses and equally open to change (e.g., Wolpe, 1978).

Therapies Based on Classical Conditioning and Extinction

Techniques that use classical conditioning and extinction are meant to change behavior by changing emotion—the extent to which certain stimuli elicit feelings of joy, fear, liking, and disliking. In behavior therapy, the client's task is often to unlearn the connection between particular stimuli and her or his maladaptive emotional responses, as in the case of a student who is debilitated by anxiety during every examination. Behavior therapy can also be directed at developing aversions to stimuli that we might like too much—such as alcohol, cigarettes, and fattening foods. Of the many different techniques that might be used, we shall discuss four: systematic desensitization, flooding, aversion therapy, and covert sensitization.

Systematic Desensitization

Perhaps the earliest example of the therapeutic use of classical conditioning was an experiment in which a little boy named Peter was cured of his fear of rabbits by being given candy and other snacks as a rabbit was gradually brought closer and closer (Jones, 1924). **Systematic desensitization**, which was developed by Joseph Wolpe (1958), is a similar procedure in which the client is gradually exposed to anxiety-producing stimuli while relaxed.

Systematic desensitization aims at the gradual extinction of anxiety, and it involves three steps. First, the therapist trains the client in deep-muscle relaxation, generally using Jacobson's progressive relaxation, which was described in Chapter 21. In the second step, the therapist and patient construct a hierarchy of fears—that is, a list of anxiety-producing situations, ranked from the least to the most feared, as shown in Table 24.1. Third, in the actual desensitization, after the client relaxes, the therapist describes the least anxiety-producing scene in the hierarchy and asks the client to imagine it. Once the client can imagine the scene without any anxiety, the therapist moves to the next scene in the hierarchy and again asks the client to imagine it. This procedure is repeated over a series of sessions until the client is able to imagine the scene that formerly produced the most anxiety without experiencing any rise in anxiety at all.

Systematic desensitization is not confined to imaginary stimuli; it can be used with real stimuli as well. The method appears to work because it indirectly encourages people to expose themselves to actual situations that they fear (Leitenberg,

Table 24.1
A graduated hierarchy of situations that elicited increasing amounts of anxiety from a client being systematically desensitized to the fear of death. A rating of 100 means "as tense as you ever are"; a rating of zero means "totally relaxed."

Ratings	Items
5	1. Seeing an ambulance
10	2. Seeing a hospital
20	3. Being inside a hospital
25	4. Reading the obituary notice of an old person
30–40	5. Passing a funeral home (the nearer, the worse)
40–55	6. Seeing a funeral (the nearer, the worse)
55–65	7. Driving past a cemetery (the nearer, the worse)
70	8. Reading the obituary notice of a young person who died of a heart attack
80	9. Seeing a burial assemblage from a distance
90	10. Being at a burial
100	11. Seeing a dead man in a coffin

Source: Wolpe, J., and D. Wolpe. *Our useless fears.* Boston: Houghton Mifflin, 1981.

1976). The technique has been extensively evaluated and has been found to be effective with phobias, recurrent nightmares, and complex interpersonal problems, such as fear of rejection and fear of behaving aggressively (Kazdin and Wilson, 1978; Rimm and Masters, 1979).

Flooding

Flooding might be described as cold-turkey extinction therapy. It has been used to treat many of the same anxieties as systematic desensitization, but **flooding** involves real, not imaginary, situations, although imagination may be used in conjunction with actual exposure. The technique has been particularly useful in the elimination of obsessive-compulsive rituals (Rachman and Hodgson, 1980). For example, if hand-washing rituals are based on the fear of contamination, flooding would require the clients actually to contaminate themselves by touching and handling dirt or whatever substance they are trying to avoid, and afterward to be prevented from carrying out their cleansing ritual. Over repeated trials, the intense anxiety elicited by "contamination" without hand washing would be extinguished. However, this treatment is intensive and requires that someone be with the client twenty-four hours a day to prevent the ritual. Thus, it is customarily used with patients who have been admitted to a hospital, where they are under constant supervision.

Aversion Therapy

When **aversion therapy** is used to change emotional responses, the client is exposed to stimuli that elicit maladaptive responses, accompanied by aversive stimuli such as electric shock or nausea-producing drugs. Through classical conditioning, the formerly attractive stimuli become repellent. Aversion therapy has been used effectively in the treatment of sexual deviations and alcoholism (Rachman and Wilson, 1980). For example, a pedophiliac is given electric shocks while being shown slides of young children, or an alcoholic is given a drug that produces nausea and is then asked to sip an alcoholic beverage. Such therapy, particularly when it involves electric shock, has been controversial, even among behavior therapists.

Covert Sensitization

One alternative to the use of painful shock is a technique called **covert sensitization**, in which clients are asked to visualize the behavior they are trying to eliminate and then to conjure up the image of an extremely painful or revolting stimulus (Cautela, 1966; 1967). For example, a therapist may instruct a smoker to close her eyes, relax, and picture herself taking out a cigarette. As she imagines lighting up and taking a puff, she is told to imagine that she feels nauseated, starts gagging, and vomits all over the floor, the cigarettes, and finally herself. The details of this scene are imagined with excruciating vividness and in minute detail. The client also practices visualizing an alternative, "relief" scene in which the decision not to smoke is accompanied by pleasurable sensations.

Covert sensitization and aversion therapy are most successful when combined with techniques aimed at teaching the client adaptive responses to replace the maladaptive responses. Thus, a problem drinker may need to learn not only how to avoid alcohol but also how to control stress more effectively and how to be more effective in relations with other people. Some of the techniques for controlling stress were discussed in Chapter 21; in the next sections we will see how therapists help clients to acquire new skills.

Therapies Based on Operant Conditioning

Therapies based on classical conditioning are extremely useful in extinguishing maladaptive responses and substituting adaptive ones. But often a client's behavior is not so much maladaptive as it is deficient or missing altogether (Goldfried and Davison, 1976). The person has never learned the appropriate response, or has been so seldom reinforced for it that it rarely occurs.

In treatments based on operant conditioning, desirable behavior is increased by reinforcement and undesirable behavior is decreased by punishment and extinction. Operant conditioning has been used effectively with many different problems to teach new skills and to increase the frequency of people's adaptive behavior in a wide variety of settings. The technique has been successfully applied in teaching retarded children to care for themselves, teaching language to autistic children, increasing the adaptive behavior of schizophrenics, increasing hyperactive children's ability to attend to schoolwork, and helping individuals who overeat, cannot sleep, or have difficulty studying.

Often therapists find it helpful to write a contract that specifies exactly what behavior will earn reinforcement. This is particularly useful in the solution of marital and family conflicts. All parties agree on exactly what behavior each desires from the other. The behavior, along with rewards and sanctions, is stipulated in the contract, which all parties sign.

Since reinforcement can so effectively change behavior, attempts have also been made to structure a person's environment so that appropriate behavior in many areas of life is reinforced while inappropriate behavior is extinguished. The result is the **token economy**, used primarily in institutions, in which a wide range of appropriate behavior is rewarded with tangible conditioned reinforcers, or tokens, that patients can use to "buy" back-up reinforcers. In the typical token economy ward, a board lists various kinds of desirable behavior and the token reward for each. Within the institution is a canteen where patients can exchange their tokens for back-up reinforcers, such as candy, toiletries, or cigarettes. In many cases, tokens can also be spent on privileges —television time, access to the telephone, overnight passes, and so forth (Kazdin, 1977).

Therapies Based on Modeling and Cognitive Restructuring

Not all behavior therapists rely on the techniques of classical and operant conditioning. Those who have been influenced by the social learning perspective place great emphasis on cognition. They believe that modeling has a powerful effect on behavioral change and that the way people interpret events in their lives is as important as what actually happens to them.

Modeling

Modeling is the process by which a person learns some new behavior by watching another person perform it; as we saw in Chapter 8, in this observational learning the model's actions are considered stimuli that act as information. Modeling has been particularly effective in the treatment of phobias (Rosenthal and Bandura, 1978). For example, researchers have been able to eliminate dog phobia in children by having them, in a number of successive sessions, watch another child (called "Fearless Peer") approach a dog, touch it, pet it, and eventually play actively with it. After observing the Fearless Peer, 67 percent of the children had overcome their fear of dogs to such an extent that they could climb into a playpen with a dog, pet it, and remain alone with the animal (Bandura, Grusec, and Menlove, 1967).

More effective than modeling alone is **participant modeling**, in which the therapist models the feared activity and then helps the client to confront and master a graduated series of threatening activities (Bandura, Jeffery, and Wright, 1974). This procedure is one we all use to learn many skills in everyday life—not simply from observing another but by practicing our imitation of the model until we have mastered the activity. When applied to social behavior, a similar procedure has been called **behavior rehearsal**. It has been includ-

ed in programs for social skills training and assertiveness training, in which people learn how to assert themselves, overcoming their passivity yet not becoming aggressive (e.g., Sarason, 1976).

Albert Bandura (1977) has proposed a comprehensive theory of behavior change. He suggests that the mechanisms by which behavior is regulated are primarily cognitive. Particularly important in his view are **efficacy expectations**—people's beliefs that they can successfully execute whatever behavior is required to produce a desired outcome. Efficacy expectations determine how hard people will try, how long they will persist, and whether they will attempt an act at all. Since success raises expectations and failure lowers them, expectations can be increased either by experiencing the sense of mastery that follows one's own successful performance or by observing the success of another. Thus, participant modeling and behavior rehearsal are likely to be effective treatments because they are powerful means of changing efficacy expectations.

Cognitive Restructuring

The process of **cognitive restructuring** focuses on the client's ways of perceiving the world and regards self-defeating behavior as a result of the client's false assumptions. Consequently, therapy aims at identifying these irrational assumptions and subjecting them to the cold light of reason. Albert Ellis (1962), for example, argues that thousands of people lead unhappy lives because of certain irrational beliefs that they hold, such as "I must be loved and approved of by everyone whose love and approval I seek" or "I must be utterly competent in everything I do." In Ellis's **rational-emotive therapy**, clients are first led to recognize the irrational nature of these previously unexamined beliefs, then are aided in establishing a more realistic cognitive framework so that they interpret events in their lives in the light of different assumptions.

An effective way to change a person's erroneous assumptions and patterns of thought has been developed by Donald Meichenbaum (1977). Meichenbaum calls his method of cognitive restructuring **self-instructional training**, and it works directly on maladaptive mental processes. Meichenbaum gives clients new ways of thinking and talking about their problems, and in concentrating on this positive "self-talk," people give up their old self-defeating ways of thought that have become self-fulfilling prophecies.

The third method of cognitive restructuring is **cognitive therapy**, a treatment devised by Aaron Beck (1976). Beck also believes that irrational thoughts and faulty assumptions can lead to emotional disorders, and he has been especially successful in treating depression. When treating depressed people with cognitive therapy, the therapist's first task is to show them that what they think determines how they feel. In the process, the therapist questions clients in such a way that they examine the connection between their own interpretations of events and their subsequent feelings. Gradually, they discover that the negative conclusions they have made about themselves and the world are not based on fact; when this point is reached, the therapist helps the clients to substitute appropriate interpretations of events and to correct the unreasonable assumptions that have led them to distort reality and are thus central to their depression (Beck et al., 1979).

In recent years interest in the use of cognitive techniques such as cognitive restructuring has increased. Cognitive therapy has almost become a separate specialty. Many therapists identify themselves as cognitive behavior therapists and their specialty as cognitive behavior therapy. One reason for the growing interest in cognitive techniques is that they seem to work. For example, in a review of forty-eight studies, Miller and Berman (1983) found that cognitive behavior therapy was substantially more effective than no treatment. However, they found therapies emphasizing cognitive techniques no more effective than those emphasizing behavioral techniques.

HUMANISTIC THERAPIES

In humanistic therapies, the concepts of illness, doctor, and patient are deemphasized. Instead, psychological treatment is viewed as a growth experience, and the therapist's task is to help clients fulfill their individual human potential. Unlike behavior therapy and psychodynamic therapies, humanistic therapies emphasize the clients' sense of freedom and their ability to choose their own future rather than their enslavement to the past. A close client-therapist relationship is

encouraged as the therapist attempts to share the client's experience while providing an uncritical atmosphere in which the client's inner strength can emerge.

Client-Centered Therapy

The best-known of the humanistic therapies is Carl Rogers' system of **client-centered therapy**, which is also referred to as **nondirective counseling**.* Rogers (1951) believes that people are innately motivated to fulfill their own individual potentials; thus, the role of the therapist is to help clients clarify their feelings and come to value their own experience in the world, thus healing the split between self and organism discussed in Chapter 19.

In order to accomplish this, the therapist must be emphathic, warm, and sincere. Thus, the therapist must have **congruence**, or genuineness, the ability to share her or his own feelings with the client in an open and spontaneous manner. In addition, the therapist must have **empathic understanding**, the ability to see the world through the eyes of the client. The therapist offers the client **unconditional positive regard**, supporting the client regardless of what she or he says or does. Instead of interpreting or instructing, the therapist clarifies the client's feelings by restating what has been said. The client-centered therapist is concerned that he or she recognize as precisely as possible what the person is trying to communicate.

Gestalt Therapy

In **gestalt therapy**, Freudian concepts are blended with humanistic philosophy and radically different therapeutic techniques. Frederick (Fritz) S. Perls (1970; Perls, Hefferline, and Goodman, 1951), who developed gestalt therapy, depended heavily on Freudian ideas concerning motivation, dream interpretation, and the influence of old, unresolved conflicts on present psychological disorder, but he rejected Freud's determinism. Gestalt (meaning "whole," "form," "pattern," or "image") therapy attempts to take all life into consideration. The organism is seen as having an

---

*In his recent writings (1980), Rogers has begun to refer to his therapy as "person-centered" rather than "client-centered" therapy, to suggest that his principles apply in all human interaction, not just in the relationship between therapist and client. "Client-centered" is still the more common term, however, and for that reason we shall retain it.

inherent capacity for growth, which is accomplished through insights and interactions with the environment. The ultimate goal is "organismic self-regulation," or balance and integration of the individual. Through awareness, imbalances can be corrected and successful integration of the different aspects of personality can be achieved and maintained.

The role of the therapist is to help the client dispense with defenses, unfold potential, increase awareness, and release pent-up feelings. The three major values of gestalt therapy are emphasis on the *now*, rather than the past or the future; focus on the *spatial*, what is present rather than what is absent; and concentration on the *substantial*, the act rather than the fantasy (Korchin, 1976).

Gestalt therapists use a variety of techniques to achieve these goals. Therapy takes place within the framework of explicit rules governing communication and language. All communication between therapist and client is focused on the present and on the client's present awareness, and it is an exchange between equals. Clients are expected to use the first-person singular ("I am," "I do," "I feel") to show that they take responsibility for their own actions and feelings (saying, for example, "I am angry," rather than "Don't you think I have a right to be annoyed?"). Some exercises are designed to heighten the client's awareness of past conflicts. As clients act out their conflicts, they assume different aspects of their personality, shifting from one role to another to experience conflicting needs and demands. The reenactment of these conflicts often becomes violent and highly emotional. Other exercises develop clients' awareness of their own movements, tone of voice, and feelings. Once clients have focused awareness on various aspects of self, they can take responsibility for their own feelings, thoughts, and actions. When dreams are analyzed, the different characters and objects in the dream are seen as fragments of the self, and the client is encouraged to imagine that she or he is each character and object and to express the feelings that accompany these roles. Such reenactments lead to acceptance and reintegration of these aspects of the self.

Nonprofessional Helpers

Most people who have a psychological problem do not seek help from a professional psychotherapist

Shapedown is a twelve-week program of weight management for teenagers, which originated at the University of California, San Francisco, and is now offered at four hundred medical centers across the country. It not only incorporates an exercise and diet regime, it teaches teens to change problem-causing habits.

(Gurin, Veroff, and Feld, 1960). This does not mean that they go without any help, however. People who lack the funds, who think their problem is not serious enough to need professional help, or who fear or distrust therapy are likely to seek some support from family and friends.

A second valuable source of help outside formal psychotherapy is self-help groups. There are many such groups, most focusing on a particular problem: Alcoholics Anonymous, Weight Watchers, support groups for cancer patients, rape victims, parents who have abused their children, and many more. These groups can be of considerable help to some people, offering social support from understanding peers and a chance to express destructive urges (such as to drink or to abuse a child) in a safe environment.

Finally, help may sometimes be offered by paraprofessionals—that is, people with some training in counseling troubled people. Paraprofessionals often work with mental health professionals in a clinic or volunteer setting. Later in this chapter we shall consider the work of crisis hot lines, which are often run by paraprofessionals. Counseling from paraprofessionals may be very effective, especially when the counselor is experienced and well trained (Hattie et al., 1984).

GROUP AND FAMILY APPROACHES

Individual therapy is both expensive and time-consuming. In addition, the therapist sees the client alone, plucked out of her or his normal environment and stripped of the human relationships that may be affecting the client's disorder. The goal of making therapy cheaper, quicker, and more relevant to the patient's daily problems has led to the increasing popularity of treating people in couples, families, or groups.

Group Therapy

The concept of group therapy can be traced to Joseph Hershey Pratt, a Boston internist who worked with tubercular patients at the turn of the century. In an attempt to relieve the debilitating effects of depression and isolation experienced by the severely ill patients, he began to arrange regular group sessions, instructing his patients to keep diaries of their weight gains and losses, everyday events of their lives, and their general emotional state (Korchin, 1976). During the next thirty years a number of psychiatrists independently experimented with group methods. In the 1930s and 1940s group methods applying psychological principles began to evolve. And after World War II the group therapy movement gained impetus when it became necessary to treat large numbers of people, both veterans and civilians, who had suffered from the social, political, and economic upheavals of the period.

Group therapy lessens the economic problem that other therapies pose by allowing more patients to be treated at lower fees. But its chief advantage is that it concentrates on and promotes better interpersonal relationships. Moreover, clients who are extremely resistant to individual therapy seem to respond to the emotional support of the group. This is particularly true when all members of the group have a common problem, such as drug addiction, alcoholism, or obesity.

Family and Marital Therapy

In marital and family therapy, the group is a natural one, formed by the bonds of kinship. Although the symptoms of one member may have brought the couple or family into therapy, the entire group is viewed as the treatment unit, and the assumption is that the group as a whole is disturbed.

There are several types of family therapy. In behavioral family therapy, family interactions are stressed, and members are made aware of the way their actions reinforce one another's behavior. Some therapists see family distress as the result of "coercion," in which each member uses aversive acts or words to influence the others' behavior (Patterson and Hops, 1972). In marital behavior therapy, for example, it is assumed that the couple have been locked into frustrating behavior exchanges for so long that they have lost sight of the effect of their behavior on each other and are unaware of the sources of their unhappiness. The therapist's aim is to shift the couple's behavior toward positive, mutually reinforcing interactions, to improve communication between them, and to improve their skills for solving problems and settling conflicts (Jacobson and Margolin, 1979).

In the communcations (Satir, 1967; Watzlawick, Beavin, and Jackson, 1967) or strategic (Watzlawick, Weakland, and Fisch, 1974) approach, it is assumed that subtle nonverbal signals that directly contradict family members' verbal signals are involved in the disorder.

In the systems approach, the assumption is that people are members of a family social system that consists of a set of interlocking roles (Ackerman, 1958; Minuchin and Fishman, 1981). In the course of living together, each couple or family, consciously or unconsciously, sets up expectations for one another and assigns roles for each person to fill. Thus there may be a "weak" member, a "strong" member, a "caretaker," a "scapegoat." When roles are inappropriate or unduly restrictive, the most fragile member of the unit may show symptoms of mental disturbance, but all members are believed to contribute to the breakdown. Indeed, some therapists contend that the role system of the nuclear family requires a sick member (Minuchin, 1974).

THE EFFECTIVENESS OF PSYCHOTHERAPY

In 1952 Hans Eysenck reviewed twenty-four studies of the outcome of psychotherapy, five concentrating on psychoanalytic treatment and nineteen on "eclectic" treatment, in which several different therapeutic approaches are combined. He concluded that psychotherapy was no more effective than no treatment at all. According to his interpretation of these studies, only 41 percent of the psychoanalytic patients improved, while 64 percent of those given eclectic psychotherapy were "cured" or had improved. But Eysenck argued that even this 64 percent improvement rate was no indication that psychotherapy had any effect, since it had been reported that 72 percent of a group of hospitalized neurotics improved without treatment (Landis, 1937). If no treatment at all produces as much improvement as psychotherapy, the obvious conclusion is that psychotherapy is ineffective. Eysenck (1966; 1967) has vigorously defended this controversial position and believes that only behavioral therapy is at all effective.

Many additional reviews and studies have been generated by Eysenck's charges. In a thoughtful review, Allen Bergin (1971; Bergin and Lambert, 1978) replied to Eysenck. First, Bergin demonstrated that when different but equally defensible assumptions about the classification of patients were made, the effectiveness of psychoanalytic treatment was much greater than Eysenck had reported; perhaps as many as 83 percent of the patients improved or recovered. Second, when Bergin and Lambert reviewed seventeen studies with untreated control groups, the rate of improvement without treatment was only about 43 percent.

Bergin's reviews question the validity of Eysenck's sweeping generalization that psychotherapy is no more effective than no treatment at all. But much of Bergin's argument is based on differences of opinion about how patients should be classified. Precise criteria for "improvement" are difficult to define and to apply. The nature of "spontaneous remission" (sudden disappearance) of symptoms in persons who have not received formal psychotherapy is difficult to assess, for these people may have received help from unacknowledged sources—friends, relatives, religious advisers, family physicians.

In an attempt to surmount some of these problems, Mary Lee Smith, Gene V. Glass, and Thomas I. Miller (1980) analyzed 475 controlled studies of psychotherapy (see Figure 24.1). They devised a statistical technique for summarizing the findings of the studies and found strong evidence for the effectiveness of psychotherapy. The average client who had received therapy scored more favorably on the outcome measures than 80 percent of the persons in untreated control groups. Smith, Glass, and Miller also assessed the effectiveness of different types of psychotherapy and found that all types of individual therapy were more effective than no treatment. In addition, group therapy was found to be as effective as individual therapy. From this evaluation, it could be concluded that psychotherapy is more effective than no treatment, and that differences in effectiveness between various forms of therapy are small.

Figure 24.1. Is psychotherapy effective? Researchers who reviewed 475 studies think the answer is yes. Clients receiving each of the types of psychotherapy shown in this graph were compared with untreated control groups. The bars indicate the percentile rank that the average treated client attained on outcome measures when compared with control subjects for each type of therapy. Thus the average client receiving psychodynamic therapy scored more favorably on outcome measures than 75 percent of the untreated controls. (Adapted from Smith, Glass, and Miller, 1980.)

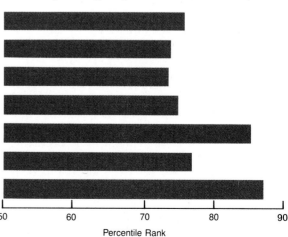

Effectiveness of Various Types of
Psychotherapy Compared to Untreated Control Groups

However, many of the studies included in Smith, Glass, and Miller's review were flawed by methodological problems. In most of them, the client's improvement was measured by the therapist's overall impression, which in turn was based on the client's own reports. Both sources of information—the therapist's opinion and the client's opinion—are extremely indirect measures of the client's actual functioning. Another difficulty with the Smith, Glass, and Miller review is that not all studies they included were done on a clinical population. Many used college student volunteers, whose problems may not have been as serious as those of other clinical patients. When Andrews and Harvey (1981) reanalyzed only the studies from the review in which "neurotics" had sought or been referred for treatment, they found that behavioral therapies had a significantly higher average effect than verbal dynamic psychotherapies.

Other studies have confirmed this finding. In a review of sixteen methodologically strong outcome studies that evaluated various therapies for "neurotic" disorders, nine showed that behavior therapy was the most effective treatment, and seven showed no difference in effectiveness between behavioral and other treatments. However, none found any other type of treatment to be more effective than behavior therapy. In addition, behavior therapy was superior for many problems not included in the review of 475 studies by Smith, Glass, and Miller. Behavior therapy was more effective than other therapies for the treatment of addiction, the institutional management of psychotic disorders, and childhood disorders such as bed-wetting and hyperactivity (Kazdin and Wilson, 1978).

Although many types of psychotherapy can be of substantial benefit, there is still much to be learned about the development of effective therapies for specific disorders. Recent years have seen efforts to integrate the various therapies, combining the insights and techniques of one or more in clinical practice. For example, Wachtel (1977) has suggested that psychodynamic therapies are particularly good at identifying the conflicts that are central to the individual, while behavioral therapies provide the techniques for helping the individual cope more effectively with those conflicts.

NEUROSCIENCE APPROACHES TO THERAPY

The various psychotherapies described in this chapter are based on psychogenic approaches to mental disorders—that is, they aim at changing behavior, emotions, or cognition. In contrast, therapies based on biogenic theories aim at altering the workings of the central nervous system. This is most commonly done with drugs, although intervention by means of electroconvulsive therapy or psychosurgery is also possible. Drug therapies are often used in conjunction with psychotherapy.

Antianxiety Drugs

Antianxiety drugs are used to reduce anxiety, apprehension, and tension. They are commonly known as tranquilizers, specifically as "minor" tranquilizers to distinguish them from the antipsychotic drugs, or "major" tranquilizers (discussed below). Antianxiety drugs are in wide use. The most popular tranquilizers are Tranxene (clorazepate); Librium (chlordiazepoxide hydrochloride); and Valium (diazepam). In fact, tranquilizers have become so popular that Valium is now the most frequently prescribed drug in the world (Ray, 1983).

One reason for the popularity of these drugs is their presumed effectiveness in helping normal people cope with difficult periods in their lives, but they are also prescribed for the alleviation of various anxiety disorders, for stress-related physical disorders, and for symptoms of alcohol withdrawal. The major effect of Tranxene, Librium, and Valium is to depress the activity of the central nervous system. While antianxiety drugs can be an important component of psychological treatment, they do have side effects. The most common are fatigue, drowsiness, and impaired motor coordination. In addition, the body develops a tolerance to the drug, so that larger and larger doses are required to produce the same effect. The problems of tolerance and subsequent dependence on the drug are particularly notable for insomnia, for which antianxiety drugs are frequently prescribed. Consequently, these drugs are better for short-term crises than for long-term chronic conditions. They may also be dangerous if taken with other depressants or with alcohol. A heavy dose of an antianxiety drug taken with alcohol can result in death.

Antipsychotic Drugs

Antipsychotic drugs, known as "major" tranquilizers, dramatically affect the symptoms of psychosis—agitation, withdrawal, thought disorder, hallucinations, and delusions. They do not affect anxiety.

Among these drugs, the most widely prescribed are the phenothiazines, including Thorazine (chlorpromazine), Stelazine (trifluoperazine), and Mellaril (thioridazine). When Thorazine was introduced in the United States in the mid-1950s, it was an immediate success. Within eight months of its appearance, it had been used by approximately 2 million patients. Because patients improved so dramatically, Thorazine led to an opening up of the mental hospitals. Fewer wards were locked, and more and more patients were returned to the community. Thus, the introduction of phenothiazines contributed considerably to the community mental health movement, which will be discussed later in the chapter. Phenothiazines have also advanced our knowledge of schizophrenia, because the effort to discover how these drugs worked led researchers to the dopamine hypothesis, which was discussed in Chapter 23.

Although antipsychotic drugs are effective, there are several drawbacks to their use. Their calming influence is accompanied by side effects that include constipation, blurred vision, dry mouth, and muscle rigidity and tremors. An additional side effect that is resistant to treatment is **tardive dyskinesia**, a muscle disorder in which patients grimace and smack their lips uncontrollably. Tardive dyskinesia usually appears in patients over forty years old after six months or more of continuous treatment with antipsychotic drugs. Since the vast majority of psychotic patients in the United States take one of the major tranquilizers on a daily basis and since the disorder does not disappear when the drug is discontinued, tardive dyskinesia presents a serious problem.

Despite their effectiveness in returning people to society, antipsychotic drugs are limited in their power. They do not cure schizophrenia, and if released patients stop taking the drugs, their symptoms generally return. Thus for many patients, chronic hospitalization has been changed

Antipsychotic drugs such as Thorazine and Stelazine help to ease the symptoms of psychotic patients.

to a "revolving-door" existence of releases, relapses, returns to the hospital, and rereleases after the drugs again take effect. In addition, patients who are taking phenothiazines usually make only a marginal adjustment to life in society.

Antidepressant Drugs

The antidepressant drugs, which are used to lift the mood of depressed patients, were discovered by accident in 1952 when Irving Selikof and his colleagues, treating patients for tuberculosis with a drug called Iproniazid, noticed that it made them cheerful and optimistic. Iproniazid interferes with the action of monoamime oxydase (MAO), an enzyme that degrades neurotransmitters, including norepinephrine and serotonin. Iproniazid was later found to cause liver damage and is no longer prescribed, but other MAO inhibitors are occasionally used. When taking a MAO inhibitor, a person must follow a highly restricted diet because the drugs interact with tyramine and can cause death. Thus, foods high in tyramine—including aromatic cheese, avocado, beer, chicken liver, cream, lox, and yeast extracts—must be eliminated from the diet.

More effective and less dangerous than MAO

inhibitors are the tricyclics, so named because their molecular structure is arranged in three rings; the major tricyclics are Tofranil (imipramine), Elavil (amitriptyline), and Sinequan (doxepin). Their effectiveness was also discovered by accident. Since they are similar in structure to the phenothiazines, the tricyclics were tried on schizophrenics, who showed an unexpected elevation of mood. Tricyclics increase the availability of serotonin and norepinephrine at receptor sites in the brain, and MAO inhibitors decrease transmitter availability; thus both classes of drug support the norepinephrine hypothesis of depression discussed in Chapter 23 (Berger, 1978).

Lithium, relatively new to the psychiatric community in the United States, is administered as a simple mineral salt, lithium carbonate. This substance was discovered to have sedative qualities by John Cade, an Australian physician, in 1949. It is used to treat manic episodes and bipolar disorders, because it effectively returns patients to a state of emotional equilibrium in which extreme swings of mood do not occur (Prien, Klett, and Caffrey, 1974; Stallone et al., 1973). It is sometimes effective in cases of major depression as well. Lithium was not introduced into the United States until the late 1960s, because it can be toxic and it has caused death. Its riskiness lies in the fact that the effective dosage is quite close to the toxic dosage. Therefore, its level in the patient's bloodstream must be closely monitored. Among the possible side effects of lithium are kidney damage, stomach upsets, and weight gain (Mendels, 1976).

Electroconvulsive Therapy

Electroconvulsive therapy (ECT) is commonly known as "shock treatment." Its primary use is in the treatment of severe depression; it usually works faster than antidepressant drugs (Greenblatt, 1977; Scovern and Kilmann, 1980). It involves administering a series of brief electrical shocks of approximately 70 to 130 volts, spaced over a period of several weeks. The shock induces a convulsion similar to an epileptic seizure. Although no one understands exactly how ECT works (Greenblatt, 1977), it is the convulsion that seems to produce the therapeutic effect; shock at levels too low to induce convulsion is ineffective.

As it is now applied, ECT entails relatively little discomfort for the patient. Before treatment, the patient is given a sedative and injected with a muscle relaxant to alleviate involuntary muscular

contractions and to prevent physical injury. Even with these improvements, however, ECT is a drastic treatment and must be used with great caution. A common side effect of ECT is memory loss, both anterograde (loss of the capacity to learn new material) and retrograde (loss of the capacity to recall previously learned material). Anterograde memory gradually returns to normal after treatment (Squire and Slater, 1978). As for retrograde memory, there is a marked loss one week after treatment with nearly complete recovery within seven months. In many cases, however, some subtle memory losses, particularly for events occurring within the year preceding hospitalization, will persist beyond seven months (Squire, Slater, and Miller, 1981). And in very rare cases (Roueché, 1974), such persisting losses are not subtle, but comprehensive and debilitating. However, the probability of memory loss is less if ECT is confined to the right hemisphere, which has less to do with language, rather than delivered to both sides of the brain (Squire and Slater, 1978).

Although ECT is effective, it remains controversial; many people view it as akin to torture. In 1982 the voters of Berkeley, California, passed a referendum making the administration of ECT a misdemeanor punishable by a fine of up to $500 and six months in jail. Although this ban was later reversed by the courts, the fact that it was passed by the voters suggests the negative feelings many people have about ECT.

Psychosurgery

Psychosurgery is the most extreme of all organic treatments. It involves serious risks for the patient, and its effects are irreversible. Modern psychosurgery began in 1935, when Egas Moniz and Almeida Lima developed the procedure known as **prefrontal lobotomy**, in which a surgical instrument is inserted into the brain and rotated to sever nerve fibers connecting the frontal lobe (thought center) and the thalamus (emotional center). It was expected that, in cases of severe mental disorder, this interruption in communication would help reduce the impact of disturbing stimuli on mood and behavior. During the next twenty years other methods of psychosurgery evolved, and operations were done on thousands of patients. Unfortunately, although some extremely disturbed patients may have benefited from the surgery, others were left in vegetative states. And some died. The discovery of antipsychotic drugs in the 1950s brought a halt to most psychosurgery.

Today the crude lobotomies of the 1940s and 1950s are no longer performed. They have been replaced by "fractional operations," which destroy very small amounts of brain tissue in precise locations (Valenstein, 1973). Such operations are sometimes performed in the United States, but only after all other modes of treatment have been exhausted. In 1976 the National Commission for the Protection of Human Subjects in Biomedical and Behavioral Research concluded that these limited procedures have been beneficial in cases of depression associated with intractable pain. Furthermore, the serious side effects and risks associated with lobotomy appear not to accompany the new techniques. The commission encouraged further research and recommended that psychosurgery be considered an experimental procedure to be used only under stringent safeguards of the patient's rights and welfare.

COMMUNITY AND MENTAL HEALTH

It is seldom easy for a person who has been hospitalized for a mental disorder to reenter society. Often released patients find themselves too far from the hospital for any supplementary care and too fragile to cope independently with the pressures of the outside world. Without community support, these patients may not be able to make a successful return to society. Some community assistance is available through community mental health centers, halfway houses, and hot lines, but the ultimate goal is the prevention of disorder.

Community Mental Health Centers

The Community Mental Health Centers Act of 1963 was designed to solve some of the problems faced by patients trying to reenter society. It mandated one mental health center for every 50,000 members of the U.S. population, to supply needed psychological services for the former patient attempting to function within the community. Other purposes of these centers were to educate community workers such as police, teachers, and clergy in the principles of preventive mental health, to train paraprofessionals, and to carry out research. Although funding for centers has been cut back, those that are in operation supply such important supports as outpatient, inpatient, and emergency services as well as community consultation.

When outpatient services are provided, people can walk into a clinic and receive therapy once, twice, or several times a week, without leaving home or giving up a job, and without feeling stigmatized as institutionalized mental patients. The centers also serve as a bridge between hospitalization and complete independence by giving aftercare and supplementary services to patients released from hospitals. It is clear that the centers meet an important need; for example, outpatient care increased twelvefold, from 379,000 to 4.6 million clinical episodes, in the twenty years from 1955 to 1975 (Kiesler, 1982).

When inpatient services are available, severely disturbed people can be hospitalized within the community. Friends and family have easy access to them, and the patients feel less isolated and more accepted. Many centers have arrangements for day hospitals, in which patients may make use of the therapy and facilities offered by a hospital during the day and go home at night. Day hospitals, first introduced at the Menninger Clinic in 1949 and now numbering over a thousand nationwide, are particularly effective at preventing full-time hospitalization (Greene, 1981; Straw, 1982). Night hospitals work in a similar way, accommodating patients at night and leaving them free to be at work or at home during the day.

When community mental health centers provide emergency services, they often take the form of storefront clinics that are open twenty-four hours to deal with such sudden crises as suicide attempts and drug overdoses. The centers may have teams of psychologically trained personnel on call, ready to go to city hospital emergency rooms and deal with psychological traumas.

When community consultation services are provided, mental health centers have qualified personnel available to advise other community workers, such as teachers, police, and clergy, on the handling of psychological problems in the classroom and within the community. Sensitivity workshops give instruction on such matters as how to intervene in potentially violent family quarrels, how to talk potential suicides out of jumping off a bridge, and how to keep truants from dropping out of school.

Halfway Houses

Halfway houses, which provide an intermediate step between the hospital and the community, are

THE HOMELESS: VICTIMS OF GOOD INTENTIONS

A woman named Judy lives at Sixty-third Street and Second Avenue in Manhattan—not in an apartment, but on the street. She spends her days sitting quietly on the sidewalk, surrounded by her possessions. But around eleven o'clock at night Judy begins to scream obscenities. Sometimes she continues for hours. At first neighbors felt sorry for the woman, but after many sleepless nights they called the police. Judy was taken to Bellevue, a psychiatric hospital. She was released the next day, however, and she returned to her corner. Judy is one of the thousands of homeless people, some of them "bag ladies," who have become a familiar sight in New York and other cities. New York City officials estimate that at least a third of the homeless have psychiatric histories and should be receiving psychiatric care. Why are they homeless? Judy and others like her are victims of well-intentioned policies that have backfired.

In the early 1960s a number of mental health and civil rights groups became concerned about the crowded conditions in state mental hospitals. Hundreds of thousands of people were confined involuntarily to mental hospitals. Well-meaning experts noted that

their confinement was unnecessary: the new tranquilizing drugs reduced psychotic episodes, making it possible for the mentally ill to function adequately in the outside world— so might it not be feasible to release many of them with proper medication? Moreover, a pilot study in Missouri showed that patients who were given intensive treatment at small, local mental health centers were released 237 days sooner than similar patients treated at large institutions.

The Joint Commission on Mental Illness and Health recommended the creation of a nationwide network of community health centers where patients could receive care without leaving their neighborhoods and families. Concerned about the rising cost of state hospitals, politicians readily agreed. So Congress passed the Community Mental Health Center Act in 1963, and many states followed up with civil rights guarantees for the mentally ill. Under New York State's mental hygiene law, for example, people cannot be hospitalized involuntarily unless they are deemed likely to cause themselves or others serious harm—that is, unless they are homicidal or suicidal.

"Deinstitutionalization" was

hailed as an enlightened, humane, and cost-effective solution to the mental health problem. In New York alone, the population of state institutions fell from 81,000 in 1965 to 21,000 in 1985. But many of the professionals who fought for deinstitutionalization now regret that more resources have not been put into deinstitutionalization. Many of those centers that have been put in place do not have the facilities or the high-quality staff that produced such stunning results in the Missouri study. In addition, the mentally ill often do not have homes or families to return to. Second, the long-term use of "miracle" drugs has negative side effects (especially uncontrollable head and neck movements); not surprisingly, many patients stop taking medication soon after their release from a hospital. Finally, there is the question of whether individuals like Judy are competent to make decisions about whether or not they need treatment. As things stand, nothing can be done for someone who refuses help.

Source: The New York Times, October 10, 1984, pp. Al, B4; October 18, 1984, pp. C1, C4.

houses in which individuals with common problems live together. The residents provide support for one another and use whatever supplementary services they need until they are able to function entirely on their own. These houses have proliferated in recent years and have been quite useful in easing the transition from hospital care to community life. Halfway houses have been successful

in the rehabilitation of drug addicts, newly released mental patients, former convicts, and alcoholics. Reports indicate that residents of small halfway houses are less likely to be rehospitalized than patients who have been returned to the community without any supplementary support system (Cannon, 1975).

In large cities, not enough true halfway houses

These boys have broken their addiction to drugs, but before returning to their communities, they are living in a half-way house. There, with support from each other and from trained counselors, they are preparing to resume "life on the outside."

exist. Instead, former mental patients are often sent to nursing homes or large, converted hotels, where no supplementary support systems are provided. Such facilities may be little more than "back wards" located within the community (Jones, 1975). To be successful, community-based care must have adequate financial support. In the absence of funds for small, high-quality facilities, the alternative method of housing former mental patients in nursing homes and hotels may simply constitute dumping them into our urban centers to survive as best they can.

Crisis Intervention: The Hot Line

Community services that involve clinics, hospitals, or halfway houses are costly and complicated to set up, but the crisis hot line provides an instant, economical, and effective way to deal with emergency situations. People who are in trouble can telephone at any time and receive immediate counseling, sympathy, comfort, and referrals to clinics and hospitals. The best known of these systems is the Los Angeles Suicide Prevention Center, established in 1958. Similar hot lines have been set up for crime victims, alcoholics, and people under stress of all kinds. Since 1960, more than 180 suicide-prevention hot lines and 600

youth and/or drug hot lines have been established in the United States (Trowell, 1979).

Prevention

The basic goals of community psychology are to prevent the development of disorder (primary prevention); to prevent the worsening of disorder (secondary prevention); and to prevent the severe effects of major disorder on the victim and on society (tertiary prevention). Primary prevention of mental disorder is desirable but difficult to accomplish. It requires changing those aspects of society and the environment that lead to psychological disturbance, and we have seen in Chapter 23 how complex the causes of disorder can be. Nevertheless, nutritional counseling, teaching effective coping skills, and designing less stressful school environments are all potentially important methods of reducing the incidence of disorder.

Secondary prevention, the early detection and treatment of problems before they become severe, is somewhat less complex, but is still no easy task. Outpatient clinics, emergency services, hot lines, and some paraprofessional programs are examples of secondary prevention. Early detection of problems usually requires a trained professional, but consultation programs with schools and law enforcement agencies are one way to expand secondary prevention.

Tertiary prevention programs include the day hospitals and night hospitals and the halfway houses described above. These programs are designed to help those who have suffered a serious disorder to resume useful roles in society and to prevent the recurrence of disorder.

The prevention of disorder is the goal of both the community mental health movement and community psychology, but some psychologists maintain that they have become preoccupied with the delivery of individual services, whereas their major effort should be to improve social conditions. Community psychologists have been urged to focus on the design of social systems that foster health and growth, thus turning their efforts to primary prevention in its broadest sense (Goodstein and Sandler, 1978). If that goal is achieved, the incidence of psychological disorder will be significantly reduced. But society cannot be changed quickly, and in the meantime those individuals affected by psychological disorder must be treated with the best methods available.

SUMMARY

1. **Psychotherapy** is a systematic series of interactions between a therapist trained to solve psychological problems and a person who is troubled or is troubling others. Its goal is to alleviate the problem, either through the patients' understanding of their motives or through directly changing behavior. Professionals who treat mental disorders may be **psychiatrists**, **psychoanalysts**, **clinical psychologists**, **psychiatric social workers**, or **psychiatric nurses**.

2. Psychodynamic therapies are closely identified with Freud and focus on a dynamic interplay of conscious and unconscious elements. During therapy, **resistance**, or attempts by the client to block treatment, must often be dealt with. **Transference neurosis**, often regarded as necessary to effective therapy, occurs when the client transfers to the analyst emotions originally directed toward the parents and reenacts early conflicts. Ego psychologists and neo-Freudians are among the psychodynamic therapists. Most psychodynamic therapy tends to emphasize present situations and is briefer and less intensive than traditional psychoanalysis.

3. Behavioral therapies that use classical conditioning and extinction are meant to change behavior by changing emotions. The techniques include **systematic desensitization**, in which a relaxed client is gradually exposed to imaginative or real re-creations of anxiety-producing stimuli; **flooding**, in which the client is exposed to real situations that produce intense anxiety; and **aversion therapy**, in which the client's exposure to stimuli that elicit maladaptive responses is accompanied by aversive stimuli (electric shock or drugs), and **covert sensitization**, in which the aversive stimuli are imagined. Therapies based on operant conditioning generally punish or extinguish maladaptive responses while reinforcing adaptive ones. Sometimes used in such therapies are behavioral contracts, written contracts that specify behavior, reinforcements, and punishments, and **token economies**, in which behavior is rewarded with tangible objects that can be exchanged for secondary reinforcers. Therapies based on **modeling**, which can take the form of **participant modeling** or **behavioral rehearsal**, place great emphasis on cognition. Bandura has proposed that cognition is responsible for behavior change and that **efficacy expectations**, the belief that one can successfully execute a behavior, are important in the process. **Cognitive restructuring**, including **rational-emotive therapy**, **self-instructional training**, and **cognitive therapy**, attempts to change a client's false perceptions and assumptions to more rational beliefs.

4. Humanistic therapies view psychological treatment as a growth experience, and the therapist helps clients to fulfill their individual potential by emphasizing a sense of freedom and the ability to choose their own future. In **client-centered therapy**, the therapist helps clients clarify feelings and come to value their own

experience of the world. Therapists must have **congruence**, the ability to share their own feelings with the client, and communicate **unconditional positive regard**, nonjudgmental acceptance of the client. **Gestalt therapy** combines Freudian concepts with humanistic philosophy. Always concentrating on the present, the therapist helps the client give up defenses, expand potential, increase awareness, and release pent-up feelings. Clients follow rules of communication that help them take responsibility for their thoughts and actions, act out conflicts, and express feelings.

5. Many people receive help with their psychological problems from nonprofessional helpers. These may be friends, family, or trusted acquaintances. Self-help groups exist to offer support to people seeking to cope with a particular problem, such as drinking. Paraprofessional counselors may also be helpful; many work in community settings in conjunction with mental health professionals.

6. Group therapy was developed as an inexpensive, quick treatment that was relevant to a patient's daily problems. Each psychotherapeutic approach has developed a form of group therapy. In family and marital therapy, the group is a natural one and the entire group is the treatment unit. In behavioral family therapy, the stress is on family interactions and an awareness of how members reinforce one another's behavior. In the communications approach, based on the double-bind theory, contradictory family communications are uncovered. In the systems approach, the role each member takes in the relationship is emphasized.

7. Based on studies of therapy, it has been contended that psychotherapy has no effect at all and that people do as well without therapy as with it. Later, more extensive reviews have found strong evidence for the effectiveness of psychotherapy; some reviews have found little difference among the various therapies in their effectiveness, and others have found behavioral

therapy to be most effective. As yet researchers have not identified the most effective method of treatment for various disorders.

8. Neuroscience therapies aim at altering the central nervous system. Antianxiety drugs (such as Valium) are mild tranquilizers that are prescribed for anxiety disorders, stress-related physical disorders, and withdrawal from alcohol. Antipsychotic drugs (such as Thorazine) are major tranquilizers used to alleviate extreme agitation and hyperactivity in psychotic patients. They have allowed many chronic patients to return to society but have serious side effects, such as **tardive dyskinesia**, a muscle disorder. Antidepressant drugs (such as imipramine) are used to regulate mood, and they have been helpful in treating depression. **Electroconvulsive therapy (ECT)**, or shock treatment, is effective in the treatment of depression; it is a drastic treatment that may be followed by loss of memory. Psychosurgery, including the procedure known as **prefrontal lobotomy**, is an extreme treatment. Lobotomies were halted by the discovery of antipsychotic drugs, but a more localized procedure, known as a "fractional operation," is still sometimes used after all other treatments have failed.

9. Community mental health programs provide transitional support for discharged mental patients, help people stay within the community, and educate community workers. They often provide outpatient, inpatient, and emergency services as well as community consultation. Halfway houses, in which people with a common problem live together, ease the transition from hospital care to community life. The crisis hot line is an instant, economical, and effective means of dealing with emergencies by telephone. The basic goals of community psychology are to prevent the development of disorder (primary prevention); to prevent the worsening of disorder (secondary prevention); and to prevent the severe effects of major disorder on the victim and on society (tertiary prevention).

KEY TERMS

aversion therapy
behavior rehearsal
client-centered therapy
clinical psychologist
cognitive restructuring
cognitive therapy
congruence
covert sensitization
efficacy expectations
electroconvulsive therapy (ECT)
empathic understanding

flooding
gestalt therapy
modeling
nondirective counseling
participant modeling
prefrontal lobotomy
psychiatric nurse
psychiatric social worker
psychiatrist
psychoanalyst
psychotherapy

rational-emotive therapy
resistance
self-instructional training
systematic desensitization
tardive dyskinesia
token economy
transference
transference neurosis
unconditional positive regard

RECOMMENDED READINGS

BERNSTEIN, D. A., and M. T. NIETZEL. *Introduction to clinical psychology.* New York: McGraw-Hill, 1980. A textbook on clinical psychology including chapters on community psychology and clinical interventions from various perspectives.

CORSINI, R. J. (Ed.). *Current psychotherapies.* Itasca, Ill.: Peacock Publishers, 1984. Most of the chapters were written by distinguished leaders of the various approaches, and major current therapies are covered. Each author follows the same format and outline, which makes comparison of therapies easier.

GARFIELD, S. L., and A. E. BERGIN. *Handbook of psychotherapy and behavior change: An empirical analysis* (3rd ed.). New York: Wiley, 1986. The most comprehensive collection of readings on psychotherapy. It contains sections on experimentation in psychotherapy, analysis of therapies, and discussions of a variety of therapeutic approaches.

HERINK, R. (Ed.). *The psychotherapy handbook.* New York: New American Library, 1980. Brief descriptions and bibliographies for 250 different psychotherapies.

KORCHIN, S. J. *Modern clinical psychology.* New York: Basic Books, 1976. A comprehensive survey of all aspects of clinical practice, with clear presentations and comparisons of various therapeutic approaches.

LAKIN, M., *The helping group: therapeutic principles and issues.* New York: Random House, 1986. This text discusses how psychotherapy and quasi-therapy (self-help, support, consciousness-raising, and growth) groups employ group techniques to ameliorate psychological distress and dysfunction. Compares group with individual therapies, discussing how to improve the therapeutic use of the group context.

WILSON, G. T., and K. D. O'LEARY. *Principles of behavior therapy.* Englewood Cliffs, N.J.: Prentice-Hall, 1980. An introductory textbook by two leading behavior therapists.

PART EIGHT

SOCIAL PSYCHOLOGY

To a scientist, the most irritating and frustrating social-psychological aberration of the day (and perhaps the most dangerous in the long run) is the current tendency for educated and sophisticated people to be antiscientific.

This tendency is perhaps more noticeable in the United States than in any other industrialized nation, and that is puzzling. Why should it be that the nation that leads the world in science and technology and that has benefited from them most in terms of national power, international influence, and high standard of living should be so intensely antiscientific?

There are a number of reasons, I think.

First, there is a confusion between science and technology. Science is a methodology, an organized system for squeezing information out of the universe and gaining knowledge and understanding. Technology is the application of the knowledge gained by science toward the solution of problems of life.

It is quite possible that such solutions create other problems that can be viewed as worse than the problems that have been "solved." Insecticides may produce resistant strains of pests; food additives may improve appearance and keeping qualities, yet cause cancer; new sources of energy may introduce radiation risks; factories manufacturing useful products may also spew forth chemical wastes.

In all these cases, is it the knowledge and the method of gaining that knowledge that is the danger—or is it the unwise application of the knowledge? Is it the scientist who makes discoveries who is responsible for evil, or the generals and politicians who apply them with only immediate military or political advantage in mind and the industrialists who do so with only short-term profits in mind?

If we grant all that, then how do we go about insuring that the world applies its knowledge wisely; that we make our decisons with forethought and with shrewd weighing of alternatives; that we resist the immediate advantage at least until we think out the possible long-term disasters?

It is important to remember that technology does not include hardware alone; it is not merely a mélange of tools and devices. Applications of knowledge can involve imponderables and intangibles, and that is where social science comes into the picture.

To understand how people behave may make it possible to devise ways of making society work more smoothly. During World War II, for instance, it was necessary to subject people to heavier taxation than hitherto. The tax collectors knew that if they waited until the end of the year and then asked for a heavy tax, it would turn out that people had already spent the money. How could they persuade people to put aside a portion of their earnings each week so that they would have enough at the end of the year to pay their taxes? Knowing how people are when it comes to money, they knew this would be impossible. Then they came up with an ingenious solution—the federal withholding tax, wherein the employers withheld a portion of every paycheck and gave it to the government. The people undergoing such a tax never actually saw the money and could freely spend what they did get. Many, in fact, received a refund at the end of the year, and that gave them something to look forward to. The simple concept of withholding made paying taxes far less painful.

Suppose our knowledge of human behavior could be applied to encourage the wise application of knowledge generally. Technology would thus be used to help cure the evils of technology.

Isaac Asimov

ATTITUDES AND ATTITUDE CHANGE

In every action we take, our perceptions, emotions, motivations, and thoughts interact in complex ways. When we are studying for an exam, our cognitive processes seem to dominate; when we are entering a dark, abandoned cave, we are intensely aware of our emotions—fear, curiosity, surprise; and when we are trying to beat a rival in a tennis match we may be driven by strong motivational factors—the wish to win, the desire to humiliate a foe. Yet even though one elementary psychological process seems to direct our actions in each situation, aspects of the other processes are present too. When we study for an exam, we are processing information *because* we are motivated to pass the course with a good grade, and obtaining a good grade would also give us pleasure —a positive feeling. Thus, when we say that some particular behavior (call it *X*) is dominated by a specific psychological process (call it *A*), we simply mean that most of the change that appears in behavior *X* is influenced by process *A*. It does not mean that the behavior is influenced by process *A* alone.

All sciences break phenomena into their basic

elements in order to study them; psychology breaks down behavior into elementary psychological processes. But understanding separate components of behavior is not enough. We also need to know how these elementary processes fit together —how they are integrated into behavior. We saw in Chapter 19 how the concept of personality integrates a person's thoughts, emotions, motives, and perceptions to explain consistencies in individual behavior. In this chapter we will see how our thoughts, emotions, and motives are integrated in attitudes.

The simplest way to think about our **attitudes** is to view them as our predispositions toward objects—predispositions that reflect our individual preferences and aversions. These predispositions affect the way we perceive these objects and think about them. And because attitudes are predispositions to *act* as well as to feel and think, motivational factors are also involved. If you have a positive attitude toward the Republican party, you will perceive Republican slogans, candidates, and activities in a favorable light, you will believe that Republican policies are good for the country, and you will be motivated to vote for Republican candidates.

The multibillion-dollar advertising industry's goal is to change your buying patterns. Thus, each ad tries to create a positive attitude toward a given brand or to make an existing attitude more positive. The targets of advertising are your perceptions, your cognitions, your emotions, your motivation, and ultimately your behavior.

THE NATURE OF ATTITUDES

Attitudes are not, of course, limited to our behavior as consumers. They are the most conspicuous aspect of our entire social lives. When you make a new acquaintance, some of the first things you talk about are your likes and dislikes. You may talk about a movie you liked, a teacher you hated, a lecture you found interesting; or about how you detest dieting, love to jog, and try to travel at every opportunity. We want to know the attitudes of new acquaintances, and we want them to know ours —because attitudes determine the course of our personal relationships. Imagine that you are a liberal feminist, and you discover that a new acquaintance strongly opposes equal pay for equal

work. If this new acquaintance also loves the teacher you hate, dislikes jogging, is bored by your favorite movie, and never wants to go out of town, chances are that the relationship will never ripen into friendship.

The Public and Private Significance of Attitudes

We have attitudes about an enormous array of subjects: political candidates, remedies for inflation, the value of a college education, shrimp, New York champagne, roommates, friends, and countless other objects and events, concrete or abstract. These attitudes, whether trivial or important, affect our personal actions. We buy the cigarettes we favor, listen to the music we like, seek out the people who interest us, and dress in clothes we consider attractive. Our attitudes are also implicated in enormously important actions involving whole societies. Wars have been fought over the centuries and continue to rage around the world, justified by religious, racist, and nationalistic attitudes.

It can be argued that wars arise from economic and political circumstances, but even those "economic" and "political" circumstances can be reduced to attitudes. A war may erupt when two nations quarrel over some scarce resource—say,

Attitudes about human rights and freedoms can spur people to risk even their lives. These Poles know that carrying the outlawed *Solidarność* banner puts them in great danger, but their feelings against repression are greater than their fears.

oil. But it was not oil that caused the war—it was people's attitudes toward one nation's possession of oil and the other's lack of it. To a handful of nationalistic fanatics in Lebanon, the wish to seek death by driving a truck filled with explosives into the U.S. marine barracks is a reasonable attitude. Attitudes toward the Polish government generated the *Solidarność* movement, a movement that recruited more than ten million people who took enormous risks even though they knew they would face retaliation and deprivation for years to come. Gangs fight each other daily in bloody battles whose only gain is pride, merely because they hold hostile attitudes toward each other. It is difficult to realize the extent to which our lives, our history, our ideas, and our actions—from those that make us snip a few inches off our hair to those that destroy nations—are under the influence of attitudes.

Because people's attitudes influence their political, economic, and social behavior, a good deal of time, money, and attention is spent on public opinion polling in an attempt to monitor public attitudes. Firms like the Gallup and Harris organizations compile thousands of responses to questions about everything from presidents to pollution. Major corporations conduct consumer surveys on people's attitudes about subjects as diverse as toothpaste preferences and banking needs. And pollsters' reports concerning our attitudes toward abortion, prayer in schools, a nuclear freeze, or "Star Wars" can have a profound effect on the actions of elected officials and the course of the nation.

What Constitutes an Attitude?

Attitudes are complicated mixtures of some basic psychological processes. One way to understand how attitudes influence our lives is to separate these complex psychological phenemona into their components: cognition, emotions, motivation, and behavior.

Cognitive Components

The cognitions we have about a particular senator —that is, what we *know* about him or her—are part of our attitude toward that person. Does the senator support or oppose school busing? What stand has the senator taken on increased defense spending or an increase in taxes? These attitudinal cognitions are what we commonly call **beliefs**, or knowledge structures about objects and events. Some beliefs are based in fact, but many beliefs are false: the belief that the national debt exceeds a trillion dollars is true, and the belief that all Russians hate Americans is false. In addition, some beliefs are verifiable, and others are not. We can readily verify our beliefs about the size of the national debt by consulting the U.S. Bureau of the Budget. But the belief many people hold that human lives are influenced by astrological patterns is not verifiable. For obvious reasons verifiable beliefs are more vulnerable to change than unverifiable beliefs; we tend to cling to unverifiable beliefs with tenacity.

Affective Components

After we have identified the cognitive components of an attitude, we still need more information to understand it. Suppose we know that our friend Sam is aware of the senator's position on busing. We still do not know Sam's attitude toward the senator, because we also need information about the *affective components* of Sam's attitude: the attraction or aversion Sam feels toward the senator. If we also know whether Sam favors busing or disapproves of it, we can guess how he feels toward the senator: people who *like* the senator's stand on busing or defense spending or tax increases will have a favorable attitude toward the senator.

Sometimes, in fact, the affective component is primary. This is especially clear in the case of attitudes formed early in life, such as food preferences that develop before we know much about what we are eating. At a young age, Mexican children develop a fondness for chili pepper, a food that produces a burning sensation, severely irritates the mouth, and can make the nose run and bring tears to the eyes. Mexican mothers give their toddlers food that contains small amounts of chili pepper and gradually increase the concentration until the five-year-old is voluntarily eating chili pepper at its full strength (Rozin and Rozin, 1981; Rozin and Schiller, 1980). These children like chili pepper not because they know it contains vitamins A and C, nor because they know that it might accelerate heat loss in a warm climate or stimulate digestion. They simply like it because they have positive emotional reactions to it.

These emotional reactions are likely to endure,

no matter what a child learns about chili pepper as he or she grows up. Our knowledge about any given object may change profoundly. We may learn the chemical structure of chili pepper; we may discover what is involved in its digestion; we may acquire sophisticated knowledge about the numerous varieties of chili pepper, about how it is raised and cured, about its many uses. But our preference for or aversion to chili pepper may not be greatly influenced by this knowledge. In most cases, the affective component of attitudes tends to be more stable than the cognitive component.

Note, furthermore, that the same *cognition* about an object may promote attraction in one individual and aversion in another. For instance, learning that a new acquaintance is homosexual may make that person attractive or unattractive to us, depending on our affective reaction to homosexuality.

Motivational Components

Attitudes are also linked to an object's importance to us. If a visitor from France hears of the senator's stand on New York State tax reform, for example, the visitor is unlikely to feel either an attraction or an aversion toward the senator. In fact, it has been suggested that we will not form an attitude toward any object—whether a person, a situation, or a behavior—unless we believe that object has attributes or consequences that are relevant to us. The *motivational components* of an attitude—the negative and positive incentives that might motivate our behavior toward the object—are crucial to our attitudes. We integrate our various beliefs to arrive at an evaluation of the object, that is, to determine how important it is to us. The net result is our attitude toward it (Fishbein and Ajzen, 1975).

In order to predict a person's behavior, then, we need more information than what the person knows about the object and how he or she feels about it. We must also know something about how the behavior is likely to be supported by motivational factors. Suppose the Red Cross asks for donations of blood. A person may recognize the useful work done by the Red Cross, may know all about the shortage of blood and the great need for it, and may favor the Red Cross program—yet this same person may refuse to give blood. Why? Because the sight of blood makes him or her faint. As this example suggests, other attitudes or emotional predispositions may either support a predicted

behavior or compete with it. Unless we know about the competing (or supporting) factors, we have no way to know whether an attitude a person holds is capable of motivating him or her to take some action.

Note that the motivational aspects of any attitude always compete against other motivations. A person may favor the election of a particular senator, yet not contribute to the senator's political campaign—because of a competing motivation to replace a failing refrigerator.

We can see why attempts to predict a person's behavior directly from attitudes are rarely successful. An attitude can produce a wide range of behavior, from a faint smile of approval or a response to a survey question, to the sacrifice of one's life.

EXPLAINING ATTITUDE FORMATION

How do we form an attraction or an aversion—and what factors can change it? Suppose you are asked to state your own attitudes toward pornography, marijuana, the military draft, or your roommate. You probably think that your attitudes toward these things come from your knowledge about them. You think you are for or against the legalization of marijuana because of what you know about the effects of the drug. You like or dislike your roommate because you believe he or she is a certain kind of person.

Research suggests, however, that this simple, rational explanation of how attitudes are formed is only a part of the actual process. Our attitude about an object may even change while the object stays the same—so attitudes obviously do not have their origin in the objects themselves. If you start with a strong aversion to snails or chili pepper but eventually grow to like them, it is not the objects that have changed, but you.

Our attitudes are influenced by many factors, including emotional associations, a desire to emulate the attitudes of people we respect and admire, expectations of reward or punishment, and a need to establish some degree of consistency between our beliefs and our behavior. In other words, attitudes about everything from tofu to nuclear war are subject to many influences.

The Effect of Repeated Exposure

Some of our attitudes are simply based on experience. If we encounter an object repeatedly, we will develop a positive attitude toward it. No reward, no reason, no belief, no goal of any sort need be connected with the object. Simple repeated encounters are all that is needed to produce a positive attitude; this phenomenon is called the **exposure effect**.

Is there a similar mechanism that can produce negative attitudes? Apparently not: simple repeated encounters do not lead to negative attitudes. Rather, negative attitudes are formed in a number of ways. First, if aversive consequences accompany the encounter so that the individual comes to connect disgust, fear, or pain with the object, he or she will acquire a negative attitude toward that object. Often we need only one negative experience to develop an aversion. (By contrast, repeated neutral encounters are necessary to develop positive attitudes from mere exposure.) In addition, negative attitudes can be formed in connection with stereotypes (see Chapter 26).

The exposure effect has been demonstrated in many experiments. In one study (Zajonc, 1968), researchers repeatedly exposed college students to various neutral but highly unfamiliar items, such as Chinese ideographs, nonsense words, or photo-

Figure 25.1. Average rated affective connotation of nonsense words and Chinese-like characters as a function of frequency exposure. (After Zajonc, 1968.)

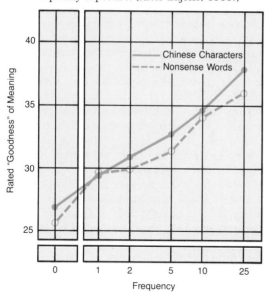

graphs of faces. They included nothing that might affect the students' attitudes toward the items. The students saw some of the items twenty-five times; they saw other items ten times, five times, or only once. The students were then shown the entire group of items and asked how much they liked each one. Included with the more or less familiar items were other similar items the students had never seen. As it turned out, the students liked the unfamiliar items least. And the more often the students had seen the other items in the series, the better they liked them (see Figure 25.1).

The effect of exposure is not limited to human beings. Rats raised to the continual strains of Mozart will, given a choice between Mozart and Schönberg, choose Mozart. And rats raised to the sound of Schönberg prefer the works of that composer to Mozart (Cross, Holcomb, and Matter, 1967).

No one has been able to explain why repeated exposure is followed by a positive attitude. We might guess that we like familiar items better because we recognize them, and the feeling of recognition is pleasant. When we hear a familiar piece of classical music, we enjoy it more than we did the first time we heard it; perhaps we recognize familiar themes, anticipate the way they are developed, and experience pleasure when our expectations are confirmed. Yet this plausible explanation does not hold up. Research has shown conclusively that people come to like things they have seen even when they cannot recognize the items—and even when they are unaware that they have ever seen them.

For example, in one study, college students watched a blank screen where polygons were flashed subliminally (so briefly that the viewers could not possibly recognize them). Afterward, the students were shown pairs of polygons; one of the pair had been flashed in front of them and the other had not. When they were asked which of the two they preferred, a majority chose the flashed stimuli—stimuli that were *objectively* familiar to the viewers even though the viewers had no *subjective* feeling of recognition (Kunst-Wilson and Zajonc, 1980). Other researchers have successfully replicated this experiment (e.g., Seamon, Brody, and Kauff, 1983), indicating that the feeling of recognition is not responsible for the liking that follows exposure. As we saw in Chapter 6, such research suggests the possibility that attitudes can be established by subliminal means.

Reinforcement Theories

Although repeated exposure to an object is the simplest way of acquiring attitudes, attitudes can also be formed by more complex processes. We acquire some of our attitudes through reinforcement—just as we acquire other habits and behavioral dispositions. Suppose a person says that capital punishment is a good idea and her friends strongly agree. Their support strengthens her attitude. But if her friends disagree vigorously with her opinion, her attitude may be weakened. When we want to know why a person is a lifelong liberal or conservative, a committed capitalist or a revolutionary, a staunch Catholic or an avowed atheist, we can find part of the explanation in the principles of learning discussed in Chapter 8—classical and operant conditioning. According to these theories, many attitudes are formed because of the rewards or punishments associated with them.

Note that when attitudes are acquired through mere exposure, no response—attitudinal or otherwise—is necessary. When reinforcement is involved, however, the person must respond in some way to the object, and this attitudinal response is either rewarded or punished. The response can be an action, a statement, or a facial expression that is reinforced or punished by others; or the reinforcement can be within the individual—the first bite of a mango is rewarded by an extremely pleasant taste sensation. Because the reinforcement is contingent on the person's response, he or she develops a tendency to react the same way the next time the attitude object is encountered.

Classical Conditioning of Attitudes

Psychologists have demonstrated that attitudes can be formed by the same conditioning process that taught Pavlov's dogs to salivate at the sound of a bell. When we repeatedly encounter a previously neutral object along with either a pleasant or an unpleasant stimulus, we eventually respond to the object itself just as we originally responded to the stimulus. In fact, in one experiment using classical conditioning, researchers succeeded in reversing women's attitudes toward specific words (Zanna, Kiesler, and Pilkonis, 1970). Fifty women were told that they would receive a series of electric shocks. For one group of women, the word "light" announced the onset of shock; the word "dark"

signaled the shock's end. The signal words were reversed for the other group. Before the experiment all the women said they liked the word "light" better than "dark," but afterward, their attitudes were affected by the way the words had been connected with shock. When "light" signaled shock and "dark" signaled relief from shock, the women's attitude toward "light" became much less favorable and their attitude toward "dark" much more so. In addition, the women generalized these attitudes to other, related words. Women who had been shocked each time they heard the word "light" also evaluated the word "white" less favorably than they had before, while those who had been shocked on the word "dark" also developed more negative attitudes toward "black."

Such findings indicate that people may form attitudes simply by associating objects with emotion-arousing circumstances. We might, for example, learn to dislike people we encounter only in hot, crowded subways, and we might be particularly drawn to ideas put forth by attractive, entertaining teachers. Many of our most emotionally laden attitudes may be acquired, at least in part, through this basic mechanism of learning. Note that when we attach a positive or negative emotional reaction to some object through classical conditioning, we do not necessarily develop a corresponding set of cognitive beliefs.

Operant Conditioning of Attitudes

In contrast to the "involuntary" responses (such as fear or pleasure) that are involved in most instances of classical conditioning, operant conditioning generally involves voluntary behavior. Operant conditioning is based on the assumption that people tend to repeat behavior that has a desirable result and tend not to repeat behavior that has an undesirable result. The person is attempting to obtain some reward or avoid some punishment.

Research confirms that attitudes can be learned through operant conditioning. Suppose that every time you mention to your friends that you believe people should make a greater effort to convert to solar energy, they respond by saying, "That's an excellent idea," or "I agree completely." Would these responses tend to make you a more ardent supporter of solar energy? Apparently so.

An experiment at the University of Hawaii (Insko, 1965) demonstrated the strength of verbal reinforcement on attitude formation. During an interview, students were complimented for expressing a favorable attitude toward Aloha Week, a celebration held by the university every autumn. About a week after these "conditioning" interviews, the students filled out a questionnaire about local issues. Included in the list of items was a question about the possibility of adding a second Aloha Week to the university's spring schedule. Students whose positive attitudes toward the festival had previously been verbally reinforced expressed more favorable attitudes toward a spring-time celebration than did a control group that had not been previously conditioned.

If our attitudes can be shaped by an unknown experimenter who simply repeats "good" every time we express a certain opinion, imagine how easily attitudes can be shaped when the rewards are highly valued ones, such as approval and affection of family and friends. In fact, the presence of such reinforcement may be one of the reasons young children so often parrot their parents' attitudes long before the children understand what they are saying. Youngsters of five or

THE STOCKHOLM SYNDROME

Some of our attitudes develop through mere exposure, while others are the result of reinforcement—we connect some object with pleasant or unpleasant experiences. But what if the two influences seem to work at cross-purposes? What if lengthy exposure is combined with repeated punishment? In very special circumstances it seems that exposure is more powerful than punishment in determining attitudes. The circumstances are those of hostage and captor, and the attitude is known as **the Stockholm syndrome.**

The syndrome got its name in Stockholm, Sweden, where a woman was taken hostage during a bank robbery a number of years ago. This woman, who had never seen her captors before, fell in love with one of the robbers. Her attachment to her captor was so strong that she later broke her engagement to another man and remained true to her captor while he served a prison term. This woman's experience, while exaggerated, has been repeated again and again in all

parts of the world. The best-known example in the United States was provided by Patty Hearst, who—while being held for ransom—joined her captors' revolutionary group and helped them hold up a bank.

The Stockholm syndrome may develop even when the captor physically mistreats the hostage. The journalist Richard Dudman was captured by guerrillas in Cambodia, who beat him. Dudman has described his own feelings toward his captors:

When they released us I felt I was leaving true friends. . . . I refused to tell intelligence officers in Saigon the exact place where we had been released. . . . In writing about the experience, I recalled with fondness the pleasures of eating roast dog and playing chess with our captors. I tried to avoid calling them guards . . . and preferred the term "escorts." My analysis at the time was that we had faced a common danger together and in a sense had become comrades. (McCarthy, 1980)

What happened to Dudman, to Hearst, and to the woman in Stockholm often happens to hostages in bank robberies

and in plane hijackings. In June 1985, a hijacked American plane was held for fifteen days on the runway of a Beirut, Lebanon, airport. The hijackers threatened several times to blow up the plane and all the hostages. Finally, the prisoners were released from the secret locations to which they had been removed in Beirut. Several hostages interviewed by journalists spoke well of their captors and their cause and defended some of their actions during the captivity.

How does exposure overcome the effects of physical and mental punishment? No one is certain, although some psychologists believe the bond may develop because the hostages are completely dependent on their captors (Sancton, 1980). The captors play a stern parental role, and the hostages' very lives rest on the whim of these "parents." Perhaps the situation is similar to that of the abused child and his or her parents. Although the parent beats the child severely, the child continues to feel love and eagerly tries to please the parent.

six enthusiastically support the Democratic or Republican candidate during every presidential election campaign, although they cannot understand either their candidate's platform or the election process. Similarly, seven- or eight-year-olds who shout racial slurs in the playground or scribble them on the schoolyard wall seldom grasp the full significance of their words. It is very likely that these children have at some time been positively reinforced for acting as if they shared their parents' attitudes. In many cases these experiences may actually instill in the child the attitude he or she has "acted out."

Changes in Attitudes

Because attitudes are an important factor in shaping behavior, psychologists, corporations, journalists, and government experts want to know not only how attitudes are formed but also why, as time passes, they occasionally change. To some extent the answers to this second question are the same as the answers to the first. Attitudes can change merely through repeated exposure to an object, and they can change because of pleasant or unpleasant consequences associated with it.

But other factors can also bring about changes in attitude. Two major sources of change have been extensively studied by psychologists. One source is persuasive communication, such as advertising, in which deliberate efforts are made to change people's attitudes. The second source of attitude change lies in attempts to resolve cognitive dissonance, which was discussed in Chapter 12. In this type of change, people are seeking consistency in the cognitive components of their attitudes. In the following pages, we look at research that explores each type of attitude change.

ATTITUDE CHANGE AND PERSUASIVE COMMUNICATION

Advertisements, sales pitches, political campaigns, lobbying efforts, and newspaper editorials are all examples of **persuasive communication** —direct, overt attempts to change people's attitudes. American business and industry alone spend about $50 billion each year on advertising. An enormous industry is devoted to discovering

better ways of changing people's attitudes (in the hope of influencing their behavior), and to using these methods in the service of business and politics. Parents and children, employers and employees, salespeople and customers also try to persuade one another; we have all been involved in arguments in which one person tries to change the other's attitudes and, ultimately, behavior. Persuasion, in its form and effects, is one of the most thoroughly studied topics in social psychology.

Influences on Persuasiveness

There is no magic formula that will enable a wily persuader to control people's attitudes toward candidates, political issues, or consumer products. But psychologists have identified a number of factors in the effectiveness of any effort at persuasion. These factors include the characteristics of the source, the contents and style of the message, and the nature of the audience. Each induces attitude change by affecting one or more of the basic elements of attitudes: cognition, emotion, and motivation.

Characteristics of the Source

The extent to which a viewer's, reader's, or hearer's attitudes are changed by persuasive communication depends as much on *who* delivers the message as on *what* that person says. And unless the source is seen as credible, the attempt is likely to fail.

Credibility If the source is a person with prestige, the message will have more credibility; the person's level of education, apparent intelligence, status, expertise on the issues involved, and professional status also affect credibility (Hastie, Penrod, and Pennington, 1982). The importance of **source credibility** was clearly demonstrated in a classic study of persuasion conducted more than thirty years ago (Hovland and Weiss, 1951). People were more convinced of the truth of a statement about the practicality of atomic submarines when they were told that the source was a noted American physicist than when they were told the source was the Russian newspaper *Pravda*. Similarly, more people were convinced by an article about antihistamine drugs when they thought it had

Credibility is very much in the eyes of the beholder. When she is speaking to a group of liberal, career-oriented women, feminist Gloria Steinem has great credibility. But were she to deliver the same speech to a group of conservative businessmen, her credibility would drop sharply.

appeared in the prestigious *New England Journal of Medicine* than when they thought it had been published in a mass-circulation pictorial magazine.

The degree to which any persuader is deemed credible also depends on whether the audience thinks he or she is trustworthy. Even an expert will be seen as lacking in credibility if the audience suspects that he or she has some ulterior motive for making the appeal. Voters know that a political candidate is specifically trying to persuade them of her or his own merits; they are likely to look to another person or organization to verify the candidate's qualifications. One manifestation of the importance of trustworthiness is the tendency for people to be more persuaded by a message if they overhear it than if it is addressed directly to them (Walster and Festinger, 1962). Apparently, when people overhear a communication, they are less likely to question the source's motive, probably because they assume from the situation that the person cannot be trying to deceive them out of self-interest.

A communicator's perceived self-interest may also tend to make the public distrust messages from certain institutions. Among social institutions, political leaders and labor unions are trusted least, and their messages tend to be regarded with skepticism. Business leaders and the media are trusted somewhat more by the public, and the military, police, and the legal system have even more credibility. Scientific, medical, and academic communicators are trusted most by the public (Etzioni and Diprete, 1979). But the general acceptance of *all* institutions and the public's trust in them have been declining steadily since the assassination of President John F. Kennedy in 1963 (Lipset and Schneider, 1982).

Attractiveness Another factor that can affect a particular communicator's persuasiveness is simply how attractive and likable the listeners find that communicator. Even height has an effect: tall individuals are more persuasive than short ones (Feldman, 1971). The football player's successful endorsement of deodorants, shaving cream, and hair tonics demonstrates that an attractive, likable source need not be knowledgeable to be persuasive. And even the ulterior motive of an attractive source may be ignored: when a football star endorses a particular product on television, everyone knows that he is being handsomely paid for his efforts, yet such testimonials persuade thousands of fans to use the product. But an unattractive, unlikable source may produce a "boomerang" effect: the audience may respond by adopting attitudes contrary to those advocated by the source.

All these patterns fit in with the principles of cognitive consistency, which was discussed in Chapter 12. Listeners tend to adapt their attitudes about the message to their attitudes about the person who delivers it. By agreeing with people we like and disagreeing with those we dislike, we maintain cognitive consistency and avoid tension. And if we agree with the attitudes of someone we like and admire, our own sense of self-worth is enhanced, for we become more similar to the admired communicator (McGuire, 1985).

The power of an attractive source became especially clear during the 1980s, when President Ronald Reagan's personality projected such a positive image that he was able to argue successfully for unpopular policies. President Reagan was able to maintain a high deficit (which drove real interest rates to an unprecedented level) and yet gain in popularity, winning reelection by a sweeping majority. During the same period, his opponent in the 1984 elections, Walter Mondale, also tried to promote an unpopular policy—raising taxes. But Mondale's attempts were followed by a decline in his own popularity.

Those characteristics of the source that influence persuasiveness produce their effects by working primarily on specific components of the audience's attitudes. For instance, expertise and trustworthiness tend to attack the cognitive component of attitudes, while attractiveness tends to attack the affective component.

Characteristics of the Message

Would-be persuaders also have to think carefully about their message: sometimes a message may have an unforeseen effect on the audience. In 1985 a very effective source was dropped by a large hamburger chain after she made a commercial for another product. Her success had depended on the shouted question, "Where's the beef?" as she looked at hamburgers sold by competing chains. But then she made a spaghetti sauce commercial, loudly trumpeting, "I've found it!" Her original sponsors began to fear viewers would decide the sponsor's own hamburgers were also long on bun and short on beef. We have no way of knowing whether that concern was misplaced, but we do know that messages vary widely in effectiveness.

Messages also aim at different aspects of attitudes. Advertisers often do this deliberately. For example, one ad may be directed at cognitive attitudinal components, appealing to your knowledge; another may aim at emotional components, connecting the product with fun and pleasure. A third may try to manipulate behavior directly, ordering you to "reach for" a particular brand of cola.

One-Sided vs. Two-Sided Arguments If you are trying to influence attitudes, is it better to avoid mentioning the other side, or should you discuss the weaknesses of the opponent while extolling your own strength? Advertisers are uncertain about this. Traditionally, they have avoided naming competing brands because they have feared giving free, even if unfavorable, exposure to a rival product. In the past, companies wanted to make sure the viewer remembered the name of their own brand, not that of their competitors. And so the pitches in most television commercials declared a certain brand of toothpaste, aspirin, or paper towel to be superior to "other leading brands," or to "the product you're currently using," or even to "Brand X." During the past several years, however, some brave manufacturers of soft drinks, cold remedies, pain relievers, automobiles, cigarettes, and other products have actually begun naming their competitors.

Which approach is more effective? The answer appears to depend on the audience for whom the message is intended. This became clear when, during World War II, researchers conducted an experiment comparing one-sided and two-sided arguments (Hovland, Lumsdaine, and Sheffield, 1949). More than 200 men received a series of radio transcripts arguing that, even after Germany surrendered, it would take at least two years to end the war with Japan. Half the men received a one-sided message that pointed only to obstacles, such as distance, plentiful Japanese resources, and a large Japanese army. The rest of the men received a two-sided message. It contained all the information in the one-sided message along with opposing evidence that pointed to such factors as the superiority of the U.S. Navy and the improved chance of Allied success when all resources could be devoted to a one-front war. Overall, the one-sided and two-sided communications produced substantially the same net change in attitudes, but important differences emerged when the men's initial opinions and education were taken into account. Those who initially believed that the war would probably continue for another two years were more influenced by the one-sided message, while those who initially thought that the war would end sooner were more influenced by the two-sided argument. Also, men who were better educated, and who would be expected to view the communications fairly critically, were more impressed with the two-sided communication, while the reverse was true for less-educated men. Thus, a one-sided argument is more effective than a two-sided one if the audience initially favors the communicator's position and is relatively poorly educated. Conversely, an audience composed of people who are initially opposed to the communicator's viewpoint and who are relatively well educated will be more influenced by a two-sided argument.

Linking Emotions with the Message Linking the message with a pleasant emotional state is another successful method of persuasion. When a television commercial shows a new car being admired by a beautiful woman or a handsome, sophisticated man, the advertisers are using this technique, as mentioned earlier. So are corporate executives when they bring prospective clients to an elegant restaurant to talk business. Research confirms that associating a point of view with positive emotions can help change the attitudes of an audience. For example, in one study (Janis, Kaye, and Kirschner, 1965) subjects who were given peanuts and Pepsi while reading a persuasive communication were more inclined than people in a control group to be convinced by the arguments they encountered. Apparently, the pleasant emotional state created by snacking on desirable food can make a message seem more agreeable.

Negative emotions can also be used to change attitudes. Fear has frequently been used as a technique of persuasion, especially in campaigns to reduce cigarette smoking, traffic fatalities, and drug abuse. A critical factor in the success of scare tactics is the amount of fear induced. A classic study (Janis and Feshbach, 1953) compared the effectiveness of three different levels of fear and found that an appeal that aroused a small amount of fear was the most persuasive. High school students watched a film on oral hygiene that stressed the importance of regular tooth brushing. A high-fear group saw the consequences of dental neglect in graphic detail, including close-ups of severely decaying teeth and unpleasant mouth infections. A second group saw more moderate cases of tooth decay. A third, low-fear group saw only diagrams, and all photographs were of completely healthy teeth. Later, 36 percent of the students exposed to the low-fear condition reported favorable changes in their dental hygiene practices—as compared with 22 percent exposed to the high-fear condition. It seems that if the fear induced by a message is too great, people attempt to reduce their anxiety by pushing the information to the back of their minds—in short, by ignoring it. This is especially true when the audience is not told how to prevent the feared consequences, or if the audience feels incapable of taking the necessary steps or believes that their actions will be ineffective (Leventhal, Singer, and Jones, 1965). For example, attempts to get people to have cancer-detection examinations may fail because the ads arouse such a high level of anxiety that many viewers repress or avoid all thoughts concerning cancer, particularly if they are dubious about the value of treatment.

However, if the audience is told how to avoid undesirable consequences and *believes* the pre-

ventive action is possible and effective, then high levels of fear will lead to substantial attitude change. In a study that met these conditions, high levels of fear were most effective in persuading university students to get tetanus inoculations (Dabbs and Leventhal, 1966). In addition, the more specific the recommendations presented for action, the greater will be the extent of change in behavior (Leventhal, Singer, and Jones, 1965). Lastly, the effectiveness of fear as a persuader apparently depends on whether the outcome is avoidable or unavoidable. Regardless of our level of fear, if we believe that a recommended change in our attitudes or behavior—or both—will help us avoid an unfavorable outcome, we are likely to make the change; if we think the change is useless, we are not likely to make it.

Making Sure the Message Is Remembered No matter how carefully a message is prepared, it will not change people's attitudes if they cannot remember it. One of the primary concerns in advertising research is whether the ad leaves the person with a memory of a product. If the viewer remembers the commercial but forgets the brand name, the ad can have little effect. Just remembering the message is not enough; the shopper must also *retrieve* the relevant information at the time he or she is choosing among products on the supermarket shelf. Short and striking messages are the most effective, primarily because they are easy to retain, but the retention of an ad can also be powerfully influenced by the emotional quality of its message. When "Mean Joe Green," bruised and battered after a game, accepted a Coke from a young boy, most people remembered both the situation and the product. This commercial was striking in its appeal to some positive emotions, and its effectiveness was probably heightened by the contrast to the aggression associated with football.

Yet even if people remember a persuasive message clearly, their attitudes may not change. When people's memory for the content of the message is compared with their overall attitude change, the correlation is usually low (Insko, Lind, and LaTour, 1976). Advertisers seem to ignore this low correlation when they spend enormous amounts of money each year in the hope of influencing behavior. In a presidential year, a great deal of talent and effort and more than half a billion dollars' worth of political advertising is devoted to changing the political behavior of Americans. Much of it may be wasted; research shows that this massive endeavor has a surprisingly modest effect on attitudes and voting (Patterson, 1980).

Characteristics of the Audience

The source and the message do not work in isolation; as we have already seen, the educational level and prior attitudes of the audience help to determine the effectiveness of persuasion. Other characteristics of the audience are equally important.

Sometimes deep psychological needs and motives affect a person's readiness to be persuaded. There is evidence, for example, that people with a strong need for social approval tend to be susceptible to social influence (Marlowe and Gergen, 1969). Other psychological reasons for persuasibility are less obvious. Ernest Dichter (1964), a motivational researcher who has engineered many commercial advertising campaigns, once lent his talents to a Red Cross drive for blood donations. He suggested that men might be reluctant to give blood because it aroused unconscious anxieties associated with the draining of their strength and virility. So he recommended that the campaign focus on masculinity, implying that each man in the audience had so much virility that he could afford to give away a little. Dichter also proposed that each man be made to feel personally proud of any suffering connected with the process. One of Dichter's strategies was to give each blood donor a pin in the shape of a drop of blood—the equivalent of a wounded soldier's Purple Heart. These tactics did in fact produce a sharp increase in blood donations by men.

An individual's susceptibility to persuasion is also related to his or her knowledge about or interest in the issue at hand: the more the person knows, the less easily he or she can be persuaded. For example, the fact that in past studies women appeared more persuasible than men may simply have been the result of researchers' choice of traditionally "male-oriented" issues, such as political and economic affairs (Aronson, 1976). This hypothesis is supported by experiments that found men easier to influence about traditionally "female-oriented" issues, such as home management or family relations, and found women more open to persuasion about traditionally "male-oriented" topics (Sistrunk and McDavid, 1971; Cacioppo and Petty, 1980). In these studies, neither gender was found to be more susceptible to persuasion than the other when allowances had been made for the subject matter. However, recent research suggests that women may be somewhat more susceptible with regard to *any* topic. In a review of 148 studies on gender differences in persuasion, Alice Eagly and L. L. Carli (1981) found that women are slightly but significantly more open to influence.

Resistance to Persuasion

Even the most compelling persuasive communication may fail because of resistance on the part of the audience. People are not passive. While they listen to a communication, they evaluate the points the speaker is making, and they may draw up counterarguments of their own. Research indicates that resistance to persuasion is strongest when counterarguments are available and weakest when there are none. Thus, factors that increase the availability of counterarguments will in turn increase people's resistance to persuasion.

"Inoculation" against Persuasion

Some beliefs are taken so much for granted that when they are strongly attacked, people find it difficult to muster effective counterarguments. How would you react, for example, if you read an extremely persuasive article arguing that monthly self-examinations have no effect on the incidence of death from breast cancer, or that regular brushing is useless in preventing tooth decay? Despite your surprise that these widely held beliefs had been attacked, you might very well end up accepting the new points of view simply because you were unprepared to defend the old ones (although they are true).

William McGuire and his colleagues have argued that people can be "inoculated" against such persuasive assaults in much the same way that we are inoculated against tetanus or diptheria (McGuire and Papageorgis, 1961). In medical inoculation a person who has never been exposed to a disease is given a weakened form of the disease-causing agent, which stimulates the body to manufacture defenses against it. If a virulent form of the disease should later attack, these defenses make the person immune to infection. An analogous principle underlies **inoculation** against persuasion. The person who has never before heard a particular point of view attacked is exposed to opposition, and is then given a dose of the counterarguments needed to defend that viewpoint.

To inoculate one group of subjects against persuasion, McGuire first exposed them to challenging arguments against a formerly unquestioned proposition (that regular brushing prevents tooth decay), then to a statement that refuted those arguments and reinforced the initial belief. A week later, the same people read another communication that challenged the same initial belief. Far fewer of the people who had received the inoculation were persuaded by the challenge than those who had not been inoculated. The inoculation had effectively stimulated their psychological defenses against a challenge and made their initial attitude more resistant to change, as shown in Figure 25.2.

Forewarning

People cannot always be armed with arguments to refute an opposing point of view, but they can sometimes be warned that their own beliefs will be challenged. Evidence on the effectiveness of such warnings is mixed. In one study (Freedman and Sears, 1965), a group of teenagers who had been warned ten minutes in advance that they would hear a speech on why young people should not be allowed to drive were more resistant to persuasion than a group who had not been forewarned. But other researchers have obtained different results. For example, people who were forewarned that they would hear arguments against their own view on the likelihood of an economic recession were the ones who displayed the greatest change in their attitudes (Hass and Mann, 1976).

One way to reconcile these seemingly contradictory findings is to take into account the level of the subjects' commitment to their initial attitude. When people are firmly committed to a particular belief, as most teenagers are about their right to drive, they become more likely to resist an opposing point of view after they are warned. However, when people are somewhat ambivalent toward a belief, as those who believed in the likelihood of a recession may have been, they become more inclined to succumb to a persuasive challenge (Kiesler and Jones, 1971).

A person's level of knowledge about the issues involved may also help explain the varying results of forewarning experiments. When people are not particularly well informed about a subject, antici-

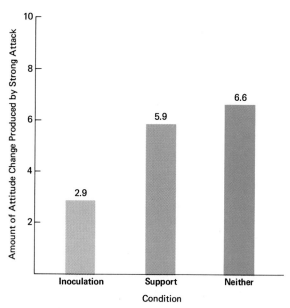

Figure 25.2. This graph shows the amount of attitude change in three groups of subjects, measured in response to a strong attack on a commonly held belief (that brushing the teeth three times daily is a good thing to do). The "inoculation" subjects were previously exposed to a weak form of the attack and were helped to defend their initial belief against the weak argument. The "support" group was given some prior support for the initial belief without any kind of attack on it. The "neither" group received no prior treatment. The "inoculation" group showed much more resistance to change in their attitudes on the subject than the other two groups. Attitude change was measured on an arbitrary scale of 1 to 10, with 10 representing a complete change of attitude. (After McGuire and Papageorgis, 1961.)

pation of an opposing argument may cause them to modify their own position in that direction. The strategy is basically taken to save face: people want to avoid being caught in a situation that would force them to defend a view they cannot intelligently support (Hass and Mann, 1976).

ATTITUDE CHANGE AND COGNITIVE DISSONANCE

The second major area of research in attitude change involves cognitive dissonance. The discussion of cognitive consistency in Chapter 12 indicated that when we hold two conflicting cognitions we are thrown into a state of dissonance, and that we will seek some way of resolving the dissonance and restoring internal harmony.

In 1984 joggers all over the world were thrown into cognitive dissonance when fifty-two-year-old Jim Fixx, whose book *The Complete Book of Running* is credited with creating millions of dedicated joggers, died from a heart attack while running. The major elements in the cognitive structure that supports jogging follow the line that jogging prevents heart disease and extends longevity. So when the most prominent promoter of jogging died of the very disease against which he had dedicated his program, each jogger had to do a good deal of cognitive work to resolve the dissonance. Jogging authorities, sports physicians, and the media rushed to supply explanations: Fixx had formerly been overweight and a heavy smoker; his heart had been damaged before he took up running; there was history of heart disease in his family. But no one is certain just how joggers across the country finally handled the task of overcoming their dissonance. If they were to keep on with their time-consuming, arduous activity, they had to integrate their understanding of Fixx's death with other beliefs they had formed to support jogging.

Dissonance can even make a disliked communicator a more effective persuader—an effect that seems to conflict with our earlier discussion of the effect of the source. If a disliked communicator can persuade a person into even temporary compliance—buying a product, voting for a candidate, taking a position on some issue—the resulting change in that person's attitude is often more permanent than if the persuader had been an admired communicator. Once an individual agrees with the communicator's proposition, he or she faces dissonance because the proposition was advocated by someone he or she dislikes or has no respect for. In order to resolve this dissonance, the individual finds other reasons to justify the change, bolstering the change and resolving dissonance (Zimbardo et al., 1965).

Post-Decision Dissonance

Leon Festinger's (1957) theory of cognitive dissonance predicts that every decision we make in our daily lives is followed by a state of dissonance. Each decision requires us to select among alternatives, and the positive features of the rejected

alternatives together with the negative features of our choice make some degree of **post-decision dissonance** inevitable. One way we can resolve the dissonance is to change our attitude toward the alternatives, either by decreasing our opinion of the items we have rejected or increasing our opinion of the item we have selected. We usually do both. Suppose you bought a Volvo even though you did not like its color and preferred the color and looks of the Oldsmobile you were considering. Afterward, you are likely to say, "Now that I've had a chance to drive my Volvo, I think its color is nicer after all."

This dual method of resolving post-decision dissonance appeared in a classic experiment. J. W. Brehm (1956) asked college students to rate eight products, such as a radio, a toaster, and a stopwatch, for attractiveness, with the understanding that they would receive one of the products for participating in the experiment. After the students have made their ratings, they were asked to choose between two of the items; then, after they had actually received their gift, they rated all eight items again. The results showed that the students had reduced their dissonance by rating the object

Figure 25.3. After deciding between two objects, students' valuation of the objects changed to resolve their dissonance, with greater changes required to resolve a higher level of cognitive dissonance. (From Brehm, 1956.)

Resolving Post-Decision Dissonance

	Rating of Chosen Object	Rating of Rejected Object	Total Change
Low dissonance (objects rated dissimilarly)	+.25	−.12	.37
High dissonance (objects rated similarly)	+.32	−.53	.85

they had chosen more favorably and the rejected object more negatively than they had the first time (see Figure 25.3). Since some of the students had chosen between a pair of objects they had rated similarly, their choice had been a difficult one. Other students had chosen between a pair of objects they had rated quite differently, which presumably made their choice easy. But both groups of students followed the predicted pattern of attitude change; moreover, in accord with dissonance theory, the shift was greater when the pair had originally been similarly valued. When the original choice is close, much greater dissonance is aroused, which in turn leads to a greater reevaluation of both items.

Cognitive Consistency versus Reinforcement

In our earlier discussion of cognitive dissonance (Chapter 12), an experiment (Festinger and Carlsmith, 1959) was described in which people were asked to lie about a task; those who received just a one-dollar reward developed more positive attitudes toward that task than those who had been given a twenty-dollar reward. In this study, people seemed to act in a manner exactly contrary to what we might expect from a reinforcement model of attitude change: the lower their reward was, the *greater* their shift in attitude was. But the relationship between attitude change and reinforcement was not a simple one—it was complicated by dissonance. People who received only one dollar experienced high levels of dissonance, which led them to change their attitudes so they no longer felt they had lied. People who received twenty dollars experienced little dissonance (they figured that they had been paid well to lie) and had no need to change their attitudes.

Subsequent investigations suggest that cognitive dissonance and reinforcement principles influence behavior under different circumstances. One factor that seems to affect whether dissonance theory or reinforcement theory is better at predicting behavior is the extent to which people have freedom of choice (Lindner, Cooper, and Jones, 1967). Students were asked to write a forceful, persuasive essay supporting a very unpopular bill. (The bill was to ban communists and people who had taken the Fifth Amendment from speaking at state-supported institutions, such as state colleges and universities.) The experiment-

ers told some students that the decision to write the essay was entirely up to them; with others, the experimenters acted as if compliance with this request were naturally expected. The amount of money offered the students also varied—a small amount for some students and a relatively large amount for others.

After completing the essay, each student was asked to indicate his or her real opinion about the speaker-ban legislation. Students who had written the essay under the "free choice" condition behaved as predicted by dissonance theory. (They were essentially in the same situation as the people in the earlier study who had lied about the dull task.) These students were more likely to have changed their attitudes and to support the ban if they had received low rewards. Students who had written under the "no choice" condition, however, were not in a situation that produces high levels of dissonance. They tended to behave as predicted by reinforcement theory: those who had received the greater reward were more likely to change their attitudes. Thus, rather than being contradictory, reinforcement and cognitive consistency models both contribute to our understanding of how people form and change their attitudes.

Do PEOPLE'S ATTITUDES PREDICT THEIR BEHAVIOR?

It should follow from the discussions in this chapter that knowing a person's attitudes will *not* allow us to predict how she or he will behave in a particular situation. Indeed, the distinction between cognition and affect suggests that the person may say one thing and actually feel another. Thus, a person's verbal behavior may give no clue to his or her actual attitudes, or to how these attitudes will be expressed in such other behavior as voting, giving to charity, or eating liver. Since most attitude measures tap primarily the cognitive component of attitudes, it would be unwise to expect these measures to predict behavior with any precision. In fact, attitudes are sometimes quite inconsistent with behavior.

This inconsistency was demonstrated by a classic study conducted a half century ago by Richard LaPiere (1934), who traveled around the United States with a Chinese couple. LaPiere expected to encounter anti-Oriental attitudes that would make it difficult for the Chinese couple to find places to sleep and eat. But this was not the case. "In something like ten thousand miles of motor travel," wrote LaPiere, "twice across the United States, up and down the Pacific Coast, we met definite rejection from those asked to serve us just once" (p. 232).

Judging by the friendly behavior of the innkeepers and tradespeople they encountered, we might conclude that Americans in the 1930s were almost entirely free of prejudice against Orientals. Our conclusion would be wrong. LaPiere followed up his travels by writing a letter to each of the 251 establishments he and his Chinese friends had visited, asking whether they would provide food or lodging to members of the Chinese race. Of the 128 who responded (who, it must be noted, were not necessarily the same people the travelers had encountered), over 90 percent answered with a flat no. Only one said yes, and the rest said their decision would depend on the circumstances. People's attitudes toward serving Chinese, then, seemed to be extremely inconsistent with the behavior they had already shown.

This discrepancy between attitudes and behavior has since been confirmed. In one study (Wicker, 1971) the attitudes of people toward their church were measured against three kinds of church-related behavior: how often they attended church, how much money they contributed to their church, and how often they participated in church activities. It seems reasonable to expect that people who expressed the strongest, most positive attitudes toward their church would be most inclined to give time and money to the church and attend service regularly. As it turned out, there was only a slight tendency in this direction. In general, the correlation between attitudes and behavior was very weak. In fact, knowledge of a person's attitude toward the church was practically useless in predicting that person's church-related behavior.

Factors that Weaken the Attitude-Behavior Link

Because the relationship between attitudes and behavior can be inconsistent, we might be tempted to abandon the concept of attitudes. After all, a concept that is a worthless predictor has little practical use. But social psychologists argue that it is unrealistic to expect attitudes to correspond perfectly to behavior. Behavior is seldom—if ever—the product of a single influence. Instead, say these social psychologists, when we evaluate people's attitudes, we must take into account factors that may weaken the relationship between their attitudes and their behavior.

First, situational factors can weaken this relationship, prompting a person to act in a manner inconsistent with her or his predispositions. LaPiere concluded that his friends were received and well treated by establishments that did not ordinarily accept Chinese because of such situational factors as the high quality of their clothing and luggage and their friendly manner, which inspired courtesy.

Second, there may be conflicts among people's attitudes. For instance, a man may hold the attitude that one should avoid trouble by minding one's own business, but he may also hold the attitude that one should help the defenseless. What does this Good Samaritan do when he sees an old man being assaulted on the street and can help the victim only by attacking the aggressor? If he stands idly by, his behavior is inconsistent with the attitude that he should help; if he attacks, his behavior is inconsistent with the attitude that he should not get involved. It is inevitable that attitudes will sometimes come into conflict with one another, resulting in at least partial inconsistency between attitudes and behavior.

Third, a single attitude can be expressed through a variety of behavior. For instance, in the study on church-related attitudes and behavior (Wicker, 1971), the researcher concluded that a person can express devotion to the church in many ways. A person who does not attend services regularly, contribute money weekly, or participate in most church activities may nevertheless be the first person to offer help when the church is damaged by fire or when it needs to be defended from the criticism of others.

Finally, the strength and importance of an attitude, the impact it has on an individual's life, helps to determine the extent to which it governs behavior. Two people may share the attitude that public education should be improved, but a parent is far more likely than a nonparent to act on that attitude by voting for school bond issues, attending hearings on education, and visiting schools.

It would be naïve, then, to expect to be consistently able to predict behavior from a particular attitude. However, when significant factors are taken into account, consistency between attitudes and behavior emerges. Mark Snyder and D. Kendzierski (1982) have clarified the attitude-consistency controversy by pointing out three factors that affect the match between attitudes and behavior. First, *people must know how they feel.* Individuals who are aware of their attitudes can more readily use them as guides to action. Second, people must perceive that the attitudes they hold are *relevant* to the action they are about to take. Third, because action is in part determined by the immediate and transitory requirements of the situation, behavior will be affected by the *extent to which individuals submit to these requirements and the extent to which they ignore them.*

The Role of Self-Monitoring

As Snyder and Kendzierski observe, attitudes serve as important guides to action for some people but are less crucial for others. Some people are particularly quick to adjust their behavior to the demands of the situation. They choose their actions carefully, so as to make a good impression. This form of vigilance is called **self-monitoring**, and Snyder (1979) has constructed a scale to measure it. The self-monitoring scale rates the extent to which individuals monitor their actions. The scale contains such items as "My behavior is usually an expression of my true inner feelings, attitudes, and beliefs" and "I can only argue for ideas which I already believe," both of which are more frequently endorsed by low self-monitors and rejected by high self-monitors. In contrast, items such as "I sometimes appear to others to be experiencing deeper emotions than I actually am" are endorsed by high self-monitors and rejected by low self-monitors. People who are high self-monitors seem to be guided more by situational demands than by their own attitudes.

If this is true, then the attitudes of high self-monitors would play a relatively small role in determining their behavior. In an attempt to find out how self-monitoring limits the relationship between attitudes and behavior, Snyder and Kendzierski (1982) asked individuals to consider a court case involving allegations about sex discrimination. (Two weeks before they took part in the experiment, all subjects' attitudes toward sex discrimination were measured.) One group of sub-

jects simply read resumes of two biologists, Mr. Sullivan and Ms. Harrison, who were ostensibly qualified to judge women's ability to do certain jobs; the subjects then made their decision and recommendations for the case. Another group of subjects were asked to "organize [their] own thoughts and [their] own views of the issue of affirmative action," a step that gave the subjects access to their own attitudes. A third group was told "Not only will your decision have implications for the parties involved, but it may also have implications for affirmative action programs," a step that made their attitudes fully relevant to their behavior.

The results indicated that self-monitoring affects the relationship between attitudes and behavior differently, depending on the situation. The attitudes and behavior of low-self-monitors correlated +.18 when they simply read the resumes, +.47 when their own attitudes were available to them, and +.45 when their attitudes were socially relevant. However, high self-monitors were greatly influenced when they believed their attitudes were relevant. When they simply read resumes, the correlation between attitudes and their decision was low (−.17); it was still low (+.18) when their attitudes were available; but it was high (+.60) when their attitudes were relevant. Clearly, the relationship between attitudes and behavior is complicated by numerous factors.

Because behavior and attitudes are not perfectly correlated, we cannot judge people's attitudes by observing their behavior. This is especially true in interpersonal relationships. Dating couples always wonder whether the other person is really "serious" about the relationship. Each of them observes the behavior of the partner toward him- or herself and toward possible competitors. Each gift, each compliment, each thoughtful gesture, each minute the partner is late for a date, each time the partner seems to enjoy talking to a potential competitor is inspected as a "key" to the partner's "true" attitudes toward the relationship. Yet, as we have seen, these acts can mean everything or nothing or something in between.

Attitudes play such an important role in our behavior that being able to predict them accurately would be of great value. Attitudes help determine where we live, how we dress, where we work, how we spend our leisure time, and whom we marry. In the next chapter, we explore the influence of attitudes on our perception of others.

SUMMARY

1. An **attitude** is an attraction or aversion toward an object, in which cognitive, affective, motivational, and behavioral processes are implicated. The attraction or aversion is the affective component of an attitude, and our **beliefs**, or knowledge structures about objects and events, are the cognitive component. The affective component is more enduring than the cognitive component, and once an attitude has been established, the cognitions that were its original basis may be abandoned. If attitudes are to produce behavior, they must be capable of motivating the person to take instrumental action.

2. Many factors influence the development of an attitude. The **exposure effect**, repeated neutral encounters with an object, can produce a positive attitude. A negative attitude will not develop unless aversive consequences are connected with the encounter, but a single negative experience can lead to an aversion. Exposure affects attitudes even when people do not recognize the objects they have previously encountered, indicating that the feeling of recognition is not responsible for the effects of exposure.

3. According to reinforcement theories, attitudes can be formed through classical conditioning (in which a positive or negative emotional reaction becomes associated with some object) or through operant conditioning (in which people tend to repeat behavior that results in something desirable and fail to repeat acts that result in something undesirable).

4. Once an attitude has formed, it can be changed by repeated exposure to an object and by the consequences of displaying the attitude. Attitudes can also be changed by **persuasive communication**—direct, overt attempts to change them. Its effectiveness depends on the characteristics of the source, the message, and the audience. The credibility of the source, which is affected by the source's prestige, education, apparent intelligence, status, expertise, professional status, and trustworthiness, affects the extent to which the message changes attitudes, as does the source's attractiveness and likability. As for the message, a one-sided argument is more effective than a two-sided argument if the audience initially favors the communicator's position and is relatively poorly educated; a two-sided argument is more effective with a relatively well-educated audience that is initially opposed to the communicator's viewpoint. Linking the message with a pleasant emotional state or arousing fear in the audience are also successful means of persuasion. Low amounts of fear often seem to be most successful at changing attitudes, although when people are given explicit ways to combat the fear and believe their actions will be effective, high levels of fear are also effective. In regard to the audience, a person's susceptibility to persuasion is determined by psychological needs and motives and decreased by knowledge about or interest in the issue.

5. Resistance to persuasion is greatest when counterarguments are available and weakest when they are unavailable. Factors that enhance the availability of counterarguments will increase resistance to persuasion. People can sometimes be "inoculated" against persuasion by being given counterarguments needed to defend their viewpoint. Forewarning is effective in making people resistant to persuasion when they have a high level of commitment to their initial attitude.

6. Attitudes may also change when a person is thrown into a state of cognitive dissonance. All decisions are followed by **post-decision dissonance**, and this state is often resolved by changing attitudes toward the original alternatives. The selected alternative is seen as more valuable that it originally appeared, and the rejected alternatives are devalued. Both dissonance theory and reinforcement theory can explain attitude change; dissonance theory seems to predict attitudes better when people have freedom of choice, and reinforcement theory seems to predict attitudes better when people feel they have little freedom to choose.

7. Attitudes and behavior are sometimes quite inconsistent. The relationship between attitudes and behavior may be weakened by situa-

tional factors, conflicts among attitudes, the possibility of expressing a single attitude in a variety of ways, or the relative unimportance of the attitude in a person's life. The **self-monitoring** scale developed by Snyder provides a basis for predicting the degree of consistency between attitudes and behavior. It assumes that individuals need to know how they feel to use attitudes as guides to action, that individuals must perceive that their attitudes are relevant to the action under consideration, and that individuals' tendency to submit to the immediate and transitory requirements of the situation or to ignore them affects the strength of the correlation between attitudes and behavior.

KEY TERMS

attitude
beliefs
exposure effect

inoculation
persuasive communication
post-decision dissonance

self-monitoring
source credibility
the Stockholm syndrome

RECOMMENDED READINGS

FESTINGER, L. *A theory of cognitive dissonance.* Stanford, Calif.: Stanford University Press, 1957. The original systematic statement of a theory that has had a major impact on attitude-change research.

FESTINGER L., H. RIECKEN, and S. SCHACHTER. *When prophecy fails.* Minneapolis: University of Minnesota Press, 1956. A fascinating account of the development of a doomsday religious cult and its members' attitudes and behavior when their prophecy of the end of the world did not come true.

FISHBEIN, M., and I. AJZEN. *Belief, attitude, intention and behavior: An introduction to theory and research.* Reading, Mass.: Addison-Wesley, 1975. The authors present their own rather attractive theory of attitude formation and change.

FISKE, S. T., and S. E. TAYLOR. *Social cognition.* New York: Random House, 1984. State of the art in the application of the cognitive science to the understanding of how we view and understand ourselves and others.

HOVLAND, C. S., I. L. JANIS, and H. H. KELLEY. *Communication and persuasion: Psychological studies of opinion change.* New Haven, Conn.: Yale University Press, 1953. A classic book, reporting the early work of the Yale Communication Research Program.

MATLIN, M. W., and D. J. STANG. *The Pollyanna principle.* Cambridge, Mass.: Schenkman, 1978. This is a very clearly written book presenting most of the research on exposure effects and other related attitude issues.

MCGUIRE, W. J. The nature of attitudes and attitude change. In G. LINDZEY and E. ARONSON (Eds.), *The handbook of social psychology* (2nd ed.). Vol. 3. Reading, Mass.: Addison-Wesley, 1969. An excellent, comprehensive review of the field. The best single source for an overview.

PETTY, R. E., and J. T. CACIOPPO. *Attitudes and persuasion: Classic and contemporary approaches.* Dubuque, Iowa: Brown, 1981. The most extensive recent summary of theories and research on attitudes and attitude change.

INTERPERSONAL PERCEPTION AND ATTITUDES

Our perceptions of the physical world determine much of our behavior: we dress warmly when icy winds blow, duck falling objects, avoid poisons, and stay out of the path of speeding trucks. Yet some of the most significant aspects of human reality are social. For example, consider the way we vary our behavior depending on whether we are interacting with a child or an adult, a male or a female, an acquaintance or a stranger, a policeman or a panhandler, a Catholic or a Christian Scientist. Or take another example: we pay more attention to the way we look than to the way we feel. Why? Because we believe that the way we feel is unlikely to have much effect on other people, but the way we look will probably influence the way other people treat us.

In sum, our perceptions of other people's feelings, thoughts, and intentions affect our behavior. Even as young children, we learn how to make countless social distinctions and how to act on them. How do we tune our social behavior so finely? How do we learn the small distinctions among the people we meet and the situations in which we meet them? As we shall see in this chapter, there is a constant interplay among our perceptions of others, our attitudes, and our behavior. The result has a strong effect on our everyday social experience—from the friends we make to the people we fall in love with.

INTERPERSONAL PERCEPTION

It would be impossible to base our interactions with each person on a special rule and our behavior in each social situation on a unique plan. Instead, we learn to group people and situations in classes and categories. As we saw in Chapter 10, categories enable us to organize our knowledge about the world so that we can think about it more efficiently. They allow us to go beyond the information that is available in any situation; thus, they enable us to make decisions and act on inferences that do not have to be validated on each new occasion.

The people in this group are dressed in the punk style, so most of us would classify them as "punk types." Such a categorization leads us into conclusions about their behaviors and beliefs which may, in fact, be false.

When we first encounter a person or even an imaginary figure, we assign this person or figure to a grouping that already exists in our mind. Then, if we want more information about the new acquaintance, we can refer to the properties that distinguish the members of that grouping from nonmembers. If, for example, all you know about a male stranger is that he is a lawyer from Philadelphia, assigning him to that category allows you to guess that he is probably quite clever, and that he is very likely to be wealthy, more than thirty years old, and highly verbal. You may even go further and guess that he wears dark suits and ties, has fair control of his emotions, speaks without a Southern accent, and works long, hard hours.

Social psychologists are especially interested in the categories we have devised for people, as opposed to inanimate objects. How are social categories formed? How do they emerge? What qualities are involved in such categories as redheads, paraplegics, geniuses, punks, teenagers, strangers, shy, stingy, industrious, or rowdy people? Some of the attributes of these categories have an objective basis. After all, redheads do have hair that contains some semblance of the color red, and teenagers can be distinguished by their age. However, each of these categories also implies subjective

features that distinguish it. In our culture, for example, redheads are generally thought of as hot-tempered and teenagers as tactless.

In addition, the social and affiliative networks through which we relate to other people have an influence on the categories we use. This basis of categorization often has nothing to do with the object itself; instead, it depends on the person making the attribution. The same individual, say, a member of Sigma Xi, will be classified as "one of us" or "one of them," depending on whether the person he is interacting with is a fraternity brother or a member of another fraternity.

Categorization is often useful. It helps us cope with the world, allowing us to organize our perceptions about other people. But it can also have negative consequences.

The Consequences of Social Categorization

Categorization frees us from the burden of attending to all the particular properties of each object we meet. And thanks to categories, we do not have to note every detail if the same object is slightly changed, or if the circumstances are slightly different. But at the same time categorization may cause us to jump to premature conclusions or even give way to prejudice. When we have a prejudice about people, we prejudge them by relegating them to a category blindly, assigning to them all the attributes of the category without first making sure that these attributes apply: "Oh, those physics majors are just a bunch of grinds," we might say. As we saw in Chapter 10, category boundaries are fuzzy; many members of a category may not have all of its distinguishing features, and many categories are extremely vague.

Once categories are created in the minds of people, they can have profound consequences —social, political, religious, economic. They can lead to stereotyping, self-fulfilling prophecies, and the division of the world into ingroups and outgroups. At times a category may even mean the difference between life and death.

Stereotyping

When we **stereotype** a member of a group, we rigidly assign to that person all the standardized attributes that we ordinarily assign to the group, making no allowances for the person's individuality. Furthermore, we *behave* toward all the members of a category according to the characteristics we associate with the category. So if we include "hot-tempered" among the properties of redheads, we might not entrust a redhead with serious responsibility; similarly, if our category of teenager includes the attribute "tactless," we would not send a teenager to resolve a touchy conflict between a newly married couple. (Whether this particular redhead was level-headed or this teenager was tactful would not influence our decision.)

A stereotype is a category, but it is a unique kind of category, because the features that determine the way we evaluate it are especially active and prominent. As soon as we stereotype someone, we place that person somewhere on the "good–bad" dimension—and usually on the bad end. Because stereotypes have this evaluative quality, they are *attitudes*—of a certain sort. As we shall see, stereotypes have the same compo-

nents as attitudes. Because they are categories, stereotypes clearly have a cognitive component. Because they generate strong feelings—usually negative—they have an affective component. And because stereotypes often guide our action, they also have motivational and behavioral components.

Racism, Sexism, and Prejudice Throughout history, stereotypes have led to **prejudices**, negatively toned attitudes and opinions that people hold about an entire group, such as a racial minority or women. In most instances the beliefs on which prejudice is based are either exaggerated or wrong. When prejudice is expressed in behavior, the result is **discrimination**; this term refers to specific practices, often institutionalized, such as excluding women or members of racial minorities from certain kinds of activities, jobs, organizations, or educational opportunities. When prejudices and discrimination are directed toward a particular ethnic group, the result is **racism**, in which the specific attitudes and behavior are based on people's belief that their own race is superior. In the case of **sexism**, people believe that their own sex is superior. As noted in Chapter 25, however, people's attitudes are not always closely linked to their behavior. A person may be prejudiced without showing discriminatory behavior; and conversely, a person who is not prejudiced may act in a discriminatory manner when he or she is subjected to group pressure.

Although there are considerable differences between sexism and racism, there are also some similarities between the two. First, there is segregation in the division of labor. Women and blacks have traditionally been more likely to work in the home—their own homes or the homes of others —than as part of the regular labor force. Second, women and blacks have each been segregated into certain occupations. Third, at times both women and blacks have been repressed by violent means. Blacks have been lynched, and women have been raped and subjected to sexual harassment and violence in the form of incest and wife abuse (Helmreich, Spence, and Gibson, 1982).

Why Do Stereotypes Persist? What happens when a member of a group clearly does not fit the stereotype? When stereotypes are disconfirmed, do they disappear? Suppose, for instance, a man considers women to be passive, quiet, and not very bright. In this case he may continue to see an

This woman's inability to walk limits her mobility, but the human tendency to stereotype limits her in other ways as well. She may be unfairly judged as being unable to do simple tasks, such as shopping, because others think that handicapped people are incompetent.

individual woman as passive, quiet, and unintelligent, no matter how aggressively and competently she behaves. Or he may consider her an exception to the rule and hang on to the stereotype. One way many men hang onto the stereotype is by attributing the accomplishments of a successful woman to her ambition and hard work. By refusing to see her as talented, the man sees her as conforming to the stereotype (Deaux, 1976; Fiske and Taylor, 1984). Another way in which the man can protect his stereotype of women is by creating a new stereotype that embraces his acquaintance's aggression and competence. He now has two stereotypes: the old stereotype that applies to women in general and a new stereotype of "castrating females" or "career women" (Taylor, 1981).

When we are able to rise above stereotypes and treat people as individuals, we usually rate them higher than we do when we treat them as members of a group. A person will be seen less favorably when he is perceived as a policeman than when we perceive him as Mr. Jackson who lives around the corner in the blue house and has three grown children. Generally, the more a group member is seen in terms of his or her own individuality, the more positive people's attitude toward that person will be (Sears, 1983).

Self-Fulfilling Prophecies

Our tendency to catergorize people may in itself induce in them certain traits that we attribute to them. **Self-fulfilling prophecies** are expectations about behavior that evoke a situation in which the expectations are confirmed. Self-fulfilling prophecies are common and can be found in all societies; they may be beneficial or harmful. Experimenter bias, which was discussed in Chapter 2, is a form of self-fulfilling prophecy.

Nearly two decades ago, social psychologists demonstrated the self-fulfilling prophecy in the classroom (Rosenthal and Jacobson, 1968). They administered a fictitious test to a sample of children in San Francisco, then informed teachers that some of these children were on the verge of a dramatic developmental leap in their intellectual ability. The intellectual bloomers had actually been picked at random by Rosenthal and Jacobson, and the information given to the teacher had no basis in fact. Yet within eight months, the bloomers' IQ scores showed a significant increase.

Why did these children show the predicted leap in intellectual ability? Probably because they were given more attention by the teachers. The teachers looked at the students more, called on them more often to answer questions, set higher goals for them, and were generally more supportive of them than they were of other children (Chaikin and Derlega, 1979). Similarly, in a study of British schoolchildren, researchers found that when teachers rated children favorably, the children were likely to show an increased level of performance (Crano and Mellon, 1978). Futhermore, this effect was even stronger than the teachers' tendency to raise their evaluation of the children after the childrens' performance had actually improved.

Self-fulfilling prophecies can be so powerful that members of the disadvantaged group may begin to believe the stereotype themselves; some may not even seek positions for which they are thought undesirable. This behavior is, of course, the essence of "fulfilling the prophecy"; disadvantaged individuals know that they have only a slight chance of landing a job for which everybody believes they are basically unsuited.

Intergroup Conflict: The World as "Us" and "Them"

Once social categorization has created groups, conflict may arise between them. If groups see their own interests and goals as different from those of other groups, hostility may develop. When people feel that they belong to a group that excludes all others, they have formed an *ingroup* ("us"). People in the excluded group belong to the *outgroup* ("them"). Members of the ingroup invest themselves primarily with valued traits and invest the outgroup with unfavorable traits (Sherif, 1976). When a group is categorized in a highly negative fashion, the consequences may be extremely harmful. The segregation of Untouchables into special quarters, of Jews and blacks into ghettos, and of the mentally ill during the Middle Ages have had damaging—in some cases fatal —consequencs for these populations.

Even so slight an incident as the chance receipt of a gift can create intergroup conflict (Rabbie and Horowitz, 1969). Groups of Dutch adolescents were invited to a laboratory, eight at a time, and divided into teams of four on a random basis. The adolescents understood that the division had been made for convenience, and that it had no intrinsic meaning. Both groups were given a few simple tasks; afterward the researcher announced that transistor radios would be given to the members of one group and that the award would be based on the flip of a coin. The radios were distributed; the adolescents were then asked to rate the members of their own group and the members of the other group. Both the outgroup as a whole and its individual members received negative ratings; the adolescents saw the other group as more hostile and less desirable than their own and saw members of the other group as less open, less responsible, and less desirable as friends. Subsequent experiments (Tajfel, 1981) have replicated these results and have shown that categorizing people on even trivial grounds, that involve neither competition nor prizes, can produce distinctions between "us" and "them." In such cases ingroup members have substantially less favorable attitudes toward the outgroup than toward the members of their own group. Even when people have no knowledge of the criteria that have been used to assign them to groups, they tend to rate members of their own group more favorably than members of other groups, even on physical traits (Doise et al., 1972).

The Effects of Segregation

A dramatic illustration of the divisive effects of segregation arose among young boys at summer camp. These boys, all of whom came from similar backgrounds, were divided into separate groups (Sherif et al., 1961). Residents of each cabin sat at their own table for meals and encountered the residents of other cabins only in competitive situations, such as intercabin races and tugs-of-war. Before long, negative stereotypes of the other group began to emerge in each group. A climate of competition and conflict developed, and overt hostility, in the form of raids and fights, appeared. Even among people with similar backgrounds, social categorizations and segregation led to intergroup conflict.

How Conflict and Competition Can Worsen "Ingroup-Outgroup" Tensions

Intergroup conflict and economic competition can also contribute to negative attitudes about racial and ethnic groups. As a racial or ethnic minority attempts to establish a more favorable position for itself in the economy and in society in general, members of that minority come into conflict with the dominant group, and the conflict leads to the development of hostility.

Can such hostility, prejudice, and discrimination be lessened? Research shows that such feelings and behavior may moderate if cooperation between groups can be established. In the study of young campers, for example, the competitive groups stopped brawling and calling one another names when their situation changed so that cooperation was essential (Sherif et al., 1961). When the boys had to work together to bring in food and to repair the water line that supplied the camp, they gradually became friends and the enmity vanished. Some years later, researchers found another way to do this. In this case, they were exploring solutions to the racial tensions created by forced busing of schoolchildren for the purpose of integrating schools. The conflict could be reduced, the researchers found, by structuring classroom activities to foster cooperation between racial groups (Aronson et al., 1975).

The "Solo Situation"

Intergroup situations exaggerate differences between groups and minimize differences within groups. Because such situations exaggerate attributes that distinguish between the groups, increasing their importance, each group strives to protect its own identity, and it becomes difficult —if not impossible—to integrate the groups.

This phenomenon becomes striking when a single outsider enters a group of otherwise homogeneous individuals. In such an arrangement, known as a **solo situation**, the other group members pay a disproportionate amount of attention to the solo individual, emphasize his or her importance in the group, exaggerate the attributes that distinguish the solo from the other members, and perceive the solo as playing out a special role in the group, frequently a stereotypical role. For example, one woman in a group of men will find herself in the spotlight of the solo situation; so will a single black in a group of whites. The woman—or the black—will generate exaggerated, stereotypic views among the other members, even if he or she behaves in a manner that conflicts with the stereotype (Taylor et al., 1978).

Clues to the Personality of Others

People seem to need to organize their perceptions about others. An accurate assessment of other people lends a measure of security to our interpersonal relationships. The ability to judge another person's personality helps us to predict what she or he may do in a range of circumstances, and this knowledge gives us some control over our future dealings with that person.

If you are sizing up your new history instructor, for example, you do not just observe that he is smoking in a no-smoking area. Rather, you attach some meaning to this action in an attempt to figure out what the behavior says about your instructor's personality. You try to decide whether he is so nervous that he has to smoke, or is simply indifferent to rules and authority. If you conclude that your instructor is indifferent to rules, you may decide that you can risk missing an assignment or coming late to class without fear that it will hurt your grade.

In a sense, we all function like detectives: we are continually gathering clues about other people's personalities from a variety of sources—their speech, posture, dress, walk, facial expressions, even whether they wear glasses. From their appearance and behavior, we tend to judge their nature. The musical *My Fair Lady* makes the point that changes in outward characteristics, especially voice and dress, can change the way others perceive a person's inner nature.

Expectations Based on Appearance

Psychologists have devoted a great deal of attention to the stereotyped expectations associated with physical attractiveness. Although we have always heard that "beauty is only skin deep," research indicates that we act as if attractiveness permeates the entire personality. In one study (Dion, Berscheid, and Walster, 1972), subjects looked at pictures of men and women and rated their personality traits. The people who were physically attractive were consistently viewed more positively than those who were less attractive. Attractive people were seen as more sensitive, kind, interesting, strong, poised, modest, and sociable, as well as more sexually responsive. Moreover, the power of beauty to create the illusion of desirable personality traits seems to begin at an early age. Children as young as three years old have been found to prefer physically attractive youngsters as friends (Dion, 1973), and adults respond more favorably to attractive children, judging them smarter and better behaved than unattractive children (Clifford and Walster, 1973).

Unattractive individuals reap all sorts of negative ratings. When college students looked at photographs of men and women, they selected unattractive individuals as being more socially deviant and politically radical, labeled the unattractive women as more likely to be lesbians, and assumed that the unattractive men probably aspired to traditionally feminine occupations (Unger, Hildebrand, and Madar, 1982). Other research has shown that in American society, obese people are considered unattractive; they are often discriminated against and stigmatized (Allon, 1975). The stigma of unattractiveness is felt in childhood. Homely children are often targets of prejudice: an unattractive child who misbehaves is more likely to be judged "bad" or "cruel" than is an attractive child who commits the same act. When women were shown pictures of attractive and unattractive children who were misbehaving, they saw the unattractive children as chronically antisocial but saw the attractive children as just "having a bad day" (Dion, 1972).

Attractive people are sought after by others and have an easier time obtaining favors from them. The life of an especially unattractive person is difficult in many ways, and the problem may be worse for women. In a study of adolescents, unattractive women were found to have significantly higher blood pressure than attractive women (Hansell, Sparacino, and Ronchi, 1982). Among adolescent men there was no relationship between attractiveness and blood pressure, nor was the relationship found among older men and women. Yet sanctions against obese women seem to continue past adolescence. Obese women are much less likely to go on to college than are nonobese women of the same intellectual ability, and obese women are much less likely to achieve a higher socioeconomic status than their parents. Similar relationships have not been found among men (Rodin, Silberstein, and Striegel-Moore, 1984).

Inferring Traits from Behavior: Attribution Theory

Although our first opinion of someone's personality is generally based on his or her physical appearance, this impression can be altered by a person's actions. In fact, some of the most important information we have about others comes from clues in their behavior. In the 1940s Fritz Heider examind the process by which our perceptions of others' actions leads us to infer their dispositions. Twenty years later other psychologists elaborated on Heider's work in a number of **attribution theories**. These theories propose to explain how people attribute personality traits to others on the basis of their behavior.

Using Apparent Motives as a Guide One version of attribution theory suggests that we use a person's motive or intention as the link between behavior and personality traits (Jones and Davis, 1965). We observe the person's actions and ask ourselves what he or she intends to accomplish by behaving in that way. If, for example, a new friend says that you look terrible in your new red sweater, you may regard the comment as an attempt to be helpful—or you may see it as an act of hostility. Depending on the motive you assign to the statement, you would attribute different personality traits to the same behavior.

Not all behavior is equally informative. Some acts are so common that they reveal little about personality. Observing a professor lecturing to students in an Elizabethan drama class and then conferring with students during office hours would enable you to deduce virtually nothing about this professor's personality, because these activities are requirements of the professorial role. They say little about him as a person, about his motives or his predispositions. But if you observed the same professor arriving a half-hour late for class every morning and refusing to set aside office hours for students, you might be able to infer a great deal about his personality. It is behavior that seems unexpected or unusual, and that can most plausibly be explained by only one motive, that provides important clues to a person's real nature (Jones and Davis, 1965).

In an experiment designed to test attribution theory (Jones, Davis, and Gergen, 1961), subjects listened to what they believed were tape-recorded interviews with applicants for training as astronauts or submariners. Beforehand, the investigator described the ideal astronaut candidate as "inner-directed"—independent, resourceful, and self-reliant—and the ideal submariner candidate in the opposite manner, as "other-directed" —obedient, cooperative, and friendly. Half of the subjects who listened to an astronaut candidate heard the applicant present himself as highly inner-directed, whereas the other half heard the candidate present himself as other-directed. Similarly, half of the subjects heard the submariner applicant present himself as closely conforming to the ideal other-directed type, while the rest heard the applicant present himself as inner-directed.

After listening to the interviews, the subjects rated the applicants according to their perceptions of the applicants' actual personalities. Consistently, applicants whose answers were contrary to what would be expected from an ideal candidate —for example, an astronaut candidate who presented himself as other-directed—received higher ratings for credibility. The people listening to the interviews assumed that a candidate would not have given a "wrong" answer unless it was true. In contrast, they reasoned that an applicant who painted himself as conforming to expectations might have been telling the truth, but it was just as likely that he was saying what would get him admitted to the training program. In the latter case there was no way to discover the applicant's real motives. These findings support attribution theory, since unusual behavior (giving an unexpected response) that could reasonably be explained by only one motive was seen as most revealing.

Situational vs. Dispositional Causes When Adolf Eichmann, who carried out the Nazi policies that led to the deaths of 6 million Jews, was accused of mass murder, he claimed that he had no personal ill feelings toward Jews. He was, he said, merely obeying the orders of his superiors. Eichmann was convicted of crimes against humanity and executed; but some observers at the trial agreed that Eichmann showed no firm convictions or any specific evil motives (Arendt, 1978), and others pointed out that the Nazi state required unconditional and uncritical submission to its leadership (Kaufmann, 1973). Were Eichmann's actions the result of his own disposition or of the situation in which he found himself?

As we saw in Chapter 19, personality theorists argue over whether our actions are affected primarily by enduring dispositions or momentary circumstances. This debate is an attempt to discover the actual causes of people's behavior. Social psychologists view the problem from a different angle; they are interested in our *perceptions* concerning the causes of people's behavior. The dis-

Figure 26.1A. This is the introduction read to the class in Kelley's experiment on person perception and one of the notes that was then handed out. Read the note and try to imagine yourself in the situation. Then look at the accompanying photo. Form an impression of the instructor and note your reactions to him. When you have done so, look at Figure 26.1B, page 633. (After Kelley, 1950.)

> Your regular instructor is out of town today, and since we of Economics 70 are interested in the general problem of how various classes react to different instructors, we're going to have an instructor today you've never had before, Mr. Blank. Then, at the end of the period, I want you to fill out some forms about him. In order to give you some idea of what he's like, we've had a person who knows him write up a little biographical note about him. I'll pass this out to you now and you can read it before he arrives. *Please read these to yourselves and don't talk about this among yourselves until the class is over so that he won't get wind of what's going on.*

> Mr. Blank is a graduate student in the Department of Economics and Social Science here at M.I.T. He has had three semesters of teaching experience in psychology at another college. This is his first semester teaching Ec. 70. He is 26 years old, a veteran, and married. People who know him consider him to be a very warm person, industrious, critical, practical, and determined.

A re-creation of the classroom scene in Kelley's experiment on person perception (see Figures 26.1A and 26.1B). Kelley was able to demonstrate in this study how strongly our impressions of people can be influenced by our expectations about them.

tinction between dispositional and situational causes of behavior is extremely important, because these judgments can have a profound effect on our lives and on the lives of others. Whether a murder is classified as homicide or involuntary manslaughter depends greatly on whether the actions of the defendant can be attributed to his or her disposition or to the circumstances—say, to self-defense. As Heider (1958) put it, we can perceive behavior as having either dispositional or situational causes. When we explain behavior in terms of a **dispositional cause**, we attribute the action to the specific person involved and to that person's disposition. When we explain it in terms

of a **situational cause**, we attribute it to conditions in the environment—to the situation.

Consider a less controversial example than Adolf Eichmann. Suppose a man is desperately trying to sleep. He fails. He tosses and turns, tries to think of boring topics, reads—but all in vain. He simply cannot go to sleep. Why? Even if you do not know anything about the man or the situation, you may be tempted to suggest that he is a chronic insomnia sufferer who never falls asleep before 5:00 A.M. You have invoked a dispositional attribution: the insomniac cannot sleep because of internal physiological causes—there is something wrong with him. But suppose this man is in a motel room, facing a steep incline on a major highway. Like everyone else in the motel, he is being kept awake by the noise of trucks. Once he is home, he will sleep without difficulty. Now you know that the cause of his sleeplessness is not in his body or in his disposition, but in the environment—the cause is situational.

When we consider our own behavior, we often attribute it to situational circumstances, especially when we are not proud of it. When we nick somebody's fender, we explain that the night was foggy or the road was slippery, or that the brakes failed momentarily. But when someone else dents our car, we explain the action in dispositional terms: the other driver was careless. These tendencies have been explained as the result of our perceptual perspective. When we are looking for the cause of someone else's behavior, we are *observers*, and we focus primarily on the other's action. But when it comes to our own behavior, we are *actors*, aware of all the environmental pressures that affect us (Jones and Nisbett, 1971).

L. D. Ross (1977) has suggested that the term **fundamental attribution error** be used to describe this tendency of observers to attribute other people's behavior to dispositional factors. When we attribute an action to a person's disposition, we are not always wrong. But the same action is often attributed to the situation when the actor judges his or her own action, yet attributed to disposition when an observer is judging the actions of others; so one of the judgments must be erroneous.

Thomas Pettigrew (1979) looked at the same phenomenon in terms of ingroups and outgroups. He noted that we tend to find dispositional causes for the misdeeds of an outgroup and the laudable achievements of an ingroup, but find situational causes for the misdeeds of an ingroup and the laudable achievements of an outgroup. When Soviet fighters shot down a Korean jetliner in 1982, there was an immediate tendency to attribute the act to Soviet hostility and aggressiveness (dispositional causes). But when American planes bombed a hospital in Grenada, we labeled the disaster an unfortunate mishap caused by poor intelligence, poor visibility due to bad weather, lack of markings on the hospital, and confusion in orders (situational causes). Pettigrew calls this tendency the **ultimate attribution error**; he believes it to be one of the basic components of prejudice toward outgroups.

Biased Inferences

Our inferences about other people and their motives do not always follow the rules of logic. The same biases in judgment that affect problem solving affect our perceptions of people; after all, figuring out a person's personality and probable behavior is a form of problem solving. As we saw in Chapter 10, a variety of biases affect our conclusions and guesses, including biases in representativeness, availability, anchoring, and hindsight.

When we make judgments about other people, we tend to be so thrown off by a resemblance to a stereotypical example that we discard any other information we might have (Kahneman and Tversky, 1973). Like other biases of judgment, the bias of representativeness is widespread; it is

found even among people who are trained in statistics and probability (Kahneman and Tversky, 1973; Nisbett and Ross, 1980).

Integrating Impressions of Others

Once we infer that a person possesses certain traits, our perceptions become more integrated and we form a lasting impression. In the process of fitting together the pieces of personality, some traits seem more important than others to the final impression.

Central Traits

Certain traits apparently have a disproportionate impact on our evaluation of people. In one experiment (Kelley, 1950), students at the Massachusetts Institute of Technology (MIT) were told that their class would be taught that day by a new instructor, whom they would be asked to evaluate at the end of the period. Before the instructor was introduced, the students were given a biographical note about him. The students did not know that two versions of the note had been distributed. Half the students read the description in Figure 26.1A, and the rest read the one in Figure 26.1B. The two sketches differed by only two words, with the first describing the instructor as "very warm" and the second calling him "rather cold." This simple change created differing sets of expectations and had great impact on how the students

Figure 26.1B. The other note in Kelley's experiment on person perception. (If you have not looked at Figure 26.1A, do so first.) Read this description, let it sink in, and then look at the accompanying photo again, noting your reactions as before.

> Mr. Blank is a graduate student in the Department of Economics and Social Science here at M.I.T. He has had three semesters of teaching experience in psychology at another college. This is his first semester teaching Ec. 70. He is 26 years old, a veteran, and married. People who know him consider him to be a rather cold person, industrious, critical, practical, and determined.

perceived the instructor. In the evaluations they filled out at the end of class, students who had read the biography that included the word "warm" rated the instructor as substantially more considerate, informal, sociable, popular, good-natured, and humorous than did students who had read the word "cold." The instructor's description as "warm" or "cold" also affected the students' response to him during a class discussion: 56 percent of the students who expected "warmth" participated in the discussion, whereas only 32 percent of those who expected "coldness" did so. (The instructor's appearance is shown in the photo on page 632.)

Solomon Asch, who conducted similar pioneering experiments in the late 1940s and early 1950s, called such traits as "warm" and "cold" **central traits** because they have such marked effects on the way other, related traits are perceived (Asch, 1946). Apparently, when we think we have detected a central trait, we build around it a cluster of expectations of additional traits the person will possess and of how she or he will behave toward other people.

The Primacy Effect

The order in which traits are perceived can also affect the impression of personality. There is evidence that the traits that are first detected influence subsequent information about the person, a process called the **primacy effect**. If, for example, your first meeting with a classmate is at a football game where the young man impresses you with his knowledge of game strategy and team standings, it may be difficult to see him as an intellectual when you later learn he is an "A" student with a major in philosophy. In your mind he will remain more the sports enthusiast than the student of Plato.

The primacy effect is so powerful because, as we saw in Chapter 19, we believe that the way a person acts during a first meeting reveals his or her personality. As information comes in successive chunks, it is absorbed in the context of that initial knowledge. If you discover that a woman is calm after you have learned that she is intelligent, you have a different image of her than if you had discovered that she is calm after you have learned that she is shrewd.

Primacy is in part a form of another inference bias—availability. As noted in Chapter 10, biases of availability lead people to give more weight to information that is most available in memory. Things that first come to mind have more impact on our judgment than information that is dredged up later (Kahneman, Slovic, and Tversky, 1982).

SELF-PERCEPTION

Of all the people we know, only one is always available for our own examination. That person is the self. How do we perceive ourselves? How do we gather information about and evaluate ourselves? When we evaluate others, we tend to make inferences from their appearance and behavior, and we often resort to stereotypes in an effort to manage the information we receive. Some psychologists argue that our perception of others and our self-perception are similar processes. As we observe our own behavior, we assign motives to our acts and sometimes infer corresponding personality traits (Bem, 1972).

Building Self-Perception

As we observe ourselves acting and consider why we do what we do, we appear to build up rich and important cognitive structures about the self called **self-schemas**—clusters of generalizations about the self based on past experiences that organize, summarize, and explain our behavior in specific domains (Markus, 1977). These self-schemas derive from specific incidents in the past ("I was fifteen minutes late for my dental appointment yesterday") and from generalizations about our behavior made by the self and others ("Sally says I'm not very dependable, but I never stand anyone up").

Once a schema is established, it helps us deal with information that is related to a particular aspect of our behavior, such as whether we are masculine, feminine, creative, dependable, independent, or obese. Studies (Markus, 1977) indicate that we develop numerous schemas, and that not all of us have the same ones. Some people have a schema about their masculinity, but others do not, so that with respect to masculinity they are "aschematic."

The way we perceive ourselves strongly affects the way we behave. The boys flexing their muscles probably think of themselves as fine physical specimens. The girls seem to be viewing their images a bit less seriously.

Impression Management

Because the way we are perceived exerts a greater influence on how we are treated than the way we "really" are, being able to influence other people's perception of ourselves may affect our lives. Conceivably, it may change the way they treat us, making us more popular and perhaps even raising our self-concepts. But in order to influence the behavior of others in this way, we have to display the sort of behavior that will lead them to make favorable attributions of our intentions, abilities, and feelings. This technique, known as **impression management**, induces others to perceive us in the most favorable light (Snyder, 1977).

Such behavior sounds insincere, and to some extent it is. But there is probably not a person alive who has not, at some time or another, adjusted his or her behavior so as to create a desirable impression on others. The adjustment need not even be conscious. We all want some affection, and few of us would reject the respect or admiration of others.

Mark Snyder (1979) believes that most people tend to act so as to make the best possible impression; he says we engage in **self-monitoring**, controlling our words, our actions, the way we present ourselves, and our nonverbal displays of emotion. Most of us are sensitive to social situations and match our behavior to the situation.

Not everyone monitors his or her behavior to the same degree; as we saw in Chapter 25, some of us are high self-monitors and others are low self-monitors. When high self-monitors are responding to Snyder's Self-Monitoring Scale, a series of twenty-five true–false statements about the self, they indicate that they find it easy to imitate the behavior of others, that they would probably make good actors, that they can argue in favor of ideas even if they do not believe them, and that their apparent friendliness may deceive people they really dislike. Other researchers (Fiske and Taylor, 1984) describe high self-monitors as more socially skilled than low self-monitors; they are quicker to adapt to new situations, better at reading the nonverbal behavior of others, and more likely to initiate conversations, and they have better self-control. In a situation that depends on the responses of another person, such as when one is trying to convince an employer to adopt a new program or trying to make an impression on a potential date, high self-monitors remember more about the critical person and confidently make inferences about their reactions.

Because high self-monitors gauge their behavior to manage the impressions of others, they show more variability from one situation to the next than do low self-monitors. In fact, when high self-monitors assess their own behavior, they are likely to make situational attributions in circumstances where low self-monitors tend to make dispositional attributions (Snyder, 1979). Susan Fiske and Shelley Taylor (1984) have identified some of the methods of impression management that are used by high self-monitors and are available to anyone who wishes to manage other people's impressions:

■ *Behavioral matching.* This method of impression management simply means doing what the other person is doing. When you are with a modest person, you are modest; with a rowdy person, you are rowdy.
■ *Conformity to situational norms.* Going to a French restaurant, you dress for the occasion and save your T-shirt and jeans for the coffee shop. You yell at a football game but not in the boss's office.
■ *Appreciating or flattering others.*
■ *Behavior-attitude consistency.* You behave so as to suggest that your attitudes are *consistent* with your behavior—even if they are not. The successful self-monitor manages impressions so as to be perceived as a sincere, modest person who is very attracted by whomever he or she is with.

We tend to view extreme cases of impression management with disdain, but we may still succumb to the strategy. Politicians are heavily engaged in impression management; in fact, they hire public-relations firms to do nothing but help them manage the impressions of voters. These firms determine what impression the candidate should project, then arrange the candidate's appearances, speeches, and publicity during a campaign so as to project that image. In 1984 President Reagan's campaign for reelection projected the image of a true American—a leader desiring peace through strength who was willing to spend money on defense (but would spend it wisely and effectively); a leader who knew what was good for the country, and whose decisions could be trusted; a man untroubled by difficulties and completely sincere in his beliefs and values. His opponent, Walter Mondale, was not successful in projecting a unified image; his campaign depended more on issues than on personality. And Mondale was defeated.

How much the outcome of the election was determined by personality is uncertain. It seems clear, however, that a candidate's personality is much more important today than it was when Franklin Roosevelt ran for his fourth term in 1944. Today television continually projects the candidate's image into every home; this process gives politicians an opportunity to manage voters' impressions and gives voters an opportunity to make attributions about the candidate's behavior.

INTERPERSONAL ATTITUDES AND FRIENDSHIP

Our perception of others is seldom a dispassionate and objective activity, in which we quietly examine the details of social information available to us. Rather, our feelings are involved. When we meet a man who is famous, we immediately experience a positive feeling toward him. When we are confronted by a woman who has just won the Boston marathon, we experience admiration. We respond to intelligence, wealth, and beauty with positive emotions and to ugliness, fraud, and stupidity with negative ones. Thus social perception and social categorization are highly evaluative processes that are accompanied by strong attitudes.

The Effects of Proximity

At the first session of a new class, what makes you decide that you would rather sit next to one person than another? At a party full of strangers, what triggers your decision to talk to one person instead of another? The answers to these questions depend upon a number of factors that determine whether a new acquaintance becomes a friend or remains distant. First impressions certainly affect the development of our attitudes toward others. But proximity is an equally important factor.

Think of your own friends. If you live in San Francisco, chances are your best friends are San Franciscans, probably people who live in your neighborhood or go to your school. You may believe that many interesting people live in Philadelphia or Atlanta, but unless you met some of them, you could not become their friends. In fact, the single most important factor in friendship is physical **proximity**—how close together people live and work.

The powerful effects of proximity were demonstrated in a study (Segal, 1974) of a police academy in which male cadets were alphabetically assigned to dormitory rooms and classroom seats. Upon entry, a cadet whose name began with A was likely to room with another cadet whose name also began with A, or with B or C, and to sit near him in class. After six weeks, the researcher asked cadets about their choices of friends among their classmates. There was a remarkable tendency for cadets to choose as friends classmates whose names began with letters near their own in the alphabet. Among the sixty-five friendships formed among the cadets, twenty-nine (45 percent) were between men next to each other in alphabetical order, and such choices were more likely to be reciprocated than were choices made out of alphabetical order. Just the accident of names predisposed Smith to become friends with Simmons rather than with Adkins and predisposed Adkins to become friends with Abelson.

Proximity is a powerful factor in friendship because the exposure effect, which was discussed in Chapter 25, depends on proximity. But proximity has other effects. People who live close to each other tend to be similar in many ways: socioeconomic status, school background, educational attainment, ethnic background, political leanings, clothing style, family structure, and so forth. Since similarity is another powerful factor in friendship formation, as we shall see in the following section, geographic proximity promotes a host of processes that combine to generate and maintain friendships. It is no accident that many people marry the person next door.

The Effects of Similarity

There is apparently a good deal of truth to the old saying "Birds of a feather flock together," for similarity is another important factor that influences the development of friendship. People tend to form relationships with others who are like themselves in a number of ways. As we saw in Chapter 17, this is as true of children as it is of adults (Hartup, 1983). One way to examine the effects of similarity is to look at the way it affects attraction between the sexes.

Similarity in Appearance

In romantic novels and movies, the handsome hero almost always ends up with the beautiful heroine. Life apparently follows fiction in most cases, with beauty attracting beauty. Studies (Murstein, 1972) of dating relationships indicate that people of similar physical attractiveness tend to pair off. For example, a study of clients of a Los

Angeles dating service showed that couples tended to sort themselves out on the basis of physical similarity (Folkes, 1982). Selection was made on the basis of information available to all subscribers; this information consisted of a questionnaire about the subscriber's occupation, age, attitudes, interests, and background, as well as a photograph and a five-minute videotape. From this information a member could express interest in meeting another member; the second member could then decide to initiate the relationship by releasing his or her surname and phone number, by initiating contact, or by actually dating. The subscribers who were studied had an average age of thirty-six years. As it turned out, the physical attractiveness of subscribers they chose to contact or date was similar to their own.

One possible explanation for this pattern is that when choosing a date, people consider not only the attractiveness of the other person but also the probability of being rejected by that person. Dating, in other words, follows the rules of the marketplace: a man calculates risks and rewards before he approaches a woman for a date. If a man considers himself to be fairly unattractive, he considers it probable that an attractive woman will reject him, so he lowers his sights to a somewhat less attractive date. Some evidence of this "matching process" has been supplied by research in which it was found that when there was no possibility of refusal, men tended to choose more attractive women for dates than they would have chosen under ordinary conditions (Berscheid et al., 1971).

Other studies, however, have produced somewhat contradictory results. In one experiment (Huston, 1973), men who rated themselves low in physical attractiveness seemed to select dates who were as attractive as those selected by men who rated themselves high in physical attractiveness. This held true even though men who gave themselves low ratings also believed they had a poorer than average chance of being accepted by the most attractive females. It is possible that men with a low evaluation of themselves were less sensitive to rejection than those who considered themselves to be attractive. Unattractive men may become accustomed to being turned down, and the chance of a highly rewarding partner may encourage them to risk refusal.

Another possible interpretation is that people will try to develop dating relationships with the most attractive partner available, regardless of the probability of rejection. But since they are rejected by those who think they can find more attractive dates, people of similar attractiveness end up paired. According to this explanation, such a "sorting process" can explain the finding that dating couples tend to be similar in physical attractiveness.

Similarity in Social Background

Not only do most couples tend to be similar in physical attractiveness, they also tend to share the same race, religion, economic status, and educational level. Young people often encounter strong social pressures, especially from parents, to marry someone with a similar social history. Such a sorting process is encouraged by proximity. As noted earlier, people of similar income levels and ethnic backgrounds generally live in the same areas and send their children to the same schools. When children and adolescents encounter only people who share their race, religion, and economic level, their friends and potential dating partners will inevitably be similar to them in social background.

Similarity versus Exposure

The proverb about birds that flock together raises a question about the relative strength of these two mechanisms of attitude formation. Which is more important in the development of attraction: mere exposure or a person's similarity to us? We have no data from human research that can provide an answer, but the situation has been explored among newly hatched chicks, where the process is not obscured by the effect of human cognition (Zajonc, Wilson, and Rajecki, 1975). When food coloring is injected into an egg between the eleventh and thirteenth days of incubation, the hatchling emerges with plumage of the injected color. Shortly after hatching, pairs of chicks dyed either green or red were placed together in otherwise isolated compartments for sixteen to eighteen hours. Members of some pairs were of the same color (birds of a feather) and other pairs were mixed (one red and one green chick). Afterward, the chicks were observed in interaction with their cagemate, with a strange bird of their own color, and with a strange bird of another color. As a test of affiliation, researchers used pecking, because chicks peck strangers much more than they peck companions. The results were clear: exposure was more important than similarity. Chicks of both colors liked their cagemates most—whether or not the cagemates resembled them—and they liked birds unlike their cagemates least. That is, red chicks raised with green chicks preferred strange green chicks to strange chicks with feathers like their own, and green chicks raised with red chicks preferred strange red chicks.

Generally, among couples, like attracts like. Men and women tend to be drawn toward people of similar backgrounds and levels of physical attractiveness.

There is a rich interplay among friendship, proximity, and similarity. Proximity can promote the formation of friendships. But it also predisposes people to become similar to each other—in language, in culture, in dress, in likes and dislikes, in political opinions, and in income. At the same time a reciprocal influence exists between friendship and proximity. Proximity determines the range of people with whom it is possible to make friends, and it ensures repeated exposure. But once friendships are formed, friends tend to remain close to each other and to maintain contact. Thus, friendship promotes proximity.

Similarity also affects the development of friendships. Like the relationship between friendship and proximity, the relationship between similarity and friendship is also reciprocal: we want our friends to share our views and tastes, and we want them to be like us in many ways. Similarity may also promote proximity. For example, people tend to move into neighborhoods that are occupied by others more or less like themselves. They seek out ethnic and religious affinity, and similarity of socioeconomic level. No one likes to be among people who are "different" and to risk the danger of being considered an "outsider." Thus, proximity, similarity, and friendship all enhance and reinforce each other.

Attraction and Attribution of Similarity

There is more to attractiveness than the interaction of proximity, outward appearance, and socioeconomic, religious, and ethnic similarity. The final element of attractiveness is in the eye of the beholder and is often determined by a number of extremely subtle behavioral cues. On the basis of these cues, we decide whether another person shares any of our personal characteristics, attitudes, or inclinations. We are all sensitive to such behavioral cues, and we seem to pick them up within a few minutes of meeting a person. For example, after a brief interaction with a stranger of the opposite sex, subjects were asked to rate the stranger's attractiveness. Each subject was also asked to respond to measures that rated his or her own self-esteem and self-consciousness. Although none of the subjects knew the other person's self-esteem and self-consciousness rating, they consistently found most attractive people who were like themselves on these measures (Lloyd, Paulse, and Brockner, 1983).

Since attractive people make desirable friends, and since one avenue of friendship formation is through similarity, we might ask just how far we would go out of our way to seek out similarities between us and an attractive stranger. Perhaps we simply hope that our behavior, tastes, and attitudes resemble those of attractive people. Perhaps we perceive ourselves as already having the qualities we see in an attractive stranger. Or perhaps we impute our own qualities—whether good or bad—to attractive people who might become our friends.

The last possibility may best describe the situation. As we have seen, when we find strangers attractive, they often turn out to resemble us in some way (Lloyd, Paulse, and Brockner, 1983). Another study indicates that we will go some distance in imputing our own qualities to an attractive stranger (Marks, Miller, and Maruyama, 1981). College students who judged both themselves and strangers on a number of personality traits assumed that physically attractive strangers were more like themselves than were unattractive strangers. The assumption was so strong that the students declared that they were similar to attractive strangers even on such undesirable traits as greed, conceit, phoniness, selfishness, and hostility (see Figure 26.2). In contrast, the students denied their close resemblance to unattractive strangers, even on such positive traits as thoughtfulness, intelligence, open-mindedness, dependability, and honesty.

Figure 26.2. Mean assumed trait similarity between self and target persons. The numbers beside each data point are mean responses. Lower numbers reflect greater assumed trait similarity. (Adapted from Marks, Miller, and Maruyama, 1981.)

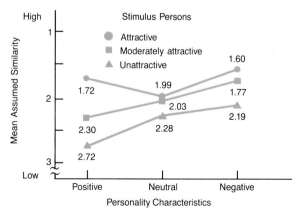

People also tend to believe that attractive people have attitudes and tastes like their own. In another study subjects assumed that attractive peers were likely to endorse their own attitudes and beliefs on an array of issues, ranging from issues that were deeply important to them, such as politics, to trivial matters, such as their preferences among cigarette brands (Marks and Miller, 1982). Subjects again distanced themselves from unattractive peers, assuming that their attitudes on important issues differed, although indicating that on trivial matters their attitudes were probably similar.

Despite our wishful assumptions of similarity, we do look for other qualities in friendship. The course of friendship is strongly affected by such rewarding aspects as approval and the compatibility of needs.

The Effects of Approval

The promise of approval from others weighs heavily in the formation of friendships. People who approve of us and show that they like us bolster our sense of self-worth.

It might be expected, then, that showering someone with praise would be the surest path to friendship. Yet some studies have shown that unquestioning approval does not produce the most favorable attitudes toward the approving person. In one study (Aronson and Linder, 1965), women overheard a series of remarks about themselves made by a confederate of the researchers. Women in one group heard only complimentary remarks, and those in a second group heard very derogatory remarks. A third group heard very derogatory remarks, which gradually became positive and at last were highly complimentary (this was called the *gain* condition). A fourth group heard comments that were at first very positive but became less favorable and finally very disparaging (this was called the *loss* condition). When each woman was asked how much she liked the confederate, the confederate who had begun by saying negative things and ended by being laudatory was liked the best. The confederate who had been uniformly positive was liked—but not as much as the one who had switched from criticism to approval. The confederate who had said consistently negative things was also preferred to the one who had begun with compliments and ended with disapproval.

As noted in Chapter 25, attitudes are influenced by many factors. In this case, the early disparaging remarks made in the gain condition may have established the genuineness and credibility of the confederate. The subject may have thought the change revealed that the confederate was a discriminating person and not easy to impress. As a result, the eventual approval may have seemed especially rewarding. When the confederate's remarks were uniformly positive, the subject may have thought that the confederate praised everyone. The remarks, therefore, were less gratifying, and the confederate was liked somewhat less. In the loss condition, the subjects who heard positive comments followed by negative ones may have experienced such a surprising and disappointing loss of self-esteem that they felt cooler toward the confederate than they would have felt toward someone who had been critical all along.

The Effects of Complementary Needs

Important as approval is, the ways in which the personalities of people mesh may be more important than the need for unstinted praise. Attempting to explain bonds of mutual interdependence between lovers, Carl Jung (whose theories were discussed in Chapter 18) suggested that people have unconscious "archetypes," or ideals, of the sort of persons who would best complement them. When someone encounters a person who corresponds to this archetype, she or he immediately becomes aware of the match and falls in love.

Other theorists (e.g., Winch, 1958) have suggested that complementary needs are a basis for attraction between friends as well as lovers. Thus, a person with the need to dominate is attracted to one with the need to be dominated; a person with a need to care for others is drawn to one with a need to be cared for. In describing a friendship between two teenage boys, psychologist Robert White provided a good example of how two personalities complemented one another:

> Ben, whose school experience had been so unstimulating that he never read a book beyond those assigned, discovered in Jamie a lively spirit of intellectual inquiry and an exciting knowledge of politics and history: Here was a whole world to which his friend opened the door and provided guidance. Jamie discovered in Ben a world previously closed to him, that of confident interaction with other people. Each

admired the other, each copied the other, each used the other for practice.

Later research suggests, however, that friendships may depend more on a compatibility of needs than on a simple complementarity. An example of compatible needs in a pair of friends is a high level of dominance in one person and a low need for autonomy (independence) in the other. A high need for dominance in one partner and a low need for dominance in the other would be complementary, but would not necessarily be compatible. The importance of compatibility appeared in an assessment of camp counselors who had worked together for at least a month and had formed friendships. There was strong evidence that counselors with compatible need structures tended to become friends (Wagner, 1975).

Compatibility of needs may be important for a harmonious marriage. When the need structures of married couples were studied, there was no evidence of any relationship between marital adjustment and simple complementarity. But couples who scored high on a scale of marriage adjustment had similar needs for affiliation, aggression, autonomy, and nurturance. Apparently, similarity in these needs makes for a harmonious marriage. A couple with similarly high needs for affiliation, for example, can socialize a great deal, while a couple who are both low in the need for affiliation can be stay-at-homes. Sharply different levels of need for affiliation would be expected to produce tension between marriage partners.

Although a knowledge of needs may be a reliable guide to friendship patterns and marital adjustment, the principles for determining need compatibility are complex and subtle. They are complicated by the fact that the social context of a relationship affects the compatibility of need structures (Wagner, 1975). Because of these complexities, the relationships of compatibility and complementarity must be examined on a trait-by-trait basis.

The Effects of Birth Order

Given the influences on friendship formation discussed so far, the fact remains that no matter what the situation, some people are obviously shy and have difficulty making friends and others are just as obviously popular and become friendly with a stranger in minutes. These inclinations affect all our social relationships, and we have little control over them. Although the precise circumstances that help to shape such traits as sociability and shyness are unknown, research suggests that family experiences may be of major importance in their development. Specifically, **birth order**, or the sequence in which children are born into a family, appears to give later-born children a social advantage, so that they tend to make friends more easily than do first-born children.

The greater sociability of later-born children develops because of what seem like disadvantages in childhood. The first-born have their parents to themselves until they acquire their first sibling, so that their first and most frequent contact as infants and young children is with adults. The later-born, however, never have their parents to themselves in early childhood, and much of their growth is dominated by interaction with an older sibling. Thus, first-born children, in contrast with those born later, acquire different conceptions about what sorts of people might be friends with them, how to get other people to do things for them, and what sorts of people have power and what sorts do not. Later-born children, on the other hand, are likely to feel powerless, because they must learn to work with—and around—other family members to achieve their goals. As a result of their birth order, the later-born develop social skills that contribute to their popularity outside the family (Markus, 1981). In fact, when researchers (Miller and Maruyama, 1976) asked a large number of children to choose from among their classmates the child they would like to play ball with during recess, the later-born were picked more often than the first-born.

The contribution of birth order to personality is the basis for a theory that predicts the probable success of adult heterosexual relationships. This **duplication hypothesis**, which was developed by Walter Toman (1976), applies the influence of similarity on attraction to experiences that accompany a person's birth order. According to Toman, marriage partners seek to duplicate their childhood sibling relationships and are happiest when they do so. Thus, a first-born woman who grew up with a younger brother would be happiest if she married a man who had an older sister. Toman used his hypothesis to predict the probability of divorce and separation, with some success, although subsequent research has failed to support his predictions.

However, if younger siblings are indeed more

sociable and outgoing than first-born children, it would follow that couples made up of the later-born should have especially satisfactory relationships. Besides developing strong social skills, the later-born learn to settle for second-best (as they often had to do at home), an ability that should lend their relationships more give-and-take and therefore greater stability. To test this idea, researchers (Ickes and Turner, 1983) observed forty male-female pairs during informal, face-to-face interaction. Both men and women with an older sibling of the opposite sex were likely to have rewarding interactions with strangers of the opposite sex. Last-born men talked more than first-born men, asked more questions, and were better liked by their female partners. Last-born women were more likely to start a conversation than were first-born women, and they smiled more at their partners. First-born women tended to be rated as strong, vain, or sensitive by their male partners, and first-born men as unassertive, unexciting, and unfriendly by their female partners. Although a five-minute conversation between a pair of strangers cannot be used to predict the stability —or even the likelihood—of marriage, the study does support the notion that the later-born have an edge in social situations.

INTERPERSONAL ATTRACTION AND LOVE

What is love? And how does it differ from liking? What causes two people to fall in love? These questions have fascinated human beings for centuries, yet only in the last few decades have psychologists begun to study them.

After studying a number of couples, George Levinger (1974) found that romantic relationships have a natural history; those that become deep pass through an inevitable series of stages. Before the relationship begins, of course, a couple has no contact. The first real stage of the relationship, called the *awareness stage,* begins when two people begin to notice each other. If the relationship progresses past mutual awareness, there will be *surface contact*; the pair become acquainted, but their interchanges are superficial and limited to impersonal matters. As the relationship develops, the couple moves into the *mutuality stage*; they share many activities and feel they can de-

pend on each other. Finally, the fully developed relationship moves into the *interdependence stage.* This stage is usually reserved for couples who live together, marry, or have childen. By now the pair's interdependence extends over most spheres of their lives; their social, economic, affectionate, sexual, religious, political, and professional lives become intertwined.

How do psychologists know whether a couple is truly in love? The subjective nature of love makes it difficult to define scientifically, but some psychologists have tried to distinguish love from liking by asking people to describe their feelings toward a lover, compared to their feelings toward a friend. For example, the individuals who comprised more than 200 dating couples from colleges in the Boston area answered a lengthy questionnaire concerning their feelings toward their boyfriend or girlfriend (Rubin, 1970). Their answers fell into two groups, with one set describing feelings that reflected what is commonly regarded as "liking" and the other describing "loving." Some of the relationships were predominately loving, and others were predominately liking.

Feelings are often expressed in behavior, and researchers have also attempted to identify behavior that is related to love. In the Boston college study, "loving" couples—couples who scored high on statements reflecting love—spent more time gazing into each other's eyes than did "liking" couples (Rubin, 1973). As various studies have shown (Hall, 1966), eye contact within extremely short distances is reserved for the expression of deep emotion. Therefore sustained eye contact reflects the strong, positive feelings that are assumed to characterize love and the intimate communication that is common among lovers.

The emotions that accompany love are complex and far from being clearly understood. They involve sexual excitement (see Chapter 13), dependency needs, joy, anxiety, jealousy, sometimes a desire for control, and many other feelings. Especially in the early stages of a relationship, people find it difficult to label these emotions and may mistake one for another. For example, when a man first met an attractive woman, he might have confused whatever emotions he was feeling with sexual excitement and sexual attraction, even though his arousal had little to do with sexuality.

Evidence for such "misattribution" of emotion comes from a study (Dutton and Aron, 1974) testing the hypothesis that arousal from a source unconnected with sexual excitement might be mistaken for sexual excitement if environmental cues about sexuality are present. In this study, male subjects met an attractive female stranger, either under fear-provoking conditions or in safety. In the fear-arousing condition, the men had just crossed an unsteady, decrepit bridge that swayed in the wind high above a rocky gorge. As they stepped from the bridge, the woman—who was a confederate of the experimenter—asked them to write a brief story for a project. The stories these men wrote contained more sexual imagery than did stories written by men in a control group who had been approached by the same woman as they crossed a solid bridge that spanned a shallow stream. The men who crossed the unsteady bridge were also more likely to telephone the attractive confederate later to be told more about the project. According to the two-factor theory of emotion,

discussed in Chapter 11, crossing the shaky, dangerous bridge frightened (and thus physically aroused) the men; at the sight of the woman, they relabeled their arousal as sexual attraction. If this interpretation is correct, perhaps other strong emotions could be appraised as love if the situation makes that appraisal possible.

Romantic attraction, then, may be based on physiological arousal, perhaps coupled with the operation of learning principles. But these explanations need not detract from the pleasures of intimate friendship and love. The sun is no less enjoyable on a warm summer day when we know that the rays are part of the electromagnetic spectrum produced by the fusion of hydrogen atoms into helium. In the same way, the pleasures of friendship and love need not be diminished by our increased understanding of them.

SUMMARY

1. Social categories enable us to organize our perceptions about people, freeing us from the burden of attending to all the characteristics of each person we meet. But categories can also result in **stereotyping**, which makes no allowances for individuality, and can lead to **racism** and **sexism**, in which specific patterns of attitudes and behavior are applied to members of particular groups. Negative attitudes toward a group are known as **prejudices**, and practices that exclude individuals because of their group membership are known as **discrimination**. Social categorization can also lead to **self-fulfilling prophecies**, in which expectations about behavior evoke situations that confirm the expectations, and to intergroup conflict. When a member of an outgroup enters a homogeneous ingroup, a **solo situation** develops, in which the solo individual is highly stereotyped.

2. Assessing another's personality helps to predict that person's behavior and provides some control in future dealings with her or him. Appearance and behavior are two major categories often used in judging a person's nature. First impressions of strangers are often formed

on appearance, and stereotypes connected with their appearance are used to infer personality. Physically attractive people are generally viewed positively and physically unattractive people are generally viewed negatively. The kindness, sociability, and sensitivity ascribed to attractive people may be the result of others' behavior toward them—behavior based on the stereotypical notion that they indeed possess these qualities.

3. According to **attribution theories**, which explain how people ascribe personality traits to others on the basis of their behavior, a person's apparent motive provides the link between behavior and action. Important clues to personality are found in unexpected behavior that can be plausibly explained by only one motive. We tend to attribute the actions of others to **dispositional causes** and our own actions to **situational causes**. The tendency of observers to prefer dispositional attributions is known as the **fundamental attribution error**, and when ingroups describe their own actions in situational terms and the actions of outgroups in dispositional terms, the tendency is known as the **ultimate attribution error**. Attributions are

sometimes wrong, because the same biases in judgment that affect problem solving also affect our inferences about people's personality.

4. After we infer another's traits, we integrate those perceptions to form a lasting impression of that person. **Central traits** have marked effects on the way other, related traits are perceived, and the detection of a central trait creates expectations about other traits and probable behavior. According to the **primacy effect**, the traits that are first perceived influence further impressions of a person. People tend to screen out, reinterpret, or assign less importance to information received after a first impression has been formed.

5. Some psychologists believe that our perceptions of others and self-perception are similar processes. As a perception of the self develops, cognitive structures are formed called **self-schemas**—clusters of generalizations about the self based on past experiences that organize, summarize, and explain our behavior in specific domains. An established schema helps in dealing with information related to that aspect of behavior. The attempt to induce others to perceive us in the most favorable light is known as **impression management**, and it is carried out by a process of **self-monitoring**, in which we control our behavior, adjusting it to various social situations, so as to create a good impression.

6. **Proximity**, or how close together people live and work, influences the development of attitudes and plays a major role in the development of friendships. Similarity is another factor in the development of attitudes, and people tend to form friendships and romantic attachments with others like themselves in level of attractiveness, race, religion, economic status, and educational level. Although the relative strengths of exposure and similarity are unknown, exposure seems to be the stronger force among newly hatched chicks.

7. The promise of approval from others affects the development of friendship, yet constant approval seems to produce less favorable attitudes than does approval that follows criticism. However, the context in which approval or criticism is received determines its effects in daily life. Need structures also play a role in attraction, with both complementary and compatible needs affecting friendships. Again, context is important; in marriage, unless certain needs are compatible, marital tension is likely to develop. Another factor that influences friendship is **birth order**, or the sequence in which children are born into a family. Later-born children develop social skills that contribute to their popularity. According to the **duplication hypothesis**, people are happiest when they re-create their birth-order position in their marital relationship.

8. Psychologists who have studied romantic love have distinguished between "liking" and "loving", and found that "loving" is sometimes reflected in such behavior as prolonged eye contact. It has been suggested that falling in love can be explained by the two-factor theory of emotion, in which physiological arousal is attributed to the presence of another and interpreted as sexual attraction.

KEY TERMS

attribution theories	impression management	self-schemas
birth order	prejudice	sexism
central traits	primacy effect	situational cause
discrimination	proximity	solo situation
dispositional cause	racism	stereotype
duplication hypothesis	self-fulfilling prophecies	ultimate attribution error
fundamental attribution error	self-monitoring	

RECOMMENDED READINGS

FISKE, S. T., and S. E. TAYLOR. *Social cognition.* Reading, Mass.: Addison-Wesley, 1984. The most recent volume on cognitive processes in social psychology. It organizes the literature by analyzing those elements that enter social cognition, and the processes whereby they are acquired, retained, and used in an ongoing interaction with others. The volume also relates cognition to affect and analyzes cognitions in the context of attitude research.

HARVEY, J. H., W. Y. ICKES, and R. F. KIDD (Eds.). *New directions in attribution research.* Hillsdale, N.J.: Erlbaum, 1976. A collection of provocative papers—the frontiers of research on person perception—by leading researchers and theoreticians.

RAJECKI, D. W. *Attitudes: Themes and advances.* Sunderland, Mass.: Sinauer, 1982. This is the most recent book on attitudes. It presents a lucid review of theory and research on attitudes. It concludes with a review of application of attitude research to the notions of self, prosocial behavior, and social stereotypes.

SCHLENKER, B. R. *Impression management: The self-concept, social identity, and interpersonal relations.* Belmont, Calif.: Brooks/Cole, 1980. Research and theory on what we do to manipulate the perceptions others have of us, how this changes what they think of us, and how this changes us.

SCHNEIDER, D. J., A. H. HASTORF, and P. C. ELLSWORTH. *Person perception* (2nd ed.). Reading, Mass.: Addison-Wesley, 1979. Extensive survey of issues in person perception, including impression formation and the interpersonal perception of nonverbal cues.

TAJFEL, H. *Human groups and social categories: Studies in social psychology.* New York: Cambridge University Press, 1981. A theoretical and empirical exploration of the problems of social categorization. How do we categorize others? What effects does categorization have on them and on us?

TVERSKY, A., and D. KAHNEMAN. Judgment under uncertainty: Heuristics and biases. *Science,* 1974, *185,* 1124–1131. A review of biases and errors people make in drawing inferences about others and about social events.

SOCIAL INFLUENCE AND GROUP PROCESSES

In October 1984, there was a riot in Detroit in which one man was shot and killed, eighty people were injured, forty-one were arrested, and more than $100,000 worth of property was destroyed (Leo, 1984). What touched off this riot? The Detroit Tigers had beaten the San Diego Padres to win baseball's World Series. In their "joy," baseball fans threw rocks and bottles; they smashed and torched police cars; with no apparent goal, they stole or destroyed anything they came across. It was a "celebrating riot." And it was not an isolated event; in recent years, Americans have begun to go in for riots of this type—fans of winning teams seem to riot automatically after championship games.

As this alarming new trend demonstrates, our behavior is highly responsive to that of other people. How we behave is affected by internal states such as our needs, memories, and beliefs, but it is also affected by external stimuli and the information we glean from them. Social scientists have looked at this pattern on several levels. Sociol-ogists often explain "meaningless" mob action like the celebrating riots in terms of broad social influences, such as economic factors. Social psychologists, by contrast, tend to look at forces that affect individuals: for example, they are likely to point out how anonymous the individual is in a crowd, or how frustrated an individual may feel if he or she fails to achieve some goal. In this chapter we will look at social influence from the viewpoint of social psychologists.

The impact of social influence can be seen in many types of behavior—not only when people join a riot, but also when they obey authority, cooperate with each other, aid a person in distress, or act in numerous other ways. Its effects range from the primitive influence exerted by the mere presence of others to the complex effects of brainwashing. In this chapter, we first explore the influences of others on a single individual. Then we turn to an examination of mutual influence as it occurs in such group processes as cooperation and competition.

SOCIAL FACILITATION

The simplest form of social influence was studied by the earliest social psychologists. At the turn of the century investigators became interested in the way the mere presence of others affected human performance. For example, an early researcher (Triplett, 1897) noted that bicycle racers do much better in competitive races than when racing alone against the clock. He decided that the presence of others performing the same task always increases a person's motivation and thus improves performance. At first it appeared that Triplett's explanation was correct. **Social facilitation**, or enhanced performance in the presence of others, was supported by a number of subsequent studies in human beings and also in many animal species (Dashiell, 1930; Travis, 1925). It was thought to be a basic, pervasive phenomenon.

But when conflicting evidence appeared, psychologists began to doubt that social facilitation always worked to improve performance. It was found that people actually took longer to solve complex problems and made more mistakes when they worked on the same task in the presence of one another (Allport, 1920), and that it took people longer to learn a complex maze when other people were around (Pessin and Husband, 1933). Similar experiments with animals were also ambiguous. Social facilitation appeared among animals that ate or drank in the presence of others: for example, a chicken allowed to eat grain until it would eat no more began eating again when it was joined by a hungry chicken (Bayer, 1929). But animals became slow at learning mazes when in groups. Furthermore, a solitary cockroach found its way through a maze much more rapidly than did pairs or groups of three cockroaches (Gates and Allee, 1933). In sum, social facilitation occurred when people or other animals worked on simple tasks or on tasks they had already mastered, but their performance worsened on complex tasks or on tasks that required them to learn new skills.

Seemingly, the findings were chaotic. Yet there was a consistency in these results that allowed psychologists to sort out the confusion. Researchers had found, in other human and animal studies, that motivation in itself also affected performance, sometimes helping it and sometimes hindering it. Zajonc (1965) made a connection between these findings and the findings in the social facilitation experiments.

The Concept of Dominant Response

The behaviorist Kenneth Spence had discovered that the differences in performance that emerge when motivation, drive, or arousal is varied are not random but quite systematic. He noted that when an individual's motivation increases, his or her performance on simple tasks improves—but performance on complex tasks deteriorates. He explained these results by invoking the concept of dominant response. **Dominant responses** are those that have been extremely well learned and are therefore most likely to be made by an organism in a given situation. For example, eating may be the dominant response when food is placed before a hungry or greedy animal, and escape may be the dominant response when an animal is threatened. In simple tasks the dominant responses are mainly correct, but when the individual is learning a new skill, such as riding a bicycle, the dominant responses are mainly wrong. Zajonc inquired: What happens when we are learning in the presence of another person? Apparently, the presence of someone else has an arousing effect, and when we are aroused, our dominant responses are enhanced. These responses will be more likely to occur and to occur more often, and each response will be more intense than it is when our arousal ebbs.

Since our dominant responses are mostly wrong when we are learning a new task, and mostly right when we are performing a task we have already mastered, the presence of others should impede learning but improve performance on well-learned tasks. Most research on social facilitation has supported this explanation (Bond and Titus, 1983; Geen and Hange, 1977; Zajonc, 1965). When people work at tasks in the presence of observers, their palms sweat, a sign of arousal (Martens, 1969). Further, although the presence of others interferes with performance when a person is just beginning to learn to trace the path through a maze with a finger, once the individual has mastered the maze, the presence of others improves speed and proficiency (Hunt and Hillery, 1973). The presence of others leads to many errors when a maze is complex, but fewer errors when a maze is simple.

Arousal in Social Facilitation

What is the nature of the arousal underlying social facilitation? One possibility is that the presence of spectators or other individuals working on the same task leads to apprehension: the person may become concerned about the way others might evaluate him or her (Cottrell, 1972). But research indicates that apprehension about other people's evaluation is not always a necessary factor in social facilitation. In one study (Markus, 1978), students who thought they were waiting to take part in an experiment were asked to change their clothes in order to resemble other subjects in the group. The students changed their outer garments either in a room by themselves or in a room occupied by a technician, who sat with his back to the students and appeared to be absorbed in repairing a piece of electronic equipment. When the students were taking off or putting on their own clothes (a well-learned task with correct dominant responses), the presence of the technician speeded their responses. But when the students were putting on the unfamiliar coats and shoes (a relatively unfamiliar task), the presence of the technician slowed their responses. This finding was surprising: after all, the simple task of changing clothes in the presence of an uninterested worker of the same sex would seem unlikely to make the students fear that they were being evaluated. Yet the students' performance showed the effects of both social facilitation and interference from the presence of others.

It turns out, however, that in some situations, evaluation apprehension *is* a significant factor. In a recent field study at the University of California in Santa Barbara, researchers timed male and female runners as they covered two 45-yard segments of a footpath (Worringham and Messick, 1983). Twelve of the runners ran both segments by themselves; another dozen ran the first segment alone, but as they ran the second segment they were watched by a woman seated on the grass near the path. A third set of twelve runners also ran the first segment alone, but as they ran the second segment, they passed a woman who sat facing away from them, engrossed in a book. Running speed during the second segment increased in just one group: the group that had been observed by the woman sitting near the path. Since all the groups were unaware that they were being timed, only the group watched by the woman could have been concerned that they were being evaluated.

CONFORMITY

Social facilitation is the simplest form of social influence; its effects are primitive because it merely slows down or speeds up behavior. In social facilitation the *direction* of behavior does not change, and the mere presence of others does not lead to the acquisition of new habits or to the extinction of old ones. By contrast, other forms of social influence that we hardly notice have more complex effects on us.

Two of these more complex forms of social influence have been of special interest. One is the way in which social pressure can induce a person to conform to a prevailing attitude or perception. The other is the process that leads people to obey commands from authoritative sources, even when it means violating their own moral standards. For example, most Americans insist that they would never have supported Adolf Hitler if they had lived in Germany during World War II. Yet millions of Germans did, and these people were not unusual in any significant respect—not particularly weak or especially open to suggestion. They were simply ordinary people, responding to extraordinary circumstances in what was apparently a very ordinary way.

Individual Conformity to Norms

The norms of a culture are social forces that exert a powerful, although often unrecognized, influence toward conformity. A **norm** is a shared standard of behavior, a guideline people follow in their relations with others. It is difficult to imagine much behavior that is not affected by social norms —the food we eat, the clothes we wear, the books we read, the movies we see, the music we listen to, the religious and political beliefs we hold, the people we like and dislike, and the way we work. If you wrote down all your behavior that is not influenced by these social factors, you would produce a tiny list, limited mostly to physiological functions. Even physiological functions, in fact, are socially influenced. For example, cultural influences determine how human wastes are eliminated, where this is done, and the hygienic rules governing the process. In some cultures elimination is a more shameful act than in others, but all cultures have norms about its conduct and train children to comply with them. For example, a child in North Africa soon learns never to put food in the mouth with the left hand because that hand is reserved for toilet functions.

Conformity to norms is the result of implicit or explicit social pressure; it can be defined as the tendency to shift one's views or behavior closer to the norms expressed by other people. When you conform, it is not necessarily because you are convinced that what you are saying or doing is right. You may simply take a particular public stance because you believe that others prefer, or even demand, that you do so.

In some cultures (for example, China or Japan), conformity has a relatively positive connotation; in the United States, conformity to less important social norms tends to be regarded as slavish imitation. Yet despite the negative connotation conformity has in this culture, norms often serve important social functions. They protect weaker members of the community and promote social integration; they assure that vital social processes, such as procreation, mating, distribution of goods, succession of authority, and preservation of property, are carried out in an orderly way, without conflict or strife.

The behavior most important to the community is generally regulated by law. Of course, law forbids us to kill, rob, or pillage, but it also ensures conformity in less critical behavior. The law forces us to go to school until we are sixteen, to pay taxes on our income, to limit ourselves to one spouse at a time, to drive on the right side of the road, and to go no faster than 55 miles per hour. Less important norms are backed by custom. Custom says that we should not break into a line of people who are waiting to buy concert tickets; we should not come to a funeral dressed as a clown; we should not smoke in a house of worship. Some norms, such as shaving or ending a meal with dessert, have functions that are difficult to determine, but even these norms may at one time have had a reasonable purpose.

The degree to which people conform to social norms is generally distributed around the mean of a normal curve: for example, the time at which people take lunch might resemble a normal curve, with the mean at a few minutes after noon. In most cases, the more powerful the social pressures to conform, the more closely people's behavior or belief is distributed around the mean. In cases where society insists on conformity, the frequency distribution rises abruptly, peaks sharply, and then rapidly drops off: the time at which students

Appropriate dress is a social norm that varies from place to place. This runner's outfit will probably slow him down, but he can still run his race. If he tried to dine at an expensive French restaurant, however, he'd be waved away.

arrive for class has a much steeper frequency distribution than the time at which people go to bed.

Of course, conforming behavior is only one aspect of uniformity of behavior, a pattern that has a much wider scope. **Uniformity** of behavior refers to common behavior shared by almost all the members of a given group or community. The fact that almost everyone sleeps lying down is an instance of uniformity, not conformity: society exerts no pressure on the individual to sleep lying down. Biological constraints are responsible for most instances of uniform behavior. By contrast, the special form of uniformity we call conformity derives from the social pressures to which individuals are subjected whenever they try to deviate from the norm.

Accepting prevailing norms is often a constructive form of behavior. Common standards make it possible for us to predict other people's behavior with some accuracy and to communicate with them without misunderstanding. In addition, conformity to norms can provide the necessary emotional support that enables a person to accomplish important goals; it can help him or her give up drugs, for example, or resist tyrannical authority.

Yet some instances of conformity have little to recommend them (Allen, 1965). People may at times renounce a belief they know to be right simply to avoid being out of step with the majority. Voting against a potential club member because other members do not like the candidate's religion and refusing to speak out against a politician because she or he is a local favorite are examples of this kind of conformity.

Conformity in an Ambiguous Case: Sherif's Experiments

There are situations where individual conformity goes beyond matters of belief and custom; social influence can even lead people to question the information received by their senses. In a classical experiment that marked the beginning of conformity research, Muzafer Sherif (1936) used a visual illusion to demonstrate the way people conform to norms even when they make judgments about perceptual phenomena. Sherif used the "autokinetic effect," in which a stationary pinpoint of light, when viewed in total darkness, appears to move. People viewed such lights by themselves and, over the course of many judgments, each arrived at a stable—but different—range of judgments concerning the distance the light "moved." Afterward, several individuals, each with a different pattern of judgment, viewed the light together and judged aloud the distance the light "traveled." In the course of making these judgments, their widely divergent estimates converged until they resembled one another closely.

The situation in this experiment differs sub- stantially from that found in social facilitation. In social facilitation, the effect is caused by the mere presence of others—their behavior provides no reinforcement and furnishes no cues as to appropriate responses. In the conformity experiment, however, the person does receive information from others. Although she or he is not required to use this information as a guide to behavior, it is available. If the person feels any compulsion to follow it, social influence has exerted an effect.

In Sherif's experiments, people who viewed the light together from the beginning made similar judgments during the first session. And people who started by making their judgments in groups, but then watched the light by themselves, were found to have adopted the social norm as their own—they persisted in giving approximately the same estimates that had been developed within the group.

Conformity in an Unambiguous Case: Asch's Experiments

Some psychologists doubted that Sherif's experiments had demonstrated the power of conformity, because the situation was so ambiguous and each viewer so uncertain of her or his judgments that the viewers eagerly accepted the only available information—the judgments of other subjects. One of those who doubted the significance of Sherif's results was Solomon Asch. Asch thought that if people could judge unambiguous stimuli under optimal conditions, the sort of convergence Sherif had found would not appear. Individuals who shifted their opinions when the facts were uncertain would not be moved when faced with reality, Asch believed. But when he tested his proposal with male college students, the results surprised him (Asch, 1951).

Each student was told that he was participating in an experiment on visual judgment in which he would compare the lengths of lines. He would be shown two white cards: one card with a single vertical line (the standard), and another with three vertical lines of different lengths (see Figure 27.1). The alleged experimental task was to determine which of the three lines on the second card was the same length as the standard.

The student sat in a room with seven other apparent subjects who were actually Asch's confederates. After unanimous judgments on the first two sets of cards, the third set was shown. Al-

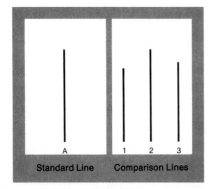

Figure 27.1. The stimuli in a single trait in Asch's experiment. The subject must state which of the comparison lines he judges to be the same length as the standard. The discrimination is an easy one to make: control subjects (those who made the judgments without any group pressure) chose line 2 as correct over 99 percent of the time.

though the correct response was obviously line 2, the first confederate declared that line 1 matched the standard. In turn, the other six confederates agreed—and with great certainty. Now the true subject was faced with a dilemma. His eyes told him that line 2 was the correct choice, but six other people had unanimously and confidently selected line 1. Confronted with a solid—but obviously wrong—majority, almost one-third of the fifty people Asch tested bowed to social influence and conformed with the obviously incorrect choice at least half the time.

Conformity to Social Roles: Zimbardo's Experiment

Social conformity of a different sort was studied when Zimbardo, Haney, and Banks (1973) advertised in newspapers for volunteers to take part in a mock prison experiment. The volunteers were randomly assigned roles as prisoners and guards. Both groups were placed in the basement of the Stanford University psychology building and given minimal instructions: they were told to assume their assigned roles and that the guards' job was to "maintain law and order." In only a few hours the behavior of one group had become sharply differentiated from the behavior of the other group, as each conformed to what was considered the "appropriate" social role. The "guards" had adopted behavior patterns and attitudes that are typical

of guards in maximum security prisons, with most of them becoming abusive and aggressive. Most of the "prisoners" had become passive, dependent, and depressed, although some became enraged at the guards. The suffering among the "prisoners" was so great that one had to be released in less than thirty-six hours; several other "prisoners" also had to be released before the experiment, intended to run for two weeks, was ended after six days.

Factors Influencing Conformity

What accounts for conformity in cases where we go against the evidence of our senses to conform? Part of the conformity that appeared in Asch's research may lie in situational factors built into the experimental design. For one thing, the judgments of the confederates were unanimous; not one of them hinted that another answer might be possible. By varying the basic experiment, Asch found that the extent of agreement was an important influence. When just one confederate gave the correct answer, thus offering implicit support for the test subject's "unpopular" view, the proportion of subjects who conformed dropped dramatically—from 32 percent to 5 percent. It appears that a single voice raised in opposition to an otherwise unanimous judgment can have a remarkable effect. Others who may be leaning toward a dissenting view but are not sure that they should express it may decide to assert themselves against the majority.

Another situational factor that influenced the conformity Asch found was the requirement that his subjects interact face to face with the confederates. Later research showed that when people can respond anonymously, they conform less often (Deutsch and Gerard, 1965).

However, the Asch experiments also included situational factors that might have actually lowered the pressure to conform. The confederates were complete strangers to the subject, with no special claim on her or his loyalty or affection. The subject had never seen them before and probably would never see them again. Consequently, she or he had little reason to fear that nonconformity would have social repercussions. The existence of this situational factor, which would logically reduce the pressure to conform, has led some psychologists to conclude that Asch's work revealed only the tip of the conformity iceberg. If the pressure to conform among strangers is so strong, it seems likely that the pressure to conform among friends is far stronger.

Social pressure to conform with inaccurate visual judgments has some limits. To assess the relative influence of social and perceptual factors, investigators (Jacobs and Campbell, 1961) subjected several "generations" of subjects to the autokinetic effect and observed the transfer of norms from one generation to the next. The first subject was led into a dark room where there were two confederates instructed to announce that the pinpoint of light moved 15 or 16 inches. (When there were no other cues and no other individuals making judgments, the average distance of the light's apparent movement was about 3½ inches.) The confederates made their judgments first. After the two confederates and the subject had judged the movement, one of the confederates was thanked for participating and replaced by a new subject. Now there were two true subjects and only one confederate. After the second set of judgments, the last confederate was replaced by a third subject, leaving no one with instructions to make obviously false judgments. On the fourth set of judgments the first naive subject was replaced by a new subject and this procedure was continued for ten generations of subjects. As shown in Figure 27.2, in the presence of confederates, subjects judged the light to make large movements, but as the confederates were replaced by true subjects, social influence decreased and perceptual influences became increasingly powerful. The judgments of the final generation were the same as those of subjects in a control group who had never been exposed to erroneous judgments.

Minority Influence

The results of conformity research bring to mind the words of John Stuart Mill, who spoke of the "tyranny of the majority," which necessarily imposes its will on the dissenting minority. Yet history provides plentiful evidence that over time minorities can change majority views. If this were not so, the United States would still be a slaveholding society, women would not be able to vote, and prohibition would not have come and gone in the land. The minority is always viewed as "dissenting"; yet researchers have wondered whether a majority and a minority exert similar social influence by means of similar processes.

The effect of majority and minority influence shows itself in different ways. The French social psychologist Serge Moscovici (1980) noted that when individuals find themselves in situations that demand conformity, their private reactions are often changed more by minority influence than by the influence of the majority. The majority is powerful in producing public compliance, in which the individual's *behavior* changes to meet

Figure 27.2. In a study using the autokinetic effect, social influences were gradually overcome by perceptual factors, but it required ten "generations" of subjects before judgments of a light's apparent motion were the same as those of a control group who had never come under social pressure to conform. (After Jacobs and Campbell, 1961.)

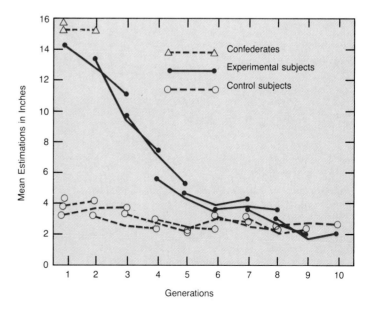

pressures to conform. But at the same time the minority often induces the individual to accept its view privately, so that people's private *attitudes* shift away from the majority position.

In a study of opinion concerning gay rights (Maass and Clark, 1983), researchers found that people's private attitudes moved toward the minority position at the same time that their public expression of attitudes followed the usual pattern of conformity to the majority view. (Expressing attitudes is, of course, a form of behavior.) In another study (Nemeth and Wachtler, 1983), the presence of a dissenting minority in a group problem-solving situation had a latent effect on an individual's subsequent private efforts to solve the problem. Individuals who had been exposed to a minority were more likely to find new solutions later and to look at the problem differently than those who had worked on their own throughout the experiment or had been exposed only to the majority view.

The moderating influence of a minority on later behavior has also been demonstrated in a study of jury decisions (Nemeth and Wachtler, 1984). Subjects who served in a mock jury, charged with deciding personal injury cases, seemed unmoved by a confederate who consistently advocated lower compensation for the victim than the majority believed was warranted. But on later personal injury cases, the influence of the minority confederate became clear. Subjects who had been ex-

posed to a minority confederate in the first case —even though they had conformed to the majority in their judgment—tended to award significantly lower compensation on later cases than subjects who had not been exposed to a minority confederate.

In all these studies researchers have assumed that the process by which minorities and majorities influence attitudes is different. Presumably, the influence of the majority is potent because of the majority's strength, immediacy, and number. By contrast, the influence of the minority presumably is effective because the minority's dissenting position makes them stand out against the crowd and attract attention, and because the minority's willingness to go against the majority proves their conviction and consistency. Seeing the minority's position, observers may be thrown into a state of cognitive dissonance (see Chapters 12 and 25) and rethink their beliefs. However, Bibb Latané and Sharon Wolf (1981) question these distinctions. They propose that the conviction and consistency of the minority simply make them appear to be stronger and more immediate in the eyes of others. According to Latané and Wolf, all social influence operates through the same factors: the strength, immediacy, and the size of the group.

As we saw in the discussion of attribution theory (Chapter 26), when someone behaves in a way that conflicts with our expectations concerning that person's role or personality, we tend to

Those demonstrating against a majority position gain influence when people in the majority begin to question their own beliefs. These women were part of an ongoing demonstration at a Cruise missile site in Greenham, England.

view the person as an especially credible source of information. The "deviant" action tells us something about the individual—perhaps about his or her convictions. The action emphasizes the strength of the person's belief, and we infer that the grounds for his or her action are valid. When this happens, we may take the minority view more seriously. It may appear to us as a carefully considered opinion that deserves further analysis—and even adoption.

Obedience to Authority

The key conflicts that emerged between the "prisoners" and "guards" in Zimbardo's experiment concerned obedience, behavior that can in some circumstances be destructive. "When you think of the long and gloomy history of man," wrote C. P. Snow (1961), "you will find more hideous crimes have been committed in the name of obedience than have been committed in the name of rebellion." **Obedience** is any behavior that complies with the explicit commands of a person in authority. The Spanish Inquisition, the Salem witch hunts, the Nazi war crimes, the massacre of Vietnamese civilians at My Lai, the mass suicides at Jonestown are historical examples of inhumane behavior resulting from obedience to authority.

Needless to say, obedience does not always have destructive results. Compliance with the demands of parents and teachers, for example, is an important part of developing into a mature, responsible adult. And compliance with the law is essential if any society is to function successfully. Nevertheless, most of the research on obedience has focused on the negative consequences of unquestioning compliance, in the hope of discovering how such destructive acts as atrocities committed during wartime could have come to pass.

Milgram's Experiments

The most dramatic and extensive investigation of obedience was conducted by Stanley Milgram (1974), who studied men of all ages and from a wide range of occupations. Each subject was paid to take part in what he was told was a study of the effects of punishment on learning. The experimenter, dressed in a white laboratory coat, instructed each subject to read a list of word pairs to a "learner" (really a confederate of the experiment-

er) whose task it was to memorize them. The learner was taken into an adjacent room, out of the subject's sight, for the duration of the experiment. Every time the learner made a mistake, the subject was to punish him by administering a shock from an impressive-looking shock generator (which, of course, was not connected). The generator had thirty clearly marked voltage levels, with switches ranging from 15 to 450 volts and labels ranging from "Slight Shock" to "Danger: Severe Shock." Whenever the learner made a mistake, the subject was to increase the voltage by one level and administer the shock.

Acting under instructions, the learners made many errors, necessitating increasingly severe shocks. When the shock level reached 300 volts, the learner pounded on the wall in protest and then fell silent. At this point, the experimenter instructed the subject to treat the silence as a wrong answer and to raise the voltage. If the subject ever asked to stop the experiment, the researcher sternly told him to go on.

Our obedience to authority is greater than most people believe. Psychiatrists, college students, and middle-class adults consulted by Milgram believed that virtually all subjects would break off the experiment before the dangerous shock levels were reached. Yet among forty subjects, twenty-six, or 65 percent, continued to obey the experimenter to the very end (see Figure 27.3). These subjects were not sadists. Many of them showed signs of extreme anxiety during the session, and they frequently told the experimenter that they wanted to stop. But despite their distress, most of them continued to obey the experimenter's commands. (At the time these experiments were conducted, the present strict guidelines for the protection of human subjects, discussed in Chapter 2, did not exist.)

Factors Influencing Obedience

Many factors influence the extent to which people will obey authority, especially when obedience means acting against their own moral standards. Of first importance is whether the person giving instructions is viewed as a legitimate authority. From the time we are children, we are taught that certain people can, by virtue of their social position, legitimately expect compliance with their wishes. When a police officer orders a driver to pull over to the side of the road or a physician requests that a patient undress, people usually do as they

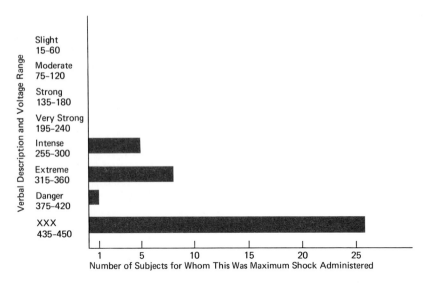

Figure 27.3. Results of Stanley Milgram's classic experiment on obedience. Subjects were told to administer increasing amounts of shock to a "learner" on the pretext that scientists were studying the effects of punishment on learning. Of forty experimental subjects, all administered shocks scaled "intense" or higher, and only fourteen refused to go all the way to the most severe, "XXX" shock level. (After Milgram, 1963.)

are told. Indeed, the sight of a person in uniform is often enough to prompt compliance. In one experiment (Bickman, 1974), researchers approached people on the streets of New York City and ordered them either to pick up a paper bag or to give a dime to a stranger. Half the researchers were dressed in neat street clothes, half in guard uniforms. Less than 40 percent of the subjects obeyed the "civilian," but more than 80 percent obeyed the "guard," even when he walked away after delivering the order and could not see whether they complied.

Gender may also affect obedience. As we saw in Chapter 25, research has confirmed the popular belief that women are more susceptible to influence than men. According to Alice Eagly (1973), this difference is rooted in inequalities of social status. Men are more likely to occupy high-status roles in society, and occupations dominated by men (such as physician) generally have higher status than occupations dominated by women (such as nurse). Eagly points out that this susceptibility, which begins in social roles, spills over into informal social groups because our expectations tend to set up a self-fulfilling prophecy (see Chapter 26), but that it disappears when women have high-status positions. For example, the woman physician or corporate executive is seen to have as much authority and influence as her male counterpart. It appears that women are more compliant than men, not because they are women, but because they have lower status and authority.

Another situational factor that affects obedience is the degree of face-to-face contact. In Milgram's original experiment (1963), the experimenter's presence encouraged compliance. Obedience dropped sharply (from 65 percent to 22 percent) in an experimental variation (1965) in which the experimenter did not remain in the room with the subject, but left the laboratory after issuing instructions and gave subsequent orders by telephone. As in the defiance of group norms, disobedience to authority seems easier when people do not have to confront authority directly.

Milgram also found that increasing the proximity of the subject to the victim increased the likelihood that the subject would defy authority. In his original study, Milgram's subjects did not see their victim, and the only audible protest was the pounding on the wall. However, when subjects were placed closer and closer to the victim, compliance dropped. In one condition, although the victim was in another room, the subject could hear the groans escalate to screams as the shocks were increased. In another arrangement, the victim and subject were in the same room—seated only eighteen inches apart. In the final condition, the subject was required to force the victim's hand onto the shock plate to administer punishment. The maximum shock delivered by subjects decreased steadily as contact with the victim increased. When the victim was remote, subjects apparently found it easier to deny the pain they were inflicting. As such denial became less possible, the victim's suffering exerted greater influence in the struggle between individual conscience and authority.

Social support for defiance is another factor

that increases people's resistance to authority. In a test of this factor (Milgram, 1965), the subject was teamed with two other "subjects" who were actually the experimenter's confederates. After the shock level had reached 150 volts, one of the confederates announced he would not continue and took a seat in another part of the room. After 210 volts, the second confederate refused to go any farther. Although the experimenter ordered the true subjects to continue, only 10 percent of them did so.

In this last condition, people were forced to choose between obedience to authority and conformity to their peers. The fact that 90 percent chose to conform to the more socially acceptable actions of their peers should not lead us to be complacent about resistance to authority. Some one person must always be first to resist, and in life, no confederates will lead the way. Also, penalties inflicted in the world for disobedience may be far more severe than the disapproval of an unknown experimenter.

The tendency toward conformity and obedience so dramatically demonstrated in the laboratory and in natural settings may strike some people as alarming. But conformity and obedience are neither good nor bad in and of themselves. They are facts of social behavior and can lead to either desirable or undesirable outcomes. Milgram believed that as we come to understand such submission better, we may learn to avoid it when necessary.

Hidden Influence

Demands for obedience and pressure for conformity to norms are not the only ways people can be made to comply. People can also be manipulated into behaving in specific ways through a variety of subtle and insidious means (see the box on page 658). On the streets of New York, a man made a successful living in selling watches at twice their cost. He paid $11 for each watch and then sold it at $22. Though $22 was a legitimate selling price, it was no bargain. But the man's watches sold like ice water in the Sahara desert—because he used a manipulative trick. He came up to each prospective buyer and offered him or her a "hot" watch for only $22. The buyers thought they were getting an expensive, stolen watch and eagerly handed over the money for this great "bargain."

One subtle way of securing compliance is by doing someone a favor. In American society we have a "rule of reciprocity," which demands that we repay in kind what someone does for us (Cialdini, 1984). So when someone does us a favor, we feel an obligation toward him or her. This rule was explored in a study at Cornell University (Regan, 1971). While a subject waited between two phases of a psychological experiment, another waiting subject (who was a confederate of the researcher) left the room for a couple of minutes and came back with two bottles of Coca-Cola. The confederate said that he had asked the researcher if it was all right to have a cold drink, and added, "He said it was okay, so I bought one for you, too." After the experiment was apparently completed, the confederate asked the subject to buy some raffle tickets on a new car. The subjects who had been given a Coca-Cola bought twice as many raffle tickets as subjects who had waited with the confederate but had not been given a Coke. The next time an airport solicitor gives you a flower and then asks for a donation to a charity or religious organization, remember the Coca-Cola experiment.

Another subtle way of securing compliance is the "foot-in-the door" technique, which was discussed in Chapter 2. With this technique, agreement to a trivial request opens the door to agreement to a much larger request. In one study (Freedman and Fraser, 1966), people agreed to display a tiny three-inch sign reading BE A SAFE DRIVER on their houses. A few weeks later, researchers asked these people to display a large, ugly sign saying DRIVE CAREFULLY on their front lawns. Only 24 percent refused; yet among people who had never been approached to display the small sign and so had not allowed the researchers to get a "foot in the door," 83 percent refused to comply. Many forms of hidden influence gain their power through a series of similar small steps. The people in Jonestown who committed mass suicide at the request of the Reverend Jim Jones had earlier complied with his many smaller but ever-growing requests. Each new request was progressively more serious and required more extensive compliance, so that when Jones asked the people to commit suicide, the action seemed only slightly less abhorrent than the last one they had complied with.

In countries that depend on their citizens' conformity and obedience, governments can use a variety of methods to produce compliance, ranging from cleverly orchestrated maneuvers to

Hidden Influence in Daily Life

When we dine at a fine restaurant, buy a car, purchase a new home, or donate money to charity, we are often the unwitting victims of hidden influence (see text). The social psychologist Robert Cialdini (1984) has studied a range of social influence by infiltrating various spheres of everyday life, such as shops, fundraising organizations, advertising, and the world of con artists.

In these settings Cialdini has observed and recorded a number of effective and subtle methods of influence. While he was working as a waiter, for example, he discovered a clever trick that guarantees high tips. First, the waiter identifies the person at the table who is likely to pay the bill. Then, when that person is handed the menu, the waiter whispers confidentially that one of the dishes—usually the most expensive one—is not up to par that day and recommends that it be avoided. Now the waiter has become a trusted advisor, and his or his suggestion of an expensive wine is heeded. Because of this "useful" and "honest" advice, the waiter is seen as deserving a larger-

than-usual tip, which is further inflated because the customer ordered an expensive wine.

Another common technique that ensures compliance is the "low ball." It is based on the fact that after a person has made a decision, he or she tends to bolster it by finding additional reasons to justify the choice; once this process is completed, a change of mind becomes difficult. Professional salespeople and con artists know that once a prospective buyer has made a commitment, he or she will find it difficult to back out of the deal, even when it suddenly becomes unattractive. When Cialdini posed as a sales trainee at a Chevrolet dealership, he noticed that experienced salesmen frequently offered the customer a bargain price, sometimes as much as four hundred dollars below the competitor's price. Although the offer was not genuine, it induced the person to decide to buy the car. Then, after the customer had decided to buy the car, the salesman set up a delay before signing the contract: purchase forms had to be filled out, financing had to

be arranged. The customer was often encouraged to drive the car a day while this process was being completed.

These activities furnished the customer with new reasons for having chosen the car, further bolstering the original choice. Suddenly, the deal would change. Sometimes the dealer discovered an "error" in the calculations: the salesman had forgotten to include the cost of the air conditioner, which added four hundred dollars to the car's price. At other times, the price was changed at the last minute: the boss rejected the salesman's price as so low the firm would lose money.

In these low-ball techniques, which exist in all spheres of life, an unusually attractive advantage is offered, and the "victim" bolsters his or her decision. Then, and just before the deal is consummated, the original advantage is deftly removed. The person still finds the purchase attractive, and he or she reasons that four hundred dollars is meaningless in a transaction involving several thousand dollars.

threats of severe punishment. For example, the workers' revolution that took place in Poland in 1980 was a movement of immense proportions: 10 million Poles deliberately defied their government at the risk of severe punishment. This movement was so massive it could not be brought down immediately, for the government had no way to imprison 10 million people. Yet within two years the movement was rendered ineffective and powerless.

How did the Polish government succeed in

destroying the resistance embodied in Solidarność ("Solidarity," the group that spearheaded the movement)? To begin with, the government cut off communication and sowed distrust among the rebels. On imposing marital law, the government's first major act was to block all private telephone lines, curtail postal service, and restrict travel. An early curfew was imposed so that people could not visit one another. And the only information Poles received was what the government chose to release and whatever thin gossip developed. Thus, the communication that would have been vital for coordinating action was virtually wiped out.

Moreover, in order to destroy people's mutual support for risky acts of defiance, the government propagated distrust. Not all of the Solidarność leaders and members were taken to prison, and many who were detained were released shortly after arrest—without apparent reason. Among people who had supported the movement, some who had committed offenses were imprisoned but others were not; among those taken to prison, some were released almost immediately. The effects were devastating. Under such conditions, when there is no access to reliable information, rumors and suspicions are rife. People began asking themselves, "Why has Mr. X not been arrested? I thought he was deeply involved in such and such a strike. Is he an 'agent provocateur'? Is he a spy? Why was Ms. Y released so soon? Is she to be trusted? What deal did she make with the police?" At the same time, the government kept economic pressures at the highest level, along with threats of punishment for antigovernment and antiparty activities. Before long, the movement was broken and 10 million defiant citizens had become obedient.

Helping

Most forms of conformity to norms are not very costly to the individual, nor do they cause particular suffering or demand effort. But there is one norm that may place the conforming person in direct danger. The norm of helping, that is, performing any act intended to benefit another individual, can require a person to save another's life at the cost of his or her own. Because helping is a special case of conformity, it is treated separately. Although many forms of helping are brought about by the pressures of ordinary social norms, some forms of helping appear universally and are believed to have a possible biological basis.

As we saw in Chapter 4, altruistic acts are those helping acts that offer no obvious rewards: making an anonymous donation to charity is altruistic, but making the same donation to secure a tax deduction is not. Risking one's life to rescue a child from a burning building is altruistic; risking one's life to earn applause from the crowd on the street is not. Although the altruistic

person may experience internal satisfaction, the motive is to help someone else in need. In addition, to be considered altruistic, an act must be intentional. Accidentally frightening a mugger away from a victim is not altruistic behavior.

Both animals and human beings behave in altruistic ways, and altruism appears to have both social and biological bases. According to the socio-biological view, which was discussed in Chapter 4, members of certain species are genetically programmed to help one another (Dawkins, 1975; Wilson, 1975). The problem with altruism is that in performing an altruistic act, an animal may have to give up its own life. But according to the concept of inclusive fitness, such an act (which removes any chance that the individual will have offspring) allows part of an individual's genes to survive by increasing the chances of survival among the individual's relatives. In this view, the individual has a greater "interest" in the persistence of its own genes than in its own life.

It is possible that such a view *may* apply to some lower animal species. And, conceivably, some forms of dangerous altruistic behavior among humans *might* be explained by these concepts. But human altruism does not quite fit these notions, and its validity among human beings has not been established. Indeed, many social scientists reject the proposition that inclusive fitness explains human altruism, for the same reason that they reject the instinct theory of human aggression. This proposition, they say, is based on questionable analogies between human and animal behavior; it ignores the role that learning plays in human social interaction, and it cannot explain variations of behavior within and between people.

In an attempt to get around some of these problems, Robert Trivers (1971) introduced the notion of **reciprocal altruism**, proposing that when a person performs an altruistic act, saving another from danger, he or she increases the chances that the person who is helped will reciprocate and may one day help either the helper or the helper's kin. If so, no direct reinforcement for the altruistic act is required—any reinforcement can be delayed. But whether or not altruism has a genetic base, there is little doubt that human beings acquire specific altruistic behavior through modeling and reinforcement. The problem for social psychologists is to explain the circumstances that evoke such behavior.

On July 31, 1983, in St. Louis, a thirteen-year-

True altruism is motivated by the wish to help another person. Here, two policemen with little regard for extreme danger risk their lives to keep a 92-year-old woman from ending hers.

old girl was raped by two youths. Several people stood by without coming to her aid; then an eleven-year-old boy rode off on his bike to get the police. This was not the first time such a thing has happened. More than twenty years ago a young woman named Kitty Genovese was savagely attacked outside her apartment building in Queens, a borough of New York City, at 3:00 A.M. She screamed for help, and although thirty-eight neighbors came to their windows, not one offered assistance. No one even called the police. The attack lasted more than thirty minutes while Kitty Genovese was attacked, stabbed, and finally killed. The murder caused a sensation, and press accounts wondered how people could be so indifferent to the fate of another human being. Many saw it as an example of the city dweller's reluctance to "get involved." Yet investigation revealed that the witnesses to the woman's murder had been far from indifferent. Her neighbors watched her ordeal transfixed, "unable to act but unwilling to turn away" (Latané and Darley, 1976, pp. 309–310).

Why do bystanders often fail to help in such

circumstances? After conducting numerous studies in an attempt to understand this phenomenon, researchers have discovered that dispositional factors alone cannot explain a person's decision not to intervene. Rather, bystanders' reactions seem to be related to several powerful situational factors. One such study was conducted by Bibb Latané and John Darley (1976). After staging a number of "emergencies" and recording the responses of bystanders, Latané and Darley concluded that the presence of other bystanders inhibits would-be altruistic bystanders from intervening to help. Latané and Darley offer three possible explanations for the failure of bystanders to respond.

The first is **audience inhibition**. When other people are present, we think twice because we are concerned about their evaluation of our behavior. Emergencies are often ambiguous. Smoke pouring from a building might signal a fire or it might be normal incinerator fumes; cries of help from the next apartment might be genuine or they might be coming from the neighbor's television set. Offering aid when none is wanted or needed places the altruistic bystander in an embarrassing situation, and the embarrassment is compounded by the presence of others who have realized that no emergency exists.

Social influence (on the interpretation of the situation), the second factor, also prevents individuals from intervening: when others are present, each person waits for the others to define the situation as an emergency by their actions. While searching for a clue as to whether the situation is serious or not, everyone tries to appear calm and collected. The result is that each bystander is taken in by the others' nonchalance and led—or misled—to define the situation as a nonemergency.

When other people are present, the need for any one individual to act seems lessened and there is a **diffusion of responsibility**. An onlooker assumes that there may be a doctor or police officer or friend or relative of the victim among the bystanders who is qualified to give aid; the sense of personal responsibility is diminished, and the onlooker can leave the scene without feeling guilty.

Latané and Darley's findings suggest that bystanders are least likely to act if all three forces

—audience inhibition, social influence, and diffusion of responsibility—are operating (see Figure 27.4). One of their experiments confirms this belief. Men who thought they were participating in a study of repression sat in cubicles equipped with television monitors and cameras; while the experimenter ostensibly went to check some equipment, the subjects filled out a questionnaire. As the men worked on their questionnaires, the experimenter staged an elaborate performance. He entered the room with the equipment and innocently picked up two wires. Immediately he screamed, threw himself in the air, hit a wall, and crashed to the floor. A few seconds later he began to moan softly. As Latané and Darley predicted, the willingness of the subjects to help the experimenter seemed to depend on the number of social forces at work.

Among those subjects who believed they were alone in the situation, 95 percent intervened almost immediately, but among those who thought that an unseen person in another cubicle had also witnessed the accident, altruism dropped to 84 percent. In this case, the difference can be attributed to diffusion of responsibility. When other

Figure 27.4. As this "decision tree" indicates, in an emergency a bystander must: (1) notice that something is happening; (2) interpret it as an emergency; and (3) decide that he or she has a personal responsibility to intervene. But the presence of others complicates this process: the presence of strangers may prevent us from concluding that the situation is an emergency; group behavior may lead us to define the situation as one that does not require action; and when other people are there to share the burden of responsibility, we may not feel obligated to aid. Thus, the more witnesses to an emergency, the less aid the victim is likely to receive. This combination of factors was what inhibited Kitty Genovese's neighbors from helping her. (After Latané and Darley, 1976.)

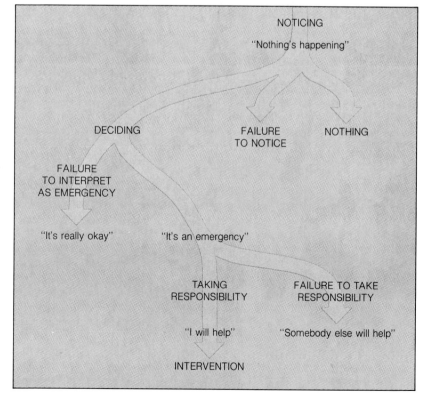

factors were added to the experimental situation, the rate of intervention decreased further. If subjects could see another person (a confederate of the experimenter) whose lack of response indicated that an emergency might not exist (social influence), or if they thought that someone was watching them (social inhibition), 73 percent offered to help. When the subject could see the confederate and believed that the confederate could also see the subject, so that all three factors affected the subject's behavior, only 50 percent of the subjects came to the experimenter's assistance.

Studies such as this are very persuasive, but under certain conditions the presence of others does not prevent bystanders from offering assistance. When bystanders have clear evidence of an emergency, the inhibiting effects of others are weakened. For example, if bystanders can gauge one another's reactions through nonverbal cues, they are likely to come to the aid of an apparent accident victim. In one experiment (Darley, Teger,

Emergencies are not the only setting for helping behavior. As we mature, helping others becomes intrinsically rewarding. Here, a grandson helps his feeble grandfather.

and Lewis, 1973), half the subjects were seated directly opposite a second subject and so could see that person's startled reaction to the sound of a heavy object falling, followed by a nearby worker's groans. In this situation, nonverbal behavior defined the event as an emergency, and subjects responded as often and as quickly as those who were alone when they heard the accident occur. And when bystanders make up a cohesive group (friends, club members, fellow employees), the larger the group, the more likely it is that someone will help, because cohesiveness among bystanders brings the norm of social responsibility to the attention of group members (Rutkowski, Gruder, and Romer, 1983).

AGGRESSION

Helping others is a universal act of conformity with clear social benefits. Its opposite, hurting others, is also universal, but it has clear social costs. Any act that is intended to cause pain, damage, or suffering to another person is an act of interpersonal **aggression**. The key attribute of an aggressive act is the intention: to be considered aggressive, an act must be deliberate—a definition that encompasses verbal attacks, such as insults and slander. Accidental injuries are not considered aggressive.

Aggression is a common feature of contemporary life. News broadcasts invariably mention some aggressive act—murder, rape, muggings, vandalism, political terrorism, or war. The broadcasts reveal alarming facts. In 1983, for example, 1,237,979 Americans were victims of reported crimes (*FBI Uniform Crime Reports*, 1984). Every twenty-five seconds one violent crime is committed in the United States. Unlike helping, aggression is controlled by a profusion of norms. These norms forbid aggression in many situations; some norms specify targets against which aggression is tolerated, but in most instances aggression violates a clear social norm.

Attempts to explain the high levels of aggressive behavior among human beings fall into three categories: biological explanations, social learning explanations, and situational explanations.

Biological Influences on Aggression

The idea that human aggression has a biological basis has a long history and many advocates.

Figure 27.5. Some researchers suggest that there is a biological origin of aggression in the oldest and most primitive parts of the human brain. Evidence from animal and human studies suggests that the hypothalamus and other structures in the temporal lobe (shown in blue) play an important role in mediating aggressive behavior. In some cases, surgical removal of the hypothalamus and amygdala has resulted in complete loss of emotional reactivity. (After Scherer, Abeles, and Fischer, 1975.)

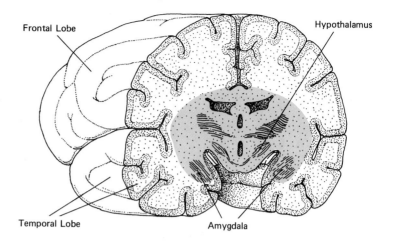

Sigmund Freud, for example, postulated that we are driven to self-destructive and aggressive behavior by a death instinct (*Thanatos*) that is at least as powerful as the life instinct (*Eros*) that impels us toward growth and self-fulfillment. According to Freud, the urge to conquer and kill is never very far beneath the surface, and the balance between our destructive and procreative impulses is, at best, uneasy. Today, psychologists generally consider Freud's concept of a death instinct highly speculative. But the underlying idea —that human aggression has a biological basis —lives on. As yet no evidence for a genetic basis of human aggression has been found. However, such evidence does exist for several animal species, including the mouse, on whose chromosomes specific gene locations for aggression have been isolated (Eleftheriou, Bailley, and Denenberg, 1974).

A number of researchers believe that biological abnormalities can explain why some individuals are especially hot-tempered and violent. For example, instead of the normal forty-six chromosomes, some men convicted of violent crimes have been found to have forty-seven, the extra chromosome being a second Y (male) chromosome (Jarvik, Klodin, and Matsuyama, 1973). Yet genetic abnormalities do not seem to account for the high levels of human aggression. The XYY chromosome pattern is exceedingly rare (it occurs at most once or twice in a thousand births), and many XYY males are upstanding citizens. A study of more than 4,000 Danish men turned up no connection between an XYY chromosome pattern and violent behavior (Witkin et al., 1976).

In other cases, violent behavior has been linked to various types of brain damage, such as an interruption in the flow of blood to the brain (which kills brain cells), injuries to the frontal or temporal lobes from falls or blows to the head, viral infections of the brain, and brain tumors (Mark and Ervin, 1970). As we saw in Chapter 3, some research has linked certain parts of the brain, shown in Figure 27.5, with human aggression. However, even granted the possibility that some damage escapes detection, brain damage cannot explain the incidence of human aggression. An estimated 10 to 15 million Americans suffer from some form of brain injury, but the majority of these people are no more aggressive than anyone else. Of greater importance is the fact that the majority of people with a history of violent behavior have no brain injury at all.

The shortcomings of biological abnormalities as a sufficient explanation of aggression become clear when we examine the case of Paul M. (Mark and Ervin, 1970). Paul admitted himself to Boston City Hospital because he was afraid he was losing his mind and could not control his violent impulses. He had, in fact, "gone wild," pulling plaster off the walls of his apartment, smashing a mirror, and badly gashing his body with a piece of the glass. Examination revealed that Paul was suffering from brain damage. An antiseizure drug was prescribed for him, and his rages stopped. On the surface, Paul's disorder appears purely biological, but a look at his history suggests other causes. One of eight children, Paul was reared in severe poverty. His father and brothers were all hot-tempered, and he was frequently beaten as a child. An older brother who had been arrested three times for armed robbery and aggravated assault was his childhood idol. Clearly, social learning was at least partly responsible for Paul's destructive and explosive behavior.

Social Learning Mechanisms

Most aggressive behavior—whether slashing with a knife, throwing a blow to the chin, setting off a pipe bomb, pulling a trigger, or shouting verbal insults—requires intricate, learned skills (Bandura, 1976). According to social learning theory, exposure to models of violent behavior and reinforcement for aggressive acts explain why people attack one another.

The Importance of Models

By observing others, we learn how and when to perform specific aggressive acts (such as how to fire a gun) as well as general strategies of aggression (such as "Stay on the offensive"). In the American culture, two of the most influential models are family members and the characters portrayed on television and in films.

Parents frequently provide powerful models of aggression for their children. Every year several hundred thousand American children are abused by adults, and some of these children grow up to become child abusers themselves (Kempe and Kempe, 1978). But violent modeling is unnecessary, and most aggressive children do not have criminally violent parents. In subtle ways, law-abiding parents who resort to "acceptable" forms of aggression to solve problems, favor coercive methods of child rearing, and are hostile toward the world in general promote aggressive behavior in their children. Such parents serve as models of aggression, not by their deeds, but by their words and attitudes (Bandura, 1976).

After watching aggressive models, children are most likely to imitate aggression if the model has been live, as Figure 27.6 shows. Nevertheless, films and television are pervasive influences on behavior. As we saw in Chapter 17, researchers have been unable to establish that violent television directly *causes* aggression, but studies consistently show that aggressive people do watch a great deal of violent television (Freedman, 1984).

Concerned by the consistent linkage of televised violence and aggressive behavior, researchers have set about finding ways to weaken the connection (Heusmann et al., 1983). They have developed techniques of intervention that reduce children's tendency to imitate the aggressive behavior they watch on their living room screens. The most promising techniques seem to involve teaching children that televised acts of violence

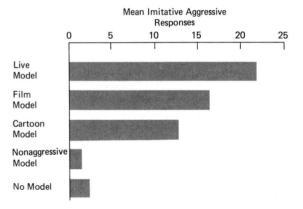

Figure 27.6. Bandura and his colleagues found that live models were more effective than either film models or cartoon characters in eliciting imitative aggressive behavior in children. (After Bandura, 1973.)

are not typical responses, that camera tricks are used to distort behavior in order to intensify its apparent aggressiveness, and that the average person solves personal problems without resorting to aggression.

Despite the possible connection between televised violence and aggression, the media are not responsible for all the violence in contemporary society. People beat, raped, and murdered one another for thousands of years before the invention of television and movies. As we saw in Chapter 8, people do not automatically perform all the behavior they learn through observation. In most cases, the behavior appears when there is some form of inducement or some expectation of reward.

The Importance of Reinforcement

According to social learning theory, people do not behave aggressively unless such behavior has "paid off" for them in the past or unless they expect it to pay off in the future. There is ample evidence that aggression *does* pay off. In one study of children, close to 80 percent of physical and verbal assaults on others produced highly rewarding results for the aggressor (Patterson, Littman, and Bricker, 1967).

Thus modeling and reinforcement interact to promote aggression. We learn aggressive behavior by watching others and refine our aggressive skills through the reinforcements that follow their practice (Bandura, 1976). Aggressive responses appear to be learned early in life and to remain fairly stable. In a twenty-two-year longitudinal study (Heusmann et al., 1984), boys' aggressiveness at age eight was a strong predictor of criminal convictions, the seriousness of criminal offenses, moving traffic violations, drunk driving, wife abuse, and the severity of punishment used with their own chidren at age thirty. Girls' aggressiveness at age eight was also correlated with criminal behavior, physical aggression, and child abuse at age thirty, although the connection was not as strong. The researchers suggest that aggressive individuals actively seek out and create situations that seem to call for their aggressive responses.

Situational Factors

The social learning explanation of aggression makes good sense. But certain situations seem so unbearable, so frustrating, that we would expect anyone to explode in anger, regardless of the consequences. Moreover, accounts abound of ordinary people being carried away and, protected by the anonymity of a crowd, engaging in behavior they otherwise might never have considered. The urban riots of the 1960s and the looting that occurred in New York City during the blackout of 1977 testify to the destructive potential of mob action. Both frustration and anonymity seem to promote aggressive behavior.

According to the **frustration-aggression hypothesis** put forward by John Dollard and his colleagues, "aggression is always a consequence of frustration" and, conversely, "frustration always leads to some form of aggression" (1939, p. 1). Dollard defined **frustration** as interference with any form of goal-directed behavior. When people are thwarted in their attempts to obtain food or water, sex or sleep, love or recognition, he and his colleagues argued, they may become aggressive.

To test this hypothesis, a team of researchers (Barker, Dembo, and Lewin, 1941) created a frustrating situation for a group of children. The children were taken to a room, showed a collection of attractive toys, and told that they could look but not touch. Later, when the children were allowed to play with the toys, they were extremely hostile —smashing them against the walls and floor. Another group of children who had not been frustrated in advance played happily and peacefully with identical toys.

One possible consequence of frustration is dis-placed aggression, which may take many forms. Since aggressive responses often bring punishment to the aggressor, a frustrated person can express aggression safely by displacing it. Thus the angry employee who has been reprimanded by his boss might kick his dog when he returns home or insult his golf partner. In dreams, aggression may be displaced to another target, especially if violence against the original target might provoke feelings of guilt. A child who has been spanked by her mother might displace an aggressive impulse against her parent by dreaming that she has harmed another authority figure, perhaps a teacher. Men may be more likely to displace aggression in this way than are women; men's dreams contain much more aggression and hostility than do the dreams of women (Winget, Kramer, and Whitman, 1972).

Aggression is only one of many possible responses to frustration, however. Some people withdraw when frustrated and others intensify their efforts to reach a goal by nonaggressive means. Nor is aggression always preceded by frustration. Most people hit back when they are attacked physically and attempt to "get even" when they are insulted or slandered. To say that a verbal or physical assault is a form of frustration is stretching the term considerably.

According to some psychologists (e.g., Berkowitz, 1962), the key to predicting aggression is not the frustration but the level of anger it arouses. In this view, frustration is neither necessary nor sufficient to provoke aggression. Anger, which may be provoked by frustration or by other experiences, such as verbal attacks, is the crucial factor (Rule and Nesdale, 1976). Among other factors that contribute to aggression is uncontrollable stress (Donnerstein and Wilson, 1976; Baron and Bell, 1976).

GROUP PROCESSES: COOPERATION AND PERFORMANCE

Each day does not bring a stranger in distress, an appeal for charity, or a situation that evokes naked aggression. Yet every day we make choices between aid and antagonism. Do you share your lecture notes with a classmate or keep them to yourself? Do you tell a prospective buyer about your car's faulty transmission or keep quiet to get a higher price for the car? Do you visit an elderly aunt to please your parents or flatly refuse to change your plans?

The choice between fullfilling only one's own needs and considering those of others underlies everything from such trivial decisions as whether to grab a seat on a crowded bus to such vital issues as deciding how the earth's limited resources will be distributed. Because so many of life's prizes —and indeed necessities—are scarce, people cannot always act in ways that maximize both their own immediate goals and those of others. The necessary choice between self-interest and cooperation, between hurting and helping, is a persistent human dilemma.

Cooperation versus Competition

Suppose that you and a friend are arrested for a petty theft. The district attorney believes that the two of you have committed a far more serious crime but does not have enough evidence to take you to court. In an attempt to get a confession for the serious crime, she has you and your friend questioned in separate rooms. If neither you nor your friend confesses, the court will send both of you to prison for one year on the petty theft charge. If both of you confess to the serious crime, the DA will recommend leniency—eight years instead of ten. If only one of you confesses to the serious crime, that person will be sentenced to only three months for turning state's evidence, but the other will go to prison for the full ten years. The dilemma is obvious. The best strategy for both of you is to stick to your alibis and refuse to confess; you will both get one year in prison, but no more. However, if you follow this strategy, but your friend does not, you will go to prison for ten years. And if you confess but your friend does not, you will get off with a three-month sentence.

The Prisoner's Dilemma game (see Figure 27.7), as this situation is called, has proved a valuable tool for discovering the conditions under which people are most likely to cooperate with each other. The experimenters explain the rules of this game, or some variation of it, to pairs of subjects. Then the game begins. Typically the experimenter runs fifteen to twenty trials. Over the long run, cooperation promises the best reward in every case. Yet blind self-interest is the most commonly chosen strategy. In most studies, between 60 and 70 percent of subjects behave

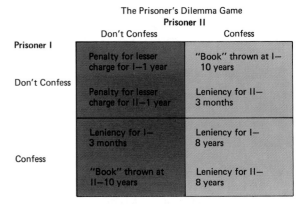

Figure 27.7. The Prisoner's Dilemma can be diagrammed as a 2 x 2 matrix. Each person must choose one of two options, prisoner I controlling the horizontal rows and prisoner II the vertical columns; the outcomes of a joint decision are given by the intersection between the row and column chosen. The best outcome is obtained by both partners cooperating with each other—in this case, by cooperating *not* to confess —but studies show that a selfish strategy is chosen more often than a cooperative one.

selfishly despite the costs involved in doing so (Oskamp and Kleinke, 1970).

The Prisoner's Dilemma game can also be used to illustrate the way various motives affect a pair of individuals in a situation involving gains and losses. As we saw, if both prisoners seek to advance their individual interests, both will get a one-year sentence. Under these conditions, the most profitable outcome for both players is "stick to their alibis," that is, to cooperate with each other, although few choose it.

Yet self-interest is not the only possible motive for the game. People also harbor additional motives such as altruism, envy, or the common good. The motives of altruism or the common good make a cooperative strategy even more rewarding because of the psychological benefits each player reaps from the other's good fortune. Only when envy is added to the motive of self-interest, so that each player derives pleasure from the other's misfortunes, does self-interest become the preferred strategy (Zajonc, 1982).

Among all the possible strategies that can be used in the Prisoner's Dilemma, only one will produce long-term stability in a social system. This fact was discovered when researchers asked game theorists in economics, sociology, political science, and mathematics to submit the best strategy for a continuing Prisoner's Dilemma game—as opposed to the one-shot version in which only a single decision is made and the individuals ostensibly never meet again (Axelrod and Hamilton, 1981). The strategies were then programmed on a computer and played out in a tournament, in which each game required two hundred moves. The winner was the Tit-for-Tat strategy, in which the person's first move is cooperative but each subsequent move is identical with the other player's last move. The Tit-for-Tat strategy begins with cooperation. Whenever the opponent makes a noncooperative move, the Tit-for-Tat strategy is quick to retaliate. But it is forgiving: it begins to cooperate again as soon as the other player makes a cooperative move.

Not all situations that are comparable to the Prisoner's Dilemma last long enough for the Tit-for-Tat strategy to become clear. As noted, a person's motives often dictate the strategy that will be used, and whether a person adopts a cooperative or competitive strategy may be affected by threats from the other player.

The Effect of Threats on Cooperation

Although altruism, the common good, and simple self-interest all favor a cooperative strategy, cooperation among players in the Prisoner's Dilemma game is rare. At the bargaining table of daily life, roommates or members of a family—like nations or labor and management—often resort to threats in an attempt to extort cooperation. Yet according to one experiment (Deutsch and Krauss, 1960), threats are not very effective.

In pairs, people played a game that is similar in structure to the Prisoner's Dilemma game. In this game, each player is in charge of a trucking company that ships goods over the routes shown in Figure 27.8. The company earns 60 cents, minus 1 cent per second in "operating expenses," for every complete trip. Hence the object of the game is to get from the starting point to the destination in the shortest possible time. Only one truck at a time can travel over the middle portion of the main route, and players can either share this road or use winding, time-consuming alternative routes. The best strategy for both players is to take turns using the main route.

To test the effects of threats, the investigators introduced two conditions. In the first, one player was given a gate that could be locked to prevent the other player from using the main route (the uni-

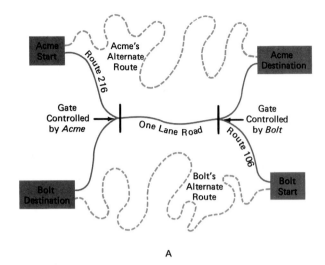

A

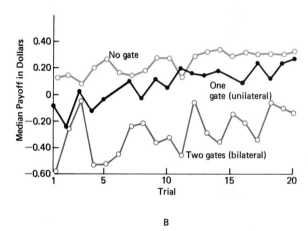

B

Figure 27.8. (A) The game used to study the effects of threat on cooperation. Each of two players (called Acme and Bolt) was told that the aim was to maximize individual profit by reaching their respective destinations as quickly as possible. The quickest route involved a shared one-lane road, and the best strategy dictated that they cooperate, taking turns using it. (B) When the variable of threat was introduced by giving only one player access to a gate which could block the road for the opponent (one gate, unilateral threat) or by giving both players access to a controlling gate (two gates, bilateral threat), cooperation was impeded. Threat was detrimental to reaching agreement, especially in the bilateral threat condition. (After Deutsch and Krauss, 1960.)

lateral threat condition). In the second, both players controlled gates (the bilateral threat condition). Cooperation, which was difficult to achieve in the no-threat condition, became even more difficult in the unilateral threat condition, and almost impossible in the bilateral threat condition. Players attempted to gain access to the main route by threatening to lock their gates. When neither player yielded, both would close their gates, use the alternative route, and incur heavy penalties. Once this pattern began, the gates were no longer simply signals or warnings, but became a means of punishment and retaliation.

Whether these results can be generalized to real life, in which the stakes are often high and the consequences serious, is debatable (Pruitt and Kimmel, 1977). For example, some argue that the fact that the United States and the Soviet Union are capable of destroying each other serves to deter each from the use of force against the other. Because of the consequences, both nations are reluctant to issue a direct threat, much less to launch an attack.

Promoting Social Cooperation

So far we have focused on choices between cooperation and competition faced by two individuals and the personal consequences of those decisions. But many individual choices between cooperation and self-interest have consequences for communities, societies, and ultimately for all humanity.

The Tragedy of the Commons

Consider what Garrett Hardin (1968) calls "**the tragedy of the commons.**" A commons is an open pasture where anyone can graze cattle. People naturally take advantage of the free grazing by adding more animals to their herds whenever they can. Disease, poaching, and war may keep the animal and human populations low so that, for a time, the system works. But eventually the day of reckoning comes: the population grows beyond the capacity of the commons to sustain it, and the overgrazed grass becomes sparse. It is only a matter of time before the once-lush pasture is barren.

Each individual herder may have some sense of this. But when she or he weighs the personal benefits of acquiring another animal against the cost of damage to the common pasture, there is no comparison. When the extra animal is sold, the herder gets all the money, but the cost of overgrazing is shared by all herders, in the form of a slight decrease in the weight of each animal. The logical course for the herder to pursue in order to maximize personal gain is to add another animal—and another, and another. Every herder comes to the same conclusion. This is the "tragedy of the commons": in pursuing individual interest, people move steadily toward eventual ruin for all.

The tragedy of the commons is an example of a **social trap**: as the result of personal decisions, people, organizations, or societies start moving in some direction or initiate relationships that later prove to be unpleasant or lethal, yet seem virtually impossible to stop (Platt, 1970).

It is easy to see how social traps develop. Behaviorists have demonstrated over and over that the immediate consequences of an action—what happens in a few seconds, hours, or days—have more impact on behavior than do long-term outcomes—what may happen in a few days, weeks, a year, or a decade. Short-term rewards are seductive. The herder is quickly rewarded for buying and selling another animal. And because punishment for overgrazing lies years in the future, it has little effect on the herder's daily behavior. Thus, in the commons and in a number of structurally similar situations, powerful psychological and social forces steadily work against cooperation.

Breaking Out of Social Traps

According to Hardin (1968), the tragedy of the commons cannot be solved by appeals to conscience, because the participants hear two conflicting messages: the norm of behaving as a responsible citizen (exercising restraint) and the value of behaving according to one's immediate self-interest (maximizing short-term personal gains). Only mutually agreed-upon coercion will get people out of social traps. By coercion, Hardin does not mean depriving people of all freedom, but simply making it so difficult or expensive to exploit the commons that few will do it.

Research suggests that there may be other ways to break out of social traps. Improving communication seems to be a promising approach, and it has been effective in the Prisoner's Dilemma (see Figure 27.9). Communication may increase cooperation for three reasons. First, communication allows individuals to become acquainted, thus increasing their concern for one another. Second, communication permits people to exchange information relevant to a cooperative decision. And

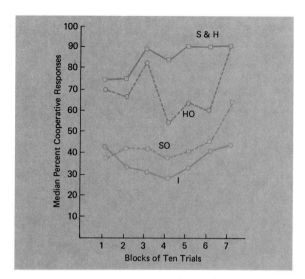

Figure 27.9. The standard Prisoner's Dilemma game does not permit communication between partners, but when the game is altered so that communication is allowed, strategies change. For example, Wichman varied the amount of communication possible in four ways: in one condition (I), isolated subjects could neither see nor hear each other; in a second condition they could hear each other (HO); in a third they could see each other (SO); and in a fourth they could both see and hear each other (S&H). As this graph shows, the more extensive the communication, the higher the rate of cooperation. (After Wichman, 1970.)

third, communication allows people to state their intentions and to assure others that those intentions are honest (Dawes et al., 1977).

Human behavior *can* change. Many people have accepted the 55-mile-per-hour speed limit on United States highways, even though the law initially met with considerable resistance. Some officials predicted that it would be impossible to enforce such a speed limit, yet the average speed on interstate highways has been considerably reduced, and few people exceed the limit by more than two or three miles per hour. Similarly, widespread support for disarmament in Europe and the United States indicates that public awareness of the nuclear threat is growing, another hopeful sign.

Group Performance

When members of a group are working cooperatively, they can clearly accomplish more than a single individual can. Indeed, some human achievements are possible only when several people participate through a group process that integrates their contributions. The economic, technological, and political complexity of contemporary society demands such diverse skills that no one can ever hope to master them all: accordingly, most industrial, scientific, and govenmental enterprises require many specialists, each contributing expertise in a different field. Moreover, as we saw in the discussion of conformity, the presence of an active minority within a group generates original solutions to problems.

As new members join a group, their effort does not always have an additive effect. Researchers studying group processes have discovered that as groups increase in size, each group member's contribution declines. But as we will see, despite this decline in individual effort, the chances of solving a problem increase when a group works on it.

Social Impact Theory and Loafing

According to **social impact theory**, the larger the group, the less pressure there is on any one member to produce, because the impact of social forces affecting the situation is spread over the entire group (Latané, 1973). Just as the presence of bystanders diffuses responsibility, so the presence of several participants in a joint endeavor reduces the individual contribution of each.

Studies have shown, for example, that when people pull together on a rope, each exerts less force than if he or she were pulling on the rope alone (Moede, 1927). Working alone, one person pulled nearly 63 kg, but two people working together pulled, not 126 kg, but 118 kg. And three pulled only 160 kg, which is about two and a half times what a single individual pulls. Apparently, individuals slacken their efforts when there are many contributors to a common task—in effect, they loaf. In groups, it seems that the members' expectations of achieving a common goal radically change their motivation and orientation.

Two Heads Are Better Than One

If each person puts out less effort when working with a group, why do the chances of reaching a solution increase dramatically when a group tackles a problem? For one thing, talent accumulates rapidly as a group grows in size. Simple mathematics shows us how a group attack increases the chance of finding a solution. Consider a problem that is so difficult it can be solved by only one person in ten. As we increase the size of the group working on the problem, the chances that it will be solved grow rapidly. Since the probability of a lone person's solving the problem is 10 percent, the chances that he or she will fail to solve it are 90 percent. But when ten people are working on the problem, the probability that all ten will fail to solve it is only 35 percent (90 percent raised to the power of 10). This means that the chances that at least one of the ten people will find the solution have increased—to 65 percent.

And even if we recognize that the presence of others results in a lessened effort by each person, groups are still more likely to solve problems than solitary individuals. Suppose that the level of individual performance is cut in half when nine others are present. The chances of each individual's solving the problem separately drop from 10 to 5 percent. Yet even with this decrement in individual performance, there is still a good prospect that the group will solve the problem, for the chances of a solution are now 40 percent.

Using a group for solving problems in this way is called the *minimal quorum* approach. In a minimal quorum situation it makes no difference how the solution is arrived at or whether more than one of the group finds it. But sometimes having a minimal quorum is not enough. In some situations, arriving at solutions or decisions may require a simple majority, or a plurality, or even a unanimity among the members before any solution is accepted.

For example, the minimal quorum is regarded as insufficient for deciding jury trials or for the deliberations of the United Nations Security Council; in both of these settings all members must come up with the same answer. When a unanimous decision is required, the size of the group no longer has a favorable effect on the answer. On the contrary, the larger the group, the less likely it will be to come up with a correct unanimous answer. When we again calculate the prospect of a solution, we find that if the chances of one person's solving the problem are 10 percent, the chances of a unanimous solution from a group of ten virtually disappear. They drop to $.1^{10}$, or .0000000001.

In some situations there is no way to identify the correct answer. Here, we generally require unanimity despite its built-in problems. In jury delib-

Table 27.1

Results of Actual Race	Predictions				
	Expert 1	*Expert 2*	*Expert 3*	*Expert 4*	Average
1	1	3	2	2	2.0
2	4	1	3	1	2.25
3	3	2	1	4	2.5
4	2	4	4	3	3.25
Correlation	.2	.4	.4	.6	1.00

erations, for example, unanimity promotes accuracy at the cost of efficiency. We do not want to punish the innocent nor let the guilty go free, and we hope that the jury will consider all possible alternatives before selecting the most accurate one. But when accuracy can be identified and verified, we are likely to adopt minimal quorum decisions, which maximize efficiency.

For some tasks, simply averaging individual decisions can generate group products that are far more accurate than those of single individuals. Consider four experts who are predicting the outcome of a race among four horses. They give us the predictions that appear in Table 27.1.

In this example, none of the experts did very well individually. Their correlations with the true order of the horses are only .2, .4, .4, and .6. But if we average their predictions, the correlation is perfect, for it ranks the horses in exactly the way the horses actually finished. As the number of judges whose decisions are being averaged increases, the correlation with the correct order also increases.

Because correlations of the average ranking are usually much higher than the correlations of any individual's judgment, we almost always do best if we go by the average ranking. If you averaged the preseason predictions of each major sportscaster and sports columnist as to National Football League rankings, the average you obtained would probably be closer to the season's outcome than the predictions of the best expert.

The kind of social-psychological research described in this chapter helps us understand some of the social influences that affect interpersonal behavior. In the next chapter, we shall examine psychological research that attempts to explain the forces that affect us at work.

SUMMARY

1. **Social facilitation**, or enhanced performance in the presence of others, occurs whenever people or animals work on simple tasks or on tasks they have already mastered. This appears to come about because the presence of others increases arousal and leads to an increase in **dominant responses**, which are the responses most likely to be made by an organism in a particular situation. On easy tasks, dominant responses are usually correct, but on difficult or new tasks, they are likely to be wrong. For this reason, the presence of others leads to poor performance on complex tasks or in the learning of new skills.

2. **Conformity** is the tendency to shift views or behavior closer to the norms followed by other people. It is the result of social pressure and can lead people to question perceptual information received by their senses. If a single person objects to the majority view or when people can remain anonymous, deviation from group norms becomes easier. **Obedience** is any behavior that complies with the explicit commands of a person in authority. In studies of obedience, people have been willing to deliver what they believed were serious or lethal shocks when ordered to do so by an authority figure. Many factors can lead to disobedience, however, including a lack of direct confrontation with authority and nearness to the victim (which makes it more difficult to deny the infliction of pain). Conformity to peers can also override the demands of authority.

3. Both animals and human beings behave in altruistic ways, and altruism appears to have both social and biological bases. According to sociobiologists, organisms are motivated to protect their genes, not their lives, so that inclusive fitness explains why animals sacrifice themselves to protect others, which share some of their genes. The application of this concept to human beings has not been established, although it may work through **reciprocal altruism**, in which reinforcement need not be direct. In emergencies, the presence of bystanders appears to inhibit people from giving aid. The explanation of this inhibiting effect includes **audience inhibition** (concern about others' evaluation of our behavior); **social influence** (waiting for others to define the situation as an emergency); and **diffusion of responsibility** (spreading the responsibility for intervening over all the bystanders). When the situation is unambiguous, however, people often intervene in emergencies.

4. Any act that is intended to cause pain, damage, or suffering to another is an act of interpersonal **aggression**. No evidence of a genetic basis for aggression has been found in humans, and biological abnormalities (such as an extra Y [male] chromosome or brain damage) cannot explain the prevalence of human aggression. Even in cases where a biological factor has been found, the expression of aggression is influenced by the environment. According to social learning theorists, exposure to violent models and reinforcement for aggressive acts explain why people so often attack one another. Situational factors also appear to play a role in aggression. According to the **frustration-aggression hypothesis**, aggression is always a consequence of **frustration** (the interference with goal-directed behavior) and frustration always leads to aggression. Frustration can also lead to displaced aggression, but aggression is not the only response to frustration. It appears that not frustration, but level of anger (which may be produced by frustration) is a necessary factor in most aggression. Uncontrollable stress also contributes to aggression.

5. The choice between cooperation and self-interest in daily life has been studied by using the Prisoner's Dilemma game. Despite the fact that a strategy of cooperation helps both players, most people choose self-interest. The most effective strategy in continuing games is Tit-for-Tat, in which, after a cooperative initial move, each subsequent move is identical with the other player's last move. Although threats are not very effective in games based on the Prisoner's Dilemma, people use threats when they are available. In games, cooperation de-

creases in a unilateral threat condition and almost disappears in a bilateral threat condition.

6. Individual choices can have serious social consequences, as in "the tragedy of the commons," which results when individual herders keep adding animals until the common pasture is destroyed by overgrazing. **The tragedy of the commons** is an example of a **social trap**: as the result of personal decisions, people, organizations, or societies start moving in some direction that later proves to be harmful or lethal, yet seems virtually impossible to stop. Social traps develop because the immediate consequences of an action (personal gain) outweigh long-term outcomes (social harm). It has been suggested by some social psychologists that only mutually agreed-upon coercion, which makes antisocial action difficult or expensive, will get people out of social traps. However, improved communication in instances when people see the possibility of long-term gain may also open social traps.

7. When working cooperatively, a group can accomplish much more than a single individual can; however, each individual group member puts out less effort in a group than when working alone. The decreased effort occurs because, as **social impact theory** predicts, the impact of social forces affecting the situation is spread out over the entire group. Whenever a solution can be verified, the minimal quorum standard is preferable; when a solution cannot be verified, unanimous agreement, though less efficient, may be necessary.

KEY TERMS

aggression
audience inhibition
conformity
diffusion of responsibility
dominant responses
frustration

frustration-aggression
   hypothesis
norm
obedience
reciprocal altruism
social facilitation

social impact theory
social influence
social trap
the tragedy of
   the commons
uniformity

RECOMMENDED READINGS

BARON, R. A. *Human aggression.* New York: Plenum Press, 1977. An excellent, up-to-date textbook that analyzes social, environmental, and individual determinants of aggression.

BERKOWITZ, L. *Aggression: A social-psychological analysis.* New York: McGraw-Hill, 1962. The successor to *Frustration and Aggression* (see below), in which the frustration-aggression hypothesis is refined and expanded.

CIALDINI, R. B. *Influence: How and why people agree to things.* New York: William Morrow, 1984. An extensive set of real-life applications of social-psychological principles.

DAWES, R. M. Formal models of dilemmas in social decision-making. In M. F. Kaplan and S. Schwartz (Eds.), *Human judgment and decision processes.* New York: Academic Press, 1975. A theoretical analysis of social dilemmas as typified by the commons problem.

DERLEGA, V., and J. GRZELAK (Eds.). *Cooperation and helping behavior: Theories and research.* New York: Academic Press, 1982. The most recent and extensive review of the current thinking about altruism, self-interest, competition, and cooperation.

DOLLARD, J., L. W. DOOB, N. E. MILLER, O. H. MOWRER, and R. R. SEARS. *Frustration and aggression.* New Haven, Conn.: Yale University Press, 1939. The classic monograph that stimulated a research effort to understand aggression that continues even today.

HARDIN, G., and J. BADEN (Eds.). *Managing the commons.* San Francisco: W. H. Freeman, 1977. Hardin popularized the tragedy of the commons as a model of resource mismanagement. In this collection of papers a variety of perspectives are brought to bear on the problem of avoiding the tragedy of resource depletion.

JANIS, I. L. *Victims of groupthink: A psychological study of foreign-policy decisions and fiascoes.* Boston: Houghton Mifflin, 1973. With great insight, Janis applies social-psychological theory to a series of historic decisions made by groups in such situations as the Bay of Pigs invasion, the Cuban missile crisis, and the escalation of the Vietnam War.

LATANÉ, B., and J. M. DARLEY. *The unresponsive bystander: Why doesn't he help?* New York: Appleton-Century-Crofts, 1970. The prizewinning report of the authors' fascinating series of experiments on the behavior of bystanders in emergencies.

MACAULAY, J., and L. BERKOWITZ (Eds.). *Altruism and helping behavior: Social psychological studies of some antecedents and consequences.* New York: Academic Press, 1970. A collection of research reports that provide useful insights into the determinants of sharing, giving, and helping.

MILGRAM, S. *The individual in a social world: Essays and experiments.* Reading, Mass.: Addison-Wesley, 1977. A stimulating excursion through Milgram's work on such varied topics as obedience, the urban experience, and the effects of television on antisocial behavior, in all of which Milgram finds similar social forces affecting behavior.

RAPOPORT, A. *Experimental games and their uses in psychology.* Morristown, N.J.: General Learning Press, University Modular Publications, 1973. A clear and concise introduction to games (like the Prisoner's Dilemma game) that are used to study competition and cooperation.

SHAW, M. E. *Group dynamics: The psychology of small group behavior.* New York: McGraw-Hill, 1976. An excellent text in which the author reviews the field, summarizes what is known, and points to problems for future research.

INDUSTRIAL/ORGANIZATIONAL PSYCHOLOGY

At the Bethlehem Steel Company, a crew of about seventy-five men handled the pig iron produced by five blast furnaces. It was heavy work—the men picked up the ninety-two-pound "pigs" and carried each one several yards away from the furnace where they dropped it onto a pile waiting to be loaded onto railroad cars. The crew's foreman was first-rate; his crew moved iron as fast and as cheaply as any other crew in the steel industry.

But one day in 1900 an American engineer named Frederick Taylor watched a group of men load "pigs." Each man loaded about twelve and a half tons a day. Taylor noted their movements and decided that, if a few simple principles were applied to their labor, productivity might be quadrupled. Taylor was right. When a hard-working and ambitious worker loaded the iron following Taylor's instructions, his productivity climbed to forty-seven and a half tons in a single day.

This study, which quadrupled production while increasing wages by only 60 percent, was a landmark study by a founding father of the new field of **industrial/organizational psychology**, or **I/O psychology**, as it is often called. I/O psychology is concerned with human behavior in the work-

Before Frederick Taylor applied his principles of scientific management to the iron and steel industry, workdays were long and hard, but productivity was low.

place. Although I/O psychology is a child of the twentieth century, its roots go back to the way people thought about man and machine a century earlier. Industry had concentrated on building new and better equipment but had paid little attention to the human beings who ran the machines. Gradually, it became clear that industry needed to consider the interaction of workers and machines. If the right conditions could be found, if human motivation and energy could be tapped, then everyone would profit.

THE DEVELOPMENT OF INDUSTRIAL/ORGANIZATIONAL PSYCHOLOGY

Three separate movements combined to produce the field of industrial/organizational psychology. One was the work of industrial engineers who used the methods of experimental psychology to redesign the workplace. The second was the work of personnel psychologists who relied on research in testing and assessment (see Chapter 20). And the third was the human relations movement, which emphasized job motivation and work satisfaction (Landy, 1985).

Frederick Taylor, who conducted the pig-iron study, was an industrial engineer. Taylor believed that it was possible to create more efficient factories, which would provide ample profits for management and higher salaries for labor. Taylor's system, known as **scientific management**, called for management to redesign work methods to make them more efficient. Under this system management would also choose the best workers for each job, train them in new methods, develop cooperation between managers and workers, and involve workers in the design and conduct of work (Muchinsky, 1983). Another expert, Hugo Münsterberg (1913/1973) was as concerned with efficiency as Taylor was, but he took a different approach to industry. Taylor had stressed the need to change people's behavior; Münsterberg, by contrast, emphasized making production more efficient by matching people to the jobs for which they were best suited. He tried to discover just what individual qualities—intelligence, personality traits, experience—contributed to people's performance in various jobs. Following Münsterberg's example, personnel experts came into

being. They tried to discover what qualities each job required, to assess each applicant's capabilities by using a range of measurement techniques, and then to fill each job with a qualified worker.

Meanwhile, another approach was also developing. In 1927 industrial psychologists conducted a series of experiments at a Western Electric plant in Illinois to discover the effect of working conditions on productivity. But what they came up with was something entirely different: no matter how they manipulated working conditions, after each intervention the workers' productivity increased. This response came to be known as the "Hawthorne effect." It led the researchers to conclude that workers' feelings affect their job performance, and that the way workers *perceive* their situation may have more influence on their performance than the objective facts of the situation (Landy, 1985).

Although some aspects of this experiment have been questioned (Rice, 1982), the Hawthorne studies caused many industrial psychologists to shift their attention from job efficiency to increasing workers' satisfaction. They concluded that feelings and motivations were as important as efficient assembly lines. They discovered that social relations among workers had a powerful influence on workers' motivation and performance.

As the field of industrial psychology grew, its interests broadened. Industrial psychologists continued to be concerned with hiring, training, and evaluating workers; they continued to investigate the social factors that affect job satisfaction and job performance. But as their research began to be applied to such organizations as hospitals, schools, and governments, "industrial" psychology no longer seemed to be an appropriate term. And so the name was changed. Since 1970 industrial psychology has been known as industrial/organizational (I/O) psychology—a name that reflects the scope of the field. In the sections that follow we will explore some of I/O psychology's major concerns.

MATCHING WORKERS TO JOBS

When you apply for a job, you are eager to put your best foot forward: to appear intelligent, capable, and highly motivated. You smile brightly and subject yourself to the selection process, conscious of

Figure 28.1. The Bennett Mechanical Comprehension Test is used to assess job applicants' understanding of mechanical principles and spatial relations. The applicant answers short questions about pictures such as the ones shown here. (Adapted from Ghiselli, 1966. Reproduced by permission from the *Bennett Mechanical Comprehension Test.* Copyright © 1942, 1967 by The Psychological Corporation. All rights reserved.)

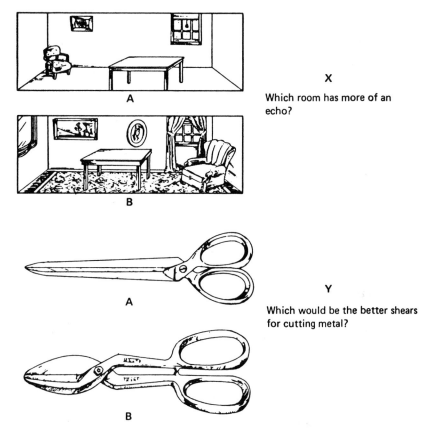

X

Which room has more of an echo?

Y

Which would be the better shears for cutting metal?

your sweaty palms, the slight tug in the middle of your stomach, and perhaps a feeling of resentment at the probing questions—some of which seem completely unrelated to the job you seek. But your potential employer also has problems. He or she must do the choosing. How is it done? And how does an employer select a person who will not quit a month later? Or one who will not have to be fired in three months for obvious incompetence?

Many employers rely on psychological tests as predictors of job performance, on nontest predictors such as interviews, or on a combination of the two.

Psychological Tests as Predictors

People differ in their traits, aptitudes, and abilities, and these differences may affect how well an individual will perform on a job. Employers use a variety of tests to identify such individual differences. Most employers believe that a person's intelligence is a good predictor of his or her job performance: intelligent employees are expected to learn a job more quickly, to perform more efficiently, and to be less likely to quit abruptly.

Hence, the need for intelligence tests in the screening of job applicants. Individual intelligence tests, such as those discussed in Chapter 20, are too expensive to be used in screening job applicants. Instead, employers use group intelligence tests that have been developed for use in personnel selection, such as the Otis Self-Administering Test of Mental Ability, which has been widely used in filling clerical or supervisory positions.

There are also other approaches to testing. For some jobs, testing a person's ability to handle words and numbers is less important than testing his or her ability to understand mechanical principles and spatial relations (see Figure 28.1); for others, testing motor ability is the key. In addition, some employers attempt to assess an applicant's personality. They may rely on self-report inventories like the ones discussed in Chapter 20. Or they may use interest inventories, which are somewhat similar but explore the person's degree of interest in various activities.

How Well Do Tests Predict Job Performance?

As we saw in Chapter 20, if a test is to be useful, it must be both reliable and valid. A useful test measures something consistently, and measures what it purports to measure. Furthermore, if a test is to be useful in screening job applicants, it should have criterion-related validity: a person's scores on the test should be related to a criterion, such as subsequent performance on a job (see Figure 28.2). In a test that correlated perfectly with success on the job (+1.0), the highest scoring applicant would do best on the job, and the higher the score, the more successful the applicant would be.

Few tests have such high validity; most are only "moderate" predictors of job success. They may correlate about +.30: tests of perceptual accuracy, for example, seem to correlate about +.30 with success in clerical occupations. Some tests are worthless as predictors. The same tests of perceptual accuracy correlate only +.05 with success in sales jobs, which may make them useless at screening applicants for such jobs (Ghiselli, 1973).

Intelligence tests seem to be moderately good predictors of job performance: they correlate about +.30 for clerical jobs, about +.29 for managerial jobs, and about +.25 for jobs in various trades and crafts (Ghiselli, 1973). Why aren't these correlations higher? In some cases the abilities measured by a given test are necessary, but not suffi-

cient, for job success. A dentist *must* have manual dexterity, so a person who fails such a test could not succeed at dentistry. However, dentistry also requires academic intelligence, diagnostic skills, and personality characteristics that keep patients coming back. In other cases a test that has validity in one employment situation is not valid for the same type of job in another workplace. This problem arises because working conditions, the tasks involved in the job, and the work force all vary from one company or industry to another.

Regardless of these limitations, some industrial psychologists still advocate the use of intelligence tests by personnel departments. Some have predicted that if the federal government used tests of cognitive aptitude for hiring, it could save $16 billion each year in labor costs, and smaller employers, such as the Philadelphia police department, could save $18 million each year (Schmidt and Hunter, 1981).

The Historical and Legal Aspects of Test Validity

The use of personality, intelligence, and aptitude tests to select or promote employees has frequently been seen as discriminatory. Such tests can be used to keep people of a particular race, color, religion, sex, or nationality out of jobs or to deny them promotion. If tests are used to discriminate against any of these groups, they are in violation of the Civil Rights Act of 1964.

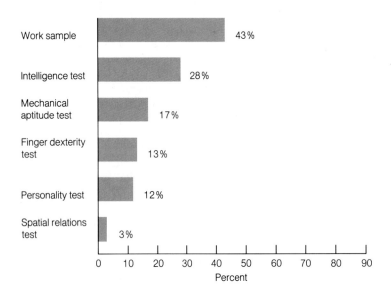

Figure 28.2. How valid are tests as predictors of job performance? This graph shows the validity of various types of tests, using job proficiency as the criterion. (Bennett, 1940.)

The discrimination need not be intentional. If the plaintiff can show statistically that use of the test has an **adverse impact** on members of a protected minority group, regardless of the employer's intentions, the courts may rule that its use violates the Civil Rights Act. How can a plaintiff prove adverse impact? By applying the "four-fifths rule." If a plaintiff can show that the proportion of minority applicants hired is less than four-fifths of the proportion of majority applicants hired, the courts consider that the test has an adverse impact on minorities. To be *without* adverse effect, a test that leads an employer to hire —let us say—10 percent of the majority applicants for a job must also lead to the hiring of at least 8 percent of the minority applicants.

But sometimes proof of adverse impact is not enough to get a ruling of discrimination. If the employer can show that the test has predictive validity, that employer can continue to use the test—unless the plaintiff can show that an alternate, but nondiscriminatory, test exists (Griffin, 1980). In this case, the issue is whether the test accurately predicts performance on the job. Even that requirement has been softened since the Supreme Court established it in 1971. First, the Court ruled that predictive validity need apply only to a training program, not to performance on the job itself (*Washington* v. *Davis,* 1976). Then the Court ruled that in some instances, content validity is enough to prove that a test is related to the job (*National Education Association* v. *State of South Carolina,* 1978).

Although the courts have relied on *criterion-related* or *content validity* in their rulings, some psychologists have suggested that valid tests are useful only for filling simple, repetitive jobs. For jobs involving complex tasks, *construct validity,* in which the test measures whatever trait or capability it claims to measure, is enough (Lerner, 1977). Note, however, that the courts are not interested in the issue of validity unless its absence leads to discrimination. Presumably, a test based on the casting of horoscopes would be accepted by the courts as long as it did not discriminate against any group specified in the Civil Rights Act.

Nontest Predictors

Most employers do not use psychological tests to screen applicants. They rely instead on such non-test predictors as interviews. The purpose of the interview is to gather information about the applicant, but it is not a simple fact-finding process. First impressions are likely to have a strong impact on an interviewer. Before the applicant has said more than a few words, the interviewer may already have categorized him or her, relying on the applicant's appearance and behavior and on information already available on an application. The applicant, who is usually aware of this tendency, has dressed to create a good impression and may be trying to present what he or she thinks the interviewer wants to see.

An interview is actually a complex, dynamic process. In fact, subjective factors play such an important role that some I/O psychologists believe the typical interview does not validly predict an applicant's potential (Thayer, 1983). Consider some of the factors that enter into the interview:

■ Most interviewers give more weight to unfavorable information than to favorable information.
■ Most interviewers have an "ideal" applicant against which they evaluate the people they interview.
■ There are wide individual differences in the cues (words, appearance, behavior) an interviewer uses to evaluate an applicant. Yet interviewers are unable to state just what cues they do use.
■ Most interviewers rely more heavily on the applicant's posture, gestures, and facial expressions than on his or her words.
■ Interviewers tend to rate more highly those applicants who are of the same ethnic background or who share the interviewer's own attitudes—although this higher rating does not seem to affect job offers (Schmitt, 1976). As Frank Landy (1985) points out, a psychological test does not measure socioeconomic status, attitude, motivation, or behavior —but an interviewer attempts to assess all of these.

The invalidity of the interview stems not just from the biases and backgrounds of the interviewer and the applicant, but from the structure of the interview itself. Because most interviews are conducted without a standardized interview guide, applicants are compared on dissimilar data. For example, if you ask one student the sum of 2 plus 2 and another the square root of 3,763, you

THE REALISTIC JOB PREVIEW

Suppose you apply for a job at a bank. The manager who interviews you describes the banking transactions you will handle, the various positions held by tellers, the pay rates, and the employee benefits; he also notes that customers must be handled with courtesy. You think it over, accept the job, and report to work with enthusiasm. On the first morning you discover that the training procedure is cumbersome and that 15 percent of new tellers are fired before its completion. You find that you have no say in your schedule, that accuracy is held to be of top importance, and that you will be required to work under pressure. You find that the customers are often rude, that pay increases are determined by an archaic system, and that your chances of moving into administration are nil. You stick it out for six months, then quit to take a job with an insurance company.

This sort of turnover costs companies money and makes workers unhappy. If you had been able to size up the job accurately beforehand, you would never have accepted it. What can companies do? Psychologists have suggested that the proportion of "revolving-door" employees could probably be reduced if employers gave applicants a **realistic job preview** (**RJP**). The realistic job preview is an honest picture of the potential job—a picture that includes the job's disadvantages.

Realistic job previews come in an assortment of forms, and some have been fairly effective. At the Marine training camp on Parris Island, South Carolina, I/O psychologists used taped interviews with recruits and other Marine Corps personnel in a film that realistically previewed Marine Corps life (Horner, Mobley, and Meglino, 1979). The film covered aspects of training and other matters that earlier recruits wished they had known about before enlisting. It also discussed acceptable recruit behavior in various situations and gave tips on how to survive training.

Not all RJPs have been so successful. Some have not increased the retention rate, although they have changed the date of departure. Among prospective bank tellers in one study (Wanous and Dean, 1984), the dropout rate after one year remained the same. However, among tellers who dropped out, those who had an RJP tended to leave during the training period; those without an RJP tended to leave after twenty-three weeks. In this case the RJP did not cut down the mismatches, but it did save the bank $1,400 on each employee who left during the training period.

After reviewing RJPs in various companies, psychologists reported that programs vary widely in their effectiveness, but that the average RJP reduces the employee turnover rate 6 percent (Reilly et al., 1981).

cannot fairly conclude that the second is worse in arithmetic—yet many interviewers do essentially this.

Worse, an interview may be as discriminatory as certain tests are if the interviewer delves deeply into aspects of the applicant's life that have no bearing on job performance. To help guard against such irrelevant probing, the Washington State Human Relations Commission has ruled that certain questions may not normally be part of an interview. The commission has forbidden interviewers to ask the applicant about arrests, citizenship, personal information (marital status, pregnancies, children, spouse's salary, child-care arrangements, whether the applicant owns or rents a house), or military discharge information (Arvey, 1979). Nor should the interviewer ask questions that are so broad that their answers are likely to provide information (such as a health condition) that is unrelated to job performance.

What, then, can be done to make interviews a useful part of the job selection process? Landy (1985) suggests that interviews are more likely to be valid under the following conditions:

▪ When the interviewer sticks to questions that reveal information pertinent to job duties
▪ When a structured interview format is used
▪ When the interviewer is trained in how to conduct an interview

■ When a panel of interviewers instead of a single interviewer is used

In addition, when interviewers are given feedback on the later success or failure of applicants they have hired, their skill in assessing candidates improves.

WORK MOTIVATION

Work motivation affects how long we stay with a company, how dependably we perform our duties, and how innovative we are on the job. Because so many aspects of our behavior at work are affected by motivation, no single theory has been able to explain them all. Instead, I/O psychologists have drawn on a number of theories to help them understand the conditions that underlie work motivation. These theories fall into three broad categories: need theories, cognitive theories, and reinforcement theory.

Need Theories of Work Motivation

Much of our behavior is motivated by needs, as we saw in Chapter 12. Several theories of work motivation have looked at performance on the job in terms of needs that are unrelated to basic drives.

Maslow's Need Hierarchy

One theory of human motives developed to explain work motivation is based on Abraham Maslow's hierarchy of needs. As we saw in Chapter 19, Maslow viewed human behavior as motivated by fundamental needs (physiological needs and safety needs), psychological needs (social needs and self-esteem needs), and metaneeds. Once a person's fundamental needs are met, he or she can focus on the next level, psychological needs, and if the psychological needs (first, for companionship and then for self-esteem) have been met, a person will be motivated by the need to fulfill his or her potential. From the standpoint of work motivation, this theory holds that a person first concentrates on pay and job security. Then with adequate pay and an assured job, the person's relationships with his or her supervisor become a matter of

concern. Then, if the work environment is satisfying, the person becomes motivated by the need to fulfill himself or herself through work (Muchinsky, 1983).

It is interesting that though Maslow's theory has had broad influence, attempts to test it in the workplace have been disappointing. In a longitudinal study of workers, researchers found that satisfaction of needs in a lower category (such as job security or friendship) did *not* diminish these needs' importance in the workers' eyes. Nor did changes in the satisfaction of needs in one category affect the importance of needs in any of the other categories (Lawler and Suttle, 1972). These researchers also found that needs seem to be divided into two categories: (1) the basic biological needs and (2) all the rest of Maslow's needs. Other psychologists have found that most research either rejects the propositions of Maslow's theory or gives them weak support at best (Wahba and Bridwell, 1976). They have concluded, however, that the theory's vagueness makes it virtually impossible to derive any testable hypotheses from it.

ERG Theory

Clayton Alderfer (1969; 1972) looked at the hierarchy of needs in a different way in an attempt to apply them to work motivation. Alderfer's **ERG theory** breaks the needs into three categories: *existence needs* (all Maslow's fundamental needs as well as fringe benefits and working conditions); *relatedness needs* (all interpersonal relationships); and *growth needs* (any of a person's needs to have a creative or productive effect on self or environment). The first letters of each category (E, R, G) form the acronym ERG.

These categories are much like Maslow's, but in ERG theory the motivation process is different. Maslow believed that the importance of a need category to an employee diminished as soon as the needs within it were met. Alderfer, however, proposed that whenever a person's attempts to satisfy higher needs were frustrated, the lower needs again became highly motivating—even though they had already been met.

Little research has been done on ERG theory, but researchers have found evidence that people tend to categorize their needs in the way Alderfer proposed (Rauschenberger, Schmitt, and Hunter, 1980). And other researchers have found, first, that the categories of needs seem to be independent of each other; and, second, that highly satisfied needs may even increase in importance (Wanous and Zwany, 1977). However, ERG theory suffers from some of the same vagueness that makes Maslow's theory difficult to test or use. As yet, researchers have found it of little help in day-to-day management practices (Wanous and Zwany, 1977).

Cognitive Theories of Work Motivation

Several theories of work motivation are based on the effects that various kinds of information have on our cognitive processes. Some of these cognitive theories focus on our expectations, some on our attempts to maintain cognitive consistency, and others on our intentions.

Expectancy Theory

According to **expectancy theory**, we are motivated not only by our goals but also by how attainable we think those goals are. Since Victor Vroom (1964) proposed expectancy theory, it has become one of the major ways of explaining work motivation. In this theory, our work motivation is determined by the interaction of three factors:

■ *Valence*—the satisfaction we anticipate from a job outcome (Say, we want a transfer to a more desirable location.)

■ *Instrumentality*—our perception of that outcome's relationship to our current job performance (Does the transfer depend on the quality of the work we are doing now?)

■ *Expectancy*—our expectations that our effort will affect performance (Can we increase our performance level by working harder?)

The valence of an outcome can be positive (a raise, a promotion) or negative (being fired or demoted). Valence can also be high or low, depending on how the person feels about an outcome.

Suppose Dennis, a beginning worker, is given a boring, low-paid, repetitive job. If there are plenty of such jobs available, Dennis may not care if he gets fired. In this case, the valence is negative but low: he has no reason to work hard. The instrumentality of the outcome is also important. If Maria assumes that the raises her company passes out each July are automatic, she will be convinced that her job performance will not affect her raise's size or arrival. Again, she will have no reason to work hard. Expectancy is perhaps the most important factor of all. If Mario works in a factory, supervising the machinery that places caps on bottles of cola, he cannot increase the number of cases that come off the line, no matter how hard he works. He can see no relationship between how much effort he puts in and his ultimate job performance. Once more, there is no reason to put out extra effort. (But if Mario were delivering cola to supermarkets and received a commission on deliveries over a certain level, he would see a close relationship between effort and performance, and his motivation would be much higher.)

A worker *should* be highly motivated when valence is high, instrumentality is clear, and expectancy is strong. And, in fact, the sort of program recommended by I/O psychologists to motivate employees uses these elements. Companies are urged to provide attractive incentives (valence) and clear descriptions of how to attain them (instrumentality), and to make certain employees know their rewards will depend on performance (expectancy) (Pritchard, DeLeo, and Von Bergen, 1976).

Expectancy theory is popular among managers for two reasons. It predicts the motivation of a good many people, and its principles are clear and relatively easy to apply in day-to-day management. How does it hold up when tested? It does a good job of predicting the behavior of people whose efforts are consciously directed toward a goal. But whenever a person's behavior is under the control of unconscious forces, expectancy theory will fail as a predictor (Miner, 1980). Personality also seems to be a factor. People who believe they have control over events in their lives generally behave in accord with expectancy theory, but people who believe that they are pawns of fate, or that their lives are controlled by powerful others, do not (Broedling, 1975).

Equity Theory

When the information we pick up from the world is inconsistent, we are thrown into an unpleasant state of cognitive imbalance. Our attempts to restore the equilibrium may affect our attitudes and our behavior. This reasoning, which underlies the various theories of cognitive consistency discussed in Chapter 12, is the basis for equity theory.

Equity theory looks at whether we believe we are being treated fairly on the job. As proposed by J. S. Adams (1965), **equity theory** says that we are motivated to remove any perceived inequities. How do we know that inequities exist? First we make a rough determination of the ratio of our own outcomes (such as pay) to our inputs (such as effort). Then we compare that ratio with the ratio we perceive to exist for others. If the two ratios are out of line with each other, we perceive an inequity and are thrown into cognitive imbalance. We are motivated to reduce this tension, and the greater the tension, the greater our motivation to do something about it.

People can restore equity in two major ways: they can change their behavior or they can change their thoughts (Muchinsky, 1983). Suppose you discover that Joan, who works at the desk next to you, is being paid $2,000 a year more than you. You and Joan both joined the company at about the same time and have similar duties. If you decide to change your behavior, you may reduce your inputs: you stop working so hard, you stretch your coffee break, you are out the door at the stroke of five. Or you may change your outcomes: you can ask for a raise. Or you may change Joan's inputs: you may maneuver the situation so that she has to work harder, perhaps by seeing that reports you would normally handle land on her desk. Or you may quit your job and go to work for a company whose salary schedule you believe is more equitable.

But you may not change your behavior at all. You may just change the way you think about the inequity. You can distort your own inputs or outcomes: you may tell yourself that you do not really work as hard as Joan. Or you can distort Joan's inputs or outcomes: you may convince yourself that she handles a number of difficult accounts and so deserves extra money. Or you can stop comparing yourself with Joan: you can begin to compare yourself with Carlos, who started work a few weeks after you came on the job.

Goal-Setting Theory

Goal-setting theory is a cognitive theory that views workers as conscious, rational creatures. This theory holds that instead of being motivated by our needs or our feelings of inequity, we are motivated by our conscious intentions to attain a specific goal. We saw in Chapter 12 that motivated behavior requires a goal; just what does goal-setting theory add to that understanding? According to Edwin Locke (1968), who developed goal-setting theory, a person must be aware of the goal and accept it. If the person accepts the goal and makes a conscious commitment to work toward it, he or she will show increased motivation in terms of effort and persistence.

Several factors can affect the intensity of our motivation (Locke et al., 1981):

- We are more motivated to work for specific goals (such as a 10 percent increase in sales) than we are to work for general goals (such as increased productivity).
- We commit ourselves more deeply to difficult goals than to easy goals or to "just do your best" situations.
- We will not be motivated unless we have the ability required to reach the goal.
- Money, titles, or other concrete rewards can increase our commitment.
- Unless we receive feedback on our performance, our motivation will decline. But when we are given accurate feedback, we can effectively adjust our strategies, our persistence, or the intensity of our efforts toward the goal (Landy, 1985).

Researchers have been testing goal-setting theory for fifteen years, and the vast majority of the studies support it (Latham and Yukl, 1975; Locke et al., 1981). Most I/O psychologists are convinced that goal setting is an effective way to increase job performance. In fact, goal setting is the basic concept behind management by objectives (MBO), a popular technique used to increase performance in corporations (see Figure 28.3).

Reinforcement Theory

Some I/O psychologists have applied operant conditioning to the workplace; there it is called **reinforcement theory**. As we saw in Chapter 8, reinforcements can change our behavior, and they do so by changing our expectancies. A wide variety of companies—fast-food chains, hospitals, and the armed forces—have tried to increase employee motivation with schedules of positive reinforcement.

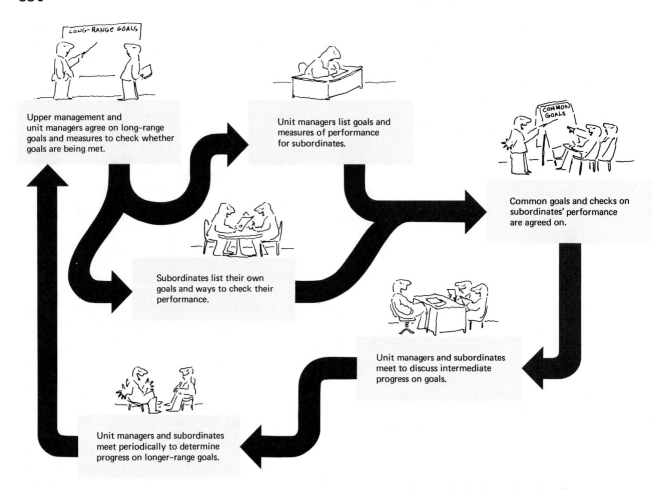

Figure 28.3. Management by objectives. In the MBO system, managers state their goals clearly and involve the appropriate workers in them from the start. The workers state their own goals too, and both workers and managers go through a cycle of discussion, review, and evaluation.

The effectiveness of reinforcement has been shown again and again. Yet there are problems with using it as a motivational technique. One emerges when a company changes the reinforcement schedule. An hourly wage is not reinforcing because the worker receives the same reward no matter how hard he or she works. But paying workers by the piece (on either a variable schedule or a fixed-ratio schedule) may lead the workers to overwork themselves, echoing the "sweatshop" conditions that were once common in the garment industry. Is it ethical for an employer to induce an employee to work to the point of exhaustion (Muchinsky, 1983)?

Another problem: what reinforces one person may not reinforce another. Individual differences among people are so great that a uniform program

of rewards is unlikely to be effective with all employees. And a final problem is that organizations sometimes institute programs and then withdraw them. If employees have been receiving special rewards (say, department store clerks are given time off with pay for meeting sales standards) and then those rewards are discontinued, workers' motivation is likely to plummet—they often become even less productive than they had been before the program began.

Work Attitudes

At least 3,000 papers have been written on the question of what makes workers happy (Locke,

1976). Why all the interest in job satisfaction? One reason is cultural: American culture portrays this country as "the land of opportunity." A second reason is practical. Common sense holds that a happy worker is a productive worker—an assumption that may not always be correct, as we will see below (Muchinsky, 1983).

What Is Job Satisfaction?

Job satisfaction is an emotional, affective orientation toward one's work. It can be measured in terms of a worker's overall satisfaction with his or her job or, alternatively, in terms of the worker's satisfaction with different facets of a job.

Conflicting and/or ambiguous roles—not knowing what we are expected to accomplish, or feeling we are subjected to contradictory demands—are major sources of job dissatisfaction. More generally, job satisfaction can be defined in terms of the match between what we want from a job and what we actually receive (McCormick and Ilgan, 1980).

Who Is Satisfied?

One of the most commonly used measures of job satisfaction is the Job Description Index (JDI). Data from the JDI can be used to determine whether certain categories of people are more satisfied with their jobs than other people are, or whether particular kinds of jobs are more satisfying than other kinds. Attempts to relate job satisfaction to such socioeconomic factors as age, race, and sex have yielded mixed results.

Dissatisfaction with pay is a major source of worker discontent. A study of managers in the United States and Canada (Dyer and Theriault, 1976) found that the amount a manager earned was the best single predictor of satisfaction with pay—hardly a surprise. Also important was the belief that the manager's supervisor was accurate in assessing his or her performance, and that the company took cost of living increases into account. In a more recent study, Weiner (1980) found that dissatisfaction with pay was a major cause of absenteeism and job turnover.

Job Satisfaction and Performance

One would think that a satisfied worker would perform better. But is this really the case? In the 1970s Mirvis and Lawler (1977) conducted a cost-benefit analysis of job satisfaction and performance. Bank tellers' attitudes and behavior were assessed before and after they took part in a job enrichment program designed to make their work more satisfying. Their job performance was measured in terms of cash shortages. The authors calculated that improved job satisfaction resulted in a *direct* saving of $17,644 a year: happy workers were much less likely to "lose" cash through carelessness and/or dishonesty. It also brought about an *indirect* saving: happy workers were also less likely to be absent or to quit. The authors calculated that the savings from not having to recruit and train new tellers amounted to $125,000 a year!

The first conclusion of the Mirvis and Lawler study—that job satisfaction has a direct effect on performance—has been questioned. Most studies find that the relationship between job satisfaction and performance, as measured by quantity of output, is weak at best (Muchinsky, 1983). Moreover, there is the question of which comes first: Does job satisfaction cause a worker to perform well, or does the feeling that he or she is doing a good job make a worker happy with the job? The debate over this point has not been closed, but evidence for the performance-causes-satisfaction view is mounting.

Research generally supports Mirvis and Lawler's second conclusion—that job satisfaction lowers absenteeism and turnover rates. Unhappy workers take more days off than do workers who like their jobs. But the correlation is smaller than we might expect—at most, $-.35$ (Muchinsky, 1983).

The more people dislike their work, the more likely they are to quit; this seems too obvious to bother reporting. But here again, the correlation is smaller than one might imagine—about $-.40$ (Muchinsky, 1983). Unhappy workers do not add up their dissatisfactions one day and walk out the door; there are intervening variables. The decision to quit, as opposed to thinking about quitting, depends on the economic climate (job availability), on the worker's specific opportunities (whether he or she has an offer or feels confident about finding other employment), and also on a cost-benefit analysis the worker performs. An unhappy worker who decides the costs of quitting are too high may engage in cognitive restructuring, reevaluating the job in more positive terms, and/or engage in indirect forms of withdrawal, such as absenteeism (Mobley, Horner, and Hollingsworth, 1978).

SOCIAL INFLUENCES AT WORK

With very few exceptions, work involves other people. Organizations are not collections of isolated individuals. Rather, they are groups of people who engage in numerous face-to-face interactions. Relationships with supervisors and co-workers can have more effect on a worker's performance and satisfaction than formal opportunities for achievement, or even the worker's personal abilities and goals (Howell and Dipboye, 1982). Here we will look first at leadership and then at work groups.

Leadership

When a movie is a box-office hit, the director (not the film and sound crews) gets the credit. Likewise, when a movie is a flop, the director takes the blame. The "cast of thousands" is all but forgotten. And so it is in business, government, and other organizations.

The impact of leadership on an organization may be somewhat exaggerated in the public mind. But managers do play a major role in shaping employees' attitudes and behavior, as well as in planning and directing work. Not surprisingly, industrial-organizational psychologists have long been interested in the question of what makes a leader effective. There are four basic approaches to this question. The first emphasizes personal traits; the second, behavior; the third, situations. The fourth and newest approach considers various combinations of these factors.

The Trait Approach

The trait approach to leadership is based on the assumption that effective leadership depends on certain stable, enduring personal characteristics. This view reflects the commonsense notion that leaders are born, not made: "Some people can lead and some can't—regardless of how hard they try, how smart they are, or how many Dale Carnegie courses they have taken" (Howell and Dipboye, 1982, p. 128). Trait theory implies that the key to running a successful organization is *selection*: find the right managers and everything else will fall into place. This approach was popular among organizational psychologists in the 1930s and 1940s, when businesses and psychologists alike had great faith in the use of psychological tests. Today, though nearly all psychologists have abandoned the trait approach, it still plays an important role in popular ideas about leadership and therefore requires examination.

What do you think of when you hear the word "leader"? You probably picture leaders as tall, well-dressed, white males who are also bright, dominant, aggressive, and charismatic. This is your own personal trait theory. Research suggests there is a grain of truth to this common stereotype —but only a grain. Physical appearance may influence first impressions, but the effect is not lasting (Dipboye, Fromkin, and Wiback, 1975). A leader must do more than "dress for success." Most people who occupy leadership roles in the United States do happen to be white males, but this is because managers tend to recruit trainees who are like themselves. Given the opportunity, females and minority-group members can be just as effective in motivating and directing people to achieve organizational goals.

There is also evidence that leadership requires intelligence, but studies of executives, middle managers, and foremen suggest that mental ability accounts for only 6 percent of the difference between effective and ineffective leaders (Ghiselli, 1976). And what about the fact that personality profiles of effective leaders generally match popular stereotypes? Effective leaders tend to be bright, aggressive, independent, and high in need for achievement (Dunnette, 1976); they like activities that involve risk, intense thought, and opportunities to dominate others (Nash, 1963); they are decisive and self-assured (Ghiselli, 1971). But taken together, these traits account for less than 10 percent of the difference between effective and ineffective leadership—leaving the other 90 percent unexplained (Korman, 1968).

The Behavioral Approach

The behavioral approach to leadership focuses on what managers do, not who they are. This view is similar to the commonsense belief that leadership is a set of techniques for managing people that anyone can learn. Whereas the trait approach suggests that organizational success lies in selecting the right people for leadership roles, the behavioral approach emphasizes training. Most of the research in this area has focused on styles of leadership.

Early studies distinguished between *democratic* and *autocratic* leadership styles. A democratic leader invites participation, sharing decisions with subordinates. An autocratic leader does not: the boss's word is law. When it was first described, democratic leadership was hailed as the modern, enlightened approach to management. It has not lived up to these early promises, however (Howell and Dipboye, 1982).

John Hemphill, Ralph Stogdill, and their colleagues (1963) have proposed a somewhat different view of leadership styles. According to these psychologists, the most significant difference is between *structure-oriented* leadership, or concern for production (sometimes referred to as "task-centered" leadership), and *consideration-oriented* leadership, or concern for people (sometimes referred to as "employee-centered" leadership). A structure-oriented manager devotes most of his or her time and energy to planning, assigning tasks, and supervising production. Achieving organizational goals comes first; people come second. But a consideration-oriented manager gives priority to establishing mutual trust, respect, and rapport with subordinates.

The Situational View

According to a third view, the effectiveness of a leader depends on the situation: on the nature of the task, the organization, and the work group. *Who* the leader is (personality traits) and *what* he or she does (behavior) are of little consequence, according to this view. The success of a business depends on economic trends, not on who occupies executive positions or how the executives run the company (Lieberson and O'Connor, 1972). The record of a major-league baseball team reflects the skill of the players, not the effectiveness of the manager (Allen, Panian, and Lotz, 1979). This approach echoes the popular saying, "Anyone can win with a winner; no one can win with a loser" (Howell and Dipboye, 1982, p. 128).

The situational view is a useful antidote to the popular view that everything depends on the individual in charge. It balances trait and behavior approaches, which may overemphasize the effects of leadership. But the majority of industrial-organizational psychologists think that developing a "leaderless" theory is equivalent to throwing out the baby with the bathwater. Today, the theories that attract the most interest are those that consider the interaction of several variables.

What makes a winning team—the manager or the players? Most likely, both are essential, as Sparky Anderson's Detroit Tigers proved in their 1984 championship season. In business, too, leadership alone cannot provide success without a group of talented, motivated workers.

Contingency Theories

Contingency theories are based on the view that effective leadership is contingent on (or depends on) particular combinations of leadership traits, behavior, and situations. Fiedler (1978) was one of the first to consider the interplay of these three factors. Fiedler holds that the most significant aspects of the work situation for a leader are: (1) the structure of the task (whether goals and means are clearly defined); (2) leader-member relations (whether the leader is respected and liked); and (3) the power associated with the leader's position (whether the organization gives the leader the power and authority to enforce decisions). The most favorable situation for a leader is one in which the task is clearly defined, the subordinates respect and like the leader, and the leader has the power to lead. Least favorable is a situation in which the task is ill defined, the relations between the leader and the other members of the group are tense, and the leader has little power. Turning to personality traits, Fiedler holds that the most significant variable is whether leaders give top priority to completing a task (directive leadership) or to maintaining good interpersonal relations (participative leadership). Directive leaders function well in unfavorable situations, for example, because their first priority is defining goals, assigning tasks, and giving the group the structure it lacks. Participative leaders are ineffective in such situations because they are more concerned with whether people like them than with the tasks at hand. Fiedler's model is controversial, but even his critics concede that his model has inspired debate about the interplay of leadership and other variables.

One of the more interesting approaches to emerge from this debate is Vroom and Yetton's model of leadership (1973). Like Fiedler, Vroom and Yetton assume that what constitutes effective leadership varies from situation to situation. But unlike Fiedler, these researchers set personality variables aside and concentrate instead on specific types of problems and specific responses and outcomes. The result is a practical decision-making procedure that managers can follow step by step. Vroom and Yetton begin by specifying five possible responses to a problem, as shown in Table 28.1. These responses range from unilateral, or autocratic, decisions (AI and AII), to collective decisions (CI and CII), to participatory decisions made by a group (GII). Next, Vroom and Yetton propose a series of questions designed to lead a manager through the decision-making tree shown in Figure 28.4. This model assumes that the appropriateness of a response depends, first, on the quality of the decision (how important it is), second, on its acceptance by subordinates (whether the decision will be accepted unanimously or provoke rebellion and/or conflict among subordinates), and third, on minimizing the time needed to decide. One strength of this model is its specificity: the precise definitions embodied in it allow researchers to take exact measurement(s) of responses and outcomes in actual work settings.

Leadership, then, does affect workers' productivity and attitudes. But workers are basically social beings, and the group in which a person works also exerts a strong influence on his or her behavior on the job.

Groups

As the Hawthorne studies mentioned earlier in this chapter showed, productivity can be influenced more by norms set by a worker's *social group* than by his or her physical surroundings. The workers in this experiment felt themselves to be part of a special group which set its own standards for productivity and other behaviors (Roethlisberger and Dickson, 1939).

Table 28.1 ■ Decision Methods for Managers

AI. You solve the problem or make decision yourself, using information available to you at the time.

AII. You obtain the necessary information from your subordinates, then decide the solution to the problem yourself. You may or may not tell your subordinates what the problem is in getting the information from them. The role played by your subordinates in making the decision is clearly one of providing the necessary information to you, rather than generating or evaluating alternative solutions.

CI. You share the problem with the relevant subordinates individually, getting their ideas and suggestions without bringing them together as a group. Then *you* make the decision, which may or may not reflect your subordinates' influence.

CII. You share the problem with your subordinates as a group, obtaining their collective ideas and suggestions. Then you make the decision, which may or may not reflect your subordinates' influence.

GII. You share the problem with your subordinates as a group. Together you generate and evaluate alternatives and attempt to reach agreement (consensus) on a solution. Your role is much like that of chairman. You do not try to influence the group to adopt "your" solution, and you are willing to accept and implement any solution which has the support of the entire group.

Source: From Vroom, V. H., and P. W. Yetton. In K. N. Wexley and G. A. Yukl (Eds.), *Organizational behavior and industrial psychology.* New York: Oxford, 1975, p. 133.

How and Why Groups Influence Their Members

If groups can be so powerful, then we need to ask some questions about the nature of that power. How do groups influence members' behavior—and why?

I/O psychologists answer the "how" part of the question by studying the kinds of signals, or stimuli, that groups send to their members. Sometimes the group transmits stimuli to an individual group member; these signals are called **discretionary stimuli** (they are sent at the discretion of the individual's peers). The group may transmit direct messages of approval or disapproval, may instruct the individual about appropriate behavior, or may model the behavior it expects. Even

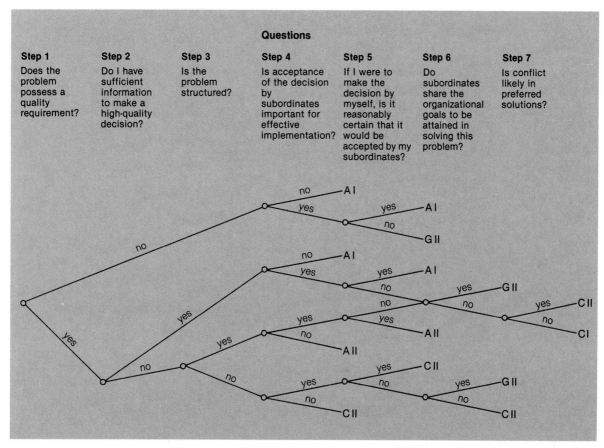

Figure 28.4. Using the Vroom and Yetton decision tree, a leader can mentally "walk through" alternative approaches to a problem before taking action. For example, if the quality of the decision is important and the leader does not have the necessary information, solution AI in Table 28.1 (the manager makes a decision with no assistance) is eliminated. If acceptance by subordinates is critical and any decision is likely to cause disagreement, then responses AI, AII, and CI are eliminated. This type of problem is best solved by bringing the group together to air their differences (CII or GII?). (Adapted from Vroom and Yetton, 1973.)

money or physical objects such as trophies may be discretionary stimuli (Hackman, 1976). In the workplace, praise, smiles, and friendly talks are all discretionary stimuli that the group uses to reinforce an individual's behavior. But should that person deviate from the group's norms, the discretionary stimuli he receives can become negative. Unfriendly remarks and cold shoulders are powerful messages of exclusion.

Why do groups use discretionary stimuli to influence their members' behavior? I/O psychologists cite three basic reasons: education and socialization, conformity, and diversity (every group needs both leaders and followers) (Hackman, 1976).

Group Effectiveness

Smiles or cold shoulders, praise or criticism powerfully influence individual group members. But they tell us only part of the story. Discretionary stimuli tell us nothing about the *external factors*. How, for example, do reward systems influence a group's effectiveness?

Rewards   As Americans, we naturally assume that rewarding individual effort will encourage even greater achievement. That may be true for individuals, but it can be a disaster for groups. If the group's task requires cooperation and interdependence, then a system that rewards individual efforts will be counterproductive. Instead of working together, group members will compete with each other, spurred on by the promise of the biggest raise or bonus.

External Pressures and Stress　A group of people in an advertising agency are working together to create a proposal for a major prospective client. Other agencies are competing for the same account, and the deadline is fast approaching. The group begins to meet frequently for long, intensive sessions, and conflicts get resolved as the goal of a winning presentation becomes stronger. The dual *external* pressures of the deadline and competition from other agencies have enhanced the group's cohesiveness and motivation.

In organizations, stress can come from within the company if one group competes with another for rewards and recognition. Again, this external stress can increase cooperation among group members, and if the group's task requires cooperation, then its performance may improve. But sometimes external stress leads to too much cooperation within a group. When this happens, the results can be disastrous, especially if the group's "task requires a high degree of information processing" (Howell and Dipboye, 1982, p. 103). According to I. L. Janis (1972), these were the conditions surrounding John F. Kennedy's tragic decision to invade Cuba's Bay of Pigs.

For some time, the Soviet influence in Cuba had been growing, and intelligence reports fed to Kennedy implied that it posed a serious threat to U.S. security. Military and intelligence advisors began to call for a radical plan to knock out the Cuban threat—an invasion of the island by way of the Bay of Pigs. Kennedy approved the plan, but the invasion was a disaster, both for the United States and for Kennedy personally. How could such a savvy, intelligent president have approved a plan that in retrospect seemed doomed to failure?

Janis's research into the decision-making processes behind the Bay of Pigs and other administrations' fiascoes suggests that a special kind of thinking, known as "groupthink," was operating. (George Orwell was the first to use this term.) According to Janis, groupthink helps a highly cohesive group—such as Kennedy's advisors —maintain its cohesiveness when under the pres-

sure of external threats. Groupthink has the following characteristics:

> the illusion among members that there is unanimous support for the decisions of the group, a distorted sense of invulnerability, a tendency to rationalize away errors in decision making, an elevated view of the group in which members believe that there is a moral justification for their decisions, and a stereotyped view of outside groups. (Howell and Dipboye, p. 103)

Members themselves fear that contradictory perceptions will destroy the group's cohesiveness, and so such thoughts go unexpressed. Fear of ridicule, too, keeps would-be critics silent.

Janis's theory has been criticized, but even if it is flawed, it does suggest that when group members suspend their own ability to think critically and independently, the group's decision-making ability is compromised.

Cohesiveness　If the members of the group find that belonging to the group helps them to achieve their goals, and if group members like each other, the group will stay together. It will be *cohesive*. What leads to high cohesiveness? It stems from a number of factors: "group success in achieving goals, small group size, external threats, and perceptions of group members that they are similar to one another in their beliefs, backgrounds, and other characteristics" (Howell and Dipboye, p. 110).

Members of highly cohesive groups will help one another and credit the group for successes, but will such groups be highly productive? Sometimes. Members of highly cohesive groups share the group's norms. If a highly cohesive group has productivity as a strongly held norm, then the group will be productive. If not, productivity will suffer.

A Multifaceted Area　Group effectiveness may also depend on a number of other factors—such as the group's size and its degree of homogeneity. Study of this aspect of workplace behavior continues; and, like many other areas of I/O psychology, it provides psychologists with interesting opportunities to apply their knowledge in a practical setting.

SUMMARY

1. **Industrial/organizational (I/O) psychology** has its roots in three separate movements: industrial engineering, personnel psychology, and the human relations movement. Fredrick Taylor, an industrial engineer, called on management to redesign work methods to make them more efficient, a system known as **scientific management.** Hugo Munsterberg emphasized making production more efficient by matching people to the jobs to which they were best suited, thus opening the way for personnel experts. And research by industrial psychologists turned attention to the effect that workers' feelings, motivations, and social relations had on productivity.

2. In matching workers to jobs, many employers rely on psychological tests as predictors of job performance, on nontest predictors such as interviews, or on a combination of the two. Psychological tests include intelligence tests; tests of mechanical aptitude, spatial relations, and motor abilities; and tests that attempt to assess an applicant's personality. To be useful, a test must be both reliable and valid. Futhermore, it should have criterion-related validity—that is, it should correlate with subsequent job performance. Most tests are only moderate predictors of success on the job. If a test has an **adverse impact** on members of a protected minority, it may be found to violate the Civil Rights Act. Interviews may lack validity because of the biases and backgrounds of the interviewer and applicant or because of the structure of the interview itself. Interviews are more likely to be valid if interviewers (1) stick to questions that reveal information pertinent to job duties, (2) use a structured format, and (3) are trained in interview techniques. Using panels of interviewers also raises validity.

3. Work motivation affects how long employees stay with a company, how dependably they perform their duties, and how innovative they are on the job. Theories of motivation can be divided into three categories: need theories, cognitive theories, and reinforcement theories. Maslow's need hierarchy views people as motivated first by fundamental needs (physiological and safety needs), then by psychological needs (social and self-esteem needs), and finally by metaneeds. Aldorfer's **ERG theory** breaks needs into three categories: existence needs, which are fundamental needs plus working conditions and fringe benefits; relatedness, or interpersonal, needs; and growth needs—the need to have a creative or productive effect on self or the environment. Cognitive theories of work motivation focus on workers' expectations, their attempts to maintain cognitive consistency, or their intentions. **Expectancy theory** states that work motivation is determined by the satisfaction one anticipates from a job outcome, the perception of that outcome's relationship to one's current performance, and expectations that one's effort will affect one's performance. **Equity theory** states that workers are motivated to remove perceived inequities. **Goal-setting theory** views workers as motivated by conscious intentions to attain a specific goal; it is the basic concept behind management by objectives (MBO). **Reinforcement theory** applies the principles of operant conditioning to the workplace; it uses positive reinforcement to increase employee motivation.

4. Job satisfaction is an emotional, affective orientation toward one's work, measured in terms of either overall satisfaction or satisfaction with different facets of work. Most studies have found that the relationship between job satisfaction and performance is weak, but that job satisfaction does lower absenteeism and turnover rates.

5. I/O psychologists take four basic approaches to the question of what makes a leader effective. The *trait approach* assumes that effective leadership depends on certain stable, enduring personal characteristics. However, since personality traits have been shown to account for less than 10 percent of the difference between effective and ineffective leaders, most psychologists have abandoned this approach. The *behavioral approach* focuses on what leaders do (their leadership styles) and emphasizes training. According to some psychologists, the most

significant difference in leadership styles is between structure-oriented leadership, or concern for production, and consideration-oriented leadership, or concern for people. The *situational view* sees the effectiveness of a leader as depending on the situation: on the nature of the task, the organization, and the work group. This approach echoes the popular saying that anyone can win with a winner; no one can with a loser. *Contingency theories* are based on the view that effective leadership is contingent on particular combinations of leadership traits, behavior, and situations. According to Fiedler, the most favorable situation for a leader is one in which the task is clearly defined, the subordinates respect and like the leader, and the leader has the power to lead. The most significant variable in terms of personality is whether a leader gives top priority to completing a task or to maintaining good interpersonal relations. Vroom and Yetton's model of leadership concentrates on specific types of problems and specific responses and outcomes, producing a practical, step-by-step decision-making procedure.

6. Norms set by the work group can stongly influ-

ence a worker's behavior on the job. Groups influence members' behavior through the use of **discretionary stimuli**—signals sent at the discretion of the individual's peers. Discretionary stimuli transmit direct messages of approval or disapproval, instruct the member about appropriate behavior, or model the behavior the group expects. Groups use discretionary stimuli to educate and socialize members, to enforce conformity, and to create and maintain diversity. When a group's task requires cooperation and interdependence, then a system that rewards individual efforts will be counterproductive, since members will compete rather than cooperate with one another. External pressures and external stress can enhance group cohesiveness and motivation, but they can sometimes lead to too much cooperation, resulting in "groupthink"—a phenomenon in which members suspend their own ability to think critically, thus compromising the group's decision-making ability. Group cohesiveness can increase productivity *if* the group has productivity as a strongly held norm. Group size and degree of homogeneity may also affect a group's effectiveness.

KEY TERMS

adverse impact
discretionary stimuli
equity theory
ERG theory

expectancy theory
goal-setting theory
industrial/organizational
 psychology (I/O psychology)

realistic job preview (RJP)
reinforcement theory
scientific management

RECOMMENDED READINGS

CASCIO, W. F. *Applied psychology in personnel management*. Reston, Va.: Reston, 1978. Comprehensive coverage of the use of tests and other means of selecting and placing people at work.

DUNNETTE, M. (Ed.). *Handbook of industrial and organizational psychology*. Chicago: Rand McNally, 1976. This scholarly work covers all aspects of I/O psychology.

PINDER, C. *Work motivation*. Glenview, Ill.: Scott, Foresman,. 1984. Coverage of work motivation and work attitudes as they relate to job performance.

SCHEIN, E. *Organizational psychology* (3rd ed.). Englewood Cliffs, N.J.: Prentice-Hall, 1980. This book gives an overview of the role of psychology in management.

The number in brackets after each entry refers to the chapter in this book in which that work is cited.

Abel, G. G., E. B. Blanchard, and **J. V. Becker.** An integrated treatment program for rapists. In R. T. Rada (Ed.), *Clinical aspects of the rapist.* New York: Grune & Stratton, 1978. [13]

Abelson, H., R. Cohen, E. Heaton, and **C. Suder.** Public attitudes toward and experience with erotic materials. In Commission on Obscenity and Pornography, *Technical reports of the Commission on Obscenity and Pornography* (Vol. 6). Washington, D.C.: U.S. Government Printing Office, 1970. [13]

Abraham, K. Notes on psychoanalytic investigation and treatment of manic-depressive insanity and allied conditions. In *Selected papers of Karl Abraham, M.D.* London: The Hogarth Press, 1948. (Originally published, 1911.) [23]

Abraham, K. The first pregenital stage of the libido. In *Selected papers of Karl Abraham, M.D.* London: The Hogarth Press, 1948 (Originally published, 1916.) [23]

Abramov, I., J. Gordon, A. Hendrickson, L. Hainline, V. Dobson, and **E. LaBossiere.** The retina of the newborn human infant. *Science,* 1982, *217,* 265–267. [14]

Abramson, L. Y., M. E. P. Selignam, and **J. D. Teasdale,** Learned helplessness in humans: Critique and reformulation. *Journal of Abnormal Psychology,* 1978, *87,* 49–74. [21]

Ackerman, N. *The psychodynamics of family life.* New York: Basic Books, 1958. [24]

Acredolo, C. Conservation-nonconservation: Alternative explanations. In C. J. Brainerd (Ed.), *Children's logical and mathematical cognition: Progress in cognitive developmental research.* New York: Springer-Verlag, 1982. [15]

Adams, J. S. Inequity in social exchange. In L. Berkowitz (Ed.), *Advances in experimental social psychology.* Vol. 2. New York: Academic Press, 1965. [28]

Adams, R. An account of a peculiar optical phenomenon seen after having looked at a moving body. *London and Edinburgh Philosophical Magazine and Journal of Science,* 1834, *5,* 373–374. [6]

Adelson, B. Problem solving and the development of abstract categories in programming languages. *Memory and Cognition,* 1981, *9,* 422–433. [10]

Adelson, J. The development of ideology in adolescence. In S. Dragastin and G. H. Elder (Eds.), *Adolescence in the life cycle.* Washington, D.C.: Hemisphere, 1975. [15]

Adler, A. Individual psychology. In C. A. Murchison (Ed.), *Psychologies of 1930.* Worcester, Mass.: Clark University Press, 1930. [18]

Adler, A. *What life should mean to you.* Boston: Little, Brown, 1931. [18]

Agnew, H. W., Jr., W. B. Webb, and **R. I. Williams.** Comparison of stage four and REM sleep deprivation. *Perceptual and Motor Skills,* 1967, *24,* 851–858. [7]

Ainsworth, M. D. S., M. C. Blehar, E. Waters, and **S. Wall.** *Patterns of attachment.* Hillsdale, N.J.: Lawrence Erlbaum, 1978. [17]

Albee, G. W. I.Q. tests on trial. *The New York Times,* February 12, 1978, p. E 13. [20]

Alcock, J. *Animal behavior: An evolutionary approach* (3rd ed.). Sunderland, Mass.: Sinauer Associates, 1984. [4]

Alderfer, C. P. An empirical test of a new theory of human needs. *Organizational Behavior and Human Performance,* 1969, *4,* 142–175. [28]

Alderfer, C. P. *Existence, relatedness, and growth: Human needs in organizational settings.* New York: Free Press, 1972. [28]

Allen, M. G. Twin studies of affective illness. *Archives of General Psychiatry,* 1976, *33,* 1476–1478. [4]

Allen, M. P., S. K. Panian, and **R. E. Lotz.** Managerial succession and organizational performance: A recalcitrant problem revisited. *Administrative Science Quarterly,* 1979, *24,* 167–180. [28]

Allen, V. L. Situational factors in conformity. In L. Berkowitz (Ed.), *Advances in experimental social psychology.* Vol. 2. New York: Academic Press, 1965. [27]

Alley, T. R. Headshape and the perception of cuteness. *Developmental Psychology,* 1981, *17,* 650–654. [17]

Allgeier, B., and **R. Allgeier.** *Sexual interactions.* Lexington, Mass.: Heath, 1984. [13]

Allon, N. The stigma of overweight in everyday life. In G. A. Bray (Ed.), *Obesity in perspective.* Washington, D.C.: U.S. Government Printing Office, 1975. [26]

Allport, F. H. The influence of the group upon association and thought. *Journal of Experimental Psychology,* 1920, *3,* 159–182. [27]

Allport, G. W. *Personality: A psychological interpretation.* New York: Holt, Rinehart & Winston, 1937. [19]

Allport, G. W. *Pattern and growth in personality.* New York: Holt, Rinehart & Winston, 1961. [19]

Allport, G. W. Traits revisited. *American Psychologist,* 1966, *21,* 1–10. [19]

Allport, G. W., and **H. S. Odbert.** Trait-names: A psycho-lexical study. *Psychological Monographs,* 1936, *47,* Whole No. 211. [19]

Allport, G. W., and **L. Postman.** *The psychology of rumor.* New York: Henry Holt, 1947. [15]

Alpert, J. L., and **M. S. Richardson.** Par-

enting. In L. W. Poon (Ed.), *Aging in the 1980s: Psychological issues.* Washington, D.C.: American Psychological Association, 1980. [17]

Altmann, S. A. Primate communication. In G. A. Miller (Ed.), *Communication, language, and meaning.* New York: Basic Books, 1973. [16]

American Association on Mental Deficiency. *Manual on terminology and classification in mental retardation* (1977 revision). Washington, D.C.: American Association on Mental Deficiency, 1977. [20]

American Cancer Society. *Cancer facts and figures, 1983.* New York: American Cancer Society, 1982. [21]

American Heart Association. *Heart facts, 1984.* Dallas: American Heart Association, 1984. [21]

American Psychiatric Association. *Diagnostic and statistical manual of mental disorders (DSM-I).* Washington, D.C.: American Psychiatric Association, 1952. [23]

American Psychiatric Association. *Diagnostic and statistical manual of mental disorders (DSM-II).* Washington, D.C.: American Psychiatric Association, 1968. [22]

American Psychiatric Association. *Diagnostic and statistical manual of mental disorders (DSM-III).* Washington, D.C.: American Psychiatric Association, 1980. [22, 23]

American Psychological Association. *Directory of the American Psychological Association.* Washington, D.C.: American Psychological Association, 1981. [1]

American Psychological Association. *Ethical principles of psychologists.* Washington, D.C.: American Psychological Association, 1981. [2]

American Psychological Association, American Educational Research Association and **National Council on Measurement in Education.** *Standards for educational and psychological tests.* Washington, D.C.: American Psychological Association, 1974. [20]

American Running and Fitness Association. *Statistical Report.* Washington, D.C.: American Running and Fitness Association, 1981. [21]

Ames, A., Jr. Visual perception and the rotating trapezoidal window. *Psychological Monographs,* 1951, *65* (7, Whole No. 234). [6]

Amoore, J. E., and **D. Venstrum.** Correlations between stereochemical assessments and organoleptic analysis of odorous compounds. In T. Hayashi (Ed.), *Olfaction and taste.* Oxford: Pergamon, 1967. [5]

Anand, B. K., G. S. Chhina, and **B. Singh.** Some aspects of electroencephalographic studies in yogis. *Electroencephalog-*

raphy and Clinical Neurophysiology, 1961, *13,* 452–456. [7]

Anastasi, A. *Psychological testing* (5th ed.). New York: Macmillan, 1982. [20]

Anders, T. F., and **H. P. Roffwarg.** The effects of selective interruption and deprivation of sleep in the human newborn. *Developmental Psychobiology,* 1973, *6* (1), 77–89. [7]

Anderson, J. R. *Cognitive psychology and its implications.* San Francisco: W. H. Freeman, 1980. [8, 10, 16]

Anderson, J. R. Interference: The relationship between response latency and response accuracy. *Journal of Experimental Psychology: Human Learning and Memory,* 1981, *7,* 311–325. [9]

Anderson, J. R. Acquisition of cognitive skill. *Psychological Review,* 1982, *89,* 369–406. [8]

Anderson, J. R. A spreading activation theory of memory. *Journal of Verbal Learning and Verbal Behavior,* 1983, *22,* 261–295. [9]

Anderson, J. R. *The architecture of cognition.* Cambridge, Mass.: Harvard University Press, 1983. [16]

Anderson, J. R., and **G. H. Bower.** A propositional theory of recognition memory. *Memory and Cognition,* 1974, *2,* 406–412. [9]

Anderson, J. R., C. F. Boyle, R. Farrell, and **B. Reiser.** Cognitive principles in the design of computer tutors. *Proceedings of the Sixth Annual Conference of the Cognitive Science Society,* 1984, pp. 2–9. [8]

Anderson, J. R., R. Farrell, and **R. Sauers.** Learning to program in LISP. *Cognitive Science,* 1984, *8,* 87–129. [10]

Andersson, B. The effect of injections of hypertonic NaCl solutions into different parts of the hypothalamus of goats. *Acta Physiologica Scandinavica,* 1953, *28,* 188–201. [12]

Andreasen, N. C., and **S. Olsen.** Negative v. positive schizophrenia: Definition and validation. *Archives of General Psychiatry,* 1982, *39.* 789–794. [22]

Andreasen, N. C., M. R. Smith, C. G. Jacoby, J. W. Dennert, and **S. S. Olsen.** Ventricular enlargement in schizophrenia: Definition and prevalence. *American Journal of Psychiatry.* 1982, *139* (3), 292–302. [22]

Andrews, G., and **R. Harvey.** Does psychotherapy benefit neurotic patients? A reanalysis of the Smith, Glass, and Miller data. *Archives of General Psychiatry,* 1981, *38,* 1203–1208. [24]

Anglin, J. *Word, object, and concept development.* New York: Norton, 1977. [15]

Appel, L. F., R. G. Cooper, N. McCarrell, J. Sims-Knight, S. R. Yussen, and **J. H. Flavell.** The development of the distinction between perceiving and memorizing. *Child Development,* 1972, *43,* 1365–1381. [15]

Arendt, H. *Life of the mind.* Vol. 1. *Thinking.* New York: Harcourt Brace Jovanovich, 1978. [26]

Aries, P. *Centuries of childhood: A social*

history of family life. New York: Vintage, 1962. [15]

Arkes, H. R., and **J. P. Garske.** *Psychological theories of motivation.* Monterey, Calif.: Brooks/Cole, 1977. [12]

Armstrong, B. Illinois judge upholds IQ test use: Departs from *Larry P. APA Monitor,* November 1980, 6–7. [20]

Armstrong, S. L., L. R. Gleitman, and **H. Gleitman.** What some concepts might not be. *Cognition,* 1983, *13,* 263–308. [10]

Arnold, M. B. *Emotion and personality.* New York: Columbia University Press, 1960. [11]

Aronson, E. *The social animal* (2nd ed.). San Francisco: Freeman, 1976. [1, 25]

Aronson, E., N. Blaney, J. Sikes, C. Stephan, and **M. Snapp.** Busing and racial tension: The jigsaw route to learning and liking. *Psychology Today,* 1975, *9,* 43–50. [26]

Aronson, E., and **D. E. Linder.** Gain and loss of esteem as determinants of interpersonal attractiveness. *Journal of Experimental Social Psychology,* 1965, *1,* 156–172. [26]

Arvey, R. Unfair discrimination in the employment interview: Legal and psychological aspects. *Psychological Bulletin,* 1979, *86,* 736–765. [28]

Asarnow, R. F., R. A. Steffy, MacCrimmon, and **J. M. Cleghorn.** An attentional assessment of foster children at risk for schizophrenia. *Journal of Abnormal Psychology,* 1977, *86,* 267–275. [23]

Asch, S. E. Forming impressions of personality. *Journal of Abnormal and Social Psychology,* 1946, *41,* 258–290. [26]

Asch, S. E. Effects of group pressure upon the modification and distortion of judgments. In H. Guertzkow (Ed.), *Groups, leadership, and men.* Pittsburgh: Carnegie Press, 1951. [27]

Aserinsky, E., and **N. Kleitman.** Regularly occurring periods of eye motility and concomitant phenomena during sleep. *Science,* 1953, *118,* 273. [7]

Ashley, F., Jr., and **W. Kannel** Relation of weight changes to atherogenic traits: The Framingham Study. *Journal of Chronic Diseases,* 1974, *27,* 103–114. [21]

Ashmead, D. H., and **M. Perlmutter.** Infant memory in everyday life. In M. Perlmutter (Ed.), *New directions in child development.* No. 10. *Children's memory.* San Francisco: Jossey-Bass, 1980. [15]

Atkinson, J. W. (Ed.). *Motives in fantasy, action, and society.* New York: Van Nostrand Reinhold, 1958a. [12]

Atkinson, J. W. Thematic apperceptive measurement of motives within a context of motivation. In J. W. Atkinson (Ed.), *Motives in fantasy, action, and society.* New York: Van Nostrand Reinhold, 1958b. [12]

Atkinson, R. C. Mnemotechnics in second-language learning. *American Psychologist,* 1975, *30,* 821–828. [9]

Attneave, F. Some informational aspects of visual perception. *Psychological Review,* 1954, *61,* 183–193. [6]

Ault, R. L. *Children's cognitive development* (2nd ed.). New York: Oxford University Press, 1983. [15]

Axelrod, R., and **W. D. Hamilton.** The evolution of cooperation. *Science,* 1981, *211,* 1390–1396. [27]

Azrin, N. H., and **R. B. Foxx.** *Toilet training in less than a day.* New York: Simon & Schuster, 1974. [8]

Babson, S. G., M. L. Pernoll, G. I. Benda, and **K. Simpson.** *Diagnosis and management of the fetus and neonate at risk: A guide for team care* (4th ed.). St. Louis: C. V. Mosby, 1980. [14]

Baddeley, A. D. Selective attention and performance in dangerous environments. *British Journal of Psychology,* 1972, *63,* 537–546. [10]

Baddeley, A. D. *The psychology of human memory.* London: Harper & Row, 1976. [9]

Baddeley, A. D., N. Thomson, and **M. Buchanan.** Word-length and time structure of short-term memory. *Journal of Verbal Learning and Verbal Behavior,* 1975, *14,* 575–589. [9]

Badia, P., J. Harsh, and **B. Abbott.** Choosing between predictable and unpredictable shock conditions: Data and theory. *Psychological Bulletin,* 1979, *86,* 1107–1131. [21]

Baer, D. M. Laboratory control of thumbsucking by withdrawal and representation of reinforcement. *Journal of the Experimental Analysis of Behavior,* 1962, *5,* 525–528. [8]

Bahnson, C.B. Stress and cancer: The state of the art. *Psychosomatics,* 1981, *22,* 207–220. [21]

Baldwin, J. D., and **J. I. Baldwin.** *Behavior principles in everyday life.* Englewood Cliffs, N.J.: Prentice-Hall, 1981. [10]

Baltes, P. B., and **K. W. Schaie.** Aging and IQ: The myth of the twilight years. *Psychology Today,* March 1974, *7,* 35–40. [15]

Bancroft, J. *Human sexuality and its problems.* New York, Churchill-Livingston, 1983. [13]

Bandura, A. Influence of models' reinforcement contingencies on the acquisition of imitative responses. *Journal of Personality and Social Psychology,* 1965, *1,* 589–595. [8, 17]

Bandura, A. *Aggression: A social learning analysis.* Englewood Cliffs, N.J.: Prentice-Hall, 1973. [17, 27]

Bandura, A. Social learning analysis of aggression. In E. Ribes-Inesta and A. Bandura (Eds.), *Analysis of delinquency and aggression.* Hillsdale, N.J.: Lawrence Erlbaum, 1976. [27]

Bandura, A. *Social learning theory.* Englewood Cliffs, N.J.: Prentice-Hall, 1977. [8, 16, 17, 19, 24]

Bandura, A. The self system in reciprocal determinism. *American Psychologist,* 1978, *33,* 344–358. [19]

Bandura, A., J. E. Grusec, and **F. L. Men-love.** Vicarious extinction of avoidance behavior. *Journal of Personality and Social Psychology,* 1967, *5,* 16–23. [24]

Bandura, A., R. W. Jeffery, and **C. L. Wright.** Efficacy of particpant modeling as a function of response induction aids. *Journal of Abnormal Psychology,* 1974, *83,* 56–64. [24]

Bandura, A., and **F. J. McDonald.** Influence of social reinforcement and the behavior of models in shaping children's moral judgments. *Journal of Abnormal and Social Psychology,* 1963, *67,* 274–281. [8]

Bandura, A., and **F. L. Menlove.** Factors determining vicarious extinction of avoidance behavior through symbolic modeling. *Journal of Personality and Social Psychology,* 1968, *8,* 99–108. [8]

Bandura, A., D. Ross, and **S. A. Ross.** Imitation of film-mediated aggressive models. *Journal of Abnormal and Social Psychology, 1963, 66,* 3–11. [8]

Bandura, A., and **R. H. Walters.** *Social learning and personality development.* New York: Holt, Rinehart & Winston, 1963. [8, 17]

Banks, M. S. The development of visual accommodation during early infancy. *Child Development,* 1980, *51,* 646–666. [14]

Banks, M. S., and **P. Salapatek.** Infant pattern vision: A new approach based on the contrast sensitivity function. *Journal of Experimental Child Psychology,* 1981, *31,* 1–45. [14]

Banks, M. S., and **P. Salapatek.** Infant visual perception. In P. H. Mussen (Ed.), *Handbook of child psychology* (4th ed.), Vol. 2, M. M. Haith and J. J. Campos (eds.), *Infancy and developmental psychobiology.* New York: Wiley, 1983. [14]

Barash, D. P. Human reproductive strategies: A sociobiologic overview. In J. S. Lockard (Ed.), *The evolution of human social behavior.* New York: Elsevier, 1980. [4]

Barber, T. X. Responding to "hypnotic" suggestions: An introspective report. *American Journal of Clinical Hypnosis,* 1975, *18,* 6–22. [7]

Barber, T. X. *Hypnosis: A scientific approach.* New York: Psychological Dimensions, 1976. [7]

Barber, T. X., N. P. Spanos, and **J. F. Chaves.** *Hypnotism: Imagination and human potentialities.* New York: Pergamon Press, 1974. [7]

Barec, L., C. MacArthur, and **M. Sherwood.** A study of health education aspects of smoking in pregnancy. *International Journal of Health Education,* 1976, *19* (Supplement 1), 1–17. [21]

Barfield, R. A., and **J. N. Morgan.** *Early retirement: The decision and the experience.* Ann Arbor, Mich.: Institute of Social Relations, University of Michigan, 1970. [17]

Barker, R. G., T. Dembo, and **K. Lewin.** *Frustration and regression: An experiment with young children.* University of Iowa Studies in Child Welfare, 1941, *18,* 386. [27]

Barlow, H. B., and **R. M. Hill.** Evidence for a physiological explanation of the waterfall phenomenon and figural aftereffects. *Nature,* 1963, *200,* 1345–1347. [6]

Barltrop, D. Transfer of lead to the human foetus. In D. Barltrop (Ed.), *Mineral metabolism in pediatrics.* Oxford: Blackwell Scientific Publications, 1969. [20]

Baron, R. A., and **P. A. Bell.** Aggression and heat: The influence of ambient temperature, negative affect, and a cooling drink on physical aggression. *Journal of Personality and Social Psychology,* 1976, *33,* 245–255. [27]

Barron, F. *Creative person and creative process.* New York: Holt, Rinehart & Winston, 1969. [10]

Barsalou, L. Ad hoc categories. *Memory and Cognition,* 1983, *11,* 211–227. [10]

Bartlett, J. C., and **J. W. Santrock.** Affect-dependent memory in young children. *Child Development,* 1979, *50,* 513–518. [9]

Bartoshuk, L. The chemical senses: I: Taste. In J. W. Kling and L. A. Riggs (Eds.), *Woodworth and Schlosberg's experimental psychology* (3rd ed.). New York: Holt, Rinehart & Winston, 1971. [5]

Bartoshuk, L., G. Dateo, D. Vandenbelt, R. Buttrick, and **L. Long.** Effects of *gymnema sylvestre* and *synsepalum dulficum* on taste in man. In C. Pfafman (Ed.), *Olfaction and taste* (Vol. 3). New York: Rockefeller University Press, 1969. [5]

Bates, E. *Language and context: The acquisition of pragmatics.* New York: Academic Press, 1976. [16]

Bates, E. *The emergence of symbols: Cognition and communication in infancy.* New York: Academic Press, 1979. [16]

Bateson, G., D. Jackson, J. Haley, and **J. Weakland.** Toward a theory of schizophrenia. *Behavioral Science,* 1956, *1,* 251–264. [23]

Battig, W. F., and **W. E. Montague.** Category norms for verbal items in 56 categories: A replication and extension of the Connecticut category norms. *Journal of Experimental Psychology Monograph,* June 1969. [10]

Bayer, E. Beitrage zur Zweikomponententheorie des Hungers. *Zeitschrift fur Psychologie,* 1929, *112,* 1–54. [27]

Beattie, G. W. Floor apportionment and gaze in conversational dyads. *British Journal of Social and Clinical Psychology,* 1978, *17,* 7–16. [16]

Beattie, G. W., A. Cutler, and **M. Pearson.** Why is Mrs. Thatcher interrupted so often? *Nature,* 1982, *300,* 744–747. [16]

Beck, A. T. *Cognitive therapy and the emotional disorders.* New York: International Universities Press, 1976. [24]

Beck, A. T. *Depression inventory.* Philadelphia: Center for Cognitive Therapy, 1978. [20]

Beck, A. T., A. J. Rush, B. F. Shaw, and **G. Emery.** *Cognitive theory of depression.* New York: Guilford Press, 1979. [23, 24]

Beck, S. J. *Rorschach's test.* Vol. 1, *Basic processes* (3rd ed.). New York: Grune & Stratton, 1961. [20]

Becker, J. V., L. J. Skinner, G. G. Abel, and **E. C. Treacy.** Incidence and types of sexual dysfunctions in rape and incest victims. *Journal of Sex and Marital Therapy,* 1982, *8* (1), 65–74. [13]

Bekesy, G. von. Current status of theories of hearing. *Science,* 1956, *123,* 779–783. [5]

Bell, A., M. S. Weinberg, and **S. K. Hammersmith.** *Sexual preference: Its development in men and women.* Bloomington: Indiana University Press, 1981. [13]

Bellows, R. T. Time factors in water drinking in dogs. *American Journal of Physiology,* 1939, *125,* 87–97. [12]

Bellugi, U. Learning the language. *Psychology Today,* 1970, *4,* 32–35 +. [16]

Belsky, J. Two waves of day care research: Developmental effects and conditions of quality. In R. Ainslie (Ed.), *The child and the day care setting.* New York: Praeger, 1985. [17]

Bem, D. J. Self-perception theory. In L. Berkowitz (Ed.), *Advances in experimental social psychology.* Vol. 6. New York: Academic Press, 1972. [26]

Bem, S. L. Sex-role adaptability: One consequence of psychological androgyny. *Journal of Personality and Social Psychology,* 1975, *31,* 634–643. [17]

Bem, S. L. Gender schema theory and its implications for child develoment: Raising gender-aschematic children in a gender-schematic society. *Signs,* 1983, *8,* 598–616. [17]

Bennett, G. K. *Test of mechanical comprehension.* New York: Psychological Corporation, 1940. Copyright 1941, renewed 1969 by the Psychological Corporation. All rights reserved. [28]

Berger, P. A. Medical treatment of mental illness. *Science,* 1978, *200,* 974–981. [24]

Bergin, A. E. The evaluation of therapeutic outcomes. In A. E. Bergin and S. L. Garfield (Eds.), *Handbook of psychotherapy and behavior change: An empirical analysis.* New York: Wiley, 1971. [24]

Bergin, A. E., and **M. J. Lambert.** The evaluation of therapeutic outcomes. In S. L. Garfield and A. E. Bergin (Eds.), *Handbook of psychotherapy and behavior change: An empirical analysis* (2nd ed.). New York: Wiley, 1978. [24]

Berkman, L. F., and **S. L. Syme.** Social networks, host resistance, and mortality: A nine-year followup study of Alameda County residents. *American Journal of Epidemiology,* 1979, *109,* 186–204. [21]

Berkowitz, L. *Aggression: A social psychological analysis.* New York: McGraw-Hill, 1962. [27]

Berlin, B., and **P. Kaye.** *Basic color terms: Their universality and evolution.*

Berkeley: University of California Press, 1969. [16]

Bernstein, I. Learned taste aversion in children receiving chemotherapy. *Science*, 1978, *200*, 1302–1303. [8]

Berntson, G. G., H. C. Hughes, and **M. S. Beattie.** A comparison of hypothalamically induced biting attack with natural predatory behavior in the cat. *Journal of Comparative and Physiological Psychology*, 1976, *90*, 167–178. [4]

Berscheid, E., K. Dion, E. Walster, and **G. M. Walster.** Physical attractiveness and dating choice: A test of the matching hypothesis. *Journal of Experimental Social Psychology*, 1971, *7*, 173–189. [26]

Bersoff, D. N. Regarding psychological testing: Legal regulation of psychological assessment in the public schools. *Maryland Law Review*, 1979, *39*, 27–120. [20]

Bertenthal, B. I., and **K. W. Fischer.** Development of self-recognition in the infant. *Developmental Psychology*, 1978, *14*, 44–50. [17]

Bertenthal, B. I., and **K. W. Fischer.** The development of representation in search: A social-cognitive analysis. *Child Development*, 1983, *54*, 846–857. [15]

Bexton, W. H., W. Heron, and **T. H. Scott.** Effects of decreased variation in the sensory environment. *Canadian Journal of Psychology*, 1954, *8*, 70–76. [6, 7]

Bickman, L. The social power of a uniform. *Journal of Applied Social Psychology*, 1974, *4*, 47–61. [27]

Bieber, I., et al. *Homosexuality: A psychoanalytic study.* New York: Basic Books, 1962. [13]

Bijou, S. W., and **D. M. Baer.** *Child development.* Vol. 2: *Universal stage of infancy.* Englewood Cliffs, N.J.: Prentice-Hall, 1965. [16]

Binet, A., and **T. Simon.** *The development of intelligence in children. (The Binet-Simon Scale).* Baltimore: Williams & Wilkins, 1916. [20]

Birch, H. B. The role of motivational factors in insightful problem-solving. *Journal of Comparative Psychology*, 1945, *38*, 295–317. [10]

Birnbaum, L., and **M. Selfridge.** Conceptual analysis of natural language. In R. C. Schank and C. K. Riesbeck (Eds.), *Inside computer understanding.* Hillsdale, N.J.: Lawrence Erlbaum, 1981. [16]

Bjork, E. L., and **E. M. Cummings.** Infant search errors: Stage of concept development or stage of memory development. *Memory and Cognition*, 1984, *12*, 1–19. [15]

Blakemore, C. The baffled brain. In R. Gregory and E. H. Gombrich (Eds.), *Illusion in nature and art.* New York: Scribner's, 1973. [6]

Blashfield, R. K. *The classification of psychopathology: Neo-Kraepelinian and quantitative approaches.* New York: Plenum Press, 1984. [23]

Bleuler, E. *Dementia Praecox or the group of schizophrenias.* New York: International Universities Press, 1950. (Originally published, 1911.) [22]

Bleuler, M. The long term course of schizophrenic psychoses. In L. C. Wynne, R. L. Cromwell, and S. Matthyse (Eds.), *The nature of schizophrenia: New approaches to research and treatment.* New York: Wiley, 1978. [22]

Bleuler, M. *The schizophrenic disorders.* New Haven, Conn.: Yale University Press, 1978. [23]

Bliss, J. C., M. H. Katcher, C. H. Rogers, and **R. P. Shepard.** Optical-to-tactile image conversion for the blind. *IEEE Transactions on Man-Machine Systems*, 1970, *11*, 58–65. [5]

Bloom, L. M. *Language development: Form and function in emerging grammars.* Cambridge, Mass.: MIT Press, 1970. [16]

Bloom, S. G. For a few scents more. *San Jose Mercury News*, March 21, 1984, pp. C1–2. [5]

Blurton-Jones, N., and **M. J. Konner.** Sex differences in behaviour of London and Bushmen children. In R. P. Michael and J. H. Crook (Eds.), *Comparative ecology and behaviour of primates.* London: Academic Press, 1973. [17]

Bohlen, J. G., J. P. Held, and **M. O. Sanderson.** The male orgasm: Pelvic contractions measured by anal probe. *Archives of Sexual Behavior*, 1980, *9*, 503–521. [13]

Bolles, R. C. *Theory of motivation.* New York: Harper & Row, 1967. [12]

Bolton, F. G., Jr. *The pregnant adolescent: Problems of premature parenthood.* Beverly Hills, Calif.: Sage, 1980. [17]

Bond, C. F., Jr., and **L. J. Titus.** Social facilitation: A meta-analysis of 241 studies. *Psychological Bulletin*, 1983, *94*, 265–292. [27]

Bootzin, R. R. *Behavior modification and therapy: An introduction.* Cambridge, Mass.: Winthrop Press, 1975. [24]

Bootzin, R. R. The role of expectancy in behavior change. In L. White, B. Tursky, and G. Schwartz (Eds.), *Placebo: Clinical phenomena and new insights.* New York: Guilford Press, 1985. [24]

Bootzin, R. R., and **J. R. Acocella.** *Abnormal psychology: Current perspectives* (4th ed.). New York: Random House, 1984. [19]

Boring, E. G. *A history of experimental psychology* (2nd ed.). New York: Appleton-Century-Crofts, 1957. [1]

Boring, E. G. Size constancy in a picture. *American Journal of Psychology*, 1964, *77*, 494–498. [6]

Borkovec, T. D., J. B. Grayson, and **K. M. Cooper.** Treatment of general tension: Subjective and physiological effects of progressive relaxation. *Journal of Consulting and Clinical Psychology*, 1978, *46*, 518–528. [21]

Borkovec, T. D., J. B. Grayson, G. T.

O'Brien, and **T. C. Weerts.** Relaxation treatment of pseudoinsomnia and ideiopathic insomnia: An electroencephalographic evaluation. *Journal of Applied Behavior Analysis*, 1979, *12*, 37–54. [21]

Borkovec, T. D., T. W. Lane, and **P. H. VanOot.** Phenomenology of sleep among insomniacs and good sleepers: Wakefulness experience when cortically asleep. *Journal of Abnormal Psychology*, 1981, *90*, 607–609. [7]

Bornstein, M. Two kinds of perceptual organization near the beginning of life. In W. A. Collins (Ed.), *Minnesota symposia on child development* (Vol. 14). *Aspects of the development of competence.* Hillsdale, N.J.: Lawrence Erlbaum, 1981. [14]

Bornstein, M. H., W. Kessen, and **S. Weiskopf.** The categories of hues in infancy. *Science*, 1976, *191*, 201–202. [16]

Bouchard, T. J. *Separated identical twins: Preliminary findings.* Invited address, annual meeting of the American Psychological Association. Los Angeles, August 1981. [14]

Bouchard, T. J., and **M. McGue.** Familial studies of intelligence: A review. *Science*, 1981, *212*, 1055–1059. [20]

Bourne, L. E., Jr. Knowing and using concepts. *Psychological Review*, 1970, *77*, 546–556. [10]

Bower, G. H. Mental imagery and associative learning. In L. W. Gregg (Ed.), *Cognition in learning and memory.* New York: Wiley, 1972. [9]

Bower, G. H. Improving memory. *Human Nature*, 1978, *1*, 64–72. [9]

Bower, G. H. Mood and memory. *American Psychologist*, 1981, *36*, 129–148. [9]

Bower, G. H. Affect and cognition. *Philosophical Transactions of the Royal Society of London (Series B).* 1983, *302*, 387–402. [10]

Bower, G. H., J. E. Black, and **T. J. Turner.** Scripts in memory for texts. *Cognitive Psychology*, 1979, *11*, 177–220. [9]

Bower, G. H., M. Clark, D. Winzenz, and **A. Lesgold.** Hierarchical retrieval schemes in recall of categorized word lists. *Journal of Verbal Learning and Verbal Behavior*, 1969, *8*, 323–343. [9]

Bower, G. H., and **E. R. Hilgard.** *Theories of learning* (5th ed.). Englewood Cliffs, N.J.: Prentice-Hall, 1981. [8]

Bower, G. H., M. B. Karlin, and **A. Dueck.** Comprehension and memory for pictures. *Memory and Cognition*, 1975, *3*, 216–229. [9]

Bower, G. H., and **M. Masling.** Causal explanations as mediators for remembering. Unpublished manuscript, Stanford University, 1978. [10]

Bower, G. H., and **T. R. Trabasso.** Concept identification. In R. C. Atkinson (Ed.), *Studies in mathematical psychology.* Stanford, Calif.: Stanford University Press, 1964. [10]

Bower, G. H., and **D. Winzenz.** Comparison of associative learning strategies. *Psychonomic Science*, 1970, *20*, 119–120. [9]

Bower, T. G. R. *Development in infancy*. San Francisco: Freeman, 1974. [15]

Bower, T. G. R. Repetitive processes in child development. *Scientific American*, 1976, *235*, 38–47. [6, 14]

Bower, T. G. R. *A primer of infant development*. San Francisco: Freeman, 1977. [6, 17]

Bowlby, J. The nature of a child's tie to his mother. *International Journal of Psychoanalysis*, 1958, *39*, 350–373. [14]

Bowlby, J. *Attachment and loss.* Vol. 1, *Attachment*. New York: Basic Books, 1969. [17]

Bowmaker, J. K., and **H. M. A. Dartnell.** Visual pigments of rods and cones in a human retina. *Journal of Physiology*, 1980, *298*, 501–511. [5]

Boyd, J. H., and **M. M. Weissman.** Epidemiology of affective disorders: A reexamination and future directions. *Archives of General Psychiatry*, 1981, *38*, 1039–1045. [22]

Boynton, R. M. *Human color vision.* New York: Holt, Rinehart & Winston, 1979. [5]

Brainerd, C. J. Learning research and Piagetian theory. In L. S. Siegel and C. J. Brainerd (Eds.), *Alternatives to Piaget: Critical essays on the theory.* New York: Academic Press, 1978. [15]

Bransford, J. D., and **J. J. Franks.** Abstraction of linguistic ideas. *Cognitive Psychology*, 1971, *2*, 331–350. [10]

Bransford, J. D., and **M. K. Johnson.** Considerations of some problems of comprehension. In W. G. Chase (Ed.), *Visual information processing.* New York: Academic Press, 1973. [9]

Brehm, J. W. Post-decision changes in the desirability of alternatives. *Journal of Abnormal and Social Psychology*, 1956, *52*, 384–389. [25]

Bremer, J. *Asexualization: A follow-up study of 244 cases.* New York: Macmillan, 1959. [13]

Bremner, J. G., and **P. E. Bryant.** Place versus response as the basis of spatial errors made by young infants. *Journal of Experimental Child Psychology*, 1977, *23*, 162–171. [15]

Breuer, J., and **Freud, S.** *Studies of hysteria.* New York: Basic Books, 1957. (Originally published, 1937.) [18]

Brewer, W. F., and **J. R. Pani.** The structure of human memory. In G. H. Bower (Ed.), *The psychology of learning and motivation: Advances in research and theory.* Vol. 17. New York: Academic Press, 1983. [9]

Brickman, P. Rational and nonrational elements in reactions to disconfirmation of performance expectations. *Journal of Experimental Social Psychology*, 1972, *8*, 112–123. [12]

Briddell, D. W., D. C. Rimm, G. R. Caddy, G. Krawitz, D. Scholis, and **R. J. Wunderlin.** Effects of alcohol and cognitive set on sexual arousal to deviant stimuli.

Journal of Abnormal Psychology, 1978, *87*, 418–430. [7]

Brines, M. L., and **J. L. Gould.** Bees have rules. *Science*, 1979, *202*, 571–573. [16]

Bringmann, W. Wundt's lab: "Humble . . . but functioning." *APA Monitor*, 1979, *10*, 13. [1]

Broadhurst, P. L. The interaction of task difficulty and motivation: The Yerkes-Dodson law revived. *Acta Psychologica*, 1959, *16*, 321–338. [19]

Brody, J. E. Remembering the Hyatt disaster: Emotional scars persist a year later. *The New York Times*, July 6, 1982, pp. C1, C4. [21]

Brody, N. *Human motivation: Commentary on goal-directed action.* New York: Academic Press, 1983. [12]

Broedling, L. A. Relationship of internal-external control to work motivation and performance in an expectancy model. *Journal of Applied Psychology*, 1975, *60*, 65–70. [28]

Bronfenbrenner, U. *Two worlds of childhood.* New York: Russell Sage, 1970. [17]

Bronfenbrenner, U., and **A. C. Crouter.** The evolution of environmental models in developmental research. In P. H. Mussen (Ed.), *Handbook of child psychology* (4th ed.). Vol. 1, W. Kessen (Ed.), *History, theory, and methods.* New York: Wiley, 1983. [17]

Brown, A. L. The development of memory: Knowing, knowing about knowing, and knowing how to know it. In H. W. Reese (Ed.), *Advances in child development and behavior.* Vol. 10. New York: Academic Press, 1975. [15]

Brown, B. B. *New Mind, New Body.* New York: Harper & Row, 1974. [7]

Brown, B. B. *Super mind: The ultimate energy.* New York: Harper & Row, 1980. [21]

Brown, P. K., and **G. Wald.** Visual pigments in single rods and cones of the human retina. *Science*, 1964, *144*, 45–52. [5]

Brown, R. *Words and things: An introduction to language.* New York: Free Press, 1958. [16]

Brown, R. *A first language: The early stages.* Cambridge, Mass.: Harvard University Press, 1973. [16]

Brown, R., and **U. Bellugi.** Three processes in the child's acquisition of syntax. *Harvard Educational Review*, 1964, *34*, 133–151. [16]

Brown, R., C. Cazden, and **U. Bellugi-Klima.** The child's grammar from I to III. In J. P. Hill (Ed.), *Minnesota Symposia on Child Development.* Vol. 2. Minneapolis: University of Minnesota, 1968. [16]

Brown, R., and **C. Fraser.** The acquisition of syntax. In C. N. Cofer and B. S. Musgrave (Eds.), *Verbal behavior and learning problems and processes.* New York: McGraw-Hill, 1963. [16]

Brown, R., and **C. Hanlon.** Derivational complexity and order of acquisition in

child speech. In J. R. Hayes (Ed.), *Cognition and the development of language.* New York: Wiley, 1970. [16]

Brown, R., and **E. H. Lenneberg.** A study in language and cognition. *Journal of Abnormal and Social Psychology*, 1954, *49*, 454–462. [16]

Brown, R., and **D. McNeill.** The "tip-of-the-tongue" phenomenon. *Journal of Verbal Learning and Verbal Behavior*, 1966, *5*, 325–337. [9]

Brownmiller, S. *Against our will.* New York: Simon & Schuster, 1975. [13]

Bruner, J. S. Nature and uses of immaturity. *American Psychologist*, 1972, *27*, 687–708. [17]

Bruner, J. S. *Under five in Britain.* London: Grant McIntyre, 1980. [17]

Bruner, J. S. *Child's talk: Learning to use language.* New York: Norton, 1983. [16]

Brunson, B. I., and **K. A. Matthews.** The Type A coronary-prone behavior pattern and reactions to uncontrollable stress: An analysis of performance strategies, affect, and attributions, during failure. *Journal of Personality and Social Psychology*, 1981, *40*, 906–918. [1, 21]

Buchanan, B. G., and **E. A. Feigenbaum.** DENDRAL and Meta-DENDRAL: Their applications dimensions. *Journal of Artificial Intelligence*, 1978, *11*, 5–24. [10]

Budzynski, T. Biofeedback and the twilight states of consciousness. In D. Goleman and R. J. Davidson (Eds.), *Consciousness: Brain, states of awareness, and mysticism.* New York: Harper & Row, 1979. [7]

Burgess, A. W., and **C. L. Holstrom.** *Rape: Victims of crisis.* Bowie, Md.: R. J. Brady, 1974. [13]

Burt, C. The genetic determination of differences in intelligence: A study of monozygotic twins reared together and apart. *British Journal of Psychology*, 1966, *57*, 137–153. [20]

Burt, C. Inheritance of general intelligence. *American Psychologist*, 1972, *27*, 174–190. [20]

Buss, A. H., R. Plomin, and **L. Willerman.** The inheritance of temperament. *Journal of Personality*, 1973, *41*, 513–524. [17]

Buss, D. M., and **K. H. Craik.** The act frequency approach to personality. *Psychological Review*, 1983, *90*, 105–126. [19]

Butcher, J. N., and **P. L. Owens.** Objective personality inventories: Recent research and some contemporary issues. In B. B. Wolman (Ed.), *Clinical diagnosis of mental disorders: A handbook.* New York: Plenum Press, 1978. [20]

Butler, R. A. Curiosity in monkeys. *Scientific American*, 1954, *190*, 70–75. [12]

Butterfield, E. C., and **G. N. Siperstein.** Influence of contingent auditory stimulation upon non-nutritional suckle. In *Proceedings of the Third Symposium on Oral Sensation and Perception: The Mouth of the Infant.* Springfield, Ill.: Charles C Thomas, 1974. [16]

Byrne, D., and **L. A. Byrne** (Eds.). *Exploring human sexuality.* New York: Crowell, 1978. [13]

Byrne, D. and **J. Lambreth.** The effects of erotic stimuli on sex arousal, evaluative responses, and subsequent behavior. Technical report of the commission on obscenity and pornography (Vol. 8). Washington, D.C.: U.S. Government Printing Office, 1971. [13]

Cacioppo, J. T., and **R. C. Petty.** Sex differences in influenceability: Toward specifying the underlying process. *Personality and Social Psychology Bulletin,* 1980, *6,* 651–656. [25]

Campbell, B. A., J. P. Misanin, B. C. White, and **L. D. Lytle.** Species differences in ontogeny of memory: Support for neural maturation as a determinant of forgetting. *Journal of Comparative and Physiological Psychology,* 1974, *87,* 193–202. [15]

Campos, J. J., S. Hiatt, D. Ramsay, C. Henderson, and **M. Svejda.** The emergence of fear on the visual cliff. In M. Lewis and L. Rosenblum (Eds.), *The origin of affect.* New York: Plenum, 1978. [14]

Cannon, M. S. The halfway house as an alternative to hospitalization. In J. Zusman and E. Bertsch (Eds.) *The future role of the state hospital.* Lexington, Mass.: Lexington Books, 1975. [24]

Cannon, W. B. The James-Lange theory of emotions: A critical examination and an alternative theory. *American Journal of Psychology,* 1927, *39,* 106–124. [11]

Cannon, W. B. Organization for physiological homeostatics. *Physiological Reviews,* 1929, *9,* 280–289. [11]

Carey, W. B. Some pitfalls in infant temperament research. *Infant Behavior and Development,* 1983, *6,* 247–254. [17]

Carlson, N. R. *Physiology of behavior* (2nd ed.). Boston: Allyn & Bacon, 1981. [3]

Carmichael, L., H. P. Hogan, and **A. A. Walter.** An experimental study of the effect of language on the reproduction of visually perceived form. *Journal of Experimental Psychology,* 1932, *15,* 73–86. [9, 15]

Carter-Saltzman, L. Biological and sociocultural effects on handedness: Comparison between biological and adopted families, 1980.

Cartwright, R. D. *Night life: Explorations in dreaming.* Englewood Cliffs, N.J.: Prentice-Hall, 1977. [7]

Carver, C. S., E. DeGregorio, and **R. Gillis.** Challenge and Type A behavior among intercollegiate football players. *Journal of Sport Psychology,* 1981, *3,* 140–148. [21]

Carver, C. S., and **C. Humphries.** Social psychology of the Type A coronary-prone behavior pattern. In G. S. Sanders and J. Suls (Eds.), *Social psychology of health and illness.* Hillsdale, N.J.: Lawrence Erlbaum, 1982. [21]

Cautela, J. R. Treatment of compulsive behavior by covert sensitization. *Psy-*

chological Record, 1966, *16,* 33–41. [24]

Cautela, J. R. Covert sensitization. *Psychological Reports,* 1967, *20,* 459–468. [24]

Cavanagh, J. P. Relation between the immediate memory span and the memory search rate. *Psychological Review,* 1972, *79,* 525–530. [9]

Ceci, S. J., and **U. Bronfenbrenner.** Don't forget to take the cupcakes out of the oven: Prospective memory, strategic time-monitoring, and context. *Child Development,* 1985, *56,* 152–164. [2]

Center for Disease Control. *Risk factor update.* Atlanta, Ga.: U.S. Department of Health and Human Services, 1980. [21]

Chaikin, A. After 15 years, still no cure for astronauts' space sickness. *San Jose Mercury News,* June 26, 1984, pp. C1+. [5]

Chaikin, A. L., and **V. J. Derlega.** Nonverbal mediators of expectancy effects in black and white children. *Journal of Personality and Social Psychology,* 1979, *37,* 897–912. [26]

Chance, J. E., and **A. G. Goldstein.** Face-recognition memory: Implications for children's eyewitness testimony. *Journal of Social Issues,* 1984, *40,* 69–85. [15]

Cherry, E. C. Some experiments on the recognition of speech with one and two ears. *Journal of the Acoustical Society of America,* 1953, *25,* 975–979. [7]

Chi, M., P. Feltovich, and **R. Glaser.** Representation of physics knowledge by novices and experts. (Technical Report). Pittsburgh: University of Pittsburgh, 1977. [10]

Chi, M. T. H. Short-term memory limitations in children: Capacity or processing deficits? *Memory and Cognition,* 1976, *4,* 559–572. [15]

Chi, M. T. H. Knowledge structures and memory development. In R. S. Siegler (Ed.), *Children's thinking: What develops?* Hillsdale, N.J.: Lawrence Erlbaum, 1978. [15]

Chomsky, N. *Language and mind.* New York: Harcourt Brace Jovanovich, 1972. [16]

Chomsky, N. *Reflections on language.* New York: Pantheon, 1975. [16]

Chomsky, N. *Language and responsibility.* New York: Pantheon, 1979. [16]

Chukovsksy, K. I. *From two to five.* Berkeley: University of California Press, 1968. [15]

Cialdini, R. B. *Influence: How and why people agree to things.* New York: William Morrow, 1984. [27]

Clancey, W. J. The epistemology of a rule-based expert system: A framework for exploration. *Artificial Intelligence,* 1983, *20,* 215–251. [10]

Claridge, G., and **G. Mangan.** Genetics of human nervous system functioning. In J. L. Fuller and E. C. Simmel (Eds.), *Behavior genetics.* Hillsdale, N. J.: Lawrence Erlbaum, 1983. [4]

Clark, A. M., and **A. D. B. Clarke.** *Early*

experience: Myth and evidence. New York: Free Press, 1979. [14]

Clark, E. V. Meanings and concepts. In P. H. Mussen (Ed.), *Handbook of child psychology* (4th ed.). Vol. 3. J. H. Flavell and E. M. Markman (Eds.), *Cognitive development.* New York: Wiley, 1983. [16]

Clark, H. H. Language use and language users. In G. Lindzey and E. Aronson (Eds.), *Handbook of social psychology* (3rd ed.). Reading, Mass.: Addison-Wesley, 1984. [16]

Clark, H. H., and **E. V. Clark.** *Psychology and language.* New York: Harcourt Brace Jovanovich, 1977. [16]

Clark, H. H., and **S. E. Haviland.** Comprehension and the given-new contract. In R. O. Freedle (Ed.), *Discourse production and comprehension.* Norwood, N.J.: Ablex, 1977. [16]

Clarke-Stewart, K. A. *Day care.* Cambridge, Mass.: Harvard University Press, 1982. [17]

Clarke-Stewart, K. A., and **G. G. Fein.** Early childhood programs. In P. H. Mussen (Ed.), *Handbook of child psychology* (4th ed.). Vol. 2, M. M. Haith and J. J. Campos (Eds.), *Infancy and developmental psychobiology.* New York: Wiley, 1983. [17]

Clausen, J. A. Men's occupational careers in the middle years. In D. H. Eichorn, J. A. Clausen, N. Haan, M. P. Honzik, and P. Mussen (Eds.), *Present and past in middle life.* New York: Academic Press, 1981. [17]

Cleckley, H. M. *The mask of sanity.* St. Louis: Mosby, 1976. [22]

Clifford, M., and **E. Walster.** The effect of physical attractiveness on teacher expectations. *Sociology of Education,* 1973, *46,* 248–258. [26]

Cobb, S. Social support as a moderator of life stress. *Psychosomatic Medicine,* 1976, *38,* 300–314. [21]

Cohen, D. B. Remembering and forgetting dreaming. In J. F. Kihlstrom and F. J. Evans (Eds.), *Functional disorders of memory.* Hillsdale, N.J.: Lawrence Erlbaum, 1979. [7]

Cohen, D. J., E. Dibble, and **J. M. Graw.** Fathers' and mothers' perceptions of children's personality. *Archives of General Psychiatry,* 1977, *34,* 480–487. [17]

Cohen, F. and **R. S. Lazarus.** Coping with the pressures of illness. In G. C. Stone, F. Cohen, and N. E. Adler (Eds.), *Health psychology—A handbook.* San Francisco: Jossey-Bass, 1979. [21]

Cohen, G. Language comprehension in old age. *Cognitive Psychology,* 1979, *11,* 412–429. [15]

Cohen, L. B. Attention-getting and attention-holding processes of infant visual preferences. *Child Development,* 1972, *43,* 869–879. [14]

Cohen, L. B., J. S. DeLoache, and **M. S. Strauss.** Infant perceptual development. In J. D. Osofsky (Ed.), *Handbook of infant development.* New York: Wiley, 1979. [14]

Cohen, S. E., and **L. Beckwith.** Preterm infant interaction with the caregiver in the first year of life and competence at age two. *Child Development,* 1979, *50,* 767–776. [17]

Colby, A., L. Kohlberg, J. Gibbs, and **M. Liberman.** A longitudinal study of moral judgment. *Monographs of the Society for Research in Child Development,* 1983, 48 (Whole No. 200). [17]

Coleman, E. Changing approaches to the treatment of homosexuality. In W. Paul, J. D. Weinrich, J. C. Gonsiorek, and M. E. Hotvedt (Eds.), *Homosexuality: Social, psychological, and biological issues.* Beverly Hills, Calif.: Sage, 1982. [13]

Colwill, R. M., and **R. A. Rescorla.** Postconditioning devaluation of a reinforcer affects instrumental responding. *Journal of Experimental Psychology: Animal Behavior Processes,* 1985, *11,* 120–132. [8]

Combs, B. J., D. R. Hales, and **B. K. Williams.** *An invitation to health: Your personal responsibility.* Menlo Park, Calif.: Benjamin/Cummings, 1980. [7]

Commission on Obscenity and Pornography. *Report.* Washington, D.C.: U.S. Government Printing Office, 1970. [13]

Condry, J. C., and **S. L. Dyer.** Fear of success: Attribution of cause to the victim. *Journal of Social Issues.* 1976, *32* (3), 63–83. [12]

Connell, D. B., J. I. Layzer, and **B. D. Goodson.** National study of day care centers for infants: Findings and implications. Paper presented at the Annual Meeting of the American Psychological Association, New York, September 1979. [17]

Connor, J. Olfactory control of aggressive and sexual behavior in the mouse (Mus musclus L.). *Psychonomic Science,* 1972, *27,* 1–3. [13]

Cooley, C. H. *Human nature and the social order.* New York: Scribner's, 1912. [14]

Cordes, C. Easing toward perfection at twin oaks. *APA Monitor,* 1984, *15,* 1+. [1]

Cordes, C. "Will *Larry P.* face the supreme test?" *APA Monitor,* 1984, *15* (4), 26–27. [17]

Coren, S., C. Porac, and **L. M. Ward.** *Sensation and perception.* San Diego, Calif.: Academic Press, 1984. [5]

Cornell, E. H. Infant's discrimination of faces following redundant presentation. *Journal of Experimental Child Psychology,* 1974, *18,* 98–106. [14]

Cornell, E. H. Developmental continuity of memory mechanisms: Suggestive phenomena. In R. Kail and N. E. Spear (Eds.), *Comparative perspectives on the development of memory.* Hillsdale, N.J.: Lawrence Erlbaum, 1984, [15]

Corso, J. F. Auditory perception and communication. In J. E. Birren and K. W. Schaie (Eds.), *Handbook of the psychology of aging.* New York: Van Nostrand Reinhold, 1977. [5]

Costanza, P. R., and **M. E. Shaw.** Con-

formity as a function of age level. *Child Development,* 1966, *37,* 967–975. [17]

Cote, L. Basal ganglia, the extrapyramidal motor system, and diseases of transmitter metabolism. In E. R. Kandel and J. H. Schwartz (Eds.), *Principles of neural science.* New York: Elsevier/North Holland, 1981. [3]

Cottington, E. M., K. A. Matthews, E. Talbott, and **L. H. Kuller.** Environmental events preceding sudden death in women. *Psychosomatic Medicine,* 1980, *42,* 567–574. [21]

Cottrell, N. B. Social facilitation. In C. G. McClintock (Ed.), *Experimental social psychology.* New York: Holt, Rinehart & Winston, 1972. [27]

Coulter, X., A. C. Collier, and **B. A. Campbell.** Long-term retention of early Pavlovian fear conditioning in infant rats. *Journal of Experimental Psychology: Animal Behavior Processes,* 1976, *2,* 48–56. [15]

Cowen, E. L., A. Pederson, H. Babijian, L. D. Izzo, and **M. A. Trost.** Long-term followup of early detected vulnerable children. *Journal of Consulting and Clinical Psychology,* 1973, *41,* 438–446. [17]

Coyle, J. T., D. L. Price, and **M. R. DeLong.** Alzheimer's disease: A disorder of cortical cholinergic innervation. *Science,* 1983, *219,* 1184–1190. [3, 15]

Coyne, J. C., and **R. S. Lazarus.** Cognitive style, stress perception, and coping. In I. L. Kutash and L. B. Schlesinger (Eds.), *Handbook on stress and anxiety.* San Francisco: Jossey-Bass, 1980. [20]

Craik, F. I. M., and **M. Byrd.** Aging and cognitive deficits: The role of attentional resources. In F. I. M. Craik and S. Trehub (Eds.), *Advances in the study of communication and affect.* Vol. 8. *Aging and cognitive processes.* New York: Plenum, 1982. [15]

Craik, F. I. M., and **R. S. Lockhart.** Levels of processing: A framework for memory research. *Journal of Verbal Learning and Verbal Behavior,* 1972, *11,* 671–684. [9]

Crano, W. D., and **P. M. Mellon.** Causal influence of teachers' expectations on children's academic performance: A cross-lagged panel analysis. *Journal of Educational Psychology,* 1978, *70,* 39–49. [26]

Creese, I., D. R. Burt, and **S. H. Snyder.** Brain's dopamine receptor—Labeling with [dopamine—H-3] and [H21 operidol—H3]. *Psychopharmacology Communications,* 1975, *I,* 663–673. [23]

Crick, F., and **G. Mitchison.** The function of dream sleep. *Nature,* 1983, *304,* 111–114. [7]

Crnic, K., A. Ragozin, M. Greenberg, N. Robinson, and **R. Basham.** Social interaction and developmental competence of preterm and full-term infants during the first year of life. *Child Development,* 1983, *54,* 1199–1210. [14]

Crockenberg, S. Infant irritability, mother

responsiveness, and social support influences on the security of infant-mother attachment. *Child Development,* 1981, *52,* 857–865. [17]

Crockenberg, S., and **C. Acredolo.** Infant temperament ratings: A function of infants, of mothers, or both? *Infant Behavior and Development,* 1983, *6,* 61–72. [17]

Crook, T. and **J. Eliot.** Parental death during childhood and adult depression: A critical review of the literature. *Psychological Bulletin,* 1980, *87,* 252–259. [18]

Cross, H., A. Holcomb, and **C. G. Matter.** Imprinting or exposure learning in rats given early auditory stimulation. *Psychonomic Science,* 1967, *7,* 233–234. [25]

Crouse, J. H. Retroactive interference in reading prose materials. *Journal of Educational Psychology,* 1971, *62,* 39–44. [9]

Crowe, S. J., S. R. Guild, and **L. M. Polvogt.** Observations on the patholoy of high-tone deafness. *Bulletin of Johns Hopkins Hospital,* 1934, *54,* 315–379. [5]

Curtis, H., and **N. S. Barnes.** Invitation to biology (3rd ed.). New York: Worth, 1981. [4]

Dabbs, J. M., Jr., and **H. Leventhal.** Effects of varying the recommendations in a fear-arousing communication. *Journal of Personality and Social Psychology,* 1966, *4,* 525–531. [25]

Daehler, M. W., and **D. Bukatko.** *Cognitive development.* New York: Knopf, 1985. [15]

Daehler, M. W., and **C. Greco.** Memory in very young children. In M. Pressley and C. J. Brainerd (Eds.), *Cognitive learning and memory in children.* New York: Springer-Verlag, 1985. [15]

Damon, W. Early conceptions of positive justice as related to the development of logical operations. *Child Development,* 1975, *46,* 302–312. [17]

Daniel, R. S. *Notes for a course in professional problems.* Unpublished manuscript, 1975. [1]

Darley, J. M., A. I. Teger, and **L. D. Lewis.** Do groups always inhibit individuals' responses to potential emergencies? *Journal of Personality and Social Psychology,* 1973, *26,* 295–399. [27]

Darwin, C. *The expression of emotions in man and animals.* Chicago: University of Chicago Press, 1967. (Originally published, 1872.) [11, 14]

Dashiell, J. F. An experimental analysis of some group effects. *Journal of Abnormal and Social Psychology,* 1930, *25,* 190–199. [27]

Dattore, P. J., F. C. Shontz, and **L. Coyne.** Premorbid personality differentiation of cancer and noncancer groups: A test of the hypothesis of cancer proneness. *Journal of Consulting and Clinical Psychology,* 1980, *48,* 388–394. [21]

Davenport, W. Sexual patterns and their regulation in a society of the southwest pacific. In F. A. Beach (Ed.), *Sex and Behavior.* New York: Wiley, 1965. [13]

Davis, J. M. Dopamine theory of schizophrenia: A two-factor theory. In L. C. Wynne, R. L. Cromwell, and S. Matthysse (Eds.). *The nature of schizophrenia: New approaches to research and treatment.* New York: Wiley, 1978. [23]

Davis, P. G., B. S. McEwen, and **D. W. Pfaff.** Localized behavioral effects of titrated estradiol implants in the ventromedial hypothalamus of female rats. *Endocrinology,* 1979, *104,* 898–903. [11]

Davison, G. C. Homosexuality: The ethical challenge. *Journal of Consulting and Clinical Psychology,* 1976, *44,* 157–162. [13]

Dawes, R. M., J. McTavish, and **H. Shaklee.** Behavior, communication, and assumptions about other people's behavior in a common dilemma situation. *Journal of Personality and Social Psychology,* 1977, *35,* 1–11. [27]

Dawkins, R. *The selfish gene.* New York: Oxford University Press, 1975. [27]

de Kleer, J., and **J. S. Brown.** Mental models of physical mechanisms and their acquisition. In J. R. Anderson (Ed.), *Cognitive skills and their acquisition.* Hillsdale, N.J.: Lawrence Erlbaum, 1981. [10]

Deaux, E. Thirst satiation and the temperature of ingested water. *Science,* 1973, *181,* 1166–1167. [12]

Deaux, K. *The behavior of women and men.* Monterey, Calif.: Brooks/Cole, 1976. [26]

DeCasper, A. J., and **A. A. Carstens.** Contingencies of stimulation: Effects on learning and emotion in neonates. *Infant Behavior and Development,* 1981, *4,* 1–17. [15]

DeCasper, A. J., and **W. P. Fifer.** Of human bonding: Newborns prefer their mothers' voices. *Science,* 1980, *208,* 1174–1176. [14]

DeCharms, R. *Personal causation: The internal affective determinants of behavior.* New York: Academic Press, 1968. [12]

Deci, E. L. *Intrinsic motivation.* New York: Plenum, 1975. [12]

DeGroot, A. D. *Thought and choice in chess.* The Hague: Mouton, 1965. [10]

DeLoache, J. S. Naturalistic study of memory for object location in very young children. In M. Perlmutter (Ed.), *New directions in child development.* No. 10. *Children's memory.* San Francisco: Jossey-Bass, 1980. [15]

Delongis, A., J. C. Coyne, G. Dakof, S. Folkman, and **R. S. Lazarus.** Relationship of daily hassles, uplifts, and major life events to health status. *Health Psychology,* 1982, *1,* 119–136. [21]

DeLora, J. S., and **Warren, C. A.** *Understanding sexual interaction.* Boston: Houghton Mifflin, 1977. [13]

Dement, W. C. *Some must watch while some must sleep.* San Francisco: Freeman, 1974. [7]

Dement, W. C. Two kinds of sleep. In D. Goleman and R. J. Davidson (Eds.), *Consciousness: Brain, state of awareness, and mysticism.* New York: Harper & Row, 1979. [7]

Dement, W. C., and **E. A. Wolpert.** The relation of eye movements, body mobility, and external stimuli to dream content. *Journal of Experimental Psychology,* 1958, *55,* 543–553. [7]

DeMonasterio, F. M. Center and surround mechanisms of opponent-color X and Y ganglion cells of retina of macaques. *Journal of Neurophysiology,* 1978, *41,* 1418–1434. [5]

Dempster, F. N. Memory span: Sources of individual and developmental differences. *Psychological Bulletin,* 1981, *89,* 63–100. [15]

DeMyer, M. K., J. N. Hingtgen, and **R. K. Jackson.** Infantile autism reviewed; A decade of research. *Schizophrenia Bulletin,* 1981, *7,* 388–541. [22]

Dennis, M. Capacity and strategy for syntactic comprehension after left and right hemidecortication. *Brain and Language,* 1980, *10,* 287–317. [2]

Dennis, M., and **H. A. Whitaker.** Language acquisition following hemidecortication: Linguistic superiority of the left over the right hemisphere. *Brain and Language,* 1976, *3,* 404–433. [16]

Dennis, W., and **M. G. Dennis.** The effect of cradling practices upon the onset of walking in Hopi children. *Journal of Genetic Psychology,* 1940, *56,* 77–86. [14]

Dennis, W., and **J. Sayegh.** The effect of supplemenary experiences upon the behavioral development of infants in institutions. *Child Development,* 1965, *36,* 81–90. [14]

Dent, H. R. The effects of interviewing strategies on the results of interviews with child witnesses. In A. Trankell (Ed.), *Reconstructing the past.* Deventer, The Netherlands: Kluwer, 1982. [15]

Dent, H. R., and **G. M. Stephenson.** Identification evidence: Experimental investigations of factors affecting the reliability of juvenile and adult witnesses. In D. P. Farrington, K. Hawkins, and S. M. Lloyd-Bostock (Eds.), *Psychology, law, and legal processes.* Atlantic Highlands, N.J.: Humanities Press, 1979. [15]

Depue, R. A., and **S. M. Monroe.** The unipolar-bipolar distinction in the depressive disorders. *Psychological Bulletin,* 1978, *85,* 1001–1029. [22]

Deregowski, J. B. *Illusions, patterns and pictures: A cross-cultural perspective.* London: Academic Press, 1980. [6]

Deutsch, M., and **H. B. Gerard.** A study of normative and informational influences on social judgment. *Journal of Abnormal and Social Psychology,* 1965, *51,* 629–636. [27]

Deutsch, M., and **R. M. Krauss.** The effect of threat upon interpersonal bargaining. *Journal of Abnormal and Social Psychology,* 1960, *61,* 181–189. [27]

DeValois, R. L. Analysis and coding of color vision in the primate visual system. *Cold Spring Harbor Symposia on Quantitative Biology,* 1965, *30,* 567–579. [5]

DeValois, R. L., and **K. K. DeValois.** Neural coding of color. In E. C. Carterette and M. P. Friedman (Eds.), *Handbook of perception,* Vol. V, *Seeing.* New York: Academic Press, 1975. [5]

deVilliers, J. G., and **P. A. deVilliers.** *Language acquisition.* Cambridge, Mass.: Harvard University Press, 1978. [16]

DeVries, R. Constancy of generic identity in the years three to six. *Monographs of the Society for Research in Child Development,* 1969, *34,* Whole No. 127. [15]

Diamond, M. Sexual identity: Monozygotic twins reared in discordant sex roles and a BBC follow-up. *Archives of Sexual Behavior,* 1982, *11* (2), 181–185. [13]

Dichter, E. *Handbook of consumer motivation.* New York: McGraw-Hill, 1964. [25]

Dickinson, A. *Contemporary animal learning theory.* Cambridge: Cambridge University Press, 1980. [8]

Dillard, J. L. *Black English: Its history and usage in the United States.* New York: Random House, 1972. [16]

Dinsmoor, J. A. Punishment: I. The avoidance hypothesis. *Psychological Review,* 1954, *61,* 34–46. [8]

Dinsmoor, J. A. Punishment: II. An interpretation of empirical findings. *Psychological Review,* 1955, *62,* 92–105. [8]

Dion, K. Physical attractiveness and evaluations of children's transgressions. *Journal of Personality and Social Psychology,* 1972, *24,* 207–213. [26]

Dion, K., Young children's stereotyping of facial attractiveness. *Developmental Psychology,* 1973, *9,* 183–188. [26]

Dion, K., E. Berscheid, and **E. Walster.** What is beautiful is good. *Journal of Personality and Social Psychology,* 1972, *34,* 285–290. [26]

Dipboye, R. L., H. L. Fromkin, and **K. Wiback.** Relative importance of applicant sex, attractiveness and scholastic standing in evaluation of job applicant résumés. *Journal of Applied Psychology,* 1975 *60,* 39–43. [28]

Dishman, R. K. Compliance/adherence in health-related exercise. *Health Psychology,* 1982, *1,* 237–267. [21]

DiVitto, B., and **S. Goldberg.** The development of early parent-infant interaction as a function of newborn medical status. In T. Field, A. Sostek, S. Goldberg, and H. H. Shuman (Eds.), *Infants born at risk.* New York: Spectrum, 1980. [14]

Dixon, N. *Preconscious processing.* Chichester, England; Wiley, 1981. [6]

Doane, J., K. West, M. J. Goldstein, E. Rodnick, and **J. Jones.** Parental communication deviance and affective style as predictors of subsequent schizophrenia spectrum disorders in vulnerable adolescents. *Archives of General Psychiatry,* 1981, *38,* 679–685. [23]

Dodd, D. H., and **R. M. White, Jr.** *Cogni-*

tion: Mental structures and processes. Boston: Allyn & Bacon, 1980. [16]

Dodge, K. A. Behavioral antecedents of peer rejection and isolation. Paper presented at the Biennial Meeting of the Society for Research in Child Development, Boston, April 1981. [17]

Dodge, K. A. Social information processing variables in the development of aggression and altruism in children. In C. Zahn-Waxler, M. Cummings, and M. Radke-Yarrow (Eds.), *The develoment of altruism and aggression: Social and sociobiological origins.* New York: Cambridge University Press, 1982. [17]

Doise, W., G. Cspeli, H. D. Dann, K. Larsen, and **A. Ostell.** An experimental investigation into the formation of intergroup representations. *European Journal of Social Psychology,* 1972, *2,* 202–204. [26]

Dollard, J., L. W. Doob, N. E. Miller, O. H. Mowrer, and **R. R. Sears.** *Frustration and aggression.* New Haven, Conn.: Yale University Press, 1939. [27]

Dollard, J., and **N. E. Miller.** *Personality and psychotherapy: An Analysis in terms of learning, thinking, and culture.* New York: McGraw-Hill, 1950. [19]

Donaldson, M. *Children's minds.* New York: Norton, 1979. [15]

Donnerstein, E., and **D. W. Wilson.** Effects of noise and perceived control on ongoing and subsequent aggressive behavior. *Journal of Personality and Social Psychology,* 1976, *34,* 744–781. [27]

Dornbusch, S. M., J. M. Carlsmith, R. T. Gross, J. A. Martin, D. Jenings, A. Rosenberg, and **P. Drake.** Sexual development, age, and dating: A comparison of biological and social influences upon one set of behaviors. *Child Development,* 1981, *52,* 179–185. [17]

Draguns, J. G. Psychological disorders of clinical severity. In H. C. Triandis and J. G. Draguns (Eds.), *Handbook of cross-cultural psychology* (Vol. 6). *Psychopathology.* Boston: Allyn & Bacon, 1980. [22]

DuBois, P. H. Review of the Scholastic Aptitude Test. In O. K. Buros (Ed.), *The seventh mental measurements yearbook.* Highland Park, N.J.: Gryphon Press, 1972. [20]

Duck, S. W., and **G. Craig.** Personality similarity and the development of friendship: A longitudinal study. *British Journal of Social and Clinical Psychology,* 1978, *17,* 237–242. [12]

Duffy, E. *Activation and behavior.* New York: Wiley, 1962. [19]

Duncan, S., Jr. Nonverbal communication. *Psychological Bulletin,* 1969, *72,* 118–137. [11]

Duncker, K. On problem solving (L. S. Lees, Trans.). *Psychological Monographs,* 1945, *58* (Whole No. 270). [10]

Dunlap, K. The role of eye muscles and mouth muscles in the expression of emotions. *Genetic Psychology Monographs,* 1927, *2,* 199–233. [11]

Dunn, J., and **C. Kendrick.** *Siblings: Love,* envy, and understanding. Cambridge, Mass.: Harvard University Press, 1982. [17]

Durkin, D. *Children who read early.* New York: Teachers College Press, 1966. [16]

Dutton, D., and **A. Aron.** Some evidence for heightened sexual attraction under conditions of high anxiety. *Journal of Personality and Social Psychology,* 1974, *30,* 510–517. [26]

Dyer, L., and **R. Theriault.** The determinants of pay satisfaction. *Journal of Applied Psychology,* 1976, *61* 596–604. [28]

Eagly, A. H. Gender and social influence: A social psychological analysis. *American Psychologist,* 1973, *38,* 971–981. [27]

Eagly, A. H., and **L. L. Carli.** Sex of researchers and sex-typed communications as determinants of sex differences in influenceability: A meta-analysis of social influence studies. *Psychological Bulletin,* 1981, *90,* 1–20. [25]

Eberhardy, F. The view from "the couch." *Journal of Child Psychology and Psychiatry,* 1967, *8,* 257–263. [22]

Eccles, J. C., M. Ito, and **J. Szentagotnaik.** *The cerebellum as a neuronal machine.* New York: Springer, 1967. [3]

Educational Broadcasting Company. Depression: The shadowed valley. From the series *The thin edge.* Educational Broadcasting Corporation, 1975. [22]

Egan, D. E., and **B. J. Schwartz.** Chunking in recall of symbolic diagrams. *Memory and Cognition,* 1979, *7,* 149–158. [10]

Ehrhardt, A. A., G. Grisanti, and **E. A. McCauley.** Female-to-male transsexuals compared to lesbians: Behavioral patterns of childhood and adolescent development. *Archives of Sexual Behavior,* 1979, *8,* 481–490. [13]

Ehrhardt, A. A., and **H. F. L. Meyer-Bahlburg.** Effects of prenatal sex hormones on gender-related behavior. *Science,* 1981, *211,* 1312–1318. [13, 17]

Ehrlich, D., I. Guttman, P. Schonbach, and **J. Mills.** Postdecision exposure to relevant information. *Journal of Abnormal and Social Psychology,* 1957, *54,* 98–102. [12]

Eichorn, D. H., J. V. Hunt, and **M. P. Honzik.** Experience, personality, and IQ: Adolescence to middle age. In D. H. Eichorn, J. A. Clausen, N. Haan, M. P. Honzik, and P. H. Mussen (Eds.), *Present and past in middle life.* New York: Academic Press, 1981. [15]

Eimas, P. D., and **V. C. Tartter.** On the development of speech perception: Mechanisms and analogies. In H. W. Reese and L. P. Lipsitt (Eds.), *Advances in child development and behavior.* Vol. 13. New York: Academic Press, 1979. [16]

Eisenberg, R. The organization of auditory behavior. *Journal of Speech and Hearing Research,* 1970, *13,* 461–464. [14]

Ekman, P. Universals and cultural differences in facial expression of emotion. In J. K. Cole (Ed.), *Nebraska Symposium* on Motivation. Lincoln: University of Nebraska Press, 1972. [11]

Ekman, P. *The face of man: Expressions of universal emotions in a New Guinea village.* New York: Garland STPM Press, 1980. [11]

Ekman, P., and **W. V. Friesen.** Constants across culture in the face and emotion. *Journal of Personality and Social Psychology,* 1971, *17,* 124–129. [11]

Ekman, P., and **W. V. Friesen.** *Unmasking the face: A guide to recognizing emotions from facial expressions.* Englewood Cliffs, N.J.: Prentice-Hall/Spectrum, 1975. [11]

Ekman, P., W. V. Friesen, and **P. Ellsworth.** *Emotion in the human face: Guidelines for research and an integration of findings.* Elmsford, N.Y.: Pergamon, 1972. [11]

Ekman, P., R. Levenson, and **W. V. Friesen.** *Science,* 1983, *221,* 1208–1210. [11]

Elder, G. H., Jr. Historical change in life patterns and personality. In P. B. Baltes and O. G. Brim, Jr. (Eds.), *Life span developmental psychology.* Vol. 2. New York: Academic Press, 1979. [17]

Elder, G. H., Jr., T. V. Nguyen, and **A. Caspi.** Linking family hardship to children's lives. *Child Development,* 1985, *56,* 361–375. [17]

Eleftheriou, B. E., D. V. Bailley, and **V. H. Denenberg.** Genetic analysis of fighting behavior in mice. *Physiology and Behavior,* 1974, *13,* 773–777. [27]

Ellis, A. *Reason and emotion in psychotherapy.* Secaucus, N.J.: Lyle Stuart, 1962. [24]

Elster, A. B., E. R. McAnarney, and **M. E. Lamb.** Parental behavior of adolescent mothers. *Pediatrics,* 1983, *71,* 494–503. [17]

Engel, G. L. Sudden and rapid death under psychological stress. *Annals of International Medicine,* 1971, *74,* 771–782. [21]

Engle-Friedman, M., E. A. Baker, and **R. R. Bootzin.** Reports of wakefulness during EEG identified stages of sleep. *Sleep Research,* 1985, *14,* 152. [7]

Epstein, A. N. Water intake without the act of drinking. *Science,* 1960, *131,* 497–498. [12]

Epstein, S. M. Toward a unified theory of anxiety. In B. A. Maher (Ed.), *Progress in experimental personality research* (Vol. 4). New York: Academic Press, 1967. [12]

Erdelyi, M. *Psychoanalysis: Freud's cognitive psychology.* New York: W. H. Freeman, 1985. [18]

Erdelyi, M. H., and **B. Goldberg.** Let's not sweep repression under the rug: Toward a cognitive psychology of repression. In J. F. Kihlstrom and F. J. Evans (Eds.), *Functional disorders of memory.* Hillsdale, N.J.: Lawrence Erlbaum, 1979. [9]

Erdelyi, M. H., and **J. Kelinbard.** Has Ebbinghaus decayed with time? The growth of recall (hyperamnesia) over days. *Journal of Experimental Psychol-*

ogy: Human Learning and Memory. 1978 4, 275–289. [18]

Erickson, R. P. On the neural basis of behavior. American Scientist, 1984, 72, 233–241. [5]

Ericsson, K. A., W. G. Chase, and **S. Faloon.** Acquisition of a memory skill. Science, 1980, 208, 1181–1182. [9]

Erikson, E. H. Childhood and society. New York: Norton, 1950. [18]

Erikson, E. H. Childhood and society. (2nd ed.). New York: Norton, 1963. [17]

Erikson, E. H. Young man Luther: A study in psychoanalysis and history. New York: Norton, 1968. [18]

Erikson, E. H. Gandhi's truth: On the origins of militant nonviolence. New York: Norton, 1969. [18]

Erikson, K. Everything in its path: Destruction of community in the Buffalo Creek flood. New York: Simon & Schuster, 1976. [21]

Ervin-Tripp, S. Is second-language learning like the first? TESOL Quarterly, 1974, 8, 111–127. [16]

Etzioni, A., and **T. A. Diprete.** The decline in confidence in America: The prime factor. Journal of Applied Behavioral Science, 1979, 15, 520–526. [25]

Evans, E. F. Neural processes for the detection of acoustic patterns and for sound localization. In F. O. Schmitt and F. G. Worden (Eds.), The neurosciences, third study program. Cambridge, Mass.: MIT Press, 1974. [5]

Evans, R. I., R. M. Rozelle, M. B. Mittelmark, W. B. Hansen, A. L. Bane, and **J. Havis.** Deterring the onset of smoking in children: Knowledge of immediate physiological effects and coping with peer pressure, media pressure, and parental modeling. Journal of Applied Social Psychology, 1978, 8, 126–135. [21]

Exner, J. E. The Rorschach: A comprehensive system. New York: Wiley, 1974. [20]

Eysenck, H. J. The effects of psychotherapy: An evaluation. Journal of Consulting Psychology, 1952, 16, 319–324. [24]

Eysenck, H. J. The effects of psychotherapy. New York: International Science Press, 1966. [24]

Eysenck, H. J. New ways in psychotherapy. Psychology Today, 1967, 1, 39–47. [24]

Eysenck, H. J. The structure of human personality. London: Methuen, 1970. [19]

Fabian, W. D., Jr., and **S. M. Fishkin.** A replicated study of self-reported changes in psychological absorption with marijuana intoxication. Journal of Abnormal Psychology, 1981, 90, 546–553. [7]

Fadiman, J. The transpersonal stance. In M. J. Mahoney (Ed.), Psychotherapy process: Current issues and future directions. New York: Plenum, 1980. [19]

Fagan, J. F. Infants' delayed recognition memory and forgetting. Journal of Experimental Child Psychology, 1973, 16, 424–450. [15]

Fagan, J. F. Infants' recognition of invariant features of faces. Child Development, 1976, 47, 627–638. [14]

Fagot, B. I. Consequences of moderate cross-gender behavior in children. Child Development, 1977, 48, 902–907. [17]

Fagot, B. I. The influence of sex of child on parental reactions to toddler children. Child Development, 1978, 49, 459–465. [17]

Fantz, R. L. Pattern vision in newborn infants. Science, 1963, 140, 296–297. [14]

Farah, M. The neurological basis of mental imagery: A componential analysis. Cognition. 1984. [3]

Farnham-Diggory, S. Learning disabilities. Cambridge, Mass.: Harvard University Press, 1978. [16]

Faust, I. M., P. R. Johnson, J. S. Stern, and **J. Hirsch.** Diet-induced adipocyte number increases in adult rats: A new model of obesity. American Journal of Physiology, 1978, E279–E286. [12]

Feigenbaum, E. A. The art of artificial intelligence: Themes and case studies in knowledge engineering. International Joint Conferences on Artificial Intelligence, 1977, 5, 1014–1029. [10]

Feldman, J. A. A connectionist model of visual memory. In G. E. Hinton and J. A. Anderson (Eds.), Parallel models of associative memory. Hillsdale, N.J.: Lawrence Erlbaum, 1981. [3]

Feldman, S. The presentation of shortness in everyday life—Height and heightism in American life. Paper presented at the Annual Meeting of the American Sociological Association, Chicago, 1971. [25]

Feldman, S. S., Z. C. Beringen, and **S. C. Nash.** Fluctuations of sex-related self-attributions as a function of the state of family life cycle. Developmental Psychology, 1981, 17, 24–35. [17]

Ferster, C. B. A functional analysis of depression. American Psychologist, 1973, 28, 857–870. [23]

Feshbach, S. The function of aggression and the regulation of aggressive drive. Psychological Review, 1964, 71, 257–272. [17]

Festinger, L. A theory of cognitive dissonance. Stanford, Calif.: Stanford University Press, 1957. [12, 25]

Festinger, L., and **J. M. Carlsmith.** Cognitive consequences of forced compliance. Journal of Abnormal and Social Psychology, 1959, 58, 203–210. [12, 25]

Fiedler, F. E. The contingency model and the dynamics of the leadership process. In L. Berkowitz (Ed.), Advances in experimental social psychology. New York: Academic Press, 1978. [28]

Field, J., D. Muir, R. Pilon, M. Sinclair, and **P. Dodwell.** Infants' orientation to lateral sounds from birth to three months. Child Development, 1980, 51, 295–298. [14]

Field, T. Affective displays in high-risk infants in early interaction. In T. Field and A. Fogel (Eds.), Emotion and inter-

action. Hillsdale, N.J.: Lawrence Erlbaum, 1982. [14]

Field, T. M., R. Woodson, D. Cohen, R. Greenberg, R. Garcia, and **K. Collins.** Discrimination and imitation of facial expressions by term and preterm neonates. Infant Behavior and Development, 1983, 6, 485–489. [14]

Field, T. M., R. Woodson, R. Greenberg, and **D. Cohen.** Discrimination and imitation of facial expressions by neonates. Science, 1982, 218, 179–181. [14]

Fielding, J. Successes of prevention. Milbank Memorial Fund Quarterly, 1978, 56, 274–302. [21]

Fine, T. H., and **J. W. Turner.** The effect of brief Restricted Environmental Stimulation Therapy in the treatment of essential hypertension. Behaviour Research and Therapy, 1982, 20, 567–570. [7]

Fischer, K. W. Illuminating the processes of moral development. In A. Colby, L. Kohlberg, J. Gibbs, and M. Lieberman, A longitudinal study of moral judgment. Monographs of the society for research in child development, 1983, 48 (Whole No. 200, pp. 97–107). [17]

Fischer, R. A cartography of the ecstatic and meditative states. Science, 1971, 174, 898. [7]

Fischer, S., and **R. P. Greenberg.** The scientific credibility of Freud's theories and therapy. New York: Basic Books, 1977. [7]

Fishbein, H. D. Evolution, development, and children's learning. Santa Monica, Calif.: Goodyear, 1976. [3]

Fishbein, M., and **I. Ajzen.** Belief, attitude, intention and behavior: An introduction to theory and research. Reading, Mass.: Addison-Wesley, 1975. [25]

Fishburne, P. M., H. I. Abelson, and **I. Cisin.** National survey on drug abuse: Main findings, 1979. Washington, D.C. National Institute on Drug Abuse, 1980. [7]

Fisher, S., and **R. P. Greenberg.** The scientific credibility of Freud's theories and therapy. New York: Basic Books, 1977. [18]

Fiske, E. B. An issue that won't go away. The New York Times Magazine, March 27, 1977, p. 58. [20]

Fiske, S. T., and **S. E. Taylor.** Social cognition. Reading, Mass.: Addison-Wesley, 1984. [26]

Fitzsimons, J. T. Drinking by rats depleted of body fluid without increase in osmotic pressure. Journal of Physiology, 1961, 159, 297–309. [12]

Fitzsimons, J. T. The role of renal thirst in drinking induced by extracellular stimuli. Journal of Physiology, 1969, 201, 349–368. [12]

Flavell, J. H. Cognitive development. Englewood Cliffs, N.J.: Prentice-Hall, 1977. [15]

Flavell, J. H., S. G. Shipstead, and **K. Croft.** Young children's knowledge about visual perception: Hiding objects from others. Child Development, 1978, 49, 1208–1211. [15]

Flynn, J. P., H. Vanegas, W. Foote, and **S. Edwards.** Neural mechanisms involved in a cat's attack on a rat. In R. E. Whalen et al. (Eds.), *Neural control of behavior.* New York: Academic Press, 1970. [11]

Flynn, J. R. The mean IQ of Americans: Massive gains 1932–1978. *Psychological Bulletin,* 1984, *95,* 29–51. [20]

Foley, M. A., M. K. Johnson, and **C. L. Raye.** Age-related changes in confusion between memories for thoughts and memories for speech. *Child Development,* 1983, *54,* 51–60. [15]

Folkes, V. S. Forming relationships and the matching hypothesis. *Personality and Social Psychology Bulletin,* 1982, *8,* 631–636. [26]

Ford, C. S., and **F. A. Beach.** *Pattern of sexual behavior.* New York: Harper & Row, 1951. [13]

Foss, D. J., and **D. T. Hakes.** *Psycholinguistics.* Englewood Cliffs, N.J.: Prentice-Hall, 1978. [16]

Fowler, C. A., G. Wolford, R. Slade, and **L. Tassinary.** Lexical access with and without awareness. *Journal of Experimental Psychology: General,* 1981, *110,* 341–362. [6]

Fox, J. L. PET scan controversy aired. *Science,* 1984, *224,* 143–144. [3]

Fozard, J. L. The time for remembering. In L. Poon (Ed.), *Aging in the 1980's.* Washington, D.C.: American Psychological Association, 1980. [15]

Frank, J. D. *Persuasion and healing: A comparative study of psychotherapy.* Baltimore: Johns Hopkins University Press, 1961. [24]

Frank, J. D. The placebo in psychotherapy. *Behavioral and Brain Sciences,* 1983, *6,* 291–292. [24]

Frankl, V. E. *Man's search for meaning.* Boston: Beacon Press, 1962. [23]

Frankl, V. E. *The unconscious god: Psychotheraphy and theology.* New York: Simon & Schuster, 1975. [23]

Franks, J. J., and **J. D. Bransford.** Abstraction of visual patterns. *Journal of Experimental Psychology,* 1971, *90,* 65–74. [10]

Fredericksen, N. The real test bias: Influences of testing on teaching and learning. *American Psychologist,* 1984, *39,* 193–202. [20]

Freedman, J. L. Effect of television violence on aggression. *Psychological Bulletin,* 1984, *96,* 227–246. [1, 17, 27]

Freedman, J. L., and **S. C. Fraser.** Compliance without pressure: The foot-in-the-door technique. *Journal of Personality and Social Psychology,* 1966, *4,* 195–202. [2, 27]

Freedman, J. L., and **D. O. Sears.** Warning, distraction and resistance to influence. *Journal of Personality and Social Psychology,* 1965, *1,* 262–266. [25]

Freud, S. *An outline of psychoanalysis.* New York: Norton, 1949. (Originally published, 1940.) [1]

Freud, S. *The Interpretation of dreams.* New York: Basic Books, 1955. (Originally published, 1900.) [7, 18]

Freud, S. Introductory lectures on psychoanalysis. In J. Strachey (Ed. and Trans.), *The standard edition of the complete psychological works of Sigmund Freud,* Vols. 15 and 16. London: Hogarth Press, 1961 and 1963. (Originally published, 1917.) [18]

Freud, S. *Civilization and its discontents* J. Strachey (Ed. and Trans.). New York: Norton, 1962. (Originally published, 1930.) [18]

Freud, S. *Jokes and their relation to the unconscious.* In J. Strachey (Ed.), *The standard edition of the complete psychological works of Sigmund Freud,* Vol. 6. London: Hogarth Press, 1962. (Originally published, 1905.) [18]

Freud, S. *New introductory lectures on psychoanalysis.* J. Strachey (Ed. and Trans.). New York: W. W. Norton, 1965. (Originally published, 1933.) [18]

Freud, S. Femininity. In J. Strouse (Ed.), *Women and analysis: Dialogues on psychoanalytic views of femininity.* New York: Dell, 1974. [18]

Friedman, M., and **R. H. Rosenman.** *Type A behavior and your heart.* New York: Knopf, 1974. [21]

Friedman, S., B. Jacobs, and **M. Werthmann.** Preterms of low medical risk: Spontaneous behaviors and soothability at expected date of birth. *Infant Behavior and Development,* 1982, *5,* 3–10. [14]

Friedrich, W., and **J. Boriskin.** The role of the child in abuse: A review of the literature. *American Journal of Orthopsychiatry,* 1976, *7,* 306–313. [14]

Frisby, J. P. *Seeing: Illusion, brain and mind.* New York: Oxford University Press, 1980. [5]

Frodi, A. M., M. E. Lamb, L. A. Leavitt, and **W. L. Donovan.** Fathers' and mothers' responses to infant smiles and cries. *Infant Behavior and Development,* 1978, *1,* 187–198. [14]

Froming, W. J., L. Allen, and **B. Underwood.** Age and generosity reconsidered: Cross-sectional and longitudinal evidence. *Child Development,* 1983, *54,* 585–593. [17]

Fromkin, V. (Ed.), *Speech errors as linguistic evidence.* The Hague: Mouton Publishers, 1973. [16]

Fromkin, V., S. Krashen, S. Curtiss, D. Rigler, and **M. Rigler.** The development of language in Genie: A case of language acquisition beyond the critical period. *Brain and Language,* 1974, *1,* 81–107. [16]

Fromm, E. *Escape from freedom.* New York: Holt, Rinehart & Winston, 1941. [18]

Fromm-Reichmann, F. *Psychoanalysis and psychotherapy: Selected papers.* Chicago: University of Chicago Press, 1974. [23]

Fuller, J. L. Ethology and behavior genetics. In J. L. Fuller and E. C. Simmel (Eds.), *Behavior genetics.* Hillsdale, N.J.: Lawrence Erlbaum, 1983a. [4]

Fuller, J. L. Sociobiology and behavior genetics. In J. L. Fuller and E. C. Sim-

mel (Eds.), *Behavior genetics.* Hillsdale, N.J.: Lawrence Erlbaum, 1983b. [4]

Furstenberg, F. *Unplanned parenthood: The social consequences of teenage childbearing.* New York: Free Press, 1976. [17]

Furth, H. *Thinking without language.* New York: Free Press, 1966. [16]

Gagnon, J. H. *Human sexualities.* Glenview, Ill.: Scott, Foresman, 1977. [13]

Galanter, E. Contemporary psychophysics. In R. Brown, E. Galanter, E. H. Hess, and G. Mandler, *New directions in psychology.* New York: Holt, Rinehart & Winston, 1962. [5]

Gallagher, J. M., and **D. K. Reid.** *The learning theory of Piaget and Inhelder.* Monterey, Calif.: Brooks/Cole, 1981. [15]

Galton, F. *Hereditary genius: An inquiry into its laws and consequences.* London: Macmillan, 1869. [1]

Galton, F. *Inquiries into human faculty.* London: Macmillan, 1883. [1]

Galton, L. *The silent disease: Hypertension.* New York: Crown Publishers, 1973. [21]

Ganellen, R. J., and **P. H. Blaney.** Hardiness and social support as moderators of the effects of life stress. *Journal of Personality and Social Psychology,* 1984, *47,* 156–163. [21]

Garcia, J. I.Q.: The conspiracy. *Psychology Today,* 1972, *6,* 40–43+. [20]

Garcia, J., F. R. Ervin, and **R. A. Koelling.** Learning with prolonged delay of reinforcement. *Psychonomic Science,* 1966, *5,* 121–122. [8]

Garcia, J., and **R. A. Koelling.** Relation of cue to consequence in avoidance learning. *Psychonomic Science,* 1966, *4,* 123–124. [1, 8]

Garcia, J., K. W. Rusiniak, and **L. P. Brett.** Conditioning food-illness aversions in wild animals: *Caveant canonici.* In H. Davis and H. M. B. Hurwitz (Eds.), *Operant-Pavlovian interactions.* Hillsdale, N.J.: Lawrence Erlbaum, 1977. [8]

Gardner, B. T., and **R. A. Gardner.** Teaching sign language to a chimpanzee. *Science,* 1969, *165,* 644–672. [16]

Gardner, B. T., and **R. A. Gardner.** Evidence for sentence constituents in the early utterances of child and chimpanzee. *Journal of Experimental Psychology: General,* 1975, *104,* 244–267. [16]

Gardner, E., *Fundamentals of neurology.* Philadelphia: Saunders, 1975. Copyright 1975 by Scientific American, Inc. All rights reserved. [3]

Gardner, H. The loss of language. *Human Nature,* 1978, *1,* 76–85. [3]

Gardner, H. *Frames of mind: The theory of multiple intelligences.* New York: Basic Books, 1984. [20]

Gardner, J. M., and **G. Turkewitz.** The effect of arousal level on visual preferences in preterm infants *Infant Behavior and Development,* 1982, *5,* 369–385. [14]

Gardner, L. I. Deprivation dwarfism. *Sci-*

entific American, 1972, *227*, 1, 76–82. [14]

Garfield, S. L. *Psychotherapy: An eclectic approach.* New York: Wiley, 1980. [24]

Garfield, S. L. Eclecticism and integration in psychotherapy. *Behavior Therapy*, 1982, *13*, 610–623. [24]

Garvey, C. *Play.* Cambridge, Mass.: Harvard University Press, 1977. [17]

Gates, A. I. Recitation as a factor in memorizing. *Archives of Psychology*, 1917, No. 40. [9]

Gates, M., and **W. C. Allee.** Conditioned behavior of isolated and grouped cockroaches on a simple maze. *Journal of Comparative Psychology*, 1933, *13*, 331–358. [27]

Gazzaniga, M. S. On dividing the self: Speculations from brain research. *Neurology*, 1977, 233–244. [3]

Gazzaniga, M. S. Right hemisphere language following brain bisection. A 20-year perspective. *American Psychologist*, 1983, *38*, 525–537. [7]

Geen, R. G., and **J. J. Hange.** Drive theory of social facilitation: Twelve years of theory and research. *Psychological Bulletin*, 1977, *84*, 1267–1285. [27]

Geldard, F. A. *The human senses* (2nd ed.). New York: Wiley, 1972. [5]

Gelder, M., and **T. Kolakowska.** Variability of response to neuroleptics in schizophrenia: Clinical, pharmacological, and neuroendocrine correlates. *Comprehensive Psychiatry*, 1979, *20*, 397–408. [23]

Gelman, R. Conservation acquisition: A problem of learning to attend to relevant attributes. *Journal of Experimental Child Psychology*, 1969, *7*, 167–187. [15]

Gelman, R., and **C. R. Gallistel.** *The child's understanding of number.* Cambridge, Mass.: Harvard University Press, 1978. [15]

Gentner, D., and **A. L. Stevens.** *Mental models.* Hillsdale, N.J.: Lawrence Erlbaum, 1983. [10]

Gentry, W. D., A. P. Chesney, H. E. Gary, R. P. Hall, and **E. Harburg.** Habitual anger-coping styles: I. Affect on mean blood pressure and risk for essential hypertension. *Psychosomatic Medicine*, 1982, *44*, 195–202. [21]

Geschwind, N. Specialization of the human brain, *Scientific American*, 1979, *241*, 180–201. [3]

Ghiselli, E. E. *The validity of occupational aptitude tests.* New York: Wiley, 1966. [28]

Ghiselli, E. E. *Explorations in managerial talent.* Pacific Palisades, Calif.: Goodyear, 1971. [28]

Ghiselli, E. E. The validity of aptitude tests in personnel selection. *Personnel Psychology*, 1973, *26*, 461–477. [28]

Giambra, L. M., and **D. Arenberg.** Problem solving, concept learning, and aging. In L. Poon (Ed.), *Aging in the 1980's.* Washington, D.C.: American Psychological Association, 1980. [15]

Gibson, E. J. *Principles of perceptual learning and development.* New York: Appleton-Century-Crofts, 1969. [14]

Gibson, E. J., and **H. Levin.** *The psychology of reading.* Bloomington: Indiana University Press, 1975. [16]

Gibson, E. J., and **R. D. Walk.** The effect of prolonged exposure to visually presented patterns on learning to discriminate them. *Journal of Comparative and Physiological Psychology*, 1956, *49*, 232–242. [6]

Gibson, E. J., and **R. D. Walk.** The visual cliff. *Scientific American*, April 1960, 64–71. [14]

Gibson, J. J. *The senses considered as perceptual systems.* Boston: Houghton Mifflin, 1966. [6]

Gilligan, C. *In a different voice: Psychological theory and women's development.* Cambridge, Mass.: Harvard University Press, 1982. [17]

Glanzer, M., and **W. H. Clark.** The verbal loop hypothesis: Binary numbers. *Journal of Verbal Learning and Verbal Behavior*, 1963, *2*, 301–309. [9]

Glass, A. L., K. J. Holyoak, and **J. L. Santa.** *Cognition.* Reading, Mass.: Addison-Wesley, 1979. [10]

Glass, D. C., B. Reim, and **J. E. Singer.** Behavioral consequences of adaptation to controllable and uncontrollable noise. *Journal of Experimental Social Psychology*, 1971, *7*, 244–257. [21]

Glass, D. C., and **J. E. Singer.** *Urban stress: Experiments on noise and social stressors.* New York: Academic Press, 1972. [21]

Glass, D. C. *Behavior patterns, stress, and coronary disease.* Hillsdale, N.J.: Lawrence Erlbaum, 1977. [1, 21]

Gleason, J. B., and **S. Weintraub.** Input language and the acquisition of communicative competence. In K. E. Nelson (Ed.), *Children's language.* Vol. 1. New York: Gardner Press, 1978. [16]

Glenberg, A. M., and **M. M. Bradley.** Mental contiguity. *Journal of Experimental Psychology: Human Learning and Memory*, 1979, *5*, 88–97. [9]

Glesser, G. C., B. L. Green, and **C. Einget.** *Prolonged psychological effects of disaster: A study of the Buffalo Creek Flood.* New York: Academic Press, 1981. [21]

Glover, J., and **A. L. Gary.** Procedures to increase some aspects of creativity. *Journal of Applied Behavior Analysis*, 1976, *9*, 79–84. [10]

Godden, D. R., and **A. D. Baddeley.** Context-dependent memory in two natural environments: On land and under water. *British Journal of Psychology*, 1975, *66*, 325–332. [9]

Goetz, E. M., and **D. M. Baer.** Social control of form diversity and the emergence of new forms in children's blockbuilding. *Journal of Applied Behavior Analysis*, 1973, *6*, 209–217. [10]

Goetz, E. M., and **M. Salmonson.** The effects of general and descriptive reinforcement on creativity in easel paint-

ing. In G. Semb (Ed.), *Behavior analysis and education.* Lawrence, Kans.: University of Kansas, 1972. [10]

Goldberg, S. Prematurity: Effects on parent–infant interaction. *Journal of Pediatric Psychology*, 1978, *3*, 137–144. [14]

Golden, C. J., J. A. Moses, Jr., and **R. Zelazowski.** Cerebral ventricular site and neuropsychological impairment in young chronic schizophrenics. *Archives of General Psychiatry*, 1980, *37*, 618–626. [23]

Goldfried, M. R., and **G. C. Davison.** *Clinical behavior therapy.* New York: Holt, Rinehart & Winston, 1976. [24]

Goldsmith, H. H., and **I. I. Gottesman.** Origins of variation in behavioral style: A longitudinal study of temperament in young twins. *Child Development*, 1981, *52*, 91–103. [17]

Goldstein, E. B. *Sensation and perception* (2nd ed.). Belmont, Calif.: Wadsworth, 1984. [5]

Goleman, D. *The varieties of the meditative experience.* New York: Dutton, 1977. [7]

Goleman, D., and **R. J. Davidson** (Eds.). *Consciousness: Brain, states of awareness, and mysticism.* New York: Harper & Row, 1979. [7]

Goodenough, F. L. Expression of the emotions in a blind-deaf child. *Journal of Abnormal and Social Psychology*, 1932, *27*, 328–333. [11]

Goodstein, L., and **I. Sandler.** Using psychology to promote human welfare: A conceptual analysis of the role of community psychology. *American Psychologist*, 1978, *33*, 888–891. [24]

Goodwin, D. W., F. Schulsinger, L. Hermansen, S. B. Guze, and **G. Winokur.** Alcohol problems in adoptees raised apart from alcoholic biological parents. *Archives of General Psychiatry*, 1973, *28*. 238–243. [4]

Gorden, H. W., and **J. E. Bogen.** Hemispheric lateralization of singing after intracarotid sodium amylbarbitone. *Journal of Neurology, Neurosurgery, and Psychiatry*, 1974, *37*, 727–738. [16]

Gottesman, I. I. Schizophrenia and genetics: Where are we? Are you sure? In L. C. Wynne, R. L. Cromwell, and S. Matthysse (Eds.), *The nature of schizophrenia: New approaches to research and treatment.* New York: Wiley, 1978. [23]

Gottlieb, G. Conceptions of prenatal development: Behavioral embryology. *Psychological Review*, 1976, *83*, 215–234. [14]

Gottlieb, G. The psychobiological approach to developmental issues. In P. H. Mussen (Ed.), *Handbook of child psychology.* Vol. 2, J. J. Campos and M. M. Haith (Eds.), *Infancy and developmental psychobiology.* New York: Wiley, 1983. [17]

Gould, R. L. The phases of adult life: A study in developmental psychology.

American Journal of Psychiatry, 1972, *129*, 521–531. [17]

Goulet, L. R., and **P. B. Baltes.** *Life-span developmental psychology: Research and theory.* New York: Academic Press. 1970. [1]

Gove, W. R. The current status of the labelling theory of mental illness. In W. R. Gove (Ed.), *Deviance and mental illness.* Beverly Hills, Calif.: Sage, 1982. [23]

Graf, P., L. R. Squire, and **G. Mandler.** The information that amnesic patients do not forget. *Journal of Experimental Psychology: Learning, Memory, and Cognition,* 1984, *10* (1), 164–178. [18]

Gratch, G. A study of the relative dominance of vision and touch in six-month-old infants. *Child Development,* 1972, *43*, 615–623. [15]

Greaves, G. B. Multiple personality: 165 years after Mary Reynolds. *Journal of Nervous and Mental Disease,* 1980, *168*, 577–596. [22]

Green, D. M., and **J. A. Swets.** *Signal detection theory and psychophysics.* New York: Wiley, 1966. [5]

Green, R. Sexual identity of 37 children raised by homosexual or transsexual parents. *American Journal of Psychiatry,* 1978, *135*, 692–697. [13]

Green, R. Patterns of sexual identity in childhood: Relationship to subsequent sexual partner preference. In J. Marmor (Ed.). *Homosexual behavior.* New York: Basic Books, 1980. [13]

Green, R. Environmental determinants of human sexuality. In D. Gilmore and B. Cook (Eds.), *Factors in mammal reproduction.* London: Macmillan, 1981. [13]

Green, R. Gender identity disorders and transvestism. In J. Greist, J. Jefferson, and R. Spitzer (Eds.), *Treatment of mental disorders.* New York: Oxford University Press, 1982a. [13]

Green, R. Relationship between "Feminine" and "masculine" behavior during boyhood and sexual orientation in manhood. In Z. Hoch and H. Lief (Eds.), *Sexology: Sexual biology, behavior, and theory.* New York: Excerpta Medica, 1982b. [13]

Greenberg, P. F. The thrill seekers. *Human Behavior,* 1977, *6* (4), 17–21. [12]

Greenblatt, M. Efficacy of ECT in affective and schizophrenic illness. *American Journal of Psychiatry,* 1977, *134*, 1001–1005. [24]

Greene, J., N. Fox, and **M. Lewis.** The relationship between neonatal characteristics and three-month mother-infant interaction in high-risk infants. *Child Development,* 1983, *54*, 1286–1296. [14]

Greene, L. R. Psychiatric day treatment as alternative to and transition from full time hospitalization. *Community Mental Health Journal,* 1981, *17*, 191–202. [24]

Greene, P. J., C. J. Morgan, and **D. P. Barash.** Hybrid vigor: Evolutionary biol-

ogy and sociology. In J. S. Lockard (Ed.), *The evolution of human social behavior.* New York: Elsevier, 1980. [4]

Greenwald, A. G. Self and memory. In G. H. Bower (Ed.), *The psychology of learning and motivation.* New York: Academic Press, 1981. [9]

Greer, L. D. Children's comprehension of formal features with masculine and feminine connotations. Unpublished master's thesis. Department of Human Development, University of Kansas, 1980 (cited in Huston, 1983). [17]

Gregory, R. L. *The intelligent eye.* New York: McGraw-Hill, 1970. [6]

Gregory, R. L., and **J. G. Wallace.** Recovery from early blindness: A case study. *Experimental Psychology Society Monograph,* 1963, No. 2. [6]

Grice, H. P. Logic and conversation. In P. Cole and J. L. Morgan (Eds.), *Syntax and semantics. Vol. 3: Speech acts.* New York: Seminar Press, 1975. [16]

Griffin, G. Legal views of test validity. Unpublished paper, Northwestern University, November 1980. [28]

Griffith, J. J., S. A. Mednick, F. Schulsinger, and **B. Diderichsen.** Verbal associative disturbances in children at high risk for schizophrenia. *Journal of Abnormal Psychology,* 1980, *89*, 125–131. [23]

Grinspoon, L. *Marihuana reconsidered* (2nd ed.). Cambridge, Mass.: Harvard University Press, 1977. [7]

Grinspoon, L., and **J. G. Bakalar.** *Cocaine: A drug and its social evolution.* New York: Basic Books, 1976. [7]

Grotevant, H. D., S. Scarr, and **R. A. Weinberg.** Patterns of interest similarity in adoptive and biological families. *Journal of Personality and Social Psychology,* 1977, *35*, 667–676. [4, 14]

Groth, A. N., and **H. J. Birnbaum.** Adult sexual orientation and attraction to underaged persons. *Archives of Sexual Behavior,* 1978, *7*, 175–181. [13]

Groth, A. N., and **A. W. Burgess.** Rape: A sexual deviation. *American Journal of Orthopsychiatry,* 1977, *47*, 400–406. [13]

Gruendel, J. M. Referential overextension in early language development. *Child Develoment,* 1977, *48*, 1567–1576. [16]

Grusec, J. E., and **E. Redler.** Attribution, reinforcement, and altruism: A developmental analysis. *Developmental Psychology,* 1980, *16*, 525–534. [17]

Gurin, G., J. Veroff, and **S. Feld.** *Americans view their mental health: A nationwide interview survey.* New York: Basic Books, 1960. [24]

Gustavson, C. R., J. Garcia, W. G. Hankins, and **K. W. Rusiniak.** Coyote predation control by aversive conditioning. *Science,* 1974, *184*, 581–583. [8]

Guthrie, E. R. *The psychology of learning.* New York: Harper & Row, 1935. [8]

Haber, R. N. Discrepancy from adaptation level as a source of affect. *Journal of*

Experimental Psychology, 1958, *56*, 370–375. [12]

Haber, R. N., and **L. G. Standing.** Direct measures of short-term visual storage. *Quarterly Journal of Experimental Psychology,* 1969, *21*, 43–45. [9]

Hagen, M., and **R. Jones.** Cultural effects on pictorial perception: How many words is one picture really worth? In R. Walk and H. Pick (Eds.), *Perception and experience.* New York: Plenum, 1978. [6]

Haier, R., D. Rosenthal, and **P. H. Wender.** MMPI assessment of psychopathology in the adopted-away offspring of schizophrenics. *Archives of General Psychiatry,* 1978, *35*, 171–175. [23]

Haith, M. M. *Rules that babies look by.* Hillsdale, N.J.: Lawrence Erlbaum, 1980. [14]

Haith, M. M., T. Bergman, and **M. J. Moore.** Eye contact and face scanning in early infancy. *Science,* 1977, *198*, 853–854. [14]

Hall, C. S. The meaning of dreams. In D. Goleman and R. J. Davidson (Eds.), *Consciousness: Brain, states of awareness, and mysticism.* New York: Harper & Row, 1979. [7]

Hall, C. S., and **G. Lindzey.** *Theories of personality* (3rd ed.). New York: Wiley, 1978. [1, 18]

Hall, E. Will success spoil B. F. Skinner? An interview with B. F. Skinner. *Psychology Today,* 1972, *6*, 65–72+. [19]

Hall, E. T. *The hidden dimension.* New York: Doubleday, 1966. [26]

Hansell, S., J. Sparacino, and **D. Ronchi.** Physical attractiveness and blood pressure: Sex and age differences. *Personality and Social Psychology Bulletin,* 1982, *8*, 113–121. [26]

Hanson, D. R., I. I. Gottesman, and **L. L. Heston.** Some possible childhood indicators of adult schizophrenia inferred from children of schizophrenics. *British Journal of Psychiatry,* 1976, *129*, 142–154. [23]

Harburg, E., J. C. Erfurt, L. S. Havenstein, C. Chape, W. J. Schull, and **M. A. Schork.** Socio-ecological stress, supressed hostility, skin color, and black-white male blood pressure: Detroit. *Psychosomatic Medicine,* 1973, *35*, 276–296. [21]

Hardin, G. The tragedy of the commons. *Science,* 1968, *162*, 1243–1248. [27]

Hardy, J. D., J. A. Stolwijk, and **D. Hoffman.** Pain following step increase in skin temperature. In D. R. Kenshalo (Ed.), *The skin senses.* Springfield, Ill.: Charles C Thomas, 1968. [5]

Hare-Mustin, R. T., and **J. E. Hall.** Procedures for responding to ethics complaints against psychologists. *American Psychologist,* 1981, *36*, 1494–1505. [2]

Hargadon, F. Tests and college admissions. *American Psychologist,* 1981, *36*, 1112–1119. [20]

Hariton, E. B., and **J. L. Singer.** Women's fantasies during sexual intercourse:

Normative and theoretical implications. *Journal of Consulting and Clinical Psychology*, 1974, *42*, 313–322. [13]

Harkness, S. The cultural context of child development. In C. M. Super and S. Harkness (Eds.), *New directions for child development*. No. 8, *Anthropological perspectives on child development*. San Francisco: Jossey-Bass, 1980. [14, 17]

Harlow, H. F. Love in infant monkeys. *Scientific American*, 1959, *200* (6), 68–74. [17]

Harlow, H. F., and **M. K. Harlow.** Learning to love. *American Scientist*, 1966, *54*, 244–272. [1, 17]

Harlow, H. F., and **M. K. Harlow.** Effects of various mother-infant relationships on rhesus monkey behaviors. In B. M. Foss (Ed.), *Determinants of infant behaviour*. Vol. 4. London: Methuen, 1969. [17]

Harlow, H. F., M. K. Harlow, and **D. K. Meyer.** Learning motivated by a manipulation drive. *Journal of Experimental Psychology*, 1950, *40*, 228–234. [17]

Harlow, H. F., M. K. Harlow, and **S. J. Suomi.** From thought to therapy: Lessons from a private library. *American Scientist*, 1971, *59*, 538–549. [17]

Harrell, J. P. Psychological factors and hypertension: A status report. *Psychological Bulletin*. 1980, *87*, 482–490. [21]

Harris, P. L. Infant cognition. In P. H. Mussen (Ed.), *Handbook of child psychology* (4th ed.). Vol. 2. M. M. Haith and J. J. Campos (Eds.), *Infancy and developmental psychobiology*. New York: Wiley, 1983. [15]

Harris, R. J. Inferences in information processing. In G. H. Bower (Ed.), *The psychology of learning and motivation: Advances in theory and research*. Vol. 15. New York: Academic Press, 1982. [9]

Hart, J. T. Memory and the feeling-of-knowing experience. *Journal of Educational Psychology*, 1965, *56*, 208–216. [9]

Harter, S. Pleasure derived by children from cognitive challenge and mastery. *Child Development*, 1974, *45*, 661–669. [15]

Harter, S. Developmental perspectives on the self-system. In P. H. Mussen (Ed.), *Handbook of child psychology* (4th ed.). Vol. 4, E. M. Hetherington (Ed.), *Socialization, personality, and social development*. New York: Wiley, 1983. [17]

Hartmann, E. The psychology of tiredness. In D. Goleman and R. J. Davidson (Eds.), *Consciousness: Brain, states of awareness, and mysticism*. New York: Harper & Row, 1979. [7]

Hartmann, E. The strangest sleep disorder. *Psychology Today*, April 1981, pp. 14–18. [7]

Hartup, W. W. Aggression in childhood: Developmental perspectives. *American Psychologist*, 1974, *29*, 336–341. [17]

Hartup, W. W. Peer relations. In P. H. Mussen (Ed.), *Handbook of child psychology*. (4th ed.). Vol. 4. E. Mavis Hetherington (Ed.), *Socialization, personality, and social development*. New York: Wiley, 1983. [17, 26]

Hass, A. *Teenage sexuality*. New York: Macmillan, 1979. [13]

Hass, R. G., and **R. W. Mann.** Anticipatory belief change—persuasion or impression management. *Journal of Personality and Social Psychology*, 1976, *23*, 219–233. [25]

Hassan, S. A. Transactional and contextual invalidation between the parents of disturbed families: A comparative study. *Family Process*, 1974, *13*, 53–76. [23]

Hastie, R., S. D. Penrod, and **N. Pennington.** *Inside the jury*. Cambridge, Mass.: Harvard University Press, 1982. [25]

Hathaway, S. R., and **J. C. McKinley.** A multiphasic personality schedule (Minnesota): I. Construction of the schedule. *Journal of Psychology*, 1940, *10*, 249–254. [20]

Hattie, J. A., C. F. Sharpley, and **H. J. Rogers.** Comparative effectiveness of professional and paraprofessional helpers. *Psychological Bulletin*, 1984, *95*, 534–541. [24]

Hawkins, R. D., and **E. R. Kandel.** Is there a cell biological alphabet for simple forms of learning? *Psychological Review*, 1984. [3]

Hayes, K. J., and **C. Hayes.** The intellectual development of a home-raised chimpanzee. *Proceedings of the American Philosophical Society*, 1951, *95*, 105–109. [16]

Haymes, M., L. Green, and **R. Quinto.** Maslow's hierarchy, moral development, and prosocial behavioral skills within a child psychiatric population. *Motivation and Emotion* 1984, *8*, 23–31. [12]

Hearnshaw, L. S. *Cyril Burt, psychologist*. Ithaca, N.Y.: Cornell University Press, 1979. [20]

Heath, R. G. Electrical self-stimulation of the brain in man, *The American Journal of Psychiatry*, 1963, *120*, 571–577. [3]

Hebb, D. O. *The organization of behavior*. New York: Wiley, 1949. [8, 14]

Hebb, D. O. The mind's eye. *Psychology Today*, May 1969, pp. 54–57+. [7]

Hebb, D. O. What psychology is about. *American Psychologist*, 1974, *29*, 71–79. [1]

Hecaen, H., and **M. L. Albert.** *Human neuropsychology*. New York: Wiley, 1978. [3]

Heider, F. *The psychology of interpersonal relations*. New York: Wiley, 1958. [12, 26]

Heilman, M. E., and **L. R. Saruwatari.** When beauty is beastly: The effects of appearance and sex on evaluations of job applicants for managerial and nonmanagerial jobs. *Organizational Behavior and Human Performance*, 1979, *23*, 360–372. [1]

Heim, N. Sexual behavior of castrated sex offenders. *Archives of Sexual Behavior*, 1981, *10*, 11–19. [13]

Heiman, J. R. The physiology of erotica: Women's sexual arousal. *Psychology Today*, 1975, *8*, 90–94. [13]

Heiman, J. R., L. LoPiccolo, and **J. LoPiccolo.** The treatment of sexual dysfunction. In A. Gurman and D. Kniskern (Eds.), *Handbook of family therapy*. New York: Bruner-Mazel, 1980. [13]

Held, R. Development of visual resolution. *Canadian Journal of Psychology*, 1979, *33*, 213–221. [6]

Held, R., and **A. Hein.** Movement-produced stimulation in the development of visually guided behavior. *Journal of Comparative and Physiological Psychology*, 1963, *56*, 872–876. [6]

Helmholtz, H. von. On the theory of compound colors. *Philosophical Magazine*, 1852, *4*, 519–534. [5]

Helmreich, R. L., J. T. Spence, and **R. H. Gibson.** Sex-role attitudes: 1972–1980. *Personality and Social Psychology Bulletin*, 1982, *8*, 656–663. [26]

Helson, H. *Adaptation-level theory*. New York: Harper & Row, 1964. [5]

Henle, M. On the relation between logic and thinking. *Psychological Review*, 1962, *69*, 366–378. [15]

Hering, E. *Zur Lehre vom Lichtsinne*. Vienna: Gerold, 1878. [5]

Herman, C. P., and **D. Mack.** Restrained and unrestrained eating. *Journal of Personality*, 1975, *43*, 647–660. [12]

Herrnstein, R. J. The evolution of behaviorism. *American Psychologist*, 1977, *32*. 593–603. [1]

Herron, J. (Ed.). *Neuropsychology of left-handedness*. New York: Academic Press, 1979. [3]

Hess, R. D. Social class and ethnic influences on socialization. In P. H. Mussen (Ed.), *Carmichael's manual of child psychology* (3rd ed.). Vol. 2. New York: Wiley, 1970. [14]

Heston, L. L. Psychiatric disorders in foster home reared children of schizophrenic mothers. *British Journal of Psychiatry*, 1966, *112*, 819–825. [23]

Heusmann, L. R., L. D. Eron, R. Klein, P. Brice, and **P. Fischer.** Mitigating the imitation of aggressive behavior by changing children's attitudes about media violence. *Journal of Personality and Social Psychology*, 1983, *44*, 899–910. [27]

Heusmann, L. R., L. D. Eron, M. M. Lefkowitz, and **L. O. Walder.** Stability of aggression over time and generation. *Developmental Psychology*, 1984, *20*, 1120–1134. [27]

Higbee, K. L. *Your memory*. Englewood Cliffs, N. J.: Prentice-Hall, 1977. [9]

Hilgard, E. R. *Hypnotic susceptibility*. New York: Harcourt Brace Jovanovich, 1965. [7]

Hilgard, E. R. A neodissociation interpretation of pain reduction in hypnosis.

Psychological Review, 1973, *80*, 396–411. [7]

Hilgard, E. R. Hypnosis. *Annual Review of Psychology*, 1975, *26*, 19–44. [7]

Hilgard, E. R. *Divided consciousness: Multiple controls in human thought and action.* New York: Wiley-Interscience, 1977. [7]

Hilgard, E. R. Hypnosis and consciousness. *Human Nature*, 1978, *1*, 42–49. [7]

Hinton, G. E., and **J. A. Anderson.** *Parallel models of associative memory.* Hillsdale, N.J.: Lawrence Erlbaum, 1981. [3]

Hiroto, D. S., and **M. E. P. Seligman.** Generality of learned helplessness in man. *Journal of Personality and Social Psychology*, 1975, *31*, 311–327. [21]

Hirshfeld, R. M. A., and **C. K. Cross.** Epidemiology of affective disorders: Psychosocial risk factors. *Archives of General Psychiatry*, 1982, *39*, 35–46. [22]

Hirst, W., U. Neisser, and **E. Spelke.** Divided attention. *Human Nature*, 1978. *1*, 54–61. [1]

Hobson, J. A., and **R. W. McCarley.** The brain as a dream state generator: An activation-synthesis hypothesis of the dream process. *American Journal of Psychiatry*, 1977, *134*, 1335–1348. [7]

Hochbaum, G. *Public participation in screening programs.* U.S. Department of Health, Education, and Welfare, Public Health Service, Publication #572. Washington, D.C.: U.S. Government Printing Office, 1958. [21]

Hochberg, J. *Perception* (2nd ed.). Englewood Cliffs, N.J.: Prentice-Hall, 1978. [5, 6]

Hofer, M. A. *The roots of human behavior.* San Francisco: Freeman, 1981. [14]

Hoffman, M. L. Personality and social development. Annual review of psychology, 1977, *28*, 295–321. [12, 17]

Holahan, C. J. *Environmental psychology.* New York: Random House, 1982. [1]

Holden, C. Identical twins reared apart. *Science*, 1980, *207*, 1323–1328. [4]

Holden, C. Scientist convicted for monkey neglect. *Science*, 1981, *214*, 1218–1220. [2]

Hollingshead, A. B., and **F. C. Redlich.** *Social class and mental illness.* New York: Wiley, 1958. [23]

Holmes, D. S. Meditation and somatic arousal reduction: A review of the experimental evidence. *American Psychologist*, 1984, *39*, 1–10. [7]

Holmes, T. H., and **R. H. Rahe.** The social readjustment rating scale. *Journal of Psychosomatic Research*, 1967, *11*, 213–218. [21]

Hook, J. The development of equity and logico-mathematical thinking. *Child Development*, 1978, *49*, 1035–1044. [17]

Hooker, D. *The prenatal origin of behavior.* Lawrence: University of Kansas Press, 1952. [14]

Hoon, P. W., K. Bruce, and **B. Kinchloe.** Does the menstrual cycle play a role in sexual arousal? *Psychophysiology,* 1982, *19*, 21–26. [13]

Horn, J. L. The theory of fluid and crystallized intelligence in relation to concepts of cognitive psychology and aging in adulthood. In F. I. M. Craik and S. Trehub (Eds.), *Aging and cognitive processes.* New York: Plenum, 1982. [15]

Horner, M. S. Femininity and successful achievement: A basic inconsistency. In J. Bardwick, E. M. Douvan, M. S. Horner, and D. Gutmann (Eds.), *Feminine personality and conflict.* Monterey, Calif.: Brooks/Cole, 1970. [12]

Horner, M. S. Toward an understanding of achievement-related conflicts in women. *Journal of Social Issues,* 1972, *28*, 157–175. [12]

Horner, S. O., S. H. Mobley, and **B. M. Meglino.** An experimental evaluation of the effects of a realistic job preview on marine recruit affect, intentions, and behavior. *Technical Report TR-9.* Columbia, S.C.: Center for Management and Organizational Research, College of Business Administration, University of South Carolina, 1979. [28]

Horney, K. *Our inner conflicts.* New York: Norton, 1945. [18]

Horney, K. *The neurotic personality of our times.* New York: Norton. 1965. (Originally published, 1937.) [18]

Horney, K. *Feminine psychology.* New York: Norton, 1967. [18]

Horowitz, G. P., and **B. C. Dudek.** Behavioral pharmacogenetics. In J. L. Fuller and E. C. Simmel (Eds.), *Behavior genetics.* Hillsdale, N.J.: Lawrence Erlbaum, 1983. [4]

Hovland, C. I., A. Lumsdaine, and **F. Sheffield.** *Experiments on mass communication.* Princeton, N. J.: Princeton University Press, 1949. [25]

Hovland, C. I., and **W. Weiss.** The influence of source credibility on communication effectiveness. *Public Opinion Quarterly,* 1951, 636–650. [25]

Howell, W. C., and **R. L. Dipboye.** *Essentials of industrial and organizational psychology.* Homewood, Ill.: Dorsey, 1982. [28]

Hoyer, W. J., and **D. J. Plude.** Attentional and perceptual processes in the study of cognitive aging. In L. Poon (Ed.), *Aging in the 1980's.* Washington, D.C.: American Psychological Association, 1980. [15]

Hubel, D. H., and **T. N. Wiesel.** Receptive fields, binocular interaction and functional architecture in the cat's visual cortex. *Journal of Physiology,* 1962, *160*, 106–154. [3, 5]

Hubel, D. H., and **T. N. Wiesel.** Brain mechanisms of vision. *Scientific American,* 1979, *241*, 150–163. [5]

Huesmann, L. R., K. Lagerspetz, and **L. D. Eron.** Intervening variables in the TV violence-aggression relation: Evidence from two countries. *Developmental Psychology,* 1984, *20*, 746–775. [17]

Hull, C. L. *Principles of behavior.* New York: Appleton-Century-Crofts, 1943. [8]

Humphrey, T. The development of human fetal activity and its relation to postnatal behavior. In H. W. Reese and L. P. Lipsitt (Eds.), *Advances in child development and behavior.* Vol. 5. New York: Academic Press, 1970. [14]

Hunt, E. Varieties of cognitive power. In L. B. Resnik (Ed.), *The nature of intelligence.* Hillsdale, N.J.: Lawrence Erlbaum, 1976. [20]

Hunt, J. McV. *Early psychological development.* Worcester, Mass.: Clark University Press, 1980. [14]

Hunt, M. *Sexual behavior in the 1970's.* New York: Dell, 1974. [13]

Hunt, P. J., and **J. M. Hillery.** Social facilitation in a coaction setting: An examination of the effects over learning trials. *Journal of Experimental Social Psychology,* 1973, *2*, 563–571. [27]

Hunt, W. A., J. D. Matarazzo, S. M. Weiss, and **W. D. Gentry.** Associative learning, habit, and health behavior. *Journal of Behavioral Medicine,* 1979, *2*, 111–124. [21]

Hurvich, L. M., and **D. Jameson.** An opponent-process theory of color vision. *Psychological Review,* 1957, *64*, 384–404. [5]

Huston, A. C. Sex-typing. In P. H. Mussen (Ed.), *Handbook of child psychology* (4th ed.). Vol. 4, E. M. Hetherington (Ed.), *Socialization, personality, and social development.* New York: Wiley, 1983. [17]

Huston, T. L. Ambiguity of acceptance, social desirability, and dating choice. *Journal of Experimental Social Psychology,* 1973, *9*, 32–42. [26]

Huxley, A. The doors of perception. In D. Goleman and R. J. Davidson (Eds.), *Consciousness: Brain, states of awareness, and mysticism.* New York: Harper & Row, 1979. [7]

Hyde, J. S. Gender differences in aggression. *Developmental Psychology,* 1984b, *20*, 722–736. [17]

Hyman, B. T., G. N. Van Hoesen, A. R. Domasio, and **C. L. Barnes.** Alzheimer's disease: Cell-specific pathology isolates the hippocampal formation. *Science,* 1984, *225*, 1168–1170. [3, 9]

Hyman, I. A. Psychology, education, and schooling. *American Psychologist,* 1979, *34*, 1024–1029. [20]

Ickes, W., and **M. Turner.** On the social advantages of having an older, opposite-sex sibling: Birth order influences in mixed-sex dyads. *Journal of Personality and Social Psychology,* 1983, *45*, 210–222. [26]

Inhelder, B., and **J. Piaget.** *The growth of logical thinking from childhood to adolescence.* New York: Basic Books, 1958. [15]

Insko, C. A. Verbal reinforcement of attitude. *Journal of Personality and Social Psychology,* 1965, *2*, 621–623. [25]

Insko, C. A., E. A. Lind, and **S. LaTour.**

Persuasion, recall, and thought. *Representative Research in Social Psychology*, 1976, *7*, 66–78. [25]

Institute of Medicine. *Marijuana and health.* Washington, D.C.: National Academy Press, 1982. [7]

Ital, T. M. Qualitative and quantitative EEG findings in schizophrenia. *Schizophrenia Bulletin*, 1977, *3*, 61–79. [23]

Iversen, S. D., and **L. L. Iversen.** *Behavioral pharmacology.* New York: Oxford University Press, 1975. [7]

Iverson, L. I. The chemistry of the brain. *Scientific American*, 1979, *241*, 134–149. [3, 7]

Izard, C. E. *The face of emotion.* New York: Appleton-Century-Crofts, 1971. [11]

Izard, C. E. *Human emotions.* New York: Plenum, 1977. [11]

Izard, C. E., E. A. Hembree, L. M. Dougherty, and **C. C. Spizzari.** Changes in facial expressions of 2- to 19-month-old infants following acute pain. *Developmental Psychology*, 1983, *19*, 418–426. [11]

Jackson, D. D. Reunion of identical twins, raised apart, reveals some astonishing similarities. *Smithsonian*, October 1980, 48–56. [4]

Jackson, M. D., and **J. L. McClelland.** Processing determinants of reading speed. *Journal of Experimental Psychology: General*, 1979, *108*, 151–181. [16]

Jacob, R., H. Kraemer, and **W. S. Agras.** Relaxation therapy in the treatment of hypertension. *Archives of General Psychiatry*, 1977, *34*, 1417–1427. [21]

Jacobs, R. C., and **D. T. Campbell.** The perpetuation of an arbitrary tradition through several generations of a laboratory microculture. *Journal of Abnormal and Social Psychology*, 1961, *62*, 649–658. [27]

Jacobs, T. J., and **E. Charles.** Life events and the occurrence of cancer in children. *Psychosomatic Medicine*, 1980, *42*, 11–24. [21]

Jacobson, E. *Progressive relaxation.* Chicago: University of Chicago Press, 1938. [21]

Jacobson, E. *Anxiety and tension control.* Philadelphia: Lippincott, 1964. [21]

Jacobson, J. L., S. W. Jacobson, G. G. Fein, P. M. Schwartz, and **J. K. Dowler.** Prenatal exposure to an environmental toxin: A test of the multiple effects model. *Developmental psychology*, 1984, *20*, 523–532. [14]

Jacobson, N. S., and **G. Margolin.** *Marital therapy: Strategies based on social learning and behavior exchange principles.* New York: Brunner/Mazel, 1979. [24]

Jacobson, S. W. Matching behavior in the young infant. *Child Development*, 1979, *50*, 425–430. [11, 14]

Jacobson, S. W. Maternal caffeine consumption prior to pregnancy. Paper presented at the Meeting of the Society for Research in Child Development. Detroit, April 1983. [14]

James, W. *The principles of psychology.* New York: Holt, 1890. [11]

Janis, I. L. *Victims of groupthink: A psychological study of foreign-policy decisions and fiascoes.* Boston: Houghton Mifflin, 1972. [28]

Janis, I. L., and **S. Feshbach.** Effects of fear-arousing communications. *Journal of Abnormal and Social Psychology*, 1953, *48*, 78–92. [25]

Janis, I. L., D. Kaye, and **P. Kirschner.** Facilitating effects of "Eating-While-Reading" on responsiveness to persuasive communications. *Journal of Personality and Social Psychology*, 1965, *1*, 181–186. [25]

Jarvik, L. F. Thoughts on the psychobiology of aging. *American Psychologist*, May 1975, 576–583. [15]

Jarvik, L. F., J. E. Blum, and **A. O. Varma.** Genetic components and intellectual functioning during senescence: A 20-year study of aging twins. *Behavior Genetics*, 1972, *2*, 159–170. [14]

Jarvik, L. F., V. Klodin, and **S. S. Matsuyama.** Human aggression and the extra Y chromosome: Fact or fantasy? *American Psychologist*, 1973, *28*, 674–682. [27]

Jellinek, E. M. *Phases in the drinking history of alcoholics.* New Haven, Conn.: Hillhouse Press, 1946. [22]

Jemmott, J. B., III, and **S. E. Locke.** Psychosocial factors, immunologic mediation, and human susceptibility to infectious disease: How much do we know? *Psychological Bulletin*, 1984, *95*, 78–108. [21]

Jenkins, J. G., and **K. M. Dallenbach.** Oblivescence during sleep and waking. *American Journal of Psychology*, 1924, *35*, 605–612. [9]

Jensen, A. R. How much can we boost I.Q. and scholastic achievement? *Harvard Educational Review*, 1969, *39*, 1–123. [20]

Jensen, A. R. *Educability and group differences.* New York: Harper & Row, 1973. [20]

Jensen, A. R. Sir Cyril Burt in perspective. *American Psychologist*, 1978, *33*, 499–503. [20]

Jensen, A. R. *Bias in mental testing.* New York: Free Press, 1980. [20]

Jessor, R. Adolescent problem drinking: Psychosocial aspects and developmental outcomes. Paper presented at the Alcohol Research Seminar held as part of the international ceremony designating the National Institute on Alcohol Abuse and Alcoholism a Collaborating Center of the World Health Organization. Washington, D.C., November 2, 1983*a*. [17]

Jessor, R. The stability of change: Psychosocial development from adolescence to young adulthood. In D. Magnusson and V. Allen (Eds.), *Human development: An interactional perspective.* New York: Academic Press, 1983*b*. [17]

John, R. S., S. A. Mednick, and **F. Schulsinger.** Teacher reports as a predictor of schizophrenia and borderline schizophrenia: A Bayesian decision analysis. *Journal of Abnormal Psychology*, 1982, *91*, 399–412. [23]

Johnson, D. M., G. R. Parrott, and **R. P. Stratton.** Production and judgment of solutions to five problems. *Journal of Educational Psychology Monograph Supplement*, 1968, *59* (6, Pt. 2). [10]

Johnson, M. K., and **M. A. Foley.** Differentiating fact from fantasy: The reliability of children's memory. *Journal of Social Issues*, 1984, *40*, 33–50. [15]

Johnson, P. J., and **J. M. Davidson.** Intracerebral androgens and sexual behavior in the male rat. *Hormones and Behavior*, 1972, *3*, 345–357. [11]

Johnson-Laird, P. N. *Mental models.* Cambridge, Mass.: Harvard University Press, 1983. [9]

Jones, E. E., and **K. E. Davis.** From acts to dispositions: The attribution process in person perception. In L. Berkowitz (Ed.), *Advances in Experimental Social Psychology.* Vol. 2. New York: Academic Press, 1965. [26]

Jones, E. E., K. E. Davis, and **K. J. Gergen.** Role playing variations and their informational value for person perception. *Journal of Abnormal and Social Psychology*, 1961, *63*, 302–310. [26]

Jones, E. E., and **R. E. Nisbett.** *The actor and the observer: Perceptions of the causes of behavior.* Morristown, N.J.: General Learning Press, 1971. [26]

Jones, M. Community care for chronic mental patients: The need for a reassessment. *Hospital and Community Psychiatry*, 1975, *26*, 94–98. [24]

Jones, M. C. A laboratory study of fear: The case of Peter. *Pedagogical Seminary*, 1924, *31*, 308–315. [24]

Jones, M. M. Conversion reaction: Anachronism or evolutionary form? A review of the neurologic, behavioral, and psychoanalytic literature. *Psychological Bulletin*, 1980, *87*, 427–441. [22]

Jouvet, M. The function of dreaming: A neurophysiologist's point of view. In M. S. Gazzaniga and C. Blakemore (Eds.), *Handbook of psychobiology.* New York: Academic Press, 1975. [7]

Judd, C. M., and **J. A. Kulik.** Schematic effects of social attitudes on information processing and recall. *Journal of Personality and Social Psychology*, 1980, *38*, 569–578. [1]

Kagan, J. The growth of the "face" schema: Theoretical significance and methodological issues. In J. Hellmuth (Ed.), *The exceptional infant.* Vol. 1. *The normal infant.* New York: Brunner/ Mazel, 1967. [14]

Kagan, J. The baby's elastic mind. *Human Nature*, 1978, *1*, 66–73. [14]

Kagan, J., R. B. Kearsley, and **P. R. Zelazo.** *Infancy: Its place in human* *development.* Cambridge, Mass.: Harvard University Press, 1978. [17]

Kahneman, D., P. Slovic, and **A. Tversky.** *Judgment under uncertainty: Heuristics and biases.* Cambridge: Cambridge University Press, 1982. [26]

Kahneman, D., and **A. Tversky.** On the psychology of prediction. *Psychological Review,* 1973, *80,* 237–251. [10, 26]

Kakihana, R., and **J. C. Butte.** Behavioral correlates of inherited drinking in lab animals. In K. Eriksson, J. D. Sinclair, and K. Kiianmaa (Eds.), *Animal models in alcohol research.* New York: Academic Press, 1980. [4]

Kamin, L. G. *The science and politics of IQ.* New York: Wiley, 1974. [20]

Kamin, L. G. Heredity, intelligence, politics, and psychology: I. In N. J. Block and G. Dworkin (Eds.), *The IQ controversy.* New York: Pantheon, 1976. [20]

Kamin, L. J. Predictability, surprise, attention, and conditioning. In B. A. Campbell and R. M. Church (Eds.), *Punishment and aversive behavior.* New York: Appleton-Century-Crofts, 1969. [8]

Kandel, D. B. On processes of peer influences in adolescence. In R. Silbereisen and K. Eyferth (Eds.), *Integrative perspectives in youth development: Person and ecology.* New York: Springer Verlag, 1984. [17]

Kandel, E. R. Small systems of neurons. *Scientific American,* 1979, *241,* 66–87. [8]

Kanisza, G. Subjective contours. *Scientific American,* 1976, *234,* 48–52. [6]

Kannel, W. B., and **T. Gordon.** Physiological and medical concomitants of obesity: The Framingham Study. In G. A. Bray (Ed.), *Obesity in America.* Washington, D.C.: National Institutes of Health Publication #79–359. U.S. Government Printing Office, 1979. [21]

Kaplan, R. M. The connection between clinical health promotion and health status: A critical overview. *American Psychologist,* 1984, *39,* 755–765. [21]

Kasamatsu, A., and **T. Hirai.** An electroencephalographic study on the Zen meditation (Zazen). *Folia Psychiatrica et Neurologica Japonica,* 1966, *20,* 315–366. [7]

Katchadourian, H. A., and **D. T. Lunde.** *Fundamentals of human sexuality* (2nd ed.). New York: Holt, Rinehart & Winston, 1975. [13]

Kaufman, B. Reaching the "unreachable" child. *New York,* February 3, 1975, 43–49. [22]

Kaufmann, W. *Without guilt and justice.* New York: Peter Wyden, 1973. [26]

Kausler, D. H. *Experimental psychology and human aging.* New York: Wiley, 1982. [15]

Kavanaugh, D. J., and **G. H. Bower** Mood and self-efficacy: Impact of joy and sadness on perceived capabilities. *Cognitive Therapy and Research,* 1985. [10]

Kazdin, A. E. *Behavior modification in*

applied settings. Homewood, Ill.: Dorsey Press, 1975. [8]

Kazdin, A. E. *The token economy: A review and evaluation.* New York: Plenum, 1977. [24]

Kazdin, A. E. History of behavior modification: Experimental foundations of contemporary research. Baltimore: University Park Press, 1978. [1]

Kazdin, A. E., and **G. T. Wilson.** *Evaluation of behavior therapy: Issues, evidence and research strategies.* Cambridge, Mass.: Ballinger, 1978. [19, 24]

Keating, D. P. Thinking processes in adolescence. In J. Adelson (Ed.), *Handbook of adolescent psychology.* New York: Wiley-Interscience, 1980. [15]

Keegan, J. *The face of battle.* New York: Viking, 1976. [10]

Keeney, T. J., S. F. Cannizzo, and **J. H. Flavell.** Spontaneous and induced verbal rehearsal in a recall task. *Child Development,* 1967, *38,* 953–966. [15]

Keesey, R. E., and **T. L. Powley.** Hypothalamic regulation of body weight. *American Scientist,* 1975, *63,* 558–565. [12]

Kelley, H. H. The warm-cold variable in first impressions of persons. *Journal of Personality,* 1950, *18,* 431–439. [26]

Kellogg, W. N., and **L. A. Kellogg.** *The ape and the child.* New York: McGraw-Hill, 1933. [16]

Kelly, D. D. Somatic sensory system IV: Central representations of pain and analgesia. In E. R. Kandel and J. H. Schwartz (Eds.), *Principles of neuroscience.* New York: Elsevier/North-Holland, 1981. [3]

Kempe, R. S., and **C. H. Kempe.** *Child abuse.* Cambridge, Mass.: Harvard University Press, 1978. [27]

Kendall, P. C., and **S. D. Hollon** (Eds.). *Cognitive-behavioral interventions: Theory, research, and procedures.* New York: Academic Press, 1979. [19]

Kendall, P. C., and **S. D. Hollon (Eds.).** *Assessment strategies for cognitive-behavioral interventions.* New York: Academic Press, 1981. [19]

Keppel, G., and **B. J. Underwood.** Remembering without awareness. *Canadian Journal of Psychology,* 1962, *1,* 153–161. [9]

Kernberg, O. F. *Borderline conditions and pathological narcissism.* New York: Jason Aronson, 1975. [18]

Kettlewell, H. B. D. Selection experiments on industrial melanism in the lepidoptera. *Heredity,* 1955, *9,* 323–342. [4]

Kety, S. S. Biochemical hypotheses and studies. In L. Bellak and L. Loeb (Eds.), *The schizophrenic syndrome.* New York: Grune & Stratton, 1969. [23]

Kety, S. S. Disorders of the human brain. *Scientific American,* 1979, *241,* 202–214. [3]

Kety, S. S., D. Rosenthal, P. H. Wender, R. Schulsinger, and **B. Jacobsen.** Mental illness in the biological and adoptive families of adopted individuals who have become schizophrenic: A prelimi-

nary report based upon psychiatric interviews. In R. Fieve, D. Rosenthal, and H. Brill (Eds.), *Genetic research in psychiatry.* Baltimore: Johns Hopkins University Press, 1975. [23]

Kiesler, C. A. Mental hospitals and alternative care. *American Psychologist,* 1982, *37,* 349–360. [24]

Kiesler, C. A., and **J. Jones.** The interactive effects of commitment and forewarning: Three experiments. In C. A. Kiesler (Ed.), *The psychology of commitment: Experiments linking behavior to belief.* New York: Academic Press, 1971. [25]

Kimball, J. P. Seven principles of surface structure parsing in natural language. *Cognition,* 1973, *2,* 15–47. [16]

Kimura, D. The asymmetry of the human brain. *Scientific American,* 1973, *228,* 70–78. [3]

Kinsbourne, M., and **F. Wood.** Short-term memory processes and the amnesic syndrome. In D. Deutsch and J. A. Deutsch (Eds.), *Short-term memory.* New York: Academic Press, 1975. [9]

Kinsey, A. C., W. B. Pomeroy, and **C. E. Martin.** *Sexual behavior in the human male.* Philadelphia: Saunders, 1948. [13]

Kinsey, A. C., W. B. Pomeroy, C. E. Martin, and **P. H. Gebhard,** *Sexual behavior in the human female.* Philadelphia: Saunders, 1953. [13]

Kirkegaard-Sorenson, L., and **S. A. Mednick.** Registered criminality in families with children at high risk for schizophrenia. *Journal of Abnormal Psychology,* 1975, *84,* 197–204. [23]

Klajner, R., C. P. Herman, J. Polivy, and **R. Chhabra.** Human obesity, dieting, and anticipatory salivation. *Physiology and Behavior,* 1981, *27,* 195–198. [12]

Klatzky, R. L. *Memory and awareness: An information-processing perspective.* New York: W. H. Freeman, 1984. [18]

Klaus, M. H., and **J. H. Kennell.** *Maternal-infant bonding.* St. Louis: C. V. Mosby, 1967. [14]

Kleck, R. E., R. C. Vaughn, J. Cartwright-Smith, K. B. Vaughan, C. Z. Colby, and **J. T. Lanzetta.** Effects of being observed on expressive, subjective, and physiological responses to painful stimuli. *Journal of Personality and Social Psychology,* 1977, *34,* 1211–1218. [11]

Kleiman, D. When abortion becomes birth: A dilemma of medical ethics shaken by new advances. *The New York Times,* February 15, 1984, pp. B1+. [14]

Klein, D. B. *A history of scientific psychology: Its origins and philosophical backgrounds.* New York: Basic Books, 1970. [1]

Klima, E. S., and **U. Bellugi.** Teaching apes to communicate. In G. A. Miller (Ed.), *Communication, language, and meaning: Psychological perspectives.* New York: Basic Books, 1973. [16]

Kline, D. W., D. M. Ikeda, and **F. J. Schieber.** Age and temporal resolution in color vision: When do red and green make yellow? *Journal of Gerontology*, 1982, *37*, 705–709. [15]

Klineberg, O. Emotional expression in Chinese literature. *Journal of Abnormal and Social Psychology*, 1938, *33*, 517–520. [11]

Knepler, A. E. Adolescence: An anthropological approach. In C. D. Winter and E. M. Nuss (Eds.), *The young adult: Identity and awareness*. Glenview, Ill.: Scott, Foresman, 1969. [17]

Kobasa, S. C. Stressful life events and health: An inquiry into hardiness. *Journal of Personality and Social Psychology*, 1979, *37*, 1–11. [21]

Koepke, J. E., M. Hamm, M. Legerstee, and **M. Russell.** Neonatal imitation: Two failures to replicate. *Infant Behavior and Development*, 1983, *6*, 97–102. [14]

Kohlberg, L. A cognitive-developmental analysis of children's sex role concepts and attitudes. In E. E. Maccoby (Ed.), *The development of sex differences*. Stanford, Calif: Stanford University Press, 1966. [17]

Kohlberg, L. Stage and sequence: The cognitive-developmental approach to socialization. In D. A. Goslin (Ed.), *Handbook of socialization theory and research*. Chicago: Rand McNally, 1969. [17]

Kohlberg, L. Stages of moral development as a basis for moral education. In C. M. Beck, B. S. Crittenden, and E. V. Sullivan (Eds.), *Moral education: Interdisciplinary approaches*. Toronto: University of Toronto Press, 1971. [17]

Kohn, M. L. The effects of social class on parental values and practices. In D. Reiss and H. A. Hoffman (Eds.), *The American family: Dying or developing?* New York: Plenum Press, 1979. [17]

Kohut, H. *The restoring of the self*. New York: International Universities Press, 1977. [18]

Kolata, G. Math genius may have hormonal basis. *Science*, 1983, *222*, 1312. [3]

Kolata, G. Why do people get fat? *Science*, 1985, *227*, 1327–1328. [12]

Kolata, G. B. Clues to the cause of senile dementia. *Science*, 1981, *211*, 1032–1033. [15]

Kolb, B., and **I. Q. Whishaw.** *Fundamentals of human neuropsychology*. San Francisco: Freeman, 1980. [3]

Kolb, L. C., V. W. Bernard, and **B. P. Dohrenwend** (Eds.). *Urban challenges to psychiatry: The case history of a response*. Boston: Little, Brown, 1969. [22]

Kolodner, J. L. Maintaining organization in a dynamic long-term memory. *Cognitive Science*, 1983, *7*, 243–280. [9]

Kolodny, R. C., W. H. Masters, B. F. Hendry, and **G. Toro.** Plasma testosterone and semen analysis in male homosexuals. *New England Journal of Medicine*, 1971, *285*, 1170–1174. [13]

Kopp, C. B. Antecedents of self-regulation:

A developmental perspective. *Developmental Psychology*, 1982, *18*, 199–214. [15]

Korchin, S. J. *Modern clinical psychology*. New York: Basic Books, 1976. [24]

Korman, A. The prediction of managerial performance: A review. *Personnel Psychology*, 1968, *21*, 295–332. [28]

Korner, A., and **R. Grobstein.** Visual alterness as related to soothing in neonates: Implications for maternal stimulation and early development. *Child Development*, 1966, *37*, 867–876. [14]

Korner, A., and **E. Thoman.** The relative efficacy of contact and vestibular proprioceptive stimulation in soothing neonates. *Child Development*, 1972, *43*, 443–454. [14]

Kraepelin, E. *Clinical psychiatry: A textbook for physicians*. New York: Macmillan, 1902. [22]

Kraepelin, E. *Textbook of psychiatry* (8th ed). New York: Macmillan, 1923. (Originally published, 1883.) [23]

Krashen, S. D. The critical period for language acquisition and its possible basis. In D. Aaronson and R. W. Rieber (Eds.), *Developmental psycholinguistics and communication disorders*. Annals of the New York Academy of Science, 1975, *263*, 211–224. [16]

Kristeller, J. L., G. E. Schwartz, and **H. Black.** The use of Restricted Environmental Stimulation Therapy (REST) in the treatment of essential hypertension: Two case studies. *Behaviour Research and Therapy*, 1982, *20*, 561–566. [7]

Kuczaj, S. A., II. Children's judgments of grammatical and ungrammatical irregular past-tense verbs. *Child Development*, 1978, *49*, 319–326. [16]

Kuczaj, S. A., II. Evidence of a language learning strategy: On the relative ease of acquisition of prefixes and suffixes. *Child Development*, 1979, *50*, 1–13. [16]

Kuffler, S. W. Discharge patterns and functional organization of mammalian retina. *Journal of Neurophysiology*, 1953, *16*, 37–68. [5]

Kuhn, D., J. Langer, L. Kohlberg, and **N. S. Haan.** The development of formal operations in logical and moral judgment. *Genetic Psychology Monographs*, February 1977, *95L*, 97–188. [17]

Kulik, J. A., R. L. Bangert-Drowns, and **C.-L. C. Kulik.** Effectiveness of coaching for aptitude tests. *Psychological Bulletin*, 1984, *95*, 179–188. [20]

Kulik, J. A., and **W. J. McKeachie.** The evaluation of teachers in higher education. In F. N. Kerlinger (Ed.), *Review of research in education*. Itasca, Ill.: Peacock, 1975. [1]

Kunst-Wilson, W. R., and **R. B. Zajonc.** Affective discrimination of stimuli that cannot be recognized. *Science*, 1980, *207*, 557–558. [6, 11, 25]

Kupfermann, I. Localization of higher functions. In E. R. Kandel and J. H.

Schwartz (Eds.), *Principles of neuroscience*. New York: Elsevier/North Holland, 1981. [3]

Kurtines, W., and **E. B. Greif.** The development of moral thought: Review and evaluation of Kohlberg's approach. *Psychological Bulletin*, 1974, *81*, 453–470. [17]

LaBerge, S. P., L. E. Nagel, W. C. Dement, and **V. P. Zarcone.** Lucid dreaming verified by volitional communication during REM sleep. *Perceptual and Motor Skills*, 1981, *52*, 727–732. [7]

Labouvie-Vief, G. V., and **M. J. Chandler.** Cognitive development and life-span developmental theory: Idealistic versus contextual perspectives. In P. B. Baltes (Ed.), *Life-span development and behavior*. Vol. 1. New York: Academic Press, 1978. [15]

Labov, W. The boundaries of words and their meanings. In C. J. N. Bailey and R. W. Shuy (Eds.), *New ways of analyzing variations in English*. Washington, D.C.: Georgetown University Press, 1973. [10]

Lachman, J. L., and **R. Lachman.** Age and the actualization of world knowledge. In L. W. Poon, J. L. Fozard, L. S. Cermak, D. Arenberg, and L. W. Thompson (Eds.), *New directions in memory and aging: Proceedings of the George A. Talland Memorial Conference*. Hillsdale, N.J.: Lawrence Erlbaum, 1980. [15]

Lagerspetz, K., M. Nygard, and **C. Strandvik.** The effects of training in crawling on the motor and mental development of infants. *Scandinavian Journal of Psychology*, 1971, *12*, 192–197. [14]

Laing, R. D. *The politics of experience*. New York: Pantheon, 1967. [23]

Laing, R. D., and **A. Esterson.** *Sanity, madness, and the family* (2nd ed.). New York: Basic Books, 1971. [23]

Laird, J. D. Self-attribution of emotion: The effects of expressive behavior on the quality of emotional experience. *Journal of Personality and Social Psychology*, 1974, *24*, 475–486. [11]

Laird, J. D., and **M. Crosby.** Individual differences in the self-attribution of emotion. In H. London and R. Nisbett (Eds.), *Thinking and feeling: The cognitive alteration of feeling states*. Chicago,: Aldine, 1974. [11]

Lamaze, F. *Painless childbirth: The Lamaze method*. New York: Simon & Schuster, 1972. [5]

Lamb, M. E. The development of mother-infant and father-infant attachments in the second year of life. *Developmental Psychology*, 1977, *13*, 637–648. [17]

Lamb, M. E. Social interaction in infancy and the development of personality. In M. E. Lamb (Ed.), *Social and personality development*. New York: Holt, Rinehart & Winston, 1978. [17]

Lamb, M. E., and **M. A. Easterbrooks.** Individual differences in parental sensitivity: Origins, components, and consequences. In M. E. Lamb and L. R. Sherrod (Eds.), *Infant social cognition*. Hillsdale, N.J.: Lawrence Erlbaum, 1981. [17]

Lamb, M. E., M. A. Easterbrooks, and **G. W. Holden.** Reinforcement and punishment among preschoolers: Characteristics, effects, and correlates. *Child Development*, 1980, *51*, 1230–1236. [17]

Lamb, M. E., R. A. Thompson, W. P. Gardner, E. L. Charnov, and **D. Estes.** Security of infantile attachment as assessed in the "Strange situation": Its study and biological interpretation. *Behavioral and Brain Sciences*, 1984, *7*, 127–171. [17]

Landesman-Dwyer, S., and **I. Emanuel.** Smoking during pregnancy. *Teratology*, 1979, *19*, 119–125. [14]

Landis, C. A. A statistical evaluation of psychotherapeutic methods. In L. E. Hinsie (Ed.), *Concepts and problems of psychotherapy*. New York: Columbia University Press, 1937. [24]

Landy, F. J. *Psychology of work behavior* (3rd ed.). Homewood, Ill.: Dorsey Press, 1985. [28]

Lang, A. R, D. J. Goeckner, V. J. Adesso, and **G. A. Marlatt.** Effects of alcohol on aggression in male social drinkers. *Journal of Abnormal Psychology*, 1975, *84*, 508–518. [7]

Lang, P. J., D. G. Rice, and **R. A. Sternbach.** The psychophysiology of emotion. In N. S. Greenfield and R. A. Sternbach (Eds.), *Handbook of psychophysiology*. New York: Holt, Rinehart & Winston, 1972. [11]

Lange, C. G., and **W. James.** *The emotions*. Baltimore: Williams & Wilkins, 1922. [11]

Langer, E. J., and **J. Rodin.** The effects of choice and enhanced personal responsibility for the aged: A field experiment in an institutional setting. *Journal of Personality and Social Psychology*, 1976, *34*, 191–198. [17, 21]

Langer, E. J., J. Rodin, P. Beck, C. Weinman, and **L. Spitzer.** Environmental determinants of memory improvement in late adulthood. *Journal of Personality and Social Psychology*, 1979, *37*, 2003–2013. [15]

Lansdell, H. A sex difference in effect of temporal lobe neurosurgery on design preference. *Nature*, 1962, *194*, 852–854. [3]

Lanyon, R. I., and **D. Goodstein.** *Personality assessment*. New York: Wiley, 1971. [20]

Lanzetta, J. T., J. Cartwright-Smith, and **R. E. Kleck.** Effects of nonverbal dissimulation on emotional experience. *Journal of Personality and Social Psychology*, 1976, *33*, 354–370. [11]

LaPiere, T. R. Attitudes vs. actions. *Social Forces*, 1934, *13*, 230–237. [25]

Larry P. v. Wilson Riles 495 F Supp 926 (N. D. Cal. 1979). [20]

Latané, B. *A Theory of social impact*. St. Louis: Psychonomic Society, 1973. [27]

Latané, B., and **J. M. Darley.** Help in a crisis: Bystander response to an emergency. In J. W. Thibaut, J. T. Spence, and R. C. Carson (Eds.), *Contemporary topics in social psychology*. Morristown, N.J.: General Learning Press, 1976. [27]

Latané, B., and **D. Elman.** The bystander and the thief. In B. Latané and J. M. Darley (Eds.), *The unresponsive bystander: Why doesn't he help?* New York: Appleton-Century-Crofts, 1970. [2]

Latané, B., and **S. Wolf.** The social impact of majorities and minorities. *Psychological Review*, 1981, *88*, 438–453. [27]

Latham, G. P., and **G. A. Yukl.** A review of research on the application of goal setting in organizations. *Academy of Management Journal*, 1975, *18*, 824–845. [28]

Lawler, E. E., and **J. L. Suttle.** A causal correlational test of the need hierarchy concept. *Organizational Behavior and Human Performance*, 1972, *7*, 265–287. [28]

Lazarus, R. S. Emotions and adaptation: Conceptual and empirical relations. In W. Arnold (Ed.), *Nebraska symposium on motivation*. Lincoln: University of Nebraska Press, 1968. [21]

Lazarus, R. S. The stress and coping paradigm. In C. Eisdorfer, D. Cohen, and A. Kleinman (Eds.), *Conceptual models for psychopathology*. New York: Spectrum, 1980. [21]

Lazarus, R. S., and **E. Alfert.** The short-circuiting of threat by experimentally altering cognitive appraisal. *Journal of Abnormal and Social Psychology*, 1964, *69*, 195–205. [11]

Lazarus, R. S. and **S. Folkman.** Coping and adaptation. In W. D. Gentry (Ed.), *The handbook of behavioral medicine*. New York: Guilford, in press. [21]

Lazarus, R. S., A. Kanner, and **S. Folkman.** Emotions: A cognitive-phenomenological approach. In R. Plutchik and H. Kellerman (Eds.), *Theories of emotion*. New York: Academic Press, 1980. [21]

Leahy, R. L. Parental practices and the development of moral judgment and self-image disparity during adolescence. *Developmental Psychology*, 1981, *17*, 580–594. [17]

Leakey, R. E., and **R. Lewin.** *Origins*. New York: Dutton, 1977. [4]

Lebowitz, M. Generalization from natural language text. *Cognitive Science*, 1983, *7*, 1–40. [9]

Lee, L. C. *Personality development in childhood*. Monterey, Calif.: Brooks/Cole, 1976. [17]

Leitenberg, H. Behavioral approaches to treatment of neuroses. In H. Leitenberg (Ed.), *Handbook of behavior modification and behavior therapy*. Englewood Cliffs, N.J.: Prentice-Hall, 1976. [24]

Lenneberg, E. H. *The biological foundations of language*. New York: Wiley, 1967. [16]

Lenneberg, E. H., and **J. M. Roberts.** *The language of experience*. Bloomington: Indiana University Press, 1956. [16]

Leo, J. Take me out to the brawl game. *Time*, October 29, 1984, p. 87. [27]

Leopold, R. L., and **H. Dillon.** Psychoanatomy of a disaster: A long-term study of post-traumatic neuroses in survivors of a marine explosion. *American Journal of Psychiatry*, 1963, *119*, 913–921. [23]

Lepper, M. R. Intrinsic and extrinsic motivation in children: Detrimental effects of superfluous social controls. In W. A. Collins (Ed.), *The Minnesota symposia on child psychology* (Vol. 14). *Aspects of the development of competence*. Hillsdale, N.J.: Lawrence Erlbaum, 1981. [12]

Lerner, B. *Washington v. Davis:* Quantity, quality, and equality in employment testing. In P. Kurland (Ed.), *The Supreme Court Review* (1976 vol.). Chicago: University of Chicago Press, 1977. [28]

Leventhal, H. and **P. D. Cleary.** The smoking problem: A review of the research and theory in behavioral risk modification. *Psychological Bulletin*, 1980, *88*, 370–405. [21]

Leventhal, H., R. Singer, and **S. Jones.** Effects of fear and specificity of recommendation upon attitudes and behavior. *Journal of Personality and Social Psychology*, 1965, *2*, 20–29. [25]

Levine, J. D., N. C. Gordon, J. C. Bornstein, and **H. L. Fields.** Role of pain in placebo analgesia. *Proceedings of the National Academy of Sciences*, 1979, *76*, 3528–3531. [2]

Levinger, G. A three-level approach to attraction: Toward an understanding of pair relationships. In T. L. Huston (Ed.), *Foundations of Interpersonal Attraction*. New York: Academic Press, 1974. [26]

Levinson, S. E., and **M. Y. Liberman.** Speech recognition by computers. *Scientific American*, 1981, *244*, 64–76. [16]

Levy, S. M. Host differences in neoplastic risk: Behavioral and social contributors to disease. *Health Psychology*, 1983, *2*, 21–44. [21]

Lewine, R. R. J. Sex differences in schizophrenia: Timing or subtype? *Psychological Bulletin*, 1981, *90*, 432–444. [22]

Lewinsohn, P. M. Clinical and theoretical aspects of depression. In K. S. Calhoun, H. E. Adams, and K. M. Mitchell (Eds.), *Innovative treatment methods of psychopathology*. New York: Wiley, 1974. [23]

Lewinsohn, P. M., W. Mischel, W. Chaplin, and **R. Barton.** Social competence and depression: The role of illusory self-perceptions. *Journal of Abnormal Psychology*, 1980, *89*, 203–212. [1]

Lewinsohn, P. M., J. M. Sullivan, and **S. J. Grosscup.** Changing reinforcing events: An approach to the treatment of depression. *Psychotherapy: Theory, Research, and Practice,* 1980, *17,* 322–334. [23]

Lewinsohn, P. M., M. A. Youngren, and **S. J. Grosscup.** Reinforcement and depression. In R. A. Depue (Ed.), *The psychobiology of the depressive disorders.* New York: Academic Press, 1979. [23]

Lewis, J. M., E. H. Rodnick, and **M. J. Goldstein.** Intrafamilial interactive behavior, parental communication deviance, and risk for schizophrenia. *Journal of Abnormal Psychology,* 1981, *90,* 448–457. [23]

Lewis, M., and **J. Brooks-Gunn.** *Social cognition and the acquisition of self.* New York: Plenum, 1979. [14]

Lewis, R. *Miracles: Poems by children of the English-speaking world.* New York: Simon & Schuster, 1966. [15]

Liben, L. S. Perspective taking skills in young children: Seeing the world through rose-colored glasses. *Developmental Psychology,* 1978, *14,* 87–92. [1]

Liberman, M. C. Single-neuron labeling in the cat auditory cortex. *Science,* 1982, *216,* 1239–1241. [5]

Liberman, R. P. What is schizophrenia? *Schizophrenia Bulletin,* 1982, *8,* 435–437. [23]

Lidz, T. *The origin and treatment of schizophrenic disorders.* New York: Basic Books, 1973. [23]

Lidz, T., et al. The intrafamilial environment of schizophrenic patients: Marital schism and marital skew. *American Journal of Psychiatry,* 1957, *114,* 241–248. [23]

Lieberman, M. A., and **A. S. Coplan.** Distance from death as a variable in the study of aging. *Developmental Psychology,* 1970, *6,* 71–84. [17]

Lieberson, S., and **J. F. O'Connor.** Leadership and organizational performance: A study of large corporations. *American Sociological Review,* 1972, *37,* 117–130. [28]

Liebeskind, J. C., and **L. A. Paul.** Psychological and physiological mechanisms of pain. *Annual Review of Psychology,* 1977, *28,* 41–60. [5]

Liem, J. H. Effects of verbal communications of parents and children: A comparison of normal and schizophrenic families. *Journal of Consulting and Clinical Psychology,* 1974, *42,* 438–450. [23]

Lindner, D. E., J. Cooper, and **E. E. Jones.** Decision freedom as a determinant of the role of incentive magnitude in attitude change. *Journal of Personality and Social Psychology,* 1967, *6,* 245–254. [25]

Linder, R. *The fifty-minute hour.* New York: Holt, Rinehart & Winston, 1955. [18]

Lindsay, P. H., and **D. A. Norman.** *Human information processing.* New York: Academic Press, 1972. [6]

Lindsay, P. H., and **D. A. Norman.** *Human information processing* (2nd ed.). New York: Academic Press, 1977. [5]

Lipset, S. M., and **W. Schneider.** The confidence gap: Business, labor, and government in the public mind. New York: Free Press, 1982. [25]

Lipsitt, L. P. The study of sensory and learning processes of the newborn. *Clinics in Perinatology,* March 1977, 4. [14]

Lisker, L., and **A. Abramson.** The voicing dimension: Some experiments in phonetics. *Proceedings of the Sixth International Congress of Phonetic Sciences,* Prague, 1968. Prague: Academia, 1970), pp. 563–567. [16]

Littman, R. A., and **H. M. Manning.** A methodological study of cigarette brand discrimination. *Journal of Applied Psychology,* 1954, *38,* 185–190. [11]

Lloyd, K., J. Paulse, and **J. Brockner.** The effect of self-esteem and self-consciousness on interpersonal attraction. *Personality and Social Psychology Bulletin,* 1983, *9,* 397–403. [26]

Locke, E. A. Toward a theory of task motivation and incentives. *Organizational Behavior and Human Performance,* 1968, *3,* 157–189. [28]

Locke, E. A. The nature and causes of job satisfaction. In M. D. Dunnette (Ed.), *The handbook of industrial and organizational psychology.* Chicago; Rand McNally, 1976. [28]

Locke, E. A., K. N. Shaw, L. M. Saari, and **G. P. Latham.** Goal setting and task performance, 1969–1980. *Psychological Bulletin,* 1981, *90,* 125–152. [28]

Locke, J. L., and **V. L. Locke.** Deaf children's phonetic, visual, and dactylic coding in a grapheme recall task. *Journal of Experimental Psychology,* 1971, *89,* 142–146. [9]

Loehlin, J. C., G. Lindzey, and **J. N. Spuhler.** *Racial differences in intelligence.* San Francisco: Freeman, 1975. [20]

Loftus, E. F. *Eyewitness testimony.* Cambridge, Mass.: Harvard University Press, 1979. [1, 16]

Loftus, E. F. *Memory.* Reading, Mass.: Addison-Wesley, 1980. [9]

Loftus, E. F., and **G. M. Davies.** Distortions in the memory of children. *Journal of Social Issues,* 1984, *40,* 51–67. [15]

Loftus, E. R. *Memory.* Reading, Mass.: Addison-Wesley, 1980. [7]

Loftus, E. R., and **G. R. Loftus.** On the permanence of stored information in the human brain. *American Psychologist,* 1980, *35,* 409–420. [7]

London, M., and **D. W. Bray.** Ethical issues in testing and evaluation for personnel decisions. *American Psychologist,* 1980, *35,* 890–901. [20]

London, P. *Behavior control.* New York: Harper & Row, 1969. [19]

LoPiccolo, J. Direct treatment of sexual dysfunction in the couple. In J. Money and H. Musaph (Eds.), *Handbook of sexology.* New York: Elsevier-North Holland Press, 1978. [13]

Lorenz, K. Die Angeborenen former moglicher Arfahrung. *Zeitschrift fur Tierpsychologie,* 1943, *5,* 233–409. [17]

Lorenz, K. *Evolution and the modification of behavior.* Chicago: University of Chicago Press, 1965. [4]

Lovass, O. I., R. L. Koegel, and **L. Schreibman.** Stimulus overselectivity in autism: A review of research. *Psychological Bulletin,* 1979, *86,* 1236–1254. [22]

Luborsky, L. B., and **D. P. Spence.** Quantitative research of psychoanalytic therapy. In S. L. Garfield and A. E. Bergin (Eds.), *Handbook of psychotherapy and behavior change: An empirical analysis* (2nd ed.). New York: Wiley, 1978. [24]

Luchins, A. S. Classroom experiments on mental set. *American Journal of Psychology,* 1946, *59,* 295–298. [10]

Luria, A. R. *The mind of a mnemonist.* New York: Basic Books, 1968. [9]

Lykken, D. T. *A tremor in the blood: Uses and abuses of the lie detector.* New York: McGraw-Hill, 1981. [11]

Lynch, J. J. *The broken heart: The medical consequences of loneliness.* New York: Basic Books, 1977. [21]

Lynch, J. J., D. A. Paskewitz, and **M. T. Orne.** Some factors in the feedback control of human alpha rhythm. *Psychosomatic Medicine.* 1974, *36* (5) 399–410. [7]

Lyons, R. D. Vietnam veterans turn to therapy. *The New York Times,* Nov. 13, 1984, pp. C1, C6. [21]

Maass, A., and **R. D. Clark III.** Internationalization versus compliance: Differential processes underlying minority influence and conformity. *European Journal of Social Psychology,* 1983, *13,* 197–215. [27]

Maccoby, E. E. Women's intellect. In S. M. Farber and R. H. L. Wilson (Eds.), *The potential of women.* New York: McGraw-Hill, 1963. [12]

Maccoby, E. E., and **C. N. Jacklin.** *Psychology of sex differences.* Stanford, Calif.: Stanford University Press, 1974. [17]

Maccoby, E. E., and **C. N. Jacklin.** Sex differences in aggression: A rejoinder and reprise. *Child Development,* 1980, *51,* 964–980. [17]

Macfarlane, A. *The psychology of childbirth.* Cambridge, Mass.: Harvard University Press, 1977. [14]

Mackay, A. V. R., L. L. Iversen, M. Rossor, E. Spokes, E. Bird, A. Arregui, I. Creese, and **S. Snyder.** Increased brain dopamine and dopamine receptors in schizophrenia. *Archives of General Psychiatry,* 1982, *39,* 991–997. [23]

Mackintosh, N. J. *Conditioning and associative learning.* Oxford: Clarendon Press, 1983. [8]

MacNichol, E. F., Jr. Three-pigment color vision. *Scientific American,* 1964, *211,* 48–56. [5]

Madden, D. J., and **R. D. Nebes.** Aging and the development of automaticity in visual search. *Developmental Psychology,* 1980, *16,* 377–384. [15]

Magoun, H. W. *The waking brain.* Springfield, Ill.: Charles C Thomas, 1963. [3]

Maher, B. A., and **W. B. Maher.** Psychopathology. In E. Hearst (Ed.), *The first century of experimental psychology.* Hillsdale, N.J.: Lawrence Erlbaum, 1979. [22]

Maher, E. A. (Ed.). *Contributions to the psychopathology of schizophrenia.* New York: Academic Press, 1977. [22]

Mahoney, K., and **B. L. Hopkins.** The modification of sentence structure and its relationship to subjective judgments of creativity in writing. *Journal of Applied Behavior Analysis,* 1973, *6,* 425–433. [10]

Malamuth, N. M., and **J. V. P. Check.** The effects of mass media exposure on acceptance of violence against women: A field experiment. *Journal of Research in Personality,* 1981, *15,* 436–446. [13]

Malamuth, N. M., and **E. Donnerstein.** The effects of aggressive-pornographic mass media stimuli. In L. Berkowitz (ed.), *Experimental social psychology.* New York, Academic Press, 1982. [13]

Maltzman, I. On the training of originality. *Psychological Review,* 1960, *67,* 229–242. [10]

Mans, L., D. Cicchetti, and **L. A. Sroufe.** Mirror reaction of Down's syndrome infants and toddlers: Cognitive underpinnings of self-recognition. *Child Development,* 1978, *49,* 1247–1250.[14]

Marañon, G. Contribution à étude de l'action emotive de l'adrenaline. *Revue Francaise d' Endocrinologie,* 1924, *2,* 301–325. [11]

Maratsos, M. Some current issues in the study of the acquisition of grammar. In P. H. Mussen (Ed.), *Handbook of child psychology* (4th ed.). Vol. 3: J. H. Flavell and E. M. Markman (Eds.), *Cognitive development.* New York: Wiley, 1983. [16]

Marcel, A. Conscious and unconscious perception: Experiments on visual masking and word perception. *Cognitive Psychology,* 1983, *15,* 197–238. [6]

Marcel, A. J. Conscious and unconscious perception: An approach to the relations between phenomenal experience and perceptual processes. *Cognitive Psychology,* 1983, *15,* 238–300. [7]

Marcia, J. E. Identity in adolescence. In J. Adelson (Ed.), *Handbook of adolescent psychology.* New York: Wiley-Interscience, 1980. [17]

Marin, B. V., D. L. Holmes, M. Guth, and **P. Kovac.** The potential of children as eyewitnesses: A comparison of children and adults on eyewitness tasks. *Law and Human Behavior,* 1979, *3,* 295–305. [15]

Mark, V. H., and **F. R. Ervin.** *Violence and the brain.* New York: Harper & Row, 1970. [7]

Markman, E. M. Realizing that you don't understand: A preliminary investigation. *Child Development,* 1977, *48,* 986–992. [15]

Markman, E. M. Two different kinds of hierarchical organization. In E. K. Scholnick (Ed.), *New trends in conceptual representation: Challenges to Piaget's theory?* Hillsdale, N.J.: Lawrence Erlbaum, 1983. [15]

Markman, E. M., and **J. Seibert.** Classes and collections: Internal organization and resulting holistic properties. *Cognitive Psychology,* 1976, *8,* 561–577. [15]

Marks, G., and **N. Miller.** Target attractiveness as a mediator of assumed attitude similarity. *Personality and Social Psychology Bulletin,* 1982, *8,* 728–735. [26]

Marks, G., N. Miller, and **G. Maruyama.** Effect of targets' physical attractiveness on assumption of similarity. *Journal of Personality and Social Psychology,* 1981, *41,* 198–206. [26]

Markus, H. Self-schemata and processing information about the self. *Journal of Personality and Social Psychology,* 1977, *35,* 63–78. [26]

Markus, H. The effect of mere presence on social facilitation: An unobtrusive test. *Journal of Experimental Social Psychology,* 1978, *14,* 389–397. [27]

Markus, H. Sibling personalities: The luck of the draw. *Psychology Today,* 1981, *15,* 35–37. [26]

Marlowe, D., and **K. J. Gergen.** Personality and social interaction. In G. Lindzey and E. Aronson (Eds.), *Handbook of social psychology* (Vol. 3, 2nd ed.). Reading, Mass.: Addison-Wesley, 1969. [25]

Marshall, G., and **P. Zimbardo.** The affective consequences of "inadequately explained" physiological arousal. *Journal of Personality and Social Psychology,* 1979, *37,* 970–988. [11]

Martens, R. Palmar sweating and the presence of an audience. *Journal of Experimental Social Psychology,* 1969, *5,* 371–374. [27]

Martin, G. B., and **R. D. Clark.** Distress crying in neonates: Species and peer specificity. *Developmental Psychology,* 1982, *18,* 3–9. [14]

Martindale, C. *Cognition and consciousness.* Homewood, Ill.: Dorsey, 1981. [7, 10]

Martorano, S. C. A developmental analysis of performance on Piaget's formal operations tasks. *Developmental Psychology,* 1977, *13,* 666–672. [15]

Marx, J. L. Autoimmunity in left-handers. *Science,* 1982, *217,* 141–144. [3]

Maslach, C. Negative emotional biasing of unexplained arousal. *Journal of Personality and Social Psychology,* 1979, *37,* 953–969. [11]

Masling, J., C. Johnson, and **C. Saturansky.** Oral imagery, accuracy of perceiving others, and performance in Peace Corps training. *Journal of Personality and Social Psychology,* 1974, *30,* 414–419. [18]

Masling, J., J. Price, S. Goldband, and **E. S. Katkin.** Oral imagery and autonomic arousal in social isolation. *Journal of Personality and Social Psychology,* 1981, *40,* 395–400. [18]

Maslow, A. H. *Motivation and personality.* New York: Harper & Row, 1954. [12, 19]

Maslow, A. H. Deficiency motivation and growth motivation. In M. R. Jones (Ed.), *Nebraska symposium on motivation, 1955.* Lincoln: University of Nebraska Press, 1955. [19]

Maslow, A. H. *The psychology of science; A reconnaissance.* New York: Harper & Row, 1966. [19]

Maslow, A. H. *Toward a psychology of being* (2nd ed.). New York: Van Nostrand Reinhold, 1968. [19]

Maslow, A. H. *The farther reaches of the human mind.* New York: Viking, 1971a. [12, 19]

Maslow, A. H. Some basic propositions of a growth and self-actualizing psychology. In S. Maddi (Ed.), *Perspectives on personality.* Boston: Little, Brown, 1971b. [19]

Mason, J. W. Specificity in the organization of neuroendocrine response profiles. In P. Seeman and G. M. Brown (Eds.), *Frontiers in neurology and neuroscience research.* First International Symposium of the neuroscience Institute, Toronto, Ontario: University of Toronto, 1974. [21]

Mason, W. A. The effects of social restriction on the behavior of Rhesus monkeys: III. Tests of gregariousness. *Journal of Comparative and Physiological Psychology,* 1961, *54,* 287–290. [11]

Masters, W. H., and **V. E. Johnson.** The sexual response cycle of the human female: III, The clitoris: Anatomic and clinical considerations. *Western Journal of Surgery, Obstetrics, and Gynecology,* 1962, *70,* 248–257. [13]

Masters, W. H., and **V. E. Johnson.** *Human sexual response.* Boston: Little, Brown, 1966. [13]

Masters, W. H., and **V. E. Johnson.** *Human sexual inadequacy.* Boston, Little, Brown, 1970. [13]

Masters, W. H., and **V. E. Johnson.** *Homosexuality in perspective.* Boston: Little, Brown, 1979. [13]

Matheny, A. P. Bayley's infant behavior record: Behavioral components and twin analyses. *Child Development,* 1980, *51,* 466–475. [17]

Matsuyama, S. S., and **L. F. Jarvik.** Genetics and mental functioning in senescence. In J. E. Birren and R. B. Sloane (Eds.), *Handbook of mental health and* *aging.* Englewood Cliffs, N.J.: Prentice-Hall, 1980. [3]

Matthews, K. A. Psychological perspectives on the Type A behavior pattern. *Psychological Bulletin, 1982, 91,* 293–323. [21]

Maugh, T. H. Marijuana justifies "serious concern." *Science, 1982, 215,* 1488–1489. [7]

Maurer, D., and **P. Salapatek.** Developmental changes in the scanning of faces by young infants. *Child Development, 1976, 47,* 523–527. [14]

Mayer, W. Alcohol abuse and alchoholism: The psychologist's role in prevention, research and treatment. *American Psychologist, 1983, 38,* 1116–1121. [21]

Mayr, E. Behavior programs and evolutionary strategies. *American Scientist,* 1974, 650–659. [4]

McArthur, L. A., M. R. Solomon, and **R. H. Jaffe.** Weight and sex differences in emotional responsiveness to proprioceptive and pictorial stimuli. *Journal of Personality and Social Psychology, 1980, 39,* 308–319. [11]

McBain, W. N., and **R. C. Johnson.** *The science of ourselves.* New York: Harper & Row, 1962. [5]

McCall, R. B. *Infants.* Cambridge, Mass.: Harvard University Press, 1979. [16]

McCall, R. B., M. I. Appelbaum, and **P. S. Hogarty.** Developmental changes in mental performance. *Monographs of the Society for Research in Child Development,* 1973, Whole No. 173. [20]

McCarthy, A. Voices of their captors. *Commonweal,* February 15, 1980, 72–73. [25]

McCary, J. L. *McCary's human sexuality* (3rd ed.). New York: Van Nostrand, 1978. [13]

McCauley, E., and **A. A. Ehrhardt.** Female sexual response: Hormonal and behavioral interactions. *Primary Care, 1976, 3,* 455–476. [13]

McClelland, D. C. *The achieving society.* Princeton, N.J.: Van Nostrand-Reinhold, 1961. [12]

McClelland, D. C. Managing motivation to expand human freedom. *American Psychologist, 1978, 33,* 201–210 [12]

McClelland, D. C. The need for power, sympathetic activation, and illness. *Motivation and emotion* 1982, 6, 31–41. [12]

McClelland, D. C., and **D. G. Winter.** *Motivating economic achievement.* New York: Free Press, 1969. [12]

McClelland, D. C., et al. The achievement motive. New York: Appleton-Century-Crofts, 1953. [12]

McClelland, J. L., and **D. E. Rumelhart.** An interactive model of context effects in letter perception, Part I: An account of basic findings. *Psychological Review,* 1981, 88, 375–407. [6]

McClintock, M. K., and **N. T. Adler.** The role of the female during copulation in wild and domestic Norway rats *(rattus Norvegicus). Behavior,* 1978, 67, 67–96. [13]

McCormick, E. J., and **D. R. Ilgan.** *Industrial psychology.* Englewood Cliffs, N.J.: Prentice-Hall, 1980. [28]

McCulloch, W. S., and **W. H. Pitts.** A logical calculus of the ideas immanent in nervous activity. *Bulletin of Mathematical Biophysics,* 1943, 5, 114–133. [3]

McGeoch, J. A. *The psychology of human learning.* New York: Longmans, Green, 1942. [9]

McGhie, A., and **J. Chapman.** Disorders of attention and perception in early schizophrenia. *British Journal of Medical Psychology,* 1961, 34, 103–116. [22]

McGlone, J. Sex differences in functional brain asymmetry. *Cortex,* 1978, 14, 122–128. [3]

McGraw, M. B. *Growth: A study of Johnny and Jimmy.* New York: Appleton-Century-Crofts, 1935. [14]

McGraw, M. B. Later development of children specially trained during infancy: Johnny and Jimmy at school age. *Child Development,* 1939a, 10, 1–19. [14]

McGuinness, D., and **K. H. Pribram.** The origins of sensory bias in the development of gender differences in perception and cognition. In M. Bortner (Ed.), *Cognitive growth and development.* New York: Bruner/Mazel, 1979. [17]

McGuire, R. J., J. M. Carlisle, and **B. G. Young.** Sexual deviations as conditioned behavior: A hypothesis. *Behaviour Research and Therapy,* 1965, 2, 185–190. [13]

McGuire, T. R., and **J. Hirsch.** Behavior-genetic analysis of *Phormia regina:* Conditioning, reliable individual differences, and selection. *Proceedings of the National Academy of Sciences, USA,* 1977, 74, 5193–5197. [4]

McGuire, W. J. The nature of attitudes and attitude change. In G. Lindzey and E. Aronson (Eds.), *Handbook of social psychology* (3rd ed.). Reading, Mass.: Addison-Wesley, 1985. [25]

McGuire, W. J., and **D. Papageorgis.** The relative efficacy of various types of prior belief—Defense in producing immunity against persuasion. *Journal of Personality and Social Psychology,* 1961, 62, 327–337. [25]

McKenzie, B., and **R. Over.** Young infants fail to imitate facial and manual gestures. *Infant Behavior and Development,* 1983, 6, 85–96. [14]

McNeil, E. B. *The quiet furies.* Englewood Cliffs, N.J.: Prentice-Hall, 1967. [22]

McNeill, D. *The acquisition of language: The study of developmental psycholinguistics.* New York: Harper & Row, 1970. [16]

Mead, G. H. *Mind, self and society: From the standpoint of a social behaviorist.* Chicago: University of Chicago Press, 1934. [14]

Mednick, M. T. S. The new psychology of women: A feminist analysis. In J. E. Gullahorn (Ed.), *Psychology and women: In transition.* New York: Wiley, 1979. [12]

Mednick, S. A. Breakdown in individuals

at high risk for schizophrenia: Possible predispositional perinatal factors. *Mental Hygiene,* 1970, 54, 50–63. [23]

Mednick, S. A. Birth defects and schizophrenia. *Psychology Today,* 1971, 4, 48–50 passim. [23]

Meichenbaum, D. H. Self-instructional methods. In F. H. Kanfer and A. P. Goldstein (Eds.), *Helping people change: A textbook of methods.* New York: Pergamon Press, 1975. [19]

Meichenbaum, D. H. *Cognitive behavior modification: An integrative approach.* New York: Plenum Press, 1977. [24]

Meichenbaum, D. H., and **M. E. Jaremko (Eds.).** *Stress reduction and prevention.* New York: Plenum, 1983. [21]

Meichenbaum, D. H., and **D. Turk.** Stress, coping, and disease: A cognitive-behavioral perspective. In R. W. J. Neufield (Ed.), *Psychological stress and psychopathology.* New York: McGraw-Hill, 1982. [21]

Meiselman, K. C. *Incest.* San Francisco: Jossey-Bass, 1978. [13]

Meltzoff, A. N., and **M. K. Moore.** Imitation of facial and manual gestures by human neonates. *Science,* 1977, 198, 75–78. [14]

Meltzoff, A. N., and **M. K. Moore.** The origins of imitation in infancy: Paradigm, phenomena, and theories. In L. P. Lipsitt and C. K. Rovee-Collier (Eds.), *Advances in infancy research.* Vol. 2. Norwood, N.J.: Ablex, 1983. [11, 14]

Mendels, J. Lithium in the treatment of depression. *American Journal of Psychiatry,* 1976, 133, 373–378. [24]

Menyuk, P., and **N. Bernholtz.** Prosodic features and children's language production. *MIT Research Laboratory of Electronics Quarterly Progress Reports,* 1969, No. 93, 216–219. [16]

Menzel, E. M. Cognitive mapping in chimpanzees. In S. H. Hulse, H. Fowler, and W. K. Honig (Eds.), *Cognitive processes in animal behavior.* Hillsdale, N.J.: Lawrence Erlbaum, 1973. [8]

Mercer, J. R. I.Q.: The lethal label. *Psychology Today,* 1972, 6, 44–47+. [20]

Mersky, H., and **F. G. Spear.** *Pain: Psychological and psychiatric aspects.* London: Baliere, Tindall, and Cassell, 1967. [5]

Merton, R. K. *On the shoulders of giants* (Vicennial ed.). New York: Harcourt Brace Jovanovich, 1985. [10]

Mervis, C. B., and **M. A. Crisafi.** Order of acquisition of subordinate-, basic-, and superordinate-level categories. *Child Development,* 1982, 53, 258–266. [15]

Messick, S. Test validity and the ethics of assessment. *American Psychologist,* 1980, 35, 1012–1027. [20]

Messick, S., and **A. Jungeblut.** Time and method in coaching for the SAT. *Psychological Bulletin,* 1981, 89, 191–216. [20]

Meyer, A. J., J. D. Nash, A. L. McAlister, N. Maccoby, and **J. W. Farquhar.** Skills training in cardiovascular health education campaign. *Journal of Consulting* *and Clinical Psychology*, 1980, *48* 129–142. [21]

Meyer, D. E., and **R. W. Schvaneveldt.** Meaning, memory structure, mental processes. In C. Cofer (Ed.), *The structure of human memory.* San Francisco: Freeman, 1976. [9]

Meyer-Bahlburg, H. F. L. Sex hormones and male homosexuality in comparative perspective. *Archives of Sexual Behavior*, 1977, *6*, 297–325. [13]

Meyer-Bahlburg, H. F. L. Sex hormones and female homosexuality: A critical examination. *Archives of Sexual Behavior*, 1979, *8*, 101–119. [13]

Michaels, R. H., and **G. W. Mellin.** Prospective experience with maternal rubella and the associated congenital malformations. *Pediatrics*, 1960, *26*, 200–209. [14]

Milgram, S. Behavioral study of obedience. *Journal of Abnormal and Social Psychology*, 1963, *67*, 371–378. [27]

Milgram, S. Some conditions of obedience and disobedience to authority. In I. D. Steiner and M. Fishbein (Eds.), *Current studies in social psychology.* New York: Holt, Rinehart & Winston, 1965. [27]

Milgram, S. *Obedience to authority.* New York: Harper & Row, 1974. [27]

Miller, G. A. The magical number seven, plus or minus two: Some limits on our capacity for processing information. *Psychology Review*, 1956, *63*, 81–97. [9]

Miller, G. A. Reconsiderations: Language, thought, and reality. *Human Nature*, 1978, *1*, 92–96. [16]

Miller, J., C. Schooler, M. L. Kohn, and **K. A. Miller.** Women and work: The psychological effects of occupational conditions. *American Journal of Sociology*, 1979, *85* (1). [17]

Miller, L. L., and **R. J. Branconnier.** Cannabis: Effects on memory and the cholinergic limbic system. *Psychological Bulletin*, 1983, 441–457. [7]

Miller, N., and **G. Maruyama.** Ordinal position and peer popularity. *Journal of Personality and Social Psychology*, 1976, *33*, 123–131. [26]

Miller, N. E. Biofeedback: Evaluation of a new technique. *New England Journal of Medicine*, 1974, *290*, 684–685. [7]

Miller, R. C., and **J. S. Berman.** The efficacy of cognitive behavior therapies: A quantitative review of the research evidence. *Psychological Bulletin*, 1983, *94*, 39–53. [24]

Miller, R. E., W. F. Caul, and **I. A. Mirsky.** Communication of affects between feral and socially isolated monkeys. *Journal of Personality and Social Psychology*, 1967, *7*, 231–239. [11]

Milner, B. Amnesia following operation on the temporal lobes. In C. W. M. Whitty and O. L. Zangwill (Eds.), *Amnesia.* London: Butterworths, 1966. [3]

Milner, B. Interhemispheric differences in the localization of psychological processes in man. *British Medical Bulletin*, 1971, *27*, 272–277. [3]

Miner, J. B. *Theories of organizational behavior.* Hinsdale, Ill.: Dryden Press, 1980. [28]

Minkowski, A. *Regional development of the brain in early life.* Oxford: Blackwell, 1967. [14]

Minuchin, S. *Families and family therapy.* Cambridge, Mass.: Harvard University Press, 1974. [24]

Minuchin, S., and **H. C. Fishman.** *Family therapy techniques.* Cambridge, Mass.: Harvard University Press, 1981. [24]

Mirvis, P., and **E. E. Lawler.** Measuring the financial impact of employee attitudes. *Journal of Applied Psychology*, 1977, *62*, 1–8. [28]

Mischel, W. A social-learning view of sex differences in behavior. In E. E. Maccoby (Ed.), *The development of sex differences.* Stanford, Calif.: Stanford University Press, 1966. [17]

Mischel, W. *Personality and assessment.* New York: Wiley, 1968. [19]

Mischel, W. Toward a cognitive social learning reconceptualization of personality. *Psychological Review*, 1973, *80*, 252–283. [17, 19]

Mischel, W. On the interface of cognition and personality: Beyond the person-situation debate. *American Psychologist*, 1979, *34*, 740–754. [17, 19]

Mischel, W. Convergences and challenges in the search for consistency. *American Psychologist*, 1984, *39*, 351–364. [19]

Mitler, M. M., C. Guilleminault, J. Orme, V. P. Zarcone, and **W. C. Dement.** Sleeplessness, sleep attacks, and things that go wrong in the night. *Psychology Today*, December 1975, pp. 45–50. [7]

Moar, I. Grid schemata in memory for large-scale environments. *Proceedings of the Fifth Annual Conference of the Cognitive Science Society*, Rochester, N. Y., 1983. [8]

Mobley, W. H., S. O. Horner, and **A. T. Hollingsworth.** An evaluation of precursors of hospital employee turnover. *Journal of Applied Psychology*, 1978, *63*, 408–414. [28]

Moede, W. Die Richtlinien der Leistungs-Psychologie. *Industrielle Psychotechnik*, 1927, *4*, 193–207. [27]

Moeser, S. D., and **A. S. Bregman.** Imagery and language acquisition. *Journal of Verbal Learning and Verbal Behavior*, 1973, *12*, 91–98. [16]

Moir, D. J. Egocentrism and the emergence of conventional morality in preadolescent girls. *Child Development*, 1974, *45*, 299–304. [17]

Molfese, D. L., and **V. J. Molfese.** Hemisphere and stimulus differences as reflected in the cortical responses of newborn infants to speech stimuli. *Developmental Psychology*, 1979, *15*, 505–511. [16]

Molfese, D. L., and **V. J. Molfese.** Cortical responses of preterm infants to phonetic and nonphonetic speech stimuli. *Developmental Psychology*, 1980, *16*, 574–581. [16]

Monagan, D. Crosscurrents: CIA seals. *Science '82*, 1983, *3*, 80. [8]

Moncrieff, R. W. *Odour preferences.* New York: Wiley, 1966. [5]

Money, J. Factors in the genesis of homosexuality. In G. Winokur (Ed.), *Determinants of human sexual behavior.* Springfield, Ill.: Charles C Thomas, 1963. [13]

Money, J. and **A. A. Ehrhardt.** *Man and woman, boy and girl.* Baltimore: Johns Hopkins University Press, 1972. [13]

Montgomery, K. C. The role of the exploratory drive in learning. *Journal of Comparative and Physiological Psychology*, 1954, *47*, 60–64. [12]

Moos, R. H., R. C. Cronkite, and **J. W. Finney.** A conceptual framework for alcoholism treatment evaluation. In E. M. Patterson and E. Kaufman (Eds.), *Encyclopedic handbook of alcoholism.* New York: Gardner, 1982. [21]

Morgan, J. L., and **E. L. Newport.** The role of constituent structure in the induction of an artificial language. *Journal of Verbal Learning and Verbal Behavior*, 1981, *20*, 67–85. [16]

Morris, N. M., and **J. R. Udry.** Pheromonal influences on human sexual behavior: An experimental search. *Journal of Biosocial Science*, 1978. [5]

Mortimer, J. T., M. D. Finch, and **D. Kumka.** Persistence and change in development: The multidimensional self-concept. In P. B. Baltes and O. G. Brim, Jr. (Eds.), *Life-span development and behavior.* Vol. 4. New York: Academic Press, 1982. [17]

Mortimer, J. T., J. Lorence, and **D. Kumka.** Work and family linkages in the transition to adulthood: A panel study of highly educated men. *Western Sociological Review*, 1982, *13*(1). [17]

Moscovici, S. Toward a theory of conversion behavior. In L. Berkowitz (Ed.), *Advances in experimental social psychology.* Vol. 13. New York: Academic Press, 1980. [27]

Moss, H. A. Early sex differences and mother-infant interaction. In R. C. Freedman, R. N. Richards, and R. L. Van de Wiele (Eds.), *Sex differences in behavior.* New York: Wiley, 1974. [17]

Mosteller, F. Innovation and evaluation. *Science*, 1981, *211*, 881–886. [10]

Mowrer, O. H. *Learning theory and behavior.* New York: Wiley, 1960. [8]

Mrazek, P. B. The nature of incest: A review of contributing factors. In P. B. Mrazek and C. H. Kempe, *Sexually abused children and their families.* New York: Pergamon, 1981. [13]

Muchinsky, P. M. *Psychology applied to work.* Homewood, Ill.: Dorsey Press, 1983. [28]

Mull, H. K. The effect of repetition upon the enjoyment of modern music. *Journal of Psychology*, 1957, *43*, 155–162. [11]

Münsterberg, H. *Psychology and industrial efficiency.* Management History Series (19). Easton, Pa.: Hive, 1973. (Originally published, 1913.) [28]

Murphy, H. B. M., E. D. Wittkower, J. Fried, and **H. Ellenberger.** A cross-cultural survey of schizophrenic symptomatology. In *Proceedings of the Third World Congress of Psychiatry* (Vol. 2). Toronto: University of Toronto Press, 1961. [22]

Murphy, J. M. Psychiatric labeling in cross-cultural perspective. *Science,* 1976, *191,* 1019–1028. [22]

Murray, F. B. Acquisition of conservation through social interaction. *Developmental Psychology,* 1972, *6,* 1–6. [15]

Murray, H. A., et al. *Explorations in personality.* New York: Oxford University Press, 1938. [12, 20]

Murray, J. P. *Television and youth: 25 years of research and controversy.* Boys Town, Nebraska: Boys Town Center for the Study of Youth Development, 1980. [16]

Murstein, B. I. Physical attractiveness and marital choice. *Journal of Personality and Social Psychology,* 1972, *22,* 8–12. [26]

Mussen, P. H., and **N. Eisenberg-Berg.** *Roots of caring, sharing, and helping: The development of prosocial behavior in children.* San Francisco: Freeman, 1977. [17]

Muuss, R. E. *Theories of adolescence* (3rd ed.). New York: Random House, 1975. [17]

Myers, J. K., and **L. L. Bean.** *A decade later: A follow-up of social class and mental illness.* New York: Wiley, 1968. [23]

Naftulin, D. H., J. E. Ware, and **F. A. Donnelly.** The Doctor Fox lecture: A paradigm of educational seduction. *Medical Education,* 1973. *48,* 630–635. [1]

Nathan, P. E. Alcoholism. In H. Leitenberg (Ed.), *Handbook of behavior modification and behavior therapy.* Englewood Cliffs, N.J.: Prentice-Hall, 1976. [8]

Nathan, P. E., P. Robertson, and **M. M. Andberg.** A systems analytic model of diagnosis. IV: The diagnostic validity of abnormal affective behavior. *Journal of Clinical Psychology,* 1969, *25* 235–242. [22]

National Center for Educational Statistics. Gainful employment among high school youth. *Bulletin,* September 1981. Whole issue. [17]

National Education Association v. State of South Carolina. 434 U.S. 1026 (1978). [28]

National Institute of Mental Health. *Television and behavior: Ten years of scientific progress and implications for the eighties. I. Summary report.* Washington, D.C.: Department of Health and Human Services, 1982. [16]

National Institute on Drug Abuse. *National household survey on drug abuse.* Rockville, Md., 1983. [7]

Natsoulas, T. Consciousness. *American Psychologist,* 1978. *33,* 906–914. [7]

Natsoulas, T. Addendum to "Consciousness." *American Psychologist,* 1983, *38,* 121–122. [7]

Needleman, H. L. Lead poisoning in children: Neurologic implications of widespread subclinical intoxications. *Seminars in Psychiatry,* 1973, *5,* 47–53. [20]

Needleman, H. L. Subclinical lead exposure in Philadelphia schoolchildren. *New England Journal of Medicine,* 1974, *290,* 245–248. [20]

Neisser, U. The control of information pickup in selective looking. In A. D. Pick (Ed.), *Perception and its development.* Hillsdale, N.J.: Lawrence Erlbaum, 1979. [15]

Nelson, C. A., and **F. D. Horowitz.** The perception of facial expressions and stimulus motion by two- and five-month-old infants using holographic stimuli. *Child Development,* 1983, *54,* 868–877. [14]

Nelson, K., L. Rescorla, J. Gruendel, and **H. Benedict.** Early lexicons: What do they mean? *Child Development,* 1978, *49,* 960–968. [16]

Nelson, K., and **G. Ross.** The generalities and specifics of long-term memory in infants and young children. In M. Perlmutter (Ed.), *New directions for child development.* No. 10. *Children's memory.* San Francisco: Jossey-Bass, 1980. [15]

Nelson, K. E. Facilitating children's syntax acquisition. *Developmental Psychology,* 1977, *13,* 101–107. [16]

Nelson, K. E., and **K. Nelson.** Cognitive pendulums and their linguistic realization. In K. E. Nelson (Ed.), *Children's language.* Vol. 1. New York: Gardner Press, 1978. [16]

Nemeth, C. J., and **J. Wachtler.** Creative problem solving as a result of majority vs. minority influence. *European Journal of Social Psychology,* 1983, *13,* 45–55. [27]

Neugarten, B. L. Adaptation and the life cycle. *The Counseling Psychologist,* 1976, *6,* 16–20. [17]

Neugarten, B. L. Personality and aging. In J. E. Birren and K. W. Schaie (Eds.), *Handbook of the psychology of aging.* New York: Van Nostrand Reinhold, 1977. [15]

Neugarten, B. L., interviewed by E. Hall. New rules for old. *Psychology Today,* 1980, *13,* 66–80. [17]

Neugebauer, R. Treatment of the mentally ill in medieval and early modern England: A reappraisal. *Journal of the History of the Behavioral Sciences,* 1978, *14,* 158–169. [23]

New York Times. Settlement offer by drug company, July 16, 1984, p. A20. [14]

New York Times, October 3, 1984, A1, D27, and *Newsweek,* October 15, 1984, 113. [22]

Newell, A., and **P. S. Rosenbloom.** Mechanisms of skill acquisitions and the law

of practice. In J. R. Anderson (Ed.), *Cognitive skills and their acquisition.* Hillsdale, N.J.: Lawrence Erlbaum, 1981. [8]

Newell, A., and **H. A. Simon.** *Human problem solving.* Englewood Cliffs, N.J.: Prentice-Hall, 1972. [10]

Newman, G., and **C. R. Nichols.** Sexual activities and attitudes in older person. *Journal of the American Medical Association,* 1960, *173,* 33–35. [13]

Nicassio, P., and **R. Bootzin.** A comparison of progressive relaxation and autogenic training as treatments for insomnia. *Journal of Abnormal Psychology,* 1974, *83,* 253–260. [21]

Nilsson, N. J. *Problem-solving methods in artificial intelligence.* New York: McGraw-Hill, 1971. [10]

Nisbett, R. E., and **L. Ross.** *Human inference: Strategies and shortcomings of social judgment.* Englewood Cliffs, N.J.: Prentice-Hall, 1980. [26]

Norman, D. A. *Learning and memory.* San Francisco: Freeman, 1982. [9, 10]

Nurnberger, J. I., and **E. S. Gershon.** Genetics. In E. S. Paykel (Ed.), *Handbook of affective disorders.* New York: Guildford Press, 1982. [22]

Office of the Surgeon General. *Television and growing up: The impacts of televised violence.* Washington, D.C.: U.S. Government Printing Office, 1972. [17]

Offir, C. W. *Human sexuality.* New York: Harcourt Brace Jovanovich, 1982. [13]

Ogilvie, B. C. Stimulus addiction: The sweet psychic jolt of danger. *Psychology Today,* 1974, *8,* 88–94. [12]

Olds, J., and **P. Milner.** Positive reinforcement produced by electrical stimulation of septal area and other regions of rat brain. *Journal of Comparative and Physiological Psychology,* 1954, *47,* 411–427. [3]

Olton, D. S., and **A. R. Noonberg.** *Biofeedback: Clinical applications in behavioral medicine.* Englewood Cliffs, N.J.: Prentice-Hall, 1980. [7]

Oncology Times. Smoking-related deaths higher for heart disease than cancer. *Oncology Times,* 1984 *6*(2), 3, 35. [21]

Orlofsky, J. L. Parental antecedents of sex-role orientation in college men and women. *Sex Roles,* 1979, *5,* 495–512. [17]

Ormiston, L. H. Factors determining response to modeled hypocrisy. Unpublished doctoral dissertation, Stanford University, 1972. [8]

Orne, M. T. The use and misuse of hypnosis in court. *International Journal of Clinical and Experimental Hypnosis,* 1979, *14,* 311–341. [7]

Orne, M. T., and **K. E. Scheibe.** The contribution of non-deprivation factors in the production of sensory deprivation effects: The psychology of the panic button. *Journal of Abnormal and Social Psychology,* 1964, *68,* 3–12. [7]

Ornstein, P. A., and **M. J. Naus.** Rehearsal processes in children's memory. In P. A. Ornstein (Ed.), *Memory development in children.* Hillsdale, N.J.: Lawrence Erlbaum, 1978. [15]

Ornstein, R. E. *The psychology of consciousness* (2nd ed.) New York: Harcourt Brace Jovanovich, 1977. [7]

Orwell, G. *Nineteen eighty-four.* New York: Harcourt, Brace, 1949. [16]

Oskamp, S., and **C. Kleinke.** Amount of reward as a variable in Prisoner's Dilemma game. *Journal of Personality and Social Psychology,* 1970, *16,* 133–140. [27]

Oswald, I. *Sleeping and waking.* Amsterdam, Elsevier, 1962. [7]

Overmier, J. B., and **M. E. P. Seligman.** Effects of inescapable shock on subsequent escape and avoidance responding. *Journal of Comparative and Physiological Psychology,* 1967, *63,* 28–33. [21]

Overton, W. F., and **H. W. Reese.** Models of development: Methodological implications. In J. R. Nesselroade and H. W. Reese (Eds.), *Life-span developmental psychology: Methodological issues.* New York: Academic Press, 1973. [19]

Paivio, A. *Imagery and verbal processes.* New York: Holt, Rinehart & Winston, 1971. [9]

Paranjpe, A. C. *Theoretical psychology: The meeting of East and West.* New York: Plenum Press, 1984. [7]

Parke, R. D., and **R. G. Slaby.** The development of aggression. In P. H. Mussen (Ed.), *Handbook of child psychology* (4th ed.). Vol. 4, E. M. Hetherington (Ed.), *Socialization, personality, and social development.* New York: Wiley, 1983. [17]

Parke, R. D., and **B. R. Tinsley.** The early environment of the at-risk infant: Expanding the social context. In D. D. Bricker (Ed.), *Intervention with at-risk and handicapped infants.* Baltimore: University Park Press, 1982. [17]

Parker, E. S., and **E. P. Noble.** Alcohol consumption and cognitive functioning in social drinkers. *Journal of Studies on Alcohol,* 1977, *38,* 1224–1232. [7]

Parkes, M. C., B. Benjamin, and **R. G. Fitzgerald.** Broken heart: A statistical study of increased mortality among widowers. *British Medical Journal,* 1969, *1,* 704–743. [21]

Parkinson, L., and **S. Rachman.** Intrusive thoughts: The effects of an uncontroled stress. *Advances in Behavior Research and Therapy,* 1981, *3,* 111–118. [6]

Parkinson, S. R., J. M. Lindholm, and **T. Urell.** Aging, dichotic memory and digit span. *Journal of Gerontology,* 1980, *35,* 87–95. [15]

Parmelee, A. H., Jr., and **M. D. Sigman.** Perinatal brain development and behavior. In P. H. Mussen (Ed.), *Handbook of child psychology* (4th ed.). Vol. 2: *Infancy and developmental psychobiolo-*

gy, M. M. Haith and J. J. Campos (Eds.). New York: Wiley, 1983. [3]

PASE v. Hannon 506 F. Supp. 831 (N. D. Ill. 1980). [20]

Patterson, G. R. Mothers: The unacknowledged victims. *Monographs of the Society for Research in Child Development,* 1980, *45,* 5 (Whole No. 186). [17]

Patterson, G. R. *Coercive family process.* Eugene, Oregon: Castalia Publishing Co., 1982. [17]

Patterson, G. R., and **H. Hops.** Coercion: A game for two: Intervention techniques for marital conflict. In R. Ulrich and P. Mountjoy (Eds.), *The experimental analysis of social behavior.* New York: Appleton-Century-Crofts, 1972. [24]

Patterson, G. R., R. A. Littman, and **W. Bricker.** Assertive behavior in children: A step toward a theory of aggression. *Monographs of the Society for Research in Child Development,* 1967, *32,* 5 (Whole No. 113). [17, 27]

Patterson, T. E. *The mass media: How Americans choose their president.* New York: Praeger, 1980. [25]

Pattie, F. A. A report of attempts to produce uniocular blindness by hypnotic suggestion. *British Journal of Medical Psychology,* 1935, *15,* 230–241. [7]

Paul, S. M. Movement and madness: Toward a biological model of schizophrenia. In J. D. Maser and M. E. P. Seligman (Eds.), *Psychopathology: Experimental models.* San Francisco: Freeman, 1977. [23]

Pavlov, I. P. *Conditioned reflexes.* London: Oxford University Press, 1927. [1, 8]

Penfield, W. The mind-brain question. In D. Goleman and R. J. Davidson (Eds.), *Consciousness: Brain, states of awareness, and mysticism.* New York: Harper & Row, 1979. [7]

Penfield, W., and **T. Rasmussen.** *The cerebral cortex of man.* New York: Macmillan, 1950. [3]

Pennington, N., and **R. Hastie.** Juror decision making models: The generalization gap. *Psychological Bulletin,* 1981. *89,* 246–278. [1]

Perlmutter, M. Learning and memory through adulthood. In M. W. Riley, B. B. Hess, and K. Bond (Eds.), *Aging in society: Selected reviews of research.* Hillsdale, N.J.: Lawrence Erlbaum, 1983. [15]

Perlmutter, M., and **E. Hall.** *Adult development and aging.* New York: Wiley, 1985. [15]

Perls, F. S. Four lectures. In J. Fagan and I. L. Shepherd (Eds.), *Gestalt therapy now: Therapy, techniques, applications.* Palo Alto, Calif.: Science & Behavior Books, 1970. [24]

Perls, F. S., R. F. Hefferline, and **P. Goodman.** *Gestalt therapy: Excitement and growth in the human personality.* New York: Julian Press, 1951. [24]

Pessin, J., and **R. W. Husband.** Effects of

social stimulation on human maze learning. *Journal of Abnormal and Social Psychology,* 1933, *28,* 148–154. [27]

Peterson, A. C., and **B. Taylor.** The biological approach to adolescence. In J. Adelson (Ed.), *Handbook of adolescent psychology.* New York: Wiley-Interscience, 1980. [17]

Peterson, L. R., and **M. Peterson.** Short-term retention of individual verbal items. *Journal of Experimental Psychology,* 1959, *58,* 193–198. [9]

Petrig, B., B. Julesz, W. Kropfl, G. Baumgartner, and **M. Anliker.** Development of stereopsis and cortical binocularity in human infants. *Science,* 1981, *213,* 1402–1405. [14]

Pettigrew, T. The ultimate attribution error: Extending Allport's cognitive analysis of prejudice. *Personality and Social Psychology Bulletin,* 1979, *5,* 461–476. [26]

Pfaffman, C. Gustatory nerve impulses in rat, cat and rabbit. *Journal of Neurophysiology,* 1955, *81,* 429–440. [5]

Pfeifer, L. A subjective report of tactile hallucination in schizophrenia. *Journal of Clinical Psychology,* 1970, *26,* 57–60. [22]

Phillips, S., S. King, and **L. Dubois.** Spontaneous activities of female versus male newborns. *Child Development,* 1978, *49,* 590–597. [17]

Piaget, J. *The child's conception of the world.* New York: Harcourt, Brace, 1929. [15]

Piaget, J. *The child's conception of number.* Boston: Routledge & Kegan Paul, 1952. [15]

Piaget, J. *The construction of reality in the child.* New York: Basic Books, 1954. [15]

Piaget, J. *The origins of intelligence in children.* New York: International Universities Press, 1966. (Originally published, 1952). [15]

Piaget, J. Needs and significance of cross-cultural research in genetic psychology. In B. Inhelder and H. H. Chipman (Eds.), *Piaget and his school.* New York: Springer, 1976. [15]

Piaget, J. *Success and understanding.* Cambridge, Mass.: Harvard University Press, 1978. [15]

Piaget, J., and **B. Inhelder.** *Le developpment des quantities chez l'enfant; conservations et atomisme.* Neuchatel: Delachaux et Niestle, 1941. [15]

Piaget, J., and **B. Inhelder.** *The child's conception of space.* London: Routledge & Kegan Paul, 1956. [15]

Piaget, J., and **B. Inhelder.** *The psychology of the child.* New York: Basic Books, 1969. [15]

Pines, M. Recession is linked to far-reaching psychological harm. *The New York Times,* April 6, 1982. [23]

Platt, J. R. *Perception and change: Projections for survival.* Ann Arbor: University of Michigan Press, 1970. [27]

Plotkin, W. B., and **R. Cohen.** Occipital

alpha and the attributes of the "alpha experience." *Psychological Physiology,* 1976, *13,* 16–21. [7]

Poeppel, E., R. Held, and **D. Frost.** Residual visual function after brain wounds involving central pathways in man. *Nature,* 1973, *243,* 295–296. [7]

Pollack, I., and **J. M. Pickett.** The intelligibility of excerpts from conversations. *Language and Speech,* 1963, *6,* 165–171. [16]

Polya, G. *How to solve problems.* San Francisco: W. H. Freeman, 1957. [10]

Pomeroy, W. B. The Masters-Johnson report and the Kinsey tradition. In R. Brecher and E. Brecher (Eds.), *An analysis of "Human sexual response."* New York: New American Library, 1966. [13]

Postman, L., and **K. Stark.** Role of response availability in transfer and interference. *Journal of Experimental Psychology,* 1969, *79,* 168–177. [9]

Prechtl, H. F. R. Regressions and transformations during neurological development. In T. G. Bever (Ed.), *Regressions in mental development: Basic phenomena and theories.* Hillsdale, N.J.: Lawrence Erlbaum, 1982. [4, 14]

Premack, D. Language in the chimpanzee? *Science,* 1971*a, 172,* 808–822. [16]

Premack, D. On the assessment of language comprehension in the chimpanzee. In A. M. Schrier and F. Stollnitz (Eds.), *Behavior of non-human primates.* New York: Academic Press, 1971*b.* [16]

Pribram, K. H. *Languages of the brain: Experimental paradoxes and principles in neuropsychology.* Monterey, Calif.: Brooks/Cole, 1971. [3]

Price, R. H. *Abnormal behavior: Perspectives in conflict* (2nd ed.). New York: Holt, Rinehart & Winston, 1978. [23]

Prien, R. F., C. J. Klett, and **E. M. Craffey.** Lithium prophylaxis in recurrent affective illness. *American Journal of Psychiatry,* 1974, *131,* 198–203. [24]

Pritchard, R. D., P. J. DeLeo, and **C. W. Von Bergen.** A field experimental test of expectancy-valence incentive motivation techniques. *Organizational Behavior and Human Performance,* 1976, *15,* 355–406. [28]

Pruitt, D. G., and **M. Kimmel.** Twenty years of experimental gaming: Critique, synthesis, and suggestions for the future. In M. R. Rosenzweig and L. W. Porter (Eds.), *Annual review of psychology.* Vol. 28. Palo Alto, Calif.: Annual Reviews, 1977, pp. 363–392. [27]

Pulkkinen, L. Self-control and continuity from childhood to late adolescence. In P. Baltes and O. Brim (Eds.), *Life-span development and behavior.* Vol. 4. New York: Academic Press, 1982. [17]

Pulkkinen, L. Youthful smoking and drinking in a longitudinal perspective. *Journal of Youth and Adolescence,* 1983, *12,* 253–283. [17]

Rabbie, J. M., and **M. Horowitz.** Arousal of ingroup-outgroup bias by a chance win or loss. *Journal of Personality and Social Psychology,* 1969, *13,* 269–277. [26]

Rachman, S. J. *Fear and courage.* San Francisco: W. H. Freeman, 1978. [21]

Rachman, S. J., and **R. J. Hodgson.** *Obsessions and compulsions.* Englewood Cliffs, N. J.: Prentice-Hall, 1980. [22, 24]

Rachman, S. J., and **G. T. Wilson.** *The effects of psychological therapy* (2nd. ed.) Oxford: Pergamon Press, 1980. [24]

Rada, R. T. Psychological factors in rapist behavior. In R. T. Rada (Ed.), *Clinical aspects of the rapist.* New York: Grune & Stratton, 1978. [13]

Radke-Yarrow, M., C. Zahn-Waxler, and **M. Chapman.** Children's prosocial dispositions and behavior. In P. H. Mussen (Ed.), *Handbook of child psychology* (4th ed.). Vol. 4, E. M. Hetherington (Ed.), *Socialization, personality, and social development.* New York: Wiley, 1983. [17]

Rauschenberger, J., N. Schmitt, and J. E. Hunter. A test of the need hierarchy concept by a Markov model of change in need strength. *Administrative Science Quarterly,* 1980, *25,* 654–670. [28]

Ray, O. S. *Drugs, society, and human behavior* (3rd ed.). St. Louis: Mosby, 1983. [24]

Regan, D., K. Beverley, and **M. Cynader.** The visual perception of motion in depth. *Scientific American,* 1979, *241* (1), 136–151. [6]

Regan, D. T. Effects of a favor and liking on compliance. *Journal of Experimental Social Psychology,* 1971, *7,* 627–639. [27]

Reich, J., R. Maier, L. Klein, and **J. Gyurke.** Effects of infant appearance and state patterns on adult perceptions. Paper presented at the International Conference on Infant Studies, New York City, April 1984. [14]

Reilly, R. R., B. Brown, M. R. Blood, and **C. Z. Malatesta.** The effects of realistic previews: A study and discussion of the literature. *Personnel Psychology,* 1981, *34,* 823–834. [28]

Reinisch, J. M. Prenatal exposure to synthetic progestins increases potential for aggression in humans. *Science,* 1981, *211,* 1171–1173. [17]

Reisenzein, R. The Schachter theory of emotion: Two decades later. *Psychological Bulletin,* 1983, *94,* 239–264. [11]

Reitman, J. S. Without surreptitious rehearsal, information in short-term memory decays. *Journal of Verbal Learning and Verbal Behavior,* 1974, *13,* 365–377. [9]

Rescorla, R. A. Probability of shock in the presence and absence of CS in fear conditioning. *Journal of Comparative and Physiological Psychology,* 1968, *66,* 1–5. [8]

Rescorla, R. A. Some implications of a

cognitive perspective on Pavlovian conditioning. In S. H. Hulse, H. Fowler, and W. Honig (Eds.), *Cognitive processes in animal behavior.* Hillsdale, N.J.: Lawrence Erlbaum, 1978. [8]

Resnik, R. B., R. S. Kestenbaum, and **L. K. Schwartz.** Acute systemic effects of cocaine in man: A controlled study by intranasal and intravenous routes by administration. *Science,* 1977, *195,* 696–698. [7]

Revelle, W., P. Amaral, and **S. Turriff.** Introversion-extraversion, time stress, and caffeine: The effect on verbal performance. *Science,* 1976, *192,* 149–150. [19]

Revelle, W., M. S. Humphreys, L. Simon, and **K. Gilliland.** The interactive effect of personality, time of day, and caffeine: A test of the arousal model. *Journal of Experimental Psychology: General,* 1980, *109,* 1–31. [19]

Rheingold, H. L., J. L. Gewirtz, and **H. W. Ross.** Social conditioning of vocalizations in infants. *Journal of Comparative and Physiological Psychology,* 1959, *52,* 68–73. [15]

Rhine, J. B. Telepathy and other untestable hypotheses. *Journal of Parapsychology,* 1974, *38,* 137–153. [1]

Rhodewalt, F., and **R. Comer.** Induced-compliance attitude change: Once more with feeling. *Journal of Experimental Social Psychology,* 1979, *15,* 35–47. [11]

Rice, B. The Hawthorne Effect: Persistence of a flawed theory. *Psychology Today,* 1982, *16,* 71–74. [28]

Rice, R. D. Premature infants respond to sensory stimulation. *APA Monitor,* November 1975. [14]

Rimm, D. C., and **J. C. Masters.** *Behavior therapy: Techniques and empirical findings.* New York: Academic Press, 1979. [24]

Ringuette, E. L., and **T. Kennedy.** An experimental study of two double-bind hypotheses. *Journal of Abnormal Psychology,* 1966, *71,* 136–141. [23]

Risley, T. R. The effects and side-effects of punishing the autistic behavior of a defiant child. *Journal of Applied Behavior Analysis,* 1968, *1,* 21–34. [8]

Robbins, M. B., and **G. D. Jensen.** Multiple orgasm in males. *Journal of Sex Research,* 1978, *14,* 21–26 [13]

Robertson, L. S. Factors associated with safety-belt use in 1974 starter-interlock equipped cars. *Journal of Health and Social Behavior,* 1975, *16,* 173–177. [21]

Rock, I. *The nature of perceptual adaptation.* New York: Basic Books, 1966. [6]

Rodin, J. Current status of the internal-external hypothesis for obesity: What went wrong? *American Psychologist,* 1981, *36,* 361–372. [21]

Rodin, J. Insulin levels, hunger and food intake: An example of feedback loops in body weight regulation. Based on Presidential Address, Division 38, American Psychological Association Meeting. Anaheim, California, August 1983. [12]

Rodin, J., interviewed by E. Hall. A sense of control. *Psychology Today*, 1984, *18*, 38–45. [12]

Rodin, J., and J. Marcus. Psychological factors in human feeding. *Pharmac. Ther.*, 1982, *16*, 447–468. [12]

Rodin, J., L. Silberstein, and R. Striegel-Moore. Women and weight: A normative discontent (in press). [26]

Roethlisberger, F. J., and W. J. Dickson. *Management and the worker: An account of a research program conducted by Western Electric Co.* Cambridge, Mass.: Harvard Business School, 1939. [28]

Roff, M., S. B. Sells, and M. M. Golden. *Social adjustment and personality development in children.* Minneapolis: University of Minnesota Press, 1972. [17]

Roffwarg, H. P., J. N. Muzio, and W. C. Dement. Ontogenetic development of the human sleep-dream cycle. *Science*, 1966, *132*, 604–619. [7]

Rogel, M. J. A critical evaluation of the possibility of higher primate reproductive and sexual pheromones. *Psychological Bulletin*, 1978, *85*, 810–830. [13]

Rogers, C. R. A Theory of personality. In S. Maddi (Ed.), *Perspectives on personality.* Boston: Little, Brown, 1971. [19]

Rogers, C. R. *A way of being.* Boston: Houghton Mifflin, 1980. [19]

Rogers, C. R. *Client-centered therapy: Its current practice, implications, and theory.* Boston: Houghton Mifflin, 1951. [24]

Rogers, C. R. *A way of being.* Boston: Houghton Mifflin, 1980. [24]

Rolls, E. T., M. J. Burton, and F. Mora. Hypothalamic neuronal responses associated with the sight of food. *Brain Research*, 1976, *111*, 53–56. [12]

Rorschach, H. *Psychodiagnosis: A diagnostic test based on perception.* New York: Grune & Stratton, 1942. [20]

Rosch, E. H. On the internal structure of perceptual and semantic categories. In T. E. Moore (Ed.), *Cognitive development and the acquisition of language.* New York: Academic Press, 1973. [10]

Rosch, E. H., and C. B. Mervis. Family resemblances: Studies in the internal structure of categories. *Cognitive Psychology*, 1977, *7*, 573–605. [10]

Rosch, E. H., C. B. Mervis, W. Gray, D. Johnson, and P. Boyes-Braem. Basic objects in natural categories. *Cognitive Psychology*, 1976, *8*, 382–439. [10]

Rose, S. *The conscious brain.* New York: Knopf, 1973. [7]

Rose, S. A. Developmental changes in infants' retention of visual stimuli. *Child Development*, 1981, *42*, 227–233. [15]

Rose, S. A., and M. Blank. The potency of context in children's cognition: An illustration through conservation. *Child Development*, 1974, *45*, 499–502. [15]

Rose, S. A., K. Schmidt, M. L. Riese, and W. H. Bridger. Effects of prematurity and early intervention on responsivity to actual stimuli: A comparison of preterm and full term infants. *Child Development*, 1980, *51*, 416–425. [14]

Rosen, G. The evolution of social medicine, In H. Freeman, S. Levine, and L. Reeder (Eds.) *Handbook of medical sociology* (2nd ed.). Englewood Cliffs, N.J.: Prentice-Hall, 1972. [21]

Rosen, W. G., and R. C. Mohs. Evolution of cognitive decline in dementia. In S. Corkin, K. L. Davis, J. H. Gordon, E. Usdin, and R. J. Wurtman (Eds.), *Aging.* Vol. 19. *Alzheimer's Disease: A report of progress in research.* New York: Raven Press, 1982. [15]

Rosenhan, D. L. On being sane in insane places. *Science*, 1973, *179*, 250–258. [22]

Rosenman, R. H., R. J. Brand, C. D. Jenkins, M. Friedman, R. Straus, and M. Wurm. Coronary heart disease in the Western Collaborative Group study: Final follow-up experience of 8½ years. *Journal of the American Medical Association*, 1975, *8*, 872–877. [21]

Rosenstock, I. M. Historical origins of the health belief model. *Health Education Monographs*, 1974, *2*, 328–335. [21]

Rosenthal, D., P. H. Wender, S. S. Kety, R. Schulsinger, J. Welner, and L. Ostergaard. Schizophrenics' offspring reared in adoptive homes. In D. Rosenthal and S. S. Kety (Eds.), *The transmission of schizophrenia.* Elmsford, N.Y.: Pergamon Press, 1968. [23]

Rosenthal, R. *Experimenter effects in behavioral research.* New York: Appleton-Century-Crofts, 1966. [2]

Rosenthal, R., and L. Jacobson. *Pygmalion in the classroom: Teacher expectation and pupils' intellectual development.* New York: Holt, Rinehart & Winston, 1968. [26]

Rosenthal, T., and A. Bandura. Psychological modeling: Theory and practice. In S. L. Garfield and A. E. Bergin (Eds.), *Handbook of psychotherapy and behavior change: An empirical analysis* (2nd ed.). New York: Wiley, 1978. [19, 23, 24]

Rosenzweig, M. R. U. S. psychology and world psychology. *American Psychologist*, 1984, *39*, 877–884. [1]

Ross, E. D., and M. Mesulam. Dominant language functioning of the right hemisphere: Prosody and emotional gesturing. *Archives of Neurology*, 1979, *36*, 144–148. [11]

Ross, E. R. The aprosodias: Functional anatomic organization of the affective components of language in the right hemisphere. *Archives of Neurology*, 1981, *38*, 561–569. [3]

Ross, L. D. The intuitive psychologist and his shortcomings: Distortions in the attribution process. In L. Berkowitz (Ed.), *Advances in experimental social psychology.* Vol. 10. New York: Academic Press, 1977. [26]

Rotter, J. B. Generalized expectancies for internal versus external control of reinforcement. *Psychological Monographs*, 1966, *80*, 1, Whole No. 609. [20]

Roueché, B. Annals of medicine: As empty as Eve. *The New Yorker*, September 9, 1974, pp. 84–100. [24]

Rovée-Collier, C. The ontogeny of learning and memory in human infancy. In R. Kail and N. E. Spear (Eds.), *Comparative perspectives on the development of memory.* Hillsdale, N.J.: Lawrence Erlbaum, 1984. [15]

Rozin, E., and P. Rozin. Culinary themes and variations. *Natural History*, 1981, *90*, 7–14. [25]

Rozin, P., and D. Schiller. The nature and acquisition of a preference for chili pepper by humans. *Motivation and Emotion*, 1980, *4*, 77–101. [25]

Rubenstein, C., P. Shaver, and L. A. Peplau. Loneliness. *Human Nature*, February 1979, *2*, 58–65. [17]

Rubin, H. B., and D. E. Henson. Voluntary enhancement of penile erection. *Bulletin of the Psychonomic Society*, 1975, *6*, 158–160. [13]

Rubin, Z. Measurement of romantic love. *Journal of Personality and Social Psychology*, 1970, *16*, 265–273. [26]

Rubin, Z. *Liking and loving: An invitation to social psychology.* New York: Holt, Rinehart & Winston, 1973. [26]

Rubin, Z. *Children's friendships.* Cambridge, Mass.: Harvard University Press, 1980. [17]

Rule, B. G., and A. R. Nesdale. Emotional arousal and aggressive behavior. *Psychological Bulletin*, 1976, *83*, 851–863. [27]

Rumbaugh, D. M. (Ed.). *Language learning by a chimpanzee: The Lana project.* New York: Academic Press, 1977. [16]

Russell, W. R., and P. W. Nathan. Traumatic amnesia. *Brain*, 1946, *69*, 280–300. [9]

Rutkowski, G. K., C. L. Gruder, and D. Romer. Group cohesiveness, social norms, and bystander intervention. *Journal of Personality and Social Psychology*, 1983, *44*, 545–552. [27]

Rutter, M. The city and the child. *American Journal of Orthopsychiatry*, 1981, *51*, 610–625. [17]

Rutter, M., and L. Lockyer. A five to fifteen year follow-up of infantile psychosis: I. Description of sample. *British Journal of Psychiatry*, 1967, *113*, 1169–1182. [22]

Rycroft, C. Introduction. In M. Prince, *Dissociation of personality.* New York: Oxford University Press, 1978. [22]

Sachar, E. J. Psychobiology of affective disorders. In E. R. Kandel and J. H. Schwartz (Eds.), *Principles of neurosci-*

ence. New York: Elsevier/North Holland, 1981. [3]

Sackheim, H. A., and **R. C. Gur.** Lateral asymmetry in intensity of emotional expression. *Neuropsychologia,* 1978, *16,* 473–481. [11]

Sackheim, H. A., R. C. Gur, and **M. C. Saucy.** Emotions are expressed more intensely on the left side of the face. *Science,* 1978, *202,* 434–436. [11]

Sacks, H., E. Schlegloff, and **G. Jefferson.** A simplest systematic for the organization of turn-taking in conversation. *Language,* 1974, *50,* 696–735. [16]

Saghir, M. T., and **E. Robins.** *Male and female homosexuality: A comprehensive investigation.* Baltimore: Williams & Wilkins, 1973. [13]

Sagi, A., and M. L. Hoffman. Empathic distress in the newborn. *Developmental Psychology,* 1976, *12,* 175–176. [14]

Sameroff, A. J., and **P. J. Cavanaugh.** Learning in infancy. In J. D. Osofsky (Ed.), *Handbook of infant development.* New York: Wiley-Interscience, 1979. [15]

Sancton, T. A. Smoothing the way. *Time,* November 17, 1980, 79. [25]

Sandberg, E. C., N. L. Riffle, J. V. Higdon, and **C. E. Getman.** Pregnancy outcome in women exposed to diethylstilbestrol in utero. *American Journal of Obstetrics and Gynecology,* 1981, *140,* 194–205. [14]

Sarason, I. G. A modeling and informational approach to delinquency. In E. Ribes-Inesta and A. Bandura (Eds.), *Analysis of delinquency and aggression.* Hillsdale, N.J.: Lawrence Erlbaum, 1976. [24]

Sarbin, T. R., and **W. C. Coe.** *Hypnosis: A social psychological analysis of influence communication.* New York: Holt, Rinehart & Winston, 1972. [7]

Satir, V. *Conjoint family therapy* (Rev. ed.). Palo Alto, Calif.: Science & Behavior Books, 1967. [24]

Savage-Rumbaugh, E. S., J. L. Pate, J. Lawson, S. T. Smith, and **S. Rosenbaum.** Can a chimpanzee make a statement? *Journal of Experimental Psychology: General,* 1983, *112,* 457–488. [16]

Savage-Rumbaugh, E. S., D. M. Rumbaugh, and **S. Boysen.** Do apes use language? *American Scientist,* 1980, *68,* 49–61. [16]

Scanlon, J., and **J. J. Chisholm, Jr.** Fetal effects of lead exposure. *Pediatrics,* 1972, *49,* 145–146. [20]

Scarr, S. *Race, social class, and individual differences in I.Q.* Hillsdale, N.J.: Lawrence Erlbaum, 1981. [20]

Scarr, S. Outline of developmental contributions to clincial psychology. Paper presented at Annual Meeting of American Psychological Association. Los Angeles, August 1981*a.* [14]

Scarr, S. *Mother care/Other care.* New York: Basic Books, 1984. [17]

Scarr, S., and **K. K. Kidd.** Developmental behavioral genetics. In P. H. Mussen (Ed.), *Handbook of child psychology* (4th ed.). Vol. 2. M. M. Halth and J. J. Campos (Eds.), *Infancy and developmental psychobiology.* New York: Wiley, 1983. [4, 16, 20]

Scarr, S., and **P. Salapatek.** Patterns of fear development during infancy. *Merrill-Palmer Quarterly of Behavior and Development,* 1970, *16,* 53–90. [14]

Scarr, S., P. L. Webber, R. A. Weinberg, and **M. A. Wittig.** Personality resemblance among adolescents and their parents in biologically related and adoptive families. *Journal of Personality and Social Psychology,* 1981, 40. [14]

Scarr, S., and **R. A. Weinberg.** IQ test performance of black children adopted by white families. *American Psychologist,* 1976, *31,* 726–739. [20]

Scarr, S., and **R. A. Weinberg.** The influence of "family background" on intellectual attainment. *American Sociological Review,* 1978*b, 43,* 674–692. [14]

Scarr-Salapatek, S. Unknowns in the IQ equation. *Science,* 1971, *174,* 1223–1228. [20]

Scarr-Salapatek, S. An evolutionary perspective on infant intelligence: Species patterns and individual variations. In M. Lewis (Ed.), *Origins of intelligence.* New York: Plenum, 1976. [14]

Schachter, S., and **J. E. Singer.** Cognitive, social and physiological determinants of emotional state. *Psychological Review,* 1962, *69,* 379–399. [11]

Schachter, S., and **L. Wheeler.** Epinephrine, chlorpromazine, and amusement. *Journal of Abnormal and Social Psychology,* 1962, *65,* 121–128. [11]

Schaefer, C., J. C. Coyne, and **R. S. Lazarus.** The health-related functions of social support. *Journal of Behavioral Medicine,* 1981, *4,* 381–406. [

Schaeffer, J., T. Andrysiak, and **J. T. Ungerleider.** Cognition and long-term use of ganja (cannabis). *Science,* 1981, *213,* 465–466. [7]

Schank, R. C. *Dynamic memory.* Cambridge: Cambridge University Press, 1982. [9]

Schank, R. C., and **C. K. Riesbeck** (Eds.). *Inside computer understanding.* Hillsdale, N.J.: Lawrence Erlbaum, 1981. [16]

Schares, G. Alzheimer's disease. *Palo Alto Weekly,* October 20, 1982, pp. 15–16. [3]

Scheerer, M. Problem-solving. *Scientific American,* 1963, *208,* 118–128. [10]

Scheff, T. J. *Labeling madness.* Englewood Cliffs, N.J.: Prentice-Hall, 1975. [23]

Scherer, K. R., R. P. Sheles, and **C. S. Kischer.** *Human aggression and conflict.* Englewood Cliffs, N.J.: Prentice-Hall, 1975. [27]

Schiff, M., M. Duyme, A. Dumaret, J.

Stewart, S. Tomkiewicz, and **J. Feingold.** Intellectual status of working-class children adopted early into upper-middle-class families. *Science,* 1978, *200,* 1503–1504. [20]

Schildkraut, J. J. The catecholamine hypothesis of affective disorders: A review of supporting evidence. *American Journal of Psychiatry,* 1965, *122,* 509–522. [23]

Schildkraut, J. J. Neuropharmacological studies of mood disorders. In J. Zubin and F. A. Freyhan (Eds.). *Disorders of mood.* Baltimore: Johns Hopkins Press, 1972. [23]

Schmeck, H. M., Jr. Implant brings sound to deaf and spurs debate over its use. *The New York Times,* March 27, 1984, pp. C1+. [5]

Schmidt, F. L., and **J. E. Hunter.** Employment testing: Old theories and new research findings. *American Psychologist,* 1981, *36,* 1128–1137. [28]

Schmitt, N. Social and situational determinants of interview decisions: Implications for the employment interview. *Personnel Psychology,* 1976, *29,* 79–101. [28]

Schneider-Rosen, K., and D. Cicchetti. The relationship between affect and cognition in maltreated infants: Quality of attachment and the development of visual self-recognition. *Child Development,* 1984, *55,* 648–658. [14]

Schuckit, M. A. Biological markers: Metabolism and acute reactions to alcohol in sons of alcoholics. *Pharmacology, Biochemistry and Behavior,* 1980 (Supplement I), *13,* 9–16. [4]

Schuckit, M. A., and V. Rayses. Ethanol ingestion: Differences in blood acetaldehyde concentrations in relatives of alcoholics and controls. *Science,* 1979, *203,* 54–55. [4]

Schultes, R. E. *Hallucinogenic plants.* New York: Golden Press, 1976. [7]

Schultz, J. H., and **W. O. Luthe.** *Autogenic therapy. Vol. I.: Autogenic methods.* New York: Grune & Stratton, 1969. [21]

Schwartz, D. J., L. N. Weinstein, and **A. M. Arkin.** Qualitative aspects of sleep mentation. In A. M. Arkin, J. S. Antrobus, and S. J. Ellman (Eds.), *The mind in sleep: Psychology and psychophysiology.* Hillsdale, N.J.: Lawrence Erlbaum, 1978. [7]

Schwartz, G. E. Psychobiological foundations of psychotherapy and behavior change. In S. L. Garfield and A. E. Bergin (Eds.), *Handbook of psychotherapy and behavior change.* New York: Wiley, 1978.

Schwartz, G. E., P. L. Fair, M. R. Mandel, P. Salt, M. Meiske, and **G. L. Klerman.** Facial electromyography in the assessment of improvement in depression. *Psychosomatic Medicine,* 1978, *40,* 355–360. [11]

Schwartz, J. H. Chemical basis of synaptic transmission. In E. R. Kandel and J. H.

Schwartz (Eds.), *Principles of neuroscience*. New York: Elsevier/North-Holland, 1981. [3]

Scollan, R. A real early stage: An unzippered condensation of a dissertation on child language. In E. Ochs and B. B. Schieffelin (Eds.), *Developmental pragmatics*. New York: Academic Press, 1979. [16]

Scott, J. P. Genetics of social behavior in nonhuman animals. In J. L. Fuller and E. C. Simmel (Eds.), *Behavior genetics*. Hillsdale, N.J.: Lawrence Erlbaum, 1983. [4]

Scott, W. E., Jr. The effects of extrinsic rewards on "intrinsic motivation": A critique. *Organizational Behavior and Human Performance*, 1975, *15*, 117–129. [12]

Scovern, A. W., and **P. R. Kilmann.** Status of electroconvulsive therapy: Review of the outcome literature. *Psychological Bulletin*, 1980, *87*, 260–303. [24]

Scribner, S., and **M. Cole.** Effects of constrained recall training on children's performance in a verbal memory task. *Child Development*, 1972, *43*, 845–857. [15]

Seamon, J. J., N. Brody, and **D. M. Kauff.** Affective discrimination of stimuli that are not recognized: Effects of shadowing, masking, and cerebral laterality. *Journal of Experimental Psychology: Learning, Memory, and Cognition*, 1983, *9*, 544–555. [25]

Searle, J. R. *Speech acts: An essay in the philosophy of language*. New York: Cambridge University Press, 1969. [16]

Sears, D. O. The person-positivity bias. *Journal of Personality and Social Psychology*, 1983, *44*, 233–250. [26]

Sedgwick, R. Antipsychiatry from the sixties to the eighties. In W. R. Gove, (Ed.), *Deviance and mental illness*. Beverly Hills, Calif.: Sage, 1982. [23]

Segal, B., H. Huba, and **J. L. Singer.** *Drugs, daydreaming and personality: A study of college youth*. Hillsdale, N.J.: Lawrence Erlbaum, 1980. [7]

Segal, M. W. Alphabet and attraction: An unobtrusive measure of the effects of propinquity in a field setting. *Journal of Personality and Social Psychology*, 1974, *30*, 654–657. [26]

Segall, M. H., D. T. Campbell, and **M. J. Herskovits.** *The influence of culture on visual perception*. Indianapolis: Bobbs-Merrill, 1966. [6]

Selfridge, O. G. Pandemonium: A paradigm for learning. In *Symposium on the mechanization of thought process*. London: HM Stationery Office, 1959. [6]

Selman, R. L. Toward a structural analysis of developing interpersonal relations concepts. In A. Pick (Ed.), *Minnesota Symposia on Child Psychology*. Vol. 10. Minneapolis: University of Minnesota Press, 1976. [17]

Selman, R. L. *The growth of interpersonal understanding*. New York: Academic Press, 1980. [17]

Selman, R. L., and **D. Jacquette.** Stability and oscillation in interpersonal awareness: A clinical-developmental analysis. In C. B. Keasey (Ed.), *Nebraska Symposium on Motivation*. Vol. 25. Lincoln: University of Nebraska Press, 1977. [17]

Serbin, L. A., K. D. O'Leary, R. N. Kent, and **I. J. Tonick.** A comparison of teacher response to the pre-academic and problem behavior of boys and girls. *Child Development*, 1973, *33*, 796–804. [17]

Seyle, H. *The stress of life*. New York: McGraw-Hill, 1956. [21]

Seyle, H. *Stress without distress*. Philadelphia: Lippincott, 1974. [21]

Seyle, H. *Stress in health and disease*. Woburn, Mass.: Butterworth, 1976. [21]

Shantz, C. U. Social cognition. In P. H. Mussen (Ed.), *Handbook of child psychology* (4th ed.). Vol. 3, J. H. Flavell and E. M. Markman (Eds.), *Cognitive development*. New York: Wiley, 1983. [17]

Shapiro, C. M., R. Bortz, D. Mitchell, P. Bartel, and **P. Jooste.** Slow-wave sleep: A recovery period after exercise. *Science*, 1981, *214*, 1253–1354. [7]

Shapiro, D., and **I. B. Goldstein.** Biobehavioral perspectives on hypertension. *Journal of Consulting and Clinical Psychology*, 1982, *50*, 841–858. [21]

Shapiro, D., and **R. S. Surwit.** Learned control of physiological function and disease. In H. Leitenberg (Ed.), *Handbook of behavior modification and behavior therapy*. Englewood Cliffs, N.J.: Prentice-Hall, 1976. [8]

Sheehan, S. *Is there no place on earth for me?* Boston: Houghton Mifflin, 1982. [22]

Sherif, C. W. *Orientation in social psychology*. New York: Harper & Row, 1976. [12, 26]

Sherif, M. *The psychology of social norms*. New York: Harper, 1936. [27]

Sherif, M., O. J. Harvey, B. J. White, W. R. Hood, and **C. W. Sherif.** *Intergroup conflict and cooperation: The robber's cave experiment*. Norman: University of Oklahoma Press, 1961. [26]

Shortliffe, E. H. *Computer-based medical consultations: MYCIN*. New York: American Elsevier, 1976. [10]

Shostak, M. *Nisa: The life and words of a !Kung woman*. Cambridge, Mass.: Harvard University Press, 1981. [21]

Siegel, R. K. Hallucinations. *Scientific American*, 1977, *237*, 132–140. [7]

Siegler, R. S. Information processing approaches to development. In P. H. Mussen (Ed.), *Handbook of child psychology* (4th ed.). Vol. 1. W. Kessen (Ed.), *History, theory, and methods*. New York: Wiley, 1983. [15]

Simmons, F. B., J. M. Epley, R. C. Lumis, N. Guttman, L. S. Frischkopf, L. D. Harmon, and **E. Zuricker.** Auditory nerve: Electrical stimulation in man. *Science*, 1965, *148*, 104–106. [5]

Siqueland, E., and **C. A. Delucia.** Visual reinforcement of non-nutritive sucking in human infants. *Science*, 1969, *165*, 1144–1146. [15]

Sistrunk, F., and **J. W. McDavid.** Sex variables in conforming behavior. *Journal of Personality and Social Psychology*, 1971, *17*, 200–207. [25]

Skinner, B. F. *Behavior of organisms: An experimental analysis*. New York: Appleton-Century-Crofts, 1938. [8]

Skinner, B. F. *Walden two*: New York: Macmillan, 1948. [1, 19]

Skinner, B. F. Superstitious behavior in the pigeon. *Journal of Experimental Psychology*, 1948a, *38*, 168–172. [8]

Skinner, B. F. *Science and human behavior*. New York: Macmillan, 1953. [8]

Skinner, B. F. *Verbal behavior*. New York: Appleton-Century-Crofts, 1957. [16]

Skinner, B. F. *Beyond freedom and dignity*. New York: Knopf, 1971. [1, 19]

Skinner, B. F. The steep and thorny road to a science of behavior. *American Psychologist*, 1975, *30*, 42–49. [19]

Skinner, B. F. Intellectual self-management in old age. *American Psychologist*, 1983, *38*, 239–244. [15]

Sklar, L. S., and **H. Anisman.** Stress and cancer. *Psychological Bulletin*, 1981, *89*, 369–406. [21]

Skodak, M., and **H. M. Skeels.** A final follow-up of one hundred adopted children. *Journal of Genetic Psychology*, 1949, *75*, 85–125. [20]

Slater, E. A review of earlier evidence on genetic factors in schizophrenia. In D. Rosenthal and S. S. Kety (Eds.), *The transmission of schizophrenia*. Elmsford, N.Y.: Pergamon, 1968. [23]

Slobin, D. I. Cognitive prerequisites for the development of grammar. In C. A. Ferguson and D. I. Slobin (Eds.), *Studies of child language development*. New York: Holt, Rinehart & Winston, 1973. [16]

Smith, A., and **O. Sugar.** Development of above-normal language and intelligence twenty-one years after hemispherectomy. *Neurology*, 1975, *25*, 813–818. [16]

Smith, C., and **B. Lloyd.** Maternal behavior and perceived sex of infant revisited. *Child Development*, 1978, *49*, 1263–1265. [17]

Smith, M. L., G. V. Glass, and **T. I. Miller.** *The benefits of psychotheraphy*. Baltimore: Johns Hopkins Press, 1980. [24]

Smith, S. B. Why TV won't let up on violence. *The New York Times*, January 13, 1985, Section 2, p. 2+. [17]

Smith, S. D., W. J. Kimberling, B. F. Pennington, and **H. A. Lubs.** Specific reading disability: Identification of an inherited form through linkage analysis. *Science*, 1983, *219*, 1345–1347. [16]

Snow, C. E., and **M. Hoefnagel-Höhle.** The critical period for language acquisition: Evidence from second-language learning. *Child Development,* 1978, *49,* 1114–1118. [16]

Snow, C. P. Either-or. *Progressive,* 1961, *25* (2), 24–25. [27]

Snyder, M. Impression management. In L. S. Wrightsman (Ed.), *Social psychology.* Belmont, Calif.: Brooks/Cole, 1977. [26]

Snyder, M. Self-monitoring processes. In L. Berkowitz (Ed.), *Advances in experimental social psychology.* Vol. 12. New York: Academic Press, 1979. [25, 26]

Snyder, S. H. Catecholamines in the brain as mediators of amphetamine psychosis. *Archives of General Psychiatry,* 1972, *27,* 169–179. [23]

Snyder, S. H. The dopamine hypothesis of schizophrenia: Focus on the dopamine receptor. *American Journal of Psychiatry,* 1976, *133,* 197–202. [23]

Snyder, S. H. The true speed trip: Schizophrenia. In D. Goleman & R. J. Davidson (Eds.), *Consciousness: Brain, states of awareness, and mysticism.* New York: Harper & Row, 1979. [7]

Snyder, S. H. Dopamine receptors, neuroleptics, and schizophrenia. *American Journal of Psychiatry,* 1981, *138,* 460–464. [23]

Snyder, S. H. Drug and neurotransmitter receptors in the brain. *Science,* 1984, *224,* 22–31. [3]

Soldatos, C. R., J. D. Kales, M. B. Scharf, E. O. Bixler, and **A. Kales.** Cigarette smoking associated with sleep difficulty. *Science,* 1980, 551–552. [7]

Solomon, R. L. The opponent-process theory of acquired motivation: The costs of pleasure and the benefits of pain. *American Psychologist.* 1980. *35,* 691–712. [12]

Sopchak, A. L., and **A. M. Sutherland.** Pyschological impact of cancer and its treatment: VII. Exogenous sex hormones and their relation to lifelong adaptations in women with metastatic cancer of the breast. *Cancer,* 1960, *13,* 528–531. [13]

Sorenson, R. C. *Adolescent sexuality in contemporary America.* New York: World, 1973. [13]

Sowell, T. New light on black I.Q. *The New York Times Magazine,* March 27, 1977, pp. 56–62. [20]

Spanos, N. P. Witchcraft in histories of psychiatry: A critical analysis and an alternative conceptualization. *Psychological Bulletin,* 1978, *85,* 417–439. [23]

Spence, J. T., J. W. Cotton, B. J. Underwood, and **C. P. Duncan.** *Elementary statistics* (3rd ed.). Englewood Cliffs, N.J.: Prentice-Hall, 1976. [2]

Sperry, R. W. The great cerebral commisure. *Scientific American,* January 1964, 110. [3]

Sperry, R. W. Left-brain, right-brain. *Saturday Review,* 1975, *2,* 30–33. [3]

Sperry, R. W. Changing concepts of consciousness and free will. *Perspectives in Biology and Medicine,* 1976, *20,* 9–19. [7]

Sperry, R. W. Bridging science and values: A unifying view of mind and brain. *American Psychologist,* 1977, *32,* 237–245. [7]

Spiker, D., and **M. Ricks.** Visual self-recognition in autistic children: Developmental relationships. *Child Development,* 1984, *55,* 214–225. [14]

Spitzer, L., and **J. Rodin.** Human eating behavior: A critical review of studies in normal weight and overweight individuals. *Appetite: Journal for intake research,* 1981, *2,* 293–329. [12]

Spitzer, R. L. More on pseudoscience in science and the case for psychiatric diagnosis: A critique of D. L. Rosenhan's "On being sane in insane places" and "The contextual nature of psychiatric diagnosis." *Archives of General Psychiatry,* 1976, *33,* 459–470. [22]

Spitzer, R. L., J. B. W. Forman, and **J. Nee.** DSM-III field trials: I. Initial interrater diagnostic reliability. *American Journal of Psychiatry,* 1979, *136,* 815–817. [22]

Spitzer, R. L., A. E. Skodol, M. Gibbon, and **J. B. W. Williams.** *Psychopathology: A case book.* New York: McGraw-Hill, 1983. [22]

Spring, C., and **C. Capps.** Encoding speed, rehearsal, and probed recall of dyslexic boys. *Journal of Educational Psychology,* 1974, *66,* 780–786. [16]

Springer, S. P., and **G. Deutsch.** *Left brain, right brain.* San Francisco: Freeman, 1981. [3, 7]

Squire, L. R., and **P. C. Slater.** Bilateral and unilateral ECT: Effects on verbal and nonverbal memory. *American Journal of Psychiatry,* 1978, *135,* 1316–1320. [9, 24]

Squire, L. R., P. C. Slater, and **P. L. Miller.** Retrograde amnesia and bilateral electroconvulsive therapy. *Archives of General Psychiatry,* 1981, *38,* 89–95. [9, 24]

Sroufe, L. A. Attachment and the roots of competence. *Human Nature,* 1977, 50–57. [17]

Stallone, F., E. Shelley, J. Mendlewicz, and **R. R. Fieve.** The use of lithium in affective disorders. III: A double-blind study of prophylaxis in bipolar illness. *American Journal of Psychiatry,* 1973, *130,* 1006–1010. [24]

Stanford Computer Science Department. *Heuristic programming project.* Stanford, Calif.: Stanford University, 1980. [10]

Stapp, J., and **R. Fulcher.** The employment of APA members: 1982. *American Psychologist,* 1983, *38,* 1298–1320. [1]

Steele, B. F., and **H. Alexander.** Long-term effects of sexual abuse in childhood. In P. B. Mrazek and C. H. Kempe (Eds.), *Sexually abused children and their families.* New York: Pergamon, 1981. [13]

Stein, A. H., and **M. M. Bailey.** The socialization of achievement orientation in females. *Psychological Bulletin,* 1973, *80,* 345–366. [12]

Steinberg, L. D., E. Greenberger, L. Garduque, M. Ruggiero, and **A. Vaux.** The effects of working on adolescent development. *Developmental Psychology,* 1982, *18,* 385–395. [17]

Steiner, J. E. Human facial expressions in response to taste and smell stimulation. In H. Reese and L. P. Lipsitt (Eds.), *Advances in child development and behavior.* Vol. 13. New York: Academic Press, 1979. [3, 14]

Sterman, M. B. Biofeedback and epilepsy. *Human Nature,* May 1978, *1,* 50–57. [21]

Stern, D. N. Mother and infant at play: The dyadic interaction involving facial, vocal, and gaze behavior. In M. Lewis and L. A. Rosenbloom (Eds.), *The effect of the infant on its caregiver.* New York: Basic Books, 1974, [14]

Stern, W. *The psychological methods of testing intelligence.* Baltimore: Warwick & York, 1914. [20]

Sternberg, R. J. *Intelligence, information-processing, and analogical reasoning: The componential analysis of human abilities.* Hillsdale, N.J.: Lawrence Erlbaum, 1977. [10]

Sternberg, R. J. Testing and cognitive psychology. *American Psychologist,* 1981, *36,* 1181–1189. [20]

Sternberg, R. J. Toward a triarchic theory of human intelligence. *The Behavioral and Brain Sciences,* 1984, *7,* 269–315. [20]

Sternberg, S. High-speed scanning in human memory. *Science,* 1966, *153,* 652–654. [9]

Sternglanz, S. H., and **L. A. Serbin.** Sex role stereotyping in children's television programs. *Developmental Psychology,* 1974, *10,* 710–715. [17]

Stevens, C. F. The neuron. *Scientific American,* 1979, *241,* 55–65. [3]

Stevens, S. S. On the psychophysical law. *Psychological Review,* 1957, *64,* 153–181. [5]

Stewart, K. Dream theory in Malaya. In C. T. Tart (Ed.), *Altered states of consciousness.* New York: Doubleday, 1972. [7]

Stoyva, J. Self-regulation and the stress-related disorders: A perspective on biofeedback. In D. I. Mostofsky (Ed.), *Behavior control and modification of physiological activity.* Englewood Cliffs, N.J.: Prentice-Hall, 1976. [3]

Stratton, G. M. Some preliminary experiments on vision without inversion of the retinal image. *Psychological Review,* 1896, *3,* 611–617. [6]

Strauss, J. S., W. T. Carpenter, and **J. J. Bartko.** The diagnosis and understanding of schizophrenia: II. Speculations on the processes that underlie schizophrenic symptoms and signs. *Schizophrenia Bulletin*, 1974, *11*, 61–76. [22]

Strauss, M. E., W. C. Foureman, and **S. D. Parwatikar.** Schizophrenics' size estimations of thematic stimuli. *Journal of Abnormal Psychology*, 1974, *83*, 117–123. [22]

Straw, R. B. Meta-analysis of deinstitutionalization in mental health. Unpublished doctoral dissertation, Northwestern University, 1982. [24]

Strayer, F. D., and **J. Strayer.** An ethological analysis of social agonism and dominance relations among preschool children. *Child Development*, 1976, *47*, 980–989. [17]

Strayer, J. Social conflict and peer group status. Paper presented at Biennial Meeting of the Society for Research in Child Development, New Orleans, March 1977. [17]

Street, R. F. A gestalt completion test. New York: Bureau of Publications, Teachers College, Columbia University, 1931. [6]

Streissguth, A. P., H. M. Barr, and **D. C. Martin.** Maternal alcohol use and neonatal habituation assessed with the Brazelton scale. *Child Development*, 1983, *54*, 1109–1118. [14]

Streissguth, A. P., S. Landesman-Dwyer, J. C. Martin, and **D. W. Smith.** Teratogenic effects of alcohol in humans and laboratory animals. *Science*, 1980, *209*, 353–361. [14]

Streissguth, A. P., D. C. Martin, H. M. Barr, B. M. Sandman, G. L. Kirchner, and **B. L. Darby.** Intrauterine alcohol and nicotine exposure: Attention and reaction time in 4-year-old children. *Developmental Psychology*, 1984, *20*, 533–541. [14]

Stunkard, A. J. From explanation to action in psychosomatic medicine: The case of obesity. *Psychosomatic Medicine*, 1975, *37*, 195–236. [21]

Stunkard, A. J. Behavioral medicine and beyond: The example of obesity. In O. F. Pomerleau and J. P. Brady (Eds.), *Behavioral medicine: Theory and practice.* Baltimore: Williams & Wilkins, 1979. [21]

Suedfeld, P. Changes in intellectual performance and in susceptibility to influence. In J. P. Zubek (Ed.), *Sensory deprivation: Fifteen years of research.* New York: Appleton-Century-Crofts, 1969. [7]

Suedfeld, P. *Restricted Environmental Stimulation: Research and clinical applications.* New York: Wiley, 1980. [7]

Suedfeld, P., C. Roy, and **P. B. Landon.** Restricted Environmental Stimulation Therapy in the treatment of essential hypertension. *Behaviour Research and Therapy*, 1982, *20*, 553–560. [7]

Sugarman, S. *Children's early thought: Developments in classification.* New York: Cambridge University Press, 1983. [15]

Suomi, S. J., and **H. F. Harlow.** Depressive behavior in young monkeys subjected to vertical chamber confinement. *Journal of Comparative and Physiological Psychology*, 1972, *80*, 11–18. [17]

Super, C. M. Environmental effects on motor development: The case of "African infant precocity." *Developmental Medicine and Child Neurology*, 1976, *18*, 561–567. [14]

Super, C. M. Cognitive development: Looking across at growing up. In C. M. Super and S. Harkness (Eds.), *New directions for child development.* No. 8. *Anthropological perspectives on child development.* San Francisco: Jossey-Bass, 1980. [15]

Surveying Crime. Report of the Panel for the Evaluation of Crime Surveys. Washington, D.C.: National Academy of Sciences, 1976. [2]

Szasz, T. S. *The myth of mental illness: Foundations of a theory of personal conduct.* New York: Harper & Row, 1961. [22, 23]

Tajfel, H. *Human groups and social categories.* Cambridge: Cambridge University Press, 1981. [26]

Talovic, S. A., S. A. Mednick, F. Schulsinger, and **I. R. H. Falloon.** Schizophrenia in high-risk subjects: Prognostic maternal characteristics. *Journal of Abnormal Psychology*, 1980, *89*, 501–504. [23]

Tart, C. T. *States of consciousness.* New York: Dutton, 1975. [7, 19]

Tavris, C. A., and **C. Offir.** *The longest war: Sex differences in perspective.* New York: Harcourt Brace Jovanovich, 1977. [17]

Taylor, D. A. *Mind.* New York: Simon & Schuster, 1982. [7]

Taylor, S. E. A categorization approach to stereotyping. In D. L. Hamilton (Ed.), *Cognitive processes in stereotyping and intergroup behavior.* Hillsdale, N.J.: Lawrence Erlbaum, 1981. [26]

Taylor, S. E. *Health psychology.* New York: Random House, 1986. [21]

Taylor, S. E., S. T. Fiske, N. L. Etcoff, and **A. J. Ruderman.** Categorical and contextual bases of person memory and stereotyping. *Journal of Personality and Social Psychology*, 1978, *36*, 778–793. [26]

Tedeschi, J. T., B. R. Schlenker, and **T. V. Bonoma.** Cognitive dissonance: Private ratiocination or public spectacle? *American Psychologist*, 1971, *26*, 685–695. [12]

Teller, D. Y. Color vision in infants. In *Development of perception.* Vol. 2. New York: Academic Press, 1981. [14]

Terman, L. M. *The measurement of intelligence.* Boston: Houghton Mifflin, 1916. [20]

Terman, L. M., and **M. A. Merrill.** *Stanford-Binet Intelligence Scale: Manual for the third revision, Form L-M.* Boston: Houghton Mifflin, 1973. [20]

Terrace, H. S., L. A. Petitto, R. J. Sanders, and **T. G. Bever.** Can an ape create a sentence? *Science*, 1979, *206*, 891–902. [16]

Thomas, E. L., and **H. A. Robinson.** *Improving reading in every class: A sourcebook for teachers.* Boston: Allyn and Bacon, 1972. [9]

Thomas, H. Unfolding the baby's mind: The infant's selection of visual stimuli. *Psychological Review*, 1973, *80*, 468. [14]

Thompson, C. R., and **R. M. Church.** An explanation of the language of a chimpanzee. *Science*, 1980, *208*, 313–314. [16]

Thompson, L. High-tech hearing aids for the deaf. *San Jose Mercury News*, June 12, 1984, pp. C1–2. [5]

Thompson, R. A., M. E. Lamb, and **D. Estes.** Stability of infant-mother attachment and its relationship to changing life circumstances in an unselected middle-class sample. *Child Development*, 1982, *53*, 144–148. [17]

Thompson, S. C. Will it hurt less if I can control it? A complex answer to a simple question. *Psychological Bulletin*, 1981, *90*, 89–101. [21]

Thorndike, E. L. Animal intelligence. *Psychological Review Monograph*, 1898, 2. [8]

Thorndike, R. L. *Reading comprehension: Education in fifteen countries.* New York: Wiley, 1973. [16]

Tinbergen, N. *The study of instinct.* New York: Oxford University Press, 1973. [14]

Tolman, E. C. Cognitive maps in rats and men. *Psychological Review*, 1948, *55*, 189–208. [8]

Toman, W. *Family constellation: Its effect on personality and social behavior* (3rd ed.). New York: Springer, 1976. [26]

Tonkova-Yampol'skaya, R. V. Development of speech intonation in infants during the first two years of life. In C. A. Ferguson and D. I. Slobin (Eds.), *Studies of child language development.* New York: Holt, Rinehart & Winston, 1973. [16]

Torgersen, A. M., and **E. Kringlen.** Genetic aspects of temperament differences in twins. *Journal of American Academy of Child Psychiatry*, 1978, *17*, 433–444. [17]

Tourangeau, R., and **P. C. Ellsworth.** The role of facial response in the experience of emotion. *Journal of Personality and Social Psychology*, 1979, *37*, 1519–1531. [11]

Trabasso, T., A. G. McLanahan, A. M. Isen, C. A. Riley, P. Dolecki, and **T. Tucker.** How do children solve class inclusion problems? In R. S. Siegler (Ed.), *Children's thinking: What develops?* Hillsdale, N.J.: Lawrence Erlbaum, 1978. [15]

Trabasso, T. R., and **G. H. Bower.** *Atten-*

tion in learning: Theory and research. New York: Wiley, 1968. [8, 10]

Travis, L. E. The effect of a small audience upon hand-eye coordination. *Journal of Abnormal and Social Psychology*, 1925, *20*, 142–146. [27]

Triplett, N. The dynamogenic factors in peacemaking and competition. *American Journal of Psychology*, 1897, *9*, 507–533. [27]

Trivers, R. L. The evolution of reciprocal altruism. *Quarterly Review of Biology*, 1971, *46*, 35–57. [4, 27]

Trowell, I. Telephone services. In L. D. Hankoff and B. Einsidler (Eds.), *Suicide: Theory and clinical aspects.* Littleton, Mass.: PSG Publishing, 1979. [24]

Tryon, R. C. Genetic differences in maze learning in rats. *Thirty-Ninth Yearbook, National Society for the Study of Education (Part I).* Bloomington, Ill.: Public School Publishing, 1940. [4]

Tuchman-Duplessis, H. *Drug effects on the fetus.* Sydney: ADIS Press, 1975. [14]

Tulkin, S. R., and **J. Kagan.** Mother-child interaction in the first year of life. *Child Development*, 1972, *43*, 31–41. [17]

Tulving, E., and **J. Psotka.** Retroactive inhibition in free recall: Inaccessibility of information available in the memory store. *Journal of Experimental Psychology*, 1971, *87*, 1–8. [9]

Tulving, E., and **D. M. Thomson.** Encoding specificity and retrieval processes in episodic memory. *Psychological Review*, 1973, *80*, 352–373. [9]

Turk, D. C., D. H. Meichenbaum, and **W. H. Berman.** Application of biofeedback for the regulation of pain: A critical review. *Psychological Bulletin*, 1979, *86*, 1322–1338. [21]

Turkington, C. The growing use, and abuse, of computer testing. *APA Monitor*, 1984, *15* (1), 7+. [20]

Tversky, A., and **D. Kahneman.** Judgment under uncertainty: Heuristics and biases. *Science*, 1973, *185*, 1124–1131. [10]

Tversky, A., and **D. Kahneman.** The framing of decisions and the psychology of choice. *Science*, 1981, *211*, 453–458. [10]

Tversky, A., and **D. Kahneman.** Extensional versus intuitive reasoning: The conjunction fallacy in probability judgment. *Psychological Review*, 1983, *90*, 293–315. [10]

Tversky, A., R. Vallone, and **T. Gilovich.** Misconception of chance processes in basketball. Submitted to *Science*, 1984. [10]

Tversky, B. Distortions in memory for maps. *Cognitive Psychology*, 1981, *13*, 407–433. [8]

Tversky, B., and **K. Hemenway.** Objects, parts, and categories. *Journal of Experimental Psychology: General*, 1984, *113*, 169–193. [10]

Ullman, C. A. Teachers, peers, and tests as predictors of adjustment. *Journal of Educational Psychology*, 1957, *48*, 257–267. [17]

Umbreit, J., and **L. S. Ostrow.** The fetal alcohol syndrome. *Mental Retardation*, 1980, *18*, 109–111. [14]

Unger, R. K., M. Hildebrand, and **T. Madar.** Physical attractiveness and assumptions about social deviance: Some sex-by-sex comparisons. *Personality and Social Psychology Bulletin*, 1982, *8*, 293–301. [26]

U.S. Bureau of the Census. *Statistical abstract of the United States, 1982–83* (103rd ed.). Washington, D.C.: U.S. Government Printing Office, 1982. [15]

U.S. Congress, Select Committee on Aging and Committee on Energy and Commerce, Ninety-Eighth Congress. Alzheimer's disease. Joint Hearing. Washington, D.C.: U.S. Government Printing Office, 1984. [3]

U.S. Department of Health and Human Services. *The fourth special report to the United States Congress on alcohol and health.* Washington, D.C.: Alcohol, Drug Abuse, and Mental Health Administration, January 1981. [22]

Valenstein, E. S. *Brain control.* New York: Wiley-Interscience, 1973. [24]

Van Kammen, D. P. Y-aminobutyric acid (GABA) and the dopamine hypothesis of schizophrenia. *American Journal of Psychiatry*, 1977, *134*, 138–143. [23]

Vance, E. B., and **N. W. Wagner.** Written descriptions of orgasm: A study of sex differences. *Archives of Sexual Behavior*, 1976, *5*, 87–98 [13]

Vernon, P. Psychological effects of air raids. *Journal of Abnormal and Social Psychology*, 1941, *36*, 457–476. [21]

Vischi, T. R., K. R. Jones, E. L. Shank, and **L. H. Lima.** *The alcohol, drug abuse, and mental health national data book.* Washington, D.C.: U.S. Government Printing Office, 1980. [14]

Vitz, P. C. Affect as a function of stimulus variation. *Journal of Experimental Psychology*, 1966, *71*, 74–79. [12]

von Senden, M. *Space and sight: The perception of space and shape in the congenitally blind before and after operations.* New York, 1960. [6]

Vroom, V. H. *Work and motivation.* New York: Wiley, 1964. [28]

Vroom, V. H., and **P. W. Yetton.** *Leadership and decision-making.* Pittsburgh: University of Pittsburgh Press, 1973. [28]

Vroom, V. H., and **P. W. Yetton.** In K. N. Wexley and G. A. Yukl (Eds.), *Organizational behavior and industrial psychology.* New York: Oxford, 1975. [28]

Vygotsky, L. S. *Thought and language.* Cambridge, Mass.: MIT Press, 1962. [15]

Wadden, T. A., and **C. H. Anderson.** The clinical use of hypnosis. *Psychological Bulletin*, 1982, *91*, 215–243. [7]

Waddington, C. H. *The strategy of the genes.* New York: Macmillan, 1957. [14]

Wagner, A. R. Stimulus validity and stimulus selection in associative learning. In N. J. Mackintosh and W. K. Honig (Eds.), *Fundamental issues in associative learning.* Halifax: Dalhousie University Press, 1969. [8]

Wagner, R. V. Complementary needs, role expectations, interpersonal attraction, and the stability of working relationships. *Journal of Personality and Social Psychology*, 1975, *32*, 116–124. [26]

Wahba, M. A., and **L. B. Bridwell.** Maslow reconsidered: A review of research on the need hierarchy theory. *Organizational Behavior and Human Performance*, 1976, *15*, 212–240. [28]

Walk, R. D., J. D. Sheperd, and **D. R. Miller.** Attention as an alternative to self-induced motion for perceptual behavior of kittens. *Society for Neuroscience Abstracts*, 1978, *4*, 129. [6]

Walker, J. I., and **J. O. Cavenar.** Vietnam veterans: Their problems continue. *Journal of Nervous and Mental Disease*, 1982, *170*, 174–180. [21]

Wallace, R. K., and **H. Benson.** The physiology of meditation. *Scientific American*, 1972, *226*, 84–90. [7]

Wallace, W. L. Review of the Scholastic Aptitude Test. In O. K. Buros (Ed.), *The seventh mental measurements yearbook.* Highland Park, N.J.: Gryphon Press, 1972. [20]

Wallas, G. *The art of thought.* New York: Harcourt Brace, 1962. [10]

Walsh, D. A. The development of visual information processes in adulthood and old age. In F. I. M. Craik and S. Trehub (Eds.), *Advances in the study of communication and affect.* Vol. 8. *Aging and cognitive processes.* New York: Plenum, 1982. [15]

Walsh, D. A. Age differences in learning and memory. In D. S. Woodruff and J. E. Birren (Eds.), *Aging: Scientific perspectives and social issues* (2nd ed.). Monterey, Calif.: Brooks/Cole, 1983. [15]

Walster, E., and **L. Festinger.** The effectiveness of "overheard" persuasive communications. *Journal of Abnormal and Social Psychology*, 1962, *65*, 395–402. [25]

Waltz, D. Generating semantic descriptions from drawings of scenes with shadows. AI-TR-271, Project MAC, Massachusetts Institute of Technology. Reprinted in P. H. Winston (Ed.), *The psychology of computer vision.* New York: McGraw-Hill, 1975. [6]

Wanous, J. P., and **R. A. Dean.** The effects of realistic job previews on hiring bank tellers. *Journal of Applied Psychology*, 1984, *69*. *[28]*

Wanous, J. P., and **A. Zwany.** A cross-sectional test of the need hierarchy theory. *Organizational Behavior and Human Performance,* 1977, *18,* 78–79. [28]

Warren, R. M. Perceptual restoration of missing speech sounds. *Science,* 1970, *167,* 392–393. [6]

Warrington, E. K., and **H. I. Sanders.** The fate of old memories. *Quarterly Journal of Experimental Psychology,* 1971, *23,* 432–442. [15]

Warrington, E. K., and **L. Weiskrantz.** New method of testing long-term retention with special reference to amnesiac patients. *Nature,* 1968, *217,* 972-974. [9]

Washington v. Davis. 426 U.S. 299 (1976). [28]

Wason, P. C., and **P. N. Johnson-Laird.** *Psychology of reasoning: Structure and content.* Cambridge, Mass.: Harvard University Press, 1972. [15]

Watson, C. G., and **C. Buranen.** The frequency and identification of false positive conversion reactions. *Journal of Nervous and Mental Disease,* 1979, *167,* 243–247. [22]

Watson, J. B. Psychology as the behaviorist views it. *Psychological Review,* 1913, *20,* 158–177. [1]

Watson, J. S. Smiling, cooing, and "the game." *Merrill-Palmer Quarterly of Behavior and Development,* 1972, *18,* 323–339. [15]

Watson, R. I. *The great psychologists: From Aristotle to Freud.* Philadelphia: Lippincott, 1963. [1]

Watzlawick, P., J. Beavin, and **D. Jackson.** *Pragmatics of human communication: A study of interaction patterns, pathologies, and paradoxes.* New York: Norton, 1967. [24]

Watzlawick, R., J. Weakland, and **R. Fisch.** *Change: Principles of problem formation and problem resolution.* New York: W. W. Norton, 1974. [24]

Waxenberg, S. E. Psychotherapeutic and dynamic implications of recent research on female sexual functioning. In G. D. Goldman and D. S. Milman (Eds.), *Modern woman: Her psychology and sexuality.* Springfield, Ill. Charles C Thomas, 1969. [13]

Waynbaum, I. *La physionomie humaine: Son mécanisme et son role social.* Paris: Alcan, 1907. [11]

Webb, L. J., R. S. Gold, E. E. Johnstone, and **C. C. Diclemente.** Accuracy of DSM-III diagnoses following a training program. *American Journal of Psychiatry,* 1981, *138,* 376–378. [22]

Webb, W. B. Sleep and dream. In B. B. Wolman (Ed.), *Handbook of general psychology.* Englewood Cliffs, N.J.: Prentice-Hall, 1973. [7]

Webb, W. B. The nature of dreams. In D. Goleman and R. J. Davidson (Eds.), *Consciousness: Brain, states of awareness and mysticism.* New York: Harper & Row, 1979. [7]

Webb, W. B., and **J. Kersey.** Recall of dreams and the probability of stage 1—REM sleep. *Perceptual and Motor Skills,* 1967, *24,* 627–630. [7]

Weber, M. *The Protestant ethic and the spirit of capitalism.* New York: Scribner's, 1904. [12]

Webster, R., M. M. Steinhardt, and **M. Senter.** Changes in infants' vocalizations as a function of differential acoustic stimulation. *Developmental Psychology,* 1972, *7,* 39–43. [14]

Wechsler, D. *Wechsler Adult Intelligence Scale manual.* New York: Psychological Corporation, 1955. [20]

Wechsler, D. *The measurement and appraisal of adult intelligence* (14th ed.). Baltimore: William & Wilkins, 1958. [20]

Weil, A. T., N. Zinberg, and **J. M. Nelsen.** Clinical and psychological effects of marijuana in man. *Science,* 1968, *162,* 1234–1242. [7]

Weiner, B. *Theories of motivation: From mechanism to cognition.* Chicago: Markham, 1972. [12]

Weiner, N. Determinants and behavioral consequences of pay satisfaction: A comparison of two models. *Personnel Psychology,* 1980 *33,* 741–758. [28]

Weingartner, H., W. Adefris, J. E. Eich, and **D. Murphy.** Encoding-imagery specificity in alcohol state-dependent learning. *Journal of Experimental Psychology: Human Learning and Memory,* 1976, *2,* 83–87. [9]

Weisberg, R. W. *Memory, thought, and behavior.* New York: Oxford University Press, 1980. [10]

Weiskrantz, L., E. K. Warrington, M. D. Sanders, and **J. Marshall.** Visual capacity of the hemianopic field following a restricted occipital ablation. *Brain,* 1974, *97,* 709–728. [7]

Weiss, J. M. Psychosomatic Disorders. In J. D. Maser and M. E. P. Seligman (Eds.), *Psychopathology: Experimental models.* San Francisco: W. H. Freeman, 1977. [21]

Wellman, H. M., K. Ritter, and **J. H. Flavell.** Deliberate memory behavior in the delayed reactions of very young children. *Developmental Psychology,* 1975, *11,* 780–787. [15]

Wellman, H. M., S. C. Somerville, and **R. J. Haake.** Development of search procedures in real-life spatial environments. *Developmental Psychology,* 1979, *15,* 530–542. [15]

Wells, G. L., and **R. E. Petty.** The effects of overt head movement on persuasion: Compatibility and incompatibility of responses. *Basic and Applied Social Psychology,* 1980, *1,* 219–230. [11]

Wendt, G. R. Vestibular functions. In S. S. Stevens (Ed.), *Handbook of experimental psychology.* New York: Wiley, 1951. [5]

Werner, A. Sexual dysfunction in college men and women. *American Journal of Psychiatry,* 1975, *132,* 164–168. [13]

Werner, J. S., and **M. Perlmutter.** Development of visual memory in infants. In H. W. Reese and L. P. Lipsitt (Eds.), *Advances in child development and behavior.* Vol. 13. New York: Academic Press, 1979. [15]

Wertheimer, M. Untersuchunger zur Lehre von der Gestalt. *Psychologisches Forschung.* 1923, *4,* 301–350. [6]

White, B. L. An experimental approach to the effects of experience on early human behavior. In J. P. Hill (Ed.), *Minnesota Symposia on Child Psychology.* Vol. 1. Minneapolis: University of Minnesota Press, 1967. [14]

White, B. L. *Human infants: Experience and psychological development.* Englewood Cliffs, N.J.: Prentice-Hall, 1971. [14]

White, S. H., and **D. B. Pillemer.** Childhood amnesia and the development of a socially accessible memory system. In J. F. Kihlstrom and F. J. Evans (Eds.), *Function disorders of memory.* Hillsdale, N.J.: Lawrence Erlbaum, 1979. [15]

Whitfield, I. C. The organization of the auditory pathways. *Journal of sound and vibration research,* 1968, *8,* 108–117. [5]

Whitlock, F. A. The aetiology of hysteria. *Acta Psychiatrica Scandinavica,* 1967, *43,* 144–162. [22]

Whorf, B. L. Science and linguistics. In J. B. Carroll (Ed.), *Language, thought, and reality: Selected writings of Benjamin Lee Whorf.* Cambridge, Mass.: MIT Press, 1956. [16]

Whybrow, P. C., and **A. J. Prange, Jr.** A hypothesis of thyroid-catecholamine-receptor interaction. *Archives of General Psychiatry,* 1981, *38,* 106–113. [23]

Wichman, H. Effects of isolation and communication in a two-person game. *Journal of Personality and Social Psychology,* 1970, *16,* 114–120. [27]

Wickelgren, W. A. *How to solve problems.* San Francisco: W. H. Freeman, 1974. [10]

Wicker, A. W. An examination of the "other variables" explanation of attitude-behavior inconsistency. *Journal of Personality and Social Psychology,* 1971, *19,* 18–30. [25]

Wicklund, R. A., and **J. W. Brehm.** *Perspectives on cognitive dissonance.* Hillsdale, N.J.: Lawrence Erlbaum, 1976. [12]

Wilkes, A. L., and **R. A. Kennedy.** Relationship between pausing and retrieval latency in sentences of varying grammatical form. *Journal of Experimental Psychology,* 1969, *79,* 241–245. [16]

Williams, B. M. Hypnosis is like a scalpel: You wouldn't want it wielded by your janitor. *Psychology Today,* November 1974, pp. 126–127. [7]

Williams, M. D., and **J. D. Hollan.** The process of retrieval from very long-term memory. *Cognitive Science,* 1981, *5,* 87–119. [9]

Williams, R. L., I. Karacan, and **C. J. Hursch.** *EEG of human sleep: Clinical applications.* New York: Wiley, 1974. [7]

Wilson, E. O. *Sociobiology: The new synthesis.* Cambridge, Mass.: Harvard University Press, 1975. [4, 5, 16, 27]

Wilson, E. O. *On human nature.* Cambridge, Mass.: Harvard University Press, 1978. [4]

Winch, R. F. *Mate selection: A study of complementary needs.* New York: Harper & Row, 1958. [26]

Wine, J., and **F. Krasne.** The cellular analysis of invertebrate learning. In T. Teyler (Ed.), *Brain and learning.* Stamford, Conn.: Greylock Publishing, 1978. [3]

Winer, G. A. Class-inclusion reasoning in children: A review of the empirical literature. *Child Development,* 1980, *51,* 309–328. [15]

Winget, C., M. Kramer, and **R. Whitman.** Dreams and demography. *Canadian Psychiatric Association Journal,* 1972, *17,* 203–208. [27]

Witkin, H. A., S. A. Mednick, F. Schulsinger, E. Bakkestrom, K. O. Christiansen, D. R. Goodenough, K. Hirchhorn, C. Lunsteen, D. R. Owens, J. Philip, D. B. Reuben, and **M. Stocking.** Criminality in XYY and XXY men. *Science,* 1976, *193,* 547–555. [27]

Wolff, P. H. The natural history of crying and other vocalizations in early infancy. In B. M. Foss (Ed.), *Determinants of infant behavior.* Vol. 4. London: Methuen, 1969. [16]

Wolff, S., and **H. G. Wolff.** *Human gastric function.* New York: Oxford University Press, 1947. [11]

Wolpe, J. *Psychotherapy by reciprocal inhibition.* Stanford, Calif.: Stanford University Press, 1958. [24]

Wolpe, J. *The practice of behavior therapy* (2nd ed.). New York: Pergamon Press, 1973. [22]

Wolpe, J. Cognition and causation in human behavior and its therapy. *American Psychologist,* 1978, *33,* 437–446. [24]

Wolpe, J., and **D. Wolpe.** *Our useless fears.* Boston: Houghton Mifflin, 1981. [24]

Woodruff, R. A., P. J. Clayton, and **S. B. Guze.** Is everyone depressed? *American Journal of Psychiatry,* 1975, *132,* 627–628. [22]

Woodworth, R. S. *Experimental psychology.* New York: Holt, Rinehart & Winston, 1938. [12]

Woolsey, C. N. Organization of the cortical auditory system. In W. A. Rosenblith (Ed.), *Sensory communication.* New York: Wiley, 1961. [3]

Worringham, C. J., and **D. M. Messick.** Social facilitation of running: An unobtrusive study. *Journal of Social Psychology,* 1983, *121,* 23–29. [27]

Wurtman, R. J. Nutrients that modify brain function. *Scientific American,* 1982, 50–59. [3]

Wynder, E. L., T. Kajitani, J. Kuno, J. C. Lucas, Jr., A. DePalo, and **J. Farrow.** A comparison of survival rates between American and Japanese patients with breast cancer. *Surgery, Gynecology, Obstetrics,* 1963, *117,* 196–200. [21]

Wynne, L. C., M. T. Singer, J. J. Bartko, and **M. L. Toohey.** Schizophrenics and their families: Recent research on parental communication. In J. M. Tanner (Ed.), *Psychiatric research: The widening perspective.* New York: International Universities Press, 1975. [23]

Yates, A. J. *Biofeedback and the modification of behavior.* New York: Plenum, 1980. [7,21]

Yerkes, R. M., and **J. D. Dodson.** The relation of strength of stimulus to rapidity of habit formation. *Journal of Comparative Neurology and Psychology,* 1908, *18,* 459–482. [19]

Yonas, A., W. Cleaves, and **L. Pettersen.** Development of sensitivity to pictorial depth. *Science,* 1978, *200,* 77–79. [14]

Youniss, J. *Parents and peers in social development: A Sullivan-Piaget perspective.* Chicago: University of Chicago Press, 1980. [17]

Zaidel, E. Language comprehension in the right hemisphere following cerebral commisurotomy. In A. Caramazza and E. Zurif (Eds.), *Langauge acquisition and language breakdown: Parallels and divergences.* Baltimore: Johns Hopkins University Press, 1978. [3]

Zajonc, R. B. Social facilitation. *Science,* 1965, *149,* 269–274. [27]

Zajonc, R. The attitudinal effects of mere exposure. *Journal of Personality and Social Psychology Monographs,* 1968, *9* (Part 2), 1–27. [11, 25]

Zajonc, R. B. Family configuration and intelligence. *Science,* 1976, *192,* 227–236. [20]

Zajonc, R. B. Altruism, envy, competitiveness, and the common good. In V. Derlaga and J. Grzelak (Eds.), *Cooperation and helping behavior.* New York: Academic Press, 1982. [27]

Zajonc, R. B. Emotion and Facial Efference: A theory reclaimed. *Science,* 1985, *228,* 15–21. [11]

Zajonc, R. B. The decline and rise of scholastic aptitude scores. *American Psychologist,* in press. [20]

Zajonc, R. B., H. Markus, and **G. B. Markus.** The birth order puzzle. *Journal of Personality and Social Psychology,* 1979, *37,* 1325–1341. [20]

Zajonc, R. B., W. R. Wilson, and **D. W. Rajecki.** Affiliation and social discrimination produced by brief exposure in day-old domestic chicks. *Animal Behavior,* 1975, *23,* 131–138. [26]

Zanna, M. P., and **J. Cooper.** Dissonance and the pill: An attribution approach to studying the arousal properties of dissonance. *Journal of Personality and Social Psychology* 1974, *29,* 703–709. [12]

Zanna, M. P., C. A. Kiesler, and **P. A. Pilkonis.** Positive and negative attitudinal affect established by classical conditioning. *Journal of Personality and Social Psychology,* 1970, *14,* 321–328. [25]

Zelnick, M., J. F. Kantner, and **K. Ford.** *Sex and pregnancy in adolescence.* Beverly Hills, Calif.: Sage, 1981. [17]

Zeskind, P. S. Cross-cultural differences in maternal perceptions of low- and high-risk infants. *Child Development,* 1983, *54,* 1119–1128. [17]

Zillman, D. Excitation transfer in communication-mediated aggressive behavior. *Journal of Experimental Social Psychology,* 1971, *7,* 419–434. [11]

Zimbardo, P. G., A. Cohen, M. Weisenberg, L. Dworkin, and **I. Firestone.** The control of experimental pain. In P. G. Zimbardo, A. Cohen, M. Weisenberg, L. Dworkin, and I. Firestone (Eds.), *The cognitive control of motivation.* Glenview, Ill.: Scott, Foresman, 1969. [12]

Zimbardo, P. G., C. Haney, and **W. C. Banks.** A Pirandellian prison. *The New York Times Magazine,* April 8, 1973, pp. 38–60. [27]

Zimbardo, P. G., M. Weisenberg, I. Firestone, and **B. Levy.** Communicator effectiveness in producing public conformity and private attitude change. *Journal of Personality,* 1965, *33,* 233–255. [25]

Zimmerman, D. W. Sustained performance in rats based on secondary reinforcement. *Journal of Comparative and Physiological Psychology,* 1959, *52,* 353–358. [8]

Zubin, J., and **B. Spring.** Vulnerability: A new view of schizophrenia. *Journal of Abnormal Pycyhology,* 1977, *86,* 103–126. [23]

Zuckerman, D. Learning: Too many sibs put our nation at risk? *Psychology Today,* 1985, *19,* 5–10. [20]

Zuckerman, M. The search for high sensation. *Psychology Today,* 1978, *11,* 30–46. [12]

Zuckerman, M., R. Klorman, D. T. Larrance, and **N. H. Spiegel.** Facial, autonomic, and subjective components of emotion: The facial feedback hypothesis versus externalizer-internalizer distinction. *Journal of Personality and Social Psychology,* 1981, *41,* 929–944. [11]

Zuckerman, M., and **L. Wheeler.** To dispel fantasies about the fantasy-based measure of fear of success. *Psychological Bulletin,* 1975, *82,* 932–946. [12]

GLOSSARY

absolute threshold—the weakest stimulus that produces a sensation. [5]

accommodation—(1) reflexive contraction of lens muscles to focus eyes on nearby objects. (2) the modification of existing schemes to incorporate new knowledge that does not fit them. [5, 15]

acetylcholine (ACH)—neurotransmitter used by the motor neurons of the spinal cord. [3]

achievement motive—the capacity to derive satisfaction by attaining some standard of excellence. [12]

achievement tests—tests constructed to assess the extent of an individual's knowledge about subjects taught in school. [20]

acquisition—(1) the process by which an organism learns the association involved in classical conditioning. (2) the process by which we initially perceive, register, and record information in our memory. [8, 9]

act frequency approach—an approach to personality that claims that we tend to add up all of a person's actions that fit a particular category, then assign a trait to the person on that basis. [19]

active phase—that stage in the course of schizophrenia in which psychotic symptoms predominate. [22]

ad hoc categories—spur-of-the-moment categories constructed to handle particular functions. [10]

adaptation—adjustment in sensory capacity. [5]

adaptive behavior—any behavior that makes an animal function better in its environment. [4]

adaptive radiation—evolutionary pattern in which a group of organisms with a common ancestor diversify so that they can move into a new environmental niche. [4]

additive color mixing—the combining of colored lights. [5]

adjacency pairs—conversational convention in which an utterance by one person tells the other which sort of response is appropriate; common pairs include question/response, summons/answer, etc. [16]

adverse impact—results when the proportion of minority applicants hired after taking an employment test is less than four-fifths of the proportion of majority applicants hired. In such an instance, the courts consider that the test has an adverse impact on minorities. [28]

affect—emotional response. [22]

affective disorder—disturbance of mood. [22]

afterimage—a sensory impression that persists after removal of the stimulus. [5]

aggression—any act that is intended to cause pain, damage, or suffering to another. [27]

agnosia—an inability to recognize sounds. [3]

algorithm—a simple set of rules arranged in a logical order that will solve all instances of a particular set of problems. [10]

altricial—helpless (referring to the young of a species) [14]

altruism—prosocial behavior showing unselfish concern springing from a combination of emotional distress at another's plight and an understanding of her or his needs. [17]

Alzheimer's disease—a debilitating brain disease characterized by increasingly serious memory disorder and deterioration of attention, judgment, and personality; most common among older adults. [3]

amnesia—partial or total loss of memory. [3, 9, 22]

amplitude—intensity of a sound wave, usually expressed in decibels. [5]

amygdala—a structure in the limbic system. [3]

anal stage—the stage in psychosexual development during which the child's attention shifts to the anus and the pleasures of holding in and pushing out feces. [17, 18]

analogy—a parallel between two systems whose parts are related in a similar way. [10]

analytic psychology—a school of psychoanalysis founded in 1913 by Carl Jung. [18]

anchoring—a bias in judgment, resulting from the effect of the starting point from which the decision was made. [10]

androgen insensitivity syndrome—the condition of a genetically male fetus whose body cells fail to respond to androgen; the baby will be born genetically male but with the external anatomy of a female. [13]

androgens—male sex hormones. [13]

androgynous—having gender roles that embrace characteristics of both sexes. [17]

anterograde amnesia—a condition in which people are unable to lay down new memories. [9]

antisocial personality. [22] See **sociopath.**

anvil—one of the ossicles. [5]

anxiety—in Freudian theory, a state of psychic pain that alerts the ego to danger; it is akin to fear. [18, 22]

anxiety disorder—a condition in which severe and persistent anxiety interferes with daily functioning. [22]

aphasia—an inability to speak or to understand spoken language. [3]

apparent movement—the perception of motion when a rapid succession of motionless stimuli mimic the changes that occur in true movement. [6]

applied science—the use of basic science to accomplish practical goals. [1]

approach-avoidance conflict—a conflict of two motives, so that satisfying one motive frustrates the other. [19]

aptitude tests—tests designed to find out about an individual's talent or capacity for particular lines of work. [20]

archetypes—in Jung's terms, ancient ideas or images common to all human beings in all eras and all regions of the world and that form the collective unconscious. [18]

arousal—a series of physiological changes, primarily in the autonomic system, that take place when an individual has an emotion. [11]

artifical intelligence (AI)—computer programming that solves problems by following steps similar to those a human being would take. [10]

assimilation—the incorporation of new knowledge through the use of existing schemes. [15]

association—a learned connection between two events. [8]

ataxia—a condition characterized by severe tremors, drunken movements, and loss of balance; due to damage to the cerebellum. [3]

attachment—an emotional bond such as one which is formed between the infant and her or his primary care giver. [17]

attitude—an attraction or aversion toward an object, in which cognitive, affective, motivational, and behavioral processes are implicated. [25]

attribution theories—theories that propose to explain how people attribute personality traits or intentions to others to explain their behavior. [26]

audience inhibition—supression due to concern about others' evaluation of our behavior. [27]

auditory cortex—the area in the temporal lobe of the brain that processes auditory information. [3]

auditory stream segregation—the auditory effect of two simultaneous lines of melody, each with a distinctive quality. [6]

authenticity—living by personal values. [23]

autistic fantasy—a state on the continuum that stretches from normal waking consciousness to dreaming; it lacks any orientation toward reality. [7]

autogenic training—a relaxation procedure that depends on self-suggestion and imagery. [21]

autokinetic movement—an illusion of movement caused by random eye movements, which make a stationary spot appear to move in the dark. [6]

autonomic nervous system—the division of the PNS that regulates the internal environment and is generally involuntary. [3]

availability—a heuristic in which predictions are based on a comparison of the current situation with past examples that readily come to mind. [10]

aversion therapy—therapy in which the client's exposure to stimuli that elicit maladaptive responses is accompanied by aversive stimuli. [24]

aversive learning—learning that relies on such techniques as punishment, escape, and the avoidance of punishment. [8]

avoidance learning—conditioning in which an organism prevents the arrival of an unpleasant stimulus by its response to a warning stimulus. [8]

axon—a long fiber of a neuron that leads away from the cell body. [3]

basal ganglia—a group of brain structures that seem to control movement and coordinate the motor cortex and thalamus. [3]

basic anxiety—in Horney's terms, anxiety arising out of a child's sense of helplessness and isolation. [18]

basic hostility—in Horney's terms, hostility arising from resentment over parental indifference, inconsistency, and interference. [18]

basic level—that level in a hierarchy that seems the most economical for cognitive manipulation; the level that provides the most information. [10]

basic needs—fundamental physiological needs and intermediate psychological needs (such as safety and self-esteem). [12]

basic science—fundamental principles that explain a broad range of facts. [1]

basilar membrane—a membrane supporting the organ of Corti. Movements of this membrane stimulate hair cells, which in turn trigger electrical activity in the auditory nerve. [5]

behavior—anything a person does or experiences, including thoughts, feelings, and dreams. [1]

behavior genetics—the study of inherited patterns of behavior. [4]

behavior rehearsal—a procedure similar to participant modeling, but applied to social behavior. [24]

behavioral medicine. [1] See **health psychology.**

behaviorism—the approach to psychology that limits its study to observable, measurable responses to specific stimuli. [1]

beliefs—knowledge structures about objects and events. [25]

binocular disparity—difference in the retinal image received by each eye; source of information for depth perception. [6]

biofeedback—the provision of a continuous flow of information regarding some physiological function by electronic devices; a person can then learn to attain voluntary control over the monitored function. [7, 21]

biogenic theory—the view that mental disorder has a physical, or organic, cause. [23]

bipolar disorder—a disorder characterized by extreme moods, beginning with a manic episode of euphoria, excitement, and activity, followed by a depressive episode. [22]

birth order—the child's rank in the sequence of births. [26]

blocking—a reliable phenomenon that occurs in all species and in most conditioning situations, in which the conditioning normally caused by CS–UCS pairings can be blocked entirely. [8]

brain stem—a part of the central core of the brain. [3]

branching—evolutionary pattern in which one evolutionary line splits off from another. [4]

Broca's aphasia—severe disturbance of speech production, brought about by damage to the rear of the left frontal cortex. [3]

cardinal trait—a single trait that directs a major portion of a person's behavior. [19]

case study—a method of collecting data in which researchers conduct an intensive investigation of one or a few individuals, usually with reference to a single psychological phenomenon. [2]

catecholamine hypothesis—the hypothesis that depression results from low levels of norepinephrine (a catecholamine) and mania results from high levels of norepinephrine in the brain. [23]

categorical perception—the inborn tendency to hear speech sounds in distinct categories. [16]

celibacy—complete abstinence from sexual activity. [13]

cell body—the part of a neuron containing the nucleus. [3]

centers—clumps of neurons in the central nervous system that function as units; also called *nuclei*. [3]

central core—the area of the brain that carries out functions necessary for survival. [3]

central nervous system (CNS)—the major control center

of behavior. It consists of the brain and the spinal cord. [3]

central traits—characteristic ways of dealing with the world that can be captured by a trait name (honest, loving, gregarious) and that have marked effects on the way other, related traits are perceived. [19, 26]

cerebellum—the area of the brain that coordinates voluntary movement and maintains physical balance. [3]

cerebral cortex—the gray matter that covers the cerebral hemispheres. [3]

cerebral hemispheres—the most prominent layer of the brain; involved in information processing. [3]

cerebrum—portion of the brain that allows us to plan, learn, and reason; includes the cerebral cortex and the tissue beneath it. [3]

chunks—clusters of information that form familiar sequences or patterns of elements; used to encode material in short-term memory. [9]

clang association—in schizophrenia, the throwing together of concepts, ideas, and symbols merely because they rhyme. [22]

classical conditioning—a process whereby a neutral stimulus, when repeatedly presented with another stimulus that normally evokes a reflexive response, comes to elicit that response when presented by itself. [8]

client-centered therapy—a humanistic therapy in which the client learns to reintegrate self and organism, to accept all experiences as genuine, and to establish an unconditional positive regard. [24]

clinical psychologist—a mental-health professional who has earned a doctorate (PhD or PsyD) in clinical psychology and has completed a one-year clinical internship. [24]

clinical psychology—the approach to psychology concerned with the study, diagnosis, and treatment of abnormal behavior. [1]

closed genetic programs—innate genetic programs for behavior; the animal is born with them and they can be changed only slightly by experience. [4]

cochlea—the portion of the inner ear containing receptors for converting acoustic energy into sound. [5]

cognition—the process of knowing; the higher mental processes that human beings engage in, including problem solving, knowing, thinking, decision making, reasoning, judging, imagining. [10]

cognitive balance theory—the theory proposing that information about people's inconsistent relationships with each other leads to a conflict that the individual seeks to resolve. [12]

cognitive control—the guidance and maintenance of behavior through self-reinforcement. [19]

cognitive dissonance theory—the theory proposing that contradictory thoughts cause a state of psychological distress known as dissonance; the individual then attempts to reestablish internal harmony. [12]

cognitive map—an internal representation of the way objects and landmarks are arranged in their environments. [8]

cognitive restructuring—a process that focuses on the client's ways of perceiving the world and regards self-defeating behavior as a result of the client's false assumptions. [24]

cognitive therapy—a method of cognitive restructuring that aims to show clients that what they think determines how they feel. [24]

cohort—a group of people of the same age. [15]

collective unconscious—in Jung's terms, a level of the unconscious; a storehouse of memories and behavior patterns inherited from humanity's remote ancestral past. [18]

color cancellation—the phenomenon occurring when complementary colors are combined and perceived as colorless. [5]

common ground—the shared knowledge of speaker and listener. [16]

common trait—a basic mode of adjustment that is approximately the same for all individuals. [19]

community psychology—a branch of clinical psychology with the primary aim of preventing mental disorders. [1]

complementary colors—pairs of colors lying opposite each other on the color wheel. [5]

complexive thinking—in cognitive development, a child's tendency to jump from one idea to another without coordinating them. [15]

compulsion—an action that a person uncontrollably performs again and again, although she or he has no conscious desire to do so. [22]

computerized tomography (CT) scan—technique that uses multiple X-ray pictures to reconstruct single cross-section pictures of the brain. [3]

concrete-operational period—the period of cognitive development characterized by logical thought—but only in regard to concrete objects. [15]

concurrent validity—the correlation of a test's scores with other existing measures and standards. [20]

conditional positive regard—the withholding of love and praise when a child does not conform to parental or social standards. [19]

conditioned reinforcer—a stimulus that signals that a primary reinforcer will soon appear. [8]

conditioned response (CR)—a response to a CS. [8]

conditioned stimulus (CS)—a new stimulus that elicits behavior after repeated association with the UCS. [8]

conditions of worth—extraneous standards whose attainment ensures positive regard. [19]

cones—receptor cells in the eye operating in bright light. Cones are responsible for detailed vision and color perception. [5]

conformity—the tendency to shift one's views or behavior closer to the norms that are expressed by other people. [27]

congruence—genuineness; the therapist's ability to share her or his own feelings with the client in an open and spontaneous manner. [24]

conjunction—classification rule in which two attributes determine membership in a group. [10]

conjunction fallacy—the fallacy of believing that an example with both a common *and* a distinctive feature is more representative than an example with only the distinctive feature. [10]

consciousness—an awareness of the thoughts, images, sensations, and emotions that flow through the mind at any given moment. [7]

conservation—the principle that irrelevant changes in

the external appearance of objects have no effect on the objects' quantity. [15]

constituent—a major subdivision of a sentence, such as a noun phrase or a prepositional phrase. [16]

construct validity—a test's measurement of the trait or theoretical construct it claims to measure. [20]

consumer psychology—a branch of industrial psychology concerned with preferences, buying habits, and responses to advertising of consumers. [1]

content validity—a test's coverage of a representative sample of the measured attribute. [20]

context—the setting in which stimuli appear; a retrieval cue for memory. [6]

continuity—a principle of grouping. [6]

continuous reinforcement schedule—a schedule of reinforcement in which the subject is rewarded for every response. [8]

control condition—in an experiment, the condition that remains unchanged, the condition to which the experimental condition is compared. [2]

conventional level—Kohlberg's stage of moral development in which the child or adult decides moral issues in terms of maintaining the social order and meeting the expectations of others. [17]

conversion disorder—disorder in which an individual develops some physical dysfunction—such as blindness, deafness, paralysis, or loss of sensation in some part of the body—that has no organic basis and apparently expresses some psychological conflict. [22]

cooperative principle—the fundamental assumption that speakers and listeners will cooperate in using language. [16]

coping—the process of managing external and internal pressures that might otherwise lead to stress. [21]

cornea—the transparent covering in front of the eye. [5]

corpus callosum—a thick band of neural fibers that carries messages between the left and right sides of the brain. [3]

correlational coefficient—the descriptive statistic indicating the degree of linear relatedness. A perfect positive correlation is indicated by the coefficient $+ 1$; a perfect negative correlation is indicated by $- 1$. [2]

correlational research—studies that investigate the systematic relationships between two (or more) characteristics of individuals. [2]

counterbalancing—a procedure for making sure that variables that are of no theoretical interest to the experimenter are evenly distributed across the variables of interest. [2]

covert sensitization—a technique in which clients are asked to visualize the behavior they are trying to eliminate and then to conjure up the image of an extremely painful or revolting stimulus. [24]

creativity—the combination of previously unconnected elements in a new and useful way. [10]

cued recall—retrieval process in which an associated piece of information guides the memory search. [9]

culture-fair test—a test whose items or methods of administration do not depend on familiarity with the cultural background. [20]

curve of normal distribution—a smooth, symmetrical bell-shaped curve; the theoretical curve that would

result if an infinite number of cases were represented. [2]

decay—erosion of memory traces with the passage of time. [9]

decibel (dB)—a unit of measurement used to express perceived sound intensity. [5]

deductive scale. [20] See **rational scale.**

defense mechanism—an intrapsychic technique to conceal the source of anxiety from the self and from the world. [18]

deferred imitation—the ability to mimic on one occasion actions observed at an earlier time. [15]

deficiency needs. [19] See **basic needs.**

delusions—irrational beliefs that are maintained despite overwhelming evidence that they have no basis in reality. [22]

demand characteristics—a methodological problem in which a subject's response is strongly determined by the research setting. [2]

dendrites—short fibers that branch out from the cell body. [3]

denial—defense mechanism in which a person refuses to recognize a threatening source of anxiety. [18]

dependent variable—the event that is being studied and that is expected to change when the independent variable is altered. [2]

depressant—a drug that retards the action of the central nervous system so that neurons fire more slowly. [7]

developmental psychology—the approach to psychology that is concerned with all aspects of behavioral development over the entire life span. [1]

diathesis-stress model—the view that genes establish a diathesis, or predisposition, to schizophrenia, but that the disorder will not develop unless the predisposition is combined with certain stressful environmental factors. [23]

dichotic listening—a process in which a person wearing a set of earphones hears two different messages played simultaneously, one in each ear. [7]

dichromats—people who have difficulty discriminating wavelengths in certain regions of the spectrum. [5]

difference threshold—the smallest change in a stimulus that produces a change in sensation. [5]

diffusion of responsibility—spreading the responsibility for intervening over all the bystanders. [27]

discreteness—a major characteristic of human language; the distinctness of the units that compose it. [16]

discretionary stimuli—signals that groups send to an individual member to either change or reinforce that member's behavior. [28]

discrimination—(1) differentiation among similar stimuli, with response to one and no response to others. (2) the behavioral expression of prejudice. [8, 26]

disjunction—classification rule in which *either* of two features determines category membership. [10]

displacement—(1) process in which new items entering short-term memory seem to crowd out earlier items. (2) a major characteristic of language; transmission of information about distant objects or events. (3) in Freud's terms, transference of psychic energy from the original object to a variety of substitute objects. [9, 16, 18]

dispositional cause—cause of behavior that is attributed to a specific person and to that person's disposition. [26]

dissociative disorder—the dissociation, or splitting off, of certain aspects of memory and identity. [22]

DNA (deoxyribonucleic acid)—twisted strings of chemical building blocks that transmit the genetic code. [4]

doctrine of specific nerve energies—sensory quality depends on the neural pathways activated by stimuli, not on the physical properties of the stimuli. [5]

dominant responses—the responses most likely to be made by an organism in a given situation. [27]

dopamine—a neurotransmitter thought to regulate emotional response and complex movements. [3]

dopamine hypothesis—the view that schizophrenia is associated with excessive activity in those parts of the brain that use dopamine to transmit neural impulses. [23]

double-bind hypothesis—the theory that mutually contradictory messages from parent to child are a strong causative agent in schizophrenia. [23]

double-blind procedure—a method of avoiding experimenter bias in which neither researcher nor subjects know which group is the experimental group and which the control group. [2]

drive—an internal motivational factor. [12]

drug—any inorganic substance that can interact with a biological system. [7]

duplication hypothesis—a theory proposing that people are happiest when they re-create their birth-order position in their marital relationship. [26]

dyslexia—disorder in which children with normal intelligence and adequate environmental opportunities have extreme difficulty learning to read. [16]

eardrum—membrane in the ear that vibrates in response to sound. [5]

educational psychology—the approach to psychology that investigates all the psychological aspects of the learning process. [1]

efficacy expectations—people's beliefs that they can successfully execute whatever behavior is required to produce a desired outcome. [24]

ego—according to Freud, a psychic component serving as mediator between the id and reality. [18]

ego identity—in Erikson's terms, an integrated, autonomous, unique "self." [18]

ego psychologist—a psychoanalytic investigator who considers herself or himself a Freudian but who elaborates on Freud's theory, emphasizing ego functions. [18]

egocentrism—in cognitive development, a child's belief that others literally see things as the child does. [15]

ejaculation—the discharge of fluid during orgasm. [13]

elaborative rehearsal—a form of rehearsal that transfers information into long-term memory so that it may later be retrieved. [9]

electroconvulsive therapy (ECT)—"shock treatment"; administering a series of brief electrical shocks of approximately 70 to 130 volts, spaced over a period of several weeks. The shock induces a convulsion similar to an epileptic seizure. [24]

electroencephalography (EEG)—technique used to record the brain's electrical activity as measured by electrodes placed on a person's scalp. [3]

electromyographic recording (EMG)—measurements of electrical activity from muscles. [11]

embryo—the developing organism in the womb from the fourth to the eighth week. [14]

empathic understanding—the therapist's ability to see the world through the eyes of the client. [24]

empirical approach—an approach to scientific investigation that employs experimentation and direct observation. [2]

encoding. [9] See **acquisition.**

encoding specificity—phenomenon in which retrieval will be poor if the retrieval situation differs greatly from the situation at the time of encoding. [9]

endocrine glands—glands that produce hormones. [3]

endocrine system—a set of glands which secretes hormones carried in the bloodstream. They influence neural and muscular tissue in other parts of the body. [3]

endorphins—a variety of neurotransmitter similar in structure to opiates; implicated in pain and pleasure. [3]

environmental niche—the particular environmental situation, including food supply, shelter, climate, and pressure from predators, to which a species is suited. [4]

environmental psychology—the approach to psychology that studies the relationship between people and their physical settings. [1]

epidemiology—the study of the range of occurrence, distribution, and control of illness in a population. [22]

epinephrine—neurotransmitter that plays a vital role in arousal of the sympathetic nervous system and the reticular activating systems of the brain. [3]

equilibration—in cognitive development, a continual search for a balance between assimilation and accommodation. [15]

equity theory—cognitive theory of work motivation stating that employees are motivated to remove any perceived inequities. [28]

erectile failure—a man's inability to achieve or maintain an erection. [13]

ERG theory—theory of work motivation based on the worker's existence needs, relatedness needs, and growth needs. [28]

erogenous zone—an area of the body that is particularly sensitive to touch; a focus of pleasure. [13, 17]

escape learning—the learning of a specific response that terminates some unpleasant stimulus, enabling the organism to escape from an unpleasant situation. [8]

ethologists—scientists who try to explain animal behavior in evolutionary terms. [4]

event-related potential (ERP)—changes in the brain's electrical activity in response to stimulation presented by a researcher. [3]

evolution—the theory that each species developed from earlier forms of life. [4]

excitatory connection—a message that causes a receiving neuron to fire. [3]

excitement phase—the first phase of sexual response. [13]

exhibitionism—sexual gratification obtained through exhibiting the genitals to an involuntary bystander. [22]

existential frustration—a major source of abnormal behavior arising from an inability to find meaning in life. [23]

expectancy theory—cognitive theory of work motivation stating that we are motivated not only by our goals but by how attainable we think they are. [28]

experience (of an emotion)—the subjective feeling that accompanies an emotion. [11]

experiment—a method of collecting data in which researchers actively control the presence, absence, or intensity of factors that may affect the behavior under study. [2]

experimental condition—in an experiment, the condition in which the factor under study is manipulated to test its effect. [2]

experimental psychology—the approach to psychology that investigates basic behavioral processes that are shared by several species. [1]

experimenter effects—biases that the experimenter unwittingly introduces into the study. [2]

exposure effect—positive attitude produced by repeated neutral encounters with an object. [25]

expression (of an emotion)—behavioral acts that are uniquely elicited by an emotion. [11]

extinction—the slow decline and eventual disappearance of a conditioned response. [8]

extrasensory perception (ESP)—the reception of knowledge about the environment that does not arrive through a known sensory channel. [1]

extrinsic motivation—the process by which external rewards lead an individual to undertake a behavior. [12]

extroversion—in Jung's terms, a major personality orientation in which the person is overly interested in the external world and thus is outgoing, sociable, and excitement-seeking. [18]

face validity—a test's appearance of validity to the people taking it. [20]

facial-feedback hypothesis—the hypothesis that our subjective experience of emotion comes from an awareness of our facial expressions. [11]

factor analysis—a statistical method that analyzes responses to a host of possible scale items and reduces them to a few underlying factors. [20]

false alarms—errors in which a subject detects a signal when none has been given. [5]

family resemblance—the more closely an instance (for example, apple) resembles many other category members (other fruits), the more typical it is judged to be. [10]

fear of success—the motive to avoid success. [12]

feature analysis—the process by which sensory information is identified according to its distinctive characteristics or features. [6]

feedback—reinforcement in the form of information about past performance that is used to alter future behavior. [8]

fetal alcohol syndrome—birth defect characterized by mental retardation and retarded growth in babies born to alcoholic mothers. [14]

fetishism—sexual gratification that is dependent on an inanimate object or some part of the body other than the genitals. [22]

fetus—the developing organism in the womb from the eighth week to birth. [14]

field experiments—studies in which researchers can introduce the independent variable but cannot control other variables and often cannot assign subjects to the experimental group. [2]

figure—in a scene, the region that represents an object. [6]

figure-ground reversal—type of visual ambiguity that arises when figure and ground alternate so that perception of the image shifts from one interpretation to another. [6]

fixation—(1) an automatic application of an inappropriate strategy and a rigid clinging to the obviously ineffective approach. (2) a halt in psychosexual development caused by failure to resolve the conflict between impulse and control. [10]

fixed interval schedule—a partial reinforcement schedule in which reinforcement comes for the first response after a specified period. [8]

fixed ratio schedule—a partial reinforcement schedule in which the subject is rewarded each time it makes a specific number of responses. [8]

fixed-action patterns—genetic programs of behavior that take the form of relatively sterotyped and often-repeated patterns of movement. [4]

flooding—an intensive extinction therapy. [24]

forensic psychology—the approach to psychology that applies psychological principles to the problems of law enforcement and the courts. [1]

formal-operational period—the culmination of cognitive development, characterized by abstract reasoning and the ability to assume artificial premises that are known to be false. [15]

fovea—the retinal area that lies almost directly opposite the pupil of the eye. It contains only cone receptors and is the area of the highest visual acuity. [5]

frame—the way a problem is phrased. [10]

fraternal twins—twins who have developed from two eggs, each fertilized by a different sperm. [4]

free association—an indirect therapeutic technique employed to study unconscious processes. The patient will say anything that comes to mind, making no attempt to produce logical statements, and the psychoanalyst will attempt to interpret the associations. [1, 18]

free (unaided) recall—retrieval process in which a memory search is undertaken with only a weak cue or an entire set of items. [9]

free-floating anxiety—an inability to specify the source of the fear. [22]

frequency—the number of waves passing a given point in a given period. [5]

frequency distribution—a representation that shows the relationship between responses and the observed frequency of those responses. [2]

frequency theory—pitch is determined by the frequency per second of neural impulses sent to the brain. [5]

frontal lobe—the area of the brain generally involved in behavior. [3]

frustration—interference with any form of goal-directed behavior. [27]

frustration-aggression hypothesis—the idea that "aggression is always a consequence of frustration" and, conversely, "frustration always leads to some form of aggression" (Dollard, 1939). [27]

fugue—a dissociative disorder in which individuals flee from the home as well as from the self. [22]

fully functioning—psychologically adjusted, open to experience, undefensive, accurately aware, unconditionally positive in self-regard, harmonious in relations with other people. [19]

functional fixedness—the inability to use a familiar object in an unfamiliar way. [10]

fundamental attribution error—the tendency of observers to attribute other people's behavior to dispositional factors. [26]

galvanic skin response (GSR)—a decrease in the resistance of the skin to electrical conduction. [11]

ganglia—collections of neuron cell bodies found principally along the spinal column. [3]

gender identity—the child's understanding that she or he is female or male and will always remain so. [17]

gender roles—attitudes and patterns of behavior that society considers acceptable for each gender. [17]

gender schema—conceptual pattern for organizing new information on the basis of gender roles. [17]

generalization gradient—rate of decrease in an organism's tendency to respond as the resemblance between a new stimulus and a conditioned stimulus becomes fainter. [8]

generalized anxiety disorder—anxiety disorder characterized by diffuse and generalized anxiety that is impossible to manage by avoiding specific situations. [22]

genes—basic units of information on the DNA string that pass along specific hereditary traits. [4]

genital stage—the final stage of psychosexual development, in which the focus is on the pleasures of sexual intercourse. [17, 18]

gestalt—a meaningful pattern or figure into which human beings group perceptual information. [6]

gestalt therapy—a blend of Freudian concepts with humanistic philosophy and radically different therapeutic techniques. [24]

given-new strategy—a decoding technique, essential to comprehending speech, in which the listener takes the new information in the utterance and integrates it with old information. [16]

glands—organs that secrete hormones. [3]

glia—structural units of the nervous system; they provide nutrients and structural support to neurons and bar certain substances from the bloodstream. [3]

goal-setting theory—cognitive theory of work motivation that views workers as motivated by conscious intentions to attain a specific goal. [28]

grammar—the structure of language. [16]

ground—in a scene, the region that represents spaces between objects. [6]

grouping—the organizing of sensory data. [6]

growth needs. [19] See **metaneeds.**

habituation—decrease in the strength of a response; occurs after a novel stimulus has been presented over a long time. [8]

hair cells—the receptors in the organ of Corti. [5]

hallucinations—spontaneous sensory perceptions—usually of sounds—that are unrelated to external stimuli. [22]

hallucinogen—a drug with the ability to produce hallucinations. [7]

hammer—one of the ossicles in the middle ear. [5]

health belief model—a model that sees attitudes, values, and knowledge as paramount in maintaining health. [21]

health psychology—area of psychology that aims at understanding the relationship between the mind and the individual's physical condition. [1, 21]

heritability—the extent to which the observed variation of a trait can be attributed to genetic differences among a specific group of individuals in a specific environment. [20]

heuristic—a rule of thumb that provides a general direction for solving problems. [10]

hindsight—a bias in judgment resulting from looking back on events after they have already occurred. [10]

hippocampus—a structure in the limbic system. [3]

homeostasis—a process of self-regulation to maintain a balanced internal environment; a state of equilibrium. [3]

homosexual—a person whose primary source of sexual gratification is members of the same sex. [13]

hormones—chemical substances used by the endocrine system to transmit messages. [3]

hostile aggression—aggression that aims at hurting another person. [17]

human-factors psychology—a branch of industrial psychology that considers the purpose of a particular machine or environment, the capabilities of the probable user, and the most efficient design that matches the two. [1]

humanistic-existential perspective—a psychogenic approach to psychological disorder that includes both humanistic and existential theories. [23]

hypnagogic state—the state lying between waking and sleep. [7]

hypochondriasis—the preoccupation with bodily symptoms as possible signs of serious illness. [22]

hypothalamus—a small structure in the brain that monitors changes in internal environment and sends signals to maintain equilibrium. [3]

hypothesis—proposition or belief to be tested. [2]

id—according to Freud, the biological drives with which the infant is born. [18]

identical twins—twins who are the product of a single fertilized egg that divided early in the course of prenatal development. [4]

identity—an individual's sense of personal sameness and continuity. [17]

identity crisis—an internal conflict that requires the adolescent to develop a new self-concept. [17, 18]

ill-defined problem—a problem that has no agreed-upon steps or rules that will produce a product generally accepted as a solution. [10]

illusion—a perception that does not correspond to a real object or event; it is produced by physical or psychological distortion. [6]

illusory aftereffects of motion—an illusion of reverse

movement that occurs after gazing at some movement for a long time, then shifting the gaze to a stationary object. [6]

impression management—displaying behavior that will lead others to make favorable attributions of our intentions, abilities, and feelings. [26]

impression management theory—the theory that maintains that a person's attitudes remain impervious to the effects of dissonance and that the insufficient reward affects only the expression of attitudes to others. [12]

imprinting—the process by which some species of birds and mammals form early social attachments. [4]

incentive—an external motivational stimulus. [12]

incest—sexual activity between closely related persons. [13, 22]

inclusive fitness—the concept that the fitness of an individual to survive is a combination of his or her own personal fitness and the fitness of his or her relatives based on their shared genes. [4]

independent variable—any factor whose change is expected to affect the event being studied. [2]

individual psychology—the school of psychology founded by Alfred Adler in 1911. [18]

individual trait—a unique way of organizing the world that cannot be applied to all people. [19]

individuation—in Jung's terms, a process of developing all parts of the personality. [18]

induced movement—an illusion in which a stationary object appears to move because its relationship to a surrounding background changes. [6]

industrial/organizational (I/O) psychology—field of psychology concerned with human behavior in the workplace. [1, 28]

inferiority complex—in Adler's terms, the feelings and actions that characterize a person with an inability to overcome a childhood sense of incompleteness. [18]

inhibited ejaculation—a condition in which men are unable to ejaculate during sexual activity. [13]

inhibitory connection—a message that prevents a receiving neuron from firing. [3]

inoculation—process of providing a person with defenses against the effects of persuasion. [25]

insight—the sudden perception of a new relationship that leads to an innovative solution. [10]

instrumental aggression—aggression that aims at acquiring or retrieving objects, territory, or privileges. [17]

instrumental conditioning. [8] See **operant conditioning.**

intelligence quotient (IQ)—the ratio of mental age to chronological age. [20]

intensity—the strength of a stimulus such as the amplitude of the air-pressure wave. [5]

interference—process in which other material in memory blocks out material that is being sought. [9]

interjudge reliability—the extent to which the scoring or interpretation of a test by different judges will produce the same results. [20]

internal consistency reliability—the extent to which different parts of a test produce the same results. [20]

internalization—the child's incorporation of society's values to such an extent that violation of these standards produces a sense of guilt. [17]

interneurons—neurons that connect only sensory and motor neurons. [3]

interposition—a monocular depth cue in which one object partially blocks the view of another object. [6]

intrinsic motivation—the process by which long-term goals or preferences lead an individual to undertake a behavior. [12]

introversion—in Jung's terms, a major personality orientation in which the person withdraws interest from the external world and consequently is quiet, reserved, and cautious. [18]

iris—the pigmented portion of the eye that surrounds the pupil of the eye. [5]

James-Lange theory of emotion—the view that emotion results from the perception of bodily changes. [11]

just noticeable difference (JND). [5] See **difference threshold.**

key-word system—mnemonic system used in foreign-language learning; an English word similar to the foreign word to be learned is used to cue the foreign word. [9]

kinesthesis—the sense of body movement and position. [5]

latency period or **stage**—the period in psychosexual development in which libidinal dynamics are more or less stabilized; children busy themselves exploring the world and learning new things. [17, 18]

latent content of dreams—according to Freud, the unconscious wishes, primarily derived from unresolved early emotional conflicts, veiled by symbolic images in dreams. [7, 18]

lateral geniculate nucleus (LGN)—a grouping of cell bodies in the thalamus. [5]

lateralization—the establishment of functions in one hemisphere or the other. [3]

learned helplessness—the acquired belief that one cannot exert any control over the environment. [21]

learning—a change in behavioral disposition that is caused by experience and not explained on the basis of reflexes, maturation, or temporary states. [8]

lens—a transparent structure behind the pupil of the eye. [5]

limbic system—the layer of the brain involved in motivational and emotional processes. [3]

linear function. [2] See **linear relationship.**

linear perspective—the apparent convergence of parallel lines in the distance. [6]

linear relationship—a relationship between variables that can be represented graphically as a straight line. [2]

linguistics—the study of language's structure. [16]

localization of function—the idea that different parts of the brain appear to be involved in different types of behavior. [3]

locus of control—degree to which persons believe that they are personally responsible for what happens to them. [20]

long-term memory—the type of memory storage capable of storing a limitless amount of information indefinitely. [9]

lucid dreams—dreams in which a person is aware that he or she is dreaming. [7]

maintenance rehearsal—a form of rehearsal to maintain information in short-term memory. [9]

major depression—one or more major depressive episodes with no intervening episodes of euphoria. [22]

manifest content of dreams—according to Freud, that level of content in dreams that is a weaving of daily events, sensations during sleep, and memories; the surface meaning. [7, 18]

marital schism—a basic family pattern, thought to produce schizophrenia, in which the parents of the schizophrenic are bitterly divided. [23]

marital skew—a basic family pattern, thought to produce schizophrenia, in which one parent of the schizophrenic totally dominates the other. [23]

masochism—sexual gratification obtained through having pain inflicted on oneself. [22]

match—to assign subjects to groups on the basis of a characteristic, so that the subjects in each condition have the same amount of the characteristic. [2]

mean—the arithmetic average of a distribution of scores. [2]

meaningfulness—a characteristic of human communication in which the relationship between a word and an object is arbitrary, depending solely on agreement among a group of people as to meaning. [16]

means-end analysis—a problem-solving strategy in which the person tries to reduce the distance between the current position and the goal. [10]

measure of central tendency—a descriptive statistic that represents the middle of a distribution of responses—the mode, mean, or median. [2]

median—the score that falls in the exact middle of a distribution, when all scores are arranged from highest to lowest. [2]

medical model—a model of abnormal behavior that views psychological problems in the same way as it views physical problems—as diseases. [22]

meditation—a retraining of attention that induces an altered state of consciousness. [7]

medulla—the part of the brain stem involved in breathing, circulation, chewing, salivation, and facial movements. [3]

memory trace—a physiological change theoretically formed in the brain to record information; as time passes, the trace decays. [9]

mental retardation—"significantly subaverage general intellectual functioning existing concurrently with deficits in adaptive behavior, and manifested during the developmental period" (American Association on Mental Deficiency, 1977). [20]

mental set—a tendency to keep repeating solutions that worked in other situations. [10]

metacognition—an understanding of the cognitive processes. [15]

metamemory—knowledge about how one's own memory system works. [9]

metaneeds—the highest motives, having to do with creativity and self-actualization. [12, 19]

metapathologies—crises (such as alienation and apathy) that result when metaneeds are not fulfilled. [19]

method of loci—mnemonic system that uses a series of places along a familiar route to organize and cue retrieval of information to be remembered. [9]

midbrain—the part of the brain stem that contains centers for visual and auditory reflexes. [3]

mild retardation—mental retardation in which the (Stanford-Binet) IQ is between 52 and 67; mild retardates can hold undemanding jobs, marry, and have children. [20]

Minnesota Multiphasic Personality Inventory (MMPI)—an empirically constructed personality inventory, valuable for diagnosing certain mental illnesses. [20]

mnemonic systems—systems that organize material so that it can be remembered. [9]

mode—a measure of central tendency; the score that most frequently appears in a distribution. [2]

modeling—the process by which a person learns some new behavior by watching another person perform it. [24]

models—persons from whom a pattern of behavior is learned by observation. [8]

moderate retardation—mental retardation in which the (Stanford-Binet) IQ is between 36 and 51; although moderate retardates can take care of themselves, they must live in sheltered workshops. [20]

monochromats—people who are totally color-blind. Monochromats see the world in shades of gray. [5]

monocular cues—information that does not require the cooperation of both eyes. [6]

moral anxiety—(1) in Freud's terms, anxiety over danger that comes from the superego. (2) generally, anxiety caused by the superego's demands for moral behavior. [18, 23]

morphemes—the smallest units of meaning within a word. [16]

motherese—the special ways in which adults speak to small children. [16]

motion parallax—differences that occur in the relative movement of retinal images when the observer moves or changes position. [6]

motivation—the process corresponding to the property of behavior called "motive." [12]

motive—the dynamic property of behavior that gives it organization over time and that defines its end states. [12]

motor cortex—the area of the frontal lobes involved in regulation of voluntary movement. [3]

motor neurons—neurons that carry messages from the spinal cord to muscles or glands. [3]

multiple orgasms—a series of orgasms that women may experience without going through the resolution phase after each orgasm. [13]

multiple personality—a division into two or more complete behavior organizations, each well-defined and highly distinct from the others; a rare dissociative disorder. [22]

myelin sheath—a fatty, whitish substance that wraps around some axons and that serves as insulation. [3]

natural category—a category made up of some class of objects in the world. [10]

natural selection—the individual's reproductive success, which is made possible by its genetic differences from other members of its population. [4]

naturalistic observations—a method of collecting data in which researchers carefully observe and record behavior in natural settings. [2]

negative correlation—a relationship between two variables in which a high rank on one measure is accompanied by a low rank on the other. [2]

negative reinforcement—the strengthening of a response by the removal or termination of a stimulus. [8] See also **escape learning.**

neodissociation theory—a theory of hypnosis based on the notion that consciousness depends on multiple systems that are coordinated through hierarchies of control, and that during hypnosis the controls shift. [7]

nerves—bundles of neuron fibers. [3]

nervous networks—a system of communication channels that spreads into every part of the body. [3]

neurons—the specialized cells in the central nervous system that transmit information by means of electrochemical impulses. [3]

neuropsychology. [1] See **physiological psychology.**

neuroscience—area of psychology that investigates the workings of the sensory systems; the effects of various brain chemicals on psychological phenomena such as memory, pain, and motivation; and the effects of brain damage on behavior. [1]

neurosis—any condition in which a person develops some maladaptive behavior as a protection against unconscious anxiety. [22]

neurotic anxiety—in Freud's terms, anxiety over danger that comes from the id. [18, 23]

neurotransmitter—a chemical stored in sacs at the tip of the axon, that transmits messages across the synapse. [3]

nondirective counseling. [24] See **client-centered therapy.**

non-REM (NREM) sleep—the stages of sleep other than REM sleep. [7]

norepinephrine—neurotransmitter that may be involved in arousal, pleasure, dreaming, and mood. [3]

norm—a normative distribution that shows the frequency with which particular scores on a test are made. [14]

normal curve of distribution—a bell-shaped, symmetrical distribution, in which mean, median, and mode are the same. [2]

norms—(1) averages derived from observing many individuals. (2) a society's rules that prescribe "right" and "wrong" behavior. [20, 22, 27]

nuclear magnetic resonance (NMR)—technique that uses radio waves on a body enclosed in a magnetic field to produce images of tissue, biochemical activity, and metabolism. [3]

obedience—any behavior that complies with the explicit commands of a person in authority. [27]

object concept—an understanding that objects have an existence of their own. [15]

object permanence—the awareness that objects continue to exist when out of sight. [15]

obsession—an involuntary, irrational thought that occurs repeatedly. [22]

obsessive-compulsive disorders—disorders characterized by rituals of orderliness or cleanliness, such as continual hand washing. [23]

occipital lobe—the area in the brain for reception and analysis of visual information. [3]

Oedipal conflict—the most important conflict in the child's psychological development, in which children perceive themselves as rivals of their same-sex parents for the affection of the parent of the opposite sex. [17]

olfaction—the sense of smell. [5]

olfactory epithelium—the sense organ for olfaction. [5]

open genetic program—a genetic program that can be modified by experience, thus permitting an animal to store more information than can be transmitted in a closed genetic program. [4]

operant conditioning—conditioning in which learning is explained by the way the consequences of behavior affect the organisms's behavior in the future. [8]

opponent-process theory—(1) the theory of color vision proposing the existence of three antagonistically organized systems, with two of the systems composed of pairs of opposite colors. (2) the theory explaining acquired motivations as the result of two opposing processes. [5, 12]

optic chiasm—the junction where the nerves meet and are rerouted. [5]

optic disc—the "blind spot" in the eye; the area on the retina through which the optic nerve passes. [5]

optic nerve—the nerve that relays visual information to the brain. [5]

optimal-level theories—theories proposing that activities seemingly unrelated to specific primary needs are based on a built-in tendency to maintain a certain level of stimulation. [12]

oral stage—that stage in psychosexual development that occupies the first year of life and during which the baby's mouth is the primary source of sensual pleasure. [17, 18]

organic brain syndromes—disorders directly traceable to the destruction of brain tissue or to biochemical imbalance in the brain. [22]

organism—the total range of a person's possible experiences. [19]

organizational psychology. [1] see **industrial/organizational (I/O) psychology.**

orgasm—the climactic phase of sexual response. [13]

orienting reflex—physiological reaction to a novel stimulus. [8]

ossicles—a series of bones in the middle ear. [5]

oval window—the flexible membrane that divides the middle ear from the inner ear. [5]

overextension—a child's tendency to extend the meanings of words to cover objects or actions for which they have no words. [16]

overinclusion—a loosening of associations, so that each sentence is generated from some mental stimulus in the preceding sentence. [22]

overregulation—extension of a grammatical rule to cases where it does not apply. [16]

ovulation—release of a mature egg from the ovary. [13]

pain thresholds—points at which pains are first perceived. [5]

pair recognition—test of memory retrieval in which the subject is asked to confirm whether a paired test item matches a previously learned pair. [9]

Pandemonium model—model of feature analysis proposing that the brain identifies unknown letter stimuli by weighing the various stimuli features that match the letter stored in memory, then summing those weighted matches over all features available in the pattern. [6]

panic attacks—episodes in which an already heightened state of tension mounts to an acute and overwhelming level. [22]

panic disorder—panic attacks preceded by no specific stimulus. [22]

paradoxical cold—the phenomenon of feeling a cold sensation when a cold spot on the skin is stimulated with a hot stimulus. [5]

parapsychology—the study of ESP; the psychology of events that go beyond what is probable. [1]

parasympathetic nervous system—the division of the autonomic nervous system that dominates in relaxed situations. [3]

parietal lobe—the area of the brain behind the central fissure. [3]

Parkinson's disease—a chronic and often progressive condition characterized by involuntary shaking of the limbs and head. [3]

partial reinforcement schedule—a schedule of reinforcement in which the subject is rewarded after only some of its responses. [8]

participant modeling—a therapeutic technique in which the therapist models the feared activity and then helps the client to confront and master a graduated series of threatening activities. [24]

pathway—"cable" made up of long, parallel axons that transmit signals in the central nervous system. [3]

pattern recognition—process through which we identify a shape or sound as similar to something we have seen before. [3]

pedophilia—sexual gratification obtained through sexual contacts with children. [22]

peg-word system—mnemonic system based on ten or more simple words that act as memory pegs or hooks. [9]

percentile system—a system of scoring tests in which the group of scores is divided into one hundred equal parts. [20]

perception—an organism's awareness of objects and events in the environment, brought about by stimulation of the organism's sense organs. [6]

perceptual constancy—the tendency to perceive objects as having certain constant or stable properties. [6]

perceptual set—the readiness to perceive stimuli in a specific way, ignoring some types of stimulation and becoming sensitive to others. [6]

peripheral nervous system (PNS)—the relay system connecting the CNS and all parts of the body. [3]

perseveration—(1) a verbal slip in which a produced sound is erroneously repeated later in the utterance. (2) a tendency to dwell on the primary association to a given stimulus. [16, 22]

personal disposition. [19] See **individual trait.**

personal unconscious—in Jung's terms, a level of the unconscious similar to the unconscious as depicted by Freud. [18]

personality—the differences among people plus the stability of any individual's behavior over long periods. [17, 18]

personality disorder—disorder involving inflexible and maladaptive personality traits that impair functioning. [22]

personality psychology—the approach to psychology in which individual differences in behavior are studied. [1]

personnel psychology—a branch of industrial psychology. Personnel psychologists screen job applicants, evaluate job performance, and recommend employees for promotion. [1]

persuasive communication—a direct, overt attempt to change attitudes. [25]

phallic stage—the third stage of psychosexual development, during which the child's attention is focused on the genitals and the pleasures of fondling them. [17, 18]

phenomenological approach—an approach in the humanistic-existential perspective that stresses the individual's own perception of events as opposed to a therapist's interpretation of hidden causes. [23]

pheromones—chemicals that trigger a behavioral reaction in other animals of the same species. [5]

phi phenomenon—an example of apparent motion in which the illusion is created by rapidly flashing still pictures. [6]

phobia—an anxiety irrationally centered on a particular object or situation. [22]

phonemes—the smallest sound units in the language. [16]

photopigment—a light-sensitive molecule. [5]

phyletic evolution—a straight-line pattern of evolution. [4]

physiological psychology—the approach to psychology that attempts to untangle the connections between the endocrine and nervous systems and behavior. [1]

physiological zero—the temperature at which there is no sensation. [5]

pitch—the attribute of tones in terms of which they may be described as high or low. This attribute is closely related to frequency of the sound waves. [5]

pituitary gland—the "master gland" of the endocrine system. [3]

place theory—the theory stating that the site of maximum displacement on the basilar membrane indicates to the brain the specific frequency of sound. [5]

placebo—a substance that has no direct physiological effect. [3, 5]

placebo effect—phenomenon in which subjects' expectations of the effect of a substance result in their experiencing the effect, even though they are actually given an inert substance. [2]

plastic—the characteristic of human behavior that makes it capable of being molded by environmental influences. [4]

plateau phase—the second phase of sexual response. [13]

pons—the part of the brain stem that connects the two halves of the cerebellum and that acts as a relay station. [3]

population—a group of interest identified by some particular characteristic or group of characteristics. [2]

position emission tomography (PET) scan—technique that provides color contour maps of brain activity through use of injected radioactive glucose. [3]

positive correlation—a relationship between two variables in which a high rank on one measure is accompanied by a high rank on the other. [2]

positive reinforcer—reward that increases an organism's tendency to repeat a response that leads to it. [8]

postconventional level—Kohlberg's stage of moral development at which an individual judges moral issues in terms of self-chosen principles and standards based on universal ethical principles and on the ideals of reciprocity and human equality. [17]

post-decision dissonance—state in which an awareness of the positive features of the rejected alternative and the negative features of the chosen alternative creates cognitive inconsistency. [25]

PQ4R method—mnemonic system used to improve memory for test material; consists of six steps: preview, question, read, reflect, recite, and review. [9]

pragmatics—the study of linguistic function. [16]

precocial—competent (referring to the young of a species). [14]

preconventional level—Kohlberg's stage of moral development in which children judge moral issues in terms of pain or pleasure or of the physical power of authority. [17]

predictive validity—a test's ability to produce scores that show a relationship to future performance on a job. [20]

prefrontal lobotomy—a surgical procedure in which a surgical instrument is inserted into the brain and rotated to sever nerve fibers connecting the frontal lobe (thought center) and the thalamus (emotional center). [24]

pregenital stage—a collective term for Freud's first three psychosexual stages. [18]

prejudice—negatively toned attitudes and opinions about an entire group, such as a racial minority or women, developed in the absence of sufficient knowledge. [26]

premature ejaculation—a condition in which men ejaculate rapidly, before they or their partners would like. [13]

preoperational period—the period of cognitive development characterized by the development of language, elaborate symbolic play, and the absence of logic; the preschool years. [15]

primacy effect—a process in which the personality traits that are detected first influence subsequent information about the person. [26]

primary appraisal—a person's initial appraisal of new or changing circumstances to determine what they mean to him or her. [21]

primary colors—in additive color mixing, the three basic colors (blue, red, and green) that can be combined to produce any other color. [5]

primary drives—internal motivational factors that seek fulfillment of basic needs. [12]

primary erectile failure—the condition of a man who has never been able to achieve or maintain an erection sufficient for intercourse. [13]

primary orgasmic dysfunction—the situation of women who have never experienced orgasm through any means. [13]

primary prevention—a method of maintaining health by encouraging people to develop a healthy lifestyle. [21]

primary reinforcer—a stimulus that fulfills some basic need. [8]

priming—presenting an item or an association to an item several seconds or minutes before memory for the item is tested, thus preparing it for subsequent retrieval. [9]

proactive interference—interference in which earlier learning blocks out subsequent learning. [9]

problem reduction—problem-solving strategy in which a large problem is broken into a number of smaller, easier-to-solve problems. [10]

problem space—a person's conception of the possible moves to be examined in solving a problem. [10]

prodromal phase—a phase of deterioration, in which a person becomes increasingly withdrawn, eccentric in behavior, and unable to carry out daily functions, before schizophrenia becomes active. [22]

productivity—a major characteristic of human language; the capacity to allow individual units to be combined into an unlimited number of messages. [16]

profound retardation—mental retardation in which the (Stanford-Binet) IQ is below 20; profoundly retarded persons usually remain in institutions but can sometimes carry out a few tasks under close supervision; some cannot speak, although they may understand simple communication. [20]

program evaluation—evaluation by psychologists of the cost and effectiveness of applied programs. [1]

progressive relaxation—a relaxation technique in which the individual tenses and then releases different muscle groups in sequence. [21]

projection—the unknowing attribution of one's own impulses or fears onto others. [18]

projective tests—tests whose overall assessment depends upon clinical interpretation. [20]

proposition—the form in which a thought occurs in our consciousness; it consists of a subject (topic) with a predicate (comment about the topic). [16]

prosocial behavior—action intended to benefit another person, taken without expectation of external reward, and generally involving some cost to the individual. [17]

prototype—a hypothetical best—or most typical—example of a category. [10]

proximity—a principle of grouping; how close together people live and work. [6, 26]

psychiatric nurse—a registered nurse who has specialized in psychiatric nursing. [24]

psychiatric social worker—a professional who has earned a master's degree in social work and has specialized in psychiatric social work. [24]

psychiatrist—a physician (MD) who specializes in the diagnosis and treatment of mental illness. [24]

psychoactive drug—a drug that interacts with the central nervous system to alter mood, perception, and behavior. [7]

psychoanalysis—the process by which Freud attempted to bring unconscious material into the patient's awareness, where it could be examined rationally. [18]

psychoanalyst—a person with special training in the technique of psychoanalysis and who has been psychoanalyzed as part of the training. [24]

psychodynamics—the interplay of conflicting forces within the personality. [18]

psychogenic theory—the view that mental disturbances result primarily from psychological factors. [23]

psychohistory—the application of psychoanalytic principles to the study of historical figures. [18]

psycholinguistics—the study of language's function; how language is used. [16]

psychological test—an objective and standardized measure of a sample of behavior that provides a systematic basis for making inferences about people. [20]

psychology—the study of behavior. [1]

psychopharmacology—the study of the relationship between drugs and behavior. [1]

psychosis—a condition in which the person's perceptions of reality are highly distorted. [22]

psychosocial—caused by both psychological and social factors. [18]

psychotherapy—a systematic series of interactions between a therapist trained to aid in solving psychological problems and a person who is troubled or who is troubling others. [24]

psychotic disorder—a disorder characterized by a generalized failure of functioning in all areas of a person's life. [22]

P300 wave—feature of the event-related potential that arises when a person's expectations are upset. [3]

puberty—the period of sexual maturation that transforms a child into a physical adult. [17]

punishment—a consequence that leads to the suppression of or to a decrease in the frequency of a behavior. [8]

pupil—the opening in the center of the eye. [5]

qualitative change—change in cognitive development, considered as involving a radical restructuring of the mind. [15]

quality—the kind of sensation a stimulus produces. [5]

quantitative change—change in cognitive development, considered as resulting from the accumulation of knowledge. [15]

quantitative psychology—the approach to psychology that specializes in measurement and statistics. [1]

racism—specific attitudes and behavior based on people's beliefs that their own race is superior. [26]

randomly assign—to assign subjects to a treatment condition in such a way that each subject has an equal chance of being placed in either condition. [2]

range—the difference between the smallest and the largest scores in a statistical distribution. [2]

rape—nonconsenting sexual intercourse with another person as the result of force, threat, or intimidation. [13, 22]

rational scale—personality test developed by defining the various constructs to be measured, then writing items that appear to fit the definitions. [20]

rational-emotive therapy—a therapy in which clients are first led to recognize the irrational nature of previously unexamined beliefs and then are aided in establishing a more realistic cognitive framework; a method of cognitive restructuring. [24]

rationalization—defense mechanism in which a person devises a plausible explanation for doing (or not doing) something that in fact he or she is doing for different reasons. [18]

reaction formation—the replacement of an anxiety-producing impulse by its opposite. [18]

reaction range—the unique range of responses to the environment possible for the genetic make-up of each person. [20]

realistic fantasy—a state on the continuum that stretches from normal waking consciousness to dreaming; it is most like normal consciousness. [7]

realistic job preview (RJP)—an honest picture of the potential job, including its disadvantages. [28]

reality anxiety—in Freud's terms, anxiety over danger that comes from the outside world. [18, 23]

receptive field—the restricted region of the retina within which a neural response may be generated by light. [5]

receptor neurons—the specialized cells that receive sensory information from the environment. [3]

reciprocal altruism—theory proposing that when a person performs an altruistic act, he or she increases the chances that the person being helped will reciprocate and may one day help either the helper or the helper's kin. [4, 27]

reconditioning—relearning of a conditioned response that has been extinguished by again pairing the CS and US. [8]

referential—use of symbols to refer to objects. [16]

reflex arc—the basic functional unit of the nervous system; a connection between sensory and motor signals. [3]

reflexes—nervous system responses that provide immediate involuntary reactions or responses to stimuli. [3]

refractory period—(1) a short period after a cell has fired, during which it cannot transmit an impulse. (2) a period of time that must pass after a man's orgasm before he can become sexually aroused again. [3, 13]

regression—defense mechanism in which a person returns to an earlier stage of development in response to some perceived threat. [18]

rehearsal—mental repetition of material we wish to retain in memory. [9]

reinforcement control—a way of regulating and maintaining behavior by rewarding an individual after he or she has behaved in a particular way. [19]

reinforcement theory—theory of work motivation that applies the techniques of operant conditioning to the workplace. [28]

relative size—the relationship between the size of the retinal image produced by an object and the apparent distance of that object from an observer. [6]

reliable—a test, measuring something consistently. [20]

REM (rapid eye-movement) sleep—a stage of sleep associated with dreams, in which the eyes move rapidly back and forth under closed eyelids. [7]

representational thought—thinking in which one mentally represents objects not directly in front of one. [15]

representativeness—a heuristic in which predictions are based on resemblances between the predicted event and a typical example. [10]

repression—the fundamental defense mechanism, one that keeps threatening thoughts and memories from consciousness and pushes them back into the unconscious. [18]

residual phase—a period following the active phase of schizophrenia in which behavior resembles that of the prodromal phase. [22]

resistance—a client's attempts to block the therapist's treatment. [24]

resolution phase—the final phase of sexual response. [13]

resting rate—the rate at which small spontaneous impulses are sent down the axon during a neuron's resting phase. [3]

retention—the maintenance of information in storage. [9]

reticular formation—the part of the brain stem that arouses higher brain areas to incoming information and maintains the sleep-waking cycle. [3]

retina—the surface at the back of the eye composed of receptors and neurons. [5]

retrieval—the ability to get encoded information out of storage and back into awareness. [9]

retrieval cue—a piece of information that helps us to retrieve information from long-term memory. [9]

retroactive interference—interference in which subsequent learning blocks out earlier learning. [9]

retrograde amnesia—a condition in which people are unable to remember events preceding some kind of brain insult. [9]

reverie—a state on the continuum that stretches from normal waking consciousness to dreaming; it consists of unrelated images, scenes, or memories. [7]

reversal—verbal slips in which sounds are exchanged. [16]

rhodopsin—a highly sensitive photopigment found in rods. [5]

rods—receptor cells in the eye responsible for vision in dim light. Rods signal information about brightness. [5]

role enactment theory—the theory that hypnosis is simply a special case of role playing. [7]

role taking—being able to imagine oneself in another's place. [17]

Rorschach Inkblot Test—a test in which a person is handed a series of symmetrical inkblots, one at a time, and is asked to report what she or he sees, using free association. [20]

round window—a membranous spot on the cochlea. [5]

sadism—sexual gratification obtained through inflicting pain on another person. [22]

sample—a representative selection of members of a defined population. [2]

scatter plot—graph on which a large number of data are plotted; used to show the range of possible relationships. [2]

schedule of reinforcement—the basis on which a subject is rewarded for a behavior. [8]

schema—organized cluster of general knowledge that we possess about any general topic. [9, 10]

schemes—action patterns that consist of whatever in an action can be repeated and generalized to other situations. [15]

schizophrenia—a group of disorders characterized by thought disturbance that may be accompanied by delusions, hallucinations, attention deficits, and bizarre motor activity. [22]

Scholastic Aptitude Test (SAT)—a test designed to measure "aptitude for college studies" rather than school achievement or general intelligence. [20]

school psychology—the approach to psychology concerned with assessment of children with learning or emotional problems. The school psychologist will then work out ways for parents and teachers to help these children. [1]

scientific management—a system for the redesign of work methods to make them more efficient. [28]

script—the schema of routine events that typically occur in a particular situation. [16]

search tree—the set of all possible moves that will lead to solution of a problem. [10]

secondary appraisal—a person's assessment of whether he or she has the resources and ability to cope with a situation. [21]

secondary erectile failure—a condition in which men who have experienced no erectile failure with a partner in the past are unable to achieve or maintain an erection in some or all sexual situations. [13]

secondary (situational) orgasmic dysfunction—the situation of women who experience orgasms sometimes, but not with their primary sexual partner or not during sexual intercourse. [13]

secondary reinforcer. [8] See **conditioned reinforcer.**

secondary trait—a characteristic mode of behavior that is less prominent than a central trait and is seen in fewer situations. [19]

second-order conditioning—a phenomenon in which a *second* neutral stimulus, when it repeatedly follows a conditioned stimulus, becomes capable of eliciting the conditioned response by itself. [8]

selective attention—the process of controlling the selection of material from sensory memory. [9]

self—the parts of the total range of a person's possible experiences that the individual recognizes and accepts. [19]

self-actualization—fulfillment of an individual's capabilities. [19]

self-fulfilling prophecies—expectations about behavior that evoke a situation in which the expectations are confirmed. [26]

self-instructional training—a method of cognitive restructuring that gives clients new ways of thinking and talking about their problems. [24]

self-monitoring—controlling our words, actions, and nonverbal displays of emotion so as to create a favorable impression. [25, 26]

self-schemas—clusters of generalizations about the self based on past experiences that organize, summarize, and explain our behavior. [26]

semen—the fluids discharged by males in ejaculation. [13]

semicircular canals—the three fluid-filled canals in the inner ear that make up the vestibular organ. [5]

sensorimotor period—the period of cognitive development in which the infant relies on action schemes; the first two years of life. [15]

sensory deprivation—alteration of consciousness by sharp reduction of all sensory stimulation. [7]

sensory memory—the momentary persistence of sensory information after stimulation has ceased. [9]

sensory neurons—neurons that carry messages from the sense organs to the spinal cord. [3]

separation distress—an infant's protesting when parted from the mother and expressing joy when the mother returns. [17]

septal area—a structure in the limbic system. [3]

serotonin—neurotransmitter believed to affect body temperature, sensory perception, and the onset of sleep. [3]

severe retardation—mental retardation in which the (Stanford-Binet) IQ is between 20 and 35; severe retardates can learn to care for some of their physical needs. [20]

sexism—attitudes and behavior based on the belief that one's own sex is superior. [26]

sex-typed behavior—behavior that is regarded as appropriate for only one sex. [17]

sexual dysfunction—any recurring problem that prevents an individual from engaging in sexual relations or from reaching orgasm during sex. [13]

shaping—a form of operant conditioning based on the reinforcement of ever-closer approximations of a desired behavior. [8]

short-term memory (STM)— the type of memory storage capable of retaining information for about fifteen seconds. [9]

sign stimulus—a particular stimulus that triggers the appearance of fixed-action patterns as well as some more complex behavior. [4]

signal detection theory—the theory proposing that there is no single absolute threshold for a stimulus. [5]

similarity—a principle of grouping. [6]

simplicity—the concept integrating all the principles of grouping. [6]

simplification—problem-solving strategy in which a solution to a similar but relatively simple problem is worked out in order to generalize the solution method to a more complex problem. [10]

single feature—the classification rule that depends on just a single attribute (for example, doctor). [10]

single-item recognition—test of memory retrieval in which subject is asked to confirm whether an item was on a previously learned list. [9]

single-unit recording—placement of an electrode to allow researchers to record the electrical activity of a single neuron. [3]

situational cause—cause of behavior that is attributed to conditions in the environment. [26]

size constancy—the tendency to perceive the size of an object as constant regardless of its distance and, hence, the size of its retinal image. [6]

slow potential—change in voltage of a receiving neuron. [3]

social behavior—any behavior that involves the interaction of two or more individuals. [4]

social cognition—the child's understanding of the social world and the process by which the child comes to understand why people behave as they do in social situations. [17]

social facilitation—enhanced performance in the presence of others. [27]

social impact theory—the theory that when social forces affect a situation, the larger the group, the less pressure on any one member because the impact of the forces is spread over the entire group. [27]

social influence—waiting for others to define the situation as an emergency. [27]

social interest—in Adler's terms, the inborn desire to strive for the public good. [18]

social learning theory—the theory proposing that learning is not simply a matter of reacting to stimuli; rather, people apply cognitive processes to the stimuli they encounter, selecting, organizing, and transforming them. [8]

social psychology—the approach to psychology concerned with the study of the behavior of people in groups. In social psychology, special attention is paid to the influence of other people on individuals. [1]

social trap—a situation in which as a result of personal decisions, people, organizations, or societies start moving in some direction or initiate some relationship whose consequences become collectively harmful or lethal but that seems virtually impossible to stop. [27]

socialization—the process of absorbing society's attitudes, values, and customs. [17]

sociobiology—the study of the genetic basis of social behavior and organization. [4]

sociopath—one who is indifferent to the rights of others. [22]

solo situation—phenomenon in which a single outsider enters a group of otherwise homogeneous individuals. [26]

somatic nervous system—the division of the PNS related to the external world and generally under voluntary control. [3]

somatoform disorder—disorder whose distinguishing feature is the persistence of symptoms that have a somatic or physical form, but in which there is no physiological malfunction. [22]

somatosensory cortex—the area of the parietal lobe involved in reception and interpretation of touch and positional information. [3]

source credibility—the extent to which the prestige of the source affects a message's believability. [25]

source trait—an underlying root or cause of a surface trait. [19]

species—a group of individuals who can mate with each other and produce offspring under natural conditions. [4]

species-specific behavior—behavior typical of a particular species whose members share a common genetic background and a common environment that provides similar influences and experiences. [4]

speech act—an utterance. [16]

spermatogenesis—the process of sperm production. [13]

spinal cord—column of neurons that bring information from the skin and muscles to the brain and send motor commands back to muscles. [3]

spontaneous recovery—temporary reappearance of an extinguished response when an organism is reintroduced to the experimental situation. [8]

stages—cognitive periods of development in which a child's thinking patterns are radically different from those of an earlier period. [15]

standard deviation (S.D.)—the preferred measure of variability. It shows how much figures in a given set of data vary from the mean. [2]

standard score system—a system of scoring tests in which standard scores represent points on a bell-shaped curve that reflects the normal pattern of distribution of scores on almost any test. [20]

standardization group—a large and well-defined group of people to which a test is given to establish the test's norms. [20]

Stanford-Binet Test—a revision of Binet's test of intelligence; devised at Stanford University. [20]

state-dependent memory—memory more easily recalled when a person is in the same physiological state as when she or he acquired the information. [9]

stereopsis—perception of depth based on binocular disparity. [6]

stereotype—to rigidly assign to a person all the standardized attributes that we ordinarily assign to the group, making no allowances for individuality. [26]

stimulant—a drug that increases heart rate, blood pressure, and muscle tension by stimulating the central nervous system. [7]

stimulus—any form of energy that can evoke a response. [5]

stimulus control—a particular behavior taking place only when a particular stimulus in the environment evokes it at the appropriate time. [19]

stimulus generalization—the tendency for a response learned in one situation to occur in response to other similar stimuli or situations. [8]

stirrup—one of the ossicles. [5]

Stockholm syndrome—the attachment that develops between a hostage and his or her captor. [25]

stress—a term without precise meaning; sometimes defined as any stimulus that places a strain on a person's physical or psychological capacity to adjust; sometimes defined as an internal response to some disruptive or disquieting situation. [21]

subjective contours—lines or shapes that appear to be part of a figure but are actually not physically present. [6]

subjects—human beings or other animals that are the source of responses in an experiment. [2]

sublimation—the diversion of emotional energy from its original source to a socially constructive use. [18]

subliminal perception—the registration of sensory information that influences behavior without producing any conscious experience of the stimulus. [6]

superego—according to Freud, that part of the personality that represents the moral standards of the society as conveyed to the child by the parents. [18]

superstitious behavior—the increase of a response owing to a coincidental relationship between the behavior and a reinforcer. [8]

surface traits—clusters of behavior that tend to go together. [19]

survey—method of collecting data in which researchers obtain information about people's characteristics, attitudes, opinions, or behavior by asking them questions. [2]

sympathetic nervous system—the division of the autonomic nervous system that dominates in emergencies or stressful situations. [3]

synapse—a small gap between neurons. [3]

synergistic—a combined action of drugs. For example, the effect of two depressants taken together is greater than the sum of the two drugs' effects. [7]

syntax—the rules for combining words to form sentences. [16]

systematic desensitization—a procedure aiming at the gradual extinction of anxiety, in which the relaxed client is gradually exposed to anxiety-producing stimuli. [24]

systematic relationship—correlation between two sets of phenomena that happen together that is significantly higher than chance. [2]

tardive dyskinesia—a muscle disorder in which patients grimace and smack their lips uncontrollably. [24]

taste buds—the structures in the mouth and tongue that contain receptor cells for taste stimuli. [5]

telegraphic speech—a child's utterances in the language-acquisition stage, characterized by two-word sentences. [16]

temperament—the individual's pattern of activity, susceptibility to emotional stimulation, response to stimuli, and general mood. [17]

template matching—theory of pattern recognition proposing that the brain recognizes patterns such as letters by comparing the stimuli to standard patterns it has stored in memory. [6]

temporal lobe—the area in the brain involved in auditory reception and processing of visual information. [3]

test-retest reliability—the extent to which repeated administration of a test to the same group of people produces the same results. [20]

texture gradient—the graduated differences in texture that occur as distance increases. [6]

thalamus—a pair of structures in the brain that provides a link between the cerebral hemispheres and the sense organs. [3]

the tragedy of the commons—an example of a social trap. [27] See **social trap.**

Thematic Apperception Test (TAT)—a test consisting of a series of cards depicting ambiguous scenes involving one, two, or three people. The subject is asked to tell a story about each picture. [20]

theory—a system of rules or assumptions about natural phenomena that can be used to predict future events or to explain how these phenomena work. [2]

theory of multiple intelligences—a theory in which equal weight is given to seven different kinds of intelligence. [20]

theory of psychosexual development—Freud's theory

that from earliest infancy people are motivated by powerful biological instincts to seek pleasure and that at different ages, different parts of the body are the focus of this pleasure. [17]

tip-of-the-tongue phenomenon—the condition of knowing that the information is known, while retrieval cues fail to produce the information. [9]

token economy—a therapeutic technique, used primarily in institutions, in which a wide range of appropriate behavior is rewarded with tangible conditioned reinforcers, or "tokens." [24]

trait—"any relatively enduring way in which one individual differs from another" (Guilford, 1959). [19]

transference—a client's transfer to the analyst of childhood feelings toward important people in his or her life, particularly the parents. [24]

transference neurosis—the stage of therapy in which the client reenacts with the analyst childhood conflicts with the parents. [24]

transsexualism—gender identification with the opposite sex. [13, 22]

transvestism—sexual gratification obtained through dressing in clothing of the opposite sex. [22]

traumatic—psychologically damaging. [18]

trichromatic theory—the theory proposing that color vision is based on three types of cones thought to be mingled in a mosaic pattern throughout the central retina. [5]

trimester—one-third of the period of pregnancy. [14]

Turner's syndrome—the condition of a fetus that has received only a single X chromosome and no Y chromosome. [13]

turn-taking conventions—signals that indicate who will be next to speak in a conversation. [16]

two-factor theory of emotion—the theory that the experience of an emotion is based on a physiological change plus a cognitive interpretation of that change. [11]

Type A behavior—a personality pattern; people who fit this pattern are highly competitive, hostile when thwarted, and their behavior shows the urgency of working against the pressures of time. [21]

ultimate attribution error—the tendency to find dispositional causes for the misdeeds of an outgroup and situational causes for the misdeeds of an ingroup. [26]

unconditional positive regard—continued support of a person (by the self or others) regardless of what the person says or does. [19, 24]

unconditioned response (UCR)—an unlearned response to a stimulus. [8]

unconditioned stimulus (UCS)—a stimulus that evokes a response without having been learned. [8]

unconscious—an aspect of personality unknown to the mind of the subject. [18]

uniformity—common features or behavior shared by almost all members of a given group. [27]

vaginismus—a condition in which involuntary muscle spasms cause the vagina to shut tightly so that penetration by the penis is extremely painful or impossible. [13]

valid—of a test, measuring what it purports to measure. [20]

variability—the degree to which a group of responses spreads out from the mean or median. [2]

variable interval schedule—a partial reinforcement schedule in which reinforcement comes at unpredictable times. [8]

variable ratio schedule—a partial reinforcement schedule in which reinforcement comes after an unpredictable number of responses. [8]

verbal encoding—naming or verbally describing material to be stored into short-term memory. [9]

vestibular sense—the sense of balance. [5]

visual cortex—area of brain most involved in receiving and analyzing visual information; located in occipital lobe. [3]

visual depth perception—the ability to tell how far away an object is. [6]

voyeurism—sexual gratification obtained through secret observations of another person's sexual activities or genitals. [22]

wariness of strangers—a baby's responding to strangers with, for example, fear or withdrawal. [17]

wavelenth—a unit of scale of the electromagnetic spectrum. [5]

Weber's law—the law stating that the amount of stimulus needed to produce a just noticeable difference is a constant fraction of the intensity of the stimulus. [5]

Wechsler Adult Intelligence Scale (WAIS)—a test for adults that measures both performance and verbal ability. [20]

Wechsler Intelligence Scale for Children (WISC)—a test of children that measures both verbal and performance ability. [20]

Wechsler Preschool and Primary Scale of Intelligence (WPPSI)—a test that measures both verbal and performance ability of children from four to six and a half years old. [20]

well-defined problem—a problem with a clear structure; one in which there is always a clear standard for deciding whether the problem has been solved. [10]

Wernicke's aphasia—loss of ability to comprehend language, brought about by damage to the left temporal cortex. [3]

working backward—a special form of means-end analysis consisting of devising a plan by working backward from the goal state. [10]

Young-Helmholtz hypothesis—color vision relies on only three basic kinds of color cones, sensitive to the three primary colors of red, blue, and green. [5]

INDEX OF SUBJECTS

Chapter One   Opener:Bill Longcore/Longcore Maciel Studio. 5:*Fingerprint Landscape* (1950), © Saul Steinberg. Collection of the artist.   9:Sepp Seitz/Woodfin Camp & Associates. 11:George N. Peet/The Picture Cube.   13:Peter Menzel/Stock, Boston.   15:Catherine Ursillo/Photo Researchers.

Chapter Two   Opener:James R. Holland/Stock, Boston. 25:Dr. Fred Espenak/Science Photo Library-Photo Researchers. 29:Bohdan Hrynewych/Southern Light.   34:John Troha/Black Star.

Chapter Three   Opener:Roger Ressmeyer/Wheeler Pictures. 56, Figure 3.3:Top left, Julius Weber; top center, Lester V. Bergman & Associates; top right, UPI/COMPIX.   62:Grey Villet/ Visions.   65:Martin M. Rotker/Phototake.   66:Top, Dan McCoy/Rainbow; bottom, NIH/Science Source-Photo Researchers.

Chapter Four   Opener:Portenfield/Chickering/Photo Researchers.   91:John Barr/Gamma-Liaison.   94:Thomas McAvoy/LIFE MAGAZINE © Time Inc.   95:Joy A. Guravich/ Photo Researchers.   97:Fred Bruemmer.

Chapter Five   Opener:Linda K. Moore/Rainbow.   104:Elyse Rieder/Photo Researchers.   118, Figure 5.9 A & B:Ishihara Color Blindness Test Charts reprinted with the permission of Graham-Field, Inc., New Hyde Park, N.Y.   126:Jean-Claude Delmas/Woodfin Camp & Associates.   130:NASA.

Chapter Six   Opener:Dean Krakel II/Photo Researchers. 144:Bottom left, *Delivery of the Keys*, Perugino, Vatican Museum. Scala/Art Resource; right, Frank Siteman/Stock, Boston. 146:Both, Random House photos by K. Bendo.   151, Figure 6.12C:*Waterfall* by M. C. Escher, © M. C. Escher Heirs, c/o Cordon Art, Baarn, Holland.

Chapter Seven   Opener:Geoffrey Gove.   167:Arthur Tress. 168:James H. Karales/Peter Arnold, Inc.   170:Detail, *Queen Katherine's Dream*, William Blake, National Gallery of Art, Washington, D.C. Rosenwald Collection.   176:Courtesy of Bernard S. Brucker, Ph.D., Director, Biofeedback Laboratory, University of Miami School of Medicine; photo by Joey Young.

Chapter Eight   Opener:James R. Smith.   200:Ken Robert Buck/The Picture Cube.   202:Ethan Hoffman/Archive. 208:Harvey Stein.   211:Suzanne Szasz/Photo Researchers.

Chapter Nine   Opener:Arthur Tress.   235:Rick Smolan.

Chapter Ten   Opener:Peter Angelo Simon/Phototake. 250:Michael Grecco/Picture Group.   265, Figure 10.6:Leonard Speier.   266, Figure 10.8:Leonard Speier.   268:Richard Pilling/Focus on Sports.

Chapter Eleven   Opener:Arthur Grace/Stock, Boston.   276:O. Franken/Sygma.   277:Harry Wilks/Stock, Boston.   283:Fredrik D. Bodin/Stock, Boston.   292:Don Ploke/Las Vegas Sun.

Chapter Twelve   Opener:Hazel Hankin.   301:Franklin/Sygma. 305:Larry Lee/West Light.   306:A. Devaney, Inc.   308:Courtesy of R. A. Butler.   311:John J. Krieger/The Picture Cube.

Chapter Thirteen   Opener:Geoffrey Gove.   326:Jaye R. Phillips/The Picture Cube.   330:Tequila Minsky.   336:Sepp Seitz/Woodfin Camp & Associates.   337:Arthur Tress. 341:Bettye Lane/Photo Researchers.

Chapter Fourteen   Opener:Craig Aurness/West Light. 351:Marcia Keegan.   354:Rick Winsor/Woodfin Cmap & Associates.   357:Courtesy of American Heart Association.

361, Figure 14.3:Courtesy of Dr. Richard Walk.   365:Suzanne Szasz.

Chapter Fifteen   Opener:Dan McCoy/Rainbow.   371:Elizabeth Crews.   372:All, George Zimbel/Monkmeyer.   374:Dr. Carolyn Rovel-Collier, Rutgers University, Department of Psychology. 377:Peter Menzel/Stock, Boston.   380:All, Steve Wells.

Chapter Sixteen   Opener:Arthur Tress.   401:Richard Kalvar/ Magnum.   403:Drawing by Stevenson; © 1976 The New Yorker Magazine Inc.   408:Alain Keler/Sygma.   417:Paul Fusco/ Magnum.

Chapter Seventeen   Opener:Alan Carey/The Image Works. 428:Allen Green/Photo Researchers.   430:Ira Berger/Woodfin Camp & Associates.   438:Frank Siteman/The Picture Cube. 441:Lawrence Frank.   444:Mary Ellen Mark/Archive. 446:Hazel Hankin.

Chapter Eighteen   Opener:Geoffrey Gove.   454:The Bettmann Archive.   462:Gary Goodman/The Picture Cube.   464:Robert V. Eckert Jr./EKM-Nepenthe.   466:Sonia Moskowitz.

Chapter Nineteen   Opener:Liane Enkelis/Stock, Boston. 482:Tannenbaum/Sygma.

Chapter Twenty   Opener:Cary Wolinsky/Stock, Boston. 495:George Hall/Woodfin Camp & Associates.

Chapter Twenty-One   Opener:Owen Franken/Stock Boston. 520:Arthur Tress.   522:Left, Dick Hanley/Photo Researchers; right, Robert Pacheco/EKM-Nepenthe.   527:Eli Reed/Magnum. 528:Ted Spiegel/Black Star.   533:Alan Carey/The Image Works. 534:Chuck O'Rear/West Light.

Chapter Twenty-Two   Opener:*Standing Man*, W. De Kooning, Wadsworth Atheneum, Hartford, Connecticut. Photo by Joseph Szaszfai 541:Barbara Alper.   544:Barbara Alper.   549:Arthur Tress.   552:*Birthday*, Marc Chagall. Oil on canvas. The Solomon R. Guggenheim Museum, New York.   553, Figure 22.4:Both, courtesy of Al Vercoutere, Camarillo State Hospital. 557:Bettye Lane/Photo Researchers.   558:Jeff Alberston/Stock, Boston.

Chapter Twenty-Three   Opener:Bill Longcore/Longcore Maciel Studio.   570:Peter Marlow/Sygma.   573:Dan Budnik/Woodfin Camp & Associates.   574:Leonard Speier.

Chapter Twenty-Four   Opener:*Transcribing the Internal Horizon* by Lorena Laforest Bass.   585:Arthur Tress.   591:Roger Ressmeyer/Wheeler Pictures.   595:Leonard Speier.   599:Joel Gordon.

Chapter Twenty-Five   Opener:Camilla Smith/Rainbow. 606:Michel Philippot/Sygma.   613:Gianfranco Gorgoni/Contact Press Images.

Chapter Twenty-Six   Opener:John Lei/Stock, Boston. 626:Peter Marlow/Sygma.   627:Sybil Shelton/Monkmeyer. 635:Alan Carey/The Image Works.   638:Tom Campbell/West Light.

Chapter Twenty-Seven   Opener:Jeffry W. Myers/Stock, Boston.   650:Peter Southwick/Stock, Boston.   654:Chris Steele-Perkins/Magnum.   660:UPI/Bettmann Newsphotos. 662:Mark Jury Communications.

Chapter Twenty-Eight   Opener:Peter Menzel.   675:Culver Pictures.   687:Adam J. Stoltman/Duomo.